Flannery O'Connor:
An Annotated Reference Guide
to Criticism

Irwin Streight
Editor

Flannery O'Connor
(1925-1964)

Flannery O'Connor:
An Annotated Reference Guide to Criticism

Compiled and Annotated by

R. Neil Scott

Ina Dillard Russell Library
Georgia College & State University

TIMBERLANE BOOKS
Milledgeville, Georgia

10 9 8 7 6 5 4 3 2 1

Timberlane Books
P.O. Box 1280, Milledgeville, Georgia 31059-1280

ISBN 0-9715428-0-5

A catalog record for this book is available from the Library of Congress
Library of Congress Control Number: 2002090969

Manufactured in the United States by BookMaster's, Inc., Ashland, Ohio

For

Sheila,

and our children

Stephanie, Sherry, and David

Also,

my father

John Taylor Scott, Jr.

Contents

Preface   ix

Acknowledgements   xi

(Mary) Flannery O'Connor: A Brief Biographical Sketch   xiii

First Editions and Related Works   1

WRITINGS ABOUT FLANNERY O'CONNOR:

     Section 1: Book-Length Criticism Prior to 1975   3

     Section 2: Book-Length Criticism, 1975-2000   9

     Section 3: Articles, Chapters, Essays, 1975-2000   77

     Section 4: Dissertations, 1961-2000   689

     Section 5: Foreign Language Criticism, 1975-1999   787

     Section 6: Master's Theses, 1961-2000   833

SUPPLEMENTAL RESOURCES:

     Appendix 1: Reviews of Principal Editions   873

     Appendix 2: Movies and Videos of Works   887

INDEXES:

     Index 1: Author Index   891

     Index 2: Name Index   922

     Index 3: Subject Index   949

About the Author and Editor   1063

Preface

Flannery O'Connor: An Annotated Reference Guide to Criticism is the product of ten years of scholarly research. It is designed to serve as a comprehensive sequel to Robert E. Golden's 1977 contribution to O'Connor scholarship, *Flannery O'Connor and Caroline Gordon: A Reference Guide* (Boston: G.K. Hall) and as a tribute to the scholarly community interested in Flannery O'Connor's life and work.

Supplementing Golden's guide, which covers O'Connor criticism published from 1952 to 1976, this present work is designed to offer readers detailed, yet succinctly written descriptive abstracts of criticism published from 1975 to 2000. In addition, the following categories include entries published before 1975: dissertations (1961-2000); a checklist of master's theses (1961-2000); and citations to reviews of book-length criticism.

Arrangement

While serious consideration was given to arranging entries chronologically, it was found, after conferring with a number of distinguished O'Connor scholars, that an alphabetical arrangement by author--divided by type of work--was preferred.

O'Connor scholars concurred that while Robert Golden's guide adequately documented the early growth of O'Connor criticism, the scholarly community has since divided into a wide variety of factions and perspectives. Consequently, many believe it is now more useful to be able to assess a colleague's collected body of work to better understand his or her position, than to view the production of O'Connor scholarship chronologically.

Book Reviews

Only those book reviews published in *The Flannery O'Connor Bulletin* or those which discuss and compare two or more books related to O'Connor are annotated. These contributions are included because they tend to focus on the *context* of the criticism instead of simply discussing the merits or faults of a single, specific work. However, for those scholars intent upon assessing the critical reception of each book, a representative list of book reviews follows each book entry.

Literary Criticism and Copyright

Abstracts written for this guide are intended to be descriptive, not evaluative. They are structured to offer enough information for the reader to make the final judgement as to whether it would be helpful to locate and read the original.

One of the inherent difficulties in compiling a bibliography of this nature, however, lies in the abstracting of book-length works. It is one task to effectively abstract and index a twenty or thirty-page article, yet another to deal with a two-hundred or three-hundred page book. Because this work can only *describe* the contents of each book cited, not summarize it, scholars are advised to carefully study the indexes of each book consulted as well.

Literary criticism is itself an art. Thus, I have often quoted the author to provide readers with a better idea of *how* something is said, in order to complement *what* is being said. It is hoped that this selective use of quoted text will allow readers to be able to judge the *quality* of the writing in the work described as well.

This use of brief, quoted excerpts is carefully weighed against fair use guidelines allowed by provisions of U.S. Copyright Law. These guidelines allow limited use of a scholarly work for research, teaching, criticism, and other similar purposes. Other factors that I have considered include the nature of the original work, the amount and substantiality of use, and the effect of quotation upon the market for the original publication.

Dissertations and Theses

Abstracts of doctoral dissertations included are based on abstracts in editions of University Microfilm's (UMI) *Dissertation Abstracts International.* However, because some institutions do not cooperate with UMI, dissertations not included in *Dissertation Abstracts* were abstracted directly from the dissertation itself (by borrowing a copy via inter-library loan or by visiting the library of an institution that owns a copy) or from information provided by the author.

Errors and Inaccuracies

Finally, despite the enormous effort that I have devoted to this project, errors and inaccuracies undoubtedly remain, and materials that I should have identified and included may be absent. For these shortcomings I take full responsibility. Please send notice of any errors, inaccuracies, or omissions to R. Neil Scott, c/o Flannery O'Connor Collection, Russell Library, Georgia College & State University, Milledgeville, Georgia, 31061.

Your comments and suggestions are appreciated and will be considered for any future editions.

R. Neil Scott
Georgia College & State University
Milledgeville, Georgia
September, 2001

Acknowledgements

Flannery O'Connor: An Annotated Reference Guide to Criticism is a product of efforts by the author and Nancy Davis Bray, Assistant Director for Special Collections and Curator of the *Flannery O'Connor Collection* at Georgia College & State University (GC&SU), to identify, procure for the Collection, and cite in this guide, criticism related to Flannery O'Connor published between 1975 and 2000.

The value of this work was recognized while completing the Library's successful *National Endowment for the Humanities (NEH) Preservation Grant*, written and submitted by Janice C. Fennell, Sarah Gordon, Nancy Davis Bray, and this author (all of GC&SU) in 1989. It was while compiling evidence of the standing of Flannery O'Connor in the scholarly community for the NEH grant that the author realized the need for this reference guide and began work on it.

Georgia College & State University Support

The author is deeply indebted to many colleagues who have helped to locate, examine, acquire, and abstract materials cited. While the list is a long one, among those to whom the largest debt is owed is Mardy Prentice, the former Associate Vice-President for Academic Affairs and Dean of Graduate Studies at GC&SU. In 1990, Dean Prentice provided funding from her own office travel funds for an initial research trip to the U.S. Library of Congress, Duke University, and the University of North Carolina at Chapel Hill to determine the feasibility of identifying and abstracting criticism for a project of the magnitude seen in this volume.

Following the initial award from Mardy Prentice, the author has received awards for travel and research from GC&SU's *Faculty Research* and *Faculty Development Committees*, the *GC&SU Foundation*, as well as Russell Library research leave and travel fund allocations. The author is grateful for this support.

The author also recognizes support provided by many of his Russell Library colleagues at GC&SU: Janice C. Fennell, Bill Richards, Mary M. Jones, Nancy Davis Bray, Laura King, Stephen Westman, Faye Heal, Carol Babyak, Linh Uong, Tara Rigsby, Christy Prince, Carol Ward, Hunter Eck, Lamonica Jenkins Sanford, Christine Zuger, Mary Kitchens and Tracy Bellew.

To each of these colleagues, I offer my thanks and gratitude.

Dissertation Research Assistance

The author wishes to acknowledge the award of a matching grant to the *Flannery O'Connor Collection* at Georgia College & State University from University

Microfilms International (UMI). Through UMI's generous support, the Russell Library was able to acquire most of the dissertations cited. Having these dissertations readily available for the compilation and writing of the "Dissertations" section of this work was most helpful.

The author also wishes to acknowledge the assistance of Sue B. Sasseen, a friend and colleague, who provided a substantial number of summary abstracts of dissertations derived largely from *Dissertation Abstracts* as part of the requirements for her doctoral studies at Texas A&M University and to Allys Dierker for her assistance in tracking citations to book reviews of O'Connor's principal editions as part of her doctoral research at Tulane University.

O'Connor Scholars

Suggestions offered by O'Connor scholars have been very helpful. My thanks to: Sarah Gordon, Editor of the *Flannery O'Connor Bulletin*; Virginia Wray, Editor of *Cheers! The Flannery O'Connor Society Newsletter*; J.J. Quinn, S.J.; Tom Frazier; Robert H. Tate; Marshall Bruce Gentry; Donald E. Hardy; Miles Orvell; Paul W. Nisly; Clif Boyer; Georgia Anne Newman; and Valerie Nye.

Foreign Language Abstracts

The author also wishes to extend his appreciation to the many colleagues who wrote abstracts of foreign language materials: Timour Abdoullin (Russian), Marguerite Bartoli (French), Eleonora Buzzo (Spanish), Jeri H. Dies (Spanish), Amedeo Fedeli (Italian), Sonia González (Spanish), Roger Noël (French, Italian and German), Hajime Noguchi (Japanese), Kathleen M. Olson (Spanish), Rönnog Seaberg (Danish, Swedish, and Norwegian), George Toth (Russian), Chikage Toyama (Japanese), and Kayoko Watanabe (Japanese).

Other Scholarly Support

Thanks to my dear friend, Marie F. Harper, of the Los Alamos National Laboratory for her good advice and help in indexing and editing. To my bright and ever energetic research assistant, Livia Regel, who assisted me with the layout of entries while completing her master's thesis for Otto-Von-Guericke University.

Also, to Donna Gautier, Library Associate at the Russell Library of Georgia College & State University, and Craig Amason, former Director of the Mary Vinson Public Library in Milledgeville, Georgia for their assistance in proofreading the manuscript.

Most of all, I tip my hat to to my good friend and editor, Irwin Streight.

Flannery O'Connor,
A Brief Biographical Sketch

Though decades have passed since Flannery O'Connor's death at 39, the many books, articles, dissertations, and theses cited and described in this guide all testify to the interest that scholars and general readers alike have in Flannery O'Connor's startling and uniquely crafted stories.

Much of this criticism focuses upon her sharp ear for Southern dialect and her use of symbolism, grotesque imagery, shocking characterization, apocalyptic violence, and bizarre, paradoxical irony, as she drives home her themes of redemption, Christian mystery, original sin, and the action of grace upon sinful humanity.

Among O'Connor's most memorable "Christ-haunted" characters are Hulga, a one-legged intellectual who holds a Ph.D. in philosophy, who is out-rationalized and loses her artificial leg to a traveling Bible salesman in a painfully funny hayloft seduction scene ("Good Country People"); The Misfit, a former gospel singer who murders a grandmother for pleasure as they discuss the resurrection of Christ ("A Good Man Is Hard to Find"); Hazel Motes, a veteran who returns home to immerse himself in sin until undergoing an agonizing transformation amid a world of complacent Christians (*Wise Blood*); and Mr. Guizac, a hard-working, efficient, farmworker from Poland, whose murder by passive consent demonstrates how evil moves into hearts where there is an absence of love ("The Displaced Person").

O'Connor's Irish Catholic Roots

Scholars are indebted to Flannery O'Connor's biographer, Sally Fitzgerald, for her 1980 account in the *Georgia Historical Quarterly* tracing Flannery O'Connor's family background to some of the first Irish settlers of Georgia and for providing a context for her Irish Catholic roots.[1]

Fitzgerald notes that O'Connor's maternal great-grandfather, Hugh Donnelly Treanor, participated in the first Catholic Mass in Milledgeville held on a piano in his hotel apartment in the 1840s, and that, years later, his widow, Johannah Harty Treanor, donated the land for the city's Catholic Church. She reports that both had emigrated to America from Ireland when they were young and settled in Milledgeville after their marriage in 1848, where Hugh owned a grist mill nearby on the Oconee River.[2]

Fitzgerald also recounts that Flannery O'Connor's maternal grandfather, Peter James Cline, son of a Latin teacher from Ireland who died at 39, was not only a successful merchant and farmer, but Milledgeville's mayor for many years as well. Her research indicates that Peter James Cline married Kate Treanor, and upon her death, her sister Margaret Ida Treanor (both daughters of Hugh and Johannah), and--by his two wives--produced sixteen children, Flannery's mother Regina being one of the youngest of the second marriage.[3]

Fitzgerald notes that Flannery O'Connor's paternal great-grandfather, Patrick O'Connor, also came from Ireland in the mid-1830s and established a wagon manufacturing company in Savannah, Georgia. One of his eleven children, Edward Francis O'Connor, Sr., who became a wealthy banker and investor, was Flannery O'Connor's grandfather, father to her own father, Edward, Jr.

Flannery O'Connor's father, Edward O'Connor, Jr. distinguished himself as an Army officer in France during World War I and as Commander of the American Legion for Georgia in 1936. While he was considered "a charming and public-spirited man," the poor business conditions of the Depression in Savannah prevented him from becoming as successful as his father in the real estate and construction businesses in which he was engaged.[4]

Childhood

Edward O'Connor, Jr. married Regina Cline in 1922, and on March 25, 1925 their beloved only child Mary Flannery O'Connor was born. Doted upon by her two devoutly Catholic parents, Mary Flannery spent her early childhood years attending St. Vincent's Grammar School and Sacred Heart Parochial School in Savannah.

Flannery received notoriety at an early age when she was filmed by a Pathé News crew with a pet chicken that she had trained to walk backwards. The news clip of the five-year-old child with her pet chicken--given to her by her aunt--was shown in theaters across the country and undoubtedly helped to establish her lifelong love of peacocks, ducks, and other fowl as pets.[5]

In March, 1938, when Flannery was only 12, her father accepted a position with the Federal Housing Administration in Atlanta. The family initially moved from Savannah to Atlanta together, but within a few months, Flannery and her mother returned to the family home in Milledgeville. The home, located on West Greene Street, and graced with tall white columns along the front, had served for a short time as the Governor's mansion when Milledgeville was still Georgia's capital. It had been purchased in 1886 by Peter James Cline, Flannery's grandfather, and had remained in the family ever since.

Flannery's father remained in Atlanta until 1940, when he became gravely ill and joined his wife and daughter in Milledgeville. Then, only a few weeks before Flannery's sixteenth birthday in 1941, he died of complications arising from disseminated lupus erythematosus and was buried only a few blocks from the family's home in Memory Hill Cemetery.

Years at GSCW and Iowa

Upon graduation from Peabody High School in 1941, O'Connor attended Georgia State College for Women (GSCW), located in Milledgeville, only a block from her Greene Street home. There she served as art editor for the college paper, *The Colonnade* (which often included her block print cartoons), and edited, during her senior year, the campus literary magazine, *The Corinthian*. She also submitted cartoons to the *New Yorker* during her undergraduate years, but none of them were accepted. Flannery graduated from GSCW in 1945 with an A.B. in Social Science.

That same year she shortened her name from Mary Flannery O'Connor to Flannery O'Connor and applied for admission to the University of Iowa's graduate journalism program. She was accepted at Iowa and began taking classes in the fall of 1945. There O'Connor met with Paul Engle, director of the University's Writer's Workshop, and applied for admission into his M.F.A. program. Initially Engle was taken aback by O'Connor's almost unintelligible Georgia accent, but upon being shown some of her work, he immediately recognized her as a talented writer and encouraged her transfer.

Flannery O'Connor kept a low profile in the Writer's Workshop. Classmates report that she rarely spoke in class and usually deferred the reading of her own work to others. Her drive and talent were recognized however, and she was greatly encouraged by the support of Engle and other faculty.

In 1946, Flannery sold her first story "The Geranium" to *Accent* and won, in the following year, the *Rinehart-Iowa Fiction Award*. This award, which brought her a $750 honorarium and gave Rinehart the option to purchase her first novel, provided the support she needed to remain at Iowa another year to complete her master's thesis, *The Geranium: A Collection of Short Stories*. O'Connor left Iowa in mid-1947 with her M.F.A. and literary contacts that were to prove helpful throughout her career.

New York, Connecticut, and the Onset of Lupus

A few months after leaving Iowa, O'Connor was invited in early 1948 to Yaddo, a prominent artists' colony in Saratoga Springs, New York. There she worked on her first novel, *Wise Blood*, which she had begun at Iowa under Engle's direction, and met poet Robert Lowell, who introduced her to her future editor Robert Giroux and to the noted translator Robert Fitzgerald and his wife Sally.

O'Connor completed several draft chapters of *Wise Blood* at Yaddo, but was disappointed with the responses of her Rinehart editor, John Selby. As a result, she asked to be released from her contract and began working with Harcourt Brace.

O'Connor left Yaddo in March, 1949, after she, Lowell, and others became embroiled in a dispute with Yaddo Center Director, Elizabeth Ames, whom Lowell had accused of being a communist sympathizer. The Board rallied to Ames's defense and several writers left, including O'Connor. She moved into a YWCA on 134th Street in New York City,[6] but accepted an offer a few months later from her new friends Robert and Sally Fitzgerald to move into their garage apartment near Ridgefield, Connecticut.

During the first few years after she left Iowa, O'Connor was hard at work. She saw three of her stories published, and completed drafts of several others that were later to become chapters in *Wise Blood*. She found living with the Fitzgeralds to be pleasant and productive, but in the fall of 1950, began feeling a heaviness in her arms while typing. A local doctor suggested she might have early signs of arthritis and urged her to undergo a medical examination during her next visit home.

Shortly thereafter, in December, 1950, during a train trip home to Milledgeville to visit her mother, 25-year-old Flannery O'Connor became critically ill. Noting the tell-tale butterfly rash across the bridge of her nose, a specialist diagnosed her as having disseminated lupus erythematosus, the same disease that had killed her father ten years earlier.

O'Connor spent much of the following year in the Emory University Hospital in Atlanta undergoing blood transfusions and shots of the experimental drug ACTH. She was released to the care of her mother during the following summer of 1951.

Due to Flannery's weakened condition, she and her mother moved to a dairy farm a few miles north of Milledgeville, on Highway 441, that her mother had inherited in 1947. Renamed *Andalusia*, the farm is vividly described by Sally Fitzgerald in an article in *Southern Living* in 1983. The two-story white farmhouse with its surrounding acreage and various out-buildings was to be Flannery's home for the rest of her life.[7]

Andalusia

Once she regained the strength to do so, Flannery O'Connor devoted her mornings to writing while her mother ran the farm. The two often ate their midday meal at the Sanford House restaurant in Milledgeville, then returned home so Flannery could rest and tend her peacocks, chickens, and other fowl, or read or paint.

Though largely house-bound and weakened from massive doses of ACTH, O'Connor was not a recluse. She enjoyed entertaining visitors and corresponding with many friends, writers, and "cranks." From groups of school children who came on school field trips to see her peacocks, burros, cows and other farm animals, to aspiring and well-known writers, reporters, members of the clergy, and friends, all were graciously greeted and welcomed at Andalusia.

Because of her frail health and her reliance upon crutches after 1953, travel for O'Connor was difficult. Still, she managed to make a trip to the healing baths of

Lourdes, France, and gained an audience with Pope Pius XII in Rome in May, 1958. She also lectured at more than a dozen colleges and universities. Drafts of those lectures, carefully crafted and usually read word for word, are scrutinized to discern O'Connor's practices as a writer and intentions for her fiction.

O'Connor's writings, her meditative life on the farm, and the devoted attention and care she received from her mother, served as the focal points for her life at Andalusia until her untimely death at 39 in Milledgeville on August 3, 1964 from complications of her recently reactivated lupus. Flannery O'Connor was buried next to her father in Milledgeville's Memory Hill Cemetery; her mother, Regina Cline O'Connor died on May 8, 1995 and was buried alongside them.

Flannery O'Connor's Writings

During her years at Andalusia, Flannery O'Connor finished her novel *Wise Blood* (Harcourt, Brace, 1952); a short story collection, *A Good Man Is Hard to Find and Other Stories* (Harcourt, Brace, 1955); another novel, *The Violent Bear It Away* (Farrar, Straus and Cudahy, 1960); the Introduction to *A Memoir of Mary Ann* (Farrar, Straus and Cudahy, 1962), and her posthumously published collection *Everything That Rises Must Converge* (Farrar, Straus and Giroux, 1965). Flannery also left portions of an unpublished novel tentatively titled *Why Do the Heathen Rage?* However, this novel is considered too fragmented to be published.

After her death, Robert and Sally Fitzgerald compiled and edited O'Connor's essays, published as *Mystery and Manners: Occasional Prose* (Farrar, Straus and Giroux, 1969), and two years later, Farrar, Straus and Giroux published *The Complete Stories*, with an introduction by Robert Giroux. Sally Fitzgerald's edited collection of O'Connor's letters, *The Habit of Being: Letters of Flannery O'Connor* (Farrar, Straus and Giroux), followed in 1979.

Other important compilations of O'Connor's work include her book reviews, compiled by Leo Zuber and edited by Carter Martin, *The Presence of Grace and Other Book Reviews by Flannery O'Connor* (U of Georgia Press, 1983); O'Connor's correspondence with Brainard and Frances Neel Cheney in the Vanderbilt University Library, edited by C. Ralph Stephens, *The Correspondence of Flannery O'Connor and the Brainard Cheneys* (UP of Mississippi, 1986); and Rosemary M. Magee's collection of O'Connor interviews, *Conversations with Flannery O'Connor* (UP of Mississippi, 1987).

The Flannery O'Connor Collection at GC&SU

The *Flannery O'Connor Collection* at Georgia College & State University (GC&SU) serves as the principal repository for O'Connor's manuscripts and letters. This collection, most of which was donated by Flannery's mother Regina Cline O'Connor in 1971, includes a wide variety of materials of interest to scholars. The catalog of manuscripts in the collection is described by Stephen G. Driggers,

Robert J. Dunn, and Sarah Gordon in *The Manuscripts of Flannery O'Connor at Georgia College* (U of Georgia Press, 1989).

The *Flannery O'Connor Memorial Room*, dedicated in 1974, contains many items donated by the family, including Victorian period furnishings from Andalusia and the several hundred books that comprised O'Connor's library at her death. These books are cited and described in Arthur F. Kinney's, *Flannery O'Connor's Library: Resources of Being* (U of Georgia Press, 1985).

Awards and Honors

Despite the opinion of some who believe that O'Connor serves as a good example of how conservative writers and thinkers are slighted, O'Connor received many awards and honors for her writing.[8] Her most prominent honors include two *Kenyon Review* Fellowships (1953, 1954); a National Institute of Arts and Letters Grant (1957); a Ford Foundation Creative Writing Fellowship (1959); O. Henry First Prize awards for "Greenleaf" (1957), "Everything That Rises Must Converge" (1963), and "Revelation" (1964); a Henry H. Bellaman Foundation award in 1964; and honorary degrees from St. Mary's College, Notre Dame (1962) and Smith College (1963). Flannery O'Connor's most significant honor, however, was awarded for her posthumously published *Complete Stories* (1971); this collection won--over Walker Percy's *Love in the Ruins* and E.L. Doctorow's *The Book of Daniel*--the National Book Award for Fiction in 1972.[9]

Television, Film, and Dramatic Productions

Two of O'Connor's stories were produced for television: "The Life You Save May Be Your Own" starring Gene Kelly (1957), and Horton Foote's adaptation of "The Displaced Person," which was included in the *American Short Story Series* in 1977.

John Huston's film version of *Wise Blood*, produced by Michael and Kathy Fitzgerald and based upon Benedict Fitzgerald's screenplay, is also noteworthy. The film stars Brad Dourif and features a cameo appearance by Huston himself. It was distributed by New Line Cinema in 1980, and is currently available in video.

Dramatic adaptations of O'Connor's works are rare; however, Cecil Dawkins used selections from five O'Connor short stories for her play *The Displaced Person*, which was produced in New York's American Place Theater in 1966 and again by the Theatrical Outfit of Atlanta in 1998.

Bibliographies and Criticism

Two previous book-length bibliographies relate to O'Connor's work: Robert F. Golden and Mary C. Sullivan's, *Flannery O'Connor and Caroline Gordon: A Reference Guide* (G.K. Hall, 1977); and, David Farmer's *Flannery O'Connor: A Descriptive Bibliography* (Garland, 1981).

Golden's guide, the first half of which describes books and articles on O'Connor's life and work to 1975, is updated by this present work. Farmer's book cites and describes the various editions and translations of O'Connor's writings, most of which he had collected and donated to the Ransom Humanities Research Collection at the University of Texas at Austin Library.[10]

For undergraduates, Martha E. Cook's bibliographical essay on O'Connor in *American Women Writers: Bibliographical Essays*, (Greenwood Press, 1983, pp. 269-96) may be helpful. *The Flannery O'Connor Bulletin*, published since 1972-- and renamed *The Flannery O'Connor Review* in 2000--should be consulted as the principal scholarly journal focusing on O'Connor's life and work.

Significance of Flannery O'Connor's Work

Although the body of fiction she published during her lifetime is small--only two novels and two collections of short stories--O'Connor's reputation is firmly established. Drawing upon the strengths of such writers as Sophocles, Dante, Henry James, Nathaniel Hawthorne, Edgar Allan Poe, William Butler Yeats, James Joyce, and William Faulkner, O'Connor has, in turn, exerted considerable influence upon the styles of such contemporary writers as Lee Smith, Walker Percy, Alice Walker, Alice Munro, Joyce Carol Oates, and Harry Crews.

Adding to O'Connor's reputation are the articles, books, dissertations, and theses cited and described in this volume, and the fact that her stories are represented in virtually every introductory literature anthology used in American universities.

While more than a few Southern writers have focused upon religious themes, none has done so in quite the manner as O'Connor. Her interest in the effect of God's grace upon the complacent Christian or reluctant convert, and her pursuit of this theme deep into the hearts and minds of her readers, has one very specific goal: to turn her reader toward Christ for guidance and redemption.

In reference to her own methods in writing fiction O'Connor once remarked, "for the hard of hearing you shout, and for the almost-blind you draw large and startling figures." O'Connor used cutting satire and grotesque imagery to support acts of violence in her work. That use, though intentional, is by no means gratuitous. Instead, she uses it to shock readers into the realization that their own intellectual abilities are far too limited to provide a clear understanding of the nature of the universe and to urge them to carefully consider Christ's offer of redemption.

Although there are scores of differing perspectives as to why O'Connor's art is so important to American literary culture, to this author, her genius appears to lie in how she uses straightforward, simple prose to draw her readers into the inner world of her characters. Once there, she hopes they will recognize their own flawed character and look to Christ for redemption and deliverance.

R. Neil Scott

References

1. Fitzgerald, Sally. "Root and Branch: O'Connor of Georgia." *Georgia Historical Quarterly* 64.4 (1980): 377-87.

2. Fitzgerald 380.

3. Fitzgerald 382-83.

4. Fitzgerald 385-86.

5. Hyman, Stanley Edgar. "Flannery O'Connor: 1925-1964." *American Writers: A Collection of Literary Biographies.* Ed. Leonard Unger. Vol. 3. New York: Charles Scribner's, 1974. 337.

6. Stephens, Martha. "Flannery O'Connor." In *Fifty Southern Writers After 1900.* Ed. Joseph M. Flora and Robert Bain. New York: Greenwood, 1987. 335.

7. Fitzgerald, Sally. "Books About the South: The Andalusian Sibyl." *Southern Living* (May 1983): 164-65.

8. Belsie, Laurent. "Literary Laurels to Reinforce Traditional Values: Ingersoll Foundation Aims to Reward Thinkers Who Have No Liberal Bias." *Christian Science Monitor* (29 Nov. 1984): 30.

9. Trimmer, Joseph F. *The National Book Awards for Fiction: An Index to the First Twenty-Five Years.* Boston: G.K. Hall, 1978. Xvii, xxii, 91, 92, 141, 200, 255-69.

10. Oram, Richard W. "Flannery O'Connor Research Holdings at the University of Texas." *Flannery O'Connor Society Newsletter* 1.1 (1993): 2.

Flannery O'Connor:
An Annotated Reference Guide to Criticism

First Editions and Related Works

1   *The Complete Stories*. New York: Farrar, Straus and Giroux, 1971.

2   *Conversations with Flannery O'Connor*. Ed. Rosemary M. Magee. Literary Conversation Series. Jackson: UP of Mississippi, 1987.

3   *The Correspondence of Flannery O'Connor and the Brainard Cheneys*. Ed. and intro. C. Ralph Stephens. Jackson: UP of Mississippi, 1986.

4   *Everything That Rises Must Converge*. Intro. Robert Fitzgerald. New York: Farrar, Straus and Giroux, 1965.

5   *Flannery O'Connor: Collected Works*. Ed. Sally Fitzgerald. New York: Library of America, 1988.

6   *A Good Man Is Hard to Find and Other Stories*. New York: Harcourt Brace, 1955. *The Artificial Nigger and Other Tales*. London: Spearman, 1957.

7   *The Habit of Being: Letters of Flannery O'Connor*. Ed. and intro. Sally Fitzgerald. New York: Farrar, Straus and Giroux, 1979.

8   "Introduction." *A Memoir of Mary Ann*, by the Dominican Nuns of Our Lady of Perpetual Help Home Atlanta, Georgia. New York: Farrar, Straus & Cudahy, 1961, 3-21.

9   *Mystery and Manners: Occasional Prose*. Ed. Sally and Robert Fitzgerald. New York: Farrar, Straus and Giroux, 1969.

10   *The Presence of Grace and Other Book Reviews by Flannery O'Connor*. Comp. Leo J. Zuber. Ed. and intro. Carter W. Martin. Athens: U of Georgia P, 1983.

11   *Three by Flannery O'Connor*. New York: Signet, 1962.

12   *The Violent Bear It Away*. New York: Farrar, Straus and Cudahy, 1960.

13   *Wise Blood*. New York: Harcourt, Brace, 1952.

14   Driggers, Stephen G., Robert J. Dunn, with Sarah Gordon. *The Manuscripts of Flannery O'Connor at Georgia College*. Athens: U of Georgia P, 1989.

I Book-Length Criticism Prior to 1975

Descriptive abstracts of the following pre-1975 book length criticism are included in *Flannery O'Connor and Caroline Gordon: A Reference Guide*, compiled by Robert E. Golden and Mary C. Sullivan. Boston: G.K. Hall, 1977.

Readers are referred to specific entries in the following manner:

See Robert E. Golden's *Guide* Year.Entry Number.

15   Browning, Preston M., Jr. *Flannery O'Connor*. Carbondale: Southern Illinois UP, 1974.

See Robert E. Golden's *Guide* 1974.A1.

Representative Reviews: Anon., *Choice* 12.1 (1975): 68; Ronald DiLorenzo, *Review for Religious* 34.4 (July 1975): 647; Melvin Friedman, *Studies in American Fiction* 3 (1975): 226-28; John L. Idol, *Studies in Short Fiction* 12.3 (1975): 303-04; J.J. Quinn, *Best Sellers* 34.20 (15 Jan. 1975): 455; Martha Stephens, *American Literature* 47.3 (1975): 483-85; Harriett Strauss, *Library Journal* 1 March 1975: 482; J.J. Quinn, *Best Sellers* 34.20 (15 Jan. 1975): 455; J.O. Tate, *Flannery O'Connor Bulletin* 5 (1976): 105-11; Ralph Wood, *Christian Century* 92.13 (1975): 360.

16   Drake, Robert. *Flannery O'Connor: A Critical Essay*. Grand Rapids, MI: Eerdmans, 1966.

See Robert E. Golden's *Guide* 1966.A1.

Representative Reviews: O.B. Emerson, *Studies in Short Fiction* 5.2 (1967-68): 207-08; Robert E. Fitch, *New York Times Book Review* 13 Nov. 1966: 46-47; Robert F. Fleissner, *Southern Review* ns 6.3 (1970): 884-89; Haydn L. Gilmore, *Christian Century* 7 Sept. 1966: 1081; Charles A. Huttar, *Gordon Review* 10.1 (1966): 44-45; Edward Krickel, *Georgia Review* 23.2 (1969): 246-47; Marion Montgomery, *Georgia Review* 22.2 (1968): 188-93.

17   Driskell, Leon V., and Joan T. Brittain. *The Eternal Crossroads: The Art of Flannery O'Connor*. Lexington: UP of Kentucky, 1971.

See Robert E. Golden's *Guide* 1971.A1.

Representative Reviews: Anon., *Booklist* 1 Jan. 1972: 377; Anon., *Choice* 9.8 (1972): 967; John Alfred Avant, *Library Journal* 96.15 (1971): 2644; Preston M. Browning, Jr., *Contemporary Literature* 16.2 (1975): 260-71; Stuart L. Burns, *Mississippi Quarterly* 27.4 (1974): 483-95; Carol Cleveland, *Review for Religious* 31.2 (1972): 304-5; Scott Donaldson, *Modern Fiction Studies* 18.2 (1972): 281-84; Louise Y. Gossett, *American Literature* 44.3 (1972): 517-19; Charles M. Hegarty, *Studies in Short Fiction* 10.1 (1973): 117-20; Frederick P.W. McDowell, *Southern Review* ns 9.4 (1973): 998-1013.

18   Eggenschwiler, David. *The Christian Humanism of Flannery O'Connor*. Detroit, MI: Wayne State UP, 1972.

See Robert E. Golden's *Guide* 1972.A1.

Representative Reviews: Anon., *Choice* 9.11 (1973): 1446; Charles A. Brady, *Commonweal* 97.4 (1972): 93-4; Preston M. Browning, Jr., *Contemporary Literature* 16.2 (1975): 260-71; Stuart L. Burns, *Mississippi Quarterly* 27.4 (1974): 483-95; John Cunningham, *Southern Humanities Review* 8.3 (1974): 375-88; Robert Drake, *Christian Scholar's Review* 3.2 (1973): 205-08; Joseph E. Jensen, *American Notes & Queries* 12.1 (1973): 14-15; Eileen Kennedy, *Best Sellers* 32.11 (1 Sept. 1972): 253-54; Thomas E. Luddy, *Library Journal* 97.17 (1972): 3159; Irving Malin, *American Literature* 45.1 (1973): 137-38; Barbara Mutkowski, *Thought* 49.193 (1975): 205-06; Paul W. Nisly, *Christianity and Literature* 25 (1976): 53-59; Patrick Henry Reardon, *Review for Religious* 32.1 (1973): 190-91.

19   Feeley, Kathleen. *Flannery O'Connor: Voice of the Peacock*. New Brunswick, NJ: Rutgers UP, 1972. New York: Fordham UP, 1982.

See Robert E. Golden's *Guide* 1972.A2.

Representative Reviews: Anon., *Choice* 9.3 (1972): 368; Anon., *Christian Century* 89.5 (1972): 150; Anon., *Publisher's Weekly* 200.21 (1971): 36; Charles A. Brady, *Commonweal* 97.4 (1972): 93-4; Preston M. Browning, Jr., *Contemporary Literature* 16.2 (1975): 260-71; Carol Cleveland, *Review for Religious* 31.3 (May 1972): 506; John Cunningham, *Southern Humanities Review* 8.3 (1974): 375-88; Robert Drake, *Christian Scholar's Review* 2.3 (1972): 245-47; Louise Y. Gossett, *American Literature* 44.3 (1972): 517-19; Mary McBride, *Library Journal* 97.7 (1972): 1326;

Frederick P.W. McDowell, *Southern Review* ns 9.4 (1973): 998-1013; Saul Maloff, *Commonweal* 90.18 (1969): 490-91; Mary Morton, *Mississippi Quarterly* 37.1 (1983-84): 89-95; Barbara Mutkoski, *America* 126.8 (1972): 212-13; John J. Quinn, *Best Sellers* (1 Feb. 1972): 483-84; Francis Sweeney, *New York Times Book Review* 13 Feb. 1972: 30.

20 Friedman, Melvin J. and Lewis A. Lawson, eds. *The Added Dimension: The Art and Mind of Flannery O'Connor*. New York: Fordham UP, 1966. 2nd rev. ed., 1977.

See Robert E. Golden's *Guide* 1966.A2.

Indicates in "Preface to the Second Edition" that the second edition contains all of the original essays except for those in the section titled "Flannery O'Connor in Her Own Words." Also, added for the second edition is "Preface to the Second Edition"; "Postscript: A Personal Note"; and an essay titled "'The Perplex Business': Flannery O'Connor and Her Critics Enter the 1970s." [Note: Friedman's essay "Flannery O'Connor's Sacred Objects" is not included in the second edition.]

Representative Reviews: Anon., *Catholic Library World* 38.5 (Jan. 1967): 344; Anon., *Critic* 25.4 (1967): 86; Richard Allen Davison, *Studies in Short Fiction* 5.3 (1967-68): 310-11; Robert F. Fleissner, *Southern Review* ns 6.3 (1970): 884-89; Louise Y. Gossett, *American Literature* 39.2 (1967): 245-46; Lois Hartley, *America* 116.2 (1967): 56-57; Jean D. Kellogg, *Christian Century* 21 Dec. 1966: 1575-77; Marion Montgomery, *Georgia Review* 22.2 (1968): 188-93; Miles D. Orvell, *Sewanee Review* 78.1 (1970): 184-92; Richard Thompson, *Library Journal* 92.3 (1967): 581; Thomas F. Walsh, *Modern Language Journal* 52.1 (1968): 32-33.

21 Hendin, Josephine. *The World of Flannery O'Connor*. Bloomington: Indiana UP, 1970.

See Robert E. Golden's *Guide* 1970.A1.

Representative Reviews: Anon., *Booklist* 67.3 (1970): 125; Anon., *Choice* 7.9 (1970): 1232; John Alfred Avant, *Library Journal* 95.13 (1970): 2479; Preston M. Browning, Jr., *Studies in Short Fiction* 8.4 (1971): 653-57; John Cunningham, *Southern Humanities Review* 8.3 (1974): 375-88; Donald Gregory, *Prairie Schooner* 46.3 (1972): 259-60; Warren Leamon, *Georgia Review* 26.3 (1972): 381-84; Frederick P.W. McDowell, *Southern Review* ns 9.4 (1973): 998-1013; Walter Sullivan, *American Literature* 43.1 (1971): 146-47; Brom Weber, *Saturday Review* 18 July 1970: 29-30.

22   Hyman, Stanley Edgar. *Flannery O'Connor*. U of Minnesota Pamphlets
      on American Writers Ser. 54. Minneapolis: U of Minnesota P, 1966; Rpt.
      in *Seven American Women Writers of the Twentieth Century: An
      Introduction*. Ed. Maureen Howard. Minneapolis: U of Minnesota P,
      1977. 311-55.

      See Robert E. Golden's *Guide* 1968.A1.

      Representative Reviews: Anon., *Choice* 3.11 (1967): 1015; Irving Malin,
      Commonweal 85.9 (1966): 269-70; Marion Montgomery, *Georgia Review*
      22.2 (1968): 188-93; Rollene W. Saal, *Saturday Review* 23 Apr. 1966: 50;
      Richard Van Der Beets, *Studies in Short Fiction* 5.1 (1967): 87-88.

23   Martin, Carter W. *The True Country: Themes in the Fiction of Flannery
      O'Connor*. 1969. Nashville: Vanderbilt UP, 1994.

      See Robert E. Golden's *Guide* 1969.A1.

      Representative Reviews: Louise Abbot, *South Atlantic Quarterly* 68.4
      (1969): 566-67; Anon., *Choice* 6.10 (1969): 1397-98; Anon., *Publisher's
      Weekly* 195.3 (1969): 261; Anon., *TLS: Times Literary Supplement* 24
      July 1969: 829; Anon., *Virginia Quarterly Review* 45.4 (1969): R-137;
      Frederick Asals, *Novel* 4.1 (1970): 92-96; Maurice Bassan, *Mississippi
      Quarterly* 22.4 (1969): 370-73; Thomas W. Cummings, *Review for
      Religious* 28.5 (1969): 859-60; John Cunningham, *Southern Humanities
      Review* 8.3 (1974): 375-88; Louise Y. Gossett, *American Literature* 41.3
      (1969): 456; Charles J. Huelsbeck, *Catholic World* 209.1252 (July 1969):
      187, 190; B.R. McElderry, Jr., *Modern Fiction Studies* 15.4 (1969): 550-
      56; Minnie Hite Moody, *Columbus (OH) Dispatch* (15 June 1969): 14;
      Elizabeth R. Nelson, *Library Journal* 94.10 (1969): 1993-94; Miles D.
      Orvell, *Sewanee Review* 78.1 (1970): 184-92; Henry Taylor, *Western
      Humanities Review* 23.4 (1969): 361-62.

24   Muller, Gilbert H. *Nightmares and Visions: Flannery O'Connor and the
      Catholic Grotesque*. Athens: U of Georgia P, 1972.

      See Robert E. Golden's *Guide* 1972.A3.

      Representative Reviews: Anon., *Choice* 10.1 (1973): 96; Anon. *Booklist*
      69.6 (1972): 271-72; Anon., *New York Times Book Review* 1 Oct. 1972:
      38; Preston M. Browning, Jr., *Contemporary Literature* 16.2 (1975): 260-
      71; Stuart L. Burns, *Mississippi Quarterly* 27.4 (1974): 483-95; John
      Cunningham, *Southern Humanities Review* 8.3 (1974): 375-88; Robert
      Drake, *Christian Scholar's Review* 3.2 (1973): 205-08; Sarah Gordon,

Christianity and Literature 24.2 (1975): 52-56; Louise Y. Gossett, *American Literature* 44.4 (1973): 697-98; Lawrence D. Joiner, *Studies in Short Fiction* 11.1 (1974): 113-14; Sammy Staggs, *Library Journal* 97.20 (1972): 3713.

25   Orvell, Miles. *Invisible Parade: The Fiction of Flannery O'Connor.* Philadelphia: Temple UP, 1972. Rpt. with new Preface, *Flannery O'Connor: An Introduction.* Jackson: UP of Mississippi, 1991.

See Robert E. Golden's *Guide* 1972.A4.

Representative Reviews of the Two Editions: Anon., *Choice* 10.6 (1973): 777; Anon., *University Press Book News* 4.2 (1992): 41; Preston M. Browning, Jr., *Contemporary Literature* 16.2 (1975): 260-71; Stuart L. Burns, *Mississippi Quarterly* 27.4 (1974): 483-95; Carol Cleveland, *Review for Religious* 33.3 (1974): 743-45; John Cunningham, *Southern Humanities Review* 8.3 (1974): 375-88; Melvin J. Friedman, *American Literature* 45.2 (1973): 313; Mary Ellis Gibson, *Mississippi Quarterly* 46.4 (1993): 639-50; J.J. Quinn, *Best Sellers* 33.5 (1 June 1973): 118; Gene W. Ruoff, *Western Humanities Review* 27.3 (1973): 312-13; Herbert E. Shapiro, *Library Journal* 98.14 (1973): 2300.

26   Reiter, Robert E., ed. *Flannery O'Connor.* St. Louis: B. Herder, 1968.

See Robert E. Golden's *Guide* 1968.A1.

Representative Reviews: Timothy A. Mitchell, *Social Justice Review* 64.3 (1971): 104.

27   Stephens, Martha. *The Question of Flannery O'Connor.* Baton Rouge: Louisiana State UP, 1973.

See Robert E. Golden's *Guide* 1973.A1.

Representative Reviews: Anon. *Choice* 11.2 (1974): 262; Preston M. Browning, Jr., *Modern Fiction Studies* 21.2 (1975): 298-99; Stuart L. Burns, *Mississippi Quarterly* 27.4 (1974): 483-95; Ronald Di Lorenzo, *Review for Religious* 33.3 (1974): 726-27; Robert J. Dunn, *Flannery O'Connor Bulletin* 5 (1976): 112-18; David Eggenschwiler, *Journal of English and Germanic Philology* 73.4 (1974): 569-72; Melvin J. Friedman, *Southern Literary Journal* 6.2 (1974): 124-29; John L. Idol, *Studies in Short Fiction* 11.4 (1974): 447-49; Claire Katz, *American Literature* 46.2 (1974): 241-42; Brita Lindberg-Seyersted, *English Studies* (Netherlands) 56 (1975): 270-72; Paul W. Nisly, *Christianity and*

Literature 25.2 (1976): 53-59; C. Shapiro, *Novel* 8.1 (1974): 78-80; Sammy Staggs, *Library Journal* 99.3 (1974): 365.

28   Walters, Dorothy. *Flannery O'Connor*. New York: Twayne, 1973. Macmillan, 1976.

See Robert E. Golden's *Guide* 1973.A2.

<u>Representative Reviews</u>: Stuart L. Burns, *Mississippi Quarterly* 27.4 (1974): 483-95; Nancy Y. Hoffman, *Studies in Short Fiction* 10.3 (1973): 294-95; J.O. Tate, *Flannery O'Connor Bulletin* 5 (1976):105-11.

29   Asals, Frederick. *Flannery O'Connor: The Imagination of Extremity.*
Athens: U of Georgia P, 1982.

Asals submits that his "overriding concern . . . is to plot out the most
significant dimensions of the imagination" seen in O'Connor's works, and
"to focus on her fascination with tensions and polarities." Observes her
use of startling and violent dualistic images and her debt to previous
writers of the grotesque. Notes the unreconciled extremes evident in
O'Connor's fiction and outlines how these elements work effectively.
Discusses in the first chapter sources and influences for some of
O'Connor's early stories: "The Geranium," "The Turkey," "The Crop,"
"The Barber," "Wildcat," and "The Train."

Focuses in the following three chapters on O'Connor's artistic practice in
her more mature stories, paying "close attention to texture," while
examining the "crucial and recurrent patterns of character and action" and
exploring "some characteristic habits of mind and the fictional strategies
that embody them." Illustrates points by drawing upon a variety of stories,
then focuses on one story in particular for each chapter. In the fifth
chapter Asals discusses *The Violent Bear It Away*, "both as a culmination
of trends in her fiction after *Wise Blood* and as a significant achievement
in its own right."

Outlines, in the final chapter, the religious dimensions of O'Connor's
imagination, focusing on her aesthetic discrimination. Maintains that
inferences related to her theology "need to be determined within the larger
imaginative structure of her fiction, not outside of it." Is dismayed to note
that studies--including his own--seem to miss "the incorrigible sense of
comedy that animates" O'Connor's creations. Finds her fiction to reflect
"a world of pain dominated by the crucified, not the resurrected Christ,
given over to sharp suffering and sudden death."

Representative Reviews: Anon. *Choice* 20.2 (1982): 262; Robert
Belflower, *Journal of American Studies* 17 (Dec. 1983): 479-80; Beverly
Lyon Clark, *Novel* 16 (1983): 265-68; Sheila Coghill, *Library Journal*
107.12 (1982): 1225; Thomas J. Corr, *College Literature* 11.3 (1984):
293-96; A.R. Coulthard, *American Literature* 55.3 (1983): 470-71;
Frederick Crews, *New York Review of Books* 37.7 (1990): 49-55; John
Cunningham, *Southern Humanities Review* 19.1 (1985): 72-3; John F.
Desmond, *Flannery O'Connor Bulletin* 11 (1982): 131-41; Kathleen J.
Feeley, *Christianity & Literature* 32.3 (1983): 63-65; Melvin J. Friedman,

Review 5 (1983): 149-54; Marshall Bruce Gentry, *Studies in the Novel* 15 (1983): 156-58; Jan Nordby Gretlund, *South Carolina Review* 16.1 (1983): 130-33; William Koon, *Studies in Short Fiction* 20 (Fall, 1983): 342; M.B. McNamee, *Review for Religious* 42.4 (1983): 624-25; Anne Marie Mallon, *Religion and Literature* 17.3 (1985): 63-8; J.R. May, *Horizons* 10.1 (1983): 199-201; William McBrien, *Times Literary Supplement* 21 Jan. 1983: 56; Mary Morton, *Mississippi Quarterly* 37.1 (1983-84): 89-95; Brian Abel Ragen, *Papers on Language & Literature* 27.3 (1991): 386-98; William J. Stuckey, *Modern Fiction Studies* 28.3 (1982): 507-18.

30   Asals, Frederick, ed. and intro. *"A Good Man Is Hard to Find": Flannery O'Connor*. Women Writers Texts and Contexts. New Brunswick, NJ: Rutgers UP, 1993.

Designed as a casebook "for both beginning and advanced students," this work provides an authoritative text of Flannery O'Connor's short story, "A Good Man Is Hard to Find," as well as a twenty-two page Introduction by the editor and a chronology of O'Connor's life and work. Includes two items by O'Connor (introductory remarks at a reading of the story and excerpts from two letters), reprints of critical essays, and a select bibliography.

Notes in Part I of the three-part Introduction that "A Good Man Is Hard to Find" is probably O'Connor's best-known work. Describes the story as one which "makes available more rapidly and obviously than anything else she ever wrote [O'Connor's] unsettling mix of comedy, violence, and religious concern that characterizes her fiction." Details the story's publication history and its place within the context of the 1950s and "Southern nostalgia."

In Part II of the Introduction, Asals discusses at length, and offers specific examples of, the criticism and analysis the story underwent after its publication in Caroline Gordon and Allen Tate's anthology, *The House of Fiction*.

Part III offers insights into the story's meaning. Discusses the design of the story's action (to close the gap between the grandmother and The Misfit), then offers a view of The Misfit as "a variation on that enduring American type, the individualistic male whose violence both expresses and substitutes for inner incompleteness." Comments on the grandmother's various roles, including her adoption at the end of an "archetypal female role." Discusses the impact and overall importance of this story within the context of American literature.

Includes ten critical essays, all reprints:

Bellamy, Michael O. "Everything Off Balance: Protestant Election in Flannery O'Connor's `A Good Man Is Hard to Find,'" Rpt. from *The Flannery O'Connor Bulletin* 8 (1979): 116-24. *See* entry 162.

Bryant, Hallman B. "Reading the Map in `A Good Man Is Hard to Find,'" Rpt. from *Studies in Short Fiction* 18 (1981): 301-07. *See* entry 238.

Doxey, William S. "A Dissenting Opinion of Flannery O'Connor's `A Good Man Is Hard to Find,'" Rpt. from *Studies in Short Fiction* 10 (1973): 199-204. *See* Robert E. Golden's *Guide* 1973.B9.

Dyson, Peter. "Cats, Crime, and Punishment: *The Mikado's* Pitti-Sing in `A Good Man Is Hard to Find,'" Rpt. from *English Studies in Canada* 14 (1988): 436-52. *See* entry 440.

Jones, Madison. "A Good Man's Predicament," Rpt. from *The Southern Review* 20 (1984): 836-41. *See* entry 804.

Marks, W.S., III. "Advertisements for Grace: Flannery O'Connor's `A Good Man Is Hard to Find,'" Rpt. from *Studies in Short Fiction* 4 (1966): 19-27. *See* Robert E. Golden's *Guide* 1966.B29.

Martin, Carter. "`The Meanest of Them Sparkled': Beauty and Landscape in Flannery O'Connor's Fiction," Rpt. from *Realist of Distances: Flannery O'Connor Revisited*. Ed. Karl-Heinz Westarp and Jan Nordby Gretlund (Aarhus, Denmark: Aarhus UP, 1987): 147-59. *See* entry 977.

Scheick, William J. "Flannery O'Connor's `A Good Man Is Hard to Find' and G.K. Chesterton's *Manalive*," Rpt. from *Studies in American Fiction* 11 (1983): 241-45. *See* entry 1366.

Schenck, Mary Jane. "Deconstructed Meaning in [`A Good Man Is Hard to Find']," [Originally published under title: "Deconstructed Meaning in Two Short Stories by Flannery O'Connor"] Rpt. from from *Ambiguities in Literature and Film*. Ed. Hans P. Braendlin (Tallahassee: Florida State UP, 1988): 125-35. *See* entry 1372.

Tate, J.O. "A Good Source Is Not So Hard to Find," Rpt. from *The Flannery O'Connor Bulletin* 9 (1980): 98-102. *See* entry 1514.

Representative Reviews: Gary R. Grund, *Studies in Short Fiction* 32.1 (1995): 121-22; John R. May, *Flannery O'Connor Bulletin* 22 (1993-94): 133-37; Charlotte Templin, *College Literature* 22.2 (1995): 151-56.

31   Bacon, Jon Lance. *Flannery O'Connor and Cold War Culture*. Cambridge
          Studies in American Literature and Culture 72. Cambridge and New
          York: Press Syndicate of the U of Cambridge, 1993.

          Suggests that because "an intertextual approach shows the pervasiveness
          of the Cold War narrative in American culture, it also sheds light on the
          literary narratives that O'Connor created." States that "by treating
          Milledgeville as a site with meaning for historians of the Cold War," one
          is able to "stress the historical contingency of O'Connor's fiction."

          Sees in O'Connor's fiction evidence of how she "dramatized `the
          combination of fright and self-righteousness' . . . attributed to many
          Americans during the Cold War." Argues that as "an American Catholic
          writing for publication during the Cold War," O'Connor "participated in
          a history both political and religious."

          Discusses O'Connor's fiction in relation to films, paintings, political
          speeches, Supreme Court decisions, sociological studies, advertising copy,
          television programs, and the illustrated narratives of comic books. Cites
          her enthusiasm for the works of Marshall McLuhan as evidence that his
          interdisciplinary and intertextual study "would hardly surprise" O'Connor.

          Works discussed include *Mystery and Manners*, "Greenleaf," "A Circle
          in the Fire," "Good Country People," "The Enduring Chill," "A Good Man
          Is Hard to Find," "The Peeler," *Wise Blood*, *The Violent Bear It Away*,
          "The Displaced Person," "A Late Encounter With the Enemy,"
          "Everything That Rises Must Converge," "Judgement Day," "The Barber,"
          "The Artificial Nigger," and "The Life You Save May Be Your Own."

          Representative Reviews: Will Brantley, *Contemporary Literature* 37.1
          (1996): 132-44; Robert H. Brinkmeyer, Jr., *Journal of American Studies*
          29.2 (1995): 259-60; Robert Donahoo, *Texas Review* 15.1-2 (1994): 97-
          99; Marshall Bruce Gentry, *Studies in Short Fiction* 32.2 (1995): 274-76;
          Thomas Schaub, *Modern Fiction Studies* 40.2 (1994): 373-75; Ralph C.
          Wood, *Religion & Literature* 26.3 (1994): 81-88.

32   Balazy, Teresa. *Structural Patterns in Flannery O'Connor's Fiction*. Seria
          Neofilologia 4. Warszawa and Poznaþ (Poland): Paþstwowe Wydawnictwo
          Naukowe, 1982.

          [In English]. Balazy states in her Introduction that while this study is
          concerned with the religious elements of O'Connor's fiction, it focuses "on
          the function and treatment of this dimension in the structure" of *Wise
          Blood*, *The Violent Bear It Away*, and selected stories. Balazy's critique
          emphasizes "the formal aspect" of the fiction over thematic concerns, and

presents "structural models that underlie this fiction as responsible for its unity and coherence."

Distinguishes between O'Connor's religious elements and aspects of the Southern grotesque and examines her views on the modern age "in the light of Christian orthodoxy." Attempts to relate these views to "specific character types and their plights in her work."

Observes that O'Connor's narrative structure constitutes a quest, whereby the "protagonist must acquire and mature in faith . . . [and] leave the profane reality of his natural condition and concern for the sacred reality of grace and redemption." Examines the quest motif in *Wise Blood*, focusing on "the questions of human autonomy and freedom as false notions and obstacles in the protagonist's quest." Discusses *The Violent Bear It Away*, in which "the quest of the protagonist . . . to become a prophet is shown as a violent progress toward true faith."

In her final chapter Balazy examines five of O'Connor's stories that offer "the most frequent patterns of the protagonist's quest." Asserts that in "A Good Man Is Hard to Find," "The Life You Save May Be Your Own," and "The River," a false concept of evil "must be corrected for the fulfillment of the quest." Concludes that in "Everything That Rises Must Converge" and "Parker's Back" protagonists "have to perceive the phenomenon of grace to relate to O'Connor's Christian universe." Ends with a brief discussion of O'Connor criticism in Poland.

33   Balée, Susan. *Flannery O'Connor: Literary Prophet of the South*. Great Achievers: Lives of the Physically Challenged. New York: Chelsea House, 1995.

A profusely illustrated young adult biography, published as part of a series focusing "on the life stories of disabled men and women who have found strength and courage to develop their special talents." Includes a wide variety of biographical details related to O'Connor's life: her interest in peacocks, chickens and other peafowl; the challenges her Lupus Erythematosus presented; her early years in Savannah and Milledgeville; her student days at Georgia State College for Women (now Georgia College & State University) and the University of Iowa's Writer's Workshop; her stay at Yaddo, including a description of the "communist" incident involving Agnes Smedley, Elizabeth Ames, Elizabeth Hardwick, and Robert Lowell; her friendship with Sally and Robert Fitzgerald; the television dramatization of "The Life You Save May Be Your Own" starring Gene Kelly; her visit to Lourdes and audience with the Pope; her work on the Introduction included in *A Memoir of Mary Ann*; and her final days working on short stories included in *Everything That Rises*

Must Converge. Offers excerpts from O'Connor's letters as well as brief outlines and discussions of *Wise Blood*, "The Geranium," "The Displaced Person," "The Artificial Nigger," *The Violent Bear It Away*, "Everything That Rises Must Converge," and "Judgement Day."

Representative Reviews: *CHEERS! The Flannery O'Connor Society Newsletter* 2.2 (1994-95): 1, 4; Sandra B. Connell, *Book Report* 14.4 (1996): 51; Carolyn Phelan, *Booklist* 91.9 (1995): 810; Phyllis Graves, *School Library Journal* 41 (Jan. 1995): 138-39; Carolyn Phelan, *Choice* 32.5 (1995): 810.

34   Baumgaertner, Jill Peláez. *Flannery O'Connor: A Proper Scaring.* Wheaton Literary Ser. Wheaton, IL: Harold Shaw, 1988; Rev. ed. Chicago: Cornerstone, 1998.

Examines O'Connor's interest in exaggerated visual representation and discusses how "sight and insight are intimately connected metaphors" in her stories. Notes how, "At key moments--often at the height of a story's crisis, sometimes at a moment of foreshadowing--O'Connor clicks the camera and catches a strange picture." Ties this technique to seventeenth-century "emblems": visual representations that "literalized a motto, epigram, or scriptural passage to provoke a new response to an old and often too familiar saying." Discusses "The Geranium," "The Barber," "The Crop," "The Turkey," "Good Country People," "The Life You Save May Be Your Own," and "The Comforts of Home" in this context.

Addresses the role of belief in the work of the Christian writer and the difficulty such writers have "in making revelatory action believable to the modern reader." Notes that "the closer and more prolonged her characters' encounters with the divine," the more frequent the appearance of emblems in O'Connor's fiction. Offers readings of "Parker's Back," "The Lame Shall Enter First," "The Artificial Nigger," "The Displaced Person," "A Temple of the Holy Ghost," "The Enduring Chill," and "The River." Also discusses O'Connor's view of sacrament and her use of symbols and images of the Holy Ghost.

Follows with biblically informed readings of "A Good Man Is Hard to Find," "A Late Encounter with the Enemy," "A View of the Woods," "A Circle in the Fire," "Everything That Rises Must Converge," "Greenleaf," and "Revelation."

Describes *Wise Blood* as the story of "a modern pilgrim who does not want to progress, who is in fact more interested in moving backwards than forwards." Explores the "allegoric and emblematic resonance in *The Violent Bear It Away*," noting that the three principal characters, "The

Christian, the Modern Man, [and] the boy," could represent "characters from a morality play, or archetypes from mythology." Closes with a close examination of "Judgement Day," noting that O'Connor hurried her revisions and was "not completely satisfied with the story."

Representative Reviews: Terrence N. Brown, *Criswell Theological Review* 4.2 (1990): 441-43; Tony Brown, *Charlotte (NC) Observer* "Book Week" 25 Sept. 1988: F5; Rebecca Roxburgh Butler, *Flannery O'Connor Bulletin* 17 (1988): 101-04; Henry Carrigan, *Publisher's Weekly* 245.46 (1998): S20; Robert Drake, *Christian Century* 105.24 (1988): 742-43; Gail McGraw Eifrig, *Cresset* 51.8 (1988): 25-28; Kathleen Feeley, *Christianity & Literature* 38.2 (1989): 78-9; Harold Fickett, *Christianity Today* 4 Nov. 1988: 50; Fan Mayhall Gates, *Christian Scholar's Review* 20.3 (1990): 315-16; Arndt Halvorson, *Book Newsletter of Augsburg Publishing House* Nov.-Dec. 1988: 10; Henrietta Ten Harmsel, *Reformed Journal* 39.1 (1989): 28-30; Linda Whitney Hobson, *Mississippi Quarterly* 43.4 (1990): 539-43; Harry L. Poe, *Review and Expositor* 87.3 (1990): 535-36; Maureen Ryan, *American Literature* 62.3 (1990): 527-29; S.W. Whyte, *Choice* 26.1 (1988): 108; Gregory Wolfe, *Eternity* Dec. 1988: 45-46; [Rev. ed.] Virginia Wray, *Flannery O'Connor Bulletin* 26-27 (1998-2000): 190-92.

35   Bloom, Harold, ed. and intro. *Flannery O'Connor*. Modern Critical Views. New York: Chelsea House, 1986.

Contends that this indexed volume brings together the best available criticism on O'Connor's fiction. Comments in the Introduction on *The Violent Bear It Away*, "A Good Man Is Hard to Find" and "A View of the Woods." Suggests that a division exists "between O'Connor's stance as a Catholic moralist, and the extraordinary thematic and narrative violence of her characteristic work."

Includes eleven essays, all reprints except for John Burt's:

Asals, Frederick. "The Double," Rpt. from *Flannery O'Connor: The Imagination of Extremity* by Frederick Asals, U of Georgia P, 1982. *See* entry 115.

Burt, John. "What You Can't Talk About." *See* entry 268.

Fitzgerald, Robert. "*Everything That Rises Must Converge*," Rpt. from "Introduction." *Everything That Rises Must Converge* by Flannery O'Connor. (New York: Farrar, Straus & Giroux, 1965.) *See* Robert E. Golden's *Guide* 1965.B30.

Fitzgerald, Robert. "The Countryside and the True Country," Rpt. from *Sewanee Review* 70.3 (1962). *See* Robert E. Golden's *Guide* 1962.B4.

Hawkes, John. "Flannery O'Connor's Devil," Rpt. from *Sewanee Review* 70.3 (1962). *See* Robert E. Golden's *Guide* 1962.B12.

Humphries, Jefferson. "Proust, Flannery O'Connor, and the Aesthetic of Violence," Rpt. from *The Otherness Within: Gnostic Readings in Marcel Proust, Flannery O'Connor, and François Villon* by Jefferson Humphries, Louisiana State UP, 1983. *See* entry 775.

Lawson, Lewis. "The Perfect Deformity: *Wise Blood*," [Originally titled "Flannery O'Connor and the Grotesque: *Wise Blood*"] Rpt. from *Renascence: Essays on Values in Literature* 17.2 (1965). *See* Robert E. Golden's *Guide* 1965.B47.

Oates, Joyce Carol. "The Visionary Art of Flannery O'Connor," Rpt. from *Southern Humanities Review* 7.3 (1973). *See* entry 1181.

Schleifer, Ronald. "Rural Gothic," [Originally titled "Rural Gothic: The Stories of Flannery O'Connor"] Rpt. from *Modern Fiction Studies* 28.3 (1982). *See* entry 1378.

Shloss, Carol. "Epiphany," Rpt. from *Flannery O'Connor's Dark Comedies* by Carol Shloss, Louisiana State UP, 1980. *See* entry 1422.

Wood, Ralph C. "From Fashionable Tolerance to Unfashionable Redemption," [Originally titled "From Fashionable Tolerance to Unfashionable Redemption: A Reading of Flannery O'Connor's First and Last Stories"] Rpt. from *The Flannery O'Connor Bulletin* 7 (1978). *See* entry 1673.

Representative Reviews: Sharon Felton, *Studies in Short Fiction* 25.4 (1988): 484-85; Brian Abel Ragen, *Papers on Language & Literature* 27.3 (1991): 386-98.

35a   Bloom, Harold, ed. and intro. *Flannery O'Connor: Comprehensive Research and Study Guide*. Bloom's Major Short Story Writers Series. Broomall, PA: Chelsea House, 1999.

"Designed to present biographical, critical, and bibliographical information" on O'Connor's most important short fiction, this volume focuses on four of her stories: "A Good Man Is Hard to Find," "Good Country People," "Everything That Rises Must Converge," and "Revelation."

Discusses, in the Introduction, the influence on O'Connor of William Faulkner's *As I Lay Dying* and Nathanael West's *Miss Lonelyhearts*, and "examines some of the perplexities evoked" by O'Connor's "rather fierce stance towards some of the protagonists in her stories."

Follows with plot summaries of each story examined, a discussion of principal characters, bibliographies of books by O'Connor and about her work, and an "Index of Themes and Ideas."

Includes excerpts from the following "critical views":

"A Good Man Is Hard to Find":

Gardiner, Harold C. "On O'Connor's Clarity of Vision." From "Flannery O'Connor's Clarity of Vision." *The Added Dimension: The Art and Mind of Flannery O'Connor*. Ed. Melvin J. Friedman and Lewis A. Lawson. New York: Fordham UP, 1966. 190-91. *See* Robert E. Golden's *Guide* 1966.B14.

Malin, Irving. "On O'Connor and the Grotesque." From "Flannery O'Connor and the Grotesque." *The Added Dimension: The Art and Mind of Flannery O'Connor*. Ed. Melvin J. Friedman and Lewis A. Lawson. New York: Fordham UP, 1966. 113-14. *See* Robert E. Golden's *Guide* 1966.B28.

Hoffman, Frederick J. "On the Search for Redemption in O'Connor's Fiction." From "The Search for Redemption." *The Added Dimension: The Art and Mind of Flannery O'Connor*. Ed. Melvin J. Friedman and Lewis A. Lawson. New York: Fordham UP, 1966. 33-34. *See* Robert E. Golden's *Guide* 1966.B19.

Kahane, Claire. "Flannery O'Connor's Rage of Vision." From *Critical Essays on Flannery O'Connor*. Ed. Melvin J. Friedman and Beverly Lyon Clark. Boston: G.K. Hall, 1985. 123-24. *See* entry 811.

Knechel, Ruthann. "On O'Connor's Episodic Tales of Sin." From *The Narrative Secret of Flannery O'Connor*. Tuscaloosa, AL: U of Alabama P, 1994. 37-38. *See* entry 55.

Brinkmeyer, Robert H., Jr. "On Asceticism and the Imaginative Vision of O'Connor." From "Asceticism and the Imaginative Vision of Flannery O'Connor." *Flannery O'Connor: New Perspectives*. Ed. Sura P. Rath and Mary Neff Shaw. Athens: U of Georgia P, 1996. 178-79. *See* entry 215.

"Good Country People":

Drake, Robert. "On O'Connor's Fiction." From *Flannery O'Connor: A Critical Essay*. William B. Eerdmans, 1966. 24-26. *See* Robert E. Golden's *Guide* 1966.B9.

Holman, C. Hugh. "On O'Connor and the Southern Literary Tradition." From "Her Rue With a Difference." *The Added Dimension: The Art and Mind of Flannery O'Connor*. Ed. Melvin J. Friedman and Lewis A. Lawson. New York: Fordham UP, 1966. 78-80. *See* Robert E. Golden's *Guide* 1966.B20.

McFarland, Dorothy Tuck. "On O'Connor's Book *A Good Man Is Hard to Find*." From *Flannery O'Connor*. New York: Frederick Ungar, 1976. 35-36. *See* Robert E. Golden's *Guide* 1976.A2.

Di Renzo, Anthony. "On the Word, the Flesh, and the Grotesque in O'Connor's Fiction." From *American Gargoyles: Flannery O'Connor and the Medieval Grotesque*. Carbondale: Southern Illinois UP, 1993. 74-75. *See* entry 41.

Reesman, Jeanne Campbell. "On Women, Language, and the Grotesque in the Work of O'Connor and Welty." From "Women, Language, and the Grotesque in Flannery O'Connor and Eudora Welty." *Flannery O'Connor: New Perspectives*. Ed. Sura P. Rath and Mary Neff Shaw. Athens: U of Georgia P, 1996. 46-47. *See* entry 1315.

McMullen, Joanne Halleran. "On Stylistic Techniques of Annihilation in O'Connor's Fiction." From *Writing Against God: Language as Message in the Literature of Flannery O'Connor*. Macon, GA: Mercer UP, 1996. 16-17. *See* entry 64.

"Everything That Rises Must Converge":

Martin, Carter W. "On O'Connor's Sacramental View." From *The True Country: Themes in the Fiction of Flannery O'Connor*. Nashville: Vanderbilt UP, 1969. 15-17. *See* Robert E. Golden's *Guide* 1969.A1.

Browning, Preston M., Jr. "On O'Connor's Book *Everything That Rises Must Converge*." From *Flannery O'Connor*. Carbondale: Southern Illinois UP, 1974. 100-02. *See* Robert E. Golden's *Guide* 1974.A1.

Dunleavy, Janet Egleson. "On Black and White Roles in O'Connor's Short Fiction." From "A Particular History: Black and White in Flannery O'Connor's Short Fiction." *Critical Essays on Flannery O'Connor*. Ed. Melvin J. Friedman and Beverly Lyon Clark. Boston: G.K. Hall, 1985.

197-98. *See* entry 435.

Kessler, Edward. "On the Violence of Metaphor in O'Connor's Fiction." From *Flannery O'Connor and the Language of the Apocalypse*. Princeton, NJ: Princeton UP, 1986. 42-44. *See* entry 56.

Desmond, John F. "On Community in History in O'Connor's Fiction." From *Risen Sons: Flannery O'Connor's Vision of History*. Athens: U of Georgia P, 1987. 63-82. *See* entry 39.

Gentry, Marshall Bruce. "On Gender Dialogue in O'Connor's Fiction." From "Gender Dialogue in O'Connor." *Flannery O'Connor: New Perspectives*. Ed. Sura P. Rath and Mary Neff Shaw. Athens: U of Georgia P, 1996. 59-60. *See* entry 587.

"Revelation":

Quinn, M. Bernetta. "On O'Connor as a Realist of Distances." From "Flannery O'Connor, a Realist of Distances." *The Art and Mind of Flannery O'Connor*. Ed. Melvin J. Friedman and Lewis A. Lawson. New York: Fordham UP, 1966. 176-77. *See* Robert E. Golden's *Guide* 1966.B31.

Schleifer, Ronald. "On the Stories of Flannery O'Connor." From "Rural Gothic: The Stories of Flannery O'Connor." *Critical Essays on Flannery O'Connor*. Ed. Melvin J. Friedman and Beverly Lyon Clark. Boston: G.K. Hall, 1985. 164. *See* entry 1378.

Gresset, Michael. "On the Audacity of Flannery O'Connor." From "The Audacity of Flannery O'Connor." *Critical Essays on Flannery O'Connor*. Ed. Melvin J. Friedman and Beverly Lyon Clark. Boston: G.K. Hall, 1985. 104-05. *See* entry 670.

Poirier, Richard. "On O'Connor's Fiction." From "If You Know Who You Are You Can Go Anywhere." *Critical Essays on Flannery O'Connor*. Ed. Melvin J. Friedman and Beverly Lyon Clark. Boston: G.K. Hall, 1985. 45-46.

Baumgaertner, Jill P. "On a Proper Scaring in the Fiction of Flannery O'Connor." From *Flannery O'Connor: A Proper Scaring*. Wheaton, IL: Harold Shaw, 1988. 114-15. *See* entry 34.

Yaeger, Patricia. "On O'Connor and the Aesthetics of Torture." From *Flannery O'Connor: New Perspectives*. Ed. Sura P. Rath and Mary Neff Shaw. Athens: U of Georgia P, 1996. 198-99. *See* entry 1701.

36   Brinkmeyer, Robert H., Jr. *The Art and Vision of Flannery O'Connor*.
Southern Literary Studies. Baton Rouge: Louisiana State UP, 1989.

Suggests that O'Connor's fiction "arises from pressure and resistance" and draws "from voices both within and without herself" to test and challenge "her self-conception and her faith." Brinkmeyer acknowledges that his approach is partially based upon "the type of dialogic encounter" seen in Mikhail Bakhtin's work. Remarks that O'Connor's ability to give "free expression to her fundamentalist voice and to other voices of her self rather than monologically suppressing them is a crucial factor behind her artistic greatness."

Explores "the crucial role that the narrator plays in the dynamic of O'Connor's fiction." Discusses *Wise Blood* and *The Violent Bear It Away*, and four stories: "Everything That Rises Must Converge," "The Artificial Nigger," "The Enduring Chill," and "The Lame Shall Enter First." Contends that "the narrator is a central figure in O'Connor's stories, and the narrator's relationship with both O'Connor and the story itself is fraught with tension." Sees the novels as displaying "an intensification of the narrator's perspective," and as having a subject matter that is openly religious and fundamentalist, resulting in "a more charged religious tone and tension." Argues that O'Connor "was pressured" by the narrator and, "as the narrator was, by the narrative, and particularly by the characters and their interactions." Notes that Bakhtin frequently discussed this dynamic and argued that "in the best fiction characters exert profound pressure on the author."

Discusses three types of O'Connor's characters: intellectuals, artists, and prophet-freaks, chosen "because they all embody aspects of O'Connor that, at their extreme, come into potential conflict with her overriding Catholic ideology." Characters discussed include: Sheppard, Rayber, Joy/Hulga Hopewell, Mrs. Hopewell, Asbury, Julian, Calhoun, Mary Elizabeth, Singleton, Old Tarwater, Lucette Carmody, Hazel Motes, The Misfit, and the grandmother.

Suggests that O'Connor had conflicting views regarding her readers, sometimes downplaying their significance while, at other times, arguing that readers "played a crucial role in artistic creation and that writers always had to be aware of, and to take account of" them. Explores these assertions and relates that because she kept her readers in mind when she wrote, O'Connor "entered into a profound interplay with aspects of herself usually suppressed by her ruling Catholicism," a process which brought her Catholic vision "under pressure and challenge."

<u>Representative Reviews</u>: Anon. *University Press Book News* 2.2 (1990): 35; Robinson Blann, *Studies in the Novel* 23.3 (1991): 384-86; Frederick

Crews, *New York Review of Books* 37.7 (1990): 49-55; Joseph Dewey, *Modern Fiction Studies* 36.4 (1990): 576-78; Marshall Bruce Gentry, *South Central Review* 8.2 (1991): 99-100; Benjamin Griffith, *Atlanta Journal Constitution* 4 Feb. 1990: L9; Ann Hulbert, *TLS: Times Literary Supplement* 3 May 1991: 20; Arthur F. Kinney, *Southern Quarterly* 28.4 (1990): 123-25; A. Robert Lee, *Notes and Queries* 39.2 (1991): 246-47; James M. Mellard, *American Literature* 63.1 (1991): 147-48; Charles C. Nash, *Library Journal* 114.19 (1989): 86; Brian Abel Ragen, *Papers on Language & Literature* 27.3 (1991): 386-98; A.G. Tassin, *Choice* 27.10 (1990): 1674; Mary Louise Weaks, *Mississippi Quarterly* 46.1 (1992-93): 149-52; Ralph C. Wood, *Religious Studies Review* 17.1 (1991): 59.

37   Chauhan, Posh Charak. *Religious Humanism in the Fiction of Flannery O'Connor.* New Delhi: Arya Book Depot [30 Naiwala, Karol Bagh, New Delhi, India-110 005], 1995. 231 pp.

Discusses O'Connor's place in American letters, focusing on the influence her Southern heritage had on her opinions and writings and how her work serves "as a manifestation of her religious humanism." Suggests that O'Connor--in such works as "A Late Encounter With the Enemy"--was aware of how Southerners' "pretensions to superiority of birth and breeding were pierced through with the guilt of treachery in the acquisition of Indian lands and the sin of black slavery." Sees O'Connor's work to reflect Faulkner in the way she focuses on "the plain folk of the South" and uses the manners of her region to create her fiction.

Explores, in Chapter 2, O'Connor's views in *Mystery and Manners* "about art, and society," and mines these views for "their aesthetic and social implications." Concludes that O'Connor belongs "to the school of thinkers and artists who believe that reality is something different from social or economic existence." Sees O'Connor's aesthetic views as "in many ways, analogous to those of T.S. Eliot," and offers examples of how she viewed her faith not as a restriction, but as a means of enlarging her sensitivity and powers of observation.

Follows, in Chapter 3, with a discussion of the six short stories O'Connor submitted for her M.F.A. thesis at the University of Iowa in 1947. Finds these stories insightful in illustrating principles which initially governed her work. Notes that none illustrates her preoccupation with religion; rather, the stories reflect her role as "an amused observer of life in her native South." Suggests that, "from the point of view of the development of her art, the thesis stories are comparable, to [T.S.] Eliot's poetry up to and including *The Waste Land.*"

Chapters 4 and 5 offer careful, detailed explications of *Wise Blood* and the stories that comprise O'Connor's collection, *A Good Man Is Hard to Find*. Sees O'Connor as concerned with the alienation of the modern individual from God, and observes that while her protagonists are typically "actively engaged with God," they also try to resist their vocation, "defy it even," and possess a "consuming passion" to attempt to define for themselves their place in the universe and their "relation to a God."

Chapter 6 offers a detailed discussion of *The Violent Bear It Away*, viewed as a tale of "the terrible initiation of a reluctant prophet." Focuses upon the roles of the principal characters: Rayber as "one of O'Connor's superb caricatures of the modern technological rationalist"; Old Tarwater as the "hero"; and Francis Marion Tarwater, whose "richly symbolic" name calls to mind Francis Marion "the `old swamp fox' of the Revolutionary War [and] Tarwater [as] a discredited folk cure all." Concludes that the novel is, for O'Connor, a "denunciation of the modern age and [a] deep rooted critique of it in theological terms."

Explicates in Chapter 7 the stories that comprise *Everything That Rises Must Converge*. Notes that in each of the stories a "self sufficient character meets his nemesis," and that "the action is presented in such a way that there is always scope for the character to be redeemed at the end." Finds three of the stories, "The Enduring Chill," "Revelation," and "Parker's Back" to be "occupied with the operation of revelation and grace upon the spirit through `suprahuman' manifestations."

Concludes with a comparison of O'Connor's "artistic practice" to that of T.S. Eliot, and offers an assessment of her central themes, reputation, and religious views. A 130-item "Works Cited" list follows at the end of the text.

38   Coles, Robert. *Flannery O'Connor's South*. Baton Rouge: Louisiana State UP, 1980. Athens: U of Georgia P, 1993.

Describes the "social scene" and the civil rights movement in Georgia during the early 1960s. Contrasts O'Connor's "northern reader"--and the perspective of the South that he or she brings to a reading--with the version of reality that O'Connor saw and portrayed in her fiction. Discusses O'Connor's view of the *grotesque*, her treatment of black characters, and the various philosophical and religious themes seen in her work. Provides a fairly close, but informal reading of "The Displaced Person." Sees it as reflective of the South as a region, and asserts that, through this story, O'Connor "pursued her main business of storytelling as a means of showing the depth of God's mysteries." Contends that the result is "a series of reminders about God's earth as well as His universe,

His Commandments: a rare and exceedingly high kind of sociology, history, [and] social psychology."

Discusses O'Connor's comment that the South's alienation was "not alienation enough," and her belief that the South was finding itself forced not only out of its sins, but its "few virtues" as well. Considers such topics as pride, intellectual conviction, practical heresies, the South's "old-time religion," and "backwoods fundamentalism" as seen in "Parker's Back," "Good Country People," and "The Artificial Nigger." Suggests that O'Connor's "own theological sophistication enabled her to connect the sights and sounds of back-country, southern twentieth-century life to a history that began in Christ's time, and even before." Illustrates with lengthy explications of *Wise Blood* and "Parker's Back."

Regards O'Connor as a "Southern intellectual" who "steeped herself" in literature, religion, art, psychology "and, in her own sharp fashion, the South's social and political matters." Sees this background evident in "her repeated jabs at social science, psychology, theorists, and . . . the entire liberal, secular world." Reads "The Lame Shall Enter First" as O'Connor's attempt "to dramatize an incompatibility she has seen about her in this modern world: intellectuals who mock traditional religion, then take a certain religious way of getting along with others."

Discusses the contrast between intellectual and spiritual knowledge in "Good Country People," "The Enduring Chill" and *The Violent Bear It Away*. Refers to works by Simone Weil, St. Thomas Aquinas, Sigmund Freud, Carl Jung, and Georges Bernanos. Concludes that O'Connor was "a writer with few peers . . . of enormous promise . . . a soul blinded by faith; hence with an uncanny endowment of sight."

Representative Reviews: Anon. *Choice* 18.3 (1980): 392; Anon. *Kirkus Reviews* 15 Apr. 1980: 548; Anon. *Publisher's Weekly* 217.9 (1980): 84; Anon. *Virginia Quarterly Review* 56.4 (1980): 127; Harold Beaver, *TLS: Times Literary Supplement* 21 Nov. 1980: 1336; John Conarroe, *American Literature* 53.1 (1981): 138-40; Edward K. Eckert, *Cithara* 21 (1982): 40-43; Melissa Conway Flannery, *Best Sellers* 40.4 (1980): 150; Melvin J. Friedman, *Southern Literary Journal* 15.1 (1982): 120-29; Edmund Fuller, *Wall Street Journal* 2 June 1980, eastern ed.: 24; Richard Gray, *Journal of American Studies* 15.2 (1981): 299-300; Patrick G. Hogan, *Studies in Short Fiction* 19.4 (1982): 395-97; Richard King, *New Leader* 8 Sept. 1980: 22-23; William Koon, *Library Journal* 105.8 (1980): 982; Diane McGifford, *Canadian Review of American Studies* 13.3 (1982): 389-96; Anne Marie Mallon, *Religion and Literature* 17.3 (1985): 66; J.J. Quinn, *America* 20 Dec. 1980: 416; William J. Stuckey, *Modern Fiction Studies* 28.3 (1982): 507-18; J.O. Tate, *National Review*

32.17 (1980): 1032-33; Margaret Wimsatt, *Commonweal* 107 (1980): 532-33; Ralph C. Wood, *Christian Century* 98.1 (1981): 25.

39   Desmond, John F. *Risen Sons: Flannery O'Connor's Vision of History*. Athens: U of Georgia P, 1987.

Explores how O'Connor's "vision of history" relates to her creative practice as a literary artist. Argues that the crucial questions "about her vision of history, about the relationship between past and present, about her artistic practice--ultimately lead back to the metaphysical foundation: her radical sense of the order of reality." Disputes assertions by critics "that O'Connor's sense of the order of reality is fundamentally Manichean." Contends instead that O'Connor's "metaphysics, historical vision, and artistic technique all derive specifically from her belief in Christ's Incarnation and Redemption of human history." Regards the impact of this belief to be so strong as to make her artistic and historical vision "inseparable within the creative act." Examines the metaphysical basis of O'Connor's art and considers her growth in sophistication and technique as a writer for the purpose of determining whether it is connected to her own theological development, thinking, and vision. Explores this issue "to emphasize the dynamic of her growth against the habit [by many critics] of seeing her thought and art in a totally monolithic way."

Representative Reviews: Robert H. Brinkmeyer, *Studies in Short Fiction* 25.2 (1988): 169-70; Elizabeth Brown-Guillory, *American Literature* 60.3 (1988): 497-98; William Burke, *Modern Fiction Studies* 34.2 (1988): 247-49; Patrick W. Carey, *Catholic World* 232.1390 (July-Aug. 1989): 183-84; Robert Drake, *Christianity and Literature* 37.3 (1988): 60-61; Sally Fitzgerald, *Religion and Literature* 21.1 (1989): 137-48; Melvin J. Friedman, *International Fiction Review* 15.2 (1988): 179-81; Michael Kowaleski, *Southern Quarterly* 27.4 (1989): 112-14; L. Lawson, *Southern Literary Journal* 23.1 (1990): 107-12; Edward Quinn, *Mississippi Quarterly* 43.1 (1989-90): 117-19; Brian Abel Ragen, *Papers on Language & Literature* 27.3 (1991): 386-98; Linda D. Schlafer, *Flannery O'Connor Bulletin* 16 (1987): 86-89; N.M. Tischler, *Choice* 25.6 (1988): 903.

40   Dibble, Terry J. *Flannery O'Connor's Short Stories: Notes*. Ed. Gary Carey. Lincoln, NB: Cliffs Notes, 1986. [Cover title: *Cliffs Notes on O'Connor's Short Stories*].

Dibble's *Cliff's Notes* are intended to provide readers with critical evaluations of eleven of O'Connor's short stories. Includes a three-page biographical sketch along with two brief essays and a list of "Suggested Essay Questions." A select bibliography refers readers to O'Connor's works, the *Flannery O'Connor Bulletin*, and sixteen critical commentaries.

Stories explicated include: "A Good Man Is Hard to Find," "The Life You Save May Be Your Own," "The River," "A Late Encounter With the Enemy," "The Displaced Person," "The Artificial Nigger," "Good Country People," "Everything That Rises Must Converge," "Revelation," "Parker's Back," and "Judgement Day."

41   DiRenzo, Anthony. *American Gargoyles: Flannery O'Connor and the Medieval Grotesque*. 1993. Carbondale: Southern Illinois UP, 1995.

Finds the roots of O'Connor's grotesque fiction "located in medieval folk art." Describes the purposes of grotesque art, focusing on its "comic shock treatment."

Sees the climactic scene of "The Artificial Nigger" as a key to understanding O'Connor's grotesque style. Describes O'Connor's art as mocking and challenging "a restricted point of view," that of idealized beauty or propriety, only to be labeled "ugly and evil." Contends that her "deranged fundamentalists" serve as freakish, crippled gargoyles who "measure `a grotesque distance' between their Christian subculture and that of `the liberal secular' world."

Outlines how O'Connor uses Christ as the ideal behind her satire, an ideal "that must be degraded as well as exalted if it is ever to be a living presence in the physical world." Offers evidence to support Stanley Edgar Hyman's claim that "Christ is the real hero" of O'Connor's fiction. Discusses, in this context, *Wise Blood*, "The Displaced Person" ("an ironic passion play"), and "Parker's Back" (a sacrilegious, "Punch-and-Judy show about the difference between religion and faith").

Finds O'Connor's regard for the body reflective of a medieval outlook and unique in American fiction, "distinguished by its candor and unflinching realism." Sees her characters as "both beautiful and ugly, impressive and ludicrous." Discusses, in this context, Mrs. Shortley of "The Displaced Person," Ruby of "A Stroke of Good Fortune," Hulga of "Good Country People," the twelve-year-old girl of "A Temple of the Holy Ghost," Tarwater of *The Violent Bear It Away*, and Nelson of "The Artificial Nigger."

Examines *The Violent Bear It Away*, focusing on Francis Marion Tarwater, "one of O'Connor's grimmest protagonists, so serious that he is unintentionally funny." Finds the work to be a mixture of "prophecy and satire, holy seriousness and unholy flippancy." Reads "A Circle in the Fire" as a disturbing religious story" in which "the meek inherit the land by burning it," and reflective of O'Connor's "complicated humor" derived from demonic elements. Considers "The River" an illustration of how blasphemy and grotesqueness can serve the same satirical purpose. Offers a twenty-eight page explication of "A Good Man Is Hard to Find," seen as O'Connor's "little masterpiece" and "a crash course in the grotesque."

Sees O'Connor as a chronicler of the collapse of the subculture of the white American South, who leaves Southern literature "`demythified.'" Discusses, in the context of this contention, O'Connor's narrator, her use of the role of carnival, and offers readings of *The Violent Bear It Away*, "A Late Encounter with the Enemy," "The Partridge Festival," "The Enduring Chill," "Judgement Day," "Revelation," and "The River."

Representative Reviews: Jill Peláez Baumgaertner, *American Literature* 66.3 (1994): 607-08; Gary M. Ciuba, *Flannery O'Connor Bulletin* 22 (1993-94): 140-43; Marshall Bruce Gentry, *Studies in Short Fiction* 32.2 (1995): 119-21; J.W. Hall, *Choice* 31.5 (1994): 778-79; David J. Knauer, *Mississippi Quarterly* 49.1 (1995-96): 127-32; Ralph C. Wood, *Religion & Literature* 26.3 (1994): 81-88.

42   Driggers, Stephen G. and Robert J. Dunn with Sarah Gordon. *The Manuscripts of Flannery O'Connor at Georgia College*. Athens: U of Georgia P, 1989.

Describes the arrangement of the manuscripts in the collection and notes that they illustrate how O'Connor "often produced dozens of variants of single episodes." Discusses in particular the large number of drafts that exist for her last two stories ("Parker's Back" and "Judgement Day"), and indicates that they "suggest the amount of rewriting O'Connor normally did and, consequently, how many of the drafts for her other fiction are missing." Entries in this catalog "describe the physical appearance of the manuscripts in the folders and files, and the plot, characters, and stylistic and formal characteristics of their contents." Details the arrangement of the 905 folders in 297 files and how they are cross-referenced to other related files. Provides an index which "shows the order of the files and folders . . . [and] how [Driggers's] file numbers differ" from Dunn's. Also included is a timeline indicating dates O'Connor is believed to have worked on each piece of fiction.

Representative Reviews: Anon. *American Literature* 62.2 (1990): 373; Anon. *Reference & Research Book News* 4.6 (1989): 29 [Listing only]; Robert Aiken, *American Reference Books Annual: 1990* 21 (1990): 488;

Gerald Becham, *Georgia Librarian* 27.1 (1990): 19-20; Valerie Macys, *Papers of the Bibliographical Society of America* 83.3 (1989): 401-03; John N. Somerville, Jr. *Mississippi Quarterly* 43.2 (1990): 249-52; Ralph C. Wood, *Flannery O'Connor Bulletin* 18 (1989): 99-105.

42a   Edmondson, Henry T., III. *Return to Good and Evil: Flannery O'Connor's Response to Nihilism.* Lanham, MD: Lexington Books, [Expected date of publication is June, 2002.]

Organizes O'Connor's fiction around her principal preoccupation, cultural and philosophical nihilism; and, by recourse to her fiction, correspondence, prose, and personal library, demonstrates how she attempts to refute the modern nihilistic threat with the theology and philosophy of St. Thomas Aquinas. [Abstract provided by the author.]

43   Enjolras, Laurence. *Flannery O'Connor's Characters.* Lanham, MD: UP of America, 1998.

Contends that O'Connor depicts the human body as "ugly" and viewed her characters as "monsters who assail" her readers. Suggests that her plots "could easily turn into nightmares" as the scenes she depicts "come to life not so much with people as with ghastly substitutes." Alleges that even when her characters are not crippled, they "appear as caricatures" because, for her, the human body is not worthy of "dignity or respectability." Closes with the suggestion that O'Connor's depiction of "physical ugliness and suffering, horrible events, and violent deaths should not distress the oversensitive reader" but be understood as opportunities for salvation.

44   Farmer, David R. *Flannery O'Connor: A Descriptive Bibliography.* Garland Reference Library of the Humanities. New York: Garland, 1981.

Describes O'Connor's published writings, including posthumously published works, from her early contributions to journals at Georgia State College for Women, through the stories and books that formed the bulk of her canon, to the letters collected in *The Habit of Being* (1979). Includes all first appearances of her work, later editions, and impressions. In addition to the descriptive list of O'Connor's books, the volume also covers books written by others and writings published in pamphlets, periodicals, book reviews, and books authored by others. Describes, in a separate section, adaptations, including films and parodies based upon her work.

Representative Reviews: Anon. *Choice* 19.3 (1981): 356; Gerald Becham, *Flannery O'Connor Bulletin* 11 (1982): 129-30; Gerald Becham, *RQ* 21.2

(1981): 197-98; Bernice Bergup, *American Reference Books Annual* 13 (1982): 659-60; George Bixby, *American Book Collector* 3-4 (1982): 48-50; Melvin J. Friedman, *Southern Literary Journal* 15.1 (1982): 120-29.

45   Fickett, Harold, and Douglas R. Gilbert. *Flannery O'Connor: Images of Grace.* Illus. Douglas R. Gilbert. Grand Rapids, MI: Eerdmans, 1986.

Part I, *Life and Work,* by Harold Fickett (pp. 1-111), offers an introductory critical-biography of O'Connor, amply illustrated with photographs. Traces her growth as a writer and believer by focusing on her artistic development and her views of sin and salvation as they apply to her work. Provides an outline of O'Connor's life, her relationship with her parents, and suggests that she developed a character that was "highly sensitive and fiercely independent." Describes her adolescent years and relates them to "A Temple of the Holy Ghost"; discusses her participation in Paul Engle's Writer's Workshop at Iowa, her year at Yaddo, and her subsequent moves to New York and Ridgefield, Conn. Reports on her attack of lupus in late 1950; her treatment with ACTH; and her move back to Milledgeville, Georgia, which "enriched her appreciation of her region dramatically." Suggests that in *Wise Blood* O'Connor "won her way through to the narrative method that characterizes her mature work." Offers a close reading of *The Violent Bear It Away* and considers her use of foreshadowing and symbolic imagery. Discusses why O'Connor wrote the Introduction to *A Memoir of Mary Ann.* Relates that because O'Connor sought to be present to readers only through her writing, she probably would not have approved of attempts to more fully understand her fiction through her letters. Contends that she would have preferred that her life be read "as a supreme example of the triumph of the imagination over individual circumstance." Offers readings of "The Displaced Person" and "Revelation," asserting that the latter is a story that "only a great artist in possession of her powers would have the audacity to write." Concludes with a discussion of O'Connor's final days.

Part II, *Images,* by Douglas R. Gilbert (pp. 112-51), provides a photographic essay consisting of thirty-three black and white photographs accompanied by selections from *Mystery and Manners* and *The Habit of Being.* Scenes convey the rural nature of O'Connor's region: its dirt roads, gardens, clear-cut and plowed fields, and people at work, leisure, and worship. Particular focus is on religious images: rural churches, Sunday worship services, a cemetery memorial, and a final photograph of a river scene accompanied by text from "The River."

Representative Reviews: Anon. *American Literature* 58.4 (1986): 676; Anon. *Christian Century* 103.32 (1986): 955; Patricia Demers, *Canadian Catholic Review* 5.3 (1987): 105-06; Joe Dewey, *Modern Fiction Studies*

33.2 (1987): 323-26; Kathleen Feeley, *Review for Religious* 46.4 (1987): 626-27; Francis Fike, *Christianity and Literature* 37.2 (1988): 60-61; Marshall Bruce Gentry, *Publications of the Arkansas Philological Association* 13.1 (1987): 83-85; Jan Nordby Gretlund, *Mississippi Quarterly* 40.2 (1987): 118-22; Peter S. Hawkins, *Christian Scholar's Review* 17.1 (1987): 82-83; Jonathan Kirsch, *Los Angeles Times Book Review* 27 July 1986: 6; Mel Lorentzen, *Eternity* 38.2 (1987): 36; J. Ramsey Michaels, *Daughters of Sarah* 13.6 (1987): 28-29; Paul W. Nisly, *Christianity Today* 30.18 (1986): 64; William J. O'Brien, *Religious Studies Review* 13.2 (1987): 163; J.J. Quinn, *Best Sellers* 46.7 (1986): 263; Tim Unsworth, *Salt* 6.9 (1986): 29-31; Ralph C. Wood, *Flannery O'Connor Bulletin* 16 (1987): 90-94.

46   Friedman, Melvin J., and Beverly Lyon Clark, eds. *Critical Essays on Flannery O'Connor*. Critical Essays on American Lit. Boston: G.K. Hall, 1985.

Includes twenty-eight reviews and critical essays related to O'Connor's life and work, all reprints except for selections by Irving Malin and Janet Egleson Dunleavy. Selections are arranged into three sections: the first offers twelve reviews dealing with O'Connor's two novels, and her collections of short stories and essays; the second provides "tributes and reminiscences"; and the third includes "a chronological record of the critical response to the writing."

Contents of the volume include:

Asals, Frederick. "[The Limits of Explanation]," Rpt. from "Flannery Row," *Novel* 4.1 (1970). *See* Robert E. Golden's *Guide* 1970.B4.

Bleikasten, André. "The Heresy of Flannery O'Connor," Rpt. from *Les Américanistes* by Ira D. and Christiane Johnson. Port Washington, NY: Kennikat Press, 1978. *See* entry 178.

Burns, Marian. "O'Connor's Unfinished Novel," Rpt. from *Flannery O'Connor Bulletin* 11 (1982). *See* entry 262.

Clark, Beverly Lyon and Caroline M. Brown "A Review of O'Connor Criticism." *See* entry 313.

Coffey, Warren. "Flannery O'Connor," Rpt. from *Commentary* (Nov. 1965). *See* Robert E. Golden's *Guide* 1965.B19.

Duhamel, P. Albert. "Flannery O'Connor's Violent View of Reality," Rpt. from *Catholic World* 190.1139 (Feb. 1960). *See* Robert E. Golden's *Guide* 1960.B22.

Dunleavy, Janet Egleson. "A Particular History: Black and White in Flannery O'Connor's Short Fiction." *See* entry 435.

Ferris, Sumner J. "The Outside and the Inside: Flannery O'Connor's *The Violent Bear It Away*," Rpt. from *Critique* 3.2 (1960). *See* Robert E. Golden's *Guide* 1960.B25.

Friedman, Melvin. "Flannery O'Connor: The Canon Completed, the Commentary Continuing," Rpt. from *Southern Literary Journal* 5.2 (1973). *See* Robert E. Golden's *Guide* 1973.B11.

Friedman, Melvin J. "Flannery O'Connor in France: An Interim Report," Rpt. from *Revue des Langues Vivantes* 43 (1977). *See* entry 561.

Gordon, Caroline. "With a Glitter of Evil," Rpt. from *New York Times Book Review*, 12 June 1955. *See* Robert E. Golden's *Guide* 1955.B16.

Gresset, Michel. "The Audacity of Flannery O'Connor," Rpt. from *La Nouvelle Revue Française* 216 (Dec. 1970). *See* entry 670.

Hawkes, John. "Flannery O'Connor's Devil," Rpt. from *Sewanee Review* 70 (1962). *See* Robert E. Golden's *Guide* 1962.B12.

Kahane, Claire. "Flannery O'Connor's Rage of Vision," Rpt. from *American Literature* 46.1 (1974). *See* entry 811.

Kazin, Alfred. "Flannery O'Connor: The Complete Stories," Rpt. from *New York Times Book Review*, 28 Nov. 1971. *See* Robert E. Golden's *Guide* 1971.B16.

Malin, Irving. "Singular Visions: `The Partridge Festival.'" *See* entry 963.

Maloff, Saul. "On Flannery O'Connor," Rpt. from *Commonweal*, 8 Aug. 1969. *See* Robert E. Golden's *Guide* 1969.B27.

Merton, Thomas. "Flannery O'Connor: A Prose Elegy," Rpt. from *Raids on the Unspeakable*. New York: Harcourt Brace, 1983. *See* entry 1066.

Poirier, Richard. "If You Know Who You Are You Can Go Anywhere," Rpt. from *New York Times Book Review*, 30 May 1965. *See* Robert E. Golden's *Guide* 1965.B62.

Porter, Katherine Anne. "Gracious Greatness," Rpt. from *Esprit* 8 (1964). *See* Robert E. Golden's *Guide* 1964.B69.

Rubin, Louis D., Jr. "Two Ladies From the South," Rpt. from *Sewanee Review* 63 (1955). *See* Robert E. Golden's *Guide* 1955.B23.

Schleifer, Ronald. "Rural Gothic: The Stories of Flannery O'Connor." *See* entry 1378.

Simons, John W. "A Case of Possession," Rpt. from *Commonweal*, 27 June 1952. *See* Robert E. Golden's *Guide* 1952.B14.

Sonnenfeld, Albert. "Flannery O'Connor: The Catholic Writer as Baptist," Rpt. from *Contemporary Literature* 13 (1972). *See* Robert E. Golden's *Guide* 1972.B39.

Stallings, Sylvia. "Young Writer With a Bizarre Tale to Tell," Rpt. from *New York Herald Tribune Book Review*, 18 May 1952. *See* Robert E. Golden's *Guide* 1952.B16.

Tate, Allen. "Platitudes and Protestants," Rpt. from *Esprit* 8 (1964). *See* Robert E. Golden's *Guide* 1964.B83.

Walker, Alice. "Beyond the Peacock: The Reconstruction of Flannery O'Connor," Rpt. from *In Search of Our Mothers' Gardens*. San Diego: Harcourt Brace, 1983. *See* entry 1572.

Warnke, Frank J. "A Vision Deep and Narrow," Rpt. from *New Republic*, 14 March 1960. *See* Robert E. Golden's *Guide* 1960.59.

Representative Reviews: Sarah Gordon, *Flannery O'Connor Bulletin* 14 (1985): 115-17; Brian Abel Ragen, *Papers on Language & Literature* 27.3 (1991): 386-98; S.W. Whyte, *Choice* 23.4 (1985): 602.

47   Gentry, Marshall Bruce. *Flannery O'Connor's Religion of the Grotesque.* Jackson: UP of Mississippi, 1986.

Focuses on the strategies O'Connor uses to move her characters toward achieving redemption. States that Mrs. Shortley of "The Displaced Person," and the grandmother of "A Good Man is Hard to Find," serve "as extreme examples of the two contrasting transformations O'Connor dramatizes." Contends that "the energy for Mrs. Shortley's redemption comes primarily from within her own psyche, while the grandmother's awakening is forced upon her." Notes that O'Connor "dramatize[s] Mrs. Shortley's peculiar sort of redemption in many works," while "the grandmother's more traditional version of redemption--requiring a conscious response to outside forces--appears rarely" in her fiction.

Groups O'Connor's stories into those which demonstrate "the positive grotesque" wherein characters "bring about their own redemption": "Revelation," "The Enduring Chill," "A Circle in the Fire," "Greenleaf," "A Temple of the Holy Ghost," "The Partridge Festival," "Parker's Back," "The Artificial Nigger," and "Judgement Day"; and stories in which "transformation comes from outside," wherein "negative grotesquerie" prevails: "A Late Encounter with the Enemy," "A Stroke of Good Fortune," "The River," and "Everything That Rises Must Converge."

Examines Mrs. McIntyre, of "The Displaced Person," and The Misfit of "A Good Man Is Hard to Find," described as characters "who do not complete a grotesque self-redemption." Notes two other stories with similar outcomes: "The Life You Save May Be Your Own" and "Good Country People."

Offers readings of O'Connor's two novels, *Wise Blood* and *The Violent Bear It Away*, demonstrating how they "constitute her most complex involvement with the grotesque." Concludes that "the reader of O'Connor is encouraged to produce an extremely personal reading," as it appears that O'Connor's "greatest act of faith as a writer [was] to assume that 'misreadings' of her work might turn out to be so many more paths to redemption."

[Note: excerpt from the introductory chapter was published as, "Tracks to the Oven of Redemption," *Flannery O'Connor Bulletin* 15 (1985): 72-79.]

Representative Reviews: Frederick Asals, *Canadian Review of American Studies* 18.2 (Summer 1987): 231-33; Nancy Bright, (Jackson, MS) *Clarion-Ledger* 27 July 1986: F3; Robert H. Brinkmeyer, *Southern Literary Journal* 20.1 (1987): 145-48; Virginia Spencer Carr, *American Literary Scholarship: An Annual 1986* (Durham: Duke UP, 1988): 269; A.R. Coulthard, *American Literature* 59.1 (1987): 146-47; Sally Fitzgerald, *Religion and Literature* 21.1 (1989): 137-48; A.J. Griffith, *Choice* 24.2 (1986): 306; Keith A. Jenkins, *South Central Review* 5.1 (1987): 104-06; Gail Mortimer, *Southern Quarterly* 26.3 (1988): 76-77; Miles D. Orvell, *Journal of Modern Literature* 13 (1986): 518-19; Brian Abel Ragen, *Papers on Language & Literature* 27.3 (1991): 386-98; Sura P. Rath, *Flannery O'Connor Bulletin* 15 (1986): 82-87.

48   Getz, Lorine M. *Flannery O'Connor: Her Life, Library and Book Reviews.* Studies in Women & Religion 5. New York: Edwin Mellen, 1980.

Divided into four parts, this indexed volume offers a perspective of O'Connor's intellectual activities, including the collected holdings of her personal library--housed in the Flannery O'Connor Memorial Room at Georgia College & State University--and reprints of her book reviews. Includes a 55-page literary biography focusing on how O'Connor's fiction reflects "her response to the influence of her societal, familial, religious, and literary milieu." Describes O'Connor's personal library, including a list of its volumes, inscriptions, and annotations. Examines the collection "to determine the literary and religious spectrum against which she developed as an intellectual and critic." Outlines O'Connor's work "as a book critic," presenting, in chronological order of publication, texts of her published reviews and lists of all her known reviews, published and unpublished.

Representative Reviews: Anon. *Choice* 18.10 (1981): 1416; Anon. *Washington Post Book World* 11.3 (1981): 8; Frederick Asals, *Flannery O'Connor Bulletin* 9 (1980): 132-36; Melvin J. Friedman, *Southern Literary Journal* 15.1 (1982): 120-29; Anne E. Patrick, *Journal of the American Academy of Religion* 50.1 (1982): 148; Linda Schlafer, *Flannery O'Connor Bulletin* 11 (1982): 43-57; June Schlueter, *Studies in Short Fiction* 19.1 (1982): 92-93; William J. Stuckey, *Modern Fiction Studies* 28.3 (1982): 514-18; 30.4 (1984): 832-34; Ralph Wood, *Religious Studies Review* 7.4 (1981): 345.

49   Getz, Lorine M. *Nature and Grace in Flannery O'Connor's Fiction.* Studies in Art and Religious Interpretation 2. New York: Mellen, 1982.

Examines the literary structures and devices O'Connor employs in her narratives to depict various types of grace: Thomistic grace in "A Temple of the Holy Ghost" and "The Artificial Nigger"; Augustinian grace in "Greenleaf" and "Everything That Rises Must Converge"; and Jansenistic grace in "Parker's Back" and "The Comforts of Home."

Discusses in detail "The Lame Shall Enter First," which is regarded as an exception to O'Connor's method and concerns in that "it portrays more the absence than the presence of grace." Suggests that O'Connor's method in this story appears "Augustinian and Jansenistic" in that she uses "literary devices in such a way as to present a new mode, analogous to a Manichaean understanding of the relation of nature and supernatural." Comments further on two other exceptions to O'Connor's narratives of grace: "The Partridge Festival" ("a narrative of `no grace'") and "Judgement Day," which "portrays nature to be so closely related to grace that no distinction between the two is possible."

This study is footnoted, indexed, and includes a bibliography of works by and about O'Connor, including some unpublished material.

Representative Reviews: W.J. Stuckey, *Modern Fiction Studies* 30.4 (1984): 832-34.

50   Giannone, Richard. *Flannery O'Connor and the Mystery of Love.* Urbana: U of Illinois P, 1989; New York: Fordham UP, 1999.

Notes a "uniformity of attitude" among critics and suggests that their focus on seeking "the source of sin" in O'Connor's characters "cramps debate." Contends that critics should, instead, focus on how O'Connor's sinners *atone* for their sins.

Examines the empowering and "joyous" aspect of O'Connor's fiction and contends that it illustrates how her writings may be viewed as a "work of intimacy and ennobled humanity." Offers careful and detailed explications of virtually all of O'Connor's fiction as reflecting O'Connor's own overlooked "great tenderness of spirit" and "controlled abandonment to love."

Representative Reviews: Anon. *Reference & Research Book News* 4.6 (1989): 29 [Listing only]; J.R. Baker, *Religion and Literature* 23.1 (1991): 103-4; Gary M. Ciuba, *Thought* 66.260 (1991): 115-17; Francis Fike, *Christianity and Literature* 39.3 (1990): 349-51; Karen Fitts, *College Literature* 18.1 (1991): 99-100; Melvin J. Friedman, *International Fiction Review* 17.1 (1990): 70-72; M. Gillan, *Choice* 27.6 (1990): 949; Lisa Honaker, *Modern Fiction Studies* 36.2 (1990): 240-42; Catherine Kenney, *Christian Century* 107.11 (1990): 344-45; Bonnie Lyons, *Studies in Short Fiction* 27.3 (1990): 425-26; Alice Hall Petry, *Southern Literary Journal* 23.2 (1991): 110-12; Brian Abel Ragen, *Papers on Language & Literature* 27.3 (1991): 386-98; Maureen Ryan, *American Literature* 62.3 (1990): 527-29; John N. Somerville, Jr., *Mississippi Quarterly* 43.2 (1990): 249-52; M.S. Stephenson, *Choice* 37.5 (2000): 930; W.J. Stuckey, *Modern Fiction Studies* 30.4 (1984): 832-34; Ralph C. Wood, *Flannery O'Connor Bulletin* 18 (1989): 99-102.

50a   Giannone, Richard. *Flannery O'Connor: Hermit Novelist.* Urbana and Chicago: U of Illinois P, 2000.

Examines O'Connor's themes of the desert life, ascetic spirituality, and self-denial. Suggests that her "reapplication of desert spirituality" from such works as *The Life of Anthony*, *The Sayings of the Desert Fathers*, and *The Lives of the Desert Fathers*, magnifies the "allure and magnificence" of her fiction. Contends O'Connor's depiction of characters amid a "desert life of solitude and trial," provided her with an ideal against which she could judge "the heart-wounding dissensions of American life."

Traces in the first chapter, "The Hermit Novelist," O'Connor's "interest in desert monastics" and finds it to flower "in the course of her artistic development." Contends that she "found a wisdom in the desert fathers (abbas) and mothers (ammas) that stirred her imagination with possibilities for replenishing our century." Follows with a discussion of the "personal, biblical, and aesthetic forces" which undergird her "evolving sympathy with the spiritual experiment of the ancient Christian East."

Focuses in chapter two, "Hazel Motes and the Desert Tradition," on how in *Wise Blood*, "renunciation guides Hazel Motes to integrity." Outlines how his "ascetic search unfolds," examines the ascetic life, and argues that *Wise Blood* may be considered "the Ur-text of O'Connor's asceticism." Concludes that, "by facing out his unbelief through bodily mortification," Hazel Motes "finds a consoling wholeness in solitude that is denied him in the broken modern world."

Discusses in the third chapter, "Sporting with Demons," five stories in *A Good Man Is Hard to Find*. Sees in each protagonist of "The Life You Save May Be Your Own," "A Stroke of Good Fortune," "A Circle in the Fire," "Good Country People," and "A Late Encounter With the Enemy" an individual "vanquished by the demonic temptation to love his or her own desire above the good of another character or above the will of God."

Turns in the fourth chapter, "Entering a Strange Country," to the remaining five stories in *A Good Man Is Hard to Find*: the title story, "The River," "A Temple of the Holy Ghost," "The Artificial Nigger," and "The Displaced Person." Finds the protagonists of these stories to be responsive "to the call of the desert," and sees them as among the few who will "survive the era's evil without being corrupted by it."

Explores in the fifth chapter, "The Prophet and the Word in the Desert," the "impulses and cultural significance of asceticism and the trials of solitude" in *The Violent Bear It Away*. Outlines the historical context that gives "meaning to religious withdrawal in the novel," and refers to the biblical and patristic sources which generate the ascetic action of Tarwater's struggle against the demons that plague him. Views the novel as "the story of the ancient Egyptian desert set in the American South." Examines "how, through the poetics of solitude," O'Connor creates "'a very minor hymn to the Eucharist' [that] comes together like a liturgical song." Sees Tarwater as destined to be "a holy terror in distributing the news that pulsates in his blood."

Considers in the sixth chapter, "Acedia *and* Penthos," two conditions discussed by ancient hermits. The first, *acedia*, one of eight categories of evil, is "a state of the soul . . . linked to solitude" and marked by "indolence, tedium, disgust, despondency, and bitterness." The second, *penthos*, is "linked to the awareness of personal sin." Individuals subject to either of these conditions mourn "for the possible loss of eternal happiness for oneself and all others." Illustrates the presence of these states of being in O'Connor's characters through explications of three stories from *Everything That Rises Must Converge*: the title story, "The Comforts of Home," and "Greenleaf."

Continues in the seventh chapter, "Vision and Vice," with explications of three more stories from *Everything That Rises Must Converge*: "A View of the Woods," "The Lame Shall Enter First," and "Revelation." Focuses on characters who "see themselves as virtuous," but who use their concern for others as "the basis for their own dignity and superiority." Suggests that O'Connor's use of the "shock of recognition" demolishes "the fabricated vision" of these individuals so they may heal "in the form of a new integrity."

Discusses in the concluding chapter, "The Power of Exile," the three remaining stories from *Everything That Rises Must Converge*: "Parker's Back," "The Enduring Chill," and "Judgement Day." Considers how solitary characters in these stories turn their loneliness into an encounter with a "divine loneliness" from which they may "draw divine light." Maintains that "in showing how God's help enters the exile's life, these stories not only tell a story but also fix a vision of grace."

In assessing O'Connor's accomplishments, Giannone remarks, "From her remote perch in Baldwin County [Georgia], O'Connor saw an America that no other writer has got right. Now we cannot see it without seeing O'Connor. From our basis of poverty in the desert, we can only be grateful for the miracle of O'Connor's correcting our vision by her perception of divine love revealing that we, greatly loved, are participants in the lasting drama crystallizing around the word uttered and acted in the desert."

Representative Reviews: Ralph C. Wood, *Flannery O'Connor Bulletin* 26-27 (1998-2000): 182-85.

51   Golden, Robert E. and Mary C. Sullivan. *Flannery O'Connor and Caroline Gordon: A Reference Guide*. Reference Guides in Literature. Boston: G.K. Hall, 1977.

Divided into two sections: the first, by Robert E. Golden, covers Flannery O'Connor; the second, by Mary C. Sullivan, covers Caroline Gordon.

Golden's section provides an indexed, comprehensive, chronological descriptive bibliography--excluding transient mentions and material contained in standard reference sources--of reviews, articles, books and other secondary materials published between 1952 and 1976 related to Flannery O'Connor. Acknowledges that the volume's descriptive annotations are not designed to be evaluative, nor do they attempt to judge the quality of an author's viewpoint. Instead, the authors have produced a convenient guide "useful for discovering the various interpretations" of O'Connor's works and "for tracing the growth and changing nature of her literary reputation." Includes some foreign language materials and a checklist of Ph.D. dissertations for the period of 1961-1975.

Representative Reviews: Anon. *Booklist* 75.13 (1979): 1111-12; Anon. *Choice* 14.9 (1977): 1192; Melvin J. Friedman, *Southern Literary Journal* 12.2 (1980): 114-24; William Koon, *Studies in Short Fiction* 16 (1979): 250-51; Sheila Pepper, *Library Journal* 102.12 (1977): 1363; Diane Tolomeo, *Review* 2 (1980): 271-86.

51a   *Flannery O'Connor: A Celebration of Genius*. Ed. Sarah Gordon. Athens, Ga.: Hill Street Press, 2000.

Provides aficionados with a unique collection of essays, fiction, and poetry in tribute to Flannery O'Connor on the occasion of her seventy-fifth birthday. Contributors include some of America's most respected literary figures, each offering a brief contribution regarding O'Connor's influence and place in their creative lives: Doris Betts, David Bottoms, Mary Ward Brown, Andrea Hollander Budy, Fred Chappell, Robert Coles, Sarah Gordon, Susan Elizabeth Howe, Mark Jarman, Greg Johnson, Madison Jones, Maxine Kumin, Brett Lott, David Madden, Nancy Mairs, Padgett Powell, Lee Smith, Kellie Wells, Miller Williams, and "Guerrilla Girl Alma Thomas."

Illustrated with a variety of photographs: O'Connor as a young child, student, and adult; her family's farm, Andalusia; her father, Edward O'Connor; and one of her beloved peacocks. [Royalties from the volume are donated to Georgia College & State University's Flannery O'Connor Collection at the Ina Dillard Russell Library.]

Representative Reviews: William A. Sessions, *Flannery O'Connor Bulletin* 26-27 (1998-2000): 196-99.

51b   Gordon, Sarah. *Flannery O'Connor: The Obedient Imagination*. Athens: U of Georgia P, 2000.

Addresses in the first chapter, "Questions of Power and Authority," O'Connor's early efforts to gain control over her writing and career.

Focuses on "The Crop" as reflective of attempts "to exert some control over her own textuality." Finds in this story O'Connor's "acute awareness of limitation, restraint, and possibility in the female artist's situation" and uses it to illustrate her views regarding her faith and writing. Offers examples of O'Connor's "refusal to allow her female protagonists to follow the script for acceptable behavior." Sees these stories as reflective of O'Connor's attempts to free herself from familial and societal pressures.

Examines in the second chapter, "The Question of the Fierce Narrator," O'Connor's narrative vision during her apprentice years. Lists Caroline Gordon and Edgar Allan Poe as sources for her style, and refers to the influence of *The New Yorker*'s "tough minded" Dorothy Parker. Explores a range of critical perspectives on O'Connor's narrative art, including feminist, deconstructionist, and Bakhtinian approaches. Highlights commentary by John Hawkes, Frederick Crews, Josephine Hendin, Robert Brinkmeyer, and Marshall Bruce Gentry. Illustrates these perspectives with continued discussion of the thesis stories, and concludes that no one perspective on O'Connor's fiction "is sufficient to present it in its fullness or complexity."

Tracks in the third chapter, "Literary Lessons: The Male Gaze, the Figure Woman," the milestones of O'Connor's literary education, and discusses how she "learned well the lessons of the New Critics," which served as "the basis for her aesthetic" of "a curious blend of the tenets of the New Criticism [with] those of Catholic Christianity." Considers Poe, Nathanael West, and T.S. Eliot as the three writers most central to her vision of the modern waste land as depicted in *Wise Blood*. Declares that Allen Tate's essay "The Man of Letters in the Modern World" provides the ideological and theological basis of the book. Insists that O'Connor defines her territory as within the constraints of New Criticism and "in the context of the Western tradition of the male quest narrative." Contends that she "had internalized the male-centered spiritual tradition of Melville, Hawthorne, and Twain." Explores evidence of Cartesian dualism in *Wise Blood*, as reflected in the development of the character of Sabbath Lily Hawks. Notes that early drafts of the novel reveal that O'Connor initially experimented with Sabbath Lily as a female prophet figure with a "struggling, questioning" faith. Sees this effort as indicative of O'Connor's "ambivalence about woman-as-object (of the male gaze) and woman-as-subject (an agent with her own gaze)" and reflective of a kind of rebelliousness. Closes with a discussion of O'Connor's "attitude toward the value of life on this earth," focusing on her "repeated use of punishment of the flesh, which she associates with the earthly and often with the female." Explores this concern through discussion of Poe's *The Narrative of Arthur Gordon Pym* and other of his stories. Finds that Poe's works along with Nathanael West's *Miss Lonelyhearts* profoundly influenced O'Connor's vision.

Outlines in Chapter 4, "The Gentleman Caller and the Anagogical Imagination," how O'Connor, like T.S. Eliot and Walker Percy, "probed the possibilities of language and its relationship to reality." Finds "the grounding for O'Connor's art in the incarnational theory of thinkers like William Lynch." Uses these positions to explore "the presence of a persistent fictional pattern--that of the gentleman caller--around which O'Connor . . . organized much of her best fiction." Sees this pattern as "an important metaphor for the soul's call to salvation," and illustrates its use through analysis of how O'Connor's female characters are metaphorically "penetrated--or, at the very least . . . entreated or `courted'"--by God through the entreaties of the gentleman caller. Outlines this pattern as evidenced in "The River," "A Temple of the Holy Ghost," "A Circle in the Fire," "The Life You Save May Be Your Own," "Good Country People," "The Displaced Person," and "Greenleaf." Concludes that O'Connor is in line with the teachings of the Church regarding "the sacredness of the human body" and its "recurrent metaphoric use of the soul as female pursued by the Divine Lover."

Considers in Chapter 5, "The Historic, the Orthodox, the Intimate," positions of a variety of critics on O'Connor's "relationship to the history of her region." Compares her vision with those presented by William Faulkner and Margaret Mitchell, and sees O'Connor as retreating from the subject of southern history in her depiction of southern characters with "foolish pride" in their ancestry. Refers to *Gone With the Wind* and Tate's *Ode to the Confederate Dead* in this context, and sees the Confederate general in "A Late Encounter with the Enemy" as a comic antihero. Argues that O'Connor rejected concerns regarding regional identity and concentrated, instead, in John Desmond's words, on a "`world-historical imagination.'" Considers *The Violent Bear It Away* in this context as representing "the full development of a complex consciousness from an internal perspective." Closes with a consideration of the Maryat Lee-O'Connor correspondence to ascertain whether O'Connor was a racist. Concludes that while O'Connor was certainly "not a saint," the "power of her fiction" is "not damaged" by such an allegation.

Offers in the *Epilogue* a rationale for the principal position taken in the book, namely, that there exists a paradox in the manner O'Connor, as a "Catholic writer creates and explores fictive worlds and yet works within the limits of faithful obedience to the hierarchial Church." Argues that O'Connor's "sense of obedience" was formed by the teachings of the Catholic Church and "by her upbringing as a white southern woman in a mannered society with high expectations for its females to `do pretty.'" Closes with an explication of "Parker's Back," seen as a story which "brings together most of the concerns of O'Connor's canon" and appears "to anticipate a new direction and a fuller acceptance of that love which, in poet Richard Wilbur's words, `calls us to the things of this world.'"

Representative Reviews: Greg Johnson, *Atlanta Journal-Constitution* (10 Dec. 2000): F6.

52   Grimshaw, James A., Jr. *The Flannery O'Connor Companion*. Westport, CT: Greenwood, 1981.

Provides summaries of O'Connor's twenty-five short stories and two novels, detailing plot, characters, themes, and symbolism. Includes a catalogue of "the 200 characters in Flannery O'Connor's published canon." Each reference is identified along with "the characters' appearances, mannerisms, and singularly descriptive expressions." Also offers synopses of her essays designed to "draw readers' attention to their applicability [to] her fiction." Further, explores O'Connor's place in 20th-century literature: as a Southerner, Catholic, and "woman writer."

Appendix One provides biographical sketches of selected "Catholics and existentialists whose works were known to O'Connor and whose ideas gave her cause to reflect on her own theological concerns." Reprints in Appendix Two O'Connor's "Introduction to *A Memoir of Mary Ann*."

Representative Reviews: Anon. *American Literature* 54.2 (1982): 313-14; Anon. *Choice* 19.9 (1982): 1240; Melvin J. Friedman, *Southern Literary Journal* 15.1 (1982): 120-29; Louise Gossett, *Christianity and Literature* 32.1 (1982): 69-70; William Bradley Hooper, *Booklist* 78.2 (1981): 87; John R. May, *Flannery O'Connor Bulletin* 11 (1982): 123-28; Mary Morton, *Mississippi Quarterly* 37.1 (1983-84): 89-95; Paul W. Nisley, *Christian Scholar's Review* 12.3 (1983): 255-57; William J. Stuckey, *Modern Fiction Studies* 28.3 (1982): 507-18.

53   Hawkins, Peter S. *The Language of Grace: Flannery O'Connor, Walker Percy, and Iris Murdoch*. Cambridge, MA: Cowley, 1983.

The four chapters which comprise this book, based on a series of lectures, focus on the "central loss of Christianity in Western culture" and what this loss has meant to the literary art produced by Flannery O'Connor, Walker Percy, and Iris Murdoch. States that the goal of these three authors, just as it was for the writers of such classics as *The Canterbury Tales*, the *Faerie Queene*, *Paradise Lost*, and *The Pilgrim's Progress*, is to inspire readers to turn from wickedness "to love and do good." Examines problems the three writers encounter as they continue in this tradition of "bringing the reader to a new state of consciousness and self-awareness."

Discusses, O'Connor's realization that "she had to discover a new language of grace in order to confront the reader with the experience of

God." Outlines her "strategy for approaching her audience," describes her "traditional Christian sensibility," and examines the context within which she considered her fiction "realistic." Discusses O'Connor's use of the bizarre and the grotesque, along with distortion and exaggeration to reach unbelieving readers; her use of biblical allusion; and her successful reliance upon her "narrational voice to suggest the ultimate meaning of her stories." Discusses the role of the narrator in John Huston's 1979 film version *Wise Blood*, "Parker's Back," "Revelation," and "The Artificial Nigger," followed by a careful reading of "A Good Man Is Hard to Find."

Devotes a chapter each to Walker Percy and Iris Murdoch. In these chapters, uses O'Connor's work to illustrate and compare how each of the three worked to communicate with their "unbelieving audience." Suggests that O'Connor provides readers with "a set of critical terms and fictional strategies" to better understand how she and other Christian writers use "clarity and mystery" to bridge the gap between themselves and readers.

Representative Reviews: Diogenes Allen, *Theology Today* 40.2 (1983): 237-38; Sheila Coghill, *Library Journal* 108.2 (1983): 131; John Cunningham, *Southern Humanities Review* 19.3 (1985): 297-99; John F. Desmond, *Christianity and Literature* 37.2 (1988): 54-56; James M. Mellard, *Modern Fiction Studies* 30.2 (1984): 417-20; A. Pollard, *Churchman: Journal of Anglican Theology* 98.1 (1984): 82-83; Royal Rhodes, *Kenyon Review* 6.2 (1984): 129-31; James C. Schaap, *Calvin Theological Journal* 20.2 (1985): 333-34; John D. Sykes, Jr. *Religious Studies Review* 9.4 (1983): 370; James J. Thompson, Jr. *Christianity and Literature* 34.4 (1983): 68-69; Mary Winifred, *Catholic Library World* 57.5 (1986): 208-9; Ralph C. Wood, *Journal of the American Academy of Religion* 51.4 (1983): 717.

54 Humphries, Jefferson. *The Otherness Within: Gnostic Readings in Marcel Proust, Flannery O'Connor and François Villon*. Baton Rouge: Louisiana State UP, 1983.

Discusses O'Connor's affinities with and indebtedness to Marcel Proust in chapter six, "Proust, Flannery O'Connor, and the Aesthetic of Violence" (pp. 95-111) and in chapter seven, "Art, Delusion, Disease, and Reality: The Apotheosis of Asbury Fox in 'The Enduring Chill'" (pp. 112-40).

Provides a close reading of "The Enduring Chill," with references to O'Connor's other stories and her two novels. Finds O'Connor's use of physical violence helpful in casting "shadows" in such a manner that they positively articulate the "negative space" that Proust explored.

Suggests that O'Connor's "The Enduring Chill" did not reach its "final form" until after she had read Proust. Contends that the story can be read

as "a parodic retelling of the `happy' tale which many readers seem
determined to read in Proust's work--that is, Marcel's discovery of art as
a vocation and his transmogrification as *artiste*--whether or not
[O'Connor] had Proust consciously in mind."

Representative Reviews: John Anzalone, *French Review* 59.6 (1986):
969-70; Anon. *American Literature* 56.2 (1984): 302; Alexander Gelley,
Library Journal 108.14 (Aug. 1983): 1484; J. Gratton, *French Studies*
40.1 (1986): 116-17; James M. Mellard, *Modern Fiction Studies* 30.2
(1984): 417-20; M. Morton, *Mississippi Quarterly* 37.1 (1983-84): 89-95.

55   Johansen, Ruthann Knechel. *The Narrative Secret of Flannery O'Connor:
             The Trickster as Interpreter*. Tuscaloosa: U of Alabama P, 1994.

Examines "the major structural elements and narrative devices O'Connor
employs to create her fictional landscape," and her use of the archetypal
trickster as "a likely guide through [her] landscape and interpreter of her
narrative secret."

Discusses the characteristics, importance, and "utility for O'Connor's
artistic and religious purposes" of the trickster figure. Suggests that these
figures not only link her stories "with diverse literatures but also open a
discourse between twentieth-century material-rationalist interpretations
of reality and ancient folklore and myth."

Describes five "narrative devices through which O'Connor shapes the
structures of stories" in *A Good Man Is Hard to Find* and *Everything That
Rises Must Converge*: her use of backwoods speech juxtaposed to biblical
allusions; incantation; doubled characters who embody the shadows and
contradictions of innocence and experience; circular narrative structures;
and her use of "ambiguous figures who move from the fringes to the
center of action" to transform characters. Discusses how O'Connor uses
"techniques of indirection" to create tension. Explores the unpredictable
and uneven role of her narrators and the challenges they pose for critics;
"how the shifting narrative voice assists the mediations of the trickster";
O'Connor's use of *as if*; and her use of irony, "which makes it possible to
hold apparently contradictory perceptions simultaneously."

Juxtaposes *Wise Blood* and *The Violent Bear It Away* to review the "array
of literary devices that animate the structure of her narratives," and uses
"the principle of analogy" to explore "how the very structures of her
novels are animated by her metaphysical views of the Incarnation."

Representative Reviews: D. Coshnear, *Choice* 32.5 (1995): 781; Sarah
Gordon, *Southern Humanities Review* 31.1 (1997): 77-80; David J.

Knauer, *Mississippi Quarterly* 49.1 (1995-96): 127-32; Anne Rowe, *Southern Literary Journal* 28.2 (1996): 121; Ralph C. Wood, *Religion & Literature* 26.3 (1994): 81-88.

56   Kessler, Edward. *Flannery O'Connor and the Language of the Apocalypse.* Princeton Essays in Lit. Princeton: Princeton UP, 1986.

Focuses on O'Connor's use of language, and sees her "in the company of apocalyptic poets like Blake and T.S. Eliot." Suggests that O'Connor's metaphors are rarely "satisfying correspondences between man and a natural order, as those of Eudora Welty and Wallace Stevens often are." Looks as well at O'Connor's use of "gestures, both physical and verbal, in order to approach the hidden truth they so often misrepresent."

Observes that although O'Connor "'spent a lot of time getting *seems* and *as if* constructions out'" of *The Violent Bear It Away*, "the stylistic tic remained." Suggests that it is "a symptom of some deeper struggle to work out her unconscious poetics." Argues that "O'Connor's metaphors, particularly her characteristic *as if*, release a power, often violent and threatening, that demands the death of understanding before the reader can begin to evolve a new consciousness."

Contends that because O'Connor rejected "a return to the human community offered by comedy" and denied that "suffering ends with tragedy," she was left with only two verbal avenues for concluding her narratives: to use irony to imply the existence of a transforming power, or to use metaphor to "show that same power acting within external nature and imaginative vision."

Argues that O'Connor's work demonstrates her belief that "the cure is neither behind us nor before us but within us." Discusses her attention to society at large; the limited value she placed on geography and place; and her intent to tell readers: "no amount of social renovation can renovate the individual self . . . other people can entertain and comfort us but [they] cannot join us in the process of discovering what may be."

Compares O'Connor to Carson McCullers, Erskine Caldwell, and Nathanael West. Concludes that metaphor "was O'Connor's instrument for accommodating transcendent vision to the traditional materials of prose fiction . . . [and] her raids on the inarticulate remain among the most powerful in contemporary literature."

Representative Reviews: Frederick Asals, *Canadian Review of American Studies* 21.1 (1990): 95-99; Robert H. Brinkmeyer, *American Literature* 59.4 (1987): 680-81; Virginia Spencer Carr, *American Literary*

Scholarship: An Annual 1986 (Durham: Duke UP, 1988): 269; Joe Dewey, *Modern Fiction Studies* 33.2 (1987): 323-26; Sally Fitzgerald, *Religion and Literature* 21.1 (1989): 137-48; Melvin J. Friedman, *Clio* 16.3 (1987): 294-96; Marshall Bruce Gentry, *Publications of the Arkansas Philological Association* 13.1 (1987): 83-85; Edward Grallafent, *Times Higher Education Supplement* (London) 748 (1987): 17; Arthur F. Kinney, *International Fiction Review* 14.1 (1987): 50-51; Brian Abel Ragen, *Papers on Language & Literature* 27.3 (1991): 386-98; Ted R. Spivey, *Christianity and Literature* 38.4 (1989): 90-92; Ralph C. Wood, *Flannery O'Connor Bulletin* 15 (1986): 88-91; D.W. Zimmerman, *Choice* 24.7 (1987): 1060.

57   Kinney, Arthur F. *Flannery O'Connor's Library: Resources of Being.* Athens: U of Georgia P, 1985.

Provides an indexed, bibliographic list of Flannery O'Connor's books, which were given to the Russell Library at Georgia College & State University by Regina Cline O'Connor. Notes that her magazines and journals are listed separately. Bibliographic annotations note whether the book is in hardcover or paperback; publication or series information; publication or copyright date; and whether editorial information is included. Bibliographic annotations are followed by descriptive acknowledgements of markings, including whether O'Connor signed or dated the book or whether any marginal linings, marginalia, underlining, check marks, or asterisks are visible. States that O'Connor's "original form and spelling have been preserved." Also includes references to reviews O'Connor wrote on the particular book and whether "any mention of a particular book, its preparation, publication, reception, or the ideas in it and O'Connor's evaluation of it," are in any of O'Connor's letters published in *The Habit of Being: The Letters of Flannery O'Connor*, edited by Sally Fitzgerald.

Provides insight into her reading interests from excerpts of letters to "A" and Janet McKane. Reports how she acquired the volumes included, notes significant gaps in the collection, and suggests titles of more than thirty works that the compiler is certain that she would have used extensively. Maintains that the collection reflects O'Connor's "staunch Catholicism" and supports those who view her as a "keen amateur theologian." Describes marginalia and various other underlined and "penciled portions of text," that serve as "direct signposts" to help readers map out O'Connor's "aesthetic theory."

Representative Reviews: Robert H. Brinkmeyer, *Mississippi Quarterly* 38.2 (1985): 143-46; Dorothy H. Brown, *Christianity and Literature* 35.1 (1985): 70-71; Melvin J. Friedman, *International Fiction Review* 13.1

(1986): 32-33; Anne Marie Mallon, *Religion and Literature* 17.3 (1985): 63-68; Eugenia E. Schmitz, *American Reference Books Annual 1986* (Littleton, CO: Libraries Unlimited, 1986): 447.

58   Kreyling, Michael, ed. *New Essays on* Wise Blood. Series ed. Emory Elliott. American Novel Ser. Cambridge: Cambridge UP, 1995.

Includes an "Introduction" by Michael Kreyling and four "specifically commissioned" essays devoted to O'Connor's *Wise Blood*, intended "to provide students of American literature and culture" with an introductory critical guide to this "widely read and studied" novel. Declares that each essay is included to present readers with "a distinct point of view," and to provide a "forum of interpretative methods and the best contemporary ideas" on this work.

Essays in this collection include:

Kreyling, Michael. "Introduction" (pp. 1-24) by Michael Kreyling. *See* entry 882.

Bacon, Jon Lance. "A Fondness for Supermarkets: *Wise Blood* and Consumer Culture." *See* entry 126.

Mellard, James M. "Framed in the Gaze: *Wise Blood*, and Lacanian Reading." *See* entry 1058.

Brinkmeyer, Robert H. "'Jesus stab me in the heart!': *Wise Blood*, Wounding, and Sacramental Aesthetics." *See* entry 218.

Yaeger, Patricia Smith. "The Woman Without Any Bones: Anti-Angel Aggression in *Wise Blood*." *See* entry 1702.

Representative Reviews: Floyd Barnett, *Mississippi Quarterly* 50.1 (1996-97): 185-88; Peter Rawlings, *Journal of American Studies* 30.3 (1996): 471-72.

59   Logsdon, Loren, and Charles W. Mayer, eds. *Since Flannery O'Connor: Essays on the Contemporary American Short Story*. Essays in Lit. 7. Macomb: Western Illinois UP, 1987.

Offers a collection of essays "dedicated to the memory of Flannery O'Connor," which focuses on the interest and activity in the short story genre in America since her short story collection *A Good Man Is Hard to Find* was published in 1955.

Observes in the Introduction that "America has seldom produced a first-rate novelist who was not also deeply interested in the story." Discusses the "strong link" between American women and the short story and the "polarizing process" that has taken place "between the traditional `realistic' story and the radical new `experimental' story."

Other authors discussed in various essays in the volume include Eudora Welty, David Barthelme, E.L. Doctorow, Cynthia Ozick, Grace Paley, Ann Beattie, Bobbie Ann Mason, Raymond Carver, John Cheever, Louise Erdrich, Gerald Vizenor, and Leslie Silko.

Includes fourteen critical essays, five of which focus on O'Connor:

Barnes, Linda Adams. "The Freak Endures: The Southern Grotesque from Flannery O'Connor to Bobbie Ann Mason." *See* entry 136.

Darretta, John L. "From `The Geranium' to `Judgement Day': Retribution in the Fiction of Flannery O'Connor." *See* entry 368.

Darretta, John L. and Richard Giannone. "Commentary by John L. Darretta and Richard Giannone." *See* entry 369.

Giannone, Richard. "Flannery O'Connor's Consecration of the End." *See* entry 608.

Lonnquist, Barbara C. "Narrative Displacement and Literary Faith: Raymond Carver's Inheritance from Flannery O'Connor." *See* entry 925.

Representative Reviews: William Burke, *Modern Fiction Studies* 34.2 (1988): 247-49; Marshall Bruce Gentry, *Flannery O'Connor Bulletin* 17 (1988): 109-11; George Monteiro, *Studies in Short Fiction* 25.3 (1988): 328-29.

59a   Martin, Regis. *Grace, Grotesquerie, and God: A Short Study in the Unsentimental Art and Faith of Flannery O'Connor.* Steubenville, OH: Franciscan UP, 1991.

Appears to be the publication of five untitled lectures on Flannery O'Connor, focusing on (1) her life; (2) an explication of "A Good Man Is Hard to Find"; (3) a discussion of "The Displaced Person" and her tendency to "write about freaks"; (4) her reputation; and (5) aspects of her life that most influenced her work.

The first section discusses, a variety of topics, including her battle with Lupus and how she learned from Père de Chardin to seek "passive diminishment" to "endure every affliction she had not the capacity to escape"; her "romance with Roman Catholicism [that] remained both ardent and uncomplicated right up to the end"; reflections of her faith, courage, and personality as seen in letters published in *The Habit of Being*; and her recognition of, and battle with, "sin in a world suddenly divested of belief in an Evil Intelligence bent on bedeviling us with its false attraction."

The second section outlines an interpretation of "A Good Man Is Hard to Find" meant to help readers to "see and to savor something of the fierce and necessary confrontation they offer with [St. Cyril's] Dragon." Focuses, on The Misfit, seen as "the only character in the story in whom . . . the utilization of sin by grace achieves final and concentrated expression. The very ardors of his poison become, in the hands of an ironic God, medicine for another's salvation." Ties this idea to O'Connor's belief that "'reality is something to which we must be returned at considerable cost.'"

O'Connor's use of freaks is the focus of the third section of this short booklet. Offers an explication of "The Displaced Person" that views Mrs. Shortley as one who "having ascended falsely and too soon . . . is doomed to fall." Contends that O'Connor intended for readers "to be drawn, if not literally to doom, then certainly to some imagined condition thereof," as her stories appear to be "meant to impart an analogous ordeal of judgement." Sees O'Connor as attempting "to rivet the reader's attention upon what remains essential . . . we have souls to save or lose."

Outlines in the fourth section O'Connor's view of human character and the impact of sentimentality upon the modern individual. Suggests that O'Connor viewed character as the culmination of choices made. Uses this perspective to consider choices O'Connor made for her own life, and suggests that her work reflects her statement, "'I see from the standpoint of Christian orthodoxy . . . for me the meaning of life is centered on our Redemption by Christ and what I see in the world I see in relation to that.'"

Closes in the fifth section with an overall assessment of O'Connor's work and influence, seeing it as "a continuing and compelling theater of instruction." Concludes that "few other artists of this century" have "lived more deeply" than O'Connor, as "so utterly at home was she with the great mysteries of her religion" that few writers have ever had their art spring "more directly from life" than O'Connor.

60   May, John R. *The Pruning Word: The Parables of Flannery O'Connor.* Notre Dame, IN: U of Notre Dame P, 1976.

Discusses in the Introduction how O'Connor's "sense of tradition in both literature and religion has caused a revolution of sorts in the American literary world." States that because she forced "contemporary criticism to witness a seemingly anachronistic wedding of art and belief," critics have had to wrestle with whether or not they "strip O'Connor's art of its distinctive meaning if . . . [they] fail to comprehend its grasp of mystery." Suggests that, "in addition to the aesthetic problem posed by the currently disturbing religious vision that O'Connor dramatizes, she has raised the practical question of the very validity of our interpretation of fiction." Uses as an example the scholarly dialogue among biblical scholars--from a wide variety of denominational beliefs--which has produced an enormous body of objective exegetical literature, and sees an opportunity for similar approach among *literary* scholars. Views O'Connor's work as fertile ground for such efforts and urges that the "critical dialogue" found in the body of criticism surrounding her work be used to produce a similar objective consensus regarding its interpretation as well. Follows with a description of the phases that such an objective consensus might require, then indicates the phases in which various scholarly efforts to interpret O'Connor's fiction to date might fit.

Focuses in the first chapter on reading O'Connor's fiction from the perspective that "the New Hermeneutic's understanding of how `word' [serves] as interpreter of human existence." Contends that O'Connor's fiction "achieves its distinctive dramatic impact through the power of language to interpret its listener rather than through its need to be interpreted by him." Uses examples from O'Connor's short story "Revelation" to point out how she uses words and gestures to articulate the meaning she intends. Sees in her work a technique similar to that of Jesus' use of parables: readers extract--from scenes of ordinary life in her fiction--meaning and wisdom relevant to "universal human existence." Recognizes that O'Connor, like Jesus, conveys her themes "through a new configuration of existing language" that forces readers to take a fresh look at their world because it makes reality live for them in a new way. Proposes that, as a result, O'Connor's readers not only read her work but *participate* in it as well.

Devotes the remainder of the book to readings and discussion of hermeneutic patterns seen in O'Connor's fiction that invite readers to participate in her depiction of reality. Considers in the second chapter O'Connor's "uncollected stories": "The Geranium," "The Barber," "Wildcat," "The Crop," "The Turkey," "The Train," "The Peeler," "The Heart of the Park," "Enoch and the Gorilla," "You Can't Be Any Poorer Than Dead," "The Partridge Festival," and "Why Do the Heathen Rage." Follows in the third chapter with explications of stories in O'Connor's two collections, *Everything That Rises Must Converge* and *A Good Man Is Hard to Find*, and in the fourth chapter with hermeneutic patterns as seen in *Wise Blood* and *The Violent Bear It Away*. Includes bibliographic notes (pp. 151-69); a "Selected Bibliography of Textual Analyses" (pp. 170-74); and, a subject index.

<u>Representative Reviews</u>: Anon. *Book Forum* 2.4 (1976): 562; Anon. *Choice* 13.8 (1976): 982; Lawrence S. Cunningham, *Horizons* 4.1 (1977): 154-55; John F. Desmond, *World Literature Today* 51.2 (1977): 284; John Ditsky, *American Literature* 48.3 (1976): 409-10; Dean Ebner, *Christian Scholar's Review* 7.2-3 (1977): 264-66; Leslie Field, *Modern Fiction Studies* 22 (1976): 624-25; Melvin J. Friedman, *Southern Literary Journal* 12.2 (1980): 114-24; Mary McBride, *Library Journal* 101.8 (1976): 1020; J.J. Quinn, *Best Sellers* 36.7 (Oct. 1976): 227; J.J. Quinn, *Theological Studies* 38.1 (1977): 209; Carl R. Sherman, *Book Forum* 3.2 (1977): 290-94; J.O. Tate, *Flannery O'Connor Bulletin* 5 (1976): 105-11; Diane Tolomeo, *Review* [UP of Virginia] 2 (1980): 271-86.

61   Mayer, David R. *Drooping Sun, Coy Moon: Essays on Flannery O'Connor*. Kyoto, Japan: Yamaguchi, 1996.

Offers a collection of ten essays written over a period of nearly twenty years and originally published in a variety of scholarly journals. The essays are arranged in three groups: the first group of three essays, titled "Belief," examines O'Connor's "explicit theological doctrines and Biblical sources." Mayer maintains that O'Connor's "literary religious imagination tends to be in large sweeps rather than specific denominational concerns." A second group of five essays, titled "Images," shows how O'Connor "takes a startling physical object and makes it reflect something of the spirit." Closes with a third group of two essays, titled "Structures," which point out "that O'Connor's way of unsettling her readers is not limited to her beliefs nor unusual images," but is also derived from how she "manipulates narrative point of view and grammatical structures to bring new patterns of perception before her readers' eyes." Includes a 116 item bibliography and a cumulative subject index.

The ten critical essays include:

Section I -- "Belief":

"Incarnate Wisdom: *Wise Blood*." Rpt. from *Academia* 24 (Feb. 1977): 15-30. *See* entry 1010.

"Apologia for the Imagination: `A Temple of the Holy Ghost.'" Rpt. from *Studies in Short Fiction* 11 (1973): 147-52. *See* Robert E. Golden's *Guide* 1974.B15.

"Conflicts of Testaments: `Parker's Back.'" Rpt. from *Bible Today* 21 (Jan. 1983): 20-24. *See* entry 1008.

Section II -- "Images"

"The Blazing Sun and Relentless Shutter: The Kindred Arts of Flannery O'Connor and Diane Arbus." Rpt. from *Christian Century* 30 Apr. 1975: 435-40. *See* entry 1007.

"*The Violent Bear It Away*: Flannery O'Connor's Shaman." Rpt. from *Southern Literary Journal* 4.2 (1972): 41-54. *See* Robert E. Golden's *Guide* 1972.B31.

"Flannery O'Connor and the Peacock." Rpt. from *Asian Folklore Studies* 35.2 (1976): 1-16. *See* entry 1009.

"Outer Marks, Inner Grace: `Tattooed Christ.'" Rpt. from *Asian Folklore Studies* 42.1 (1983): 117-27. *See* entry 1012.

"`Ain't Adjusted to the Modern World': Flannery O'Connor and the Automobile." Rpt. from *Kansas Quarterly* 21.4 (1989): 67-74. *See* entry 1005.

Section III -- "Structures"

"Shifts of Allegiance: `A Good Man Is Hard to Find.'" Rpt. from *Academia* 26 (1979): 1-11. *See* entry 1013.

"`Like Getting Ticks Off a Dog.'" Rpt. from *Christianity and Literature* 33.4 (1984): 17-34. *See* entry 1011.

62   McFarland, Dorothy Tuck. *Flannery O'Connor*. New York: Frederick Ungar, 1976.

Discusses O'Connor's artistic concern with "how the realm of the Holy interpenetrates this world and affects it." Comments that O'Connor's use of the grotesque serves as "an offshoot of the fictional form that Hawthorne designated as `romance' to distinguish it from the traditional novel." Remarks that her use evokes "a world empty of meaning" and expresses "the incommensurability between the divine and the human."

Discusses the style, techniques, themes, characters, and mystery found in O'Connor's stories in *A Good Man Is Hard to Find*. Offers an explication of the title story which focuses on how she reveals "the hollowness of the protagonist's conventional understanding of order, of destroying the conventional order," and how she suggests "the existence of a profound but appallingly demanding order beneath it." Offers less detailed analyses of the other stories in the collection.

Sees the stories in O'Connor's second collection, *Everything That Rises Must Converge* as reflecting her interest in Teilhard de Chardin's hypothesis that "evolution, far from stopping with the emergence of *homo sapiens*, continues to progress toward higher levels of consciousness." Notes that her characters in these stories "typically resist this kind of rising and the spiritual convergence with others that accompanies it."

Finds *Wise Blood*, though "strong and strikingly original," a bizarre novel with a "starkness of style and flatness of characterization" that prevent it from being easily accessible. Outlines the plot and discusses how "despite his protestations of disbelief in Jesus, Haze is nevertheless obsessed with him." Discusses how Haze's "condition" of not having a home and his fierce committment "to the belief that he has no soul" affect his actions throughout the novel. Includes a discussion of the role of vision in the novel and how the ending "reflects Haze's progress from alienation, isolation, and imprisonment," to a final stage of union--through death-- with God.

Outlines the plot of *The Violent Bear It Away* and explores the motivation for Tarwater's actions. Contrasts Tarwater's efforts to transform himself "completely into a mechanical man" in the beginning and middle of the novel with the focused and determined prophet he has become by the end. Closes with a comparison of O'Connor's two novels, and concludes that both works embody "a paradox in that their theological content is offset by a tone that begins in comedy and becomes increasingly dark, violent, and horrifying." Suggests in closing that O'Connor viewed herself "as a prophet," with her art serving as the medium for her "prophetic message."

Representative Reviews: Anon. *Choice* 13.5-6 (1976): 664; Eileen Baldeshwiler, *Studies in Short Fiction* 15.3 (1978): 340-42; Melvin J. Friedman, *Southern Literary Journal* 12.2 (1980): 114-24; Mary McBride, *Library Journal* 101.8 (1976): 1020; J.O. Tate, *Flannery O'Connor Bulletin* 5 (1976): 105-11.

63   McKenzie, Barbara. *Flannery O'Connor's Georgia*. Foreword by Robert Coles. Athens: U of Georgia P, 1980.

Offers eighty-nine annotated black-and-white photographs intended to provide readers with a visual perspective of Flannery O'Connor's fictional world. The photographs present a wide variety of typical middle-Georgia scenes: house trailers, signs with fundamentalist slogans, junk yards,

yards, "artificial niggers," Stone Mountain, old barns, country stores, and a "pig parlor." Features a number of photographs of O'Connoresque individuals relaxing, socializing, worshiping, or working in agricultural settings. Includes photographs of the interior and exterior of O'Connor's home in Milledgeville and nearby family farm Andalusia.

A twenty-page introduction to O'Connor's life precedes the main body of photographs, with an additional twenty-one photographs of Flannery, her parents, and friends.

Representative Reviews: Anon. *AB Bookman's Weekly* 67.3 (1981): 359; Anon. *American Literature* 53.2 (1981): 343; Anon. *Booklist* 77.11 (1981): 742; Anon. *Choice* 18.7 (1981): 950; Anon. *Critic* 39.12 (1981): 4; Anon. *Virginia Quarterly Review* 58.1 (1982): 17; Anon. *Washington Post Book World* 21 Dec. 1980: 12; Martha Chew, *Southern Quarterly* 20.1 (1981): 85-88; Diana Williams Combs, *Flannery O'Connor Bulletin* 9 (1980): 120-24; Melvin J. Friedman, *Southern Literary Journal* 15.1 (1982): 120-29; A. Alling Jones, *Flannery O'Connor Bulletin* 9 (1980): 124-26; Diane McGifford, *Canadian Review of American Studies* 13.3 (1982): 389-96; Thomas L. McHaney, *South Atlantic Review* 46.3 (1981): 75-76; Mary Morton, *Mississippi Quarterly* 37.1 (1983-84): 89-95; Donald R. Noble, *Southern World* 3.1 (1981): 73-79; William J. Stuckey, *Modern Fiction Studies* 28.3 (1982): 507-18; Ruth M. Vande Kieft, *Georgia Review* 36.1 (1982): 226-28.

64   McMullen, Joanne Halleran. *Writing Against God: Language As Message in the Literature of Flannery O'Connor*. Macon, GA: Mercer UP, 1996.

Contends that a linguistic analysis of O'Connor's fiction reveals, more than other critical approaches, the depth of her talent. Suggests that readers "must be explicitly coached if [their] interpretations are to match O'Connor's explications." Explores O'Connor's literary style of using simple sentences, meaningful grammatical construction, and "naming techniques that obscure or minimize personal worth." Addresses her use of symbols, suggesting that her inconsistent use of symbolic "hats, sunglasses, eyes, eyeglasses, colors, wood, animals, and machinery" poses problems for her readers.

Discusses the negation present in O'Connor's fictional world signalled by her use of "negative words, negative verbs, anagrams, the concept of suffering, mysterious concealments, and directional metaphors," which McMullen argues work "to negate the action of grace presumably available to her characters."

Suggests as well that O'Connor's "images of the Georgia landscape, familial relationships, the Christ figure, inanimate objects, death, and

Christian humanism take on unexpected meanings, and on close inspection appear not to support her stated Catholic views." Outlines the "Catholic concept of a sacramental marriage, the Church's stance on birth control, and the sanctity of the family," and compares these positions to O'Connor's conflicting "private comments."

Representative Reviews: Timothy P. Caron, *American Literature* 72.1 (2000): 209-10; Sally Fitzgerald, *Religion and the Arts* 2.4 (1998): 519-29; Marshall Bruce Gentry, *Flannery O'Connor Bulletin* 24 (1995-96): 129-32; Anthony G. Tassin, *Choice* 34.3 (1996): 457.

65   Montgomery, Marion. *Why Flannery O'Connor Stayed Home.* Prophetic Poet and the Spirit of the Age 1. La Salle, IL: Sherwood Sugden, 1981.

Discusses, over thirty-one chapters, a wide range of topics, characters, works, and ideas which define, illustrate, and outline O'Connor's vision of the world. Offers comment on her various writings including her book reviews and the marginalia in her personal library, while focusing on *Wise Blood* and "A Good Man Is Hard to Find."

Explores how O'Connor's role as a prophet "reveals much to us of our general cultural countryside at the crossroads of time and the timeless." Ties her writing to her concern that our age appears to reject history, "except in so far as it may be turned to satisfactions of the appetite for sentimentality." Concludes that O'Connor set "herself exacting standards, in her love of the truth, to be measured by the outer limits possible to her gift, and, like Dante, she should "be numbered among the eminent who have left their marks upon the community of man through their art."

Representative Reviews: Anon. *Choice* 19.3 (1981): 382; Anon. *Virginia Quarterly Review* 58.1 (1982): 7-8; John F. Desmond, *World Literature Today* 56.2 (1982): 345; Robert Drake, *Christianity and Literature* 31.3 (1982): 87-89; James B. Graves, *Conservative Digest* 15.3 (1989): 63-64; Michael Jordan, *Reflections* 1.3 (1982): 1; Lewis A. Lawson, *Modern Age* 27.3-4 (1983): 319-21; Anne Marie Mallon, *Religion and Literature* 17.3 (1985): 66-67; Ralph McInerny, *American Spectator* 16.7 (1983): 22-23; Paul W. Nisley, *Christian Scholar's Review* 12.3 (1983): 255-57; T.H. Pickett, *Southern Humanities Review* 18.4 (1984): 372-73; William A. Sessions, *Georgia Review* 39.3 (1985): 629-34; William J. Stuckey, *Modern Fiction Studies* 28.3 (1982): 507-18.

66   Montgomery, Marion. *Why Hawthorne Was Melancholy.* Prophetic Poet and the Spirit of the Age 3. LaSalle, IL: Sherwood Sugden, 1984.

This third volume of Montgomery's trilogy offers a lengthy discussion of Nathaniel Hawthorne's fiction focussed on "the special mode of existence of the world in our intellect." Includes dozens of references to Flannery O'Connor works, characters, remarks, and religious beliefs. Ties O'Connor's efforts to serve as a "'realist of distances'" and her view of writing as "'incarnational'" to Hawthorne's art. Includes, in the chapter titled, "Technometria Darkening the Green World," a discussion of "Hawthorne's disquiet over the Manichean roots of Puritanism that O'Connor notices in him," a disquiet that Montgomery claims is a theme in O'Connor's own fiction as well.

Considers how O'Connor's religious beliefs affected her approach to writing fiction. Contrasts her remark that "where there is no belief in the soul, there is little drama," with Hawthorne's uncertainty in his treatment of evil. Suggests that O'Connor "shares Hawthorne's interest in the Satanic, but without his uneasiness." Compares O'Connor's characters, Bishop and Rayber of *The Violent Bear It Away* with Hawthorne's Pearl and Dimmesdale of *The Scarlet Letter*.

Representative Reviews: William A. Sessions, *Georgia Review* 39.3 (1985): 629-34.

67   Montgomery, Marion. *Why Poe Drank Liquor*. Prophetic Poet and the Spirit of the Age 2. LaSalle, Ill: Sherwood Sugden, 1983.

This second volume of Montgomery's trilogy offers a thirty chapter exploration of Edgar Allan Poe's thought and fiction with contextual discussion of O'Connor's theology and literary art throughout. Argues that Poe's influence upon O'Connor's fiction not only is "more considerable than the scant mention suggests," but "lies at a deeper level than that of humor." Focuses upon differences between these two writers' humor and world view. Discusses O'Connor's fascination with Poe's successful use of exaggeration, and contends that "there is in Poe's territory, a Devil of which he is aware," against which O'Connor and others have fought long and hard.

Declares that "it is a Poe-like mind that Miss O'Connor dramatizes as central to her fiction." Supports this contention with an discussion of "Poe's imputed cousin, Hazel Motes" of *Wise Blood*, whom O'Connor created to be, like Poe, "tormented by that larger world which is not of his own making." Finds O'Connor's fiction, unlike Poe's, to reflect "a confident reading of her place in creation such as allowed her to value herself and creation in general with a steady, direct eye, and hence with a disturbing eye." Concludes that it "is as if Poe, catching a glimpse of the abyss, lacks the courage to name it," and because he cannot, death becomes only "an end" for him, whereas it is only a beginning for O'Connor's characters.

Representative Reviews: Michael Jordan, *Reflections* 2 (Fall, 1983): 27; T.H. Pickett, *Southern Humanities Review* 20.2 (1986): 201-3; Ron Rash, *South Carolina Review* 16.2 (1984): 140; William A. Sessions, *Georgia Review* 39.3 (1985): 629-34.

68   O'Connor, Flannery. *Conversations with Flannery O'Connor*. Ed. Rosemary M. Magee. Literary Conversations. Jackson: UP of Mississippi, 1987.

Offers a compilation of twenty-two "conversations" with Flannery O'Connor, interviews that originally appeared in a variety of publications. Magee's Introduction describes O'Connor's responses to her interviewers and suggests that these responses illustrate her interaction with others. Outlines O'Connor's varied approaches in dealing with reporters, participants of literary discussions, panels, and literary critics. Includes a chronology and index.

Interviewers include: Harvey Breit, Celestine Sibley, Betsy Lochridge, Margaret Turner, Robert Donner, Richard Gilman, Katherine Fugin, Faye Rivard, Margaret Sieh, Betsy Fancher, Granville Hicks, Joel Wells, Frank Daniel, Richard P. Frisbie, Gerard E. Sherry, and C. Ross Mullins, Jr.

The twenty-two interviews include:

"May 15 Is Publication Date of Novel by Flannery O'Connor, Milledgeville." Rpt. from *The Union-Recorder* [Milledgeville, GA] 24 April 1952, p. 1. *See* Robert E. Golden's *Guide* 1952.B3.

Breit, Harvey. "Galley Proof: *A Good Man Is Hard to Find.*" Rpt. from transcript of *Galley Proof* filmed by WRCA-TV (NBC) in New York, May 1955.

Breit, Harvey. "In and Out of Books: Visitor." Rpt. from *The New York Times* 12 June 1955, p. 8. *See* Robert E. Golden's *Guide* 1955.B10.

Sibley, Celestine. "Baboons Differ with Giraffes." Rpt. from *The Atlanta Constitution* 13 Feb. 1957, p. 24.

"*Motley* Special: Interview with Flannery O'Connor." Rpt. from *The Motley* [Spring Hill College, Mobile, AL] 9 (Spring 1958): 29-31. *See* Robert E. Golden's *Guide* 1958.B1.

"A Symposium on the Short Story." Rpt. from *Esprit* [U of Scranton] 3 (Winter 1959): 8-13.

"An Interview with Flannery O'Connor and Robert Penn Warren." Rpt. from *Vagabond* [Vanderbilt U] 4 (Feb. 1960): 9-17. *See* Robert E. Golden's *Guide* 1960.B35.

Lochridge, Betsy. "An Afternoon with Flannery O'Connor." Rpt. from *The Atlanta Journal and Constitution Magazine*, 1 Nov. 1959, pp. 38-40. *See* Robert E. Golden's *Guide* 1959.B4.

Turner, Margaret. "Visit to Flannery O'Connor Proves Novel Experience." Rpt. from *The Atlanta Journal and Constitution*, 29 May 1960, p. G2. *See* Robert E. Golden's *Guide* 1960.B57.

Donner, Robert [Richard Gilman], "She Writes Powerful Fiction." Rpt. from *The Sign* 40 (March 1961): 46-48. *See* Robert E. Golden's *Guide* 1961.B3.

Gilman, Richard. "On Flannery O'Connor." Rpt. from *The New York Review of Books*, 21 Aug. 1969, pp. 24-26. *See* Robert E. Golden's *Guide* 1969.B18.

Fugina, Katherine, Faye Rivard, and Margaret Sieh. "An Interview with Flannery O'Connor." Rpt. from *Censer* [College of St. Teresa, Winona, MN] Fall 1960: 28-30. *See* Robert E. Golden's *Guide* 1960.B28.

"Recent Southern Fiction: A Panel Discussion." Rpt. from *Bulletin of Wesleyan College* [Macon, GA] 41 (Jan. 1961).

Fancher, Betsy. "Authoress Flannery O'Connor is Evidence of Georgia's Bent to the Female Writer." Rpt. from *The Atlanta Constitution* 21 April 1961, p. 27. *See* Robert E. Golden's *Guide* 1961.B4.

Hicks, Granville. "A Writer at Home with Her Heritage." Rpt. from *Saturday Review* (12 May 1962): 22-23. *See* Robert E. Golden's *Guide* 1962.B14.

Wells, Joel. "Off the Cuff." Rpt. from *The Critic* 21 (Aug.-Sept. 1962): 4-5, 71-72. *See* Robert E. Golden's *Guide* 1962.B23.

Daniel, Frank. "Flannery O'Connor Shapes Her Own Capital." Rpt. from *The Atlanta Journal and Constitution* 22 July 1962, p. C2. *See* Robert E. Golden's *Guide* 1962.B3.

Frisbie, Richard P. "King of the Birds." Rpt. from *Plymouth Traveler* 3 (Aug.-Sept. 1962): 16-17.

Sherry, Gerald E. "An Interview with Flannery O'Connor." Rpt. from *The Critic* 21 (June-July 1963): 29-31. *See* Robert E. Golden's *Guide* 1964.B23.

Mullins, C. Ross, Jr. "Flannery O'Connor: An Interview." Rpt. from *Jubilee* 11 (June 1963): 32-35. *See* Robert E. Golden's *Guide* 1963.B14.

"Southern Writers are Stuck with the South." Rpt. from *Atlanta Magazine* 3 (Aug. 1963): 26, 60, 63. *See* Robert E. Robert E. Golden's *Guide* 1963.B2.

Fancher, Betsy. "My Flannery O'Connor." Rpt. from *Brown's Guide to Georgia* 3 (March/April 1975): 16-22. *See* entry 475.

Representative Reviews: Frederick Asals, *Canadian Review of American Studies* 21.1 (1980): 95-99; B.L. Clark, *Resources for American Literary Study* 18.1 (1992): 113-16; Blanche Farley, *Flannery O'Connor Bulletin* 16 (1987): 82-87; Sandra Havener, *Women's Studies International Forum* 11.1 (1988): 87; Patrick Kelly, *Canadian Catholic Review* 5.3 (1987): 107; William Monroe, *South Central Review* 5.1 (1988): 101-03.

68a   O'Connor, Flannery. *"A Good Man Is Hard to Find": Flannery O'Connor.* Ed. Laura Mandell Zaidman. Harcourt Brace Casebook Series in Literature. Fort Worth, TX: Harcourt College Publishers, 1999.

Designed to provide students with "a convenient, self-contained reference tool that they can use to complete a research project for an introductory literature course," this volume offers a reprint of, and supportive scholarly materials for, one of O'Connor's most notable stories, "A Good Man Is Hard to Find."

Opens with an introductory essay titled "The World of Flannery O'Connor" that discusses O'Connor's habit of sending amusing news items to friends; describes the cold war backdrop of her stories, the domestic environment, and the Civil Rights struggles of the her times; refers to the popular culture of the 1950s; and closes with a discussion of O'Connor's views on violence and religious issues in the South.

Follows with the reprint of the story itself, preceded by a short biographical sketch describing O'Connor's background, professional career, writings, and awards. Concludes this section with several questions and suggestions for term paper topics related to the story.

Provides twelve essays reflecting a range of critical perspectives on the story:

Asals, Frederick. "The Aesthetics of Incongruity." Rpt. from *Flannery O'Connor: The Imagination of Extremity*. Athens: U of Georgia P, 1982. 142-54. *See* entry 29.

Bellamy, Michael O. "Everything Off Balance: Protestant Election in Flannery O'Connor's `A Good Man Is Hard to Find.'" Rpt. from *Flannery O'Connor Bulletin* 8 (1979): 116-24. *See* entry 162.

Bryant, Hallman B. "Reading the Map in `A Good Man Is Hard to Find.'" Rpt. from *Studies in Short Fiction* 18 (1981): 301-07. *See* entry 238.

Butler, Rebecca R. "What's So Funny About Flannery O'Connor?" Rpt. from *Flannery O'Connor Bulletin* 9 (1980): 30-40. *See* entry 270.

Coulthard, A.R. "Flannery O'Connor's Deadly Conversions." Rpt. from *Flannery O'Connor Bulletin* 13 (1984): 87-98. *See* entry 349.

Highsmith, Dixie Lee. "Flannery O'Connor's Polite Conversation." Rpt. from *Flannery O'Connor Bulletin* 11 (1982): 94-107. *See* entry 740.

Jones, Madison. "A Good Man's Predicament." Rpt. from *Southern Review* 20 (1984): 836-41. *See* entry 804.

O'Connor, Flannery. "From *The Habit of Being: Letters of Flannery O'Connor*." Ed. Sally Fitzgerald. New York: Farrar, Straus & Giroux, 1979.

O'Connor, Flannery. "On Her Own Work." From *Mystery and Manners: Occasional Prose*. Ed. Sally and Robert Fitzgerald. New York: Farrar, Straus & Giroux, 1969. 107-14.

Tate, J.O., Jr. "A Good Source Is Not So Hard to Find." Rpt. from *Flannery O'Connor Bulletin* 9 (1980): 98-103. *See* entry 1514.

Walker, Alice. "Beyond the Peacock: The Reconstruction of Flannery O'Connor." Rpt. from *In Search of Our Mothers' Gardens: Womanist Prose*. San Diego: Harcourt, Brace, Jovanovich, 1975. 42-59. *See* entry 1572.

Green, Eddie. "A Good Man Is Hard to Find." [Lyrics].

Concludes with a reprint of a sample student research paper, "Sin and Punishment According to Flannery O'Connor," by Renae Martin, with descriptive marginal notes, an extensive bibliography, and an abbreviated "Guide to MLA Documentation Style."

Representative Reviews: Valerie Nye, *Flannery O'Connor Bulletin* 26-27 (1998-2000): 193-95.

69   O'Connor, Flannery. *The Presence of Grace and Other Book Reviews by Flannery O'Connor*. Comp. Leo J. Zuber. Ed. and intro. Carter W. Martin. Athens: U of Georgia P, 1983.

Martin's Introduction summarizes the "broad range of works" O'Connor chose to review, including biographies, saints' lives, sermons and theology, fiction, literary criticism, and works related to psychology, philosophy, science, and history. Discusses why O'Connor contributed reviews to the particular publications she chose and "recurrent concerns that emerge as themes in the reviews." Emphasizes her focus on and committment to books "'about religion.'" Concludes that these reviews confirm that O'Connor's art "arose from the religious convictions that she subjected to intense scrutiny not only in her heart but in her mind as well."

Provides an author and title index. Some selections were previously published in "'Reader, Look for Yourself': Recovered Book Reviews." *Georgia Review* 37.2 (1983): 371-82.

Representative Reviews: Anon. *American Literature* 56.1 (1984): 136; Anon. *Virginia Quarterly Review* 60.1 (Winter 1984): 7; John L. Casteel, *Review for Religious* 42.6 (1983): 937-38; Sheila Coghill, *Library Journal* 108.14 (Aug. 1983): 1484; Thomas J. Corr, *College Literature* 11.3 (1984): 293-96; John F. Desmond, *Modern Age* 28.2-3 (1984): 296-98; Patrick Jordan, *Commonweal* 110.20 (1983): 637-38; Joan Leonard, *Journal of the American Academy of Religion* 52.4 (1984): 793; Rosemary M. Magee, *Christianity and Literature* 33.3 (1984): 76-77; Anne Marie Mallon, *Religion and Literature* 17.3 (1985): 64-65; W.J. Stuckey, *Modern Fiction Studies* 30.4 (1984): 832-34; John Sykes, *Religious Studies Review* 13.1 (1987): 63-64; Ralph Wood, *Flannery O'Connor Bulletin* 12 (1983): 117-21.

70   O'Connor, Flannery and Brainard Cheney. *The Correspondence of Flannery O'Connor and the Brainard Cheneys*. Ed. and intro. C. Ralph Stephens. Jackson: UP of Mississippi, 1986.

An indexed, annotated, chronological compilation of the correspondence between Flannery O'Connor and Brainard and Frances Neel Cheney, donated by Brainard Cheney to the Vanderbilt University Library. Dates of the letters included range from February 8, 1953 to July 16, 1964.

The volume includes a foreword by Brainard Cheney, a seventeen-page introduction by Stephens providing useful biographical and other related details, and four Appendices: Frances Neel Cheney's review of *A Good Man Is Hard to Find*; Brainard's reviews of *Wise Blood* and *The Violent Bear It Away*; and Brainard's response to an article by John Hawkes.

Editor states that all 188 of the letters, except five from O'Connor, are presented "transcribed whole and uncut." They deal with a wide variety of topics, including their writing projects; news of friends and family; invitations to visit and comments related to recent visits; farm news (including incidents at Andalusia); O'Connor's notes on her peacocks and other birds; and various theological discussions.

[Note: The material deleted from three of the five letters (6, 84 and 87) relates to racial issues, while the other two (90 and 151) have a single name deleted from each. Originals are located in the "Brainard Bartwell Cheney Papers" in the Special Collections Department of the Jean and Alexander Heard Library, Vanderbilt University, (Box 6, Folders 58-62). Readers are also referred to Terrye Newkirk's 1984 M.A. thesis, also located in Vanderbilt's Special Collections: "Cheers: Letters of Flannery O'Connor to Brainard and Frances Neel Cheney, 1953-1958."]

Representative Reviews: Anon. *Kirkus Reviews* 54.9 (1 May 1986): 711; Frederick Asals, *Canadian Review of American Studies* 18.2 (Summer 1987): 231-33; Robert H. Brinkmeyer, *Southern Literary Journal* 20.1 (1987): 145-48; Virginia Spencer Carr, *American Literary Scholarship: An Annual 1986* (Durham, NC: Duke UP, 1988): 269; Beverly Lyon Clark, *New York Times Book Review* 24 Aug. 1986: 19; John F. Desmond, *Modern Age* 30.3-4 (1986): 331-33; Joe Dewey, *Modern Fiction Studies* 33.2 (1987): 323-26; Stephen G. Driggers, *Southern Humanities Review* 22.2 (1988): 291-92; Sarah Gordon, *Flannery O'Connor Bulletin* 15 (1986): 92-95; Jan Nordby Gretlund, *Mississippi Quarterly* 40.3 (1987): 349-52; Darlene Kelly, *Canadian Catholic Review* 5.3 (1987): 106-07; Russell Kirk, *Reflections: The Wanderer Review of Literature, Culture, and the Arts* 7.1 (Winter, 1988): 8; Loxley F. Nichols, *National Review* 19 Dec. 1986: 54-55; Miles D. Orvell, *Journal of Modern Literature* 13 (1986): 519; N.M. Tischler, *Choice* 24.3 (1986): 479; Lawrence Willson, *Sewanee Review* 96.2 (1988): 283-86.

71   Paulson, Suzanne Morrow. *Flannery O'Connor: A Study of the Short Fiction*. Twayne's Studies in Short Fiction Ser. 2. Boston: G.K. Hall, 1988.

Described by Paulson as a "book on modernism and Flannery O'Connor," this work examines "O'Connor's `modern consciousness' to explain why her work at first glance seems `different' and to suggest a more balanced approach than the strictly theological one that dominates most criticism on O'Connor today."

The book is divided into three parts. Part 1, "The Short Fiction: A Critical Analysis," outlines the variety of themes and literary techniques displayed in her short fiction. Paulson identifies a predominant character type-- "Death-Haunted Questers"--and four recurring types of conflict in O'Connor's stories: Male/Female, Class, Racial, and Good/Evil.

Part 2, "The Writer: Selected Comments by O'Connor, Her Friends, Her Mentors, Her Editors, and Her Critics," provides readers with "a selection of O'Connor's own comments on her art, her reader, and her community." These selections are included to illustrate "interesting interrelationships" of authorial commentary. Considers O'Connor's Introduction to *A Memoir of Mary Ann* as the most important excerpt in this section.

Part 3, "The Critics," includes reprints and excerpts of 25 critical essays, a chronology of O'Connor's life, honors and work, and a bibliography of primary and secondary sources. The 25 essays included are intended not only for readers "familiar with *The Complete Stories* but [also for those] just beginning a study of the criticism." Declares that selections were chosen "to reconcile some of the differences in the critical canon" as well as to provide "thoughtful interpretations representing diverse judgements about O'Connor's short fiction." Includes the following selections:

Quinn, Sister M. Bernetta. "Flannery O'Connor and the Catholic Writer": (154-56). Rpt. of "View From a Rock: The Fiction of Flannery O'Connor and J.F. Powers." *Critique: Studies in Modern Fiction* 2.2 (1958): 19-27. *See* Robert E. Golden's *Guide* 1958.B6.

Lévy, Maurice. "Catholic Writing and Universal Themes of Suffering": (157-59). Rpt. of "L'écriture Catholique de Flannery O'Connor." *Revue française d'Études américaines* (1976): 125-33. *See* entry 2088.

Curley, Dan. "Flannery O'Connor and Moral Relativism": (159-61). Rpt. of "Flannery O'Connor and the Limitless Nature of Grace." *Revista de Letras* 7 (1970): 371-84.

Fitzgerald, Robert. "Flannery O'Connor and the Modern Consciousness": (161-64). Rpt. of "Introduction." *Everything That Rises Must Converge* by Flannery O'Connor. (New York: Farrar, Straus & Giroux, 1965). *See* Robert E. Golden's *Guide* 1965.B30.

Eggenschwiler, David. "Wholeness, Incompleteness, and Estrangement: Flannery O'Connor and Christian Humanism": (164-68). Rpt. of "The

Whole House." *The Christian Humanism of Flannery O'Connor*. (Detroit: Wayne State UP, 1972). *See* Robert E. Golden's *Guide* 1972.A1.

Myers, David A. "Fragmentation and Angst in `The Displaced Person'": (169-70). Rpt. of "A Galaxy of Haloed Suns: Epiphanies and Peacocks in Patrick White's *A Woman's Hand* and Flannery O'Connor's `The Displaced Person.'" *Literatur in Wissenschaft und Unterricht* 14.4 (1981): 214-24.

Le Clézio, J.M.G. "The Parent's Fear of Death in Modern Civilization": (170-72). Rpt. from the "Preface." *Et ce sont les violents qui l'emportent.* Trans. C. Frederick Farrell, Jr. and Edith R. Farrell. [Paris]: Editions Gallimard, 1965. *See* Robert E. Golden's *Guide* 1965.B48.

Heller, Arno. "The Developing Self in the Modern World": (172-73). Rpt. from "`Experienced Meaning': Wirkungästhetiche Betrachtungen zur Kurzprosa Flannery O'Connor." *Forms of the American Imagination: Beitrage zur neueren amerikanischen Literatur*. Ed. Sonja Bahn, et al. Innsbruck: Institut fur Sprachwissenschaft de Universitat Innsbruck, 1979. 165-79. *See* entry 2060.

Klug, M.A. "Flannery O'Connor and the Artist" (173-75). Rpt. of "Flannery O'Connor and the Manichean Spirit of Modernism." *Southern Humanities Review* 17.4 (1983): 303-13. *See* entry 863.

Gresset, Michel. "Flannery O'Connor and the South" (176-77). Trans. C. Frederick Farrell, Jr. and Edith R. Farrell. Rpt. from "Le Petit Monde de Flannery O'Connor," *Mercure de France*, série moderne (Jan. 1964): 141-43. *See* Robert E. Golden's *Guide* 1964.B41.

Gordon, Sarah. "Flannery O'Connor and Realism" (177-80). Rpt. from "Flannery O'Connor and the Common Reader." *Flannery O'Connor Bulletin* 10 (1981): 38-45. *See* entry 631.

Rubin, Louis D., Jr. "Flannery O'Connor and Southern Fiction" (180-82). Rpt. from "Flannery O'Connor's Company of Southerners: or `The Artificial Nigger' Read as Fiction Rather than Theology." *Flannery O'Connor Bulletin* 6 (1977): 47-71. *See* entry 1344.

Driskell, Leon V. and Joan T. Brittain. "Flannery O'Connor and the Bible" (182-84). Rpt. from *The Eternal Crossroads: The Art of Flannery O'Connor*. Lexington: UP of Kentucky, 1971. *See* Robert E. Golden's *Guide* 1971.A1.

Bleikasten, André. "Flannery O'Connor, Freud, and Lacan" (185-88). Rpt. from "Writing on the Flesh: Tattoos and Taboos in `Parker's Back.'"

Southern Literary Journal 14.2 (1982): 8-18. *See* entry 179.

Jones, Bartlett C. "Flannery O'Connor and Depth Psychology" (188-90). Rpt. from *Midcontinent American Studies Journal* 5.2 (1964): 50-56. *See* Robert E. Golden's *Guide* 1964.B50.

[Kahane], Claire Katz. "Flannery O'Connor's Sadistic Wit." (191-95). Rpt. from "Flannery O'Connor's Rage of Vision," *American Literature* 46.1 (1974): 54-67. *See* Robert E. Golden's *Guide* 1974.B14.

Westling, Louise. "Feminine Identity." (195-98). Rpt. from *Sacred Groves and Ravaged Gardens: The Fiction of Eudora Welty, Carson McCullers, and Flannery O'Connor*. Athens: U of Georgia P, 1985. *See* entry 80.

Browning, Preston M. "O'Connor's Clinical Understanding of Neurosis." (199-210). Rpt. from *Flannery O'Connor*. Carbondale: Southern Illinois UP, 1974. *See* Robert E. Golden's *Guide* 1974.A1.

Morton, Mary L. "O'Connor and Jung." (201-03). Rpt. from "Doubling in Flannery O'Connor's Female Characters: Animus and Anima." *Southern Quarterly* 23.4 (1985): 57-63. *See* entry 1124.

Asals, Frederick. "The Terrifying, the Comic, and the Melodramatic." (204-07). Rpt. from *Flannery O'Connor: The Imagination of Extremity*. Athens: U of Georgia P, 1982. *See* entry 29.

Currie, Sheldon. "Flannery O'Connor's Comic Imagery." (207-09). Rpt. from "Freaks and Folks: Comic Imagery in the Fiction of Flannery O'Connor." *Antigonish Review* 62-63 (1985): 133-42. *See* entry 364.

Kessler, Edward. "Flannery O'Connor's Poetic Imagery." (209-13). Rpt. from *Flannery O'Connor and the Language of Apocalypse*. Princeton, NJ: Princeton UP, 1986. *See* entry 56.

Richard, Claude. "Flannery O'Connor and Narratology." (213-18). Rpt. from "Desire and Destiny in Flannery O'Connor's `A Good Man Is Hard to Find.'" *Delta* 2 (1976): 61-74. *See* entry 2131.

Drake, Robert. "Flannery O'Connor's Compassion." (218-19). Rpt. from *Flannery O'Connor: A Critical Essay*. Grand Rapids, MI: Eerdmans, 1966. *See* Robert E. Golden's *Guide* 1966.A1.

Walters, Dorothy. "The Lack of Beauty in Flannery O'Connor's Work." (220-23). Rpt. from *Flannery O'Connor*. Boston: G.K. Hall, 1973. *See* Robert E. Golden's *Guide* 1973.A2.

Representative Reviews: Robert H. Brinkmeyer, Jr., *Mississippi Quarterly* 43.2 (1990): 257-58; Melvin J. Friedman, *International Fiction Review* 16.2 (1989): 139-42; Marshall Bruce Gentry, *Studies in Short Fiction* 26.2 (1989): 208-09; Arno Heller, *AAA-Arbeiten Aus Anglistik und Amerikanistik* 16.1 (1991): 109-10; Paul W. Nisley, *Christianity and Literature* 39.1 (1989): 107-08; Ted R. Spivey, *Christianity and Literature* 38.4 (1989): 90-92; Louise Westling, *Flannery O'Connor Bulletin* 17 (1988): 98-100.

72   Quinn, John J., ed. *Flannery O'Connor: A Memorial*. Scranton, PA: U of Scranton P, 1995.

This volume is based upon a special O'Connor commemorative edition of *Esprit*, a small campus journal published by the University of Scranton. The issue [8.1 (1964)] was published shortly after O'Connor's death. Noting the "heavy demand from around the country for copies of this special edition," the University of Scranton Press issued "this tribute" as a way to commemorate the 30th anniversary of O'Connor's death.

Readers are directed to Robert E. Golden and Mary C. Sullivan's *Flannery O'Connor and Caroline Gordon* [Boston: G.K. Hall, 1977] for Golden's citations and abstracts of articles that appeared in the original issue. However, a comparison of this volume with the original issue reveals some differences.

The following items from the original volume are not included: Nine drawings by Paul W. Lowry and Anthony R. Cannella depicting various O'Connor characters; several photographs (mostly of Andalusia), which had illustrated Katherine Anne Porter's essay, "Gracious Greatness"; and essays or poems by Rudolph Fara, John F. Judge, Jr., John Connolly, Robert C. Gredlicks, Joseph C. Townend, Paul D. Liesman, Kenneth Zeiss, Richard W. Quinn, Frank Kelly, and Bernard A. Yanavich, Jr.

A number of items are added to the 1995 reissued edition: a letter from Flannery O'Connor to Fr. Quinn in which she ranks short stories submitted by students for a contest; O'Connor's remarks at a University of Scranton symposium in which she defines what a short story is and offers advice to those who might wish to become short story writers; her remarks upon receiving the Georgia Writers' Association Scroll; and two concluding essays by Fr. Quinn: a review of *The Violent Bear It Away* and a discussion of the influence of Joseph Conrad and William F. Lynch on O'Connor's work. An index is also included.

Representative Reviews: Marshall Bruce Gentry, *Studies in Short Fiction* 34.2 (1997): 260-61; Sura P. Rath, *Flannery O'Connor Bulletin* 24 (1995-96): 138-40.

73 Ragen, Brian Abel. *A Wreck on the Road to Damascus: Innocence, Guilt, and Conversion in Flannery O'Connor*. Chicago: Loyola UP, 1989.

Explores how O'Connor uses the automobile and other elements of popular culture "to embody the idea of perfect freedom." Sees her use "as an emblem for the philosophies" that celebrate this freedom, and observes O'Connor's focus on "the figure of the solitary man, who is burdened by no past, forms no ties in the present, and is always able to create himself anew and assume a fresh identity." Outlines how O'Connor's treatment shows that an individual must choose between the illusory promise of perfect freedom or the real offer of redemption.

Contends that the effectiveness of O'Connor's fiction lies in how she fuses elements from popular culture with biblical stories and images of violence. Suggests that O'Connor developed a theory of fiction based upon the idea that "a work can convey many meanings, including the most spiritual, by accurately describing the physical world."

Discusses how essential Christian doctrines, such as Original Sin, salvation and the Incarnation, serve as a foundation for O'Connor's work. Offers readings of "Parker's Back," "The Life You Save May Be Your Own," and a lengthy, detailed explication of *Wise Blood*. Contends that in each, the main character's "reaction to the awful offer of grace is tightly bound up with O'Connor's exploration of Christian mysteries and her attack on recent intellectual movements."

Explores O'Connor's use of distortion "to write on what she called the anagogical level," and the significance of "an action or a gesture" to reveal the spiritual meaning of a story.

Representative Reviews: Anon. *University Press Book News* 1.4 (1989): 24; Gerald T. Cobb, *Theological Studies* 51.2 (1990): 380-81; Kathleen Feeley, *Christianity and Literature* 39.3 (1990): 347-49; Edward Halsey Foster, *Small Press* 8.1 (1990): 34; A.J. Griffith, *Choice* 27.5 (1990): 800; Catherine Kenney, *Christian Century* 107.11 (1990): 344-45; Sheryl L. Meyering, *American Literature* 63.1 (1991): 148-49; John N. Somerville, Jr. *Mississippi Quarterly* 43.2 (1990): 249-52; Ralph C. Wood, *Flannery O'Connor Bulletin* 18 (1989): 99-105.

74 Rath, Sura and Mary Neff Shaw, Eds. *Flannery O'Connor: New Perspectives*. Athens: U of Georgia P, 1996.

Contends that the essays included in this collection represent the range of new critical perspectives on O'Connor and attest to the directions in which

O'Connor scholarship has moved over the last decade and a half. Remarks in the Introduction that while some of the essays "probe issues that, until recently, had been ignored," others address "longstanding debates in light of new critical insights from gender studies, rhetorical theory, dialogism, and psychoanalysis." Essays feature discussions of O'Connor's early stories, her canonical status, and the feminist undertones in her use of the grotesque. Of particular interest is the volume's 200+ item bibliography and its cumulative index.

Along with Rath's ten-page "Introduction," the volume includes the following essays:

Brinkmeyer, Robert H., Jr. "Asceticism and the Imaginative Vision of Flannery O'Connor." *See* entry 215.

Fodor, Sarah J. "Marketing Flannery O'Connor: Institutional Politics and Literary Evaluation." *See* entry 536.

Gentry, Marshall Bruce. "Gender Dialogue in O'Connor." *See* entry 587.

Giannone, Richard. "Displacing Gender: Flannery O'Connor's View from the Woods." *See* entry 606.

Gordon, Sarah. "'The Crop': Limitation, Restraint, and Possibility." *See* entry 630.

Kennelly, Laura B. "Exhortation in *Wise Blood*: Rhetorical Theory as an Approach to Flannery O'Connor." *See* entry 830.

Paulson, Suzanne Morrow. "Apocalypse of Self, Resurrection of the Double: Flannery O'Connor's *The Violent Bear It Away*." *See* entry 1245.

Reesman, Jeanne Campbell. "Women, Language, and the Grotesque in Flannery O'Connor and Eudora Welty." *See* entry 1315.

Shaw, Mary Neff. "'The Artificial Nigger': A Dialogical Narrative." *See* entry 1410.

Yaeger, Patricia. "Flannery O'Connor and the Aesthetics of Torture." *See* entry 1701.

Representative Reviews: Morgan S. Grether, *Women's Studies* 28.2 (1999): 235-38; M.S. Stephenson, *Choice* 34.1 (1996): 125; Virginia Wray, *Flannery O'Connor Bulletin* 24 (1995-96): 133-37.

75 Saunders, Kay. *Letters From the Other Side: The Gift of Flannery O'Connor*. Appleton, WI: Saunders, 1998.

A collection of fourteen original poems written from the perspective of "what Flannery might say if she were able to continue her letter writing after her death." Inspired by O'Connor's letters published in *The Habit of Being*, Saunders states that she has "borrowed [O'Connor's] words, misspellings and all" to "help others discover the gift of Flannery O'Connor." Poems focus upon a variety of topics, including O'Connor's lupus, her use of crutches, her relationship with and admiration for her father [Edward F. O'Connor, Jr.], and the role others played in supporting her literary efforts.

75a Scott, R. Neil and Valerie Nye. *Postmarked Milledgeville: A Guide to Flannery O'Connor's Correspondence in Libraries and Archives*. Ed. Sarah Gordon and Irwin Streight. Ms. Milledgeville, GA: Flannery O'Connor Collection, Russell Library, Georgia College & State U, 2001.

"Designed to help scholars fill in the gaps of O'Connor's published correspondence," this guide "may be viewed as a literary map, pointing out known collections of O'Connor's correspondence in libraries and archives."

Refers scholars to O'Connor's correspondence held in collections of 24 libraries and archives, most notably: Georgia College & State University, Duke University, Emory University, Harvard University, Kenyon College, New York Public Library, Princeton University, Syracuse University, University of Maryland, University of North Carolina at Chapel Hill, University of Tulsa, Vanderbilt University, and Washington & Lee University.

Offers descriptions of the content and locations of correspondence between O'Connor and the following individuals: Olive Bell Davis, Allan Nevins, Mack Buckley Swearingen, Thomas F. And Louise Gossett, James McCown, Katherine Anne Porter, Roslyn Barnes, Ethel Daniell, Ben Griffith, Laurence Perrine, Elizabeth McKee, Leo Zuber, Sally Fitzgerald, Fred Darsey, Joel Wells, David Estes, Marvin Whiting, Frank Daniel, Dora Byron, Helen Soul, J.L. Mazzaro, Madison Jones, Betty Hester, Paul Barrus, George Beiswanger, James Bonner, Brainard and Francis Neel Cheney, O.B. Emerson, Betty Ferguson, Robert Giroux, Caroline Gordon, Gussie Harrison, Mary Virginia Harrison, DeVene Harrold, Alta Haynes, Caroline Ivey, Edward Kessler, William Koon, Roberta Lawrence, Maryat Lee, Betty Boyd Love, Allen Maxwell, John Selby, Paul Engle, Marion Montgomery, Martha Pennington Null, Joan O'Connor, Marion Peterman Page, Rebekah Poller, Richard Russell,

Virginia Satterfield, Jessie Trawick, Katherine Scott, Marcus Smith,
Grace Terry, Shirley Abbott Tomkievicz, Rosa Lee Walston, Eileen Hall,
Robert Lowell, John Hawkes, John Crowe Ransom, Anne Brooks Murray,
Paula Diamond, Elizabeth Aimes, Ashley Brown, Allen Tate, Whit
Burnett, Albert Fowler, Granville Hicks, William Van O'Connor, Richard
B. Allen, Frank Daniel, John Donald Wade, Grace Van Wormer, Louis
Dollarhide, Ward Allison Dorrance, Lockwick Charles Hartley, Louis
Rubin, Walker Percy, Gordon Lish, Andrew Lytle, Alice Morris, Harding
Lemay, Cecil Dawkins, Thomas Henry Carter, and G. Roysce Smith.

75b   Seel, Cynthia. *Ritual Performance in the Fiction of Flannery O'Connor.*
Studies in American Literature and Culture. Rochester, NY: Camden
House, 2000.

Argues for an intensive look at ritual as structure (or aesthetic frame) and
as transforming action (or performance) as a way of illuminating
O'Connor's method and the impact of her art.

Utilizes performance theory, cultural and literary studies, Catholic
theology, and psychoanalytic theory, along with feminist criticism of
O'Connor's canon to demonstrate how an archetypal feminine energy
serves as the nexus of change in O'Connor's ritual performances. Presents,
in this process, an alternative reading to feminist critiques that cast
O'Connor's stories as hostile to or indifferent to women.

Suggests that an "individuation process," as defined by Carl Jung, serves
as the psychological event that supports these performances, even as a
ritual pattern delineates the perimeter and sacramental action fires the
transformation. Views O'Connor's characters as individuals compelled by
a ritually-induced change of Being.

Argues that while this impetus often appears in masked, grotesque, or
even violent forms--all means of presentation typical of traditional ritual
performances--O'Connor's ultimate aim is to re-awaken and return
repressed or split-off aspects of the Self (particularly with respect to a
degradation of the feminine) and to ready the cultural ground and the
individual soul for the interpretation of the divine and profane realms, and
thereby to regenerate the splintered modern temperament.

Surveys, in the Introduction, O'Connor criticism, clarifies terms and
theoretical views, and offers insight into the history and culture of
O'Connor's region. Finds certain aspects of the Southern psyche to be
especially contingent to the distinctive role played by Southern women.
Explores O'Connor's knowledge of and position on these conditions.
Discusses O'Connor's own considerable scholarship, and includes

selections from her remarks, essays, letters, and marginalia. Notes that Mircea Eliade, Teilhard de Chardin, and Carl Jung, among others, may have influenced her thought, and thus her art.

Discusses the positions of more recent scholars in the field of ritual studies, such as Victor Turner, Tom Driver, and Malidoma Somé. Examines specific ritual practices in the Catholic Church and from the ancient Mysteries at Eleusis for their possible presence in the fiction as well.

Lays the theoretical groundwork of the study, then proceeds with an in-depth discussion of six of O'Connor's short stories: "A Circle in the Fire," "The Artificial Nigger," "The Lame Shall Enter First," "The River," "A Temple of the Holy Ghost," and "A Stroke of Good Fortune."

Concludes with a discussion of the extreme theatricality of O'Connor's ritual performances, and compares her work to such avant-garde dramatists as Samual Beckett and Antonin Artaud. Calls for a live staging of O'Connor's stories, and imagines new revelations and the sheer pleasure which might thereby be evoked. (From author's abstract).

76   Shloss, Carol. *Flannery O'Connor's Dark Comedies: The Limits of Inference*. Southern Literary Studies. Baton Rouge: Louisiana State UP, 1980.

Addresses O'Connor's use of rhetorical devices to infer "secondary levels of implication" in her stories. Argues that, because of the "pointed relationship between the conclusions of inference and the mental resources of the perceiver," O'Connor carefully considered her reader's ability to understand and infer from her text. Cites evidence that O'Connor "addressed herself precisely to those who were untutored in religious belief," and argues that "it is in terms of those readers" that critics ought to "evaluate the success of her rhetoric."

Contends that because O'Connor frequently violates "the commitment to represent the concrete world with fidelity," and because she "did not think that reality was Reality," using the term *realism* to describe her fiction is inaccurate. Offers as evidence O'Connor's own comments, which point out how, for O'Connor, reality was "not the tangible world encountered without delusion, but a dimension of perception . . . transcending the substantial field of sense impressions." Uses these discussions as background for examining O'Connor's use of symbols, Christian myth, similes, metaphor, and her "romantic tendency to analogize" in order to "dehumanize and distance the human life rendered" in her fiction. Follows with explications of "Greenleaf" and "The Displaced Person," to illustrate how O'Connor's "analogies begin with the concrete world as theme," and using the process of inference, lead the reader "not directly to the spirit, but to an expanded sense of the physical environment."

Explicates *The Violent Bear It Away* and contends that while the allusions in this novel are clear, O'Connor intrudes at the end and "defines the precise ordering of values on which a reader's judgement depends, even when biblical references are clearly presented." Looks at O'Connor's manipulation of the reader's sympathy toward old Tarwater, and argues that the novel's characters serve merely as "a portrayal of monomania." Remarks that because O'Connor's "manipulation of attitude toward Tarwater and the boy is [both] complex and ambiguous," O'Connor ultimately fails "to provide clear guidance" to the reader. Concludes, however, that despite O'Connor's hesitancy "to `tell' enough to make textual meanings unambiguous to the nonreligious," her fiction "retains a weight of human concern that makes the reading [of her fiction] a disturbing encounter, valuable to readers of any persuasion because its haunting truth rests on sharable experience rather than prohibitive religious allusion."

Representative Reviews: Anon. *American Literature* 53.2 (1981): 343; Anon. *Choice* 18.6 (1981): 799; Anon. *Virginia Quarterly Review* 57.2 (1981): 54; John Cunningham, *Studies in Short Fiction* 18.3 (1981): 332-33; Elizabeth Evans, *Flannery O'Connor Bulletin* 10 (1981): 93-96; Melvin J. Friedman, *Southern Literary Journal* 15.1 (1982): 120-29; Louise Y. Gossett, *South Atlantic Quarterly* 81.2 (1982): 243; Richard Gray, *Journal of American Studies* 15.2 (1981): 309-10; William Koon, *Library Journal* 105.15 (1980): 1736; Diane McGifford, *Canadian Review of American Studies* 13.3 (1982): 389-96; Anne Marie Mallon, *Religion and Literature* 17.3 (1985): 67-68; Mary Morton, *Mississippi Quarterly* 37.1 (1983-84): 89-95; David Seed, *Notes and Queries* 29 (1982): 276-77; William J. Stuckey, *Modern Fiction Studies* 28.3 (1982): 507-18; Ralph Wood, *Religious Studies Review* 7.4 (1981): 345.

77   Spivey, Ted R. *Flannery O'Connor: The Woman, the Thinker, the Visionary*. Macon, GA: Mercer UP, 1995.

Describes meeting O'Connor in 1958 and offers impressions and details of their correspondence. Notes the belief O'Connor shared with T.S. Eliot and William Butler Yeats, that "a new dark age was about to descend upon mankind," and supports this view with Sally Fitzgerald's comment that O'Connor "was, at times, a kind of modern sibyl." Remarks on O'Connor's "profound emotional and visionary quality" and her "pessimism" rooted in "a Southern stoicism" adopted by pre-Civil War Southern gentry.

Explores, O'Connor's "intellectual life in the context of her life in the South." Identifies the three intellectual viewpoints O'Connor adhered to: "that of Southern Agrarianism, of a strictly orthodox Thomism, and of an apocalyptic Catholicism." Compares O'Connor to Walker Percy and finds her "both a profounder thinker and artist." Notes O'Connor's attraction to "religious existentialists," such as Martin Buber and Gabriel Marcel and her use of the "rebellious individual" character in *Wise Blood* and *The Violent Bear It Away*.

Discusses O'Connor's status as "a woman of letters" and comments on the portrayal of O'Connor as "a kind of recluse." States that James Joyce meant more to O'Connor "than any other writer," and that she turned to his and Hemingway's work "for inspiration." Ties her work to Joyce's in "her first chief theme: the individual who cannot free himself from Jesus," and in her "profound concern with art in all its manifestations." Includes a lengthy explication and discussion of *Wise Blood* showing links with Joyce's *A Portrait of the Artist as a Young Man*. Argues that even though O'Connor "was a gifted critic, thinker, artist and even woman of letters, she was primarily a literary visionary not unlike Joyce or even Dostoevsky." Reads "A Good Man Is Hard to Find" and "The Displaced Person" as O'Connor's "profoundest visions of the destruction of paralyzed worlds." Offers, as well, explications of "The River," "Good Country People," and "The Artificial Nigger." Praises O'Connor's deep visionary insight in *The Violent Bear It Away*, especially in "her characterization of old Tarwater in terms of his suffering, his prophetic insights and actions, his alienation in an unbelieving world, and his fraternal association with several blacks . . . who make up a cadre of believing Christians."

Considers O'Connor's "vision of the growth of a new communal association of humanity," based upon influences of Teilhard de Chardin and Thomas Merton. Discusses how this theme is evidenced in "Revelation" and "The Enduring Chill." Contends that de Chardin served as "only" an inspiration for O'Connor, "not a revered master like Saint Thomas Aquinas." Notes similarities between O'Connor and Thomas Merton, and illustrates how O'Connor labored through her work to show "how, through suffering and evil, human beings learn to realize the essential human core in themselves and others." Concludes with discussion of several stories from O'Connor's second collection: "The Lame Shall Enter First," "The Enduring Chill," "Greenleaf," "The Comforts of Home," "A View of the Woods," "Parker's Back," and "Judgement Day."

Representative Reviews: Marshall Bruce Gentry, *Southern Quarterly* 34.2 (1996): 149-50; M.S. Stephenson, *Choice* 33.2 (1995): 296.

78   Westarp, Karl-Heinz, comp. *Flannery O'Connor: The Growing Craft.*
                Southern Literary Ser. 4. Birmingham, AL: Summa, 1993.

                Offers a synoptic variorum edition of four stories: "The Geranium"
                (1946), "An Exile in the East" (1954), "Getting Home" (1964) and
                "Judgement Day" (1964). Declares that because the four are rewritings of
                much of the same material, the synoptic, collated arrangement offers
                readers an opportunity to compare various sections of text and to "follow
                at close range O'Connor's artistic development from beginning to end."

                The stories are preceded by Westarp's thirty-one page Introduction, which
                describes the manuscripts for each story in the *Flannery O'Connor
                Collection* of the Russell Library at Georgia College & State University,
                the publication history of each story, and an outline of significant
                differences between them.

                Representative Reviews: Marshall Bruce Gentry, *Flannery O'Connor
                Bulletin* 22 (1993-94): 138-39; David J. Knauer, *Mississippi Quarterly*
                49.1 (1995-96): 127-32; Tom Noyes, *American Studies International* 35.3
                (1997): 97.

79   Westarp, Karl-Heinz, and Jan Nordby Gretlund, eds. *Realist of Distances:
                Flannery O'Connor Revisited.* Aarhus, Denmark: Aarhus UP, 1987.

                This volume is intended to offer "critical essays celebrating Flannery
                O'Connor's unique vision of the convergence of the temporal and the
                eternal." Notes that while some essays "point out that her fiction is
                grounded in the particularities of the South and her awareness of her
                immediate world," others focus on her "literary integrity and offer an
                evaluation of her literary impact." States that the essays all treat O'Connor
                as "the prophetic poet, the *realist of distances*, who tried to recall us to our
                largely forgotten relation to the world and each other." Remarks that the
                essays were all originally presented at a symposium held during August
                1984 at Sønderborg, Denmark.

                In addition to Sally Fitzgerld's "Degrees and Kinds: Introduction," the
                volume's essays are grouped into five sections:

                Section I: Developing Artist:

                Brown, Ashley. "Flannery O'Connor: A Literary Memoir." *See* entry 224.

                Drake, Robert. "`The Lady *Frum* Somewhere': Flannery O'Connor Then
                and Now." *See* entry 428.

Westarp, Karl-Heinz. "Flannery O'Connor's Development: An Analysis of the `Judgement Day' Material." *See* entry 1614.

Schlafer, Linda. "Pilgrims of the Absolute: Léon Bloy and Flannery O'Connor." *See* entry 1376.

Section II: Narrator:

Feeley, Kathleen. "`Mine is a Comic Art . . .': Flannery O'Connor." *See* entry 484.

Ashley, Jack Dillard. "Throwing the Big Book: The Narrator's Voice in Flannery O'Connor's Stories." *See* entry 121.

Gentry, Marshall Bruce. "Narration and the Grotesque in Flannery O'Connor's Stories." *See* entry 590.

Section III: Image Maker:

Currie, Sheldon. "Comic Imagery in the Fiction of Flannery O'Connor." *See* entry 364.

Blasingham, Mary V. "Archetypes of the Child and of Childhood in the Fiction of Flannery O'Connor." *See* entry 177.

Garson, Helen S. "Cold Comfort: Parents and Children in the Work of Flannery O'Connor." *See* entry 580.

Washburn, Delores. "The `Feeder' Motif in Flannery O'Connor's Fiction: A Gauge of Spiritual Efficacy." *See* entry 1585.

Section IV: Aesthete:

Beck, Christiane. "Flannery O'Connor's Poetics of Space." *See* entry 156.

Martin, Carter. "`The Meanest of Them Sparkled': Beauty and Landscape in Flannery O'Connor's Fiction." *See* entry 977.

Muzina, Matej. "Inescapable Lucidity: Flannery O'Connor's Gift and Most Terrible Affliction." *See* entry 1135.

Zacharasiewicz, W. "From the State to the Strait of Georgia: Aspects of the Response by Some of O'Connor's Creative Readers." *See* entry 1716.

Section V: Thinker and Believer:

Ireland, Patrick J. "The Sacred and the Profane: Redefining Flannery O'Connor's Vision." *See* entry 714.

Gretlund, Jan Nordby. "The Side of the Road: Flannery O'Connor's Social Sensibility." *See* entry 676.

Ebrecht, Ann. "`The Length, Breadth, and Depth of the World in Movement': The Evolutionary Vision of Flannery O'Connor and Teilhard de Chardin." *See* entry 442.

Mott, Sara. "Flannery O'Connor's Unique Contribution to Christian Literary Naturalism." *See* entry 1127.

Montgomery, Marion. "Flannery O'Connor: Realist of Distances." *See* entry 1102.

<u>Representative Reviews</u>: Manuel Brito, *Revista canaria de estudios ingleses* (Spain) 15 (1987): 214-16; Sharon Felton, *Mississippi Quarterly* 41.1 (1987/88): 119-22; Laura B. Kennelly, *South Central Review* 5.1 (1988): 103-04; Arthur F. Kinney, *Southern Quarterly* 26.3 (1988): 77-80; J.O. Tate, *Flannery O'Connor Bulletin* 16 (1987): 95-97.

80   Westling, Louise. *Sacred Groves and Ravaged Gardens: The Fiction of Eudora Welty, Carson McCullers, and Flannery O'Connor*. Athens: U of Georgia P, 1985.

Examines the roles expected of Southern women and suggests how these roles may have shaped the lives and art of Eudora Welty, Carson McCullers, and Flannery O'Connor. Discusses how each reacted to the expected place of women, using evidence found in their letters, fiction, and lives. Sees each as having countered an "ambiguous" inheritance "by creating [her] own rich matriarchal traditions" through art. Suggests that, collectively, their fiction serves as a denial of "the patriarchal version of Southern life" presented by such authors as William Faulkner, John Crowe Ransom, Allen Tate, and William Styron.

Concentrates on these writers' concerns as women, specifically "their treatment of the problems of identity, on attitudes toward the mother, on the ways in which men are perceived, and on the distinctly female uses of place and symbol in their stories." Argues that whereas Welty celebrates womankind, O'Connor and McCullers struggle against it.

Sees O'Connor's "sour and resentful" children "as emblems of their mothers' debilitating power" who "set themselves at odds" with them "in resistance to femininity." Observes that, of all the daughters O'Connor created, only retarded Lucynell Crater is "at ease with her feminine self."

Includes careful explications of "A Temple of the Holy Ghost" (with comparisons to McCuller's *The Member of the Wedding*) and "Good Country People"; a discussion of the "sexual dimension" of O'Connor's stories and her use of religious solutions "to the problem of feminine identity"; differences between O'Connor's male ("aggressive and vindictive") and female ("rendered passive by punishment") characters; and, the influence of the hostile legal and business environment faced by post-Civil War Southern widows on O'Connor's portrayal of them. Characterizes O'Connor's mother-daughter relationships in discussions of "The Life You Save May Be Your Own," "Why Do the Heathen Rage," "A Circle in the Fire," "Revelation," and "A Stroke of Good Fortune."

Notes O'Connor's familiarity with Thomas Bulfinch's *Mythology*, comparative mythology, and Greek tragedy (through Robert Fitzgerald's work), and suggests that this knowledge influenced her fictional landscapes and her depiction of groves, meadows, pastures, and the protective woods surrounding farms ruled by women. Ties men's incursions onto these farms to sexual imagery and seduction patterns, arguing that the "pattern and tone of action in O'Connor's farm stories" is close to "the archetypal rape images of Greek mythology." Discusses "Greenleaf" and "A Circle in the Fire" to illustrate why the persistent appearance of fertility myths "creates tensions in the stories which O'Connor's craft cannot resolve." Concludes that while O'Connor's fiction "is an achievement of the first order in literary terms, O'Connor also wrote stories "where problems of female sexual identity twist plots away from their intended shapes and where feminine assertion is continually punished by masculine assaults which distort ancient mythic patterns associating women with the landscape."

Representative Reviews: William L. Andrews, *Contemporary Literature* 27.2 (1986): 257-64; Frederick Asals, *Flannery O'Connor Bulletin* 14 (1985): 111-14; Robert H. Brinkmeyer, Jr. *American Literature* 58.2 (1986): 301-02; Virginia Spencer Carr, *American Literary Scholarship: An Annual 1986* (Durham, NC: Duke UP, 1988): 268; Beverly Lyon Clark, *Novel* 20.2 (1987): 188-90; Jim Elledge, *Booklist* 81.7 (1985): 1230-31; Marshall Bruce Gentry, *South Central Review* 2.4 (1985): 106-08; A.J. Griffith, *Choice* 23.3 (1985): 454; Claire Kahane, *JEGP: Journal of English and Germanic Philology* 85.4 (1986): 595-98; G.W. Koon, *Studies in Short Fiction* 23.1 (1986): 132; Nöel Polk, *Studies in the Novel* 18.4 (1986): 456-57; Diane Roberts, *Essays in Criticism* 36.2 (1986): 180-86; Nancy M. Tischler, *Christianity and Literature* 35.4 (1986): 46-47; Mary Louise Weaks, *Mississippi Quarterly* 40.1 (1986-87): 64-69; Stephen J. Whitfield, *Florida Historical Quarterly* 64.4 (1986): 473-74.

81   Whitt, Margaret Earley. *Understanding Flannery O'Connor: New Perspectives.* Understanding Contemporary American Fiction. Columbia: U of South Carolina P, 1995.

Written as a guide or companion to O'Connor's work "for students as well as good nonacademic readers." Provides an overview of O'Connor's life, professional career, and status as a writer. Suggests that "two essential components . . . drive her fiction": the fact that she "was both Southern-- ripe with its manners--and Roman Catholic--replete with its mystery." States that it is the blend and weaving together of these components-- manners and mystery--that make O'Connor's stories so "strikingly, stridently different."

Offers close readings of all of O'Connor's fiction. Discusses the fourteen essays included in O'Connor's collection of "occasional writings," *Mystery and Manners*, and the collection of O'Connor's letters, *The Habit of Being.* Devotes the final chapter to a discussion of the nine stories that are included in *The Complete Stories*, published in 1971.

Supplies, throughout the volume: reference notes at the end of each chapter; information related to date and place of publication of materials; criticism by contemporary reviewers; and comments by O'Connor herself, gleaned from her letters and essays. Concludes with a seventeen-page classified bibliography. A comprehensive index to the main body of the book is also provided.

Representative Reviews: Jill Peláez Baumgaertner, *Choice* 33.2 (1995): 297; John F. Desmond, *American Literature* 68.4 (1996): 871-72; Marshall Bruce Gentry, *Southern Quarterly* 34.2 (1996): 149-50; Gary R. Grund, *Studies in Short Fiction* 34.3 (1997): 421-23; Saranne Weller, *Journal of American Studies* 33.3 (1999): 558-59.

82   Abbot, Louise H. "Remembering Flannery." *Flannery O'Connor Bulletin* 23 (1994-95): 61-82.

Revision of a previously published memoir by Abbot (*Southern Literary Journal* 22 (1970): 3-25), concerning her friendship with O'Connor. Recounts their meetings in Milledgeville from 1957 until Flannery's death in 1964, with descriptions of O'Connor, Andalusia, and the farmhouse (including Flannery's bedroom and the "back parlor"). Topics discussed include her observations of the notice taken of Flannery by members of the local community versus that of her family and local college friends; being with Flannery while she entertained others; Flannery's participation in "a Wednesday night reading and discussion group" at Andalusia; and, her recollections of Flannery's final hospitalization, death, and funeral service. Alludes to "something terrifying" she sometimes "glimpsed" in O'Connor, and suggests that many found her "spiritual health" and "her radical honesty, humility, and courage" to be "disquieting."

83   Adair, Sally. "Flannery O'Connor." *Athens Magazine* Aug. 1991: 56-60.

Offers recollections of O'Connor by various residents of Athens, Georgia. Presents comments by participants of a writer's workshop held at the University of Georgia in 1957, including Sue Fan Tate, Margaret Miller, Ann Orr Morris, and English professors Robert West and Marion Montgomery.

84   Aiken, David. "Flannery O'Connor's Portrait of the Artist as a Young Failure." *Arizona Quarterly* 32.3 (1976): 245-59.

Discusses four references to James Joyce in O'Connor's "The Enduring Chill." Describes the work as a satiric portrait of the "self-conscious artist-hero." Suggests that Stephen Dedalus is caricatured by Asbury, who, like Joyce's hero, views his family, home, and religious tradition as limitations to be defied in the name of art. Attributes Asbury's failure as an artist to "faulty character." Reminds readers of O'Connor's view that a narrative is flawed if the author fails to reveal a clear moral judgment, and argues that O'Connor herself mars this work with her own heavy-handedness and over-writing.

84a   "ALA '99 Paper Abstracts." *Cheers! The Flannery O'Connor Society Newsletter* 7.1 (Spring/Summer 1999): 3.

Provides brief abstracts of O'Connor-related papers presented at the 1999 meeting of the American Literature Association: Sarah Gordon's "Revelatory Moments: Flannery O'Connor and Elizabeth Bishop"; Marshall Bruce Gentry's "Loving the Alien: Alice Munro's `Save the Reaper' as a Response to Flannery O'Connor's `A Good Man Is Hard to Find'"; and Sarah Fodor's "No Literary Orthodoxy: O'Connor, the New Critics, and Jacques Maritain."

85   Albert, John. "Andalusia: For Mary Flannery O'Connor (1925-1964)." *John Albert Poems II*. Ed. and intro. by Patricia A. Schwab. Bergenfield, NJ: John Otto Schwab, 1994. 143-44.

A poem offering an impressionistic perspective of Flannery O'Connor, her home at Andalusia, and the "mystery" she attempted to convey. Her influence on the poet is also acknowledged.

86   Alessio, Carolyn. "A Writer's Writers: Lee Smith's Short Fiction About Aspiring Authors and Other Unconventional Characters." *Chicago Tribune* 30 Nov. 1997, sec. 14: 14+

Notes that writer-protagonists in two of Lee Smith's short stories, collected in *News of the Spirit* (Putnam, 1997), "claim to adore" Flannery O'Connor.

87   Alexander, Alice. "The Memory of Milledgeville's Flannery O'Connor is Still Green." *Atlanta Journal* 28 March 1979: B1, B3.

Offers a biographical sketch based upon recollections from a number of O'Connor's friends, James and Mary Barbara Tate, Louise Abbot, Margaret Uhler, Mary Virginia Russell, Reynolds and Dick Allen, Fannie White, and Mary Jo Thompson. Dick Allen recounts an occasion he took Mary Flannery to a local country club on a date, "bought her a Co'Cola," and remembers O'Connor saying "`My damn foot's gone to sleep.'"

88   Alexander, Benjamin B. "`The Connections of Kin' in the Writings of Andrew Lytle." *Modern Age* 31.1 (1987): 7-20.

Includes brief, passing references to Flannery O'Connor, including a discussion of the difference in critical attention paid to Lytle versus O'Connor, one of "his more famous students." Comments that the "explicitly religious texture" of Lytle's *A Wake for the Living*, resembles O'Connor's work "in the sense that the religious issue" becomes a dominant theme in Lytle's writing as well.

89   Alexander, Benjamin B. "The Continuing Relevance of Andrew Lytle." *South Carolina Review* 24.2 (1992): 173-77.

Contends that A.E. Elmore's article in the Fall, 1990 issue of *South Carolina Review* is unfairly critical of the work of Andrew Lytle. Includes a discussion of the "curious question that suggests that Miss O'Connor is somehow more palatable than her teacher [Lytle] to Elmore because he admires the fact that Miss O'Connor's distinction is rooted in her art." Notes also that "she, unlike Lytle, on a superficial level of analysis did not leave a legacy of disturbing social and political opinions." Argues that for Elmore "to pursue the tortured logic of praising Flannery O'Connor on the one hand, while suggesting Lytle `was on the losing side of history,' is simply to ignore the considerable impact that the agrarian writings had in creating the intellectual climate that gave rise to modern Southern literature." [See: Elmore, A.E. "A.E. Elmore Replies." *South Carolina Review* 24.2 (Spring 1992): 177-78, for his response.]

90   Alexander, Benjamin B. *Flannery O'Connor and Dante's Divine Comedy.* Heritage Lectures 204. Washington, D.C.: Heritage Foundation, 1989.

A fourteen-page published version of a paper presented to the Heritage Foundation on May 24, 1989. Examines the similar theological and religious visions that Flannery O'Connor and Dante Alighieri shared, and focuses upon examples and patterns which indicate Dante's influence-- through the *Divina Commedia*--upon O'Connor and her work. Argues that O'Connor and Dante's "situations in relation to their audiences are nearly reversed."

91   Alkire, Leland G., Jr., comp. *The Writer's Advisor.* Ed. Cheryl I. Westerman. Detroit: Gale, 1985. 5, 89, 105, 122.

Offers bibliographic references to guide books on writing. Mentions O'Connor in the sections which deal with writing novels, short stories, and fictional technique.

92   Allen, Reynolds. "Writer Delighted in the World of the Absurd." *Union-Recorder* [Milledgeville, GA] 1 Aug. 1991: 4.

Biographical sketch by a community columnist of the Milledgeville, Georgia community paper. Briefly reviews O'Connor's life, writing style, and sense of humor. Refers to her difficulties with her editor at Rhinehart, John Shelby; her successful effort to recover the *Wise Blood* manuscript from that publisher; and her subsequent contract with Harcourt-Brace, "who accepted it without reservations."

93   Allen, Suzanne. "Memories of a Southern Catholic Girlhood: Flannery O'Connor's `A Temple of the Holy Ghost.'" *Renascence* 31 (1979): 83-92.

Analyzes O'Connor's sacramental view and comments on the destructiveness of her Southern evangelical characters who "have no sacramental system." Notes two allusions in the story that "introduce sexual and spiritual initiation" for the girl entering "both Southern womanhood and Christian adulthood." Relates that the first allusion deals with the story's two "good women"--the child's mother and the black cook--and their role as Christian examples. Contends that the second is how the carnival freak displays "all human imperfections, limitations which can be overcome through Incarnated Love, the Holy Eucharist." Concludes that it is through her acceptance of the carnival freak that the girl finds her path from innocent childhood to Christian womanhood, "whereas her evangelical Southern counterparts come only to sorrow and destruction because of their inability to accept the physical world."

94   Allen, Walter. "Welty, McCullers, Taylor, Flannery O'Connor." *The Short Story in English*. Oxford: Clarendon, 1981. 310-28.

Allen offers his views on the American short story gleaned from his lectures delivered at the British Academy and graduate seminars in various universities. Gives outline explications of "Good Country People" and "A Good Man Is Hard to Find." Suggests that in "Good Country People," "Pointer's obsession with women's glass eyes and wooden legs is something more than a symptom of a merely psychological disability or neurotic disorder." Sees it instead as "the dramatic expression in symbolic form of a disability, an incongruity, a *grotesquerie*, at the heart of things." Comments that the central concern of "A Good Man Is Hard to Find" is "The Misfit's relation to Christ and his conviction that `Jesus thrown everything off balance.'" Concludes that O'Connor is "probably nearer to Dostoevsky than to any Southern writer," and that her stories "are so absolutely of their own kind that any of them will lead directly into the world and values she creates."

95   Allen, William Rodney. "The Cage of Matter: The World as Zoo in Flannery O'Connor's *Wise Blood*." *American Literature* 58.2 (1986): 256-70.

Offers a brief review of criticism related to *Wise Blood*, then details O'Connor's use of animal imagery to intensify the novel's themes. Suggests that O'Connor shows "that the world, without its spiritual dimension, is merely a prison for an odd collection of inmates--a zoo for the human animal."

96   Allen, William Rodney. "Mr. Head and Hawthorne: Allusion and Conversion in Flannery O'Connor's `The Artificial Nigger.'" *Studies in Short Fiction* 21.1 (1984): 17-23.

Remarks that O'Connor referred to herself as one of Nathaniel Hawthorne's descendants and demonstrated intimate knowledge of his works. Suggests that she drew heavily from his sketch, "The Custom House" (preface to *The Scarlet Letter)* for "The Artificial Nigger." Discusses the conversion experience and moonlight imagery in each story; the fact that both stories feature men who cling to their provincial worlds; and the shared major theme of each story: the handing down of guilt from one generation to the next.

97   Allen, William Rodney. *Walker Percy: A Southern Wayfarer*. Jackson: UP of Mississippi, 1986. 38, 79, 91, 102, 104.

Offers brief references to O'Connor's life and work in relation to Percy's novels: the presence in *The Moviegoer* of "an echo of the imagery of Hazel Motes's train ride in *Wise Blood,*" and Robert H. Brinkmeyer's observation that Percy adopted a new strategy from O'Connor's use of violence in *The Violent Bear It Away*. Allen's analysis of Percy's *Lancelot* begins with Hazel Motes's remark, "`The only way to the truth is through blasphemy,'" and Allen remarks that Lancelot "joins such fascinating demoniacal literary precursors" as Hazel Motes in O'Connor's *Wise Blood*.

98   Allison, John M. "James Wilcox (1949-)." *Contemporary Fiction Writers of the South: A Bio-Bibliographical Sourcebook*. Ed. Joseph M. Flora and Robert Bain. Westport, CT: Greenwood, 1993. 468-78.

Includes a brief discussion of O'Connor's influence on Wilcox's work. States that his mother, "an avid reader who encouraged her children to explore books," encouraged her son to read O'Connor's short stories after she had attended a reading by O'Connor at nearby Southeastern Louisiana University. Reports that James Wilcox now "identifies O'Connor's short stories as an influence on his writing, noting that they gave him the courage to write novels."

98a   Als, Hilton. "The Unvanquished: Sally Mann's Portrait of the South." *New Yorker* 27 Sept. 1999: 98-102.

Discusses O'Connor's efforts "to pit her irony against her times" and considers her as one of the few Southern writers who attempted "to tell the truth of their experience, to debunk the magnolia-strewn myths of the region by confronting its history of industrial and political folly." Uses O'Connor's artistic intentions as background and context to discuss the photographic art of Kentucky-born Sally Mann in her book of black-and-white photographs, *At Twelve: Portraits of Young Women* (1988).

99   Alther, Lisa. "Introduction" to *A Good Man Is Hard to Find* by Flannery O'Connor. London: Women's Press, 1980. 2-8.

Attempts to "place" O'Connor as "a Southerner, a Catholic, and a woman," and asserts that "each hated category has a bearing on her writing." Discusses the types of characters found in O'Connor's work; her efforts to describe "a poverty of the soul not confined to any one geographical region"; and O'Connor's identity as a woman writer. [Rpt. in *Friendship and Sympathy: Communities of Southern Women Writers.* Ed. Rosemary M. Magee. Jackson: UP of Mississippi, 1992. 187-92.]

100   Anastaplo, George. "Can Beauty 'Hallow Even the Bloodiest Tomahawk'?" *Critic: A Catholic Review of Books and the Arts* 48.2 (1993): 1-18.

Discusses Ernest Hemingway's "The Killers," O'Connor's "A Good Man Is Hard to Find," and the 1991 Academy Award-winning film, "The Silence of the Lambs." Examines the three to see what "glimpses into the human soul" they might provide. Provides excerpts from the two stories and relies upon critical assessments by Carl and Mark Van Doren to provide a context for discussing the artistic depiction of violence. Compares "A Good Man Is Hard to Find" with "The Killers," citing comments by Martha Foley, Thomas Merton, and Caroline Gordon. Focuses on the stories' settings, the approach used by each author to killing, and the perspective from which Hemingway's killers might view O'Connor's. Sees O'Connor as being influenced by Hemingway, and suggests that while there is "more nobility" in his story than in hers, O'Connor's view that there is "no human remedy or solution offered for the human condition" appears to be "the more popular today."

101   Anderson, Roger K. "Back to the Terrible Secret: Unblinking Novel From Martin Amis." Rev. of *Time's Arrow. Houston Chronicle* 5 Jan. 1992: 13.

Refers to O'Connor as a writer "who believes that an unblinking look at the horrors that men do can make us see the darkest seeds that reside in us, seeds that, without the corrections of morality, produce horrors unthinkable, but which need thinking on nonetheless."

102   Andreas, James. "'If It's a Symbol, to Hell with It': The Medieval Gothic Style of Flannery O'Connor in *Everything That Rises Must Converge*." *Christianity & Literature* 38.2 (1989): 23-41.

Contends that O'Connor's Gothic perspective is derived "directly from original medieval theological and aesthetic sources." Describes her Gothic style and grotesque humor, and her interest in medieval theology, philosophy, and aesthetics as evidenced in *Everything That Rises Must Converge*.

102a   Andretta, Helen R. "A Thomist's Letters to `A.'" *Flannery O'Connor Bulletin* 26-27 (1998-2000): 52-72.

Examines O'Connor's correspondence to "A" (Betty Hester) for insights into her knowledge of Thomas Aquinas and how she applied Thomistic philosophy to her own life and art. Remarks in particular, on O'Connor's interest in the writings of Jacques Maritain. Closes with a discussion of how "Maritain's works on the relationship between art and Thomistic philosophy [appear to have] guided O'Connor in an understanding of her writing in the light of her faith and of Aquinas."

103   Angle, Kimberly Greene. "Flannery O'Connor's Literary Art: Spiritual Portraits in Negative Space." *Flannery O'Connor Bulletin* 23 (1994-95): 158-74.

Describes how the application of "negative-space theory" can be applied to all of O'Connor's short fiction. Suggests that it provides "an explanation of how a spiritual dimension can co-exist with the obviously violent and bizarre nature of her stories." Declares that "within the `outer sketch' of her stories, in which characters are void of spirituality, O'Connor, like the negative-space artist, simultaneously creates an `inner sketch' of the nature of redemption and grace that is the fulfillment of that void." Refers to ideas of Betty Edwards, Edward B. Lindaman, and Alan Watt and offers readings of "The Enduring Chill" and "The Comforts of Home" to show how O'Connor uses this concept.

104   "Announcement: The Third Flannery O'Connor Symposium." *Flannery O'Connor Bulletin* 12 (1983): 3.

Announces that the Flannery O'Connor Board and Georgia College & State University will sponsor "the third O'Connor symposium, a weekend of thoughtful and lively lectures, films, and tours of the writer's terrain." Reports that Ralph Wood, J.O. Tate, and Frederick Asals will present papers and that Sally Fitzgerald will be presenting the *Flannery O'Connor Memorial Lecture* "from the forthcoming biography."

104a   "Announcing the *Flannery O'Connor Review.*" *Flannery O'Connor Bulletin* 26-27 (1998-2000): 135.

Announces that the inaugural issue of *The Flannery O'Connor Review*, "a new journal building on the strengths" of the *Flannery O'Connor Bulletin*, will feature, among other topics, "a section on southern preaching." Notes that the date of the first volume will be "Fall 2001."

105   Arbery, Glenn Cannon. "Victims of Likeness: Quadroons and Octoroons in Southern Fiction." *Southern Review* 25.1 (1989): 52-71.

Discusses the role of partially black characters in Southern literature, focusing on William Faulkner's *Absalom, Absalom!*, Allen Tate's *The Fathers*, and George Washington Cable's "Madame Delphine." Includes a discussion of "the problem of bastardy" in O'Connor's *Wise Blood* (in regard to Sabbath Hawks).

106   Archer, Emily. "Naming in the Neighborhood of Being: O'Connor and Percy on Language." *Studies in the Literary Imagination* 20.2 (1987): 97-108.

Asserts that an examination of the writings of Walker Percy and Flannery O'Connor reveals that both shared many of the same preoccupations. Among their mutual concerns is their focus on language as a basis for a "diagnosis of the twentieth century" and as an instrument for its healing. Discusses each author's focus on the "act of naming": Percy's belief that the best he could hope for was "finally only an attempt at asking the right questions"; and O'Connor's quest, which focused on her search for words that might transform nature and illustrate her penetrating vision. Concludes that the "strength of O'Connor and Percy's art rests largely on their commitment to stalk the created world for the accurate, incarnational name of things."

107   Archer, Emily. "`Stalking Joy': Flannery O'Connor's Accurate Naming." *Religion and Literature* 18.2 (1986): 17-30.

Describes the importance that O'Connor places upon "the craft of constructing names for [her] fictional characters." Asserts that for O'Connor, naming is "inextricable with seeing, and seeing with truth." Suggests that naming provides O'Connor with a way to affirm and participate in the mystery of the Divine life and is an important aspect of her artistic technique.

108   Archer, Jane Elizabeth. "'This Is My Place': The Short Films Made from Flannery O'Connor's Short Fiction." *Studies in American Humor* 1.1 (1982): 52-65.

Briefly reviews O'Connor's place in literary criticism, examining both her intentions as well as the various labels used by critics to "place" her work. Argues that in view of their secular and doctrinal traditions, "the place Flannery O'Connor's fiction holds in film" inhabits a similar "literary landscape for critics and filmmakers." Suggests that filmmakers have generally used her stories as blueprints and "filmed her stories by exchanging shot for descriptive sentence . . . transposing film sequence for bits of narrative action." Analyzes film versions of "A Circle in the Fire," "The Displaced Person," "The Comforts of Home," and "Good Country People," and summarizes similarities, focal points, and themes.

109   Arnold, Edwin T. "The Canonization of Jesse Stuart." *Appalachian Journal* 13.1 (1985): 28-33.

A review essay on H. Edward Richardson's biography, *Jesse: The Biography of an American Writer--Jesse Hilton Stuart*, which contains references to O'Connor. Reports O'Connor's remark after meeting Stuart at a symposium at Vanderbilt in 1959: "Jesse Stuart's ego was like the light on the front of a train but as [Robert Penn] Warren remarked, we probably all have that much but just know how to keep it under better cover." Mentions O'Connor's "amazed recounting" of an incident in which Stuart told O'Connor that her story "A Good Man Is Hard to Find" simply did not end right and suggested to O'Connor that she "'should have kept it going until the cops got there and saved the grandmother!'"

110   Arnold, Marilyn. "*Nickel Mountain*: John Gardner's Testament of Redemption." *Renascence* 30.2 (1978): 59-68.

Includes a brief comparison of Gardner's work with that of O'Connor: "With the exception of Flannery O'Connor, John Gardner may well be America's only major writer of fiction since Faulkner to speak boldly and explicitly in public about the moral obligations of the artist as a shaper of values." Remarks that, however, "unlike Flannery O'Connor, who was trying mainly to convince a hard-headed audience that the redemption of Jesus Christ is real, John Gardner prefers to seek out human models of goodness and suggest that they too have redemptive powers."

111   Arnold, Marilyn. "Sentimentalism in the Devil's Territory." *Literature and Belief* 17.1-2 (1997): 243-58.

Contends that O'Connor "regarded the comic as her first line of defense against sentimentalism and that she thought religious institutions were especially vulnerable to emotional infection." Observes how O'Connor's use of "playful satire" in her letters and stories, "along with her obvious choice of the grotesque, serves to divert both O'Connor and her correspondents and readers from potential overblown tenderness." Notes that while O'Connor "could talk seriously enough about doctrinal matters and art . . . she retreated behind a shield of comedy, or scorn, whenever sentiment raised its head." Discusses O'Connor's references to the devil in her fiction and in letters to "A," Cecil Dawkins, and other correspondents; O'Connor's belief that sentimentality and pornography were linked; differences between O'Connor's work and Eudora Welty's; and the observation that O'Connor "intended her art to be an antidote to the romantic mentality of the times," which she saw as fostered by the devil "to divert us from faith's stony realities." Follows with discussions of her use of "holy violence," using excerpts from *Wise Blood* and *The Violent Bear It Away* to argue that O'Connor believed that "violent grace" serves as "a manifestation of divine mercy offered to the redeemable."

112   Arnold, Marilyn. "*The Violent Bear It Away*: Flannery O'Connor's Reluctant Compromise with Mercy." *McNeese Review* 28 (1981-82): 25-33.

Discusses the scriptural basis and religious significance of O'Connor's *The Violent Bear It Away*. Indicates that while many readers admire her writing ability, they also "cringe at the deftness with which she practices terminal grace," as well as "her insistence on the `violence of love' and the violence of religious experience."

113   Arnold, Marilyn. "*Wise Blood*: Flannery O'Connor's Lonely Gospel of Hope." *Drew Gateway* 46.1-3 (1975-76): 78-84.

Asserts that while O'Connor's world may be violent and grotesque, unlike most contemporary fiction it does not depict modern life as hopeless. Contends that O'Connor forces her readers to confront "Western man's oldest and sometimes only hope--ultimate redemption through Jesus Christ." Finds *Wise Blood* to be O'Connor's clearest statement of humanity's need for redemption. Contends that because Hazel Motes blames himself, the reader understands that he will join the multitude of O'Connor's other characters "who are granted the moment of grace, the moment of self-revelation and God-recognition--and hence, the moment of hope, for redemption is real."

114   Asals, Frederick. "Differentiation, Violence, and the Displaced Person." *Flannery O'Connor Bulletin* 13 (1984): 1-14.

Explores O'Connor's use of "mystery and manners" through some of the ideas of René Girard, "particularly those developed in his provocative book *Violence and the Sacred*." Outlines Girard's speculations on "the mechanisms of ritual sacrifice" and violence, and ties them to O'Connor's "Everything That Rises Must Converge," "Judgement Day," and her "several tales of women owners of small farms." Focuses on "the most revealing and inclusive tale" of this latter group, "The Displaced Person," and offers a detailed explication. Suggests that Girard's view of violence as endemic to man, "so endemic . . . that it constantly threatens to burst through all social orders, to consume the community itself as well as its individual members," offers a vantage point from which one might better understand O'Connor's use of violence in "The Displaced Person." Sees this, and O'Connor's other stories of this type, as springing from the fact that the "post-World War II South of her fiction is a society in which traditionally clear separations . . . seem to have wobbled, become unstable, [and] blurred in such ways as to release an ever mounting anxiety until, under the pressure of a tale's action, it bursts into violence."

115   Asals, Frederick. "The Double." *Flannery O'Connor: Modern Critical Views*. Ed. Harold Bloom. New York: Chelsea House, 1986. 93-109.

An edited and shortened version of Asals's essay originally published as "The Double in Flannery O'Connor's Stories," in *The Flannery O'Connor Bulletin* 9 (1980): 49-86. This version leaves out the portion of the text that offers a reading "The Comforts of Home." [Rpt. as "The Double," in *Flannery O'Connor: The Imagination of Extremity*, by Frederick Asals (Athens: U of Georgia P, 1982. 95-123).]

116   Asals, Frederick. "The Double in Flannery O'Connor's Stories." *Flannery O'Connor Bulletin* 9 (1980): 49-86.

Examines O'Connor's use of the double figure, asserting that as "an expression in character and action . . . the pattern recurs so often that it can only be called obsessive." Sees her use as taking two forms: "either one character discovers that another is a replica of himself," or "more often, one character is presented as the alter ego of another." Cites a variety of characters with double figures, and notes O'Connor's use of terms such as "double, replica, twin, brother, negative image, [and] mirror" as indicative of the "classic language of the doppelgänger motif." Offers readings of "A View of the Woods" and "Good Country People" to illustrate how O'Connor uses the double motif "in almost directly contrary ways." Contends that one story shows the disastrous effect of a character refusing to recognize his double figure, while in the other, the comic climax is brought about by the character's "inability *not* to recognize him." Further explores the double motif with a reading of "The Comforts of Home," which Asals regards as "surely one of the least convincing [stories] O'Connor ever devised." Observes that it "seems to demand a `psychological reading.'" Remarks that O'Connor clearly viewed the unconscious not only as a repository of "repressed sexual and aggressive urges, but as a realm of inherent theological dimension from which could come intimations [doubles] of the demonic and divine." Concludes that, because O'Connor "could not still that ironic voice that questions and contradicts," her integrity and use of the double motif enable her projection of "these conflicts in her fiction, dramatizing and exploring the clash without pretending to a spurious reconciliation she could not feel."

117   Asals, Frederick. "`Obediah,' `Obadiah': *Guys and Dolls* and `Parker's Back.'" *Flannery O'Connor Bulletin* 21 (1992): 37-42.

Finds coincidences in a section of dialogue of Sky Masterson in *Guys and Dolls* and O.E. Parker in "Parker's Back." Observes that both occur at the climax of the work, deal with a pious wife, and involve a demand by that wife from her husband that he state his real name (a variation in spelling of the same name, "Obediah")--the utterance of which allows "full entry into the religious life." Suggests that both works "share a comic stylization . . . [especially] in their presentations of Protestant evangelism and their protagonists' journeys toward some manner of `conversion.'" Concludes that *Guys and Dolls*, as a musical comedy, does not reflect the "darker tones that `Parker's Back'" and later musicals such as *West Side Story* and *Gypsy* employ. "What O'Connor does is take popular conventions--boy-meets-girl, how-I-found-God-and-became-a-happier-person--and evolve them until they express a more disturbing vision."

118   Asals, Frederick. Rev. of *Flannery O'Connor: Her Life, Library, and Book Reviews*, by Lorine M. Getz. *Flannery O'Connor Bulletin* 9 (1980): 132-36.

Suggests that while O'Connor's writings represented in this volume "do not have the charm, depth, nor general interest of the writings in *Mystery and Manners*, or *The Habit of Being*," this volume "will prove an indispensable work for O'Connor scholars in the foreseeable future." Contends that her reviews "deepen and extend our knowledge of her views on a number of subjects," and reflect her charitable work as a reviewer. Outlines Getz's literary biography of O'Connor and her descriptive list of O'Connor's library at Georgia College & State University. Quibbles with Getz's view "that O'Connor must be seen against both her Catholic and Southern backgrounds."

119   Asals, Frederick. Rev. of *Sacred Groves and Ravaged Gardens: The Fiction of Eudora Welty, Carson McCullers, and Flannery O'Connor*, by Louise Westling. *Flannery O'Connor Bulletin* 14 (1985): 111-14.

Focuses on the two chapters devoted to O'Connor's work. Reminds readers that while O'Connor made "abruptly dismissive remarks" on "`the feminist business,'" Westling's work provides "the most sustained attempt to bring O'Connor's corpus within the purview of feminist criticism." Questions Westling's decision to "concentrate on female characters and relationships and the landscapes traditionally associated with them" instead of "on the more general condition of `feminization' in O'Connor's fiction." Cites other concerns regarding "Westling's finding `confusion' in several stories," and wishes that she "had made some discriminations in her argument that O'Connor rejects the traditional identification of the landscape with the feminine." Concludes that the book "is clearly written and cogently argued, tactful in its handling of biographical matters, [and] never less than interesting."

120   Asals, Frederick. "Some Glimpses of Flannery O'Connor in the Canadian Landscape." *Flannery O'Connor Bulletin* 23 (1994-95): 83-90.

Discusses the influence of Flannery O'Connor on Canadian writers by outlining similarities, pointing out parallels and using quotes from interviews of the writers discussed and their work to illustrate connections. Refers to a wide variety of Canadian writers, including: Deborah Joy Corey, Alice Munro, Leon Rooke, Barry Callaghan, Jack Hodgins, Hugh Hood, Isabel Huggan, Joan MacLeod, and Helen Porter. Also refers to scholarly work on O'Connor in Canada by J. Peter Dyson, Linda Munk, and Irwin Streight. Concludes that "it is safe to say--as it is said of Jesus and Elvis--that in Canada, `Flannery Lives!'"

121   Ashley, Jack Dillard. "Throwing the Big Book: The Narrative Voice in
        Flannery O'Connor's Stories." *Realist of Distances: Flannery O'Connor
        Revisited.* Ed. Karl-Heinz Westarp and Jan Nordby Gretlund. Aarhus
        (Denmark): Aarhus UP, 1987. 73-81.

        Asserts that "O'Connor's omniscient narrator's voice . . . is a complex
        aggregate: the comic and ironic voice of the eiron; the rational and moral
        voice of the chorus; [and] the prophetic and apocalyptic voice of the
        oracle." Suggests that it is the eiron that creates, the chorus that judges,
        and the oracle that condemns, though sometimes it redeems.

122   Association of American Book Publishers. *America Through American
        Eyes: An Exhibit of Recent Books That Reflect Life in the United States.*
        Moscow: Moscow International Book Fair, 1979. 74.

        Provides an entry and short description of O'Connor's *The Complete
        Stories* in the category "Our Current Literature: Fiction." Refers to
        O'Connor as "One of our best Southern writers, dealing with Christianity,
        evangelical religion, prophets, madness, the land, growing up, and the
        mysteries of feeling." Adds that her letters have been compared with those
        of D.H. Lawrence and Lord Byron.

123   "Author's Beloved Peacocks Come to Violent End." *Charleston (SC) Post
        and Courier* 29 Nov. 1991: B10.

        Reports that the last of O'Connor's peacocks was eaten by a silver fox near
        Lake Lorelei in southern Ohio. Recounts O'Connor's love for peacocks,
        the symbolic role they play in her work, and how they were dispersed
        after her death in 1964.

124   Aycock, Wendell. "The American Short Story into Film." *Studies in Short
        Fiction* 18.3 (1981): 324-26.

        Discusses *The American Short Story* film series that first appeared, in its
        original form, on PBS in the spring of 1977. Lists and describes the films
        included in the first series, then the eight new adaptations shown in 1980
        and 1981. Includes a brief comment regarding O'Connor's "The Displaced
        Person."

125   Babinec, Lisa S. "Cyclical Patterns of Domination and Manipulation in
        Flannery O'Connor's Mother-Daughter Relationships." *Flannery
        O'Connor Bulletin* 19 (1990): 9-29.

Offers a study "of mother-daughter relationships from a feminist perspective." Refers to O'Connor's comments to "A"; discusses whether O'Connor "lacks feminist sensitivity"; and sets out to use "contemporary feminist theory to ascertain whether or not feminist readings can be drawn" from her fiction. Analyzes "Good Country People," "Revelation," and "A Circle in the Fire." Considers "four damaging aspects of mother-daughter relationships: the pattern of maternal domination, failed expectations, the effects of manipulation, and the ready acceptance of the masculine work ethic." Suggests that the works of Marianne Hirsch and Sara Ruddick provide the best critical purview from which to discuss "'maternal thinking.'" Uses their work "to determine the cyclical patterns that evolve from attempts at domination and manipulation and to ascertain why mothers and daughters fail to interact successfully." Concludes with an overview "of the mother-daughter action/reaction" in an effort to "provide possible reasons for O'Connor's presentation of abusive family relationships."

126   Bacon, Jon Lance. "A Fondness for Supermarkets: *Wise Blood* and Consumer Culture." *New Essays on Wise Blood*. Ed. Michael Kreyling. New York: Cambridge UP, 1995. 25-49.

Suggests that the portrayal of Joy-Hulga in "Good Country People" reflects "a strong affinity" between O'Connor and Marshall McLuhan. Refers to McLuhan's use of body parts (legs) in *The Mechanical Bride*, and remarks that "Like McLuhan, O'Connor relates the imagery of body parts to the idea of selfhood." Argues that when Manley Pointer steals Joy-Hulga's leg, "she succumbs to the `cultural dynamics' identified by McLuhan -- the dynamics of `replaceable parts.'" Discusses how salesmen make "frequent appearances" in O'Connor's work, and indicates that for each, "salesmanship means the deferment of true selfhood." Relates how this relationship--between salesmanship and selfhood--"receives its fullest treatment" in *Wise Blood*, and describes how the book serves as O'Connor's "critique of American consumer culture, whose period of greatest expansion coincided with her literary career." Claims that the techniques of advertising and marketing serve a scenic function on one level, and "have significance for individual identity" on another. Describes, the manner in which O'Connor identifies Enoch with consumerism and how, he "exemplifies the `public helplessness' that McLuhan hoped to remedy by analyzing advertising." Explores the idea "that a salesperson would have to identify herself with the product being sold," the "rise of a `personality market,'" and O'Connor's use of Solace Layfield and Hoover Shoats as examples. Concludes that O'Connor's work illustrates her view that America's consumer society would disappoint all who believe that a material product might bring self-realization. Strives to show that she viewed the social norm of her day as "decidedly offensive," and that the "American way" was antithetical to Catholicism and fundamentalism. Refers to David Riesman's *The Lonely Crowd*, William H. Whyte's *The Organization Man*, C. Wright Mills's *White Collar*, Vance Packard's *The Hidden Persuaders*, Will Herberg's *Protestant - Catholic - Jew*, Norman Vincent Peale's *The Power of Positive Thinking*, and discusses points made by Louis Kronenberger, Newton Arvin, Frances Cheney, John H. Marion, A. Roy Eckardt, and John C. Bennett.

127   Bain, Robert, Joseph M. Flora and Louis D. Rubin, Jr. *Southern Writers: A Biographical Dictionary*. Baton Rouge: Louisiana State UP, 1979. 329-30.

         Offers a brief biographical article on O'Connor. Lists her major works and mentions the original publications of her early stories. Asserts that O'Connor's acclaim is "hardly matched by any other writer of her time."

128   Baker, J. Robert. "Flannery O'Connor's Four-Fold Method of Allegory." *Flannery O'Connor Bulletin* 21 (1992): 84-96.

         Discusses O'Connor's use of allegory and her view of the difficulty allegory poses for modern readers. Suggests that "O'Connor's own alert and earnest view of the concrete and the literal led her" to its use, and "as she focused on manners, she created a fiction deeply rooted in the medieval four-fold method of exegesis." Offers a reading of *The Violent Bear It Away* based upon the premise that "the allegorical mode is intrinsic" to a proper reading of the novel. Contends that the "obsessed and driven" characters O'Connor created for this work are "more types and personifications than personalities." Notes that their repetitive actions resolve "into a psychomachia played out in the protagonist Tarwater and in his uncles, Mason and Rayber." Argues that images of "Baptism and the Bread carry the tropological and anagogical significations of the novel." Further, insists that "the sacrament with its conversion of the individual enacts the moral choice that any human being, even a reader, faces: the dull and often enervating practice of belief as opposed to the fascinating but finally lethal lure of evil." Regards Tarwater's vision of redeemed souls eating loaves of bread and fish as "an anagogical portrait of the human soul opened by violence--particularly by the violence of God's apocalyptic mercy--to redemption."

129   Baker, William and Kenneth Womack. *Recent Work in Critical Theory, 1989-1995*. Bibliographies and Indexes in World Literature, No. 51. Westport, CT: Greenwood, 1996. 82, 316-17, 405-06.

Provides an annotated bibliography of articles and books on critical theory published between 1989 and 1995. Three citations refer to Flannery O'Connor: Robert Penn Warren's *Talking With Robert Penn Warren*, edited by Floyd C. Watkins, John T. Hiers, and Mary Louise Weaks (Athens: U of Georgia P, 1990); *The Female Tradition in Southern Literature*, edited by Carol S. Manning (Urbana: U of Illinois P, 1993); and, Paul Giles's *American Catholic Arts and Fictions: Culture, Ideology, Aesthetics* (Cambridge UP, 1992).

130   Balazy, Teresa. "External Mediation in Flannery O'Connor's *Wise Blood*." *Studia Anglica Posnaniensia* (Poznan, Poland) 9 (1977): 169-95.

Asserts that O'Connor may be distinguished from humanist existentialist writers by her emphasis on sin and grace in relation to the mystery of redemption, as exemplified in *Wise Blood*. Argues that O'Connor sees existentialists as influencing the modern individual to distrust the "existence of transcendent Christian reality." Suggests that O'Connor's believers deny--but seek--God. Adapts René Girard's concept of "external mediation," and sees that O'Connor's protagonist must be brought to recognize "redemption as his real desire and Christ as his only true mediator."

131   Baldanza, Frank. "O'Connor, Mary Flannery." *The Encyclopedia of Southern History*. Ed. David C. Roller and Robert W. Twyman. Baton Rouge: Louisiana State UP, 1979. 533, 727, 935-36.

Offers a biographical sketch and description of O'Connor's works. Quotes Caroline Gordon on O'Connor: "`she was the first fiction writer of outstanding talent to look at the rural South through the eyes of Roman Catholic orthodoxy.'" Suggests that O'Connor's typical characters were "protestant fundamentalist fanatics," and that her two novels depict "God-obsessed BIBLE BELT prophets [who] suffer hideous anguish in struggling with vocations in the context of an urban secular society permeated with religious apathy, humanism, science, and materialism." Asserts that O'Connor's short stories reflect "a pattern in which supernatural grace . . . erupts violently within the experience of ordinary rural people." Submits that O'Connor "was acutely aware of the dilemma of presenting essentially medieval Catholic assumptions to a body of secularized readers." Concludes that O'Connor uses "macabre caricature, vicious satire, and violently ludicrous comedy to shock complacent readers into a recognition of her own sense of urgency to accept certain traditional views of Christ, the devil, death, and salvation."

132   Baldwin, Dean, and Gregory L. Morris. "Flannery O'Connor (1925-1964)." *The Short Story in English: Britain and North America, An Annotated Bibliography.* Magill Bibliographies. Metuchen, NJ: Scarecrow, 1994. 242-57.

Offers descriptive summaries (100-120 words each) of books and articles related to O'Connor. Items are divided into three categories: "General Biographical and Critical Studies" (26 abstracts); "Selected Titles: Collections" (1 abstract); and, "Selected Titles: Individual Stories" (12 abstracts).

133   Balée, Susan. "Flannery O'Connor Resurrected." *The Hudson Review* 47.3 (1994): 377-93.

Recounts a visit to Milledgeville, Georgia in April, 1994 to attend Georgia College & State University's "Habit of Art" celebration in honor of O'Connor. Refers to her own young-adult biography of O'Connor and states that because she had more questions than answers, she came to the conference to immerse herself "in Flannery's home country . . . to grasp somehow, finally, the truth of her life." Finds the sight of Flannery's mother's "decrepit" house in town "depressing," and offers a running commentary on her activities while attending the conference: meeting Cecil Dawkins, Barry Moser, Louise Westling, Claire Shepard, and Louise Erdrich; her discussion and outline of her interview with Sally Fitzgerald (focusing on O'Connor's love life); and her description of the "most important" session of the conference, the panel discussion--with Ralph Wood, Willie Jennings, and Henry Russell--which focused on O'Connor's position and attitude on "the race issue."

134   Bamberg, Marie Louise. "A Note on the Motif of Midday Crisis in Flannery O'Connor's *The Violent Bear It Away.*" *AN&Q: American Notes & Queries* 23.1-2 (1984): 19-21.

Explores the motif of sun imagery as illustrative of midday crisis in *The Violent Bear It Away*. Suggests that noon is "a moment of suspense between time past and time to come . . . a turning point . . . the hour of physical and spiritual crisis." Refers to Tarwater's awakening to his need for redemption as a reminder "that in the Christian tradition, Christ's agony on the cross gives noon its positive force."

135   Bandy, Stephen C. "'One of My Babies': The Misfit and the Grandmother." *Studies in Short Fiction* 33 (1996): 107-17.

Reports that "criticism of Flannery O'Connor's fiction, under the spell of the writer's occasional comments, has been unusually susceptible to interpretations based on Christian dogma." Discusses "A Good Man Is Hard to Find" and argues that while "the concerns of this story are the basic concerns of Christian belief: faith, death, salvation . . . if one reads the story without prejudice, there would seem to be little . . . to inspire hope for redemption of any of its characters." Offers a reading of the story, focusing on the actions and intentions of the Grandmother and The Misfit. Concludes that the message of the story is "profoundly pessimistic and in fact subversive to the doctrines of grace and charity, despite heroic efforts to disguise that fact."

135a   Banner, Keith. "In Flannery O'Connor's Footsteps."Interview with Brian Bouldrey. *Lambda Book Report* 7.8 (1999): 6-8.

Bouldrey interviews novelist and short story writer, Keith Banner, who expresses his admiration for Flannery O'Connor and the "Christian" love she had for her characters. Describes this love as a "spiritual love" that "values people," even though it "is not really a sentimental or even emotional love." States that he sees her as "not encumbered by religion, [but] freed by it . . . to see the truth behind the facades people put up in order to lie to themselves."

136   Barnes, Linda Adams. "The Freak Endures: The Southern Grotesque from Flannery O'Connor to Bobbie Ann Mason." *Since Flannery O'Connor: Essays on the Contemporary American Short Story.* Ed. Loren Logsdon and Charles W. Mayer. Macomb: Western Illinois UP, 1987. 133-41.

Introduces a discussion of the grotesque in Southern fiction by isolating, then summarizing, three elements of O'Connor's version of the grotesque: her use of it as an instructional tool; her objective of comic effect; and her role as a "writer of realism who is a spokesman of and to her age." Contends that, just as the South has changed since O'Connor's death, "the Southern grotesque has changed with it." Refers to William Peden's, "A Mad World, My Masters," and Lewis A. Lawson's 1967 essay, "The Grotesque in Recent Southern Fiction" along with his 1984 collection of essays on post-World War II Southern writers, *Another Generation,* to frame a discussion of the use of the grotesque in post-O'Connor Southern fiction. Makes a case for Bobbie Ann Mason's grotesque as being "firmly rooted in the tradition of Flannery O'Connor." Then, offers a work-by-work discussion of Mason's use of the grotesque, relating it to her view of the situation in the modern South, and as a tool with which "to speak to and about her own generation."

137   Bart, Robert S. "The Miraculous Moonlight: Flannery O'Connor's `The Artificial Nigger.'" *St. Johns Review* 37.2-3 (1986): 37-47.

Offers an extensive analysis of "The Artificial Nigger," with emphasis on sources of imagery in the Bible, Dante's *Divine Comedy*, and on meanings related to images of "blackness." Explores the role and involvement of the black characters; the meaning of the plaster figure (the "artificial nigger"); and the significance of moonlight. Concludes that the "black light" restores "true dignity not only to Nelson and Mr. Head, but to all the insulted, degraded, and abused, while setting them free not only of their chains, but of their hate, their fear, and their wounded pride."

138   Bartley, Numan V. "Society and Culture in an Urban Age." *A History of Georgia*. Ed. Kenneth Coleman, et al. 2nd ed. Athens: U of Georgia P, 1991.

Cites the works of Flannery O'Connor and Carson McCullers as examples of how the Southern literary renaissance continued after World War II. Offers a brief biographical sketch, refers to O'Connor's "powerful religious orientation," and states that she "peopled her South with grotesque characters too dissolute and unrepentant to attain salvation."

139   Bass, Eben. "Flannery O'Connor and Henry James: The Vision of Grace." *Studies in the 20th Century: A Scholarly and Critical Journal* 14 (Fall, 1974): 43-67.

Considers how O'Connor learned from Henry James's practice and theory of fiction and adapted his methods, particularly his use of point of view, to suit her own purposes. Suggests that O'Connor "does not restrict point of view for simplicity's sake," but, like James, believes that "the ricochet of viewer and his reactions is crucial to the tale." Proposes that what characters in both James and O'Connor's fiction "see and fail to see are much more true to the story, the true country, than are the `incidents' [in the stories] themselves." Recognizes and classifies a variety of points of view found in O'Connor's fiction: the "indignant young watcher," the "inept male intellectual," "males with smothering mothers," characters involved in parent-child conflicts, "strong-minded matriarchs," and characters with "unwelcome emotional ties." Illustrates O'Connor's uses of point of view with reference to practically all of her major short fiction.

140   Bassett, Beth Dawkins. "Converging Lives." *Emory Magazine* 58.4 (1982): 17-23.

Discusses how Sally Fitzgerald met Flannery O'Connor through Robert Lowell in the spring of 1949. Provides Fitzgerald's recollections of O'Connor's physical characteristics, including her gaze, which Fitzgerald describes as being "so penetrating I always wondered how anyone dared to speak out very openly around her." States that after Fitzgerald read "The Train," she developed a close friendship with the young writer, one that became even closer when she moved into the Fitzgerald's garage apartment in Connecticut. Relates that it was during this time that O'Connor worked on the raw material of *Wise Blood*, and read Nathaniel Hawthorne, Gustave Flaubert, Balzac, Eudora Welty, William Faulkner, and other novelists. Reports that after 1950 O'Connor's lupus forced her to stay in Georgia, and outlines Fitzgerald's brief description of this period of her life. Mentions that at the request of O'Connor's mother, Regina Cline O'Connor, Sally Fitzgerald agreed to write Flannery's biography.

141   Bassett, Beth Dawkins. "Fitzgeralds Assist Filming `Wise Blood.'" *Emory Magazine* 58.4 (1982): 23.

Describes the set design and other contributions of Sally Fitzgerald and her two sons, Michael (producer) and Benedict (script writer), for the filming of John Huston's "Wise Blood." Mentions Huston's remark that, along with "The African Queen" and "The Maltese Falcon," "Wise Blood" was "among his top three most critically acclaimed films."

142   Batts, Martin. "Flannery O'Connor: Good and Evil in a Relativistic World." *Proceedings of the Northeast Regional Meeting of the Conference on Christianity and Literature, Regis College, 10-12 October 1996*. Ed. Joan F. Hallisey and Mary-Anne Vetterling. Weston, MA: Regis College, 1996. 8-11.

Sees O'Connor as one of the few modern writers who "dares to assert that the business of fiction is to embody transcendent mystery through earthly manners." Describes how she depicts a vision "of evil which sees the devil as a real spirit with a specific personality battling against a real, transcendent good." Explicates "A Good Man Is Hard to Find" in this context, focusing upon "the incongruity between The Misfit's kindly manners . . . and his cruel actions." Argues that this contrast "shows his inability to make polite behavior fit with fundamental states of good and evil," and leaves him alienated and disillusioned "in a universe which is viewed as having no meaning or objective standards."

143   Bauer, Margaret D. "Alice Walker: Another Southern Writer Criticizing Codes Not Put to `Everyday Use.'" *Studies in Short Fiction* 29.2 (1992): 143-51.

Discusses parallels between stories in Walker's *In Love and Trouble* and the fiction of William Faulkner, Katherine Anne Porter, Flannery O'Connor, and Eudora Welty. Contends that "the disjointedness, the presence of a gorilla, and the grotesque god" in Walker's "Entertaining God," parallel aspects of O'Connor's *Wise Blood*. Also suggests that Walker's use of a "superior-minded child looking down on her mother's simplicity, and, in effect, the simplicity of her heritage" may remind readers of O'Connor's "Good Country People," "Everything That Rises Must Converge," and "The Enduring Chill."

144   Baumbach, Jonathan. "The Acid of God's Grace." *The Landscape of Nightmare: Studies in the Contemporary American Novel*. New York: New York UP, 1965. 87-100.

Explores the ritual configuration in *Wise Blood*, focusing on its reversal of the "rite of passage." Concentrates on O'Connor's first novel, but suggests that *The Violent Bear It Away* and *A Good Man Is Hard to Find* also share the same "rigidly defined religious concerns." Attributes O'Connor's creation of "claustrophobic reality" to a "lack of breadth and depth" in her fictional world.

145   Baumgaertner, Jill P. "'The Meaning Is in You': Flannery O'Connor in Her Letters." *Christian Century* 23-30 Dec. 1987: 1172-76.

Suggests that *The Habit of Being* demonstrates O'Connor's belief that the only worthy subject of literature is that of the conversion experience and losses associated with that experience. Traces the relationship between O'Connor's belief as a conservative Catholic and her fictional method. Suggests that her own "self-abandonment" to her characters while writing is analogous to an abandonment of self in Christianity. Remarks that "the universal experience of unbelief, which O'Connor considered the necessary starting point of faith," brings her fundamentalist protesters closer to the Catholic Church than they realize.

146   Bawer, Bruce. "Under the Aspect of Eternity: The Fiction of Flannery O'Connor." *New Criterion* 7.5 (1989): 35-41.

Review essay on the Library of America edition of O'Connor's *Collected Works*. Refers to O'Connor's steadily growing reputation and expresses the opinion that her career, like those of Nathaniel Hawthorne, Edgar Allan Poe, Stephen Crane, and Henry James before her, constitutes a major chapter in the history of the American short story." Outlines plots and themes of *Wise Blood* and *The Violent Bear It Away*, and discusses reasons O'Connor's novels are considered less effective than her stories. Concludes that O'Connor's stories are "in the most urgent sense, works of moral compulsion: they compel one to look critically into one's heart, to question one's most long-settled assumptions about oneself." [Also included in Bruce Bawer's, *The Aspect of Eternity: Essays*. St. Paul, MN: Graywolf, 1993. 309-20.]

147   Beacham, Walton, ed. "Flannery O'Connor, 1925-1964." *Research Guide to Biography and Criticism: 1990 Update*. Washington, D.C.: Beacham, 1990. 367-70.

Updates David C. Dougherty's essay in the 1985 edition by the same title [Wash., D.C.: Research Publishing, 867-70]. Divided into three sections ("Autobiographical Sources," "Evaluation of Selected Criticism," and "Other Sources"), this work offers excerpts of major book-length criticism on O'Connor.

148   Beasley, David. "Flannery O'Connor Compels Scholars, Fans." *Atlanta Journal and Constitution* 17 June 1984: 2C.

Discussion of why readers visit Milledgeville, based upon short interviews with Sarah Gordon (English Professor), Robert Gorman (Coordinator of Information Services in the Russell Library) and Regina O'Connor (Flannery's mother). Reports that in the O'Connor Room visitors see Flannery O'Connor's personal library, furniture, and an original painting. Refers to John Kennedy Toole, author of *A Confederacy of Dunces* (winner of the 1981 Pulitzer Prize), who committed suicide on his way home from a visit in 1969, during a time when he was working on a doctoral thesis related to O'Connor.

149   Beauchamp, Wilton and David Matchen. "The Cheney-O'Connor Letters." *Publications of the Missouri Philological Association* 9 (1984): 78-85.

Notes that none of the letters between O'Connor and the Brainard Cheneys were included in *The Habit of Being*, probably due to space limitations. Contends that they are still useful to scholars as examples of her humor and the "helping hand" she often offered to other writers. Briefly describes Cheney's life and work, noting that both O'Connor and Cheney were Catholic and natives of Georgia; then describes and provides excerpts from some of the fifty letters they exchanged. Reports that the correspondence is now located in the Brainard Cheney Collection at the Joint Universities Libraries in Nashville, Tennessee. Concludes with Cheney's description of O'Connor's funeral mass.

150   Beaver, Harold. "On The Verge of Eternity." *Times Literary Supplement*
             21 Nov. 1980: 1336.

             Tribute to O'Connor and her work. Offers a biographical summary,
             discusses her letters ("an incomparable American work"), her sense of
             humor, and presents a few anecdotes. Refers to O'Connor's dislike of
             Carson McCullers, and her exasperation with literary critics and their
             obsession with her use of symbolism. Concludes with a negative review
             of Robert Coles's *Flannery O'Connor's South.*

151   Beaver, Harold. "A Southern Diptych: Faulkner and O'Connor." *The
             Great American Masquerade.* Totowa, NJ: Barnes and Noble, 1985. 175-
             95.

             Discusses Faulkner and O'Connor as contemporaries, though with quite
             different aesthetics. Suggests that while O'Connor's orthodoxy was
             "essential" to her life and work, she was still neither a "regional" writer,
             which her Catholicism prevented, nor simply a "Catholic" writer, which
             her Southern nature prevented.

152   Becham, Gerald. "The Flannery O'Connor Collection: GC's Vital
             Legacy." [Georgia College & State University] *Columns* 20.2 (1975): 3-5.

             Offers a history and description of the Flannery O'Connor Collection at
             Georgia College & State University (GC&SU) in Milledgeville. Outlines
             its contents, including the manuscripts and private library, and notes that
             forty-four scholars have used the materials "in the short time the
             manuscripts have been available." Reports on the role of the Alumni
             Association in supporting the planning, construction, and furnishing of the
             Flannery O'Connor Room; how the Alumni Association co-sponsored
             with the English Department and Library, the *Flannery O'Connor
             Bulletin*; the success of the College's symposium, "Flannery O'Connor: A
             Celebration" which in 1974, brought 292 participants from 16 states and
             Canada; Walter Sullivan's educational film, "The World of Flannery
             O'Connor" aired in 1974 by educational stations throughout the South;
             and Robert Dunn's efforts to sort and catalog the manuscript collection.
             Also, refers to the roles that Dorrie Neligan, Lucy Nell Cunningham
             Smith, Henry Green, Rosa Lee Walston, Mary Barbara Tate, Sarah
             Gordon, Caroline Gordon, Robert Drake, Frederick Asals, and Marion
             Montgomery have had in the continued support of O'Connor's legacy.
             Includes photographs of furniture in the Flannery O'Connor Room.

153   Becham, Gerald. Rev. of *Flannery O'Connor: A Descriptive
             Bibliography*, by David Farmer. *Flannery O'Connor Bulletin* 11 (1982):
             129-30.

Describes this bibliography as "a complete, comprehensive listing of everything Flannery O'Connor produced in print, as well as adaptations and translations of her works." Outlines the volume's contents and types of materials cited in each section. Refers readers to Lorine M. Getz's *Flannery O'Connor: Her Life, Library and Book Reviews* (Edwin Mellen Press, 1980); Leo Zuber and Carter Martin's upcoming book, *The Presence of Grace and Other Book Reviews by Flannery O'Connor* (U of Georgia P, 1983); and commends Farmer's decision to include O'Connor's linoleum-block cartoons and section on film and television adaptations. Concludes that, along with Robert Golden and Mary C. Sullivan's *Flannery O'Connor and Caroline Gordon: A Reference Guide* (G.K. Hall, 1977), this book serves as an essential and important contribution to O'Connor scholarship.

154   Becham, Gerald. Rev. of *The Manuscripts of Flannery O'Connor at Georgia College*, by Stephen G. Driggers, Robert Dunn, and Sarah Gordon. *Georgia Librarian* 27.1 (1990): 19-20.

Offers insight into how the 4,000 pages of Flannery O'Connor's manuscripts were initially sorted and arranged. Describes how Gerald Becham of Georgia College and Father Charles M. Hegarty first sorted the collection; further sorting efforts by Robert J. Dunn during 1975-1978 resulted in more detailed and useful files. Dunn's later final arrangement with cross references was completed by Steve Driggers and Sarah Gordon and eventually published.

155   Beck, Charlotte. "Caroline Gordon and Flannery O'Connor: An Empowering Anxiety of Influence." *Flannery O'Connor Bulletin* 25 (1996-97): 194-213.

Discusses the "possibility that Caroline Gordon was, in the Bloomian sense, the strong precursor whom O'Connor had, first, to please but ultimately to resist in asserting her own autonomy." Suggests that toward the end of her life, O'Connor's relationship to Gordon involved "an empowering anxiety of influence." Contends that while Gordon's suggestions for improvement of her manuscripts served as "a `master class' in the writing of fiction," O'Connor's own "additions and revisions seem to outdistance Gordon's suggestions [to] produce a vastly more artistic result than her mentor envisioned." Illustrates this discussion with examples from *Wise Blood* and stories that comprise *A Good Man Is Hard to Find* and *Everything That Rises Must Converge*. Focuses upon "The Artificial Nigger," with less attention to "The Enduring Chill," "The Comforts of Home," "The Lame Shall Enter First," "The Partridge Festival," and "Parker's Back." Notes Sally Fitzgerald's remark that "The

Enduring Chill" was to serve as the nucleus for O'Connor's unfinished novel, *Why Do the Heathen Rage?* Concludes that, even until the end, O'Connor "apparently wanted freedom from Gordon's `strictures'" but was unable to detach herself.

156   Beck, Christiane. "Flannery O'Connor's Poetics of Space." *Realist of Distances: Flannery O'Connor Revisited.* Ed. Karl-Heinz Westarp and Jan Nordby Gretlund. Aarhus (Denmark): Aarhus UP, 1987. 136-46.

Examines O'Connor's use of space, color, light, and movement in her stories as related to her "imaginary creation" of "spatial figures." Attempts to "bring out the texture of various connotations that contribute to make of a space a subjective, existential experience of the characters and/or of the narrator." Sees a pervasive hostility of space in O'Connor's works, usually based upon her treatment of the sun. Contends that this two-dimensional use of space parallels the flatness of her fictional characters.

157   Becker, Isidore H. "Flannery O'Connor's Satiric Humor." *Selected Essays: International Conference on Wit and Humor, 1986.* Ed. Dorothy M. Joiner. Carrollton: West Georgia College, 1988. 9-13.

Discusses "Greenleaf" and "A Temple of the Holy Ghost" as examples of the "profound wit, satire and irony" deriving from the "varied existential predicaments" of O'Connor's characters. Suggests that the satirical portrait of Mrs. May in "Greenleaf" targets "social attitudes based on pride, prejudice, folly and ignorance," leading to condescending attitudes toward children and blacks. Contends, that the satiric tone in "A Temple of the Holy Ghost" is more humorous because the hermaphrodite is an example of the "unsympathetic satire on inhumane treatment of people by an adult society that feeds upon the degradation of unfortunate human beings." Refers to O'Connor's "Godlike tolerance and understanding" of freaks.

158   Becker, Leslee. "A Million Dollars' Worth of Entertainment." *Flannery O'Connor Bulletin* 24 (1995-96): 82-84.

Offers recollections and impressions of having watched "The Life You Save May Be Your Own" on television as a child and of visiting Milledgeville--at age fifty--many years later. Mentions O'Connor's own impression of the television show as noted in letters collected in *The Habit of Being*, and discusses writing a story of her own "about a retarded girl who disappears during a punishing winter and whose body is found in the spring." Outlines ties this story has to O'Connor's. Refers to a visit to Yaddo at which time she was told "about a peculiar writer, a loner at

Yaddo, who had died under mysterious circumstances" who "was a hermaphrodite," and suggests that "surely, O'Connor returned to Milledgeville with stories in her head."

159   Beeching, Paul Q. "Same Belfry, Different Bats." *National Catholic Reporter* 18 July 1986: 9.

Compares and contrasts the writings of O'Connor and J.F. Powers. Focuses on the suddenness of O'Connor's salvation, the "moment in which to feel the presence of grace and accept it or reject it." Suggests that perhaps O'Connor herself became sentimental "despite her obvious literary skill--sentimental in that Gothic, violent way" Edgar Allan Poe and William Faulkner were sentimental. Points out the gap between the religion of individual Christians, such as O'Connor, and that of the Church as a whole. Declares sardonically, "short of an appearance of the Blessed Virgin Mary, the last thing any bishop wants in his diocese is an outpouring of grace. Grace makes people saints, and saints resemble O'Connor's Misfit."

160   Behrendt, Stephen C. "Knowledge and Innocence in Flannery O'Connor's `The River.'" *Studies in American Fiction* 17.2 (1989): 143-55.

Declares that the "expansion of spirit through the action of grace," a recurring theme of O'Connor's, "finds its parallel in the expansion of consciousness [in] which readers find themselves made to participate against their wills" as each story comes to a violent conclusion. Refers to O'Connor's comment that her approach is meant "'to jar the reader into some kind of emotional recognition.'" Analyzes "The River" and points out examples of O'Connor's attempt to "jar the reader's sensibilities," in order to understand the "mystery" she presents. Relates examples from William Blake's *Songs of Innocence* to show how another literary artist "offers a particularly instructive perspective" on the same "mystery" as that in "The River." Concludes that the works of Blake and O'Connor similarly examine the conflict between adult skepticism and the faith and vision of children.

161   Beiswanger, George. "From `The Office of Fiction.'" *Flannery O'Connor Bulletin* 25 (1996-97): 175-82.

Offers a two-part essay, the first of which discusses the liberties and limitations that fiction writers face when creating characters, the world in which they inhabit, and the order of events in which their stories unfold. Using Taulkinham from *Wise Blood* as an example, the author explores how O'Connor creates a "geography" for readers. Follows by contrasting this process with the reassessment of realism that occurred in the nineteenth century, and defends the writer's right to create such landscapes. Considers, in the second part of this essay, O'Connor's use of metaphor and symbolic meaning in her depiction of "eyes" and "seeing" in *Wise Blood*. Outlines examples of the difficulties that writers face in "using words to make human action and its scene somehow visible." Concludes with a comment on the uniqueness of O'Connor's artistry in the extent to which she devoted herself to using the qualities of the words she chose, not for their verbal effect, but to enhance the visibility of her tale.

162   Bellamy, Michael O. "Everything Off Balance: Protestant Election in Flannery O'Connor's `A Good Man Is Hard to Find.'" *Flannery O'Connor Bulletin* 8 (1979): 116-124.

Takes issue with Robert Milder's article, "The Protestantism of Flannery O'Connor," not because he associates O'Connor's writings with Protestantism, "but rather because, at least in the case of `A Good Man,' he does not go far enough." Suggests that readers can "learn something significant about this story," and its author's religious views, by considering the extent to which it "reveals the conflict between Flannery O'Connor's avowed Catholicism and her tendency to view religious experience in the context of Protestant Election." Discusses how the story reflects the "spiritual allegory of the Protestant pilgrim" after the manner of Bunyan's *A Pilgrim's Progress*. Points out the presence of inversions reflective of demonology in the story and carefully considers the grandmother's conversion experience. Alleges that if readers view O'Connor's works in the context of her beliefs, the "most significant struggle" is not a Manichean conflict between good and evil, but the conflict between her "tendency to conceive of the human condition in terms of stark polarities, and . . . to view mankind in the context of a middle way." Concludes that it is because of her views that "the world of her fiction appears to The Misfit, to the Catholic humanist in Flannery O'Connor, and . . . readers as well, as off-balance, almost at times in fact, as grotesque."

163   Belsie, Laurent. "Literary Laurels to Reinforce Traditional Values: Ingersoll Foundation Aims to Reward Thinkers Who Have No Liberal Bias." *Christian Science Monitor* 29 Nov. 1984: 30.

Cites Flannery O'Connor as a novelist who never received the credit she deserved. Uses the fact that she never won a Pulitzer Prize and received the National Book Award only posthumously as an example of how conservative writers and thinkers are slighted.

164   Ben-Bassat, Hedda. "Flannery O'Connor's Double Vision." *Literature &*
Theology 11.2 (1997): 185-99.

Discusses O'Connor's "double vision," which springs from her approach
to writing as "`a Catholic peculiarly possessed of the modern
consciousness.'" Suggests that this "peculiar duality" not only grants her
a perception of "the contemporary situation at the ultimate level," but
"creates in her a `conflict between two sets of eyes.'" Submits that while,
on the one hand, O'Connor addresses contemporary readers by including
in her fiction "the rendering of `adequate psychology,' `the economic
situation,' `hazy compassions,' and `the joy of life itself,'" she also uses the
ironic method to address her "ideal readers whom she wants to shock into
existence." Recognizes O'Connor for challenging "the self-consciousness
of contemporary fiction which presents, with nihilistic skepticism, a sense
of disparity between self and the world," and praises her ability to
juxtapose her own vision to that of her contemporary readers and her ideal
readers in order "to open (violently if necessary) the pair of eyes they
prefer to keep blindfolded." Offers a reading of "The Displaced Person"
in the context of this dual vision.

164a   Ben-Bassat, Hedda. "Vision Without Prophets: ViolenceWithout Fission
of Subjectivity in Flannery O'Connor." *Prophets Without Vision:*
Subjectivity and the Sacred in Contemporary American Writing.
Lewisburg, PA: Bucknell UP, 2000. 65-86.

Offers a chapter devoted to O'Connor which combines "old traditions with
new political and historical awareness" to consider examples of "crises of
ideology and identity" in contemporary American fiction. Finds
O'Connor's work to invite an "explicitly theological reading," and outlines
the positions of such critics as Emily Miller-Budick, Claire Katz-Kahane,
Richard Giannone, Harold Bloom, and writer John Updike for context.
Discusses her use of "double" figures, "prophecy" as a vocation, and the
"psychology and theology of grace," which frame her "constructions of
violently split and shattered selfhood." Offers explications of *Wise Blood*
and *The Violent Bear It Away* and finds that "there is nothing sublime
about O'Connor's not merely diminished but grotesquely deformed
prophets." Compares *Wise Blood* to Melville's *Moby Dick* and considers
how she uses "strategies of apocalyptic violence to produce in the reader
a shattering openness to the experience of self-under-Judgement." Finds
O'Connor's "psychologically violent breakdown of Huck Finn-like
individuals" to reflect her "deliberate strategy for carrying the reader to
the threshold of death and Judgement." Carefully considers O'Connor's
views regarding her readers, the type of devil figure she sought to create,
her use of competing voices as an "antidote to American illusionism and
dream-culture," and the role of grace and violence in her fiction.

165   Benoit, Raymond. "The Existential Intuition of Flannery O'Connor in *The Violent Bear It Away.*" *Notes on Contemporary Literature* 23.4 (1993): 2-3.

Suggests that both Sören Kierkegaard and O'Connor "monitor the unrelenting and glacially leveling advance of secularism down from the height of the Enlightenment into every preserve of the human spirit." Pairs Kierkegaard's *Either/Or* and *The Present Age* with O'Connor's *The Violent Bear It Away.* Quotes Thomas Merton's remark in *Mystics and Zen Masters,* "`I can think of no American writer who has made a more devastating use of existential intuition.'" Focuses on, and discusses, O'Connor's truck driver character, who picks up Tarwater and insists that he constantly talk to keep him awake. Finds the "tragic/comic dialogue" to indicate that the driver "wants to be kept awake but not to be awakened." Concludes that Rayber, Tarwater, and the homosexual, "as they hate, love, and sin, are absolved alongside this vacuum in the truck driver where nothing exists."

166   Beppu, Keiko. "The Fallen Idol and Southern Women Writers: Mother and Daughter in Flannery O'Connor's Stories." *Women's Studies Forum* [Kobe Jogakuin University] (Japan) 3 (1989): 13-29.

Analyzes the mother-daughter relationships in "The Life You Save May Be Your Own" and "Good Country People." Claims that in traditional Christianity, women are regarded as "not clean" and are "separated" from redemption. O'Connor dares to draw such women as the Lucynell Craters and the Hopewells as ugly and detestable characters and permits them, paradoxically, to receive God's unlimited love, resulting in a "modified paradigm." (Abstracted by Kayoko Watanabe).

167   Bergstrom, Robert F. "Discovery of Meaning: Development of Formal Thought in the Teaching of Literature." *College English* 45.8 (1983): 745-55.

Offers examples of how to encourage students to develop the "mental structures" needed to successfully read modern literature, such as Joseph Conrad's *Heart of Darkness*, F. Scott Fitzgerald's *The Great Gatsby*, John Fowles's *The Magus*, and Flannery O'Connor's *Wise Blood*. For O'Connor's work, exercises are described which are used to lessen students' "sense of distance from the characters" and help them explore the "strange behavior by the characters." Finds that students often conclude that Hazel Motes's actions "are quite understandable in view of his background" and that "they can see themselves reacting to events in his upbringing as he does." Argues that these exercises enable students "to see the world through Motes's eyes, an intellectual and emotional step without which the book is simply unintelligible."

168   Bergup, Bernice. Rev. of David Farmer's *Flannery O'Connor: A Descriptive Bibliography*. *American Reference Books Annual 1982*. Vol. 13. Ed. Wynar, Bohdan, Susan C. Holte and Janet Littlefield. Littleton, CO: Libraries Unlimited, 1982. 659-60.

Cites, describes, and evluates David Farmer's *Flannery O'Connor: A Descriptive Bibliography* (New York: Garland, 1981). Concludes that "scholars and aficionados alike will welcome Farmer's contribution to the study of Flannery O'Connor's work."

169   Berret, Anthony J. "Religion and Comedy in Recent Fiction." *New Catholic World* 225.1350 (1982): 254-56.

Examines the depiction of religious concerns in several modern novels, including O'Connor's *Wise Blood*. Notes that while O'Connor "cherished her Catholic heritage, she drew the characters and scenes of her stories from the Low Church, Bible Belt South." Sees as her motivation, her belief that "Catholic symbols--seasons, statues, vestments, and rituals-- had become too abstract . . . so holy that they were set apart from ordinary life and reality," and "their effects became mechanical rather than creative." Offers a reading of *Wise Blood* and contends that it reflects her attempt to "choose symbols that would restore the wild, haunting, and ridiculous aspects of the nature-grace connection." Other works examined include Frederick Buechner's *Lion Country*, J.F. Powers's *Morte D'Urban*, and Mary Gordon's *The Company of Women*.

169a   Beringer, Cindy. "'I Have Not Wallowed': Flannery O'Connor's Working Mothers." *Southern Mothers: Fact and Fictions in Southern Women's Writing*. Ed. Nagueyalti Warren and Sally Wolff. Baton Rouge: Louisiana State UP, 1999. 124-41.

Admires how O'Connor develops characters "drawn from the red clay of southern agrarian life," blending "humor, irony and satire" to create individuals "whose lives are thwarted and misguided." Sees families in her fiction as existing "in a grotesque state of permanent hostility," with offspring exhibiting "such a lack of civilizing influence" that readers are often relieved when "God exacts his mercy" through violence. Finds similarities between O'Connor's personal circumstances and situations presented in her fiction, and notes that many critics consider "the sometimes vicious, often emotionally lacking offspring" in her works as possible "self-parodies." Comments that because O'Connor's mothers treat their children "as pawns in the socioeconomic struggle," the children are "forced into roles of both tyrant and infantile manipulator" setting them up for "an unhealthy cycle of mutual dependency, disrespect, and conflict." Follows with careful explications of "The Enduring Chill," "Good Country People," and "Greenleaf" focusing on the conflicts seen between Mrs. Fox and Asbury, Mrs. Hopewell and Joy-Hulga, and Mrs. May and her two sons, Wesley and Scofield.

170   Betts, Doris. "Daughters, Southerners, and Daisy." *The Female Tradition in Southern Literature*. Ed. Carol S. Manning. Urbana: U of Illinois P, 1993. 259-76.

Suggests that there is truth to Gail Goodwin's statement, "`I believe our lives shape our fiction just as much as our fiction shape our lives.'" Illustrates this suggestion with a discussion of biographical details of a number of contemporary writers. Offers brief references to O'Connor, including the observation that "not many Southern choirgirls have grown up to profess in the 1980s' novels [reflecting] the commitments of Flannery O'Connor." Comments that O'Connor "put her finger on `the business of being a storyteller'" when she observed that whereas her Boston cousins "`discuss problems,'" Southerners "`tell stories.'"

171   Betts, Doris. "The Fingerprint of Style." *Black Warrior Review* 10 (1983): 171-84.

Discusses and outlines various categories of literary style, comparing them to religions and personalities exhibited by biblical prophets. Contends that while readers may attempt to categorize writers in some general way, such efforts are impossible because there exists a "`fingerprint of style'" for each writer. Includes brief references to O'Connor, noting the religious nature of art and how the seriousness of her work has influenced her own.

172   Betts, Doris. "Talking to Flannery." *Flannery O'Connor Bulletin* 24 (1995-96): 77-81.

Reflects on O'Connor's influence upon her life and work. Outlines initial differences regarding views on Christianity, marital status, and health, and then describes how she came to a better understanding of O'Connor's work through discussions with Louise Abbott and C. Hugh Holman. Considers the impact of O'Connor's writings upon undergraduates in her classes, and notes that most students no longer have a religious background adequate for understanding biblical allusions. Discusses different perceptions of humor between black and white students in some of O'Connor's stories, such as "The Enduring Chill" and "Everything That Rises Must Converge," and remarks how her own attitudes toward O'Connor and her work changed through reading the stories. Describes how she sometimes carries on a monologue with O'Connor's spirit, and closes with a discussion regarding her decision to return to the Church.

173   Betts, Glynne Robinson. *Writers in Residence: American Authors at Home*. New York: Viking, 1981.

Conveys through photographs and descriptive narrative, the homes and work areas of more than forty authors. Briefly describes, on pages 110-115, O'Connor's interest in peacocks, her writing habits, and the influence of religion upon her life and work. Includes several photographs taken by the author during a visit with Regina Cline O'Connor [Flannery's mother]: Flannery's home at Andalusia; out-buildings on the property; a peacock and donkey ["Ernest"] near the front gate; a view of rocking chairs on the front porch; the living room of the residence with Flannery's self-portrait above the couch; and a view of an unoccupied tenant farmer's house on the property.

174   Beutel, Katherine Piller. "Flannery O'Connor's Echoing Voices in *The Violent Bear It Away*." *Journal of Contemporary Thought* 4 (1994): 23-36.

Suggests that O'Connor's work contains an echo of "masculine and authoritative voices, especially a `voice' of religious orthodoxy." Offers a reading of *The Violent Bear It Away* that suggests O'Connor's narrative voice functions in a way similar to the role of Ovid's mythological Echo. Discusses Tarwater's conflict in responding to authority. Suggests that this conflict is shown using "echoing voices on the narrative level and also, by textual implication, on an authorial level, wherein O'Connor herself can be seen as Echo, especially of the voice of religious authority that was central to her life." Remarks that some of the novel's "subversive echoes are voices and words that emerge independent of speakers," spilling out "without the person's conscious choice to utter them." Refers to attempts "to give the text a `prophetic' reading . . . to locate the Devil's voice as consistently `other' and evil," in commentary by Jill Baumgaertner, John Hollander, John Hawkes, Mary Buzan, Zhong Ming, Claire Kahane Katz, Susan Hardy Aiken, Kate Ellis, Ronald Schleifer, and André Bleikasten. Concludes that "it becomes impossible to label one voice as authority and one voice as rebellion; the source of any one voice remains unknowable."

Thus, by "leaving the clash of authoritative and subversive echoes to dominate . . . O'Connor creates a disturbing text that remains ambiguous about the proper response to authority."

174a   Bieber, Christina. "Called to the Beautiful: The Incarnational Art of Flannery O'Connor's *The Violent Bear It Away.*" *Xavier Review* 18.1 (1998): 44-62.

Outlines through an explication of *The Violent Bear It Away* how O'Connor presents a "spiritual reality [that] her readers would rather ignore" and contrasts it with the concrete world they usually find more acceptable. Notes that because her work "re-enacts the word become flesh, the mystery made visible, the universal born into a particularity," O'Connor "came to describe her own work as `incarnational art.'" Contends that the language O'Connor uses to describe Tarwater's call to become a prophet "bears a striking similarity to that which she uses to describe her own vocation as an artist," and finds the novel to be "a picture of the struggles and pitfalls that face the modern artist." Suggests that Old Tarwater and Rayber have "surprisingly limited influence as teachers" as Tarwater's decision to follow his calling is his own. Refers to views of the city; the meaning of the characters' names; young Tarwater as a symbol of John the Baptist and Bishop as a symbol of God and O'Connor's incarnational art; why Old Tarwater considered his spiritual vision a burden while young Tarwater felt his was a gift; Rayber's love for Bishop and his "error" of trying "to make reality conform to his abstractions." Also discusses the influence of St. Thomas Aquinas and Jacques Maritain. Concludes that the success of the novel lies in how "the mystery of God's call opens up," not only inside Tarwater's blood, but "inside the reader's mind" as well.

175   Binding, Paul. "The Travels: In Georgia." *Separate Country: A Literary Journey Through the American South.* New York: Paddington, 1979. 149-70.

Binding, a British citizen, discusses views of individuals met during his travels in Georgia, including Southern men's views of Southern women; perspectives on Atlanta (including those of James Dickey and Marion Montgomery); and comments on such Southern writers as Flannery O'Connor. Discusses O'Connor's literary reputation, and asserts that "she is, Faulkner excepted, the Southern writer most known and respected in the outside world." Examines O'Connor's use of the South as setting, and the influence of her Catholic beliefs on her work, noting that the South is "perhaps the staunchest and most fanatically protestant community in the world." Criticizes O'Connor's "unconcealed contempt" for humanists.

States that he dislikes her vision, and contends that it is "perfectly legitimate to suggest that . . . [O'Connor's] elaborate cruelties . . . are features not of God's world but of Flannery O'Connor's private one." Applauds her literary art but is not convinced "that psychologically she knew what she was doing." Argues that O'Connor "does not concede (how could she?) that her imaginative gravitation to the bizarre and deformed is due to a strong vein of sadism." Expresses disappointment in O'Connor's "contempt for the healthy, the well-adjusted and the socially integrated," and her dismissal of events and feelings which play a role in most lives, such as "sexual love, work, social relations, family life, friendship and the pleasures of the senses." Offers a reading of *The Violent Bear It Away*, and finds it to be "a deeply sick document, a neurotic travesty of existence." Concludes that, in spite of criticisms noted, O'Connor's "artistic fidelity to her vision" is worthy of respect as is also "the fine character of the woman who left behind her such a glowing memory."

176   Blanch, Mae. "Joy and Terror: Figures of Grace in Cather and O'Connor Stories." *Literature and Belief* 8 (1988): 101-15.

Asserts that despite differences in their treatment of the "grace theme," both Flannery O'Connor and Willa Cather draw upon the traditional Christian meaning: "the free and unmerited gift of God's favor to humanity as demonstrated in the atonement of Christ for the salvation of repentant sinners." States that O'Connor focuses on humanity's sinful nature and need for grace to achieve salvation. Notes that she uses violence to shock both her characters and her readers into recognizing their sinful nature, and once commented "'their heads are so hard that almost nothing else will work.'" Discusses Cather's protagonists and suggests that they "are more impoverished than sinful, and their encounters with grace are gentle and gradual rather than violent and abrupt." Suggests that this leads to a spiritual enrichment that comes with God's gift of grace. Examines O'Connor's "A View of the Woods," and "Revelation"; and Cather's "The Best Years" and "Jack-a-Boy."

177   Blasingham, Mary V. "Archetypes of the Child and of Childhood in the Fiction of Flannery O'Connor." *Realist of Distances: Flannery O'Connor Revisited*. Ed. Karl-Heinz Westarp and Jan Nordby Gretlund. Aarhus (Denmark): Aarhus UP, 1987. 102-12.

Observes that O'Connor's work contains many children from a wide range of backgrounds. Proposes that their presence is integral to her message: while real in the "literal dimension," they may also be interpreted archetypically as "myth-children, symbolic rather than humanized, and therefore 'divine' in the psychological use of the term."

178   Bleikasten, André. "The Heresy of Flannery O'Connor." *Les Américanistes: New French Criticism on Modern American Fiction*. Literary Criticism Series. Ed. Ira D. and Christiane Johnson. Port Washington, NY: Kennikat, 1978. 53-70.

Examines the difficulty that writers such as O'Connor have in taking the position of serving the two "uneasy bedfellows" of religion and literature. Notes that what has helped such so-called Christian writers as Georges Bernanos, François Mauriac, and T.S. Eliot "from becoming trapped in apologetics" is that--in their best work--"the demands of writing clearly prevailed over their private preconceptions." Discusses a variety of O'Connor's views and methods, notably her concept of the Devil as a being who sees a "soulless" world "transfixed in a fiendish grimace"; her use of humor and laughter; her "penchant for freaks, idiots, and cripples, her fascination with the morbid, macabre, and monstrous"; her use of "landscapes of nightmare"; and her "heavy reliance on grotesque effects and how she expected her readers to respond to them." Refers to the Christian references and parallels in O'Connor's fiction, and emphasizes "the possibility of more than one reading of her fiction," with illustrative examples from *Wise Blood* and *The Violent Bear It Away*. Finds that the "truth of O'Connor's work is the truth of her art, not that of her church," and concludes that although she was a Catholic, she was "not a Catholic novelist . . . as a writer she belongs to no other parish than literature." [Rpt. in *Critical Essays on Flannery O'Connor*. Ed. Melvin J. Friedman and Beverly Lyon Clark. Boston: G.K. Hall, 1985. 138-58.]

179   Bleikasten, André. "Writing on the Flesh: Tattoos and Taboos in `Parker's Back.'" *Southern Literary Journal* 14.2 (1982): 8-18.

Argues that "Parker's Back" is a "uniquely intriguing" story that should be read and interpreted as if by a first-time reader. Contends that doing so allows the reader to feel the strangeness and wonder as it startles and shocks. Suggests that this perspective also allows the reader to focus more clearly on the story's most surprising feature, which startles most modern readers: Parker's penchant for tattooing. Offers an explication of the story and concludes that not only is Parker O'Connor's fictional double, but that she may have viewed her works as a metaphor of one tattoo after another, "hoping that in the end they would cohere into a beautiful design."

180   Bloom, Harold, ed. *Modern Critical Views: Eudora Welty*. New York: Chelsea House, 1986. 6, 72, 77, 150.

In the Introduction, Bloom argues that Eudora Welty is a more "genial" writer than O'Connor, and classifies her story "The Burning" as belonging--along with O'Connor's "A Good Man Is Hard to Find"--to "the dark genre of Southern Gothic." O'Connor is briefly mentioned by three contributors: Joyce Carol Oates suggests that, unlike Welty's stories, O'Connor's "are populated by beings not quite human"; Reynolds Price comments that unlike characters in O'Connor and Carson McCuller's fiction, Welty's characters are "almost never freaks"; and Raad Cawthon asserts that only O'Connor matched Welty's "uncanny ability to put onto paper the way people actually speak."

181   Blythe, Hal and Charlie Sweet. "Darwin in Dixie: O'Connor's Jungle." *Notes on Contemporary Literature* 21.2 (1991): 8-9.

Suggests a reading of "A Good Man Is Hard to Find" in which rural Georgia is "a part of the Darwinian universe; in which human beings are basically animals, and life is a jungle where only the strongest survive." Concludes that O'Connor's intent is to demonstrate that in this modern world, with its noted absence of Christ, "people are driven by an animalistic nature, and it doesn't matter whether they are full of grace or graceless." Contends that, in this view, the South becomes a naturalistic universe where the strongest brutes--not the meek--inherit the earth.

182   Blythe, Hal and Charlie Sweet. "The Misfit: O'Connor's `Family' Man as Serial Killer." *Notes on Contemporary Literature* 25.1 (1995): 3-5.

Suggests that O'Connor "uses several parallels to imply that Bailey's family is like The Misfit's," which--in turn--serves as an explanation as to why the grandmother recognizes The Misfit as one of her own children. Concludes that O'Connor's depiction of The Misfit "offers a unified explanation for a serial killer: he is produced by a dysfunctional family."

183   Blythe, Hal and Charlie Sweet. "O'Connor's `A Good Man Is Hard to Find.'" *Explicator* 50.3 (1992): 185-87.

Contends that O'Connor's "A Good Man Is Hard to Find" contains many allusions to William Butler Yeats's poem, "The Second Coming." Provides specific examples of parallels between the two works and concludes that O'Connor's story "is a fulfillment of Yeats's prophecy." Sees The Misfit as "the beast, its hour come round at last, that arrives in the chaotic modern world to usurp the authority of civilized Christianity. The future belongs to the brutes."

184   Blythe, Hal and Charlie Sweet. "O'Connor's `A Good Man Is Hard to Find.'" *Explicator* 55.1 (1996): 49-51.

Contends that O'Connor "inserts several specific elements" from Geoffrey Chaucer's *Canterbury Tales* into "A Good Man Is Hard to Find." Remarks that "the resulting contrast between medieval characters, frames, settings, and motifs and their modern day counterparts creates a powerful commentary on the declining role of religion in twentieth-century society."

185   Bolton, Betsy. "Placing Violence, Embodying Grace: Flannery O'Connor's `Displaced Person.'" *Studies in Short Fiction* 34.1 (1997): 87-104.

Explores "the relationship between vision and violence, what is suffered and what beheld" in "The Displaced Person." Considers how O'Connor structures the story "around a newsreel image of the Holocaust--the momentary frozen picture of a room piled high with bodies--and . . . attempts to make sense of that vision and the proliferation of violence that image seems to produce." Argues that "the technology of O'Connor's storytelling offers a (still violent) alternative to the violent technology of images the story explicitly thematizes." Uses Walter Benjamin's essays "The Work of Art in an Age of Mechanical Reproduction" and "The Storyteller," to "frame the kinds of technology at work." Suggests that "the story presents a film image (of horrific death) as the mystery requiring repeated confrontation," and proposes that O'Connor seeks to use this image "to alter the beliefs of her readers through an appeal to their senses." Submits that O'Connor's goal is to make her readers so uncomfortable with the "threat of displacement and the violence that accompanies it," that they will embody it "by reducing it literally to an experience of the senses."

186   Bolton, Philip. "Author O'Connor Not Simply a Recluse." *Macon (GA) News* 21 Dec. 1978: B1.

Refers to Sally Fitzgerald's work in compiling O'Connor's letters for *The Habit of Being*, recollections of their first meeting, and O'Connor's initial attack of lupus.

187   Bolton, Philip. "*Wise Blood* Film Based on O'Connor Novel." *Macon (GA) News* 21 Dec. 1978: B6.

Reports on preliminary plans for the filming of John Huston's version of *Wise Blood*.

188   Bond, Adrienne. "Renewal." *Flannery O'Connor Bulletin* 15 (1986): 34.

A poem dedicated to Flannery O'Connor using the imagery of botanical growth overcoming a man-made house contrasted with bodily pain.

189   Bonetti, Kay. "An Interview with Harry Crews." *Missouri Review* 6 (Winter 1983): 143-64.

Offers a lengthy interview of Harry Crews in question-and-answer format. Crews states that he is flattered to be compared with O'Connor in his use of the Gothic and grotesque, and that he believes, like O'Connor, that he knows "how people talk, and the dialect, and their tendency to do one thing or another thing."

190   Bongartz, Roy. "Yaddo at 60." *Publisher's Weekly* 13 June 1986: 32-35.

Describes Yaddo, the 400-acre retreat for artists and writers where O'Connor wrote much of *Wise Blood*. O'Connor is mentioned in passing.

191   Bonney, William. "The Moral Structure of Flannery O'Connor's *A Good Man Is Hard to Find*." *Studies in Short Fiction* 27.3 (1990): 347-56.

Argues that the ten stories in O'Connor's *A Good Man Is Hard to Find* "circumscribe a moral and thematic center." Suggests that the first and last stories--"A Good Man Is Hard to Find" and "The Displaced Person"-- establish this circumscription, and "are technically and ethically definitive." Comments on the collection of stories as a whole and maintains that it "is profoundly hopeful in its suggestion that the fallen world of pride and materialism can be transcended by at least a few."

192   Boos, Florence and Lynn Miller. *Bibliography of Women and Literature: Vol. I: Articles and Books (1974-1978) By and About Women From 600 to 1975.* New York: Holmes & Meier, 1989. 331-36.

Provides a list of citations to articles, dissertations, and books related to Flannery O'Connor which were published between 1974 and 1978.

193   Booth, Mark. Introduction. *Christian Short Stories: An Anthology.* New York: Crossroad, 1984. 9-19.

Offers an bibliographical essay on the art of the Christian short story, focusing on how such stories serve the purpose of "recommending the Christian view of life." O'Connor's "The Artificial Nigger" is included in a collection of sixteen stories by Christian writers. Closes with a reading of "The Artificial Nigger," and contends that it "epitomizes what the short story does better than any other genre; [because] it describes the impinging of the divine on the mundane." Concludes that O'Connor "brilliantly elucidates the insufficiency of common sense when it comes to dealing with the everyday," as "she holds a microscope to apparently insignificant corners of a decaying world to show it to be a battleground of good and evil."

194   Booth, Stanley. "Crying in the Wilderness: The Life and Work of Flannery O'Connor." *Gadfly* (Dec. 1998): 16-21.

Offers a profile of the life and work of Flannery O'Connor, illustrated with photographs of four O'Connor-related paintings by Laura Lasworth. Discusses a wide variety of background details: the Pathé News film clip of five-year-old Mary Flannery O'Connor with her chicken that walked backwards; the impact of her illness and how she dealt with its complications; her education and reading; and the role O'Connor's faith played in her life and work. Follows with descriptions and explications of *Wise Blood*, the title story of *A Good Man Is Hard to Find*, and *The Violent Bear It Away*. Concludes with details of O'Connor's work with the Dominican Nuns of Our Lady of Perpetual Help Cancer Home in Atlanta to assist in publishing their book, *A Memoir of Mary Ann*. Sidebar notes provide explanations of the context of Lasworth's paintings.

195   Boren, Mark. "Flannery O'Connor, Laughter, and the Word Made Flesh." *Studies in American Fiction* 26.1 (1998): 115-28.

Argues that O'Connor uses "an ambivalent, even abusive, social laughter . . . with images of self-contained, isolated figures characteristic of our own modern age" to generate the power "that lies at the heart of her [grotesque] fiction." Regards her laughter as "directed neither at someone nor aligned with someone," but as "a general laughter of `the situation' and of partial knowledge." Submits that this laughter, which "is neither positive nor negative but supremely accepting," permeates her writing and is "aimed directly at the human condition" in a manner that is "antithetical to the excesses of sentimentality." Refers to laughter in "Parker's Back," "Good Country People," "A Good Man Is Hard to Find," "The Enduring Chill," "Everything That Rises Must Converge," and *Wise Blood*.

196   Borgman, Paul. "Three Wise Men: The Comedy of O'Connor's *Wise Blood.*" *Christianity & Literature* 24.3 (1975): 36-48.

Suggests that an examination of the conflict between the three main characters in *Wise Blood* reveals "widely varying modes of seeing life and reacting to it." Declares that it is these differences which produce the "comic drama" of the work. Describes Mrs. Flood as one of O'Connor's most memorable characters, "eccentrically individual in her characterization and crucial in her dramatic role," and contends that she "serves the author's anagogical purposes as the culminating definitive touch to a mode of seeing things . . . which Hazel must resist."

197   Bourne, Paul. "My Friendship with Flannery O'Connor." *Flannery O'Connor Bulletin* 17 (1988): 81.

Brief essay by Bourne, a Trappist monk, who describes his "best-remembered impressions" of Flannery O'Connor. States that while he found O'Connor to be "one of the few unique persons" he ever encountered, she was also an "entirely human person, influenced by human prejudices." Recollects that "Flannery seemed to find comfort in writing" to him "of both her problems and her successes."

198   Bowen, Rose. "Baptism by Inversion." *Flannery O'Connor Bulletin* 14 (1985): 94-98.

Contends that "the theme of grace, pervasive in O'Connor's fiction, is often perceived not by its joyful presence, but rather by its tragic absence." Ties this absence and O'Connor's concept of original sin to the stories included in *A Good Man Is Hard to Find,* focusing on "Good Country People." Suggests that "Good Country People" serves as "a conscious echo of the baptismal rite." Discusses parallels in Joy/Hulga's "faith and commitment to herself" and contrasts this commitment to the profession of faith, rites, and ritual of the baptismal candidate's affirmation of "personhood in the image and likeness of God." Concludes that Hulga "qualifies as paradigm for the human condition in the absence of grace as well as for its potential under the absence of grace."

199   Bowen, Rose. "Christology in the Works of Flannery O'Connor." *Horizons* 14.1 (1987): 7-23.

Argues that Christology and ecclesiology, which serve as essential elements to O'Connor's perspective, are reflected mostly in her book reviews, correspondence, and essays. Notes that "the reviews in particular

(69 of the 143 titles reviewed pertain to subject matter that is religious or theological) attest to the range, depth, and vitality of her own theological investigation." Declares that by 1961 O'Connor's religious views had become heavily influenced by Karl Adam, Romano Guardini, Pierre Teilard de Chardin, and Francis Durrwell. Suggests that readers can follow the influence of these theologians in her nonfiction writings.

200   Bowman, Michael S. "Performing Literature in an Age of Textuality." *Communication Education* 45.2 (1996): 96-101.

Refers to "recent debates over the literary canon," and wonders whether "oral interpretation could be construed as one of those `operations' that defines and protects the literary status of a certain kind of text, while relegating others to the periphery or to the ghetto of the non-literary." Includes, in this brief discussion, concern regarding "whether the popularity . . . of writers [such as] Flannery O'Connor and Eudora Welty should be taken as evidence of their value as artists, or as evidence that their writing matches or conforms to our value-based preselection of an ideal literary-performance experience."

201   Box, Terry. "A Resurrection for The Misfit in Flannery O'Connor's `A Good Man Is Hard to Find.'" *Lamar Journal of the Humanities* 17 (1991): 51-54.

Asserts that The Misfit's references to Jesus and the resurrection arouse such a sense of compassion and "a sense of their common humanity" in the grandmother that she is spiritually resurrected. States that The Misfit rejects the grandmother's "act of compassion because it does not fit in with his notion of the unreality of good, and therefore puts everything out of order." Concludes that "The Misfit's only order is evil."

202   Boyd, L.M. [Untitled]. *Prince George's (MD) Express* 9-10 May 1996: B1.

Paragraph of apparent filler that may, indirectly, be related to O.E. Parker's tattoo in "Parker's Back." States that sailors of three hundred years ago sometimes had a crucifix tattooed on their back to counter the punishment of 24 lashes customarily given for being drunk while on duty. Suggests that the general idea was that not only would the person administering the lashing "be reluctant to swing full tilt," but that the whip itself might "curl back from the holy symbol."

203   Boyles, Mary. "Self-Discovery as Salvation in Flannery O'Connor's Fiction." *Selected Essays From the International Conference on Work and the World of Discovery, 1992*. Ed. Gerald Garmon. Carrollton: Dept. of English, West Georgia College, 1994: 14-20.

Discusses how O'Connor's fiction, "with its bizarre characters, its macabre situations, [and] its unrelieved devastation of one human on another," serves as an "agent of grace for her readers." Contends that O'Connor's stories "break through the carefully-laid insulation which keeps us from seeing the world and ourselves as we really are." Offers explications of "Good Country People," "A Good Man Is Hard to Find," and "Everything That Rises Must Converge" in this context. Concludes that while the comedy in O'Connor's fiction "arises from the grotesquerie, [and] the exaggeration of her characters' actions and responses," her approach is purposeful in showing how her characters are like her readers, who stand "in continual need of some . . . freak to ravage [their] complacence and redirect [their] vision."

204   Boyum, Joy Gould. "'Wise Blood': Wise Choices." *Double Exposure: Fiction Into Film*. New York: Universe, 1985. 175-82.

Discusses John Huston's film adaptation of *Wise Blood*. Remarks that "if one were to accept traditional notions of what is possible for the screen, the work of Flannery O'Connor might seem utterly, unequivocally unfilmable." Offers a summary of the plot and notes that "it is precisely this hero [Hazel Motes] and his weird quest" that Huston adapted. Provides a range of examples which illustrate that "not only was O'Connor filmable, but there was much about her work that transferred to the screen with remarkable ease." Examines differences between the book and film, the treatment of O'Connor's characters and symbolic texture, and Huston's strategies to push viewers "away from the literal level."

205   Bracken, James K. "Flannery O'Connor (1925-1964)." *Reference Works in British and American Literature: Vol. II English and American Writers*. Englewood, CO: Libraries Unlimited, 1991. 199.

Cites and descriptively annotates bibliographies, handbooks, and journals related to O'Connor. Includes David Farmer's *Flannery O'Connor: A Descriptive Bibliography* and Robert E. Golden's *Flannery O'Connor and Caroline Gordon: A Reference Guide* as bibliographic sources; James A. Grimshaw Jr.'s *The Flannery O'Connor Companion* as a useful handbook; and *The Flannery O'Connor Bulletin* (published by Georgia College & State University) as a related journal for O'Connor scholars.

206   Bradbury, Malcolm. *The Modern American Novel*. New York: Viking,
         1992. 121, 162, and 273-74.

         Includes brief references to Flannery O'Connor. Bradbury comments how
         "the whole still-active landscape of Southern Gothic fiction--in the work
         of writers like Carson McCullers and Flannery O'Connor, and then James
         Purdy and James Dickey--would hardly be conceivable without Faulkner's
         work." Notes the "marked revival of Gothic writing" during the forties
         and fifties as seen in the writings of McCullers, Eudora Welty, and
         O'Connor, who "all mixed a formal experimentalism with a dark vision
         of decadence and evil, producing a Gothic vision that has persisted
         powerfully in more recent women's writing." Remarks on the impact of
         O'Connor and her contemporaries on modern women writers.

207   Brandolino, Gina. "Flannery O'Connor's South." *Georgia Journal* 16.2
         (1996): 12-17.

         Provides an introductory essay which briefly outlines biographical details
         of O'Connor's life, describes the "strange characters" who inhabit
         O'Connor's fictional world, and examines these grotesque fictional people
         whose "oddities all stem from some factor of traditional Southern
         ideology that they have either taken to extremes or gone to extremes to
         defy--or both--in a desperate attempt to define themselves." Follows the
         initial descriptive part of the essay with recollections of an automobile trip
         from Chicago to St. Petersburg, Florida. Uses the sights seen and
         individuals met in comparison and contrast to O'Connor's fictional
         Southern world. Includes photographs of O'Connor and a small color
         picture of the Gordon-Cline-O'Connor house in Milledgeville.

208   Brantley, Richard E. Rev. of *The Comedy of Redemption: Christian Faith
         and Comic Vision in Four American Novelists*, by Ralph C. Wood.
         Flannery O'Connor Bulletin 17 (1988): 105-08.

         Characterizes Wood's book as a "forthright, fresh perspective" on the
         works of O'Connor, Percy, Updike, and DeVries. Finds that each support
         the Christian view of the "Good News," that humanity surely does not
         "flail in a void . . . that we are upheld by sheer grace, [and] that we stand
         on Christ the solid rock." Suggests that "comedy, for Wood, derives from
         the hope and joy announced by the Gospel to the world," and that "the
         deepest comedy . . . is `the unilateral and uncompromising comedy of
         God's grace.'" Asserts that the theology of this "`comedy of redemption'"
         is based upon the view of Karl Barth that God "is the gracious Person who
         decided both to create the world and to redeem it." Discusses Wood's
         examination of O'Connor's biography, regionalism, and Catholicism, his

"Barthian perspective" on O'Connor, and the seemingly "audacious point of view . . . that O'Connor explains rather than dramatizes what mercy means." Concludes that this "full-scale interrelation of comic theory, theology, and fiction is more than the usual bland, cautious, and `objective' writing of the academic world." It is, instead, "the fully matured result of a quarter-century of teaching by a Baptist Southerner with keen theological intelligence."

209   Brantley, Will. "O'Connor, Porter, and Hurston on the State of the World." *Contemporary Literature* 37.1 (1996): 132-44.

Discusses three books--Jon Lance Bacon's *Flannery O'Connor and Cold War Culture*, John Lowe's *Jump at the Sun: Zora Neale Hurston's Cosmic Comedy*, and Janis P. Stout's *Katherine Anne Porter: A Sense of the Times*--in the context of "the contemporary revolution in literary theory and criticism" and to address fears that such a revolution might "bypass the domain of Southern studies." Affirms that the three books "add significantly to the current movement to deprovincialize the study of the South" and contribute to discussions of how these writers "responded to the shaping forces and issues of their times."

210   Bray, Nancy Davis. "`How Do I Get to the Flannery O'Connor Collection?'" *Flannery O'Connor Bulletin* 17 (1988): 90-91.

Describes some of the rules and regulations governing use of the *Flannery O'Connor Collection* of the Russell Library of Georgia College & State University in Milledgeville, Georgia. Discusses restrictions related to photocopying, types of users, arranging tours, and other "requirements" of policies and procedures designed "to assist the library staff in developing schedules, arranging appointments, and enabling scholarly research to progress."

211   Brewer, Nadine. "Christ, Satan, and Southern Protestantism in O'Connor's Fiction." *Flannery O'Connor Bulletin* 14 (1985): 103-10.

Addresses criticism that O'Connor incorrectly depicts the Protestant South and writes "only about freaks." Contends that the problem may be that of "misunderstanding on the part of the reader, not the writer." Focuses on the paradox of why O'Connor "has been so widely misread, despite the probability that no other `Southern' writer has written of her own country with more perspicacity and scrupulous realism." Confirms O'Connor's use of regional religious perspectives through discussion of how her Catholicism--like the religion of the typical Southerner--reflects her tie to "original sin, redemption through Christ and the last judgement," and the belief that "the human soul is a battleground for Christ and the devil." Comments on the influence of O'Connor's Irish heritage in regard to Southern and Irish views of demon possession, and how readers may be confused by O'Connor's "symbols of Christ and the devil" when her demons become "instruments of divine revelation, [and] agents of grace." In this context, refers to textual evidence in "The River," *Wise Blood*, "A Good Man Is Hard to Find," "Parker's Back," "A Circle in the Fire," "The Lame Shall Enter First," "The Life You Save May Be Your Own," and "The Displaced Person."

212   Brewton, Butler. "The South and Border States." *Literary Guide to the United States*. Ed. Stewart Benedict. New York: Facts on File, 1981. 129-58.

Surveys geographic places reflected in American literature. Brewton provides a brief discussion of O'Connor's life and work, and argues that O'Connor, who "lived on a country estate called Andalusia, and heaped up honors for her literary activity," should be regarded as "among the most accomplished American writers." Illustrations: a map of "The South & Border States" identifying the homes of nineteen authors of the region.

213   Bridges. Phyllis. "Katherine Anne Porter on Her Contemporaries." [Paper presented at the Annual Meeting of the National Women's Studies Association. Towson, MD, June 14-18, 1989.] 11 pp. [ERIC Document ED 315 770].

Describes personal experiences, judgements, and comments that Katherine Anne Porter recorded in her essays, letters, and conversations about a variety of contemporary writers, including Earnest Hemingway, William Faulkner, Saul Bellow, Virginia Woolf, D.H. Lawrence, Eudora Welty, Norman Mailer, Betty Friedan, and Flannery O'Connor. Reprints from Porter's *Collected Essays* her praise and admiration for O'Connor: "'She came up among us like a presence, a carrier of a gift not to be disputed but welcomed. She lived among us like a presence and went away early, leaving her harvest perhaps not yet all together gathered, though, like many geniuses who have small time in this world, I think she had her warning and accepted it.'"

214   "Brigham Young Symposium Offered Numerous Papers." *CHEERS! The Flannery O'Connor Society Newsletter* 3.2 (1995-96): 5-6.

States that 55 papers were delivered at the three-day "Flannery O'Connor and the Christian Mystery Seventieth Birthday Symposium" at Brigham

Young University, November 9-11, 1995. Provides an alphabetical list of contributors, institutional affiliation, and title of the paper presented.

215   Brinkmeyer, Robert H., Jr. "Asceticism and the Imaginative Vision of Flannery O'Connor." *Flannery O'Connor: New Perspectives*. Ed. Sura P. Rath and Mary Neff Shaw. Athens: U of Georgia P, 1996. 169-82.

Sally Fitzgerald's comment, "`Flannery seemed fated to asceticism,'" is used to introduce a discussion of O'Connor's commitment to her vocation. Suggests that her statements "on the necessity of disciplined routine call to mind the strict regulations of cenobitic monasticism practiced by monks who live entirely regimented lives in isolated communities." Discusses a variety of related topics: the influence of Jacques Maritain's aesthetics and view of the artist upon O'Connor's thinking; her acceptance of Teilhard de Chardin's "concept of `passive diminishments'"; the debt that modernist writers owe (in the context of viewing "the artistic vocation in religious terms") to Gustave Flaubert; T.S. Eliot's "extolling the virtues of the artist's impersonality"; and the threat "to the artist and artistic activity" of egoism and "the exclusive passion for art." Closes with a discussion of how Maritain's aesthetics and Geoffrey Galt Harpham's "reading of asceticism" are helpful in understanding O'Connor's aesthetics and imaginative life. Sees her as an embodiment of their ascetic artist.

216   Brinkmeyer, Robert H., Jr. "Borne Away by Violence: The Reader and Flannery O'Connor." *Southern Review* 15.2 (1979): 313-21.

Discusses O'Connor's strategy of shocking readers and assaulting their rationalism with violence. Suggests that she does so to convey her religious vision. Explains that O'Connor's plots are carefully structured "to shake the reader's confidence in his own rational abilities, and . . . to make him see Christ's suffering and man's redemption as basic facts of human life." Considers O'Connor's strategy as a method of communication in *The Violent Bear It Away*, and concludes that the violence in this and other works "bears us away, beyond the limitations and distortions of our modern rationalism, to a new vision of what she felt the center of life really is."

217   Brinkmeyer, Robert H., Jr. "A Closer Walk With Thee: Flannery O'Connor and Southern Fundamentalists." *Southern Literary Journal* 18.2 (1986): 3-13.

States that O'Connor felt that she owed a debt to her native protestant South and its fundamentalist preachers since the traditions they provided "quickened her imagination and brought a weight and fullness to her Catholic vision that it might otherwise have lacked." Argues that the Old South, the middle Georgia humor of Augustus Baldwin Longstreet, Joel Chandler Harris, "Bill Arp," and William Tappan Thompson--combined with stories of comic escapades of rural folk versus "city slickers"--also provided a foundation for the structure of O'Connor's work.

218 Brinkmeyer, Robert H., Jr. "'Jesus, Stab Me in the Heart!': *Wise Blood*, Wounding, and Sacramental Aesthetics." *New Essays on Wise Blood*. Ed. Michael Kreyling. New York: Cambridge UP, 1995. 71-89.

Discusses the controversy regarding whether or not O'Connor effectively communicated her Christian vision in *Wise Blood*. Notes how early reviewers "focused almost exclusively on the bizarre qualities of the novel," while later readers--aided by her letters, comments, essays, and note to the second edition--viewed the novel as a significant religious work. Examines O'Connor's prophetic (sacramental) vision and her attempt to write as an artist with "two sets of eyes, the artist's and the Church's." Offers a reading of *Wise Blood* which addresses "the problem of how to explain, in light of O'Connor's professed sacramental aesthetics and vision, the utterly degraded world of the novel, a world so fallen as to appear unredeemable." Refers to interpretations of asceticism, the significance of Enoch's "moves toward pure bestiality," Haze's "world-ridding" self-inflicted violent acts, and the Yahwist "wounding of O'Connor's characters." Refers to relevant comments by John Desmond, J. Hillis Miller, Frederick Asals, William Rodney Allen, Ben Griffith, Betty Boyd Love, Geoffrey Galt Harpham, Josephine Hendin, Elaine Scarry, Cecil Dawkins, Herbert Schneidau, and Henri Frankfort.

219 Brinkmeyer, Robert H., Jr. *Three Catholic Writers of the Modern South*. Jackson: UP of Mississippi, 1985. ix-x, 99, 105, 148, 161, 171-72.

Offers passing references to O'Connor in this study of three novelists: Allen Tate, Caroline Gordon, and Walker Percy. Suggests that these converts to the Catholic Church were, like O'Connor, "nourished" by their Southern roots. Asserts that each was "molded" by "Old South" traditions and a sense of community. Compares, in the Introduction, their relationship to their faith to that of O'Connor, who was a "born Catholic." Notes that each of the three was "acutely aware that the South of their childhoods was falling prey to the ravages of twentieth-century society, and that the old ways bore little relevance to modern culture." Argues that it was the conflict of these two cultures that shaped these three writers' imaginations, and that this conflict was partially responsible for their turning to the Church "to restore myth, meaning, and mystery" to "a morally irresponsible modern world."

220   Brittin, Ruth L. "Harry Crews and the Southern Protestant Church." *A Grit's Triumph: Essays on the Works of Harry Crews*. Ed. David K. Jeffrey. Port Washington, NY: Associated Faculty, 1983. 79-99.

Discusses how Crews's fiction always, "'in some way concerns itself with man's relationship to God.'" Includes brief, introductory comments regarding how Crews's focus on "the unique, popular Southern religion and its preacher" in his novel *The Gospel Singer* may be traced back to "the tradition of Southern writers from the Old Southwestern Humorists to such moderns as Flannery O'Connor, Erskine Caldwell, and Madison Jones." Contends that in his combining of "the hilarious humor of the Old Southwestern Humorists and Erskine Caldwell with the high-serious, psychological studies in O'Connor and Jones, Crews presents the most authentic picture of all."

221   Brodhead, Richard H. "A Life of Letters." *Yale Review* 69.3 (1980): 451-56.

Review essay of *The Habit of Being*. Declares that O'Connor's confinement due to illness makes her correspondence "acts of communication in the fullest sense," and that the letters display her full command of language and exhibit how her life was pared to essentials: Catholicism, writing, and daily living at Andalusia. Suggests that the letters serve as more than a "skeleton key" to her work; they are instead "the richest volume of correspondence by an American author to have appeared in many years."

222   Brooks, Cleanth. "The Crisis in Culture as Reflected in Southern Literature." *The American South: Portrait of a Culture*. Ed. Louis D. Rubin, Jr. Baton Rouge: Louisiana State UP, 1980. 171-89.

Contends that a fissure has developed between "man's inner and outer life," and that the resulting fragmentation has created a "crisis in culture." Sees the bridging of this rift as one of the principal endeavors of generations of literary artists, and describes representative efforts by prominent twentieth-century Southern writers. Among those whose efforts are discussed in some detail are John Crowe Ransom, Allen Tate, Robert Penn Warren, William Faulkner, and Walker Percy. O'Connor is mentioned only in passing at the end of the essay, along with Caroline Gordon and Andrew Lytle, as one of those who also "deal with the theme of the terrible division of the age" and who "benefit from their Southern experience and heritage."

223   Brooks, Cleanth. *The Language of the American South*. Mercer U Lamar
        Memorial Lectures, No. 28. Athens: U of Georgia P, 1985.

        In these published lectures, Brooks pays tribute to the character and
        distinctiveness of Southern language. He offers examples from the works
        of a variety of Southern writers to demonstrate that "the strength of even
        the most formal Southern writers stems from their knowledge of, and
        rapport with, the language spoken by the unlettered." Discusses
        O'Connor's, "The Enduring Chill" as an illustrative example of such
        "expressive language," focusing on her use of "`country idiom.'"

224   Brown, Ashley. "Flannery O'Connor: A Literary Memoir." *Realist of
        Distances: Flannery O'Connor Revisited*. Ed. Karl-Heinz Westharp and
        Jan Nordby Gretlund. Aarhus (Denmark): Aarhus UP, 1987. 18-29.

        Discusses Brown's friendship with O'Connor, which dated back to 1952
        when he corresponded with her regarding *Wise Blood*'s episodic format
        and Brainard Cheney's 1952 review of the novel for *Shenandoah*.
        Outlines O'Connor's reading interests during the 1950s and mentions
        Caroline Gordon, Allen Tate, and J.P. Bishop.

225   Brown, Ashley. "An Unwritten Drama: Susan Jenkins Brown and
        Flannery O'Connor." *Southern Review* 22.4 (1986): 727-37.

        Reprints portions of letters between Susan Jenkins Brown and Flannery
        O'Connor--with commentary by Ashley Brown--regarding the possibility
        of Susan Brown developing a play from one of O'Connor's works.
        Considered were "The Enduring Chill," "A Good Man Is Hard to Find,"
        and "The River," among others. Sue Brown was an editor who had gained
        experience with the Provincetown Players. She counted such established
        figures as Malcolm Cowley, Kenneth Burke, Hart Crane, Allen Tate, and
        Caroline Gordon as friends, and her friendship with O'Connor developed
        from a relatively brief visit by Caroline Gordon and O'Connor to "Robber
        Rocks," Brown's farmhouse on the New York/Connecticut border, in early
        June, 1955. Notes that while O'Connor knew little about the theater, a
        number of her contemporaries, such as William Faulkner, Eudora Welty,
        Robert Penn Warren, Carson McCullers, Brainard Cheney, and Peter
        Taylor were trying to become more involved in it. Concludes, "this little
        episode, though it came to nothing, was altogether typical of the period."

226   Brown, Hugh R. "`Friends' Welcome New members and Visitors."
        Flannery O'Connor Society Newsletter 1.1 (1993): 2.

Brown discusses the purchase of Flannery O'Connor's childhood home (207 East Charlton Street) in Savannah by the President and two faculty members of Armstrong State College in 1989 and its subsequent use as a literary center and memorial to O'Connor.

227   Brown, Hugh R. "Savannah Landmark: Flannery O'Connor's Childhood Home." *Flannery O'Connor Bulletin* 18 (1989): 43-45.

Describes the fund-raising efforts of a foundation formed by the author, Bob Strozier, and President Bob Burnett--all of Armstrong State College-- to purchase Flannery O'Connor's childhood home located at 207 Charlton Street in Savannah, Georgia. Reports on Armstrong State's "Flannery O'Connor Day" celebration and the foundation's successful campaign to raise the necessary funds for a down payment of $32,500. Describes the group's continuing efforts and its plans to use the house as a "museum/literary center." Illustrated with photographs of the historic marker, the front of the home, the entrance to the parlor floor from Charlton Street, and the walled garden in the back yard.

228   Brown, Jerry Elijah. Introduction. *The Family*. Literary Classics of Alabama Series. Tuscaloosa: U of Alabama P, 1991. vii-xvii.

Provides an overview of Caroline Lawson Ivey's life and offers comments on how--in this book--the "South comes to represent the America emerging after World War II," especially in terms of how "the metaphor of an atomic bomb shook the sills of a society never remote from the changes in the wider world." Discusses Ivey's friendship with O'Connor, including their meeting through Rosa Lee Walston; their "warm correspondence"; O'Connor's appreciation of Ivey's "sympathetic reading of her stories"; and O'Connor's comments on Ivey's unpublished 800-page second novel.

229   Brown, Jerry Elijah. "The War Between the Tates." *South Carolina Review* 23.1 (1990): 158-66.

A review essay that includes brief, passing references to O'Connor: Caroline Gordon's advice and encouragement of O'Connor and Walker Percy and Allen Tate's remark that O'Connor's idiom was "'too flat-footed to catch the Holy Ghost.'"

230   Brown, Mary Ward. [Untitled]. *Flannery O'Connor Bulletin* 24 (1995-96): 123-24.

Remembers reading "A Late Encounter With the Enemy" in a 1953 issue of *Harper's Bazaar* and being electrified and feeling "a stab of pure envy." Felt O'Connor's use of Southern speech and her depiction of characters "were so real, familiar, funny, and tragic," that she may well have "split contemporary American fiction into some kind of Before and After." Describes rereading O'Connor's work, including stories such as "The Comforts of Home" and "The Partridge Festival" (which seemed "a little forced") and subsequently "trying to write fiction" to save her soul.

231   Brown, Rosellen. "On DuBose Heyward's *Peter Ashley. Classics of Civil War Fiction.* Ed. David Madden and Peggy Bach. Jackson: UP of Mississippi, 1991. 117-30.

Discusses DuBose Heyward's novel, *Peter Ashley*, and suggests that the author's "own ambivalence about what mattered most to a man, his independence of mind or the mindless demands of his `heritage,' coupled with an outmoded conception of plot, confuse the picture" and make the book interesting, but "far less interesting than it could have been." Includes a brief reference to Julian's mother in O'Connor's "Everything That Rises Must Converge," stating that Heyward serves as a model for the type of Southerner embodied in the mother as his life, like hers, mirrored the South's "helpless fall from grace" and confirmed that members of the Southern gentry "could be in reduced circumstances but `never forget who they were.'"

232   Brown, Thomas H. "O'Connor's Use of Eye Imagery in *Wise Blood*." *South Central Bulletin* 37 (1977): 138-40.

Analyzes the compositional style of *Wise Blood*, which draws heavily for its imagery upon the concrete, the immediate, the sensuous, and the particularity of detail." Notes O'Connor's almost overwhelming use of eye imagery and suggests "that the naked eye is not to be trusted . . . true knowledge of the nature and reality of God and Man is also intuitive and emotional, not merely intellectual."

232a   Brown, Tony. "Flannery: It All Belongs to O'Connor, Not Just the South." *Savannah Morning News* 2 May 1982: G1+.

Profiles Flannery O'Connor's life and works using quotes from an interview with Sally Fitzgerald. Discusses O'Connor's intentions, how she viewed her art, and her childhood in Savannah. Includes Fitzgerald's comments on the religious nature of O'Connor's work; how she viewed her fiction as being "so compact that it qualified as poetry"; and the rise of O'Connor's reputation to the point that she is now "mentioned in tandem with William Faulkner" as being one of the South's foremost writers. Notes Fitzgerald's comment that while only 5,000 copies of *The Habit of Being* were initially bound, the publisher has sold 50,000 copies to date. Reports Fitzgerald's comments on the making of John Huston's version of *Wise Blood*, and reveals that, when *Wise Blood* was published, "one family member reported that she burned the book . . . [while] others passed it around in a brown paper sack." Concludes with Fitzgerald's opinion that *Wise Blood* is based upon the story of St. Paul, and that Tarwater in *The Violent Bear It Away* is really a thinly disguised "Jonah figure." Includes brief discussion of O'Connor's early childhood in Savannah based upon comments from her babysitter, Janey Oetgen, of Atlanta.

233   Brown, W. Dale. "Will Campbell By the Fire." *Southern Quarterly* 31.2 (1993): 164-86.

In an interview, Campbell offers his assessment of Flannery O'Connor's writings. Campbell says that he likes O'Connor's work and wishes he could have met her. He relates that he initially thought she was "making fun of my people," and laments O'Connor's early death.

234   Browning, Preston M., Jr. "Flannery O'Connor's Devil Revisited." *Southern Humanities Review* 10 (1976): 325-33.

Reviews John Hawkes's essay, "Flannery O'Connor's Devil," [*Sewanee Review* (Summer 1970): 395-407]. Notes that in his article, Hawkes argues that "O'Connor's practice often suggests a 'diabolical' authorial voice." Discusses characters in O'Connor's works which represent the devil, the multiplicity of forms and guises the devil employs, and apparent intentions. Concludes that O'Connor was following the tradition of Nathaniel Hawthorne, Dostoevsky, Baudelaire, and Gide when she allowed the devil such a conspicuous role in her fiction. Suggests that just as Freud had to "'play the Devil'" to fully understand how human thought can be so devious, O'Connor was also forced to do the same.

235   Browning, Preston M., Jr., et al. "Flannery O'Connor and the Grotesque Recovery of the Holy." *Adversity and Grace: Studies in Recent American Literature*. Ed. Nathan A. Scott, Jr. Chicago: U of Chicago P, 1968. 133-61.

Asserts that Flannery O'Connor defies every attempt to place her in any school or tradition. Analyzes a variety of her works, using traditional methods such as thematics and characterization. Draws an analogy between O'Connor's works and those of Dostoevsky.

236   Bruss, Neal H. "Lacan & Literature: Imaginary Objects and Social Order." *Massachusetts Review* 22 (Spring 1981): 62-92.

Offers a discussion of Jacques Lacan's interpretation of Sigmund Freud's theories regarding the various stages of human development, the Oedipal complex, and the distinction between the "Symbolic, Imaginary and Real." Applies these ideas to readings of Homer's *The Iliad*, Marcel Proust's *Remembrance of Things Past*, and William Shakespeare's *Hamlet*. Contends that each of these works "end[s] in the same way, by putting their major characters in new relations to the Symbolic." Includes a brief reference to O'Connor, listing her among the writers to whom the statement applies: "The Symbolic also explains that part of the writer which is totally dedicated to being a writer, to getting it right, [and] to mastering the resources of language."

237   Brussat, Frederic and Mary Ann. "A Viewer's Guide: Flannery O'Connor's `The Displaced Person.'" *The American Short Story*. New York: Cultural Information Service, 1979. 26-27.

Refers to the thirteen-week film series, "The American Short Story," which aired on the Public Broadcasting System (PBS), and offers this booklet as a study guide useful for individual groups of viewers. Discusses the short stories and the series in general, offering a brief biography of each author and a list of questions and answers about the film and story. Refers to "The Displaced Person" and provides a brief, basic summary, including two quotes from O'Connor concerning "image[s] of ultimate reality" and "that sense of mystery which cannot be accounted for."

238   Bryant, Hallman B. "Reading the Map in `A Good Man Is Hard To Find.'" *Studies in Short Fiction* 18.3 (1981): 301-07.

Analyzes O'Connor's use of real place names in "A Good Man Is Hard to Find." Suggests that they were chosen most significantly to foreshadow and "augment the theme of the story." States that because all of the places mentioned--with one exception, the town of "Timothy"--actually exist, the reader is able to estimate the distance the family travels. Discusses place names mentioned in detail and concludes that "the family's wayward lives are given direction in their final moments, and . . . [they] are at last on the right road."

239   Bryant, J.A., Jr. "A Renaissance in Full Swing: Women Extend Fiction's Range." *Twentieth-Century Southern Literature*. UP of Kentucky, 1997. 137-54.

Offers a brief biographical sketch and considers O'Connor's reputation and place in American literature. Follows with a discussion of *Wise Blood*, suggesting that at the time of publication what saved the novel, "and with it O'Connor's budding career," was "the powerful vitality of the work." States that because readers in the 1950s more readily acknowledged the place of religious faith in literature, "almost as soon as *Wise Blood* came out, Flannery O'Connor began to assume willy-nilly the status of a cult figure." Provides a brief explication of *The Violent Bear It Away* and notes that some critics consider this novel to be O'Connor's masterpiece. Concludes that taken together, O'Connor's work deserves "a place of distinction in America's literary annals, although the exact degree of that distinction is still difficult to predict."

240   Bryfonski, Dedria, ed. *Contemporary Literary Criticism*. Vol. 10. Detroit: Gale Research, 1980. 416-23.

Offers a compilation of short critical essays by Kenneth Frieling, Robert Midler, Thomas LeClair, Josephine Hendin, J.O. Tate, Michael True, and Robert Towers. Subject matter includes an examination of the realistic elements of O'Connor's work; her use of the grotesque; and the balance between religious and non-religious aspects of her fiction. Includes reviews of *The Habit of Being*.

241   Bryfonski, Dedria, ed. *Contemporary Literary Criticism*. Vol. 13. Detroit: Gale Research, 1979. 364-372.

Provides a number of essays, including one by Patricia D. Maida based upon the premise that "vision functions as the dynamic principle" in O'Connor's work. Another, by David Aiken, asserts that O'Connor's Asbury Porter Fox "corresponds" with James Joyce's Stephen Dedalus. A final longer essay, by André Bleikasten, discusses the religious and grotesque concerns seen in O'Connor's fiction.

242   Buchalter, Gail. "`I'm Optimistic -- It Creates Possibilities.'" *Macon [GA] Telegraph Parade Magazine* 8 June 1997: 4-6.

Offers a biographical sketch of Tommy Lee Jones, an Academy Award winning actor from Texas. Mentions that Jones majored in English at Harvard, where he "did his senior tutorial on the writer Flannery O'Connor and graduated cum laude."

243   Buchanan, James H. "The Face of the Wolf." *Patient Encounters: The Experience of Disease.* Charlottesville: UP of Virginia, 1989. 131-49.

A medical essay divided into four parts. Part one focuses on the symptoms, characteristics, and diagnosis, of Disseminated Lupus Erythematosus, using O'Connor as a case study. The second part focuses on O'Connor's career as a writer and the impact of this disease upon her work. The third describes "the elaborate and complex process of dying her death." The final part is a description of what O'Connor's final days, hours, and minutes were probably like.

244   Buck, Claire. "O'Connor, Flannery." *The Bloomsbury Guide to Women's Literature.* New York: Prentice Hall, 1992. 871-72.

Offers a brief biographical sketch, a listing of O'Connor's works, and a citation to one critical work about her writings (Marion Montgomery's *Why Flannery O'Connor Stayed Home*). Contends that "like the daughters in *A Good Man Is Hard to Find and Other Stories* (1955), O'Connor rebelled against the role of the Southern lady, criticizing Southern pride for its false piety and moral blindness." Suggests that she featured "grotesque characters to emphasize how pride perverts the self."

245   Buckley, James J. "A Field of Living Fire: Karl Barth on the Spirit and the Church." *Modern Theology* 10.1 (1994): 81-102.

Explicates and uses Flannery O'Connor's story "Revelation" to better understand those "arguments in conversation with Barth which have thus far been, by and large, *outside*" his theology. Sees the story as "a delightful parable of the critically consoling fire of God" which serves as "what Barth might call a `secular parable' of the relationship between the Holy Spirit and the Church." Suggests that "the grammar of the story" judges the reader. Refers to Ralph Wood's comment that in "Revelation" "`divine wrath is couched wholly within the terms of divine mercy. It is a mercy that is like a refiner's fire--cleansing rather than consuming.'"

246   Budick, Emily Miller. "`American Israelites': Literalism and Typology in the American Imagination." *Biblical Patterns in Modern Literature.* Brown Judaic Studies, 77. Ed. David H. Hirsch and Nehama Aschkenasy. Chico, CA: Scholar's Press, 1984. 187-208.

Discusses evidence of the Old Testament story of "the sacrifice of Isaac" in the works of five prominent American authors: Charles Brockton Brown, Nathaniel Hawthorne, Herman Melville, Sherwood Anderson, and

Flannery O'Connor. Examines works, including "A View of the Woods," to review uses of biblical materials and to explain "what the stories may be concluding about a certain quality of American imagination and its conception of self and nation." Remarks that O'Connor's stories "reflect on the causes and consequences of American materialism and relate that materialism to elements of America's antitypological and historical literalism."

247   Budick, Emily Miller. "Art and the Female Spirit: Flannery O'Connor." *Engendering Romance: Women Writers and the Hawthorne Tradition.* New Haven: Yale UP, 1994. 162-80.

Argues that in O'Connor's *The Violent Bear It Away* the male characters attempt to live in a "world of the purely intellectual and spiritual, in disrelation to the world of biology, sexuality, and women." Outlines how their attempts to do so negate their ability to "produce viable offspring." Explores the "the femininity of Christ" as related to the purpose of the story, and suggests that "the Tarwaters' desire to eliminate sexuality and women from their world coincides with their desire to be their own purely masculine Christs." Refers to comments by or about David Eggenschwiler, Richard Chase, Leo Steinberg, and Wolfgang Iser, and incorporates discussion of William Faulkner's *Absalom, Absalom* and *The Sound and the Fury*, Carson McCuller's *The Heart Is a Lonely Hunter*, Harriet Beecher Stowe's *Uncle Tom's Cabin*, and Nathaniel Hawthorne's "Roger Malvin's Burial."

248   Budick, Emily Miller. *Fiction and Historical Consciousness: The American Romance Tradition.* New Haven: Yale UP, 1989. 19, 38-39, 62, 65-68, 80-81, 221n6.

Examines works which may be categorized as American historical romance, focusing on the "relationship between this tradition's emphatic rejection of mimetic modes of representation and its equally strong insistence on specified settings in place and time." Categorizes O'Connor's "A View of the Woods" as among those works that use the typological "sacrifice of the son by the patriarchal father" as a structure for investigating the relationship between history and romance. Compares the story to Sherwood Anderson's *Winesburg, Ohio*. Sees the Grandfather as refusing to admit that "the climax of Christian history has already occurred," and offers a three-page discussion of O'Connor's suggestion that our "'view of the woods' is the only fortune we possess and that we inherit it from God as the medium of salvation." Sees O'Connor as among the select group of authors who acknowledge and accept "the burdens and errors of American history" and use their writings to "provide the possibility of self-aware reflection, which could ultimately effect the revision of American history."

249   Budy, Andrea Hollander. "Redemption." *Flannery O'Connor Bulletin* 24 (1995-96): 119-20.

A poem that considers the question of what would have happened if The Misfit had believed the grandmother in "A Good Man Is Hard to Find" and turned his head with her to hear "this other music."

250   Buechner, Frederick. "Flannery O'Connor." *The Clown in the Belfry: Writings on Faith and Fiction*. San Francisco: Harper Collins, 1992. 2-3, 67-71.

An essay originally written as an introduction to Jill Baumgaertner's, *A Proper Scaring*. Buechner describes his visit to O'Connor's hometown, Milledgeville, Georgia, and compares her work to his own. Concludes that O'Connor's work was original and extraordinary "because her corner of the territory [of Christendom] was one that no other writer . . . could possibly work."

251   Bukovinsky, Janet. "Flannery O'Connor." In *Women of Words: A Personal Introduction to Thirty-Five Important Writers*. Illus. Jenny Powell. Philadelphia: Running Press, 1994.

The author's intention is to provide readers with an opportunity to "meet a woman, read about her life, sample her work, and search for clues to her personality and motivations in the portraits which accompany each section." The profile of O'Connor includes a brief biographical introduction to O'Connor's life and work, an excerpt from her story "Everything That Rises Must Converge," and a color portrait of O'Connor sitting with her arms resting in her lap.

252   Bunch, Cedile Dianne. "Images of Imperfection: Flannery O'Connor's Young Intellectuals." *Kinjo Gakuin Daigaku Ronsyu* (Japan) 119 (1987): 117-32.

Analyzes and compares O'Connor's characters Asbury Fox, Julian, and Calhoun. Argues that all of them move from self-assuredness to self-doubt and insecurity in the face of a more powerful divine authority. (Abstracted by Kayoko Watanabe).

253   Burke, Daniel. "Flannery O'Connor: Pride and Prejudice in `The Artificial Nigger.'" *Beyond Interpretation: Studies in the Modern Short Story*. Troy, NY: Whitson, 1991. 145-61.

Argues that "The Artificial Nigger" presents a reversal of the "traditional pattern of initiation stories," in that O'Connor has "the elder instructor achieving more wisdom than the child initiate." Includes a brief comparison with Nathaniel Hawthorne's "My Kinsman, Major Molineux." Then, describes how, "in the seesawing antagonism of the two main characters, betrayal, the consciousness of sin, and the agony of guilt," both Mr. Head and Nelson have been able to "overcome their pride" and absolve "their prejudice for one another."

254   Burke, William. "Displaced Communities and Literary Form in Flannery O'Connor's `The Displaced Person.'" *Modern Fiction Studies* 32.2 (1986): 219-27.

Suggests that while most criticism to date of "The Displaced Person" follows Robert Fitzgerald's interpretation, which involves "reading the story as a product, as a kind of achieved metaphor," the story should still be explored on a dramatic level as well. Argues that it should be carefully read as "a sequence of developments--as a displacement of community, and on the rhetorical level as a displacement of literary strategies." Uses this perspective to carefully analyze the story.

255   Burke, William. "Fetishism in the Fiction of Flannery O'Connor." *Flannery O'Connor Bulletin* 22 (1993-94): 45-52.

Suggests that there is "a gallery of fetishists" in O'Connor's fiction. Contends that these characters "are obsessed not only by private curiosities like glass eyes and wooden legs but also by socially acceptable interests such as the acquisition of property and concern with cleanliness." Defines "fetishism" and delineates its use by O'Connor. Refers to Sigmund Freud's and Ernest Becker's views and uses the term to discuss situations in O'Connor's works in which characters place such value upon "some object or condition . . . that it is raised `to the level of the absolute,'" and becomes "a profane interest [which] occupies the place of the sacred." Argues that while a sexual or psychological aspect may be present, "these characters are essentially responding to a spiritual malady in which the fetish guards against the anxiety about death." Analyzes "Good Country People" in this context and finds the story to have "clear Freudian overtones." Discusses Mrs. Turpin's preoccupation with cleanliness in "Revelation;" the automobile as fetish in "The Life You Save May Be Your Own" and *Wise Blood*; and O'Connor's "most pervasive and sinister fetish," property, which is illustrated so aptly by Mr. Fortune in "A View of the Woods." Concludes that the appearance of fetishism in O'Connor's work reflects her interest in the problem of "human impoverishment or limitation" of the spirit and how it is so often concealed so as to distract a character from facing the true reality "of a poverty fundamental" to all of humankind.

256   Burke, William M. "Protagonists and Antagonists in the Fiction of Flannery O'Connor." *Southern Literary Journal* 20.2 (1988): 99-111.

Observes that many of O'Connor's stories "involve two characters in conflict, a relation of protagonist and antagonist central to the dramatization and development of her themes." Suggests that these antagonistic relationships can be categorized as reflecting the contrast between metaphor and metonymy. Discusses and analyzes metonymic relationships in a variety of O'Connor's stories, including "Good Country People" and "Parker's Back" and then focuses on the use of metaphor in "Revelation" and "A Good Man Is Hard to Find."

257   Burkle, Howard R. "The Child in Flannery O'Connor." *Flannery O'Connor Bulletin* 18 (1989): 59-69.

Suggests that Flannery O'Connor uses the child character in her works to call attention "to some moral-spiritual flaw" that she wishes to "hold up to judgement." States that she censures this flaw implicitly "by depicting the child as its innocent victim," while, at other times--such as with Mary Grace's assault on Mrs. Turpin--O'Connor does so more obviously. Maintains that literary critics have simplistically concluded that O'Connor's child characters are symptomatic of her own "unresolved psychological problems." Concedes that while such psychological interpretations may, be helpful in some ways, O'Connor's child characters also "speak as much about humanity's relation to the transcendent--about the conflict between God and humanity--as about conflict within O'Connor's psyche and between O'Connor and her society." Notes that "because in her heart she is the most traditionally religious of O'Connor's children," the child in "A Temple of the Holy Ghost" is deserving of study. Offers a close reading of the story, and finds the child to be "almost prophetic" in how she "mediates judgement." The child is for O'Connor's readers, in many ways, a point of contact where the transcendent intersects the human plane of existence and challenges its ways. Outlines observations of the roles and effect of children in a variety of selected works and finds that while they appear to vary in their spiritual qualities, most "play an important part in O'Connor's effort to make readers conscious of their spiritual needs."

258   Burkman, Katherine H., and J. Reid Meloy. "The Black Mirror: Joseph Conrad's *The Nigger of the `Narcissus'* and Flannery O'Connor's `The Artificial Nigger.'" *Midwest Quarterly* 28.2 (1987): 230-47.

Suggests that both Conrad's crew of the "Narcissus" and Mr. Head and Nelson of "The Artificial Nigger" participate in spiritual quests and "find a measure of salvation through their encounters with a black double." Contends that both Conrad and O'Connor shared the same artistic goal of "using art as a mirror that would faithfully reflect the universe as they perceived it."

259   Burns, Dan G. "Flannery O'Connor's `Parker's Back': The Key to the End." *Notes on Contemporary Literature* 17.2 (1987): 11-12.

Asserts that because O'Connor's ironic images depend upon biblical types, a close reading of the biblical text related to Parker's Christian names reveals keys to better understanding the story's plot and its enigmatic conclusion. Contends that Parker's tears at the end of the story express a sense of ecstasy at his redemption.

260   Burns, Margie. "A Good Rose Is Hard to Find: `Southern Gothic' as Social Dislocation in Faulkner and O'Connor." *Works and Days* 6.1-2 (1988): 185-201.

Asserts that William Faulkner's "A Rose for Emily" and Flannery O'Connor's "A Good Man Is Hard to Find" are "premier examples" of the Southern Gothic literary mode. States that both stories "achieve their full horror through intense comedy, a black humor which largely accounts for the place of `Southern' relative to `Gothic.'" Claims that the Southern Gothic approach serves as a distancing method, by mystifying the matter presented, "removing it into an `atmosphere' detached from social actuality, and engineering a response alienated and unsympathetic." Examines the narratives of each story in light of these contentions. [Rpt. in *Image and Ideology in Modern/Post Modern Discourse*. Ed. David B. Downing and Susan Bazargan. Albany, NY: SUNY Press, 1991. 105-23).]

261   Burns, Marion. "The Chronology of Flannery O'Connor's `Why Do the Heathen Rage?'" *Flannery O'Connor Bulletin* 11 (1982): 58-75.

Traces the history of O'Connor's work on her unfinished novel, "Why Do the Heathen Rage?" using information from *The Habit of Being* and evidence found in the manuscripts in the *Flannery O'Connor Collection* of the Russell Library at Georgia College & State University in Milledgeville. Concludes that the evidence reveals that O'Connor wrote the manuscripts for the novel "between 1960 and 1963, most of it in fact in 1963." This statement "controverts the conclusion of Stuart L. Burns" that at the time of O'Connor's death, she "'had been working on 'The Heathen' for at least seven, and possibly as long as ten years.'" Describes Burns's proposition and counters his position point by point, scene by scene, and offers opinions as to why evidence is contrary to his assertions. Discusses the unfinished novel's characters, O'Connor's clipping describing the tattoos on a man, and refers to a number of her other works, including: "The Enduring Chill," "An Exile in the East," *The Violent Bear It Away*, "The Artificial Nigger," and "Greenleaf." Also discusses several of O'Connor's correspondents, including "A" [Betty Hester], Allen Tate, Alice Morris, Maryat Lee, T.R. Spivey, Ashley Brown, Cecil Dawkins, Robert Giroux, Sister Mariella Gable, and Janet McKane.

262   Burns, Marion. "O'Connor's Unfinished Novel." *Flannery O'Connor Bulletin* 11 (1982): 76-93.

From the fragments available in the *Flannery O'Connor Collection* of the Russell Library at Georgia College & State University, Burns examines the composition of O'Connor's incomplete third novel--which she tentatively titled "Why Do the Heathen Rage?" Speculates on how the novel might have been structured, compares it to *Wise Blood* and *The Violent Bear It Away*, and notes that it posed "many technical problems for the author." Discusses Walter Tilman, the protagonist, and focuses on: the meaning of his name; how he, like Hazel Motes and Francis Marion Tarwater, finds Christ (but adopts "a distinctly pre-Reformation Christianity"); and how he resembles "a Christian monk" like St. Jerome, and demonstrates a knowledge of Church philosophy and politics similar to that of a scholar. Contends that Walter's "Catholicism and medievalism are what determine him in the novel, and what ultimately determine the shape of the novel, [and] its structure and theme." Reports that "The Heathen" started out as a sequel to "The Enduring Chill," which "was to feature Asbury, whose conversion . . . was originally to have been the premise for the third novel." Observes that the manuscripts reflect that O'Connor dropped this idea, and turned Walter into "a susceptible personality, already intellectually converted to an early form of Christianity, but yet to undergo spiritual conversion." Follows with an outline and discussion of problems O'Connor encountered with scenes she developed for Walter's revelation and conversion, and questions of characterization, theme, structure, symbolism, and the plot itself. Closes with a discussion of why "there are reasons enough to suppose that, even had O'Connor lived much longer, 'Why Do the Heathen Rage?' would never have been published as a novel." Notes that remarkable similarities exist between this work and John Kennedy Toole's *A Confederacy of Dunces*. [Rpt. in *Critical Essays on Flannery O'Connor*. Ed. Melvin J. Friedman and Beverly Lyon Clark. Boston: G.K. Hall, 1985. 169-80.]

263   Burns, Shannon. "Flannery O'Connor: The Work Ethic." *Flannery O'Connor Bulletin* 8 (1979): 54-67.

Sees O'Connor's characters as falling into two categories: those similar to Hazel Motes, Francis Marion Tarwater, and The Misfit, who have based their lives "on a denial much like Carlyle's Everlasting No," and those "who have already established or inherited a comfortable niche in the order of the universe, a way of life insistently based on the American work ethic." Maintains that O'Connor's view of characters of this second type reflects four influences of the American work ethic: "the Calvinist regard of material prosperity as a sign of salvation"; Ben Franklin's view of an individual's worth being equated with material success from honest, hard work; Longfellow's views expressed in "A Psalm of Life"; and the general American belief "that virtually anything can be accomplished by dint of hard work." Applies O'Connor's perspective of the American work ethic to readings of "Everything That Rises Must Converge," "The Displaced Person," "Greenleaf," "Revelation," and "A View of the Woods." Refers to comments by Miles Orvell, and discusses O'Connor's use of class structure to describe "rigid rules set down by those who describe the ethic." Concludes that O'Connor's work reflects her view that the work ethic in America is "a limiting and spiritually barren vision, if pursued in and of itself."

264   Burns, Shannon. "The Literary Theory of Flannery O'Connor and Nathaniel Hawthorne." *Flannery O'Connor Bulletin* 7 (1978): 101-13.

Discusses the literary kinship between O'Connor and Nathaniel Hawthorne, and suggests that many critics--with the exception of Miles Orvell--have "limited their vision" of O'Connor by focusing too narrowly upon her Christian concerns. Asserts that not only do O'Connor's statements about her own literary approach "quite literally" echo Hawthorne, but that her "central artistic concern" seems "virtually identical" to his. Refers to a variety of Hawthorne's works to illustrate parallels: *The House of Seven Gables*, *The Blithedale Romance*, *The Marble Faun*, "Rappaccini's Daughter," "The Custom House," "Young Goodman Brown," "Roger Malvin's Burial," "The Snow-Image," and "Main Street." Considers how both authors plead for "readers who will endeavor to take, or be shown, the proper point of view in reading and judging their works" and be willing see how "some higher truth, some supra-reality, might exist." Through readings of Hawthorne's "The Snow

Image" and O'Connor's "A Good Man Is Hard to Find." Burns explores how both writers attempt to shatter their reader's concept of reality and "create a world in which the reader is able to wonder, to speculate, even to doubt." Concludes that the core of both O'Connor's and Hawthorne's fiction "is the same," as both attempted "to show the reader that `reality' holds many dimensions." Consequently, "O'Connor emerges not as a Catholic or even Christian writer, but as an artist of complex vision working . . . out of Hawthorne's own tradition."

265   Burns, Stuart L. "How Wide Did `The Heathen Range?'" *Flannery O'Connor Bulletin* 4 (1975): 25-41.

Considers whether the 378 pages of manuscript for O'Connor's unfinished novel, "Why Do the Heathen Rage," might "promise something publishable in the future" similar to that of James Agee's *A Death in the Family* or F. Scott Fitzgerald's *The Last Tycoon*. Regretfully reports that "there is . . . no novel there at all," but relates how the manuscript "affords clear insight" into O'Connor's writing methods and offers "sobering . . . clues regarding the evolution of the unfinished novel." Contends the material suggests that "while O'Connor *wanted* to write novels, she was best able to exercise her talents through the medium of the short story or the short story cycle." Remarks that "writing--especially the writing of a novel--was, for O'Connor, a slow, painful and frustrating experience"; and while "the manuscript suggests that O'Connor was not embarked in any new direction in her unfinished novel," there is evidence to hint that she may have been trying to develop a "family chronicle--a sort of Georgia counterpart to the works of Faulkner." Discusses O'Connor's use of symbols and describes plot fragments of the manuscript, tying them to sections of other works, including "The Enduring Chill," "Everything That Rises Must Converge," "The Partridge Festival," "Greenleaf," "Judgement Day" (and its earlier version, "An Exile in the East"), "The Artificial Nigger," and "Parker's Back."

266   Burr, Nelson R. "New Eden and New Babylon: Religious Thoughts of American Authors, A Bibliography: Flannery O'Connor: Southern Anomaly." *Anglican and Episcopal History* 56.1 (1987): 87-107.

Discusses the wide variety of arguments and perspectives that critics have used to examine O'Connor's works. Cites thesis statements of thirty dissertations, twenty articles, and six books.

267   Burr, Nelson R. "New Eden and New Babylon: Religious Thoughts of American Authors, A Bibliography: Flannery O'Connor: Take Heaven by

Violence." *Historical Magazine of the Protestant Episcopal Church* 55.3 (1986): 213-47.

Suggests that "probably no novelist has appreciated the religious and moral agony of the Calvinistic South, in such vivid style, as has Catholic Flannery O'Connor." Cites thesis statements of six dissertations, one article, and one book.

268   Burt, John. "What You Can't Talk About." *Flannery O'Connor: Modern Critical Views*. Ed. and intro. by Harold Bloom. Modern Critical Views. New York: Chelsea House, 1986. 125-43.

Uses the story of Satan's setting Jesus upon the pinnacle of the Temple of Jerusalem as a starting point for examining "The Turkey" (later called "The Capture") and "Parker's Back" in Part I of a two-part essay. Suggests that while O'Connor's desire to convey a sense of the transcendence of God to unbelievers was one of the most difficult tasks she could undertake, these two stories convey two different perspectives of O'Connor's attempt to do so. Focuses on the "Something Awful" which chases Ruller in "The Turkey," and views it as an illustration of how difficult it is to explain what "faith has faith in." Then examines in "Parker's Back" Parker's attempt to satisfy Sarah Ruth, on the one hand, and to convert his tattoos "into a flowing arabesque," on the other. Sees the "parodic epiphany" scene as a demonstration of how enlightenment is often not recognized for what it is. Concludes Part I by noting how the two stories "seem to repel each other." Argues that "either we can comprehend God through symbols or we cannot." Asserts that readers may be left thinking that they are either like Ruller, who is "absolutely shut out of the secret of the story," or like Parker who is "beaten from pillar to post." Examines, in Part II, how Hazel Motes, in *Wise Blood*, lives through both "the consequences of his errors" and his nihilism with enough integrity to transcend himself. Sees his power and integrity as lying not in what he accomplishes, but in what he fails to do. Notes that, unlike in "The Turkey" and "Parker's Back," O'Connor "has it both ways" in *Wise Blood*: she "rejects the inward power which her characters take as their sole authority" while recognizing how this inward power "seems not only to redeem Haze" but to win the "grudging respect of both author and reader." Concludes that the novel leaves O'Connor and Haze "in a perilous but acutely balanced standoff."

269   Butler, Rebecca Roxburgh. Rev. of *Flannery O'Connor: A Proper Scaring*, by Jill P. Baumgaertner. *Flannery O'Connor Bulletin* 17 (1988): 101-04.

Review essay which finds Baumgaertner's book to be "a specifically Christian reading of O'Connor's collected letters, selected short stories, and novels." Questions whether the book is truly necessary and wonders if "the catch is too big for the boat." Reports the book to be an attempt to examine O'Connor's "life, faith, and writing for evidence that will explain the strangeness of the fiction and, at the same time, document the congruence of O'Connor's theology and her artistic talent." Suggests that while some of the critical references and biblical parallels appear to be somewhat randomly selected, or "to support only the thesis under discussion," the readings are well organized and "perceptive and sensible." Concludes that the work "is a worthy attempt at a coherent understanding of the diverse and peculiar beauties of O'Connor's fiction."

270   Butler, Rebecca R[oxburgh]. "What's So Funny About Flannery O'Connor?" *Flannery O'Connor Bulletin* 9 (1980): 30-40.

Notes that in spite of O'Connor's remarks that many of her stories are "too funny to read before an audience," many readers and critics fail to see the humor in her work. Argues that, as a result, early critics emphasized the religious or psychological dimensions of her fiction. Suggests myriad ways by which the humor of her work can be best appreciated: "one-sided" readings in the historical context of Western comedy; O'Connor's use of the middle Georgia humor of Joel Chandler Harris and Augustus Baldwin Longstreet; her use of peculiar and zany titles, characters, and place names; comic dramatizations; and the "rhythm and lilt" of her comic dialogue. Focuses on her use of "the sense of threat, of danger, of violence," to suggest how her work, like "all accomplished comedy contains or rests upon some deeply serious or horrifying repugnant reality." Contends that her use of shock tactics, "trouble," and the "Great American Joke" (which allows for the "triumph of the banal"), serve "as an antidote to that mind-dulling sentimentality that O'Connor attacked at every opportunity."

271   Butler, Rebecca Roxburgh. "*Wise Blood*'s Joy In Contradiction." *Flannery O'Connor Bulletin* 10 (1981): 23-28.

Suggests that while "the pointedly foolish contradiction of the title," *Wise Blood*, and "the furious self-division" of Hazel Motes "suggest that contradiction dominates" this work, "the joy that accompanies that contradiction may not be so obvious." Discusses how Hazel Motes serves as "a caricature of a romantic hero," and uses O'Connor's own comments in the Preface to the second edition on "the nature of joy" to introduce a discussion of her "method and manner in the novel." Sees O'Connor's "characteristic parallel style" as "very much in evidence in the paired opposition of the comic and the serious," and notes that the various types of contradiction that structure and adorn *Wise Blood* "range from the briefest double negative or denial to more complex verbal wit and nonsense to lengthy arguments and staged conflicts." Offers a reading of the novel in the context of the contradictions noted and concludes that their use reflects O'Connor's choice of "a rhetorical technique that both suited her own experience and talent and that gave the fiction simplicity, clarity, and strength."

272   Butler, Robert James. "Visions of Southern Life and Religion in O'Connor's *Wise Blood* and Walker's *The Third Life of Grange Copeland.*" *CLA Journal* 36.4 (1993): 349-70.

Points out the coincidence that Flannery O'Connor and Alice Walker--two of America's most noted Southern, women authors--lived just a few miles apart (indeed, on the same road), but never met. Recounts their differences, then focuses on similarities based upon "the fact that both women were Southern writers responding to similar pieces of Southern geography and culture." Describes each author's "`double vision'" of the South and asserts that this split view helped each write about the region in an unsentimental way while still holding up its sense of place and "`close community.'" Contends that both authors' fiction converged on the region's religious traditions and suggests that "at the heart of their visions [is] a religious preoccupation" with the "transformation of the self into a radically new life." Argues that this interest is revealed most dramatically in their first novels: O'Connor's *Wise Blood* and Walker's *The Third Life of Grange Copeland.* Offers a detailed reading and explication of the two novels and finds that each portrays the South "as a severely `fallen world' which imposes tremendous hardship on its people but also as a region which, paradoxically, offers the possibility of salvation because it has kept alive a religious tradition centered in the conversion experience." Concludes that, while they criticized many aspects of Southern culture, both O'Connor and Walker "were able to transcend the determinism and despair which characterizes so much of Southern literature" by focusing on the "affirmative vision" of the region's religious traditions.

273   Butterworth, Nancy K. "Flannery O'Connor." *American Novelists Since World War II: Fourth Series.* Ed. James R. and Wanda H. Giles. Dictionary of Literary Biography. Vol. 152. Detroit: Gale Research, 1995. 158-81.

Cites work by O'Connor and states that although she completed "only a small corpus of fiction during her brief life . . . her stunning talent was immediately recognized and her reputation has grown enormously since her death." Refers to comments by Caroline Gordon, O'Connor's own comments from "The Fiction Writer and His Country," and remarks by Sally and Robert Fitzgerald from the introductions to *The Habit of Being* and *Mystery and Manners*. Provides a biographical sketch which offers details of her childhood in Savannah and Milledgeville, her student days, and dates of publication. Includes brief critical summaries of her stories and novels. Follows with discussions of her method of writing, influences, her battle with lupus erythematosus, reactions to *Wise Blood*, her lectures, publication of *A Good Man Is Hard to Find*, her disillusionment with her readership, her vision and use of violence, irony and the grotesque to convey her message. Comments on O'Connor's "doctrinal differences from Protestants," the relationship between her work and that of the "social and realities of the South" during years she wrote, the "negative parent-child dynamics" noted in her work, her use of violence to bring her characters to redemption, how she addressed "structural and narrative difficulties" in her novels, Teilhard de Chardin's influence upon her during her last two years of life, and how readers "are finding narrowly religious interpretations" of her work "repetitive and restrictive." Concludes with an overview of critical commentary, and suggests areas where further study may be worthwhile. Offers a useful list of references to critical interpretation and includes a number of photographs: O'Connor in 1962 and in 1953; O'Connor with the 1944-45 staff of the Georgia State College for Women's literary quarterly (*The Corinthian*); the dust jackets for *Wise Blood* and *The Violent Bear It Away*; O'Connor with Katherine Anne Porter in 1958 and with Brainard Cheney in 1959; and, of the poster advertising *The Habit of Art* symposium held at Georgia College & State University in 1994.

274   Buzan, Mary. "The Difficult Heroism of Francis Marion Tarwater." *Flannery O'Connor Bulletin* 14 (1985): 33-43.

Contends that Tarwater's metamorphosis in *The Violent Bear It Away* "affirms the novel's Dantesque vision of spiritual mysteries, more especially of the mystery of love." Sees Mason's love, reflected in Bishop, as teaching Tarwater "self-respect and self-love." Suggests that Tarwater's "feelings, retaught by Bishop's redemptive, Christ-like death and violated but strengthened by the rape, empower" and assist him in gaining victory over the stranger. Argues that when Tarwater accepts his role as prophet, after having dealt with the devil "as does Dante crawling down Satan's back," he is acting on "his own sense of divine mercy and grace, dedicating himself to . . . an all-encompassing love."

275   Byars, John. "Mimicry and Parody in *Wise Blood*." *College Literature* 11.3 (1984): 276-79.

Argues that O'Connor effectively communicates irony in *Wise Blood* through "Hazel's confrontations with projections of himself which he fails to recognize as such." Suggests that O'Connor uses this pattern so readers can see how people, animals, and objects "mimic and parody Hazel's simultaneous flight from, and pursuit of God." Cites Hazel Motes as a classic example of a comic character according to Henri Bergson's theory of comedy. Then, discusses patterns of replication, metaphors of characters with animals, and incidents serving as mirroring devices.

276   Byars, John. "Prophecy and Apocalyptic in the Fiction of Flannery O'Connor." *Flannery O'Connor Bulletin* 16 (1987): 34-42.

Observes that while examples of the crucial role that O'Connor assigns to her false and real prophets are obvious, critics and readers have found it difficult to understand the "nature and shape" of her fiction as prophecy. Reviews the perspective offered by Miles Orvell and suggests that O'Connor presents readers with two contradictory prophetic images. The first is that of a society with such a deeply embedded evil nature that total destruction will be required. The second, reflects a view that even though a portion of the community may be deeply flawed, individuals may find possibilities for regeneration. Asserts that O'Connor's contradictory images reflect a tension between the imminence of total destruction and the possibility of restoration. Cites Edwin Honig's definitions of prophetic and apocalyptic modes of vision, reviews related biblical scholarship, and then offers a detailed look at examples of the two in a wide variety of O'Connor's works. Also examines O'Connor's dramatic closures. Notes that while her apocalyptic visions "move the reader from the constricted world of the protagonist to a sense of cosmic grandeur and immensity," they also raise important questions regarding her views of judgement and revelation.

277   Byars, John A. "W.B. Yeats and *Wise Blood*." *Flannery O'Connor Bulletin* 14 (1985): 88-93.

Suggests that "a collection of folklore published by W.B. Yeats in 1891 [*The Celtic Twilight*] may have contained the seeds for two scenes in Flannery O'Connor's *Wise Blood*." Focuses on Yeats's "The Last Gleeman," a sketch in which a poet is impersonated in a manner which resembles scenes in *Wise Blood* (where Hazel Motes confronts Onnie Jay Holy and later Solace Layfield). Lists and describes similarities and differences in the tone, style, and plots of the two works. Relates that insight "may be gained by looking at the pattern of Hazel Motes's development in light of certain crucial ideas about self-realization expressed by Yeats." Contends, on the basis of evidence presented, that

O'Connor "at one time may have read the Yeats sketch and that some of these features later surfaced, probably not deliberately, in *Wise Blood*."

278   Byerman, Keith E. "Intense Behaviors: The Use of the Grotesque in *The Bluest Eye* and *Eva's Man*." *College Language Association Journal* 25 (June 1982): 447-57.

Discusses how Toni Morrison's character, Pecola, of *The Bluest Eye*, and Gayl Jones's character, Eva, of *Eva's Man*, are used to examine "grotesqeries of American society." Specifically, Pecola is seen as epitomizing "the American obsession with whiteness," and Eva with "society's fixation on sexual dominance." Includes a brief reference to, and application of, O'Connor's definition of the grotesque.

279   Byrd, Rudolph P. *Jean Toomer's Years with Gurdjieff: Portrait of an Artist, 1923-1936*. Athens: U of Georgia P, 1990. 122-23.

Examines Jean Toomer's interest in George Ivanovich Gurdjieff's teachings. Includes a discussion of shortcomings in his story "Transatlantic," using comments made by Flannery O'Connor on characteristics of writing that might mark it as amateurish. Concludes that while Toomer was certainly not a beginning writer when he penned "Transatlantic," he was, "in his role as social critic and spiritual reformer," guilty of the indiscretions that O'Connor had identified. Contends that in all Toomer's fiction written after *Cane*, "it becomes painfully evident that Toomer was far more interested in ideas and problems than in character development, or in what O'Connor called the `texture of existence.'"

280   Byrd, Rudolph P. "Sound Advice From a Friend: Words and Thoughts from the Higher Ground of Alice Walker." *Callaloo* 6 (Spring-Summer 1983): 123-29.

Discusses Walker's fiction, focusing on her essays in *In Search of Our Mothers' Gardens*. Contends that readers "should feel both excitement and gratitude" for this "collection of essays written over the past seventeen years in such magazines as *Ms.* and *Essence*." Includes brief references to how Walker "examines, with respect and admiration," the fiction of other writers such as Flannery O'Connor. States that like O'Connor, Walker "believes in the restorative powers of laughter."

281   Byrne, Mary Ellen. "Flannery O'Connor's Moments of Grace." *Teaching English in the Two Year College* 15.4 (1988): 250-54.

Asserts that "instructors of introductory literature courses can teach [students] how to analyze content and meaning through a pervading theme." Uses three of Flannery O'Connor's stories ("Revelation," "Everything That Rises Must Converge," and "A Good Man Is Hard to Find") as examples. Focuses on the "moment of grace" in each story, and demonstrates how to "discuss its central importance in the work." Discusses a variety of related topics: the role of Catholicism in O'Connor's work; the concept of grace; Alice Walker's view of what O'Connor was "about"; the significance of her story titles (which signify spiritual intent); similar characteristics and devices used in each story; and the language, violence, and use of light in O'Connor's moments of grace. Concludes that for students to gain insight from O'Connor's stories and more fully to understand their "mystery," teachers should "draw attention to these crucial moments in her stories," discuss O'Connor's role as a Catholic writer, and "define the aspects of her Catholicism which vitalize these stories, namely, grace as essential for salvation and . . . as a divine offering to each human being."

282   Calisch, Richard. "Dante and Oedipus Go to Atlanta, Georgia." *English Journal* 70.7 (1981): 63-66.

Discusses influences in O'Connor's "The Artificial Nigger": "First, the profusion of references to Dante's *Inferno*; second, a wealth of analogies to *Oedipus Rex*; [and] third, a less developed series of parallels to the story of Tobias and the Archangel Raphael as told in the *Apocrypha*." Concludes that the Dante theme "cries out to be noticed" in the story and should be carefully considered.

283   Campbell, Debra. "'Flannery O'Connor Is Not John Updike.'" *American Quarterly* 43.2 (1991): 333-40.

Review essay of several books that discuss the "current identity crisis" of American Catholics. Outlines the historical background of the crisis and focuses on the theological positions of writers and others influencing opinions. Includes a brief reference to O'Connor, through a remark by Andrew Greeley regarding the boundary between Catholic and Protestant Americans: "'Flannery O'Connor is not John Updike.'" Suggests that Greeley's remark encapsulates "the difference between the Catholic imagination and the Protestant imagination" in a "palpable, yet esoteric" way.

284   Canfield, John. "A Conversation with Shirley Ann Grau." *Southern Quarterly* 25.2 (1987): 39-52.

An interview in which Grau offers an assessment of O'Connor's artistic achievement in relation to that of Carson McCullers. States that McCullers's work attracts her because of McCullers's "underrated" position as a writer and the "element of legend-making" seen in her work. Applauds McCullers's ability to make her characters "bigger than life." Suggests that O'Connor tried the same approach, but contends that "in her case the theological input kind of overloads it." Follows with the observation that O'Connor's work is "so concentrated that the symbols pile on top of each other, and it kind of wastes itself."

285   Caro, Frances A. de. "Proverbs and Originality in Modern Short Fiction." *Western Folklore* 37 (1978): 30-38.

Argues that proverbs are a useful way to simplify communication, both verbally and by writers who wish to use them to inform aspects of their literary work. Speculates that modern literary critics frown upon their use leaving the fiction writer "to an indirect or partially ironic use in order to be able to reap their communicative benefits." Suggests that this speculation is "borne out" by illustrations from four stories discussed: Katherine Mansfield's "Bliss," J.F. Powers' "The Valiant Woman," Ruth Suckow's "A Start in Life," and O'Connor's "A Good Man Is Hard to Find." Contends that O'Connor's work presents readers with "a proverb being used as the title, and . . . again by a character in a perfectly direct manner to comment upon the terrible state of modern society." Offers a reading of the story and examines the dual use of the proverb. Suggests that, "on the one hand it can be taken at face value . . . indeed a good man *is* hard to find, if the people in the story are representative of humanity." Notes also how "O'Connor plays with the proverb, contradicting it, showing how easy it can be to find a good man if one refuses to face up to the reality of evil." Finds that O'Connor "could not have used the proverb at face value without also working the ironic contradiction."

286   Carr, Pat. "Flannery O'Connor." *American Women Writers: A Critical Reference Guide from Colonial Times to the Present.* Ed. Lina Mainiero and Langdon Faust. Vol. 3. New York: Frederick Ungar, 1981. 287-91.

Uses O'Connor's own critical comments to analyze her work, providing general summaries of her major works and a short bibliography. Concentrates on O'Connor's use of the grotesque.

286a   Carroll, Rachel. "Foreign Bodies: History and Trauma in Flannery O'Connor's `The Displaced Person.'" *Textual Practice* 14.1 (2000): 97-114.

Contends that "history and the irrational are revealed to exist in intimate proximity in O'Connor's texts: the past haunts the present by returning through the unconscious." Ties Freud's definition of the "uncanny" to O'Connor's use of historical subject material to suggest that the "violent disruptions" seen in "The Displaced Person" tend to "reveal their imprint on the unconscious in the form of trauma." Relates how O'Connor's use of the Holocaust fulfills Cathy Caruth's definition of trauma and is "mediated through two central signifiers of modernity: the cinema and the railway." Discusses the statelessness of the Displaced Person and contrasts his situation with the "rootedness of identity" so important to Southerners and with the mechanism of false witness: a mechanism to which "the foreign body of the displaced person . . . falls victim."

287   Carson, Ricks. "O'Connor's *Wise Blood*." *Explicator* 49.3 (1991): 186-87.

Discusses Enoch Emery's obsession with the woman who appears at the swimming pool. Suggests that Enoch "bears a startling likeness to an incubus . . . demon spirits [who] were believed to desire sexual intercourse with sleeping women." Notes that the woman herself "has a generally lewd air and `sharp teeth protruding from her mouth,'" and states that O'Connor later "turns her into a succubus, the female counterpart of an incubus." Concludes that in the context of Hazel Motes's "nose for the devil, the incubus and succubus images provide subtle and brilliant examples of O'Connor's art of characterization, as well as keys to her moral vision."

287a   Carter, David. "Memories of Flannery O'Connor." *Savannah News-Press* (13 Aug. 1989): F1+.

Offers a biographical sketch covering O'Connor's life from her early childhood days in Savannah to her later years living at the family dairy farm, Andalusia, just north of Milledgeville, Georgia. Discusses views of her writing held by family and her family's Milledgeville friends, the two men with which she was in "love" (Marine sergeant John Sullivan and Harcourt Brace salesman Erik Langkjer), and the circumstances of her death from lupus in August, 1964.

288   Casey, Roger N. "Driving Miss Flannery: Automobiles in O'Connor's Short Stories." *Journal of Contemporary Thought* 4 (1994): 85-97.

Examines O'Connor's use of the automobile as a symbol, a "metaphorical `engine' under the hood" of many of her short stories. Acknowledges J.O. Tate's "seminal scholarly analysis" of the role of Hazel Motes's Essex in

Wise Blood. Suggests that Tate's assertion--that "O'Connor found the perfect symbol for her novel"--applies to O'Connor's short stories as well. Remarks that, "one will find that every short story written after *Wise Blood* contains an automobile used in some fashion, while her works prior to the novel contain scarcely a reference to a car." Proceeds to discuss, in some detail, the role of the automobile in "The Life You Save May Be Your Own," "Parker's Back," "A Good Man Is Hard to Find," "The Displaced Person," and "Greenleaf." Briefly refers to vehicles in "The Comforts of Home," "A Temple of the Holy Ghost," "Good Country People," and "The Partridge Festival." Refers to writings by Joel Wells, J.O. Tate, Melvin J. Friedman, Mircea Eliade, and Brian Abel Ragen. Concludes that O'Connor realized the importance and the usefulness of the automobile as a "fictional tool," as her works "demonstrate an overwhelming understanding of the prominence automobility was attaining in the post-war culture, particularly in the South."

289   Cash, Jean W. "The Flannery O'Connor-Andrew Lytle Connection." *Flannery O'Connor Bulletin* 25 (1996-97): 183-92.

Offers a profile of the Southern Agrarian writer and creative writing teacher, Andrew Lytle, and discusses his working relationship with, and opinion of, Flannery O'Connor. Includes details of his appointment as temporary Director of the Iowa Writer's Workshop, which, in turn, led to his becoming O'Connor's teacher in the spring of 1947 and advisor for her master's thesis which became part of her first novel, *Wise Blood*. Relies on details provided in Lytle's correspondence and interviews as well as recollections by James B. Hall, Robie Macauley, and Merrill Joan Gerber, to offer insight into the working relationship of Lytle and O'Connor and the respect they had for each other. Concludes with Lytle's comment on O'Connor, only two years before his own death, that "`She was one of the best and she will live, I think. It's the real thing.'"

290   Cash, Jean W. "Flannery O'Connor: Art `Demand(s) Celibacy.'" *Postscript: Publication of the Philological Association of the Carolinas* 15 (1998): 23-32.

Contends that while questions regarding O'Connor's "sex life or lack thereof" may be "intrusive and irrelevant," scholars examining her background have no choice but to face them and offer "speculation and conclusions." Discusses evidence found in correspondence to and from "A", Maryat Lee, Betty Boyd, and Stephen Wilbers; in the unpublished journals of Maryat Lee and Alta Ramsey; and in interviews with Robert E. Lee, Andrew Lytle, James B. Hall, Helen I. Greene, Robie Macauley and Walter Sullivan. Concludes "it seems clear that, despite some minor heterosexual interest during her young adulthood, O'Connor never actively pursued either a heterosexual or a homosexual relationship."

291   Cash, Jean W. "Flannery O'Connor as Lecturer: ` . . . a secret desire to rival Charles Dickens.'" *Flannery O'Connor Bulletin* 16 (1987): 1-15.

Describes O'Connor's attitude and work related to the "nearly sixty public lectures and readings" she presented between 1955 and 1963. Argues that the sheer number "undercuts the traditional view that O'Connor languished in Milledgeville." Suggests that these lectures and readings were a natural extension of her writing career which provided her with an opportunity to meet other prominent writers, brought intellectual stimulation, and offered yet another opportunity "to guide the nonbelievers of her generation toward redemption through grace." Indicates that O'Connor's lectures helped her self-confidence and provided much-needed financial support. Discusses her lectures, including "The Fiction Writer in the South," "The Freak in Modern Literature," and "The Catholic Novelist in the Modern South." Offers a list of personal appearances, and provides the date, location, and the subject or title of each lecture. Concludes that "without her public career, O'Connor would have lived a far more limited life--both as a writer and as a human being."

292   Cash, Jean W. "Maryat and `Flanneryat': An Antithetical Friendship." *Flannery O'Connor Bulletin* 19 (1990): 56-72.

Draws on the one hundred and sixty-one largely unpublished letters from Flannery O'Connor to Maryat Lee, other letters Lee wrote, and Lee's private journals (1956-65) to explore the close friendship between the two. Offers background related to the circumstances of their meeting, their extensive correspondence, and Lee's visits to Milledgeville. Provides excerpts from letters and journal entries to substantiate biographical details and to compare and contrast the two close friends. Focuses on such topics as their differences in "living a physically complete life"; the role of their religious faith and its influence on their vocations as writers; Flannery's use of Lee's letters to keep up with the New York scene; their Southern background and family connections; their sense of humor; their views on race issues; Flannery's relationship with her mother Regina; and their mutual concern with personal health problems. Mentions Lee's husband David Foulkes-Taylor; O'Connor's love for Erik Langkjaer; her "socially prominent Savannah cousin, Kate Flannery Semmes"; Father James McCown; and Ralph C. Wood's analysis of O'Connor's attitude on race. Accompanying the essay are a photograph of Maryat Lee and her caricature of Flannery.

293   Cash, Jean W. "Milledgeville 1957-1960: O'Connor's `pseudo-literary &
             theological gatherings.'" *Flannery O'Connor Bulletin* 18 (1989): 13-27.

             Provides background and descriptions of the participants, subjects,
             authors, and titles discussed at the regular gatherings at the O'Connor's
             family farm (Andalusia), between late 1957 and 1960. Relying upon
             letters, interviews, and recollections, the author pieces together an
             assessment and description of the level of participation of each attendee,
             to what extent and in what manner each interacted with the others, and
             Flannery's own perspective. Refers to participants William Kirkland,
             George Beiswanger, James and Mary Barbara Tate, Mary and Lance
             Phillips, Elizabeth Ferguson, Paul Cresap, Stephen Kramer, Mary Sallee,
             Maryat Lee, and Russell Green. Concludes that the gatherings provided
             O'Connor with an opportunity to discuss ideas relevant to her own work
             and added variety to her life. In addition, they "helped the Milledgeville
             community to understand and appreciate O'Connor as a serious writer."

294   Cash, Jean W. "O'Connor as Distinguished Alumna: Wit and Wisdom."
             English Language Notes 29.1 (1991): 67-70.

             Reprints O'Connor's acceptance speech, after being selected as a
             Distinguished Alumni Award recipient, given on May 15, 1957 during
             Honor's Day ceremonies at the Georgia State College for Women.
             Reviews her attitudes and humor related to having to give "two pages of
             thanksgiving" and shake "the soggy paws of citizens from all over the
             state." Refers to the reaction of community and family members to the
             televised version of "The Life You Save May Be Your Own," and "the
             insincere regard of celebrity-seekers . . . after *Time* magazine reviewed
             her collection of short stories in 1955." Finds that O'Connor's remarks
             given on this occasion reflect "her concerns, both serious and comic, as
             a literary artist practicing her craft in 1957."

295   Cash, Jean W. "O'Connor in the Iowa Writers' Workshop." *Flannery
             O'Connor Bulletin* 24 (1995-96): 67-75.

             Provides comments about O'Connor by her fellow students and teachers
             during the time she attended the Writer's Workshop at the University of
             Iowa. Includes recollections by Paul Engle, Andrew Lytle, Kay Burford,
             Mary Mudge Wiatt, James B. Hall, Herbert Nipson, Hank Messick,
             Charles Embree, Jean Williams Wylder, and Gene Brzenk.

296   Cash, Jean W. "O'Connor on `Revelation': The Story of a Story." *English
             Language Notes* 24.3 (1987): 61-67.

Contends that excerpts from letters in *The Habit of Being* show O'Connor "in an act of personal revelation, telling the story of her story . . . `Revelation.'" States that the letters provide insight into the story's genesis and completion, and offer a look "into the process and techniques of her writing."

297   Cash, Jean W. "O'Connor on *The Violent Bear It Away*: An Unpublished Letter." *English Language Notes* 26.4 (1989): 67-71.

Provides excerpts from letters to John Hawkes and Elizabeth Fenwick Way which discuss the final episode in *The Violent Bear It Away*. Declares that a letter from O'Connor to Grace Terry written in the summer of 1962 offers the best insight into this episode in which Tarwater accepts the existence of absolute evil and his responsibility to evangelize against it. The letter is reprinted, and in it O'Connor explains her intentions of portraying the homosexual as the devil.

298   Castex, Peggy Hanemann. "Demonic Grotesque in Flannery O'Connor's `The Displaced Person': An Exercise in Subversive Ambiguity." *Le Sud et autres points cardinaux: actes du colloque de 1984*. Centre de Recherches et Littérature et Civilisation Nord-Américaines. Ed. Jeanne-Marie Santraud. Paris: Presses de l'Université de Paris-Sorbonne, 1987. 7-20.

Describes the nature and use of the grotesque in O'Connor's works. Asserts that she resorted to the extreme means of conveying her vision through "the *terrible* or *demonic* grotesque . . . [which] is based on the constraint of fear and the release of laughter." Illustrates O'Connor's technique by examining "The Displaced Person," and suggests that thematically it reflects conflicting topical elements and patterns. Finds that O'Connor's "attitudes broaden into a study in multiple discourse and multiple vision climaxing in the bedrock dichotomy between the practical or human view versus the theological or divine view." Discusses the symbolism of the peacock, and contends that it "is a feathered stand-in for Guizac," as both "are exotic and therefore displaced." Reminds readers that O'Connor herself admitted that the story's ending was confusing as she "resorted to a form of understatement in an effort to make her arcane and decidedly Catholic message accessible to a broader audience." Suggests that the story has a double structure, an overstatement apparent "round the Catholic currents audible throughout the story," and an understatement that "emanates from deeper, inner rhythms which follow the cyclical patterns of the Old Testament."

299   Castronovo, David. "`The Glamour of High Things': The Southern
              Gentleman in Modern Literature." *The American Gentleman: Social
              Prestige and the Modern Literary Mind*. New York: Continuum, 1991.
              146-87.

              Discusses O'Connor's "Everything That Rises Must Converge." Suggests
              that the story presents a "complex view of the disease of gentility" as
              Julian, "a finely drawn loser," unsuccessfully attempts "to buoy himself
              up with pathetic notions of his gentility and intellectual superiority." Cites
              the story as "a brilliant exploration of how little people struggle to be big."

300   Cavnar, Cindy M. "Flannery O'Connor: *A Memoir of Mary Ann*." *New
              Covenant* 11.3 (1981): 24-27.

              Offers an introductory essay followed by a reprint of O'Connor's
              "Introduction to *A Memoir of Mary Ann*." Suggests that O'Connor's
              "Introduction" offers a good look at "the Christian view of death,
              suffering, and the grotesque." Reviews O'Connor's views regarding the
              use of violence and the opportunities she offers to characters to respond
              to God within evil circumstances.

301   Chamlee, Kenneth D. "Cafés and Community in Three Carson McCullers
              Novels." *Studies in American Fiction* 18 (Autumn 1990): 233-40.

              Discusses McCullers's frequent use of the interior settings of cafés in *The
              Ballad of the Sad Café, The Heart Is a Lonely Hunter*, and *The Member
              of the Wedding*. Suggests that these settings, and the "parade of deformed
              and confused people" in them, who are "seeking human connections . . .
              ultimately provide a false sense of emotional security and fail to give
              characters the lasting acceptance and feeling of community they desire."
              Includes a brief, passing reference to the settings ("the deltas, forests, and
              worn-out farms") used by O'Connor and Eudora Welty.

302   Chapin, John D. "Flannery O'Connor and the Rich Red River of Jesus'
              Blood." *Christianity and Literature* 25.3 (1976): 30-35.

              Asserts that O'Connor's work reflects a bizarre method of what Christian
              life entails: she writes not of "guilt or innocence, nor about ritual per se.
              Rather, she presents a metaphor for the process of salvation . . . "
              Analyzes "The River" in this context, describing it as outlining "what is
              required before the `long, gentle hand' will firmly grasp the sinner and
              move him to the Kingdom of Christ."

303   Chappell, Fred. "Fantasia on the Theme of Theme and Fantasy." *Studies in Short Fiction* 27.2 (1990): 179-89.

         Discusses the "difficulty in handling theme in short stories which employ as a prominent element of their construction some aspect of the fantastic." Refers to O'Connor's comment that the Gothic mode in fiction "was a kind of shorthand," which "allowed the writer to address his idea with extreme efficiency, without sinking into a quagmire of humdrum and sometimes groveling detail."

304   Charney, Mark J. *Barry Hannah*. New York: Twayne, 1992. vii, 2, 23, 24.

         A chronologically arranged literary biography of Barry Hannah that examines his "preoccupation with unconventional narrative form" and his use of thematic shifts "from violence and isolation to peaceful alternatives and community acceptance." Includes brief, passing references to his literary kinship with O'Connor. Hannah's honesty, vision, and narrative voices have been compared to O'Connor's, and it is noted that he drew from writers such as O'Connor to emphasize "the influence of the South upon a series of grotesque, eccentric, and violent characters" in *Geronimo Rex*.

305   Cheatham, George. "Jesus, O'Connor's Artificial Nigger." *Studies in Short Fiction* 22.4 (1985): 475-79.

         Discusses Mr. Head's assessment of the statue: "They ain't got enough of the real ones here. They got to have an artificial one." Argues that the statement is neither irony nor artistic lapse, but instead represents the theological essence of the story: "an explanation once and for all of the mystery of existence." Concludes that O'Connor's true meaning is that humankind needs "one more sufferer, one more `nigger,' an artificial one." Suggests that O'Connor created the statue as a symbol that God has, through his son Jesus Christ, become an `artificial nigger' to bring redemption to the world.

306   Cheney, Lynne V. "A Conversation With Robert Coles." *Humanities* 12.2 (1991): 4-9.

         Coles mentions O'Connor in passing. States that she was an influential figure who helped him more fully understand what he believes in and what "matters."

307   Chew, Martha. "Flannery O'Connor's Double-Edged Satire: The Idiot
           Daughter Versus the Lady Ph.D." *Southern Quarterly* 19.2 (1981): 17-25.

           Asserts that an analysis of O'Connor's characterization of Southern
           women reveals a complex, double-edged satire of Southern traditions and
           attitudes. States that Lucynell Crater in "The Life You Save May Be Your
           Own" and Hulga Hopewell in "Good Country People" are perhaps the
           clearest examples of satirical portraits of daughters who represent
           different responses to the Southern woman's traditional role. Contends
           that these two stories reflect her perspective that "there is not much
           difference between the idiot daughter and the lady Ph.D."

307a   Childress, Mark. "Shirley Anne Grau: A Southern Writer Who Isn't."
           Southern Living July 1980: 48.

           Profiles the life and work of the Pulitzer Prize winning New Orleans
           novelist and short story writer, Shirley Anne Grau. Grau states that the
           label "Southern writer" annoys her, and she assesses O'Connor's writing
           as "`devious-minded and hollow.'" Illustrations: Photographs of Grau at
           her typewriter and a posed portrait.

308   Chow, Sung Gay. "`Strange and Alien Country': An Analysis of
           Landscape in Flannery O'Connor's *Wise Blood* and *The Violent Bear It
           Away*." *Flannery O'Connor Bulletin* 8 (1979): 35-44.

           Suggests that O'Connor's "views on the use of the grotesque" extend "to
           her description of the landscape," which "is depicted in such a way as to
           create atmosphere, to evoke an emotional response in the reader, [and] to
           achieve what Poe calls a unity of effect." Discusses the function of
           landscape in *Wise Blood* and *The Violent Bear It Away*. Contends that
           O'Connor "draws a sombre, dismal picture," with urban landscapes
           depicted as nasty places with "dirty side streets and dark alleys,"
           residential areas colored with a monotonous yellow or gray, and a
           countryside which is naturally ugly. Argues that her purpose is to convey
           a "sinister and menacing world" where everything is "disjointed, distorted,
           [and] disordered." Concludes that O'Connor uses landscape to not only
           establish mood and tone, but to offer the most suitable environment for
           characters who are "grotesque, deformed, and ugly." Refers to comments
           by Jane Hart, Daniel F. Littlefield, Jr., and Carter Martin.

309   Church, Joseph. "An Abuse of the Imagination in Flannery O'Connor's `A
           Good Man Is Hard to Find.'" *Notes on Contemporary Literature* 20.3
           (1990): 8-10.

Observes that all the characters in "A Good Man Is Hard to Find," except the grandmother, are "superficial, inward-turning people." Notes that only the grandmother is given the ability "to transform the natural world into meaningful terms." Upon closer examination, however, this ability comes up short as its limitations illustrate her "self-serving aestheticism." Concludes that O'Connor uses the grandmother to urge readers to condemn such aestheticism and to "use our imagination to establish responsible--not picturesque--connections with a needful world."

310   Ciuba, Gary M. "The Fierce Nun of *The Last Gentleman*: Percy's Vision of Flannery O'Connor." *Flannery O'Connor Bulletin* 15 (1986): 57-66.

Suggests that Walker Percy "sees in O'Connor a model for the novelist as believer." Notes that in interviews and writings, he cites her "with a frequency second only to his references to Faulkner." Contends that both Percy and O'Connor focus on "spiritual wayfaring," and that Percy "reads O'Connor as exemplifying the theological aesthetic of his own work." Suggests that O'Connor revealed to Percy "how a renewal of religious language can reach an indifferent audience." Contends that Percy's *The Last Gentleman* not only reflects O'Connor's influence, but "also pays fictional tribute" to her. Offers a reading showing how Val Vaught serves as "Percy's dense and mysterious portrait of the fellow novelist who made language once again new so that it might bear the good news."

311   Ciuba, Gary M. "From Face Value to the Value in Faces: *Wise Blood* and the Limits of Literalism." *Modern Language Studies* 19.3 (1989): 72-79.

Notes that in *Wise Blood* O'Connor avoids portraying all the features of her characters' faces, "preferring to concentrate on striking and invariably ugly physical characteristics." Contends that while her "extreme selectivity and exaggeration turn characters into spiritual cartoons," and her "gaze obliterates much," her work "leaves the essentials of the soul to be seen in the distorted outlines of the body." Concludes that O'Connor's artistry reflects the perspective that "seeing the face of a man in all its graciousness could be like beholding the very countenance of God."

311a Ciuba, Gary [M.] "`Like a Boulder Blocking Your Path': Scandal and Skandalon in Flannery O'Connor." *Flannery O'Connor Bulletin* 26-27 (1998-2000): 1-23.

Evaluates O'Connor's concern that the "scandal" she presented in her fiction "might lead her readers to suffer a radical loss of grace." Sees her apprehension as based upon her belief "that recent novelists had largely withdrawn themselves from their work," which "caused readers to be involved in passionately intense experiences without the usual moral perspective provided by writers in the past." Refers to O'Connor's essay "Total Effect and the Eighth Grade" and her position that some authors might exploit "the vulnerability" of young readers' "tender imaginations." Follows with a discussion of René Girard's thesis, referred to as "'the skandalon' mimetic desire," whereby the self seeks "to overcome its emptiness by imitating a model who seems to have attained fulfillment." Uses this theory to carefully explicate the relationships between Mason Tarwater, Young Tarwater, Rayber, Bishop, Buford Munson, and "the lavender-eyed stranger" in *The Violent Bear It Away*.

312   Ciuba, Gary M. Rev. of *American Gargoyles: Flannery O'Connor and the Medieval Grotesque*, by Anthony Di Renzo. *Flannery O'Connor Bulletin* 22 (1993-94): 140-43.

Suggests that because O'Connor "often seemed to find her place in the twentieth century by way of the middle ages," Di Renzo's book offers readers a worthy perspective. Notes how O'Connor's work reflects the many contradictions seen in the artistic endeavors of the late Middle Ages and that Di Renzo finds "telling analogues for the unlikely unions at the heart of O'Connor's faith and aesthetics." Comments that Di Renzo persuasively establishes "O'Connor's deep pleasure in deformity" and "convincingly argues" that O'Connor shared with the artists of the medieval grotesque "not simply a vision of the world based on complexity and conjunction but a repertory of devices . . . that ground theology in a humbled rhetoric of the earth." States that Di Renzo is on-target with his discussion of how O'Connor "revels in juxtaposing opposites, inverting hierarchies, and underwriting ambiguities" to create an "inclusive art that embraces not just sinners and saints but [also] sinful saints and saintly sinners." Affirms Di Renzo's view of O'Connor's humor, her rhetoric, and her "exposure of folly," but expresses disappointment in how "some of the terror and tenderness in her art" is overlooked, especially as seen in *The Violent Bear It Away*.

313   Clark, Beverly Lyon and Caroline M. Brown. "A Review of O'Connor Criticism." *Critical Essays on Flannery O'Connor*. Ed. Melvin J. Friedman and Beverly Lyon Clark. Boston: G.K. Hall, 1985. 202-21.

Offers a chronological, carefully annotated bibliography of twenty-two books and articles that reflect some "of the best and most innovative criticism on Flannery O'Connor." Included are works by: M. Joselyn, Sr., C. Hugh Holman, Stanley Edgar Hyman, Martha Stephens, Frederick Asals, Josephine Hendin, Sister Kathleen Feeley, Miles Orvell, Preston M.

Browning, Jr., David Aiken, John R. May, Dorothy Tuck McFarland, Claude Richard, Louis D. Rubin, Jr., Claire Kahane, Louise Westling, Renata R. Mautner Wasserman, and Robert Coles.

314   Clark, John R. and William E. Morris. "Ah, Similitudo! Notes on Southern Humor." *Mississippi Folklore Register* 17.2 (1983): 67-80.

Discusses the use and geographic limitations of the simile in Southern humor. Argues that "it is deliberately regional and definitely reflective of Southern people and Southern ways, their conditions, [and] their outlook." Asserts that the simile is a basic strategy for conveying Southern wit which renders "brilliant the surface of tale-telling and just plain talk." Submits that Southern similes come out of the daily life, traditions, jokes and stories of Southerners who are all "rural at heart." Illustrates this argument with examples from Eudora Welty's "Powerhouse," William Faulkner's "A Rose for Emily," and Flannery O'Connor's "The River."

315   Clark, Michael. "Flannery O'Connor's `A Good Man Is Hard to Find': The Moment of Grace." *English Language Notes* 29.2 (1991): 66-69.

Considers whether the grandmother's final act in "A Good Man Is Hard to Find," (reaching out and touching The Misfit), is a "token of true, divine grace and spiritual insight." Notes that while O'Connor herself stated that the act was such a token, critics remain unconvinced. Suggests that references to two books of the *Bible*, *I* and *II Timothy*, "can explain the crux of the story . . . [and] provide a subtext for the general and problematic episode of O'Connor's story, the grandmother's moment of grace."

316   Clasby, Nancy T. "`The Life You Save May Be Your Own': Flannery O'Connor as a Visionary Artist." *Studies in Short Fiction* 28.4 (1991): 509-20.

Reminds readers of O'Connor's reservations concerning psychoanalytic interpretations of her work and suggests that these reservations may be "based in part on an accurate perception of the limits of Freudian thought as applied to the image-making activity of the artist." Contends that, in spite of O'Connor's reservations, "a Jungian hermeneutics offers a way of opening up O'Connor's extraordinary image structures." Suggests that "O'Connor's grotesques link her with such artists as Blake, Goethe, and Hoffman, whom Jung called `visionary artists' because, in his view, their imagery emerges in an almost unfiltered rush from the collective unconscious." Finds O'Connor's "The Life You Save May Be Your Own" to be "particularly rich in symbols of interacting masculine and feminine elements and in images of the sacred child." Attempts "to show how a Jungian reading can illuminate matrices of imagery that often remain obscure in Freudian readings." Concludes that by "stripping her characters of ordinary social context and realistic detail, O'Connor reveals the archetypes underlying the narrative. [Thus,] `The Life You Save May Be Your Own' presents us with a tableau of grotesque forms acting out the central modern psychomachia of the wasteland."

317   Clayton, Lauren. "The Theme of Redemption in Selected Short Stories by Flannery O'Connor." *New Generation 80: A High School Humanities Review* [Florida State U] 2 (1980): 21-28.

Compares similar characters found in four works by Flannery O'Connor. Notes that in each story "there is one character who emerges with both good and evil qualities." Examines the mother in "Everything That Rises Must Converge," the grandmother in "A Good Man Is Hard to Find," Mr. Paradise in "The River," and the Bible salesman in "Good Country People."

318   Cleary, Michael. "Environmental Influences in Flannery O'Connor's Fiction." *Flannery O'Connor Bulletin* 8 (1979): 20-34.

Examines how O'Connor uses the contrast of country and city environments to "affect our understanding of her characters and themes." Suggests that she "presents the country as a positive force, a superior environment to the city," by depicting the country locale "as a truly Edenic representation of a world of natural beauty, innocence, harmony, and isolation." Argues that O'Connor uses the country as "a refuge for suffering Man After the Fall," as "a haven from the corrupting influences of the city," and "as the required setting for a religious awakening." Follows with a discussion of her depiction of the city as "an overpowering, negative influence, spawning negative attitudes and values in those who reside there or journey there." Then, examines how the characters, plots and themes exhibit the presence of city-country, and Edenic contrasts in *Wise Blood, The Violent Bear It Away,* "A Circle in the Fire," "A Good Man Is Hard to Find," "The Lame Shall Enter First," "Judgement Day," "The Artificial Nigger," "Good Country People," and "A Stroke of Good Fortune." Concludes that O'Connor's work ties together American Romantic and religious traditions, by using "the country" as a touchstone, an "Edenic paradise for the innocent or sanctuary for the repentant sinner," and as a place where individuals can "rely on the inspiration and comfort of the country rather than on the dogma of formal religion."

319   Clift-Pellow, Arlene. "Literary Criticism and Black Imagery." *Images of Blacks in American Culture: A Reference Guide to Information Sources.* Ed. Jessie Carney Smith. New York: Greenwood, 1988. 139-89.

Offers a bibliographical essay that focuses on the appearance and depiction of African-Americans in literature. Lists and describes important contributions arranged by time period, followed by lists of references by genre and topic. Concludes with a cited list of criticism by author, including two essays focused on O'Connor's work: Turner F. Boyd's, "Ironic Dimensions in Flannery O'Connor's `The Artificial Nigger'" [*Mississippi Quarterly* 21 (1968): 243-51]; and, Melvin G. Williams's "Black and White: A Study in Flannery O'Connor's Characters" [*Black American Literature Forum* 10 (1976): 130-32].

320   Cline, Peter. "Flannery." *Terminus* [Atlanta: St. Pius High School] (March 1976): 5.

Short essay by a relative of Flannery O'Connor. Cline asserts that O'Connor "would have found all the devotion and searching for meaning in her work as funny."

321   Coale, Samuel Chase. "Faulkner, McCullers, O'Connor, Styron: The Shadow of the South." *In Hawthorne's Shadow: American Romance From Melville to Mailer.* Lexington: UP of Kentucky, 1985. 63-101.

Discusses Flannery O'Connor in a chapter shared with twentieth-century writers, William Faulkner, Carson McCullers, and William Styron. Compares her writing to that of Nathaniel Hawthorne, and states that both writers "knew the dungeon of the heart, the demonic, godlike power of the creative artist, the scent of old Adam's sins, the scorn of rationalist, self-sufficient men . . . and viewed the world in stark polarities." Offers a reading of O'Connor's *The Violent Bear It Away* that demonstrates her affinities with Hawthorne's romances. Observes that O'Connor's "dark woods, that place of mystery with its mysterious rim and edge, its atmosphere of lightning and dense shadow, its black caves and swollen red sun, suggest Hawthorne's romantic settings." Discusses criticism and perspectives of O'Connor's work which suggests that "her world is so grotesque, her characters so programmed to act as demonic grace compels them to, that any Christian vision shatters and collapses." Follows with the argument that O'Connor worked very hard to structure her work to firmly establish "in her hard-edged landscape . . . the possibility of ambiguity, and in such a modern Manichean maze, in so secular and physically visible a place, ambiguity becomes an act of reconciliation, a revelation of the possibility of spiritual powers and forces."

322   Coale, Samuel [Chase]. "Styron's Disguises: A Provisional Rebel in
           Christian Masquerade." *Critique: Studies in Modern Fiction* 26.2 (1985):
           57-66.

           Discusses William Styron's fiction, focusing on how "the problem of evil
           haunts him at all levels," and why his writing is generally regarded as
           being "in the tradition of the Southern Gothic romance." Includes a brief,
           indirect comparison of Styron's work to O'Connor's, arguing that both
           writers have been influenced by Edgar Allan Poe.

323   Cobb, James C. "Southern Writers and the Challenge of Regional
           Convergence: A Comparative Perspective." *Georgia Historical Quarterly*
           73.1 (1989): 1-25.

           Outlines how the themes and public statements of a wide variety of
           Southern writers were in reaction to changes taking place in the South.
           Includes a discussion of Robert Coles's interpretation of O'Connor's "The
           Displaced Person" as a story reflective of "many of the concerns about
           economic modernization expressed by the Nashville Agrarians and other
           Southern writers." Other references to O'Connor include her concern that
           the South was becoming too much like the rest of the country; her use of
           Julian in "Everything That Rises Must Converge" as an "overeducated
           ne'er-do-well liberal"; and how Eudora Welty and Walker Percy joined
           her in confronting, through their writing, "the cultural consequences of
           economic modernization."

324   Cobb, Joann P. "Pascal's Wager and Two Modern Losers." *Philosophy
           and Literature* 3.2 (1979): 187-98.

           Reviews the reasoning behind Blaise Pascal's "wager" to the unbeliever
           (that if the odds for the existence of God are at least a 50-50 chance, and
           if one chooses to believe that God does exist, one gains everything by
           believing and loses nothing if he does not). Then examines two stories
           which "present wagerers who lose": Katherine Anne Porter's Granny
           Weatherall in "The Jilting of Granny Weatherall" and The Misfit in
           O'Connor's "A Good Man Is Hard to Find." Contends that The Misfit in
           "A Good Man Is Hard to Find" is more than "just another rationalizing
           outlaw"; he is a man who recognizes the need for the Pascalian wager and
           wagers "eternal loss" believing that "Jesus didn't do what he said."

325   Coles, Robert. "Flannery O'Connor: Letters Larger Than Life." *Flannery
           O'Connor Bulletin* 8 (1979): 3-13.

Offers comments on *The Habit of Being* as "a biography of sorts," noting that O'Connor's "strength of personality is constantly evident" in her letters, and reveal her to be "a warm, sensitive, responsive person; such a woman of give and take . . . a sound and knowing overseer of herself and those she knew and loved." Discusses the "intriguing spiritual relationship" between Flannery O'Connor and Simone Weil. Comments on her views of Weil as found in her letters, and explores what she meant when she describes Weil as a "'remarkable woman'" whose ideas intrigued her, though she found them "'ridiculous.'" Quotes from the letters, especially those to "A," and suggests that her comments on Weil's courage serve as "an utterly tell-tale insight into the essential nature" of her own courageous life.

326   Coles, Robert. "Flannery O'Connor: A Southern Intellectual." *Southern Review* 16.1 (1980): 46-64.

Discusses O'Connor's attitude toward intellectuals, both in her fiction and in real life. Contends that "she caricatures them in her stories; she condemns them in her essays; [and] she gives them the back of her hand, repeatedly, in her letters." Offers detailed comments on "Good Country People," "The Enduring Chill," and *The Violent Bear It Away*. Discusses O'Connor's work in light of the influences of Simone Weil, Sigmund Freud, Carl Jung, and Georges Bernanos.

327   Coles, Robert. "Flannery O'Connor's Lupus: A Commentary on Her Collected Letters, *The Habit of Being*." *JAMA: The Journal of the American Medical Association*. 26 Sept. 1980: 1441-42.

Outlines O'Connor's career and early life in Savannah and Milledgeville, Georgia, and in Iowa and New York. Briefly discusses her lupus and the effects of her cortisone treatments. States that O'Connor's letters portray her as a radical conservative whose suffering is "endured with a calm and knowing dignity." Suggests that *The Habit of Being* might be worthy as a text for those students, physicians, and patients "interested in a writer's effort to understand this Life." Closes with the observation that O'Connor's faith was so strong that she never felt the need for psychological counseling to understand or accept her medical predicament.

328   Coles, Robert. "Flannery O'Connor's South." *Atlanta Journal-Constitution*, Atlanta Weekly, 29 June 1980: 22-27.

Offers a close reading of "The Displaced Person" as a religious drama which powerfully portrays the issues of O'Connor's native South.

Concludes that O'Connor used her story-telling to show the depth of God's mysteries; to ground readers in "the Southern land"; and "to draw upon its inhabitants knowingly, surely, [and] suggestively" in order to remind readers about the interrelationship between people, races, and God's universe and commandments.

329   Coles, Robert. "Flannery O'Connor's *Wise Blood*." *New Republic* 10 May 1980: 26-28.

Discusses critical reaction to and O'Connor's own retrospective views of *Wise Blood*, noting that "O'Connor had a good deal of trouble" with both of her novels, but felt pleased with this one. Proposes that the "down-home existentialism is not offered in the tones of fashionable 20th-century despair . . . Haze is a prophet denouncing what prophecy has come to, hereabouts and now." Concludes that it "is a truly radical novel - full of scorn for the `principalities and powers' so many of us worship blindly: Mammon, Caesar, and not least, Satan set up in his digs as the local minister." Argues that the book demonstrates O'Connor's lean, powerful, and "brilliantly suggestive" writing. Contends that the wild humor, and familiar landscapes of "ominous black skies, those stars that puzzle us so, the silver streaks of clouds, an occasional fiery sun, and the dark woods that loom in the distance of so many scenes" is all "so appropriate in its caustic attention to a range of our 20th-century obsessions." Illustrations: reproduction of a charcoal sketch of O'Connor.

330   Coles, Robert. "Gatsby at the B School." *New York Times Book Review* 25 Oct. 1987: 1, 40-41.

Coles outlines the seminar he has taught at the Harvard Business School: "The Business World: Moral and Social Inquiry Through Fiction." Lists the books discussed in class and considers the impact of the fiction upon his students. Includes a discussion of O'Connor's "The Displaced Person," focusing on how the story may be seen as "an account of what happens to a Southern landowner as she tries to run a tighter business operation."

331   Coles, Robert. "Instances of Modernist Anti-Intellectualism." *Modernism Reconsidered*. Ed. Robert Kiely. Cambridge: Harvard UP, 1983. 215-28.

Discusses anti-intellectual themes found in works by William Carlos Williams and in James Agee's *Let Us Now Praise Famous Men* as assaults on the "supposedly sterile, self-important academy." Devotes the final paragraph of the essay to O'Connor, suggesting that her use of anti-intellectualism was "a variant of self-examination, self parody--and an indirect call for mercy, an appeal for forgiveness in the Christian tradition." Contends that her intellectual characters, such as Hulga of "Good Country People," Asbury of "The Enduring Chill," and Julian of "Everything That Rises Must Converge," need "no gratuitous psychiatric interpretation from us," but should be viewed as individuals who, by the end of the story, are offered transcendence through self-recognition and shame in their role as intellectuals.

332   Coles, Robert. "A Literature of Soul Searching." *Theology Today* 45 (July 1988): 200-07.

Outlines a course titled "'A Literature of Christian Reflection'" that the author, a professor of Psychiatry and Medical Humanities, team-teaches at Harvard University with Robert Kiely, a professor of English. Coles applauds how O'Connor, one of the authors whose works are studied, "gave stunning fictional incarnations to Christian, or more precisely, Catholic doctrine." Sees each of her works as "an effort to take Biblical dogma into the realm of Southern story-telling."

333   Coles, Robert. "Mystery and Flannery O'Connor." *Harvard Diary: Reflections on the Sacred and the Secular.* New York: Crossroad, 1988. 13-15.

Remarks that O'Connor was a marvelous storyteller to be appreciated for her use of symbolism, humor, and Southern dialect, "all in the service of a complex philosophical and theological presentation." Discusses her view of the social sciences and the human need for mystery. Suggests that she viewed mystery as "a gift of God," and "only wanted us to understand where the water's edge begins."

334   Coles, Robert. "Reflections." *Religion and Intellectual Life* 1.4 (1984): 11-13.

Mentions "constantly pressing" the works of Flannery O'Connor and Walker Percy upon his Harvard class "The Literature of Social Reflection." Argues that each of these "morally haunted if not possessed [authors], offer an edifying example to any of us who might worry that a respectable and productive intellectual life ought to be kept apart from a person's religious interests."

335   Coles, Robert. *That Red Wheelbarrow: Selected Literary Essays.* Iowa City: U of Iowa P, 1988. 213-54.

This collection includes reprints of five of Coles's essays on O'Connor, the originals of which are cited and abstracted individually in this guide:

"Flannery O'Connor's Roots," rpt. from the Preface to *Flannery O'Connor's Georgia*, by Barbara McKenzie. *See* entry 63.

"Flannery O'Connor: A Southern Intellectual," rpt. from *Southern Review* 16.1 (1980): 46-64. *See* entry 326.

"Flannery O'Connor's *Wise Blood*," rpt. from *New Republic* 10 May 1980: 26-28. *See* entry 329.

"Letters Larger Than Life," rpt. from the *Flannery O'Connor Bulletin* 8 (1979): 3-13. *See* entry 325.

"*The Habit of Being*: Flannery O'Connor's Illness and Collected Letters," rpt. from *JAMA: Journal of the American Medical Association* 26 September 1980: 1441-42. *See* entry 327.

336   Collins, Glenn. "From Memory to Page, Or How Pete Dexter Wrote a Prize Winner." *New York Times* 5 Dec. 1988: C13.

Offers a biographical profile of Pete Dexter, which includes memories of his childhood years in Milledgeville, and his admiration for O'Connor. Notes his recollection of visiting Andalusia with his mother to see Flannery O'Connor's peacocks, then closes with his remark that he had wanted to name his daughter "Flannery," but had been overruled by his wife, who "bridled at the idea that [their daughter would have] go through life with a handle like that."

337   Collum, Danny Duncan. "Nature and Grace: Flannery O'Connor and the Healing of Southern Culture." *Sojourners* 23.10 (1994-95): 22-24.

Collum states that as a Southerner from the deep South, raised as a Southern Baptist, and later converted to Catholicism, O'Connor speaks to his condition. Discusses how the South's identity, as O'Connor observed, "results from beliefs and qualities . . . absorbed from the scriptures and from her own history of defeat and violation: a distrust of the abstract, a sense of human dependence on the grace of God, and a knowledge that evil is not simply a problem to be solved, but a mystery to be endured." Finds that characteristics of Southernness are clearly evident in O'Connor's stories. Discusses her deep-seated hostility toward the city, and asserts that O'Connor "could not have understood and dramatized the things that she did about the South without the critical distance of

Catholicism." Suggests that the South displays "a joyous biracial culture" amid a setting of natural beauty, while its inhabitants insist "that things of this world are irredeemably evil." Finds that this assessment results in a "cultural schizophrenia" that serves to torment Southern artists. Concludes that it was O'Connor's Catholicism that provided her--and Walker Percy-- with "a way to think through these contradictions and emerge with some vision of wholeness."

338   Combs, Diana Williams and A. Alling Jones. "Two Views." Rev. of *Flannery O'Connor's Georgia,* by Barbara McKenzie. *Flannery O'Connor Bulletin* 9 (1980): 120-26.

Offers two divergent reviews of the same book: Combs's is sharply critical while Jones's review is positive and supportive. Combs asserts that McKenzie "has fallen short of the mark," and infers that her work is "characteristic of inept photographers," includes multiple contradictions, and is fundamentally marred by her "limitation in understanding the region." Points out problems with the format, size, and placement of the photographs, and concludes that McKenzie "displays little `tact, intelligence, or originality.'" Jones counters, arguing that McKenzie's work "presents a sensitive, personal vision deeply touched and guided" by O'Connor's writings. Sees the photographs as "bold and full of contrasts," and as a work which crystallizes "the visual imagery evoked by O'Connor's stories." Concludes that because the landscape of O'Connor country is "rapidly passing from view," McKenzie's "documentation of concrete particulars must be valued by serious readers of Flannery O'Connor's fiction."

339   Combs, Richard E. and Nancy R. Owen. *Authors: Critical and Biographical References.* 2nd. ed. Metuchen, NJ: Scarecrow, 1993. 185.

Provides citations to commentaries--six pages or longer--on the lives and works of 3,317 authors from more than 11,000 English-language books. Includes citations to 13 books containing material related to the life and work of Flannery O'Connor: Louis D. Rubin's *A Gallery of Southerners* (Louisiana State UP, 1982); Charles Alva Hoyt's *Minor American Novelists* (Southern Illinois UP, 1970); Stephanie Kraft's *No Castles on Main Street* (Rand McNally, 1979); Joyce Carol Oates's *The Profane Art: Essays and Reviews* (E.P. Dutton, 1983); Robert Coles's *That Red Wheelbarrow* (U of Iowa P, 1988); Theodore Solotaroff's *The Red Hot Vacuum* (Atheneum, 1970); Jeffery Steele's *The Representation of the Self in the American Renaissance* (U of North Carolina P, 1987); Harry S. Mooney and Thomas F. Staley's *The Shapeless God* (U of Pittsburgh P, 1968); Walter Allen's *The Short Story in English* (Oxford UP, 1981);

Richard Pearce's *Stages of the Clown* (Southern Illinois UP, 1970); V.S. Pritchett's *The Tale Bearers* (Random House, 1980); Josephine Hendin's *Vulnerable People* (Oxford UP, 1978); and Bettina L. Knapp's *Women in Twentieth Century Literature* (Pennsylvania State UP, 1987).

340   Cook, Martha E. "Flannery O'Connor." *American Women Writers: Bibliographical Essays*. Ed. Maurice Duke, Jackson R. Bryer, and M. Thomas Inge. Westport, CT: Greenwood, 1983. 269-96.

Offers an extensive bibliographic description of available scholarly materials which are worthy of consultation for studying the life and works of Flannery O'Connor. The book is divided into a series of short bibliographic essays which treat the following: bibliographies of criticism and editions; repositories of manuscripts and letters; biographical sources; book-length criticism and pamphlets; and articles, essays, and "parts of books." Offers an evaluative analysis of each source cited aimed at the scholar-reader in mind. Questions Sally Fitzgerald's "principle of selection" and scholarly method used in the compilation of O'Connor's letters published in *The Habit of Being*.

341   Cook, Martha E. "Flannery O'Connor's *Wise Blood*: Forms of Entrapment." *Modern American Fiction: Form and Function*. Ed. Thomas Daniel Young. Baton Rouge: Louisiana State UP, 1989. 198-212.

Agrees with those critics who contend that *Wise Blood* is not "easy reading," but suggests that the ambiguity of the work is one that "challenges, and not merely confuses, her reader." Offers an explication of the novel based upon the idea that the "form of the novel is circular: Hazel moves around, but he continues to come back to the same place either literally or symbolically." Argues that while he seeks the security of a place or home, Hazel stays "on the move" to escape what he sees as the entrapment of the religious faith that is his heritage." Submits that Hazel is able to see, understand, and believe again only after he is blind; it is with this faith that he finds "his true identity and his true spiritual home." Concludes with a discussion of the early negative critical response to the publication of *Wise Blood*, and comments on O'Connor's preface to the second edition. Contends that while reading reviews and criticism of the novel may be interesting and valuable, "all one needs to do is give *Wise Blood* a close, careful, sophisticated reading" to understand it.

342   Cooper, Stephen. "Literal Silences, Figurative Excess: `Jhon' Huston's *Wise Blood*." *Flannery O'Connor Bulletin* 17 (1988): 40-50.

Reprints O'Connor's "introductory `Author's Note to the Second Edition" of *Wise Blood* and discusses how her comments "remain remarkable for the range of their suggestiveness." Evaluates John Huston's 1979 film adaptation in relation to O'Connor's intentions. Focuses on the use of light, the intentional misspelling of Huston's first name ("Jhon"), and suggests that O'Connor's use of the "as if" is interpreted by Huston through his use of the "relation between camera and face." Attempts, "as a modest homage to the doubled aspect of *Wise Blood*," to show how "the loss of metaphor that occurs in the adaptation of the novel into film is compensated, even over compensated for, by, among other things, an excessive insistence on the face as a purveyor of otherwise invisible information . . . " Refers to filmmaking theories of Sergei Eisenstein, George Bluestone, Kristin Thompson, and Béla Balázs. Concludes with a discussion of the "film's astonishing gallery of perfect casting: the dull but fixated face of Dan Shor as Enoch Emory; the goofy, salacious face of Amy Wright as Sabbath Lily; the rubescent good-ol-boy face of Ned Beatty as Onnie Jay Holy/Hoover Shoats."

342a   Copeland, Jennifer. "Friend and Editor of Flannery O'Connor Dies at 83." *CHEERS! The Flannery O'Connor Newsletter* 8.1 (2000): 1.

Reports that Sally Fitzgerald, "editor and close friend" of Flannery O'Connor, "died of complications of cancer" in Cambridge at age 83. Refers to Sarah Gordon's remark that Fitzgerald's editing of *Mystery and Manners* and *The Habit of Being* were "`landmarks of achievement in O'Connor scholarship" and Bill Sessions's assessment that "the O'Connor the world knows today would not be the same" without Fitzgerald's work.

343   Core, Deborah. "Caroline Gordon, Ford Madox Ford: A Shared Passion for the Novel." *Southern Quarterly* 28.3 (1990): 33-42.

Includes a discussion of Caroline Gordon's influence upon O'Connor, citing Rose Ann C. Fraistat's suggestion in *Caroline Gordon as Novelist and Woman of Letters* (Baton Rouge: Louisiana State UP, 1984), that Gordon had taught O'Connor more about writing than anyone else.

344   Core, George. "Poetically the Most Accurate Woman Alive." *Southern Review* 20.4 (1984): 951-57.

Offers a review essay of Albert J. Devlin's *Eudora Welty's Chronicle: A Story of Mississippi Life* (Jackson: UP of Mississippi, 1983) and Eudora Welty's *One Writer's Beginnings* (Cambridge: Harvard UP, 1984). Includes a brief comparison of Welty's career with that of O'Connor, noting the "meteoric rise" of O'Connor's literary reputation. Remarks that O'Connor, like Welty, had to deal with a "long crippling illness."

345   Corn, Alfred. "An Encounter With O'Connor and `Parker's Back.'" *Flannery O'Connor Bulletin* 24 (1995-96): 104-18.

Describes impressions of Flannery O'Connor when she gave an informal talk to undergraduates at Emory University in 1962. Discusses the content of the talk and provides transcripts of two letters written by O'Connor to the author during the same year regarding how she "with her sharp and cultivated mind, had retained her faith" and "how free will" might be better understood. Follows with a detailed explication of "Parker's Back," seeing it as "a fable, perhaps even a parable, because its investment in symbolic values far exceeds . . . its fidelity to naturalistic demands." Explores the "central drama of the story," and discusses why, after receiving the tattoo, Parker can never go back to his old life. States that O'Connor's use of the tattoo is "one of the most daring fictional renderings of incarnational theology ever imagined." Explores "symbolic resonances" of the story and ties it to Mircea Eliade's *Patterns in Comparative Religion*, Teilhard de Chardin's *The Phenomenon of Man*, and Gustave Weigel's *The Modern God*. Closes with a discussion of how "tattooing, however negative its social connotations and however little authorized by tradition, could serve to enact spiritual truths not different in kind from those symbolized in Baptism, the Eucharist, Marriage, and Ordination."

346   Corse, Larry B. and Sandra Corse, comp. *Articles on American and British Literature: An Index to Selected Periodicals, 1950-1977*. Chicago: Swallow Press and Ohio UP, 1981. 130.

Includes a bibliographical index to 39 periodical essays or articles on Flannery O'Connor's life and work.

347   Coulthard, A.R. "The Christian Writer and the New South: Or, Why Don't You Like Flannery O'Connor?" *Southern Humanities Review* 13 (1979): 79-83.

Coulthard observes that most students in his classes range from indifferent to antagonistic toward O'Connor's works. Concludes that the problem lies in the generation gap between O'Connor and modern college students and in the "tough-minded absolutism" of O'Connor contrasted to his students' "sentimental moral relativism." Reminds readers that while her work is humorous and delightful, the work was also written "to save our souls."

348   Coulthard, A.R. "Flannery O'Connor's Backtracking Muse." *Studies In American Fiction* 11.2 (1983): 247-53.

Argues that O'Connor repeated herself "with a frequency that seems inconsistent with her otherwise fertile imagination." Points out numerous examples: her "conversion" theme; the depiction of redemption; protagonists kept from salvation by their own intellectual pride; stories which conclude with "quasi-violence"; generational conflicts; the irony of kin against kin; and the "husbandless woman who owns a farm." Contends that there are indications in her last story, "Parker's Back," that suggest that "had she lived, she was prepared to give even freer play to her comic imagination," and that "only death kept O'Connor's muse on a familiar track."

349   Coulthard, A.R. "Flannery O'Connor's Deadly Conversions." *Flannery O'Connor Bulletin* 13 (1984): 87-98.

Contends that while O'Connor believed that the fiction writer could not "'move or mold reality in the interests of abstract truth,'" she distorts reality "in the interest of theology" in "Greenleaf" and "The River." Examines both of these stories, along with "A Good Man Is Hard to Find," in regard to the death of the protagonist, and questions whether his or her conversion is convincing enough. Finds Mrs. May's goring in "Greenleaf" to be "more contrived than inevitable" and Harry's drowning in "The River" to be "only slightly less so." Refers to O'Connor's statement that converts should "see themselves in a `blasting annihilating light,'" and argues that "callowness rules out the possibility of such a vision for the young protagonist of `The River.'" Finds this vision to be "absent from `Greenleaf' to the extent that Mrs. May ends up an unconvincing symbol . . . rather than a changed human being." States that "only in `A Good Man Is Hard to Find' is the death of the protagonist inevitable and her conversion made convincing by dialogue and action."

350   Coulthard, A.R. "Flannery O'Connor's Names." *Southern Humanities Review* 18.2 (1984): 97-105.

Calls attention to letters in which O'Connor quibbled about the misspelling of certain characters' names and, yet, accused critics of "straining the soup too thin" for asking questions about the meaning of other names. Argues that the names are indeed symbolic and comically ironic, and that most point directly to issues such as psychopathological behavior, ironic reversals of biblical characteristics, artifices of grandiose social status, and sexual perversions.

351   Coulthard, A.R. "Flannery O'Connor's `A View of the Woods': A View of the Worst." *Notes on Contemporary Literature* 17.1 (1987): 7-9.

Contends that O'Connor's "A View of the Woods" is one of "only three clunkers" among the nineteen stories in her two published collections. Coulthard suggests that it is her only published story "which totally fails to either delight or instruct" and "is her worst piece of fiction." Argues that the story's thematic strands are never woven together, that it offers poor characterization which fails to evoke either sympathy or respect for its character, and provides only "muddled symbolism" with "virtually no humor." Concludes that just as O'Connor herself, "just prior to its first publication," said that she was "`thoroughly sick of it,'" O'Connor's fans and readers "should feel no guilt or remorse at sharing that emotion."

352   Coulthard, A.R. "From Sermon to Parable: Four Conversion Stories by Flannery O'Connor." *American Literature* 55.1 (1983): 55-71.

Discusses four of O'Connor's stories in which the protagonist has the opportunity to "live" after experiencing conversion. Contends that O'Connor did not "always live up to her dictum that `In the greatest fiction, the writer's moral sense coincides with his dramatic sense.'" Concludes that while "A Temple of the Holy Ghost" and "The Artificial Nigger" are "relative failures," "Revelation" and "Parker's Back" show that O'Connor had "gained the confidence to unblinkingly train her comic-ironic eye on humanity, even in the experience of grace."

353   Cox, James M. "On Flannery O'Connor and `The Displaced Person.'" *The American Short Story*. Ed. Calvin Skaggs. New York: Dell, 1979. 337-45.

Contends that "The Displaced Person" is an excellent "entry to Flannery O'Connor's work, for this story is a true introduction to her world." Remarks that "she was a writer, not a saint . . . her form was fatally secular, and her profound religious sense of herself caused her to be permanently estranged from the public identity she knew she was determined to have." Continues with a close, lengthy reading of "The Displaced Person." Sees it as a story which "exposes the bigotry of the South's poor whites (the Shortley's) and shabby gentility (Mrs. McIntyre) as they are threatened by the Displaced Person (Mr. Guizac)." Suggests that the "ignorant suspicion, self-complacency, and vicious fear with which Mrs. Shortley contemplates the presence of Mr. Guizac disclose her as the American version of that mentality which we would rather attribute to those in Europe who had put Mr. Guizac in a concentration camp." Argues that the story's meaning is clear: that each character "is somehow a displaced person." Concludes that the "moral violence of the modern world" is just as prevalent in O'Connor's "`backward' region of the rural South" as elsewhere.

354   Crews, Frederick. "The Power of Flannery O'Connor." *New York Review of Books* 26 April 1990: 49-55.

Offers a lengthy review essay of O'Connor's *Collected Works*, Robert H. Brinkmeyer, Jr.'s *The Art and Vision of Flannery O'Connor*, Ralph Wood's *The Comedy of Redemption*, and Frederick Asals's *Flannery O'Connor: The Imagination of Extremity*. Notes that "O'Connor had no cause to disprize university writing programs, for she herself . . . was the first prominent American author to have been significantly shaped by one." Suggests that publication of her *Collected Works* forces critics to face the issue of O'Connor's lack of plentitude, and realize that "for all their brilliance [her work] cannot conceal a certain narrowness of emphasis and predictability of technique." Discusses views of James M. Mellard and Miles Orvell and explores Freudian influences. Refers to Brinkmeyer as "an old-fashioned thematic critic" whose work appears to be "a parallel effort to save the author from her announced values" who, in turn, relies implausibly upon Mikhail Bakhtin's "idea of `the dialogic imagination.'" Compares O'Connor's statements to Roman Catholic teachings. Asserts that Wood's book, which examines O'Connor as a "fundamentally comic writer . . . deriving from the good news of Catholic Eschatology," offers "some of the best informed and most discerning theological criticism O'Connor has yet received." Refers to John Hawkes's suggestion that O'Connor "was of the Devil's party without knowing it," and indicates that Wood must contend with critics who support Hawkes's argument, such as André Bleikasten. Praises Asals for seeing "O'Connor as a master of tension." Touts his book as helpful in tracing O'Connor's "growth toward the relative serenity of her later work." Concludes that "it is a measure of her success that we are still grasping at formulas that might explain, or even explain away, [her] electrifying power." [Rpt. as "The Critics Bear It Away," in *The Critics Bear It Away: American Fiction and the Academy*. New York: Random House, 1992. 143-67.]

355   Crocker, Michael W., and Robert C. Evans. "Faulkner's `Barn Burning' and O'Connor's `Everything That Rises Must Converge.'" *CLA Journal* 36.4 (1993): 371-83.

Suggests that O'Connor "shared many of the same values and attitudes as Faulkner," including his "lack of pretense and his identification with his native region." Declares also that O'Connor may have felt a sense of intimidation and an "`anxiety of influence.'" Notes a wide variety of similarities between Faulkner's "Barn Burning" and O'Connor's "Everything That Rises Must Converge," including the fact that both stories deal with a central character's initiation and maturity to a higher level of consciousness, while "the crucial moment of initiation of the youthful central character is postponed," and is sudden and abrupt when it does happen. Reviews the two stories and declares that their differences "do not seem merely accidental." Concludes that the similarities and differences between the two stories indicate that O'Connor may have been subtly influenced by Faulkner when she wrote "Everything that Rises Must Converge."

356   Cronin, Gloria L. "Immersions in the Postmodern: The Fiction of Allegra Goodman." *Daughters of Valor: Contemporary Jewish American Women Writers*. Ed. Jay L. Halio and Ben Siegel. Newark: U of Delaware P, 1997. 247-48.

Discusses Allegra Goodman's interest in "the current conditions of the contemporary American spiritual pilgrimage." Offers a brief discussion of the similar approaches that Goodman and Flannery O'Connor share. In particular, just as O'Connor combined traditions of the Protestant Bible Belt, her Roman Catholic heritage, and the Christian traditions of the agrarian South to create her "religious seeking" characters, Goodman drew from "the combined traditions of university-educated discourse communities, Yiddish comedy, and urbane *New Yorker* satire." Notes that Goodman, unlike O'Connor, "is less concerned with the visible or invisible manifestations of grace than she is with its comic human obstacles."

357   Crowley, J. Donald. "O'Connor (Mary) Flannery." *Reference Guide to Short Fiction*. Ed. Noelle Watson. Detroit: St. James, 1994. 394-96.

Provides an encyclopedic entry which outlines biographical details of O'Connor's life, lists her publications, cites twenty-eight booklength critical studies, and provides a six-paragraph assessment of her contribution to American literature. States that she is "recognized as one of the most distinguished and distinctive writers of modern American fiction." Notes that rarely "has a writer with so relatively small a corpus attracted such intense and sustained critical engagement and controversy" as has O'Connor. Discusses the role of "sanctifying grace" in her work; her use of the Southern Gothic, the Grotesque, and violence in certain named characters; and how the violent and sacramental merge in O'Connor's vision. Offers the assessment that, given the "deeply problematic relationship her aesthetic and her practice prompt with the unbelieving reader, O'Connor's stature is astonishing."

358   Crowley, Sue Mitchell. "*The Thanatos Syndrome*: Walker Percy's Tribute
to Flannery O'Connor." *Walker Percy: Novelist and Philosopher*. Ed. Jan
Nordby Gretlund and Karl-Heinz Westarp. Jackson: UP of Mississippi,
1991. 225-37, 248.

Refers to O'Connor's essay on the problem of human suffering published
as the Introduction to *A Memoir of Mary Ann*. Contends that--without
initially realizing it--Walker Percy took this work as the primary motif in
his last novel, *The Thanatos Syndrome*. Suggests that he "so absorbed
O'Connor's ethical attitudes and apocalyptic vision, and the actual
language in which she couches these," that they became his own. States
that O'Connor's influence on Percy may be seen in "the linguistic
coincidence of opposites; the jeremiad against contemporary secularism;
the comic, grotesque exaggeration that covers a deeply theological subject
matter; and . . . the symbolism that emerges from a sacramental sense of
the world." Considers the possibility that "O'Connor's `Mary Ann theme'
has been present in Percy's thought from the beginning." Concludes that
O'Connor and Percy were both "`newsbearers,'" who understood that the
ultimate intention of their work was "revelation."

359   Crowley, Sue Mitchell. "Walker Percy's Wager: *The Second Coming*."
Critical Essays on Walker Percy. Ed. J. Donald Crowley and Sue Mitchell
Crowley. Boston: G.K. Hall, 1989. 225-43.

Discusses Percy's *The Second Coming*, with brief references to O'Connor
and her work. Compares Percy's "play on the word `grace'" to O'Connor's
"brand of salvific humor," and his similar use of the sun as a symbol and
view of nature as sacramental.

360   Cunningham, David S. "The Transfiguration of Time: Flannery
O'Connor's Disorienting Fiction." *Sojourners* 23.10 (1994-95): 40-41, 43-
44.

Offers comments on the modern linear view of time and contrasts it with
that of the "circular" view held by early Christians. Contends that rituals
such as the "regular cycles of Christian prayer, the repeating scripture
readings and feast days, and even the circular nature of the worship
service . . . are small reflections of the Christian understanding of time in
its cosmic scale." Refers to Saint Augustine's view that such circular
rituals reflect humanity's longing to return to God's presence and contends
that he "could not have hoped for a more brilliant 20th-century
commentator on this aspect of the human condition than Flannery
O'Connor." Using Mrs. May in "Greenleaf" and Mason Tarwater in *The*

Violent Bear It Away as examples, outlines how O'Connor's knowledge of "the distinctively Christian scheme of things" helped her to "bring time's circularity to life" in her stories. Concludes that O'Connor's fiction "transfigures time; it reminds us that we depend upon God for everything we have, and that we ultimately return everything--including ourselves--to God."

361   Cunningham, John. "Recent Works on Flannery O'Connor: A Review-Essay." *Southern Humanities Review* 8.3 (1974): 375-88.

Discusses six critical studies related to Flannery O'Connor, focusing on "the major problems which confront the critic, which Cunningham describes: the interpretation and meaning of the violence and outcome of her stories; the significance of O'Connor's freaks; the role of the natural world; "the unwillingness of secular critics to understand stories about the sacred and the apparently insuperable temptation to go hankering after the fleshpots of existentialism." The six works examined are Miles Orvell's *Invisible Parade: The Fiction of Flannery O'Connor*; David Eggenschwiler's *The Christian Humanism of Flannery O'Connor*; Gilbert Muller's *Nightmares and Visions: Flannery O'Connor and the Catholic Grotesque*; Carter Martin's *The True Country: Themes in the Fiction of Flannery O'Connor*; Sister Kathleen Feeley's *Flannery O'Connor: Voice of the Peacock*; and Josephine Gattuso Hendin's *The World of Flannery O'Connor*.

362   Cunningham, Lawrence S. "The World Redeemed: Flannery O'Connor." *The Catholic Heritage: Martyrs, Ascetics, Pilgrims, Warriors, Mystics, Theologians, Artists, Humanists, Activists, Outsiders, and Saints*. New York: Crossroads, 1983. 140-43.

Sees O'Connor's art as similar to that of Gerard Manley Hopkins: it reflects a "Christian aesthetic emphasis by which the very things of creation in themselves shine forth the reality of God if only viewers . . . [are] able `to see' with the eyes of faith." Considers O'Connor the "most articulate exponent" of this "sacramental view of the world in our century." Examines her method of shocking readers out of their "ordinary way of thinking" to get them to come around to hers, and discusses how, "despite the violence in her stories, the oddities of her characters, and the backwoods humor of her narrative, there is always something more solemn at work." Concludes that O'Connor's importance lies in the fact that she pushes her characters and readers to "see mysteries at the edge of things," and in the "tactile sacramentality" in her work that "stands in tension with much of literary modernism."

363   Current-García, Eugene. Rev. of *Lost in the Cosmos*, by Walker Percy. *Southern Humanities Review* 19.2 (1985): 191-92.

Includes comparison of Percy's approach to writing fiction with that of Flannery O'Connor, focusing on "Judgement Day" and "The Lame Shall Enter First."

364   Currie, Sheldon. "Freaks & Folks: Comic Imagery in the Fiction of Flannery O'Connor." *Antigonish Review* 62-63 (Summer-Fall 1985): 133-42.

Using Hazel Motes, Enoch Emery, Hulga, and Mr. Shiftlet as examples, along with discussions of car and animal imagery, and Hulga's wooden leg, the author contends that O'Connor's stories illustrate Henri Bergson's theory of comic laughter. Includes explications of "The Life You Save May Be Your Own," "Good Country People," and *Wise Blood*. [Rpt. as "Comic Imagery in the Fiction of Flannery O'Connor," in *Realist of Distances: Flannery O'Connor Revisited*. Ed. Karl-Heinz Westarp and Jan Nordby Gretlund. Aarhus (Denmark): Aarhus UP, 1987. 94-101.]

365   Currie, Sheldon. "A Good Grandmother Is Hard to Find: Story as Exemplum." *Antigonish Review* 81-82 (Spring-Summer 1990): 143-56.

Offers a close reading of "A Good Man Is Hard to Find" that focuses on the meaning of the grandmother's crossed legs; how both The Misfit and grandmother appear to be "spiritual twins"; the meaning and implications behind O'Connor's description of The Misfit as "a different breed of dog"; and The Misfit's moral criteria for measuring behavior. Addresses the meaning of the metaphor of the "cloudless, sunless sky," and whether or not the grandmother finally makes the "leap" at the end to become a good woman. Refers to possible influences on O'Connor by such authors as T.S. Eliot, Charles Baudelaire, Nathaniel Hawthorne, Ernest Hemingway, and W.H. Auden.

366   D'Evelyn, Thomas. "Grace in the Grotesque." *Christian Science Monitor* 24 Aug. 1988: 17-18.

Review essay of *Collected Works* by Flannery O'Connor, edited by Sally Fitzgerald and published as part of The Library of America series. States that "despite her reputation for black humor, O'Connor's vision is biblical [and] prophetic." Suggests that while "it is tempting to see her as a complex of paradoxes," she was a "craftsman," indeed "one of the best." Refers to O'Connor's respect for Henry James's work, her sense of humor, and her dialogue. Provides a brief explication and discussion of "Revelation" to illustrate her talent and perspective.

367   Daniel, Dan. "Amazing Crossroads in *Love and Work.*" *Reynolds Price: From A Long and Happy Life to Good Hearts.* [Proceedings of the Seventh Annual Southern Writers' Symposium, Methodist College, April 15-16, 1988.] Ed. Sue Leslie Kimball and Lynn Veach Sadler. Fayetteville, NC: Methodist College Press, 1989. 46-53.

Discusses Reynolds Price's *Love and Work* and *A Long and Happy Life.* Includes a brief comparison of Eborn, of *Love and Work,* with O'Connor's Rayber of *The Violent Bear It Away.* Contends that both characters "relentlessly pursue the past within family relationships only to be victimized by their failure to comprehend its essence." Suggests that "Price's ghosts and O'Connor's grotesques are used to condemn the smug self-assurance of the materialist and the desperate humanism of the existentialist." Concludes that where O'Connor's "*telos* is union with God," Price's "is union within the human community."

368   Darretta, John Lawrence. "From 'The Geranium' to 'Judgement Day': Retribution in the Fiction of Flannery O'Connor." *Since Flannery O'Connor: Essays on the Contemporary American Short Story.* Ed. Loren Logsdon and Charles W. Mayer. Macomb: Western Illinois UP, 1987. 21-28.

Suggests that O'Connor's story, "'The Geranium' introduces the predominant concern of her life's work -- the concept of retribution," and that "Judgement Day," her final story, reveals how "within the twenty-year span of her writing career, O'Connor's idea of retribution had expanded." Contends that while O'Connor's original use of the concept was "a personal and familial one; her final concept shows an interest that is eschatological." Discusses how retribution expresses her creativity as a writer and "defines the contour of her achievement as an artist." Examines how O'Connor develops the themes and forms of retribution in her fiction, and comments that she "kept doing things over and over until they not only came out but came out right." Finds that O'Connor's view of and use of retribution in her fiction "reveals the foundation of her theological thinking: one is paid back for the evil one does or for the failure to do good." Compares O'Connor's "traditional" view of retribution to that of Dante, noting that she believes, like he, that "'the penalty of sin is to dwell in it. Man is punished *by* his sins rather than *for* them. Hell is to live in the evil character one has made for himself.'"

369   Darretta, John L[awrence] and Richard Giannone. "Commentary by Darretta and Giannone." *Since Flannery O'Connor: Essays on the Contemporary American Short Story*. Ed. Loren Logsdon and Charles W. Mayer. Macomb: Western Illinois UP, 1987. 29-31.

Giannone offers comments on Darretta's essay, "From `The Geranium' to `Judgement Day': Retribution in the Fiction of Flannery O'Connor;" and Darretta comments on Giannone's essay, "Flannery O'Connor's Consecration of the End." [Both published in this volume on pages 21-28 and 9-20, and cited and abstracted individually in this guide.]

370   Dart, Bob. "Historian's Pick Nation's Most Influential Women." *Atlanta Journal-Constitution* 17 March 1993: B5.

Ranks the most influential women of the twentieth century in nine fields. O'Connor is listed sixth in the "literature" category. Results are based upon a survey of 300 professors from the fields of history, American studies, and women's studies by the Siena Research Institute in cooperation with the National Women's Hall of Fame in Seneca Falls, New York. Other writers ranked were: 1. Willa Cather, 2. Edith Wharton, 3. Pearl S. Buck, 4. Toni Morrison, 5. Gertrude Stein, 7. Eudora Welty, 8. Zora Neale Hurston, and 9. Adrienne Rich.

371   Daunt, Chris. "The Engraver's Preface to the Pictures." *Flannery O'Connor Bulletin* 22 (1993-94): 74.

Daunt states that he was introduced to O'Connor's work while studying for a literature degree at Newcastle University and--as a former art student--"responded readily" to her "vivid visual language." Comments that because he is a Catholic, he "recognized that the curious and comic figures" O'Connor created in her works "were acting out the great themes of sin and redemption." Mentions meeting and corresponding with Ralph Wood. Discusses his desire to produce engravings for an illustrated edition of O'Connor's works, and describes the process and technique of producing copper engravings. Illustrated with reproductions of four engravings titled: "Lucynell Crater and Lucynell Crater"; "Wise Blood"; "Sarah Ham"; and "Everything That Rises."

372   Daunt, Chris. "Flannery O'Connor." *Flannery O'Connor Bulletin* 25 (1996-97): viii.

Daunt offers a reproduction of a woodcut portrait of Flannery O'Connor, "characterized by angular cuts and strong design."

373   "Davie County Arts Council Celebrated Southern Fiction." *CHEERS! The Flannery O'Connor Society Newsletter* 6.1 (1998): 4.

Reports that the celebration of the literary arts, Southern Fiction REVIVAL: Literary Adaptations in Theatre and Film, held in Mocksville, North Carolina, October 9-11, 1998, included a showing of John Huston's film adaptation of *Wise Blood* and "a biographical play on Flannery O'Connor," directed by John Rushton, titled *Shouting to the Deaf.*

374   Davies, Horton. "Anagogical Signals in Flannery O'Connor's Fiction." *Thought* 55.219 (Dec. 1980): 428-38.

Asserts that O'Connor's stories are parables worth probing for both their religious insights and brilliant observations about humanity. Suggests that "the obscurity in their anagogical interpretation will be lessened for those within the tradition of the Catholic Church" and those well-acquainted with the Bible. Discusses "theological pointers" found in O'Connor's work, including "incompleteness," "the use of eyes and spectacles," "liturgical colors," and "the clue offered by the formulaic `As if.'"

375   Davies, Horton and Marie-Helene Davies. "The God of Storm and Stillness: The Fiction of Flannery O'Connor and Frederick Buechner." *Religion in Life* 48.2 (1979): 188-96.

Asserts that Flannery O'Connor and Frederick Buechner are "prophetic voices crying in the wilderness of our modern secular society" who insist that "Christ is the only oasis in that desert." States that while the religious focus for each author is the crucifixion of Christ and a firm belief in the afterlife, "their lives, the genres of fiction they employ, and their theological emphases are radically different." Asserts that their differences may be based upon the fact that one writer is a Catholic, the other a Protestant.

376   Davis, Alan. "The Faith of Fiction: Symbolism in Flannery O'Connor's `A Good Man Is Hard to Find.'" *Teaching Composition with Literature: Writing Exercises and Ideas.* ["A Special Supplement to Accompany *Literature: An Introduction to Fiction, Poetry, and Drama.*" 6th ed.]. Ed. Dana Gioia. New York: Harper-Collins, 1995. 46-50.

Offers a brief reading of "A Good Man Is Hard to Find" and describes a "teaching approach" to the story "which begins with small-group readings" followed by "readings structured by an O'Connor quotation" and concludes with "each student writing an essay that is both a critical response to group discussion and an appraisal of O'Connor's story." Suggests that this collaborative approach to the story "keeps students honest and demonstrates that a symbol must be earned by writer and reader alike before it can be claimed." Contends that "A Good Man Is Hard to Find" is, in fact, "so full of technique and craft in the service of vision and theme, that it sometimes seems . . . to be the perfect `teaching' story."

377   Davis, Cynthia J. and Kathryn West. *Women Writers in the United States: A Timeline of Literary, Cultural, and Social History*. New York: Oxford UP, 1996. 282-83, 294, 300, 308, 317, 339.

Under the column "Texts," notes the publication date of O'Connor's works: her story, "The Geranium," in 1946; her first novel, *Wise Blood*, in 1952; her collection of short stories, *A Good Man Is Hard to Find and Other Stories*, in 1955; her second novel, *The Violent Bear It Away*, in 1960; and her posthumous collection of short stories, *Everything That Rises Must Converge*, in 1965. Reports that *Flannery O'Connor: The Complete Stories* won the National Book Award for 1972. Highlights of the cultural and social history at the time of each publication are provided in an adjacent column labeled "Context."

378   Davis, Joseph K. "Time and the Demonic in William Faulkner and Flannery O'Connor." *Studies in the Literary Imagination* 20.2 (1987): 123-43.

Examines relationships between O'Connor's work and that of William Faulkner. Focuses on their dramatization of "modern obsessions with time and the demonic." Suggests that in Faulkner's works, characters use blocks of time to brood and agonize. Finds conversely, that O'Connor accepts time within the context of the Catholic Church; that is, her characters encounter "apocalyptic time" as God intervenes and offers grace. Indicates that while Faulkner sees the evil of this world as the result of individual failure(s) to transcend selfish ego-centered desires, O'Connor dramatizes the theological Devil/Satan of the Bible in an effort to convey how the demonic figure attempts to "name" (and therefore reveal) himself.

379   Davis, Rebecca and Susan Mesner, ed. "Suffering." *The Treasury of Religious & Spiritual Quotations: Words to Live By*. Pleasantville, NY: Reader's Digest, 1994. 540.

Includes a quote from O'Connor, taken from the Introduction she wrote in 1962 to *A Memoir of Mary Ann*: "One of the tendencies of our age is to use children's suffering to discredit the goodness of God . . . In this popular pity, we mark our gain in sensibility and our loss in vision. If other ages felt less, they saw more."

380   Davis, Thadious M. "Race and Religion." *The Columbia History of the American Novel.* Ed. Emory Elliott. New York: Columbia UP, 1991. 407-36.

Argues that O'Connor was uncomfortable in representing "the African American in her rural world," and was "one of the few Southern writers of her generation to acknowledge the difficulty of entering into the consciousness of characters of a different race." Briefly compares O'Connor's work to that of Shirley Ann Grau, noting differences in each writer's treatment of race and region. States that while neither *Wise Blood* nor *The Violent Bear It Away* treat race as a significant aspect of the region, O'Connor did--with her stories--finally turn "to an exploration of racial integration just as the Civil Rights movement began to change the face of the South."

381   Davis, William V. "'Large and Startling Figures': The Place of 'Parker's Back' in Flannery O'Connor's Canon." *Antigonish Review* 28 (1977): 71-87.

Offers a reading of "Parker's Back" which focuses on O'Connor's "Christian concerns" as illustrated to the reader through her protagonist, O.E. Parker. Argues that O'Connor's focus on a single character in such an intense manner may be the principal reason that her novels are so flawed. Declares that O'Connor "finds it difficult to sustain complex or extended action or control a number of characters in an even way or on a large canvas." Discusses a variety of related topics, including: the scriptural basis for Parker's name; his obsessive quest for tattoos; implications of the tattoo of the "stern Byzantine Christ" on his back; and the redemptive and eschatological nature of her work.

382   Dawkins, Cecil. Interview with Kay Bonetti. Audiocassette. Columbia, MO: American Audio Prose Library, 1983.

In an interview conducted in February, 1983 by Kay Bonetti, in Columbia, Missouri, Dawkins talks about growing up in the South, characters and themes in her works, and her friendship with Flannery O'Connor. [1 sound cassette, 57 min.].

383   Dawson, Jan C. "Flannery O'Connor's `Sisters.'" *Southern Studies* 4.2 (1993): 157-70.

Draws on a discussion by Flannery O'Connor, Caroline Gordon, and Katherine Anne Porter with Louis Rubin and Madison Jones at Wesleyan College, Macon, Georgia in October, 1960, to illustrate the three writers' common views and sisterly support of each other. To substantiate the deep affinities Porter and Gordon felt for each other and with O'Connor, "despite the generational difference and the uniqueness of the 1960 Wesleyan gathering," Dawson offers details of each writer's personal situation as women and Southerners and suggests that "Catholicism had shown them how to live in both worlds at once." Concludes that "Catholicism opened up to these three Southern writers a world in which there was no spiritual conflict between being a woman and being a literary person." Refers to Robert H. Brinkmeyer's *Three Catholic Writers of the Modern South*, Sister Kathleen Feeley's *Flannery O'Connor: Voice of the Peacock*, and Louise Cowan's 1956 article in *Critique*, "Nature and Grace in Caroline Gordon" to illustrate points made.

384   Day, Susan M. "*Flannery O'Connor Bulletin*, Vol. 24: An Issue Well Worth the Wait." *CHEERS! The Flannery O'Connor Society Newsletter* 4.2 (1996/97): 2-3.

Finds the poetry and prose in the 1995-96 issue of the *Flannery O'Connor Bulletin* to be of particular interest and the critical essays of high quality. Focuses on Jane Hannon's essay, "The Wide World of Her Parish: O'Connor's All-Embracing Vision of the Church," praising her "nuanced description of O'Connor's sometimes elusive and perplexing experience of the church." Compares essays by Doreen Fowler and Henry M.W. Russell on the question of race in O'Connor's work, asserting that "despite their different approaches to this question, the two studies succeed in transcending some of the narrow, ideological assumptions about `O'Connor the racist.'" Praises Fred R. Thiemann for his article on "the clichés that both shape and order Hulga and Mrs. Hopewell's world in `Good Country People.'" Follows with somewhat briefer discussions of other articles, personal tributes, and poems included in the issue.

385   Day, Susan M. "Moral Vision and the Grotesque: Another Look at Flannery O'Connor's Novel *Wise Blood*." *Grail: An Ecumenical Journal* (Canada) 13.3 (1997): 11-27.

Contends that O'Connor "recognized that while the South provided her with the religious landscape for her fiction," the perception of this landscape's "religious history was changing, and in fact diminishing."

Suggests that because this "common measure was disintegrating," O'Connor faced the arduous task of "writing in and for a world that did not share her vision of reality." Sees O'Connor's "moral vision" as reflected in her use of "sometimes violent literary means to get her vision across to a hostile audience," and categorizes this strategy as a use of the grotesque to portray the "spiritual disorder in the life of modern human beings." Offers a reading, in this context, of *Wise Blood*, focusing on the moral implication of Hazel Motes's blinding himself. Concludes that O'Connor used the grotesque to address society's loss of vision and that, assuming a prophetic role, she moved the souls of her audience, who were "unaware" of her intentions. Refers to St. Cyril of Jerusalem and his story of the dragon sitting beside the road, Thomas Aquinas's *Summa Theologica*, and Philip Keane's *Christian Ethics and Imagination*.

386   Deeken, Agnese. "The Apprehension of Natural and Supernatural Reality in Flannery O'Connor's `A Good Man Is Hard to Find.'" *Seirei Women's Junior College Bulletin* (Japan) 9 (Dec. 1981): 14-18.

387   Delattre, Edwin J. "Pushing Against the Age." *Bostonia* 1 (1994): 36-43.

Delattre describes a trip to Milledgeville, Georgia to pay respects to O'Connor's "memory." Relates how he was "shocked to find no references to her or her work in the various brochures on sights to see in the area" or on the historic marker outside Milledgeville's Catholic Church. Outlines his difficulties in finding the O'Connor farm, describes its appearance, and relates his disappointment in finding the Georgia College & State University Library and its *Flannery O'Connor Collection* closed. Reports that the O'Connor-Cline House and grounds "look as if they belong in a Grade B horror movie." Relates that he was told that Regina Cline O'Connor, Flannery's mother, lives in the house as "a virtual recluse." Expresses disappointment that O'Connor is "so little remembered in her own home town," and sees this as a sad "and a dangerous sign."

388   Demory, Pamela H. "Violence and Transcendence in *Pulp Fiction* and Flannery O'Connor." *The Image of Violence in Literature, the Media, and Society: Selected Papers [from the] 1995 Conference [of the] Society for the Interdisciplinary Study of Social Imagery*. Ed. and intro. Will Wright and Steven Kaplan. Pueblo, CO: Society for the Interdisciplinary Study of Social Imagery, 1995: 187-94.

Suggests that readers may "profitably borrow from O'Connor scholarship and O'Connor's own analyses of her work as a way to interpret the meaning of Quentin Tarantino's enigmatic film," *Pulp Fiction*. Discusses the setting, themes, and mood of the film, then compares Tarantino's characters, Jules and Vincent, with O'Connor's The Misfit in "A Good Man Is Hard to Find." Focuses on the issue of how viewers might reconcile Tarantino's depiction of "the blood-riddled corpses of three young men in an apartment with spiritual transcendence," and considers the purpose of each writer's use of religious elements, banality, and violence with grotesque humor. Offers a "religious reading" of O'Connor's story and Tarantino's film, and addresses the objections of those who see the operation of grace in each work as irrational and implausible. Discusses "the connection between violence and redemption," seen as "central to O'Connor's view of Christianity and to her fiction." Concludes that while O'Connor's purpose is to convince readers "of the powerful force of evil in the world and of our great need for grace," Tarantino seeks "to demonstrate that in spite of everything we have seen in his film--all the violence, degradation, death, crime, amoral behavior--grace is still possible; there might still be a God who doesn't judge us on merit."

389   Denham, Robert D. "The World of Guilt and Sorrow: Flannery O'Connor's `Everything That Rises Must Converge.'" *Flannery O'Connor Bulletin* 4 (1975): 42-51.

Offers a reading of "Everything That Rises Must Converge" that illustrates how O'Connor's views on short story form "closely parallel R.S. Crane's Neo-Aristotelian argument about casual inquiry as a method of criticism." Outlines how readers might "account for the form which gives the story meaning by beginning with the plot as experienced." Focuses on the final scene and submits that O'Connor carefully controls the reader's feelings about Julian and his mother, only to turn these feelings (which are tied to the reader's experience) upside down. Sees the reader's experience with this story as "primarily a reversal" of his or her "expectations and desires for the principal characters and a change in attitude toward them." Concludes that the story is Julian's, as "his mother's death becomes the terrible means by which he can grow toward maturity."

390   Desmond, John F. "Flannery O'Connor and the History Behind the History." *Modern Age* 27.3-4 (1983): 290-96.

Considers the value of O'Connor's work and her place "in the tradition of modern Southern letters." Discusses criticism that asserts that O'Connor's work "does not adequately represent the complexities of the modern consciousness." Suggests that this criticism requires a discussion of the relationship between O'Connor's art and her religious convictions. Argues that this discussion must include a judgement related to the question of whether O'Connor's "history behind the history" or vision of the "transcendent order of reality" is valid. Concludes that O'Connor gave readers the ability to see and experience, in their own minds, "the complex dynamic between eschatology and history, and to live as creators of history and not simply as its victims."

391   Desmond, John F. "Flannery O'Connor and the Idolatrous Mind." *Christianity & Literature* 46.1 (1996): 25-35.

Argues that O'Connor's fiction reflects her belief that the modern mind is preoccupied with self-created idols and that her "business as a writer" was "to `pulverize' the idolatrous minds of her characters and readers through force." Suggests that she believed that this approach would, at least, open these individuals to "new ways of seeing by shattering the many false hierarchies her culture had given itself over to." Provides background regarding "the nature and history of idol-making," explores O'Connor's understanding of it, and offers a reading of "The Artificial Nigger" in the context of this discussion. Includes references to Owen Barfield's *Saving the Appearances: A Study in Idolatry*; Walker Percy's essay, "Notes for a Novel About the End of the World"; and O'Connor's own essay, "The Nature and Aim of Fiction."

392   Desmond, John F. "Flannery O'Connor, Henry James, and the International Theme." *Flannery O'Connor Bulletin* 9 (1980): 3-18.

Examines how O'Connor "was able to appropriate several dominant Jamesian themes and transfigure them within her larger religious vision" by taking the most salient aspects of formalist technique to "serve the higher technical ends of her `incarnational art.'" Notes O'Connor's admiration for Henry James, especially his "deep respect for mystery and abiding sense of evil," and suggests that she adapted his "International Theme" for use in illustrating her own "redemptive conception of history." Offers readings of "A Good Man Is Hard to Find," "A Circle in the Fire," "The Displaced Person," and "Greenleaf" in the context of "the theme of the clash between America and Europe," recast "within the larger framework of a specifically Christian redemptive conception of history." States that "the model for her treatment" of this theme is clearly suggested in "A Good Man Is Hard to Find," is advanced--"in both thematic and technical complexity"--in "A Circle in the Fire," is "most explicit" in "The Displaced Person," and is achieved in the most refined and subtle manner in "Greenleaf."

393   Desmond, John [F]. "Flannery O'Connor in Denmark." *Flannery O'Connor Bulletin* 13 (1984): 77-79.

Reports on the *Flannery O'Connor Commemorative Symposium*, jointly sponsored by the University of Aarhus and Odense University and held at Sandbjerg, Denmark August 2-5, 1984. Describes topics of papers presented and states that while many were "a familiar rehearsal of critical interests," some broke new ground. Offers brief comments on presentations by Sally Fitzgerald, Ashley Brown, Ann Ebrecht, Linda Schlafer, Marion Montgomery, Kathleen Feeley, Sheldon Currie, Marshall Bruce Gentry, Patrick Ireland, Mary V. Blasingham, Christiane Beck, Henry Blackwell, John Desmond, Robert Drake, Carter Martin, Dolores Washburn, Jan Gretlund, Mary Frances Hopkins, Beverly Long, and Robert Overstreet. Concludes that the Conference demonstrates that O'Connor's "position in modern American letters is firm but still unsettled." [Note: Essays from this gathering were published in *Realist of Distances: Flannery O'Connor Revisited.* Ed. Karl-Heinz Westarp and Jan Nordby Gretlund. Aarhus (Denmark): U of Aarhus P, 1987.]

394   Desmond, John F. "Flannery O'Connor's Sense of Place." *Southern Humanities Review* 10 (1976): 251-59.

Suggests that, like Eudora Welty, O'Connor uses relation to place as a distinguishing mark of her character's spiritual condition. Asserts that her characters attempt to sustain a false innocence, an innocence which is eventually shattered and replaced by a "true sense of reality." Sees this innocence often symbolically represented by Florida, a "topographical symbol for man's attempt to deny the fall, his link with the natural order and history, and by extension his need for a divine redeemer."

395   Desmond, John F. "Mr. Head's Epiphany in Flannery O'Connor's `The Artificial Nigger.'" *NMAL: Notes on Modern American Literature* 1.3 (1977): Item 20.

Provides an analysis of Mr. Head's epiphany in which the full extent of his sins against humanity and God are fully realized. States that it is through the "mysterious presence of the artificial nigger" that Mr. Head is reconciled with his grandson Nelson after they have returned to the country from the city. Contends that the journey parallels the one in Dante's *Divine Comedy;* both include a journey through Hell and Purgatory and both end "with a return to the Earthly Paradise, symbolized . . . by the return to the country." Suggests that "not until the state of innocence has been recovered can sin be apprehended in its full horror."

396   Desmond, John F. Rev. of *Flannery O'Connor: The Imagination of Extremity,* by Frederick Asals. *Flannery O'Connor Bulletin* 11 (1982): 131-41.

Finds Asals's study to be "a superb and penetrating analysis of O'Connor's
mind and art, well-unified, argued with skill and cogency, and cleverly
written." Discusses the main thrusts of Asals's analyses: how O'Connor's
imagination is "essentially empowered by a Manichean dualism that gave
her a `rich passion . . . for extremes'"; the role and purpose of "tension" in
her work; the influence of Edgar Allan Poe and Nathanael West's *Miss
Lonelyhearts* on O'Connor as she developed her "`ironic voice, grotesque
perception, and the theme of religious quest'"; Asals's "probing [of] the
underlying psychological tensions that inform the structure, image
patterns, motive, and action" of her art; O'Connor's use of a "`doubling'
of symbolic devices"; and her additional use of a "theological dimension
to the psychological." Uses examples from *Wise Blood*, "Good Country
People," "Revelation," "The Artificial Nigger," and *The Violent Bear It
Away* to illustrate points made. Concludes that Asals's work "marks a
significant advancement in the critical understanding of O'Connor's
fiction."

397   Desmond, John F. Rev. of *Flannery O'Connor: An Introduction*, by Miles
Orvell. *Flannery O'Connor Bulletin* 20 (1991): 117-20.

Reports that--except for the new preface--this book is a reissue of the
author's previous study, *Invisible Parade: The Fiction of Flannery
O'Connor*. Questions the republication, noting that since its original
appearance, "exemplary studies of O'Connor's fiction" and *The Habit of
Being: Letters of Flannery O'Connor* have been published. Examines the
publisher's claim that "the `book continues to garner appreciation for its
sound insights,'" and questions whether the opportunity to revisit Orvell's
views of O'Connor's world is necessary. Concludes that the book is an
"early, tentative" probe at understanding O'Connor's work that should
have been carefully revised to consider later criticism to prevent it from
being more than "a critical anachronism."

398   Desmond, John F. Rev. of *The Narrative Secret of Flannery O'Connor*,
by Ruthann Johansen. *Flannery O'Connor Bulletin* 23 (1994-95): 184-87.

Categorizes Johansen's book as another contribution by a scholar who--
like others--has "struggled with the central paradox of trying to elucidate
a body of fiction that is grounded in the fundamental experience of
mystery." Observes how she makes this attempt by "examining
O'Connor's narrative strategies in relation to her intentions as a prophetic
artist." Outlines Johansen's view of O'Connor's fiction and her analysis of
O'Connor's "intent to shatter her reader's conventional modes of thought
. . . " Then, describes how Johansen "argues that the workings of the
trickster as both actor . . . and interpreter . . . are the key to O'Connor's

design of mystery, the point where narrative strategy and the Incarnation intersect." Compliments Johansen on her use of an "impressive array of critical tools . . . including narrative theory, intertextuality, myth and anthropology, and . . . insights from the Biblical prophetic tradition and Christian theology," but questions whether such an approach might run "the risk of diluting the central subject--the unique mystery of the Incarnation--by subsuming it under the broad patterns of cultural myth." Concludes with a discussion of why, "for all its erudite and stimulating critical exegesis," the book "seems a mixed achievement."

399   Desmond, John F. Rev. of *Possum and Other "Receits" for the Recovery of "Southern" Being*, by Marion Montgomery. *Flannery O'Connor Bulletin* 16 (1987): 79-81.

Declares that Montgomery "attempts to define the nature of `Southern' being, contrast it with an aberrant, gnostic form of existence, and offer `receits' for a recovery of authentic being." Describes his definition of "*Southernness*," how he "traces the root of his idea," and how "`Southern' being" can be recovered. Suggests that underlying Montgomery's view is the concept of "a shared community of nature and being which is prior to reason's activity." Asserts that Montgomery contends that the Southern Fugitives--among others--recognized our "decayed state of modern being and attempted to combat it." Concludes that Montgomery believes that the task to be completed in order to recover from man's present state of spiritual decay, is "to restore rhetoric to its proper authority as articulator of being, because language can clarify the mind's action and prevent the disintegration of community."

400   Desmond, John F. "Risen Sons: History, Consciousness, and Personality in the Fiction of Flannery O'Connor." *Thought* 59.235 (1984): 462-82.

Examines the question of whether O'Connor's vision and characters are "sufficiently complex enough to deal with the subtle nuances of the modern mind's spiritual struggles." Discusses criticism of this nature by Lewis P. Simpson in his *The Brazen Face of History: Studies in the Literary Consciousness in America* [Baton Rouge: Louisiana State UP, 1980], and explores O'Connor's theological and philosophical roots that form the basis of her Christology. Reviews the "intellectual paths" of thinkers whose works may have influenced O'Connor, including Eric Voegelin, Mircea Eliade, Etienne Gilson, Jacques Maritain, Karl Jaspers, William Lynch, Claude Tresmontant, and William Thompson. Applies the theories and conceptual explanations of the development of consciousness of these thinkers to O'Connor's fiction, focusing on *The Violent Bear It Away*. Concludes that many of O'Connor's characters, including Tarwater, are complex dramatic visions of her mind and her "engagement with history . . . in all its ultimate extensions of meaning."

401   Desmond, John F. "The Shifting of Mr. Shiftlet: Flannery O'Connor's `The Life You Save May Be Your Own.'" *Mississippi Quarterly* 28.1 (1974/75): 55-59.

Offers a reading of "The Life You Save May Be Your Own" that focuses on the nature and development of the complex protagonist, Tom T. Shiftlet. Explores "the intricate dramatic development of the story and its profound analysis of spiritual malaise." Concludes that Shiftlet is like Young Goodman Brown in the way that he "refuses to `fall' into the ambiguous human community." Suggests that while Shiftlet may save his life by refusing to acknowledge and die into the mystery of existence, "the self he saves is a false and sterile parody of the redeemed creature, endlessly questing for pure transcendence, endlessly unable to die."

402   Desmond, John F. "Signs of the Times: Lancelot and The Misfit." *Flannery O'Connor Bulletin* 18 (1989): 91-98.

Asserts that "in spite of their considerable differences," there is evidence "to indicate a strong affinity of vision" between Walker Percy's work and O'Connor's. Suggests that Percy's novels "often echo O'Connor's ideas, as in his allusion to `the violent bear it away' . . . or his extensive use of the theme that `tenderness [cut off from the source of tenderness] leads to the gas chamber.'" States that while Percy had a much longer career, both mined "a similar core of beliefs and responses to modernity," most clearly evident in their "portrayals of two prophetic anti-heroes--The Misfit and Lancelot Lamar." Examines the two characters' similar philosophical positions on "alternatives of belief and action available to post-Christian man." Concludes that while both characters suffer from despair, "that condition is the ground for hope, a paradox that accounts in part for their subversive appeal as modern anti-heroes."

403   Desmond, John F. "Violence and the Christian Mystery: A Way to Read Flannery O'Connor." *Literature and Belief* 17.1-2 (1997): 129-47.

Suggests that O'Connor's use of violence serves as "both an attraction and a stumbling block," as the "mysteries of violence her stories create often lead us to question the nature of our own fascination." Contends that her use of violence is "based always on her reading of the Scriptures and her Catholic faith." Remarks that the outward violence in O'Connor's stories is meant to reflect "the spiritual violence of inner thought and attitude engraved in the heart and from which acts of murder, deception, rivalry, and stigmatizing erupt." Argues that her use of violence is complicated by the New Testament teaching that unconditional love and charity are the elements that violently "wrench human beings out of their `natural' existence and into the `unnatural' world of Christian commitment." Ties O'Connor's views to René Girard's *Violence and the Sacred*, which "presents an anthropological explanation for the origins of religious rites . . . rooted in the problem of violence." Includes a reading of *The Violent Bear It Away*, focusing on Tarwater's role as a prophet.

404   Desmond, John F. "Walker Percy, Flannery O'Connor, and the Holocaust." *Southern Quarterly* 28.2 (1990): 35-42.

Discusses the similarity between Walker Percy's Father Smith of *The Thanatos Syndrome* and his argument on the significance of the Holocaust, and Flannery O'Connor's "Introduction" to *A Memoir of Mary Ann*. Focuses on O'Connor's view of the Holocaust "as a horrifying example of modern sentimentality, which she . . . sees as rooted in an ethic of tenderness that is divorced from the meaning of Christian redemption." Suggests that both O'Connor and Percy's Father Smith expressed the idea that "language contains not only the power to name truth but to an almost unimaginable power for deception . . . all manner of atrocities and betrayal can be committed in the name of love, benevolence, and idealism." Concludes that O'Connor and Percy saw the Holocaust as a symbol of the much greater drama of the human struggle with evil and quest for eternal salvation.

405   Dessommes, Nancy Bishop. "O'Connor's Mrs. May and Oates's Connie: An Unlikely Pair of Religious Initiates. *Studies in Short Fiction* 31.3 (1994): 433-40.

Compares and contrasts aspects of O'Connor's "Greenleaf" to Joyce Carol Oates's "Where Are You Going, Where Have You Been?" Finds Oates's story "fraught with religious overtones and nightmarish imagery" in a manner similar to O'Connor's. Argues that Oates's Connie is similar to Mrs. May in that both characters "are forced, in a moment of self-realization, to recognize the divine presence in the world; they must, if only for an instant, come to terms with moral responsibility and concern for affairs other than those of self." Concludes that the ordeals of Connie and Mrs. May offer each "a moral insight, or revelation, one that elevates the ordinary woman to the state of religious hero."

406   Dettelbach, Cynthia Golomb. *In the Driver's Seat: The Automobile in American Literature and Popular Culture*. Westport, CT: Greenwood, 1975. 101-06.

Explores the car imagery in O'Connor's *Wise Blood* and "The Life You Save May Be Your Own." Suggests that while Hazel Motes's car in *Wise Blood* initially functions as his home, pulpit, and mode of transportation, later, as the plot progresses, the car is transformed from a possession to his "symbolic possessor--his spiritual Father and God." Asserts that even after the Essex is destroyed "its spiritual effect on Motes" shows that he follows a similar path "to a . . . gratuitous martyrdom at the hands of the police." Declares that in "The Life You Save May Be Your Own," Tom Shiftlet's car "functions in Manichean ways," first as a devil or tempter that prompts remorse for his sinful acts, and later as a vehicle taking him to "Mobile (a name which suggests cars) [and] implies that more false gods await Shiftlet."

407   Detweiler, Jane A. "Flannery O'Connor's Conversation With Simone Weil: *The Violent Bear It Away* as a Study of Affliction." *Kentucky Philological Review* 6 (1991): 4-8.

Points out O'Connor's interest, as expressed in her correspondence, in writing a comic novel based upon the French, Jewish intellectual, Simone Weil. Suggests that while O'Connor may have differed with Weil on church doctrine, she still tries to answer Weil's "questions" through her "treatment of mystery" in *The Violent Bear It Away*. Discusses Weil's belief that "affliction . . . is the soul's profound sense of the absence of God," and ties this concept to the fact that all of the characters in O'Connor's novel are intentionally afflicted to respond to Weil's "questions."

408   Dillard, Annie. "The State of the Art: Fiction and Its Audience." *Massachusetts Review* 23 (Spring 1982): 85-96.

Offers an excerpt from *Living By Fiction* (Harper & Row, 1982) which addresses the question: Why are some writers "still concentrating on traditional virtues like deepened characters and dramatic story-telling?" Includes a brief discussion of O'Connor's reputation, comparing her with John Steinbeck. Contends that, unlike Steinbeck's, O'Connor's reputation "seems to be high at the moment."

409   Dillard, Gail P. "Flannery O'Connor: An Overview of Criticism 1975-1985." Ms. *Flannery O'Connor Collection*, Russell Library, Georgia College & State University, Milledgeville, GA, 1986.

Agrees with Stuart L. Burns that much of the O'Connor criticism is redundant. Observes that instead of consensus, some topics have created polarities among scholars and "led to an unusual amount of criticism of other criticism." Concedes that there is still "useful scholarship being done," and provides a descriptive bibliography in narrative form of book-length works of criticism published between 1975 and 1985. Asserts that much of the work is circular, leading back to many of the same points with few breaking new ground. Concludes that "the complexity of [O'Connor's] fictional technique" is "there to ponder," and it is "in this direction that the most promising possibilities for criticism seem to lie."

410   Dillard, Martha. "The Genesis of the O'Connor Paintings." *Flannery O'Connor Bulletin* 21 (1992): 74.

Describes how, when "faced with a deadline for an exhibit of abstract paintings," the author found inspiration in O'Connor's short stories. Reports that her approach was to visualize the image that each story evoked, sketch it, and continue reading. States that she continued this process for several weeks and then painted for another several months. Contends that "O'Connor's eye for the visual . . . is everywhere apparent in her succinct descriptions of people and places." Illustrations: color photographs of four paintings titled *That Gentleman*, *Asbury's Vision*, *Converging*, and *Revelation*.

411   Dinger, Ed. *Seems Like Old Times*. Ed. Ed Dinger. Iowa City: Iowa Writer's Workshop, 1986. 13-14, 15, 83-88, 125.

A collection of reminiscences submitted by alumni and friends of the Iowa Writers' Workshop for the Workshop's 1986 Golden Jubilee. Those which mention O'Connor include submissions by James B. Hall, Charles Embree, Jean Wylder, and Allan Gurganus. The most extensive of the submissions is that by Wylder, which was excerpted from "Flannery O'Connor: A Reminiscence and Some Letters," published in the Spring, 1970 issue of *North American Review*.

412   Ditsky, John. "The Figure in the Linoleum: The Fictions of Alice Munro." *Hollins Critic* 22.3 (1985): 1-10.

Reports that Canadian writer, Alice Munro, names four American women writers as her literary mentors: Katherine Porter, Eudora Welty, Flannery O'Connor, and Carson McCullers. Declares that O'Connor's influence may be found in Munro's "A Trip to the Coast," "Thanks for the Ride," "Age of Faith," and "Baptizing."

413   Doll, Howard D. *Oral Interpretation of Literature: An Annotated Bibliography with Multimedia Listings*. Metuchen, NJ: Scarecrow, 1982. 332, 381, 447.

Provides references to cassette recordings of the works of O'Connor, and to film adaptations of "The Comforts of Home", "Good Country People," and "Revelation."

414   Donahoo, Robert. "25th Anniversary *Flannery O'Connor Bulletin* Reviewed." *CHEERS! The Flannery O'Connor Society Newsletter* 6.1 (1998): 1-2.

Congratulates the editor, Sarah Gordon, for "putting together an issue that is intellectually and emotionally satisfying," admirably reflecting the gamut of the "various newly hot literary `isms'" that continue to dominate academic circles. Finds articles by Sue Walker and Joseph Torchia to be particularly useful and provocative for those interested in "that most slippery of O'Connor subjects: her illness." Recognizes Sarah Fodor's essay undermining "the truism that O'Connor's education and early writings were steeped in the ideology of New Criticism," then refers to articles by Dennis P. Slattery and Kathleen Sullivan Porter as two examples. Commends Slattery's article on animal imagination in "Revelation" as the stronger of the two. Reports that articles by Matthew Gamber, Jean W. Cash, and Charlotte Beck "touch clearly on historical aspects of O'Connor studies," but wishes that the three "had spun out the implications of their discoveries." Finds articles by Ralph C. Wood and Robert C. Evans, which reflect "the mainstream tradition of O'Connor criticism," both "insightful and persuasive." Regards the excerpt from George Beiswanger's essay, "The Office of Fiction" useful for the way it provides readers with "a sense of how O'Connor was understood by at least one fellow resident of Milledgeville." Concludes that readers should regard the volume with "gratitude and appreciation" as it "suggests that the study of O'Connor's life and work is . . . alive: continuing to develop, deepen, possibly even to mature."

415   Donahoo, Robert. "Healing the Cultural Divides: Reading `A Good Man Is Hard to Find.'" *Journal of Contemporary Thought* 4 (1994): 7-21.

Notes a shift in O'Connor criticism in recent years, from thematic and philosophical concerns toward a context which considers the impact of history on her work. Refers to contributions by Marshall Bruce Gentry, Thomas Hill Schaub, and Jon Lance Bacon as examples. Focuses on the American reader of the 1940s and 1950s, discussing the "fractured nature of that culture." Uses Richard Brodhead's description of types of readers during Louisa May Alcott's career. Ties the "story papers" of Alcott's day to the "confessional" and men's "police-reporter" magazines of O'Connor's; the "familiar domestic fiction offering moral and social direction" in the 19th century to 1950s magazines such as *Ladies' Home Journal* and *McCall's*; and notes the difficulties confronting serious writers of both periods. Refers to Cleanth Brooks and Robert Penn Warren's textbook *Understanding Fiction*, Brooks's *An Approach to Fiction*, and O'Connor's own essays in *Mystery and Manners* to delineate "literature" from these other classes of writing and the impact that such a delineation had on O'Connor's work. Provides "a culturally aware reading of `A Good Man Is Hard to Find'" which contends that O'Connor addressed the expectations of "a tripartite cultural division similar to Brodhead's picture." Describes three ways the story can be read and notes the context of each perspective as it relates to Brodhead's framework. Concludes that the story "serves both to reveal a perceived historical cultural situation, even as it attempts to alter--if only for the duration of the text--that situation." Further, "Like any good miracle, the text contains not just spiritual insight but historical, cultural conditions."

416   Donahoo, Robert. "O'Connor's Ancient Comedy: Form in `A Good Man Is Hard to Find.'" *Journal of the Short Story in English / Les Cahiers de la nouvelle* (France) 16 (Spring 1991): 29-40.

Argues that an examination of the form and mechanics of "A Good Man Is Hard to Find" reveals that the story is not merely idiosyncratically created, but patterned according to classical models developed by Dante and Aristophanes. Offers a reading of the story in this context and concludes that O'Connor's depiction of the Grandmother's "change"--from merely exhibiting good manners through words to showing love through action--conforms to the *agon* of Aristophanes's comedies. Declares that the dialogue between The Misfit and Grandmother exhibits the characteristics "of a debate which develops elements of both trial and duel" as in a Greek *agon*. Observes that O'Connor has shunned the use of "instantaneous conversion" as a literary device and has chosen to "conform to the Dantean pattern of comic illumination achieved through a descent into a Hell."

417   Donahoo, Robert. "O'Connor's Catholics: A Historical-Cultural Context." *Literature and Belief* 17.1-2 (1997): 101-13.

Reviews popular images of Catholics during the late 1940s and 1950s and examines how O'Connor sought, through her fiction, "to alter those images in ways that enhance perceptions of Catholicism." Uses Catholic settings and characters found in "A Temple of the Holy Ghost," "The Enduring

Chill," and the 1954 *Sewanee Review* version of "The Displaced Person" as supporting evidence. Concludes that while none of the discussions of these stories "demands that we construct totally new readings of the tales themselves," it is recognized that "they do add a level of complexity."

418   Donahoo, Robert. "The Problem With Peelers: *Wise Blood* as Social Criticism." *Flannery O'Connor Bulletin* 21 (1992): 43-57.

Suggests that because "the world of *Wise Blood* is one in which something is desperately wrong," readers may wish to go beyond theology and consider the novel "as a criticism of the culture it represents." Uses the scene in which all the main characters are focusing on a mechanical potato peeler to propose that "for all its simplicity and surface inanity, the potato peeler serves as a metaphor for a type of action that O'Connor saw as prevalent in her culture: re-creations of evangelical-style conversions." Refers to descriptions of conversions by William James, John Wesley, and B.J. Leonard; literary uses by Johnson Jones Hooper, William Faulkner, and William Styron; and O'Connor's views as well. Submits that the peeler seems emblematic of the evangelical Protestant view of conversion as being an "unexpected, instantaneous transformation," a view rejected by O'Connor. Discusses O'Connor's link of "potato-conversion to economic exploitation." Concludes that in this story, "O'Connor demonstrates that the American tendency to address a problem by changing its appearance-- mixing the power of money with the hope of conversion--proves not just a mistake, but the initial step in spiritual and social damnation."

419   Donahoo, Robert. "Review of the FO'C Bulletin, Vol. 22." *CHEERS! The Flannery O'Connor Society Newsletter*. 2.2 (1994-95): 2-3.

Offers introductory comments which contend that--until recently--the O'Connor scholarly community could be divided into two groups: those who "disparage O'Connor's writing and achievement largely in light of its Catholic-Christian ideology," and "those who accept O'Connor as canonical and seek to explicate and underscore her aesthetic achievement and philosophical statements." Offers examples of scholars positioned in each category and concludes that--until recently--"with the exception of the occasional historical and biographical foray, it's difficult to find much outside these bounds." Reports that the *Flannery O'Connor Bulletin*'s volume 22 issue serves as evidence that critical commentary is now "changing." Suggests that "O'Connor scholarship is moving into the confusing and uncertain world of contemporary literary criticism . . . a world marked by diverse methods and interests that refuses to consistently value form, unity, and complexity." Observes that scholars are not asking "what O'Connor means or how her writing 'rates,' but rather how it works as language and what it does in the world." Comments on positions taken and content of four articles in the issue: Irwin Streight's "Is There a Text in This Man?: A Semiotic Reading of `Parker's Back'"; Val Larsen's "A Tale of Tongue and Pen: Orality and Literacy in `The Barber'"; William Burke's "Fetishism in the Fiction of Flannery O'Connor"; and, Ralph Wood's "Where Is the Voice Coming From?: Flannery O'Connor on Race." Concludes that O'Connor scholars are now "following the theoretical paths now made hard and firm by those in other fields" and entering "a volatile critical scene where `with wandering steps and slow'" they must make their way.

420   Donahoo, Robert. "Tarwater's March Toward the Feminine: The Role of Gender in O'Connor's *The Violent Bear It Away.*" *CEA Critic* 56.1 (1993): 96-106.

Considers O'Connor's status among American feminists and reports that she "is cited as an example of a woman hiding her sex behind an androgynous name." Asserts that she stands accused "of creating women characters who are `punished for unfeminine arrogance.'" Questions the validity of claims that O'Connor "somehow supports, endorses, or even acquiesces to masculine values." Offers a detailed reading of *The Violent Bear It Away* supporting a "picture of the feminine" that may serve as a model for viewing many of her other works as well. Refers to the theory of Hélène Cixous to support an argument for O'Connor's "interest in and use of the feminine," and suggests that "if we read O'Connor's texts with eyes not only for individual women but also for the feminine, the feminine emerges as a controlling force." Focuses on Jungian feminine and masculine aspects of Lucette Carmody (the child evangelist) and young Tarwater. Also discusses, in this context, O.E. Parker's role in "Parker's Back." Refers to critical comments by Susan Gubar, Jane Tomkins, John Hawkes, Rosamond Rosenmeier, Louise Westling, Elaine Showalter, Ann Belford Ulanov, and Nancy K. Miller. Concludes that "in interlacing her Christian theology with Jungian theory and female experience, in telling her feminine story through males such as Tarwater and O.E. Parker," O'Connor protects and arms the reader "against the privileging, the hypostatizing, ultimately the essentializing, of our own limited sense of what goes with what."

421   Donnelly, Daria. "Flannery O'Connor in Reverse--*Jesus' Son*: Stories by Denis Johnson." *Commonweal* 13 Aug. 1993: 23-24.

Contends that Denis Johnson "has been carrying on an edgy romance with Catholicism and O'Connor ever since the demonic rapist Ned Higher-and-Higher appeared in his first novel, *Angels*. Suggests that Ned may have been created by Johnson to upstage O'Connor's malevolent violet-eyed stranger in *The Violent Bear It Away*. Remarks that Johnson's *Jesus' Son* "owes much to O'Connor's spiritual vocation for the grotesque." Outlines the kinds of "Catholic images" used and argues that "Where[as] O'Connor writes from certitude," Johnson's work "emerges from his incertitude." Concludes that, with this book, Johnson gives the reader "a narrator who is of God's party without knowing it"; his "'Maniac Drifter' whizzes by O'Connor's Milledgeville, Georgia, with a spiritual longing and narrative power born of hope and doubt."

422   Donohue, Agnes McNeill. "The Numenous [*sic*] Vision of Flannery O'Connor." *Critic* 34.3 (1976): 32-42.

Discusses impressions of O'Connor after rereading her writings twelve years after her death. Asserts that "Jonathan Edwards's `Sinners in the Hands of an Angry God' is not so distant as one would think from Flannery O'Connor's ambiance." States, "no thinking reader can escape her mordant ironic-comic orchestrating as she grills us over her Southern hellish barbecue pit first on one side, then on the other. She is God-awful tough on her characters, herself, and on all of us." Provides a biographical sketch, discusses critical reaction to her work, and offers brief summaries of the plots of *Wise Blood*, *The Violent Bear It Away*, and most of her short stories. Concludes that after reading an O'Connor story "We are left uneasy because the artistic ambiguity summons up the most frightening dilemmas of human existence, presents them with an explosive dramatic tension, but leaves us to face multi-leveled ironic explorations of the human psyche that are capable of endless extensions of meaning." Illustrations: Photographs of O'Connor standing in front of her self-portrait, and standing on the steps of Andalusia, the family farm, near Milledgeville, Georgia.

423   Dorsey, James E. "Carson McCullers and Flannery O'Connor: A Checklist of Graduate Research." *Bulletin of Bibliography & Magazine Notes* 32.4 (1975): 162-67.

States that this checklist supplements earlier bibliographies on O'Connor published in the September-October 1967, January-April 1968, May-August 1968, and October-December 1973 issues of this same journal.

424   Dougherty, David C. "Flannery O'Connor 1925-1964." *Research Guide to Bibliography and Criticism*. Ed. Walter Beacham. Vol. 2. Washington, D.C.: Research Publishing, 1985. 867-870.

Provides a chronology of important events in Flannery O'Connor's life; a bibliography of her work; an overview and evaluation of biographical sources; an overview of literary criticism; and an evaluation of important critical sources, including entries in selected dictionaries and encyclopedias. Critical works cited and abstracted include Sally Fitzgerald's *The Habit of Being*; Lorine M. Getz's *Flannery O'Connor: Her Life, Library and Book Reviews*; Dorothy A. Walter's *Flannery O'Connor*; Frederick Asals's *Flannery O'Connor: The Imagination of Extremity*; Sister Kathleen Feeley's *Flannery O'Connor: The Voice of the Peacock*; Melvin J. Friedman and Lewis A. Lawson's *The Added Dimension: The Art and Mind of Flannery O'Connor*; Josephine Hendin's *The World of Flannery O'Connor*; and Carol Shloss's *Flannery O'Connor's Dark Comedies: The Limits of Inference*. [See also entry for the 1990 update: Walton, Beacham, ed. "Flannery O'Connor, 1925-1964." *Research Guide to Biography and Criticism: 1990 Update*. Wash., D.C.: Beacham Publishing, 1990. 367-70.]

425   Douglas, Thomas E. "Interview: Denise Giardina." *Appalachian Journal* 20 (Summer 1993): 384-93.

Offers an introduction and interview, edited into a narrative format, of writer Denise Giardina. Giardina briefly discusses Flannery O'Connor's influence upon her work.

425a   Downs, Gene. "Simply O'Connor: Progress Made in Preserving Flannery O'Connor Home." *Savannah Morning News* 9 Nov. 1993: B1+.

Describes the success of the Flannery O'Connor Home Foundation in Savannah despite its "hand-to-mouth" financial situation. Quotes founding member Hugh Brown throughout, as he reflects on how the Foundation first purchased the home in 1989 and then began restoring it. Notes that Brown finds the upkeep of the home--which dates back to 1855--to be an "eternal dilemma," as O'Connor herself had learned when she inherited the home in 1959 only to find that it needed a new roof. Outlines the Foundation's 1994 "wish list," and remarks that O'Connor herself would "be amused to know that the ceiling still has a leak."

426   Drake, Robert. "Eudora Welty's Country--and My Own." *Modern Age* 23.4 (1979): 403-09.

Drake discusses the influence of Eudora Welty and Flannery O'Connor upon his own efforts to write fiction. States, "it was Miss Welty who first awakened me to the possibilities, for fictional purposes, of the time and place I had been living in all my life; and it was Miss O'Connor who later on intensified whatever convictions I had managed to acquire about what my fictional country was and what I owed to it and myself." Compares Welty's geographic sense of place with O'Connor's Christian perspective of humanity's "true country." Notes the various meanings O'Connor intended, and her belief that "the artist--or mankind--ignores his true country at his peril."

427   Drake, Robert. "Flannery O'Connor." *Religion and Modern Literature: Essays in Theory and Criticism.* Ed. G.B. Tennyson and Edward E. Ericson, Jr. Grand Rapids, MI: William B. Eerdmans, 1975. 393-406.

Discusses O'Connor's "Christian commitment as an artist," using remarks from her essay: "The Fiction Writer and His Country" collected in *The Living Novel: A Symposium*, edited by Granville Hicks. Uses these remarks to frame O'Connor's approach to her writing and examine her dramatization of religious themes. Follows with brief discussions of "The Displaced Person," *The Violent Bear It Away*, *A Memoir of Mary Ann*, "The Artificial Nigger," "A Temple of the Holy Ghost," and "A Good Man Is Hard to Find." Also comments on O'Connor's use of symbolism, the grotesque, and the idea that our "true country" lies beyond this world. [Note: This essay is an excerpt from Drake's *Flannery O'Connor: A Critical Essay* (Grand Rapids, MI: William B. Eerdmans, 1966).]

428   Drake, Robert. "The Lady `Frum' Somewhere: Flannery O'Connor Then and Now." *Modern Age* 29.3 (1985): 212-23.

Drake recalls reading *A Good Man Is Hard to Find* in 1957. Offers biographical insights and describes how it altered his perspective of "Southern Gothic," of her later works, and led to his subsequent friendship with O'Connor. [Rpt. in *Realist of Distances: Flannery O'Connor Revisited*. Ed. Karl-Heinz Westarp and Jan Nordby Gretlund. Aarhus (Denmark): Aarhus UP, 1987. 30-45.]

429   Drake, Robert. "Three Southern Ladies." *Flannery O'Connor Bulletin* 9 (1980): 41-48.

Discusses parallels and common causes of Katherine Anne Porter, Eudora Welty, and Flannery O'Connor. Asserts that each of the three "are simply good writers, even perhaps minor great writers," and that their most common attribute is that they are "trying to tell the truth." Sees Porter as a perfectionist whose work is "first-rate" and whose technique is as finely honed as that of Henry James and Gustave Flaubert. Contends that Welty's view merely dramatizes the paradox of the "stress and counter-stress" of life, and "provides no answers." Suggests that O'Connor's work "may be more of a problem," as she is "narrower both in theme and in terrain." Because *"belief* is a central matter in her work," O'Connor is "'controversial' in a way that Miss Porter and Miss Welty are not." Argues, however, that O'Connor "is not trying to convert anybody to anything, and certainly some of the members of her own church were misguided in implying that she was a sort of Roman-Catholic writer-in-residence." Believes that living in the South gave each of these three writers "a place, a time, a community, a *there*," which enabled each to have "done her own thing and done it well."

430   Driggers, Stephen G. "The Catalog of the Flannery O'Connor Manuscripts at Georgia College." *Flannery O'Connor Bulletin* 14 (1985): 59-61.

Discusses and offers details related to Robert J. Dunn's efforts to organize the files, separate papers, and group "related sets of manuscripts together" for the purpose of producing a catalog of Flannery O'Connor's manuscripts in the Library of Georgia College & State University in Milledgeville. Explains why Dunn's catalog, which he intended to have published in 1977, never appeared, and outlines how obstacles were overcome to complete his catalog (primarily through the use of subsequently published books, such as *The Habit of Being, Mystery and Manners, The Presence of Grace*, and *Flannery O'Connor's Library: Resources for Being*). [*The Manuscripts of Flannery O'Connor at Georgia College*, edited by Stephen G. Driggers and Robert J. Dunn, with the help of Sarah Gordon of Georgia College & State University, was published by the University of Georgia Press in 1989.]

431   Duckworth, C. Victoria. "The Redemptive Impulse: *Wise Blood* and *The Color Purple*." *Flannery O'Connor Bulletin* 15 (1986): 51-56.

Suggests that O'Connor and Alice Walker may be linked by their common concern with personal redemption. Sees both authors as using "characters caught in a violent--sometimes grotesquely violent--world . . . struggling toward their own redemption, many without any conscious knowledge of what impels them." Outlines and discusses the plot and action of O'Connor's *Wise Blood* and Walker's *The Color Purple*. Sees *Wise Blood* as the story of "a man whose `vision' has blurred," and who is on a journey "to correct his religious astigmatism." Contends that *The Color Purple* has a similar theme, but one which is presented in a more joyous manner: as the story of Celie's redemption and resurrection "through one of the most unlikely saviors in recent fiction, Shug Avery." Refers to interpretive comments by Gilbert H. Muller and Peter S. Prescott. Concludes that "both novels are finally concerned with the triumph of vision and the possibility of redemption."

432   Duke, Maurice, Jackson R. Bryer, and M. Thomas Inge, eds. *American Women Writers: Bibliographical Essays*. Westport, CT: Greenwood, 1983. 269-96.

Offers an extensive bibliographical essay discussing O'Connor and her work in terms of biography, bibliography, editions, manuscripts and letters, lengthy and shorter critical materials.

433   Dukes, Thomas. "`Place in Fiction': Marjorie Kinnan Rawlings and Eudora Welty." *Marjorie Kinnan Rawlings Journal of Florida Literature* 3 (1991): 7-18.

Examines Rawlings's work to determine whether she should be mentioned "in the same breath" as such writers as Flannery O'Connor, Eudora Welty, Katherine Anne Porter, Ellen Glasgow, and Margaret Mitchell. Focuses on comparing Rawlings's "concern with place to Eudora Welty's poetic of place." Concludes that Rawlings "belongs to a specifically pastoral tradition of southern writers," and contends that her work, with its reliance upon the Southern sense of place, should be considered alongside that of Welty, O'Connor, and other major Southern women writers.

434   Dunaway, John M., ed. *Exiles and Fugitives: The Letters of Jacques and Raïssa Maritain, Allen Tate, and Caroline Gordon*. Baton Rouge: Louisiana State UP, 1992. 6, 57, 79, 83-84, 86, 89, 91.

Offers a compilation of letters between Jacques and Raïssa Maritain and Allen Tate and Caroline Gordon, which "reveal a rich tapestry of mutual respect, of intellectual fervor, [and] of constructive criticism." Notes that Jacques Maritain probably "owed much of his familiarity with the author of *Wise Blood* to Caroline Gordon," and includes several letters with references to O'Connor.

435   Dunleavy, Janet Egleson. "A Particular History: Black and White in Flannery O'Connor's Short Fiction." *Critical Essays on Flannery O'Connor*. Ed. Melvin J. Friedman and Beverly Lyon Clark. Boston: G.K. Hall, 1985. 186-202.

Addresses attitudes toward black Americans in O'Connor's work. Offers an overview of the social history of blacks during her lifetime and contends that by the time she graduated from Georgia State College for

Women (GSCW) in 1945, "the scene had been set for the demonstrations and legal challenges that were to rock Southern society in the last decade of her life." Examines similarities between "The Geranium" and "Judgement Day" and compares the characters in both stories. Follows with extensive summaries of the plots of "The Train," "Wildcat," "The Barber," "The Enduring Chill" and "Everything That Rises Must Converge." Refers to O'Connor's remark about the manners of the "`uneducated Southern Negro,'" and finds it "reaffirmed in her fiction not only by George, Randall, and Morgan, but also by Astor and Sulk." Concludes that the evolution of the Negro's "new code of manners" is reflected in Mrs. Turpin's "Boethian soliloquy" in "Revelation."

436   Dunn, Joe P. and Howard L. Preston, eds. *The Future South: A Historical Perspective for the Twenty-first Century*. Urbana: U of Illinois P, 1991. 159, 168-69, 172, 179, 227, 228.

Discusses the South's attitude toward its own future. Includes several brief references to O'Connor, most notably James Dickey's comment that women writers in the South were given the choice of writing about a historic subject or "could deal with the eccentric village types such as Carson McCullers and Eudora Welty frequently do and Flannery O'Connor does to the extreme." Refers to James C. Cobb's use of O'Connor's scene of The Misfit shooting the grandmother in "A Good Man Is Hard to Find" to describe how the South, "`under the gun' of national scrutiny and assessment," continues to behave.

437   Dunn, Robert J. "The Manuscripts of Flannery O'Connor at Georgia College." *Flannery O'Connor Bulletin* 5 (1976): 61-69.

Describes problems encountered in cataloging and arranging the manuscripts donated by Regina Cline O'Connor to the *Flannery O'Connor Collection* of Georgia College & State University in 1970. Details previous efforts by Catherine Garner, David Estes, Robert N. Smith, Gerald Becham, and Charles M. Hegarty. Then, outlines the issues faced, and solutions developed to bring the project to completion. Remarks how certain "characters, episodes, motifs, and themes appear, disappear, and reappear" in the manuscripts, and offers helpful hints as to how O'Connor developed her stories, "doggedly pursued" them, and often reworked her material to fit stories for which it was not originally intended.

438   Dunn, Robert J. "A Review of Martha Stephens' *The Question of Flannery O'Connor* and Dorothy Walters' *Flannery O'Connor*." *Flannery O'Connor Bulletin* 5 (1976): 112-18.

Noting that the number of books to date on O'Connor has grown to thirteen, and that "the number of articles has proliferated exponentially," Dunn finds it "surprising that there should have appeared close upon one another two works so markedly different." Comments that though they each explore the "same basic issues"--"the aesthetic difficulty posed by the informing philosophy of the fictions, the function of the grotesque in expressing that philosophy, the role of the comic, [and] the influence of diseases and relative confinement upon O'Connor's view of the world"--in Dunn's view Stephens's book falls far short of Walters's. Offers a thoughtful analysis of the perceived shortcomings of Martha Stephens's book and concludes that it "represents rather haphazard scholarship used in an attempt to explain fiction for which the author lacks fundamental sympathy." Focuses on Stephens's "failure to study O'Connor's theology," her lack of research on forms of the grotesque, and her failure to use a systematic approach to O'Connor's fiction. Sees Dorothy Walters's book as "certainly one of the best critical overviews of O'Connor yet produced," representing "the work of a thoughtful, careful scholar and reader who understands and may even share the philosophy and vision" of O'Connor. Lauds Walters' clear, intelligent, formalist methodology, her "solid and knowledgeable understanding of the relevant theology," and her "full awareness of the operations of the grotesque."

439   Dyer, Joyce C. "'Something' in Flannery O'Connor's *Wise Blood*." *Notes on Contemporary Literature* 15.5 (1985): 5-6.

Contends that O'Connor relates the word "something" with the hidden, haunting, invisible forces that do not allow Hazel Motes rest until his last few days of life as a prophet. Asserts that it is this "something" that deepens the reader's understanding of Hazel Motes's external quest. Finds that the association of the word "with the Enoch Emery sub-plot accentuates the perversity of the idea of a new Jesus."

440   Dyson, J. Peter. "Cats, Crimes, and Punishment: The 'Mikado's' Pitti-Sing in 'A Good Man Is Hard To Find.'" *English Studies in Canada* 14.4 (1988): 436-52.

Points out and discusses "some of the numerous and complex *Mikado* echoes in 'A Good Man Is Hard to Find.'" Argues that both works utilize major elements of humor and "explore thematically the significance of the mysteriously arbitrary design by which characters and situations are moved despite themselves." Mentions Josephine Hendin, Sir William S. Gilbert, and focuses on the role of Pitty Sing.

441 East, Charles. "The Dream-Career of James Prewitt." *Southern Review* 29.3 (1993): 465-80.

Discusses James Prewitt, a largely unpublished writer from New Orleans. Focuses on entries in Prewitt's journal, which include his July 6, 1967 notes on O'Connor: "'Now there's a writer that beats us all. So *hard-eyed*.'" Prewitt comments on O'Connor's `tough-minded faith that never expected reward,'" and expresses his view that O'Connor would have been greatly affronted "'if at Lourdes a miracle *had* cured her of her illness.'"

442 Ebrecht, Ann. "'The Length, Breadth, and Depth of the World in Movement': The Evolutionary Vision of Flannery O'Connor and Teilhard de Chardin." *Realist of Distances: Flannery O'Connor Revisited*. Ed. Karl-Heinz Westarp and Jan Nordby Gretlund. Aarhus (Denmark): Aarhus UP, 1987. 208-16.

Asserts that the protagonists in "A View of the Woods" and "Everything That Rises Must Converge" adopt approaches to the physical world similar to those described by Teilhard de Chardin. States that one approach is that the world is too vast for humankind to truly count, and the second is that the world is too beautiful to be ignored, and should instead be adored. Contends that O'Connor found Teilhard de Chardin's theories to be attractive and similar to her own beliefs.

443 Edelstein, Mark G. "Flannery O'Connor and the Problem of Modern Satire." *Studies in Short Fiction* 12.2 (1975): 139-44.

Asserts that O'Connor used her characters to develop a world, "fantastic in a different way," which "brilliantly satirizes contemporary man." Argues that for O'Connor, the stupidity of the modern rejection of God's plan of salvation resulted in a social order that was grotesque and therefore fit subject for satire. Suggests that O'Connor's satire often goes unrecognized by readers because it is not based "on the kind of moral standard her readers might readily accept." Refers to the literary theory of Northrup Frye and discusses "The Life You Save May Be Your Own," "The Artificial Nigger," "A Circle in the Fire," and *Wise Blood*. Concludes that O'Connor's success as a satirist can be attributed to how she surprises readers "by the very peculiarity of her characters."

443a Edmondson, Henry T., III. "Flannery O'Connor's Teaching on the Nature of Evil in `The Lame Shall Enter First.'" Unpublished essay, 2000. [To be published in *Faith, Reason, and Political Life Today*. Ed. Peter A. Lawler and Dale McConkey. Lanham, MD: Lexington Press, 2000.]

Offers a careful and detailed explication of "The Lame Shall Enter First" as presenting O'Connor's view of the nature of evil. Suggests that O'Connor intended the story "to awaken the spiritual consciousness of a world consumed by rationalist thought" and indicates that she "seems to have reached deep within her own reservoir of wisdom and talent to teach [her readers] something." Compares O'Connor's views regarding the nature of evil with those of John Hawkes, and submits that O'Connor wisely teaches that evil "cannot be understood except in a context infused with a religious understanding." Sees the story as demonstrating that while "humanitarianism without faith may be the cruelest kind of kindness . . . benevolence inspired by the transcendent is goodness indeed." Follows with a discussion of O'Connor's admiration of Joseph Conrad's work and concludes that "an absence of faith in the transcendent brings with it a double curse: not only are we deprived of belief in inspiration and guidance outside of ourselves, [but] even more perversely, we are oblivious to the reality of evil in its many disguises."

444   Edmunds, Susan. "Through a Glass Darkly: Visions of Integrated Community in Flannery O'Connor's *Wise Blood*." *Contemporary Literature* 37.4 (1996): 559-85.

Offers a reading of *Wise Blood* that challenges critics--such as Frederick Crews and Claire Kahane--who take O'Connor's fiction to task "for its failure to endorse the historical struggle for racial integration and equality." Remarks that while O'Connor "responded negatively to civil rights activists' daring and highly effective use of the mass media," sheis perceived as joining "other integrationists in actively tracing out points of correspondence" between "contemporary history and Christ's Second Coming." Describes how Martin Luther King, Jr. "made Paul's eschatological vision of integrated community a crucial point of reference in the struggle to achieve racial integration on earth," and uses numerous examples from *Wise Blood* to illustrate how O'Connor reflected King's belief that "through `brotherly' acts of love which recognize and foster the unity of all God's children, each individual or community on earth may realize in part the redemptive narrative of history, which Christ will make whole at the end of time." Considers her use of mirrors to reflect the "mysterious images of racial and gender mixing which . . . reconstruct Haze's notions of family, community, and selfhood" and how her "representations of race and gender relations emerge and the discursive formations through which many of us read these representations today."

445   Edwards, Bruce L. "Flannery O'Connor." *Critical Survey of Long Fiction: English Language Series*. Ed. Frank N. Magill. Englewood Cliffs, NJ: Salem, 1983. 2033-40, 3270-73, 3336-39.

Refers to *Wise Blood* as a "memorable and piercing postmodern delineation of Western society's anxiety over God's absence." Contends that O'Connor did not succeed in "making Christianity more palatable but in making its claims unavoidable." Includes a brief biographical sketch, a review of her novels, and a few critical references. A brief discussion of "The Displaced Person" is also provided in the section titled "The Novella," by Charles E. May, which provides a list of anthologies in which this story is published.

446   Edwards, Bruce L., Jr. "Flannery O'Connor: Defamiliarizing the Mystery of Godliness." *Literature and Belief* 4 (1984): 69-78.

Discusses how O'Connor communicated her orthodoxy to the modern reader, attempts by critics to "pigeonhole" her fiction, and her vision of Christ. Outlines how she avoided "mere tractarianism" and propagandizing, and how she forces her readers to "confront the gospel." Suggests that "an appropriate measuring stick of O'Connor's craft" might be that of her success in defamiliarizing the concepts underlying the gospel, especially conversion and discipleship. Refers to Walker Percy and C.S. Lewis, and discusses the concept of "defamiliarization" as defined by Russian formalist critic Victor Shkovsky.

446a   Egan, Kimberly. "Ruby Turpin in Flannery O'Connor's `Revelation.'" *Notes on Contemporary Literature* 28.2 (March 1998): 8-9.

Contends that Ruby Turpin in "Revelation" is a difficult, despicable character who spends her life "viciously criticizing and labeling other people, while setting herself apart as superior." Argues, however, that it is this very "air of superiority" that "makes her transformation at the end of the story even more moving." Concludes that, despite the position of those critics who believe that Ruby is destined for hell, the "cricket choruses" indicate that "there is hope for her yet; even if she has not yet been changed by her revelation, she still has a chance to learn from it."

447   Ehrlich, Eugene and Gorton Carruth. *The Oxford Illustrated Literary Guide to the United States*. New York: Oxford UP, 1982. 90, 169, 254-60, 349, 458.

Lists authors who have resided in the United States. Describes Saratoga Springs, New York; Atlanta, Savannah, and Milledgeville, Georgia; and Iowa City, Iowa-- all places Flannery O'Connor lived during some part of her lifetime.

448   Eifrig, Gail McGrew. "A Proper Knowing." *Cresset* 51.8 (1988): 25-28.

Discusses the paradox noted by those "who read a lot of fiction" that "there is a lot about a given situation in the text that the text is revealing, but not saying." Refers to those readers "who know, accept, and even enjoy this fact" as "knowing readers." Explores "this knowing/unknowing quality of reading" using Mark Twain's *Huckleberry Finn* and O'Connor's "A Good Man Is Hard to Find," before proceeding to offer a review essay of Jill Baumgaertner's *Flannery O'Connor: A Proper Scaring* (Harold Shaw Publishers, 1988). Suggests that O'Connor's work often baffles and puzzles her readers and that Baumgaertner's work "quite successfully answers the questions posed by such baffled readers." Focuses on Baumgaertner's approach to O'Connor's work through the use of seventeenth-century "emblem literature." Then describes how she provides interested readers with "a tour of the O'Connor territory . . . arranging the stories according to the theological emphasis which must be perceived if the story is to be clear as revelation."

449   Eigen, Michael. "The Sword of Grace: Flannery O'Connor, Wilfred R. Bion and D.W. Winnicott." *Psychoanalytic Review* 72.2 (1985): 335-46.

Analyzes writings by Flannery O'Connor, D.W. Winnicott, and Wilfred R. Bion. States that each writer project is not a static, psychoanalytic selfhood, but one whose very existence is opened and expanded at any given moment by the knowledge and revelation of that moment. Psychoanalyzes some of O'Connor's characters in what he refers to as a radically new mode, one which is no longer "reductionistic." Discusses them in current psychoanalytical terms. Refers to various theorists and how their concepts take into consideration "faith" and "mystery." Positions O'Connor in the midst of these analysts, while acknowledging her as primarily a fiction writer who felt the analyses of spirituality to be beyond the reaches of psychology.

450   Elkins, Mary J. "*Wise Blood*: Definition and Discovery." *Confrontation* 35.3 (1987): 177-85.

Contends that the key concept in O'Connor's sense of Hazel Motes's integrity lies in her interpretation of free will as "'many wills conflicting in one man.'" Asserts that *Wise Blood* is a story of a man making his first individual decisions and choices, free to accept or reject the definitions of family and faith. Suggests that because underlying each of Motes's decisions are certain crucial definitions, *definition* is a central concept. Finds his self-definition, for example, to be that of a non-believer in a world without Jesus. Sees positive and negative definitions woven together to the extent that by the end of the novel Haze understands the "inseparability of Jesus and not-Jesus, [and] the term and its negation." Concludes that his words and actions merge and become "perceptions informed by faith."

451   Elliott, Emory. "Gesture and Style in *The Moviegoer*." *Walker Percy's Feminine Characters*. Ed. Lewis A. Lawson and Elzbieta H. Oleksy. Troy, NY: Whitston, 1995. 34-49.

Mentions, in passing, that critics have tended to overlook Percy's debt to other American writers. Focuses on Percy's own acknowledgment that he admired the works of a wide variety of American writers, including those by Flannery O'Connor.

452   Ellis, Grace W. "UnSouthern Times." *Southern Exposure* 11 (Jan.-Feb. 1983): 65-67.

Describes Microfilming Corporation of America's microfiche-based product, "50 Great American Writers." Examines the criteria for inclusion of writers by this New York Times subsidiary, and finds evidence that *The New York Times* has discriminated not only "against women, blacks, and poets," but also against Southern writers. Examines news and reviews related to Flannery O'Connor's works and finds only 22 entries, far short of the 40 to 60 entries originally required for inclusion in the set. Discusses how Southern writers' books were reviewed by *The New York Times Book Review* and notes evidence that the editorial staff appeared more interested in literary style than in substance and concern with "place." Concludes that *The New York Times* under Richard Gilman's influence showed favoritism to white, male writers who focused on "style" simply because "it's a matter of New York regionalism."

453   Ellis, James. "Watermelons and Coca-Cola in `A Good Man is Hard to Find': Holy Communion in the South." *Notes on Contemporary Literature* 8.3 (1978): 7-8.

Asserts that Edgar Teagarden is "a Southern myth counterpart to the grandmother and her preoccupation with being a lady." Discusses the significance of his carving "EAT" in the watermelons; Teagarden being "present at the first offering of Coca-Cola stock;" and the use of the name "Teagarden" as a contrast to the Garden of Gethsemane. Concludes that the grandmother's story is O'Connor's "analogue to Holy Communion."

454   Ellis, Juniper. "O'Connor and Her World: The Visual Art of *Wise Blood*." *Studies in the Humanities* 21.2 (1994): 79-95.

Offers an explication of *Wise Blood* in the context of "the visual nature of [O'Connor's] world." Suggests that her depiction of grotesque scenes parallels Roman wall paintings, and "'that movement of modern art which called itself Surrealism.'" Remarks that O'Connor's own drawings "evince the playful and violent disruption of order" and utilize qualities of "distortion, humor, and exaggeration." Illustrates, from a wide variety of examples, how her characters "appear in grotesque, visual terms," and suggests that her depiction of "human characters in terms of animals and objects," creates "a severe edge to the humor of her distorting descriptions." Notes that even in their interactions they seem distorted, as "their speech communicates little more than trite, hackneyed sentiments and their pleas for money or sex." Concludes that "the repeated patterns of studies in O'Connor's work . . . arise because critics too often focus on O'Connor's theology rather than her art." Refers to critical positions of Frederick Asals, Gilbert Muller, Carter Martin, James Mellard, Marshall Bruce Gentry, and Frederick Crews; the art of Salvador Dali, Hieronymous Bosch, and Giuseppe Arcimboldo; and comments by Mikhail Bakhtin, Wolfgang Kayser, and Ewa Kuryluk. Includes four woodblock print illustrations by O'Connor originally published in the Georgia State College for Women (GSCW) *Colonnade* and *Spectrum*.

455   Elrod, John W. "The Social Dimension of Despair." *International Kiergegaard Commentary: The Sickness Unto Death.* Ed. Robert L. Perkins. Macon, GA: Mercer UP, 1987. 107-19.

Discusses Sören Kierkegaard's concept of the "actualized self" and the suffering required to become "self-conscious" in the context of his ethical-religious theory. Uses O'Connor's "Everything That Rises Must Converge" to illustratehis theory of "small-mindedness." Suggests that the black mother's rage is based upon her "denial of the social arrangements of white supremacy." Contends that the identity of Julian's mother and the inherited white tradition require "the continuing servitude of the blacks." Finds that it is the conflict between these two identities that constitutes Kierkegaard's "notion of the spiritual ground of cultural and class conflict."

456   Emerick, Ronald. "Hawthorne and O'Connor: A Literary Kinship." *Flannery O'Connor Bulletin* 18 (1989): 46-54.

Suggests that "the territory of influences upon O'Connor has been insufficiently explored." Reviews influences mentioned by a wide variety of critics and/or O'Connor herself, and asserts that "the influence of

Nathaniel Hawthorne . . . is possibly the most pervasive of all." Offers numerous examples of her "deep interest" in Hawthorne's life and writings, including the link between herself and Hawthorne in "Introduction to *A Memoir of Mary Ann*"; her view that they both shared a similar approach and subject matter; and their mutual concern with the definition and development of the moral romance.

457   Emerick, Ronald. "*Wise Blood*: O'Connor's Romance of Alienation." *Literature and Belief* 12 (1992): 27-38.

Argues that both of O'Connor's novels, as well as all of her short stories, "participate in the genre of the American romance" as defined and reflected by Hawthorne. Contends that *Wise Blood* contains similar "cornerstones of romance: mood, setting, and character," as well as "distortion of reality to reveal essential truths, and . . . obsessed, alienated protagonists." Suggests that O'Connor views "the romance as a borderland between two worlds, the natural and the supernatural, a land suffused with truth and mystery." Discusses O'Connor's definition of romance as spiritual mystery, reflecting "the deeper realism and essential truths which the romance writer seeks to portray." Offers a reading of *Wise Blood* and compares Hazel Motes to Hawthorne's Arthur Dimmesdale and Reuben Bourne. Notes that Enoch Emery parallels Haze's career, but "on a more comic and equally grotesque level." States that Enoch is a victim of irresistible compulsions, his own loneliness, and shares with Haze the problem of searching for a meaningful existence. Concludes that Haze and Enoch are similar to Hawthorne's obsessed and guilt-ridden protagonists and serve as forerunners to O'Connor's later characters, such as O.E. Parker and Francis Marion Tarwater. Remarks that some of O'Connor's later characters also portray another typical Hawthorne-like protagonist: "the man or woman consumed with intellectual pride." Refers to André Bleikasten, Sister Kathleen Feeley, and Lewis A. Lawson.

458   Emerson, Bo. "The Secret Life of Betty Hester." *Atlanta Journal-Constitution* ("Dixie Living") 28 Mar. 1999: M1-M2.

Profiles the friendship and 250-letter, nine-year correspondence between Flannery O'Connor and Hazel Elizabeth Hester, the anonymous correspondent referred to in *The Habit of Being* as "A." Offers biographical details and compares physical and personal charactersistics that the two women had in common. Follows with a discussion of Hester's intellectual interests, religious views, and lifestyle. Includes illustrations: drawings of both Hester and O'Connor.

459   Emerson, O.B., and Marion C. Michael, comps. and eds. *Southern Literary Culture: A Bibliography of Masters' and Doctors' Theses.* University: U of Alabama P, 1979. vii, 117-21.

Provides references to 88 Master's theses and Doctoral dissertations related to O'Connor's work.

460   Emmett, Paul J. "Manifest Details and Latent Complexities in Flannery O'Connor's `A Good Man Is Hard to Find.'" *Transactions of the Wisconsin Academy of Sciences, Arts and Letters* 77 (1989): 65-75.

Cites passages from O'Connor's essay "The Nature and Aim of Fiction" that "suggest O'Connor's insistence upon the details of fiction." Asserts that scholars have not been thorough in analyzing the details of O'Connor's works, suggesting that her "subtle details are even more subtle and detailed than has been supposed." Examines "A Good Man Is Hard to Find" from the perspective that "every word is important and every detail increases the story's depth in numerous directions." Claims that the work "has, in fact, the density of a dream." Makes frequent use of Freudian theory to "penetrate the details" of the story, asserting that "the final scene cannot be accounted for until we account for the vivid details that precede it." Argues that the story's climactic scene "is a most violent rejection of the grandmother as mamma and of the maternal breast." Concludes that the story becomes one of "the ultimate defeat of the Great Mother," and that The Misfit's shooting of the grandmother is his "desperate attempt to shore up his tenuous and threatened masculinity." Notes that even as The Misfit shoots her, "at the latent level he succumbs to her" and thus "the grandmother smiles in death."

461   Emmens, Carol A. *Short Stories on Film.* Littleton, CO: Libraries Unlimited, 1978. 220-21.

Directory of films listing the following O'Connor short stories: "A Circle in the Fire," "The Comforts of Home," "The Displaced Person," and "Good Country People."

462   Engell, John. "Hawthorne and Two Types of Early American Romance." *South Atlantic Review* 57.1 (1992): 33-51.

Contends that Nathaniel Hawthorne combined "two types of early American `romance,' traditionally labeled `Gothic' and `historical,'" to create "a hybrid American `romance'--more complex and malleable than its predecessors." Includes a passing reference to O'Connor, including her among a list of distinguished writers who belong "to 'the school of Hawthorne,'" those writers who follow him "in synthesizing the disparate types and elements of early American romance in their psychological, moral, social fictions."

463   England, Eugene. "Wilderness as Salvation in Peterson's *The Canyons of Grace." Western American Literature* 19.1 (1984): 17-28.

Discusses Levi Peterson's fiction and contends that his work is the first "to explore for the American West the ancient myth of wilderness as context for explicitly religious trial and decision." Suggests that his success is due, to some extent, to being able "to do as a Mormon what Flannery O'Connor has done as a Catholic: write imaginative and skillful visions of the possibilities and paradoxes of his *theology* . . ." Compares Peterson's depiction of grace to that of Franz Kafka and O'Connor, and finds his unique in that it "has less of Kafka's absurd dream-like rationality and none of O'Connor's unconditional joy in the irrational intrusion of grace."

464   Enser, A.G.S. *Filmed Books and Plays: A List of Books and Plays From Which Films Have Been Made, 1928-1986.* Brookfield, VT: Gower, 1987. 561.

Refers to a film version of *Wise Blood* entitled "The Artificial Eye."

465   Ensor, Allison R. "Flannery O'Connor and Music." *Flannery O'Connor Bulletin* 14 (1985): 1-13.

Discusses music in O'Connor's life and examples of her "recognition of music as an important part of the lives of some of her characters," focusing on those in "A Temple of the Holy Ghost," "A Good Man Is Hard to Find," and "Revelation." Reviews her experience with musical instruments, her use of records sent to her by Thomas Stritch in 1964, references to music in her nonfiction, and songs which "would intrude into her brain" as a result of her medication. Notes that both Tom T. Shiftlet in "The Life You Save May Be Your Own" and The Misfit in "A Good Man Is Hard to Find" had been gospel singers; Enoch Emery in *Wise Blood* plays mouth organ and sings hymns he learned as a child; Onnie Jay Holy, also in *Wise Blood*, plays the guitar and had hosted a radio program; H.C. in "The Displaced Person" has a "'sweet voice for hymns'"; and Bevel Summers in "The River" sings at the baptismal service. Also briefly describes the use of music in "Enoch and the Gorilla," *Wise Blood*, "The Lame Shall Enter First," "The Enduring Chill," "Wildcat," "A Stroke of Good Fortune," and "A Late Encounter With the Enemy."

466   "Essayist Says Being Black or White Isn't So Simple." Narr. Coleman, Korva. *Weekend Edition-Sunday*. PBS. 27 Nov. 1994.

PBS host Korva Coleman reports on the controversy surrounding the publication of *The Bell Curve*. Refers to the author's "assertion that black people score lower than whites on I.Q. tests, partly because of genetic differences." Introduces guest Patricia Raybon who discusses how, in her own family, because some of her own ancestors bore children of white, African, and Indian fathers, assertions such as the author's are not so simple. Maintains that "our racial picture . . . calls into question our common labels" of black and white, and further states, "this thing called race . . . leads to goofy theories and bad science and wobbly notions of racial purity." Declares that Flannery O'Connor "wrote of our dilemma" in "The Artificial Nigger," and describes the scene in which the boy does not recognize the "nigger" because the grandfather had told him that "niggers" were black, ("the black man the boy had seen was tan"). [Television transcript # 1099-16; 804 words. A copy of this transcript has been donated to the *Flannery O'Connor Collection* in the Russell Library at Georgia College & State University.]

467   Ettin, Andrew V. "The Pastoral as Genre and Mode." *Literature and the Pastoral*. New Haven: Yale UP, 1984. 58-74.

Discusses the characteristics "of works that fit comfortably into the pastoral genre," contending that doing so "will tell us something about the work in question, if only by giving us a standard by which to measure the work's variances from convention." Examines a wide variety of literary works, including O'Connor's "A Circle in the Fire." Offers a reading of the story and suggests that it "is a more complex and less immediately recognizable modal version of the pastoral . . . [because] the pastoral qualities are natural (as in Whitman) rather than societal (as in Schiller)." Concludes that Mrs. Cope attempts to possess the pastoral world of her home, and for this attempt she pays a price: "first by not being able to enjoy what she had when she had it, and second by being forced to give up the stewardship that she interprets as ownership."

468   Evans, Elizabeth. *Anne Tyler*. New York: Twayne, 1993. 10, 11, 23, 74, 145-46.

Discusses Tyler's literary contributions as a novelist, short-story writer, and literary critic. Contains passing references to O'Connor. Comments that though the distinctive Southern accent and gesture are interesting to outsiders, it is the *ability* and quality of their writing that make writers such as Eudora Welty, Anne Tyler, and Flannery O'Connor important and enduring. Contains a paragraph comparing O'Connor's Onnie Jay Holy in *Wise Blood* to Anne Tyler's character, Brother Hope.

468a   Evans, Elizabeth. "A Note on 'A Late Encounter with the Enemy'." *Flannery O'Connor Bulletin* 26-27 (1998-2000): 136-38.

Refers to J.O. Tate's article in the 1979 issue of the *Flannery O'Connor Bulletin* titled "O'Connor's Confederate General: A Late Encounter," and his assertion that real-life "General" William Jordan Bush of Fitzgerald, Georgia served as O'Connor's model for "General" Tennessee Flintrock Sash in "A Late Encounter with the Enemy." Discusses O'Connor's use of details gleaned from Milledgeville's *Union-Recorder* and the *Atlanta Journal-Constitution* "as a ready source for the ridiculous and sublime" in her fiction. Suggests that the *Atlanta Constitution*'s "lavish" coverage of the premier of *Gone With the Wind* in December, 1939 may have influenced O'Connor to use this event as background for this story. Closes with a discussion of General Sash's vision and how the story reflects O'Connor's theme of "the action of grace and the revelation of a character's true self at the moment of death."

469   Evans, Elizabeth. Rev. of *Flannery O'Connor's Dark Comedies: The Limits of Inference*, by Carol Shloss. *Flannery O'Connor Bulletin* 10 (1981): 93-96.

Evans discusses Shloss's thesis that O'Connor failed in her efforts to write anagogical fiction "because of difficulty in second-guessing the perception of her secular readers and in anticipating how much `telling' to incorporate in the text." Suggests that those who are experienced in teaching O'Connor's fiction, "can testify that readers respond with sensitivity and understanding to the religious themes and concede the working of mystery and grace within the stories." Outlines concerns related to Shloss's analysis of O'Connor's use of the grotesque and "allusion and analogy to `establish a private topology," her method in joining "the extremes of New Criticism"; and factual errors noted in the book. Concludes that Shloss's contention that O'Connor failed as an anagogical writer reflects her own misreading of O'Connor's fiction.

470   Evans, Robert C. "Poe, O'Connor, and the Mystery of the Misfit." *Flannery O'Connor Bulletin* 25 (1996-97): 1-12.

Offers examples of the "widely divergent interpretations" of O'Connor's The Misfit, then compares him to Edgar Allan Poe's character Bon-Bon. Agrees with J.O. Tate's assumption that in creating The Misfit O'Connor was influenced by newspaper accounts of a real-life criminal, but also suggests that she was perhaps equally influenced by reading Poe's story "Bon-Bon." Lists similarities between Bon-Bon and The Misfit, then compares the underlying structures and catalogs parallels in the plots and physical details of the stories. Argues that while Poe's depiction of Satan in "Bon-Bon" is a humorous caricature of evil whom readers cannot easily take seriously, The Misfit not only threatens readers but *haunts* them.

471   Evans, Robert C., Anne C. Little, and Barbara Wiedemann. *Short Fiction: A Critical Companion.* West Cornwall, CT: Locust Hill, 1997. 181-98.

Intended to aid students assigned to read short fiction, this volume includes detailed descriptive summaries "of some of the most interesting analyses these works have provoked." Among the forty stories analyzed-- based upon being "most frequently included in classroom anthologies"-- are O'Connor's "A Good Man Is Hard to Find" (21 abstracts) and "Everything That Rises Must Converge" (16 abstracts). Provides indexes arranged "by critical approach," topic, and critic. Critics whose works are excerpted, include: Frederick Asals, Michael O. Bellamy, Robert H. Brinkmeyer, Jr., Joan T. Brittain, Preston M. Browning, Jr., Hallman B. Bryant, Michael W. Crocker, John F. Desmond, Anthony Di Renzo, William S. Doxey, Leon V. Driskell, Robert C. Evans, Kathleen Feeley, Doreen Ferlaino Fowler, Marshall Bruce Gentry, Richard Giannone, Josephine Hendin, Mary Frances Hopkins, David Jauss, Patricia Dinneen Maida, John V. McDermott, Carter W. Martin, John R. May, Marion Montgomery, Kurt R. Niland, Miles Orvell, Alice Hall Petry, Mary Jane Schenck, Martha Stephens, J.O. Tate, and Dorothy Walters.

472   Ewell, Barbara C. "Discontinuities of Region, Gender and Genre: The Short Stories of Chopin, Welty, O'Connor and Walker." *Women's International Forum* 10.5 (1987): 34.

Provides an abstract of a paper, (moderated by Suzanne Jones), which suggests that Kate Chopin, Eudora Welty, Flannery O'Connor, and Alice Walker "share the discontinuous experiences of being female, being Southern and writing in a `fragmented' genre, the short story." Examines selected stories by each author and explores "the consequences of this confluence of marginalities, of discontinuities as they converge on a subject viewed as central to female identity: motherhood." Finds that these authors' portrayals reflect "the larger concerns of the discontinuity of human experience in the modern world, where patriarchal obsessions with abstraction, control and homogeneity have decentered the experience of connectedness that motherhood implies, thus making the margins that these writers address critical to our self-understanding."

473   "Exhibit Shows Cards From O'Connor." *Union-Recorder* [Milledgeville, GA] 16 Dec. 1983: B1.

Describes the display of 14 Christmas cards sent by Flannery O'Connor to friends shown in the Special Collections Department of the Russell Library at Georgia College & State University.

474   Fairbanks, Carol. *More Women in Literature: Criticism of the Seventies.* Metuchen, NJ: Scarecrow, 1979. 269-70.

Short bibliography of articles which analyze O'Connor's depiction of women. Limited to those published in periodicals during the 1970s.

475   Fancher, Betsy. "My Flannery O'Connor." *Brown's Guide to Georgia* 3.2 (1975): 16-22.

Personal reminiscences by the author of *Blue River*, and subsequent book editor of the *Atlanta Journal-Constitution*. Describes O'Connor as "a writer who probed, in a distinctly Southern idiom, the mysterious outer reaches of reality that are the province of the prophet and poet." Relates their last meeting, one week before O'Connor's death, and their chance encounter with a drunk "prophet freak."

476   Fanknitz, Mark A.R. "Raymond Carver and the Menace of Minimalism." *CEA Critic* 52.1-2 (1989-90): 62-73.

Briefly discusses Carver's debt to O'Connor, including Barbara Lonnquist's remark "that `perhaps [Carver's] final inheritance from Flannery O'Connor has been her invincible faith.'"

477   Farley, Blanche. "Echoes of Poe, in Sawmill and Loft." *Flannery O'Connor Bulletin* 14 (1985): 14-24.

In response to Sally Fitzgerald's remark that Edgar Allan Poe and Flannery O'Connor were "radically divided in ways philosophic, spiritual, and aesthetic," Farley contends that a look at the humor they used in their work will "reinforce already established links." Compares and points out similarities in content and style between Poe's "The Gold Bug," and O'Connor's "Judgement Day." Then, relates visual similarities of "Judgement Day" to Poe's "The Spectacles." Discusses O'Connor's "inclination to juxtapose rustic country sounds with a more sophisticated speech," and suggests that both O'Connor and Poe owe a debt to "a long line of Middle Georgia humorists," including Augustus Baldwin Longstreet. Refers to their common ability to skillfully handle "the comic and the terrible within a single story," and focuses on O'Connor's expert balancing of these in the hayloft scene of "Good Country People." Argues that the leg-stealing is more shocking than violent and sets up a tension that "can perhaps be attributed to the comic effects which precede this last section so that the sense of the terrible merges with the comic . . . " Sees similarities in the "comic and terrible features" of "Good Country People" and Poe's "The Man That Was Used Up." Concludes with an exploration of the theme of vision and the use of "two archetypes: the trickster and the taboo." Refers to critical commentary by Allen Tate, Louis D. Rubin, Jr., Henri Bergson, Jack Matthews, Sigmund Freud, and Brainard Cheney.

478   Farley, Blanche. Rev. of *Conversations with Flannery O'Connor*, by Rosemary Magee. *Flannery O'Connor Bulletin* 16 (1987): 82-85.

Describes interviews and reminiscences included in Magee's collection. States that O'Connor's "'terse but careful and thoughtful replies,' fall refreshingly on our ears, and we find it instructive to consider again these occasions of the fifties and sixties when many journalists seemed at a loss to discuss her work on its own terms . . . " Suggests that the encounters show her as "the young, vulnerable, still-struggling artist, who sometimes came across as shy and reticent, whose most telling remarks . . . could be muffled by the scream of a fellow panelist's ego or cut short by a Harvey Breit." Farley refers to her own memory of hearing O'Connor speak at a luncheon, and suggests that the pieces in the book ring true as spontaneous exchanges and "a record of their times." Focuses on the pieces by Betsy Fancher, Richard Gilman, and Richard Frisbie.

478a   Farley, Blanche. Review of Mab Segrest's *My Mama's Dead Squirrel: Lesbian Essays on Southern Culture. Off Our Backs: A Woman's Newsjournal* 26.4 (1986): 23-24.

Disagrees with Segrest's assessment of Flannery O'Connor's "Good Country People." Contends that she "fails to equate O'Connor's humor with the religious views so central to her work."

479   Farmer, Joy A. "Mary Hood and the Speed of Grace: Catching Up with Flannery O'Connor." *Studies in Short Fiction* 33.1 (1996): 91-99.

Discusses O'Connor's influence on Mary Hood as reflected in her fiction. Focuses on the "powerful spiritual dimension" in each writer's work and their mutual "interest in evil and the human response to it." Points out parallels to O'Connor's *The Violent Bear It Away* in Hood's "Something Good for Ginnie." Follows with a detailed explication of Hood's "How Far She Went," noting similarities with O'Connor's "The Artificial Nigger": how the plots of both stories center on an adult denying his or her offspring; the child's "revenge" in each story; each author's allusions to Dante's *Inferno*; the depiction of "the city" as an evil place; and how the lawn ornament in O'Connor's story has a counterpart in the grandmother's dog in Hood's story.

480   Farnham, James F. "Further Evidence for the Sources of `Parker's Back.'" *Flannery O'Connor Bulletin* 12 (1983): 114-16.

Provides additional information related to Karl-Heinz Westarp's "investigation into sources for `Parker's Back'" (published in Vol. 11 of the *Flannery O'Connor Bulletin*). Reviews Westarp's findings and suggests additional facts related to the existence of an interview of an Augusta, Ga. tattoo artist--Ted Don Inman, Sr.--who told of tattooing the image of Christ on a man's back. Suggests that the article in the newspaper that O'Connor read was probably published during the spring of 1963 instead of 1960, as Westarp suggests, and probably in a newspaper other than the *Augusta Chronicle*. Recounts O'Connor's remark related to reading about the tattoo and states that he realized later that he had "witnessed an important stage in the gestation of the story."

481   Farnham, James F. "Six Unpublished Letters of Flannery O'Connor With a Commentary." *Flannery O'Connor Bulletin* 12 (1983): 60-66.

Offers the text of six unpublished letters and two Christmas cards, along with brief critical commentary. Suggests that they contain "authenticity and integrity about self, strong personal conviction and judgment, and the usual O'Connor wit." Reports that their correspondence began in the spring of 1959, when Farnham wrote O'Connor about her work, which enabled Farnham to publish an article of critical commentary. [See, "The Grotesque in Flannery O'Connor" *America* 13 May 1961: 277-81.] O'Connor's letters to Farnham deal with "the workings of divine grace" in her stories; the "nature" of her audience and how it affects her use of the grotesque; her view that both Hazel Motes and Tarwater are "saved"; her approval of Farnham's "idea that the people who take redemption literally are usually the ones who are saved"; Farnham's gifts; her response to his invitation to come to St. Francis College; and an "injunction that the job of the artist is to produce art, not to talk about art or the creative process." Refers to: William Faulkner, *To Kill a Mocking Bird*, Sister Alice ("a Dominican nun at a home for incurable cancer patients in Atlanta"), Norman Mailer, James Baldwin, C. Vann Woodward, and Hannah Arendt.

482   "February, of course is a slow month . . . " *Friends of Flannery*
       [Newsletter]. 1.3 (March 1992): 1.

       Reports a visit to Flannery O'Connor's childhood home in Savannah, GA,
       by Mrs. Lois Doner of Winnisquam, NH. Notes that Doner was a student
       with O'Connor at the Iowa writing school in 1946 and recalls her as being
       "a quiet student who even then gave promise of greatness."

483   Feeley, Kathleen. "Flannery O'Connor's Use of the Southern Literary
       Tradition." *Insight* [Journal of Notre Dame Women's College] (Japan) 14
       (1982): 1-14.

       Discusses Southern writing as a fusion of the tragic with the comic, and
       locates O'Connor's art in a tradition of Southern literature. Comments on
       "Parker's Back" to illustrate O'Connor's method of infusing mystery into
       the events of ordinary life. (Abstracted by Kayoko Watanabe).

484   Feeley, Kathleen. "`Mine is a Comic Art . . . ': Flannery O'Connor."
       Realist of Distances: Flannery O'Connor Revisited. Ed. Karl-Heinz
       Westarp and Jan Nordby Gretlund. Aarhus (Denmark): Aarhus UP, 1987.
       66-72.

       Discusses O'Connor's wry understatement, "mine is a comic art, but that
       does not detract from its seriousness." Suggests that her art consisted of a
       sketching out with words, of "a vision of reality which measures what is
       and what could be, and laughs at the infinite distance between them."

485   Feeley, Kathleen. "The Peacock and the Pole: A Tale of Displacement."
       Canadian Catholic Review 5.3 (1987): 101-04.

       Offers a reading of "The Displaced Person" that illustrates "how O'Connor
       fused the visible and the invisible worlds in her writing." Discusses the
       story in three sections. In the first, Feeley comments on the intransigence
       of Mrs. Shortley and the impact of the arrival and performance of Mr.
       Guizac. Picks up after Mrs. Shortley's death, in the second section, and
       probes Mrs. McIntyre's background and character. Suggests that she
       appears to be "an independent, self-centred woman who believes she has
       complete control of her environment." Examines the lack of understanding
       between Mrs. McIntyre and Mr. Guizac and notes that this foreshadows
       the ending. Concludes that it is "the silent collusion of Mrs. McIntyre, Mr.
       Shortley, and Sulk" which results in the death of the Pole. Declares that
       the incident "illuminates the spiritual country of the Pole and the
       displacement of Mrs. McIntyre in that faith-impregnated world." Closes

with a brief discussion of the black figures, the symbolic meaning of the peacock, and the observation that O'Connor's real achievement--illustrated by this work--is that she could tell a good story.

486   Feeley, Margaret Peller. "Flannery O'Connor's *Wise Blood*: The Negative Way." *Southern Quarterly* 17.2 (1979): 104-22.

Examines *Wise Blood* as "a Christian *commedia* in which the action begins at the low level of comedy but becomes increasingly other-worldly." Contends that the path that Hazel Motes walks as a Christian pilgrim, is "a well-worn one, a comic version, sometimes inversion, of the Negative Way (*via negativa*) or the way of rejection." Suggests that the Negative Way merges with the "Way of Affirmation," as O'Connor again "seems to dangle the possibility of salvation in front of her characters and then, with a bitter twist, snatch life away."

487   Felder, Deborah G. "Flannery O'Connor." *The 100 Most Influential Women of all Time: A Ranking of Past and Present*. Secaucus, NJ: Carol Pub. Group, 1996. 285-88.

Offers a biographical sketch of O'Connor along with a photograph of her sitting in a rocking chair and a familiar quote from an essay in *Mystery and Manners* regarding her focus in writing upon "'the action of grace in territory held largely by the devil.'" The author ranks O'Connor 80th on her list of 100 most influential women, and regards her as "one of the most important fiction writers of post-World War II American literature." Finds her fiction to be "some of the most original and provocative writing of the twentieth century." [In her introductory remarks, Felder states that her ranking reflects results of a survey of "women's studies department chairs and professors in American colleges and universities."]

488   Fennell, Janice C., Nancy Davis Bray, Sarah E. Gordon and R. Neil Scott. "Proposal for the Preservation and Conservation of the Flannery O'Connor Manuscripts (with Performance Reports)." Ms. Nov., 1989, *Flannery O'Connor Collection*, Russell Library, Georgia College & State University, Milledgeville, GA.

Proposal and reports related to Georgia College & State University's successful application for a "Preservation Grant" from the National Endowment for the Humanities. Describes how, under the direction of Janice C. Fennell, Project Director, grant funds were to be used to make duplicate preservation copies of 7,000 pages of O'Connor manuscripts and galley proofs; microfilm copies of the manuscripts and other materials indexed in the Driggers Catalog (excluding *Habit of Being* materials); and to deacidify, treat, and encapsulate 5,925 pages of O'Connor manuscripts. Georgia College & State University provided matching funds for the award from the NEH and the project was completed in 1991--largely through work by Nancy Davis Bray, Curator of the *Flannery O'Connor Collection* at Georgia College & State University.

489   Fennick, Ruth. "First Harvest: Flannery O'Connor's `The Crop.'" *English Journal* 74.2 (1985): 45-50.

Asserts that high school literature anthologies usually do not include works by O'Connor because they are often considered "not sufficiently `classic,'" too violent, or "too theologically narrow." Urges teachers to consider using some of O'Connor's early stories. States that these "generally lack the extreme violence, the shockingly grotesque characters and the somewhat heavy dose of `redemption through grace.'" Submits that "The Crop" is particularly appropriate as it previews qualities found in her later fiction in its symbolism, characters, comic style, and themes of "self-deception if not self realization." Offers an extensive analysis of the story, and cites critical assessments by Mary Lambert Warner, Frederick Asals, and Stuart L. Burns.

490   Fenster, Valmai Kirkham. *Guide to American Literature*. Littleton, CO: Libraries Unlimited, 1983. 173-75.

Offers undergraduate and graduate students a descriptively annotated guide to materials on American literature published through May 1982. The *Guide* is divided into two parts: the first outlines a strategy for using the library for literary research, including citations and descriptions of selected sources. The second lists primary and secondary materials related to 100 "literary authors," including Flannery O'Connor. Provides in the Part II entry for O'Connor, titles and the date of publication for her writings in both separate and collected edition format; reference to the "extensive collection" of papers in the Russell Library archives of Georgia College & State University in Milledgeville; bibliographic citations for fifteen books of criticism; reference to bibliographies on O'Connor's work (by Robert E. Golden and David Farmer); and suggests that readers view the *Flannery O'Connor Bulletin* as "a clearinghouse for bibliographical and critical contributions" related to O'Connor's life and work.

491   Ferguson, Paul F. "By Their Names You Shall Know Them: Flannery O'Connor's Onomastic Strategies." *Literary Onomastics Studies* 7 (1980): 87-109.

States that O'Connor used names to "reveal the things of God . . . and the concrete nature of evil." Discusses the significance of namelessness and lists categories of names in O'Connor's fiction, including those drawn from the Old and New Testaments and history, with a final category for "those which are metaphorical or paronomasic." Concludes that "Onomastics for O'Connor is . . . not merely an ornamental device but is the most vital aspect of her art."

492   Ferguson, Paul F. "Onomastic Revisions in Flannery O'Connor's *Wise Blood*." *Literary Onomastics Studies* 13 (1986): 97-110.

Discusses the appearance and publication dates of O'Connor's early stories. Defends *Wise Blood* as being more than "a number of `short stories strung together to form a novel,'" as alleged by Melvin J. Friedman. Examines the onomastic revisions O'Connor made between writing the short stories and the novel. Suggests that because the given names of some of the characters do not change, there appears to be "a common thematic link" between the stories and *Wise Blood*. Analyzes each name, its possible meanings and associations, and notes the biblical origins for particular names. Concludes that what O'Connor "learned about names and naming in the process of revising *Wise Blood* contributed significantly to her development as a mature writer."

493   Ficken, Carl. "Flannery O'Connor: `Parker's Back.'" *God's Story and Modern Literature: Reading Fiction in Community*. Philadelphia: Fortress, 1985. 120-30.

Describes O'Connor's Christian perspective and how she attempted to express her faith in her writing. Asserts that "though her literary production was relatively small, she is widely recognized as one of the most important Southern writers of the past half-century and one who made a significant contribution to our national literature." Finds her work is particularly relevant in how "she understood Christianity, its relation to culture, and the function of the believing writer in that context." Examines and offers a careful reading of "Parker's Back." Focuses on its explicit Christian references and how it reaches beyond allusion toward theological substance. Concludes that O'Connor offers readers a double opportunity in this story. First, readers can "apply all the principles of literary criticism--analyzing style, characterization, allusion, structure and other elements of fiction--just as we would with any other writer" and enjoy O'Connor's work as a story. Further, Christian readers may wish to explore the implications of the image of Christ on Parker's back, the meaning behind Parker's full name, and "consider what it might mean if Parker were O'Connor's representation of a modern disciple."

494   Ficken, Carl. "Theology in Flannery O'Connor's *The Habit of Being*."
            Christianity & Literature 30.2 (1981): 51-63.

Using an *Atlantic* reviewer's comment on *The Habit of Being* as a starting
point, Ficken argues that the letters might indeed "'take readers further
into the forests of theology than most non-Catholics will want to travel.'"
Interprets the "forests" analogy as a positive one, rich in variety and
surprises. Comments on O'Connor's context, her orthodoxy, methodology,
and expression of Christian Realism.

495   Fickett, Harold. "Flannery O'Connor: Guardian Angel." *Reality and the
            Vision*. Ed. Philip Yancey. Dallas: Word, 1990. 70-79.

The author describes the influence that O'Connor's writings have had on
his own literary efforts and personal beliefs. Finds that O'Connor's
presence gives him "hope that one could be [both] a believer and a writer
of serious fiction." Refers to O'Connor as a "guardian angel," one who
helped him examine his own ideas and history to more fully understand
how to live simultaneously in both the religious and secular worlds.
Discusses John Hawkes's correspondence with O'Connor and his
acknowledgement of the role of her Christian belief in her art; the author's
own sense of apartness, which stemmed from growing up as a
fundamentalist in Los Angeles; the humor in O'Connor's fiction and his
"identification with her times"; O'Connor's perspective on her art as "a
form of thinking" that did not allow it to be "'used' to convey messages";
her use of an epiphany to illustrate a character's moment of insight; and the
role of O'Connor's art in helping the author shape his own work. Reviews
patterns in O'Connor's fiction, noting "how the human will to power--and
the pride that becomes the personality of this will--extends its deadly
consequences into social and even international affairs." Discusses "The
Displaced Person," *Wise Blood*, "The River," and "Parker's Back."
Concludes that because readers "experience the need for God in
O'Connor's work," they find themselves opening up to the possibility of
God's presence. [Rpt. in *The Classics We've Read, The Difference They've
Made*. Ed. Philip Yancey. New York: McCracken, 1993. 93-105.]

496   Field, James A. "Preparing for Liturgy: Part Two, A Timely Whack on the
            Head." *Today's Parish* 25.6 (1993): 31-33.

Discusses the results of a Gallup poll which indicated that "a staggering
two-thirds of active Catholics do not believe with the church in regard to
the real presence of Christ in the Eucharist." Suggests that this finding
"represents a mortal danger" to church members' life together and is "a
force undermining the deepest foundations" of the traditions of the church.

Includes a discussion of "A Temple of the Holy Ghost," finding it to be a story "about the brokenness of humanity" and how "the radical assent to humanity [is] accomplished for us by Christ." Suggests that the story "is deeply autobiographical," and that there is "no finer reflection on the real presence around." Contends that O'Connor broaches the topic of the presence of Christ "in such a subversive manner that the story can be received with enthusiasm by a seminar room full of atheists at sophisticated universities," a group whose members "might think this a tale of psychological integration rather than a parable of salvation." Explicates the story and argues that it illustrates how O'Connor "understood with every fibre of her being what has been called 'the Catholic thing,' this sense that we are all broken vessels, all wounded, all in need of healing and wholeness, and it is precisely in our brokenness that we are most loved by God."

497   Fincher, Cheryl. "Flannery's Writing is Still Siren Song to Believers." *Macon (GA) Telegraph* 15 Nov. 1998: 1E, 6E.

Discusses Georgia College & State University's role as the center of Flannery O'Connor studies, and focuses upon its support of "the longest-running publication in the United States to a female writer," the *Flannery O'Connor Bulletin.* Quotes comments by *Bulletin* editor Sarah Gordon that O'Connor would probably be "very amused" at all the O'Connor "seekers" who come to Milledgeville to visit. Refers to novelist Joseph Torchia's admiration for O'Connor and notes that O'Connor's more renowned fans include actors Tommy Lee Jones and Holly Hunter, singer Bruce Springsteen, and movie director John Waters.

498   Finholt, Richard. "Northrop Frye's Theory of Countervailing Tendencies: A New Look at the Mode and Myth Essays." *Genre* 13 (Summer 1980): 203-57.

Includes a discussion of "A Good Man Is Hard to Find," focusing on how "the shattering impact" of the story is derived from O'Connor's refusal to provide the reader "with anyone, besides The Misfit, who might represent anything approximating a reliable point of view."

499   Finley, Mitch. *Season of New Beginnings*. Mineola, NY: Resurrection Press, 1997. 13-14, 20-21, 27-28, 34-35, 41-42, 48-49, 55-56, 61-62, 63.

Intended to serve as "a spiritual compass" for readers during the forty-day season of Lent, this slim volume offers daily "mini-meditations" which begin with "a brief quotation" from the writings of such influential figures as Flannery O'Connor, Saint Augustine of Hippo, Dorothy Day, Vincent van Gogh, Saint Teresa of Avila, and John Henry Newman. All of O'Connor's quotes are taken from her correspondence published in *The Habit of Being*, edited by Sally Fitzgerald.

500   Finn, James. "Personal Perspective 2: Alice Walker & Flight 007." *Christianity and Crisis* 31 Oct. 1983: 397-98.

Discusses Alice Walker's essay "Beyond the Peacock: The Reconstruction of Flannery O'Connor," published in her collection *In Search of Our Mothers' Gardens*. Reviews the parallel literary lives of these two authors; comments on Walker's appreciation of O'Connor; then takes issue with Walker's comments that the Catholic church is annoyed that in O'Connor's stories "not only does good not triumph, it is usually not present." Argues that Walker's statement "has struck a false note," which passes another stereotype on to her readers. Compares Walker's response to that of stereotypes found in many political discussions such as those related to the downing of Korean Air Lines flight 007, and urges readers to remember that it is better to "start with the facts" not with stereotypes.

501   Fiondella, Maris G. "Augustine, the `Letter,' and the Failure of Love in Flannery O'Connor's `The Artificial Nigger.'" *Studies in Short Fiction* 24.2 (1987): 119-29.

Argues that "The Artificial Nigger" is best viewed as a study of narcissism presented ironically, and discusses the story "in light of Augustine's writings on sin and the `letter.'" Suggests that O'Connor's stories illustrate attempts by characters to secure a "`place' that allows them to dominate or master others." Discusses how several begin with a solitary character surveying the landscape, implying a perspective based on an assumption that "the world can be possessed and manipulated through discourse." Suggests that the principal irony found in her stories is the clash between an omniscient perspective and the content of the narrative sentences. Claims that this discrepancy calls attention "to matters of language (rhetorical figuration, verbal mood) that reveal how meaning is formed." Proposes that O'Connor "addresses religious allusion to readers above the heads of the characters, offering a metalanguage that comments on Mr. Head's viewpoint or subject-position." Finds Mr. Head to be "a divided subject who has denied ego and identified with an ideal whose language has the power to constitute a world." Declares that there is an element of irony in the self-imputed redemption in that readers are forced "to disidentify with Mr. Head's viewpoint and to become reflexive." Submits that the "nigger" becomes a scapegoat for Mr. Head and "is finally `artificial' because it represents a type of signification that permits any subject, including readers, to exchange self-knowledge for a more desirable representation and to act on that basis in reality." Concludes that through this story O'Connor allows readers to recognize and embrace difference, both in the world and in written text, and "construe meaning `as if'" for themselves.

501a   Fishman, Jane. "Where People Go When They Just Can't Get Enough." *Savannah Morning News* 28 Feb. 1997: D1+.

Describes the fascination that visitors to the Flannery O'Connor Room at Georgia College & State University have regarding Flannery O'Connor's life and the many questions they ask regarding her childhood in Savannah. Recounts the establishment of the Flannery O'Connor Home Foundation and the efforts of Hugh Brown, Robert Burnett, and Robert Strozier to purchase--through the Foundation--the Savannah townhouse on East Charlton Street in which O'Connor lived during the first twelve years of her life. Outlines their plans for the home to be turned into "a cultural center for the arts." Includes a photograph of the home with the State historic marker in the foreground.

502   Fitzgerald, Robert. "Flannery O'Connor: A Memoir." *The Third Kind of Knowledge: Memoirs & Selected Writings*. Ed. Penelope Laurans Fitzgerald. New York: New Directions, 1993. 105-24.

Offers an essay, divided into six sections, originally published as Fitzgerald's "Introduction" to *Everything That Rises Must Converge* [New York: Farrar, Straus & Giroux, 1966. vii-xxxiv]. Provides extensive details regarding Flannery O'Connor's life and work from the time she moved in with Robert and Sally Fitzgerald in 1949 at the age of twenty-four until her death in 1964. Also includes considerable information about her childhood and home in Milledgeville, Georgia. Discusses her father, Edward F. O'Connor; her grandfather, Peter Cline; her mother, Regina Cline O'Connor; and a variety of other family members, including Mrs. Hugh Treanor, Kate L. Treanor, and Margaret Ida Treanor. Also refers to the pen drawings of George Price; Andrew Lytle's article and Flannery's work with Caroline Gordon; Dr. Arthur J. Merrill's efforts to pull Flannery through her first bout with Lupus and her subsequent setbacks with the disease and various medication and treatments; Isaac Rosenfeld's review of *Wise Blood* in *The New Republic*; her correspondence with the Fitzgerald's about her work; the award to her of a Kenyon Fellowship; her trip to Europe (funded by "Cousin Katie" of Savannah) and audience with Pope Pius XII; Fitzgerald's comments regarding "the beauty" in her writing; O'Connor's parody of the Existentialist point of view as described by Brainard Cheney in his article in *Sewanee Review*; the similarity of her work to that of T.S. Eliot; and, closes with critical comments on a number of the stories included in *Everything That Rises Must Converge*. Includes a portrait-style photograph of Flannery O'Connor taken about 1946. [Note: Selections rpt. in *Women Writers of the Short Story: A Collection of Critical Essays*. Ed. Heather McClave. Englewood Cliffs, NJ: Prentice-Hall, 1980. 124-35.]

503   Fitzgerald, Robert. Interview. "The Art of Translation I: Robert Fitzgerald." By Edwin Frank and Andrew McCord. *Paris Review* 94 (1984): 38-65.

Edited transcript of an interview with Robert Fitzgerald which focuses on his background, mentors, and work. Fitzgerald quotes O'Connor regarding his "moments of vision as a young man," referring to her statement that "'the church is custodian of the sense of life as a mystery.'" Fitzgerald also responds to a question near the end of the interview concerning how he came to know Flannery O'Connor. States that he met O'Connor when she came to New York to visit them with Cal (Robert) Lowell, whom she met at Yaddo: "they'd been at Yaddo and there was a dustup at Yaddo in which I'm afraid Lowell had begun to go off his trolley." Recalls that they "met Flannery in the course of that," and developed a friendship with her "independently of Lowell." When asked by the interviewer if he had served as "something of a counselor" to O'Connor, Fitzgerald responds, "No, no, she knew what she was about." He states, however, that he supplied O'Connor with her title "The Life You Save May Be Your Own" from a road sign he saw, and also suggested revisions for *The Violent Bear It Away*, which she incorporated. Refers to her a "a good friend" whose work was "always great fun to see."

504   Fitzgerald, Sally. "The Andalusian Sibyl." *Southern Living* 18.5 (1983): 164-65.

Describes "Andalusia," O'Connor's family farm, located just outside Milledgeville, Georgia. Offers a description of the interior of the farmhouse during the time that Flannery lived there.

505   Fitzgerald, Sally. "Assumption and Experience: Flannery O'Connor's `A Temple of the Holy Ghost.'" *Cross Currents* 31 (Winter 1981-82): 423-32.

Discusses O'Connor's beliefs as a Catholic and how these beliefs relate to her fictional art. Analyzes "A Temple of the Holy Ghost," asserting that it is the only O'Connor story which "openly examines the experience of a Catholic." Contends that the story also appears to have been written "from what had been both accepted and experienced" by O'Connor herself. Suggests meanings for the protagonist's actions and discusses the symbolism of the sun, the hermaphrodite, and the Sacred Host. Offers two interpretations as to why O'Connor chose the hermaphrodite as the focal character: the freak may be a "holy figure," to represent "the holiness of sexuality in human life"; or the hermaphrodite may symbolize the celibacy of those who accept religious vows.

506   Fitzgerald, Sally. "Degrees and Kinds: Introduction." *Realist of Distances: Flannery O'Connor Revisited*. Ed. Karl-Heinz Westarp and Jan Nordby Gretlund. Aarhus (Denmark): Aarhus UP, 1987. 11-16.

Describes the location and circumstances of the August, 1984 gathering of European and American scholars near Sonderborg, Denmark, which resulted in the collected essay volume edited by Westarp and Gretlund. Reviews trends in O'Connor criticism and comments on what O'Connor would have probably thought of "all this scholastic uproar."

507   Fitzgerald, Sally. *Flannery O'Connor and Her Unwritten Sacred History*. Birmingham, AL: Oxmoor House, 1984.

Essay written to serve as an introduction to O'Connor for purchasers of the "Southern Classics Library" edition of *Everything That Rises Must Converge*. Describes O'Connor's Georgia roots and cultural heritage, her use of local rural dialect, how her Catholic faith provided her with a "point of view" from which to write, and her attitude toward her characters. Provides brief, insightful summaries of *Wise Blood*, *A Good Man Is Hard to Find*, *The Violent Bear It Away*, and *Everything That Rises Must Converge*. Illustrations: O'Connor at ages three and seven; of her reading a newspaper on her front porch later in life; and her self-portrait with a pheasant cock.

508   Fitzgerald, Sally. "Flannery O'Connor: Four Letters to a Stranger." *Canadian Catholic Review* 5.3 (1987): 85-90.

Discusses O'Connor's willingness and critical method used to analyze and respond to the manuscripts writers sent to her for comment. Refers to various other requests as well, including those of the "spiritually bewildered." Reprints four letters sent to Alfred Corn, a freshman in college at the time, who had heard her speak to an English class at Emory University in May, 1962. Suggests that the letters are those of a believer to one experiencing fear of losing his faith. Notes that Corn later became a respected writer who produced several books of poetry.

509   Fitzgerald, Sally. "Flannery O'Connor: Patterns of Friendship, Patterns of Love." *Georgia Review* 52.3 (1998): 407-25.

Fitzgerald offers a biographical sketch, drawing upon personal recollection, interviews, and correspondence from many of O'Connor's close friends and literary colleagues. Suggests that during the course of her life O'Connor "gathered to herself a great flock of friends, as various as they were devoted, to whom she in turn dedicated almost as much time and energy as she did to her fiction." Adds that, because some of the letters published in *The Habit of Being* raised questions in some readers' minds, it is appropriate (in this article) "to introduce those of Flannery's friends who might most interest--and inform--her readers" and to try to correct "some misconceptions in the process." Finds evidence "to suggest a recurring pattern of pain and disappointment in O'Connor's deepest emotional relationships" (particularly with the few men she admired enough to consider pursuing a romantic relationship). Notes that she seemed to have been blessed with a series of friends and guardians "provided especially to further her efforts" and "to see that she reached the hands of the next appointed guardian." Refers to and describes her relationships with a wide variety of friends, mentors, and colleagues, in particular, Betty Boyd, John Sullivan, George Beiswanger, Robie Macauley, Paul Griffith, Clifford Wright, Elizabeth Fenwick, Edward Maisel, Robert Lowell, Robert Fitzgerald, Erik Langkjaer, "A," and Maryat Lee.

510   Fitzgerald, Sally. "Flannery O'Connor's Letters." *Second Century Radcliffe News* 1.1 (1980): 14-15.

Discusses the compilation and selection of O'Connor's letters for *The Habit of Being*. Describes them as "celebrations of life and of work, of faith and of friendship, and . . . what these things meant to her." Provides a brief biographical sketch, focusing on her lupus erythematosus, then reviews the difficulties of the *Habit of Being* book project. Characterizes the process of gathering the correspondence as an unsystematic "treasure hunt" in which the widely scattered letters were traced following clues and word-of-mouth referrals. Concludes with an overview of the working relationship she developed with Flannery's mother, Regina Cline O'Connor, and their differing perspectives related to Flannery's letters.

511   Fitzgerald, Sally. "The Habit of Being." *Flannery O'Connor Bulletin* 6 (1977): 5-16.

Sally Fitzgerald discusses the circumstances of, and her thoughts on, the publication of Flannery O'Connor's letters in *The Habit of Being*. States that the idea had originally been suggested to her and her husband, Robert Fitzgerald, that O'Connor's letters be included in a volume of her non-fiction writings. However, because they felt that "the time had not come for the publication of her correspondence," only selections of her non-fiction work were included in *Mystery and Manners*. Reports that later, after observing how "misinterpretations proliferated" and how O'Connor remained to readers "a somewhat mysterious figure . . . still vulnerable to distant guesses on the nature of her work, to say nothing of the nature of her being," the Fitzgeralds felt that "the time had come to make her voice heard again." Acknowledges the support of O'Connor's publishers and her mother, Regina Cline O'Connor, in granting her the "privilege" of selecting letters. Offers her opinion on how the letters may serve to convey O'Connor's "living presence," and serve as "a self-portrait in words." Then, outlines various areas of content and insights offered in the letters: the impression the letters provide of O'Connor possessing "a *joie de vivre*, rooted in her talent and the possibilities of her work"; how, while the "world of the absurd delighted her," and she "could write fine country talk," she could just as easily "set forth with strength and clarity, and in enviable English style, a theological insight that shed light in every direction"; her correspondence with, and reliance upon those "whose literary judgement she respected"; her discussions, in the letters, of books with friends; and how her "real love for the Church" and "impatience with fatuity and obtuseness among Catholics" is evident. Closes with a discussion of Flannery's move home to Georgia; the impact of her "permanently curtailed life"; reasons "The Artificial Nigger" is particularly important; and how a passage from Jacques Maritain's *Art & Scholasticism* suggested the title, *The Habit of Being*, for the collection.

512   Fitzgerald, Sally. "Happy Endings." *Image: A Journal of the Arts and Religion* 16 (Summer 1997): 73-80.

Contends that while many readers may think that things "end badly" for many characters in O'Connor's fiction, when viewed in the context of O'Connor's faith, these same characters have instead "happy endings." Discusses death in the "larger context of ongoing life, both in eternity, and in space and time," and how O'Connor's faith taught her that "both death and life must be understood in the context of divine love." Uses these ideas as a structure for an explication of "A Good Man Is Hard to Find." Comments on how O'Connor found the "germ of the story" in newspaper articles in 1953: one of a little girl who had won a prize for performing the song "A Good Man Is Hard to Find"; a second of a "small-time robber who called himself 'The Misfit'"; and a third about the criminal "'aloose' in the region" named James Francis "(Three-Gun)" Hill. Offers a summary of the events that occur in the story and comments on how each reflects tenets of O'Connor's religious views and faith. Sees the family as benefitting from the "`terrible mercy'" of God and the grandmother's death as an "unquestionably `a happy death,' something the author, like all Catholics, had been taught to pray for every day of her life."

513   Fitzgerald, Sally. Introduction. *The Habit of Being*. Ed. Sally Fitzgerald. New York: Farrar, Straus and Giroux, 1979.

Fitzgerald offers an essay which provides a useful framework for readers so that they might better appreciate the letters included in *The Habit of Being*. Refers to a remark by Katherine Anne Porter that photographs of Flannery "show nothing of her grace," and suggests that perhaps O'Connor's true likeness "will be painted by herself, a self-portrait in words . . . in her letters." Offers recollections of the time when Flannery lived with Robert and Sally Fitzgerald in Connecticut, noting the importance that letters held for her, especially the daily correspondence she carried on with her mother. Then, uses the letters to generalize aspects of O'Connor's work and life: her personality and sense of humor; her continued reliance upon friends "whose literary judgement she respected"; her reputation for answering "any letter someone had taken the time to write to her"; and her respect for the Church. Discusses O'Connor's reluctance to return to the South, her eventual acceptance of this necessity, her work habits, and love for peafowl while living at Andalusia. Closes with a discussion of "The Artificial Nigger" and Jacques Maritain's *Art and Scholasticism*. Suggests that Maritain influenced O'Connor's thinking regarding the concept of the "habit of art." Concludes that the letters reflect O'Connor's taking the "habit of art" one step further, to become a "habit of being."

514   Fitzgerald, Sally. Introduction. *Three by Flannery O'Connor*." *Three by Flannery O'Connor*. New York: Signet-NAL, 1983. vii-xxxviv.

A three-part essay offering a well-rounded, insightful introduction to O'Connor's *Wise Blood*, *The Violent Bear It Away*, and *Everything That Rises Must Converge*. Part I describes O'Connor's arrival in Iowa in 1945, Paul Engle's initial reaction to her work, and how her Iowa Writers Workshop colleagues "found her affable and friendly." Lists writers she read during those years and comments on her interest in Nathaniel Hawthorne, Henry James, Joseph Conrad, Edgar Allan Poe, and T.S. Eliot in particular. Offers evidence that suggests *Wise Blood* and "The Train" may have been intended as part of a trilogy whose hero was based upon the speaker in Eliot's *The Waste Land*. States that by the time the book was completed, however, only traces of Eliot's work remained. Recounts the disappointing reception that *Wise Blood* received, but notes that other writers--such as Robert Lowell, John Crowe Ransom, Caroline Gordon, and J.F. Powers--"greatly admired it, and recognized the emergence of a strong and original talent." Part II focuses on the implications for O'Connor's writing of her struggle with lupus erythematosus. Suggests that her decision to "`write about folks'" instead of freaks, her move to Georgia to live with her mother, and her reliance upon stories in the local newspaper and the conversations heard from her fellow townspeople instead of "literary sources," were all a result of this "reversal." Refers to "You Can't Be Any Poorer Than Dead," and offers a reading of *The Violent Bear It Away*, for which this story served as the basis for the first chapter. Outlines O'Connor's religious concerns reflected in the book and follows with a discussion of O'Connor's essay, "The Fiction Writer and His Country." Part III describes the first chapter of the third novel O'Connor hoped to complete but never did. Uses it to speculate on the direction O'Connor's art may have taken. Closes with comments on stories from her posthumously published collection, *Everything That Rises Must Converge*, including, "Everything That Rises Must Converge," "Greenleaf," "A View of the Woods," "The Enduring Chill," "The Comforts of Home," "The Lame Shall Enter First," "Revelation," "Parker's Back," and "Judgement Day."

515   Fitzgerald, Sally."The Invisible Father." *Christianity & Literature* 47.1 (1997): 5-18.

Discusses Flannery O'Connor's parents and how their roots, religious beliefs, and general social and economic circumstances may have influenced her sense of self and personality. Defends O'Connor's writings against contentions that "repressed rage against her mother" might have been a "motivating drive in her writing life." Pieces together anecdotes from family members and friends which illustrate family circumstances, including those from Caroline Gordon, Regina O'Connor, a family baby-sitter, and Edward O'Connor's sister. Considers the impact of her father's death upon Flannery, and offers evidence from letters and a notebook of how much she adored him. Finds in Flannery's view of her father, Edward Francis O'Connor, "the background for the divine imagery that was such a factor in the formation of her mind and sense of life," and that, in turn, provided her with "the substructure of her imagination."

516   Fitzgerald, Sally. "A Letter From Flannery O'Connor About *Wise Blood*." *Katallagete* 9 (Summer 1985): 5-13.

Fitzgerald provides remarks edited from a tape of a class discussion at Berea College in March, 1985. Focuses on a letter written by O'Connor in 1954 to the editor of *Epoch* in which she discusses *Wise Blood*. Fitzgerald offers insights related to O'Connor's view of Catholicism; Hazel Motes's actions in *Wise Blood*; and the symbolic meaning of his car. Refers to Father Feeney of Boston's Saint Paul's Church and *The Violent Bear It Away*. Following the lecture, Fitzgerald supplies excerpts of answers to fifteen *Wise Blood*-related questions posed to her.

517   Fitzgerald, Sally. "Letter Watching." [Georgia College & State University] *Columns* 24.1 (1979): 4-7.

Following a brief biographical sketch provided by the editor in the introduction, Fitzgerald reflects upon her lifelong interest in studying people, her experience during World War II as a "censor of cables," and laments how "communication is quickly becoming ethereal, air-borne, [and] telephonic." She then voices her pleasure in knowing that Flannery O'Connor's time preceded this modern age of electronic communication and describes how her letters were acquired for *The Habit of Being*. Specifically mentioned is correspondence held by Elizabeth McKee, Maryat Lee, Robert Giroux, and the anonymous correspondent referred to in the volume as "A." Contends that the letters from O'Connor to "A" form "the backbone of the collection." Notes that Caroline Gordon Tate had loaned her correspondence from O'Connor to a graduate student "who simply never returned them." Concludes that the opportunity to collect the letters for the volume was a privilege. Concludes that the letters "show once and for all that she [O'Connor] was a fine, funny, kind and friendly girl of genius and of deep faith."

518   Fitzgerald, Sally. "Letters of Flannery O'Connor." *Sign* 58.8 (1979): 18-22.

Selected excerpts of letters from *The Habit of Being* detailing correspondence between O'Connor and an anonymous friend who was outside the Church. Letters relate to the woman being drawn into the Church by O'Connor, and then subsequently leaving. Fitzgerald provides a brief introduction, describing O'Connor in the letters as "`calm, slow, funny, courteous, both modest and very sure of herself, intense, sharply penetrating, devout but never pietistic, downright, occasionally fierce, and honest in a way that restores honor to the world.'"

519   Fitzgerald, Sally. "A Master Class: From the Correspondence of Caroline Gordon and Flannery O'Connor." *Georgia Review* 33.4 (1979): 827-46.

Reprints letters between O'Connor and Caroline Gordon [Tate] focusing on Gordon's suggestions for improving *Wise Blood*--letters that had not been available for inclusion in *The Habit of Being*. Declares that the correspondence serves as a "kind of Master Class" between a generous and brilliant teacher and a "student of genius." Refers to Robert Fitzgerald, Robert Giroux, Walker Percy, Franz Kafka, Anton Chekhov, Marcel Proust, Stephen Crane, Gustave Flaubert, and Henry James.

520   Fitzgerald, Sally. "O'Connor, Flannery." *Notable American Women: The Modern Period*. Vol. 4. Ed. Barbara Sicherman and Carol Hurd Green. Cambridge, MA: Harvard UP, 1980. 512-15.

Provides an insightful biographical sketch of O'Connor: the impact of her father's death; the onset and progression of her illness; and a brief synopsis of her two novels. Closes with the observation that O'Connor's focus and concern was primarily on other individuals, not the social concerns of groups. Declares that O'Connor "gave to her lonely, freakish, often maimed, and usually violent characters a dignity and significance that can never again be denied them."

521   Fitzgerald, Sally. "Other Peoples' Mail: Collecting Letters." *Bunting Institute Working Papers*. Cambridge, MA: Mary Ingram Bunting Institute, Radcliffe College, 1979.

Fitzgerald describes her experiences related to the publication of letters written by Flannery O'Connor in *The Habit of Being*. Focuses on her collaboration with Regina Cline O'Connor, Flannery's mother, to select letters appropriate for publication, and outlines the process by which she located, identified, and contacted a number of O'Connor's correspondents, including: Janet McKane, O'Connor's "longtime literary agent" [Elizabeth McKee], an unnamed "earnest young movie-maker," the "Director of the Iowa Writer's Workshop" [Paul Engle], Robert Lowell, the anonymous correspondent referred to in *The Habit of Being* as "A," and Caroline Gordon. Acknowledges the difficulties that Regina Cline O'Connor overcame, related to her own private, reticent nature, to work in a cooperative manner with Fitzgerald on this publication project. Closes with brief remarks on a few of the letters that "got away or remained hidden in the shadows."

522   Fitzgerald, Sally. "The Owl and the Nightingale." *Flannery O'Connor Bulletin* 13 (1984): 44-58.

Outlines and discusses possible influences on O'Connor's work, including: Franz Kafka's *Collected Stories*; Nathanael West's *Miss Lonelyhearts* and *A Cool Million*; Joseph Conrad's "The Heart of Darkness"; Edgar Alan Poe's "wild, black `comedy'" and tales of the macabre; Stephen Crane's

The Red Badge of Courage and "The Open Boat"; and T.S. Eliot's *The Waste Land*. Cites evidence--some of which is acknowledged as from J.O. Tate's dissertation--to support the suggestion that O'Connor "found in T.S. Eliot perhaps the most important mentor of all." States that she "read and absorbed everything he wrote" and was heartened by "the very fact of his existence on the literary scene." Ties *Wise Blood* to *The Waste Land*, showing parallels in the plot and use of similar characters. Concludes that while Poe may have "'set her going,'" and West "greatly helped to release the power that emerges for the first time in the finished *Wise Blood*, "it was Eliot and his *Waste Land* who provided for her the first impetus to write such a book as *Wise Blood* at all."

523   Fitzgerald, Sally. "The Penetration of Experience: Permutations in the Fiction of Flannery O'Connor." *Bunting Institute Working Papers*. Cambridge, MA: Mary Ingram Bunting Institute, Radcliffe College, 1980.

Suggests that O'Connor was a writer who not only "knew that real and enduring excitement lay in the penetration of experience, more than in its mere accumulation," but one who used meaning derived from "the smallest things, as well as tremendous events . . . as building material" for the "complex, multidimensional structures" that comprised her literary art. Offers examples to support this contention: how hearing a reference to "'an artificial nigger' on the lawn" of a house led to her use of the phrase as "a symbol or metaphor for something far larger and more mysterious"; how the death of her father when she was fifteen, may have influenced her to have so few "whole" families in her stories; how growing-up with "much older" relatives allowed her to observe the conflicts that develop between generations, as seen and depicted in her work; how her Catholic faith influenced her creation of characters, episodes, and themes; how her own experience of arriving by train from the North, deathly ill from her first bout with Lupus, informed her description of Asbury's arrival in a similar manner in "The Enduring Chill"; and how she drew from her own confinement and dependence upon her mother to create similar scenarios for her own characters. Makes brief reference to "A View of the Woods," "The River," "The Lame Shall Enter First," *The Violent Bear It Away*, and *Wise Blood*, and offers more extensive discussions of "The Artificial Nigger," "The Enduring Chill," "Good Country People," and "A Temple of the Holy Ghost." Concludes that O'Connor's life is reflected in her fiction: it is "the tragedy--or comedy--of the individual, as a microcosm of the region, or of mankind, while remaining very much himself, in very real and natural circumstances," confronting the mystery of God's love.

524   Fitzgerald, Sally. "Rooms With a View." *Flannery O'Connor Bulletin* 10 (1981): 5-22.

Compares O'Connor with Trappist monk Thomas Merton, whom she never met. States that both O'Connor and Merton would have probably "delighted in the downrightness, the humor, and the self-mockery, to say nothing of the high intelligence and invincible faith, of the other." Discusses their differences in personality, character, and experience; how "their calls to religious life came in very different ways"; and how their circumstances--solitude, exile, chronic illness, connection to place--influenced their careers. Describes O'Connor's home in Milledgeville, Georgia, her surroundings at the writer's colony at Yaddo and while living with Sally and Robert Fitzgerald "on the Redding Ridge," in Connecticut. Suggests that, without having lived on her family's isolated farm outside Milledgeville, "in the ever-present shadow of death--it is unlikely that Flannery O'Connor would have peered so deeply into the implications of that faith, that, as she said, she could not abandon even if she wanted to." Refers to *Wise Blood*, provides a quote from George Meredith's poem, "Lucifer in Starlight," and refers to comments by Cecil Dawkins, Caroline Gordon, Monica Furlong, Pierre Emmanuel, and Marianne Moore. [Originally presented as the Thomas Merton Memorial Lecture at Columbia University, on November 13, 1981.]

525   Fitzgerald, Sally. "Rooms With a View." *Katallagete* 8.1 (1982): 4-11.

Slightly edited version of the author's Thomas Merton Memorial Lecture given at Columbia University, November 13, 1981. [This address was published under the same title in *The Flannery O'Connor Bulletin* 10 (1981): 5-22.]

526   Fitzgerald, Sally. "Root and Branch: O'Connor of Georgia." *Georgia Historical Quarterly* 64.4 (1980): 377-87.

Offers an essay based on a paper the author presented to the Georgia Historical Society at Milledgeville in October, 1980. Provides not only a detailed chronicle of Flannery O'Connor's family history but also explores the role of Irish Catholics in early Georgia. One of the few articles which discuss Flannery O'Connor's father, Edward O'Connor, Jr.

527   Fitzgerald, Sally and Ralph C. Wood. "Letters to the Editor." *Flannery O'Connor Bulletin* 23 (1994-95): 175-83.

Sally Fitzgerald writes (15 April 1995) "to correct an unfortunate error of fact" presented by Ralph C. Wood in his "keynote address for the panel `O'Connor and Race'" in 1994 at Georgia College & State University, later published--in revised form--in *The Flannery O'Connor Bulletin.*

Following Fitzgerald's letter, two letters from O'Connor to John Crowe Ransom and another from Ransom to O'Connor are published as evidence for Fitzgerald's assertion. These three letters from 1955, are in turn, followed by a response from Ralph C. Wood (27 April 1995). Fitzgerald focuses on Wood's contention that when Ransom, "asked Flannery to consider changing the title of . . . `The Artificial Nigger,' to accord with the journal's [*Kenyon Review*] longtime practice of avoiding the use of that offensive word in a title, `She refused.'" Fitzgerald argues that while it is true that Ransom "suggested a possible change in the title . . . it is *not* true that she refused to comply." Fitzgerald then discusses Wood's "prosecutorial mode of presentation"; his source for the "charges"; O'Connor's probable reasons for declining the alternative title proposed; "her metaphorical intentions" for using "the battered form of the plaster figure"; and the fact that the journal editors made the final decision to use O'Connor's title. Fitzgerald accepts blame for not pointing out Wood's error and other statements he made that should have been challenged. Refers to Philip Blair Rice, Peter Taylor, Caroline Gordon, John Howard Griffin, William Sessions, Father James McCown, James Baldwin, Lillian Smith, Sarah Gordon, and Carson McCuller's *Clock Without Hands*. Ralph Wood states--in his brief response--that Flannery "must be hooting and hurrawing" in paradise over this matter. Declares that "`I stood out for my title' cannot be interpreted as a *refusal* to change it," and indicates disappointment in the manner that the letters "heretofore held private" are being used.

528   Fitzpatrick, Ruth McDonough. "Tossing the Mighty From Their Thrones." *National Catholic Register* 25 April 1997: 2.

Briefly discusses O'Connor's "Revelation." Uses the teenage girl's action of throwing her book at the "Bible-thumping, smug Christian woman" as the basis for a homily on "`the politics of otherness.'"

529   Flaig, Bonnie. "*A Good Man Is Hard to Find*." *Masterplots II: Women's Literature Series*. Vol. 3. Ed. Frank N. Magill. Pasadena, CA: Salem, 1995. 944-47. 6 vols.

Categorizes and discusses the stories in O'Connor's collection, *A Good Man Is Hard to Find*. Sees one group--of five stories--as focused on "strong Southern women whose `sins' range from simple smugness to pride in one's physical and material attributes as virtues." Included in this group are "A Good Man Is Hard to Find," "Good Country People," "A Stroke of Good Fortune," "A Circle in the Fire," and "The Displaced Person." Contends that the five stories in the second group--"The River," "A Temple of the Holy Ghost," "A Late Encounter With the Enemy," "The

Life You Save May be Your Own," and "The Artificial Nigger"--appear "to center around the theme of spiritual initiation." Notes that O'Connor was "the first woman to be compared with the great male Southern writer William Faulkner," and argues that "by taking her art seriously, and working hard during her tragically short life to achieve the status of a great American writer, O'Connor set a standard and paved the way for women writers to come."

529a "Flannery O'Connor / Sally Fitzgerald to Speak About Author." *Savannah Morning News* 11 April 1982: G3.

Announces Fitzgerald's lecture "The Vision of the Night: Prophecy and Poetry of Flannery O'Connor," to be delivered on April 23, 1982 at Savannah's Telfair Academy of Arts and Sciences, sponsored by the Georgia Poetry Society and the Telfair's Gilmer Lecture Series. Describes the plots and critical acclaim of O'Connor's two novels (*Wise Blood* and *The Violent Bear It Away*) and offers a brief biographical sketch of Fitzgerald, noting that she is "at work on `Mansions of the South,' a biography of Miss O'Connor."

530 "Flannery O'Connor's Fans Try To Buy Author's Home." *Atlanta-Constitution* 6 July 1989: D3.

Reports that Hugh Brown at Armstrong State College and two of his colleagues are planning to purchase Flannery O'Connor's childhood home on Lafayette Square in Savannah, Georgia. Notes that the group must raise $50,000 by 1 August 1989 to complete the purchase.

531 Fleissner, Robert F. "Conrad, Hardy, O'Connor and the Monomyth." *Notes on Contemporary Literature* 9.2 (1979): 2-5.

Explores the concept of the Monomyth, "the myth that mythically subsumes all myths," and applies it to short stories, including Thomas Hardy's "The Three Strangers," Joseph Conrad's "The Lagoon," and Flannery O'Connor's "Everything That Rises Must Converge." Asserts that O'Connor's story "involves a desecration of the initiation rite." Suggests that as they enter the bus the mother "is the neophyte being helped by her son, who functions as the tutelary guide." Concludes that the interaction of the black mother and child forces the ceremony to be "desecrated."

532 Fleming, Thomas J. "An Unbroken Circle." *Modern Age* 29.3 (1985): 265-68.

A review essay of M.E. Bradford's *Generations of the Faithful Heart: On Literature of the South* (La Salle, IL: Sherwood Sugden, 1983); and Lewis A Lawson's *Another Generation: Southern Fiction Since World War II* (Jackson: UP of Mississippi, 1984). Discusses how Lawson's volume is devoted "to the postwar generation of Southern writers and their search for `some transcendent controlling principle' to replace the old certainties of place and kin." Outlines Lawson's view that Southern writers became obsessed with the postwar "social disintegration" and began to focus on "personal survival and even, as in the case of Flannery O'Connor and Walker Percy, with salvation." Argues that while his use of the legend of St. Anthony to illuminate *Wise Blood* might resemble a "scouting expedition through unexplored territory," Lawson is correct in pointing out that O'Connor's objective in writing the novel was to "expose the perils of ecstatic fundamentalism."

533   Flora, Joseph M. and Robert Bain, ed. *Contemporary Fiction Writers of the South: A Bio-Bibliographical Sourcebook*. Westport, CT: Greenwood, 1993. Passing references xi, 5, 7, 22, 24, 63, 64, 106-07, 115, 120, 163, 169, 181-82, 185, 216, 242, 261, 280, 282-83, 287, 289, 292, 322, 335, 337, 364, 369, 376, 434, 437, 469, 491, 510.

Uses essay profiles of contemporary Southern authors to offer "a report on the flurry of good books Southerners have written in the last two or three decades." Each essay provides a biographical sketch, a discussion of the author's major themes, an assessment of reviews and scholarship, a chronological list of the author's works, and a bibliography of selected criticism. O'Connor is mentioned as being read by, or an influence on, twenty-one of the forty-nine authors profiled: Lisa Alther, Larry Brown, Harry Crews, Andre Dubus, Clyde Edgerton, Kaye Gibbons, Ellen Gilchrist, Marianne Gingher, Barry Hannah, William Humphrey, Madison Jones, Bobbie Ann Mason, Cormac McCarthy, Berry Morgan, Helen Norris, Charles Portis, Padgett Powell, John Kennedy Toole, James Wilcox, Sylvia Wilkinson, and John Yount.

534   Flower, Dean. "Eudora Welty Come From Away." *Hudson Review* 38.3 (1985): 473-80.

Includes a brief reference to O'Connor as part of a discussion of Welty's use of Southern or regional voice. Suggests that when O'Connor wrote a letter or wrote narrative that included her characters' conversations, the voice remained "essentially the same." Contends that Welty, in contrast, often used colloquial voices in a manner that was significantly different than that of "the inward voice of the story itself."

535   Flower, Dean. "Fiction Chronicle." *Hudson Review* 35.2 (1982): 274-89.

Offers reviews of ten books, including Doris Betts's *Heading West*, which, along with Ella Leffland's *Last Courtesies and Other Stories*, is seen as being heavily influenced by the style and characterization of Flannery O'Connor. Discusses Betts's book and compares her character, Dwight Anderson, to O'Connor's The Misfit from "A Good Man Is Hard to Find."

536   Fodor, Sarah J. "Marketing Flannery O'Connor: Institutional Politics and Literary Evaluation." *Flannery O'Connor: New Perspectives*. Ed. Sura P. Rath and Mary Neff Shaw. Athens: U of Georgia P, 1996. 12-37.

In a five-part essay, the author outlines and discusses a range of topics: (1) support by the literary academy for O'Connor's fiction, focusing on the role of the New Critics and New York intellectuals; (2) how reviewers and critics evaluate O'Connor's work and classify it in the context of region, religion, and gender; (3) positions and methods that O'Connor's critics and supporters have used to critique and defend her reputation; (4) the impact of "institutional politics" on the canonization of O'Connor's work, focusing on the battle between the New Critics and the New York intellectuals; (5) the literary history of her work, the proliferation of critical approaches, and the transition of the reception of O'Connor's work from Southern Gothic, Catholic and "masculinely powerful" into broader frameworks. Mentions film adaptations and a wide variety of critics and reviewers: Frederick Crews, Willard Thorpe, Paul Lauter, Paul Engle, John Crowe Ransom, Robert Penn Warren, John Palmer, Monroe Spears, Alfred Kazin, Philip Rahv, Robert Lowell, William Phillips, John Simons, Sylvia Stallings, W.K. Wimsatt, Monroe C. Beardsley, Granville Hicks, Donald Davidson, Louis Rubin, William Goyen, Sandra Gilbert, Susan Gubar, Caroline Gordon, Andrew Lytle, Robert Fitzgerald, John Hawkes, John Aldridge, Irving Howe, R.W.B. Lewis, Ihab Hassan, James Justus, Ben Satterfield, Raymond Federman, Malcolm Bradley, and Larry McCaffrey.

537   Fodor, Sarah J. "Outlaw Christian: An Interview with Reynolds Price." *Christian Century* 22-29 Nov. 1995: 1128-31.

An interview with Reynolds Price in question-and-answer format, which includes a discussion of his admiration for O'Connor's fiction. Remarks that while he considers O'Connor's story "Revelation" to be "one of the greatest ever written by anyone," he does not regard her as one of his favorite writers because, in his opinion, O'Connor "had a mean streak. She was a saint, but saints have lots of mean streaks."

538   Fodor, Sarah. "Proust, `Home of the Brave,' and *Understanding Fiction*:
               O'Connor's Development as a Writer." *Flannery O'Connor Bulletin* 25
               (1996-97): 62-80.

               Contends that before readers cast young Flannery O'Connor, about to enter
               the Iowa Writer's Workshop, as "an eager, unformed and uninformed
               novice" who needed to be socialized "into the prevailing ideology of New
               Criticism," they should "take into account the years prior to her studies at
               Iowa in which she had already begun to develop a characteristic subject,
               style, and voice." Discusses the early influences upon O'Connor of Ogden
               Nash, William Faulkner, Marcel Proust, Edgar Allan Poe, and Nathaniel
               Hawthorne, and the later influence of such contemporaries as Caroline
               Gordon, Maryat Lee, and Paul Engle. Reviews her early writing "to show
               how her work calls on diverse literary traditions, and contends that it
               offers no evidence "that she wrote by following prescriptions for creative
               writing, new critical or otherwise." Follows with a discussion of her
               writing while an undergraduate at Georgia State College for Women,
               including her 1943 story "Home of the Brave," and argues that in this
               piece O'Connor "not only provides a well-crafted story, pleasing to new
               critical tastes, but also addresses psychological, social, political, and
               ethical issues." Concludes that the originality of O'Connor's writing resides
               in her ability, "evident throughout her writing career, to confront readers
               in her [own] idiosyncratic way with recognizable versions of social,
               economic, political, and religious realities."

539   Fodor, Sarah J. "Review of *The Flannery O'Connor Bulletin* Vol. 23."
               CHEERS! The Flannery O'Connor Society Newsletter 3.2 (1995-96): 2-3.

               Reviews the 1994-95 issue (Vol. 23) of the *Flannery O'Connor Bulletin*.
               Applauds the collection of articles for the extent to which they show "an
               awareness of the cultural studies movement, of the intertextuality of
               writing, and of interrelations among individuals and communities which
               impact composition . . . " Then, discusses each article, paying particular
               attention to contributions by Virginia Wray, Marshall Bruce Gentry, and
               Karl Martin which "open up possibilities for reading and understanding
               O'Connor in new ways."

540   Fodor, Sarah J. "`A world apparently without comment' or Shouting at the
               Reader: Narrative Guidance in O'Connor's Fiction." *Literature and Belief*
               17.1-2 (1997): 217-29.

               Contends that while O'Connor's "preference for the dramatized scene
               reflects the aesthetics she shared with New Critics and writers in the
               Jamesian tradition . . . her experimentation with statements that guide

interpretation indicates that Christian meaning was so important to her fiction that she was willing to violate the principles of `show, don't tell' in order to get that meaning across." Describes the goals of New Critics such as Allen Tate, Cleanth Brooks, and Caroline Gordon and ties these goals to O'Connor's attempts to have her narration occur "`through the minds and eyes'" of her characters. Follows with a discussion of "the tension evident in O'Connor's fiction, between New Critical values of indirection, objectivity, and ambiguity, and her concern that the reader understand her ideas, particularly the Christian dimension of her stories." Illustrates this aspect of O'Connor's narrative technique in "A Good Man Is Hard to Find," "The Artificial Nigger," "Revelation," and "Parker's Back," demonstrating how she "manages to shout at the reader while constructing a world apparently without comment."

541   Folks, Jeffrey J. "`The Enduring Chill': Physical Disability in Flannery O'Connor's *Everything That Rises Must Converge.*" *University of Dayton Review* 22.2 (1993): 81-88.

Contends that problems related to O'Connor's lupus "gradually became essential to her sense of her own being and were `usefully' . . . translated into her fiction." Finds that O'Connor "returned increasingly to the metaphors of physical disability . . . until in the final collection of stories, *Everything That Rises Must Converge*, her fictional world is permeated with illness and accident." Suggests that examples of O'Connor's daily dealings with "emotional and psychological responses to disability" abound in letters published in *The Habit of Being*. Describes O'Connor's "metaphoric system," the influence of her illness on her approach to writing and view of the grotesque, and finds parallels between events in her own life and the characters and events in her stories. Discusses "The Enduring Chill," "The Lame Shall Enter First" and O'Connor's "Introduction" to *A Memoir of Mary Ann*. Refers to comments and criticism by Mary Barbara Tate, John F. Desmond, Edward Kessler, Ted Spivey, Claire Katz, Bruce Bawer, James M. Mellard, Karl-Heinz Westarp, and Lee Sturma. Concludes that O'Connor's illness "resulted in penetrating psychological and thematic insights, [and] a consciousness of mortality and change," especially in the stories in *Everything That Rises Must Converge.*

542   Folks, Jeffrey J. "Ernest Gaines and the New South." *Southern Literary Journal* 24.1 (1991): 32-46.

Discusses Ernest Gaines's depiction of the New South in his stories. Focuses on how his works "couple a highly realistic depiction of technological change with an insistence on the value of connection with the past and the responsibility of the individual to communal needs." Includes a variety of comparisons between Gaines's work and Flannery O'Connor's, focusing on how they each rely upon "a highly developed Southern literary tradition that suggests conventional responses to mechanization." Mentions O'Connor's *Wise Blood* and "The Life You Save May Be Your Own." Concludes that for both writers, "the machine connotes neither the ultimate destructiveness nor the seductive attraction" that it suggested for William Faulkner or Richard Wright.

543   Folks, Jeffrey J. "An Interview with Robert Drake." *Mississippi Quarterly* 43.2 (1990): 221-33.

Drake discusses his own fiction and impressions of a wide variety of writers. Includes comments on O'Connor, whom he finds to be "a very great comic artist." States that he has taught "several seminar courses on her fiction," and found that students "love her work." Notes that in one seminar, which covered the fiction of Allen Tate, William Faulkner, Walker Percy, and Flannery O'Connor, the students "overwhelmingly preferred" O'Connor's work over that of other writers.

544   Folks, Jeffrey J. "The Mechanical in *Everything That Rises Must Converge*." *Southern Literary Journal* 18.2 (1986): 14-26.

Argues that "one can trace the tension in O'Connor's writing between the traditionalist eager to decry the abuses of modernization . . . and the sophisticated modern, aware of the latest advances in psychiatry and philosophy." Discusses how "A View of the Woods" serves as a "vision of progress" that surveys the South's transition toward the "industrial New South," and suggests that O'Connor's purpose in doing so "is not to satirize the industrialization . . . but to explore the necessity of the mechanical element in human society." Another version of this essay--by the same title--was published in Folks's *Southern Writers and the Machine: Faulkner to Percy* (New York: Peter Lang, 1993. 81-101).

545   Fontes, Montserrat. "`Sometimes--there's God--so quickly!'" *Flannery O'Connor Bulletin* 24 (1995-96): 88-90.

Offers recollections of an NEH-funded independent study trip made to Milledgeville during the summer of 1985 to study O'Connor's typescripts in the Flannery O'Connor Collection. States that O'Connor interested her "as a writer and as a Catholic," and that she "was sure that Catholicism would prove to be the reason why" both she and O'Connor "resorted so freely to violence" in their fiction. Describes her arrival at the Atlanta airport, her drive to Milledgeville, and how the process of her work led her from O'Connor's finished, polished work to focus on "the labor involved in reaching that product." Relates that what she found, as she examined the typescripts, were examples of O'Connor's "raw, naked endurance." Remarks, "the word *loneliness* occurred to me. Yes, that was the price." Finds how the typescripts show how O'Connor "forced her illness to work for her" as she used the loneliness and isolation she dealt with to search for and describe "truth." Relates that while her interest in O'Connor initially "began with her use of the grotesque," she learned more about "the veritable grotesqueness of a writer's life" and what lay in store for herself.

546   Forkner, Ben, and J. Gerald Kennedy. "An Interview with Walker Percy." *Delta* (France) No. 13 (Nov. 1981): 1-20.

Percy comments regarding what O'Connor might say about the use of the novel to encourage "salvation through language," and recalls how Caroline Gordon begin encouraging both of their careers. Follows with questions and answers in which Percy discusses O'Connor's *Wise Blood*, "The Artificial Nigger," and "Everything That Rises Must Converge."

547   Foster, Shirley. "Flannery O'Connor's Short Stories: The Assault on the Reader." *Journal of American Studies* (Great Britain) 20.2 (1986): 259-72.

Suggests that O'Connor's fragmented and unpredictable style and her use of paradox instead of balance, was based upon her "Christian belief that `grace' is offered ... chiefly in extreme and unexpected situations where [readers] may be shocked into spiritual insight." Discusses single versus multiple points of view in "A Good Man Is Hard to Find," "Greenleaf," "The Enduring Chill," and "Good Country People."

548   Foust, Ronald E. "The Rules of the Game: A Para-Theory of Literary Games." *South Central Review* 3.4 (1986): 5-14.

Presumes "that `a detailed theory of literature can be developed on the model of game-playing' and that the absence of such a `hypothetical model of description' constitutes a major obstacle in our attempt to establish an inclusive literary poetics." Contends that "such a theory would clarify the problem of the relation between fiction and fact and thus aid in our understanding of the social role that literature plays as a cultural institution." Offers a brief, passing reference to O'Connor's novel *Wise Blood* as an example of the type of work that underscores "the relation between fiction and fact by placing the acts of story telling, reading, and writing . . . in the fiction's foreground." Sees this action as "playing with words," and part of a literary game.

549   Fowler, Doreen [Ferlaino]. "Deconstructing Racial Difference: O'Connor's 'The Artificial Nigger.'" *Flannery O'Connor Bulletin* 24 (1995-96): 22-32.

Finds "The Artificial Nigger" to be "deeply puzzling," as even the "racial slur in the title is problematic." Suggests that the "troubling title carries a scarcely veiled symbolic meaning" as the use of the words "artificial" and "nigger" appear to enforce each other. Sees "the word, *nigger,* [as] a term used to revile the racial other," an artificial "fiction invented by the patriarchal structure to enforce otherness and thereby make possible the 'high estate' of the white male." Refers to Ferdinand de Saussure's theory that if "all meaning is relational," then "a sign has meaning only because of its differences from other signs." Suggests that this story deconstructs "the myth of white male superiority," revealing that "the difference between white and black is a matter of language and social construction." Further, that "the racial other on whose otherness white male superiority depends is not other but the same, and that the boundaries that divide white from black must be continuously and strenuously reinforced culturally, because without this cultural reinforcement, they collapse back into one another and form one whole, one humanity." Implies that the story also dissects patriarchy, "exposing the workings of patriarchal culture through the power relations of two white men, a grandfather and grandson." Sees the statue as signifying "' the mystery of existence,'" and that it helps the two to experience "the inadequacy of patriarchal culture to represent in its divisions and boundaries the boundless universe."

550   Fowler, Doreen Ferlaino. "Mrs. Chestny's Saving Graces." *Flannery O'Connor Bulletin* 6 (1977): 99-106.

Reports that critics of "Everything That Rises Must Converge" have traditionally "seen little to like in Julian's mother." Notes that critics typically "brand her as the archetypal, small-minded, Southern bigot and a chief object of Flannery O'Connor's scorn." Argues that while the mother does indeed stand "convicted of undisguised feelings of superiority to the majority of the human race," she is "not merely a grotesque, one-dimensional caricature of typically Southern vices," but "a highly complex character who exhibits both the weaknesses and the strengths of the old Southern tradition." Offers a reading of the story which ties together "two closely related image patterns: the imagery of martyrdom and childhood." Sees O'Connor's use of these as helping to define "those qualities which provide Julian's mother with avenues of grace." Challenges those critics who view Julian's mother as "the real villain of the piece" by pointing out that where O'Connor "is merciless" in her treatment of Julian, her treatment of his mother "is merciful." Concludes that O'Connor "reserves her harshest judgement for Julian, the story's protagonist and a member of Miss O'Connor's own generation." Insists that O'Connor "subdues her satire and creates a composite, even paradoxical, portrait of exasperating vices mixed with redeeming graces" for Julian's mother, and sees her as a member of "that older generation, a generation still dazzled by visions of waving Confederate banners and white-porticoed mansions."

550a   Fowler, Jennifer. "Team Searches for O'Connor Letters, Writings." *[Milledgeville, GA] Union-Recorder* 27 May 1999: A1+.

Reports that R. Neil Scott and Valerie Nye of Georgia College & State University (GC&SU) are "searching the nation for pieces of O'Connor's lesser-known writings--her private letters." Describes how the two scholars have located "600 to 700 letters in 35 different archival collections all over the country," including archives at Duke University, University of North Carolina at Chapel Hill, University of Tulsa, University of Iowa, Emory University, Harvard University, and the New York Public Library. States that a reference guide with citations to these collections and descriptions of their contents will be published later in the year. [Note: Scott and Nye expect to see this work, tentatively titled *Postmarked Milledgeville: A Guide to Flannery O'Connor's Correspondence in Libraries and Archives*, published in 2001.]

551   Fowlie, Wallace. "Faith and Narrative in Dante." *Notre Dame English Journal* 15.2 (1983): 67-76.

Claims that Dante's *Inferno* "is a leading model for our modern novel of the self," and that the *Divine Comedy* is a clear "record of faith." Describes Dante's objective as being "concerned with leaving after him a work that would never betray him." Utilizes *Wise Blood* as an example of how Dante's *Inferno* influenced modern narratives which portray a journey through life. Argues that the difference between O'Connor and Dante is that she addresses the action of grace "to characters who are indifferent to it because they live in a world ruled by Satan," while Dante's sinners know they are sinners. Suggests that *Wise Blood* is "not an imitation of the *Inferno* but rather a parody both gentle and serious at the same time." Asserts that both authors "attempt to explain why a man's salvation is a drama . . . played out" with a devil "determined to demonstrate his own supremacy." Concludes that O'Connor attempted to take the reader "beyond the point that can be accounted for by the psychologist," whose approach to the devil, "never explains the irrationality of malice in the world that now threatens its own destruction each day."

552   Fraistat, Rose Ann C. *Caroline Gordon as Novelist and Woman of Letters*.
           Baton Rouge: Louisiana State UP, 1984. 5, 23-24, 26-33, 101-02, 164,
           168.

           Offers brief references to Flannery O'Connor's life and work, including
           comparisons of O'Connor's work with that of Gordon and Truman Capote,
           and the way in which Gordon portrayed herself in her correspondence with
           O'Connor. Follows with a discussion of Gordon's role as one of
           O'Connor's most influential, helpful, and trusted critics, especially in the
           writing of *Wise Blood* and *A Good Man Is Hard to Find*, and suggests that
           Gordon's fiction may have provided O'Connor "with worthy models to
           emulate." Also refers to O'Connor's use of the grotesque and her "own
           mythical system."

553   Freedman, James O. "Honoring Talent for Glowing Prose." *Des Moines
           Sunday Register*, 28 Sept. 1986: n.p.

           From the author's remarks to the University of Iowa's Foundation Board
           of Directors, on the appointment of Marvin Bell to the Flannery O'Connor
           Professorship in Letters. The President of the University offers a
           biographical sketch of O'Connor, including a description of her
           educational background; her first meeting with Paul Engle (Director of the
           Iowa Writer's Workshop); her quiet demeanor in the Workshop's classes;
           the "cold, drafty boardinghouse" she lived in while attending classes at
           Iowa; her move to Yaddo in New York, then on to Ridgefield, Connecticut
           to live with Sally and Robert Fitzgerald, and later back home to Georgia;
           descriptive remarks about her writings and lectures; and remarks focused
           on the critical acclaim her writings have received.

554   Freeman, Mary Glenn. "Flannery O'Connor and the Quality of Sight: A
           Standard for Writing and Reading." *Flannery O'Connor Bulletin* 16
           (1987): 26-33.

           Asserts that O'Connor's ability to translate "her attentive eye into sensory
           detail for fiction," is similar to that of such masterful authors as Henry
           James, Joseph Conrad, Ford Madox Ford, and Gustave Flaubert. Discusses
           the influence of Jacques Maritain and suggests that O'Connor herself
           believed, that "for the writer, a first step in acquiring the habit of art is
           improving his quality of seeing . . . [then] the author must, ultimately,
           write--that is, translate into words his particular vision for the reader."
           Outlines Caroline Gordon's influence on O'Connor's work and offers
           specific examples from passages taken from *Wise Blood*. Declares that
           these passages illustrate how Gordon helped O'Connor develop more
           "effective means of making characters and scenes more visible." Argues

that the *reader* has a responsibility, too; if one wishes to truly "see and understand a writer's work, the reader must learn that art is selective and that the writer chooses details for a purpose." Closes with discussion of the role of "the glorious peacock tail" which serves as a suitable symbol for the eye, or quality of seeing.

555   Freeman, Mary G[lenn]. "Medical Documentation: An English Composition Professor's Perspective." *ERIC Document* (1989) ED 321 798 [21 pp.].

Discusses O'Connor's advice to aspiring writers that they should learn "to stare" and "acquire `the habit of seeing deeply.'" Asserts that this advice is particularly useful for nurses learning medical documentation skills. Recounts examples from the current nursing literature that reflect common medical documentation problems and notes that O'Connor's advice "to avoid unsupported generalities turns out to be useful for medical documenters, too." Contends that O'Connor's advice, if followed, will help nurses gain better observational skills that will be untainted by predispositions of motivation, personality, or emotional perspectives.

556   Freibert, Lucy M. "Southern Song: An Interview with Margaret Walker." *Frontiers* 9.3 (1987): 50-56.

Walker refers to Flannery O'Connor, Carson McCullers, and Alice Walker, as writers with a similar "Gothic imagination." States that she is "repelled" by O'Connor's "The Artificial Nigger," and contends that none of the three writers stand "the great test of an artist"--that of producing literature that readers want to read over and over again.

557   French, Patricia Ross. "Reader Response Theory: A Practical Application." *Journal of the Midwest Modern Language Association* 20 (Fall 1987): 28-40.

The author reflects upon her experience with reader-response theory applied to teaching a high school class which discussed, among other stories, "The Artificial Nigger" and "A Good Man Is Hard to Find." Presents the theoretical model upon which the teaching was based, describes what the students and teacher actually did in class to utilize the theory, and discusses and evaluates the class's various reader-response based activities. Outlines her "feelings of inadequacy" for teaching "The Artificial Nigger," her discomfort with the use of the word "nigger," and the students' response and discussion of the story. States that she was "amazed at how the class worked to overcome the problem" of what the term "nigger" meant to African-Americans. Concludes that because "the discussion was free, forthright, and full," the students "had accomplished superbly" what she, as teacher, "could not have done" on her own.

558   French, Warren. "Fiction vs Film, 1960-1985." *Contemporary American Fiction*. Ed. Malcolm Bradbury and Sigmund Ro. London: Edward Arnold, 1987. 107-22.

Discusses a wide variety of film versions of fiction by prominent writers, viewing the process as "a war between words and images that has left behind it a litter . . . of winding miles of discarded film and heaps of debauched books." Included in this discussion is John Huston's "hell-fire version" of O'Connor's *Wise Blood*, described as being "too strong medicine for attenuated American sensibilities."

559   Friedman, Melvin J. "Dislocations of Setting and Word: Notes on American Fiction Since 1950." *Studies in American Fiction* 5.1 (1977): 79-98.

Includes a two-page discussion of O'Connor's work, focusing on *Wise Blood* and *The Violent Bear It Away*, and finds them to be "patterned, with the same sure sense of design that Flaubert (whom she admired a great deal) and E.M. Forster possessed." Refers to how much French readers have been drawn to O'Connor's work, noting that *A Good Man Is Hard to Find* was added to the country's *agrégation* list in 1975. Contends that "despite her lack of experimentation and the numbing sameness of her themes and preoccupations, Flannery O'Connor is probably the best of the Southern writers after Faulkner."

560   Friedman, Melvin J. "Flannery O'Connor." *Biographical Dictionary of Contemporary Catholic American Writing*. Ed. Daniel J. Tynan. New York: Greenwood, 1989. 221-24.

Offers a biographical sketch that briefly outlines details of Flannery O'Connor's life, then focuses upon her work and reputation in both the United States and abroad. As evidence that O'Connor's position abroad is clearly as secure as it is in the United States, cites David Farmer's *Bibliography*, which lists the various translations of her work, and the fact that *A Good Man Is Hard to Find and Other Stories* was added to the required reading list for all advanced graduate students in English and American literature in France. Mentions Henry James, Gustave Flaubert, and Caroline Gordon as positive influences upon her work.

561   Friedman, Melvin J. "Flannery O'Connor in France: An Interim Report."
Revue des Langues Vivantes: Tijdschrift Voor Levende Talen 43.5 (1977):
435-42.

Describes the acceptance and appreciation by the French reading public
of the works and translations of works by such Southern writers as Edgar
Alan Poe, William Faulkner, John Dos Passos, Sherwood Anderson,
William Styron, and Flannery O'Connor. Discusses Maurice-Edgar
Coindreau's 1959 translation of *Wise Blood*; Michael Gresset's
"sophisticated review" of the French translation of *A Good Man Is Hard
to Find* by Henri Morisset (who also translated *Everything That Rises
Must Converge*); Andre Simon's 1975 translation of *Mystery and
Manners*; and Claude Fleurdorge's translations of a number of O'Connor's
M.F.A. thesis stories. Examines examples of the "translator's craft" and
suggests that O'Connor's idiom easily adjusts to the French language.
Concludes with discussion of special issues of French journals devoted to
O'Connor and university centers with particular interest in Southern
Literature and O'Connor's work. [Rpt. in *Critical Essays on Flannery
O'Connor*. Ed. Melvin J. Friedman and Beverly Lyon Clark. Boston: G.K.
Hall, 1985. 130-37.]

562   Friedman, Melvin J. "Flannery O'Connor's *Via Extrema et Negativa*."
Review 5 (1983): 149-54.

Discusses Jerome Klinkowitz's "unencouraging" assessment of O'Connor
scholarship. Pointedly remarks that Frederick Asals's book *Flannery
O'Connor: The Imagination of Extremity* will not likely be viewed by
Klinkowitz as "mediocre and repetitious." Discusses each chapter of the
book in a review essay. Concludes that the book "is a careful,
discriminating, original study."

563   Friedman, Melvin J. "'The Human Comes Before Art': Flannery O'Connor
Viewed Through Her Letters and Her Critics." *Southern Literary Journal*
12.2 (1980): 114-24.

A review essay that treats a number of critical works: Sally Fitzgerald's
The Habit of Being; Robert E. Golden and Mary C. Sullivan's *Flannery
O'Connor and Caroline Gordon: A Reference Guide*; John R. May's *The
Pruning Word: The Parables of Flannery O'Connor*; and Dorothy Tuck
McFarland's *Flannery O'Connor*. Offers comments on O'Connor's
reservations about Caroline Gordon, from letters in *The Habit of Being*,
and mentions O'Connor's discussions of other contemporary writers. Says
the letters to "A" come closest to being engaging in the spiritual and
literary sense, with those to Cecil Dawkins following shortly behind.

Others, popular though they may be, "seem forced." Commends Robert Golden's *Reference Guide*, though laments the absence of a promised follow-up. Says May's book counters Hendin's *The World of Flannery O'Connor*, the two books offering "the extreme possibilities of commentary" on O'Connor. Remarks that McFarland's book is "sane . . . knowing . . . [and] less demanding than May's" as it observes and explores O'Connor's obsession with "incongruities."

564   Friedman, Melvin J. "Introduction." *Critical Essays on Flannery O'Connor*. Ed. Melvin J. Friedman and Beverly Lyon Clark. Boston: G.K. Hall, 1985. 1-15.

Offers a three-part introductory essay that provides a context for the criticism included in this collection. Explores in the first part O'Connor's life and credentials as an "Agrarian-nurtured" rural Southerner whose Catholicism was "linked to her `habit of being.'" Notes the "disturbed rumblings" about the proliferation of commentary about her fiction. Then, places her work as occurring between "the neatly patterned, mythically ordered texts" of modernism and the "`disruptive' gestures of the so-called postmodernists." Outlines in the second part several significant contributions to the criticism of O'Connor's work. States the essence of each article or book referred to: John Hawkes's article in *Sewanee Review* in 1962 and his other in the Winter 1964 issue of *Esprit*; Martha Stephens's *The Question of Flannery O'Connor*; Josephine Hendin's *The World of Flannery O'Connor*; Carol Shloss's *Flannery O'Connor's Dark Comedies: The Limits of Inference*; and essays by Claire Kahane and André Bleikasten. Devotes remarks in the third part to comments by reviewers and critics of *The Habit of Being*, edited by Sally Fitzgerald, and *The Presence of Grace and Other Book Reviews*, edited by Leo J. Zuber and Carter W. Martin. Suggests that while "Like Flaubert's correspondence, the contents of *The Habit of Being* offer an essential passageway" to O'Connor's art, the letters "do not . . . belong in the company of the masters of the form." Discusses her letters to "A," Maryat Lee, Cecil Dawkins, John Hawkes, and Caroline Gordon. Closes the third section with remarks on *The Presence of Grace and Other Book Reviews*, Miles Orvell's *Invisible Parade: The Fiction of Flannery O'Connor*, Kathleen Feeley's *Flannery O'Connor: Voice of the Peacock*, Lorine M. Getz's *Flannery O'Connor: Her Life, Library and Book Reviews*, and David Farmer's *Flannery O'Connor: A Descriptive Bibliography*.

565   Friedman, Melvin J. "`The Perplex Business': Flannery O'Connor and Her Critics Enter the 1970s." *The Added Dimension: The Art and Mind of Flannery O'Connor*. Melvin J. Friedman and Lewis A. Lawson. 2nd. ed., Rev. New York: Fordham UP, 1977. 207-34.

Offers "an overview of recent developments in O'Connor criticism and editing," with emphasis on book-length works. Notes in the book's Preface that portions previously appeared in different form in the *Journal of Modern Literature, American Literature, Southern Literary Journal*, and *Studies in American Fiction*. Provides one-to-three-page critical discussions of the following: Josephine Hendin's "naughty, irreverent" *The World of Flannery O'Connor*; Sally and Robert Fitzgerald's *Mystery and Manners: Occasional Prose*; O'Connor's *The Complete Stories of Flannery O'Connor*, and her two collections, *A Good Man Is Hard to Find* and *Everything That Rises Must Converge*; Carter Martin's *The True Country: Themes in the Fiction of Flannery O'Connor*; the "unprepossessing" and "low-keyed" *Flannery O'Connor Bulletin*; Kathleen Feeley's *Flannery O'Connor: Voice of the Peacock*; David Eggenschwiler's "perceptive" *The Christian Humanism of Flannery O'Connor*; Gilbert Muller's "unpretentious" *Nightmares and Visions: Flannery O'Connor and the Catholic Grotesque*; Miles Orvell's *Invisible Parade: The Fiction of Flannery O'Connor*; Dorothy Walters's "penetrating" contribution to the Twayne's United States Authors Series, *Flannery O'Connor*; Martha Stephens's "usefully irreverent" and "best book we have," *The Question of Flannery O'Connor*; and Preston Browning's *Flannery O'Connor*.

566   Friedman, Melvin J. "Preface to the Second Edition." *The Added Dimension: The Art and Mind of Flannery O'Connor*. Melvin J. Friedman and Lewis A. Lawson. 2nd ed. Rev. New York: Fordham UP, 1977. 1-31.

Notes that while a decade has passed since the publication of the first edition, the positive response of reviewers and scholars suggested to Fordham University Press that this second edition was needed. Acknowledges that the editors did not see the need to update the bibliography and made only "minor corrections and adjustments" to the essays themselves. Provides a listing, with brief commentary, of other bibliographies of criticism and editions available to scholars, making special mention of Robert E. Golden and Mary Sullivan's *Flannery O'Connor and Caroline Gordon: A Reference Guide* and David Farmer's *A Descriptive Bibliography of the Works of Flannery O'Connor*. Reports the addition to this edition of Friedman's essay, "'The Perplex Business': Flannery O'Connor and Her Critics Enter the 1970s." States that copyright considerations prevented the inclusion of "Flannery O'Connor in Her Own Words," which had appeared in the first edition.

567   Friedman, Melvin J. "Robert Coles's South and Other Approaches to Flannery O'Connor." *Southern Literary Journal* 15.1 (1982): 120-29.

Reviews Coles's credentials and discusses his *Flannery O'Connor's South* and *Walker Percy: An American Search*. States that Coles "seems to bring to Flannery O'Connor's South an Emersonian brightness and optimism." Remarks that he approaches her work "with a freshness and gentle persuasiveness absent from much O'Connor criticism." Other essay reviews follow, which discuss Carol Shloss's *Flannery O'Connor's Dark Comedies: The Limits of Inference*; David Farmer's *Flannery O'Connor: A Descriptive Bibliography*; Barbara McKenzie's *Flannery O'Connor's Georgia*; Lorine Getz's *Flannery O'Connor: Her Life, Library and Book Reviews*; and James Grimshaw's *The Flannery O'Connor Companion*. Concludes that these works "indicate that critics are not ready as yet to declare a moratorium" on O'Connor scholarship, and that critical works such as these, and especially Coles's, "are well worth having."

568   "The *Friends of Flannery* newsletter is published . . . " *Friends of Flannery* [Newsletter]. (April 1997): 3.

Reports that the *Friends of Flannery* newsletter is published "occasionally" in support of the "Flannery O'Connor Childhood Home Foundation," by the Department of Languages, Literature and Dramatic Arts, Armstrong Atlantic State University. The address and telephone number for the Foundation is 11935 Abercorn Street, Savannah, GA 31419. (912) 927-5289.

569   Fromm, Harold. "Genius or Fudge? The Clouded Alembics of Magister Poe." *Hudson Review* 45.2 (1992): 301-09.

Considers "the serious limitations of Poe's individual productions" through a discussion of his commitment to art versus that of Flannery O'Connor. Observes that, unlike O'Connor, Poe "was heavily dependent upon a laboratory of manipulative alchemies that served as surrogates for `authenticity.'" Commends O'Connor for her commitment "to identify and represent the enigmas of human life," and her efforts "to expose the varied but self-deluding subterfuges her protagonists employed to justify themselves in relation to these enigmas."

570   Frost, Wendy and Michele Valiquette. *Feminist Literary Criticism: A Bibliography of Journal Articles: 1975-1981*. New York: Garland, 1988. 220, 326-327, 450-451, 747.

Bibliographical reference with keyword indexes for each entry. Lists three articles (by Martha Chew, Alice Walker, Claire Kahane) that offer a feminist approach to O'Connor's work.

571   Fuglie, Gordon. "Postmodern Mystic: The Art of Laura Lasworth." *Image: A Journal of the Arts & Religion* (Fall 1997): 63-72.

Discusses Lasworth's interest in Flannery O'Connor's writings, which, in turn, led Lasworth to paint a second series of works depicting characters and situations from O'Connor's stories and novels. Includes illustrations of five paintings: *St. Thomas and Mr. Eco*; *St. Thomas Aquinas Baptizing Umberto Eco*; *The Ascension of Hazel Motes*; *The Light and Dark Church*; and, *The Donkey with Red Garden Boots*.

572   Fultz, James R. "*Wise Blood*: O'Connor-Huston's Dark, Divine Comedy." *Proceedings of the 5th Purdue University Conference on Film*. West Lafayette, IN: Purdue UP, 1980. 117-23.

Offers a detailed review of Huston's film of O'Connor's *Wise Blood*. Reports that viewers will not be disappointed, seeing it as Huston's best film in years and as a brilliant adaptation of O'Connor's book. Praises Benedict Fitzgerald's screenplay as one which "carefully preserves the letter and spirit of the novel." Details how Huston draws upon a variety of comic traditions to bring the book to screen. Focuses on how "O'Connor's oddly comic slant on the world of *Wise Blood* is realized by the resources of the cinema." Provides an episodic review of the plot and a description of the book's mixed reception as shown by its original reviews in 1952. Then discusses Huston's cinematic technique, dialogue, and framing of shots. Outlines how Hazel Motes's character and others are filmed. Concludes that because Huston "has masterfully used the language of film to recreate Flannery O'Connor's dark, divine comedy," viewers may be provoked to "look into the novel."

573   Gale, Steven H., ed. *Encyclopedia of American Humorists*. New York: Garland, 1988. 283.

Mentions O'Connor's "grotesque humor" and compares it to that of William Faulkner and Erskine Caldwell.

574   Gallagher, Michael Paul. "The Drama of Grace." *The Tablet* 29 July 1989: 864.

Discusses why O'Connor's death at such an early age was such "an enormous loss to literature and to Catholic writing in particular." Contends that O'Connor "was probably the most theologically equipped of fiction writers in English since George Eliot," and indicates how her stories, "which seem like grotesque thrillers, conceal an element of comic-cum-religious shock." Lists religious thinkers O'Connor studied, her perspective on the South and its influence on her work, and outlines her views of modern culture and the "securities of the secular imagination." Describes how her sense of humor influenced both her writing and view of life, and argues that the "wit of her fiction was more ambitiously aimed at the defense mechanisms of atheistic pride in the modern world." Refers to Irish novelist Brian Moore; explicates "Revelation"; and concludes that while O'Connor "was a serious woman, a proud Southerner, a demanding Catholic, a sharp critic of nonsense . . . she was a joyous comedian as well, someone for whom `happiness' was bigger than `non-misery.'"

575   Gallagher, Michael Paul. "Prophetess in Fiction." *The Way: A Review of Contemporary Christian Spirituality* 27.2 (1987): 117-23.

Claims that O'Connor possessed "possibly the greatest Catholic imagination in English-language fiction." Suggests that the distinguishing characteristic between O'Connor and other Catholic and Christian writers was her level of understanding of theological writings: she not only possessed an appreciation of the prophetic, she understood its scriptural basis as well. Examines O'Connor's "prophetic vision," refers to her review of Bruce Vawter's *The Conscience of Israel*, her readings of Thomas Aquinas's *De veritate*, and reminds readers that O'Connor's "approach to fiction was to be comically faithful to the visible universe and at the same time `go through it into an experience of mystery.'" Indicates that O'Connor was, "`deconstructing' the spiritual limitations of bourgeois readers, enticing them to enlarge what they understood by realism and reality." Discusses the type of action found in her stories, her use of the grotesque, her limitations, her attitude toward Southern tradition and her sense of evil. Offers a reading of "The Artificial Nigger," and declares that the closing of the story is unique among O'Connor's works, in that--through Mr. Head--"she allows herself a more extended and indeed eloquent commentary on the spiritual drama than elsewhere."

576   Galloway, Lewis F. "The Sacrament of Suffering: The Religious Vision of Flannery O'Connor." Ms. Kosmos Club Papers. South Caroliniana Library, U of South Carolina, Oct. 1992. [14 pp.]

Discusses Flannery O'Connor's religious faith as reflected in her novels, stories, nonfiction, and book reviews. Provides a biographical sketch, and outlines O'Connor's beliefs regarding redemption, "the extreme nature of humanity's social and spiritual alienation," and "aspects of the prophetic, apocalyptic and sacramental forms of religious expression" seen in her work. Follows with a discussion of religious themes in her work as evidenced in *Wise Blood*, *The Violent Bear It Away*, "Parker's Back,"

"Revelation," "A Good Man Is Hard to Find," and "A Temple of the Holy Ghost." Suggests that O'Connor's fiction reflects her conviction that "the world in which men and women live is a holy place," often unseen because "the human illusion of self-sufficiency and the radical character of human sin lead to . . . alienation and despair." Concludes that O'Connor sought to use her fiction to show how "redemptive love of God for creation is most often experienced in those moments of suffering," times when the "human spirit sees clearly, for the first time perhaps, the terrifyingly beautiful mercy of God."

577   Gamber, Matthew T. "Flannery O'Connor and the U.S. Catholic Press: Apprehending a Literature of Grace." *Flannery O'Connor Bulletin* 25 (1996-97): 105-37.

Discusses the response of the Catholic press in the United States to O'Connor's published writings from 1952 until 1966. Provides, in chronological order, excerpts from specific reviews, and then considers "the reactions that usually followed." Concludes that there was, indeed, "a slow and steady growth in appreciation for the work of Flannery O'Connor in the Catholic press of the fifties and sixties," and that this appreciation "centered on the fact that she was somehow trying to offer a `literature of grace.'" Includes a fifty-three item bibliography.

578   Gandolfo, Anita. *Testing the Faith: The New Catholic Fiction in America.* Contributions in American Studies, 100. New York: Greenwood, 1992. 12, 15.

Contains two brief references to O'Connor, both dealing with her comment that "`in the last four or five centuries we in the Church have over-emphasized the abstract and consequently impoverished our imagination and our capacity for prophetic insight.'" Uses her comment to support the argument that Catholic theologians were so "`impoverished'" that they were "unaware of the sociological and psychological impact of the changes in worship decreed" by the Second Vatican Council.

579   Garbett, Ann D. "*Wise Blood.*" *Masterplots II: Women's Literature Series.* Vol. 6. Ed. Frank N. Magill. Pasadena, CA: Salem, 1995. 2478-2482. 6 vols.

Identifies and describes the principal characters of O'Connor's *Wise Blood,* then discusses the plot, theme and origins of the novel. Sees this work as "intended to articulate [the] religious truths that O'Connor, writing from her faith as a Roman Catholic, took very seriously." Refers to her disinterest in civil rights, women's rights, and other social issues and finds that her "best contribution to American literature . . . was her combination of the comedic and the serious, a combining that was quite in keeping with her intense belief in the saving power of divine love."

580   Garson, Helen S. "Cold Comfort: Parents and Children in the Work of Flannery O'Connor." *Realist of Distances: Flannery O'Connor Revisited.* Ed. Karl-Heinz Westarp and Jan Nordby Gretlund. Aarhus (Denmark): Aarhus UP, 1987. 113-22.

Considers the parent-child relationships in a variety of O'Connor's short stories, noting that more than half of her stories deal with the relationship between parents and children. Reports that rarely are both parents present, almost always there is only one child, and "in all her work, parents and children want and expect things of each other that can never be given." Offers readings that examine parent-child relationships in "The River," "The Lame Shall Enter First," "Good Country People," "Revelation," "A Good Man Is Hard to Find," "Greenleaf," "The Enduring Chill," "The Comforts of Home," and "Everything That Rises Must Converge." Notes that "as one critic has said of her general approach, `she found the human heart to be a pretty dark place.'" Her children find no escape from the ties that bind them to their parents, and become trapped and "dependent emotionally or physically because of age, or inability, or malaise, or illness." Concludes that the child in O'Connor's stories "struggles in a circle from which there is no way out except death."

581   Gatta, John. "*The Scarlet Letter* as Pre-text for Flannery O'Connor's `Good Country People.'" *Nathaniel Hawthorne Review* 16.2 (1990): 6-9.

Suggests that *The Scarlet Letter* "offers a kind of Satanic pre-text for the spiritual confrontation O'Connor presents in her comically devastating tale of `Good Country People.'" Asserts that both works "show the devil doing God's work, despite his destructive designs," and that both also "demonstrate how intellectual pride and distortions of language can obscure the truths of the human heart." Concludes with discussion of how aspects of O'Connor's "Introduction to *A Memoir of Mary Ann*" parallel Hawthorne's "The Birthmark." [Rpt. in *Hawthorne and Women: Engendering and Expanding the Hawthorne Tradition.* Ed. John L. Idol and Melinda M. Ponder. Amherst: U of Massachusetts P, 1999.]

582   Gay, Julie Lane. "The Literary Apologetic of Flannery O'Connor." *Crux: A Quarterly Journal of Christian Thought and Opinion* (Canada) 19.4 (1983): 27-32.

Asserts that while O'Connor is recognized as a master of the modern short story by the literary world, recognition and appreciation by Christian readers has been slow in coming due to the confusing nature and intent of the stories. Contends that "many readers sense an inexcusable discrepancy between O'Connor's intentions and the actual effect of her stories on the reader." Suggests that this discrepancy is based upon the fact that full understanding, as O'Connor intended, "might demand both literary and theological sophistication." Urges Christian readers to "reevaluate what they expect of fiction writers who are Christians."

583   Geng, Veronica and Garrison Keillor. "A Good Man Is Hard to Keep: The Correspondence of Flannery O'Connor and S.J. Perelman." *New York Times Book Review* 2 April 1995: 15-16.

Reported to be "imaginary letters" which were read at the Authors Guild Foundation's benefit dinner, on February 27, 1995 at the Metropolitan Club in New York. Veronica Geng played Flannery O'Connor, and Garrison Keillor played S.J. Perelman. Illustrated with a caricature by Robert Grossman of O'Connor holding S.J. Perelman's hands.

584   Gentry, Marshall Bruce. "ALA 1997 Panel Discussion: `Flannery O'Connor and the Maryat Lee Letters." *CHEERS! The Flannery O'Connor Society Newsletter* 5.2 (1997-98): 3.

Summarizes presentations for a panel that "was conceived primarily as an investigation into the issue of race in O'Connor's correspondence with the writer Maryat Lee." Expresses surprise that the participants "generally agreed that the charge that O'Connor was racist . . . has been overstated." Outlines Virginia Wray's contention that the correspondence between the two writers appears to have "caused O'Connor to soften her scathing critique of liberals" to the extent that her unfinished novel, *Why Do the Heathen Rage?*, appears to end "with a surprising defense of liberalism." Follows with a discussion of Robert Donahoo's comment that "interpretations tending toward accusing O'Connor of racism, are examples of literalism pushed to a dangerous extreme" and Henry Russell's observation that--because many of the letters Lee wrote are missing--"we cannot understand fully O'Connor's words on race." Considers Jean W. Cash's remarks about Lee and O'Connor's shared interest in writing and how each may have affected the other and Norman McMillan's recognition of the two writers' very different "centripetal and centrifugal personalities." Concludes with Margaret Whitt's assertion that O'Connor "let Lee loosen her up when it came to thinking radically" about her lupus, as there appears in the correspondence "a large amount of discussion of eastern medicine as it might apply to O'Connor's illness."

585   Gentry, Marshall Bruce. "The Eye vs the Body: Individual and Communal
         Grotesquerie in *Wise Blood*." *Modern Fiction Studies* 28.3 (1982):
         487-93.

         Examines various definitions of the grotesque and comments on their
         impact on O'Connor criticism. Focuses on *Wise Blood* with an in-depth
         analysis of Hazel Motes. Concludes that "the grotesque is positively
         disruptive as well as a result of disruption." Sees the grotesquerie of Motes
         as a result of his community's oppression, "an attack on what is
         unsatisfactory to Hazel in that community," and a type of inner coherence
         which leads him "out of himself and into a rejuvenated community."

586   Gentry, Marshall Bruce. "Flannery O'Connor's Attacks on Omniscience."
         Southern Quarterly 29.3 (1991): 53-61.

         Questions "the correctness of labeling O'Connor as a modernist." States
         that doing so may not necessarily open her writing to new critical insights,
         but simply reaffirm a standard reading. Discusses the narrator's ridicule in
         "The Enduring Chill" and offers, "when we look at . . . works by O'Connor
         as involving an attack on omniscience (rather than as attempts at
         omniscient narration that do not quite work out), we see them as better
         works of literature." Offers a variety of points of view on the topic of
         narrator's voice from critics, including: Edward Kessler, Suzanne Morrow
         Paulson, Thomas O. Sloane, Mark Caldwell, Shirley Foster, Jefferson
         Humphries, Louise Westling, and Sally Fitzgerald. Concludes with
         discussion of the gender of O'Connor's consciousness, and suggests that
         "perhaps, in O'Connor's works we see the gender battle producing the
         attacks on omniscience that make the author seem to be a modernist."

587   Gentry, Marshall Bruce. "Gender Dialogue in O'Connor." *Flannery
         O'Connor: New Perspectives*. Ed. Sura P. Rath and Mary Neff Shaw.
         Athens: U of Georgia P, 1996. 57-72.

         Discusses O'Connor's views on gender, her use of irony directed at her
         narrator (uses examples from "The Crop" and "Parker's Back"), and her
         treatment of her male writers and mostly female story-tellers. Suggests that
         O'Connor's narrator might be considered as "a composite figure: a female
         narrator espousing patriarchal, masculine values." Observes how
         O'Connor's narrators "who represent patriarchal authority have their
         authority undercut; the characters they mock are capable of strength and
         self-transformation that the narrators underestimate and misinterpret."
         Explores how Mikhail Bakhtin's views might be applied to the feminist
         struggle, and indicates how the struggle against the narrator's patriarchy
         "must be carried on unconsciously" by O'Connor's characters. Discusses

examples of characters who resemble O'Connor's narrator in "A Circle in the Fire" (Mrs. Pritchard), "Good Country People" (Mrs. Freeman), and "A Temple of the Holy Ghost" (the nun at the end). Considers a variety of related issues and topics: O'Connor's openness "to the raising of questions about gender"; her "presentation of women"; her creation "of female characters who achieve masculine strength" or are "associated with masculine divinity"; and how O'Connor "made many of her females into versions of Christ and other male religious figures." Offers brief readings in the context of these discussions of *The Violent Bear It Away*, "The Lame Shall Enter First," and *Wise Blood*. Refers to critical comments by Louise Westling, Frederick Crews, Ruth Fennick, Robert H. Brinkmeyer, Jr., Dale M. Bauer, Thelma J. Shinn, Claire Kahane, Kathryn Lee Seidel, Martha Chew, Karen Fitts, Jean W. Cash, Michael Holquist, Peter Stallybrass, and Allon White.

588   Gentry, Marshall Bruce. "The Hand of the Writer in 'The Comforts of Home.'" *Flannery O'Connor Bulletin* 20 (1991): 61-72.

Lists characters in O'Connor's fiction who depict her lack of respect for writers. Cites remarks in "The Nature and Aim of Fiction" that indicate her views were based upon ideas of St. Thomas. Discusses her belief that most writers rely too heavily upon technique and too little upon "vision." Suggests that "this problem" is connected to O'Connor's view that "any writer inherently commits the error of producing a text that cannot quite be the Text, that cannot duplicate scripture." Offers a reading of "The Comforts of Home" to show how "when one writes a lie, one may sneak up on truths that the proud consciousness rejects." Focuses on the character of Thomas: "images relating to the power of the hand" and how they fulfill his unconscious desires; indications that Sarah Ham is symbolically his sister; the role of Thomas's lies and his father's influence upon his actions; his embarrassment and spiritual progress experienced upon "being caught red-handed"; and a comparison of O'Connor's Thomas to St. Thomas. Asserts that the story is concerned with "the blending of genders." Concludes with a discussion of Frederick Crews's assessment that O'Connor is overrated because she "never departs from 'the regnant Creative Writing mode,' and . . . that [even] 'the most impressive and original of her stories adhere to the classroom formula of her day.'"

589   Gentry, Marshall Bruce. "Letters to the Editor." *CHEERS! The Flannery O'Connor Newsletter* 3.1 (1995): 2.

Responds to Robert Donahoo's review of volume 22 of the *Flannery O'Connor Bulletin* published in the previous issue of *CHEERS! The Flannery O'Connor Society Newsletter* [2.2 (1994-95): 2]. Agrees that the

Bulletin's articles "are becoming increasingly sophisticated in terms of theoretical approach," and contends that those who represent the *Bulletin* are just as "pleased to see this shift as happening" as readers such as Donahoo. Disagrees with Donahoo regarding his contention that Ralph Wood's essay on O'Connor's position on race is irrelevant "because it is based on outmoded premises about literature." Reminds readers that a very large audience turned-out to hear Ralph Wood present the paper the essay was based upon, and that the local [Milledgeville, GA] paper--the following day--noted his presentation with a headline "about O'Connor being called a racist by a visiting scholar." Gentry states that while he understands Donahoo's position, he believes that Wood's paper should be considered "the first in a long series of discussions about the significance of the not-yet-published Maryat Lee letters now stored at the Georgia College [& State University] Library." Concludes with remarks that the *Bulletin* would be pleased to see and publish "more essays on how O'Connor is linked to other writers," and is "increasingly open to feminist treatments on O'Connor."

590   Gentry, Marshall Bruce. "Narration and the Grotesque in Flannery O'Connor's Stories." *Realist of Distances: Flannery O'Connor Revisited.* Ed. Karl-Heinz Westarp and Jan Nordby Gretlund. Aarhus (Denmark): Aarhus UP, 1987. 82-91.

States that in a typical story, O'Connor "sets up a battle between an authoritarian narrator and a character who sees the world grotesquely." Contends that this battle is "often won by the character's unconscious maneuvers for redemption." Illustrates this contention with a brief discussion of "A Good Man Is Hard to Find," highlighting readers' doubts about the grandmother's redemption. Indicates the need for strategies "about the character's psyche so that redemption becomes believable." Suggests two strategies used by O'Connor: use of "completely innocent characters such as Harry-Bevel Ashfield in 'The River;'" and the use of "sophisticated and corrupt characters" to give "the grotesque a deeply psychological dimension . . . transforming an obstacle to redemption into a means of redemption." Discusses theories of Mikhail Bakhtin and Wolfgang Kayser regarding "the use of the grotesque as a mode of representation and . . . perception." Suggests a model similar to that of "Bakhtin's model of the novelistic literary text as a battleground, where characters fight the authoritarian narrator's rigid standards." Offers readings of "Revelation" and "Good Country People" to demonstrate how O'Connor's characters often use grotesque processes in a positive manner to move them toward redemption. Concludes with a clarification and interpretation of O'Connor's use of the word "redemption," a summation of the "new explanation" presented as to "how O'Connor is a Catholic writer," and the assertion that "a psychological approach to O'Connor's works is compatible with a theological one." Adapted from the author's *Flannery O'Connor's Religion of the Grotesque* (UP of Mississippi, 1986).

591   Gentry, Marshall Bruce. "O'Connor's Legacy in Stories by Joyce Carol Oates and Paula Sharp." *Flannery O'Connor Bulletin* 23 (1994-95): 44-60.

Sees Joyce Carol Oates and Paula Sharp as inspired by O'Connor's writings and as "sophisticated readers of her fiction." Discusses O'Connor's influence, focusing on Oates's "Where Are You Going, Where Have You Been?" and stories from Sharp's *The Imposter: Stories About Netta and Stanley*, including: "A Meeting on the Highway" and "Joyriding." Contends that Oates and Sharp "respond creatively to O'Connor's fascination with our secret desires for trespass and with the mysterious connections between danger and salvation." Submits further, that by studying stories by Oates and Sharp, readers will read O'Connor's "A Good Man Is Hard to Find" "with a new eye." Claims that Sharp and Oates are inspired by O'Connor's "Philosophical Criminal with a Car," such as The Misfit in "A Good Man Is Hard to Find," Tom T. Shiftlet in "The Life You Save May Be Your Own," and Hazel Motes in *Wise Blood*. Refers to comments by Larry Rubin, Ellen G. Friedman, A.R. Coulthard, D.F. Hurley, J.O. Tate, Victor Lasseter, Philip Roth, Suzanne Morrow Paulson, Madison Jones, Frank R. Cunningham, Greg Johnson, Nancy Bishop Dessommes, David Gratz, Marilyn Wesley, Jack Butler, and Thomas Hill Schaub. Concludes with the suggestion that just as Oates and Sharp "use the psychology of projection to discuss love," if readers will "reread O'Connor with projection and love in mind" they may "find an insight into `A Good Man Is Hard to Find.'"

592   Gentry, Marshall Bruce. Rev. of *American Fiction in the Cold War*, by Thomas Hill Schaub. *Flannery O'Connor Bulletin* 21 (1992): 144-47.

States that Schaub examines ways in which "American liberalism redefined itself during the Cold War era," and "convincingly reveals the politics behind apparently apolitical assertions about aesthetics." Indicates that O'Connor is discussed in the chapter, "Christian Realism and O'Connor's *A Good Man Is Hard to Find*." Finds Schaub's work "a sensitive and original reading of O'Connor's fiction." Outlines his thesis: that O'Connor's revision of "The Train" for *Wise Blood* reveals her as "turning away from `humanist, liberal explanations of behavior.'" Relates Schaub's conclusion that "part of the reason for O'Connor's success was that her critique of all liberalism came along at a time when most American liberals were inclined to be critical of liberalism." Highlights

Schaub's focus on "Good Country People" and "A Good Man Is Hard to Find," and his discussion of how "Hulga/Joy Hopewell and The Misfit become O'Connor's caricatures of foolish liberals." Acknowledges his suggestion that the "`ironic reversal' of O'Connor's stories is . . . another quality congenial to the revisionist liberal spirit." Concludes that Schaub "does not underestimate the religious sincerity behind O'Connor's writing, but he does reveal the extent to which there were political reasons for Original Sin to become fashionable."

593   Gentry, Marshall Bruce. Rev. of *Flannery O'Connor: The Growing Craft*, by Karl-Heinz Westarp. *Flannery O'Connor Bulletin* 22 (1993-94): 138-39.

Reports that Westarp is an expert on the manuscripts of O'Connor's "Judgement Day," recounts the various versions of the story, and contends that existent critical commentary comparing the versions of the story may need to be reexamined in view of the results in this book. Describes the format of Westarp's comparative texts and discusses the complexity of the variant works. States that such an examination may leave the reader "feeling fully persuaded of two somewhat contradictory conclusions: that O'Connor considered the alternatives to every word she wrote and that she was always on the lookout for another way to tell her story." Refers to Jan Nordby Gretlund's introduction to "An Exile in the East" in *The South Carolina Review* [11 (Nov. 1978): 3-21], Westarp's introduction to this work reviewed, and questions whether "in order to honor O'Connor's craft as she changed as a writer, we must assert that she consistently and steadily became a better writer."

594   Gentry, Marshall Bruce. Rev. of *Since Flannery O'Connor: Essays on the Contemporary American Short Story*, by Loren Logsdon and Charles W. Mayer. *Flannery O'Connor Bulletin* 17 (1988): 109-11.

States that this work is intended to offer thirteen essays which examine "the development of the American short story since the publication of *A Good Man Is Hard to Find* in 1955." Discusses Logsdon and Mayer's Introduction to the collection, differences in perspective on O'Connor in the first two essays by Richard Giannone and John L. Darretta, and comparisons by Linda Adams Barnes and Barbara C. Lonnquist of O'Connor to Bobbie Ann Mason and Raymond Carver in the last two. Reports that other authors treated in the book include Eudora Welty, John Cheever, Donald Barthelme, Ann Beattie, E.L. Doctorow, Cynthia Ozick, Grace Paley, Louise Erdrich, Gerald Vizenor, and Leslie Marmon Silko. Gentry declares, "although O'Connor goes unmentioned in many of these essays, I was surprised to discover that essays on competing ideologies in

Jewish or Native American stories could suggest interesting comparisons with O'Connor's works." Concludes that in spite of "a mass of typographical errors," and some misquoting, "there is much to admire" in this volume.

595   Gentry, Marshall Bruce. Rev. of *Writing Against God: Language as Message in the Literature of Flannery O'Connor*, by Joanne Halleran McMullen. *Flannery O'Connor Bulletin* 24 (1995-96): 129-32.

Sees McMullen's book as making "a strong case that most of O'Connor's explanations of the religious significance she thought readers should find in her fiction fail to account for the power of the fiction and even mislead." Suggests that the book "is reminiscent of criticism by John Hawkes, Martha Stephens, and Carol Shloss, who see the implications of O'Connor's fiction as running counter to wholesome intentions or as too vague and confused to be interpreted with confidence." Discusses her analysis of O'Connor's choice of character names and her findings regarding O'Connor's preference for nouns over verbs, her emphasis on pronouns, use of various verb tenses and passive constructions, and the "significance of her prepositional phrases and adjectival forms." Notes McMullen's study of O'Connor's use of symbolism, in particular, hats, eyeglasses, "the circularity of time," and the possibility (originally raised by Sarah Liggett) that the name Hulga may be "an anagram for the word `laugh.'" Applauds her coverage "of a reasonable amount of territory," (including *The Violent Bear It Away*, *Wise Blood*, "A Stroke of Good Fortune," "The Displaced Person," "The Lame Shall Enter First," "Greenleaf," "A Good Man Is Hard to Find," and "Good Country People") and how she "manages to bring up a number of questions that critics could continue to investigate for years." Comments that McMullen "seems confused about the relation of religion to the quality of O'Connor's art" and "distressed by the multiplicity of readings O'Connor's works have produced." Concludes with a discussion of McMullen's conclusion that O'Connor's "`passion for religion detracts from her artistic strength.'"

596   Gentry, Marshall Bruce. "`The River.'" *Masterplots II: Short Story, Supplement*. Ed. Frank N. Magill. Pasadina, CA: Salem, 1996. 3914-16.

Discusses O'Connor's "The River," offering a list of the principal characters, an overview of the story, a discussion of the story's theme and meanings, and an opinion regarding O'Connor's style and technique.

597   Gentry, Marshall Bruce. "Tracks to the Oven of Redemption." *Flannery O'Connor Bulletin* 14 (1985): 72-79.

Contends that Robert E. Golden "correctly identifies the foremost issue in O'Connor criticism as the relation between O'Connor's stated religious intent and the realization of that intent within the fiction." Outlines positions of various critical schools and their view of O'Connor's work and sees O'Connor's theology as being relevant to her fiction. Argues that "most critics who discuss theology have underestimated her reinterpretations of dogma," then outlines how her works exhibit "a shared fantasy and a pattern of imagery" that suggest an explanation for the redemptive experiences of O'Connor's characters. Observes how some characters "imagine themselves transported toward the site of their death," often "in a boxcar to join a pile of dead bodies to be burned in an oven." Discusses in this context definitions of the word "redemption"; the significance of the words "ideal" and "community"; the "explicit imagery of tracks toward physical annihilation"; the applicability of Bakhtin's "theory of novelistic narration" and Dorrit Cohn's views of Bakhtin's "character zone"; and how these patterns of imagery suggest "that it is the characters themselves who prepare for and bring about the revelatory religious experiences they undergo." Discusses, as examples, Mrs. Shortley of "The Displaced Person," Ruby Turpin of "Revelation," Mrs. Cope of "A Circle in the Fire," Asbury Fox's sister's comment in "The Enduring Chill," and Joy Hopewell's use of the assumed name, Hulga in "Good Country People." [An excerpt from Gentry's introductory chapter to *Flannery O'Connor's Religion of the Grotesque* (Jackson: UP of Mississippi, 1986).]

598   "Georgia Writers: Past and Present." *Georgia Journal* 5.6 (1985): 13-16.

Offers a brief biographical profile of a variety of Georgia authors, including O'Connor. Describes her childhood in Savannah and notes, "she was precocious and independent and pleased that she was an only child. At an early age she kept journals, composed poems, stories and essays." Cites awards O'Connor received and provides a brief description of her career. Does not attempt to estimate her position within the literary canon, but suggests that "she has a permanent place in American literature."

599   Gerald, Kelly S. "'Thank God for the shoe!': The Emblematic Shoe in O'Connor's Fiction." *Flannery O'Connor Bulletin* 23 (1994-95): 91-118.

Finds "147 distinct mentions of shoes" in O'Connor's fiction, with functional uses repeated from one story and character to the next. Claims that "categories of use overlap to reveal sometimes unexpected patterns of association," including "ritualistic use of shoes to indicate acts of penance, baptism, burial, and purgation"; to illustrate spiritual or profane situations; "to indicate the sexual character and situation of the wearer"; "to indicate the social class of her characters, reflecting the behavior and personality of the wearer"; and as a focal point in her cartoons for the GSCW newpspaper, *The Colonnade*. Considers O'Connor's views on Emerson's "sermon on the Lord's Supper," her interest in peacocks, and sees her use of the shoe as "a metaphor for the corruption of human pride and materialism." Carefully examines how her use of the shoe might serve "as an emblem to Martin Heidegger's thought on the nature of art." Includes illustrations and commentary on three of O'Connor's cartoons, and refers to or cites remarks by Steven Olson, Margaret Whitt, A.R. Coulthard, Alan J. Fletcher (on the parable of the peacock's feet), Ralph Waldo Emerson, Martin Heidegger, William Sessions, Stefan Schimanski, Beverly Brunson, Baron von Hügel, and Ralph C. Wood.

600   Gernes, Sonia. "Belief is the Engine: Faith and the Art of Flannery O'Connor." *New Catholic World* 228.1366 (1985): 162-66.

Edited version of "Faith and Art: The Vocation of Flannery O'Connor," published in the *Notre Dame Magazine* 10.4 (1981): 8-13, with different photographs as illustrations.

601   Gernes, Sonia. "Faith and Art: The Vocation of Flannery O'Connor." *Notre Dame Magazine* 10.4 (1981): 8-13.

Remembers reading "A Good Man Is Hard to Find" and noting how quickly her own laughter turned to horror, all of which left a lasting impression. Recalls also her own, and the audience's reaction, to the movie version of *Wise Blood*. Defends O'Connor with her own words--that "distortions" surround the Catholic in the modern world, and it is the fiction writer's job to make those distortions (which have become commonplace) appear "unnatural." Discusses "The Artificial Nigger" in these terms and estimates O'Connor's position in the canon of post-war writers. Concludes with a biographical sketch.

602   Gernes, Sonia. "To Flannery, with Thanks." *Flannery O'Connor Bulletin* 24 (1995-96): 85-87.

Offers a personal recollection of how she became familiar with O'Connor's writings while taking classes as an undergraduate at a Catholic college soon after two years of novitiate training. Remembers, years earlier, being required to write a letter of condolence to Regina Cline O'Connor upon Flannery's death and later, as an undergraduate, trying to understand why Flannery as "a Catholic writer" chose morally objectionable scenes and subjects for her fiction. Contrasts having to practice "custody of the eyes" during her training as a nun with O'Connor's interest in seeing and rendering the world as it is. Compares her own concerns as to what her own family would think of some of the content of her first novel (*The Way to St. Ives*) with O'Connor's remarks in *The Habit of Being*. Wonders what Regina thought of "that batch of letters written by sophomoric Midwestern hands," and states that were she to write Flannery now, her letter "would simply say, `Thank you.'"

603   Giannone, Richard. "`The Artificial Nigger' and the Redemptive Quality of Suffering." *Flannery O'Connor Bulletin* 12 (1983): 5-16.

Discusses the various interpretations of "The Artificial Nigger," and notes that the fascination the story holds for readers "runs counter to O'Connor's enthusiasm." Contends that "the history of its popularity is a history of discontent, especially over the way the action ends." Outlines and footnotes various readings, including remarks made by O'Connor herself. Considers the controversy and states that "such quarrels are instructive." Suggests that they tell readers "something about the assumptions O'Connor's art contends with and they invite us to consider just what signals in the story are evident to O'Connor but equivocal to her audience." Offers a detailed and lengthy explication of the story, primarily from a theological perspective, and within the context of what O'Connor probably intended in regard to the issue of racism. States that "the essential point to be made . . . concerns how a writer with a theological habit of mind works." Argues that a major clue to understanding O'Connor's perspective, especially in regard to racism, is to understand that a "spiritual writer not only takes shortcuts through social history but reverses the direction of analysis." Sees racism in the story as rising, "not out of any direct contact with blacks" but out of a "condition of unexpressed feeling."

604   Giannone, Richard. "Bobbie Ann Mason and the Recovery of Mystery." *Studies in Short Fiction* 27.4 (1990): 553-66.

Includes a brief comparison of Mason's work with that of O'Connor, referring to Linda Adams Barnes's contention that Mason is the "heiress to O'Connor's legacy."

605   Giannone, Richard. "The City: Flannery O'Connor's No Kind of Place." *Thought* 62.246 (1987): 311-28.

Sees O'Connor as "exploring the city through the experience of country fugitives . . . [which] serves a conscious moral strategy." Contends that

O'Connor's work brings out the city's inclination to offer only evil alternatives and no encouragement to resist it. Concludes that "static gruesomeness is the given" of O'Connor's cityscape.

606   Giannone, Richard. "Displacing Gender: Flannery O'Connor's View from the Woods." *Flannery O'Connor: New Perspectives.* Ed. Sura P. Rath and Mary Neff Shaw. Athens: U of Georgia P, 1996. 73-95.

Contends that, despite her "fidelity to a patriarchal church and culture," O'Connor, "in her treatment of gender . . . may turn out to be a feminist." States that "the usual dichotomy between female weakness and male toughness does not give final shape to O'Connor's action"; her characters' "cruel exercise of power fills her short stories and novels without harsh burdens falling along gender lines." Explores how "family life generates the conflicts in O'Connor's fiction" regardless of the characters' gender; the lack of gender-bonding by characters; and how--in situations in which "divine intervention corrects human perception"--the "supreme truth disarranges the roles assigned by gender and age so as to overturn the power wielded by these differences." Argues that "by driving the story toward a sacred view of human violence, O'Connor drastically dislocates our usual sexist way of seeing," because, for O'Connor, "the cancellation of any division by sex marks the fulfillment of God's promise." Closes with a lengthy, careful, and detailed reading--in the context of this discussion of gender--of "A View of the Woods." Sees the story as focused on the devaluation of a child (Mary Fortune) "under mortal patriarchal domination by two male parents." Concludes that though Mary Fortune "is battered and killed by a rigid male system out of control," O'Connor disregards her gender and has her share equally in destruction when she seizes power to defy the system.

607   Giannone, Richard. "Flannery O'Connor Tells Her Desert Story." *Religion & Literature* 27.2 (1995): 47-67.

Asserts that the "contradictory legacy" of World War II influenced thousands to follow Thomas Merton into the cloister to become monks. Suggests that this "resurgence of Christian asceticism," in turn, influenced others, including Flannery O'Connor, to take up "the ascetic spirit in their workaday lives." Describes the general goals of those who participated in this post-World War II movement, and ties the movement, and Flannery O'Connor, to "the desert fathers and mothers of the fourth century [who] fled to the sandy wastes and steep crags of Egypt and Palestine" to escape the despotic Roman world and find meaning within themselves and draw closer to God. Sees O'Connor's interest as being greatly influenced by her medical condition. Relates that it forced her "to withdraw from the vital literary and intellectual relations that were her natural context," to live in confinement in rural Georgia with her mother. Indicates that, like the primitive ascetics, O'Connor was faced with learning "how to convert her unbidden dislocation and disease into human growth," and "transform the trials of medicine and faith into art" while living in the "Georgia desert." Offers a close, detailed, and carefully crafted reading of "The Artificial Nigger," intended to help readers better "appreciate the poignancy with which O'Connor brings the still voice of the primitive desert into contemporary fiction." Introduces the story in the context of the conservative period during which it was written, and recounts how O'Connor regarded this story about racism more highly than others. Discusses how she uses this story to make a case against racism, uses ideology "to give her political drama spiritual vitality," and presents it "as a modern analogue of the late antique story of reversed discipleship."

608   Giannone, Richard. "Flannery O'Connor's Consecration of the End." *Since Flannery O'Connor: Essays on the Contemporary American Short Story.* Ed. Loren Logsdon and Charles W. Mayer. Macomb: Western Illinois UP, 1987. 9-20.

Uses remarks from an unpublished lecture of 1956 related to James Joyce's *A Portrait of the Artist as a Young Man* as an example of how O'Connor "has a knack for imbedding self-disclosure in her appreciations of other writers." Suggests that these comments are "always informal and grounded in a problem that she is tackling in her own work at the moment." Contends that while O'Connor looked to the poetry of T.S. Eliot as being "ideal of craft infused with knowledgeable witness to Christian faith," she herself was "transformed by the act of writing hammered on the habit of feeling." Argues that the more truthfully she "as storyteller renders what she sees and not what she thinks she ought to see, the closer she approaches the most ancient pattern of all--the biblical cycle of guilt and transcendence." Considers and offers a discussion of features of versions of the story titled "The Geranium," "Judgement Day," and "Exile in the East." Asserts that if one examines the features of early versions of this story and then compares them to "the distinctive moral force of the last draft, we can appreciate the odyssey that O'Connor undertakes." Concludes that "'Judgement Day' does not pretend to dramatize the full mystery of redemptive peace. Rather it shows how the new dispensation comes to each of us personally when the divine act of dying and rising reaches us through small acts of love."

609   Giannone, Richard. "'Greenleaf': A Story of Lent." *Studies in Short Fiction* 22.4 (1985): 421-29.

States that most critics view "Greenleaf" as a failed effort; that O'Connor was unable to "master the technical challenge and embody fundamental meaning in physical action." Gives favor to O'Connor's own comments and feelings of success about it. Works through the story point by point, commenting on such issues as the bull's "relationship as lover," Mrs. May's belief that the world "owes" her for the hardships that she suffers, and Mrs. May's own atheism. Argues that Mrs. May's conversion is evident in her facial changes, and even within (in terms of "rebirth") her name. Closes with an analysis of the connection between *Psalm* 22 and the story. Concludes with the suggestion that, though she was killed by the bull, Mrs. May is finally "loved" for the first time.

610   Giannone, Richard. "The Lion of Judah in the Thought and Design of *The Violent Bear It Away.*" *Flannery O'Connor Bulletin* 14 (1985): 25-32.

Considers the role and function of the stone lion, the fountain, and the concrete circle of the fountain in the park scene of the sixth chapter of *The Violent Bear It Away*. Offers a reading of this chapter, focusing on how O'Connor uses the lion as "an anagogical signpost, which, like the lawn statuary in 'The Artificial Nigger,'" is intended to guide readers' interpretation of the story. Sees the lion as "a monument to God's bold presence and in that service marks a vantage from which the reader can see all three sojourners through the park in relation to their ultimate need." Suggests that O'Connor uses the park scene to bring the novel to its midpoint, "not with explanation but through revelation." Suggests that she uses the lion, the fountain, and the park's landscape, to impart "several lessons in spiritual evolution." Contends that "the mysterious pull that Tarwater feels toward Bishop emanates from the lion"; that, just as the lion tested Daniel, "it also tested the loyalty of Mason when he was thrown into the insane asylum"; and that "the gentle side of the lion reconstitutes what is a lion's den for Tarwater into a sacred font for Bishop."

611   Giannone, Richard. "Paul, Francis, and Hazel Motes: Conversion at Taulkinham." *Thought* 59.235 (1984): 483-503.

Defends *Wise Blood* as a story worth telling because it goes out of its way to "explore extreme boundaries of conversion," and "turns in full seriousness to God." Draws out the parallels between Hazel Motes and St. Paul, and discusses the religious significance of minute details--October 4 being both the date of Hawk's sacrifice as well as the day of the feast of St. Francis of Assisi. Says O'Connor uses fear, rebellion, and injured pride to generate the hero's "acute, inner conflict." Argues that the novel's theology is embodied in the twisting of reality which critics call "the grotesque in O'Connor's art." States that the fourteen chapters of the novel suggest that Hazel, though in retreat, is moving along the fourteen stations of the cross. Analyzes this analogy in detail, chapter by chapter, breaking Hazel's behavior into two phases: first, his rejection of a righteous family; and second, a reaction against the grimness of day-to-day life in Taulkinham. Labels Hazel "a martyr" because "he crawls and digs his way to the cross . . . sealed in his own suffering and unwise blood."

612   Giannone, Richard. "Stabbing the Heart: *Catanyxis* and *Penthos* in Flannery O'Connor's `Greenleaf.'" *Christianity and Literature* 45.3-4 (1996): 331-44.

Discusses how O'Connor uses "the eremitic experience of *catanyxis* or sudden shock that puts a new feeling in the soul and . . . the stark recognition of *penthos*, the tears that flow from the inner shock" of *catanyxis*, in her short story, "Greenleaf." Defines these terms, outlines interpretations of their meanings, and provides a detailed reading of this story to illustrate how O'Connor uses these concepts as part of her "one-woman war against the age's moral blindness." Recalls that O'Connor referred to herself as "`a hermit novelist,'" and uses this statement to bolster arguments that many of her characters may be viewed as "living out the radical simplicity of eremitical solitude and ascesis" as they "grapple with their demons." Refers to Andrew Delbanco's *The Death of Satan: How Americans Have Lost the Sense of Evil*, O'Connor's correspondence with John Hawkes regarding their different views of the devil, and the sayings of Anthony the Great.

613   Giannone, Richard. "Warfare and Solitude: O'Connor's Prophet and the Word in the Desert." *Literature and Belief* 17.1-2 (1997): 161-89.

Examines the "primary impulses and cultural significance of asceticism in *The Violent Bear It Away*." Suggests that its historical context gives "rise and meaning to the religious withdrawal in the novel, and the biblical and patristic sources generating the novel's ascetic action." Offers evidence from O'Connor's letters, published in *The Habit of Being*, of her "sympathy for asceticism," and discusses why she chose to set the novel's "climactic events" between 1938 and 1952. Sees Powderhead as the "boundary between a world hostile to life and a sphere of true human order fostering dignity and holiness." Suggests that "the demonic invasion of Tarwater's body captures perfectly the patristic-monastic understanding of *logismos*," and discusses how, during his stay with Rayber, "every experience dilates to Tarwater's inner disorder." Concludes that this is a "story of the ancient Egyptian desert set in the American South."

614 Gibson, Mary Ellis. "Introduction." *New Stories by Southern Women.* Columbia: U of South Carolina P, 1989. 3-12.

Comments on the variety and quality of the twenty-one stories by women writers included in this anthology and reflects upon the meaning and context of what being a present-day Southern woman writer means. Includes passing references to O'Connor: a comparison of her prominence as compared to present-day women writers; her being one of a group of women writers who benefitted from the efforts of a previous generation; influence, along with that of Zora Neale Hurston and Eudora Welty, on Alice Walker's work; and, acknowledges that the violence of the stories included is less than that typically found in those by O'Connor.

615 Gidden, Nancy Ann. "Classical Agents of Christian Grace in Flannery O'Connor's `Greenleaf.'" *Studies in Short Fiction* 23.2 (1986): 201-02.

Examines the use of the "sun" and "bull" as symbols from classical mythology in "Greenleaf" in "the service of Christian conversion." Concludes that by identifying the sun and bull as Apollo and Dionysus readers may resolve the difficulties presented by their complex roles.

616 Gilbert, Rick. "Laura Lasworth at [Santa Monica, CA] Hunsaker/Schlesinger Gallery." *Artweek* (Jan. 1998): 54.

Reviews Lasworth's showing of a suite of 15 paintings titled, *The Habit of Being: A Portrait of Miss Mystery and Manners*, which "derives its inspiration from the writings of Flannery O'Connor." Comments that the paintings included in this show reflect Lasworth's "long preoccupation with the religious experience . . . inherent in O'Connor's fictional realm of fanatical itinerant salvationists, lurking epiphany, and quiet revelation." Includes an illustration of one of Lasworth's paintings titled, *Tarwater's Seed-like Eyes*.

617 Gilbert, Sandra M. and Susan Gubar. *No Man's Land: The Place of the Woman Writer in the Twentieth Century: Vol. 1, The War of the Words.* New Haven: Yale UP, 1988. 112, 241.

Mentions O'Connor in discussion of authors who "responded to male attacks with accounts of female freakishness, male willfulness or brutality, female guilt, and female sacrifice." Also mentioned her as among those who "wanted to repudiate a stereotypically feminine gender identity."

617a   Gilbert, Susanna. "`Blood Don't Lie': The Diseased Family in Flannery O'Connor's *Everything That Rises Must Converge*." *Literature and Medicine* 18.1 (1999): 114-31.

Argues that "O'Connor's struggle with lupus makes its way into her fiction not only literally--through images of blood, disease, death, and twisted parent-child relationships--but figuratively as well." Contends that stories in O'Connor's final collection, *Everything That Rises Must Converge*, "replicate not only the dynamics of her relationship with her parents but, more interestingly, the dynamics of her disease--its omnipresent symptoms; sudden, surprising ferocity; and, most importantly, its grotesque drama of the self against the self." Sees the "dominating presence" of O'Connor's lupus as offering an explanation for "the darkness" in her work "that has puzzled so many critics for so long." Discusses how the disease forced her to give up her independent life, dictated how her daily life was organized, and "seems to have fueled much of her fiction." Notes her remark that "Hulga, the sullen, crippled heroine of `Good Country People,'" was a projection of herself. Examines O'Connor's preoccupation with blood imagery and how the violence in her work may be an unconscious reflection of her fragile circumstances. Discusses "A View of the Woods" and "The Lame Shall Enter First," and concludes that O'Connor's "almost obsessive narrative repetition" of images of disease, disability, and death suggests that she may have been trying "to tell the story of her illness . . . to `detoxify' herself." [Rpt. in *Literature and Medicine: Writers With Chronic Illness*. Ed. Marilyn Chandler McEntyre. Baltimore: Johns Hopkins UP, 1999.]

618   Giles, Paul. *American Catholic Arts and Fictions: Catholic Ideology, Aesthetics*. New York: Cambridge UP, 1992. 23, 24, 25, 60, 118, 135, 159, 198, 206, 212, 283, 327, 332, 353-93, 394-96, 435, 449, 488, 498, 507, 509, 522, 528.

Suggests that the work of authors such as Mary McCarthy and Flannery O'Connor "can reveal more about the Catholic experience in the United States than many wearisome issues of the *Catholic Digest*" while also telling readers "a considerable amount about the development of twentieth-century Catholicism in the United States." Refers to O'Connor as one of several writers who could be said to comprise an "antiromantic `Catholic' tradition" of American literature. Notes O'Connor's observation of Ernest Hemingway's "`hunger for a Catholic completeness in life,'" and contends that her use of "one of the commonest myths of Catholicism" ("how the grace of the Catholic church knows no temporal boundaries and can work for everybody equally"), parallels "America's political rejection of . . . archaic social hierarchies of Europe." Notes O'Connor's emphasis upon "radical piety" and how her "impoverished outcast or rebel can be nearer to divine grace than the smug patriarch" living with the "rewards of an arduous secular life." Finds in this an illustration of how "within the American Catholic tradition . . . the American Dream is often represented in its barest functional outlines: as a game, a boxing ring, a football pitch, a pool hall, a gaming table." Observes how Robert Lowell's "figurative constructions in *Lord Weary's Castle* resemble those in Flannery O'Connor's stories," and compares her work with that of Alfred Hitchcock. Discusses the "tension between art and dogma" in O'Connor's work and in Catholic literature in general. Examines in Chapter 15, "The Rewriting of Theology: Katherine Anne Porter, Flannery O'Connor, Walker Percy, Donald Barthelme," the "development from Modernist to postmodernist conceptions of literature and theology" as seen in the works of these writers. Refers in this chapter to Evelyn Waugh, Caroline Gordon, Mario Praz, Pope Leo XIII, Philip Gleason, Ralph Wood, André Bleikasten, Jean Genet, Graham Greene, William Lynch, Allen Tate, Edward Kessler, Walter J. Ong, Karl Rahner, David Tracy, and David Burrell.

619   Gillespie, Michael Patrick. "Baroque Catholicism in Southern Fiction: Flannery O'Connor, Walker Percy, and John Kennedy Toole." *Traditions, Voices, and Dreams: The American Novel Since the 1960s.* Ed. Melvin J. Friedman and Ben Siegel. Newark: U of Delaware P, 1995. 25-47.

Discusses how each of these three writers, "in a highly idiosyncratic manner, draws elements of Roman Catholic belief and ritual into various aspects of his or her narratives," to infuse a unique view distinctly different from the fictional world of the South created by William Faulkner. Outlines how each writer's "concept of dogma and ritual unfold[s] as extravagant elaborations that often border on caricature," and sees their work as challenging "the more traditional concepts of faith by depicting them as delusions or as willful deceptions." In this context, offers a reading of O'Connor's "A Good Man Is Hard to Find," followed by a shorter discussion of *The Violent Bear It Away.* Proposes that while O'Connor appears to suppress "a Catholic perception of events" in her fiction, she focuses "with a graphic bitterness, on the claustrophobic environment that both nurtures and corrupts Southern Protestant fundamentalist beliefs." Concludes that O'Connor's strategy is intended to force her readers "to confront the unsatisfactory manifestations of faith and agnosticism that one finds" in Protestantism and to turn to Catholic dogma as a "coherent alternative" to "the perverse religious beliefs" that inadequately sustain her characters. Concludes, however, that Catholicism operates "least overtly" in O'Connor's fiction, appears somewhat more ambiguously in Percy's, and exists "in its most straightforward manner" in Toole's novel, *A Confederacy of Dunces.*

620   Gilman, Richard. "Salvation, Damnation and the Religious Novel." *New York Times Book Review* 2 Dec. 1984: 7+.

Gilman reflects upon a period of his life, thirty years previous, in which he had "surrendered" himself to "the large, general world of fiction," especially "fiction by Catholics." Among the variety of authors discussed is Flannery O'Connor, whom Gilman views as "the only American Catholic writer . . . whose work is about religious experience instead of, as in J.F. Powers or Edwin O'Connor, about the sociology of religion." Finds O'Connor's faith "there to see, behind the pages" of her fiction.

621   Gohdes, Clarence and Sanford E. Marovitz. *Bibliographical Guide to the Study of the Literature of the U.S.A.* 5th ed. Durham, NC: Duke UP, 1984. 123-24, 220, 232.

Refers to two works on O'Connor by W. Frohock and I. Malin. Then, under Principle Biographies, lists Dorothy Walters's, *Flannery O'Connor*.

622   Goldfield, David R. *Black, White, and Southern: Race Relations and Southern Culture, 1940s to Present.* Baton Rouge: Louisiana State UP, 1990. 43-44, 138-39.

Provides a synopsis of O'Connor's "The Displaced Person" as part of a discussion of "the darker side" of how "the outside world was penetrating the South." Focuses on Guizac's offer of his young cousin in marriage to one of the black tenants. Suggests that the incident serves as an intrusion upon Southern manners and customs which, though Guizac is killed in the process, eventually destroys the cultural milieu upon which the situation is based. O'Connor's remark that she uses violence to return her characters to reality and to prepare them to accept God's offer of grace, is used to illustrate Martin Luther King, Jr.'s concurring belief that the shedding of blood would probably be necessary to redeem the South and the region from the blight of segregation.

623   Goldstein, Bill. "PW Interviews: Mark Childress." *Publisher's Weekly* 7 Sept. 1990: 68-69.

Offers a profile of the author of *Tender, A World Made of Fire,* and *V for Victory.* Includes remarks regarding O'Connor's influence and his thoughts after reading her story, "Everything That Rises Must Converge" during his freshman year at Louisiana State: "`I couldn't believe someone had written a story so close to my family, to what I had experienced . . . it blew me away that fiction could apply even to the life you were living.'"

624   Gombar, Christina. "Flannery O'Connor: Writer of Violence and Vision."
            Great Women Writers, 1900-1950. American Profiles. New York: Facts
            On File, 1996. 145-62.

Offers a biographical sketch that describes O'Connor's childhood,
education at Georgia State College for Women (GSCW) and the Writer's
Workshop at the University of Iowa, and her battle with lupus while
"living under the constant threat of death." Follows with discussions of the
plot, themes, and main characters of "A Good Man Is Hard to Find," *Wise
Blood*, "The Artificial Nigger," "Good Country People," "The Displaced
Person," *The Violent Bear It Away*, "Everything That Rises Must
Converge," and "The Lame Shall Enter First." Mentions that William
Faulkner and Robert Penn Warren were among the visiting professors at
Iowa who "critiqued her early work." Contends that O'Connor
"transcended the boundaries of her daily experience with a far-reaching
imagination and a masterful ability to relate the local to the cosmic."
Reports that "critical interest and analysis of her work has been growing
since her death," and concludes that O'Connor's "two novels and twenty
stories achieved insights into human fallibility and the meaning of
existence that are unparalleled in American literature today."

625   Gonzales, Sarah. "A Forum in Flannery's Honor." (Georgia College &
            State University) *Alumni News Quarterly* (Summer 1988): 5.

Announces establishment of the "Flannery O'Connor Writer's Forum," for
having "distinguished writers to the [Georgia College & State University]
campus in honor of Flannery O'Connor." Notes that 1989 was both the
25th anniversary of the death of O'Connor, "the college's most celebrated
alumnus," and the centennial year of the university. Reports that James
Dickey--whom O'Connor had encouraged during his early writing career--
had visited the campus as the "first guest of the Forum."

626   Gorak, Jan. *God the Artist: American Novelists in a Post-Realist Age*.
            Urbana: U of Illinois P, 1987. 107-08, 109, 125.

Challenges "two irreconcilable ideas of the artist that have emerged in
some influential modern criticism": the view of the literary artist "as
symbolist, [and] maker of images . . . omnipotent in mind, careless of
matter, [and] oblivious of his audience," versus "the naturalist in his
various transformations . . . so crushed by power structures and language
systems, the wonder is he manages to write at all." Discusses John
Hawkes's work, including, "Flannery O'Connor's Devil," in *Sewanee
Review*; compares his originality to O'Connor's; and suggests that her
"imaginative strength was too much for her Catholic orthodoxy.

627   Gordon, Mary. "Flannery O'Connor: *The Habit of Being.*" *Good Boys and Dead Girls and Other Essays.* New York: Viking, 1991. 37-44.

Slightly altered version of Gordon's article, originally published as "The Habit of Genius," in *Saturday Review* 14 April 1979: 42-45.

628   Gordon, Mary. "The Habit of Genius." *Dialogue* 52.2 (1981): 56-59.

Slightly edited version of Gordon's article by the same title in *Saturday Review* 14 April 1979: 42-45.

629   Gordon, Mary. "The Habit of Genius." *Saturday Review* 14 April 1979: 42-45.

Under the guise of a book review of *The Habit of Being*, Gordon provides a loosely woven biographical article that discusses a variety of topics: the Catholic writer's place in society, his or her difficulty as an artist, and his or her burden as a writer/Catholic--all implied by O'Connor's idea that the "Church" has little to do with most people and more to do with "Grace." Discusses O'Connor's illness, writers O'Connor admired, her letter to her editor at Rinehart dismissing his criticism, and the general contents of letters which she concludes are a treasure and "a grace." Laments the fact that O'Connor's reputation has not been revered as it should be. Illustrations: Photograph of Flannery O'Connor's "Self-Portrait" (1953).

630   Gordon, Sarah. "`The Crop': Limitation, Restraint, and Possibility." *Flannery O'Connor: New Perspectives.* Ed. Sura P. Rath and Mary Neff Shaw. Athens: U of Georiga P, 1996. 96-120.

Suggests that while O'Connor would have been "chagrined" to see "The Crop," from her master's thesis, included in *The Complete Stories*, it "may well be the most important story in the thesis collection" and "noteworthy as a revelation of O'Connor's acknowledgement of the forces over which the female artist must have control." Remarks that "The Crop" suggests "many of the dilemmas of the southern female artist in the middle of the twentieth century in terms of range, form, and content." Then, discusses a variety of related issues: how O'Connor "indirectly attacks . . . social and economic realism, especially as exemplified in the work of fellow Georgian Erskine Caldwell"; how Miss Willerton appears to be the "first of the `comic authorial self-projections' presented throughout O'Connor's fiction"; how the story "constitutes a dialogue with herself . . . the author's attempt to exert control over her own textuality"; the response to her work by family and community; the societal pressure upon O'Connor, as a

Southern woman, to "'act pretty'"; and the fact that O'Connor was separated from her mother for only a few years. Concludes that "The Crop" "can be read . . . as subversive of niceness and propriety." In this story Flannery O'Connor "is defining for herself what a woman writer is by delineating what she is not or cannot be." Further, the work shows O'Connor's attempt "to establish her own textual territory apart from the expectations of appropriate female behavior, or questions of female power and control."

631   Gordon, Sarah. "Flannery O'Connor and the Common Reader." *Flannery O'Connor Bulletin* 10 (1981): 38-45.

Addresses the issue of whether "the instincts of the Common Reader" can be "trusted," and suggests that--whether one is a teacher of freshman English, an undergraduate, or an O'Connor "specialist"--all who approach her stories are "Common Readers." Contends that the principal problem faced is that of having to peel away "our 'educated' or 'trained' responses" so that we might better understand the text. Offers an explication of "Revelation" to illustrate O'Connor's method of drawing readers "into a world we *think* we know," and leading them "to a place that is disturbing in its unfamiliarity." Notes that, in "Revelation," it is her "reader's dangerous smugness and self-congratulations which are hit square in the eye by O'Connor." Argues that examining O'Connor as a realistic writer, or a regional humorist, or comparing her to such known writers as William Faulkner and Eudora Welty, is useful, but only "to a point." Concludes that for readers to understand Flannery O'Connor's work they must "see in the form and the content of her fiction an immersion in the real so profound that it moves beyond realism to the final shape and essences of our ultimate being."

632   Gordon, Sarah. "Flannery O'Connor, the Left-Wing Mystic, and the German Jew." *Flannery O'Connor Bulletin* 16 (1987): 43-51.

Notes that in her letters to "A," published in *The Habit of Being,* O'Connor indicates her great interest in, and respect for, Simone Weil and Edith Stein. Suggests that O'Connor found in these two figures "the extremes of religious response which interested her most." Provides brief biographical sketches of the two women, as well as summaries of, and excerpts from, O'Connor's letters. Points out evidence of their influence, including the character of Joy/Hulga Hopewell, "who bears a striking comic resemblance to Simone Weil," and the images of the holocaust in "The Displaced Person." States that the radical nature of the quest of these sensitive and intelligent women drew O'Connor, who "was always moved by the extreme tests to which passionate belief or search for belief is put."

633   Gordon, Sarah. ["Flannery O'Connor's Families: Dysfunction and
               Disgrace": Part I] "O'Connor Letters Found in East Baldwin County."
               CHEERS! The Flannery O'Connor Society Newsletter 3.1 (1995): 4.

               First installment of a paper delivered by Gordon at the "Homeplace: A
               Celebration of Family Conference" held in Athens, GA, on April 22, 1995.
               Offers fictional, humorous letters supposedly released for publication by
               their owner, the great-nephew of Francis Marion Tarwater, "a street
               preacher in Atlanta and Fulton County," who "claims to have no
               knowledge of the identity of the correspondents," Flannery O'Connor and
               Sally Virginia Cope. The hypothetical exchange refers to characters and
               scenes in "A Good Man Is Hard to Find."

634   Gordon, Sarah. ["Flannery O'Connor's Families: Dysfunction and
               Disgrace": Part II] "More East Baldwin County Letters." *CHEERS! The
               Flannery O'Connor Newsletter* 3.2 (1995-96): 3-4.

               Second installment of a paper titled "Flannery O'Connor's Families:
               Dysfunction and Disgrace," delivered by Gordon at the 1995 "Homeplace:
               A Celebration of Family Conference." Focuses upon fictitious letters
               between Flannery O'Connor and Sally Virginia Cope which deal with the
               meaning of the interaction between the grandmother and The Misfit in "A
               Good Man Is Hard to Find" and Harry Ashfield's baptism and death in
               "The River."

635   Gordon, Sarah. ["Flannery O'Connor's Families: Dysfunction and
               Disgrace": Part III] "More East Baldwin County O'Connor Letters."
               CHEERS! The Flannery O'Connor Society Newsletter 4.1 (1996): 2-3.

               Third installment of a paper titled "Flannery O'Connor's Families:
               Dysfunction and Disgrace," delivered by Sarah Gordon at the 1995
               "Homeplace: A Celebration of Family Conference." Continues with
               fictitious letters between O'Connor and Sally Virginia Cope focusing on
               O'Connor's child characters and her portrayal of parents in "The Life You
               Save May Be Your Own," "Good Country People," "The River," "A Good
               Man Is Hard to Find," and "A Temple of the Holy Ghost."

636   Gordon, Sarah. "From the Editor." *Flannery O'Connor Bulletin* 22 (1993-
               94): i-ii.

               Describes Georgia College & State University's successful symposium,
               "The Habit of Art: An Interdisciplinary Celebration of the Legacy of
               Flannery O'Connor," held April 13-16, 1994, in Milledgeville. Outlines

events, readings, and names major participants. States that in addition to papers by Ralph Wood and Louise Westling, published in this issue of the *Flannery O'Connor Bulletin*, other papers presented may be published in future issues. Reports the illness and retirement of Mary Key Ferrell who had served as editor of the *Bulletin* and announces the appointment of Jane A. Rose as Associate Editor.

637   Gordon, Sarah. "From the Editor." *Flannery O'Connor Bulletin* 24 (1995-96): i.

Describes how a number of writers were approached to offer tributes to O'Connor regarding to the importance of her fiction to their own work and urged to provide "statements testifying to O'Connor's influence and staying power." Discusses the reaction and contributions of Lee Smith, Mark Jarman, Paul Mariani, Doris Betts, Alfred Corn, Josephine Jacobsen, and Andrea Hollander Budy. Reports that the issue also contains two articles on the subject of "O'Connor and race" and photographs by Blaine Speigel that "underscore O'Connor's continuing legacy in diverse art forms."

637a   Gordon, Sarah. "From the Editor." *Flannery O'Connor Bulletin* 26-27 (1998-2000): i-iii.

Thanks readers "for their patience in waiting for this combined [1998-2000] issue" and introduces the content of the issue: the Flannery O'Connor Photography contest; the "haunting paintings of Laura Lasworth"; and the diversity of views presented in the "prose content" of the issue. Follows with the announcement that "*The Flannery O'Connor Bulletin* is undergoing a metamorphosis--in content, format, and even title!" Reports that while the new journal will still focus on Flannery O'Connor, it will be titled *Flannery O'Connor Review*, and "include articles on related writers and material . . . and will feature a larger format, a handsome color cover, artwork of all kinds." Mentions examples of topics that would be of interest for publication and closes with a statement of the aim of the new journal: to offer "a broader and deeper reading of O'Connor's terrain, a fuller understanding of its southern and Catholic contexts, and a more thorough examination of O'Connor's thematic and spiritual relationships with other writers, thinkers, and artists."

638   Gordon, Sarah, [Moderator]. "From the Panel Discussion." *Flannery O'Connor Bulletin* 13 (1984): 59-72.

Provides excerpts, transcribed by Deborah Mosley, "of highlights" from the panel discussion which took place during the third O'Connor symposium held at Georgia College & State University in Milledgeville, "Of Time and Place and Eternity," April 14-15, 1984. Sarah Gordon moderated the discussion, with Sally Fitzgerald, J.O. Tate, Ralph Wood, and Frederick Asals serving as panelists. Questions and discussion addressed: stereotyping and caricature in O'Connor's work, in particular, blacks and social scientists; "O'Connor's idea that the South is `Christ-haunted'"; the "relationship between O'Connor and the historical South"; Alice Walker's antihistorical "urge to burn down Flannery O'Connor's house"; O'Connor's use of the term "manners"; and her holocaust imagery (for example, in "Revelation"). Included are portions of Sally Fitzgerald's response to Ralph Wood's presentation (she contends that he offered "a distorted impression of Catholic practices" in regard to Hazel Motes's self-mutilation), and his retort. Concludes with Fitzgerald, Tate, and Asals responding to the question, "Did Flannery O'Connor have a problem with the Catholic idea of paying."

639   Gordon, Sarah. "From the Senior Editor." *Flannery O'Connor Bulletin* 20 (1991): i-ii.

Notes that this issue marks the twentieth anniversary of the founding of the *Flannery O'Connor Bulletin*. Briefly outlines its history and discusses its future. Discusses the reproductions of six works of art in this issue by Douglas Powers. Concludes with acknowledgement of the establishment of *The Flannery O'Connor Society* by Sura Rath of LSU-Shreveport.

640   Gordon, Sarah. "Maryat and Julian and the `not so bloodless revolution.'" *Flannery O'Connor Bulletin* 21 (1992): 25-36.

Examines the correspondence between O'Connor and Maryat Lee. Discusses Lee's letters, donated to Georgia College & State University's *Flannery O'Connor Collection* in 1991, and comments on Lee's friendship with O'Connor, their similar Southern backgrounds, dedication to their vocation as writers, sense of humor, and views on--the "most pervasive subject" of the correspondence--"the matter of race." Offers excerpts describing two incidents in which Lee encountered blacks (on a subway and a bus). Suggests that her descriptions offered O'Connor situations for use in "Everything That Rises Must Converge." Contends that, in view of O'Connor's illness and dependence upon her mother, a psychoanalytic and autobiographical reading of the story may partially reflect her "wrestling with a sense of powerlessness." States her belief that O'Connor's creation of Julian was her "way of working through all that Maryat Lee represented of social liberalism and . . . coming to terms with her own responsibilities and obligations as a writer." Describes a reading of the story by Josephine Hendin, and offers another which focuses on Julian's liberalism, rage, and powerlessness. Refers to Sally Fitzgerald's defense of O'Connor's racial views in her introduction to *The Habit of Being*. Concludes that all three characters in the story--the black woman, the mother and Julian--"constitute O'Connor's retort to those, including Maryat Lee herself, who offer simple solutions to the matter of human imperfection."

641   Gordon, Sarah. "Milledgeville: The Perils of Place as Text." *Flannery O'Connor Bulletin* 20 (1991): 73-87.

Describes Alice Walker's visit to Georgia College & State University in 1977 and discusses her "use of Andalusia and the Milledgeville locale *as text*." Refers, in a similar manner, to Barbara McKenzie's description of "rural middle Georgia" in *Flannery O'Connor's Georgia*, and Robert Coles's view of the South--in general--in his book, *Flannery O'Connor's South*. Compares these works to Arthur Kinney's 1983 essay, "In Search of Flannery O'Connor" and Michael Pearson's *Imagined Places: Journeys into Literary America*. Kinney's essay, in which he describes a visit to Milledgeville during the 1980s to catalog O'Connor's library, is analyzed and discussed at length. Focuses on the use of writing as a response to place; the reactions of local residents; factual errors; and sights and stories that Gordon herself recognizes in the Milledgeville community that might relate to this issue. Refers also to Alice Walker's *The Temple of My Familiar*; Eudora Welty's 1956 essay, "Place in Fiction"; and O'Connor-related poetry by Adrienne Bond ("Renewal"), Paul Mariani ("As Mirandola Had It, the Mirror of the Soul"), and Maxine Kumin ("Visiting Flannery O'Connor's Grave"). An analysis of Pearson's work follows. Concludes that if Walker and Kinney "came to Milledgeville to see what O'Connor saw nearly as possible as she saw it," they both failed "to get beyond the proverbial cover of the book" in making their judgements.

642   Gordon, Sarah. "The News From Afar: A Note on Structure in O'Connor's Narratives." *Flannery O'Connor Bulletin* 14 (1985): 80-87.

Discusses the relationship between Walker Percy's work and the philosophies of Soren Kierkegaard and Gabriel Marcel, and how Percy's story "The Message in the Bottle" not only "illumines the condition of modern man," but also "provides a means by which the Christian message can be understood." Contends that O'Connor, like Percy, was constantly preoccupied with the displacement of the modern individual especially in the awareness of that displacement comes to him in the form of "news from afar," the life-saving "message in the bottle." Discusses how this preoccupation is reflected in the structure of "a number of" O'Connor's works, then carefully examines the theme in "The Displaced Person" and "The Lame Shall Enter First." In the first story, sees the Displaced Person as the bearer of Christ's message, the priest as the interpreter of that news, and Mrs. McIntyre as "beginning to accept" the news only after participating in the newsbearer's (Guizac's) death. Suggests that, in "The Lame Shall Enter First," Sheppard serves as "a castaway whose acceptance of the `news' comes too late to save his neglected son." Concludes with a listing and discussion of Percy's "three criteria by which the castaway verifies the news which comes to him," and describes O'Connor herself as "a newsbearer through her art."

643   Gordon, Sarah. "O'Connor, Flannery." *Dictionary of Georgia Biography*. Vol. 2. Ed. Kenneth Coleman and Charles Stephen Gurr. Athens: U of Georgia P, 1983. 757-59.

Offers commentary regarding O'Connor's life, work, perspective, and religious orientation. Sees her as "a devout believer whose small but impressive body of fiction presents the soul's struggle with `the stinking mad shadow of Jesus.'" Lists her works, awards, honors, and discusses and offers an assessment of O'Connor's contribution to American letters. Discusses O'Connor's close relationship with her father; how she was "an avid reader with a fine sense of humor"; her artistic contributions as an undergraduate; the effects and impact of disseminated lupus erythematosus; how her "ear for the language" along with "a true sense of comic timing" enabled her to "produce some of the finest of American humor." Refers to the influences of Andrew Lytle, Robert and Sally Fitzgerald, and Carolyn Gordon. States that her letters, selected and edited by Sally Fitzgerald, and published as *The Habit of Being*, may well "prove to be as significant as her fiction in the history of American ideas."

644   Gordon, Sarah. "O'Connor, Flannery (1925-64)." *Handbook of American Women's History*. Ed. Angela Howard Zophy. Garland Reference Library of the Humanities, No. 696. New York: Garland, 1990. 446-47.

Provides an encyclopedic entry which describes O'Connor's types of characters, her publications, awards, and a biographical sketch. Offers an assessment of her place in American literature. States that "O'Connor was largely concerned with southern fundamentalist Protestants and the integrity of their search for salvation." Asserts that she "described a world in which technology and progress inevitably fail to satisfy the deepest human needs, a world in which, as she put it, `the good is under construction.'" Concludes that O'Connor "is now acknowledged as one of America's foremost writers of the short story."

645   Gordon, Sarah. "Retrospective." *Flannery O'Connor Bulletin* 7 (1978): 84.

A twenty-six line poem "for Flannery's friend, Louise Abbot" that offers a memorable image of Flannery on the "sloping porch" at Andalusia amid her "yard hens and bright birds."

646   Gordon, Sarah. Rev. of *Critical Essays on Flannery O'Connor*, by Melvin J. Friedman and Beverly Lyon Clark. *Flannery O'Connor Bulletin* 14 (1985): 115-17.

Opens with a reference to Friedman's comment on the "abundance of criticism on O'Connor's works," his view that much of it is "repetitious and often mediocre," then applauds his introductory essay as being "among the best in the collection." States that Friedman's essay is "balanced and thorough" in its treatment of the history of O'Connor criticism and that it "points incisively to the tough questions now being raised about the fiction." Reports that this volume is "Friedman and Clark's attempt `to represent the dissenters as well as the orthodox acceptors.'" Finds the religious metaphor of this objective unsettling, but recognizes the merit in their attempt to include a "broad range of approaches to the fiction over the years." Gordon reviews the essays, citing them by title, author, and original date of publication. Finds Ronald Schleifer's and Janet Egleson Dunleavy's essays to be "of questionable value," and reports that while "their attempt to indicate the variety of responses is commendable" there are "significant omissions," especially in the section entitled "A Review of O'Connor Criticism." Questions the inclusion of "Reminiscences and Tributes" in a volume intended to offer "critical essays."

647   Gordon, Sarah. Rev. of *Flannery O'Connor's South*, by Robert Coles. *Flannery O'Connor Bulletin* 9 (1980): 127-31.

Contends that because Coles is among those readers who are attracted to the spiritual appeal of O'Connor's work, his book is "a testament to the influence of O'Connor's fiction." Suggests that while O'Connor, "would certainly be amused, if not shocked, by Coles's devotion," she would undoubtedly "be pleased by the sincerity and honesty" of his response. Sees the book as a personal tribute to Flannery O'Connor. Reports that while it discusses "only a few works in great detail," it is a unique work from a "sensitive reader who constantly relates O'Connor's depiction of the South and the modern sensibility to his own experiences as observer, social worker, and therapist." Concludes with a discussion of Coles's observations that many "see the solution to life's problems solely in terms of the powerful human intellect" and "deny the presence of Mystery," Coles' view of the "use, or abuse, of language in his profession," and O'Connor's "concern with the `attraction for the Holy.'"

648   Gordon, Sarah. Rev. of *The Language of Grace: Flannery O'Connor,*
           Walker Percy, & Iris Murdoch, by Peter S. Hawkins. *Flannery O'Connor*
           Bulletin 13 (1984): 99-104.

           Finds Hawkins's book to be "a refreshingly lucid approach to matters of
           language, audience, and belief," and far superior to another work with a
           similar focus: Jefferson Humphries's *The Otherness Within: Gnostic*
           Readings in Marcel Proust, Flannery O'Connor and François Villon.
           Reports that, in his readings of Percy and O'Connor, Hawkins "focuses on
           the most crucial . . . dilemma: the portrayal of the possibility of salvation
           in a time when, for many, God is dead and, for most, the language of ʻthe
           old words of grace' has been devalued." Compares the two authors'
           approaches, focusing on their use of the familiar world and their reader's
           need for a theological frame of reference to fully understand and
           appreciate the author's intentions. Suggests that Hawkins's choice of "A
           Good Man Is Hard to Find" may not have been particularly useful;
           "Everything That Rises Must Converge" and "Greenleaf" might have been
           better examples. Considers whether readers and teachers must rely upon
           O'Connor's own comments too heavily to teach and understand her works.
           Finds Percy to be "the more canny of the two writers in that, often through
           humor and understatement, he *underwhelms* the reader: He does not
           assume what this age would have him prove." Commends the book for its
           insight and clarity, finding it to be thoughtful and incisive, an "excellent
           commentary on the dilemma of the twentieth-century writer with
           transcendent concerns."

649   Gordon, Sarah. "ʻA Stroke of Good Fortune': *The [Flannery] O'Connor*
           Collection at Georgia College." Ms. [Paper presented at the Society of
           American Archivists Meeting, 1 Oct. 1988].

           Describes Regina Cline O'Connor's donation of the bulk of her daughter's
           "literary legacy" to the Russell Library of Georgia College & State
           University in 1970. Outlines how the 5,000 pages of handwritten drafts
           and other related materials were initially sorted, arranged, and cataloged.
           Reports that galley proofs for her two novels, personal correspondence, a
           scrapbook, report cards, photographs, awards, a drawing and a painting,
           one of O'Connor's early notebooks, and O'Connor's personal library of 709
           books and journals were also given. States that after the initial evaluation,
           a series of individuals then sorted and cataloged the Collection, including
           Robert Dunn--whose manuscript catalog was the one first used by scholars
           for the Collection for the period 1976-1988--and Stephen Driggers, who
           completed his catalogue of the Collection in 1986 (published by the
           University of Georgia Press in 1989). Reports that while the original deed
           of gift stipulated that reproduction of the papers was not permissible, it
           was amended in 1984 to allow for the reproduction of the papers for

preservation purposes, and again in 1987 to add "the proviso that the reproduced manuscripts may be shared through interlibrary loan." Acknowledges that during the first years that the Collection was available, scholars had extreme difficulty gaining permission to quote from materials in the Collection, but their difficulties were eased in the late 1970's when O'Connor's literary executor "established a clear demarcation between scholarly and non-scholarly rights to publication." Reports, however, that the problem *does* continue to plague those who seek to dramatize her work. Reviews how the Collection has expanded and expresses opinion that an institution must be worthy of a gift of this nature, "educated to its value, determined about its future, and creative in providing for that future." [A copy of this paper was donated by the author to the *Flannery O'Connor Collection* at Georgia College & State University.]

650   Gordon, Sarah. "To O'Connor's Milledgeville: ` . . . by bus or by buzzard.'" *Macon Magazine* 4.3 (March-April 1990): 34-37.

Chronicles the history of O'Connor's literary production while exploring the essence of why people (Gordon calls them "pilgrims") visit O'Connor's hometown. Comments that most who come searching--from places as varied as Guatemala and Denmark--come for religious purposes, though many are resistent rather than embracing of the Christian perspective. Randomly discusses some of the fiction in its Christian/secular terms, and concludes that O'Connor's works are, as she herself had hoped, rightfully making an "uncomfortable" impression on the world.

651   Goss, James. "The Double Action of Mercy in `The Artificial Nigger.'" *Christianity and Literature* 23.3 (1974): 36-45.

Notes that critics often overlook Mr. Head's second encounter with grace, which occurs as he steps off the train after visiting the city. Explores why O'Connor included "two experiences of grace." Suggests that the two experiences "correspond to the conscious and unconscious dimensions of 'sin' from which [Mr. Head] needs redemption.'" Concludes that the two experiences may be based upon O'Connor's "Roman Catholic tradition that distinguishes the act of justification from that of sanctification." Briefly discusses possible Jungian interpretations.

652   Goss, James. "O'Connor's Redeemed Man: `Christus et/vel Porcus?'" *Drew Gateway* 44 (Winter/Spring 1974): 106-19.

Examines the "swine" imagery in three of O'Connor's works--*Wise Blood*, "The River," and "Revelation"--and suggests that O'Connor's imagery is not consistent. Recalls Jung's idea that Christ as image of one's self "lacks wholeness . . . since it does not include the dark side of things." Contends that O'Connor uses the images of "hogs" to portray the dark element in the self, but forces characters in *Wise Blood* and "The River" to choose between the two aspects, while Mrs. Turpin in "Revelation" obtains salvation by admitting the "swinish" elements within her being. Concludes that those who favor an anthropological dualism of good and evil will find support in the characters of *Wise Blood* and "The River," while those who favor a monistic, Jungian view, will approve of "Revelation."

653   Gossett, Louise Y. "Flannery O'Connor." *The History of Southern Literature*. Ed. Louis D. Rubin, Jr., et. al. Baton Rouge: Louisiana State UP, 1985. 489-93.

Discusses "place" in O'Connor's fiction and suggests that the Southern landscape figures vividly in her works. Contends that O'Connor did not "expand and build themes from one work to another as she learned to select and deploy details with increasing exactness." Cites O'Connor's central theme as the need to recognize the danger of damnation. Argues that her characters hear but do not listen, and when they persist in their actions, and then attempt to flee, they are "struck down" by their own conceit for resisting God's will. States that this "hound-of-heaven" paradigm describes the course of action in O'Connor's fiction. Discusses Tarwater of *The Violent Bear It Away*, Mrs. McIntyre of "The Displaced Person," characters in the stories in *Everything That Rises Must Converge*, and O'Connor's essays in *Mystery and Manners*. Concludes that O'Connor was unique in American literary history because of "the power with which she dramatizes her orthodox Catholic vision of redemption" and made Georgia as memorable as Faulkner and Welty did Mississippi.

654   Gossett, Thomas F. "Flannery O'Connor's Humor With a Serious Purpose." *Studies in American Humor* 3.3 (1977): 174-80.

Discusses O'Connor's "uproarious and sometimes inward and ironic" humor. Describes seeing her humor during visits to Andalusia with Father James McCown and again, with a literature class from Wesleyan College in Macon. Focuses on her readings of "Good Country People" and "A Good Man Is Hard to Find." Relates how she laughed "long and heartily" at Hulga Hopewell and the traveling Bible salesman. Then, comments on her humor and seriousness in her tale of The Misfit. Suggests that while humor in "The Enduring Chill" may be less dramatic, it is still shocking. Finds O'Connor's humor to spring "not from skepticism but faith . . . faith specifically in the Christian religion." Indicates that because O'Connor's faith was so strong, she may have believed that others didn't recognize

God out of "willful perversity"; as a result, these individuals were--for O'Connor--fair game for comedy.

655 Gossett, Thomas F. *"No Vague Believer*: Flannery O'Connor and Protestantism." *Southwest Review* 60.3 (1975): 256-63.

Reaffirms the assertion that O'Connor's "beliefs as a Catholic were both firm and definite" and that she saw "'from the standpoint of Christian orthodoxy.'" Describes examples of relationships and situations in which O'Connor dealt with Protestants, and concludes that she "was a friendly, knowledgeable, and principled critic of Protestant beliefs and practices."

656 Goyen, William. "Unending Vengeance." *Delta* (France), 2 (March 1976): 31-32.

Reprint of Goyen's review of *Wise Blood*, which originally appeared in the May 18, 1952 issue of the *New York Times Book Review*.

657 Graulich, Melody. "'They Ain't Nothing But Words': Flannery O'Connor's *Wise Blood*." *Flannery O'Connor Bulletin* 7 (1978): 64-83.

Suggests O'Connor uses distortion to hit "the mulish reader over the head to get his attention" and to confuse him "into looking for truth in unexpected places." Contends that in *Wise Blood*, O'Connor uses ambiguity, paradox, and distortion to express truth indirectly. States that even though "truths will appear distorted, even absurd, and definitely funny when they come from the mouths of grotesques," we should still accept them as truths. Discusses how the central characters of the novel "are all wordsmiths, preachers who use words self-consciously"; the book's anti-theme of "seeing-is-believing"; Enoch's use of words as tools, and how the discrepancy between his words and actions emphasizes "the failure of words to convey faith, even perverted faith." Suggests that the novel has a place "in the tradition of American religious works" as "a spiritual biography, chronicling Haze's movement from doubt to faith, from spiritual blindness to visionary belief." Fimds that while O'Connor's use of language is her strength, it is through the use of "distortion, indirection, `gaps,' negations, and ambiguous language" that she suggests the spiritual truths she is trying to convey.

658 Gray, Dabney. "The Emerging Shadow: Character Reversal in Flannery O'Connor's `The Displaced Person.'" *Publications of the Mississippi Philological Association* (1993): 44-49.

Discusses O'Connor's "gift of revealing the universal by showing the specific," and her investigation of spirituality in "The Displaced Person." Offers a Jungian view, contending that "first for Mrs. Shortley, and later for Mrs. McIntyre, Guizac is the one to whom they resign their shadow sides. He becomes their exterior devil. In him they see mirrored the evil they cannot recognize in themselves." Concludes that Mrs. McIntyre's bedridden, decimated condition at the end of the story reflects how she has become "the victim of a devil whose face is her own."

659   Gray, Jeffrey. "'It's Not Natural': Freud's `Uncanny' and O'Connor's *Wise Blood*." *The Southern Literary Journal* 29.2 (1996): 56-68.

Suggests that Freud's essay on "The Uncanny" provides "a superlative instrument for an analysis of *Wise Blood*." Offers a reading of the novel in this context and finds that Freud's "definition and typology of the uncanny opens up the novel" to allow readers to "sense not so much its meaning," but "its power to disturb." Discusses the surface violence in the novel, O'Connor's "frequent description of human physical ugliness," the "seeming lack of moral center among the characters," and her use of doubles. Finds that, despite O'Connor's views of Freud and her view of Hazel Motes as a sort of "tortured saint rising toward divine light," Freud's views in "The Uncanny" provide O'Connor's readers with an excellent understanding of why she is so effective in horrifying readers into considering their own spiritual situation. Concludes that James Mellard is correct in contending that Freud may be O'Connor's "true Other."

660   Gray, Paul. "The Belle: Magnolia and Iron." *Time* 27 Sept. 1976: 96-97.

Provides a brief social history of women's roles in the South and how women were expected to act in order to fit into Southern culture. Includes a brief reference to Flannery O'Connor, with Josephine Hendin's remark that Southern women of O'Connor's generation were expected to live their lives with "a Southern `politeness that engulfs every other emotion.'"

661   Gray, Paul. "Yoknapatawpha Blues." *Time* 27 Sept. 1976: 92-93.

Discusses the work and impact of several contemporary Southern writers, including Flannery O'Connor. Refers to her as "a Catholic whose brilliant short stories lacerated characters to get at their souls." Quotes O'Connor as saying that her literary purpose was "`To observe our fierce and fading manners in the light of our ultimate concern.'"

662   Gray, Richard. "Aftermath: Southern Literature since World War II." *The
            Literature of Memory: Modern Writers of the American South*. Baltimore,
            MD: Johns Hopkins UP, 1977. 257-305, 321-24.

Contains a sub-chapter titled "Comedy, Mystery, and the Bible Belt:
Flannery O'Connor" [274-84], which suggests that O'Connor brought to
readers an image of the South that was very unlike McCullers's. Asserts
that while McCullers's personal perceptions were hidden and operating as
hints below the surface, O'Connor foregrounded her Roman Catholic faith,
her "fully developed sense of universe," and integrated these religious
beliefs with her Southern experience. Cites evidence that O'Connor
believed that the South was "not just an acceptable location for the
Catholic writer" but "almost the perfect one." Discusses O'Connor's
grotesque characters and analyzes *Wise Blood*. Mentions Carson
McCullers, Erskine Caldwell, T.S. Eliot, and Jane Austen. Concludes that
while O'Connor's Southern inheritance helped to join her moral and
dramatic senses, "the pity of it . . . [was] that her `act of seeing' was (like
Carson McCullers's) such a very eccentric one."

663   Gray, Richard. *Writing the South: Ideas of American Region*. Cambridge:
            Cambridge UP, 1986. 186, 286.

Contains two brief references to Flannery O'Connor and her work: the first
in regard to a scene of macabre drama reminiscent of O'Connor's style; the
second placing O'Connor in the company of William Faulkner, Thomas
Wolfe, Erskine Caldwell, and Mark Twain.

664   Greenberg, Paul. "I Still Miss Flannery O'Connor." *Flannery O'Connor
            Bulletin* 24 (1995-96): 91-95.

Offers "a few words for what would have been Flannery O'Connor's
seventieth birthday." States that "No matter what you say about Flannery
O'Connor, you can't say anything better or truer or more concisely than she
did in her own writing. That was her genius: she didn't write *about* things;
she told the things themselves in her stories." Suggests that just as
O'Connor recognized Faulkner's genius and "sensibly suggested that other
writers take a siding when he was passing through," anyone writing about
O'Connor "might do better just to get out of the way, too, and let her
explain herself." Offers examples of O'Connor's comments on her gift of
writing, discusses the plain simplicity of her comments and remarks, and
admires how her "throw-away lines" have "such a no-nonsense air, such
a definitive authority." Summarizes O'Connor's views "on the nature of the
Southern religious sensibility," and reflects that O'Connor "did a beautiful
dissection of the academic tendency to over-interpret."

665   Greenburg, Paul. "Picking the Cream of the South." *Washington Times* 30
            April 1990: F3.

            Greenburg picks out his favorite Southern literary works for a *Southern
            Living* survey. Discusses works by William Faulkner, Flannery O'Connor,
            and Douglas Southall Freeman. Cites "Enoch and the Gorilla" as one of
            his favorite works, focusing on its "perfect, unspoken elucidation of the
            assumption that all you need to do is slip on the right persona and the
            world is yours."

666   Greene, Helen I. "Mary Flannery O'Connor: One Teacher's Happy
            Memory." *Flannery O'Connor Bulletin* 19 (1990): 44-48.

            Describes memories of O'Connor, whom the author knew from the age of
            twelve, when Flannery moved to Milledgeville, until apparently, the end
            of Flannery's life. Remarks that O'Connor "got her feel for local dialect
            speech" from living in a large family. Reports on O'Connor's school
            activities, how she took overloads as an undergraduate, went to school
            year-round, and that she submitted artwork to campus publications.
            Recalls having her as a student in a "survey of European history" course,
            "happy times" at the family farm (Andalusia), and remarks on the
            influence of George Beiswanger in O'Connor's decision to attend the
            University of Iowa. Relates O'Connor's comments related to atheists and
            communists that she encountered at Yaddo. Refers to the historian Allan
            Nevins, and describes visiting O'Connor with members of the Russell
            family on one occasion, and a young Danish student, Erik Langkjaer, on
            another. Concludes that while many of those O'Connor associated with
            were scholars, she had a very devoted family and mother who "made her
            life not only satisfying but happy."

667   Greenhouse, Karen. "Death--A Form of Life in Flannery O'Connor."
            Suicide and Life Threatening Behavior 8.2 (1978): 118-28.

            Analyzes O'Connor's own psychology: her fear and isolation, the
            emotional scars from having watched her father die, her disease, and her
            "obvious" problematic relationship with her mother. States that O'Connor's
            work often exemplifies repression; characters either have oversimplified
            emotional states or lack fully developed emotional qualities altogether.
            Argues that O'Connor's fixation with deformity and grotesqueness, and her
            inability to have any close relationships (except through letters), point to
            her low self-esteem and fearfulness. Contends that O'Connor and her
            mother were at odds with O'Connor's stereotypical female characters,
            especially the overbearing and insensitive mother.

668   Gregory, Donald. "Enoch Emery: Ironic Doubling in *Wise Blood*." *Flannery O'Connor Bulletin* 4 (1975): 52-64.

Contends that *Wise Blood* remains one of O'Connor's "most perplexing and enigmatic works," partly on account of the character of Enoch Emery. Suggests that O'Connor's purpose for including Enoch is twofold: first, "by doubling her presentation of Haze in her portrayal of Enoch, she indicates clearly her belief that the isolation which moves both characters to violence and murder is not unique"; and second, the doubling of "circumstances and events in Haze's life provides a comic counterpart which heightens the reader's awareness of the tragic dimensions of Haze's quest." Discusses a variety of related topics, including: biblical allusions for Haze and Enoch that partially define their functional roles; how psychological portraits of the two are similar; and how in their childhood both characters "had traumatic experiences associated with religion" that also had sexual overtones. Examines how O'Connor presents their experiences in Taulkinham "in parallel terms," provides each "with singular objects which heighten their anger and frustration," and allows the two to "attempt to take refuge in ritual as a way of giving meaning to their lives." Concludes that because Enoch's "`wise blood' is without wisdom and has played him false," the reader's understanding of Hazel Motes's destiny as a "tragic hero" is heightened by Enoch's role as "comic fool."

669   Greiff, Louis K. "J.D. Salinger's `Teddy' and Flannery O'Connor's `The River': A Comparative Analysis." *Flannery O'Connor Bulletin* 9 (1980): 104-11.

Reports that "a striking relationship exists between J.D. Salinger's `Teddy' and Flannery O'Connor's `The River.'" Describes the "remarkably similar protagonists," seen as two dynamic and "exceptional children surrounded by singularly unexceptional adults," and examines whether the two boys-- "who face common frustrations in their lives"--achieve parallel resolutions. Discusses how these two "spiritual journeyers" must deal "with parents whose materialism and passive sterility define the failures of the adult world"; how the "parent-world in both stories" serves as an "extension of Eliot's Waste Land and of [F. Scott] Fitzgerald's Valley of Ashes"; how both writers exploit the images conjured up by the use of cigarette butts and ashes; and how a comparison of the endings of both stories reveals similarities, especially in regard to how each boy approaches death. Concludes that despite the many similarities, the endings of each story are quite different: only Bevel's death, not Teddy's, "is rendered through images which suggest mystery, liberation, and progress toward the infinite."

670   Gresset, Michel. "The Audacity of Flannery O'Connor." Trans. T.G.
            Bernard-West. *Critical Essays on Flannery O'Connor*. Ed. Melvin J.
            Friedman and Beverly Lyon Clark. Boston: G.K. Hall, 1985. 100-08.

            Sees O'Connor's novels *Wise Blood* and *The Violent Bear It Away* as
            belonging "in a genre that the author virtually invented: not tragicomedy
            but a narrative whose tone is located at once beyond that of comedy, in
            farce, and outside that of tragedy, in a spiritual drama." Praises O'Connor's
            work and sees her fiction as flowing from her "remarkable gift for
            audacity." Uses scenes from *The Violent Bear It Away* and "Revelation"
            to illustrate this point, and compares her method with that of Joseph
            Conrad in *The Nigger of the Narcissus*. Discusses O'Connor's use of satire
            and finds her work to be "on one level a pitiless satire that, like that of
            William Faulkner, echoes in three kinds of space: Southern, American and
            universal." Observes that much of O'Connor's satire is aimed at women:
            "in a good third of her stories we read of sons rebelling against their
            mothers or against a mother figure," while "it is the mother who pays,
            often with her life, for her total incomprehension of the inner life of her
            child." [Originally published, in French, in *La Nouvelle Revue Française*
            No. 216 (Dec. 1970): 61-71.]

671   Gretlund, Jan Nordby. "Flannery O'Connor and Katherine Anne Porter."
            Flannery O'Connor Bulletin 8 (1979): 77-87.

            Reminds readers of O'Connor's claim that she was not familiar with the
            works of William Faulkner, Eudora Welty, and Katherine Anne Porter
            until she attended the Iowa Writer's Workshop. Lists Porter's works in
            O'Connor's personal library in the Flannery O'Connor Room at Georgia
            College & State University and O'Connor editions in the Katherine Anne
            Porter Room in the McKeldin Library at the University of Maryland.
            Summarizes the contents of letters and provides the text of two letters by
            O'Connor to Porter. Describes Porter's marginalia in her copies of
            O'Connor's *A Good Man Is Hard to Find*, *The Violent Bear It Away*, and
            Everything That Rises Must Converge. Declares that while the personal
            relationship between Porter and O'Connor "developed into a friendship
            based upon mutual admiration," this friendship developed too late in each
            of their careers "for critics to posit any significant literary influence."
            Concludes that the value of this friendship, "from a literary point of view,
            rests in the criticism they offered of each other's work in their essays,
            letters, and even their marginalia." Includes four photographs taken by
            Thomas Gossett of Porter visiting O'Connor at Andalusia.

672   Gretlund, Jan Nordby. "Flannery O'Connor's `An Exile in the East': An
            Introduction." *South Carolina Review* 11.1 (1978): 3-11.

Presents an introduction to O'Connor's previously unpublished story, "An Exile In the East" (published in the same issue on pages 12-21). Contends that the story was intended to be included in *A Good Man Is Hard to Find*, but was pulled in favor of "Good Country People" at the "last possible moment not by choice but by necessity." States that while O'Connor considered the story "finished," it appears to have evolved out of "The Geranium" and eventually became "Judgement Day." Suggests that the story belongs to O'Connor's "middle period [during which] she wrote highly realistic stories." Provides side-by-side passages of text for comparison to "Judgement Day." Concludes that the story illustrates that O'Connor not only "could be sociological as well as theological," but "could accomplish both themes at once."

673   Gretlund, Jan Nordby. "The Last Agrarian: Madison Jones's Achievement." *Southern Review* 22.3 (1986): 478-88.

Includes two brief references to O'Connor in this discussion of Madison Jones's life and work: O'Connor's comment to Jones regarding her admiration for his novel, *A Buried Land* (1963); and how his later novel, *Passage Through Gehenna* (1978) resembles the "the savage ironic humor usually associated" with O'Connor's writing.

674   Gretlund, Jan Nordby. "Mr. Shiftlet, Chapter Two: An Introduction to `The Shiftlet Fragment.'" *Flannery O'Connor Bulletin* 10 (1981): 70-77.

Discusses the contents of several manuscript fragments in the *Flannery O'Connor Collection* at Georgia College & State University that deal with the character Mr. Shiftlet and alternative endings of "The Life You Save May Be Your Own." Focuses on manuscript Dunn 156a, referred to as "The Shiftlet Fragment," contending that this work is an "attempted continuation of the story." Uses the content of this fragment to "place the story in context and to comment on other `Shiftlet' material in the manuscripts. Suggests that one of the manuscript passages "is perhaps the best illustration of how close she is to the traditional Southern humor of Johnson Jones Hooper, who lived and wrote in nearby eastern Alabama." Postulates that O'Connor may have based Tom T. Shiftlet on Hooper's character Simon Suggs, a "frontier confidence man," in *Some Adventures of Captain Simon Suggs* (1846). Outlines the plot of the published story, and relates how O'Connor stylized her writing in the tradition of popular Southern humor "to the point of caricature, keeping her poise and avoiding sentimentality." Finds both the fragments and the final story to be "hilariously tragi-comic." Indicates that the fragment is useful for developing a psychological explanation of Mr. Shiftlet's interest in automobiles, and illustrates O'Connor's style as a caricaturist (especially in her characterization of the phrenologist). Reports that O'Connor's humor "is often that of a social satirist," who was "always concerned about giving as realistic a picture as possible." Concludes that the "Shiftlet Fragment" provides information that sheds light on Mr. Shiftlet, "makes him more psychologically interesting," and indicates how he takes on "mythic dimensions." [Note: A reproduction of "The Shiftlet Fragment" follows this article, pp. 78-86.]

675   Gretlund, Jan Nordby. Rev. of *Season of the Strangler*, by Madison Jones. *Georgia Review* 37.1 (1983): 219-21.

Review essay of Jones's stories, *Season of the Strangler*. Includes a discussion of how Jones's ironic humor may remind readers of O'Connor, most notably in "Self-Portrait," seen as a "story in the O'Connor vein."

676   Gretlund, Jan Nordby. "The Side of the Road: Flannery O'Connor's Social Sensibility." *Realist of Distances: Flannery O'Connor Revisited*. Ed. Karl-Heinz Westarp and Jan Nordby Gretlund. Aarhus (Denmark): Aarhus UP, 1987. 197-207.

Considers the social experience that O'Connor displayed through her work. Reports that "for a writer whose social concern is not supposed to have been notably pronounced, O'Connor displays a remarkable social sensibility." Sees O'Connor's career "as a development from an early stereotyping tendency to the allegorizing skill of her final years." Focuses on her social concern and sensibility in works completed during her "creative middle period," which began with the publication of "A Stroke of Good Fortune" (1949) and ended with "The Artificial Nigger" (1955). Notes some of O'Connor's social concerns: "A View of the Woods" (1955) may be seen as recording humankind's desecrational nature; "Everything That Rises Must Converge" as "one of the best fictional accounts of the breakdown in the late 50s of the old order of the South"; "Revelation" as a description of "social stratification of Southern society"; and her "most astringent social comment," the "glimpse of starvation" seen in "Parker's Back." Describes the origins of some of her story ideas, including newspaper headlines for "A Good Man Is Hard to Find," "A Late Encounter With the Enemy," and "The Displaced Person." Then, offers a close reading of the latter to demonstrate her "social sensibility." Sees "The Displaced Person" as representing Mr. Guizac's "foreign social behavior" threatens the stratification of Southern society. Concludes that, to appreciate O'Connor's work, readers "must take into account her rendition of her time and place and the people there."

677   Griffin, Julie Lynn. "Novelist Mark Childress: Listening to His Characters." *Society for the Fine Arts Review* [U of Alabama, College of Arts and Sciences] 9.3 (1987): 12-15.

Profiles Alabama novelist Mark Childress, whose first novel, *A World Made of Fire*, is described as "a cross between Flannery O'Connor Southern Gothic and supernatural ghost stories." Reports that Childress considers O'Connor to be "a major influence," and describes the acclaim and comments received from Harper Lee, Eudora Welty, and others.

678   Griffith, Benjamin. "After the Canonization: Flannery O'Connor Revisited." *Sewanee Review* 97.4 (1989): 575-80.

Review essay of the Library of America edition of O'Connor's *Collected Works* that includes Griffith's own recollections of his visits to Andalusia and correspondence with O'Connor. Discusses Alice Walker's perspective on O'Connor. Excerpts letters that display O'Connor's rural wit and acknowledges her sense of Faulkner's presence. Explores O'Connor's position in regard to race relations, including her refusal to change the title of "The Artificial Nigger" to "They Had to Have an Artificial One" for John Crowe Ransom's *Kenyon Review*. Discusses her attempts to address the "race relations" issue in other stories, such as "Everything That Rises Must Converge" and "Revelation." Concludes that the volume "will stand sturdily" alongside those for Hawthorne, Melville, and Twain.

679   Griffith, Benjamin. "O'Connor's Fictional Method, Catholicism Studied." *Atlanta Journal-Constitution* 4 Feb. 1990: L9.

Review essay of Robert H. Brinkmeyer's *The Art and Vision of Flannery O'Connor*. Declares that O'Connor thought of her stories as "'gateways to vision.'" Griffith cites evidence that she was conscious of her readers, whom she saw as perversely stubborn: "'When I sit down to write . . . a monstrous reader looms up who sits down beside me and continually mutters, I don't get it, I don't see it, I don't want it.'" Concludes that while Brinkmeyer's book "is not easy reading," it is a valuable and "creative work of criticism, offering new insights into Ms. O'Connor's fictional method as well as her Catholicism."

680   Grimes, Ronald L. "Anagogy and Ritualization: Baptism in Flannery O'Connor's *The Violent Bear It Away*." *Religion and Literature* 21.1 (1989): 9-26.

Outlines the plot of *The Violent Bear It Away* and discusses the response readers are likely to have to its subject matter. Suggests that the "central gesture" of the book is "baptism and its related imagery of water and fire." Argues that two points of view--anagogical and ritological--can best help the reader to explore views of baptism. Asserts that O'Connor uses anagogical symbolism to jolt readers "off the track of moralizing, psychologizing, and playing social worker." Constructs a theoretical framework in which to analyze the novel, using Northrop Frye's discussion of anagogy, Jonathan Z. Smith's definition of ritual, and Volney Gay's interpretation of baptism.

681   Grimshaw, James A., Jr. "`Le Mot Juste': Hazel Motes's Name." *NMAL: Notes on Modern American Literature* 3.3 (1979): Item 14.

Suggests that O'Connor's choice of names reflects her concern with *le mot juste*, choosing just the right word. Discusses interpretations of the meaning of Hazel Motes's name.

682   Grimshaw, James A., Jr. "The Mistaken Identity of Rufus [Florida] Johnson." *NMAL: Notes on Modern American Literature* 1.4 (1977): Item 31.

Notes that scholars are referring to a character named "Rufus Florida Johnson," who appeared in early drafts of *The Violent Bear It Away* and was quoted by Robert Fitzgerald as mentioned in an early 1953 letter from O'Connor. Reports that the character did not appear in the published version. Contends that critics who continue to refer to the character "have conjured a literary ghost which, if not dispelled, could lead to some unsubstantiated explications of O'Connor's fiction."

683   Grimshaw, James A., Jr. "Onomastics in Flannery O'Connor's `Parker's Back.'" *Notes on Contemporary Literature* 24.3 (1994): 6-8.

Offers an explication of "Parker's Back," suggesting that the title may be read as either "a possessive or as a contraction." Discusses how "Parker *is* back": to the image of the tattooed man at the fair, to his home and wife after being away for a couple of days, and to himself after experiencing the salvation of God's grace. Outlines the story's structure and plot, then carefully analyzes the meanings of the characters' names. Suggests that O'Connor combines in Parker the character of a prophet upon whom violence is inflicted as grace, in a story about human grotesqueness.

684   Grobel, Lawrence. "Blood Ties." *The Hustons*. New York: Charles Scribner's, 1989. 695-726.

Reports on Michael Fitzgerald's role in the making of John Huston's film of *Wise Blood*. Reviews how Fitzgerald initially tracked Huston down, got him interested in directing the film, and raised the necessary funds to get the project off the ground. Focuses on the choice of actors, their interpretation of what the film was about, and the impact that the film and working with Huston had on Fitzgerald's career. Discusses roles of Brad Dourif (as Hazel Motes), Harry Dean Stanton (as Asa Hawks), Amy Wright (as Sabbath Lily), Ned Beatty (as Hoover Shoates), and Dan Shor (as Enoch Emory). Describes an incident which took place during the filming of the picture: while he was on location in Macon, Georgia, a woman sent to Huston a package with a "golden hunting horn wrapped in black velvet and a nineteenth-century poem, `The Hound of Heaven.'" States that during the following week, the woman showed up and told Huston that she had dreamed that he was dying and that God had told her to go and tell Huston, "`I am going to spare him, because he has got something important to do before he dies. You find him and tell him that.'" Relates that the woman told Huston this and left, and that he never heard from her again.

685   Groover, Joel. "O'Connor's Correspondent Dies." *Atlanta Journal-Constitution* 30 Dec. 1998: B1+.

Offers details regarding the suicide, by self-inflicted gunshot wound, of O'Connor's correspondent Elizabeth Hester on Dec. 26. States that Hester, 75--referred to as "A" in the *Habit of Being*--had "struggled with periodic bouts of depression throughout her life." Notes that Hester and O'Connor had exchanged almost 300 letters over a nine-year period. Hester, who also corresponded with Iris Murdoch, is praised by William Sessions, who commented "`She lived . . . an obscure life, yet the quality of her mind was such that she had two of the century's most famous women writers correspond with her.'"

686   Guest, David. "Truman Capote's *In Cold Blood*: The Novel as Prison." *Sentenced to Death: The American Novel and Capital Punishment.* Jackson: UP of Mississippi, 1997. 104-30.

Discusses Capote's depiction of cold-blooded killers, suggesting that his characters appear to be based more upon "popular images of the psychopath than [upon] details of a particular case, perhaps because Capote wanted to stress the danger they represented." Suggests that Capote draws upon the words of O'Connor's The Misfit from "A Good Man Is Hard to Find," and uses him as a "model psychopath."

687   Gunton, Sharon R. and Gerard J. Senick, eds. Contemporary *Literary Criticism*. Vol. 21. Detroit: Gale Research, 1982. 254-79.

Provides an extensive collection of excerpts related to O'Connor's life and work, including those by: William Esty; Caroline Gordon; Robert McCown; Sumner J. Ferris (relates the novels to the short stories); Robert O. Bowen (*The Violent Bear It Away*); Maurice Bassan; Brainard Cheney; Warren Coffey (novels as underdeveloped); Bob Dowell (says Christ-haunted figures are principle subject matter); Robert Drake (asserts O'Connor's only philosophical framework to be Christian orthodoxy and says Jesus Christ is O'Connor's principle character); V.S. Prichett; Walter Sullivan; Abigail Ann Hamblen (discusses "A Good Man Is Hard to Find"); Michael D. True (establishes O'Connor as a modern day prophet); Josephine Gattuso Hendin; Preston M. Browning, Jr. (claims religious concerns fortified O'Connor's artistic integrity); Diane Tolomeo (discusses the universal nature of the work); and Harold Beaver (also discusses the universal qualities of the work).

688   Gunton, Sharon R. and Laurie Lanzen Harris, eds. *Contemporary Literary Criticism*. Vol. 15. Detroit: Gale Research, 1980. 408-13.

Provides excerpts of criticism related to Flannery O'Connor by: Elizabeth Hardwick; Elizabeth Bishop; Robert Fitzgerald (discusses "religious knowledge"); Frederick J. Hoffman (concerned with redemption, the search for Jesus, meaning of prophecy); Caroline Gordon (connects Henry James's use of a "revolutionary" technique with O'Connor's); Kathleen Rout (analyzes the character of Mrs. May); Stephen R. Portch; and Hermione Lee (British response to O'Connor).

689   "The Habit of Art: An Interdisciplinary Celebration of the Legacy of Flannery O'Connor." *CHEERS! The Flannery O'Connor Society Newsletter* 2.1 (1994): 1-2.

Reports that 516 individuals from 30 states and 6 foreign countries attended the "The Habit of Art" symposium held at Georgia College & State University April 13-16, 1994. Reprints the program and notes that "unlike the previous symposia in 1974, 1977, and 1984, The Habit of Art offered an interdisciplinary program, including music, dance, visual art, and creative readings, as well as academic papers and panels."

690   Hair, William Ivey, James C. Bonner and Edward B. Dawson. *A History of Georgia College*. Milledgeville, GA: Georgia College, 1979. 149, 203-04, 208, 265.

Notes that O'Connor served as editor of *The Corinthian*, "a campus literary magazine designed to encourage student creativity." Mentions some of her teachers and their impressions of her work. Describes her block prints in the *Spectrum* yearbook. Refers to O'Connor's fictional character General George Poker Sash, and offers details about the real-life individual on whom he was probably modeled--"General" William Bush, who attended GSCW's 1951 commencement. Also describes Regina Cline O'Connor's gift of her daughter's manuscripts to the Russell Library.

691   Hall, Donald, ed. *The Oxford Book of American Literary Anecdotes*. New York: Oxford UP, 1981. 336

Includes an anecdote from Josephine Hendin's *The World of Flannery O'Connor* (1970) about O'Connor remaining standing, "scowling," with her back against the wall, while everyone else attending a wedding shower sat down for lunch. Suggests the event serves as an example of her "relationship with Milledgeville society."

692   Hallissy, Margaret. "Review of *Music Lesson*." *Studies in Short Fiction* 21.4 (1984): 410-11.

Suggests that Martha Lacy Hall's collection of short stories, *Music Lesson*, "may remind the reader of Flannery O'Connor without theology." Sees the work of the two writers as being similar in that both are comic writers who treat "serious subjects gently but not superficially."

693   Halsall, Jalaine. "An Interview with Rosemary Daniell." *Chattahoochee Review* 17.3 (1997): 75-101.

Offers an edited interview with Rosemary Daniell, author of *The Woman Who Spilled Words All Over Herself*, *The Hurricane Season*, *A Sexual Tour of the Deep South*, and *Fatal Flowers*. Discusses a variety of topics, including her poem, "Of Jayne Mansfield, Flannery O'Connor, My Mother and Me." Daniell refers to her visit to the Flannery O'Connor Room at Georgia College & State University, where her mother had attended, and her mother's admiration for Flannery O'Connor's lifestyle and writing.

693a   Hamelman, Steven. "A Good Man Is Easy to Find (a fiction)." *Flannery O'Connor Bulletin* 26-27 (1998-2000): 155-68.

Fictional story of six professors being driven on a tour from "the grounds of the spanking-new Flannery O'Connor Museum in Milledgeville," to the spot near Toomsboro, Georgia, "where, in `A Good Man Is Hard to Find,' a nameless family is slaughtered by The Misfit and his gang." Uses this contrived situation to have each passenger present an interpretation of the story from exaggerated scholarly perspective. The six scholars include: a New Critic, a Feminist, a New Historicist-Marxist, a Freudian, a Multiculturalist, and a Deconstructionist.

694   Hamilton, Barbara Tunnicliff. "Flannery in Iowa City." Unpublished essay, 1987. *Flannery O'Connor Collection*, Georgia College & State University, Milledgeville, GA.

Recalls living with O'Connor at the "Graduate House" at the University of Iowa September, 1946 to June, 1947. Names roommates, describes the house, and indicates that she and O'Connor were close friends and frequently took walks together. Declares that those "who lived with Flannery were a little in awe of her what-you-might-call sense of destiny." States that she typed O'Connor's M.F.A. thesis, describes how they kept in touch as the years passed, and remarks that she learned of O'Connor's death from reading her obituary in *Time* magazine.

695   Hammen, Scott. "Wise Blood." *John Huston*. Twayne's Filmmakers Series. Boston: Twayne, 1985. 127-40.

Discusses John Huston's films of 1972 to 1983, including *Wise Blood*. Contends that because the film "was shot by a close-knit group of family and friends working for very little pay in a remote unglamorous Southern town," it "could have been proclaimed a brilliant repudiation of the outmoded traditions of the commercial film industry." Sees the strength of the film as coming from the novel itself. Provides an account of Michael Fitzgerald's acquisition of the rights to the book, how he approached Huston to direct the film, and worked hard to gain the financial support needed to produce it. Describes the casting as "faultless," then refers to the innovative camera techniques used, and concludes that the film is a work reflecting a "very fine director with gifted performers and compelling material."

696   Hampl, Patricia. "The Lax Habits of the Free Imagination." *New York Times Book Review* 5 March 1989: 1+.

Discusses O'Connor's approach to writing "Good Country People" and her remark that she often "did not know where she was going when she sat down to write a short story." States that would-be writers must learn to recognize and accept the fluidity of the art of writing and endure "the fits and starts" of the process so that they might learn to "`caress the detail'" and "fight the fevers and fidgets" at the core of learning *how* to write.

697   Han, Jae-Nam. "O'Connor's Thomism and the `Death of God' in *Wise Blood*." *Literature and Belief* 17.1-2 (1997): 115-27.

Contends that O'Connor "tempered her mission as a Christian writer with the knowledge that the Nietzschean notion of the Divine Death was prevalent in her time." Contends that in *Wise Blood*, O'Connor "used the Bible as a text for critiquing death-of-God theology and its interpretation of scripture." Discusses how O'Connor "drew on the medieval hermeneutic, especially that of St. Thomas Aquinas," to accomplish her purpose. Examines "similarities in the approach to Scripture between death-of-God thinkers and Hazel Motes before his conversion." Then considers her "adoption of a Thomistic reading of the Bible," and outlines how she uses a literal reading of the scripture to drive the plot of *Wise Blood*. Concludes that by having Hazel Motes achieve salvation "through his participation in Christ's suffering," the novel is used as a means to "condemn those who follow the doctrines of death-of-God theology."

698   Handa, Sakae. "Flannery O'Connor's *The Violent Bear It Away*: Another Testimony to Spiritual Conversion." *Sei Katarina Women's Junior College Bulletin* (Japan) 22 (June 1989): 15-30.

699   Handa, Sakae. "Flannery O'Connor's *Wise Blood*: A Testimony to Spiritual Conversion." *Sei Katarina Women's Junior College Bulletin* (Japan) 21 (May 1988): 222-38.

700   Hanke, Toney. "Seeing It Whole." *Flannery O'Connor Bulletin* 6 (1977): 82.

A poem dedicated to O'Connor on "the purity we want."

701   Hannon, Jane. "The Wide World Her Parish: O'Connor's All-Embracing Vision of Church." *Flannery O'Connor Bulletin* 24 (1995-96): 1-21.

Asserts that O'Connor "had much to say about the nature and structure of the Catholic Church." Argues that "she pointed out the limiting and confining nature and structure of the parish life of her day and challenged American Catholics to take responsibility for building true Christian communities." Contends that O'Connor urged Catholics to explore their rich, neglected intellectual heritage and to contribute to discussions of issues facing the twentieth-century church. Explores O'Connor's "vision of the church" as reflected in her fiction, occasional papers and letters, book reviews, and interviews. Discusses O'Connor's "disdain for the opportunities for church involvement open to her and her criticism of the Catholic parish life of her day." Follows with explications of "Revelation" and *The Violent Bear It Away* to show how her fiction "presents a vision of [the] church that is spiritual and ecumenical rather than institutional and parochial." Concludes that through her ability to see the church from a "broad historical and spiritual perspective and with a deep personal love," O'Connor was able "to formulate constructive suggestions as to how the church . . . could better fulfill its duties to God and others."

702   Hannon, Patrick. "Bread Everlasting." *US Catholic* 63.6 (1998): 35-36.

Uses O'Connor's comment to Mary McCarthy during a party--regarding whether the Eucharist was only a symbol or truly the Body of Christ--as context for a discussion of the significance of the Eucharist to Christians.

703   Hardwick, Elizabeth. "Southern Literature: The Cultural Assumptions of Regionalism." *Southern Literature in Transition: Heritage and Promise.* Ed. Philip Castille and William Osborne. Memphis, TN: Memphis State UP, 1983. 17-28.

Discusses the regional identity of Southern writers, noting that the South "has produced a large, inchoate cluster of images about itself and its place in America." Focuses on William Styron's *Sophie's Choice* and Walker Percy's *The Moviegoer*, but includes a brief discussion of O'Connor's use of freaks and The Misfit in her story, "A Good Man Is Hard to Find." Considers O'Connor's freaks to be genuine, "driven by greed, blasphemy, and low cunning": dangerous men who "assault the sentiments and the "'good country people'" banalities and devastate the countryside." Argues that because O'Connor's "vision is never conventional and is instead transforming, altering the ground of expectation," her work "is the finest, and most original to come out of the South in the last three decades."

704   Hardy, Donald E. "The Dialogic Repetition of Free Indirect Discourse in Oral and Literary Narrative." *Repetition in Dialogue.* Ed. Carla Bazzanella. Tübingen, West Germany: Max Niemeyer Verlag, 1996. 90-103.

Explores the function of repetition in free indirect discourse and related types of speech and thought representation in oral and literary narrative and conversation. Includes an analysis of O'Connor's 1947 story "The Turkey." Provides support for the idea that literary uses of free indirect discourse are elaborations of oral strategies.

705   Hardy, Donald E. "Free Indirect Discourse, Irony, and Empathy in Flannery O'Connor's `Revelation.'" *Language and Literature* (American version) 26 (1991):37-53.

Discusses the literary function of free indirect discourse, a form of represented speech and thought that is a mixture of direct speech and indirect speech. Remarks how its presence in O'Connor's "Revelation" invites both sympathy with and ironic distance from the major character, Mrs. Turpin. Suggests that a pragmatic interpretation of free indirect discourse in this story demonstrates how O'Connor manipulates the distance between Mrs. Turpin and readers, leading readers to the revelation that they, like Mrs. Turpin, are in danger of falling into self-satisfaction. Observes that O'Connor relies on her social and cultural background, especially attitudes towards racism, in her manipulation of the sympathies of readers through free indirect discourse, and shifts between free indirect discourse and direct discourse. (From author's abstract).

706   Hardy, Donald E. "Narrating Knowledge: Presupposition and Background in Flannery O'Connor's Fiction." *Language and Literature* (Great Britain) 6.1 (1997): 29-41.

Examines clausal presupposition in O'Connor's fiction and shows how it contributes stylistically to her explorations of the fallibility of human knowledge. Suggests that marked presuppositional constructions--those in which the narrator and the narratee do not share the background knowledge of the presupposition--are attempts on the part of the narrator to put into a shared Gestalt background contested knowledge. States that these attempts have three main effects: 1) an ironic attempt on false knowledge held by a character; 2) a displacement of knowledge from a character's awareness; 3) an empathetic response to a character's knowledge of mystery or destiny. Leaves open the question whether all authors whose narrators use contested presuppositions are as concerned with the fallibility of human knowledge. (From author's abstract).

707   Hardy, Donald E. "Why Is She So Negative?: Negation and Knowledge in Flannery O'Connor's `A Good Man Is Hard to Find.'" *Southwest Journal of Linguistics* 17.2 (1998): 61-81.

Examines analytic negation in O'Connor's "A Good Man Is Hard to Find" in comparison to the Brown fiction corpus, and finds the frequency of analytic negation in O'Connor's fiction significantly higher than the frequency of analytic negation in Brown's. Accounts for the higher degree by correlating negation with dialogism, a modification of Tottie's (1991) account of higher degrees of negation in oral versus written language. (From author's abstract).

708   Hardy, Donald E., and David Durian. "Grammar and Seeing in Flannery O'Connor's Fiction: The Stylistics of Syntactic Complements." *Style* [pre-publication abstract].

Examines finite and non-finite syntactic complements to the verb *see* in O'Connor's fiction (e.g., I *saw* him running) and discusses how they contribute to O'Connor's explorations of the fallibility of human knowledge. Contends that a statistical analysis of O'Connor's fiction and the general fiction subcorpus of the Brown corpus demonstrates that her fiction has a greater concentration of *see* tokens, resulting in focalization through character reflectors rather than the narrator. Contends that further statistical analysis shows that O'Connor's fiction and the Brown corpus do not differ significantly in the distribution of the four types of complements examined: finite (I saw that he had left), bare-stem (I saw him leave), past participial (I saw him left at the doorstep), and present participial (I saw him leaving). Submits that qualitative analysis of both intuitive examples and examples from O'Connor's fiction demonstrates: 1) that the boundaries between each of the pairs semantics--pragmatics, physical perception--cognitive perception, and implication--presupposition are porous, 2) that the foreground / background gestalt distinction is multi-leveled, and 3) that the multi-leveled nature of foreground / background helps to explain the pragmatics of complements to the verb *see*. Concludes that, the porous nature of these boundaries is central to her use of these complements to show that physical and cognitive seeing are revealing of human limitations and revelatory of God's will and grace. (From author's abstract).

709   Hardy, John Edward. "No Place Like Home: The World of Walker Percy's Fiction." *New Orleans Review* 16.4 (1989): 73-81.

Examines how Walker Percy creates a sense of place in his fiction. Concludes with a brief discussion of O'Connor's comment that "'sickness is a place,' and that she herself had `never been anywhere but sick.'" Ties this comment to Percy's approach to writing.

710   Harmon, Justin, et. al. "O'Connor, Mary Flannery." *American Cultural Leaders: From Colonial Times to the Present.* Santa Barbara, CA: ABC-CLIO, 1993. 357.

Offers an assessment of O'Connor's life and work. Contends that "despite the brevity of her career, she has become known as one of the finest short-story writers of the twentieth century." Observes how her work "uses grotesque characters and bizarre situations to frame conflicts that are profoundly religious." Notes her deep concern "with the problem of redemption in a society that had moved beyond traditional religious faith."

711   Harmsel, Henrietta Ten. "Getting Kilt: Death in the Stories of Flannery O'Connor." *Reformed Journal* 37.10 (1987): 13-15.

Discusses O'Connor's preoccupation with death as seen in her fiction. Recalls her comment on another short story writer's works: "I don't like them. Nobody gets kilt in them." Surmises that the macabre and multitudinous deaths in O'Connor's stories are meant to be startling, yet not meaningless. Analyzes "The River," "A Good Man Is Hard to Find," "Greenleaf," and "The Displaced Person" to show how the deaths of the characters serve as their entrance into the "true country." Believes that O'Connor's theory of death is informed by St. Paul's letter to the Corinthians, in which he says "[in] dying, behold we live."

712   Harris, Laurie Lanzen. *Characters in 20th-Century Literature*. Detroit: Gale Research, 1990. 294-99.

Summarizes the plots and offers a brief assessment of *Wise Blood*, "A Good Man Is Hard to Find," "The Displaced Person," *The Violent Bear It Away*, and "Everything That Rises Must Converge."

713   Harris, Laurie Lanzen and Sheila Fitzgerald, ed. *Short Story Criticism: Excerpts from Criticism of the Works of Short Fiction Writers*. Vol. 1 Detroit: Gale Research, 1988. 333-73.

Offers a bibliographic essay with excerpts from works by Caroline Gordon, Louis Rubin, Robert Fitzgerald, Flannery O'Connor (her Hollins College introduction to "A Good Man Is Hard to Find"), Thomas Merton, Richard Poirier, Naomi Bliven, Stanley Edgar Hyman, Robert Drake, Josephine Hendin, Kathleen Feeley, Gilbert Muller, Martha Stevens, Alice Walker, Robert Coles, Andre Bleikasten, and Russell Kirk.

714   Hart, James D. *The Oxford Companion to American Literature*. 5th ed. New York: Oxford UP, 1983. 550.

Provides a short biography and listing of works by O'Connor.

715   Hart, Patrick, ed. *The Literary Essays of Thomas Merton*. New York: New
           Directions, 1981. 159-61.

           Merton relates O'Connor not to contemporary writers or philosophers but
           to Sophocles. Contends that it is the key word "respect" that informs the
           reading of her work.

716   Hashizume, Yumiko. "Arrival at the Verge of God's Mysterious World: A
           Study of Flannery O'Connor's Would-be Writers." *Kiyo* [Akenohoshi
           Women's Junior College, Urawa, Japan] 8 (Mar. 1990): 99-117.

           Explores O'Connor's use of intellectual would-be writers as characters, and
           their burden of "modern consciousness" in relation to faith. Offers
           readings of "The Enduring Chill," "The Partridge Festival," and
           "Everything The Rises Must Converge" in this context. Argues that by
           "taking up the motif of would-be writers repeatedly," she "demonstrates
           her humble understanding of the inadequacy of men's [sic] intellect in the
           presence of God's Mystery."

717   Hashizume, Yumiko. "The Last Quest for a True Catholicism: A Study of
           Flannery O'Connor's `Parker's Back.'" *Sophia English Studies* [Sophia
           University] (Japan) 14 (Oct. 1989): 73-91.

           Discusses O'Connor's position as a Catholic writer. Observes that she
           continued to use Protestant believers in her stories until the end of her
           short life. Analyzes "Parker's Back" as a tale of "the protagonist's
           unconscious quest for salvation." Then, discusses O.E. Parker's tattoos, the
           Common Prayer Book, Sarah Ruth, fundamentalist theology, and the
           "evangelical tradition of the South." Concludes that "Parker's Back"
           demonstrates that before her death, O'Connor "arrived at a well-balanced
           understanding of Catholics in the Protestant South. A step toward a true
           Catholicism was just about to be made."

718   Hashizume, Yumiko. "Urban Experience in Flannery O'Connor's `The
           Artificial Nigger.'" *Sophia English Studies* [Sophia University] (Japan) 11
           (Oct. 1986): 41-58.

           Discusses O'Connor's portrayal of the city as a necessary evil: a place her
           characters must pass through before they are granted a revelation; "an evil
           place" where Mr. Head and Nelson go astray and "through which they
           must proceed despite fatigue and hunger, fear and despair." Contends that
           the city symbolizes hell, and the trip, their soul's progress. Compares the
           similarities between the story and Dante's *Inferno* in the *Divine Comedy*.

Discusses the "dragon" of St. Cyril of Jerusalem, Northrop Frye's "U-shaped pattern to explain the narrative structure of the Bible, and the fact that agrarian Southerners "must face up to the reality of urban life." (Abstracted by Kayoko Watanabe).

719   Hatcher, Lint. "O'Connor Manuscripts Deteriorating With Age." *Georgia College Colonnade* 2 Sept. 1984: 1.

Reports on the condition of manuscripts in the *Flannery O'Connor Collection* of the Russell Library at Georgia College & State University (GC&SU). Discusses fundraising efforts to support preservation efforts, the materials in the collection, and stipulations accompanying the deed of gift prohibiting reproduction.

720   Havazelet, Ehud. "Our Own Light." *Flannery O'Connor Bulletin* 24 (1995-96): 96-98.

Comments on how O'Connor--like Chekhov, Faulkner, Malamud, Paley, and Munro--articulates a vision of the world in her stories and novels. Remarks that this vision reflects "an acceptance of this world, a valuing of its creatures, keenness of perception beyond the workaday lapses and failings of our creed." Discusses misinterpretations of O'Connor's interest in "human misery, human idiocy and brutishness." Contends that she "did not write of us as we should be but as we are, fallen . . . groping for the light with all the violence and anguish of our need for it." Observes that all of her characters are "running from Christ only to find at the end, they've been running headlong toward him all along." Refers to her remarks about Joseph Conrad's intention "to render the highest possible justice to the visible universe," which serves "as a reflection of the invisible universe." Concludes that O'Connor had the same ideal as Conrad in how she deployed her characters and watched them "with great tenderness and wisdom, sounding them by the depthlessness of their need and their nobility of effort in striving to meet it."

721   Havely, Cicely Palser. "Two Women Novelists: Carson McCullers and Flannery O'Connor." *The Uses of Fiction: Essays on the Modern Novel in Honour of Arnold Kettle*. Ed. Douglas Jefferson and Graham Martin. Milton Keynes (Great Britain): Open UP, 1982. 115-24.

Observes that Carson McCullers and Flannery O'Connor have been largely neglected in Britain. Remarks that both "achieved in their writing a degree of balance between the inner life and the public world." Discusses O'Connor's "Greenleaf" and notes that Mrs. May places her inner life in the context of her immediate world. Then, examines McCullers's *Clock Without Hands* and concludes that her work, like O'Connor's, shows that women writers are capable of describing "vividly realized inner lives . . . firmly set in a well observed and well analyzed social context."

721a   Havighurst, Craig. "That's All Folk: On Disk--Compass Records." *Wall Street Journal* 2 Dec. 1998: A20.

Discusses the music produced by Compass Records of Nashville, Tennessee. Refers to songs by Mississippi-born songwriter Kate Campbell as "versified short stories of peculiar Southern lives . . . likened to [fiction by] her heroes Flannery O'Connor and Eudora Welty."

722   Havird, David. "The Saving Rape: Flannery O'Connor and Patriarchal Religion." *Mississippi Quarterly* 47.1 (1993): 15-26.

Suggests that while none of O'Connor's female characters "invite assault," her strategy in "Greenleaf," "Revelation," and "Good Country People" is "to knock these proud female characters down a notch . . . by forcing upon them, in a sexually humiliating and often violent way, the humbling knowledge that they are after all women." Argues that O'Connor does this to assert that "it is not simply that they are merely human while God is divine; it is rather that they are female while God is male." Sees O'Connor insisting that female characters "surrender their pride, which has been masculine in its configuration, to Christ and that the dramatization of this abasement takes the form of sexual submission." Offers readings, in this context, of "The Enduring Chill," "Greenleaf," "Revelation," and "Good Country People." Finds her use of "Flannery O'Connor" instead of "Mary Flannery O'Connor" to be an example of her "'anxiety of authorship.'" Concludes that her "female characters become scapegoats . . . whose sin of authorship is greater even than their own prideful rejection of woman's conventional role as angel of the house."

723   Hawkins, Peter S. "Faith and Doubt First Class: The Letters of Flannery O'Connor." *Southern Humanities Review* 16.2 (1982): 91-103.

Examines O'Connor's correspondence for evidence of her "gift for taking other people's religious life seriously." Focuses on her letters to Alfred Corn, Louise Abbot, T.R. Spivey, Cecil Dawkins, and "A."

724   Hawkins, Peter S. "Flannery O'Connor: What's New?" *Religion and the Arts* 1.3 (1997): 111-19.

Examines O'Connor's letters in *The Habit of Being*, small circulation periodicals, and those known to exist in private hands, to consider what "this growing body of O'Connor's writing" might mean to critics and to the direction of O'Connor scholarship. Expresses concern that statements in her correspondence may be quoted out-of-context and challenges scholars "to respect the limits of O'Connor's letters for their sheer specificity." Refers to her correspondence with Youree Watson, "A," Mel Lorentzen, Alfred Corn, Carl Hartman, and Louise Abbott; and to Sally Fitzgerald's biography in progress, tentatively titled *The Mansions of the South*.

725   Hawkins, Peter S. "Problems of Overstatement in Religious Fiction and Criticism." *Renascence* 33 (1980): 36-46.

Discusses two prevailing attitudes about religion and literature and promotes a reader-response analysis. Labels the first attitude, which the church often adopts, as a "naive" assertion that literature serves religion to "win souls." Discusses the "literature-as-witness" approach as the other familiar alternative. Suggests that this approach seeks to expose the theological roots of thinkers such as Tillich, Whitehead, and Heidegger. Argues that O'Connor's works should be read for their "story" instead of their "mirrored religion." Contends that through this approach, the reader will undergo a new experience: "an opportunity to understand fallen nature and its restoration as though one were hearing something for the first time." Sees over-interpretation as a problem in O'Connor scholarship, and offers a reader-response analysis of "The Artificial Nigger" that seeks to avoid the typical criticism.

726   Haykin, Marti and Marc Snyder. "A Note on the Prints." *Flannery O'Connor Bulletin* 25 (1996-97): 103-04.

Discusses six O'Connor-related prints and describes the intaglio printmaking technique used to make the 8" x 10" originals. Reproductions are included: "How am I a hog and me both?" "Bevel," and "Tom T. Shiftlet" by Marti Haykin; and "Hazel," "Taulkinham," and "Enoch" by Marc Snyder.

727   Heher, Michael. "Grotesque Grace in the Factious Commonwealth." *Flannery O'Connor Bulletin* 15 (1986): 69-81.

Describes how O'Connor based her writing on experience not doctrine, and crafted this experience so readers might find revealed "some experience of Mystery." Argues that she wrote slowly not for perfection, but as part of her struggle "to locate the precise ambit" of her revelation.

Explores how her work reflects broken humanity and her characters are "not `irredeemable' but struggling toward greater freedom." Argues that "in the midst of their limited freedom, they [still] find redemption offered to them." Focuses on two biblical preoccupations in O'Connor's work: "moral judgement" and doctrine. Looks at "the work of the messenger, Mary Grace" and O'Connor's theme of biblical freedom in "Revelation." Finds the story to be "a fully enfleshed hermeneutic gloss on the passage "`Judge not, lest ye be judged.'" Concludes that O'Connor "attempts not to predict the specific actions of God so much as to encourage those in present trial to persevere against particular evils with the knowledge that the ultimate goal of history . . . is not in doubt."

728   Heine, Max. "`Because I'm Good': A *Phoenix* Interview with Dr. Robert Drake." *Phoenix* [U of Tennessee] (Winter 1976): 2-3.

Offers an interview with Robert Drake, a professor and writer, who met O'Connor and whose writing so impressed her that she introduced him to her agent in New York and helped him get his first book published. Drake describes O'Connor as "`a quiet person, but the type of quiet that you felt she could scream your head off if she wanted.'" Declares, "`she was very honest . . . she only told one story, and she told it over and over, but she did it well each time.'" Reports how Drake recounts O'Connor's response when asked why she wrote: "he lifted his nose, mocking the face of a disgusted woman, and said `Because I'm good.'"

729   Helmer, Shane, "Stumbling Onto the Spirit's Signposts." *Sojourners* 23.10 (1995-96): 18.

Discusses O'Connor's use of metaphor and her approach to the mystery and truth of "our redemption through God's grace." Suggests that while she "works the same territory as philosophers and theologians," O'Connor uses "fiction rather than exegesis."

729a   Helprin, Mark. "Contrivance: A Theory of Everything." *Forbes ASA*P 4 Oct. 1999: 244+.

Discusses Teilhard de Chardin's theory and statement that "everything that rises must converge,"commenting that his "great accomplishment was to confound the hapless nihilism based on the misapplication of the idea of entropy . . . with an exposition of how elemental physical forces are conducive to aggregation and, thus, higher form." Concludes with a discussion of O'Connor's "Everything That Rises Must Converge" as a critique of his ideas. Argues that, although O'Connor "would never know temporal glory, or be rewarded in this world," and "died without husband or children," she still "knew the simple truth that salvation is ultimately a matter of grace." Sees her position as representing the idea that "when all is said and done, man is simply unable to construct the higher parts of his destiny, and must know this to survive even the simpler challenges he is expected to meet."

730   Hemming, Roy. *Video Review's Movies on Video.* New York: Viare, 1983. 295.

Reviews John Huston's film version of *Wise Blood*. Credits O'Connor's original story and rates the film as "good."

731   Hendin, Josephine. "On and Off the Treadmill." *Vulnerable People: A View of American Fiction Since 1945.* New York: Oxford UP, 1978. 146-69.

Describes O'Connor as having a "gift for silence" and a talent for concealing "passion or fury in an outward calm." Attributes this silence to being raised in the deep South "where women are taught from childhood . . . to conceal inner turmoil behind a facade of feminine mildness." Compares O'Connor's perspective to that of Joyce Carol Oates. Describes the scene from "A Good Man Is Hard to Find" in which the grandmother is shot by The Misfit, then asks, "Was Flannery O'Connor a Misfit or Lady?" Describes incidents from O'Connor's life, a letter to Richard Stern, and other evidence that support the claim that O'Connor may have been a lonely woman who hid behind a facade of the "rigorous code of genteel Southern womanhood." Suggests that this code, which requires the individual to "not fuss" and not tell anyone about one's own "business," is widely reflected in her characters and in her own ability to "divorce behavior from feeling." Concludes that while O'Connor and her characters were always proper, the inner rage at would-be mothers and others is always present.

732   Herring, Gina. "Filming Hazel Motes: John Huston's Interpretation of *Wise Blood.*" *Journal of Contemporary Thought* 4 (1994): 71-84.

Compares and contrasts John Huston's film version of *Wise Blood* with O'Connor's novel. Discusses the aesthetic of each artist and their perspective and treatment of the novel's main character, Hazel Motes. Suggests that although both sought to use "the realistic backdrop of the modern South" and show it as an illusion, O'Connor hoped that her personal vision would obliterate the words "in favor of the spiritual world." Indicates that Huston did not share the same view, and that he saw the film instead as a "psychological, not theological," work, portraying a story "of human loneliness, rather than spiritual alienation." Finds the idea that Huston may have successfully translated O'Connor's "decidedly orthodox Christian vision into a humanist vision" to be "particularly ironic," as O'Connor "continually derided what she perceived to be the falsity, sentimentality, relativity, and ineffectuality of modern humanism." Concludes that the only way to understand and know *Wise Blood* "is to experience it directly."

733   Herrscher, Walter. "O'Connor's `The Displaced Person': The Problem of Doing Good." *Notes on Contemporary Literature* 14.1 (1984): 5-7.

Suggests that readers consider Mrs. McIntyre of "The Displaced Person" not as a selfish, worldly bigot but "as a practical individual struggling to do good, eventually destroyed by forces set in motion by her original act of kindness." Considers the priest as illustrating "the shortcomings of Christian humanitarianism unconcerned with practicality or with consequences." Presents Mr. Shortley's dilemma as a practical question: Is it right for "lower-middle-class Americans" to lose scarce jobs to those of "the overflow of other countries" who bring with them social conflict and societal disruption? Sees the work as an examination of good and evil in this world, and of the adage that "A good deed never goes unfinished."

734   Hewitt, Avis. "`Sniveler[s] After the Ineffable': Salvific Suffering in Flannery O'Connor's Sullen Sons of the South." *Proceedings of the Northeast Regional Meeting of the Conference on Christianity and Literature, Regis College, 10-12 October 1996.* Ed. Joan F. Hallisey and Mary-Anne Vetterling. Weston, MA: Regis College, 1996. 55-60.

Offers readings of "The Enduring Chill," "The Comforts of Home," and "Everything That Rises Must Converge" that focus upon how the young male protagonist in each story exemplifies "a self-love and an arrogant reliance upon [his] homemade conception of worldliness and sophistication that is aptly addressed by Proverbs 16:18, `Pride goeth before destruction, and a haughty spirit before a fall.'" Discusses common elements in each of the stories: the fact that Asbury, Thomas, and Julian "live at home with their mothers after having been away to college" and "see themselves as artists and intellectuals"; how O'Connor depicts the "distortion of the parent-child relationship in which indulgence and contempt have replaced kindness and honor"; and how each child desires "to teach his mother a lesson." Concludes that each of these young men meets with a form of punishment, as each in his own way, violates the fifth commandment, "`Honor thy father and mother.'"

735   Hewitt, Eben. "Diapsalmata and Numinous Recapitulation: The Tropology of `Parker's Back.'" *Proceedings of the Northeast Regional Meeting of the Conference on Christianity and Literature, Regis College, 10-12 October 1996.* Ed. Joan F. Hallisey and Mary-Anne Vetterling. Weston, MA: Regis College, 1996. 61-64.

Considers the challenge that faced Sören Kierkegaard and Flannery O'Connor: "how does one write `about something of which he himself says one cannot intelligibly speak, namely that Abraham's intention to sacrifice Isaac should be an act of faith.'" Suggests that this spiritual dilemma is "richly and subtly rendered" in "Parker's Back." Contends that O.E. Parker "plays a dual role in that he is both an embodiment of a hesitant, ambivalent Christ whose struggle to recognize the numinous forces in his life recapitulates the human necessity for 'acts of faith,'" while serving at the same time as an "exemplary vehicle for O'Connor's own compendious aesthetic and theological doctrine." Explicates the story in this context, focusing on the underlying suggestion of the presence of the Father, Son and Holy Ghost; the importance of Parker's name and his final recognition of, and faith in, the God that his name represents; and how, in the end, Obadiah Elihue Parker finds himself "reborn in the Garden of Eden." Concludes that O'Connor's purpose is to affirm "that it is simply the Biblical Word of God we must obey and cherish, and though we are imperfect, we cannot truly know God until we know ourselves."

736   Heymann, C. David. *American Aristocracy: The Lives and Times of James Russell, Amy, and Robert Lowell.* New York: Dodd, Mead, 1980. 366-68, 437.

Includes comments related to O'Connor's friendship with Robert Lowell while at Yaddo during the winter of 1948 (she "seemed to be attending Lowell with nothing less than rapture"); her response to Lowell's interest and involvement with anti-communist causes and discussions; and how peacock feathers from O'Connor were used to decorate Elizabeth Hardwick's "library-living room," which she used for writing.

737   Higdon, David Leon. "Flannery O'Connor's Sentence Titles." *Studies in American Fiction* 17.2 (1989): 227-34.

Reports that sentence titles, which "are unusual in short fiction and perhaps even more unique in long fiction," make up seven of O'Connor's thirty-one titles. Asserts that they reflect "a stylistic, thematic, and even metaphysical bent." Discusses two examples, "A Good Man Is Hard to Find," which exists as a philosophical assertion, as well as a direct quote from Eddie Green's 1917 blues hit popularized by Sophie Tucker; and

"Everything That Rises Must Converge" from Pierre Teilhard de Chardin's scientific-sounding philosophical proposition. Concludes that O'Connor's sentence titles function "as complex pointers" reflecting the ambiguities or multiple levels of punning" she sought for in her writing.

738   Higgs, Robert J. "Southern Humor: The Light and the Dark." *Thalia: Studies in Literary Humor* 6 (Fall-Winter 1983): 17-27.

Discusses the diversity of Southern mountain humor, focusing on how backwoods humor is preserved within it. Points out and outlines ten identifiable characteristics and how it has developed since the early nineteenth century and influences modern literary and commercial country humor. Includes brief discussions of O'Connor's work: how her ironic literary humor serves as an example of the "dark" side of mountain humor; how the oral tradition of backwoods humor survives in her work and that of William Faulkner and Eudora Welty; her remarks on the absurd and the grotesque in "Some Aspects of the Grotesque in Southern Fiction"; and how her humor compares with Mark Twain's.

739   Higgs, Robert J. "Sut Lovingood and the Hard No in Appalachian Literature: Part II." *Appalachian Heritage* 22 (Winter 1993): 6-18.

Categorizes a variety of Appalachian writers using Leslie Fiedler's "Hard No" classification. Discusses the way the "modern eclectic Appalachian novelist intersects the sacred and the secular, the Hard No and the Hard Yes." Contends that while O'Connor "does not fit comfortably into Fiedler's theory," her work does "exhibit a number of its features." Examines how she uses symbols of light and dark to affirm mystery, and uses cites from *Mystery and Manners* to illustrate her interest in Appalachian themes of divine mystery and humor. Suggests that while O'Connor's themes have influenced contemporary Appalachian writers, the themes have been present in Appalachian texts since George Washington Harris published *Sut Lovingood Yarns* in 1867.

740   Highsmith, Dixie Lee. "Flannery O'Connor's Polite Conversation." *Flannery O'Connor Bulletin* 11 (1982): 94-107.

Contends that, in O'Connor's work, "cliché, popular sayings, and slogans can become stepping stones for the reader into the world of spiritual concerns." Describes Jonathan Swift's *Polite Conversation*, and discusses how O'Connor, like Swift, uses meaningless, polite, shallow conversation as representative of humanity's "denial of ultimate concerns." Compares her use with Walker Percy's, and finds that "to both writers, language has a kind of supernatural dynamism that can reveal to us what we are essentially while it illuminates a larger reality." Refers to Miles Orvell's study of O'Connor's use of language in *Invisible Parade*, and offers careful explications of "A Good Man Is Hard to Find" and "Good Country People" in the context of the polite conversation of O'Connor's characters. Concludes that just as Percy "considers language a reflection of a reality larger than simple human perception, so O'Connor suggests that even the dead language of the cliché can be revitalized by the mystery of grace."

741   Hill, Dorothy Combs. *Lee Smith*. New York: Twayne, 1992. 122, 127-28.

Mentions O'Connor in a discussion of how the national press compares Lee Smith's work with that of William Faulkner, Eudora Welty, and Carson McCullers. Sees such comparisons as oversimplifications and stereotypical. Compares Smith's work with O'Connor's and suggests that both are concerned with restoring "human wholeness denied by the rational, the scientific, the materialistic, the moralistic, [and] the pornographic modern mind." Reviews O'Connor's themes, the influence of her Catholic faith, and her efforts to shock readers into realizing the pervasive influence of materialism in their lives. Notes that, unlike O'Connor, Smith does not write from a central creed, because "the religion available to her characters is so corrupted that it offers nothing but hollowness and cynicism." Finds both Smith and O'Connor mistrustful of "the cult of progress." Concludes that while O'Connor believed in the Church as "a channel of grace in the world," Smith is still "searching for the spirit in *female* flesh."

742   Hillis, Charlton. "Flannery O'Connor: A `Prophet Is Not Without Honor . . .'" *Chattanooga (TN) News-Free Press* 7 May 1992: D1+.

Describes a visit to the Flannery O'Connor Room at the Russell Library of Georgia College & State University, to Andalusia (the O'Connor family farm outside Milledgeville), and to O'Connor's childhood home in Savannah. Notes that Milledgeville's lack of recognition for O'Connor reflects her mother's desire for privacy. Mentions Hugh Brown's efforts to acquire the childhood home at 207 East Charlton Street in Savannah. Includes illustrations of Andalusia and O'Connor's childhood home.

743   Hines, Melissa. "Grotesque Conversions and Critical Piety." *Flannery O'Connor Bulletin* 6 (1977): 17-35.

Responds to a suggestion by Marion Montgomery that, for many critics, an examination of O'Connor's work "is often `an act of piety toward the work.'" Discusses this statement to determine the nature of such piety, whether the unsettled responses of readers might be seen as an "act of exorcism," and ways such piety "serves the sacredness of the fictional mystery." Offers an outline of the origin, history, use, and meaning of the Grotesque, and ties O'Connor's use to this subject--the conversion experience. Refers to Helen Adolf's "On Medieval Laughter" to substantiate the claim that "it is the vibrantly comprehensive spirit of the Catholic Middle Ages that speaks through Flannery's fiction." Offers a reading of "Parker's Back" to show how O'Connor used the "Grotesque structure of experience" to goad readers to try to solve what they cannot understand to regain their "worldly equilibrium." Alleges that her work haunts readers "with glimpses of a meaning whose mysterious life is as real as it is elusive," and pushes readers into being "possessed into piety." Insists that readers who "reject the exacting demands of meaning" in her stories may find themselves mysteriously fulfilling its purposes.

743a   "Historical Marker Urged for O'Connor Birthplace." *Savannah Evening Press* 22 April 1975: 1+.

Reports that the Old Capital Historical Society in Milledgeville, Georgia "has begun a project to place a historical marker on the birthplace of American author Flannery O'Connor at 207 East Charlton Street" in Savannah. Acknowledges Dorrie P. Neligan's efforts "to secure permission from the present owners for the plaque." Outlines O'Connor's career and awards, and notes Georgia College's Alumni Association adopting "as a project underwriting a $50,000 display room to be added to the college library to house the O'Connor collection." Illustrations: Photograph of the front of the house on Charlton Street.

744   Hobson, Fred C. "Odum, Davidson, and the Sociological Proteus." *Tell Us About the South: The Southern Rage to Explain*. Baton Rouge: Louisiana State UP, 1983. 180-243.

Discusses the crusade against the discipline of Sociology conducted by Donald Davidson and others during the 1930s. Contends that because he saw Sociology as "the most abstract of disciplines" that "studied people in the mass," it was "the most dangerous." Argues that Davidson saw it as a discipline committed to changing and reforming Southerners, "to taking the color and vitality out of their lives and reshaping them in the standardized American mold." Contains a passing reference to O'Connor's character, Rayber, in *The Violent Bear It Away*, as an example of "the epitome of the secularist committed to the analysis of man."

745   Hobson, Fred. Rev. of *With All My Might: An Autobiography*, by Erskine
            Caldwell. *South Atlantic Review* 53.1 (1988): 171-72.

            Discusses how Caldwell's autobiography "displays the virtues and flaws"
            of his work as a whole. Comments that while Caldwell "demonstrated the
            same attraction to the lurid and depraved in southern life that characterized
            the work of William Faulkner and Flannery O'Connor," in the end, he was
            "far from being either Faulkner or O'Connor."

746   Hobson, Fred. "The Savage South: An Inquiry Into the Origins,
            Endurance, and Presumed Demise of an Image." *Virginia Quarterly
            Review* 61.3 (1985): 377-95.

            Discusses George B. Tindall's essay, "The Benighted South: Origins of a
            Modern Image," published in *The Virginia Quarterly Review* in 1964.
            Compares his 1964 views of the South with the current situation (1985).
            Refers to O'Connor as an example of an author who was a leading
            practitioner of the Southern Gothic during the 1940s.

747   Hobson, Fred. *The Southern Writer in the Postmodern World*. Mercer
            University Lamar Memorial Lectures No. 33. Athens: U of Georgia P,
            1991. 4, 9, 21, 25-26, 32, 44, 57.

            Refers to aspects of O'Connor's life, work, and beliefs: how, along with
            Faulkner, she expresses displeasure at the use of abstraction and sociology
            in contemporary society; how most recent Southern writers are no longer
            under Faulkner's influence, but are instead influenced by Eudora Welty,
            Walker Percy, and O'Connor; the manner in which O'Connor's wrote
            approvingly of plain, poor, white Southerners; the similarities between Lee
            Smith's Jennifer in *Oral History* and O'Connor's Rayber in *The Violent
            Bear It Away*; Larry McMurtry's comment that Barry Hannah is "`the best
            fiction writer to appear in the South since Flannery O'Connor'"; and how
            some of Richard Ford's characters talk like O'Connor's.

748   Hobson, Fred. "Surveyors and Boundaries: Southern Literature and
            Southern Literary Scholarship After Mid-Century." *Southern Review* 27.4
            (1991): 739-55.

            Outlines changes in the nature of Southern literature and the critical
            approaches to its study. Credits Louis D. Rubin, Jr., Lewis P. Simpson, C.
            Hugh Holman, Thomas Daniel Young, and Walter Sullivan as
            instrumental in founding Southern literature "as a modern academic
            discipline." Refers to O'Connor as among the century's major Southern

writers and observes that many contemporary writers "now operate not under the shadow of Faulkner but under that of O'Connor and Welty." Notes the acceptance of O'Connor's work "into the canon" along with that of Eudora Welty, Katherine Anne Porter, Caroline Gordon, and Carson McCullers. Urges the modern Southern writer to "observe *his* contemporary South, not Faulkner's or O'Connor's or Richard Wright's."

749   Hobson, Linda Whitney. "A Good `Rotation.'" *Mississippi Quarterly* 43.4 (1990): 539-43.

Review of Jill P. Baumgaertner's *Flannery O'Connor: A Proper Scaring* and Bettina L. Knapp's *Women in Twentieth Century Literature: A Jungian View*. Finds both carefully researched, interesting, and worthwhile reading. Remarks on the scholars' divergent discussions of "Everything That Rises Must Converge." States that "Knapp's Jungian reading of the story contrasts substantially with Baumgaertner's more sanguine reading."

750   Hobson, Linda Whitney. "An Interview with Walker Percy, April 19, 1984, Covington, Louisiana." *Xavier Review* 4.1-2 (1984): 1-19.

Offers a brief introduction and a transcript of an interview with Percy in question-and-answer format. Percy refers to O'Connor's remarks "on the need for unsentimentality in race relations as an antidote to condescension or what used to be called paternalism."

751   Hoffman, Daniel. *Harvard Guide to Contemporary American Writing*. Cambridge, MA: Belknap, 1979. 49, 156, 179-80, 184, 244, 255-57, 287, 354-55, 365, 374.

Offers essays to serve as a survey of significant writing in the United States from the end of World War II to the end of the 1970s. Essays are included to encourage "informed discussion of the vital dialectic of themes, forms, and values which that writing embodies." Includes passing comments on O'Connor's work by Alan Trachtenberg, Lewis P. Simpson, Josephine Hendin, Nathan A. Scott, Jr., and, Elizabeth Janeway. Hendin's remarks on how O'Connor "took the traditional concerns of Southern fiction and exploded them in a new direction" are the most extensive, as they include discussions of "The Life You Save May Be Your Own," "The River," "A Good Man Is Hard to Find," and "Revelation."

752   Hogan, Michael. "Grammatical Tenuity in Fiction." *Language and Style* 14.1 (1981): 13-19.

Discusses "the significance of the progressive verbal aspect, *be* + *ing*, in prose fiction." Focuses on how "it offers good examples of the sense in which a writer's choice of grammatical form is a stylistic decision," and how "it frequently creates a certain number of stylistic effects in narrative prose." Includes examples from works by William Faulkner, William Gass, Ralph Ellison, Sean O'Faolain, Carson McCullers, and Flannery O'Connor. Notes that "free modifiers of a main clause in the form of a Verb Phrase containing the progressive" are notable in O'Connor's story "The Artifical Nigger."

753   Holfeltz, Heidi. "A Self-Portrait in Words: The Letters of Flannery O'Connor." *Literature and Belief* 2 (1982): 59-68.

Offers a biographical essay constructed from information in *The Habit of Being*. Touches on most aspects of O'Connor's life, including her life in and outside of Georgia, her relationship with her mother and other close friends, and her theological beliefs and creative impulse.

754   Hollandsworth, Linda P. "'A Good Man Is Hard to Find': Return to Reality and Acceptance of Grace Through Violence." Ms. 1995. *Flannery O'Connor Collection*, Georgia College & State University.

Argues that Flannery O'Connor is the preeminent Southern fiction writer who subscribes to the belief that violence, in life as well as in fiction, is *the* conductor to the reader's perception of truth. Suggests that she purposely uses violence and the grotesque to underscore her belief that each human being's salvation can only be achieved through moments of grace that are the results of violence. Discusses how this idea is illustrated in "A Good Man Is Hard to Find" through the characters of The Misfit and the grandmother. Sees them as representing the futility in denying Christ and their sins. Sees O'Connor's frustration with human duality in "A Good Man Is Hard to Find," which presents "a format in which to reconcile human transgressions through redemption." (From author's abstract. Presented during the Flannery O'Connor 70th Birthday Symposium held at Brigham Young University, Nov. 8-11, 1995.)

755   Holman, Clarence Hugh. "Detached Laughter in the South." *Windows on the World: Essays on American Social Fiction*. Knoxville: U of Tennessee P, 1979. 27-47.

Reviews the "traditional comic writing" of Augustus Baldwin Longstreet, Joseph Glover Baldwin, Johnson Jones Hooper, George Washington Harris, and Thomas Bangs Thorpe. Describes their "literal reporting of the strange and wonderful things of the natives, colored by a certain amount of amused extravagance." Contends that "in this century, the South has produced essentially two kinds of humor . . . the novel of manners or of urbane fantasy" and "a raucous, ribald, and extravagant humor which is the realist's way of dealing with the unbearable or the intolerable aspects of life without shifting into the tradition of the Gothic or the tragic." Cites James Branch Cabell, Ellen Glasgow, Robert Molloy, and Josephine Pinckney as examples of the first type of humor, and refers to William Faulkner's ability to describe characters without resorting to Gothic horrors or sentimental sympathy. Examines the "traditional detached comedy" evident in the writing of Erskine Caldwell and Flannery O'Connor. Observes that O'Connor's uniqueness is found in the comic detachment and sympathy shown in how she dealt with "tortured, tormented, and distorted people." Notes her method in "Good Country People" in which Hulga finds "in the young Bible salesman precisely what she has sought all her life, and it has betrayed her and left her without the means to move or see." Claims that Caldwell and O'Connor inherited "a long southern tradition of detached humor, and they employed it on the same kinds of people in many of the same locales, but for radically different purposes." Also in *Comic Relief: Humor in Contemporary American Literature*. Ed. Sarah Blacher Cohen. Urbana: U of Illinois P, 1978. 87-104.

756   Holman, C[larence] Hugh. "O'Connor, (Mary) Flannery." *American Writers Since 1900*. Ed. James Vinson and D.L. Kirkpatrick. Chicago: St. James, 1980. 425-26.

Appears to be a reprint of Holman's bio-bibliographical essay in *Novelists and Prose Writers*, Ed. James Vinson and D.L. Kirkpatrick. New York: St. Martin's, 1979. 918-20.

757   Holman, C[larence] Hugh. "O'Connor (Mary) Flannery." *Novelists and Prose Writers*. Ed. James Vinson and D.L. Kirkpatrick. New York: St. Martin's, 1979. 918-20.

Bio-bibliographical essay: includes awards, primary sources, a list of bibliographies, and a critical summary. Asserts that because much of O'Connor's work was produced after the onset of lupus, "a great deal of her best fiction is concerned with death, and often with death as a release or means of salvation." Suggests that though she worked with "a limited theme, and the range of her work often seems distressingly narrow," she worked "within the limits of her art with great commitment, artistic integrity, high technical skill, and frequent success." Concludes that while O'Connor will remain a minor literary figure, her work represents that of "enormous challenge, subtlety, and accomplishment." Also in *American Writers Since 1900*. Ed. James Vinson and D.L. Kirkpatrick. Chicago: St. James, 1980, 425-26.

758   Holmes, John R. *"Everything That Rises Must Converge." Masterplots II: Women's Literature Series*. Vol. 2. Pasadena, CA: Salem, 1995. 6 vols. 694-698.

Offers a brief summary of the plot of each of the stories included in O'Connor's collection *Everything That Rises Must Converge*, followed by a discussion of her themes, regional perspective, use of distortion and caricature, and reliance upon "the domineering mother and artistic or scholarly daughter" as character types throughout her fiction.

759   Holsen, Ruth M. "O'Connor's `Good Country People.'" *Explicator* 42.3 (1984): 59.

Sheds light on the derivation of the name "Hulga," a Norwegian name meaning "holy." Explains the impulse of O'Connor's character in terms of her choice of this name over her given one, and establishes Joy/Hulga as a person "longing for innocence, for purification."

759a   Homans, Michael. "Admirers Raise $42,180 to Get O'Connor Home." *Savannah Evening Press* 31 July 1989: 11+.

Reports that "Less than seven weeks after an effort to raise $50,000 toward the purchase price of the [Flannery O'Connor childhood] home began, $42,180 has been donated or pledged." Offers details of meetings with bankers, realtors, and the current owner (Mary Runyan) regarding the sale of the property at 207 East Charlton Street in Savannah, and quotes Bob Strozier of Armstrong State College concerning efforts to refurbish the house and reduce the remaining debt.

759b   Homans, Michael. "O'Connor Fans Can Have Tea in Writer's Refurbished Home." *Savannah Evening Press* 12 April 1990: 1.

Reports that the Flannery O'Connor Home Foundation has opened O'Connor's childhood home "to weekend visits, readings and teas." States that the parlor room of the 1855 home at 207 East Charlton Street has been refurbished in a 1930s-style decor that O'Connor would have recognized. States that "several readings of Miss O'Connor's most popular works have been scheduled for upcoming Sundays." Illustrations:

Photograph of Joe Morris and Reginald Cooper of Armstrong College painting interior walls of the O'Connor home.

759c   Homans, Michael. "O'Connor House Restoration Campaign Has Hit an Impasse." *Savannah Evening Press* 8 Nov. 1989: 23+.

Reports that efforts to raise $ 35,000 to restore the interior of Flannery O'Connor's childhood home have reached an impasse. Quotes Hugh Brown as stating that despite dozens of grant applications sent to a wide variety of philanthropic organizations, the group has not been successful in raising the additional needed funds.

759d   Homans, Michael. "Restoration Begins At O'Connor Home." *Savannah Evening Press* 12 Dec. 1989: 23+.

Interviews Hugh Brown regarding the restoration of the O'Connor's childhood home in Savannah. Reports that Cynthia Stillwell is helping to locate "period furniture, curtains and decorations for the parlor floor of the house," and that members of the foundation who purchased the home for $132,500 would attend a party celebrating their progress the following · day. Requests that "anyone with photographs or memorabilia from Miss O'Connor's childhood in Savannah contact the foundation." Illustrations: Photograph of Hugh Brown in the parlor of the home.

760   Hood, Mary, Cecil Dawkins, and Josephine Jacobsen. "Brief Testimonies." *Flannery O'Connor Bulletin* 24 (1995-96): 121-22.

Mary Hood, Cecil Dawkins, and Josephine Jacobsen offer brief comments on O'Connor's life and work. Hood describes the impact of visiting the Flannery O'Connor Collection at Georgia College & State University; Dawkins refers to Hannah Arendt's comments on "`the banality of evil'" and wonders what O'Connor would be like at age seventy; and Jacobsen recounts an incident which took place at Notre Dame College in which a member of the audience asked Flannery "why she didn't write anything that raised her heart," to which O'Connor replied "if your heart was where it's supposed to be, it would be raised."

761   Hopkins, Mary Frances. "Julian's Mother." *Flannery O'Connor Bulletin* 7 (1978): 114-15.

The author states that having, "for some years now," performed as Julian's mother in "Everything That Rises Must Converge," she is "almost offended to see her referred to as Mrs. Chestny." Contends that she "is not," and offers logical arguments in support of her assertion. Declares that the inaccurate naming of Julian's mother "blurs our concept of the character and weakens the ethos of the critic."

762   Hopkins, Mary Frances. "The Rhetoric of Heteroglossia in Flannery O'Connor's *Wise Blood.*" *Quarterly Journal of Speech* 75.2 (1989): 198-211.

Addresses two questions which perplexed readers pose: (1) "How can unrelieved violence be . . . humorous?" and (2) "How can such an avowedly religious author take such an unforgiving view of people and the world in general?" Contends that the answer to the first is apparent to readers who read the text aloud, because by doing so, the humor becomes readily apparent in "the irony in the narrative voice and the buffoonery of the characters." Asserts that the answer to the second lies in the impact of her rhetoric. Disputes analyses of *Wise Blood* by Marshall Bruce Gentry, Steven Weisenburger, and Edward Kessler and suggests that readers can develop a deeper understanding of the work using Mikhail Bakhtin's conceptual definitions of heteroglossia as an analytical tool. Contends that it is O'Connor's use of heteroglossia--more than grotesque images, use of metaphors or apocalyptic language--that lays bare the conflicting ideologies underlying her work.

763   Horton, James W. "Flannery O'Connor's Hermaphrodite: Notes Toward a Theology of Sex." *Flannery O'Connor Bulletin* 23 (1994-95): 30-42.

Reports that while O'Connor's fiction "does not usually lend itself to a discussion of sex or gender," "A Temple of the Holy Ghost" is a notable exception. Contends that critics "have neglected the sexual nature" of the hermaphrodite and concentrated "solely on the religious nature of his/her meaning and place in O'Connor's collection of grotesques." Argues that the story "contains a persistent structure of subject/object relationships that can be interpreted as a foundation for human sexuality and for God/human relationships as they are thought of within a Christian context." Considers the "theme of subject/object relations" as "highlighted by the story's concentration on the child's point of view." Discusses how the "child's raucous mockery [which] takes place at a table serves to reinforce her nature as a consuming subject"; and how the functions of intelligence and "the head" are highlighted by the child's conversation with the cook and the contrast between the child and the beauty of the other girls. Views the story as "a critique of a purely subject-oriented spirituality in which the human being sees himself or herself purely as subject and not as object."

764   Howard, Maureen. "Can Writing Be Taught in Iowa?" *New York Times Magazine* 25 May 1986: 34-36, 38, 45-46, 48-49.

Offers passing references to O'Connor: *Wise Blood* as an example of a novel "worth reading" produced by a student attending the Iowa Writer's Workshop; O'Connor's "perhaps apocryphal" comment that the Workshop did not discourage "enough" young writers; and Paul Engle's recollection of her appearing in his office "to announce she wanted to write fiction."

764a   Howard, Rosanne. "Move Under Way to Buy Flannery O'Connor Home." *Savannah Morning News* 11 June 1989: A1+.

Describes the efforts of Robert Burnett, Bob Strozier, and Hugh Brown of Armstrong State College to establish a non-profit foundation for the purpose of purchasing Flannery O'Connor's childhood home at 207 East Charlton Street in Savannah. States that the present owner, Mary Runyan, had purchased the home from Regina Cline O'Connor in 1966 as part of Flannery O'Connor's estate (who had, herself, inherited the home from her wealthy cousin Mrs. Raphael Semmes). Offers a brief biographical sketch of O'Connor, refers to the grandmother in "A Good Man Is Hard to Find" as representative of O'Connor's characters, and outlines plans to turn the home into a museum with a gift shop. Mentions that O'Connor had corrected page proofs of *Wise Blood* while visiting Mrs. Semmes in the home in 1952, and recounts Sister Jude Walsh's memory of young Flannery O'Connor arriving at Sacred Heart School in one of the two electric cars in Savannah at the time. Illustrations: Posed sitting portrait of O'Connor and a photograph of Burnett, Brown, and Strozier standing in front of the home.

765   Howarth, William. "Itinerant Passages: Recent American Essays." *Essays on the Essay: Redefining the Genre* Ed. Alexander J. Butrym. Athens: U of Georgia P, 1989. 241-49.

Suggests that in post-1965 American essays, "two forms of motion often exist in jostling opposition." The first, the "recurring process, invokes order and certainty, the successions that establish traditional patterns"; the second, a "unique process, is eccentric and finite, coming to a definite end." Cites and discusses variety of examples of each, including Alice Walker's, "Beyond the Peacock: The Reconstruction of Flannery O'Connor." Submits that in this essay, in which Walker poses "herself and O'Connor as racial and cultural opposites," Walker "eventually comes to acknowledge their shared values." Focuses on the conversation between Alice Walker and her mother related to the peacocks and implies that the "passage has the force of revelation, like `the shock of recognition' that

Melville felt on first reading Hawthorne." Concludes that "to understand the peacocks, she learns to see `beyond' them to the transcendent values they incarnate."

766   Howe, Irving. "Flannery O'Connor's Stories." *Celebrations and Attacks: Thirty Years of Literary and Cultural Commentary*. New York: Horizon, 1979. 97-101.

Reviews *Everything That Rises Must Converge* and asserts that readers should hesitate to heap praise on her work. Finds "a recurrent insecurity of tone, [with] jarring sentences in which Miss O'Connor slips from the poise of irony to the smallness of sarcasm." Offers that "one can only suppose that it is a hostility rooted in Miss O'Connor's own experience and the kind of literary education she received." Suggests that O'Connor "associates the values she respects with an especially obnoxious kind of youthful callowness, while reserving some final wisdom of experience for the foolish and obtuse." Acknowledges that while she is in control of her work, there is something missing, "a moment when the unexpected happens, a perception, an insight, a confrontation which may not be in accord with the writer's original intention." Maintains that only at the end of her life did O'Connor master the means to achieve this "release"--in "Revelation" and "Parker's Back"--and begin "to break past the fences of her skill and her ideas." [A version of this article appeared in *The New York Review of Books* 30 September 1965: 16-17.]

767   Howe, Susan Elizabeth. "An Interview with Sally Fitzgerald." *Literature and Belief* 17.1-2 (1997): 1-20.

Interview of Sally Fitzgerald in question and answer format, preceded by a brief biographical sketch. Fitzgerald comments on a variety of topics, including: references to Catholicism in "A Temple of the Holy Ghost" and "The Enduring Chill"; the meaning of Hazel Motes's actions in *Wise Blood*; Christ imagery in "A View of the Woods"; the influence of O'Connor's artistic background upon her writing; Fitzgerald's access to two of O'Connor's personal "notebooks"; O'Connor's interest in T.S. Eliot's *The Waste Land*; O'Connor's views regarding other religions and whether "you have to be baptized to enter the kingdom of heaven"; O'Connor's use of violence; ways in which O'Connor might be viewed as a "prophetic figure"; and Fitzgerald's opinions regarding O'Connor's personality and romantic interests.

768   Howell, Elmo. "The Developing Art of Flannery O'Connor." *Arizona Quarterly* 29.3 (1973): 266-76.

Argues that O'Connor's work is overrated, especially in terms of its sophistication, and examines the "shift in interest" seen in stories in *Everything That Rises Must Converge*. Sees O'Connor returning to ordinary experience and realities of home, and notes that liberal-mindedness becomes her most persistent and important theme.

769   Hubert, Linda. "To Alice Walker: Carson McCullers's Legacy of Love." *Pembroke Magazine* 20 (1988): 89-95.

Examines the "nature of love as Carson McCullers reveals it in her work," focusing on her legacy as seen in Alice Walker's *The Color Purple*. Includes a reference to O'Connor as being an influence on Walker's work.

770   Hughes, Richard E. "The Christ Myth." *The Lively Image: 4 Myths in Literature*. Cambridge, MA: Winthrop, 1975. 177-220.

Discusses how O'Connor's *Wise Blood* serves as a reflection of "the literary values of St. Matthew's narrative of Christ." Then offers a reprint of "Greenleaf" in its entirety as an "interlude" to allow readers "to play with each of the myths in a new costume" and understand how they may help to "edge the imagination over into new perceptions." Sees St. Matthew's Christ as "voracious" and O'Connor's purpose in writing *Wise Blood* as her attempt to depict the impact upon a man "who expends himself entirely, in accordance with the myth." Offers an explication of the novel, focusing upon Haze as a character with "Jeremiac intensity" and Enoch Emory as a simple-minded man who "dumbly and instinctively knows that there is a dimension of reality beyond the material" but-- because "he is afflicted with the allure of the easy and the partial"--gets "entangled in easy rituals, false formulas, and God-searches that do not involve his real self." Includes discussion of the potato peeler as a symbol of a "redemption machine" ("the crank turns, the soul comes out white"); Enoch's attempted transformation into a gorilla as acting-out the Jacob and Esau story, "courting the blessing of redemption [while] not in his own skin"; and Haze as symbolic of Saul of Tarsus, "struck down and blinded on the road to Damascus."

771   Hulbert, Dan. "'Person' Works Better in O'Connor's Words." *Atlanta Journal-Constitution* 27 March 1998: P7.

Reviews Cecil Dawkins's "slack 1960s stage adaptation" of O'Connor's "The Displaced Person," presented in Atlanta by Theatrical Outfit's 14th Street Playhouse. Contends that Dawkins's script makes O'Connor's religious symbolism "even harder to understand," and concludes that the play demonstrates how "fiercely resistant" Southern fiction is to being adapted as drama.

772   Hulick, Diana Emery. "Ralph Eugene Meatyard: *The Family Album of Lucybelle Crater.*" *History of Photography* 16 (Winter 1992): 379-83.

Review essay and explication of Meatyard's book of photographs, *The Family Album of Lucybelle Crater*. States that the book may be traced to Meatyard's fascination with O'Connor's "The Life You Save May Be Your Own," whose main characters include a Lucynelle Crater and her daughter by the same name. Contends that Meatyard imitated O'Connor's repetitive use of name by repeating his version of the name throughout his work as well. Argues that "the central metaphor of the O'Connor story suggests that no one can understand the human heart even if it is dissected," and ties this to the relationships seen in Meatyard's photographs.

773   Humphries, Jefferson. "Art, Delusion, Disease, and Reality: The Apotheosis of Asbury Fox on 'The Enduring Chill.'" *The Otherness Within: Gnostic Readings in Marcel Proust, Flannery O'Connor, and François Villon*. Baton Rouge: Louisiana State UP, 1983. 112-40.

Discusses "The Enduring Chill" to show how one might "squeeze from it some greater understanding of what 'art,' 'delusion,' and 'reality' mean, to Flannery O'Connor, to Proust," and to the author himself. Suggests that Asbury Fox "is the closest thing in all her work to a Charles Swann, an individual of creative temperament but who produces nothing." Discusses how Asbury "also bears strong resemblance to [Proust's] Marcel who, after all, is a failure until the end of his story, which is also a story of 'arty delusions' lost."

774   Humphries, Jefferson. *Metamorphoses of the Raven: Literary Overdeterminedness in France and the South Since Poe*. Baton Rouge: Louisiana State UP, 1985. 12-15, 22, 34, 58-59, 113, 165-72.

Discusses the "interlinguistic transfusion" between writers from the American South and France. Includes references to O'Connor: the role of Catholicism in the "transfusion" between the two groups; her explanation for "the Southern writer's penchant to grotesquerie as a phenomenon of loss, of a sense of displacement, exile, unwholeness"; her view of the Aristotelian tradition; the suggestion that the "most celebrated exponent in Southern literature" of the "kind of accursed and nihilistic stoicism" proposed by Jean Paul Sartre might be O'Connor's Misfit"; and discussion of the symbolism and meaning of the peacock in "The Displaced Person."

775   Humphries, Jefferson. "Proust, Flannery O'Connor, and the Aesthetic of Violence." *The Otherness Within: Gnostic Readings in Marcel Proust, Flannery O'Connor, and François Villon*. Baton Rouge: Louisiana State UP, 1983. 95-111.

Observes that while Proust "does not concern himself much with simulating `objective' realities or observe unities of time, place or even character," O'Connor could serve "as an exemplary case of the writer who observes those principles scrupulously." Sees "a profound kinship" between the two writers. Discusses a variety of topics, including their mutual concern over the practice of their art and spirit; the relationship between O'Connor's use of distortion and aesthetic violence to Maurice Blanchot's "idea of communication" and Georges Bataille's "idea of writing as transgression"; O'Connor's reply to John Hawkes about the role of the devil in her work; and how the sacred might serve "as a negation of a negation" in O'Connor's work. Suggests that O'Connor's fiction "can be read as a catalog of the unbeliever in his many incarnations," and reflects both O'Connor's and Proust's fascination "with sickness, with disabilities of mind, spirit, and matter." Discusses evil "as the unwitting servant of the good it despises" in "The River," "A Good Man Is Hard to Find," and "Good Country People." [Rpt. in *Flannery O'Connor: Modern Critical Views*. Ed. Harold Bloom. New York: Chelsea House, 1986. 111-24.]

776   Hurd, Myles Raymond. "The Misfit as Parricide in Flannery O'Connor's `A Good Man Is Hard to Find.'" *Notes on Contemporary Literature* 22.4 (1992): 5-7.

Refers to O'Connor's response to a query from John Hawkes in which she "rejects a direct identification of The Misfit with the devil" and insists that he is still redeemable. Examines how O'Connor linked The Misfit to ancient Roman law, focusing on Pompeian punishment for those who murdered "blood-related" kinsmen. Refers to how these criminals were tossed into the sea in a sack containing the live criminal along with a cock, a dog or ape, and snakes. Notes that each of these animals (or their equivalent) are cited in "A Good Man Is Hard to Find": the monkey is seen at Red Sammy Butts's restaurant; the parrots on Bailey Boy's shirt; The Misfit's recollection of his father saying that he was "'a different breed of dog'"; and The Misfit springs back "'as if a snake had bitten him.'" Suggests that even the grandmother's "sachet" suggests this link, as the "French *sachet* is commonly translated as `bag' or `sack' in English."

777   Hurst, Mary Jane. "Parent-Child Discourse." *The Voice of the Child in American Literature: Linguistic Approaches to Fictional Child Language*. Lexington: UP of Kentucky, 1990. 64-94.

Discusses O'Connor's "The Lame Shall Enter First," along with William Faulkner's *Light in August*, Henry Roth's *Call It Sleep*, and Langston Hughes's "Father and Son" as works which "illustrate the problems of father-son communication in multicultural settings."

778   Hyman, Stanley Edgar. "Flannery O'Connor." *Seven American Women Writers of the Twentieth Century: An Introduction*. Ed. Maureen Howard. Minneapolis: U of Minnesota P, 1977. 311-55.

Reprint from the "University of Minnesota Pamphlets on American Writers" series. Offers a biographical sketch followed by explications of O'Connor's principal works, including *Wise Blood*, "The Artificial Nigger," "Good Country People," "The Displaced Person," *The Violent Bear It Away*, and "Parker's Back." Suggests "certain preoccupations that seem almost obsessional": images ("flaming suns, the mutilated eyes, the `Jesus-seeing' hats," etc.); recurrent symbols (blue suits, black hats, peacocks, Faulknerian families, etc); and dysfunctional family relationships. Describes recurrent themes of "the mysteries of sex and religion"; the "perverse mother"; concepts of "change of identity, transformation, death-and-rebirth," denial and "naysaying"; and the "`God-intoxicated' world." Explores O'Connor's radical Christian dualism, her choice of Protestant Fundamentalism as a metaphor for her Catholic vision, and the "profound spiritual meaning" seen in her Negro characters. Concludes that O'Connor's symbolic action has a purging effect on readers, leaving them serene and devout.

779   Hynes, Joseph. "The Fading Figure in the Worn Carpet." *Arizona Quarterly* 42.4 (1986): 321-30.

Discusses Evelyn Waugh's novel *Brideshead Revisited* and the character of Sebastian Flyte. Relates O'Connor's Hazel Motes in *Wise Blood* and The Misfit in "A Good Man Is Hard to Find" to Sebastian. Finds that each character neither believes nor disbelieves in the supernatural elements of a Christian culture. Analyzes parallels with the characters of Henry James, Saul Bellow, and Walker Percy. Finds that all demonstrate "the working of grace in various ways, to humanly unforseen ends, in a manner making compatible divine plan, proximate causality, and free will."

780   Idol, John L., Jr. "Edna Earle Ponder's Good Country People." *Southern Quarterly* 20.3 (1982): 66-75.

Discusses Eudora Welty's Edna Earle Ponder from *The Ponder Heart*, focusing on her "small town pugnacity and self-conceit, [and] her image of herself as a member of the landed gentry now absorbed into the life of a small Southern town." Offers a brief comparison of Edna Earle to O'Connor's Hulga (Joy) Hopewell from "Good Country People." Suggests that, unlike O'Connor's Hulga, Edna Earle "would not even think of trying to show Manley Pointer . . . how meanly hypocritical he is."

780a   "In Memoriam Sarah Morgan (Sally) Fitzgerald 1917-2000." *Flannery O'Connor Bulletin* 26-27 (1998-2000): 24.

Eulogizes Sally Fitzgerald as a scholar whose contributions to O'Connor scholarship were not only "incomparable and invaluable," but whose editing and compilation of O'Connor's essays for *Mystery and Manners* and correspondence for *The Habit of Being: Letters of Flannery O'Connor*, "broadened readers' understanding of O'Connor as southerner, Catholic, friend, and artist."

781   Inge, Tonette Bond, ed. *Southern Women Writers: The New Generation.* Tuscaloosa: U of Alabama P, 1990.

Offers fifteen essays which assess post-World War II Southern women writers with references to O'Connor, including the editor's note regarding the critical attention given to O'Connor, Carson McCullers, and Eudora Welty; her assertion that O'Connor, like Welty and many of her colleagues, was a "daring" writer; and how O'Connor recognized change in the South through such incidents as the KKK illuminating their crosses with light bulbs. Other references include Elsa Nettels's note that when *The Stories of Elizabeth Spencer* was published, critics ranked Spencer as being in the company of Katherine Mansfield, O'Connor, and Welty; Linda Wagner-Martin's recognition that Shirley Ann Grau's work is included in the canon of Southern American fiction in spite of the "unexpected critical reaction" that her work, like O'Connor's, has received; Dorothy M. Scura's assertion that critics have ranked Doris Betts's short stories "in the exalted company" of O'Connor; Anne Cheney's observation that Gail Godwin has studied the fiction of, "among other Southern masters," Flannery O'Connor; Susan Gilbert's suggestion that Anne Tyler shares O'Connor's defensiveness on the topic of Southern eccentrics; Harriette Buchanan's comparison of Lee Smith's work with that by Faulkner, McCullers, O'Connor, and Welty; and Buchanan's contention that Smith's reading of these authors led to her realization that "the stuff of everyday life in the South could be the source of good fiction."

782   Ingram, Forrest L. "Theological Vision and Fictional Structure: Correspondence Between Pierre Teilhard de Chardin and Flannery

O'Connor." *Actes du VII Congrès de l'Association Internationale Literatures of America.* Ed. Milan Dimié and Juan Ferraté. Stuttgart (Germany): Bieber, 1979. 169-72.

[Cited in *Bibliography of Women and Literature, Vol. I: Articles and Books (1974-1978) By and About Women From 600 to 1975.* New York: Holmes & Meier, 1989. p. 333.]

783   Ireland, Patrick J. "The Place of Flannery O'Connor in Our Two Literatures: The Southern and National Literary Traditions." *Flannery O'Connor Bulletin* 7 (1978): 47-63.

Argues that O'Connor's remarks on the realism of the Southern Renaissance provided "substance to the powerful and sweeping thesis" of Renato Poggioli, who had asserted "that all avant-garde or post-Romantic art is inherently romantic, whether we call it Realism or even Naturalism." Outlines O'Connor's "notion that Southern fiction, indeed all modern fiction, proceeds from the romantic assumptions of the artist's relative or subjective point of view." Suggests that, because she believed that "realistic fiction must deal with the probable, not the possible," O'Connor's view meant that "such romantic relativism produces a kind of fiction in Southern literature which, though it mimics romance, makes for eminently successful novels of realism." Illustrates O'Connor's "comprehension of the relation between the Southern literary tradition and the traditional mainstream of American literature," through readings of "A Good Man Is Hard to Find," "Revelation," "The Displaced Person," "Parker's Back," and "Everything That Rises Must Converge."

784   Ireland, Patrick J. "The Sacred and the Profane: Redefining Flannery O'Connor's Vision." *Realist of Distances: Flannery O'Connor Revisited.* Ed. Karl-Heinz Westarp and Jan Nordby Gretlund. Aarhus (Denmark): Aarhus UP, 1987. 186-96.

Reminds readers of O'Connor's view of the "use of the term `grotesque' in mainstream American responses to Southern literature." Discusses how the use and view of the term have changed, including how Joyce Carol Oates, John Irving, Larry Woiwode, and Donald Barthelme view it. Suggests that the difference in use between writers of the Southern Renaissance and later mainstream writers is "a difference in culture rather than in sympathies." Identifies O'Connor's position as she, herself, explained it to John Hawkes and as interpreted by Jefferson Humphries and Robert Coles. Contends that, for O'Connor, "evil is at the root of all things grotesque," and "the grotesque is merely the conflict's phenomenological effect on reality."

785   Irving, Janet. "To the Strange Red Earth: Anagogy and Descent in Flannery O'Connor's South." *Proceedings of the First Conference of the Cape American Studies Association, 4 July 1996*. Ed. Lesley Marx, Loes Nas, and Lara Dunwell. Bellville, South Africa: U of the Western Cape, 1997. 146-56.

Explores "one dimension of Flannery O'Connor's `medieval vision': that of anagogy." Outlines how the term *anagogy* is derived "from the Greek word-stems *up* and *lead* (to elevate)" and ties this derivation to "hermeneutical theory of the middle ages." Refers to O'Connor's own comments on anagogy and how her beliefs are reflected in her own writings. Focuses upon evidence of her position through a careful explication of "The Enduring Chill," seen as one of her "more lighthearted" stories. Notes that the story opens with the main character's "movement across state boundaries," an action that has "destabilising implications" and foreshadows impending "conflict, change, and, significantly, spiritual confrontation" for Asbury. Follows with a discussion of how elements of the Prodigal Son narrative, allusions to James Joyce's *A Portrait of the Artist as a Young Man*, and the symbolic landscape and tree-line serve as foundations for the story. Contends that the American "South, like Sinai, signifies a region of potential encounter with creative impulses: [both] light and dark." Concludes that the "`fierce bird with spread wings'" seen on Asbury's bedroom ceiling symbolizes for reader's that he is "pinioned--not by familial stabs, social needling, or even his own self-incriminating shortcomings--but by the penetrating Truth from above."

785a   Jackson, O. Kay. "Flannery O'Connor's Childhood Residence Ready for Visitors." *Savannah Evening Press* 13 April 1990: 1.

Reports that Flannery O'Connor's childhood home in Savannah has been restored and is open to the public for weekend visits and readings of O'Connor's "most popular works." Notes that the four-story row house built in 1855 faces St. John the Baptist Cathedral, "where Miss O'Connor attended church" while living in the home from 1925 until her move to Atlanta, then Milledgeville, Georgia in 1938.

786   Jacobsen, Josephine. "The Mexican Peacock: (For Flannery O'Connor)." *New Yorker* 24 June 1972: 40.

A poem that examines O'Connor's intellect and emotions--love, shame--and her obsessions, especially with the peacock.

787   "James A. Grimshaw." *Flannery O'Connor Bulletin* 6 (1977): 16.

Reports that James A. Grimshaw, of the U.S. Air Force Academy, served
as the Flannery O'Connor Visiting Professor at Georgia College & State
University during the summer of 1977. Discusses his interest in Robert
Penn Warren and his encouragement of students to compare the works of
Warren to O'Connor. States that the students enjoyed the Flannery
O'Connor Collection, films, and a visit to Andalusia.

788   Janowski, Lawrence. "Flannery O'Connor: For the Deaf, For the Blind."
       The Critic: A Journal of American Catholic Culture 48.4 (1994): 2-14.

Discusses presentations on race in O'Connor's writings during "The Habit
of Art" celebration held at Georgia College & State University, April 13-
16, 1994. Contends that what emerged "was a sometimes disturbing, yet
more complete picture of the artist, her times, her work, and the
relationship that sustained and challenged her." Focuses on Ralph C.
Wood's paper on "The Artificial Nigger" and "Revelation," in relation to
remarks O'Connor made to her friend Maryat Lee in "previously
unreleased letters." Reports that Wood's paraphrasing revealed them to
include "tasteless jokes, racial slurs, the peppering of the letters with the
word 'nigger,' a suspicious, cynical view of Yankee liberalism, and an
acknowledgement that blacks made her uncomfortable." Discusses other
perspectives by scholars Henry Russell, Aleid Imthorn, Sharyn Dowd,
Willie James Jennings, Jane Rose, and her friends Sally Fitzgerald and
Cecil Dawkins. Illustrations: Close-up photograph of O'Connor's face;
O'Connor's home in Milledgeville, Georgia; and a cover photograph of a
portion of O'Connor's self-portrait.

789   Janssen, Marian. *The Kenyon Review 1939-1970: A Critical History.*
       Baton Rouge: Louisiana State UP, 1990. 173-74, 240-43, 294-95, 324.

Discusses the *Kenyon Review* fellowships, one of which O'Connor was
awarded in 1953 and again in 1954. Refers to her comment that the
financial support of these awards enabled her to focus on her writing.
Notes that O'Connor was recommended by Robert Fitzgerald, Allen Tate,
and Peter Taylor; that she was the only Fellow ever to receive a renewal;
and that the decision to award the renewal was based upon "the brilliance
of the stories she submitted to *The Kenyon Review*." Refers to John Crowe
Ransom's belief that O'Connor "was 'probably the best short story writer
in the country.'" Mentions Kenneth Burke's correspondence with Ransom
regarding the "sexually symbolic dimension" of "Greenleaf," and the fact
that O'Connor and Howard Nemerov "were among the few fiction writers
who [were] published for the first time in *The Kenyon Review*."

790   Jarman, Mark. "Unholy Sonnet." *Flannery O'Connor Bulletin* 24 (1995-
            96): 99.

            Sonnet which describes God's point of view of an incident between
            "victims" and a killer. Resolves that despite horror being "dreamed and
            brought into being," God "maintains His vigil and His power."

791   Jarrett, Beverly. "John Kennedy Toole (1937-1969)." *Contemporary
            Fiction Writers of the South: A Bio-Bibliographical Sourcebook*. Ed.
            Joseph Flora and Robert Bain. Westport, CT: Greenwood, 1993. 432-40.

            Includes two brief references to O'Connor: a quote from a letter in
            O'Connor's correspondence in *The Habit of Being*, along with Martha
            Stephens's observation that, unlike Toole, who was concerned over the
            "loss of faith," O'Connor "`was never in doubt as to what her purposes
            were'"; and how it was "perhaps doubly ironic" that Toole "had
            supposedly set out to visit the place where O'Connor lived and worked in
            January 1969" when he killed himself. Suggests that Toole "seems to have
            longed for but never found the faith that so empowered O'Connor."

792   Jarvis, Thea. "Flannery O'Connor--Georgia's Own." *Georgia Bulletin:
            Catholic Archdiocese of Atlanta* 8 May 1980: 2.

            Reports on a lecture at Emory University by Sally Fitzgerald that
            repudiated "the myth of the 'lonely artist' . . . [and] characterized her
            longtime friend [Flannery O'Connor] as totally integrated within the
            communities of her origin--the South, the Catholic Church, and the
            Cline/O'Connor clan--despite the fact that these communities didn't always
            understand the relationship." Discusses remarks by Bill Sessions, made
            during a follow-up panel discussion, that "Flannery was never bitter about
            her physical condition or the condition of the world at large. 'Amazement
            was more her attitude,' he remembers, 'not bitterness.'" Reminds readers
            that when O'Connor was twelve years old, "she created a mischievous
            study of her family entitled 'My Relatives,'" in which "no one was spared"
            and most refused to recognize themselves. Suggests that her later works
            were equally insightful, "peopled with real live members of the human
            race who invariably acted in ways that polite Southern Christian society
            did not care to acknowledge." Illustrations: Photograph of O'Connor on
            the steps at Andalusia looking at a peacock.

793   Jarvis, Thea. "Scholar Studies Racial Courtesies: Writings of Flannery
            O'Connor." *Georgia Bulletin: Catholic Archdiocese of Atlanta* 14
            November 1996: 11.

Reports on the "Midwest gathering of the Conference on Christianity and Literature" held in Dayton, Ohio in October, 1996. States that speakers focused on the "racial dimension in the work of O'Connor . . . and the anti-Semitism in the political and social writings of G.K. Chesterton." Discusses Ralph Wood's keynote speech, quoting him as saying that "far from being a racist writer, as `an increasing tribe' of critics would contend, O'Connor took her cues from racial courtesies she observed in her native Georgia." Notes his remarks regarding O'Connor's position on "the subtleties of mannerly behavior between the races," her views on "charity," and the role that the issue of race plays in "Judgement Day."

794   Jasnowski, Tony. "The Writer as Holy Fool: A Virtue of Stupidity." *Writing on the Edge* 4.2 (1993): 25-40.

Refers to O'Connor's remark that "there's a certain grain of stupidity that the writer of fiction can hardly do without,'" and ties her comment to Robert Kugelmann's assertion that "`If one can stay in the muck of appearances long enough . . . without abstracting, without categorizing,' then ultimately the true nature of any object under scrutiny `shows itself.'" Suggests that both O'Connor and Kugelmann are referring to the same aspect of "stupidity" that brings the writer to a state of deep contemplation and stillness that allows "the imagination the time and the opportunity to work." Finds O'Connor's suggestion "very imaginative, creative and sophisticated," but still lacking in explanation. Uses her comment to describe how a writer's journey into "the dangerous province of absurdity and stupidity" is really one of faith, and contends that "it is possible and appropriate to equate the stupidity demanded of the writer . . . with the stupidity characteristic of virgins, saints, and martyrs, the traditional fools found in almost all religions."

795   Jauss, David. "Flannery O'Connor's Inverted Saint's Legend." *Studies in Short Fiction* 25.1 (1988): 76-78.

Contends that the name "Julian" in "Everything That Rises Must Converge" is an "ironic allusion to St. Julian Hospitator." Argues that because of these "subtly ironic parallels" the story becomes charged with spiritual significance not only in Julian's relationship and love for his mother, but for his salvation. Concludes that O'Connor inverts this saint's legend to relate to Julian's "failure to achieve redemption."

796   Jeffrey, David K., and Donald R. Noble. "Harry Crews: An Interview." *Southern Quarterly* 19.2 (1981): 65-79.

Includes four references to Flannery O'Connor: O'Connor's remark that a writer cannot hope to fully understand the mystery of his subject, "only to deepen" it; Crews's admiration of her work; his reliance upon O'Connor's advice when reviewing students' work; and, his attempt to follow O'Connor's advice to be sure to "show the skull behind the smile" to his readers. [Rpt. in *A Grit's Triumph: Essays on the Works of Harry Crews*. Port Washington, NY: Associated Faculty Press, 1983. 140-51.]

797   Jensen, Gendron. "Flannery's Angel." (Sketch) *Flannery O'Connor Bulletin* 12 (1983): 4.

A reproduction of a sketch of Flannery O'Connor's desk, made by Jensen while on a visit to the Flannery O'Connor Collection in 1983. Reports in the "Notes on Contributors" that he is a "Minnesota artist noted for his meticulously detailed pencil drawings" which "have been exhibited throughout the country."

798   Jevens, Lisa. "Watchwords." *Chicago* 47.1 (1998): 19.

Reports that six new quotations will be added to the 26 already inscribed on the walls of the Chicago Tribune Tower, including one by O'Connor.

799   Jewell, Elizabeth. "Is Flannery O'Connor a Nonsense Writer?" *Soundings* 73.2-3 (1990): 273-302.

800   Johansen, Ruthann Knechel. "Flannery O'Connor: The Artist As Trickster." *Flannery O'Connor Bulletin* 21 (1992): 119-39.

Argues that the "capacity for negation" was important to O'Connor as it made it possible for her "to `see through,' [and] to move beyond the surfaces and closer to the essences of mystery." Describes "symbolic inversion," "ways of knowing" and the role of the "trickster," using definitions and observations from Barbara Babcock-Abrahams, William Doty, Henry Louis Gates, Jr., Mircea Eliade, Henri Bergson, Roger D. Abrahams, and Robert Pelton. Contends that the "cultural significance of the classical trickster . . . is important to understanding Flannery O'Connor's narrative secret." States that O'Connor's striving to embody-- through Southern fundamentalists--the mystery "she found in the midst of contradictions and violence led her to create variants of trickster figures." Offers The Misfit in "A Good Man Is Hard to Find" as a prime example, along with characters from "A Circle in the Fire" and "Greenleaf." Declares that O'Connor was a master of using "estranged and haunted characters," and metaphors ("like glasses and eyes, fish and seeds, blood and fire") to expose "the inner states of her characters." Indicates that her use of symbols and metaphors enabled her to turn her characters "toward Biblical antitypes and their conditions to historical-mythological ones." Discusses O'Connor's use of language to expose illusions, her shifting of the narrator's voice, the interplay of her narrative technique, her framing, and her reinforcement of the sense of movement and other "trickster-like manipulations." Concludes that through the use of the trickster, O'Connor "reveals to us that nobility and folly share the same space and that freedom lies in being bonded to our true image."

800a   Johnson, Greg. "Flannery at 75." *Atlanta Journal-Constitution* 19 March 2000: M1+.

Offers a profusely illustrated profile of Flannery O'Connor's life and work in celebration of her 75th birthday. Contends that while Margaret Mitchell has "sold more books," Carson McCullers "lived a more flamboyant life and garnered more publicity," and Alice Walker's *The Color Purple* has "won the Pulitzer prize and achieved spectacular commercial success," Flannery O'Connor remains "the greatest of Georgia writers." Includes a biographical sketch, an annotated list of her books, and discussions of the controversies surrounding her religious and racial themes and use of violence. Includes several of O'Connor's remarks regarding her views on writing, criticism, religion, and her personal life, as well as quotations from O'Connor scholars Robert Brinkmeyer, Jr., William Sessions, and Louise Abbot. Illustrations: Pastel portrait with a peacock-feather background by Elizabeth Landt; and photographs of the farmhouse at Andalusia, O'Connor sitting below her self-portrait, the covers of her books, and O'Connor sitting on the front porch reading a newspaper.

800b   Johnson, Gregory R. "Pagan Virtue and Christian Charity: Flannery O'Connor on the Moral Contradictions of Western Culture." *The Moral of the Story: Literature and Public Ethics*. Ed. Henry T. Edmondson, III. Lanham, MD: Lexington Press, 2000. 237-53.

Discusses how O'Connor's "Revelation" illustrates "the tension in Western political thought between the ideal of equality and the necessity of hierarchy or class structure and social distinction." Contrasts the idea "of the equal dignity of all men" as derived from the Christian belief "that God is infinitely distant from creation and . . . all created beings," with "the politically realistic acceptance of social hierarchy" derived from pagan Greek thought. Contends that although O'Connor "was deeply committed to the Christian vision" of charity, "she also recognized the genuine moral intelligence of the pagan viewpoint and was not, therefore, quick to dismiss it." Outlines the story's plot, discusses the "pagan virtues" of Ruby Turpin (most notably classic magnanimity), notes O'Connor's use of irony, and considers the "intelligence" of Mrs. Turpin's snobbery and Christian conscience. Closes with a careful discussion of Mrs. Turpin's moment of grace, seen as undermining her "smug conviction of her own salvation and her obsession with distinctions of class."

801   Johnson, Mark. "*Lancelot*: Percy's Romance." *Southern Literary Journal* 15.2 (1983): 19-30.

Prefaces a reading and analysis of Walker Percy's *Lancelot* with comments by O'Connor taken from her essay in *Mystery and Manners*, "Some Aspects of the Grotesque in Southern Fiction." Focuses on her views as to why Hawthorne wrote romances instead of novels, and the expectations of readers and critics who "`have set up for the novel a kind of orthodoxy." Suggests that they "demand a realism of fact which may, in the end, limit rather than broaden the novel's scope.'" Follows with O'Connor's comment that "the writer's `true country' is `what is eternal and absolute,' which `covers considerable territory.'" Concludes that while "*Lancelot* is not Percy's best book, only reading it properly--as a romance--grants us entry into its true country."

802   Johnson, Rob. "`The Topical Is Poison': Flannery O'Connor's Vision of Social Reality in `The Partridge Festival' and `Everything That Rises Must Converge.'" *Flannery O'Connor Bulletin* 21 (1992): 1-24.

Relates how Pete Dexter and Flannery O'Connor each handled facts from a murder case--which took place in Milledgeville, Georgia in 1953--in *Paris Trout* and in "The Partridge Festival." Refers to Isaac Rosenfeld's view that Southern writers have difficulty using local materials, and suggests that "what O'Connor leaves out of her story is as interesting as what Dexter puts in." Contends that O'Connor's "use of documentary material . . . raises the question" of her views on racial issues. Uses Toni Morrison's conceptual framework of "`the impact that race has on narrative,'" to examine drafts of O'Connor's story; indicates that she failed to effectively handle this material. Alleges that this failure challenged O'Connor "to rethink her use of the `topical' issue of desegregation in her next story, `Everything That Rises Must Converge,'" and that her "success at combining the topical and the timeless" signaled the beginning of another creative period" for her. Considers that "perhaps the most perplexing challenge for an artist such as O'Connor, whose theory of realism is predicated on distortion, omission, and the unseen, is the very strength of the material for fiction she has located in a social reality that needs little or no distorting." Concludes that these two stories by

O'Connor, and her use of the topical in them, appear "to mark the limit of her ability to incorporate the social reality of a desegregating South into a fictional vision meant to be true both to `time and eternity.'" Refers to comments by Brainard Cheney, Maryat Lee, John McCown, Roslyn Barnes, "A," Robert Coles, Irving Howe, and Toni Morrison.

803   Jones, Madison. "Cause for Wonder." *Flannery O'Connor Bulletin* 8 (1979): 18-19.

Recounts Madison Jones's friendship with O'Connor "over a period of nearly seven years," which was deepened by their correspondence and his visits to Andalusia. Reports that despite their friendship, he had failed to perceive what "an astonishing woman" O'Connor was until the publication of her letters in *The Habit of Being*. Discusses how surprised he was by "the uncommon force and clarity of the writing itself," and how this collection of letters serves as a "portrait of great integrity." Contends that those critics who held to "the notion that her work is lacking in real human compassion," misread her goodness and depth of love.

804   Jones, Madison. "A Good Man's Predicament." *Southern Review* 20.4 (1984): 836-41.

Explication of "A Good Man Is Hard to Find" that challenges the validity of a number of interpretations. Suggests that the story is straightforward and that all the characters are portrayed explicitly in terms of their vices; thus, the closest to a "good man" the story offers is The Misfit himself. Argues that The Misfit kills the grandmother because she tries to include him in her own decadent group of people, a group to which he is actually superior. Admits O'Connor's interpretation in *Mystery and Manners* is at odds with his own, but feels justified in taking this position because the author's interpretation is always only one of many to be considered.

804a   Jones, Philip. "'The Poor, Sick, Ugly, Raving Lunatic': Early Response to Flannery O'Connor's *Wise Blood*: An Animated Bibliography." *Southeastern Librarian* 48.2 (1998): 57-63.

Offers a "sampling of early reviews and criticism" of *Wise Blood*. Contends that although the novel "sparked reviews and critical attention in popular and scholarly publications," many readers and critics were baffled as they encountered O'Connor's "method of conveying Christian mystery through comedy and violence." Outlines the novel's route to publication, and discusses O'Connor's differences with her editor at Rinehart, John Selby. Describes the sample reviews and articles as "a glimpse of the errant, the insightful, but primarily the humorous: [as] reviewers and critics alike [were left] in a sometimes befuddled, sometimes successful search for meanings" of the novel. Concludes that while O'Connor may have "suffered under the pen" of reviewers who did not have a literary background or who "wrote in haste to meet deadlines," once her work began to receive "indepth consideration, often by scholars, informed and favorable opinions began to emerge."

805   Jones, Sonya. "Religious Studies." *Flannery O'Connor Bulletin* 24 (1995-96): 100-01.

A thirty-four line poem in seven stanzas prefaced by the statement, "In a 1953 letter to Sally and Robert Fitzgerald, O'Connor said that she thought poetry was a `filthy habit' for a fiction writer to acquire." Ties theme to Ruby Turpin of "Revelation" and Hazel Motes's "rat-colored car" from *Wise Blood*.

806   Jordan, Michael. "Flannery O'Connor's Hard Comedy." *University Bookman* 29.1 (1989): 9-12.

Offers a review of *The Correspondence of Flannery O'Connor and the Brainard Cheneys*. Cites from some of the more entertaining and informative of the letters, establishing the consistency with which the correspondence illustrates O'Connor's humor, "her Christian vision, and her inclinations as a writer and speaker."

807   Jorgenson, Eric. "A Note on the Jonah Motif in `Parker's Back.'" *Studies in Short Fiction* 21.4 (1984): 400-02.

Discusses similarities between Parker and the biblical Jonah, established from the scene in the story in which Parker is thrown from the pool hall by his cronies because his tattoo of the Byzantine Christ causes havoc there. Suggests that Parker cannot, just as Jonah could not, escape his calling as a prophet of God, though he is in flight from God.

808   Kadlecek, Jo. "`Revelation': A Short Story by Flannery O'Connor Adapted to Stage." Unpublished play script, n.d. *Flannery O'Connor Collection*. Georgia College & State University.

Script for a two-act stage production of "Revelation." Presents the following characters: Claud and Ruby Turpin, a six or seven year old boy, his mother and grandmother, an "old man," a "pleasant lady," a doctor, nurse, patient, and delivery boy, "Miss Finley," an "old black woman and a young black man," and "Mary Grace."

809   Kahane, Claire. "The Artificial Niggers." *Massachusetts Review* 19 (1978): 183-98.

Analyzes "The Artificial Nigger," "Everything That Rises Must Converge," "Judgement Day," and "The Displaced Person" (among others) for their theme--recurrent in O'Connor's work--that we are all impotent and dependent, and can be saved only through a submissive reconciliation with divine power. Recalls Leslie Fiedler's recognition in Southern literature of a "longing for a pre-lapsarian fraternity between blacks and whites," which ultimately produces racial stereotypes (for example, the passive, long-suffering negro). Contends that O'Connor's negroes are depicted more ambiguously, usually as "negative racial stereotypes," ignorant, lazy, conventional comic accessories. Uses O'Connor's critical comments concerning "the negro" to defend her portrayals as "masks" used by her blacks to insure protection and privacy. Says O'Connor's targets are not only the Southern racists but also the Northern self-serving pietists. Explores O'Connor's understanding of how psychologically devious the relationships between black and white are, and her gift for seeing the intricate patterns of rage, guilt, and dependency which keep blacks and whites chained to history.

810   Kahane, Claire. "Comic Vibrations and Self-Construction in Grotesque Literature." *Literature and Psychology* 29 (1979): 114-19.

Uses various sources to define the genre of the "grotesque." Concentrates on the use of Freudian terminology to describe what actually takes place during the reading of this literature. Argues that this experience results in an "oscillation between the comic and the fearful response." Suggests that the comic is usually overpowered by the fearful response, to "threaten the integrity of self." Discusses *Wise Blood* and Faulkner's *As I Lay Dying* in this context. Believes that while O'Connor's characters Hazel and Enoch begin at the same point, Enoch moves within a totally comic spectrum, while Hazel moves along the "uncanny pole of the grotesque."

811   Kahane, Claire. "Flannery O'Connor's Rage of Vision." *Critical Essays on Flannery O'Connor*. Ed. Melvin J. Friedman and Beverly Lyon Clark. Boston: G.K. Hall, 1985. 119-30.

Discusses O'Connor's use of violence, and argues that it is "so intense that her characters are rendered helpless, passive victims of a superior power."

Explores O'Connor's use of violence as inflicted by her narrator. Observes how it is the narrator who "plays the role of scourge" to penetrate to the very soul of O'Connor's characters. Focuses upon the "sadistic quality" of her narrator, seen as "a primitive internalized image of the parent forcing the characters through the triadic ritual of sin, humiliation, and redemption by wit as well as by plot structure," and concludes that, at the center of O'Connor's work "is a psychological demand which overshadows her religious intent, shaping plot, image, and character as well as her distinctive narrative voice."

812   Kahane, Claire. "The Gothic Mirror." *The (M)other Tongue: Essays in Feminist Psychoanalytic Interpretation.* Ithaca, New York: Cornell UP, 1985. 334-51.

Argues against the traditional psychoanalytic approach, which examines man's flight from the womb and his Oedipal tendencies, while ignoring the female child's ambivalence to and aggression toward mother. Discusses how the Gothic tradition embodies fear of separation and focuses on "dead or displaced mothers" to achieve "another angle of vision on the Gothic which has been virtually ignored." Sees as "repeatedly locked into the forbidden center of the Gothic . . . the spectral presence of a dead-undead mother, archaic and all-encompassing, a ghost signifying the problematics of femininity which the heroine must confront." Suggests that O'Connor is "perhaps the most exemplary writer of the Gothic-grotesque in recent times," and explores how her interest in "'staring at the Unnameable'" produced in her writings "a sideshow of freakish figures." Discusses O'Connor's ability in such works as *Wise Blood*, "A Stroke of Good Fortune," and "A Temple of the Holy Ghost" to use words to provide readers with a grotesque visual interpretation of the "truth 'at the dark secret center'" of the "Gothic paradigm."

813   Kahane, Claire. "Gothic Mirrors and Feminine Identity." *Centennial Review* 24 (1980): 43-64.

Uses feminist and Freudian theory to explore the nature of female identity in Gothic literature. Says that, unlike males who may reject the mother's authority on the basis of sexual difference, females suffer a complexity of confusions as a result of role establishment and projection. Suggests that Gothic literature addresses these confusions in particular. Explores the evidence of female Gothic and the grotesque in a variety of O'Connor's works, including *Wise Blood*, "A Stroke of Good Fortune," and "A Temple of the Holy Ghost."

814   Kahane, Claire. "The Maternal Legacy: The Grotesque Tradition in
       Flannery O'Connor's Female Gothic." *The Female Gothic*. Ed. Juliann E.
       Fleenor. Montreal: Eden, 1983. 242-56.

       Offers Freudian interpretations of O'Connor's fiction that reject standard
       Oedipal readings in favor of ones that explore mother-child relationships
       and imagery. Suggests that O'Connor's stories can be categorized as
       "Female Gothic" literature, which gains its tensions from the ambivalence
       between children and mothers. Uses examples from *Wise Blood*, "A
       Temple of the Holy Ghost," "A Stroke of Good Fortune," and "Good
       Country People" to illustrate patterns of the genre. Concentrates on acts
       of aggression and suppression by female characters.

815   Kane, Richard. "Positive Destruction in the Fiction of Flannery
       O'Connor." *Southern Literary Journal* 20.1 (1987): 45-60.

       Argues that O'Connor's work emanates from a shared awareness among
       Southerners of human limitation and a sense of mystery that would not
       have been possible without the figurative "fall" of the Civil War. Suggests
       that in O'Connor's stories, violence, destruction, and evil may be agents for
       good. Discusses how this theme is manifested in "A Good Man Is Hard to
       Find," "The Displaced Person," *The Violent Bear It Away*, "The Artificial
       Nigger," "A Circle of Fire," and *Wise Blood*.

816   Kaplan, Carola. "Graham Greene's Pinkie Brown and Flannery O'Connor's
       Misfit: The Psychopathic Killer and the Mystery of God's Grace."
       Renascence: Essays of Values in Literature 32.2 (1980): 116-28.

       Discusses the role of violence in literature and draws distinctions between
       various views, including the existentialist's view of violence in the world
       (Jean-Paul Sarte, Albert Camus); the alienated writer's view (Thomas
       Pynchon, Joseph Heller, Donald Barthelme, and Kurt Vonnegut, Jr.); and
       the spiritual writer's assessment (William Golding, Bernard Malamud,
       Flannery O'Connor, and Graham Greene). Says the true world of
       O'Connor's and Greene's characters is that which is "eternal and absolute."
       Discusses the two writers' psychopathic characters, Pinkie Brown and The
       Misfit, in terms of their redeemability and ability to redeem others. Shows
       how Greene and O'Connor each elicit sympathy for their killers. Contends
       that O'Connor's work is more successful than Greene's because her
       characters are more dramatically realized and, indeed, "changed."
       Concludes that O'Connor is more effective than Greene in focusing on
       human evil as pointing the way to eternal truth.

817   Kaplan, Fred, ed. *The Reader's Advisor: A Layman's Guide to Literature.*
        13th ed. Vol. 1. New York: R.R. Bowker, 1986. 556-57, 712.

        Offers a brief bibliographical essay. Mentions both *Wise Blood* and *The
        Violent Bear It Away* with a short summary of each. Comments on "A
        Good Man Is Hard to Find," "Good Country People," and "Everything
        That Rises Must Converge."

818   Karam, Sharon. "Flannery O'Connor: A Modern Apocalyptic." *Bible
        Today* 18 (1980): 182-86.

        Comments on, and offers three possible interpretations of, the meaning of
        Matthew 11:12, the verse from which O'Connor took her title *The Violent
        Bear It Away.* Argues that O'Connor firmly believed that humanity must
        choose between God's way or the Devil's, and that to make such a choice,
        "one must either be in touch with the violence of the love of God, or be
        swept into the violence of a vacuum created by evil." Contends that
        O'Connor "created a modern apocalyptic style which must be reckoned
        with in both literary and theological terms." Offers a summary of *The
        Violent Bear It Away*, and discusses O'Connor's purpose in creating the
        "stranger-friend." Finds Rayber's "struggle against his violent self" to be
        "an analog for the struggle going on in young Tarwater." States that only
        after the boy has been raped, and has "experienced the dark power of
        evil[,] can he be ready ground for the action of grace." Concludes that the
        power of O'Connor's stories lies in "her insistence that the struggle
        between a violent self and a rational self, between prophecy and demonic
        activity, between seeing the world as an unbalanced equation or as a
        symbol of the beyond," is a struggle reserved not only for her characters,
        but for all people, including her readers, here and now.

819   Karl, Frederick R. "The Faulknerian Presence in Contemporary American
        Fiction." *Conjunctions* 10 (1987): 287-302.

        Views William Faulkner as "the pre-eminent American novelist of our
        time," and comments on his presence and influence upon contemporary
        American writers. Suggests that Flannery O'Connor "first used him as an
        influence, and then passed through his presence to her own talent."
        Discusses how O'Connor's work may first appear saturated with Faulkner
        lore, verbiage, and fictional vision," but, upon closer examination, is
        actually very different. Outlines how Faulkner's presence and "influence,
        pressure, [and] force are all dissipated by O'Connor's special gift." Ties
        Robert Stone and James Purdy to Faulkner "by way of" O'Connor, and
        refers to "The Enduring Chill," "A Good Man Is Hard to Find," "The
        Lame Shall Enter First," and *The Violent Bear It Away.*

820   Karl, Frederick R. "Some Pictures From an Exhibition." *American Fictions 1940-1980: A Comprehensive and Critical Evaluation*. New York: Harper & Row, 1983. 229-53.

Declares that Flannery O'Connor had "perhaps the most singularly unique voice" of the fifties. Contends that "her mixture of wit, irony, paradox, and traditional belief in the devil and God gave her prose a maturity that belied the age at which much of her fiction was written." Cites Teilhard de Chardin's influence, then discusses her style of Gothic compared to that of William Faulkner. Concludes that the roots of her fiction lie in the works of Nathaniel Hawthorne and Herman Melville.

821   Kass, Jerome. "Flannery O'Connor's *Wise Blood*: A Screenplay." Hollywood: Script City, [1978], 1990.

A 133-page motion picture script based upon O'Connor's novel, *Wise Blood*. [From *U.S. Copyright File* database at U.S. Library of Congress.]

822   Kazin, Alfred. *A Writer's America: Landscape in Literature*. New York: Alfred A. Knopf, 1988.

Considers how a wide variety of authors created a place, through their use of imagination and recollection, where their fictional characters might live and be believed by readers. Includes a discussion of O'Connor's "A Good Man Is Hard to Find" and "Greenleaf." Suggests that she "wrote as if she had been locked up in Milledgeville with some extraordinarily painful people and had been forbidden to write about anything" but "people remarkably committed to pettiness of heart and the grotesque situations they fall into." Refers to original sin, the defeat of the South during the Civil War, the "burden of slavery," and O'Connor's illness to suggest that all of this and more was "enough to furnish her with story after story of misfits" who "seemed to have been born in a state of rage." Contends that O'Connor "wrote in little drops of acid" about people who "have a crazy disposition to error." Concludes that O'Connor was a talented, uncompromising writer whose "positively imprisoned sense of locale gave her a fixity on Southern landscape that no reader can forget."

823   Kazin, Alfred. *Writing Was Everything: The William E. Massey, Sr. Lectures in the History of American Civilization 1994*. Cambridge, MA: Harvard UP, 1995. 123, 135-36, 139-42.

Kazin offers stories of his own life, his perspective of social history and political events, and his perspective of the literary developments of his time. Recounts memories of a wide variety of contemporary writers, artists, poets, and others whom he met and befriended from his extensive literary circles. States, in a discussion of Robert Lowell, that Lowell expected adoration, and he found such emotion not only in "the many confessional women poets in the Boston area," but from Flannery O'Connor at Yaddo as well. Considers O'Connor further in his discussion of the deep-rooted religious convictions shown by her and Saul Bellow. Sees these two as the only American writers, whom he knew, who had "a sense of the radical evil that had burst upon the century." Refers to a visit he made to O'Connor in Milledgeville, remembering, "She was so inflexible in her standards that her own parish priest . . . remained in the car . . . saying that her disapproval of his usual light reading matter made him afraid to see her out of church." Considers O'Connor's faith, the importance of *The Complete Stories of Flannery O'Connor*, and the creative art of her work. Finds the work to be relentless in its dramatic reflection of O'Connor's absolute faith.

824   Kearns, Katherine. "The Nullification of Edna Pontellier." *American Literature* 63.1 (1991): 62-88.

Discusses Kate Chopin's *The Awakening*, focusing on how Edna's struggle throughout the novel illustrates the dilemma women face as they open their eyes "to the non-domestic world of masculinely defined values." Includes a comparison of Edna to O'Connor's "Ph.D. philosopher Hulga" of "Good Country People." Contends that, for Hulga, "the relative value of nothing is illustrated by the place where her leg once was," while for Edna "it is illustrated in the proliferation of her body parts into children."

825   Kehl, D.G. "Flannery O'Connor's Catholicon: The Source and Significance of the Name `Tarwater.'" *Notes on Contemporary Literature* 15.2 (1985): 2-3.

Explores the derivation of Tarwater's name. Believes it originated with an eighteenth-century remedy, one which--during that time--was said to have properties akin to divine healing. Says the term was a "ready-made metonym and metaphor for O'Connor's fictive purposes." Emphasizes her insistence on viewing Old Tarwater as hero of *The Violent Bear It Away*.

826   Kehl, D.G. "Flannery O'Connor's `Fourth Dimension': The Role of Sexuality in Her Fiction." *Mississippi Quarterly* 48.2 (1995): 255-76.

Contends that many critics have failed to appreciate the rich diversity of O'Connor's fiction, including the presence, extensiveness, and significance of sexuality in her work. Lists, describes, and discusses how sexuality "serves at least eight distinct functions" in O'Connor's fiction, including "sexual images, sexual tension, and a wide variety of sexual aberration." Works referred to include "The Crop," *The Violent Bear It Away*, "Why Do the Heathen Rage?" "A Circle in the Fire," "The Life You Save May Be Your Own," "Good Country People," "Parker's Back," "The Comforts of Home," *Wise Blood*, "A Stroke of Good Fortune," "Greenleaf," "The Lame Shall Enter First," and "A Late Encounter With the Enemy." Notes that "scattered references" appear in criticism "by a few critics," such as Richard Giannone, Marshall Bruce Gentry, Claire Kahane, and Louise Westling. Ties into the discussion Vladimir Nabokov's *Lolita*, J.D. Salinger's *The Catcher in the Rye*, Norman Mailer's *The Deer Park*, and T.S. Eliot's *The Waste Land*. Refers to comments by Eileen Hall, D.H. Lawrence, Katherine Anne Porter, Josephine Hendin, Sigmund Freud, William Faulkner, John R. May, Nathaniel Hawthorne, Jacques Lacan, Cleanth Brooks, Hans Küng, Frederick J. Hoffman, and Norma Rosen.

827   Keller, Karen. "Flecks of Fairy Tales in a Story by O'Conner [sic]." *CCTE: Conference of College Teachers of English Studies* 47 (September 1982): 40-44.

Acknowledges the Christian mythological elements in "A Good Man Is Hard to Find," but proposes that the story also includes fragments and hints of fairy tales. Focuses on the evidence of "Big Bad Wolf" characteristics and argues that the inversion (The Misfit, or Big Bad Wolf wins) adds an element of dark humor to the comic thrust of the story.

828   Kennedy, Arthur L. "A Hope Embodied in Story: Flannery O'Connor's Vision." *Lonergan Workshop*. Ed. Fred Lawrence. Vol. 4. Chico, CA: Scholar's Press, 1983. 69-85.

Raises issues about the process of transformation in O'Connor's work and discusses the "new reality" which results from that process. Contends that as story teller and interpreter of her own art, O'Connor encourages the reader to follow the same line of self-appropriation. Argues that O'Connor seeks to unveil the "hope of transformation" in her readers, specifically "a redemption of the act of reading" in "A Good Man Is Hard to Find."

829   Kennedy, J. Gerald. "Place, Self, and Writing." *Southern Review* 26.3 (1990): 496-516.

Explores "what it means to `dwell' in a place," and the question "of how place functions in the formation of identity." Applies these existential problems to writing and notes how "place often operates as a mirror, allowing the writer to represent identifying qualities through a putatively external scene." Offers a passing reference to O'Connor, noting that she and Ralph Ellison "may be seen as figures of domestic exile, projecting into their fiction a contradictory, often hostile relationship to place."

830   Kennelly, L[aura]. B. "Exhortation in *Wise Blood*: Rhetorical Theory as an Approach to Flannery O'Connor." *South Central Review* 4.1 (1987): 92-105.

Explains the term "exhortation" in accordance with Edwin Black's definition in *Rhetorical Criticism: A Study in Method,* (U of Wisconsin P, 1978). Asserts that the term defines the opposite of traditional neo-Aristotelian types or works that use emotion as an adjunct in appeals to reason. Contends that in this type of discourse, emotion does not bias the reader's judgment; instead, it precedes the writing because it precedes belief. Relates O'Connor's work in *Wise Blood* to the work of Jonathan Edwards and William Lloyd Garrison. States that evidence that the novel employs similar rhetoric comes from O'Connor's non-fiction (the idea of her estrangement from society, for example) and from the precise, realistic descriptions that O'Connor includes in her fiction. [Rpt. in *Flannery O'Connor: New Perspectives*. Ed. Sura P. Rath and Mary Neff Shaw. Athens: U of Georgia P, 1996. 152-68.]

831   Ketchin, Susan. "Narrative Hunger and Silent Witness: An Interview with Reynolds Price." *Georgia Review* 47.3 (1993): 522-42.

An abridged version of a 1992 interview with Reynolds Price that offers a brief biographical sketch and discussion of a variety of topics, including his views on Flannery O'Connor's writings. Notes Price's comment that O'Connor seemed to send her characters to hell by the end of each of her works (hell meaning that the character is "one of those people in Georgia who has to sit down and listen to your mother talk to you all day and night, and you're ugly and peglegged and must hear your mother go on about 'niggers' till doomsday"). Follows with his assertion that "the spectacle of belief in O'Connor is so radiant as to be potentially lethal. God in O'Connor seems almost like a nuclear plant out of control." Contrasts her work with that of Graham Greene and Walker Percy, and concludes "there's a mean streak in Flannery O'Connor which delights in the suffering of at least her characters, if not in that of other human beings."

832   Ketchin, Susan. "When I'm Fog on a Coffin Lid: An Interview with Allan Gurganus." *Southern Review* 29.4 (1993): 645-62.

Interview of Gurganus at his residence in Chapel Hill, North Carolina in September, 1991 which focuses on the impact of his religious background on his fiction. Includes two discussions of O'Connor in his responses to questions: the first related to how much O'Connor accomplished in her short lifetime, and the second related to her emphasis on the contrast between "godless modernity versus ancient mysteries." Gurganus remarks, "if martyrdom must come, I would like to be nailed to a cross near Miss O'Connor's." He comments further regarding the "absolute urgency" he sees in O'Connor's work and "her willingness to face up comically to the darkest questions about responsibility and salvation."

832a   Khawaja, Mabel. "Rhetoric of Irony and Prejudice in Flannery O'Connor's "A Good Man [Woman] Is Hard to Find." *Xavier Review* 15.2 (1995): 55-63.

States that "all forms of irony encompass the interplay between the expected outcome and the unexpected occurrence that culminates in a moment of ironic revelation." Uses this idea to examine "the rhetoric of irony" in "A Good Man Is Hard to Find." Sees O'Connor's use of irony in this story as serving to empower "the reader to bring together contrasting viewpoints into a meaningful whole." Suggests that D.C. Muecke's definition of irony may be used to provide "a clear framework for delineating the boundaries of prejudice in O'Connor's fiction." Further proposes that Mikhail Bakhtin's "dialogic interplay" also serves to illustrate how O'Connor's "isolated boundaries of cultural prejudices" may be contrasted "with the double consciousness of a perceptive reader." Focuses on how the contrasting viewpoints of The Misfit and the grandmother are "exposed in ironic layers." Concludes that whether the grandmother "dies as a crazy old woman or a child of grace, she seems liberated from the boundaries of her previous prejudices."

833   Kidd, Hariett. "About Flannery O'Connor." Interview by Kim Hollinshead. [Milledgeville, GA] *Union-Recorder* 19 Nov. 1988: A4.

Kidd recounts two stories about her friendship with Flannery O'Connor. In the first, she remembers borrowing O'Connor's donkey, Earnest, for a role in the Christmas pageant at the local Methodist Church. When told that Earnest had frozen still when he saw the crowd, Flannery joked that it was really because "'He found out he was in a Protestant church and he's Catholic!'" In the second story Kidd recalls an occasion when, as head of the local blood bank at the hospital, she obtained a pint of blood for O'Connor. She remembers telling O'Connor about the blood, only to be asked, "'Is it wise?'"

834   Kiell, Norman. *Psychoanalysis, Psychology, and Literature: A Bibliography*. 2nd ed. Metuchen, NJ: Scarecrow, 1982. 1026, 1084-85 (Indexes).

Offers a bibliographic index to psychoanalytical studies of O'Connor's work. Provides a detailed subject index.

835   Kiely, Robert J. "Reflections on the Novel: A Guide to Postwar Fiction." *Harvard Magazine* 79.3 (1976): 62-67.

Offers examples of important literature that has emerged since the Second World War. O'Connor's *The Violent Bear It Away* is on the suggested reading list. Includes a picture of O'Connor at Andalusia with one of her peacocks, and a reference to her and Walker Percy as being the "two most original Catholic writers in America."

836   Kiernan, Robert. "Flannery O'Connor." *Encyclopedia of World Literature in the Twentieth Century*. Ed. Leonard S. Klein. New York: Frederick Ungar, 1983. 415-16.

Provides a short bio-bibliographical article in which it is asserted that O'Connor's stories are more successful than her novels. Suggests that *The Habit of Being* indicates O'Connor's conscious craft and sophistication. Offers brief comments on the novels and a few of the stories.

837   Kikkawa, Junichi. "A Study on the Grotesque in Creative Activities Through the Works of Flannery O'Connor." *Sell* [Kyoto Gaikokugo University Bulletin] (Japan) 2 (Oct. 1985): 7-20.

Asserts that for O'Connor the word *grotesque* is not so much an abhorrent or detestable notion as a means of constructing deeper meaning to make people aware of the truth in this world. Contends that the grotesque is an adroit agent and an able emissary for a short story writer such as O'Connor, who does not have "such big weapons" as plots and actions to attract the reader's attention. (Abstracted by Kayoko Watanabe).

838   Kilcourse, George. "Flannery O'Connor: Evil and Hope in the Catholic Imagination." *Proceedings of the Annual Convention of the Catholic Theological Society of America, New York City, 1995: Theology and Modern Literature*. Ed. P. Crowley. New York: Catholic Theological Society of America, 1995. 225-28.

Outlines presentations by three scholars in a workshop held during the 1995 Annual Convention of the Catholic Theological Society that focused upon "Evil and Hope" in O'Connor's work. Moderated by Diana Culbertson, presenters summarized their research by highlighting their formal papers. Annette Moran's paper, "Meditation on Hope: Violence in Flannery O'Connor," focuses upon Rene Girard's theory of mimetic violence to examine O'Connor's use of violence and the role of the bull in "Greenleaf." Irwin Streight's paper, "Christ's Back: The Turn to Evil or Grace," examines "A Late Encounter With the Enemy," "A View of the Woods," and *The Violent Bear It Away* to consider John Hawkes's remark that O'Connor was "a writer `on the devil's side.'" George Kilcourse's paper, "Everything Off Balance: Flannery O'Connor's Christ," examines "The Lame Shall Enter First," "Good Country People," "Revelation," "The Displaced Person," and "Everything That Rises Must Converge" to consider O'Connor's use of "metaphoric revelatory moments of conversion and grace" that enable her characters to lose their "`balance'" and become "symbolically opened to a radical change of boundary or horizon in terms of their reorientation to the mystery of Christ."

839   Kilcourse, George. "O'Connor and Merton: Icons of the True Self in a `Christ-Haunted World.'" *Flannery O'Connor Bulletin* 23 (1994-95): 119-36.

Asserts that while Flannery O'Connor and Thomas Merton never met or corresponded, they appear to share a "deep spiritual and literary kinship." Compares the two and discusses how their "kindred spirituality" served as "the catalyst for their literary imaginations." Focuses on the "profoundly contemplative gifts" which enabled them to "dispel illusions and to summon the true self to replace spiritual impersonations"; how their Christ-focused imaginations "found expression in irony" so that their writing might yield "surprising insights into Christ's unique presence within our human experiences of vulnerability, poverty, and woundedness"; and how each used exaggeration "to precipitate the religious conversion of people loitering in a `post-Christian' world." Outlines how their "imaginations converge" and suggests that Merton's appreciation of O'Connor's fiction, especially of *Wise Blood*, "contributed to his own efforts to address the post-Christian world with a distinctly Christ-centered hope," most notably in his *Cables to the Ace*. Refers to remarks by Robert Giroux, Sally Fitzgerald, Ralph Wood, John Howard Griffin, and Robert Lax, and considers the influence of Jacques Maritain upon both writers. Concludes that the "imaginations of both O'Connor and Merton have given us ironic new icons of Christ, drawn in `large and startling figures' for the near-blindness of our post-Christian world."

840   Kilcourse, George. "`Parker's Back': `Not Totally Congenial' Icons of Christ." *Literature and Belief* 17.1-2 (1997): 34-46.

Examines O'Connor's "Parker's Back" in terms of her use of the grotesque and as an "ironic imagination's portrayal of Christ." Contends that O.E. Parker comes to see that he is in a state of original sin, "only through the grace of conversion. And that [this] grace becomes visible through the process of tattooing the icon of Christ" upon his back. Suggests that O'Connor's use of eye imagery "reaches a new level in `Parker's Back,'" and points out parallels between O.E. Parker and Hazel Motes of *Wise Blood*. Comments that the concluding scene may remind readers of Ralph C. Wood's view of "The Artificial Nigger"--that in O'Connor's fiction "showing becomes more effective than telling." Discusses the symbolic meaning of Parker's anchor and cross tattoos and O'Connor's use of naming to depict his "progress toward a true identity." Concludes that "Parker's Back" reflects O'Connor's "insistence upon the divinity of Christ, in the kenotic sense of the Catholic tradition," and shows how she confronts us "in the none-too-subtle icons of her grotesques."

841   Kilmer, Anne. "Flannery O'Connor." *Commonweal* 111.8 (1984): 239.

A poem which compares and contrasts O'Connor's battle with lupus with her efforts as a writer to create strange and clever characters who peopled the "dusty clay roads" and "backwoods" of her homeland.

842   Kim, Chrysostom. "A `Do-It-Yourself Religion' and the Grimly Comic in Flannery O'Connor." *American Benedictine Review* 31.3 (1980): 263-89.

Explores O'Connor's connection with Robert Lowell and Elizabeth Hardwick. Discusses Hardwick's critical statements on O'Connor and outlines aspects of her fiction, including her use of symbolism; a consideration of the emotional versus the intellectual in religion; the failure of organized religion; and the complexity of her grotesque humor. Considers the relationship between O'Connor's Catholicism and her being Southern. Refers to Walker Percy, Allen Tate, and William Faulkner.

843   Kimmey, John L. "Flannery O'Connor." *Experience and Expression: Reading and Responding to Short Fiction.* Glenview, IL: Scott, Foresman, 1976. 499.

Offers a brief biographical sketch of O'Connor, including highlights of her personal and professional life and a listing of her published writings. States that "few writers can portray grotesque characters and weird situations with such power and grim humor" as O'Connor, and suggests that her power and vision might "stem from the fact that she was a Catholic in a Protestant region." Sees her as a writer struggling with a crippling disease who wrote "a series of strange, disturbing tales about the South, most of them colored with religious significance and her own sense of distorted reality."

844   King, Chris Savage. "Wise Blood: *The Complete Stories, Flannery O'Connor.*" *New Statesman* 8 Feb. 1991: 37-38.

Uses a book review format to offer observations on O'Connor's writings. Sees her work as being "as bracing as a cold shower, at one with the spiritually cleansing function the work is supposed to perform." Contends that while she "ruthlessly cuts the crap and simply transcends her gender," her "underlying Catholicism is so gnarled and thunderous, it strips bare everything it lays its eyes on." Describes her characters, her "fine-tuned irony," her view of God, use of violence, and the presence of racism in her work. Discusses how she puts "all kinds of liberal certitudes through the threshing machine." Finds her work "always a quite sensational read" and an expression of "a heartfelt search for, and test of, spiritual values."

845   King, Josephine. Rev. of *Flannery O'Connor: Literary Prophet of the South*, by Susan Balée. *Flannery O'Connor Bulletin* 23 (1994-95): 192-94.

Expresses regret that this book is not "The Biography" of Flannery O'Connor, reminding readers that it was written as "a book directed to juvenile readers in a series entitled `Great Achievers: Lives of the Physically Challenged.'" Criticizes the cover art (painted from a photograph of O'Connor as a child) and Jerry Lewis's "pedestrian introduction." Points out "the graceless political correctness of the series title," the omission of "proper documentation of sources," and questions the amount of space given for coverage of Savannah's history, Catholicism in Georgia, the position of blacks in Southern history, and the political antics of the Talmadges. Finds Balée's introduction to Flannery O'Connor "serviceable," notes the presence of a reading list, chronology and index, and finds the choice of photographs included interesting. Concludes that Balée's work covers O'Connor's life story "sufficiently," in the way it "presents a prophet, not a saint," shows her "acerbic sense of humor," and "does not overlook attitudes that some might term racist."

846   King, Richard. "Eleanor Dickinson: Religion and the Southern Artist." *Woman's Art Journal* 3.1 (1982): 1-5.

Compares the work of Eleanor Creekmore Dickinson with that of O'Connor. States that O'Connor's perspective differs from the usual preoccupation of Southern writers, with the fear, guilt and hypocrisy of Southern religion. Distinguishes Dickinson's work from O'Connor's and asserts that Dickinson was influenced by O'Connor's letters and fiction.

847   King, Richard. "Politics and Literature: The Southern Case." *Virginia Quarterly Review* 64.2 (1988): 189-201.

Defines "politics" and "political fiction," and finds it "curious" that "political ideas and ideologies" are absent in Southern writing. Includes a page-long discussion of Anne Jones's contention that women writers, such as Eudora Welty, Katherine Anne Porter, and Flannery O'Connor, may be "read politically as `deconstructing gender.'" Contends that such a reading "works against the dominant intentions of these writers" and suggests that very little written by Welty, Porter, and O'Connor "calls for or rewards a political reading."

848   King, Robert W. and Daniel P. Sheridan. "An Interview with Barry Hannah." *North Dakota Quarterly* 56.2 (1988): 40-52.

An interview with Hannah conducted during his 1985 visit to the University of North Dakota's Sixteenth Annual Writer's Conference. Hannah expresses his views on regional writing, his practice as a writer, and his preferences in fiction. Includes two brief, passing references to O'Connor: his comment that critics "always go to Flannery O'Connor when they talk about grotesques," and "comparisons to O'Connor and Faulkner and `Gothic' and `grotesque' come up every time I get a review."

849   King, Thomas Mulvihill. "The Milieux Teilhard Left Behind." *America* 30 Mar. 1985: 249-53.

Discusses the influence of Pierre Teilhard de Chardin, the noted priest and paleontologist, upon a wide number of influential theologians, scientists, political figures, artists and writers--including Flannery O'Connor. Notes that O'Connor "often recommended Teilhard to her correspondents," took one of his statements as the title of one of her collections of her short stories (*Everything That Rises Must Converge*), and "used his passages on diminishment to understand her own approaching death."

850   Kinnebrew, Mary Jane. "Language From the Heart of Reality: A Study of Flannery O'Connor's Attitudes Toward Her Non-Standard Dialect and Her

Use of It in *Wise Blood, A Good Man Is Hard to Find,* and *The Violent Bear It Away.*" *Linguistics in Literature* 1.3 (1976): 39-53.

Concentrates on O'Connor's use of non-standard dialect to make characters "real" and "grotesque." Contends that it is important that readers realize that O'Connor regarded the whole world as non-standard because of its failure to live up to Christian ideals. Argues that, in this respect, her view of what grotesque was different than that of most people. Indeed, one of her greatest examples of perversion was the "Northern intellectual," self-confident and disdainful of "outmoded" beliefs in God. Points out that characters who use "faultless grammar" are as much freaks as any other in her fiction, because their language accentuates their superficial nature. Discusses in detail the language patterns of Rayber, the grandmother in "A Good Man Is Hard to Find," Hulga, Tarwater, Hazel Motes, and Enoch Emery to show how O'Connor exalts the non-standard speaker to emphasize the superficiality of "knowledgeable" America, seen as diseased with spiritual apathy.

851   Kinney, Arthur F. "Flannery O'Connor and the Art of the Holy." *Virginia Quarterly Review* 64.2 (1988): 215-30.

Asserts that O'Connor's drive and determination was based upon her "persistent need and concern" to write in such a manner that suggests "'both the world and eternity.'" Draws upon books found in her library, her letters, quotes written and/or attributed to her, and her fiction. Discusses how O'Connor developed "a conscious aesthetic for grotesquerie, creating an art of distortion, eccentric characters, even freaks, hoping to show how malformed the `normal' [sinner] must appear . . . from the perspective of Christ." Contends that she found that "the secular and sensual world contains--and also requires--perceptual transpositions. Objects and events [that] demand metamorphosis into higher apprehensions of Reality." Concludes that what moves the reader "so intensely in her work is not merely the fear and trembling which, sharing, she writes of so feelingly; it is the awesome uncertainty, the insecurity of human life that is the corollary." Refers to John Hawkes, Mircea Eliade's *The Sacred and the Profane,* Jacques Maritain, Maurice Coindreau, Father Leonard Mayhew, T.R. Spivey, St. Augustine, Pierre Teilhard de Chardin, Robert Drake, Cyril of Jerusalem, and Robert Coles.

852   Kinney, Arthur F. "Flannery O'Connor and the Fiction of Grace." *Massachusetts Review* 27.1 (1986): 71-96.

Questions whether O'Connor's depiction of grace is grotesque and whether or not she has "got the notion of grace all wrong." Contends that the function of O'Connor's fiction is to identify sin and to get the reader to recognize and condemn it. Argues that her subject is the action of grace and its manifestation in conversion. Identifies the chief problem in reading O'Connor's fiction as differing concepts of grace, especially between Protestant and Catholic believers. Seeks to interpret definitively the concept of grace expressed in many of O'Connor's works.

853   Kinney, Arthur F. "In Search of Flannery O'Connor." *Virginia Quarterly Review* 59.2 (1983): 271-88.

Describes his visit to Milledgeville, Georgia "to catalog the library [O'Connor] left behind, [and] to see what it was that may have informed and guided her vision and her writing." Mentions names of those he met, comments on their memories and assessments of O'Connor, and narrates his impressions and experiences during his two-week stay. Kinney's work resulted in the publication of *Flannery O'Connor's Library: Resources of Being*. Athens: U of Georgia P, 1985.

854   Kirk, Russell. "Memoir by Humpty Dumpty." *Flannery O'Connor Bulletin* 8 (1979): 14-17.

Describes meeting Flannery O'Connor in 1955, while visiting Brainard and Frances Cheney at their house, "Cold Chimneys," in Smyrna, Tennessee. States that although he had not read any of O'Connor's works, he views their meeting "as one of Eliot's Timeless moments," and remarks that spending "a day or two with Flannery O'Connor made such an enduring impression as might have required a decade of acquaintance with someone else." Concludes that she was so "far in advance" of him, that it wasn't until he was sixty that he began "to understand truths which Flannery discerned at the age of thirty." Refers to comments by Donald Davidson, T.S. Eliot, Nelson Algren, Paul Valéry, and George Scott Moncrieff.

855   Kirkland, William M. "Baron von Hügel and Flannery O'Connor." *Flannery O'Connor Bulletin* 18 (1989): 28-42.

Offers recollections of O'Connor, whom the author met while serving as rector of St. Stephen's Episcopal Church in Milledgeville, Georgia. Discusses at length the writings of Baron Freidrich von Hügel and their possible influence on O'Connor's work. Examines von Hügel's views and suggests that they "enlarged O'Connor's humanist perspective." Comments on O'Connor's reviews of von Hügel's work for the diocesan newspaper. Outlines von Hügel's position on scientific progress, his efforts to reconcile his humanist views with his "love for the Church," and his concern for others wrestling with many of the same issues. Suggests that von Hügel's legacy had an even more profound effect on O'Connor's personal than her artistic life, and asserts that his work supported O'Connor's religious faith as she battled lupus. Concludes that while the devout humanism of the two writers is different--"because of divergent understandings, hopes, and presuppositions about the modern world, about the nature of good and evil, and about the basis of hope itself"--O'Connor "continued to draw hopeful insights" from von Hügel and other humanists.

856   Kirkpatrick, D.L., ed. *Reference Guide to American Literature*. 2nd ed. Introduction by Lewis Leary and Warren French. Chicago: St. James, 1987. 417-18.

Provides a short bibliographical essay by C. Hugh Holman that lists primary sources and selected critical studies. Offers a thematic summary of the body of work which he considers to be "narrow in range and subject . . . [but] pursued with great distinction and force."

857   Kissel, Susan S. "Voices in the Wilderness: The Prophets of O'Connor, Percy, and Powers." *Southern Quarterly* 18.3 (1980): 91-98.

Examines the relationship among three Catholic writers: Flannery O'Connor, Walker Percy, and J.F. Powers. Suggests that Percy's similarities to the other two are evidenced in the publication of his fourth novel, *Lancelot*. Compares the "coldness" Lancelot confesses to the priest with the similar consciousness and cold-bloodedness of Hazel Motes and Tarwater, and Powers's Father Urban (*Morte D'Urban*). Contends that all the characters turn away from "the Sodom of Modern America" and continue a solitary existence. Notes that even Father Urban decries his original philosophy, "`that charity towards all . . . is always better than holier-than-thou singularity.'" The characters eventually reject the wickedness of the world as they had once renounced Christ and begin to deliberately spend the rest of their lives "in the struggle against human wickedness." Also included in *Walker Percy: Art and Ethics*. Ed. Jac Tharpe. Jackson: UP of Mississippi, 1980. 91-98.

858   Klein, Michael. "Visualization and Signification in John Huston's `Wise Blood': The Redemption of Reality." *Literature-Film Quarterly* 12.4 (1984): 230-36.

Uses selections from O'Connor's critical commentaries to establish the congruence between O'Connor's layering of reality in art and the world with that promoted by John Huston in his filming of *Wise Blood*. Contends that the background effects in the film (the groundwork for which O'Connor has already established in the novel), have as much signifying property as any other of its elements. Points to four images in the film that function as tropes: the C.T. Lord Highway--Milledgeville to Toombsboro; a sign for Harmony Baptist Church which contains an advertisement for Coca Cola; a faded mass-produced wall hanging of the Lord's Supper; and the Dairy Queen Brazier sign displaying "Repent and Be Baptized in Jesus Name." [See photograph in Barbara McKenzie's *Flannery O'Connor's Georgia*. Athens: U of Georgia P, 1980.]

858a   Kleppe, Sandra Lee. "Memory, Perception and Imagination in Flannery O'Connor's `Wildcat.'" *Flannery O'Connor Bulletin* 26-27 (1998-2000): 124-34.

Contends that in O'Connor's early story "Wildcat," sound imagery "pierces the consciousness of its protagonist--the blind, elderly, black Gabriel--in his most terrifying hour." Notes that "the title, the climax, and the concluding lines all foreground the animal cry that stalks and haunts" him. Suggests that "given the importance O'Connor placed on redemption in her life and art, it seems plausible that the image of the screaming wildcat may be an early expression of the religious concerns that would become the hallmark of her mature fiction." Reads the story in the context of Gaston Bachelard's theory of reality as perceived through daydreams.

859   Kleppe, Sandra Lee. "The Vertical Sense of Place in the Fiction of Barry Hannah and Flannery O'Connor." *Proceedings of the Writing and a Sense of Place Symposium, Tromsø, Norway:, 15-18 August 1996*. [Humanities Faculty, U of Tromsø, 1997]. *Nordlit* (Norway) 1 (1997): 185-200.

Applies Mikhail Bakhtin's "vertical chronotope, one of the many time-place schemes he outlines in . . . `Forms of Time and of the Chronotope in the Novel,'" to better understand the "kind of space" Barry Hannah and Flannery O'Connor construct in their fictions. Discusses how work by these authors exhibits a "literary use of space that spreads the world out along a vertical axis, blotting out linear time and twisting horizonal space into a right angle with the earth." Includes discussion of O'Connor's *The Violent Bear It Away*, "Revelation," "The Artifical Nigger," and "The Lame Shall Enter First." Briefly discusses the theme of gluttony in "The Lame Shall Enter First" in the concluding paragraph.

860   Klevar, Harvey. "Image and Imagination: Flannery O'Connor's Front Page Fiction." *Journal of Modern Literature* 4.1 (1974): 121-32.

Reminds readers that "whenever Flannery O'Connor spoke of the serious writer's art, she almost always emphasized the author's dependence upon the surrounding world for working materials." Suggests that O'Connor "practiced what she preached," since it is apparent that she "gained the inspiration for a chapter of *Wise Blood*," and her stories "A Late Encounter With the Enemy" and "The Displaced Person," from articles that appeared in her hometown newspaper, the Milledgeville, Georgia *Union-Recorder*. Provides reproductions of two of the articles and compares and contrasts the newspaper articles with the fictional works they inspired. Concludes that O'Connor used the "concrete reality" of the articles and transformed that reality "into metaphors for understanding" the "larger reality of the Sacred mystery."

861   Klinkowitz, Jerome. "Fiction -- The 1950s to the Present: Flannery O'Connor and Walker Percy." *American Literary Scholarship: An Annual/1979*. Ed. James Woodress. Durham, NC: Duke UP, 1981. 287-89.

States that while O'Connor scholarship was advanced by the publication of *The Habit of Being*, "even the best of this year's essays on Flannery O'Connor repeat familiar themes (very little given to technique) of the grotesque, the personal, and the visionary within the sphere of her Catholicism and Southern womanhood." Comments on articles by: Charles W. Mayer, Cheryl Z. Oreovicz, Suzanne Allen, Steven T. Ryan, and Barbara McKenzie.

862   Klinkowitz, Jerome. "Fiction: The 1950s to the Present." *American Literary Scholarship: An Annual/1980*. Ed. J. Albert Robbins. Durham, NC: Duke UP, 1982. 301-50.

Features a section on "Flannery O'Connor, Walker Percy, and the South." States that O'Connor and Percy criticism "may be having a Greshman's Law effect on literary scholarship of the American South: the most useful work on each of them having been done several years ago." Asserts that "mediocre and repetitious criticism is smothering their reputations in banality and allowing precious little room for either genuinely new interpretations or for much consideration at all of other Southern writers." Comments, in negative terms, about Robert Cole's *Flannery O'Connor's South*, and more positively about Carol Shloss's *Flannery O'Connor's Dark Comedies*. Follows with critical assessments of a number of articles.

863   Klug, M.A. "Flannery O'Connor and the Manichean Spirit of Modernism." *Southern Humanities Review* 17.4 (1983): 303-14.

Contends that O'Connor's contempt for the "modern age" and her antagonism toward it went beyond the artist's usual "scorn of science, technology, [and] middle-class values." Suggests that she saw "the modern consciousness . . . [as] corrupted by the Manichean predisposition `to separate spirit and matter,'" and believed that these led to the modern sense of alienation. Discusses Hazel Motes of *Wise Blood* and Young Tarwater of *The Violent Bear It Away*, and concludes that O'Connor uses her powers, the "power of her vision . . . to restore us to full sight," to "melt the modern glance, frozen in objectivity, detachment, [and] indifference."

864   Knapp, Bettina L. "Flannery O'Connor's `Everything That Rises Must Converge': Sacrifice, a Castration." *Women in Twentieth Century Literature: A Jungian View*. University Park: Pennsylvania State UP, 1987. 87-101.

Suggests that "Everything That Rises Must Converge" may be viewed as a story that presents "a religious ritual which discloses the dark side of the human experience." Contends that "Sacrifice" serves as the core of the story, and "the Parasitic/castrating relationship between a mother and son, its essence." Finds autobiographical elements in the locale, and in Julian's dependence upon his mother. Submits that while O'Connor's relationship with her mother "made terrible inroads" on her emotional life, rather than allow herself to be destroyed in spirit, she "transfigured what festered within her" into such artistic creations as this story. Offers a close reading, focusing on the sacrificial feelings that both Julian and his mother harbor for the other, and how they may correspond to "paradigms of the destructive and vengeful nature of the Great Mother's primitive side." Remarks that Julian's joy at seeing his mother embarrassed "indicates the degree of his involvement in her world," and his rage "projected outward onto her, is unconsciously focused on himself." Sees the black child as representing the white mother's infantile ways; and the black mother as "a paradigm" of Julian's "shadow, Mother Earth," signifyng "the unredeemed feminine principle existing within him." Concludes that the death of his mother--described as a `kratophany' which lends a sacred value to the event--does not free Julian from the patterns of behavior set by her. Informs rather, that Julian's feelings of guilt and sorrow "will provide him with the emotional sustenance needed to prolong the regressive pattern of behavior set forth by his sacrificing/castrating mother."

865   Knauer, David J. "Flannery O'Connor: `A Late Encounter' with Poststructuralism." *Mississippi Quarterly* 48.2 (1995): 277-89.

Challenges remarks by Frederick Crews in his essay "The Power of Flannery O'Connor" (in the *New York Review of Books*, April 26, 1990, p.

54). Suggests that Crews "disparages poststructural work on O'Connor as 'critical tampering' without defining tamper-proof criticism." Further contends that Crews "decries 'the recent revival of forthrightly ideological habits of reading' without defining ideology-free habits of reading, and implying that less forthright habits might be preferable." Counters Crews's position with views of O'Connor's "A Late Encounter With the Enemy," using "the post-structural modes of cultural materialism, Lacanian psychoanalysis, and deconstruction."

866   Knauer, David J. "The Incarnations of Flannery O'Connor." *Mississippi Quarterly* 49.1 (1995-96): 127-32.

Offers comparative reviews of three books to illustrate how "the confounding event of the Incarnation haunts Flannery O'Connor's fiction." Contends that for O'Connor, "the Incarnation brought with it an inescapable spiritual obligation," while "she also recognized the artistic obligation of a more prosaic incarnation." Finds that "both types of incarnation--divine revelation or creative process--are the subjects of the three books" under review: Karl-Heinz Westarp's *Flannery O'Connor: The Growing Craft* (Birmingham, AL: Summa, 1993); Ruthann Knechel Johansen's *The Narrative Secret of Flannery O'Connor: The Trickster As Interpreter* (Tuscaloosa: U of Alabama P, 1994); and Anthony Di Renzo's *American Gargoyles: Flannery O'Connor and the Medieval Grotesque* (Carbondale: Southern Illinois UP, 1993).

867   Knutson, Roslyn Lander. "A Faust in Eastrod Tennessee?" *Publications of the Arkansas Philological Association* 5.2-3 (1979): 16-22.

Argues that O'Connor's "literary kinsmen" are writers such as Marlowe and Goethe, who use Christian morality themes to express eternal truths. States that the stories of all three writers are not concerned with secular, sociological themes, but focus on characters who are battling for their mortal souls. Recognizes that there is no evidence that O'Connor had any direct influence from Marlowe or Goethe, but suggests that because *Wise Blood* represents a universal theme (choosing between salvation or damnation) and "works with the same literary conventions that the Faust myth uses, there is sufficient invitation to read the novel as a plausible variation." Reviews both the Marlowe and Goethe versions of the Faust legend, then offers parallels to *Wise Blood*, focusing on a view of both Hazel and Faustus as characters seeking "to prove that there's no such thing as sin by sinning as much as they can." Concludes that O'Connor's principal concern, like that of the Faust legend, is that "the choice between salvation and damnation matters, and the devil cannot be trusted to make the choice clear."

868   Koch, Claude. "Prophetic Vision and the Writer." *Four Quarters* 5.1
            Second Series (1991): 37-41.

            Addresses the question, "Should a journeyman writer and teacher have
            anything at all to say about prophecy . . . or vision?" Suggests that
            considering this question sends one back to a humbling examination of
            Flannery O'Connor's letters, stories, and occasional prose. Sees O'Connor
            as an exceptional writer who may be "an instrument through whose
            sensibility and embodied voice a vision, a revelation of what Christians
            have held to be true, may be majesterially unveiled." Asserts that
            O'Connor "spoke for, revealed, [and] bore witness to a truth beyond
            herself . . . as she dramatized distressing ambiguities *that* reality assured."
            Offers a discussion of how O'Connor, as "a poet," found her voice, and
            how "the realities of her faith infused her art." Refers to Robert Frost,
            Janus, Sir Philip Sidney, and the 15th-century artist Robert Champin.

869   Koelb, Clayton. "The Rhetoric of Ethical Engagement." *Inventions of
            Reading: Rhetoric and the Literary Imagination*. Ithaca, NY: Cornell UP,
            1988. 187-242.

            Discusses Flannery O'Connor's "The River," Hans Christian Andersen's
            "The Shadow," and Giovanni Boccaccio's *Decameron* to illustrate how
            "the ethical status of rhetoric [is] thematized to some extent." Sees each
            of these works as "particularly concerned with the effect of intention on the
            moral quality of an action." Focuses on how, in "The River," O'Connor
            uses "two conflicting alternative understandings of the same utterance" to
            open up "the space in which the story moves." Concludes that this story
            "is memorable because it questions the morality of acts whose moral
            character might not otherwise be open to question by forcing the reader to
            compare in each case the intention of an action with its effect."

870   Koenenn, Connie. "Shortcuts: In *The Dogs of Winter*, Kem Nunn Delves
            Deep Into the Primordial Pulls of Good and Evil." *Los Angeles Times* 18
            Apr. 1997: 3E.

            Essay review of Kem Nunn's *The Dogs of Winter*, with the comment that
            Nunn "is a third-generation Californian whose chronicles of the mania and
            delusions of the American West, underlined by a sense of pervasive evil,
            have been compared to the works of . . . Flannery O'Connor."

871   Kolar, Carol Koehmstedt, comp. *Plot Summary Index*. 2nd ed. Rev.
            Metuchen, NJ: Scarecrow, 1981. 86, 107, 189, 257, 296, 307.

An index of sources for plot summaries of *Everything That Rises Must Converge*, *A Good Man Is Hard to Find*, *Mystery and Manners*, *The Violent Bear It Away*, and *Wise Blood*.

872   Kolb, Harold H., Jr. *A Field Guide to the Study of American Literature*. Charlottesville, VA: UP of Virginia, 1976. 47.

Cites C. Hugh Holman's *The Roots of Southern Writing: Essays on the Literature of the American South*, which includes an essay on O'Connor.

873   Kolin, Phillip, ed. *American Playwrights Since 1945: A Guide to Scholarship, Criticism, and Performance*. New York: Greenwood, 1989. 175, 509, 567.

Sees O'Connor as an influence on Beth Henley and Tennessee Williams.

874   Koon, G.W. "O'Connor, Flannery." *Encyclopedia of Southern Culture*. Ed. Charles Reagan Wilson and William Ferris. Chapel Hill: U of North Carolina P, 1989. 890-91.

Offers a biographical sketch and assessment of Flannery O'Connor's life and work. States that while O'Connor worked with traditionally Southern themes and characters, "because of her specifically religious view, she seemed to find new meaning in them as she focused on postlapsarian existence." Refers to, or discusses her grotesques, her child characters, "the vanity of aristocratic backgrounds," the accumulation of land and other material possessions, the industrialization of the South, and the role of the automobile. Concludes that while religion has always been of concern to Southern writers, "no successful writer of the region has treated it as specifically and as thoroughly as O'Connor."

875   Koon, William. "'Hep Me Not To Be So Mean': Flannery O'Connor's Subjectivity." *Southern Review* 15.2 (1979): 322-32.

Argues that while O'Connor may have portrayed the "grimmest parts of the South," by transforming traditional Southern themes into Christian themes, her work stands as "a carefully orthodox, Christian statement." Discusses themes of land, automobiles, farms and fertility, with examples drawn from *Wise Blood* and a "A Temple of the Holy Ghost." Suggests that while O'Connor is "sternly Catholic," she is also "wildly comic, often at her own expense," as she turns her own "thinly veiled" experiences into fiction.

876   Koontz, Christian. "Flannery O'Connor." *Great Lives from History:*
          American Women Series. Ed. Frank N. Magill. Vol. 4. Pasadena, CA:
          Salem, 1985. 1369-73.

          States that O'Connor "created a small but significant body of fiction and
          nonfiction unique in American Literature, Southern literature, Catholic
          literature, and feminist literature." Offers a biographical sketch which lists
          O'Connor's influences, assesses her place in American literature, and
          provides an annotated list of eleven books of literary criticism related to
          her life and work. Concludes that "the future will surely recognize her
          significant contribution in at least three areas: the understanding of the
          human condition, the appreciation of the relationship between art and
          religion, and the valuing of women as writers."

877   Koster, Donald N., comp. *American Literature and Language: A Guide*
          to Information Sources. Detroit: Gale Research, 1982. 23, 28, 174, 200-
          03, 390.

          Selected bibliography of major critical studies of O'Connor. Includes a
          modest subject index.

878   Kowalewski, Michael. "Flannery O'Connor: Violence and the Demands of
          Art." *Deadly Musings: Violence and Verbal Form in American Fiction*.
          Princeton, NJ: Princeton UP, 1993. 194-221.

          Uses comments about Flannery O'Connor by Alice Walker to open a
          discussion of the "greatness" of her work, referring to an excerpt from
          "The Lame Shall Enter First" for emphasis. Finds that a charged
          "metaphoric atmosphere . . . permeates O'Connor's writing," resembling--
          in this context--the works of Nathanael West and Stephen Crane.
          Compares her work to Robert Frost's: "In the work of both . . . writers
          there is a complicated relationship between the desire to be understood by
          and humanely connected to others and the wish to prove worthy in the
          eyes of God or a literary tradition." Acknowledges the frequent use of
          violence in O'Connor's work, and discusses Rayber's attempt to drown
          Bishop in *The Violent Bear It Away* and O'Connor's plausible violence,
          which strives for effects beyond the scope of plausibility in "Greenleaf."
          Relates Joyce Carol Oates's opinion that O'Connor's work may be too
          blunt, impatient and fanatical to be psychologically realistic, and discusses
          the implications of reading the works as parables instead. Concludes with
          a careful explication of Hazel Motes's murder of Solace Layfield in *Wise*
          Blood, and suggests that O'Connor's use of similes displaces the authorial
          voice and provides "the violent undertow . . . that seems responsible for
          the violence done by and to various characters." Refers to criticism by a

wide variety of O'Connor scholars, including Louise Westling, Arthur Kinney, Steven Weisenburger, Frederick Crews, John Hawkes, Robert Coles, Joyce Carol Oates, Frederick Asals, Louise Gossett, Carol Shloss, Martha Stephens, Gilbert Muller, and André Bleikasten. [States in Acknowledgements that "much of the argument" of this essay appeared in his article published in *Raritan* titled "On Flannery O'Connor."]

879   Kowalewski, Michael. "On Flannery O'Connor." *Raritan* 10.3 (1991): 85-104.

Argues that the words of literary critics do not effectively convey the full power of O'Connor's fiction. Suggests that the evocative power of the "metaphoric atmosphere" she creates in her works helps readers to gain an understanding of spiritual grace, revelation, and damnation that cannot be conveyed effectively by other means. Declares that her greatness lies not in her choice of subject ("sin, damnation and prophecy") but in the *manner* in which she wrote. Contends that readers must "resist the temptation to tame or explain away . . . [her work's] tempestuous, eruptive power or to dull the sharpness" of her humor. Discusses *Wise Blood* extensively. Mentions a wide variety of writers: Alice Walker, Robert Frost, Joyce Carol Oates, Louise Westling, Robert Coles, Steven Weisenberger, Robert Fitzgerald, Claire Katz [Kahane], Arthur Kinney, and Gilbert Muller.

880   Kraft, Stephanie. "Flannery O'Connor: Redemption in Slash Pine Country." *No Castles on Main Street: American Authors and Their Homes*. Chicago: Rand-McNally, 1979. 171-76.

Provides a biographical sketch of O'Connor and describes the family's "white frame house on Green Street," and the family's farm in Milledgeville, Georgia--Andalusia. Briefly describes Flannery's daily life, themes of her work, and her battle with lupus. Illustrations: O'Connor's home on Green Street in Milledgeville; the farmhouse at Andalusia; and peacocks strolling at Andalusia.

881   Kreyling, Michael. "Fee, Fie, Faux Faulkner: Parody and Postmodernism in Southern Literature." *Southern Review* 29.1 (1993): 1-15.

Discusses how O'Connor's story, "A Late Encounter With the Enemy" serves as a parody of "public fondness for replicas or representations ('sheer images' and 'pseudo-events') of Southern history." Follows with a discussion of how the protagonist's killing of a peacock in Barry Hannah's *Geronimo Rex* and then covering the carcass with lime is "anything but gratuitous" violence, as the act symbolizes "the signature of

O'Connor" being killed and covered with "lime left over from Hazel Motes's self-blinding." Alludes to Welty's "The Burning" and Peter Taylor's "In the Miro District" to illustrate discussion, and includes remarks by Lewis Simpson, Linda Hutcheon, Julius Rowan Raper, Fred Hobson, Fredric Jameson, Reynolds Price, and Louis D. Rubin, Jr.

882   Kreyling, Michael. "Introduction." *New Essays on Wise Blood.* Ed. Michael Kreyling. New York: Cambridge UP, 1995. 1-24.

States that this collection of essays on *Wise Blood* "has been assembled not to reinforce the consensus on Flannery O'Connor's literary reputation, but to shake it a little out of complacent habits." Suggests that, just as O'Connor learned to write fiction in the New Critical tradition, readers and critics tend to read her in the same predictable context. Further, her fiction is "interpreted with such solid consensus" because many do not doubt "her own testimony as to its Christian meaning." Argues that because there has been such an enormous body of criticism of *Wise Blood*--produced in a relatively brief period of time--"the orthodox line is narrow, deep, and resistant to revision." Finds that "the historical context of O'Connor's work has been the least-explored critical territory." Relates that the essays in this volume attempt "to open new ways of seeing and understanding the novel, and the critical establishment that guards the meaning." Concludes with an extensive bibliographic essay that describes most of the book-length criticism related to O'Connor's life and work, including books by Robert Drake, Sister Kathleen Feeley, Caroline Gordon, John R. May, John F. Desmond, Marshall Bruce Gentry, Robert Brinkmeyer, Melvin J. Friedman, Josephine Hendin, Miles Orvell, Robert Coles, Frederick Asals, Dorothy Walters, Martha Stephens, Carol Schloss, Claire Kahane, James Mellard, and Louise Westling. Also refers to criticism by Robert Towers, John Hawkes, Isaac Rosenfeld, R.W.B. Lewis, Oliver LaFarge, Frederick Crews, Mikhail Bakhtin, John W. Aldridge, and Louis D. Rubin, Jr.

883   Kreyling, Michael. "A Southern Dissensus?" *Southern Literary Journal* 19.2 (Spring 1987): 102-07.

Offers a review essay of *A Modern Southern Reader*, edited by Ben Forkner and Patrick Samway; Richard Gray's *Writing the South: Ideas of an American Region*; and Ted R. Spivey's *Revival: Southern Writers in the Modern City.* Includes two brief references to O'Connor: the comment that, in *A Modern Southern Reader*, "she and her ally Walker Percy, are interpreted as the twin prophets of southernism in the modern age"; and the remark that Spivey has "nothing much" to say that truly associates O'Connor with Atlanta.

884   Kuehl, John. "The Grotesque and the Devil." *Alternate Worlds: A Study of Postmodern Antirealistic American Fiction.* Intro. James W. Tuttleton. New York: New York UP, 1989. 144-57.

Reviews examples of the grotesque tradition by practitioners in American literature from Colonial times to present. Focuses on Flannery O'Connor, John Hawkes, Nathanael West, Marguerite Young, Alexander Theroux, and William Gaddis. Compares O'Connor's *Wise Blood* (1952) with Hawkes's *The Cannibal* (1949), and argues that the two works bear crucial resemblances: both offer mutilated characters, animal imagery, grotesque situations, and "inanimate objects distorted through human or animal analogies." Discusses John Hawkes's essay, "Flannery O'Connor's Devil" (1962) which compares O'Connor's work with that of Nathanael West, and reviews the correspondence between the two writers regarding Hawkes's "conviction that Miss O'Connor used a diabolical voice." Offers a reading of "Good Country People" as an example of a brilliant display of "O'Connor's vision of evil, the devil, action, and grace." Concludes that O'Connor's "genial and glib" arch-deceiving devil changes identities to pierce the pretensions of readers.

885   Kugelmann, Robert. "Imagination and Stupidity." *Soundings* 70 (Spring-Summer 1987): 81-93.

Discusses the characteristics and nature of "stupidity." Describes how poetry, fairy tales, and literature are useful vehicles for illustrating the human fear of "being contaminated by it" while still longing for its comfort. Offers a selection of critical comments, including a quote from O'Connor (taken from *Mystery and Manners*), in which she describes how "the writer of fiction" must stare at something to transcend the obvious until "the thing shows itself."

886   Kumin, Maxine. "Visiting Flannery O'Connor's Grave: Milledgeville, Ga, 1988." *Georgia Review* 44.1-2 (1990): 30-31.

Offers a poem about the author's trip to Eatonton and Milledgeville, Georgia, to visit Andalusia, the O'Connor family farm. Describes driving past Georgia College & State University, the family home on Green Street, and on to Memory Hill Cemetery to pay respects to Flannery O'Connor at her grave site.

887   Kunkel, Francis L. "Wrestlers With Christ and Cupid." *Passion and the Passion: Sex and Religion in Modern Literature.* Philadelphia: Westminster, 1975. 129-56.

Contends that "the trademark of Nathanael West and Flannery O'Connor is religious fanaticism coupled with sex." Sees a connection "between getting high on Christ and sexual inhibition, sometimes perversion" in the work of both writers. Offers a reading of West's *Miss Lonelyhearts*, focusing on Miss Lonelyhearts' preoccupation with female suffering, subliminated homosexual desire, Freudian implications, and his "Christ dream: to heal the sick, to mend the wounded." Suggests that West was an "unbeliever obsessed with the search for belief, [who] wrote about sophisticated Jesus freaks and gang-bang nightmares." Comments that O'Connor was a believer "who mocked the notion that Christ `doesn't matter,'" and focused on "Bible Belt Jesus freaks and satanic sodomists." Describes O'Connor's religious beliefs and lack of enthusiasm for improving human society. Then, provides readings of *Wise Blood* and *The Violent Bear It Away* to illustrate how her fiction "is replete with heroes whose personalities are shaped by their attitudes toward the supernatural and sex." Sees Hazel Motes as "guilt-riven, not faith-driven . . . less a sanctified sinner whose anguish expresses a thirst for transcendental certainty than an irreligious self hater permanently in the grip of a paranoiac obsession with solitude and death." Sees similar motifs in "The Lame Shall Enter First," "Good Country People," and "A Temple of the Holy Ghost."

888   Kurmmel, Fusako. "The Comic-Violent Aspect: Flannery O'Connor's Rebels Against God in *Wise Blood* and Other Stories." *Keisen Jogakuen College Bulletin* (Japan) 20 (March 1987): 113-31.

Focuses on the comic-violent aspect of Flannery O'Connor's rebel characters in *Wise Blood* and selected short stories. Argues that Hazel is an "Everyman" who desperately tries to reject the notion of Jesus as redeemer so as to escape from the inner anxiety of confronting his own mortality. Like Hazel, The Misfit in "A Good Man Is Hard to Find" is fiercely serious. Consequently, they are both absurd, comic figures. (Abstracted by Kayoko Watanabe).

889   Kusaka, Yosuke. "Patterns of Symbolic Meaning in Flannery O'Connor's *The Violent Bear It Away*." *Bulletin of Gumma Prefectural Women's College* (Japan) 8 (March 1988): 55-63.

Locates and discusses patterns of imagery and symbolism in *The Violent Bear It Away*. Comments that Young Tarwater's clothes and his hat are symbols of his old, defiant self, while the corkscrew bottle-opener is an emblem of his new, Rayber-influenced self. Discusses imagery of sight, eyes, water, "the role of the earth," and fire. (Abstracted by Kayoko Watanabe).

890 Labrie, Ross. "Flannery O'Connor (1925-1964)." *The Catholic Imagination in American Literature*. Columbia: U of Missouri P, 1997. 211-32.

Focuses on O'Connor's writing in the context of her Catholic beliefs. Sees her as "identified with the Southern Fundamentalist's knowledge of, and deference to, Scripture, distrust of the abstract, and emphasis on the pervasive reality of evil." Draws upon her own words to illustrate how she "believed that the sting of defeat experienced by the South was its badge of spiritual awareness," which opened Southerners' eyes to their need for God. Discusses O'Connor's use of allegory, myth, realism, and irony, and compares her with Nathaniel Hawthorne, noting that both were adept at creating "bold allegorical scenes and memorable characters who are propelled by radical psychological and spiritual forces." Comments on the roles she "assigned to the devil" and the "paradoxical dependence of evil upon good" in her stories. Notes use of "the theme of God's rescue from damnation of the chosen soul" in *Wise Blood* while being somewhat indifferent to the fates of some of her lesser characters. Discusses the depiction of "the sterility of empirical rationalism" in her fiction and her concomitant interest in the effect of skepticism upon a person's faith. Offers explications and discussions of "A Good Man Is Hard to Find," "The Artificial Nigger," "A Circle in the Fire," "The Temple of the Holy Ghost," "The River," "Good Country People," "The Life You Save May Be Your Own," "The Enduring Chill," "The Lame Shall Enter First," "Parker's Back," *Wise Blood*, and *The Violent Bear It Away*. Concludes that "among Catholic American writers, O'Connor seems the most open to violence as a defense against evil," and that "apart from her consummate artistry, she is among the most universal in revealing the spiritual hunger of her characters and in her conviction . . . that the problem of evil will never be dealt with adequately by social scientists."

891 Landy, Robert. "The Image of the Mask: Implications for Theatre and Therapy." *Journal of Mental Imagery* 9.4 (1985): 43-56.

Includes a discussion of the photography of Ralph Eugene Meatyard, focusing on his "most ambitious work," *The Family Album of Lucybelle Crater*, inspired by Flannery O'Connor's character Lucynelle Crater in "The Life You Save May Be Your Own."

892 Lane, Belden C. "Grace and the Grotesque." *Christian Century* 14 Nov. 1990: 1067-69.

Applies O'Connor's statement, "'sickness before death is a very appropriate thing and I think those who don't have it miss one of God's mercies'" in a reflection on his mother who is dying of cancer. Describes the "peculiar, unanticipated comfort" that O'Connor's fiction brings, and suggests that O'Connor's characters are true-to-life in how they convey that "God's grace seldom comes in a form" one might welcome. Urges readers to consider that "the art of the grotesque--in literature and in life--can suggest to those who embrace it a healing spirituality of brokenness." Views the grotesque as "a daring exercise in summoning the absurd, making fun of what is feared." Mentions German critic Wolfgang Kayser, photographer Diane Arbus, the founder of l'Arche communities Jean Vanier, and author, Michael Downey.

893   Lang, John. "`Close Mystery': Wendell Berry's Poetry of Incarnation." *Renascence* 35.4 (1983): 258-68.

Compares the Christian views of Wendell Berry to those of Flannery O'Connor. Contends that while both writers are concerned with Christian aspects of mystery and "to disclose to the reader a world infused with grace," O'Connor focused "on what she calls `mystery as it is incarnated in human life,'" while Berry's poetry centers "upon the mystery incarnate in nonhuman life: the river and ocean, horse and hawk, [and] of God's questions to Job." Examines Berry's work and finds it to be "profoundly incarnational," stating that it "assumes the presence of spirit in matter and witnesses to this mysterious conjunction." Suggests that unlike O'Connor, "who aligned herself unequivocally with orthodox Christianity," Berry "often contrasts his own position with what he considers traditional Christian views." Argues that, "unlike O'Connor, Berry withholds final assent to Christianity."

894   Langland, Elizabeth. "Existence Beyond: Reality in Brontë and O'Connor." *Society in the Novel*. Chapel Hill: U of North Carolina P, 1984. 168-86.

Relates Emily Brontë's novel *Wuthering Heights* to O'Connor's *The Violent Bear It Away*. Argues that both share the reality of an "existence of yours beyond you"; in other words, the "preoccupation with the uselessness of our creation if we are `entirely contained here.'"

895   Langman, Larry. *Writers on the American Screen: A Guide to Film Adaptations of American and Foreign Literary Works*. New York: Garland, 1986. 161.

Includes citation to the film adaptation of *Wise Blood* by New Line.

896   Larsen, Val. "Manor House and Tenement: Failed Communities South and North in `The Geranium.'" *Flannery O'Connor Bulletin* 20 (1991): 88-103.

Outlines critical assessments of O'Connor's "The Geranium." Contends that some critics are guilty of a "rush to judgement," and tend to adopt "the role of a *reviewer* before completing the task of a *critic*." Asserts that the story is "both more integral than [Stuart L.] Burns and [Virginia] Wray have assumed and more pithy than dismissive reviewers" have assessed it. Suggests that O'Connor displays "ideological ambivalence, her unwillingness to embrace without reservation either liberalism . . . or racist conservatism" while clarifying her perspective. Finds artistry in how O'Connor "unifies the story by placing Dudley in the North" and "evoking the South through his memory of and longing for home." Maintains that the story is bound together with "interwoven themes, [and] images and forms, all of which pertain to the central focus: the inescapably social character of human beings." Implies that this focus "finds thematic expression in O'Connor's criticism of racism and ethical false consciousness, modes of social being that disconnect *I* and *thou*." Further, her position "finds formal expression in ubiquitous doublings . . . and in a correlated opening and closing." Follows assertions with a close reading of the story, including a Freudian interpretation of Dudley's role. Concludes that while Dudley finds the north offers nothing for him, "by negating New York and the Yankee black man, Dudley transforms himself into a New Yorker, the unfriendly, uncommunicative, isolated New Yorker he sees mirrored in the window as the story concludes."

897   Larsen, Val. "A Tale of Tongue and Pen: Orality and Literacy in `The Barber.'" *Flannery O'Connor Bulletin* 22 (1993-94): 25-44.

Reports that O'Connor's MFA Thesis story "The Barber" has received little attention. Finds it to be "O'Connor's first and fullest meditation on language and the linguistic coding of culture." Outlines the plot and asserts that the political disagreements of the story are "only the surface manifestation of a larger conflict between antagonistic social classes and their distinct language traditions." Contends that the deeper issue is that both principal characters (Rayber and Joe) seek to validate through their discussions "the patterns of perception, thought, and action that characterize them and their class." Compares and contrasts the nature of oral language versus that of the written word, and discusses implications such a comparison may have on the story. Explores the issue of community, and looks at O'Connor's use of irony to undercut both characters. Also discusses the role of racial conflict in the story, O'Connor's use of nursery rhymes--such as those from *Mother Hubbard* and *Boy Blue*--and Rayber's alienation and "disconnectedness." Refers to comments by Miles Orvell, Walter J. Ong, J. Goody, I. Watt, and Jesse Jackson. States that "Joe's restrained response" to Rayber's angry blow reflects that Joe "has the best claim to being a man who thinks." Concludes that because O'Connor embraced neither character's behavior, her skeptical view, which is not yet specifically Christian, "keeps her disconnected from both parties and open to some third mode of thought and action that transcends the dichotomy explored in this story."

898   Lasseter, Victor. "The Children's Names in Flannery O'Connor's `A Good Man Is Hard To Find.'" *NMAL: Notes on Modern American Literature* 6.1 (1982): Item 6.

Discusses allusions and parallels that suggest that O'Connor named John Wesley and June Starr after two of America's most notorious criminals, John Wesley Hardin (1853-93) and Belle Starr (1848-99). Observes that both were misfits: Hardin's racism was well known, and it was alleged that Starr had aristocratic ancestry--two themes that are evidenced in the story, particularly in the character and actions of the grandmother. Suggests that the children are used "to emphasize the idea of original sin" and reminds readers that O'Connor herself referred to her first collection of stories as "`nine stories about original sin.'"

899   Lasseter, Victor. "The Genesis of Flannery O'Connor's `A Good Man Is Hard To Find.'" *Studies in American Fiction* 10.2 (1982): 227-32.

Traces the possible influences of newspaper stories in the *Atlanta Constitution* on O'Connor's story "A Good Man Is Hard to Find." Supports the argument by referring to a local news item in the Milledgeville, Georgia, *Union Recorder* that informed "A Late Encounter with the Enemy," as confirmed by O'Connor's comments in *The Habit of Being*. Discusses in particular the news stories on the felon James Frances Hill, nicknamed "Maniac Hill," the probable prototype for The Misfit.

899a   Lasworth, Laura. "Reflections on the Pilgrimage." *Flannery O'Connor Bulletin* 26-27 (1998-2000): 105-12.

Artist Laura Lasworth describes the effect that reading O'Connor's works has had upon her development as an artist, her "understanding of theology and philosophy," and her pursuit of "a life of faith." Attesting to O'Connor's "mysterious involvement" in her life and work, she states that O'Connor has taught her "more about composition and the rules of art than any painting instructor." Sees in O'Connor's stories an indication of her "keen emotional awareness of--and capacity for--love, especially for children." Acknowledges being "struck by O'Connor's ability to render the emotional life of children." Illustrations: Photographs of four oil paintings by Lasworth: "O.E. Parker's Epiphany, 1997"; "The River, 1997"; "Bishop, 1997"; and "Tarwater's Seed-like Eyes, 1997."

900   Lawson, Lewis A. "Tom More: Cartesian Physician." *Delta* (France) 13 (Nov. 1981): 67-82.

Offers a reading of Walker Percy's *Love in the Ruins*, focusing on how the main character Tom More "is a thoroughgoing gnostic" who, by the end of the book, "is celebrating the Incarnation, even making confession." Discusses O'Connor's "Introduction" to *A Memoir of Mary Ann* and notes the similarities between O'Connor's frank appraisal of the grotesqueness of Mary Ann's cancer and Percy's depiction of Samantha's brain tumor.

901   Lawson, Lewis A. "*Wise Blood* and the Grotesque." *Another Generation: Southern Fiction Since World War II*. Jackson: UP of Mississippi, 1984. 22-37.

Discusses unconventional form in *Wise Blood*. Notes that O'Connor feels free to use absurdity, paradox, and illogicality to the extent that they effectively convey her vision of the "reality of Christianity." Sets the work within the school of the grotesque, and regards O'Connor's use of the religious hyperbole as her contribution to that genre.

902   Lawson, Lewis A. and John Auchard. *Articles on American Literature: 1968-1975*. Durham, NC: Duke UP, 1979. 391-95.

Extensive, though not comprehensive listing of critical periodical articles from the period 1968-1975.

903   Lawson, Lewis A. and Victor A. Kramer, ed. *Conversations with Walker Percy*. Jackson: UP of Mississippi, 1985. 11, 34, 41, 42, 47, 69, 88, 98, 99, 162-63, 165, 168, 192, 196, 214, 219, 231, 232-34, 240, 300, 309, 314-15.

Provides a compilation of interviews with Walker Percy, arranged in chronological order. Thirteen of the interviews offer brief, passing references to Flannery O'Connor; only one--previously published in the November, 1981 issue of *Delta* (Vol. 13, pp. 1-20), titled "An Interview with Walker Percy," conducted by Ben Forkner and J. Gerald Kennedy-- offers anything substantive on O'Connor.

904   Leary, Lewis, comp. *Articles on American Literature: 1968-1975.*
            Durham, NC: Duke UP, 1979. 391-96.

            Lists articles of criticism related to O'Connor.

905   Leckey, Dolores. "Spirit Moves Disabled Saints." *Florida Catholic* 17
            June 1983: 16.

            Describes the disabilities and difficulties that British scientist Stephen
            Hawking and Flannery O'Connor dealt with on a daily basis, while
            remaining creative and productive. Both are held up as "examples of how
            illness sometimes impels a person to concentrate on living in a more
            creative way." Concludes with discussion of the ideas of Swiss physician
            Paul Tournier on the relationship of illness and behavior.

906   LeClair, Thomas. "Flannery O'Connor's *Wise Blood*: The Oedipal Theme."
            Mississippi Quarterly 29.2 (1976): 197-205.

            Discusses the appropriateness of Hazel's self-blinding in *Wise Blood*.
            Argues that though the Oedipal solution is potentially hackneyed and
            feeble, the theme offers a consistent resolution to Hazel's struggle. Focuses
            on the stripper in the casket at the carnival, at which point Hazel's sexual
            guilt and eventual guilt over his mother's death become fused. Examines
            the Oedipal elements that continue to be the driving force in Hazel's life,
            a force which reaches its culmination in his own self-destruction.

907   Lee, Maryat. "Flannery, 1957." *Flannery O'Connor Bulletin* 5 (1976): 39-
            60.

            Lee describes meeting Flannery O'Connor in December, 1956, and
            recreates, through a review of her correspondence with O'Connor, an
            account of their friendship during 1957. States that before meeting
            O'Connor, she had no knowledge of her writings or reputation. Outlines,
            in detail, her thoughts and emotions from their initial meeting at
            Andalusia, and describes their friendship over the following seven years,
            punctuated with twice-monthly correspondence and visits once or twice
            each year. Appended to the article are the texts of nine letters from
            Flannery to Maryat--slightly edited--written during 1957.

908   Leitch, Addison H. "Reality in Modern Literature." *The Christian
            Imagination: Essays on Literature and the Arts.* Ed. Leland Ryken. Grand
            Rapids, MI: Baker Book House, 1981. 193-96.

Explores the difficulty and challenges that Christian artists face in portraying "reality." Discusses whether Christian artists should portray saints or sinners, or good pagans or bad Christians, and how these artists should approach the "ugliness, brutality, vice, and plain meanness" of the world. Refers to Flannery O'Connor to illustrate that "When [Christians in the arts] tell it like it is, they seem too plain (or maybe too anxious) in depicting sin and entirely too vague (or maybe too apologetic) in depicting redemption." Notes O'Connor's insistence that grace is at work in all her stories, but finds that "the grace is sometimes very hard to find." Offers brief comment on Hulga's seduction by the Bible salesman in "Good Country People," and concludes that "in order to make our total depravity plain, O'Connor makes too many of her characters bizarre."

909   Leitch, Thomas M. "The Debunking Rhythm of the American Short Story." *Short Story Theory at a Crossroads*. Ed. Susan Lohafer and Jo Ellyn Clarey. Baton Rouge: Louisiana State UP, 1989. 130-47.

Discusses how, especially in the American short story, "the reader's movement from bewilderment to authoritative revelation, from ignorance to knowledge, is complemented by what we might call the debunking rhythm of the short story, a rhythm that depends on a special use of antithesis." Suggests that O'Connor's work, like that of Edgar Allan Poe, "constitutes a thoroughgoing attack on the very notion of the self as stable, discrete, and knowable." Contends that most of O'Connor's principal characters encounter a pivotal moment of grace, a moment in which their certainties and self-concept are challenged, and they are offered the opportunity to accept or reject that grace. Notes that "in almost every case . . . acceptance is literally annihilating." Includes, as examples, passing references to Julian in "Everything That Rises Must Converge," the Grandmother in "A Good Man Is Hard to Find," Mrs. Cope in "A Circle in the Fire," Mrs. Shortley and Mrs. McIntyre in "The Displaced Person," Hulga in "Good Country People," Thomas in "The Comforts of Home," O.E. Parker in "Parker's Back," and Mr. Head and Nelson in "The Artificial Nigger."

910   Leithauser, Brad. "A Nasty Dose of Orthodoxy." *New Yorker* 7 Nov. 1988: 154-58.

Offers a biographical/analytical essay review of Library of America's *Flannery O'Connor: Collected Works*, edited by Sally Fitzgerald. Argues that O'Connor's psychology and spiritual vision stem not from her ongoing battle with disseminated lupus erythematosus, but more so from her lack of oneness with "the modern, sick, unbelieving world" to whom she felt compelled to give a "nasty dose of orthodoxy." Argues that the intertwining of her religious and aesthetic beliefs is convincing because of the fiction which she produced in accordance with it. Holds up "The Artificial Nigger" for particular scrutiny, and equates O'Connor with Evelyn Waugh and Elizabeth Bishop. Says "A Good Man Is Hard to Find" is O'Connor's masterpiece and reveres her as someone who, unlike other writers, deeply "satisfies" the reader.

911   Leon, Philip W. "Styron's Fiction: Narrative as Idea." *The Achievement of William Styron*. Ed. Robert K. Morris and Irving Malin. Athens: U of Georgia P, 1981. 124-46.

Remarks that William Styron's writings place him "in the ranks of such thinking writers" as Flannery O'Connor and Robert Penn Warren, "who are capable of telling us a good story about the complexities and difficulties inherent in the Age of Anxiety." Focuses on the "bond between all of Styron's novels as they consistently employ an artistically complex narrative method to reveal the author's central idea." Includes a brief reference to O'Connor's mastery of "the device of using secondary characters to counterbalance and reveal central figures" as with Enoch Emery and Hazel Motes in *Wise Blood*.

912   Leonard, Douglas Novich. "Experiencing Flannery O'Connor's `A Good Man Is Hard to Find.'" *Interpretations* 14 (Spring 1983): 48-54.

Offers a detailed explication of "A Good Man Is Hard to Find." States that O'Connor "employed grotesqueness and violence in her stories to illustrate the workings of grace on her characters, but more profoundly she was attempting to simulate the workings of grace in the sensibility of the reader, that rare reader who would go deeper." Argues that the story serves as an excellent example of "the dynamics between O'Connor's art and the reader," and suggests that O'Connor thought so as well, "since she spent more time explaining this story than any other . . . as if she were indulging herself in elucidating a single story as a model for the interpretation of others." Examines the passage which deals with the grandmother's "moment of grace" for meaning and interpretation, and explores the role of The Misfit and the meaning behind his name. Assesses critical interpretation of the story by Clara Claiborne Park and W.S. Marks III. Comments on the perspective that a Protestant view of the story's action of grace might offer. Refers to O'Connor's statement that "the meaning of her story should `go on expanding' in the mind of the reader," and asserts that "A Good Man Is Hard to Find" offers the reader "a simulation of the experience of grace."

913   Leonard, Joan. "Flannery Revisited." *Georgia Bulletin: Catholic Archdiocese of Atlanta* 24 April 1980: 2.

Reports that the Graduate Institute of Liberal Arts of Emory University will sponsor a program April 30, 1980, titled "The Communities of Flannery O'Connor: The Enigma of a Georgia Writer." States that the program will have two parts: for the first, the principal speaker Sally Fitzgerald will speak on the topic, "Georgia's Flannery O'Connor--Stranger in Her Homeland"; and for the second part, Elisabeth Lunz of the Emory English department will moderate a follow-up panel discussion. Scheduled to participate on the panel are William Sessions, Professor of English at Georgia State, to present "Flannery O'Connor: A Displaced Person?"; William Mallard, Professor of Theology at Candler School of Theology, presenting "Flannery O'Connor: A View From the Woods"; and Elisabeth Stevenson, on the faculty of Emory's Graduate Institute, who will address "The Artist's Vocation." Illustration: Photograph of Sally Fitzgerald.

914   "Letters Added to O'Connor Collection." (Georgia College & State University) *Alumni News Quarterly* (Fall 1990): 3.

Announces the gift to the Alumni Association of 164 letters from the correspondence of Flannery O'Connor to Maryat Lee. States that the gift is comprised of 88 handwritten and signed letters, 73 typewritten and signed letters and 3 handwritten and signed cards. Notes that many of the letters include drawings by O'Connor and that the last letter written by her was to Maryat Lee.

915   Levy, Andrew. *The Culture and Commerce of the American Short Story.* Cambridge: Cambridge UP, 1993. 5-6, 126, 133-34.

Contains a "probably fictitious anecdote" about Flannery O'Connor's attitude toward her classmate's criticism of her own work while she attended the University of Iowa's Writer's Workshop. Purportedly, O'Connor would sit politely while her stories were "ravaged by her fellow students" in Workshop sessions. However, when these same stories were submitted as her M.F.A. Thesis, her advisor was surprised to see that "she had not changed a word." The advisor returned the thesis to O'Connor "on the condition that she carefully consider the suggestions offered by her peers, and revise her stories accordingly." Supposedly, O'Connor did so, and then "resubmitted her stories a short time later, without altering a word." Notes that it was "these same stories [which] eventually earned O'Connor her fame." Refers, in the "Notes," to other discussions of O'Connor's stay at the Writer's Workshop, by Ed Dinger, Maureen Howard, and Jean Wylder.

916   Lhamon, W.T., Jr. "Chuck Berry and the Sambo Strategy in the 1950s."
           Studies in Popular Culture 12.2 (1988): 20-29.

           Argues that Sambo figures from minstrel shows "employed powerlessness
           in order to achieve an ultimate compromised victory." Discusses the
           explicit use of the Sambo doll in Ralph Ellison's *Invisible Man,* and
           O'Connor's use of a Sambo icon "to alter the perceptions of ridiculously
           racist white characters" in "The Artificial Nigger." Contends that both
           Ellison and O'Connor "could stick their Sambo figures into situations that
           peeled away their minstrel masks, baring the strings behind the smiles."

917   Lhamon, W.T., Jr. *Deliberate Speed: The Origins of a Cultural Style in
           the American 1950s.* Washington, DC: Smithsonian Institution, 1990. 6,
           17, 72, 90-91, 149, 248.

           Offers, an explication of O'Connor's "The Artificial Nigger" in the context
           of a discussion of the "Sambo" personality. Includes several other brief
           references to O'Connor's work as the author explores the "art, ideas,
           movements, and technological innovations, and distinctive lore of the
           fifties" in America.

918   Lindroth, James R. "A Consistency of Voice and Vision: O'Connor as
           Self-Critic." *Religion & Literature* 16.2 (1984): 43-59.

           Discusses the criticism of O'Connor's narrative voice and denies the
           accusation that her own voice cannot be distinguished from the narrator's.
           Labels her works as Christian Realism, and analyzes four stories and *The
           Violent Bear It Away* for their pitting of the "rhetorics of faith and
           despair." Refers to the correspondence to John Hawkes (from *The Habit
           of Being*) to establish O'Connor's theory of types of devils, in particular the
           type which goes about "piercing pretensions." Says Hawkes incorrectly
           labels the narrative voice in certain works as the light, comic type (which
           he aligns with O'Connor's) when the devil she is portraying is the powerful
           "Lucifer," who seeks to destroy God's divine plan.

919   Lindsey, William D. "Order as Disorder: *Absalom, Absalom!*'s Inversion
           of the Judaeo-Christian Creation Myth." *Faulkner and Religion: Faulkner
           and Yoknapatawpha, 1989.* Jackson: UP of Mississippi, 1991. 85-102.

           Explores the link between colonial New England and post- Reconstruction
           Mississippi seen in William Faulkner's fiction. Focuses on Faulkner's use
           of imagery and rhetoric to depict the Judaeo-Christian creation myth in
           Absalom, Absalom! Includes a brief discussion of O'Connor's view of the

"Southern experience of evil and guilt" in a section which deals with how the "Southern intellectual tradition's rejection of the philosophy of atomistic individualism" serves "simultaneously [as] a rejection of the myth of innocence."

920   Lindsey, William D. "Parable and Apologia: Flannery O'Connor's Literary-Apologetic Strategy." *CCICA Annual 1990: Catholic Writers.* Ed. Konrad Schaum. Notre Dame, IN: Catholic Commission on Intellectual and Cultural Affairs, 1990. 85-105.

Refers to works by a wide variety of O'Connor scholars in this extensively documented study of how "a *parabolic* reading of O'Connor's fiction allows one to take seriously her apologetic design and to understand her fictional technique in light of that design." Contends that O'Connor's "penchant for parable arises out of the fusion of two perspectives in her intellectual background--her Southern and Catholic perspectives." Outlines how her short fiction exhibits "a number of significant affinities with the parables of the Christian gospels." Concludes that while O'Connor's intentions are to involve readers "in a story that appears innocuous . . . by a sudden twist [they] become confrontive [sic]."

921   Linehan, Thomas M. "Anagogical Realism in Flannery O'Connor." *Renascence* 37.2 (1985): 80-95.

Argues that O'Connor's fiction is often misread because--according to O'Connor herself--it is read as realism or naturalism, whereas its true concern is with mystery. The methods for interpreting her fiction can be found in Christian scriptural hermeneutics, according to Linehan. Such an approach concentrates on the anagogical (rather than the allegorical or tropological) for the meaning of the literal level of the sacred text. Argues that this anagogical dimension is evidenced in O'Connor's depiction of the sun, moon, and woods as "skyscape,"where heaven and earth meet.

922   Liu, Dilin. "*A Good Man Is Hard to Find*: The Difference Between the Word and the World." *Short Story* 2.2 (1992): 63-75.

Contends that O'Connor "touches repeatedly on the issue of `words,' or more accurately, `the war of words,'" in stories in *A Good Man Is Hard to Find*, and confronts "the problem of signification . . . the insurmountable gap between the word and the world, or, in a broader sense, between the signifier and the signified." Outlines Terence Hawkes's contention that "language functions merely to help us constitute our own sense of reality," and because it is only "a system `which a society constructs in order to sustain and authenticate its sense of its own well being,'" there will never be a "truly objective or one-to-one relationship between the word and the world." Offers, in this context, explications of "A Good Man Is Hard to Find," "The River," "The Temple of the Holy Ghost," "A Late Encounter With the Enemy," "Good Country People," and "The Artificial Nigger." Concludes that O'Connor was acutely aware of humankind's inability to overcome "the gap between language and reality" which may be seen as "a gap which we create, consciously or unconsciously," and one "in which we human beings are forever trapped."

923   Logan, Jan H. "Flannery O'Connor and Flaubert: A French Connection." *Notes on Contemporary Literature* 13.5 (1983): 2-5.

Traces and provides examples of the influences of Flaubert's work, especially *Trois Contes*, on three stories by O'Connor: "Revelation," "Everything That Rises Must Converge," and "The Enduring Chill." Concludes that underlying O'Connor's good-humored appreciation of Flaubert's work is the more serious matter of her literary debt, which she uses to deepen the texture of her stories.

924   Long, J.V. "Clerical Character(s)." *Commonweal* 125.9 (1998): 11.

Discusses the short stories and novels of J.F. Powers, focusing on how his characters balanced their roles in the clergy with the challenges they faced during times of social and cultural change. Includes O'Connor's assessment of his work: "Powers's stories can be divided into two kinds--those that deal with the Catholic clergy and those that don't. Those that deal with the clergy are as good as any stories being written by anybody; those that don't are not so good."

925   Lonnquist, Barbara C. "Narrative Displacement and Literary Faith: Raymond Carver's Inheritance From Flannery O'Connor." *Since Flannery O'Connor: Essays on the Contemporary American Short Story*. Ed. Loren Logsdon and Charles W. Mayer. Macomb: Western Illinois UP, 1987. 142-50.

Explores ties and parallels between the art and work of Raymond Carver and Flannery O'Connor, focusing on his collection of short fiction, *Cathedral*. Discusses Carver's "respect for the intensity of O'Connor's vision," and points out how he "invokes patterns and images" from her work, and how the narrative strategy in *Cathedral* appears to be "laced with signs" of O'Connor's spirit. Refers to O'Connor's "Good Country People," "The Artificial Nigger," and "The Displaced Person" in *A Good*

Man Is Hard to Find. Recognizes both authors' use of the peacock as a key image, and agrees with Mark Facknitz's observation that both authors have their protagonists "'taken from behind by understanding.'" Offers readings of Carver's "A Small, Good Thing" and "Cathedral," paying careful attention to how he displaces and refocuses the narrative and uses the title of the latter story to provide "a summarizing metaphor for the narrative mode employed throughout." Concludes that Carver's collection illustrates how his inheritance of O'Connor's "invincible faith" helps him to celebrate "the power of short stories to locate . . . the lyricism of ordinary life."

926   Loomis, Jeffrey B. "Miltonic Patterns in Flannery O'Connor's *A Good Man Is Hard To Find.*" *Cithara: Essays in the Judaeo-Christian Tradition* 24.1 (1984): 41-58.

Notes affinities between Flannery O'Connor and John Milton. Asserts that her collection of stories in *A Good Man Is Hard to Find* "imitates the chronological order of events in *Paradise Lost* [and] shares . . . many of the Biblical allusions which Milton employs; and . . . emphasizes Milton's ultimate theme: the importance to human relations of Christlike charity." Suggests that while Milton's Calvinist theology stands in contrast to O'Connor's Catholicism, O'Connor, like Milton, uses her writing as a "tool for awakening readers to their need of the `paradise within.'"

927   Lopez, Enrique Hank. *Conversations with Katherine Anne Porter: Refugee from Indian Creek*. Boston: Little, Brown, 1981. 23-24, 131, 134, 139-40, 268, 302-03.

A biographical study which relies heavily upon Lopez's tape-recorded interviews with Porter. Offers passing references to O'Connor, including how Porter was often reminded of O'Connor's Hazel Motes of *Wise Blood* when her friends discussed such matters as the afterlife and religion; her offhand remark that O'Connor probably would not have cared for a meal of snails and champagne; her interest in the astrological sign of her literary friends, noting that O'Connor was an Aries; Porter's inclusion of O'Connor on her list of "brilliant women writers who were gifted with a `just cruelty'"; discussion of the Pulitzer Prize and the National Book Award to Porter for *Ship of Fools* instead of posthumously to O'Connor for *Everything That Rises Must Converge*; and a description of a "friendly visitation" by O'Connor's spirit, two or three years after O'Connor's death.

928   Lopez, Hank. "A Country and Some People I Love." *Katherine Anne Porter: Conversations*. Ed. Joan Givner. Jackson: UP of Mississippi, 1987. 120-34.

Includes two passing references to O'Connor: Porter's comment that O'Connor was "greatly gifted" and that her death was "a dreadful loss to us all" and a brief discussion as to whether O'Connor may have been influenced by Porter's work, possibly "Noon Wine." [Rpt. from *Harper's Magazine* (Sept. 1965): 58-68.]

929   Love, Betty Boyd. "Recollections of Flannery O'Connor." *Flannery O'Connor Bulletin* 14 (1985): 64-71.

Memoir written by Betty Boyd Love submitted to the *Flannery O'Connor Bulletin* by her husband, Jim Love, after her death. Love describes the nature of her friendship with Flannery, beginning with their freshman year at the Georgia State College for Women (GSCW), during the three years they went to school together, and over another two decades during which they corresponded. Reports that while few of their letters survived, she can offer "some small bits to the information about Flannery herself, as well as sharing some portions of her letters." Offers recollections of Flannery's personality and sense of humor; Sunday dinners at the Cline home in Milledgeville; Flannery's mother Regina Cline O'Connor and aunts, Miss Mary and Miss Katie Cline; Flannery's bedroom in the Cline house; her linoleum-block cartoons; her initials formed into a caricature of a chicken; Flannery's thoughts on her stay at Yaddo and New York City; and her interest in ads sent by Love to her from the *Los Angeles Times*. Concludes that "aside from her formidable talent," O'Connor was "a genuinely unusual individual . . . [who] knew who she was, and what she was, and was neither over-pleased nor disturbed by either." Found her to be "unfailingly delightful company," and faults those who throw barbs at Flannery's mother (Regina) as being among those who fail to understand the South and its ways. Illustrations: Portrait style yearbook pictures of Flannery and Betty Boyd Love, and a photograph of Love standing at a podium while serving as president of the Student Government Association at GSCW in 1945.

930   Ludwig, Richard M. and Clifford A. Nault, Jr., ed. *Annals of American Literature 1602-1983*. New York: Oxford UP, 1986.   309 (index) et passim.

Provides a copious index of primary publications, listed chronologically, with a list of major events for the purpose of providing readers with the historical, social and cultural background for authors included. Lists for O'Connor, *Wise Blood*, 1952; *A Good Man Is Hard to Find*, 1955; *The Violent Bear It Away*, 1960; *Everything That Rises Must Converge*, 1965; *Mystery and Manners: Occasional Prose*, 1969; *The Complete Stories*, 1971; and *The Habit of Being*, 1979.

931   Ludwin, Deanna. "O'Connor's Inferno: Return to the Dark Wood."
        Flannery O'Connor Bulletin 17 (1988): 11-39.

        Offers a close reading of "The Artificial Nigger" and compares it to *The
        Divine Comedy*. Reminds readers of the controversial nature of the work,
        focusing on O'Connor's statement that the statue is symbolic "of `the
        redemptive quality of the Negro's suffering for us all' and that Mr. Head
        is charged with grace at the end of the story." Suggests that it is "the ironic
        narrator's language, as well as the work's setting . . . [which] invite the
        reader to anticipate ironic workings throughout the story." Argues that
        while this "backwoods's version of a romantic quest" has been compared
        to *The Divine Comedy* and *The Inferno*, it is not simply "a peculiar,
        modern version of Dante's work;" it is, instead, "a mockery of the Dantean
        quest for the right path." Discusses O'Connor's intention for the statue to
        serve as a symbol, and asserts that this meaning is, unfortunately, not
        clearly communicated. Declares that while "black figures take on more
        and more meaning to the Heads and to us, the statue itself remains
        ambiguous and multi-leveled," which results in the wide variety of
        interpretations by critics and readers. Concludes that the story did, indeed,
        contain more than O'Connor herself understood, and instead of being a
        failure, "we may consider it an ironic masterpiece."

932   Luker, Ralph E. "To Be Southern--To Be Catholic: An Interpretation of
        the Thought of Five American Writers." *Southern Studies* 22.2 (1983):
        168-76.

        Discusses "a group of writers, who . . . share a Southern regional
        background and a Catholic religious tradition." Suggests that Flannery
        O'Connor, William Alexander Percy, Allen Tate, Walker Percy, and Garry
        Wills all "share a discernable pattern of values." Remarks that they are all
        "deeply critical of all abstraction." Notes that they "affirm a strong sense
        of place," seem to "yearn for a more organic, communal, or hierarchial
        society," and "are critical of liberalism's progressive view of history and
        seem to espouse a more complex, Janus-faced attitude."

933   Lundmark, Leonard. "Flannery O'Connor's Wrestling With Love." *Bulletin
        of the Faculty of Education, Wakayama University* (Japan) 38 (Feb.
        1989): 101-15.

        Asserts that *The Violent Bear It Away* is a love story: of a man fleeing
        from and then recognizing the power and meaning of the love of God, as
        well as the conquering power of that love. (Abstracted by Kayoko
        Watanabe).

934   Lyons, Bonnie. "The Contrasting Visions of Malamud and O'Connor."
            Studies in American Jewish Literature 12.2 (1993): 79-86.

Seeks to appraise the stature of the work of Bernard Malamud by
comparing and contrasting it with that of Flannery O'Connor. Finds both
authors to be brilliant short story writers and attempts to measure their
"strengths, limitations, and narrative strategies . . . by placing their work
side by side." Suggests that in spite of their contrasts, "much unites them.
There is little overt interest in psychology or sexuality in their work, and
in their fictive worlds nature is mostly background. Both wrote out of and
against what they conceived of as pervasive nihilism." Argues that "the
essential difference is their absolutely contrasting attitudes toward human
beings, and growing from this, their equally opposite approaches toward
their characters and readers." Whereas O'Connor saw an "overwhelming
sense of human depravity, of basic worthlessness," Malamud assures us
that "there are unseen virtues all around us." Discusses a variety of works,
focusing on Malamud's "The Magic Barrel" and O'Connor's "A Good Man
Is Hard to Find."

935   Lyons, Grant. "The Habit of Being Flannery." *Magazine of San Antonio*
            3.8 (1979): 82-84.

Expresses admiration for O'Connor's work through an indirect book
review of *The Habit of Being*. Discusses the book in the context of an
interview with Father James McCown at the St. Louis Church Rectory in
Castroville, Texas. Reports that McCown befriended O'Connor in January
of 1956 when he lived in nearby Macon, Georgia. Indicates that McCown
became both her "religious counselor" and friend. Discusses Flannery's
relationship with her mother Regina, talks about the "Catholic Index of
Forbidden Books," and how McCown arranged for O'Connor to publish
her essay "The Church and the Fiction Writer" in *America*. States that in
the published version of this essay, the editor "inserted a badly written and
contradictory sentence which made Flannery furious." Declares that in her
stories, Flannery O'Connor placed her mother "barely disguised, as a
comic and rather desperately vain and unconscious woman who comes to
various inglorious ends."

936   Lytle, Andrew. "Literary Portraits: Flannery O'Connor." *Southerners and
            Europeans: Essays in a Time of Disorder*. Library of Southern Civilization
            Series. Baton Rouge: Louisiana State UP, 1988. 187-88.

Recounts reading one of O'Connor's stories to students in her class while
she was enrolled at the University of Iowa. States that he knew
immediately that the work was written by a gifted Southerner since "the

idiom for her characters rang with all the truth of the real thing . . . [and] resembled in tone and choice of words all country speech" he had ever heard. Maintains that O'Connor had an "authentic voice," and that she combined this talent with her knowledge of Southern manners to focus on the "imperiled plight" of Christendom in our time. States that while her method resembled allegory, her stories are more aptly defined as morality plays. Refers to her own illness, and suggests that she had to "fight against her self so that her work might get done. The personal annililation is the habit of all serious writers, to die in one way and be revived in another."

937   MacKethan, Lucinda H. "Hogpens and Hallelujahs: The Function of the Image in Flannery O'Connor's Grotesque Comedies." *Bucknell Review* 26.2 (1982): 31-44.

Remarks that a dependency on "laughter and comic sense" characterizes O'Connor's fiction and Christian vision. Argues that though "why we laugh when experiencing a grotesque work of art" cannot be answered in a satisfactory manner, the action may be "an effect enshrouded in the mysterious workings of the human response." Discusses extensively the relationship of O'Connor's grotesque fiction to "images that affect the senses." Includes analysis of "The Artificial Nigger" and "Revelation" and demonstrates how O'Connor's comic grotesque method relies upon images from the real, concrete world to represent invisible truth.

938   MacKethan, Lucinda H. "*I'll Take My Stand*: The Relevance of the Agrarian Vision." *Virginia Quarterly Review* 56.4 (1980): 577-95.

Outlines the agrarian principles expressed in *I'll Take My Stand*, and affirms their relevance for modern Southern writers. Includes an anecdote from Flannery O'Connor's essay "The Regional Writer" about one of her friends from the north who is told by an Atlanta real estate broker that the buyer will enjoy the neighborhood because there aren't any Southerners around for miles. Sees this comment as making a "serious point about the matter of Southern identity" and reflecting the Agrarian's concern that the "Southerner's sense of identity was `obscured and in doubt.'"

939   MacKethan, Lucinda H. "Redeeming Blackness: Urban Allegories of O'Connor, Percy, and Toole." *Studies in the Literary Imagination* 27.2 (1994): 29-39.

Uses Hugh Holman's comment that "`The southerner approaches the city as a foreign land and to some extent a hostile one'" to examine O'Connor's use of the big city as a place where "good country people" must confront "a symbolic urban darkness." Sees O'Connor's representation as complicating the "traditional southern agrarian denunciation of the city," and contends that her view laid the framework for later "post-Southern-renaissance portrayals of the city, particularly those by fellow Catholics Walker Percy and John Kennedy Toole." Explores the satirical role that the city plays "as the necessary antidote to rural pride, smugness, and blind self-righteousness . . . richly embodied in `wiseblooded' modern white southerners" in O'Connor's "The Artificial Nigger," Percy's *The Moviegoer*, and Toole's *The Confederacy of Dunces*. Offers interpretive readings of these works, and refers to comments by William Rodney Allen, David McNeil, Hugh Ruppersburg, and Elizabeth S. Bell. Closes with a discussion of Toni Morrison's contention that American writers often use a black character or an "Africanist presence" as a "'surrogate and enabler,'" and suggests that O'Connor, Percy, and Toole all use such encounters for their own "white pilgrims."

940   Maddux, Stephen. "Flannery O'Connor and the Christian Pharisee." *Communio: International Catholic Review* 11.4 (1984): 335-49.

Retells the parable of the Pharisee to illustrate "means by which the self-righteous Christian eventually passes from one kind of vision (accurate, but earthly) to another." Asserts that O'Connor deals with this theme of "change of spiritual perspective" in "Revelation," and discusses how her characters resist their spiritual self until the moment that grace and vision are offered. Describes O'Connor's character types, focusing on the structure and meaning of "Revelation." Notes that O'Connor often relied upon the same fictional elements and techniques. Concludes with a discussion of how, in "the heavenly scheme . . . one must be divested of everything one has before one can understand" God's true nature.

941   Magee, Rosemary M., ed. *Friendship and Sympathy: Communities of Southern Women Writers*. Jackson: UP of Mississippi, 1992. 39-59, 63-65, 66-67, 68-69, 70-77, 78-80, 81-93, 172-86, 187-92.

Offers a compilation of reviews, essays, interviews, speeches, and recollections of women writers related to their own and their colleagues' work. Focuses on contributions which demonstrate the need for women writers to recognize and support a sense of friendship, understanding, and community among themselves. Covers a wide variety of women writers, with nine contributions (mostly reprints from 1950s and 1960s material) related to Flannery O'Connor:

"Recent Southern Fiction: A Panel Discussion," Rpt. from the *Bulletin of Wesleyan College* 41 (Jan. 1961).

Gordon, Caroline. "With a Glitter of Evil: Review of *A Good Man Is Hard to Find* by Flannery O'Connor." Rpt. from the *New York Times Book Review* 12 June 1955. *See* Robert E. Golden's *Guide* 1955.B16.

O'Connor, Flannery. "Review of *The Malefactors* by Caroline Gordon." Rpt. from *The Presence of Grace and Other Book Reviews by Flannery O'Connor*. Comp. Leo J. Zuber. Ed. Carter W. Martin. Athens: U of Georgia P, 1983 and, *The Georgia Bulletin* 31 Mar. 1956.

O'Connor, Flannery. "Review of *How to Read a Novel* by Caroline Gordon." Previously unpublished.

Gordon, Caroline. "Flannery O'Connor's *Wise Blood.*" Rpt. from *Critique* (Fall 1958). *See* Robert E. Golden's *Guide* 1958.B4.

Porter, Katherine Anne. "Gracious Greatness." Rpt. from *Esprit* 8 (1964). *See* Robert E. Golden's *Guide* 1964.B69.

Gordon, Caroline. "An American Girl." Rpt. from *The Added Dimension: The Art and Mind of Flannery O'Connor*. Ed. Melvin J. Friedman and Lewis Lawson. New York: Fordham UP, 1966. *See* Robert E. Golden's *Guide* 1966.A2.

Walker, Alice. "Beyond the Peacock: The Reconstruction of Flannery O'Connor." Rpt. from *In Search of Our Mothers' Gardens*. New York: Harcourt, 1983; and, *Ms.* (Dec. 1975). *See* entry 1572.

Alther, Lisa. "Introduction to *A Good Man Is Hard to Find* by Flannery O'Connor." Rpt. from "Introduction" to *A Good Man Is Hard to Find* by Flannery O'Connor. London: Women's Press, 1980. *See* entry 99.

942   Magill, Frank N., ed. *Critical Survey of Short Fiction*. Englewood Cliffs, NJ: Salem, 1981. XLII (index), et passim.

Provides a short annotated reference to O'Connor's essay "Writing Short Stories" in *Mystery and Manners*. Discusses "Greenleaf" in a section on reliability and location of narrative voice. Agrees with critics who contend that O'Connor has placed the short story within the romance tradition. Quotes Charles E. May and offers a lengthy essay by Ben Forkner arguing that the American short story has become a predominantly Southern genre.

943   Magill, Frank N., ed. *Great Women Writers*. New York: Henry Holt, 1994. 380-84.

Offers an overview of the life and work of Flannery O'Connor. Notes that despite her "small literary output, O'Connor has received an enormous amount of attention." Considers her to be "one of the most important American writers of the short story" and notes that she is "frequently compared with William Faulkner as a writer of short fiction." Suggests that O'Connor's life and work were "uncharacteristic for her age," in that she "seems better suited to the Middle Ages in her rather old-fashioned and conventional Catholic and Christian conviction that the central issue in existence is salvation through Christ." Characterizes her short stories, discusses their themes, and offers brief outlines and analyses of several, including, "A Good Man Is Hard to Find," "The Artificial Nigger," "Good Country People," and "The Displaced Person" from *A Good Man Is Hard to Find,* and "Everything That Rises Must Converge," "Greenleaf," "Revelation," "Parker's Back," and "Judgement Day" from *Everything That Rises Must Converge.*

944   Magill, Frank N., ed. *Masterplots: 2,010 Plot Stories & Essay Reviews from the World's Fine Literature.* Rev. ed. Englewood Cliffs, NJ: Salem, 1989. 6937-38, 7192-94.

Provides descriptive essay reviews of Flannery O'Connor's *Wise Blood* and *The Violent Bear It Away*, focusing upon their narrative structures. Discusses each novel's major characters and themes, and assesses each work's contribution to literature. Finds that the "most powerful effect" of *The Violent Bear It Away* is "its examination of the impulses of religion and of love, and the strange and terrible forms which they can assume." In a similar manner--because "man's free will is simply a conflict of many wills or desires . . . resolved only when a man abandons his desires and accedes to the will of God and allows it to be imposed on him"-- O'Connor's intention in *Wise Blood* is to show the folly of a man's attempt to follow his own free will.

945   Magill, Frank N., ed. *Masterplots II: Short Story Series.* Englewood Cliffs, NJ: Salem, 1986. XVIII (index), et passim.

Provides plot summaries of a variety of O'Connor's short stories. Includes a list of principle characters, first publication date, time and setting of the story, and thematic and stylistic analysis. Stories for which summary essays are provided include "The Artificial Nigger" and "The Displaced Person" (by Marjorie Smelstor); "The Enduring Chill" and "Good Country People" (by Bruce L. Edwards); "Everything That Rises Must Converge" and "Greenleaf" (by Katherine Snipes); "A Good Man Is Hard to Find" (by Carola M. Kaplan); "Parker's Back" (by Thomas Becknell); and "Revelation" (by Rob Geimer).

946   Magill, Frank N., ed. *Survey of Contemporary Literature*. Rev. ed.
        Englewood Cliffs, NJ: Salem, 1977. XVII (index), et passim.

        Includes updated reprints of essay-reviews from *Masterplots* and
        supplements. Includes essays on O'Connor's stories by Panthea Reid
        Broughton; *Everything That Rises Must Converge* by Richard Pearce;
        Mystery and Manners by Dorothy A. Lukas; and two uncredited essays on
        The Violent Bear It Away and *A Good Man Is Hard to Find*.

947   Magill, Frank N. "*The Violent Bear It Away*." *Masterplots*. Rev. ed.
        Englewood Cliffs, NJ: Salem Press, 1976. 6937-38.

        Reports publication details (eg. type of work, time, locale, and publication
        date) and provides a two-page summary of *The Violent Bear It Away*.

948   Magill, Frank N. "*Wise Blood*." *Masterplots*. Rev. ed. Englewood Cliffs,
        NJ: Salem Press, 1976. 7192-94.

        Reports publication details (eg. type of work, time, locale, and publication
        date) and provides a three-page summary of the plot of *Wise Blood*.

949   Magill, Frank N., and Stephen L. and Patricia King Hanson. *Magill's
        Bibliography of Literary Criticism*. Englewood Cliffs, NJ: Salem, 1979.
        1542-49.

        Offers a selective bibliography of literary criticism arranged alphabetically
        by author and organized by individual works. Lists the following works for
        Flannery O'Connor, "The Artificial Nigger," "The Displaced Person,"
        "Everything That Rises Must Converge," "Good Country People," "A
        Good Man Is Hard to Find," *Mystery and Manners*, *The Violent Bear It
        Away*, and *Wise Blood*.

950   Magistrale, Tony. "An Explication of Flannery O'Connor's Short Story `A
        View of the Woods.'" *Notes on Contemporary Literature* 17.1 (1987): 6-7.

        Contends that O'Connor's fiction serves as a reminder of the dangers
        "inherent in a culture that deliberately remains blind to the spiritual life in
        favor of immediate monetary profit." Argues that in "A View of the
        Woods," Mr. Fortune's "commercial self is under fierce assault from his
        spiritual self." Concludes that, because he refuses to acknowledge the
        struggle between his two selves, "he destroys himself and his grandchild
        because of his own negligence."

951   Magistrale, Tony. "Flannery O'Connor's Fractured Families." *Journal of American Studies* (Great Britain) 21.1 (1987): 111-14.

Discusses O'Connor's use of characters from fragmented families, often with parental figures missing. Suggests that the inability of these characters to cohabit with each other reveals their "selfish, mean-spirited temperament." Contends that these characters only become complete when forced to do so because of some tragic event introduced "to bring the protagonist to a vision of deeper insight and clarity."

952   Magistrale, Tony. "Francis Tarwater's Friendly Fiends: The Role of the Stranger in *The Violent Bear It Away*." *Notes on Contemporary Literature* 15.3 (1985): 4-5.

Summarizes the plot of *The Violent Bear It Away* and argues that "each of Satan's representatives--the `friendly strangers' Tarwater meets along the road, and even Rayber himself"--should be viewed "as physical variations of an identical corrupting force." Contends that it is only after Tarwater is raped that he is able to see clearly that "the friendly fiends have merely reflected his own darkest urgings."

953   Magistrale, Tony. "`I'm alien to a great Deal': Flannery O'Connor and the Modernist Ethic." *Journal of American Studies* (Great Britain) 24.1 (1990): 93-98.

Declares that O'Connor's greatest skill is "her ability to detail the dynamics of conflict, and to pose a dialectic of belief that directly challenges the secular spirit of her time." Sees her characters as "liberated from their trance of self" and moving from an initially stable world of self-knowledge "to a volatile realm of bewilderment and radical insight." Contends that her stance as a Southern Catholic "intensified her literal approach to religious dogma as it highlights her own personal isolation." Reports that her beliefs "often grated against what contemporary men and women most passionately believe." Argues that many readers have difficulty--not with the complexity of her work--but with her repudiation of "modernity's complacent conviction that God had died a Victorian."

954   Magistrale, [Tony] Anthony S. "O'Connor's `The Comforts of Home.'" *Explicator* 42.4 (1984): 52-54.

Argues that while O'Connor herself would have vehemently objected to a Freudian analysis to her work, "several of her stories present excellent opportunities for successful application of psychoanalytic theory." States that O'Connor "often relies on elements of modern psychology, although in her stories the psychological is always shown at odds with and inferior to the religious." Contends that "The Comforts of Home" is a good illustration, summarizes the storyline, and suggests that Thomas's "attachment and neurotic dependence [upon his mother] clearly reveal his own inability to resolve Freud's Oedipus complex." Submits that because Thomas is unable "to resolve the psychic conflict within himself by identifying with his dead parent," and "unable to control the two women in his home," he turns to the sheriff for advice, regarding him as a father figure. Notes that while Thomas has successfully repressed the physical, he is still very troubled by Star's sexuality. Submits that "it is out of his psychosexual conflict and perplexity that he reacts with hostility and disgust" toward Star and begins to plot with the sheriff for her arrest. Describes the sexual imagery of the gun and Star's purse, and offers a Freudian interpretation of the action at the end of the story. [Rpt. in *Explicator* 43.1 (1984): 57-59.]

955   Magistrale, Tony. "O'Connor's `The Lame Shall Enter First.'" *Explicator* 47.3 (1989): 58-61.

Discusses O'Connor's use of food imagery and eating in "The Lame Shall Enter First," as "metaphors to mirror the spiritual conditions of the characters." Suggests that her references to gluttony and starvation measure the psychological well-being of her characters and provide insight into their level of "spiritual malnourishment."

956   Magistrale, Tony. "Patterns of Spiritual Revelation in the Stories of Flannery O'Connor." *Lamar Journal of the Humanities* 12.1 (1986): 53-58.

Argues that because O'Connor's stories exhibit a similar pattern of revelation, it is important for readers "to acknowledge the consistent relationship that exists in her work between plot structure and the development of a character's identity." Suggests that readers carefully consider two distinctive personality types in O'Connor's work: the "Southern reactionary" and the young "intellectual." Describes and compares how each is used to convey the "ironic `lesson'" of each work. Examines also the "mechanics" of O'Connor's plots; her use of the "religious demon" personality type; situations in which her characters views of reality are called into question so they might have "a vision of deeper insight and clarity"; and how her work "achieves its affirmative form" through the realities of life's tragedies.

957   Magliola, Robert. "Grounds and Common(s), and a Heideggerian Recension." *Papers on Language and Literature* 17.1 (1981): 80-87.

Uses O'Connor's "The River" to discuss principles of Heideggerian hermeneutics as compared to interpretations by Christian critics.

958   Magliola, Robert. "Permutation and Meaning: A Heideggerian *Troisieme Voie.*" *The Philosophical Reflection of Man in Literature: Selected Papers From Several Conferences Held by the International Society for Phenomenology and Literature in Cambridge, Massachusetts: The Yearbook of Phenomenological Research*, Vol. 12. Ed. Anna-Teresa Tymieniecka. Boston: Dordrecht Reidel, 1982. 353-83.

Offers a summary of O'Connor's "The River" and suggests that because it can be interpreted in a variety of ways, the story lends itself to be used as a model for considering a variety of hermeneutical problems. Describes Christian and secularist interpretations of the story and explores the Heideggerian theory of being, which asserts that readers can accept conflicting interpretations of works as equally correct. Refers to theories of Chang Chung-yuan, E.D. Hirsch, Martin Heidegger, and Henry James. [Note: Discussion of this paper by Eugene F. Kaelin follows on pages 385-89 of this volume.]

959   Maida, Patricia D. "Light and Enlightenment in Flannery O'Connor's Fiction." *Studies in Short Fiction* 13 (1976): 31-36.

Asserts that "vision functions as the dynamic principle" in O'Connor's fiction, and suggests that she portrays characters who are "morally blind," who project their true character "through the physical quality of their eyes --through color, shape, and intensity." States that O'Connor's reader enters this world through the characters, a world of natural imagery with recurring images of "the treeline, the sun, and the color purple." Discusses a variety of topics, including how O'Connor's "tree-line" represents that line between the known and unknown; the sun, which "reflects light or enlightenment"; and her use of the color purple, which "indicates bruising and pain." Suggests that on the metaphysical level the three represent "an existential awareness and a spiritual process." Concludes that O'Connor's "fusion of character, situation, and imagery culminates in a unique experience, a metaphysical awakening, a spiritual illumination."

959a   Mairs, Nancy. "Nancy Mairs Writes to Flannery O'Connor." *Women's Review of Books* 16.10/11 (1999): 33-34.

The writer compares and contrasts her own background with that of Flannery O'Connor using information gleaned from *The Habit of Being*. Focuses on O'Connor's "Southernness," Catholic faith, and disability.

960   Makowski, Elizabeth. "Women and Role Models." *North American Review* 270 (June 1985): 60-61.

Comments on the value of looking to women writers, such as Virginia Woolf, as role models. Includes a discussion of Alice Walker's admiration for the life and work of Flannery O'Connor and Zora Neale Hurston.

961   Makowsky, Veronica A. *Caroline Gordon: A Biography*. New York: Oxford UP, 1989. 185, 196-97, 216-17.

Contains brief references to Flannery O'Connor, including a comment O'Connor made to Sally Fitzgerald about Gordon's *The Malefactors*; a discussion of Gordon's efforts to teach O'Connor and Walker Percy "their craft" (focuses on *Wise Blood*); Gordon's move to Atlanta, allowing her to visit O'Connor in the hospital shortly before her death; and her focus on the work of O'Connor and Ford Maddox Ford during the late 1960s.

962   Male, Roy R. *Enter, Mysterious Stranger: American Cloistral Fiction*. Norman: U of Oklahoma P, 1979. 25-26, 29-30, 49, 51, 68-71, 99, 101-17.

Discusses fiction in which the arrival of a "mysterious stranger" affects the community, focusing on such works as Mark Twain's "Mysterious Stranger," William Faulkner's "Spotted Horses," and Flannery O'Connor's "The Displaced Person." Notes O'Connor's use of the fully developed character who typically serves as "a receptor intelligence," one "who mediates between the stranger and the crowd or else receives alone the full impact of the intrusion," citing Mrs. Shortley and Mrs. McIntyre of "The Displaced Person" as examples. Suggests that O'Connor also mastered the use of the sinister stranger as well in each of her cloistral stories ("A Circle in the Fire," "Good Country People," "The Life You Save May Be Your Own," and "The Displaced Person"). Uses Tom Shiftlet's self-introduction to Mrs. Crater in "The Life You Save May Be Your Own" as a preface to a discussion of "the most obvious and profound problem inherent in cloistral fiction--man's curiosity set over against limits of rational human knowledge." Cites O'Connor's "The Displaced Person" as an example of fiction that examines the relationship between workers and their employers, and uses the story to introduce Herman Melville's "Bartleby the Scrivener" and "salesman stories." Briefly explicates O'Connor's "The

Life You Save May be Your Own" and "Good Country People." Closes with a twelve-page examination of two different versions of "The Displaced Person."

963   Malin, Irving. "Singular Vision: `The Partridge Festival.'" *Critical Essays on Flannery O'Connor*. Ed. Melvin J. Friedman and Beverly Lyon Clark. Boston, MA: G.K. Hall, 1985. 180-86.

Discusses "The Partridge Festival," focusing on O'Connor's choice of adjectives which are used to describe Calhoun, his activities, his automobile, and his intentions. Finds the story "profoundly troubling." Concludes that while O'Connor seems to suggest that "art can never completely capture spiritual worlds," she--through this story--is also celebrating this failure: "It is, if you will, a celebration of earthly (artistic) defeat--and supernatural victory."

964   Mallard, William. "O'Connor and Religion." *Encyclopedia of Southern Culture*. Ed. Charles Reagan Wilson and William Ferris. Chapel Hill: U of North Carolina P, 1989. 1324-25.

Describes O'Connor's fascination with "backwoods religious folk" and how she "investigates the concrete, regional scene . . . in order to touch a deeper, wider reality." Suggests that her contribution "to the knowledge of religion in the South and to contemporary understanding of the Christian faith grounded in Southern experience" is as important as her contribution to literature. Asserts that "the religious level of her work follows readily upon the artistic because of her sensitivity to the region."

965   Mallon, Anne Marie. "Mystic Quest in *The Violent Bear It Away*." *Flannery O'Connor Bulletin* 10 (1981): 54-69.

Reports that O'Connor owned key texts on mysticism and that "her letters reveal the certain traces of her constant interest in and concern with the mystic consciousness." Examines how in *The Violent Bear It Away* "this spiritual tradition seems to become most clearly fused with [her] fictive imagination." Contends that "mystic structures, themes, and imaginary resonate throughout the novel" and indicate that it was not O'Connor's "deliberate intention to make the novel's meaning dependent on an external parallel, but rather her own artistic assimilation of the many rich resources which fueled both her belief and her vision." Discusses Evelyn Underhill's *Mysticism*, St. Catherine of Siena's *Dialogue*, Tarwater's "mystic journey," and such mystics as St. John of the Cross, St. Theresa of Avila, St. Catherine of Siena, and Thomas Merton."

966   Maloney, Anne M[arie]. "Flannery O'Connor: Apostle to the Blind For Those Who Believe God Is Dead." *Crisis: A Journal of Lay Catholic Opinion* 12.10 (1994): 26-29.

Relates memories of reading the *Gospel of Matthew* as an undergraduate and feeling--like her present students--"ignorant of her faith and starved for meaning." Describes how students in her course on philosophy and literature read works by Walker Percy and O'Connor and relates how pleased she is by their positive response. Finds O'Connor's work to be especially supportive for readers interested in their Catholic faith. Uses O'Connor's letters to "A" as evidence of the faith and the strength O'Connor found in the Church. Contends that O'Connor had to grapple with words--"in a world where words no longer signify"--to describe God's grace and nature. Discusses "The Lame Shall Enter First" as an example of "writing a story about the central mystery of the Catholic faith," and how O'Connor comes "to terms with Baptism" in "The River."

967   Mann, Susan Garland. *The Short Story Cycle: A Genre Companion and Reference Guide.* New York: Greenwood, 1989. 157-71.

Discusses *Everything That Rises Must Converge* in terms of its unifying forms and "cycles." Contends that, though O'Connor was still working on the collection at the time of her death, it possesses artistic and stylistic control. Discusses parent-child relationships, imagery and doubling, conflict that leads to violence, the possibility of enlightenment.

968   Mariani, Paul. "As Mirandola Had it, the Mirror of the Soul." *Flannery O'Connor Bulletin* 15 (1986): 67-68.

A poem on the theme of how eyes reflect the soul. Describes the gaze of one inmate convicted of murdering four homosexuals as he compares Jesus to a fruitbat; the transfixing stare of another who murdered the owner of a liquor store; then, the look of two convicts, to the "downcast eyes" of a minister seeking public hearings for death row inmates.

969   Mariani, Paul. *Lost Puritan: A Life of Robert Lowell.* New York: Norton, 1994. 175, 177-80, 182, 225, 231, 233, 277, 281, 326-27, 433, 480-81.

Makes passing references to Flannery O'Connor's stay at Yaddo; offers insights on Lowell's life and work from O'Connor's correspondence; and presents Lowell's view of O'Connor.

970   Mariani, Paul. Rev. of *The Third Kind of Knowledge: Memoirs and
Selected Writings*, by Robert Fitzgerald. *Flannery O'Connor Bulletin* 21
(1992): 148-52.

Discusses Robert Fitzgerald's accomplishments as a translator and poet
and outlines how these memoirs offer biographical details related to his
childhood, his education at Harvard and his experiences in the Pacific
theater during World War II. Refers to Fitzgerald's friendships with such
luminaries as Vachel Lindsay, James Agee, Robert Lowell, Randall Jarrell,
Ezra Pound, and Flannery O'Connor. Comments on O'Connor's
introduction to the Fitzgeralds and the period in which she lived with them
in Connecticut. Suggests that because Flannery O'Connor lived "in
Georgia's Protestant, anti-Catholic Bible Belt . . . [she] came to rely on
Fitzgerald's example, as she did on the example of other `Catlick' writers
like Katherine Anne Porter, J.F. Powers, [and] Walker Percy."

971   Mariani, Paul. "Study in Black and White." *Flannery O'Connor Bulletin*
24 (1995-96): 125-26.

A fifty line poem in ten stanzas inscribed "for Flannery, who showed the
way, on her seventieth" [birthday]. Focuses on aspects of growing up "in
Mineola"; working at a Sinclair station with his father; and recollections
of an alcoholic named "Butch" who lived in a "`41 woodtrimmed Chevy
wagon up on blocks" behind a diner down the street.

972   Marinovich, Sarolta. "The Discourse of the Other: Female Gothic in
Contemporary Women's Writing." *Neohelicon: Acta Comparationis
Litterarum Universarum* (Budapest, Hungary) 21.1 (1994): 189-205.

Views Gothic literature "not so much as a specific genre in literary history
but as a mode of writing." Sees it also "as a sub-mode in novels that have
generally been called realistic." Examines Margaret Atwood's "Giving
Birth," and Doris Lessing's *The Fifth Child*, as examples of Gothic texts
that "deal with traditionally taboo, unladylike topics . . . i.e. the female
body and its functions: pregnancy, childbirth, [and] maternity." Refers to
Simone de Beauvior's "concept of women as the `Other,' the alien and
outsider in a society in which only men are recognized as subjects, [to
illustrate] why the estranged world of the Gothic appealed so strongly to
the female imagination." Explicates "A Stroke of Good Fortune" as a
Gothic parody wherein "a literal pregnancy becomes a Gothic horror,
imprisoning its reluctant victim [Ruby Hill] in a biological identity with
her mother which is perceived as tantamount to death." Concludes that
O'Connor uses the story both to illuminate "a central figure of the Female
Gothic and [to] ridicule the ignorance of a woman who bears its burden."

973   Marinovich, Sarolta. "The Divided Self: Women in the Mirror."
        Americana & Hungarica. Ed. Charlotte Kretzoi. Budapest (Hungary):
        Dept. of English, L. Eotvos University, 1989. 79-88.

        Examines the role of the mirror as "a key motif in women's literature."
        Finds that "twentieth-century women writers confront the vision of the
        divided self in the mirror," affirm it as common and specific, and "gain a
        voice of their own to express this female experience." Briefly reviews
        O'Connor's "A Stroke of Good Fortune" along with a variety of fairy tales
        and other literary works. Suggests that O'Connor's theme is "the fantasy of
        entrapment by the maternal body . . . by images of the womb as the
        mummy's tomb, of penetration, impregnation and childbirth as female
        terrors committing women to an imprisoning biological destiny that denies
        the autonomy of the self." Asserts that Ruby's moment of understanding
        occurs when she sees her mother's face instead of her own when looking
        in the mirror. Also discusses *Snow White*, Christina Rossetti's *Goblin
        Market*, Mary Elizabeth Coleridge's "The Other Side of a Mirror," Shirley
        Jackson's and Isak Dinesen's stories, Anais Nin's *A Spy in the House of
        Love*, and Angela Carter's "Wolf-Alice."

974   Marston, Jane. "Epistemology and the Solipsistic Consciousness in
        Flannery O'Connor's `Greenleaf.'" *Studies in Short Fiction* 21.4 (1984):
        375-82.

        Suggests that it is "the untrustworthiness of the senses [which] helps
        explain the ambiguity of the ending of `Greenleaf.'" States that the narrator
        cannot determine whether Mrs. May has "experienced a moment of grace"
        or not. Contends that because both the narrator and Mrs. May exist in a
        world of "appearances" it is the "scope and nature of human knowledge
        [which] emerge as thematic centers of the story." Discusses the work's
        similes, symbolism, and sexual overtones. Comments on O'Connor's
        interest in limitations to sensory knowledge and understanding, Mrs. May's
        isolation from God and nature, and "the narrator's own epistemological
        uncertainty." Concludes that, "in spite of her professions to the contrary,
        O'Connor reveals a profound affinity with those of her characters who
        dwell within the isolation of the mind."

975   Martin, Carter. "Comedy and Humor in Flannery O'Connor's Fiction."
        Flannery O'Connor Bulletin 4 (1975): 1-12.

        Suggests that those who read O'Connor's work alongside that of William
        Faulkner, might detect "echoes" of his work in hers. Contends that both
        share the Southern locale and the common ground of a "comic-cosmic
        view of man." Notes that while O'Connor's humor has often been subject

to "rejection, puzzlement, and confusion," she is simply receiving the same treatment as Faulkner, whose comic sensibility was also very misunderstood. Submits that "the reader who understands and accepts *As I Lay Dying* as a comic novel should have no trouble accepting the O'Connor canon" because her typical story "is characterized by a texture" very similar to his. Outlines various sources of comedy, and describes how comedy is often used to portray "the transition from poverty-adversity to felicity." Argues that O'Connor's fiction "is anything but peculiar, unique, or baffling," because "it is, in fact, comic and therefore as serious" as comedy has been "from the first." Outlines O'Connor's theory of comedy and then ties it to the classical theory of the comic and how it is designed to present "unpleasantness or grotesqueness as a feature of affirmation or correction rather than malice or mere invective." Claims that the "most troublesome critical problem for O'Connor readers . . . is the justification of the laughter which her work most assuredly does arouse." Refers to comments by or about Ben Jonson, George Meredith, Alexander Pope, Henri Bergson, Aristophanes's *The Frogs* and *The Birds*, Petronius Arbiter's *Satyricon*, Northrop Frye, and James Joyce. Concludes that O'Connor's comedy returns to a form "more primitive than that of Aristophanes"; in fact she returns "to the very source of comedy."

976		Martin, Carter. "The Genesis of O'Connor's `The Partridge Festival.'" *Flannery O'Connor Bulletin* 10 (1981): 46-53.

Outlines the contents of the manuscripts of "The Partridge Festival" in the *Flannery O'Connor Collection* in the Russell Library of Georgia College & State University and describes how "they clearly show the genesis of the story from Flannery's first thrust." Suggests that "the actual inception of the story" probably occurred during Milledgeville's sesquicentennial celebrations in 1953, during which time two local citizens, Marion Ennis and Thomas Bivins, were shot and killed. Describes details of these events, and discusses their influence on the contents, characters, plots, and actions of the various drafts of the manuscript. Refers to Lloyd West, Cecil Dawkins, "A," Caroline Gordon, Leon Driskell, Robert Giroux, and Ashley Brown. Concludes that the later versions of the story "move toward expression" of O'Connor's views of spiritual growth and atonement, but once the "comic-satiric intent is abandoned, the redemptive revelatory theme succumbs to the dictates of aesthetic tastes . . . " Finds the resulting story not "effectively demanding."

977		Martin, Carter. "`The Meanest of Them Sparkled': Beauty and Landscape in Flannery O'Connor's Fiction." *Realist of Distances: Flannery O'Connor Revisited.* Ed. Karl-Heinz Westarp and Jan Nordby Gretlund. Aarhus (Denmark): Aarhus UP, 1987. 147-59.

Contends that even though many readers are aware of the fact that O'Connor enjoyed painting and drawing, and that her work is highly visual, little has been written about the "beauty" in her work. Discusses the "pattern of beauty" in her fiction, which serves as "an important part of the rhetorical structure." Sees it as occurring casually, in an understated manner, and "characterized by the spareness of *ascesis* . . . usually surrounded by ugliness, banality, or violence." Examines forms of beauty found in "The Life You Save May Be Your Own," "A Good Man Is Hard to Find," and in *The Violent Bear It Away*. Focuses on O'Connor's vivid landscapes, noting that they occur in many of her stories. Concludes that though these landscapes "are the sights she saw outside her door in rural Georgia, they are the universal, archetypal landscapes of eternity in which the beauty of this world converges and becomes one with the beauty of God." Refers to Robert Fitzgerald, Friedrich Nietzsche, T.S. Eliot, Mariella Gable, Gerard Manley Hopkins, Emily Dickinson, Robert Browning, W.H. Auden, Ezra Pound, Thomas Aquinas, Martin Heidegger, Nikolaevich Tolstoy, William Blake, William Faulkner, *The Iliad*, and the medieval drama, *Everyman*.

978 Martin, Carter. "*Wise Blood*: From Novel to Film." *Flannery O'Connor Bulletin* 8 (1979): 99-115.

Offers an edited transcript, with a short introduction, of a personal interview with Benedict Fitzgerald, which took place in Macon, Georgia on March 1, 1979 (during the filming of *Wise Blood*), and was completed in April, 1979 in Cambridge, Massachusetts. Touches upon a wide variety of subjects related to the filming of *Wise Blood*, including the choice to film *Wise Blood* instead of *The Violent Bear It Away*; how John Huston arrived at his decision to serve as director; how the script for the film was written; and what parts or aspects of the book were left out. Remarks on the controversial nature of the film and the "theological debates" it sparked. Concludes that this "important, very controversial film," has no hero as "the figure of Jesus Christ steals the show." Indeed, the role of Jesus is so pervasive that Huston commented that the characters appear "`Christ-bitten' people, in that almost vampiric sense."

979 Martin, Karl. "Flannery O'Connor's Prophetic Imagination." *Religion & Literature* 26.3 (1994): 33-58.

Discusses ideas of theologian Walter Brueggemann in relation to the role of the prophet in our culture, and attempts to "place the theologians O'Connor studied in the larger framework of Old Testament scholarship." Discusses O'Connor's statements on the nature of her own work, contends that a careful study of her work confirms the legitimacy of her claim that her work functions prophetically. Finds O'Connor's fiction "closely related to, and informed by, her systematic study of the role of the prophet in culture." Refers to comments and works by wide variety of theologians and critics: Walter Brueggemann, Gerhard F. Hasel, Gerhard von Rad, Richard Nelson, J.C. Chaine, Eric Voegelin, Langdon Gilkey, Claude Tresmontant, Gustave Weigel, Dorothy Walters, Martha Stephens, Frederick Asals, J.O. Tate, Harold Bloom, John Desmond, P. Albert Duhamel, Michael D. True, Robert Drake, Leon Driskell, Joan Brittain, Miles Orvell, John May, Daniel Littlefield, Russell Reising, Anne Patrick, Wayne Booth, Gerald Graff, Paul Tillich, and Martin Buber.

980   Martin, Karl. "The Prophetic Intent of O'Connor's `The Displaced Person.'" *Flannery O'Connor Bulletin* 23 (1994-95): 137-57.

Offers a reading of "The Displaced Person" in support of an argument that it is "her most complete critique of post-World War II American culture." Contends that in this story O'Connor "challenges the superficial beliefs, oppressive political practices, and abusive economic structures of post-war America." Sees Mrs. Shortley as "a victim of an oppressive social system" and Mrs. McIntyre as "one of the proponents." Suggests that while their circumstances may have differed "in style and intensity," their perspectives "contain sharp criticism of the social system under which they live." Refers to O'Connor's disapproval of American social structures in her essays "The Fiction Writer and His Country" and "Some Aspects of the Grotesque in Southern Fiction," then contends that her prophetic message can be best understood within the context of Gerhard F. Hansel's thematic-dialectal method and supported by Walter Brueggemann. Claims that this method fits O'Connor's prophetic message, in that Mrs. McIntyre's farm "exhibits a politics of oppression and an economics of affluence undergirded by a religion of immanence." Discusses the symbolic nature of the peacock and the sun in the story, considers the images that Mrs. Shortley and Mrs. McIntyre see in their dreams and visions, and focuses on the nature of responsibility these characters have towards Mr. Guizac and others who are suffering. Concludes that those readers "who hope to understand her unique power" should carefully consider the prophetic aspects of her work because, "when O'Connor claimed that her vision was essentially prophetic, she was quite serious."

981   Martin, Regis. "Flannery O'Connor--Twenty Years After." *Center Journal* 4.1 (1984): 29-37.

Reviews the circumstances of O'Connor's lupus and asserts that the "rare and terrible disease . . . failed utterly to diminish the grace of her spirit." Discusses O'Connor's faith and "intense certitude" in God's grace, and how "completely her mind and soul found their way" into her characters. Refers to *The Habit of Being*, and concludes that though her letters may be highly valued for a number of reasons, "it is the evidence they present concerning the quality of her soul that principally commends them to us."

982   Martin, Regis. *Grace, Grotesquerie, and God: A Short Study in the Unsentimental Art and faith of Flannery O'Connor*. Steubenville, OH: Franciscan UP, 1991.

[Cited in *WorldCat* database; 25 pp.]

983   Martin, Regis. "Remembering Flannery O'Connor." *National Review* 19 Oct. 1984: 52-55.

Attempts to convey a sense of who O'Connor was and what her presence among us meant. States that she was "clearly someone of special distinction, perhaps of blessedness even." Discusses with admiration her courage, fortitude, and unhesitating belief in the existence and influence of "the Evil One." Suggests that O'Connor saw life as a mysterious journey past St. Cyril's Dragon, a struggle, a "decisive human drama" against "`an evil intelligence determined on its own supremacy.'" Remarks that O'Connor meant for her works "to awaken, and thus to mobilize, all in whom the drama of salvation has grown dim." Argues that O'Connor reveals more than a finely honed craft in her work; she bares her very soul. Implies that the characters O'Connor created reflect both events in her own life and her own character. Concludes that O'Connor's life constituted "a continuing and compelling theater of instruction" where readers will find the essence of "her moral style."

984   Martin, W.R. "The Apostate in Flannery O'Connor's `Everything that Rises Must Converge.'" *AN&Q: American Notes & Queries* 23.7-8 (1985): 113-14.

Suggests that O'Connor's character Julian is based upon the "Roman Emperor Julian (361-363 A.D.), known as the Apostate," instead of St. Julian the Hospitaller, as suggested by Marion Montgomery. Contends that the association is suggested both by details of the story as well as by the circumstances of the relationship between Julian and his mother.

985   Martin, W.R. "A Note on Ruby and Revelation." *Flannery O'Connor Bulletin* 16 (1987): 23-25.

Supports Forrest L. Ingram's argument that O'Connor intended "Revelation" "to be the culmination of the cycle" of stories in *Everything That Rises Must Converge*. Suggests that although they are excellent stories, "Parker's Back" and "Judgement Day" do not belong with the group. Discusses O'Connor's use of the colors red, pink, and purple, and Christian meanings implied by use of the name "Ruby." Contends that-- "since it flushes an angry face"--blood serves as an indicator of human weakness. Concludes that Mrs. Turpin's "blood-red human nature has made her guilty of at least one of the deadly sins, pride, but it has also, with earnest self-examination and remorse, qualified her for salvation."

986   Martinez, Inez. "Flannery O'Connor and the Hidden Struggle of the Self." *Flannery O'Connor Bulletin* 16 (1987): 52-61.

Declares that there is "such consistency of theme, tone, and style in O'Connor's fiction that it is difficult not to succumb to her self portrait." Contends that a psychological reading of how O'Connor treated weakness and vulnerability--based upon the theories of Harry Guntrip--offers useful reading of her work. Provides a brief summary of Guntrip's theories and offers a list of characters and description of their fates as examples of the existence of the "antilibidinal ego" in O'Connor's works. Challenges the traditional interpretation of these situations as being a "moral judgement" of "God's `terrible mercy,'" and states that they are instead better explained by Guntrip's "libidinal-antilibidinal dynamic." Claims that this perspective offers an excellent psychological framework from which to better understand O'Connor's canon. Offers a detailed explication of "Good Country People," focusing on Joy-Hulga's repressed dependence and vulnerability, and submits that instead of a positive transformation, the more likely outcome would be Hulga's deepened self-hatred and hatred others. Concludes that while her "religious vision may have been shaped by the psychological struggle of the libidinal and antilibidinal egos," this perspective "in no way negates the value of her work."

987   Martyn, J. Louis. "From Paul to Flannery O'Connor With the Power Grace." *Katallagete* 7.4 (1981): 10-17.

Confronts the question "What does it mean to have inherited both triumphant `Hallelujah Chorus' and the suffering world?" Contends that from a theological perspective it is evident that "it was never God's intention to redeem this world." In addition, "thisworldliness" also relevant; that is, "to confess Jesus as the Messiah . . . is to pledge oneself to *work* for the Kingdom of God on Earth." Discusses O'Connor's artistry in the context of this question, focusing on "Revelation" to illustrate theological framework. Concludes that for O'Connor, as for the Apostle

Paul, "the crucifixion is the invading apocalypse of God's unconditional grace which brings us to life in the midst of death."

988   Maschinot, Michael. "Wondering at a Freak Occurrence." *Atlanta Journal-Constitution* 19 May 1996: L8.

Contends that Ed McClanahan's themes and characters in his short story collection *Congress of Wonders* (Counterpoint, 1996) will remind readers of Flannery O'Connor, William Faulkner, and Garrison Keillor. Describes his odd assortment of characters: "All the men are deformed killers or drunken frauds, the women are prostitutes or gullible victims, and the children have at least a chance at redemption until they fall into the grown-up's clutches." Reports McClanahan's world of phoney tent preachers, prophetic hermaphrodites, and stuttering underdogs bears "resemblance to Garrison Keillor on a horrible day."

989   Mason, Michael. "Motes, Pongils and *Wise Blood*." *Times Literary Supplement* 11 Jan. 1980: 36.

Discusses John Huston's role as director of the film version of O'Connor's *Wise Blood*. Sees the film as a "close rendering" of the novel, with the result that "the peculiarities of the author's view of things [has] the effect of cramping or sealing off Huston's film." Contends that his attempt to depict O'Connor's "kind of religious irony is apt to strike non-Catholics as dull . . . and distasteful." Discusses how the novel's symbolism is "reproduced with great fidelity," and comments that Huston's direction enhances "the sense of deficient understanding" in O'Connor's characters.

990   Matchen, David E., and Wilton Beauchamp. "Enoch Emery: Flannery O'Connor and Junigan Psychology." *Publications of the Mississippi Philological Association* 1 (1982): 1-7.

Describes Enoch Emery in Jungian terms as "the primitive man whose `unconscious psyche life' is concrete and objective." Explains his behavior as what Jung called "projected sensuous form," that is, controlled by unconscious forces rather than awareness. For Enoch, the archetypes of the collective unconscious have not been sublimated. They remain central, sacred. Thus the "divine presence of the mummy" becomes ritualistic, magical, as do any of Enoch's fixations. When none of them regenerates him, Enoch finally turns to the final "religious experience": the gorilla. Comments on McCown's estimation that O'Connor rejects Jung's "dangerous" conclusion--that religion is merely symbol, but a necessary one--by mocking Jung's idea in the form of the ludicrous Enoch Emery.

991   Matchie, Thomas. "Flannery O'Connor and Louise Erdrich: The Function of the Grotesque in Erdrich's *Tracks*." *Papers Presented to the Linguistic Circle of Manitoba and North Dakota 1989-1993*. Ed. Harold J. Smith and Gaby Divay. Fargo: North Dakota State U, 1996. 67-78.

        Contends that O'Connor uses the grotesque to give "'life to the ugly' in order to expose the moral limitations of 'modern man.'" Observes in her fiction how the "mysteriously beautiful terrain" of middle Georgia, the region's trees and land, serve "as a vehicle of grace" for O'Connor. Follows with a careful, in-depth reading of Erdrich's *Tracks*, focusing on the symbolic meaning of her characters' relationships. Points out striking similarities between Erdrich's and O'Connor's use of the grotesque, and finds particular registers in Erdrich's work of *Wise Blood*, "A Circle in the Fire," "A Stoke of Good Fortune," "The Artificial Nigger," "The River," "The Life You Save May Be Your Own," "A Temple of the Holy Ghost," and "The Displaced Person." Concludes that in her use and depiction of the grotesque, "Erdrich is a true disciple of O'Connor."

992   Matsumoto, Fusae. "An Interpretation of Flannery O'Connor's 'Good Country People' and 'The Enduring Chill.'" *Seinan Jogakuin Junior College Bulletin* (Japan) 25 (Dec. 1978): 61-72.

993   Matsumoto, Fusae. "Introduction to Flannery O'Connor and Milledgeville, Georgia." *Seinan Jogakuin Junior College Bulletin* (Japan) 27 (Dec. 1980): 79-87.

994   May, John R. "The Art of Steering: Theological Literary Criticism After Three Decades." *Religion & Literature* 21.1 (1989): 1-7.

        Discusses the "possibility of writing about the meaning of literary texts," noting that such an approach "has been under attack in American critical circles now for so long." Discusses a wide variety of authors and their works to illustrate the value of this approach, including O'Connor's *The Violent Bear It Away*.

995   May, John R. "Blue-Bleak Embers: The Letters of Flannery O'Connor and Youree Watson." *New Orleans Review* 6.4 (1979): 336-56.

        Offers critical comments on correspondence between O'Connor and Youree Watson, a Jesuit priest who was teaching philosophy at Spring Hill College in Mobile, Alabama at the time. The letters, which were not included in *The Habit of Being*, are reprinted. They include discussions of a wide variety of works, including "The Enduring Chill," *The Violent Bear It Away*, *Wise Blood*, and "The Partridge Festival."

996   May, John R. "Flannery O'Connor: Critical Consensus and the `Objective' Interpretation." *Renascence* 27.4 (1975): 179-92.

Characterizes O'Connor's theory and practice as reactionary, but recognizes that "the sense of tradition in both religion and literature that she possessed has caused a revolution in the American literary world." Suggests that O'Connor's greatest contribution is how she used her art and belief to reintroduce Christian concerns into contemporary American literature. Discusses comments by E.D. Hirsch, Allen Grossman, David Eggenschwiler, Allen D. Lackey, Miles Orvell, Preston M. Browning, Jr., Josephine Hendin, Martha Stephens, and Kate Chopin, in relation to the evaluative context of O'Connor's work.

997   May, John R. "Flannery O'Connor." *Dictionary of Literary Biography: American Novelists Since World War II*. Vol. 2. Detroit: Gale Research, 1978. 382-87.

Offers a biographical review of O'Connor's personal and literary life. Asserts that she "wrote brilliant stories that brought the issue of religious faith into clear dramatic focus." Describes plots of her works and her major characters, symbolism, and trends. Illustrations: O'Connor with her self-portrait. [Updated in "The New Consciousness, 1941-1968" in *Concise Dictionary of American Literary Biography*, Ed. Matthew J. Bruccoli and Richard Layman. Detroit: Gale Research, 1987. 399-407.]

998   May, John R. "Flannery O'Connor: Southerner and Catholic." *New Catholic World* 224.1344 (1981): 261-64.

Reviews O'Connor's works and observes that her formative years "as a thinker and writer . . . coincided with the period immediately before the Second Vatican Council." Sees her Catholicism as "decidedly progressive, but responsibly informed," and her faith as "both Catholic and orthodox for the times." Suggests that *The Habit of Being* offers a "privileged view" of her faith and theological awareness. States that while literary critics "conditioned by the European Catholic tradition of Greene, Mauriac, and Bernanos have had a hard time discerning what was specifically Catholic about her fiction," others set aside this concern for the "more perplexing question of her place in the mainstream of Southern writers." Discusses the "religious dimension of her fiction," and the "failure of readers to distinguish . . . levels of religious meaning." Remarks that O'Connor's fiction addresses questions common to all major religions, including the nature of evil, "the inner experience of transformation," and the "enduring patterns of Christian experience that are the bases respectively of faith and of prophetic mission." Refers to his own work, *The Pruning Word: The Parables of Flannery O'Connor*, and states, "Whereas O'Connor's own literary theory is principally concerned with the relationship between the work of art and external reality . . . her fiction achieves its distinctive dramatic impact through the power of language to interpret its listener rather than through its need to be interpreted by him." Concludes that in spite of O'Connor's intellectual debts to others, "there can be no doubt about the effect of her fiction. She clearly wanted her characters and her readers to remain aware of their radical poverty in the face of life's mysteries." Illustrations: Includes photographs of O'Connor standing in front of her self-portrait; on crutches on the steps at Andalusia with a peacock; and of the cover of *The Habit of Being*.

999   May, John R. "The Methodological Limits of Flannery O'Connor's Critics." *Flannery O'Connor Bulletin* 15 (1986): 16-28.

Finds methodologies developed from "the interdisciplinary dialogue between theology and literature [to] offer a surer context--than realization of religious intent--for gaining some perspective on the diversity of critical opinion that has engulfed O'Connor's modest *oeuvre*." Attempts to show "how O'Connor's critics' conscious or unconscious assumptions about that relationship have inevitably shaped and limited the conclusions they have reached in analyzing her works." Acknowledges and discusses a debt to Paul Tillich for terms used, and to T.S. Eliot for his essay "Religion and Literature." Then, outlines approaches to O'Connor's work by Marshall Bruce Gentry, Marion Montgomery, Martha Stephens, Dorothy Walters, Carter Martin, Dorothy McFarland, Kathleen Feeley, Lorine Getz, Josephine Hendin, David Eggenschwiler, Preston Browning, Leon Driskell, Joan Brittain, Gilbert Muller, Frederick Asals, Louise Westling, Miles Orvell, Carol Shloss, and Peter S. Hawkins. Concludes that "the time has come . . . for the serious critic of O'Connor, believer or unbeliever, to focus exclusively on the dimensions of her religious world view and the manner in which it is achieved."

1000   May, John R. Rev. of *The Flannery O'Connor Companion*, by James A. Grimshaw. *Flannery O'Connor Bulletin* 11 (1982): 123-28.

Describes the arrangement and content of *The Flannery O'Connor Companion* and discusses Grimshaw's "evaluative reflections on O'Connor's growth as an artist." Notes that the author's intended audience is "first-time readers, devotees of various sorts, and those who come to

O'Connor's fiction already introduced to her through the growing number of film adaptations of her works." Criticizes Grimshaw's tentative and modest explications, especially in regard to his handling of O'Connor's "religious dimension." Finds Grimshaw's work to reflect a "severely limited insight into the religious perspective of O'Connor's stories." Asserts that the "alphabetical list of characters should have been trimmed considerably" and finds errors "in fact and interpretation." Concludes, however, that the book--"within the limits" set for it-- still serves as a "clear, balanced, and effective introduction" to O'Connor's work.

1001   May, John R. Rev. of "*A Good Man Is Hard to Find*," by Frederick Asals. *Flannery O'Connor Bulletin* 22 (1993-94): 133-37.

Describes the contents of Asals's casebook and expresses disappointment in the final product. Points out editorial mistakes, the limited selection of essays, and questions why a deconstructionist reading is included while a close reading of the story is not. Finds it odd that--since the book is part of "a series on women writers"--only one woman's contribution is included. Faults Asals's editorial decisions (specifically his choice of confusing and illogical essays) and questions where he aligns himself in relation to other O'Connor critics. Offers comments regarding the usefulness of contributed essays, discusses "abuses of evidence" in them, and cites other essays that might have been more useful.

1002   May, John R. "Stalking Joy, *The Habit of Being*: A Review of the Reviews." *Horizons* 7 (1980): 95-99.

Lists O'Connor's works, and briefly describes their reception by Catholic readers. Discusses the importance of her letter-writing, and how her disease influenced the number of letters she wrote and their content. Offers an overview of reviewers responses to *The Habit of Being*.

1003   Mayberry, Susan Neal. "A Study of Illusion and the Grotesque in Tennessee Williams's *Cat on a Hot Tin Roof*." *Southern Studies* 22.4 (1983): 359-65.

Offers a reading of Williams's *Cat on a Hot Tin Roof*, focusing on his depiction of "the feelings and consequences of greed, frustration, guilt, desire, and hypocrisy," and "the conflict between appearance and reality and its resolution in truth." Includes a discussion of O'Connor's definition and use of the grotesque and suggests that Williams "makes use of the O'Connor grotesque in the minor characters of his play, figures whose absurd appearance reflects a deformed soul."

1004   Mayer, Charles W. "The Comic Spirit in `A Stroke of Good Fortune.'"
          Studies in Short Fiction 16.1 (1979): 70-74.

          Discusses "A Stroke of Good Fortune," and compares it to its original text,
          which was published in 1949 as "Woman on the Stairs." Argues that
          O'Connor's changes and additions indicate that she "was striving for purely
          comic effect." Remarks that O'Connor urges the reader to "be aware of the
          spirit of comedy" and "how readily life triumphs over those who would
          deny its energy and vitality." Attempts to illustrate "descriptive
          improvements" by comparing portions of each text. Concludes that Ruby
          "substitutes sterile illusions and pretense for all reality in her existence."

1005   Mayer, David R. "`Ain't Adjusted to the Modern World': Flannery
          O'Connor and the Automobile." *Kansas Quarterly* 21.4 (1989): 67-74.

          Contends that O'Connor appropriates the automobile to use as an image
          of corrupted American society. In her view, Mayer argues, if one chooses
          to be "modern," one also chooses "to possess an automobile and with it,
          mobility, power, status, freedom, and, as it were, a sense of self-destiny."
          Claims this sense of "self-destiny" is corrupting, and that the automobile
          becomes "an instrument of the devil" in a variety of O'Connor's works.
          Examples and explications, in this context, are offered from *The Violent
          Bear It Away*, "The River," "A Circle in the Fire," "A View of the
          Woods," "Greenleaf," "The Displaced Person," "The Lame Shall Enter
          First," "A Good Man Is Hard to Find," "The Life You Save May Be Your
          Own," and, most extensively, *Wise Blood*. Notes that some of the images
          "seem to come from O'Connor's Agrarian sympathies--a recoiling against
          the `progress' represented by the northern car industry." Concludes that
          just as the Tower of Babel symbolized humanity's alienation from God,
          self, family, and fellow being, "in O'Connor's stories the automobile
          symbolizes the pride of a civilization which trusts its machines and reason
          to support individual desires and destiny." Illustrations: Photographs of a
          1923 Essex Coach Model A.

1006   Mayer, David R. *The American Neighborhood Novel*. Nanzan University
          Academic Publication Series. Nagoya (Japan): U of Nagoya P, 1986. 11,
          30, 38-40, 74-5, 77-80, 85, 87-8, 108, 110, 120-22.

          Examines O'Connor's suspicion of the evil influence that society has upon
          individuals, the mystery that each person possesses, and revelations in her
          short stories that hint of the mystery of the unknown and death. Suggests
          that Catholic writers tend to utilize visual cues in their work, especially
          color and movement, as in O'Connor's "Parker's Back." Asserts that
          Catholic writers also tend to present characters with the opportunity to

make a change. Finds O'Connor to be most interested in the moral dimensions of literature and the problem of belief.

1007   Mayer, David R. "The Blazing Sun and the Relentless Shutter: The Kindred Arts of Flannery O'Connor and Diane Arbus." *Christian Century* 30 April 1975: 435-40.

Contends that Diane Arbus's photographic work "could mirror O'Connor's fiction," as both share a "kindred approach to their respective arts." Asserts that they both insist on seeing life directly and concentrate on "the bizarre, the empty, [and] the ugly." Argues that they focus on freaks in an effort to urge readers/viewers to see the various vanities in themselves. Cites examples from both artists' works to support similarities, but concludes that "O'Connor's stories provide more indications of our human destiny because she adds the dimension of faith."

1008   Mayer, David R. "Conflicts of Testaments: New and Old." *Bible Today* 21 (Jan. 1983): 20-24.

Examines "Parker's Back" as "a particularly interesting example of Flannery O'Connor's use of the Bible." Suggests that it depicts both "the Jewish reverence for the transcendence of God as well as the Christian proclamation of the immanence of God in the Incarnation." Outlines the story, examines Sarah Ruth (who "might be said to represent the Hebrew Scriptures"), discusses Parker's Byzantine Christ tattoo and his role as "representative of Christian scriptures," and discusses the conflict between Sarah Ruth and Parker to illustrate the clash of the two testaments. Concludes that "Parker is a representative of those who accept God's revelation in Jesus Christ . . . [and it is] through the mannerisms of such a strange man as Parker [that] O'Connor leads us to the shocking mystery of the incarnation."

1009   Mayer, David R. "Flannery O'Connor and the Peacock." *Asian Folklore Studies* 35.2 (1976): 1-16.

Compares the Hindu perspective of looking for that which is pleasing and beautiful to the "'tendency of the English mind to seize what seems to it grotesque or ungainly in an unfamiliar object.'" Suggests that these differing perspectives, which combine the grotesque with humor, and reveal beauty in ugliness, "aptly [apply] to the subject matter and the technique of Flannery O'Connor's fiction." Argues that by using unpalatable characters and violence, O'Connor successfully shows the action of grace in this world. Describes the habits of peacocks, their cultural and symbolic importance upon religions through the ages, and suggests that O'Connor's view of them "involves language and ideas which easily fit into . . . [her] personal observations of the peacock and her religious beliefs about God's ways of revealing Himself to man." Analyzes "The Displaced Person" as an example of O'Connor's "most impressive use of the peacock." Contends that "The King of the Birds" provides a commentary on the story "by showing the peacock's potential religious symbolism and especially by presenting the different reactions the peacock causes, just as Christ's coming into the world does." Concludes that O'Connor's own personal affection for the peacock "led her to face her readers and create a moving and deeply-rooted religious symbol in spite of a prevailing contrary tradition."

1010   Mayer, David R. "Incarnate Wisdom: Flannery O'Connor's *Wise Blood*." *Academia* (Nanzan U, Japan) 24 (Feb. 1977): 15-30.

Builds upon Sr. Kathleen Feeley's observation that when O'Connor created the "new Jesus" in *Wise Blood*, she created a way for the two plot lines (Enoch and Hazel's stories) to converge. Emphasizes the literal and figurative use of the Incarnation in analyzing the plot of *Wise Blood*. Defines the term "Incarnation," and remarks that "as a consequence of the Incarnation, matter has been taken up into the divine . . . [and] becomes a channel of spiritual grace." Observes that O'Connor insists "on the presence of matter, the value of individual people (deformities notwithstanding), and God working through the events of history to make his offerings of grace." Remarks that in *Wise Blood*, "these religious concerns appear in the characters of Enoch and Haze, in the objects connected with them, and especially in their relation to mystery." Finds O'Connor "concerned not so much with mysticism or its approaches but with the very basic Christian truth that God died for the sins of the world, and with the way this redemption touches individual lives."

1011   Mayer, David R. "'Like Getting Ticks Off a Dog': Flannery O'Connor's 'As If.'" *Christianity and Literature* 33.4 (1984): 17-34.

Discusses O'Connor's use of the "as-if" construction to introduce a comparison. Comments that this signal phrase allows those readers who wish to view only the obvious in the story to do only that, but also "signifies deeper truths for those who are willing to accept them." States that she uses "as-if" in a manner similar to Hawthorne and Welty: to establish and/or strengthen themes, to present the unusual, to point toward unknown realms and new knowledge, and to suggest reality in these new areas. Adds that O'Connor also utilizes various patterns of as-if construction to indicate that a character will undergo significant change.

1012   Mayer, David R. "Outer Marks, Inner Grace: Flannery O'Connor's Tattooed Christ." *Asian Folklore Studies* 42.1 (1983): 117-27.

Relates O'Connor's interest in the tattoo to its context in other cultures and shows "how in her individualistic way she transformed this fascination into a work of literature." Suggests that her source was probably George Burchett's *Memoirs of a Tattooist*, which she bought from the Marboro bookstore in New York. Discusses her use of materials outside of mainstream Christian sources that others might refer to as associated with folk religions. Looks at a Japanese story titled "The Tattooer" (1910) that examines the effect of a tattoo on its wearer, and outlines the traditions and reasons people have had themselves tattooed through the ages. Reviews the tattoos Parker has acquired over time and their significance as well as the reasons he still feels unfulfilled until he has the Byzantine Christ tattooed on his back. Concludes that "Parker's Back" is "one of the most amusing of O'Connor's works," and "shows how unerring Flannery O'Connor's sense of basic human drive was, and how appropriately she selected tattooing . . . to mediate her criticism of two opposite approaches to the divine-- the rationalistic, `modern,' unbeliever, and the righteous, complacent `believer.'"

1013   Mayer, David R. "Shifts of Allegiance: Flannery O'Connor's `A Good Man Is Hard to Find.'" *Academia* (Nanzan U, Japan) 26 (1979): 1-11.

Confronts the questions, "`Who is a good man?'" and "`Why is he so hard to find?'" Suggests that O'Connor's first story, "A Good Man Is Hard to Find," initiates the reader's search for a good man and presents the pattern for the rest of the stories in the collection bearing the same title. Reviews the history of and words to the song "A Good Man Is Hard to Find," and suggests that its chorus "is especially important for the story because it foretells the appearance of The Misfit and warns about impressions of people--they may be `the other kind.'" Examines the role and personalities of the grandmother and The Misfit to determine which qualifies for O'Connor's "good man." Observes that she forces the reader to shift points of view from the grandmother to The Misfit and then back to the grandmother, then discusses what critics think about this ploy. Concludes that this strategy forces readers to "accommodate criminals and cripples, psychotics and fanatics" into their frame of reference and have obtain "a clearer perception of the world." Argues that, as with the grandmother, the reader is asked to give up a personal good opinion of himself or herself and "reach out to the less desirable person and consider him an equal."

1014   Mayer, David R. "Straddling the Worlds: Modern American Catholic Fiction." *Academia* (Nanzan U, Japan) 25 (Feb. 1978): 165-81.

Examines how the religious beliefs of Catholic writers stimulate their imaginations. Attempts to convey an understanding of "the state of modern American Catholic fiction" by examining "qualities of the Catholic imagination," surveying Catholic writing in America, and describing the works of J.F. Powers, Walker Percy, and Flannery O'Connor. Remarks of O'Connor that, "very seldom do the rituals and customs of Catholicism enter her fictional world; her characters rise not from her religion but from her region, the South." Explicates "Parker's Back" as an example of her work, which "consists of Southern Protestant characters and yet still contains strong elements of the Catholic imagination." Mentions T.S. Eliot, C.S. Lewis, Louis D. Rubin, Jr., John Pick, Orestes Brownson, Isaac Hecker, Abram Ryan, John Banister Tabb, Mary McCarthy, Theodore Dreiser, F. Scott Fitzgerald, James Farrell, Ernest Hemingway, Katherine Anne Porter, John R. Powers, Susan Cahill, Caryl Rivers, John Gallahue, Ralph McInerny, James Carroll, Jimmy Breslin, Pete Hamill, Edward Hannibal, and Willa Cather.

1015   Mayer, Suzanne. "Daring the Dragon: The Prophetic Voice and Vision of Flannery O'Connor and Thomas Merton." *Spiritual Life* 40 (Winter 1994): 230-38.

Compares and contrasts the life and work of Flannery O'Connor with that of Thomas Merton. Examines "how much each of their lives touched the other" and the "key themes and concerns" they shared. Refers to comments by Harold Fickett on O'Connor's use of images, quotes from a poem by Jessica Powers ("There Is a Homelessness"), and touches upon other comments by their publisher, Robert Giroux. Suggests that while their "points of contact" were rare, "there is something almost prophetic in the lives, personalities, and vision of each of these twentieth-century religious figures." Outlines their shared prophetic stance and contends that they, "like the classic prophets of Old Testament fame," were called from among their contemporaries "to speak to and for the people." Considers their mutual concern regarding Merton's "developing notion of the true and false self" as illustrated by O'Connor's use of this theme in "Revelation." Concludes that, like many of their characters, O'Connor and Merton faced the dragon, only to discover that the truth "lies within."

1016   Mayer, Suzanne. "Flannery O'Connor." *English Journal* 79.3 (1990): 91.

A fifteen-line poem that explores O'Connor's interest in peacocks.

1017   McAlexander, Hubert H., ed. *Conversations with Peter Taylor.* Jackson: UP of Mississippi, 1987. 8-9, 86, 116.

Offers a collection of largely previously published interviews mostly from the 1980s. A wide variety of authors are referred to, including O'Connor. In Stephen Goodwin's interview conducted in 1973, Taylor suggests that while William Faulkner was an influence on Eudora Welty's work, it was Welty--in turn--who "made it possible for Flannery O'Connor to write." States that it was Welty who "introduced the kinds of subjects in her fiction . . . that created a field for Flannery." Refers to Welty's "The Petrified Man" and "Keela, the Outcast Indian Maiden" as examples that O'Connor "could take and make her own." To J. William Broadway's question, "What do you think of O'Connor's work?" Taylor comments that he admires her work and--describing an incident during her student days at the University of Iowa--states that he enjoys her straightforward sense of humor. Another brief remark, in an interview conducted by McAlexander, refers to this same incident.

1018   McBride, Anne K. "Flannery O'Connor's Popularity Evidenced at College Seminar." *Georgia Bulletin: Catholic Archdiocese of Atlanta* 11 Oct. 1979: 7.

Reports that Sally Fitzgerald taught Georgia College & State University's 1979 Flannery O'Connor summer seminar. Describes the friendship between O'Connor and Fitzgerald, Fitzgerald's teaching method, her explanation of the meaning behind "The Artificial Nigger," *Wise Blood*, and the phrase "the habit of being." Cites changes in Milledgeville since O'Connor's death. Mentions *Mystery and Manners*, John Huston's version of *Wise Blood*, and O'Connor's peacocks. Illustrations: Flannery on crutches looking at a peacock atop the front steps of Andalusia.

1019   McBride, Mary. "Paradise Not Regained: Flannery O'Connor's Unredeemed Pilgrims in the Garden of Evil." *South Central Bulletin* 40.4 (1980): 154-56.

Notes that some of O'Connor's "evil pilgrims represent the vast capacity of unredeemed man for grotesque cruelty." Argues that these characters are selfish, disturbed, immoral, and sometimes physically violent--all to "depict the vileness of naturalistic man without redemption." Suggests that O'Connor, "by shouting the cruelty of evil, proclaims the benevolence of good." Discusses The Misfit in "A Good Man Is Hard to Find," Tom T. Shiftlet in "The Life You Save May Be Your Own," Mr. Shortley in "The Displaced Person," and the Bible salesman in "Good Country People."

1020   McCaffery, Larry, ed. *Postmodern Fiction: A Bio-Bibliographical Guide*. Vol. 2. New York: Greenwood, 1986. 180, 314, 481, 588.

Mentions O'Connor's use of Gothic form, "a favorite for women in the twentieth century." The work of Jayne Anne Phillips and Harry Crews is compared to O'Connor's.

1021   McCarthy, Coleman. "Iowa's Engle: Poet and Developer of Genius." *Des Moines Sunday Register* 14 Aug. 1983: 1C, 3C.

Discusses the role of Paul Engle, Director of the University of Iowa's Creative-Writing Workshop, in recognizing and promoting the talent and careers of dozens of recognized writers, including Flannery O'Connor. Reviews Engle's career and fundraising success, and declares that "one of the earliest signs that Engle was onto something special at the Workshop was Flannery O'Connor." States that the two held in common the fact that both were "rural" and "had their doubts about cities." Recounts an incident after a class in 1946 when Engle told O'Connor that an attempted seduction scene in one of her early chapters of *Wise Blood* "`just is not correct.'" O'Connor replied, "`Oh no, don't, not here!'" The two then went to a nearby parking lot and got into Engle's car. There he explained to her "that a sexual seduction didn't take place quite the way she had written." States that Engle suspected that O'Connor's incorrect description was most likely "`from a lovely lack of knowledge.'"

1022   McCombs, Phil. "Century of Thanatos: Walker Percy and His `Subversive Message.'" *Southern Review* 24.4 (1988): 808-24.

Includes four references to O'Connor: how both her work and Percy's are informed by their Catholic background; her use of "active evil in her work"; her remarks on "writing edifying novels" and how such practice is tied to a novelist's "moral courage"; and Percy's recollection of meeting O'Connor when she lectured at Loyola University in New Orleans.

1023   McCorkle, Jill. "Listening to Flannery." *Flannery O'Connor Bulletin* 24 (1995-96): 127-28.

Offers comments regarding the value of O'Connor's writings as a touchstone for writers and teachers of fiction. Refers to "A Good Man Is Hard to Find" and states that with each reading she comes "away each and every time feeling shocked and awed all over again." States that the story is "complex and genuine" and "offers up such a bundle of emotions that it would take all of eternity to sit and neatly unknot and wind each one up." Sees O'Connor's essay "The Nature and Aim of Fiction" in *Mystery and Manners* as a goldmine of "good solid advice that is about as blunt and to the point as any could ever be." Remarks that her classroom discussions often focus on the commercial appeal of a story instead of its technique and content, and how she often uses O'Connor's quote on Henry James ("`I know of no writer who was hotter after the dollar than James was, or who was more of a conscientious artist'") as a point of illustration in these discussions. Closes with a recollection of visiting O'Connor's hometown of Milledgeville, Georgia and finding it "alive and well and filled with her spirit."

1023a   McCormick, Patrick. "Looking for Grace." *U.S. Catholic* Nov. 1999: 26-29.

Offers a selection of "the best of the best" Catholic novels, focusing upon those Catholic storytellers who "have sparked our budding imaginations and challenged us to think about questions of sin and grace in ways that religion class or Sunday homilies rarely did." Discusses a wide variety of writers, including O'Connor, who is seen as representative of "an earlier generation." States that "authors like Flannery O'Connor, J.F. Powers, and Walker Percy showed American audiences that being a Catholic novelist wasn't an oxymoron but a vocation." Refers to O'Connor's remark, "`When people have told me that because I am Catholic, I cannot be an artist, I have had to reply, ruefully that because I am a Catholic I cannot afford to be less than an artist.'"

1024   McCown, James H. "Remembering Flannery O'Connor." *America* 1-8 Sept. 1979: 86-88.

Reminiscence by James H. McCown, who in the 1950s was Assistant Pastor of St. Joseph Catholic Church in nearby Macon, Georgia. Recounts O'Connor as saying, when visited by McCown, that he was the first Catholic who had called on her in the interest of her writing. Remembers her interest in François Mauriac, Georges Bernanos, Léon Bloy, Julien Green, Evelyn Waugh, Muriel Spark, Walker Percy, and J.F. Powers--all the authors who "so excited Catholics at the time." McCown states that he corresponded and visited often, and was so impressed with O'Connor that he wrote Harold Gardiner, then literary editor of *America*, about her work, which led to publication of O'Connor's "The Church and the Fiction Writer." Oddly, though the text became seminal, the most quoted sentence--"what leads the writer to salvation may lead the reader to sin, and the Catholic writer who looks at the possibility directly looks at the Medusa in the face and is turned into stone"--was "edited in," a fact which "made Flannery furious." Also quotes an Atlanta novelist as saying, "Flannery certainly is a great writer, but you know, there is no `love' in her writing," to which O'Connor later responded, "she's right."

1025   McDermott, John V. "Dissociation of Words With the Word in *Wise Blood*." *Renascence* 30.3 (1978): 163-66.

Argues that in *Wise Blood* a polarization exists between words and the Word and between what a character says and what he truly believes. This discrepancy of "fragmented man" is related to O'Connor's theory of "man's `conflicting wills.'" Contends that Enoch Emery has a fragmented personality in which he says one thing and then does the opposite. He serves as a contrast to Hazel Motes, "who becomes a totally integrated man as the story concludes."

1026   McDermott, John V. "Julian's Journey into Hell: Flannery O'Connor's Allegory of Pride." *Mississippi Quarterly* 28.2 (1975): 171-79.

Argues that Julian Chestny of "Everything That Rises Must Converge" has lost his faith and "runs vainly from his soul's imminent dissolution as the story reaches its inevitable climax." Recognizes that this perspective conflicts with that of Leon V. Driskell and Joan T. Brittain, who conclude that Julian will acknowledge his own weaknesses which, in turn, means that "`the moment of truth can offer nothing but hope.'" Analyzes the story in the context of this negative view and concludes that Julian is "at the end a man without a `voice' . . . or `identity,'" who becomes "`nothing' where it elicits the deepest pain--in his own mind."

1027   McDermott, John V. "Listening and Speaking: Byways to Action--Human and Divine--in O'Connor's `Greenleaf.'" *NMAL: Notes on Modern American Literature* 7.1 (1983): Item 2.

Suggests that "Greenleaf" presents a subtle tale which frames Christ's final moments through Mrs. May, who "has her own crucifixion, death, and resurrection." Argues that O'Connor's theme "is that man is saved through his own choice by listening for the sound of . . . Christ's voice, the same sound as `steady chewing.'"

1028   McDermott, John V. "O'Connor's `A Stroke of Good Fortune.'" *Explicator* 38.4 (1980): 13-14.

Contends that while few critics have examined Ruby's husband's role and whether or not he truly "slipped," Bill B. Hill "had a change of heart" and wanted children. Suggests that the "logical extension of this idea [is] that his change of attitude will affect in Ruby a change of spirit."

1029 McDermott, John V. "Voices and Vision in Tarwater's Odyssey." *Renascence* 32.4 (1980): 214-20.

Suggests that as *The Violent Bear It Away* concludes, Tarwater's "refractory vision becomes synchronized in an orbit of perfect vision" and his "vacillating will, symbolized by the conflicting voices that taunt and haunt him . . . becomes one with the Lord's." Discusses Tarwater's "divided will" (the rationalizing self and the self-indulgent, sensual self), and images of circling, seeing, hearing voices, and evil.

1030 McDonald, Henry. "The Moral Meaning of Flannery O'Connor." *Modern Age* 24.3 (1980): 274-83.

Briefly outlines critical approaches to religious fiction, then discusses O'Connor's religious commitment. Contends that she attempted to communicate her vision and theme of "the whole man" in all her fiction, but most notably through Rayber in *The Violent Bear It Away* and O.E. Parker in "Parker's Back." Sees these works as illustrating the importance O'Connor placed upon an individual's ability to integrate the natural and social world with his or her spiritual world, "not merely united but made to serve as the basis for one another." Mentions or discusses O'Connor's work in relation to St. Augustine, St. Thomas Aquinas, Friedrich Nietzsche, Manichaeism, and free will. Concludes with a discussion of the similarity of thought between the works of O'Connor and Nietzsche.

1031 McDonald, Russ. "Comedy and Flannery O'Connor." *South Atlantic Quarterly* 81.2 (1982): 188-201.

States that O'Connor's stories are comic in both the formal and ideological sense as "her mature works move through difficulties to a happy ending" that encourages "an affirmative vision of human experience." While the climax of each work is often violent or fatal, O'Connor regards such endings as "a stroke of good fortune." Discusses her characters and how they move from confusion to understanding and experience some form of salvation because "the spirit of God intervenes to save them."

1032 McDonnell, Thomas P. "O'Connor, Emerson, and the Lord's Supper." *University Bookman* 28.2 (1988): 3-5.

Recounts O'Connor's comment regarding the Eucharist at a party hosted by Mary McCarthy ("'Well, if it's a symbol, to hell with it'"), then compares her view and position with that of Ralph Waldo Emerson. Notes O'Connor's comment during a symposium on religion and art in 1963 that "'when Emerson decided in 1832 that he could no longer celebrate the Lord's Supper unless the bread and wine were removed, an important step in the vaporization of religion in America had taken place.'"

1033   McEntyre, Marilyn Chandler. "Mercy That Burns: Violence and Revelation in Flannery O'Connor's Fiction." *Theology Today* 53.3 (1996): 331-44.

Argues that the difference between O'Connor's use of violence and that of other writers, is "how she upends and indicts the cliches, the trivalization of violence, and the sentimentalities that soften our vision and confuse our judgement of it." Contends that O'Connor attempts "to restore to a largely jaded audience the capacity for shock and the possibility of recognizing evil, our involvement in it, and our need for redemption." Discusses characters in "Revelation," "Greenleaf," *The Violent Bear It Away*, and "The Lame Shall Enter First." Concludes that, while none of them are "likeable," and there are none with whom "any respectable reader would readily and wholeheartedly identify," O'Connor uses them "to illuminate" for readers her belief that "all have sinned . . . [and] there is none righteous, no not one."

1034   McFague, Sallie. "The Parabolic in Faulkner, O'Connor, and Percy." *Notre Dame English Journal* 15.2 (1983): 49-66.

Suggests that aspects of New Testament parables may be found in the works of Faulkner, Percy, and O'Connor. Contends that their presence "accounts . . . for the novelty of each author's vision of the really real, or the way to be in the world, or essential reality." Argues that O'Connor's parables point indirectly through events and circumstances "to what she believes is essential reality, the power of God through salvation." Discusses the nature of New Testament parables, the internal tension they exhibit as the listener's expectations are reversed, and notes these features in the works of Faulkner, O'Connor, and Percy. Focuses on O'Connor's *The Violent Bear It Away* calling it "a christian parable of reality." Mentions Paul Ricoeur, John Dominic Crossan, Jacques Derrida, Michel Foucault, Hayden White, Nathaniel Hawthorne, and Brainard Cheney.

1035   McFee, Michael. "Reading a Small History in a Universal Light: Doris Betts, Clyde Edgerton, and the Triumph of True Regionalism." *Pembroke Magazine* 23 (1991): 59-67.

Discusses Doris Betts's "The Spies in the Herb House" and Clyde Edgerton's *Raney* and *The Floatplane Notebooks*. Includes passing references to O'Connor that focus on how Edgerton's writing in *Raney* reflects her views on regional writing.

1036 McGifford, Diane. "Inference, Image, and Inspiration: Three About Flannery O'Connor." *Canadian Review of American Studies* 13.3 (1982): 389-96.

Integrated essay review of Robert Coles's *Flannery O'Connor's South*, Barbara McKenzie's *Flannery O'Connor's Georgia*, and Carol Shloss's *Flannery O'Connor's Dark Comedies: The Limits of Inference*. Argues that the three are uneven and betray the limits of discipline and author. States that when "read as a group they persuade the reader" that an interdisciplinary approach to O'Connor's work yields results "greater than the sum of its parts" and is perhaps the most fruitful method in "elucidating the central mystery in O'Connor's fiction." Concludes that "without meaning to denigrate the three works . . . O'Connor's art remains more powerful than the critics' abilities to penetrate it . . . her labyrinthine vision still awaits its critical Theseus."

1037 McGowan, Cecilia. "The Faith of Flannery O'Connor." *Catholic Digest* (Feb. 1983): 74-78.

Provides a biographical sketch of O'Connor. Reviews details of her childhood, study at the University of Iowa, friendship with Sally and Robert Fitzgerald, her battle with Lupus, habits, self-discipline, humor, and religious views and faith. Discusses her contemplative life, and suggests that despite O'Connor's denial, she was a mystic. Concludes that O'Connor produced "some of the most powerful literature of our century" and that she "practiced a resignation that recognized that suffering could become the touch of the divine hands, the influence of the will of God upon our lives." Condensed from *Desert Call* (Summer 1992).

1038 McInerny, Ralph [M.]. "Flannery O'Connor, Hillbilly Thomist." *American Spectator* 16.7 (1983): 22-23.

Discusses O'Connor's view that the writer's vision should be an anagogical one, and that he or she "must seek a vision of human life which sees the deeds of creatures in relation to God." Offers an indirect review of Marion Montgomery's *Why Flannery O'Connor Stayed Home*, and refers to O'Connor's statements in *Mystery and Manners* as part of an examination of the relationship between O'Connor's work and her Catholicism. Argues that O'Connor did not look "condescendingly on her troubled believers," and believed instead that individual human lives really do matter as "the deeds of everyday, are fraught with an eternal significance. The world of O'Connor could not be more concrete."

1039   McInerny, Ralph M. "A Good Woman Now Easy to Find." *Crisis* 6 (Oct. 1988): 42-43.

Review essay of *Flannery O'Connor's Collected Works*. Lists the works included, provides a biographical sketch, and discusses O'Connor's preface to *A Memoir of Mary Ann*. Describes O'Connor's preface as being "overwhelmingly powerful," and contends that it conveys "much about this wise and good woman." Reviews the connections between the Our Lady of Perpetual Help Free Cancer Home, Mary Ann, Nathaniel Hawthorne, and Hawthorne's daughter, Rose. Concludes that O'Connor's work "is that of a woman who knew she was dying. This concentrated her mind, lent a seriousness to her sense of vocation, enlivened her wit and humor, and led . . . not only to wisdom but to holiness."

1040   McInerny, Ralph M. "The Haunting Voice of An American Original." *National Catholic Register* 30 Jan. 1994: 1.

Profiles O'Connor as one of a number of Catholic writers who have contributed to the Catholic faith's "vast heritage" of literature. Cites Hazel Motes, with his visualization in *Wise Blood* of Jesus as "`a wild ragged figure motioning him to turn around and come off into the dark',," as representative of her Christ-haunted characters. Discusses the relationship between her work and her being "a cradle Catholic," and her debt to Jacques Maritain's "Art and Scholasticism." Contends that she "is by general consensus one of the great American writers of the 20th century." Concludes that "the girl from Milledgeville, Georgia, not only practised her faith but lived in an imaginative and intellectual Catholic ambience."

1041   McKenzie, Barbara. "The Camera and *Wise Blood*." *Flannery O'Connor Bulletin* 10 (1981): 29-37.

Offers two hypotheses on the nature of making novel-based films in order to provide insights into the "strengths and weaknesses of the film adaptation of *Wise Blood*." The first hypothesis, based upon Siegfried Kracauer's *Theory of Film*, relates to the idea that "every `medium has a specific nature which invites certain kinds of communication while obstructing others.'" Contends that while O'Connor's realistic touch left her novel with a "violent and comic and wild" look about it, the naturalistic style of the film adaptation of *Wise Blood* left it "too sanitized and a little less believable." The author's second hypothesis, based upon George

Bluestone's *Novels into Film*, focuses on the differences between film and the novel--namely, that the two media are "`overtly compatible, [but] secretly hostile.'" Suggests that though O'Connor was an exceptionally visual writer, she relied heavily "on figures of speech and on the internalization of external data." States that, because of the inability of film to convey O'Connor's "similes, metaphors, personifications, and other figurative devices" in visual form, the end result is a "flattened visual effect" in the film. Concludes that, "in spite of certain resemblances," the film adaptation of *Wise Blood* is an entirely different entity from O'Connor's novel.

1042   McKenzie, Barbara. "Flannery O'Connor and `The Business of the Purified Mind.'" *Georgia Review* 33.4 (1979): 817-26.

Observes that too often O'Connor's readers "have been more persistent in trying to find the autobiographical element in her fiction than in recognizing the craft that transformed the autobiographical." Suggests that her photographs contribute to this problem, and comments on her attitudes toward photographers and their invasion of her privacy. Provides a brief biography of O'Connor, comments on photographs which accompany the article, and on the establishment of the Flannery O'Connor Memorial Room at the Russell Library of Georgia College & State University.

1043   McKenzie, Barbara. "Flannery O'Connor Country: A Photo Essay." *Georgia Review* 29.2 (1975): 328-62.

Offers a brief biographical essay followed by twenty-seven black and white photographs and excerpts from several O'Connor works: "The Fiction Writer & His Country," "A View of the Woods," *Wise Blood*, "The Lame Shall Enter First," "The Displaced Person," and "The River." The introductory essay discusses "seeing" and O'Connor's reaction to being called a "regional writer."

1044   McKenzie, Barbara. "Flannery O'Connor Country on Film: A Photo Essay." *Georgia Review* 31.2 (1977): 404-26.

Provides photographs of scenes from the film adaptation of "The Displaced Person," directed by Glenn Jordan, in an attempt to translate O'Connor's "Gothic quality" into visual terms. Additional photographs of other "roadside images" are included "as a visual corollary to the complications and contradictions" of the story and film. Outlines O'Connor's career and sense of place, and describes the impact of the filming on the Milledgeville, Georgia community in June of 1976.

1045   McKenzie, Barbara. "Photographs." *Flannery O'Connor Bulletin* 9
            (1980): n.p. [Between pp. 119-20].

            Offers five photographs reproduced from the author's book *Flannery*
            O'Connor's Georgia, published by the University of Georgia Press in
            1980. Includes scenes from middle Georgia which reflect O'Connor's
            fictional characters or perspective.

1046   McKeon, Zahava. "Novels--Translative: A Discussion of Comparative
            Analysis." *Novels and Arguments: Inventing Rhetorical Criticism.*
            Chicago: U of Chicago P, 1982. 177-228.

            Uses three works by O'Connor to illustrate how rhetorical criticism
            "enables us to formulate a context for the comparative analysis of two or
            more separate named texts, and provides the method for carrying out
            comparative analysis." Offers detailed readings of *The Violent Bear It*
            Away, "The Lame Shall Enter First," and "Parker's Back" to give the
            reader a sense of the "world of Flannery O'Connor."

1047   McLellan, Amy Louise. "A Return to the South." Ms. 1989.

            Unpublished dramatic production based upon Flannery O'Connor's
            personal letters. [Cited in the *Copyright Monograph File* of the U.S.
            Library of Congress, registration PAu-1-216-880.]

1048   McMahon, Patrick. "Night Class." *Teaching English in the Two-Year*
            College 19 (May 1992): 98-99.

            Briefly describes the types of students enrolled in a community college
            and their response to O'Connor's short story, "The Displaced Person."
            Finds the story to be an example of how, "in O'Connor's work, the eternal
            intersects with the momentary." Concludes that "the rural paradise
            becomes a Fallen World because the people don't act charitably toward the
            displaced people who need their help."

1049   McMillan, Norman [R.] "Dostoevskian Vision in Flannery O'Connor's
            `Revelation.'" *Flannery O'Connor Bulletin* 16 (1987): 16-22.

            Notes that O'Connor was an avid reader of Dostoevsky and considered
            him one of her favorite authors. Observes similarities in O'Connor's
            "Revelation" and Dostoevsky's *Crime and Punishment*. Suggests that the

main characters in each--Ruby Turpin for O'Connor and Marmeladov for Dostoevsky--seek to "demonstrate the failure of earthly standards as a means of judging heavenly ones," and each present "a vision of pride as the great damning sin." Explicates sections which support the assertion that both "present judgmental human pride as running counter to the charity and generosity of the vision they embrace." Sees both authors as writing in such a manner that their "readers who begin their encounter with Marmeladov and Mrs. Turpin feeling greatly superior to them . . . finally have to face their own lack of vision."

1050   McMillan, Norman [R.] "Flannery -- A Life in Words, Adapted From the Published Letters of Flannery O'Connor." Ms. *Flannery O'Connor Collection*, Russell Library, Georgia College & State University, Milledgeville, GA. 1986.

A thirty-three page, typewritten, monologue which appears to be based upon excerpts from *The Habit of Being*. The "action of the play takes place in Flannery O'Connor's bedroom at Andalusia, the family home in Milledgeville, Georgia. The events . . . are not chronological, but all of Miss O'Connor's words were written between 1948 and 1964."

1051   McMillan, Norman R. "Mrs. McIntyre, Mrs. Shortley, and the Priest: Empathic Understanding in Flannery O'Connor's `The Displaced Person.'" *Philological Papers* 31 (1985-86): 97-103.

Suggests that although O'Connor would object to a critic using an "empathic understanding" to read her stories, doing so "would seem to open up an interesting approach." Examines "The Displaced Person" to illustrate this conceptual approach and finds that this story takes O'Connor "quickly beyond the social world and into the realms of morality and religion." Argues that each of the story's main characters "represent this failure of empathic understanding in distinct ways, ranging from comic xenophobia to tragic blindness." Analyzes each misunderstanding and failure to empathize with the Displaced Person. Concludes that while Mrs. McIntyre grasps the truth that spiritual matters are far more important than material concerns, the story does not end in a manner that adequately suggests to readers that she had been given hope for redemption.

1052   McMullen, Joanne Halleran. "The Verbal Structure of Infinity." *Language and Literature* 21 (1996): 45-64.

Discusses linear and circular patterns seen in O'Connor's depictions of time. Contends that her "verbal structures parallel the time references inherent in her fictional representations," and that "through her verb choices, verb forms and tense decisions, she masterfully suggests the enfolding of linear human time into the circle of eternal time." Offers in this context, explications of *Wise Blood*, "A Stroke of Good Fortune," "Greenleaf," "A View of the Woods," "Everything That Rises Must Converge," "Good Country People," "A Circle in the Fire," and "The Displaced Person." Concludes that "though her stories move through the linear development of plot, O'Connor's style both episodically and syntactically lends credence to her belief in an eternal circle of time rather than an evolutionary historical view."

1053   McNiff, John and Marcella Hickey. "Flannery O'Connor: The Art of Revelation." *Likha* (Philippines) 10.2 (1988-89): 24-56.

Discusses O'Connor's literary art and how it was based upon her religious beliefs and geographic region. Attempts to outline her artistic "vision," stating that for her the essence of humanity extended "beyond the ordinary, concrete world into the realm of ultimate mystery." Contends that O'Connor's paramount concern was "illuminating the relationship between finite human beings and the infinite, absolute reality, God." States that she viewed her purpose like that of the Old Testament prophets--to present a revelation--and that her stories resemble New Testament parables symbolizing the relationship between God and humankind. Remarks that because she consistently emphasized violence and abnormality, O'Connor's work may be categorized as grotesque. Describes a variety of her characters, their spiritual alienation and pride; and comments on their biblical foundation. Examines stories in *A Good Man Is Hard to Find*, focusing on "A Good Man Is Hard to Find," "Good Country People," and "The River," and comments as well on "Revelation" from *Everything That Rises Must Converge*. Finds O'Connor's constant theme to be humanity's fallen condition and potential for conversion, and "the potential for the resolution of spiritual alienation through the action of grace."

1053a   Meehan, Elizabeth. "Flannery O'Connor: The Voice of Southern Gothic." *Twentieth-Century American Writers*. San Diego: Lucent Books. 74-86.

Offers a biographical sketch of O'Connor, recounting her childhood years in Savannah and Milledgeville; her education at Savannah's St. Vincent's Catholic School, Milledgeville's Peabody High School, Georgia State College for Women (GSCW), and the University of Iowa; her literary career and her battle with Lupus. Illustrations: photographs of O'Connor, Lafayette Square in Savannah, historic homes of Milledgeville, the front of the main building at Yaddo, a Southern riverside baptism, and writers Robert Lowell and O. Henry.

1054 Meek, Kristen. "Flannery O'Connor's `Greenleaf' and the Holy Hunt of the Unicorn." *Flannery O'Connor Bulletin* 19 (1990): 30-37.

Discusses "one of the most disturbing events . . . in all of modern fiction," O'Connor's bull in "Greenleaf"--which "abruptly and violently gores a woman to death." Contends that while the "action is potent with the symbolism and undeterring vision of O'Connor's strong Roman Catholic beliefs," it also parallels the unicorn legend and "the Christian allegory known as the Holy Hunt." Refers to critical commentary by John C. Shields, Arthur F. Kinney, and James Andreas, then offers a close review of background elements of the unicorn's story. Alludes to occurrences in the King James version of the *Old Testament*, translation of the word "unicorn" from the Hebrew, and the symbolic meaning of the unicorn as related to Christ. Outlines similarities between the unicorn legend and Mrs. May's story. Comments on the unicorn's symbolic function in presenting "dual images of Christ and Satan, redemption and destruction . . . [the] interplay of chastity and lust," and the role of the virgin. Concludes that the unicorn and the bull are complex and ambiguous figures that represent Christ. Submits further that as the bull "sinks in surrender, simultaneously victim and victor (as the Christlike unicorn surrenders in the story of the Holy Hunt), this identity passes from him to Mrs. May . . . [who] experiences redemption and rebirth on the horn of the Greenleaf bull."

1055 Meese, Elizabeth A. *Crossing the Double-Cross: The Practice of Feminist Criticism.* Chapel Hill: U of North Carolina P, 1986. 37, 38, 121.

Includes passing references to O'Connor: her refusal to see James Baldwin in Georgia, due to the racist traditions of the middle Georgia society; and, the inclusion of O'Connor's name among a list of "distinguished women writers who have remained childless" or never married at all, possibly as a "notion of sexual resistance."

1056 Mehl, Duane P. "Sex and Sacrament in Contemporary Literature: The Incarnation as Method." *Currents in Theology & Missions* 10 (Dec. 1983): 351-64.

Contends that American novelists have among their ranks those who "have written a body of literature profoundly influenced by the doctrine of the incarnation, the hypostatic unity of natures in the person of Christ, and the Sacraments of the Church Catholic." Argues that during the last 75 years there has been more of a trend among authors and critics to "recognize in the incarnation the basic metaphor underlying all of reality." Discusses "incarnational writers" who have "proven their ability to survive even the fiercest onslaughts of scientific realism." Examines methods used by these writers and "indicates some of the curious and exhilarating results they have achieved in characterization and plot development." States that while O'Connor "meant to startle both characters and readers into a recognition of human sin, of God's judgement, and possible grace in Christ . . . she manages much of the time merely to startle . . . her own fictional characters." Offers insights summarized from a variety of critics, then discusses "Parker's Back" as an example of her use of an incarnational or metaphorical method with spectacular results. Other authors discussed include Nathaniel Hawthorne, Edgar Allan Poe, Herman Melville, William Faulkner, John Hawkes, Bernard Malamud, and John Updike.

1056a   Meindl, Dieter. *American Fiction and the Metaphysics of the Grotesque.* Columbia: U of Missouri P, 1996. 12, 136, 162-67, 208-10.

Discusses how "the grotesque has empowered American stories, story cycles, and novels and generally has been conducive to both the continuity and the experimentalism of American fiction." Traces how the modernist grotesque is approached by a variety of authors, including O'Connor, of whom he states, "No study of the grotesque . . . can ignore the achievement of Flannery O'Connor." Examines O'Connor's "A Good Man Is Hard to Find," and sees it as a "blood-curdling example of [how] the modernist-grotesque can yield a decidedly positive, benign view of life." Comments on the "mental suffering and travail that activated the good" in the grandmother and her family. Then points out how O'Connor uses a sardonic authorial voice to signal a satirical use of the grotesque "aimed at middle-class tastes and values, American roadside civilization, and such assorted attitudes as jingoism, condescension towards African-Americans, and yammering about the bad times." Refers to Heidegger's "Letter on Humanism" and Jung's exploration of the unconscious in reference to The Misfit's motivations to commit senseless crimes.

1057   Mellard, James M. "Flannery O'Connor's *Others*: Freud, Lacan, and the Unconscious." *American Literature* 61.4 (1989): 625-43.

Notes that O'Connor has been among the most favorably received modern American authors. Asserts that part of this success may be attributed to O'Connor's successful efforts in telling readers how she wanted them to interpret her work. Declares that she was concerned that her work might be interpreted "otherwise," with Sigmund Freud being the most significant "other." Suggests that O'Connor feared that Freud's "methodology-- psychoanalysis--and what it entails--the unconscious," might displace theology as a path of spiritual orientation. Declares that O'Connor found a place for Freud's psychoanalytic unconscious within her theological views, and that yet another "other," the "other" of Lacanian theory, turns out to be a vindication for her. Offers a reading of "A View of the Woods" to illustrate how Jacques Lacan's theories are manifested "in ways crucial to understanding" the story. Focuses on O'Connor's use of the "double" or "mirror image" in the story. Contends that this use illustrates Lacan's theory of narcissism as seen in the "identificatory and/or aggressive relations" of Mary Fortune Pitts and the old man.

1058   Mellard, James M. "Framed in the Gaze: Haze, *Wise Blood*, and Lacanian Reading." *New Essays on Wise Blood*. Ed. Michael Kreyling. New York: Cambridge UP, 1995. 51-69.

Contends that although many critics have questioned the integrity of *Wise Blood*, when "read within the framework of the post-Freudian psychoanalytic theory of Jacque Lacan," the novel demonstrates that O'Connor's fictional instincts "are virtually flawless." Offers a Lacanian reading that illustrates the foundation for Hazel's characterization, explains details of the text, and "reveals the perfectly symmetrical structure of the narrative." Further, the author's Lacanian reading attempts to explain Hazel's pathology, track "the expressions of that pathology in his preoccupations with others," and show how many specific details of the novel "are more than merely stylistic or idiosyncratic." Provides an assessment of Hazel at the expense of other characters, especially Enoch Emery. Addresses questions such as, "Why does Hazel behave as he does?" "What Drives him?" and "What is the etiology of his pathology?" Discusses the role of eyesight, specifically "the function of the gaze," visual space, dream images, and "images of the eye that function as a lure or as a screen for the gaze." Concludes with an examination of ways "this modernist novel can speak to a postmodernist epoch," including how-- when read in modernist terms--it "offers 'symptomal' meanings."

1059   Mellard, James M. "Lacan and Faulkner: A Post-Freudian Analysis of Humor in the Fiction." *Faulkner & Humor: Faulkner and Yoknapatawpha 1984*. Ed. Doreen Fowler and Ann J. Abadie. Jackson: UP of Mississippi, 1986. 195-215.

Focuses on Faulkner's *Sanctuary*, emphasizing how Popeye may serve as a "paradigm for virtually every important character" in the novel and "perhaps of all Faulkner's questing characters throughout" his fiction. Offers a brief comparison between Popeye and O'Connor's The Misfit (from "A Good Man Is Hard to Find") suggesting that "he could be, as well, Flannery O'Connor's 'Misfit.'"

1060   Mellard, James M. "Reading `Landscape' in Literature." *Centennial Review* 40.3 (1996): 471-90.

Discusses "A View of the Woods" and *Wise Blood* as presenting "ironic landscapes." States that in O'Connor's fiction "often as not we detect a rather `naive' or `primitive' allegorization that reminds [one] of the origins of landscape painting outlined by [Kenneth] Clark." Suggests that she often uses one image of landscape ironically to displace another," while just as often she presents "landscape images that support, indeed even create an ironic vision within a character." Notes her use of landscape in "A View of the Woods" to portray how the "old man's notion of his own goodness and salvation is tragically wrong." Then, discusses the scene in *Wise Blood* in which Hazel Motes watches as the patrolman pushes his car down an embankment. Contends that this scene is "very complex in its significations," especially in how it forces Motes to understand that "he is a free-floating agent in empty space," whose eyes reflect "a world empty, inhuman, filled, if with anything, with emblems of death."

1061   Mellard, James M. "Tropologies of Space: Metaphoric and Metonymic Places in Literature." *Mississippi Quarterly* 45.2 (1992): 195-200.

Review essay of a collection of essays titled, *Where? Place in Recent North American Fiction*, edited by Karl-Heniz Westarp, and published by the Department of English of Aarhus University (Denmark) in *The Dolphin* 20 (Spring 1991). Argues that Westarp's essay on O'Connor "too readily" converts places into "metaphors and symbols," and that his analysis of "The Displaced Person" falls "to the all-too-easy metaphorical transformation of physical places into metaphysical themes or ideas."

1062   Melville, Annabelle M. "Biography as Church History: Some Contrasts Between the 1950s and the 1980s." *Catholic Library World* 56.1 (1984): 38-43.

Refers to Sally Fitzgerald's efforts to produce a biography of O'Connor as a "harbinger of the perennial blooming of biography as a benefactor of church history." Briefly reviews a presentation by Fitzgerald on March 8, 1984, at Bridgewater State College. States that Fitzgerald traced both the O'Connor family and Catholicism in Georgia "back to the days of John Carroll in the eighteenth century."

1063   Menendez, Albert J. Introduction. *The Catholic Novel: An Annotated Bibliography*. New York: Garland, 1988. ix-xix.

States that Flannery O'Connor is not included because she is best known as a writer of short stories which are outside the scope of the bibliography. Reports further that while "both of O'Connor's superb novels draw upon the fundamentalist Protestant heritage of her native Georgia," they are not included because they do not "deal with the Catholic subculture." Reports that the interpretation of O'Connor's writings "has become a virtual cottage industry of late."

1064   Menides, Laura Jehn. "John Huston's `Wise Blood' and the Myth of the Sacred Quest." *Literature/Film Quarterly* 9.4 (1981): 207-12.

Suggests that John Huston's film version of *Wise Blood* "acknowledges-- and also emphasizes and expands--the mythic qualities" of O'Connor's novel. States that while Huston remained "faithful to the spirit" of the book, he also introduced "a repertory of his own powerful visual effects, images which call forth startling associations with other art forms, such as painting and sculpture, as well as with other films." Asserts that Huston's images "reverberate in the mind, suggest patterns and repetitions in human behavior, and serve to place the experiences of the film where they are in the book, in the realm of the mythic." Compares Huston's *Wise Blood* to John Ford's *The Grapes of Wrath*, and notes similar scenes, and examines the heroes of each film. Focuses on the Madonna scene in Huston's film in which Sabbath Hawkes holds the shrunken mummy, which "graphically portrays the film's point: Mote's quest . . . for a sacred, not a secular savior." Discusses Huston's "links with the Oedipus myth that are barely hinted at in the novel," and differences in the automobile symbolism between the novel and movie.

1065   Méras, Phyllis. "Talking to Writers." *Pages: The World of Books, Writers, and Writing*. Ed. Matthew J. Bruccoli and C.E. Frazer Clark, Jr. Detroit: Gale Research, 1976. 156-71.

Offers recollections of interviews and personal impressions of a wide variety of literary figures in both Europe and in the United States, including Flannery O'Connor. States that two peacock feathers given to her by O'Connor and kept in a vase in her own home, always remind Meras of O'Connor's comment that "good writing should have a concrete approach to life." Describes her visit to Milledgeville in May, 1964, at which time she found O'Connor to be "frail, but filled with a radiant joy." Follows with a descriptive summary of the interview, including O'Connor's comments on the responsibility of "sensitive, Christian-oriented" writers; the importance--to O'Connor--of using situations from her own small community to inspire her writing; and her preference for writing short stories instead of novels.

1066   Merton, Thomas. "Flannery O'Connor--A Prose Elegy." *The Literary Essays of Thomas Merton*. Ed. Patrick Hart. New York: New Direction, 1981. 159-61.

Writing in memory of Flannery O'Connor, Merton reviews some of the more common themes of O'Connor's work and states, "I will write her name with honor, [and] with love for the great slashing innocence of that dry-eyed irony that could keep looking the South in the face without bleeding or even sobbing." Asserts that "the key word to Flannery's stories is `respect,'" which for her was a touchstone as she carefully examined the South's ambiguities and decay. Discusses the types of characters O'Connor developed in her works and the way she developed plots by pulling together all the "elements of unreason and letting them fly slowly and inexorably at one another." Concludes with the tribute, "when I read Flannery I don't think of Hemingway, or Katherine Anne Porter, or Sartre, but rather of someone like Sophocles. What more can be said of a writer?" [Rpt. in *The Book of Eulogies*. Ed. Phyllis Theroux. New York: Scribner, 1997. pp. 39-41; and in *Critical Essays on Flannery O'Connor*. Ed. Melvin Friedman and Beverly Clark. Boston: G.K. Hall, 1985. pp. 68-71.]

1067   Merton, Thomas. "The Other Side of Despair." *Women Writers of the Short Story*. Ed. Heather McClave. Englewood Cliffs, NJ: Prentice-Hall, 1980. 145-49.

Considers the "`good' and the `bad' people" in O'Connor's work to better appreciate her existentialist perspective. Examines the grandmother in "A Good Man Is Hard to Find" and Rayber in *The Violent Bear It Away*, and reports that O'Connor's "moral evaluations seem to be strangely scrambled. The good people are bad and the bad people tend to be less bad than they seem." Further, her crazy characters, while indeed crazy, "turn out to be governed by a strange kind of sanity." Sees "the mild, agnostic, and objective teacher" in *The Violent Bear It Away*, "not so much evil as pure void." States that it is through him that readers can better understand existentialism as a form of "passionate resistance against the positivist outlook." [Rpt. from *Critic* 24 (Oct.-Nov. 1965):12-23 and in Merton's *Mystics and Zen Masters*.]

1068   Meurs, Jos Van, and John Kidd. *Jungian Literary Criticism, 1920-1980: An Annotated, Critical Bibliography of Works in English*. Metuchen, NJ: Scarecrow, 1988. 341 (index), et passim.

Bibliography with annotations of Jungian criticism of O'Connor's works.

1069   Meyer, Alvis. "Hazel Motes--From Tree to Tree." *Flannery O'Connor Bulletin* 11 (1982): 36-42.

Suggests that "the dark gaze" of Hazel Motes not only "permeates" Flannery O'Connor's work and "colors" her vision, but can be seen in many of the fictional characters she created. Finds aspects of Motes's character in The Misfit, June Star, and John Wesley of "A Good Man Is Hard to Find"; Tom T. Shiftlet of "The Life You Save May Be Your Own"; General Tennessee Flintrock Sash of "A Late Encounter With the Enemy"; Mr. Head of "The Artificial Nigger"; Manley Pointer and Mrs. Hopewell of "Good Country People"; Tarwater of *The Violent Bear It Away*; and Mrs. Turpin of "Revelation." Refers to a wide variety of relevant comments by critics Preston M. Browning, Robert Drake, and Martha Stephens.

1070   Meyer, William E. "The American Religion of Vision." *Christian Century* 16 Nov. 1983: 1045-47.

Asserts that in modern American culture "the divine word has been usurped by the divine vision." Offers quotations from a variety of American authors that describe "the elevation of vision over verbalization," including Ralph Waldo Emerson, William Bradford, Edward Taylor, Walt Whitman, Ernest Hemingway, Henry James, F. Scott Fitzgerald, Thomas Wolfe, and Flannery O'Connor. Focuses on O'Connor's views and states that it is understandable that she would "feel a real rapport with the Protestant fundamentalists about whom she writes: she has intuited that both religious traditions face a foe of unbelievably tremendous and subtle power in the American religion of vision." Discusses how she confronted Catholicism's "veneration for the sacred image" and how this met "its match in the American iconization of all visible things." Argues that this "apotheosis of vision" was frustrating to O'Connor "precisely because of the confusion surrounding, and the ultimate takeover of, the American religion of vision."

1071   Meyer, William E.H., Jr. "American Literature: The Aesthetics of Solitude." *University of Windsor Review* 22.2 (1989): 22-44.

Defines "American literature," and discusses how its origins and background encouraged so many American authors to use "solitary or lonely characters." Includes discussion of a wide variety of authors and works, including O'Connor's emphasis on vision and seeing through her "solitary star" in *Wise Blood*, Hazel Motes.

1072   Meyer, William E.H., Jr. "Edwards, Emerson and Beyond: The
        Hypervisual American Great Awakening." *Massachusetts Studies in
        English* 10 (Spring 1985): 24-45.

        Relies upon literary and historical documents to outline how the "New-
        World Great Awakening" manifested itself during "each `revival' of
        American self-consciousness." Contends that this event was based upon
        "the conviction that reality is essentially visual, not verbal or even
        `logical.'" Includes a brief discussion of how O'Connor's Hazel Motes, "the
        `grotesque saint' and blasphemous `revivalist'" of *Wise Blood*, symbolizes
        America's shift "from Biblical to visual truth." Suggests that it is for this
        reason that Motes "not only murders his `double' as a false prophet
        because the latter really does . . . `believe in Jesus,'" but also "shouts out
        in agony of `surprising conversion': `What you see is the truth! . . . I've
        seen the only truth there is!'"

1073   Meyer, William E.[H.], Jr. "Flannery O'Connor's `Two Sets of Eyes.'"
        Southern Studies 25.3 (1986): 284-94.

        As background, argues that "the literary criticism in America needs to be
        profoundly changed" because "the eye has usurped the place of the ear."
        Asserts that "we must recognize that our authors, our `prophets' and `word-
        smiths,' are engaged in a tremendous struggle, both within themselves and
        against New World norms, to strike a balance between the `tyrannous eye'
        and the European ear or traditional word." Suggests that O'Connor
        recognized this dilemma as a tension between "the `blind eye' of faith" and
        "Emersonian/American hypervisualization." Claims that this tension
        "creates the essence of her work and provides the key to understanding her
        grotesquerie, her ironies and revelations of hypocrisies, and her devilish
        `grace.'" Discusses groupings of O'Connor's characters: "`Displaced'
        Visionaries" (Mr. Guizac in "The Displaced Person," The Misfit in "A
        Good Man Is Hard to Find," and Hazel Motes in *Wise Blood*); "Children
        of the Sight-Faith" (Harry Ashfield in "The River" and the twelve-year-old
        girl in "A Temple of the Holy Ghost"); "Judgmental Female Observers"
        (Mrs. Flood in *Wise Blood*, Ruby Turpin in "Revelation," and Mrs.
        Shortley in "The Displaced Person"); and "Intellectual Eyeballs" (Rayber
        in *The Violent Bear It Away*, Sheppard in "The Lame Shall Enter First,"
        and Hulga in "Good Country People").

1074   Meyer, William E.H., Jr. "From *The Sun Also Rises* to *High Noon*: The
        Hypervisual Great Awakening in American Literature and Film." *Cithara*
        32.1 (1992): 39-59.

Argues that "the *aesthetic* sense is the primary determiner of culture," and that "the New World is dominated by the *hypervisual* impulse, while the Old World is controlled by the *hyperverbal* ideal." Uses examples from American literature and film "to reveal this assumption at work," including Hazel Motes's emphasis on sight in O'Connor's *Wise Blood.*

1075   Meyer, William E.H., Jr. "Melville and O'Connor: The Hypervisual Crisis." *Stanford Literature Review* 4.2 (1987): 211-29.

Compares *Moby-Dick* to *Wise Blood.* Considers other O'Connor short stories and follows the author's thesis that these works are not "amenable to Old-World methods of literary criticism."

1076   Meyers, Bertrande. "Four Stories of Flannery O'Connor." *Gleanings, Sister Bertrande Meyers, Daughter of Charity: An Anthology of Published Articles and Addresses.* Ed. Beatrice Brown. Hicksville, NY: Exposition, 1976. 29-48.

Admits that O'Connor's works are "not easy reading unless one is satisfied with the casual horror-story approach," and expresses hope that "the more thoughtful reader" will discern how she "uses her brilliant gifts for a specific purpose based on a particular plan." Offers quotations from O'Connor's essay "The Fiction Writer and His Country" to define her objectives and purpose, and uses this framework to discuss and offer interpretive readings of "The Partridge Festival," "The Comforts of Home," "The Enduring Chill," and "A View of the Woods." Reprint from *Thought* 37 (1962): 410-26.

1077   Meyers, Bertrande. "Sister Bertrande Meyers' Contribution to `Flannery O'Connor - A Tribute.'" *Gleanings, Sister Bertrande Meyers, Daughter of Charity: An Anthology of Published Articles and Addresses.* Ed. Beatrice Brown. Hicksville, NY: Exposition, 1976. 49-53.

Offers a tribute to O'Connor, noting that she had friends and foes alike. Sees her as "not a predominant figure, but one whose prominence was heightened by the controversial opinions aroused by her writings." Suggests that "both foe and friend missed the point and purpose" of her "`message' until she herself supplied the key in her essay, `The Fiction Writer and His Country.'" Suggests that her statements in this essay were taken by her friends and fair critics, "at face value and used as a sort of Rosetta stone after 1957."

1078   Michaels, J. Ramsey. "Images of Grace in Flannery O'Connor's Strong Women." *Daughters of Sarah* 16.1 (1990): 27-30.

Examines several "strong women" characters who appear in O'Connor's stories and states that they "could well be described as feminists before their time." Asserts that O'Connor's strong women are typically "widows left with the responsibility of running a farm in rural Georgia or Tennessee . . . self-sufficient women, devoted firmly to a work ethic, but not particularly religious." Characters discussed include Hulga Hopewell, Mary Grace, Mrs. Turpin, Mrs. May, Mrs. McIntyre, Mrs. Cope, and three "sidekick" characters or "confidantes": Mrs. Shortley, Mrs. Greenleaf, and Mrs. Pritchett. Discusses the nature and "individual peculiarities" of the various characters. Finds Mrs. Turpin of "Revelation" different from the others in that she is not a widow, has "no other woman as her partner or foil," and "fulfills the roles of both Mrs. McIntyre and Mrs. Shortley, [and] of Mrs. May and Mrs. Greenleaf." Discusses male protagonists, Hazel Motes and Francis Marion Tarwater, and suggests that "what makes the two novels work is that these two young men are *not* strong enough to resist the call of God." Reminds readers that the strongest men in many of O'Connor's stories are often dead, and while they still exert influence on other characters, her world "is to a considerable degree a woman's world." Argues that O'Connor's "most profound feminist short story" is "A Temple of the Holy Ghost."

1079   Michaels, J. Ramsey. "'The Oldest Nun at the Sisters of Mercy': O'Connor's Saints and Martyrs." *Flannery O'Connor Bulletin* 13 (1984): 80-86.

Explores the significance of O'Connor's choice to name "'the oldest nun at the Sisters of Mercy,'" Sister Perpetua in her short story "A Temple of the Holy Ghost." Reminds readers of the advice the nun gave, outlines her namesake's place in Catholic tradition--based upon the document *The Martyrdom of Perpetua and Felicitas*--and, ties the historical Sister Perpetua to O'Connor's character. Focuses on the Perpetua's visions: fighting beasts, changing sex and becoming a man, and encountering a dragon that one must fight. Follows with a discussion of "the sense of vocation as disciple or prophet or martyr" in *The Violent Bear It Away*. Ties Mason Tarwater to an early Christian martyr, Polycarp--based upon the *Martyrdom of Polycarp*--and, concludes that through O'Connor's characters, the saints and martyrs of the past are "'still speaking.'"

1080   Middleton, David L. "Meaning Through Form: A Study of Metaphorical Structure in Flannery O'Connor's *Wise Blood*." *Texas Review* 5.1-2 (1984): 47-57.

Argues that an examination of O'Connor's fiction "in terms of its southern regional significance" defines her concerns "as rather narrowly provincial." Suggests that *Wise Blood* "is an inward looking novel, more nearly concerned with personal than with regional meaning." Contends that before Hazel Motes "can see himself truly in relation to his God," he must "realize what kind of creature he is; he must come to know himself in a religiously absolute sense." Maintains that the best way to grasp the meanings O'Connor intended is by analyzing the novel's form and Hazel's "complementary character," Enoch Emory. Claims that O'Connor uses these two characters to dramatize "the opposite and awesome spiritual possibilities open to man . . . Enoch ultimately comes to represent a `freak' or grotesque character in the condition of damnation, Haze a `whole man' in the state of grace." Declares that the narrative construction of the novel "is neatly symmetrical" and is informed by the theological view of Creation as a Great Chain, with humankind in the middle. Examines the novel's structural parallelism and its use of characters in opposition. Concludes that O'Connor need not have worried that she would be classified as simply another regional Southern writer: "when examined in relation to the Chain of Being, *Wise Blood* is an intelligently conceived and tightly constructed first novel that clearly places Flannery O'Connor not in a local or regional but in a universal brotherhood of writers, including Shakespeare, Dante, and even Aristotle."

1081   Middleton, Robert. "Humorous American Literature and the Film: A Bibliography." *Studies in American Humor* ns 4.3 (1985): 183-91.

A checklist of articles and essays "relevant to the study of humorous American literature which has been filmed." Focuses upon those items which "are funny in themselves and intended to generate a laughing response in readers, as well as selections which are more broadly comic in theme and form." Includes O'Connor among the 20 authors featured, listing six references to reviews and discussions of John Huston's film of O'Connor's *Wise Blood*.

1082   Milder, Robert. "The Protestantism of Flannery O'Connor." *Southern Review* 11.4 (1975): 802-19.

Reviews articles and essays in *Mystery and Manners* in an attempt to "systematize" O'Connor's theory of fiction and evaluate her writings about Protestants. Concludes that O'Connor's vision insisted "on the corruption of all secular works and the divisiveness and irresistibility of grace" and is "virtually indistinguishable from the Fundamentalist Protestantism of the South." Suggests that O'Connor focused even more on *how* the Fundamentalist believed: "Armed only with the Bible and his own invincible faith, the Fundamentalist went forward to a life of incessant battle against the temptations of the world." Argues that although O'Connor often caricatured characters such as her Protestant backwoods prophets, she was always "inexorably drawn back to them by the sheer intensity of her belief."

1083   Mills, Jerry Leath. "Cormac McCarthy." *Contemporary Fiction Writers of the South: A Bio-Bibliographical Sourcebook.* Ed. Joseph M. Flora and Robert Bain. Westport, CT: Greenwood, 1993. 286-94.

Offers a biographical sketch of Cormac McCarthy, an outline of his themes, and examines of his literary art "in the context of influence and traditions in Southern fiction, especially traditions of the Gothic and the grotesque." Notes that both McCarthy and O'Connor "experienced a Roman Catholic childhood in the Protestant South." Offers brief comments on O'Connor's influence on McCarthy's work, including: how, in both, "there seems to lie a belief in the objective existence of evil, an existence not amenable to clarification by psychology or correction by social means." Refers to, in the discussion of ties with O'Connor, McCarthy's *Child of God* (1984), *Outer Dark* (1968) and *Suttree* (1986), and Joseph Conrad's *Victory* (1915).

1084   Mills, Jerry Leath. "Samburan Outside of Toomsboro: Conrad's Influence on `A Good Man Is Hard to Find.'" *South Atlantic Quarterly* 84.2 (1985): 186-96.

States that O'Connor admired Joseph Conrad and read "just about everything he wrote," which in turn, affected her work "in extensive and felicitous ways." Lists "affinities in the works of the two" and speculates that Conrad's structure, setting, and conception of characters in his novel *Victory* (1915) appears to have influenced O'Connor as she wrote her most "Conradian story, `A Good Man Is Hard to Find.'"

1085   Mills, William. "Risking the Bait: John William Corrington, 1932-1988." *Southern Review* 25.3 (1989): 586-94.

Offers a biographical sketch and a discussion of Corrington's literary interests and career. Examines his poetry and each of his novels and argues that "the best of Corrington's work can compare" to that of Flannery O'Connor, William Faulkner, and Ernest Hemingway. Notes how his "The Actes and Monuments" seems to have striking similarities to O'Connor's "A Good Man Is Hard to Find."

1086   Ming, Zhong. "Designed Shock and Grotesquerie: The Form of Flannery O'Connor's Fiction." *Flannery O'Connor Bulletin* 17 (1988): 51-61.

Observes that O'Connor discards the use of "cause-effect links" in her fiction and favors instead "the more illusive, contingent form that enables her to exploit the diverse accidents of life." Asserts that this method is most appropriate to "transmit her theological themes and make her works aesthetically enjoyable." Argues that her "fictional organization" falls into the categories of either "qualitative progression" or "repetitive form." Discusses each of the two concepts, offers readings with examples--"A Circle in the Fire" for the first, and *The Violent Bear It Away* for the second--and, suggests that the most appropriate generic category for *Wise Blood* is that of the "picaresque novel." Concludes that while "O'Connor owes much of her success to her 'prophetic vision,' she owes just as much, or even more, to her skillful handling of the material." Believes that her unique way of handling the incidents, of accumulating power for the final impact through structural repetitions, and of strategically placing the central action deserves to be called "the O'Connor Technique."

1087   Mitchell, Garry. "Priest Recalls O'Connor and the Georgia Days." *Associated Press Release for Sunday, May 5, 1985*, 1985. 2 pp.

Reports recollections of O'Connor by James McCown, a 74-year old Jesuit priest at Spring Hill College in Mobile, Alabama. McCown remarks, "'Flannery was anything but snooty . . . [she] was a person intensely interested in everybody she met--white or black, Catholic or Protestant, rich or poor, educated or uneducated. She was just not effusive--not at all.'" Quotes McCown as saying, "'I became sort of a spiritual confidant. She wrote me about some problems she was having, mostly about prayer, temptation of the flesh and things like that. Her moral problems were those of a 16-year-old convent girl . . . I think writing was a religious expression on her part.'" Comments on the fact that he does not see himself reflected in the several priest figures in O'Connor's stories. Recounts the time that he suggested that she consider Catholic polemical writing: "Her answer was instant and tart, 'That ain't my dish of tea.' And I learned a lesson about integrity in art."

1088   Moddelmog, Debra A. "Reading Myths and Mythemes After Freud: From Oedipal Incest to Oedipal Insight." *Readers and Mythic Signs: The Oedipus Myth in Twentieth-Century Fiction*. Carbondale: Southern Illinois UP, 1993. 86-104.

Discusses psychological fiction by Flannery O'Connor, Max Frisch, and Albert Moravia. Examines "the appropriation of the Oedipus myth by psychoanalysis and the consequences of that appropriation . . . for those reading and writing after Sigmund Freud." States that all three writers depart from Freud's view of the Oedipus myth "by refusing to privilege the child's attraction to a parent." Instead, for each of these writers, "the power of a desire to overwhelm and control an individual takes precedence over the origin of the desire." Suggests that their use of the self-blinding mytheme "helps to support the view that contemporary society has moved away from Freud's reading of the myth as a paradigm for childhood development." Argues that "instead of presenting blindness as punishment for incest . . . these three writers use it to confirm the Sophoclean point that the blind man can see more clearly than the man with perfect vision . . . lack of sight represents insight."

1089   Mogen, David. "Frontier Myth and American Gothic." *Genre* 14 (Fall 1981): 329-46.

Discusses the "Gothic atmosphere of our native frontier literature," tracing its development through examination of works by a variety of American writers. Includes passing references to O'Connor. Discusses how Gothic frontier narratives "developed into the complex psychological metaphor" employed by Hawthorne, Poe, and Melville, and have, in turn, influenced a number of modern American writers, including O'Connor.

1090   Moirai, Catherine Risingflame. Rev. of *The Habit of Being: Letters of Flannery O'Connor*, ed. Sally Fitzgerald. *Feminary* 12.1 (1982): 129-46.

Uses the framework of a review of *The Habit of Being*, to discuss memories of attending church with Flannery O'Connor in Milledgeville, Georgia during the late 1950s. Considers "similarities" between their two lives and offers excerpts of letters to focus attention on a wide variety of O'Connor-related topics: O'Connor's perspective on recognizing freaks; her self-concept; her confinement--due to her Lupus--to Milledgeville, and her dependent relationship with her mother; her views on racial justice and integration (including the integration of the public library and Catholic Church in Milledgeville); how many of her views were framed by, and conformed to, the traditional Southern views found in Milledgeville; and her ambivalent feelings toward "her own sex." Refers to Sally Fitzgerald's work and the general opinion of O'Connor and her work by members of the Milledgeville community. Concludes with a personal observation that the letters in *The Habit of Being* made her think "of what `home' in the patriarchy meant . . . : the loneliness, the repression, the internal and external violence . . . [and] how hard it is to leave home emotionally, even if we can move away physically."

1091   Monroe, William F. "Bringing the Script to Life: The Case of Flannery O'Connor." *Journal of Medical Humanities* 15.2 (1994): 101-11.

Contends that while "O'Connor's world might seem an unlikely theater in which to celebrate health and vitality," her purpose in writing was "not to condemn this diseased world of broken minds and bodies, but to give it life and death and meaning." Offers details regarding O'Connor's childhood, education, and family; then, describes her battle with Lupus as reflected in her fiction and letters. Suggests that the "surreal sequence of physical grotesques, degenerate relationships, and bestial characters" in *Wise Blood* reflects her fascination at the time with "the notion of escaping the world and the flesh by means of ascetic denial and the mortification of the body." Follows with an explication of "Parker's Back," finding in it an "affirmation of physical health and wholeness." Concludes that, at the end of her life, O'Connor "resisted the impulse to glorify confinement or to revel in disease as a source of insight." Relates how her genius lay in her "ability to see value, even surpassing goodness, in the physically damaged or diseased, the morally reprobate and vainglorious, [and even] in the meanest human form," to affirm "the more complex and profound goodness of the body, not as a locus of desire and gratification, a site of political contestation and negotiation, or a commodity for consumption-- but as an embodied symbol, a fleshy-and-bloodied icon, an incarnation of suffering and redemption."

1092   Monroe, William F. "Flannery O'Connor and the Celebration of Embodiment." *The Good Body: Asceticism in Contemporary Culture.* Ed. Mary G. Winkler and Letha B. Cole. New Haven, CT: Yale UP, 1994. 171-88.

Suggests that while many readers focus on O'Connor's interest in spiritual matters, her work also displays "an abiding concern with corporeality and embodiment: tastes, colors, [and] sensations." Contends that O'Connor's fiction often explores answers to the rhetorical question, "What is a morally desirable attitude toward the body?" Follows O'Connor's "artistic journey," from her first novel (*Wise Blood*) in which she "is tempted to turn to purification and ascetic denial as a means of escaping the world's `poisonous looks' and `evil smiles'," to "Parker's Back" her last story, in which she demonstrates that she "has turned unmistakably toward a motif of embodiment, a celebration of physicality and even carnality." Explicates and offers detailed discussions of these two works, demonstrating how O'Connor "abandons the penitential way, the gnostic way of negation, dualism and renunciation." Uses this discussion to decipher "clues to the varieties of asceticism now permeating late twentieth-century culture." Follows with a close look at O'Connor's battle with Lupus. Cites a wide variety of authors and scholars: Judith Andre,

Kenneth Burke, Caroline Walker Bynum, Hans Jonas, Ihab Hassan, Harold Bloom, Paul Zweig, Cleanth Brooks, John Desmond, Elaine Pagels, Rosemary Radford Ruether, Elizabeth Cady Stanton, Gertrude Stein, James E. Miller, Frederick Asals, John Stone, Regina Cline O'Connor, Eudora Welty, Sally Fitzgerald, and Brian Abel Ragen.

1093   Monroe, W[illiam] F. "Flannery O'Connor's Sacramental Icon: `The Artificial Nigger.'" *South Central Review* 1.4 (1984): 64-81.

Refers to difficulties in teaching O'Connor's "The Artificial Nigger," focusing on her use of the word "nigger." Contends that O'Connor is not a didactic writer, but a rhetorical one: "she wants to move us through an experience rather than teach us a proposition." Argues that "The Artificial Nigger" offers a critique of "the propositional and abstract propensities of both secular rationalism and iconoclastic Christian fundamentalism." Claims that O'Connor uses linguistic and dramatic means to link "both of these knowledge-centered ideologies, these `gnostic religions,' with racism and with spiritual pride." Explicates the story and concludes with the suggestion that she "moves us . . . to challenge our secular rationalism as well as our tendencies to only look within natural selves, to depend on what we have already learned and therefore `know' about."

1093a   Monroe, William F. "The `Mountain on the Landscape' of Flannery O'Connor." *Chronicle of Higher Education: The Chronicle Review* (15 Dec. 2000): B14, B16.

Considers how Flannery O'Connor's imagination may have been influenced by the presence of Central State Hospital, "the world's largest insane asylum," in her hometown of Milledgeville, Georgia. Suggests that she "maintained a sympathetic awareness of the social, political, and cultural function" of the Hospital and points to "explicit references to an asylum" in *The Violent Bear It Away*, "The Partridge Festival," and "Revelation." Considers O'Connor's views of evil and maladjusted individuals, then ties these views to societal ostracism and "prisons as warehouses for society's misfits and mistakes."

1094   Monteiro, George. "The Great American Hunt in Flannery O'Connor's `The Turkey.'" *Explicator* 51.2 (1993): 118-21.

Suggests that "The Turkey," like "The Lame Shall Enter First" and "Parker's Back," "is carefully plotted to reveal the spiritual peculiarities" of its central character. Comments that while the "outward action" in the story is "deceptively simple and direct" its "true drama . . . plays itself out in the boy's mind, a drama in which he does or does not discover God, does or does not experience grace, and performs a charitable act that may or may not be truly an act of charity." Outlines the plot and discusses how the story points toward some of O'Connor's religious concerns, brings other "hunt stories" to mind (such as Herman Melville's *Moby-Dick* and stories by Thomas Bangs Thorpe), and deals with "man's nature." Concludes that while it may be difficult to fully understand O'Connor's true meaning for the story, the theft of the turkey may have been the one event that would bring Ruller to confront God's grace and presence.

1095 Montgomery, Marion. "Afterword: Looking Before and After." *The Men I Have Chosen for Fathers: Literary and Philosophical Passages.* Columbia: U of Missouri P, 1990. 232-38.

Reflects on Richard Weaver's essay "Up From Liberalism," published in *Modern Age*. Contains only passing reference to O'Connor as a Southern writer who was concerned with many of the same issues.

1096 Montgomery, Marion. "The Artist as `A Very Doubtful Jacob': A Reflection on Hawthorne and O'Connor." *Southern Quarterly* 16.2 (1978): 95-104.

Discusses Nathaniel Hawthorne's puritan heritage and suggests that he "found himself possessed of a tradition" which he honored but at the same time from which he "found something vital . . . excluded." This missing "something" Montgomery regards as the ability to see humanity and nature differently. As a result, Hawthorne was compelled "to move more cautiously, out of an uncertainty about his calling such as we do not find in Flannery O'Connor." Concludes that Hawthorne's "uncertainties about himself as prophetic poet" were proper for a Protestant, as such uncertainty might be the voice of the Devil; "When the Protestant hears what he supposes to be the voice of the Lord, he follows it" regardless. Catholics, however, believe such voices come "from the Devil unless it is in accordance with the teaching of the Church." Mentions Eric Gill's "Art and Prudence" and St. Thomas Aquinas.

1097 Montgomery, Marion. "Cleanth Brooks and the Life in Art." *The Men I Have Chosen for Fathers: Literary and Philosophical Passages.* Columbia: U of Missouri P, 1990. 39-51.

Discusses Cleanth Brooks's works, focusing on *William Faulkner: First Encounters* (1983), which may prove "helpful in the attempt to recover literature as a civilized pleasure rather than a professional specialty."

Refers to the concern of C.S. Lewis and Brooks that "in the academy since World War II . . . there has tended to be a crippling separation of literature from life." Offers observations on the current state of teaching literature, attempts to clarify Brooks's "Southernness" in relation to characterizations of him "as a `New Critic,'" and refers to his *Understanding Poetry*, coauthored with Warren. Examines O'Connor's reviews collected in *The Presence of Grace and Other Book Review by Flannery O'Connor*. Suggests that the reader sees in this work a confirmation of O'Connor's "understanding of art and history as healthful to that body of which she is a member." States that Lowell "could not come to terms with his calling as poet," and refers to Lowell, John Berryman, Randall Jarrell, Delmore Schwartz, and Theodore Roethke as "a second `Lost Generation'" who "were burdened by discovering themselves most immediately heirs of Henry Adams." Sees O'Connor as sharing with these poets the same teachers, but reaching a different understanding of what they were saying concerning "life's relation to art." Argues that these poets confused themselves with God and "the consequences of the error in the poet is that pathetic self-consumption toward nothingness." Concludes that the "sad incompleteness" of their works "is why it is important to value art as praised and practiced by Cleanth Brooks and Flannery O'Connor."

1098   Montgomery, Marion. "Eric Voegelin as Prophetic Philosopher." *Southern Review* 24.1 (1988): 115-33.

Discusses the philosophy of Voeglin and notes how his many arguments relate to the writings of T.S. Eliot, Ezra Pound, and other writers, most especially O'Connor. Voegelin's "Quod Deus dicitur" is analyzed, as well as O'Connor's review of Voegelin's work *Order and History*. Says O'Connor and Voegelin often share as a focus St. Thomas Aquinas, and that neither the "poet" (as he calls O'Connor) nor the philosopher were trying to "prove" anything about Christianity with their writings. [Rpt. in *The Men I Have Chosen for Fathers: Literary and Philosophical Passages* (Columbia: U of Missouri P, 1990, 194-212).]

1099   Montgomery, Marion. "Flannery O'Connor and Onnie Jay Holy and the Trouble With You Innerleckshuls." *Studies in the Literary Imagination* 20.2 (1987): 67-76.

Considers Hulga, The Misfit, Hazel Motes, Onnie Jay Holy, and other characters in relation to O'Connor's theme of showing the "devastating effect of mercy upon seemingly backwoods gnostics." Notes that while some might see her as anti-intellectual, O'Connor's true intent is to show readers that their "dominant weakness is a pride of intellect."

1100   Montgomery, Marion. "Flannery O'Connor and the Jansenist Problem in Fiction." *Southern Review* 14.3 (1978): 438-48.

Observes that O'Connor's critics often detect a Jansenist taint in her work, with some, such as Warren Coffey, outraged over the possibility of the writer "corrupting those who are not able to understand what he is doing." Outlines certain defense positions, but is concerned with "consider[ing] the conflict necessary to the art of fiction as dividing the question of Jansenism in Miss O'Connor herself." Relates the Kierkegaardian dilemma of either/or and his metaphor of Job to an analysis of Hazel Motes. The argument centers on O'Connor's acceptance of "free will" and her absorption in the fiction with "inexorable" grace, a position which seems heretically Jansenist--somewhere between "John Calvin . . . and Rome." The problem, Montgomery says, is to acknowledge a relationship between the two worlds without sacrificing one to the other. Suggests that "free will" is not one but many wills at conflict with each other, thus arguing against determinacy. But concludes that in fiction, for the sake of dramatic movement, one will must come to dominate.

1101   Montgomery, Marion. "Flannery O'Connor, Eric Voegelin, and the Question That Lies Between." *Modern Age* 22.2 (1978): 133-43.

Comments on O'Connor's interest in Voegelin's *Order and History*, as her reviews and "heavy markings" in the volumes of her library attest. Says Voegelin's fourth volume brings up questions that are pivotal both for O'Connor and Voegelin, and also for other great thinkers--St. Paul, Plato, Heidegger, Edgar Allan Poe, Nathaniel Hawthorne, T.S. Eliot, and Sartre. Explores aspects of the spiritual progression of humanity and relates O'Connor's works to the questions raised by these observations.

1102   Montgomery, Marion. "Flannery O'Connor: Realist of Distances." *Realist of Distances: Flannery O'Connor Revisited*. Ed. Karl-Heinz Westarp and Jan Nordby Gretlund. Aarhus (Denmark): Aarhus UP, 1987. 227-35.

Notes that "one of the most popular critical assumptions in our century," especially among intellectuals, is that the realist's art is incompatible with that of a spiritual vision. Explores "why our unreal modernist world should inherit and treasure this disease of the intellect" and how Flannery O'Connor recognized and addressed it. Describes how O'Connor "argues for a reassociation of sensibilities that goes much deeper than literary categories," and insists that "the artist's primary responsibility is to the thing he makes." Argues that, for O'Connor, "reason and imagination are complementary aspects of a fundamental gift--namely, *being, existence* itself." Describes her Thomism and how her "mutual accommodation of reason and imagination" relate to her comment that "`art is reason in making.'" Then, addresses O'Connor's "vision of community" and summarizes her position regarding "the necessary responsibility of the artist." Refers to Jacques Maritain's *Art and Scholasticism*, Saint Thomas Aquinas, Dante, John Milton's *Lycidas*, Cardinal Spellman's novel *The Foundling*, J.R.R. Tolkien, Gerard Manley Hopkins, and John Donne.

1103   Montgomery, Marion. "Flannery O'Connor's Sacramental Vision." *This World* 4 (Winter 1983): 119-28.

Asserts that "one of the most popular critical assumptions in our century [is] that the realist's art is incompatible with a spiritual vision . . . [and that] an artist professing an orthodox Christian vision cannot adequately deal with the `real world.'" Refers to this assumption as a "disease of the intellect" which must be examined when considering Flannery O'Connor. Argues that O'Connor urged readers to return to a larger reality as she found evidence of a "reduction of reality in our separating *reason* from *imagination, judgement* from *vision*, and . . . *nature* from *grace.*" States that O'Connor is a realist and "the epithet *realist of distances* is one she embraces directly out of her fundamental Thomism. Argues that Jacques Maritain's *Art and Scholasticism* is "the primary source this side of Saint Thomas's own work for anyone exploring Miss O'Connor's aesthetic vision." Suggests that "the anagogical, the level of grace in relation to nature, is the very center of her dramatic concern." Urges that the reader "recognize Aristotelian dimensions" in her work. Examines O'Connor's views on "the Catholic writer's responsibility"; her belief "that what is good in itself glorifies God"; and her approach to "questions of reality with a piety toward creation" as reflected in her artistic work. Claims that O'Connor's faith "that existence has meaning, however deep the mysteries of existence," enables her to respond to the world by imitating "its creative activity, under the guidance of reason." Compares O'Connor to Swift and James Joyce, and claims that "in engaging in the particular" her vision coincides with that of Gerard Manley Hopkins. Concludes that what O'Connor urges as the artist's responsibility is that he must "believe, and look where you will--so long as the actions of nature are not violated by the actions of art; so long as one sees clearly; so long as one does not distort his seeing by the arrogation of final judgement or by the presumption of rejecting the complexity of existence in which the mysteries of good and evil are in contention." [Rpt. in *The Men I Have Chosen for Fathers* (Columbia: U of Missouri P, 1990, 28-38).]

1104   Montgomery, Marion. "Flannery O'Connor's Shocking Manners." *Modern Age* 21.4 (1977): 407-13.

Examines the influence upon O'Connor of the South's traditional hospitality "with its elaborate formalities called manners." Suggests that when the reader compares The Misfit's manners against his actions in "A Good Man Is Hard to Find," it is evident that O'Connor "is very deliberately revealing a process of decay in community." Comments on "Faulkner's very careful use of terms of address . . . [to] reveal both the degree to which manners have decayed in the South between Faulkner's time and Flannery O'Connor's and to show additionally a heightened concern for manners as they relate to a spiritual dimension in Miss O'Connor's thinking." Discusses Faulkner's "A Rose for Emily," the influence of the Civil War on the South, the role of the "prophetic writer," and O'Connor's *Wise Blood.*

1105   Montgomery, Marion. "Grace: A Tricky Fictional Agent." *Flannery O'Connor Bulletin* 9 (1980): 19-29.

Comments that "it is a daring adventure for the poet to engage the agency of grace in dramatic art," and suggests that the consideration of grace in O'Connor's fiction is not simply an aesthetic problem. Compares O'Connor's use of grace to that of Edgar Allan Poe, Nathaniel Hawthorne, Nathanael West, and Sophocles. Remarks that O'Connor's use of grace is unusual in that there is "not simply an intrusion of grace at a crucial moment but a constantly active presence waiting the protagonist's responses." Contends that because O'Connor "insists upon the reality of the transcendent as the source of her imitational art," she makes the "problem" more difficult for contemporary readers. Argues that "the dimension of prophecy" in O'Connor's fiction, lies in how she recalls readers to "'known but forgotten truths' by the dramatic action" in her fiction. Relates that readers "cannot, it seems, read her fiction closely and not be engaged by the metaphyscial dimensions of her art." Refers to comments by John Hawkes that O'Connor "is on the Devil's side," and by Oscar Cargill on "her use of 'fallen nature'" as "a species of 'naturalism.'" Mentions Eric Voegelin's exploration of intellectual history; Jacques Maritain's view of "the displacement of the spiritual by the intellect"; and applications of these views as they relate to The Misfit in "A Good Man Is Hard to Find."

1106   Montgomery, Marion. "Imagination and the Violent Assault Upon Virtue." *Modern Age* 27.2 (1983): 120-31.

Includes a lengthy discussion of The Misfit from O'Connor's "A Good Man Is Hard to Find," focusing on The Misfit's use of violence "practiced in the name of social progress out of deterministic premises."

1107   Montgomery, Marion. "In Defense of Evil." *The Men I Have Chosen for Fathers: Literary and Philosophical Passages*. Columbia: U of Missouri P, 1990. 9-27.

Uses quotations from O'Connor to support arguments that "art . . . bears an appreciable relation to reality beyond itself." Compares differences between the "visions radiated by the God-haunted" and "man-haunted" Southern writers, and argues that the Southern writer "is misunderstood by that postnaturalist mind, which is so heavily at home in the academy, particularly by those who see literature as a sector of our intellectual estate to be seized by the pseudosciences of sociology and psychology and turned to social and political ends." Examines the Southern writer's approach to reality, his "version of community" and "sense of place," his suspicion "of any appeal to Progress as substitute for a profound technological object," and his interest in "this problem of evil in man." Refers to Faulkner and a variety of other Southern writers in passing, and examines the concept of human evil in Richard Weaver's *Ideas Have Consequences*, Hannah Arendt's *The Life of the Mind*, Donald Campbell's remarks to fellow psychologists, and Walter Bern's 1979 article on evil in *Harper's*. Closes with the allegation that it "is only through a blinding pride . . . that we are able to deny our kinship to such arresting figurings of man as Miss O'Connor's Misfit." Concludes that by learning from the Southern writer, we--misfits all--are more fully able to participate in community, "the living body of humanity."

1108   Montgomery, Marion. *The Men I Have Chosen for Fathers: Literary and Philosophical Passages*. Columbia: U of Missouri P, 1990. 9-51, 194-212, 232-38.

Selections from the author's essays published over the past twenty-five years, which have been "somewhat" revised. States that the central theme "holding these pieces together" is his belief "that we are each born provincial, but with gifts of being sufficient to become regional." Offers six essays related to O'Connor, each of which has been abstracted under the original article citation: "In Defense of Evil"; "Flannery O'Connor's Sacramental Vision"; "Cleanth Brooks and the Life in Art"; "Solzhenitsyn as Southerner"; "Eric Voegelin as Prophetic Philosopher"; and "Afterword: Looking Before and After."

1109   Montgomery, Marion. "Of Cloaks and Hats and Doublings in Poe and Flannery O'Connor." *South Carolina Review* 11.1 (1978): 60-69.

Examines the use of the "double" by Poe and O'Connor. Suggests that "imaginistic details are of crucial importance" to her because "they reveal the presence of an external world to the character, a world which Poe is at pains always to deny." Argues that, unlike Poe, O'Connor does more than just "[stir] a reader to a fleeting emotional horror." Instead she presents images that "are anchored in the real world of the senses," and which create a panic in both the character and reader that may lead to spiritual revelation. Discusses Poe's "William Wilson," and O'Connor's *The Violent Bear It Away, Wise Blood*, and "Everything That Rises Must Converge." Finds that whereas Poe must gain the reader's attention by "melodrama, effected by diction and by typography used like musical notes to sustain a tone," O'Connor uses sentence structure and metaphors to weave an "intricate pattern of imagery" to communicate her theme of spiritual love to readers. Suggests that O'Connor's characters reflect the double presence of "the small world of their wayward selves" and the larger world around them. Refers to O'Connor's symbolic use of eyeglasses, seeing, and the hat.

1110   Montgomery, Marion. "The Poet and the Disquieting Shadow of Being: Flannery O'Connor's Voegelinian Dimension." *Intercollegiate Review* 13.1 (1977): 3-14.

Discusses O'Connor's role as "a `prophetic poet,' and the complexities of such a claim in a specialized age such as ours, in which intellect is fragmented and the fragments seized and elevated to absolute authority." Asserts that this role "points to the difficulty of valuing not only her claim but her accomplishment as artist as well." Refers to Eric Voegelin's *From Enlightenment to Revolution* and *Order and History,* and Josef Pieper's *In Tune With the World: A Theory of Festivity and Leisure: The Basis of Culture* to explore O'Connor's interest "in the effect of Enlightenment thought upon the `popular spirit of each succeeding age.'"

1111   Montgomery, Marion. *Possum and Other Receits for the Recovery of "Southern" Being*. Mercer University Lamar Memorial Lectures No. 30. Athens: U of Georgia P, 1987. 4, 8, 9, 13-14, 17, 24, 26, 30-31, 34, 39-40, 44-46, 72, 86, 92, 107, 117, 119, 121, 125-26, 130, 133, 141.

Montgomery refers to O'Connor and her fiction in brief, scattered references throughout this work. Contends that, if nothing else, the reader brings from O'Connor's work the single lesson that "if the life we save is to be our own, we'd better pay attention again to the words we say about that life." Discusses O'Connor's remark about Southern writers who deal with the grotesque "because they still recognize that which is grotesque" in the context of knowing and recognizing--"in a somewhat larger context"--"those who are given to willful, aggressive pretenses to innocence." Offers a brief reading of *The Violent Bear It Away*, using it as an example of writing which shows "evidence that `Southernness' is still alive in the South"; and shows "something of its universality" as a "local incarnation." Notes O'Connor's description of fiction as being "an `incarnational art'" and discusses some of the types of characters in her works. Examines James Joyce's and Flannery O'Connor's sense of "epiphany" as a way of comparing to and understanding that of William Faulkner. Delves into O'Connor's sense of mystery and the "mystery of grace" (described as "the principal antagonist to her characters"). Suggests that O'Connor shares with Faulkner a sense that her characters are "actual," and concludes that Faulkner "comes very near to O'Connor's understanding of the prophetic role of the past."

1112   Montgomery, Marion. "The Prophetic Poet and the Loss of Middle Earth." *Georgia Review* 33 (1979): 66-83.

Asserts that O'Connor used the "wilder grotesque" to shock readers awake and give modern readers "a larger vision of reality" than that offered by "strict empirical law." Discusses the prophetic implications of works by Nathaniel Hawthorne, D.H. Lawrence, J.R.R. Tolkien, C.S. Lewis, Jonathan Swift, G.K. Chesterton, and American novelist Sylvester Judd.

1113   Montgomery, Marion. "Prudence and the Prophetic Past: Reflections on Art From Hawthorne to Gill." *Southwest Review* 65.2 (1980): 141-54.

Discusses the religious value of art, art in relation to community, and the "artist's responsibility as workman" to "call into being through his gift" a reflection of spiritual revelation. Includes several references to Flannery O'Connor: her views on Catholic fiction; her "aesthetic and spiritual position"; the modern hero and his alienation from his community as seen in *Wise Blood*; the Catholic's vision of the cross versus that of Hawthorne; "the importance of place and community to the problem" of materialism; the need to draw "`large and startling pictures'" to awaken one's audience; and her assertion that "good art" is by nature "prophetic."

1114   Montgomery, Marion. "Solzhenitsyn as Southerner." *The Men I Have Chosen for Fathers: Literary and Philosophical Passages*. Columbia: U of Missouri P, 1990. 146-71.

States that, in a sense, Solzhenitsyn is a cousin to Southerners, as both attempt to recall "ancestral virtues now heavily besieged by the forces of modernism" and share "certain principles as central to the meaning of individual and community life." Argues that Southerners should welcome "this displaced person from the East." Discusses Solzhenitsyn's reputation, writings, and speeches, refers to the Agrarians and the book *I'll Take My*

Stand, and uses a variety of quotes from "that perceptive defender of the Southern vision, Flannery O'Connor."

1115   Montgomery, Marion. "Some Reflections on Miss O'Connor and the Dixie Limited." *Flannery O'Connor Bulletin* 5 (1976): 70-81.

Contends that in "poets" like T.S. Eliot and Flannery O'Connor "there is a firm commitment to those romantic inclinations that have become a cliché in the definitions of romanticism," that is, how "the romantic reveals himself by looking to the past . . . manifesting that fascination with the Middle Ages one finds so generally in early nineteenth-century letters." Suggests, however, that instead of only looking back to the Middle Ages, O'Connor and Eliot look "all the way back to Bethlehem" to "actively affirm a confidence in the intersection of time by the transcendent, the Incarnation, which rescues in their confidence the individual soul from both the trap of fallen nature and the treachery of language." Refers to O'Connor's "Some Aspects of the Grotesque in Southern Fiction" and "The Nature and Aim of Fiction"; James Joyce's *Finnegan's Wake*; Ezra Pound's *Cantos*; Nathaniel Hawthorne's "The Custom House"; and William Faulkner's *The Unvanquished, The Hamlet*, and "The Bear" and "Delta Autumn" in *Go Down, Moses*. Closes with a discussion of Faulkner's vision compared to that of O'Connor. Contends that O'Connor does not necessarily reject Faulkner's vision, but "sees rather that in his vision lies a ground out of which spiritual discovery and recovery may be drawn." Suggests that *Wise Blood* may be viewed "not as Faulknerian, but as reaching beyond Faulkner's world, though it shares in details of the local, regional, [and] historical." Concludes that O'Connor's fiction "is a corrective to the Manichean confusions that separate heart and head, body and mind, idea and matter."

1116   Montgomery, Marion. "Southern Letters in the Twentieth Century: The Articulation of a Tradition." *Modern Age* 24.2 (1980): 121-33.

Examines the place of the Southern writer, how he practices his art, his sense of place, his view of writing as being different from science, philosophy or theology, and his hunger for "completeness of self." Refers to O'Connor's writings as evidence of characteristics noted: Hazel Motes of *Wise Blood* discussing "sense of place;" O'Connor's recognition of humanity's need for the "shared experience" offered by storytelling; and her assertion that "the cost of evil to the individual is an absolute beyond all worldly inflations." Discusses Southern "God-haunted" writers as contrasted to those more "Man-haunted"; how the universe may be reflected in the "postage stamp" sized areas described by authors such as Faulkner and others; O'Connor's and Faulkner's communities as "spiritual organisms . . . fallen from fullness"; similarities between Southern writers and Soviet dissidents; and the utilization by Southern writers of the theme of original sin. Refers to Hannah Arendt's *The Life of the Mind* and her attempts to better understand the evil deeds of Adolf Eichmann, and discusses the evil of Hitler, Jim Jones, Charles Manson, and others-- including The Misfit. Argues that "the relation of manners to mystery is a constant one in Southern literature as it attempts to rescue cliché in its origins." Concludes that the Southern writer "bears witness beyond the limits of art's projections of man's struggle within the *metaxy*, the `In-between'. He knows this in his blood if not in his head."

1117   Montgomery, Marion. "Southern Reflections on Solzhenitsyn." *Modern Age* 19.2 (1975): 190-97.

Compares the spiritual questions posed by Solzhenitsyn to the beliefs that O'Connor attempted to convey in her writings. Finds the two to be similar in many ways and suggests that both serve as "prophet and witness of the human spirit." Concludes with an examination of Solzhenitsyn's beliefs and finds his message to be similar to The Misfit's: "either Christ *is* what he said he *is*, or he *was* a liar."

1118   Montgomery, Marion. "Vision and the Eye for Detail in Poe and O'Connor." *Flannery O'Connor Bulletin* 6 (1977): 36-46.

Sees parallels in how Edgar Allan Poe turns "traditional, though fading, concepts of good and evil upside down" to elicit sympathy for his "evil genius" narrator in "William Wilson," with O'Connor's rendering of The Misfit in "A Good Man Is Hard to Find." Follows with a discussion of Poe's use of his "CONSCIENCE" epigraph in "William Wilson," and compares it to Hazel Motes's confrontation with his own conscience-- through Silas Layfield--in O'Connor's *Wise Blood*. Concludes that because Poe substitutes a "unity of voice" for "the traditional unities of time, place, and action," O'Connor is far more effective in her utilization of "imagistic detail" in *Wise Blood* than Poe is in "William Wilson."

1119   Montgomery, Marion [Moderator], Sally Fitzgerald, Louis D. Rubin, Jr., Rosa Lee Walston, and Sarah Gordon. "Panel Discussion." *Flannery O'Connor Bulletin* 6 (1977): 72-81.

Edited comments from a panel discussion held at Georgia College & State University on April 3, 1977. Includes a note that Sally Fitzgerald's comments regarding her friendship with O'Connor, were omitted, as she "is giving a full treatment of that subject in her forthcoming book."

Questions discussed include Rubin's "criticism of the religious study" of O'Connor's work and his suggestion that readers look beyond seeing her work simply as theological statements; Walston's comments on the types of articles submitted to *The Flannery O'Connor Bulletin*; Gordon's suggestion that "many of Flannery's stories are flattened" because of readers' overzealous pursuit of religious allegory and themes; and Fitzgerald's comments that O'Connor's religious focus was, "for a long time . . . very much misunderstood," and that the amount of religious criticism may be due, in part, to O'Connor's own remarks. Panel members answer a number of questions posed by lay members of the audience: To Fitzgerald, "How much would Miss O'Connor share her writings" of *Wise Blood* with her? "How did [O'Connor] react to children?" And, would she "comment on the effect of some of the other aspects of Catholicism" that she and O'Connor "grew up with?" To Gerald Becham (Curator of the O'Connor Collection), "Is it possible to have a record made from the tapes of Flannery's reading of her stories?" And, to Gordon, "Is there any feminist criticism that might give us a fresh view of O'Connor?"

1120   Moore, Brian. "Making a Case for Distortion." Rev. of *Flannery O'Connor: Collected Works*, ed. Sally Fitzgerald. *New York Times Book Review* 21 Aug. 1988: 1, 30-31.

Offers examples of O'Connor's literal belief in heaven, hell, and the "Devil among us." Discusses the role of her Catholic faith in her artistic endeavors, and states that while O'Connor "is not a `great' writer . . . she is the master of a small highly circumscribed universe that, when we enter it, leads us inexorably toward a larger truth." Reminds readers of O'Connor's own words related to her method: "'I am interested in making a good case for distortion . . . as I am coming to believe it is the only way to make people see.'" Provides selected story lines which reflect her perspective. Offers brief biographical details, suggests Catholic influences upon her life and work, and concludes that O'Connor ultimately "resembles an Old Testament prophet, crying out in our modern wilderness," whose characters could easily have been "such figures as Charles Manson, John Hinckley, and Patty Hearst." A sidebar article by Amy Edith Johnson titled "Saying Little, Seeing Everything" offers information on Sally Fitzgerald, editor of *Flannery O'Connor: Collected Works*. Illustrations: Photograph of O'Connor on crutches at her home in Milledgeville, GA, 1962 by Jay Leviton; Photograph of O'Connor in 1945 as senior editor of the Georgia State College for Women literary quarterly, *The Corinthian*.

1121   Moore, Susan. "The Art of Flannery O'Connor: *The Habit of Being*." *Quadrant* (Australia) 30.7-8 (1986): 111-13.

Observes that while Sally Fitzgerald's edited volume of O'Connor's letters, *The Habit of Being,* was usually "greeted with enthusiasm by . . . distinguished organs of opinion in America and England," it received little attention in Australia. Refers to Olga Masters and Karl Schmude as two of the "small group of Australian writers and intellectuals who know and admire" O'Connor. Remarks that O'Connor is "an accomplished regional writer, better at evoking the religious consciousness of the American South than anyone else." Offers biographical details, and states that O'Connor's fiction blends in an unusual way "the intelligence behind the stories," which are "earthy, tough, funny, shrewd and serene, devotional, [and] sacramental." Contends that "because O'Connor's realism is informed by absolute religious conviction and sureness of touch, she is not an easy writer for our secular age to comprehend." Mentions O'Connor's "spiritual guides," her influence on writer Peter Carey, and finds that O'Connor "demands that we bring to the reading of her fiction an intuitive strength, an imaginative power, and a moral grasp which will enable us to see precisely what is needed to restore the order which has been violated."

1122   Moose, Ruth. "Flannery O'Connor's Letters: Reading Them, You Become a Part of Her World." [Georgia College & State University] *Columns* 24.1 (1979): 2-3.

Offers a review of the *Habit of Being: Letters of Flannery O'Connor,* edited by Sally Fitzgerald, previously published in the *Charlotte* (NC) *Observer* (March 18, 1979). Comments that this review is the one Regina O'Connor "seemed most delighted with." Describes "poking around in" the Flannery O'Connor files at Georgia College" and coming upon the sealed envelope of letters from O'Connor to her literary agent Elizabeth McKee. Praises Fitzgerald for never intruding as an editor and suggests that her "touches of explanation and sparse footnotes are so hostess-gracious and courteous that the whole book reads as a unit, smooth as polished wood." Laments that O'Connor's correspondence with Caroline Gordon, "her teacher at Iowa, mentor, and lifelong critic," is not included.

1123   Morse, Pamela. "Intriguing Play on Flannery O'Connor Has Feel of `Belle of Amherst.'" *Birmingham (AL) News* 25 Feb. 1992: 3C.

Review of a two-act play about Flannery O'Connor by Samford University Professor, Sam Killinger. Titled *The Mistress of Milledgeville,* the production premiered February 23, 1992 on the Samford University campus. Suggests that the play is structured "much like . . . the *Belle of Amherst,* the beautiful one-woman play about poet Emily Dickinson." Finds the play to be "a bit long" and suggests that a "little judicious editing might make this intriguing play even more pleasing." Remarks that for "a first production of a new work, Killinger's script seems remarkably polished." Describes the play's plot, the lighting, props, and the acting of Melanie MacQueen, who "captures the feisty spirit of O'Connor well." Concludes that Samford's play offers a portrait of O'Connor that is "endearing and funny . . . much like the self-portrait that adorns the set."

1124   Morton, Mary L. "Doubling in Flannery O'Connor's Female Characters: Animus and Anima." *Southern Quarterly* 23.4 (1985): 57-63.

Contends that O'Connor's stories "dramatize the ludicrosity [sic] of women who have denied the spirit of femininity." Sees them as "angular, [and] ludicrous . . . who scorn any belief in mystery or interest in creation." These are contrasted to their doubles, the "fat women of the earth." Suggests that O'Connor's careworn, joyless, humorless, angular female characters (such as Mrs. Cope, Mrs. May, and Mrs. McIntyre) lack any qualities of the *anima*. Their fat doubles (sharecroppers' wives), are fascinated by mystery and "show close affinity with mother earth." Explicates "A Circle in the Fire," "Greenleaf," and "The Displaced Person" to illustrate double figures.

1125   Morton, Mary [L.] "Flannery O'Connor in the 1980s." *Mississippi Quarterly* 37.1 (1983-84): 89-95.

Notes that "interest in Flannery O'Connor remains keen," and surveys book-length scholarship related to O'Connor from 1980 to 1983. Offers introductory remarks to O'Connor by discussing David Farmer's *Flannery O'Connor: A Descriptive Bibliography* and Carter W. Martin and Leo J. Zuber's *The Presence of Grace and Other Book Reviews by Flannery O'Connor*. Provides one-to-two paragraph reviews of Kathleen Feeley's *Flannery O'Connor: Voice of the Peacock*, Barbara McKenzie's *Flannery O'Connor's Georgia*, James A. Grimshaw's *The Flannery O'Connor Companion*, Carol Shloss's *Flannery O'Connor's Dark Comedies: The Limits of Inference*, Frederick Asals's *Flannery O'Connor: The Imagination of Extremity*, and Jefferson Humphries's *The Otherness Within: Gnostic Readings in Marcel Proust, Flannery O'Connor, and Francois Villon*. Suggests that while O'Connor's genius has engendered critical division, her technical perfection will continue to attract critics.

1126   Moss, William M. "Postmodern Georgia Scenes: Harry Crews and the Southern Tradition in Fiction." *A Grit's Triumph: Essays on Harry Crews*. Ed. David K. Jeffrey. Port Washington, NY: Associated Faculty, 1983. 33-45.

Contends that, despite Harry Crews's own objections, his writings place him "squarely in a venerable Southern tradition." Focuses on the importance of storytelling in his childhood and on his approach to writing. Includes several references to O'Connor, including her storytelling ability; her comment that writers become most familar with "`the region that most immediately surrounds'" them; Crews's frequent references to and respect for O'Connor and Erskine Caldwell ("two writers with whom he is most often compared"); his use of the grotesque in a manner similar to O'Connor; and how the sense of the mystery that served as O'Connor's theme differs from Crews's.

1127   Mott, Sara. "Flannery O'Connor's Unique Contribution to Christian Literary Naturalism." *Realist of Distances: Flannery O'Connor Revisited.* Ed. Karl-Heinz Westarp and Jan Nordby Gretlund. Aarhus (Denmark): Aarhus UP, 1987. 217-26.

Discusses O'Connor's identity as a Southerner and a Catholic "to show how these `givens' influence her treatment of . . . Christian literary naturalism." Describes stereotypic Southerners found in O'Connor's works: "the matriarchal Southern woman," the itinerant jack-of-all-trades, migrant farm workers, and the "oftentimes shiftless, but faithful black farmhands." Then, briefly explores her Southern sense of place and the implications in her work of living and working as a Catholic in the fundamentalist Bible Belt of the South. Develops a definition of literary naturalism based upon one offered by Jerold Savory and reinforced by Henry Weiman. Applies it to O'Connor's essays and fiction, and points out examples of "natural events" in a number of her works that illustrate its applicability. Asserts that "Revelation" fits Savory's tenets of Christian literary naturalism and offers a reading of the story in this context. Argues that it illustrates how, "in the natural order of things, there is an observable pattern of birth-death-rebirth, a cycle that is at the heart of the Christian belief in resurrection." Observes that in O'Connor's work, natural events, some times violent ones, appear to "operate in human life to save man from evil and bring him to the greatest good." Concludes that Christian literary naturalism "provides a critical approach to a broader frame of interpretation of O'Connor's fiction." Uses comments from a wide variety of scholars to support this approach to reading O'Connor, including Marion Montgomery, Robert Coles, Josephine Hendin, Louis Rubin, Walter Sullivan, Preston Browning, Miles Orvell, Dorothy Walters, Irving Malin, and Gilbert Muller; as well as O'Connor's own comments to John Lynch, Father John McCown, and Elizabeth Bishop.

1128   "Mrs. O'Connor Dies at Age 99." *CHEERS! The Flannery O'Connor Society Newsletter* 3.1 (1995): 1.

Reprints--from the Milledgeville, GA *Union-Recorder*--the obituary for Flannery's mother, Regina Cline O'Connor, who died in Milledgeville in May, 1995. Provides a biographical sketch and reports tributes by her close friend, Tallulah Schepis, and Georgia College & State University faculty, Sarah Gordon and Lorene Flanders.

1129   Mulder, Karen, comp. "Networking: Contemporary and Classic Books on Arts & Faith." *Christianity Today* 5 Feb. 1996: 45.

Includes Flannery O'Connor's *Mystery and Manners* among a list of seventeen books considered to be contemporary classics on the topic of "Arts & Faith." Suggests that the book serves as a "classic consideration of literary creativity."

1129a   Mullen, Christopher. "The Compassionate Tears of Mrs. Kempe and Mrs. Greenleaf: Heaven's Daughters, Earth Mothers." *Flannery O'Connor Bulletin* 26-27 (1998-2000): 97-123.

Considers the basis for O'Connor's "unmistakable ambivalence toward overtly pious, emotional, and fundamentalist manifestations of Christianity." Focuses on her readings and understanding of the "fiery, personal yet communal, unashamed, [and] compassionate" brand of Catholicism practiced in the Middle Ages. Ties characteristics and issues of these "Christ-haunted" medieval Catholics to the tension seen between Mrs. Greenleaf and Mrs. May in "Greenleaf." Sees in Mrs. Greenleaf's "own contemplative mysticism and familiar discourse with God . . . strong echoes of her spiritual foremother, Margery Kempe." Both women-- fictional and historical--embody "the mystery of the transcendent God made immanent through compassionate tears, [and] a mystery that defies all psychologizing (in both medieval and modern forms) that their peers can muster against them." Refers to books in O'Connor's Library or among those she had reviewed that may have influenced her method of characterization, including studies of mystics and saints (St. Catherine of Genoa, St. Catherine of Siena), and *The Book of Margery Kempe.*

1130   Munk, Linda. "Shouting at the Lord Across a Hogpen: Flannery O'Connor's `Revelation.'" *Theology* 97 (July-Aug. 1994): 283-92.

Cites a letter from O'Connor in which she describes Ruby Turpin as "`a country female Jacob'" and asserts that during the last two years of her life she was "taken with the struggle between Jacob and the Lord." Explores how Jacob is "`marked'" in the Bible, the blessings he extracts from the Lord, and how his struggle typifies "the purgatorial vision of O'Connor's

Mrs. Turpin." Refers to Geoffrey Hartman's interpretation of the scripture which focuses on "the name change--from Jacob to Israel" and how the change "`denotes a character change or an inner change of Jacob's previous life breaking through.'" Explicates "Revelation," and agrees with Richard Poirier's view that the story "`belongs with the few masterpieces of the form in English.'" Compares Mary Grace's attack on Mrs. Turpin to Jacob's wrestling with God to receive God's grace. Refers to Roland Barthes's structural analysis of Jacob's crossing of the river Jaboc, and notes that just as Jacob's "crossing" involved water, so does Ruby Turpin's. Closes with a discussion of possible sources for Mrs. Turpin's "vision in the hogpen."

1131   Munk, Linda. "Understanding Understatement: Biblical Typology and `The Displaced Person.'" *Journal of Literature & Theology* 2.2 (1988): 237-53.

Offers definitions of typology by Northrop Frye, Joseph Galdon and others, and asserts "that the typological method of biblical exegesis is the implicit structural principle" of "The Displaced Person." Refers to a letter by O'Connor in which she stated her objectives for the story, and her belief that she had failed to communicate the "`under-statement'" adequately. Reviews Frye's "visual metaphor for biblical typology . . . [as] a double mirror," and suggests that "typology is `a specialized form of the repeatability of myth.'" Argues that the text of "The Displaced Person" assumes "the conventions of and anticipates a typological reading." Discusses the Shortleys' automobile (as ark); Mrs. Shortley's moment of salvation; O'Connor's linkage of Mrs. McIntyre to the biblical city of Tyre, to Lot's wife, "the Great Whore of Babylon," and as a "giant wife of the countryside"; Mr. Shortley as "a dying vegetation god"; the use of the color red; Mrs. McIntyre's first husband, the Judge, and his office, as "a perversion of Solomon's temple"; and Mr. Guizac and Astor as "antitypes of the suffering servant" since they "are not and cannot be `Christ figures.'" Submits that a typological reading "plays on the dialectic of concealment and revelation, mystery and epiphany, closure and disclosure." Suggests that "the brilliance of O'Connor's typological `understatement'" in this story "is that it conceals its own exegesis, its out-writing, from those without."

1132   Murphy, Carol R. *Four Women: Four Windows on Light*. Pendle Hill Pamphlet 236. Wallingford, PA: Pendle Hill, 1981.

A 26-page pamphlet which reviews biographical details and describes religious insights of four women: Mary Baker Eddy (1821-1910), Evelyn Underhill (1875-1941), Simone Weil (1909-1943), and Flannery

O'Connor (1925-1964). Quotes O'Connor on reading Weil, her illness, her dependence upon her mother, her "loneliness in her vocation as a thoughtful writer," her perspective on orthodoxy, the Eucharist, prayer, and the civil rights struggle. Raises questions of O'Connor "from a Quaker standpoint" regarding religious dogma, "`Do-It-yourself' Protestantism," and the Eucharist as a symbol.

1133   Murphy, George D. and Caroline L. Cherry. "Flannery O'Connor and the Integration of Personality." *Flannery O'Connor Bulletin* 7 (1978): 85-100.

Addresses the question of why O'Connor's works, "so apocalyptically Christian, have become so popular within a critical community largely comprised of those whose secular values it specifically attacks?" Suggests that the answer lies with those critics who "have discerned that her religious preoccupations, though very real, have little to do with the most basic *effect* of her art, which is the evocation of certain states of feeling." Outlines "the extent to which a number of Flannery O'Connor's most powerful short stories reveal a kind of psycho-drama of the dynamics of personality," seen as "a chronically unresolved conflict between the conscious and the unconscious elements of the mind." Claims that many of O'Connor's stories "convey to the psychologically oriented reader" the impression that she is "bringing together these two ingredients of personality," in "what in psychoanalytical jargon is called the *integration of personality*." Suggests, however, that this integration is never sustained and that it "typically breaks down into an intensification of tension or into her signatory violence." Ties O'Connor's psychodynamic symbolism to that of Nathaniel Hawthorne, and refers to comments by Josephine Hendin, Stanley Edgar Hyman, Carter Martin, Robert Fitzgerald, and Louis Rubin. Offers illustrative psychoanalytical readings of "The Partridge Festival" and "The Comforts of Home," and somewhat briefer related comments on "Greenleaf," "A Circle in the Fire," "A Good Man Is Hard to Find," "Revelation," "A View of the Woods," and "Everything That Rises Must Converge."

1134   Murphy, John J. "Another Way of Seeing: Editor's Foreword." *Literature and Belief* 17.1-2 (1997): iv-viii.

Recounts meeting Flannery O'Connor during her visit to the College of Saint Teresa in Minnesota in 1960. States "No one, certainly no fiction writer, made clearer our individual absurdity and collective need for redemptive grace. No one dramatized so emphatically the psychological operation of grace and the miserable condition of the territory where grace operates." Follows with brief descriptions of O'Connor-related articles published in this special issue of *Literature and Belief*. Notes that many were originally presented at the Flannery O'Connor Symposium hosted by Brigham Young University in November, 1995.

1135   Mužina, Matej. "Inescapable Lucidity: Flannery O'Connor's Gift and Most Terrible Affliction." *Realist of Distances: Flannery O'Connor Revisited.* Ed. Karl-Heinz Westarp and Jan Nordby Gretlund. Aarhus (Denmark): Aarhus UP, 1987. 160-70.

Examines how O'Connor uses language to show the contrast between her "ordinary people and her demonic, violent, destructive or self-destructive freaks." Offers examples of Karl Jaspers's term *Grenzsituationen,* to describe O'Connor's "demonic doubters." Illustrates this assertion with selective readings of portions of *Wise Blood* and "Good Country People." Sees the contrast to be between the "repetitive babble, false conversations, or *Ersatz* communication" of ordinary people who are shut inside an inauthentic world, living a false life, and the "experience and language of her demonic characters." Contends that "although [the demonic characters] move and act in the same physical universe as the mentally inert ordinary people, theirs is another world, the world of last things, of sin and death and the horror of existence." Discusses the ideas of José Ortega y Gasset, Wolfgang Kayser, Carl Jung, George Santayana, and Erich Fromm, as well as O'Connor's own views of Simone Weil, Saint Thomas, and Saint John. Outlines O'Connor's reasons for disliking intellectuals, including her belief that they "have taken over from the Church the task of illuminating people's minds, consoling and directing them." Sees O'Connor's intellectual characters as occupying a position midway between the ordinary and the demonic. Suggests that O'Connor herself is "in the company of her demonic figures" because she, too, "is conscious to the superlative degree and characterized by incessant awareness."

1136   Mužina, Matej. "`A Reasonable Use of the Unreasonable'--Flannery O'Connor and Leonid Andreev." *Studia Romanica et Anglica Zagrabiensia* (Yugoslavia) 23.1-2 (1978): 273-302.

Compares the "nature, themes, and subject matter of the stories of Flannery O'Connor and Leonid Andreev." Asserts that these authors' works "belong to the category of the literature of extreme situations." Offers evidence for this assertion by providing "a cursory survey of the adverse literary criticism of both authors which takes as its starting point and its norm the suppositions of social criticism and social realism." Examines representative works of each author, focusing on their use of the grotesque, violence, freaks, and demonic figures "which are nearly always an image of the authors themselves in their attempt to activate the intellectual powers of an indifferent and hostile audience that would prefer to be left in their forms of `dreaming innocence.'" Contends that both authors "strive after clarity of intellectual and moral judgement and not after any . . . emotional state, whether it be pity or compassion."

1137   Myers, David A. "A Galaxy of Haloed Suns: Epiphanies and Peacocks in Patrick White's `A Woman's Hand' and Flannery O'Connor's `The Displaced Person.'" *Literatur in Wissenschaft und Unterricht* 14.4 (1981): 214-24.

Compares the function of religious epiphany in the short stories of Patrick White and Flannery O'Connor. Views both "as inheritors of western civilization's enduring religious crisis that began with the Christian existentialism of Kierkegaard and rose to a climax with Darwin's empirical challenge to Christian metaphysics and Nietzsche's aphoristic satire on Christian ethics." Describes the similarities of their "religio-fictional" methods, their mutual use of epiphanies, the peacock as a symbol, and rational humanist characters. Offers a detailed comparison of "The Displaced Person" and White's "A Woman's Hand." Concludes that "both writers are primarily concerned with the spiritual mystery of the irrational and with the tragic tension between empirical reality and spiritual truth. Both see epiphanies as brief religious illuminations that stand out in grotesque relief against a vain and ignorant society."

1138   Myers, Michael. "*Wise Blood* and the Japanese *Yūgen* Aesthetic." *Flannery O'Connor Bulletin* 21 (1992): 58-72.

Defines the Japanese term "Yūgen" and states that this medieval, Buddhist-influenced term relates to "the Japanese love of shadow, nuance, and empty space." Reports that the concept is attaining popularity again based upon the short novel by Jun'ichiro Tanizaki, *Portrait of Shunkin*. Submits that because both authors attempt to widen "medieval presuppositions to include contemporary relevance through an existential leap of faith," Tanizaki's novel is comparable to O'Connor's *Wise Blood*. Maintains that, "The centering of yūgen in Zen Buddhism and *Wise Blood* in Christianity provides a forum for exploration of questions of artistic and religious values, existence and nonexistence, and freedom and nihilism." Uses the concept of yūgen as a basis for a reading of both novels, and through a structural analysis, compares the roles of art and religion in the Buddhist and Christian worlds. Argues that "a discussion of the denouement of the narratives . . . leads to deconstruction of the distinction between the aesthetic and spiritual and reconstruction of a radical (but complex) freedom and an existential leap of faith." Contends that as a result of this leap, "Yūgen as aesthetic ideal becomes transformed into yūgen as experienced reality."

1139   Napier, James J. "Another Look at Flannery O'Connor's Opinions of Other
Writers." *Antigonish Review* 46 (1981): 95-101.

Contends that although O'Connor had "scant interest" in literary theory
and little "philosophical sophistication" regarding fiction, her views of
other writers "reveal the person we know [and] surprise at times with a
glimpse of other aspects of her independent mind." Notes that she "came
late to writers many an undergraduate takes for granted," and suggests that
this may be the reason she often "put on a country tone . . . and why she
lacked confidence in some of her critical appraisals." Discusses her
opinion of authors she read from "the nineteenth century, the modern, and
the contemporary," including Leo Tolstoy, Henry James, Nathaniel
Hawthorne, Nelson Algren, James Gould Cozzens, Ayn Rand, William
Faulkner, Katherine Anne Porter, Caroline Gordon, Marshall McLuhan,
Joseph Conrad, Marcel Proust, Franz Kafka, Vladimir Nabokov, André-
Georges Malraux, James Joyce, J.F. Powers, Truman Capote, Tennessee
Williams, Joseph Heller, William Styron, James Baldwin, Norman Mailer,
James Purdy, Elizabeth Bishop, and John Hawkes.

1140   Napier, James J. "'The Artificial Nigger' and the Authorial Intention."
Flannery O'Connor Bulletin 10 (1981): 87-92.

Questions the conclusions of Paul W. Nisly (in his article "The Prison of
the Self: Isolation in Flannery O'Connor's Fiction") and Kenneth Scouten
(in "'The Artificial Nigger': Mr. Head's Ironic Salvation"). Addresses
Nisly's argument that O'Connor's stories "deal with characters caught in
the isolation of the self," and Scouten's contention that--in "The Artificial
Nigger"--Mr. Head's salvation appears questionable. Focuses on how the
two scholars "pinpoint the 'ambiguous' within the 'literal' yet leap
categorically to the opposite of the literal." Summarizes the "'literal'
meaning of the ending" of "The Artificial Nigger" using comments found
in O'Connor's letters, including those to Ben Griffith and "A." Concludes
that O'Connor's remarks "do not suggest a continued 'isolation' for the
characters, nor do they allow . . . Scouten's point that Nelson was capable
of a spiritual effort of abasement in the presence of the black woman."

1141   Napier, James J. "The Cave-Waiting Room in O'Connor's 'Revelations.'"
["Revelation"]. *NMAL: Notes on Modern American Literature* 5.4 (1981):
Item 23.

Discusses O'Connor's use of the "light-shadow motif" and suggests that
although Josephine Hendin and other critics have expressed
disappointment at O'Connor's "supposed failure" to "develop the motif of
Plato's cave parable," the analogy can still be made. Follows with a

discussion of metaphorical parallels between Plato's "description of the prisoner's release from the cave" and Ruby Turpin's leaving the "cave-waiting room."

1142   Napier, James J. "Flannery O'Connor's Last Three: `The Sense of an Ending.'" *Southern Literary Journal* 14.2 (1982): 19-27.

Contends that O'Connor's final stories are of interest because they serve as a summation of the work of her "illness" phase and reveal new techniques and perspectives within the tragicomic mode. Sees the stories as presenting a closing coherence of outlook and "reveal a readiness to portray black characters more confidently . . . and move . . . closer to the center of her fictional stage." Examines "Revelation," "Parker's Back," and "Judgement Day."

1143   Napier, James J. "In `Parker's Back': A Technical Slip by Flannery O'Connor." *Notes on Contemporary Literature* 11.4 (1981): 5-6.

Analyzes the double flashback scenes in "Parker's Back" and argues that O'Connor appears to have forgotten to relate the opening scene back to her flashback. Concludes, however, that the action was instinctually correct and that O'Connor deliberately "flouted narrative convention."

1144   Napier, James J. "Tragic and Comic Interplay in O'Connor's `A Good Man Is Hard to Find.'" *CEA Forum* 12.2 (1981): 3-6.

Attempts to reconcile the labels of "tragic" and "comic" as applied to O'Connor's work. Utilizes definitions of the two terms offered by Walter Kerr and uses "A Good Man Is Hard to Find" as "a test." Attempts to demonstrate that the work contains both tragic and comic elements that "provide tonal guidance in the unfolding of incident and effect." Suggests that this story illustrates how O'Connor "moves from the `commonness' of comedy to the `pity and terror' of tragedy." Examines the story in three parts and argues that the final scenes of the third part offer "the conflicting value content of comedy and tragedy . . . in clearest relief." Concludes that it is The Misfit's "fall from the demands of tragedy that drops him into the commonness, the `meanness' of comedy."

1145   Nash, Jay Robert and Stanley Ralph Ross. *The Motion Picture Guide: W-Z 1927-1984.* Chicago: Cinebooks, 1987. 3880.

Review of John Huston's "Wise Blood." Rated three stars (good). Credits include the phrase "Based on the novel by Flannery O'Connor."

1146   Natoli, Joseph and Frederik L. Rusch, comps. *Psychocriticism: An Annotated Bibliography*. Westport, CT: Greenwood, 1984. 213.

Includes a short annotated bibliography of psychoanalytical studies of O'Connor's work.

1147   Neligan, Patrick, Jr. and Victor Nuñez. "Flannery and the Film Makers." *Flannery O'Connor Bulletin* 5 (1976): 98-104.

Neligan reports on Matthew Herman's NEH film project, the filming of "The Displaced Person" for the 1977 PBS television season. Describes Herman's meeting with Regina Cline O'Connor to gain permission to shoot at Andalusia and the fourteen days of location work, during which time "more than two hundred brow-sweating, marathon hours" were spent in oppressive heat as "tempers rose and unseemly language filled the air." Profiles Irene Worth as Mrs. McIntyre, Shirley Stoller as Mrs. Shortley, John Huston as Father Flynn, and Robert Earl Jones as Astor. Nuñez describes his reasons for wanting to film "A Circle in the Fire," the shortcomings of "doing a film with limited means," and the exciting and memorable challenges he faced in attempting to be faithful to O'Connor's story. Closes with a descriptive list of film adaptations of O'Connor's work, including "The World of Flannery O'Connor," narrated by Walter Sullivan and produced by Jim Spitler in 1974 for WDCN-TV of Nashville and the Nashville Public Television Council; "The Comforts of Home," produced in 1974 by Leonard Lipson for Sholip Productions and directed by Jerome Shore; and "Good Country People," adapted by Jeff Jackson (whose address is provided for ordering).

1148   Nelson, Ed[ward B.]. "Lenten Message 1976, Title: `The Tattooed Christ' Based on O'Connor Short Story: `Parker's Back.'" n.p. [1976].

Offers a reading of "Parker's Back" which examines the role and meaning of O.E. Parker's tattoos. Relates Parker's tattoo of a Byzantine Christ etched into his back to passages in the Bible and to how Southerners typically view profanity. Contends that the moral of this tale is that "whether it be a profane oath, or the manipulation of the Lord's Name for social approval, psychological identity, or self-aggrandizement, it is as sinful to manipulate and use Christ's name under religious sham as it is to utter sacrilege." Concludes that Parker was a religious phony, "not because God was unreal, or that he drank too much," nor "because he visited the pool hall; he was a sham because he `used' Jesus' Name and Face for himself--his *opus tattoo*." [Copy in the *Flannery O'Connor Collection*, Russell Library Georgia College & State University, Milledgeville, GA.]

1149   Nelson, Edward B. "Memorial Tribute." Ts. [1975].

A tribute in memory of Flannery O'Connor presented at the Old Capital Historical Society and Georgia College Architectural Seminar in Savannah, June 14, 1975. States that O'Connor wrote unapologetically "as a Christian existentialist" and as a realist accentuating the biblical themes of "Original Sin, Fall of Man, Judgement of God, Divine Grace, and Supernatural Redemption." Concludes that in O'Connor, readers "find an enlightened soul and transcendent spirit" who reflected the faith she possessed "in Jesus Christ as the absolute Lord of History." [Copy in the *Flannery O'Connor Collection*, Russell Library, Georgia College & State University, Milledgeville, GA.]

1150   Nelson, Ed[ward B.]. "A Religious Experience With Flannery O'Connor." ["A Wesley Tract"]. n.p. [1975].

Pamphlet of a sermon given by the author during homecoming festivities on April 20, 1975 at Georgia College & State University in Milledgeville, Georgia. Suggests that O'Connor "was empowered with the talent to unmask phoniness, to overturn the tables, and mirror ourselves before God--and everybody." Refers to comments by Robert Fitzgerald, and to O'Connor's "Introduction" to *A Memoir of Mary Ann*. Observes how, in O'Connor's religious literature, "mystery" serves as her vehicle for suspense, and that "her narratives reflect 'what is,' embracing reality." Illustrates her intentions and technique through a discussion of Rufus Johnson in "The Lame Shall Enter First." Focuses on scripture that supports the contention that "life is going to be different in Christ's Kingdom" because "the order will be reversed." Reminds readers that those who followed Jesus on the ass on Palm Sunday were the "hunchbacks, dwarfs, freaks, lame, blind, deaf, mentally ill, deformed, lepers, cripples, those ugly and grotesque--every conceivable child, youth, and adult face hidden in our state mental hospitals and prisons." Concludes that "We are akin to Rufus Florida Johnson in that we know that 'Jesus Saves,' but we cannot bring ourselves 'to repent' and trust him for our ultimate redemption. This is our real spiritual club foot." [Rpt. as "Flannery O'Connor." (Georgia College & State University) *Columns* 20.2 (1975): 6-8.]

1150a   Nesbitt, Laurel. "Reading Place in and around Flannery O'Connor's
              Texts." *Post Identity*. (U of Detroit Mercy) 1.1 (1997): 145-77.

              Contends that "any gainful reading of O'Connor requires that we expand
              our notion of `place' beyond the physical to acknowledge the ways" she
              addresses "(and is addressed by) the concept herself." Argues that, for
              O'Connor, "place becomes a metaphor for position," particularly in the
              three stories "The Displaced Person," "The Artificial Nigger," and
              "Everything That Rises Must Converge." Offers readings of these stories
              informed by comments from her letters and lectures. Contrasts O'Connor's
              theology with her social sensibility, discusses critical opinions of "the
              ways in which she uses black characters and racial issues in two-
              dimensional ways to bring about the development and redemption of her
              white characters," and reviews discussion among scholars as to whether
              O'Connor was a racist. Concludes that she "not only comments on place"
              and "stands on and defends particular ground herself," but that scholars
              have positions "that monitor and limit our reading of her . . . legitimating
              particular critical approaches." Urges critics to find ways "to appreciate
              the *inconsistency* that so often presents itself" in O'Connor's writings, "not
              in an attempt to point out the hypocrisy or the racism inherent in . . . [her]
              work, but in an effort to see her as placed within the mire of racial, social,
              and spiritual upheaval about which she speaks so powerfully."

1151   Neubauer, Alexander. "The Writing Class Revisited or Can Fiction
              Writing Still Be Taught?" *Poets & Writers Magazine* (March-April 1996):
              42-53.

              Invokes O'Connor's "deep criticisms" of creative writing programs as a
              context within which to discuss whether the writer's workshop "is the *best*
              place to acquire" the writer's art and craft. Recounts her opinion, to such
              a class, that while writing programs may produce writers who can "`write
              a competent story'" many of such students should be stifled because they
              still do not possess the "`vision to go with it.'" Reminds readers that
              O'Connor herself was a product of the University of Iowa's Writer's
              Workshop and notes that her words were spoken "some years before the
              flood of graduate and undergraduate writing programs across the country"
              came into existence. Includes discussion of O'Connor's views on the role
              of one's life experiences in writing and what criticisms a writing teacher
              can offer to students that may be helpful.

1152   Neuleib, Janice Witherspoon. "Comic Grotesquerie: The Means of
              Revelation in *Wise Blood* and *That Hideous Strength*." *Christianity &
              Literature* 30.4 (1981): 27-38.

Offers a brief introduction to the comic novel, then compares O'Connor's *Wise Blood* to C.S. Lewis's *That Hideous Strength*. States that both authors created "comic novels which use grotesques [to] create worlds of twisted and distorted beings so that the readers see by contrast the true shapes behind the distortions." Argues that both reveal truths through vivid suggestion and use their grotesques to "force an awareness of the healthy norm that contrasts with bent images many humans have come to accept as reality." Notes both authors' concern with how easy it has become "to suppress the internal moral promptings of conscience in a world that bombards the senses with countless trivial messages," blurring the distinction between right and wrong. Compares O'Connor's Leora Watts and Lewis's Fairy Hardcastle as examples of how the authors convey a sense of a character's inner evil through appearance and action without "preaching" to the reader. Discusses O'Connor's Hazel Motes and difficulties readers have had in interpreting O'Connor's intentions with this character. Comments on Lewis's use of contrasting characters, and how Lewis "shows characters caught in the middle trying to choose sides." Concludes that the difference between the two novels may be found in the author's choice of perspective: whereas O'Connor "chooses to chill the reader with her view of fallen man and not to go beyond into the possible effects of grace in the here and now," Lewis offers two or three views of humanity and "invites the reader inside the minds of the main characters giving the chance to choose between bent and true images."

1153   "New Books." *CHEERS! The Flannery O'Connor Society Newsletter* 2.1 (1994): 3.

Reviews Jon Lance Bacon's *Flannery O'Connor and Cold War Culture* (Cambridge: Cambridge UP, 1993) and Karl-Heinz Westarp's *Flannery O'Connor: The Growing Craft* (Birmingham, AL: Summa, 1993). Sees Bacon's work as revealing O'Connor to be "an artist deeply concerned with the issues that engaged other producers of American culture from the 1940s to the 1960s: national identity, political anxiety, and intellectual freedom." Follows with praise of Westarp's edition for making variations of O'Connor's short story "Judgement Day" available to readers, and for the way the volume--"by means of its synoptic arrangement"--offers critics "a new form of O'Connor research which permits a much easier analysis and comparison of textual variants."

1154   Newman, Georgia A. "Wanting Grace." *Flannery O'Connor Bulletin* 25 (1996-97): 193.

A thirteen-line poem, prefaced by a quotation from O'Connor in which she refers to the difficulty of writing for an audience unfamiliar with grace. In the unfulfilled lust of men observing women dancing in an adult entertainment club located along an interstate, Newman finds Christ imagery to point readers toward the one source that *will* "satisfy."

1154a   "News From Georgia: *Flannery O'Connor Bulletin* to Become *Flannery O'Connor Review*." *Cheers! The Flannery O'Connor Society Newsletter* 7.2 (Fall/Winter 1999-2000): 1.

Announces that the title of Georgia College & State University's scholarly journal devoted to Flannery O'Connor, *The Flannery O'Connor Bulletin*, will be changed to *The Flannery O'Connor Review* after publication of the combined volumes 26 and 27 in spring of 2001. States that the journal will have "an expanded format and somewhat larger scope" and that Sarah Gordon "will continue as editor, and the editorial board will remain essentially the same."

1154b   "News From Georgia: Party and Book Mark O'Connor's 75th Birthday." *Cheers! The Flannery O'Connor Society Newsletter* 7.2 (Fall/Winter 1999-2000): 1.

Reports on The Flannery O'Connor 75th birthday celebration held by Georgia College & State University, March 25, 2000, at nearby Lockerly Hall in Milledgeville. Notes that the occasion "also marked the publication of *Flannery O'Connor: In Celebration of Genius*, edited by Dr. Sarah Gordon and published by Hill Street Press of Athens."

1154c   "News From Georgia: Second Annual Festival at GC&SU." *Cheers! The Flannery O'Connor Society Newsletter* 7.2 (Fall/Winter 1999-2000): 1-2.

Describes events of the second annual Georgia Festival of Arts & Letters held March 6-11, 2000 at Georgia College & State University in Milledgeville. Reports that the program in honor of Flannery O'Connor held March 10, featured a showing of O'Connor's 1950s interview for the television show "Galley Proof"; a panel discussion on O'Connor's work and influence led by Sarah Gordon, featuring Jaimy Gordon, Judith Ortiz Cofer, and Miller Williams; "readings, talks, exhibitions and other events"; the performance of "Augustina," by Arthur Meryash; and the debut of the third issue of the University's journal *Arts & Letters*.

1155   "News from the O'Connor Collection." *Flannery O'Connor Society Newsletter* 1.1 (1993): 1.

Announces that microfilmed copies of O'Connor's manuscripts from the Flannery O'Connor Collection are now available to scholars via interlibrary loan. Reports receipt of a gift of additional letters from the estate of Maryat Lee, "a playwright, civil rights activist, artist, and friend of Flannery O'Connor."

1156   Nichols, Loxley F. "Flannery O'Connor's `Intellectual Vaudeville': Masks of Mother and Daughter." *Studies in the Literary Imagination* 20.2 (1987): 15-29.

Notes that in her letters, O'Connor "moves subtly into a third-person point of view, transforming herself into `the other one.'" Contends that while this shows her as something of a comic figure with unusual self-control and restraint, it also proved to keep even her closest friends at a distance, and shows that she was a "`writer' all the time" and "a performer who was *never* off stage."

1157   Nichols, Loxley. "The Hen, the Goose, and the Wren." *National Review* 19 Dec. 1986: 54-55.

Offers a review of *The Correspondence of Flannery O'Connor and the Brainard Cheneys*, edited by C. Ralph Stephens (UP of Mississippi, 1986. 220 pp.).

1158   Nichols, Loxley. "Keeping Up With Dr. Crane." *Flannery O'Connor Bulletin* 20 (1991): 22-32.

Discusses O'Connor's interest in the writings of George W. Crane, an author and syndicated newspaper columnist who held doctoral degrees in both medicine and psychology. Provides excerpts of O'Connor's letters related to Crane's column *The Worry Clinic*, which appeared in the *Atlanta Constitution* on a regular basis. Offers examples of his advice and contends that he was--for O'Connor--"An absurd self-parody of American secularism." Submits that because Crane was "Anti-intellectual, xenophobic, smug, provincial, capitalistic, sentimental, mechanistic, reductive, commercial, and ludicrously Protestant," he provides readers "a composite portrait of what O'Connor satirizes in her fiction." Offers examples of possible "manifestations of his thinking in O'Connor's own psychologists": Sheppard of "The Lame Shall Enter First" and Rayber of *The Violent Bear It Away*. Concludes that Crane represented for O'Connor "a refreshing joke as well as a formidable, even threatening Zeitgeist."

1159   Nichols, Loxley. "Shady Talk and Shifty Things." *Flannery O'Connor Bulletin* 14 (1985): 44-58.

Describes how O'Connor relies heavily upon presenting and cataloging "things," and notes that her fiction often contains "long lists of junk in every form . . . echoing clichés and inane ideas." Suggests that this technique conveys "the tawdriness of a modern secular world," and shows humanity's inability to make "the transient permanent." Contends that O'Connor conveyed the secular world as banal and depicted it with "comic vulgarization" to make the reader the "butt of the joke." Supports this assertion with discussions of how O'Connor's work "provides numerous examples of attempts to improve on nature by beautifications intended to halt the passage of time"; has characters defile religious terms and practices for secular purposes; and uses characters who talk and act as though they "can determine human history through sheer personal will." Remarks how the banal is evidenced in displays of violence that lead to the "loss of personal identity and class distinction," and in the misuse of religious language and ritual "as a shield" against displacement and to preserve class distinctions. Closes with a discussion tying O'Connor's technique to a comment by John Crowe Ransom on T.S. Eliot's *The Waste Land*. Concludes that "O'Connor's rendition of lust in all its manifestations" speaks "most eloquently of our own secularized national values in the American waste land she saw about her to the north, south, east, and west."

1160   Niederauer, George H. "The Church Listens to Flannery O'Connor." *Literature and Belief* 17.1-2 (1997): 21-33.

Focuses on O'Connor's views on faith and the Church as reflected in her letters: "the experience of being a believer, a disciple of Christ; the cost of discipleship; the power of grace in the experience of the believer; and the experience of the church as the setting of that life of faith and discipleship." Contends that while O'Connor "defended her church against superficial and unfair judgements, she was neither a whitewasher nor a fatalist, and she was an implacable foe of complacency." Concludes that O'Connor "thought that the name of Jesus, the reality of Jesus, belonged everywhere, indeed, was everywhere," and of the teachings of the Christian religion, "she believed all of it was true."

1161   Nielsen, Erik. "The Hidden Structure of *Wise Blood*." *New Orleans Review* 19.3-4 (1992): 91-97.

Offers a psychological study of O'Connor's *Wise Blood*, focusing on Hazel Motes's descent toward atheism, his transformation to genuine nihilist, and his eventual redemption. Discusses critical comments by Kathleen Feeley; the "incestuous and Oedipal contents" of Haze's dream on the train; O'Connor's use of shadow and vision to illustrate Haze's darker side and his mother's influence; and his self-blinding as a "final attempt to eliminate his `conscience' and his . . . past with its burden of religious `evil.'" Argues that it is "the contrast between *the profane* and *the sacred* [that] constitutes the fundamental contrast in *Wise Blood*." Concludes with a discussion of O'Connor's probable meaning for the phrase, "`pin point of light.'" Argues that "the word `light' refers to the novel's frequent use of the idea of a `shadow,'" and that it signifies "that Haze has ended his journey by returning to the divine world."

1162   Nifong, D. Michael. "Casting Strange Shadows: A Photographic Essay." *Flannery O'Connor Bulletin* 23 (1994-95): 43.

States that during his ten years of living in Milledgeville, he has enjoyed rambling--with camera in hand--through Memory Hill, a "*real* cemetery." Offers six photographs taken in the cemetery as a tribute to Flannery O'Connor and her writing.

1163   Niland, Kurt R. and Robert C. Evans. "*A Memoir of Mary Ann* and `Everything That Rises Must Converge.'" *Flannery O'Connor Bulletin* 22 (1993-94): 53-73.

Argues that O'Connor's involvement in the editing, promotion, and publication of *A Memoir of Mary Ann* during the period shortly before writing "Everything That Rises Must Converge" may have had a significant impact on the conceptual formulation of this story. States that "consciously or not, O'Connor seems to have been influenced by her strong admiration for the heroic, fun-loving, and compassionate [Mary Ann] when she came to write her story about a prematurely embittered young man." Finds the story to be one of O'Connor's most memorable and representative works, a portrayal of "bitterness, cynicism, and pride rooted in Julian's inability . . . to appreciate properly both his mother and the vital life-force she seems to embody." Comments on the role of the black child, Carver. Discusses O'Connor's allusions to sainthood in the story, and the irony in her choice of "Julian" as the main character's name; examines her use of tonal variation and her preoccupation with death; and discusses Teilhard de Chardin's influence on O'Connor's "Introduction." Concludes with a discussion of the description of Mary Ann's and Julian's mothers' deaths, focusing on the use of the eye in the text of both, and the assertion that the theme of sainthood seen in *A Memoir of Mary Ann* "is also strongly emphasized in O'Connor's story."

1164   Nilsen, Don Lee Fred. *Humor in American Literature.* New York: Garland, 1992.

Cites and offers descriptive abstracts for articles by Jane Elizabeth Archer, Isidore H. Becker, and Thomas F. Gosset on humor in O'Connor's work.

1165   Nisly, Paul W. "'Faith is not an Electric blanket.'" *Christianity Today* 17 May 1985: 21-24.

Criticizes the common view of O'Connor's works as "tricky tracts" to be wrestled with for spiritual messages, and says to read them in this manner is reductionistic and unworthy of her art. Constructs a spiritual biography of O'Connor from her letters to various associates and friends, including Cecil Dawkins, John McCown, Maryat Lee, "A," and others. Accentuates, among other things, O'Connor's determined belief in Catholic dogma, stating that it was for her, "the guardian of mystery." Includes a discussion of her early and continued skepticism and her vision of "grace."

1166   Nisly, Paul W. "A Good Book is Hard to Find." *Christianity and Literature* 25 (1976): 53-59.

Review essay of *The Eternal Crossroads: The Art of Flannery O'Connor* by Leon V. Driskell and Joan T. Brittain, and *The Question of Flannery O'Connor* by Martha Stephens. Criticizes the first book as reductionistic, primarily in its unyielding attempt to present a spiritual thematic for every story. Prefers Stephens's book, stating that it is less sympathetic to theology and offers important insights for "humanists to find basic goodness in human nature and who are naturally distressed with O'Connor's calculated affronts to humanistic thought."

1167   Nisly, Paul W. "The Mystery of Evil: Flannery O'Connor's Gothic Power." *Flannery O'Connor Bulletin* 11 (1982): 25-35.

States that in O'Connor's fiction, "evil is not some generalized force, or sociological trend, or psychological tendency: evil is concrete and tangible." O'Connor's evil is "clothed in flesh and stalks the unwary `good' people who may either deny its power or be completely oblivious to the reality of its presence." Ties her depiction to Gothicism, and discusses "The Comforts of Home," "A View of the Woods," and "The Life You Save May Be Your Own." Follows with an explication of the impact of evil upon the main characters in "A Good Man Is Hard to Find" and "The Lame Shall Enter First." Refers to comments by Robert L. Platzner, Robert D. Hume, Frederick Asals, Thomas Merton, and Richard

Chase. Relates that O'Connor "shows the terrible need for redemption by portraying characters who either glory in evil or--even worse--are entirely oblivious to its presence." Concludes that though O'Connor was obviously a devout Catholic who "surely believed in the ultimate triumph of good over evil . . . as a Gothic fictionist she left the outcome in doubt."

1168 Nisly, Paul W. "A Portrait of the Artist as a Young Southerner: Flannery O'Connor's `The Enduring Chill.'" *CLA Journal* 24.1 (1980): 42-47.

Compares O'Connor's Asbury Fox of "The Enduring Chill" to James Joyce's Stephen in *A Portrait of the Artist as a Young Man*. Reviews the plot of O'Connor's work and notes similarities between the two principal characters: both are young men who intend to be artists, both "wish to break away from their mothers; neither believes in traditional Christianity; [and] each hopes to create a new life as an artist." Examines Asbury's preoccupation with death, his "liberal attempt to cross the racial barrier through sharing a cup of milk," and his vision of the fierce bird descending from his bedroom ceiling. Asserts that it is unlikely that Asbury "has had the `last film of illusion' stripped from him"; and states, "his `feeble cry, a last impossible protest,' seems little more than another histrionic gesture." Concludes that instead of being freed--like Joyce's Stephen--"the narcissistic Asbury will evidently continue to be paralyzed by his worship of self, reflected in the mirror of Art. Flannery O'Connor offers no romantic escape."

1169 Nisly, Paul W. "The Prison of the Self: Isolation in Flannery O'Connor's Fiction." *Studies in Short Fiction* 17.1 (1980): 49-54.

Comments on Richard Chase's observation of the romance tradition in American Literature, that many American writers portray "the solitary individual who defiantly or fearfully faces the knowledge of his isolation." Relates his observation to O'Connor, contending that many of her characters are lonely individuals, isolated from others. Discusses Hazel Motes, Enoch Emery, and explicates the roles of Mr. Head and Nelson in "The Artificial Nigger" as illustrative examples. Observes that in much of O'Connor's work we find the quester creating his own prison.

1170 Nisly, Paul W. "Transforming Images." *Christianity Today* 12 Dec. 1986: 64.

Comments on a question asked by first-time readers of O'Connor's work: "`Was this woman really a Christian? What kind of person would write stories like these?'" Cautions against attempting "to extrapolate a life from

O'Connor's violent stories, and then . . . reinterpret the stories based on [a] reconstruction of her life." Refers to O'Connor's remarks on this strategy and then reviews Harold Fickett and Douglas Gilbert's book, *Flannery O'Connor: Images of Grace* (Eerdmans, 1986). Finds that Fickett "has generally succeeded well in presenting `images' of both the life and work of this major Christian author" and Gilbert did equally well in providing "wonderfully evocative black-and-white photographs of Georgia."

1171   Nisly, Paul W. "Wart Hogs From Hell: The Demonic and the Holy in Flannery O'Connor's Fiction." *Ball State University Forum* 22.3 (1981): 45-50.

Contends that O'Connor uses the conflict between "the Holy" and the demonic as her focus in the "serious matter" of writing novels. Suggests that an exploration of this nature may force the writer "to make the `descent through the darkness of the familiar' in order to discover his `region.'" Interprets John Hawkes's assessment of O'Connor's "Devil." Discusses a number of characters and stories, including Joy Hopewell in "Good Country People," Shiftlet in "The Life You Save May Be Your Own," Ruby Turpin in "Revelation," Mary Elizabeth and Calhoun in "The Partridge Festival," Old Dudley in "The Geranium," and Tanner and his daughter in "Judgement Day."

1172   Noble, Donald R. "Flannery O'Connor: A Georgian's Perspective." *Southern World* 3.1 (1981): 73-79.

Review essay of Barbara McKenzie's *Flannery O'Connor's Georgia* and Sally Fitzgerald's collection of O'Connor's letters, *The Habit of Being*, using the latter work as an introduction to an extended discussion of O'Connor's life and work. Compares McKenzie's work to Walker Evans's *Let Us Now Praise Famous Men*, and states that McKenzie "has used her fine photographic eye to show us what O'Connor was looking at . . . and was able to write about so powerfully." Offers a biographical sketch, including details related to O'Connor's childhood in Savannah and Milledgeville, Georgia, her academic career at the Georgia State College for Women and the University of Iowa, her years in the North, the onset of Lupus in December of 1950, and her relationship with her mother and farmhands who lived on the family farm (including the black couple, "Shot and Louise"). Provides brief sketches of "A Good Man Is Hard to Find" and "Good Country People." Relates O'Connor's assessment of several contemporary writers, her thoughts on "original sin," the usefulness of deformed characters "as representations of our inner, emotional and spiritual deformities," and the impact of her illness on her beliefs and writing. Illustrations: Charcoal portrait of O'Connor by Steve Sweeny.

1173 Nolan, Mary Lou. "Southern Roots, Timeless Voices." *Kansas City Star*
25 June 1989: I1+.

Examines the "hometown haunts" of four Southern writers: Faulkner's
Oxford, Mississippi; Welty's Jackson, Mississippi; O'Connor's
Milledgeville, Georgia; and Zora Neale Hurston's Fort Pearce, Florida.
Offers a brief biographical sketch, and describes each author's roots to
readers. Illustrations: Photographs of each author; Hurston's grave;
Faulkner's and O'Connor's homes; and a park pavilion near Welty's house.

1174 Norman, Geoffrey. "The FYI Library: The Ten Essential Books Of Or
About the American South." *Forbes* Winter 1997: 186.

O'Connor's *A Good Man Is Hard to Find* appears on Norman's list of "ten
books notable for their connection to the American South." Praises
O'Connor for her "distinctive, totally unsparing voice," and for her "spare,
razor-sharp prose style." The other nine include: *Absalom, Absalom!*, by
William Faulkner; *Other Voices, Other Rooms*, by Truman Capote; *Lie
Down in Darkness*, by William Styron; *Car*, by Harry Crews; *All the
King's Men*, by Robert Penn Warren; *Look Homeward, Angel*, by Thomas
Wolfe; *The Last Gentleman*, by Walker Percy; *Their Eyes Were Watching
God*, by Zora Neale Hurston; and *The Civil War*, by Shelby Foote.

1175 Norton, Jody. "History, Rememory, Transformation: Actualizing Literary
Value." *Centennial Review* 38.3 (1994): 589-602.

Draws on theories of the aesthetics of reading by Wolfgang Iser, Hans
Robert Jauss, and M.M. Bakhtin to propose a theory of "reader/text
relation": "In order to be usable for a reader as literature, a text must both
repeat and anticipate some structurally significant event in the reader's
life." Illustrates this theory through explications of Sandra Cisnero's *The
House on Mango Street* and Flannery O'Connor's "The River."

1176 Noya, José Liste. "Flannery O'Connor's `Demons': Intentionality and
Literary Meaning in `The Artificial Nigger.'" *REDEN* (Spain) 5.8 (1994):
29-44.

Sees O'Connor's secular audience as a sort of "literary `demon' with which
she struggled, wary of its incomprehension, hostility, or its potentially
more damaging `misconstrual' of her fiction." Acknowledges that, "at
times, the unbending harshness of the `ultimate reality' which O'Connor
attempted to dramatize in her fiction would prove to be a stumbling block
for many of her readers." Discusses her "uncompromising engagement

with the darker, `demonic' side of human nature," as readers find O'Connor using "murder, suicide, sodomy, arson, and a host of minor offenses" to force her protagonists to an "epiphanic crisis-point or `moment of grace.'" Explores O'Connor's "passage from authorial intention to narrative realization" through a detailed explication of "The Artificial Nigger." Includes discussions of the symbolic meaning of the statue (the "artificial nigger"), the "conflictive spheres of racial attitudes, sexuality (particularly the figure of maternity and the threat of feminine seduction), and [the] unconscious or irrational impulses [seen as] underlying human personality." Concludes that, in this "exquisitely crafted story," O'Connor's intended "spiritual implications do not exhaust the story's meaning." Instead, these implications provide for a far deeper meaning, "which goes on expanding for the reader the more he thinks about it."

1177   Nuwer, Hank. "The Writer Who Plays with Pain: Harry Crews." *South Carolina Review* 18.1 (1985): 63-73.

Offers a brief introduction to and interview with Harry Crews. Crews remarks that while he "can't count" O'Connor as an influence, he has read everything she has written.

1177a   Nye, Valerie. "Flannery O'Connor's Written Conversations: The Correspondence in the *Flannery O'Connor Collection* at Georgia College & State University." *Flannery O'Connor Bulletin* 26-27 (1998-2000): 25-42.

Offers a brief biographical sketch followed by a descriptive overview of the contents of the *Flannery O'Connor Collection*. Refers to, "among the sixty books published about O'Connor," *The Manuscripts of Flannery O'Connor at Georgia College* by Stephen Driggers, Robert J. Dunn and Sarah Gordon (Athens: U of Georgia P, 1989) and *Flannery O'Connor's Library: Resources of Being* by Arthur F. Kinney (Athens: U of Georgia P, 1985), noting that "neither focuses on the wide range of correspondence held in the collection." States that the collection holds O'Connor's collected correspondence with more than thirty individuals, ranging from the briefest of notes to extensive, thoughtfully written letters to her closest friends and colleagues. Concludes that, "by investigating the complete handwritten, typed, and signed letters . . . researchers may glimpse fully a portion of O'Connor's life and [better] understand the significance O'Connor placed on her writing, her friendships, and her faith." Lists the individuals whose correspondence to or from O'Connor is found in the Collection: Paul Barrus, George Beiswanger, James Bonner, Brainard and Francis Neel Cheney, O.B. Emerson, Betty Ferguson, Robert Giroux, Catherine Carver, Denver Lindley, Caroline Gordon, De Vene Harrold,

Alta Haynes, Caroline Ivey, Edward Kessler, William Koon, Roberta Lawrence, Maryat Lee, Betty Boyd Love, Allen Maxwell, Elizabeth McKee, Mavis McIntosh, Candida Donadio, Jeanne Minor, Rhoda Solomon, Paul Engle, Marion Montgomery, Martha Pennington Null, Joan O'Connor, Regina Cline O'Connor, Marion Peterman Page, Rebekah Poller, Mimi (Miriam) Johnson, Katherine Anne Porter, Richard Russell, Virginia Satterfield, Jessie Trawick, Katherine Scott, Marcus Smith, Grace Terry, Shirley Abbott Tomkievicz, Rosa Lee Walston, Leo Zuber, and Eileen Hall.

1177b [Nye, Valerie]. "O'Connor/Dawkins Correspondence Available in Tulsa." *Cheers! The Flannery O'Connor Society Newsletter* 7.1 (Spring/Summer 1999): 1-2.

Reports that the collection of letters from Flannery O'Connor to Cecil Dawkins is in the *Flannery O'Connor Correspondence Collection* at the University of Tulsa. Adds that Tulsa purchased the collection from Joseph the Provider Books in 1979. Notes that while 64 of the 99 letters appear in *The Habit of Being*, those selected for inclusion were generally "heavily excerpted," with "only five appearing in their entirety." Describes the content of the letters, themes and topics covered by the two writers, refers readers to a "finding aid" produced by Tulsa archivists on the Internet, and suggests that there is "much to be learned about O'Connor, her beliefs, and her close friendships by reading the set of correspondence in its uninterrupted entirety."

1177a Nye, Valerie. Rev of *The Harcourt Brace Casebook Series in Literature: "A Good Man Is Hard to Find,"* Ed. Laura Mandell Zaidman. *Flannery O'Connor Bulletin* 26-27 (1998-2000): 193-95.

Notes that this casebook is intended to offer high school, freshman college students, and other readers "historical information and criticism" of O'Connor's classic story, "A Good Man Is Hard to Find." Praises Zaidman for keeping "discourse on critical theory to a minimum" and successfully balancing "the need to provide students with relevant criticism with the need to warn them against dissecting the story word by word."

1178 Nyren, Dorothy, and Maurice and Elaine Fialka, comps. and eds. "O'Connor, Flannery." *Modern American Literature*. Vol. 4. Supp. to 4th ed. New York: Frederick Ungar, 1976. 339-40.

Excerpts criticism by Caroline Gordon and Ruth M. Vande Kieft from the Spring, 1968 issue of *Sewanee Review*; Leonard Casper's essay from *The*

Shaken Realist, edited by Melvin J. Friedman; and Richard H. Rupp's essay from *Celebration in Postwar American Fiction*.

1179   Oates, Joyce Carol. "The Action of Mercy." *Kenyon Review* 20.1 (1998): 157-60.

Provides an introduction to "The Artificial Nigger," reprinted "as it was originally written for the *Kenyon Review*" in this same issue. Describes it as a "graceful, parable-like" short story, unique in O'Connor's oeuvre because, unlike her "more characteristic prose fiction [which] bristles with cruel and sometimes savagely funny observations," it ends, "not with violent death, nor even in devastating irony, but with tenderness." Sees Mr. Head and Nelson as "genial cartoonish figures, country bumpkins," set up to suffer "O'Connor's typical ritual of humbling, unmasking, and redemption." Suggests that it is "a highly artificial, self-consciously wrought story in the mode of 1950s symbolic prose" whose opening lines seem "to have been written for academic New Critics of the era . . . to decode." Considers whether the story succeeds even though many readers may be unaware of, or even unsympathetic to, O'Connor's Christian sub-text. Concludes that because it "moves with its own dramatic momentum" and allows readers to sense the Christian imagery rather than be directly aware, it does work. [Mentions in a note that, "There is at least one distinguished American university in which a large-enrollment literature class petitioned successfully to have `The Artificial Nigger' removed from its syllabus as a racist text."]

1180   Oates, Joyce Carol. "Flannery O'Connor: A Self Portrait in Letters." *The Profane Art: Essays and Reviews*. New York: Dutton, 1983. 195-203.

Review essay of *The Habit of Being*. Finds the reading O'Connor's letters to be somewhat disturbing as well as "tonic, provocative, [and] intriguing." Asserts that while the letters--on one hand--"give life to a wonderfully warm, witty, generous, and complex personality," on the other, they reveal a "curiously girlish, childlike, touchingly timid personality." Suggests that while some letters reveal O'Connor to be a docile and conservative Catholic intellectual, others illustrate her to be "a hilariously witty observer of the grotesque, the vulgar, and the merely silly in this society." Finds and discusses "five distinctly different Flannery O'Connors" revealed in the correspondence. Also, comments on her talent for assessing the quality of her own work, the fullness of her life and friendships, and her relationship with her mother. Concludes that O'Connor "seems to have lived one of the most circumscribed lives ever lived by a distinguished artist" and enjoyed "a prolonged childhood which was never ravaged by adolescence or the complications of `adult' life."

1181   Oates, Joyce Carol. "The Visionary Art of Flannery O'Connor." *Fiction by American Women: Recent Views*. Ed. and intro. Winifred Farrant Bevilacqua. Port Washington, NY: Associated Faculty, 1983. 91-99.

Suggests that allusions to Teilhard de Chardin's work in *Everything That Rises Must Converge* do not imply--on O'Connor's part--an ultimate irony. Contends instead, that the book offers "a collection of revelations" and "points to a dimension of experiential truth that lies outside the sphere of the questing, speculative mind, but which is nevertheless available to all." Reports that each story in the collection "addresses itself to the problem of bringing to consciousness the latent horror, making manifest the Dream of Reason--which is of course a nightmare." Argues that O'Connor "sees the world as an incarnation of spirit," a world in which "people are not quite whole until violence makes them whole." Notes a connection between Kafka's "The Penal Colony" and O'Connor's "Parker's Back," and offers a reading of "The Lame Shall Enter First." Also offers interpretive readings of sections of "The Enduring Chill" and "Revelation." Explores O'Connor's sympathy with Teilhard's view that "the humanitarian impulse . . . is an egoistic activity," and comments on the starkness of O'Connor's writing and insistence that readers distinguish between "what Augustine would call the City of Man and the City of God." Closes with comments on "Revelation" and O'Connor's concern with revelations as related to "the mystic origin of religious experience, absolutely immune to any familiar labels of `good' and `evil.'" (Originally published in *Southern Humanities Review* 7 (1973): 235-46. Also in *New Heaven, New Earth: The Visionary Experience in Literature*. NY: Vanguard, 1974, 143-76; *Women Writers of the Short Story*. Ed. Heather McClave. Englewood Cliffs, NJ: Prentice Hall, 1980, 150-63; and *Flannery O'Connor: Modern Critical Views*. Ed. and intro. Harold Bloom. NY: Chelsea House, 1986, 43-53.)

1182   O'Brien, Geoffrey, Stephen Wasserman, and Helen Morris, eds. *The Reader's Catalog: An Annotated Selection of More Than 40,000 of the Best Books in Print in 208 Categories*. New York: Jason Epstein, 1989. 265, 334.

A list of O'Connor-related books still in print. Contains brief descriptions of her *Collected Works* and *The Complete Stories*. Cites one secondary source, *Flannery O'Connor's South* by Robert Coles.

1183   "Occasionally, we run across a story . . ." *Friends of Flannery* [Newsletter]. 2.4 (Sept. 1993): 2.

Recounts a story told by Ms. Pat Persse, O'Connor's cousin, about Flannery bringing home a report card with grades that would have been higher had her spelling been better: "The story is that one day she came home with her report card and despite her obvious brilliance the grades were not too good. She explained to her mother . . . that in history she had gotten an 85 but that `sister said it would have been 100 except for my spelling'; in geography the grade was 92 and also would have been 100 `except for my spelling'; and, finally, the 60 in spelling `would have been 100 except for my spelling.'"

1184   Ochshorn, Kathleen G. "A Cloak of Grace: Contradictions In `A Good Man Is Hard to Find.'" *Studies in American Fiction* 18.1 (1990): 113-17.

Reviews O'Connor's reactions to reader interpretations of "A Good Man Is Hard to Find" that contradict her intended meaning. Notes that "generally, O'Connor chalked up all the misreadings and confusion to the spiritual shortcomings of the modern reader," but argues that the discrepancies "cannot simply be explained by her theology of grace or by the lack of religious feeling among readers." Suggests, however, that her art is "not diminished by the contradictions between her work and her explanations of her work; she is made richer." Discusses the grandmother and The Misfit, and claims that despite their differences, the two "are bound by their concern with appearances and superficial respectability." Concludes that the story "speaks for an angry outsider, a person without illusion or sentimentality." Asserts that in this story, "a world of propriety and illusion is laid low by wrath, not redeemed by grace."

1185   O'Connor, Flannery. "`Be a Skeptic.'" *Christianity Today* 17 May 1985: 24.

Excerpt of a letter sent to Alfred Corn by O'Connor, reprinted from *The Habit of Being*. States that her letter was sent in response to one sent by Corn following a talk given by O'Connor to an English class at Emory University. O'Connor refers to the apostle Peter's prayer, "`Lord, I believe. Help my unbelief,'" and then states that "it is the most natural and most agonizing prayer in the Gospels, and I think it is the foundation prayer of faith." Sees the letter as offering guidance in confronting new ideas, meeting "intellectual difficulties," and the need for faith. O'Connor urges Corn to learn what he can and to also "cultivate Christian skepticism."

1186   O'Connor, Flannery. "The Coat." *Doubletake* 2.3 (1996): 38-41.

First appearance in print of this story. The plot focuses upon Rosa, a black woman who takes in clothes to wash and iron, and her husband Abram. Rosa stumbles upon a coatless corpse of a white man frozen with his outstretched arms forming a cross in the red clay. Later, her husband comes home drunk, with money taken from the pocket of a coat he had found and sold to a storekeeper in town. She assumes her husband has killed the man and advises him to bury the corpse, which leads to his violent, undeserving death at the hands of a band of white hunters. The story closes with a revelation that Rosa has suspected falsely and thus brought about Abram's death.

1187   O'Connor, Flannery. "An Exile in the East." *South Carolina Review* 11.1 (1978): 12-21.

First appearance in print of this story. The main character is Old Tanner, "a heavy old man" in poor health who has been brought by his daughter to live with her and her husband in their lower-class apartment in a poor section of New York City. The old man, who is so weak that he can barely walk, resents having to spend his last days in exile from the South, reduced to finding meaning in the smallest of incidents: watching a neighbor put out and take-in a small geranium plant each day. He misses Coleman, an alcoholic black companion that he had known back home for more than forty years, and remembers an incident from their first meeting that framed how the two viewed each other thereafter. The old man recalls with respect the bond the two shared as they lived together in the "shack made entirely of tin and crates" that the daughter found them in. She is fearful that her father may become friendly with the black man moving into the apartment next door and attempts to persuade the old man that the way to get along with "niggers" was to mind one's own business and to "live and let live." The elderly Southern father confronts his daughter on the issue but is unable to change her opinion. The story closes with Old Tanner meeting the black man in the stairwell of the apartment and, later, talking across the alleyway with the owner of the Geranium about the plant. [Note: The story is preceded by Jan Nordby Gretlund's essay, "Flannery O'Connor's `An Exile in the East': An Introduction" (pp. 3-11), which offers a comparison of the story with "The Geranium" and "Judgement Day."]

1188   O'Connor, Flannery. "Flannery O'Connor: Letters to Maurice-Edgar Coindreau (1958-1964)." *Delta* (France) 2 (Mar. 1976): 13-25.

Provides the text of ten letters--with notes--written by Flannery O'Connor to translator Maurice-Edgar Coindreau. Includes various invitations to Coindreau to visit Milledgeville; her advice against including an introduction to the French edition of *Wise Blood*; O'Connor's statement that she has never heard an "itinerant preacher" preach; references to clippings about traveling evangelists O'Connor sent to Coindreau; passing comments by O'Connor on Caroline Gordon's divorce; O'Connor's enthusiastic response to *La Sagesse Dans Le Sang*; a reference to Rev. Billy Graham being dared to participate in a "healing contest" by a Moslem leader; and her medical condition in mid-May, 1964.

1189   O'Connor, Flannery. "Novelist and Believer." *The Christian Imagination: Essays on Literature and the Arts*. Ed. Leland Ryken. Grand Rapids, MI: Baker Book House, 1981. 315-25.

Offers a "summary of Flannery O'Connor's attitude toward the Christian as writer." Provides a six-point summary of O'Connor's topics: "1) The task of the Christian writer, which begins by capturing concrete human experience and sees that experience in the light of Christian belief. 2) The direct influencea writer's world view has on his writing. 3) The spiritual climate of unbelief in which a Christian writer now writes, and how he must recognize the secular assumptions in his audience. 4) The sociological and psychological biases of our time that have produced impoverished understandings of literature and life. 5) The specific Christian doctrines that are crucial for a Christian writer: sin, creation, the centrality and transcendence of God, redemption, judgement, Satan. 6) The respect that a Christian writer must show for the literary craft." [Rpt. from O'Connor's collection of essays, *Mystery and Manners*.]

1190   O'Connor, Flannery. "Peacocks Are a Puzzle." *Reader's Digest* Mar. 1975: 205-07, 209.

Condensed from the original in *Mystery and Manners* in which O'Connor describes her interest in, and love for, her flock of more than 40 peacocks. Recounts how she had ordered an original family of one peacock and one hen with four 7-week-old peabiddies from a Florida farmer who had advertised them in the Florida *Market Bulletin*, and her sense of awe upon seeing them for the first time. Informs readers of the birds' strutting habits, their calls, and problems she encountered from their habit of "eating everything" in sight, including her mother's flowers, her uncle's figs, and the peanuts off the peanut hay stored in the family barn loft.

1191   O'Connor, Flannery. "`Reader Look For Yourself' Recovered Book Reviews." *Georgia Review* 37.2 (1983): 371-82.

Offers a sampling of O'Connor's book reviews to "illustrate not only O'Connor's famous wit and sound judgement but also her high standards of literary quality and her refusal to compromise" to meet the expectations of her audience. Describes the variety of books reviewed and mentions Leo J. Zuber, her book review editor during "many of those years."

1192 O'Connor, Flannery. ["The Shiftlet Fragment."] *Flannery O'Connor Bulletin* 10 (1981): 78-86.

Reproduction of O'Connor's marked-up typescript, referred to by Jan Nordby Gretlund as "The Shiftlet Fragment," and identified as "Dunn 156a." See also Jan Nordby Gretlund's "Mr. Shiftlet, Chapter Two: An Introduction to "The Shiftlet Fragment," in *Flannery O'Connor Bulletin* 10 (1981): 70-77.

1193 O'Connor, Flannery. "Six Cartoons." *Flannery O'Connor Bulletin* 11 (1982): N. pag. [after p. 57.]

Provides reproductions of six block print cartoons created by Flannery O'Connor. The cartoons depict humorous views of student life at Georgia State College for Women (G.S.C.W.)--O'Connor's alma mater. [The name was later changed to Georgia College & State University.]

1194 O'Connor, Flannery and Robert Penn Warren. "An Interview with Flannery O'Connor and Robert Penn Warren." *Talking with Robert Penn Warren.* Ed. Floyd C. Watkins, John T. Hiers, and Mary Louise Weaks. Athens: U of Georgia P, 1990. 52-67.

A transcript of a discussion that took place during the 1959 Vanderbilt Literary Symposium April 23, 1959, originally published in 1960 in the Vanderbilt University student magazine, *The Vagabond.* The discussion, in question and answer format, covers a wide variety of topics: whether the authors used an outline; their process of writing; whether they had an ending in mind when they began; whether it is possible "to write from a definite theological point of view"; O'Connor's view that the South was becoming "more and more city and less country"; the idea that "dehumanization" was a legitimate concern; and O'Connor's use of "freaks" in her fiction.

1195 O'Connor, Margaret Anne. "O'Connor, Flannery." *The Oxford Companion to Women's Writing in the United States.* Ed. Cathy N. Davidson and Linda Wagner-Martin. New York: Oxford UP, 1995. 641-42.

States that O'Connor's work reflects the tension of the time and conditions in which she lived: as a Roman Catholic in the years preceding the changes wrought by Vatican II, and as a Southerner during the upheaval of integration and the Civil Rights Movement. Reports that her humorous writings have been labeled by some as "black humor, southern Gothic, or southern grotesque . . . despite the tragedy or pathos of her plots." Lists her works, provides a biographical sketch, and offers brief, descriptive readings of her two novels and collections of short fiction. Concludes with a review of her themes and focus, and asserts that it is because none of her characters "receives the polite sympathy from the stories' narrators" that critics and readers find her work so fascinating and worthy of attention.

1196   O'Connor, Patricia. "The Faith of Flannery O'Connor." *Our Sunday Visitor* 25 July 1982: 12-13.

Offers biographical details, and discusses O'Connor's "faith" and the influence of her faith on the "orthodox Catholic point of view" presented in "A Good Man Is Hard to Find" and *The Violent Bear It Away*. Asserts that O'Connor "was a blunt woman, an honest woman" and that "her Christian point of view . . . was far from pious, or even obvious. Her stories are as blunt as she was, though far more harsh." Answers the rhetorical question Why didn't O'Connor end "A Good Man Is Hard to Find" with The Misfit "dropping the gun, realizing he is loved, and sobbing into the grandmother's skirts?" with the assertion that, "O'Connor writes about life as it is, and not about happy endings that we wish, sentimentally, would happen." Refers to the grandmother's murder and states, "God didn't promise protection from all evil, but salvation to those who believe. Evil exists. [O'Connor] explained that to make the redemption, to make the grace believable, she had to make the evil believable, too." Refers to O'Connor's correspondence with Alfred Corn as a testament of her faith, and ties her advice to the young student to an analysis of *The Violent Bear It Away*, concluding that O'Connor "grieved over the Raybers of this world, educated but empty."

1197   "O'Connor and the Contemporary Art Scene: Art Exhibition in California, 8 November-20 December." *CHEERS! The Flannery O'Connor Society Newsletter* 5.2 (1997-98): 1.

Reprints excerpts from a press release issued by Hunsaker Schlesinger Fine Art Gallery in Santa Monica, California announcing that an exhibition of paintings by Laura Lasworth, titled *The Habit of Being: A Portrait of Miss Mystery and Manners*, would be exhibited from November 8 - December 20, 1997. Reports that Lasworth, who was introduced to O'Connor's work in 1984, is exhibiting 13 "delicately rendered paintings," based upon, and inspired by O'Connor's fiction.

1198   "O'Connor and the Contemporary Art Scene: `The Displaced Person' Staged Again." *CHEERS! The Flannery O'Connor Newsletter* 5.2 (1997-98): 1.

Reports that Atlanta-based *Theatrical Outfit* will present Cecil Dawkins's dramatic adaptation of Flannery O'Connor's "The Displaced Person" during the 1997-98 season. Notes that Dawkins "is the only playwright to whom O'Connor gave permission to adapt her work," and that this production is the first performance "since it was staged at the American Theater in NYC in 1968."

1198a   "O'Connor's Alma Mater Draws Visits From Scholars, [and] Readers." *Savannah Morning News* 18 June 1984: C4.

Reports that though it has been two decades since Flannery O'Connor's death, scholars and "`groupies'" alike continue to visit her hometown of Milledgeville. Notes that the visitors' register for the Flannery O'Connor Room at Georgia College & State University reflects the geographic diversity of these visitors, and that her works have now become "a staple in college literature classes." Refers to John Kennedy Toole, posthumous winner of the Pulitzer Prize for his novel *A Confederacy of Dunces*.

1199   "O'Connor Trust Established." *CHEERS! The Flannery O'Connor Society Newsletter* 3.2 (1995-96): 1.

Reports that instructions in Regina Cline O'Connor's will directed that the "Mary Flannery O'Connor Charitable Trust" be established in her memory. Notes that the will "specifically states Mrs. O'Connor's `desire that the Trust use its assets to encourage and promote the development of creative writing skills through grants to schools, professors, teachers or instructors, scholarships for students, and any other means consistent with the charitable purposes of the trust.'" States that Flannery O'Connor's first cousins, Louise Florencourt of Milledgeville, GA ("who inherited the Green St. house") and Margaret Florencourt Mann of Lexington, MA (who "inherited the farm house Andalusia and 21 surrounding acres") will serve as trustees for the Trust.

1200   O'Donnell, Patrick. "The World Dactylic: Flannery O'Connor's *Wise Blood*." *Passionate Doubts: Designs of Interpretation in Contemporary American Fiction*. Iowa City: U of Iowa P, 1986. 95-115, 173-74.

Asserts that *Wise Blood* "is most often viewed just as O'Connor wished it to be: as the odyssey of a modern-day Antichrist who becomes a `Christian *malgré lui*.'" Contrasts Pynchon's *Gravity's Rainbow* with O'Connor's *Wise Blood*. Suggests that a contrast of the authorial presence of the two points out the crucial hermeneutic battle enacted in O'Connor's novel--"a battle where the singularity of an authorial intention is placed against the ironies

generated by the signs O'Connor employs in fulfilling that intention."
Finds that the "cultural dialectic of *Gravity's Rainbow* becomes, in *Wise
Blood*, a dialectic of authority, as the novel puts into question the intention
of its author's prefatory remarks and asks us to consider another dimension
of the desire for meaning." Offers a detailed, explication of *Wise Blood* in
the context of stated assertions. Explores O'Connor's use of language as "a
commodity that additively, supplementarily generates `meaning.'" States
that *Wise Blood* "inculcates a dramatic textual desire to create a certain,
certified impression, an `explanatory system' that will persuade us to
accept the conditions of the protagonist's destiny, no matter how extreme."
Mentions Milan Kundera, John Hawkes, Paul de Man, Ludwig
Binswanger, and Jacob Needleman.

1201   Ōe, Kenzaburo. "Japan, the Ambiguous, and Myself: Nobel Lecture, 7
        December 1994." *Georgia Review* 49.1 (1995): 335-43.

        Ōe uses O'Connor's words and cites her in his Nobel Prizefor Literature
        lecture. The reference appears on page 341 of this reprint of his speech:
        "This is what has become 'my habit of life'. . . through being a writer in
        my profession."

1202   "Of Interest to Scholars: The O'Connor Collection." *Flannery O'Connor
        Bulletin* 19 (1990): 74-76.

        A three-part article about the *Flannery O'Connor Collection* in the Russell
        Library of Georgia College & State University. Describes, in the first part,
        the Library's acquisition of 168 letters that O'Connor wrote to Maryat Lee
        during their close friendship between 1957 and 1964 and their availability
        to scholars. Reports, in the second part, on the College's successful efforts
        to raise funds from the National Endowment for the Humanities (NEH)
        and private donors to fund its $86,000 project to preserve and make more
        accessible the Library's O'Connor manuscripts. Concludes, in the third
        part, with a report of the Library's acquisition of 154 doctoral dissertations
        and master's theses related to Flannery O'Connor and her work as a result
        of R. Neil Scott's successful grant proposal to University Microfilms
        International (UMI).

1203   Okeke-Ezigbo, Emeka. "Three Artificial Blacks: A Reexamination of
        Flannery O'Connor's `The Artificial Nigger.'" *CLA Journal: College
        Language Association* 27.4 (1984): 371-82.

        Asserts that "The Artificial Nigger" is one of the "most powerful fictional
        commentaries of the race problem" during the time that O'Connor lived.

Suggests that the commentary is subtle, cryptic, and often missed. Discusses the metaphor of artificialness as related to the two principal characters and the statue, the "unawareness" which "is the mainspring of the story's delicate irony," and the characters' growing awareness that brings them to human naturalness. Concludes that the self-knowledge gained through painful lessons is that "the world operates in concentric circles and we cannot escape one another . . . black and white are complementary realities to those . . . who have cast off their dead weight of artificialness."

1204   Oliver, Bill. "Faith and Fiction in a Secular Age." *U.S. Catholic Historian* 6 (Spring-Summer 1987): 117-39.

States that America's most important Catholic novelists--Flannery O'Connor, J.F. Powers, and Walker Percy--each spoke of the supernatural in a conscious and deliberate manner because readers tend to "regard traditional religious symbols and structures with indifference, skepticism, or even hostility." Discusses Powers's *Morte D'Urban*, O'Connor's "A Good Man Is Hard to Find," and Walker Percy's *The Second Coming*. States that Powers "invites the reader to ponder what ideally a priest should be, and by extension what a good steward should be"; O'Connor forces readers to look directly into the "mysterious approach" of death and eternity; and Percy produces through his characters "`a comic catharsis'" by discharging "through laughter, the emotions of pity and fear . . . and in the process . . . restores our faith in the value of the concrete particular." Concludes that because these three writers believed "that `the old words of grace' are powerless to influence," they had to "explore strategies of storytelling that might open the reader to dimensions of life [that have] become inaccessible to many and remote to most."

1205   Oliver, Bill. "Flannery O'Connor's Compassion." *Flannery O'Connor Bulletin* 15 (1986): 1-15.

Reports that, according to many critics, "compassion is the quality that O'Connor's fiction" tends to lack. Refutes this contention by stating that she did indeed have compassion, but of the type that "does not deny the facts of sin and guilt." Outlines how O'Connor's compassion "grows out of the conviction that all men, though fashioned in God's image, are sinners and therefore need the aid and comfort of their fellows." Describes how she found the pride of her characters intolerable, especially those "who not only set themselves above the `niggers' and the `white-trash' but above God himself." Discusses four stories as illustrative examples of this "quality of mercy": "A Temple of the Holy Ghost," "The Artificial Nigger," "Parker's Back," and "Judgement Day." Declares that these stories illustrate how O'Connor tempered her satire with sympathy, and "in a voice at once disapproving and gentle . . . convey a viewpoint more complex and humane than we sometimes associate with her."

1206   Ollman, Leah. "Reflecting on Flannery O'Connor's Themes." *Los Angeles Times* 28 Nov. 1997: F30.

Reviews new paintings by Laura Lasworth based upon the writings of Flannery O'Connor, at the Hunsaker/Schlesinger gallery in Santa Monica, California. Finds them to be "self-sufficient--visually and emotionally lush still lifes, landscapes and portraits" that "resonate with O'Connor's texts more than they illustrate them." Concludes that these paintings, "like O'Connor's writing . . . can leave you breathless."

1207   Olschner, Leonard M. "Annotations on History and Society in Flannery O'Connor's `The Displaced Person.'" *Flannery O'Connor Bulletin* 16 (1987): 62-78.

Comments on historical developments and social trends that contributed to the shaping of post-World War II Southern attitudes recognized in "The Displaced Person." Describes the documentary news series *The March of Time* with its concluding slogan of "`Time marches on!'" Quotes from an article in *Life* on the plight of European displaced persons, and relates the background of hostility toward Catholics in the South. Describes the "ladies of the Old South" and interracial relations between white men and black women during that period; reports on the passing of the Displaced Persons Act of 1948 and reactions by Southerners to the resulting influx of foreign refugees. Ties these events and trends to Mrs. Shortley's views on religion, Mr. Guizac's arrival, presence, death, her black workers, and her resentment toward the impact that events in Europe were having on the social order of the South. Concludes that Mr. Guizac is an unwitting "moral intruder" and "an agent of change challenging Southern identity." Asserts that O'Connor's "point" is that "no one this side of heaven possesses a `place,' an ultimate home-country within time and custom, no matter how insistent and ubiquitous regional custom and manners might be. All of us are, in fact, DPs."

1208   Olson, Steven. "Tarwater's Hats." *Studies in the Literary Imagination* 20.2 (1987): 37-49.

Asserts that O'Connor's art is always grounded in the concrete and the literal before entering the abstract, theological and/or the symbolic. Suggests that whether or not Hulga's wooden leg, a character's hat, or other material objects become symbolic depends upon the physical transformations the items undergo. Refers to discussion of symbolism in Leon Driskell and Joan Brittain's *The Eternal Crossroads* and Miles Orvell's *Invisible Parade*. Focuses on O'Connor's use of hats as symbols in "A Good Man Is Hard to Find," "The Artificial Nigger," "Everything That Rises Must Converge," and *The Violent Bear It Away*. Concludes that O'Connor "gradually came to recognize the presence of a symbol" and "used them with great effectiveness."

1209   O'Mara, Phil. "Part of the Literary Context of the Work of Flannery O'Connor." *Publications of the Mississippi Philological Association* 1 (Summer 1982): 39-49.

Explores the "personal and literary context of Flannery O'Connor's achievement" and finds that "the dramatic tension, intellectual confidence, all-encompassing comedy, and compassionate exactness" of her rendering of modern life are better understood when placed "in the context of the literary and personal renewal of Catholic spirit." Lists Catholic writers of the 1940s and 1950s, recounts her Catholic heritage, and compares the approaches that O'Connor and poet Robert Lowell shared. Suggests that O'Connor realized that "her Christian perspective constituted a large part of the difficulty" in her unsuccessful negotiations with the Rinehart publishing company, and offers a detailed discussion of how her works were received by the scholarly and popular Catholic press. Explores and discusses O'Connor's interests as represented in her book reviews reprinted in *Flannery O'Connor: Her Life, Library and Book Reviews* by Lorine M. Getz, and finds that the reviews "show how fully religious, cultural and literary issues were unified" in O'Connor's mind. Asserts that "it is obvious that French Catholicism was on the whole the strongest literary and intellectual influence on her from outside the American literary tradition," and that she was "deeply concerned for the authenticity of Catholic life," which resulted in a stance that appears "to be founded on standards derived from the intellectual and artistic achievements of European Catholicism." Discusses O'Connor's "Introduction" to *A Memoir of Mary Ann* and her admiration for the work done by the Dominican Sisters for the Relief of Incurable Cancer at the St. Rose's Home.

1210   "On October 20, 1976, Regina Cline O'Connor presented a substantial gift to Georgia College . . . " *Flannery O'Connor Bulletin* 5 (1976): 69.

Reports that Regina Cline O'Connor presented a gift to Georgia College & State University that would be used to establish "the Flannery O'Connor Scholarship Fund." States that the fund would support an annual award to a Georgia College & State University student "who showed outstanding literary promise." Indicates that the first O'Connor Award would be given during the College's next Honor's Day.

1211   Opdahl, Keith. "The Nine Lives of Literary Realism." *Contemporary American Fiction*. Ed. Malcolm Bradbury and Sigmund Ro. London: Edward Arnold, 1987. 1-16.

Includes O'Connor's name among the twelve writers of the 1950s who "certainly produced . . . accomplished fiction."

1212   Oram, Richard. "Flannery O'Connor Research Holdings at the University of Texas." *Flannery O'Connor Society Newsletter* 1.1 (1993): 2.

Describes the collection of Flannery O'Connor-related materials given to the Harry Ransom Humanities Research Center at the University of Texas at Austin by David R. Farmer. Comments on Farmer's method of assembling the materials in preparation for his *Flannery O'Connor: A Descriptive Bibliography* (Garland, 1981), outlines the type and nature of editions held (some 125 books and an equal number of periodical issues), and the files of reviews of O'Connor's work, articles about her, and criticism through the early 1970s. Reports that manuscript holdings are "slight": six typed letters from O'Connor to Robie Macauley and five more to Caroline Gordon and Loretta Lish.

1213   Oreovicz, Cheryl Z. "Seduced by Language: The Case of Joy-Hulga Hopewell." *Studies in American Fiction* 7.2 (1979): 221-28.

Discusses characters and motivations in "Good Country People," focusing on Joy-Hulga's "real" world -- a world of the mind "shaped and organized not just by the thought but the `truth' of the language and syntax of a [Nicolas] Malebranche or a [Martin] Heidegger." Suggests that Joy-Hulga is surprised that the Bible salesman is "another who consciously manipulates or perverts words and epithets to convey multiple or symbolic statements." Concludes that O'Connor's "careful linking of language and perception for each character points to the central position of cognitive theory as theme and technique" in the story.

1214   O'Rourke, William. "Morphological Metaphors for the Short Story: Matters of Production, Reproduction, and Consumption." *Short Story Theory at a Crossroads*. Ed. Susan Lohafer and Jo Ellyn Clarey. Baton Rouge: Louisiana State UP, 1989. 193-205.

Includes in the discussion O'Connor's claim that "`The major difference between the novel as written in the eighteenth century and the novel as we usually find it today is the disappearance from it of the author.'"

1215   Orr, John. *The Making of the Twentieth-Century Novel: Lawrence, Joyce, Faulkner and Beyond.* New York: St. Martin's, 1987. 92, 169, and 186-87.

Offers a survey of passion and compassion in nineteenth and twentieth-century fiction. Includes brief comments related to Flannery O'Connor, including her belief that the "thematic emphasis on the lower middle classes, poor whites, black servants and laborers, and the socially outcast" by Southern writers was being misread by critics and seen, instead, "in terms of demented `Southern Gothic' or the `grotesque'"; the view that *Wise Blood* serves to dissolve the "traditional vision of the South as an arcadian repository of Christian value" and that her works, along with those of Richard Wright, Ralph Ellison, Thomas Wolfe and William Styron, "at times prophesy the erosion of historical differences between North and South as center and periphery of Modern American life"; and a brief explication of *Wise Blood* as a charting of "the disintegration of Christian compassion and belief in the same way that Faulkner charted the disintegration of honor."

1216   Osborn, Chris. "Prophecy--the `Most Terrible Vocation': God's Pursuit of the Reluctant Prophet in the Novels of Flannery O'Connor." [87 pp.] Ms. 1992.

Discusses and reviews the stories of biblical prophets who were "an integral part of O'Connor's Catholic heritage" and are of such significance to O'Connor that they "comprise essential elements of her fiction." Examines and explicates *Wise Blood*, "the story of Motes's effort to develop his own counter-Christian religion and challenge the influence of Christian teachings on society." Notes that through his encounters with others in Taulkinham, Hazel Motes works out his denial "with a passion," and that in the end, he "cannot escape the influence of the faith which he tries so assiduously to destroy." Offers an explication *The Violent Bear It Away* and contends that it is O'Connor's "investigation of the lives of a few of the violent, unnatural prophets produced by the `do-it-yourself' religion of the rural South." Asserts that Mason and Francis Marion Tarwater are modern Christian prophets who have to work out their faith dramatically and "violently shout forth the message of the revelations which God has given them." Examines George Rayber and the Devil in *The Violent Bear It Away*, and finds Rayber to be "a prototype of the modern intellectual skeptic who doubts anything which he cannot prove or observe to be true," inspired by a Devil "well-schooled . . . in classical rational nihilist thought." Concludes that, like her reluctant prophets, O'Connor "confronts humanity with its depravity and with a powerful vision of the radical, life-altering, often violent nature of God's love, which she believed to be the only hope for man's salvation." [Copy in the *Flannery O'Connor Collection*, Georgia College & State University.]

1217   Osborne, Linda Payne. "Two Generations of Southern Womanhood in Flannery O'Connor: Mothers, Daughters, Mystery, and Manners." *Mid-Hudson Language Studies* 8 (1985): 71-81.

Observes that many of O'Connor's women are on their own, do not have male support, and are facing a life "without magnolia blossoms." Suggests that O'Connor's fictional settings reflect the imprint of her own life and were chosen because she knew them and the rural South so intimately. Asserts that they fit her intentions well: "to show the mystery of life--the unknown, the poetry, or, as she says it, the touch of God's grace--in the context of the concrete, everyday life expressed through manners." Discusses characters in stories that focus on Southern women--often "mannered women blind to their own salvation"--faced with confronting the mystery of God's salvation. Examines four stories "set on farms run by women left alone to raise a daughter: "Good Country People," "A Circle in the Fire," "The Life You Save May Be Your Own," and "A Temple of the Holy Ghost"; mothers in "The Enduring Chill" and "Revelation"; and daughters in "A Good Man Is Hard to Find" and "A View of the Woods."

1218   Osinski, Bill. "Literary Giants Hail From Small Slice of Georgia." *Atlanta Journal-Constitution* 22 Mar. 1998: D9.

Provides biographical sketches of Flannery O'Connor, Alice Walker, and Joel Chandler Harris. Mentions their most prominent works and describes the context of their childhoods growing up within only a few miles of the other, but during different generations. Notes that there are few reminders of the three prominent authors in their hometowns of Milledgeville and nearby Eatonton. Includes photographs of the three authors and a fourth of Ruth Walker Hood, Alice's sister, standing in front of the small country church she attended with her sister as a child.

1218a   Osinski, Bill. "Milledgeville Celebrates Its Home-Grown Genius." *Atlanta Journal-Constitution* 12 March 2000: G4.

Describes events planned by Georgia College & State University to celebrate Flannery O'Connor's 75th birthday. Reports that the University is sponsoring a birthday celebration on March 25th; a series of public seminars during the year featuring invited speakers on Southern culture; and an exhibit of paintings by Laura Lasworth inspired by O'Connor's works. Refers to comments by Sarah Gordon regarding the *Flannery O'Connor Bulletin* and her two the forthcoming books, *Flannery O'Connor: In Celebration of Genius* and *Flannery O'Connor: The Obedient Imagination*. Includes comments by South Carolina author Brett Lott regarding O'Connor's essay "The Nature and Aim of Fiction," Robert Coles on why he teaches O'Connor to medical students, and Nancy Mairs on O'Connor's battle with Lupus.

1219   Osinski, Bill. "O'Connor's Orphan Birds Fanned Out with a Squawk." *Atlanta Journal-Constitution* 29 Sept. 1991: M1+.

Reports on O'Connor's interest in and admiration for peacocks. Quotes from her essay "The King of the Birds," and recounts the lives of her last three pair, which were taken after her death from the O'Connor farm (Andalusia) outside Milledgeville, Georgia. One pair was given to Stone Mountain Park, another pair to Our Lady of Perpetual Help cancer hospice in Atlanta, and the third to the Monastery of the Holy Ghost near Conyers, Georgia. States that the pair at Stone Mountain fell prey to predators; the second pair were sent on to the Monastery to join the third pair--where they stayed for two decades--and then, because they disturbed the Monastery's guests, were given in 1983 to Frank Reindl, who took them to his home on Lake Lorelei near Cincinnati, Ohio. Notes that "everything went along fine until somebody who lives up here started trying to keep a silver fox for a pet . . . the fox would escape periodically--and do what comes naturally to foxes that come across penned up birds . . . the fox got the last of the peafowl last winter." Illustrations: photographs of O'Connor admiring her peacocks. [Rpt. with a different photograph in the *Milledgeville (GA) Union-Recorder* 6 Dec. 1992: B1-B2.]

1220   Ostrander, Betty. "Flannery O'Connor (1925-1964)." *Georgia's Literary Heritage: Biographical and Publishing Histories of Selected Georgia Authors*. Athens, GA: Agee, 1986. 17.

Concise one-hundred word biographical sketch followed by a listing of O'Connor's works. States that O'Connor's stories "are marked by a curious blend of religion, grotesqueness, and violence with which she delves into the relationship between man and God."

1221   Owens, Collie. "Diagnosing the Disease: O'Connor's Non-Lover's Quarrel With the World." *Chattahoochee Review* 12.1 (1991): 64-78.

Contends that an essay written by Ben Satterfield in *Studies in American Fiction* (Spring 1989) is an indication of "an ideological assault on the religious themes" in O'Connor's work, and that such essays are "thinly disguised as aesthetic evaluation." States that the "mean-spirited attack exhibited in this article goes beyond the critical reevaluation that every author undergoes in due time," and that Satterfield's judgements "are slanderously absurd." Suggests that articles such as Satterfield's "are a symptom of the vacuum of moral and spiritual values in the modern world, the void that is, in fact, the prime target of O'Connor's satire, a critique that is *necessarily* informed by her Christian world view." Discusses O'Connor's satirical indictment of modernism in detail, offering examples of rationalists, irrationalists, and "true believers in the weird and mysterious," from *The Violent Bear It Away*, "The Lame Shall Enter First," *Wise Blood*, "Good Country People," "The Artificial Nigger," "A Good Man Is Hard to Find," "A Circle in the Fire," "The Displaced Person," "Greenleaf," and "A View of the Woods." Concludes that if critics "wish to take issue with Flannery O'Connor's religious viewpoint, they must do so on moral/theological grounds, not on the basis of ersatz aesthetics or name-calling."

1222   Owens, Mitchell. "The Function of Signature in `A Good Man Is Hard to Find.'" *Studies in Short Fiction* 33.1 (1996): 101-06.

Discusses O'Connor's use of signatures to represent the conflict between "the ascendancy of the mercantile and the decline of the gentility" in "A Good Man Is Hard to Find." Notes that the grandmother has, throughout her life, "been struggling with the shift from the ante-bellum values of lineage and gentility to those of a cash-oriented culture, and with the implications this shift has for the assumptions that underwrite her vanishing system of beliefs." Explicates the sections of the story which deal with Mr. Edgar Atkins Teagarden carving his initials into the side of the watermelon and The Misfit's refusal "to recognize the power of any signature other than his own." Concludes with a discussion of the symbolic meaning of The Misfit donning Bailey's colorful shirt and "how the concept of familial linkage has become attached to the signifier-shirt by Bailey's wearing of it."

1223   Owens, Virginia Stem. "Fiction and the Bible." *Reformed Journal* 38 (July 1988): 12-15.

Attempts to answer the rhetorical question, "Why do we `teach' literature?" Suggests that "we in fact got the whole idea of literature as something to be taught and studied because we had already developed the habit with the Bible." Asserts that novelists do not write for those who teach, and quotes O'Connor as saying when asked if the novel was a dying art form: "'The health of the novel is one thing that just doesn't interest me a bit. That's for English teachers to talk about.'" Points out the "paradox of modern fiction that requires the writer to conceal a story's meaning," and uses quotes from O'Connor to support her discussion. Notes that where critics, such as Annie Dillard, appear "impatient both with the process of making the meaning disappear into the material and then with having to retrieve it again, O'Connor understands this process as the *only* way to make a modern story work."

1224   Ower, John. "The Penny and the Nickel in 'Everything That Rises Must Converge.'" *Studies in Short Fiction* 23.1 (1986): 107-10.

Argues that the designs of the Lincoln penny and the Jefferson nickel are tied--as symbols--to the social, religious, and racial themes of "Everything That Rises Must Converge."

1225   Ozaki, Shunsuke. "A Short Essay on Flannery O'Connor's *Wise Blood*." *Colloquia* (Japan) 7 (Sept. 1987): 34-46.

Asserts that Hazel's rebellion against God is very similar to that of Jonah. Argues that O'Connor's novel gradually changes from absurdity to mystery, a "trick" engineered through O'Connor's use of the "as-if" construction. Concludes that O'Connor lets her readers think that *Wise Blood* is a comic novel, and all of a sudden confronts them with a mystic vision. (Abstracted by Kayoko Watanabe).

1226   Ozer, Jerome S. "*Wise Blood*." *Film Review Annual, 1981*. Ed. Jerome S. Ozer. Englewood, NJ: J. Ozer, 1982. 1067-75.

Offers reprints of eleven reviews of John Huston's film of O'Connor's *Wise Blood*. Reprinted are those by David Sterritt, *Christian Science Monitor* (7 March 1980); Rob Edelman, *Films in Review* (Jan. 1980); Charles Champlin, *Los Angeles Times* (12 December 1979); Geoffrey Nowell-Smith, *New Statesman* (18 Jan. 1980); David Denby, *New York* (10 Mar. 1980); Archer Winsten, *New York Post* (18 Feb. 1980); Alex Keneas, *Newsday* (18 Feb. 1980); David Ansen, *Newsweek* (17 Mar. 1980); Tim Pulleine, *Sight and Sound* (Winter 1979-80); Frank Rich, *Time* (25 Feb. 1980); and Andrew Sarris, *Village Voice* (25 Feb. 1980).

1227   Pace, Barbara G. "The Textbook Canon: Genre, Gender, and Race in US Literature Anthologies." *English Journal* 81.5 (1992): 33-38.

Reviews "five commonly used US literature anthologies from major publishers" to develop "a *textbook canon*" of authors appearing in three of the five books. Examines this canon to determine how women and people of color are represented "as characters and as writers." Includes O'Connor in the "Story/Novel Excerpt" category, and expresses concern that, in addition to her story "The Life You Save May Be Your Own," only four other fictional works by women are contained in the canon. Finds "all of the female characters in these stories [to be] physically weak and passive" and "voiceless victims of negative experiences with men." Concludes that "the female experience presented" in these stories falls "within a narrow social spectrum," and contain "culturally encoded structures of power and stereotyping in their historical perspectives."

1228   Pachmuss, Temira. "Dostoevsky and America's Southern Women Writers: Parallels and Confluences." *Poetica Slavica: Studies in Honor of Zbigniew Folejewski*. Ed. J. Douglas Clayton and Gunter Schaarschmidt. Ottawa: U of Ottawa P, 1981. 115-26.

Compares works of Dostoevsky, Carson McCullers, and O'Connor. Sees parallels in their "dramatization of the agony of the human soul," their dreamlike atmosphere and affinity for the grotesque, and their vision, tension, and concern for religion. Concerned primarily with Dostoevsky's *The Possessed*, McCuller's *The Heart is a Lonely Hunter* and *Member of the Wedding*, and O'Connor's *Wise Blood* and *The Violent Bear It Away*.

1229   Paige, Linda Rohrer. "White Trash, Low Class, and No Class at All: Perverse Portraits of Phallic Power in Flannery O'Connor's *Wise Blood*." *Papers on Language & Literature* 33.3 (1997): 325-33.

Observes that O'Connor's rural "low class," Southern "'white trash'" characters, who are "marked not only by their libidinous appetites" but their violent nature, paradoxically "seem privy to a spiritual vision denied to other characters." Examines the characters in *Wise Blood* and points out that they demonstrate a "capacity for vision, despite their tendency to embark on perilous journeys in pursuit of truth's opposite." Presents examples of how "the phallus becomes the vehicle that drives" Hazel Motes "on his journey into falsehood, and paradoxically, toward truth," including the stick that his mother beat him with as a child ("God's phallic rod"); Mrs. Watts as a symbol of "a type of 'phallic power'"; and--when he can no longer find satisfaction with either Mrs. Watts or Sabbath Lily-- his purchase and use of "the ultimate phallic weapon, an old Essex." Points out how O'Connor even has the Essex imitating the sexual act, as she describes it as drivable by going backwards and then forward again "'a succession of times rapidly.'"

1230 Palmer, Louis H., III. "Southern Gothic and Appalachian Gothic: A Comparative Look at Flannery O'Connor and Cormac McCarthy." *Journal of the Appalachian Studies Association* 3 (1991): 166-76.

Examines and compares "Appalachian Gothic" to "Southern Gothic" to determine if Appalachian Gothic is a sub-group of the latter. Uses Irving Malin's "paradigm" to compare the two categories, and states that Malin "defines the gothic mode in terms of the isolation and narcissism of its protagonists and their antagonistic relations with the primary unit, the family." Discusses Malin's three recurring images in Gothic literature: "the mirror, the voyage, and the house, which reinforce the themes of self-love and rejection of family." Uses Malin's critical assertions to examine and compare O'Connor's *Wise Blood*, and Cormac McCarthy's *Suttree*, chosen "because of their obvious similarities of setting--the `underside' of Southern urban life in the immediate postwar period--and because they provide some interesting contrasts." Utilizes Malin's themes, symbols, and views of the natural world to show that "this treatment is where, in this and other cases, one can distinguish between the two Gothics."

1231 Parini, Jay. "Blowing Through the Ram's Horn: Berry, Ozick, and Others." *New England Review and Bread Loaf Quarterly* 6.4 (1984): 630-38.

Includes, in a discussion of *In Search of Our Mother's Garden*, comment on Alice Walker's "deep sympathy for Flannery O'Connor, who peppered her correspondence with the word `niggers' and wrote from an explicitly Catholic position."

1232 Park, Clara Claiborne. "Crippled Laughter: Toward Understanding Flannery O'Connor." *American Scholar* 51.2 (1982): 249-57.

Describes O'Connor's writing as a "thicket of paradoxes" whose directness and precision "give almost physical pleasure." Contends that even though she was unusually aware of her readers, O'Connor still "left Southern readers indifferent," developed saintly backwoods characters unrecognizable to Catholic readers, and had to explain her work in her letters, public lectures and readings. Suggests that throughout her career readers, fellow writers, and friends, "missed the point or, worse mistook it." Contends that while O'Connor "was not well served" by her mentors, Paul Engle and Caroline Tate, her letters shine with a "humorous virtue that converted intelligence into a premature and touching wisdom." [Note: In a "Letter to the Editor" in *American Scholar* 51.3 (1982): 587, Suzanne Morrow Paulson contends that Park's criticism of O'Connor's work is "too simple."] [Rpt. in *Rejoining the Common Reader: Essays, 1962-1990*. Evanston, IL: Northwestern UP, 1991, 146-63.]

1233   Park, Clara Claiborne. "A Personal Road." *Hudson Review* 34.4 (1981-82): 601-05.

Reviews *The Stories of Elizabeth Spencer*, focusing on her "sense of place." Refers to O'Connor's comments as to why a writer should remain in his or her own region and the distance Spencer's South "has come from that history of defeat which for O'Connor taught the reality of the Fall." Applauds Spencer's art and states: "It is pleasant to know that in the dread and boisterous country of Faulkner and O'Connor," she "has for more than thirty years been walking her own path, with quiet tread."

1234   Parker, Peter, ed. "(Mary) Flannery O'Connor 1925-1964." *A Reader's Guide to Twentieth-Century Writers*. New York: Oxford UP, 1996. 555-56.

Offers a biographical sketch of O'Connor with discussion of the impact of disseminated lupus upon her life and work. States that "in her birth in Georgia, Gothic literary output, and short, unhealthy life, O'Connor resembles another Southern Renaissance writer, Carson McCullers." Suggests that the two are "sometimes confused, not least because of the similar forms their names take." Provides brief summaries of O'Connor's two novels and offers the assessment that her short stories are her "finest work." Praises O'Connor's ability to bring her "grotesque, even freakish, and often strangely inspired characters" to life.

1235   Parker, Susan. "Good Quotes Not Hard to Find in Flannery O'Connor's Works." *Macon (GA) Telegraph* 15 Dec. 1991: E10.

Admonishes compilers of *Bartlett's Familiar Quotations* for including only four quotations from O'Connor, three of which are "comparatively dry . . . and lack the humor that pervades so much of what O'Connor said and wrote." Offers 39 other "quotes missing from *Bartlett's*" along with a biographical sketch. Illustrations: Photograph of O'Connor at Andalusia leaning on a picket fence with a straw hat in her hand.

1236   Parks, Cynthia. "Recognition for Flannery O'Connor Came Late." *Florida Times-Union/Jacksonville Journal* 2 Sept. 1984: E8.

Notes that when Sarah Gordon came to teach at Georgia College in 1968, O'Connor's writings were not sold in the campus bookstore. Observes that this has changed in recent years as her works have won numerous awards and been included in "all the literature books." Offers a brief biographical sketch, describes Milledgeville, GA, O'Connor's mother Regina Cline

O'Connor, and the O'Connor Room and campus of Georgia College & State University.

1237   Parks, John G. "Losing and Finding: Meditations of a Christian Reader." *Christianity and Literature* 38.2 (1989): 19-23.

Asserts that the "predicament of the Christian reader" is analogous to the crisis of O'Connor's characters. Contends that what happens to her characters must happen to us, and observes that "despite our scholarly essays, bulletins, and critical studies on her fiction, we have not succeeded in domesticating the terror or taming the raw, primitive power of her work." Observes that "nearly all" of her stories "are stories of vision--of things we see and things we don't see, of things we try to see and things we refuse to see but, most importantly, of things we see *at last*." Discusses O'Connor's "clear-eyed" villains and maintains that the real villainy she depicts is that of the "distortions of the modern world, a world rendered unable to tell straight from crooked and blind to its own idolatries." Suggests that the "many physical, intellectual, and spiritual grotesques in O'Connor's fiction are metaphors for the distortions of the modern [Promethean] willful self." Refers to David Tracy's book, *Plurality and Ambiguity: Hermeneutics, Religion, Hope* (1987) and concludes that the distinctiveness of being a Christian reader "is the awareness and experience of the decentered self, which comes paradoxically as a gift."

1238   Parlato, Salvatore J., Jr. *Film Ex Libris: Literature in 16mm and Video.* Jefferson, NC: McFarland, 1980. 219, 221.

Provides 1,410 entries encompassing 1,012 literary works by 645 authors. Each entry includes the film's title, a short plot summary, the producer/distributor, running length, date and an indication as to whether the film is in black-and-white or color. Includes entries for "A Circle in the Fire," "The Comforts of Home," and "The Displaced Person."

1239   Parrish, Tim. "The Killer Wears the Halo: Cormac McCarthy, Flannery O'Connor, and the American Religion." *Sacred Violence, A Reader's Companion to Cormac McCarthy: Selected Essays from the First McCarthy Conference at Bellarmine College, Louisville, Kentucky, October 15-17, 1993.* Ed. Wade Hall and Rick Wallach. El Paso: Texas Western Press, 1995. 25-39.

Discusses O'Connor and McCarthy's fiction in the context of Rene Girard's statement that "violence and the sacred are inseparable" and Harold Bloom's "explication of the `emptiness' of the American soul" in *The

American Religion. Acknowledges that "critics of O'Connor and McCarthy have invariably had to wrestle with the peculiar combination of violence and redemption that suffuses each writer's fiction, seeking the former's extinction in the latter." Focuses upon O'Connor's use of violence in *Wise Blood* and *The Violent Bear It Away*, and McCarthy's use in *Blood Meridian.* Concludes that, "for O'Connor, the devil clarifies the American soul's polar choices: self-deification or nihilism."

1240   Passaro, Vince. "Dragon Fiction." *Harper's* Sept. 1996: 64-71.

Examines "the phenomenal growth" of the Christian thriller, and discusses how this genre "shares not only an acceptance of the magic of . . . faith, but also a hard belief in some other significant, latter-twentieth-century American myths." Outlines the plot and themes of Charles Colson and Ellen Vaughn's *Gideon's Torch*, Joseph Bayly's *Winterflight*, and Frank Peretti's *The Oath*, and finds them to be "dramatically unconvincing" and "flat, bilious, and tedious." Discusses how these works pale in comparison to works by such legitimate Christian authors as Dostoevsky, G.K Chesterton, Graham Greene, Francois Mauriac, George Bernanos, Nathaniel Hawthorne, and Flannery O'Connor. Then devotes several paragraphs to descriptions of how O'Connor's fiction "centered on deeper and more spiritual issues" serves to illustrate how one may "accept Roman Catholic dogma and still manage to exercise the freedom of vision, association, and thought that are the requirements of art."

1241   Patterson, Margaret C. *Author Newsletters and Journals: An International Annotated Bibliography of Serial Publications Concerned with the Life and Works of Individual Authors.* Detroit: Gale Research, 1979. 230.

Cites *Flannery O'Connor Bulletin*, published in Milledgeville, with a short annotation, index, and cross-references.

1242   Patterson, Margaret C. "Research Project A: Flannery O'Connor." *Literary Research Guide.* Rev. ed., New York: Modern Language Assn. of America, 1984. xvi-xxv.

Offers a bibliographic essay which considers the problems student researchers face in gathering information related to the life and work of Flannery O'Connor. Outlines how one might assemble facts, choose reputable reference sources, verify facts and information, and decide how much background reading may be required to complete an assigned literary project focused on O'Connor. Describes "quick" reference sources, literary handbooks, and the methods used to locate relevant books, special publications, "`reviews of research'," bibliographies and a wide variety of other sources.

1243   Patterson, Tom. "O'Connor Country: Tom Patterson Interviews Biographer, Sally Fitzgerald." *Brown's Guide to Georgia* 7.11 (1979): 22-23, 25-27.

Narrative interview of O'Connor's closest friend, Sally Fitzgerald, in Milledgeville, Georgia, where Fitzgerald was teaching a summer term class on O'Connor's writings. Describes the Georgia College & State University campus, discussion by students in Fitzgerald's class of O'Connor's "Revelation," and the script-writing and production of John Huston's *Wise Blood* in nearby Macon. Fitzgerald describes meeting O'Connor, the two years O'Connor lived with her and her husband in Ridgefield, Connecticut, and impressions Milledgeville residents and literary critics had of O'Connor's work. Fitzgerald provides helpful biographical information and personal recollections. Illustrations: Portrait-style photographs of O'Connor and Fitzgerald.

1244   Patterson, Tom. "A Tour of the Flannery O'Connor Memorial Room." *Brown's Guide to Georgia* 7.11 (1979): 24-25.

Describes the layout of the Flannery O'Connor Room in the Russell Library of Georgia College & State University. Points out the variety of materials available in the display case of the room, contents of file cabinets, and book shelves of criticism and photographs. Offers a fairly detailed description of books O'Connor had in her personal library. Illustration: Line-drawing of O'Connor Room layout.

1245   Paulson, Suzanne Morrow. "Apocalypse of Self, Resurrection of the Double: Flannery O'Connor's *The Violent Bear it Away*." *Literature and Psychology* 30.3-4 (1980): 100-11.

Analyzes *The Violent Bear It Away* and argues that even O'Connor herself acknowledged that a Freudian interpretation would be in order. Applies "the psychology of the divided self and some Freud . . . to suggest new possibilities for all her works." Examines Francis Tarwater, Mason, and Rayber, and concludes that the value of this novel "rests with its insights into human nature, not least with what it reveals about the psychology of the divided self." [Revised version included in *Flannery O'Connor: New Perspectives*. Ed. Sura P. Rath and Mary Neff Shaw. Athens: U of Georgia P, 1996. 121-38.]

1246   Paulson, Suzanne Morrow. "The Reader Replies: Flannery O'Connor."
            American Scholar 51.3 (1982): 587.

            Disagrees with Clara Claiborne Park's conclusion in her article "Crippled
            Laughter: Toward Understanding Flannery O'Connor" [*American Scholar*
            51.2 (1982): 249-57]. Argues that "Park's conclusion that O'Connor
            `consistently failed to convey to her fallen readers the meanings she
            intended' because she followed `the neo-critical orthodoxy of the self-
            sufficiency of the work' is too simple."

1247   Payne, David H. "Compelling Truths Behind the Fiction of *Paris Trout*."
            Atlanta Journal and Constitution 11 Dec. 1988: K10.

            Compares and contrasts Pete Dexter's depiction in *Paris Trout*, of the
            1953 murders in Milledgeville of Carl Bonner, Emma Johnekin, Marion
            Ennis, and Stephen T. "Pete" Bivins, with that in Flannery O'Connor's
            story, "The Partridge Festival." Notes that whereas O'Connor went to great
            lengths to disguise her version, Dexter's fidelity to the events "borders on
            the obsessive," as he include many historic details with only slight changes
            in his 1988 National Book Award winning novel.

1248   Payne, David H. "Flannery O'Connor." *Modern Women Writers*. Ed.
            Matthew J. Bruccoli and Judith S. Baughman. New York: Facts on File,
            1994. 36-43.

            Provides citations to works by and about O'Connor. States that while her
            "reputation as a writer of religious themes now seems permanently
            assured," her "position in the history of American literature" appears to be
            "not yet fixed." Includes the following categories and number of works in
            each: "Bibliographies" (2); "Books" (6); "Letters" (2); "Other" (1);
            "Collections" (3); "Manuscripts & Archives" (1); "Biographies" (3);
            "Articles" (7); and "Interviews" (2). Follows with a section on "Critical
            Studies," which includes: "Books" (21); "Collections of Essays" (4);
            "Special Journals" (6); "Book Sections" (7); and "Articles" (53).

1249   Payne, Ladell. *Black Novelists and the Southern Literary Tradition*.
            Athens: U of Georgia P, 1981. 6, 14, 34, 47-48, 52-53, 71, 73, 76, 79, 86,
            100.

            Examines the literary relationship between Southern African-American
            writers and white Southern writers, focusing on how they use "common
            sources and illustrate common values." Contains passing references to
            O'Connor's work, including mention of O'Connor among other novelists

(black and white) who are largely responsible for a Southern literary renascence; comparison of Mr. Head's discovery of pride in "The Artificial Nigger," to John Walden's loss of innocence by reading law books in Charles Waddell Chesnutt's *The House Behind the Cedars*; how Jean Toomer's "Box Seat" contains elements of the grotesque similar to that depicted by O'Connor and Carson McCullers; and how Toomer tapped the same sources of Southern cultural heritage. O'Connor is mentioned, along with several others, as asserting through her work that there is "a moral purpose in the universe." Mentions Richard Wright's lectures of 1951 in Genoa and Rome in which he "`traced the literature of the South from Faulkner to Flannery O'Connor,'" and comments how in *Native Son* Wright draws upon a Southern Gothic tradition similar to that of Carson McCullers, Truman Capote, William Faulkner, and Flannery O'Connor. Remarks that O'Connor's "A Late Encounter With the Enemy" attacks "the present validity of the white southern myth" and Ralph Ellison's *Invisible Man*, "annihilates the black one."

1250   Payne, Nancy. "Indian Nun Comes to Teach and Learns of U.S." *The* (Lancaster, PA) *Intelligencer Journal* 16 May 1994: B4.

Profile of Sister Flavia Mariapragasam, a member of the Franciscan Missionaries of Mary and the "undergraduate head of the English department at Stella Maris College of the University of Madras." States that Mariapragasm had completed a third doctoral-level dissertation on O'Connor in India shortly before her visit. Describes her interest in O'Connor, impressions of Georgia College & State University's 1994 O'Connor symposium, "The Habit of Art," and her efforts to teach American students about O'Connor's work.

1251   Pearson, Michael. "A Good Writer is Hard to Find: O'Connor's Georgia." *Imagined Places: Journeys Into Literary America*. Jackson: UP of Mississippi, 1991. 125-59.

Provides observations from a visit to Milledgeville, GA to interview local citizens about O'Connor and to visit O'Connor-related sites. Gives impressions of Milledgeville's Bureau of Tourism and Trade, the O'Connor Room at Georgia College & State University, the Old Governor's Mansion, and the Holiday Inn across from the O'Connor family farm (Andalusia). Discusses the "town's apparent unwillingness to honor O'Connor's name more forcefully." Offers comments regarding his meetings and interviews with a wide variety of local citizensg: Jan Fennell and Nancy Davis Bray of the Georgia College & State University Library; Mary Barbara Tate, a former Georgia College & State University English faculty member and part of O'Connor's Andalusia reading group; Jack

Thornton, who discusses Pete Dexter's *Paris Trout*; a Georgia Historian, James Bonner; Louise Florencourt, O'Connor's first cousin, who provided a tour of the town and Andalusia; and Regina Cline O'Connor, Flannery's mother. Includes an extensive biographical sketch of Flannery O'Connor that covers her professional accomplishments and offers details regarding her region and the family. Illustrations: Photographs of Andalusia, two of Louise Florencourt, and one of Regina Cline O'Connor at home.

1252   Pearson, Michael. "Language and Love in Walker Percy's *The Second Coming*. *Southern Literary Journal* 20.1 (1987): 89-100.

Suggests that Will Barrett's toothache in Walker Percy's *The Second Coming* reflects "a mild version of Flannery O'Connor's technique of shock and distortion."

1253   Pearson, Michael. "Rude Beginnings of the Comic Tradition in Georgia Literature." *Journal of American Culture* 11.3 (1988): 51-54.

Asserts that the relationship between the city of Atlanta as a symbol of progress and sophistication and the "rural outreaches, holding tenaciously against culture and economic development," constitutes the tension "at the heart of Georgia comedy." Contends that this tension can be traced back to Augustus Baldwin Longstreet's comic sketches in *Georgia Scenes* (1835), which dramatize the cultural gap between the dandy and the ruffian. Submits that reflections of Longstreet's work may be found in Erskine Caldwell's *Tobacco Road* (1932) and *God's Little Acre* (1933), and that both Longstreet's and Caldwell's characters may, in turn, be the prototype for O'Connor's country folk. Compares O'Connor's comedy with that found in *God's Little Acre* and suggests that "it is easy enough to see O'Connor's Georgia as another tobacco road, half-paved perhaps, but much the same nevertheless." Includes discussion of O'Connor's "Greenleaf," "Revelation," and "A Good Man Is Hard to Find."

1254   Pearson, Michael. "Stories to Ease the Tension: Clyde Edgerton's Fiction." *Hollins Critic* 27.4 (1990): 1-8.

Offers a profile of Clyde Edgerton, focusing on how his three novels, *Raney, Walking Across Egypt*, and *The Floatplane Notebooks* reflect his belief that storytelling is "intricately connected to a sense of history, the importance of family, the debate over race, and the idioms of tradition." Includes brief references to O'Connor: her love for the South and "her sense that the virtues and vices of Southern culture provide an ironic source for a creative writer"; Edgerton's awareness of O'Connor's comments regarding the changing nature of the South; the "faint echo" of O'Connor's "A Good Man Is Hard to Find" in Edgerton's *Walking Across Egypt* (in "a lighter, less violent chord"); and the assessment that Edgerton's "understanding of the South and the people who live in it is as keen as Flannery O'Connor's."

1255   Peat, Isie and Diane Young. "`What a Wonderful Century and More We Have Had.'" *Southern Living* May 1990: 87-92.

Considers the most influential Southern works, ranking those by William Faulkner, Walker Percy, Robert Penn Warren, Eudora Welty, Shelby Foote, and Flannery O'Connor in the top ten. Novelist Kaye Gibbons remarks on the *Collected Works of Flannery O'Connor*, "'I believe that O'Connor looked at humanity dry-eyed, without flinching, and she filtered what she saw and heard through her wild imagination and gave us back our own stories of redemption and grace.'" Writer Geoffrey Norman adds, "'Now if you are going to understand the South, you first must get your fingers around the idea of sin. Real, sure enough, doomed from the garden, sweaty, unstoppable sin. For that . . . Flannery O'Connor."

1256   Pelfrey, David. "Spooky Stories." *Santa Fe Reporter* 25-31 Oct. 1995: 5.

"The Lame Shall Enter First" is included in this annotated list of eight "scary short stories" for readers who wish to fully enjoy the Halloween season by reading some of the "very best of horror literature." Rufus is described as "a lanky, sociopathic, dead-end kid with a grotesque club foot" who enjoys quoting passages on hellfire and damnation from the Bible. States that when a "social worker gives this monster a key to his home . . . such benevolence . . . only fan coals of hatred behind the boy's eyes." [Reprinted from the Alabama publication *Black and White*.]

1257   Pepin, Ronald E. "Latin Names and Images of Ugliness in Flannery O'Connor's `Revelation.'" *ANQ: American Notes and Queries* 6.1 (1993): 25-27.

Examines "Revelation" and suggests that O'Connor "bestowed on her fictional characters significant names with Latin etymologies, and in so doing made them archetypes of bigotry." Focuses upon the "ugliness" which "pervades" the story and outlines how "physical repulsiveness is used extensively to mirror the baseness and bigotry of the characters." Refers to works by Bob Dowell, David Jauss, and Carter Martin that discuss the origin and meanings of symbolic names for O'Connor's characters and examine the story's swine motif.

1258   Pepperdene, Margaret W. *Flannery O'Connor's Incarnational Art.* The
        Whitworth-Muldrow Lecture for 1989. Rome, GA: Shorter College, 1989.
        [18 pp.].

        Contends that while "no writer has ever taken such pains to explain, to
        clarify, to interpret her work," O'Connor's work is still "persistently
        misunderstood." Suggests that readers simply "do not understand the
        world of her stories--the physical place where they happen, the
        metaphysical reality to which they refer, and the personal sensibility which
        shaped them." Discusses the influence of living in the "Bible Belt South,"
        O'Connor's reliance upon her Catholic faith, and the fact that she was
        "mortally ill all of her mature life." Sees the influence of Southern
        manners, "the authentic cadence and rhythms of backwoods Southern
        speech," and the constant underlying threat of violence as enabling factors
        that O'Connor drew upon to depict her characters. Finds her Christian
        vision to be the "living truth at the heart" of her fiction, and indicates that
        "her faith differed, in essential dogma, *not one whit* from that of her
        fundamentalist preachers and backwoods prophets." States that O'Connor's
        fiction is also smitten with God's influence and grace. Closes with a
        discussion of how her illness imparted "a sense of detachment from the
        world's `fever' and `fret,'" and provided her with "a perspective which
        gives all her stories that sense of seeing every event, every situation, and
        every human being in them under the aspect of eternity."

1259   Percy, Walker. *Conversations With Walker Percy.* Ed. Lewis A. Lawson
        and Victor A. Kramer. Jackson: UP of Mississippi, 1985. 11, 34, 41-42,
        47, 69, 88, 98, 99, 162-63, 165, 168, 192, 196, 214, 219, 231-34, 240,
        300, 309, 314-15.

        Offers twenty-seven interviews of Walker Percy which are compiled,
        edited and indexed in this single compact volume. Most references to
        Flannery O'Connor are brief, serving only as an example of a writing style
        or as a comparison to a particular genre or region. However, Percy's
        assessment of O'Connor's works ("I like all of them very much") on pages
        232-34 and his discussion of Thomas Merton and O'Connor on pages 314-
        15 are somewhat longer and more useful.

1260   Percy, Will. "Rock and Read: Will Percy Interviews Bruce Springsteen."
        Doubletake Spring 1998: 36-43.

        Notes in introductory remarks that in 1989 Walker Percy had penned a fan
        letter to Bruce Springsteen, "praising the musician's `spiritual journey' and
        hoping to begin a correspondence between them." Reports that while
        Springsteen did not reply, the letter prompted him to read *The Moviegoer*

and other writings by Percy, which "have had a most profound impact" on his songwriting. During the course of the interview, Springsteen mentions his interest in O'Connor's writings, stating, "There was something in those stories of hers that captured a certain part of the American character that I was interested in writing about. They were a big, big revelation." Notes his admiration for how O'Connor "got to the heart of some part of meanness that she never spelled out" that was "at the core of every one of her stories." Relates that he sensed "some dark thing--a component of spirituality" in her fiction that set him off to explore characters of his own. Comments that he was "deep into O'Connor" just prior to recording his 1982 album, *Nebraska*. Springsteen concludes that O'Connor "knew original sin--knew how to give it the flesh of a story. She had talent and she had ideas, and the one served the other."

1261   Perisho, Steve. "The Structure of Flannery O'Connor's `Revelation.'" *Notes on Contemporary Literature* 20.4 (1990): 5-7.

Contends that the "careful reader of Flannery O'Connor's `Revelation' is, [at] the opening of the story, assaulted by references to the size of the waiting room." Notes that the motif is dropped after the doctor's office waiting room incident and then only "pops up for a final time" when Ruby Turpin lifts her head from the "pig parlor" to see the "`vast horde of souls'" marching heavenward. Suggests that the waiting room can be viewed as a "pen full of hogs" because Mrs. Turpin initially "considers herself too good for the human swine all around." Asserts that Mrs. Turpin eventually comes to realize that she is indeed, "the worst kind of pig, a disgustedly self-righteous hog `with warts on its face and horns coming out behind its ears.'" States that the pig parlor becomes a waiting room for the heaven-bound, including even Mrs. Turpin who, "even *more* that the rest[,] is `from hell.'" Concludes that O'Connor intended readers to realize that it is only through "the merciful economy of God [that] even such as the last of these get in."

1262   Permut, Joanna Baumer. *Embracing the Wolf: A Lupus Victim and Her Family Learn to Live With Chronic Disease.* Atlanta, GA: Cherokee, 1989. 58, 62, 95, 124.

Contains passing references to Flannery O'Connor's struggle with Lupus in the context of the author's own battle with the disease.

1263   Petry, Alice Hall, ed. *Critical Essays on Anne Tyler.* New York: G.K. Hall, 1992. 21, 97, 139, 236-37.

Includes passing references to O'Connor and her work, including in a discussion of Southern women writers, how O'Connor and Eudora Welty "are regarded as high priestesses by the literary set"; how Anne Tyler's poor characterization in *Morgan's Passing* is "a bit as if Flannery O'Connor were writing in a fog"; how O'Connor was more successful at writing about sympathetic characters than Tyler; and using O'Connor's discussion of detail in Flaubert's *Madame Bovary*, the assertion that Tyler may be considered to be a master in the use of detail as well.

1264   Petry, Alice Hall. *A Genius in His Way: The Art of Cable's "Old Creole Days."* Cranbury, NJ: Fairleigh-Dickinson, 1988. 20, 99, 73-74, 88, and 140n.28.

Includes passing comments on O'Connor, most interestingly, evidence that supports the argument that Cable may have been "an unrecognized but absolutely vital influence" on her mind and art, and how O'Connor, like Cable, used "unlikely characters" such as The Misfit, the Displaced Person and the bull in "Greenleaf"--"as agents of Christian conversion." References comments by William Rodney Allen and Frederick Asals concerning Nathaniel Hawthorne's influence on O'Connor.

1265   Petry, Alice Hall. "Julian and O'Connor's *Everything That Rises Must Converge*." *Studies in American Fiction* 15.1 (1987): 101-08.

Suggests that the omission of a name for Julian's mother was not an oversight by O'Connor, but a statement in itself. Refers to, and agrees with, Josephine Hendin's suggestion that Julian's name signals his yearning for the "`old Gods'" as symbolized by the career of emperor Julian the Apostate, "remembered to this day for his vigorous campaign to rid the Roman Empire of its official religion, Christianity, and to reinstate the paganism of the ancient Greeks." Asserts that Hendin's suggested connections "help to guide the reader's responses to this story," but stop short in their implications for readers. Finds that "from the traditional Christian perspective, the ending of the story is insistently affirmative in that the Galilean has triumphed once again," and that the close connections between the two Julians "have implications for other works by O'Connor."

1266   Petry, Alice Hall. "Miss O'Connor and Mrs. Mitchell: The Example of `Everything That Rises.'" *Southern Quarterly* 27.4 (1989): 5-15.

Asserts that O'Connor incorporated into her fiction references to Margaret Mitchell's *Gone With the Wind*. States that these references serve as "echoes" that are "sometimes transparent and sometimes subtle, sometimes parodic and sometimes serious." Lists Julian's mother's hat, the issue of ladyhood, and O'Connor's "presentation of Julian's blue-eyed mother" as similarities between "Everything That Rises Must Converge" and *Gone With the Wind*. Concludes that O'Connor used these echoes "to help guide our responses" to her "often enigmatic fiction."

1267   Petry, Alice Hall. "O'Connor's 'Everything That Rises Must Converge.'" *Explicator* 45.3 (1987): 51-54.

Recognizes O'Connor's ability to "utilize detail symbolically," and suggests that it is evident that Julian's mother's destination, the YWCA, "serves as a gauge of the degeneration of the mother's Old South family and . . . of the breakdown of old, church-related values."

1268   Petry, Alice Hall. "O'Connor's 'Parker's Back.'" *Explicator* 46.2 (1988): 38-43.

Contends that critics have not paid sufficient attention "to the multiplicity of meanings surrounding O'Connor's title, "Parker's Back." Asserts that it is one of her "most richly suggestive titles," and that the frequent occurrence of the word "back" suggests a message-laden pattern, a blatant sign from God that (a) the tattoo 'had to be' on Parker's back . . . and that (b) paradoxically, Parker can move forward spiritually only by moving backwards physically." Concludes that O'Connor's ambiguity in this title may be deliberate on her part in order to urge readers to "deepen their penetration of these things."

1269   Petry, Alice Hall. *Understanding Anne Tyler*. Columbia: U of South Carolina P, 1990. 11-12, 159, 180n.

Refers to Tyler's indebtedness to O'Connor, Eudora Welty, Carson McCullers, and William Faulkner; epiphanies in Tyler's works that remind readers of O'Connor's fiction; and in an endnote, mentions a review of Tyler's *Morgan's Passing* by Eva Hoffman, who wrote that Tyler's style in this book might be compared to Flannery O'Connor "writing in a fog."

1270   Phillips, D.Z. "The Devil's Disguises: Philosophy of Religion, 'Objectivity' and 'Cultural Divergence.'" *Objectivity and Cultural Divergence*. Ed. S.C. Brown. London: Cambridge UP, 1984. 61-77.

Discusses O'Connor's "problem of how to convey a religious perspective in literature in a pervasively secular American culture; Robert Coles's observations of O'Connor's South and her "Georgian censure of Northern attitudes"; and correspondence with John Hawkes regarding "evil." Examines "The Lame Shall Enter First," and states that "from a religious perspective, the social worker's confidence in his explanatory categories is an aspect of the Devil's victory." Remarks that the story offers insight on how philosophers may need to consider that "they may be in the grip of the very superstitions they take themselves to be attacking." Compares the goal of the "philosopher of religion" with those of O'Connor and asserts that both are attempting to reach the same audience--those who think "God is dead." Reviews "A Good Man Is Hard to Find" paying particular attention to the differing perceptions between O'Connor and her audience regarding the use of the grotesque and mystery for effect and "the way in which The Misfit has distorted religious truths." Concludes with discussion of "reasons why neither the literary artist nor the philosopher can be complacently confident of their methods."

1271   Phillips, D.Z. "Mystery and Mediation: Reflections on Flannery O'Connor and Joan Didion." *Images of Belief in Literature.* [National Conference on Literature and Religion Papers. (Sept. 23-25, 1982)]. Ed. David Jasper. New York: Macmillan, 1984. 24-41.

Notes remarks by Simone Weil, M. O'C. Drury, Joan Baez, and Peter Winch in an introduction to a discussion of O'Connor's "Revelation" and excerpts from Didion's essays. Focuses on the idea that "mysteries must be mediated . . . without the mediation of mysteries in human life, their sense as mysteries is lost or distorted." Refers to O'Connor's remark that writers are "'seekers and describers of the real, [and] the realism of each novelist will depend on his view of the ultimate reaches of reality.'" Asserts that O'Connor worked "through the surface phenomena to the experience of mystery itself" and asserts that, for that mystery to have any sense for her, it had to "be mediated through manners, through the details of people's lives." Contrasts O'Connor with Didion, who "concludes that she has little confidence in anything that has wider pretensions to be anything more than loyalty to loved ones, a shared sense of adversity, or primitive reactions to the rights and wrongs of a shared social code."

1272   Phillips, D.Z. "A Realism of Distances." *From Fantasy to Faith.* New York: St. Martin's, 1991. 212-21.

Offers brief biographical sketch of O'Connor, recounting her remarks related to the peacock's cry in her essay "The King of the Birds," and asserts that "at the center of her fiction is the conviction that this world is a place of exile and that . . . man lives at a distance from his true home." Discusses human resistance to mystery and asserts that this resistance is based upon the fact that "we tend to give primary place to explanation" yet only religion and acceptance of God's will focuses our attention "on the limits of human existence." Discusses how O'Connor "shows the distance between man and God realistically by showing grace and mystery at work in human life." Explicates "The Artificial Nigger," and explores the relationship between Mr. Head and Nelson; states that it is a relationship that changes "when mystery and grace enter into it."

1273   Phillips, K.J. "Bowing to the Bull." *Dying Gods in Twentieth Century Fiction.* Lewisburg, PA: Bucknell UP, 1990. 65-81.

Discusses the tradition of the dying god in bull form as evidenced in O'Connor's "Greenleaf" and Hemingway's *The Sun Also Rises.* Says both writers mimic the animal's violent rites to reflect the violence in their world. Asserts that the two writers do not pit bulls against humans, as might be expected, but depict the two as mirror images. Discusses the "vegetation god" aspects in "Greenleaf." Likens Mrs. May to the bull.

1274   Pici, Frances Anne. "'The Habit of Being': A Solo-Biographical Drama on Flannery O'Connor." (Dramatic Presentation). Georgia State University Players, Georgia State U, January 11-12, 1991. Directed by Shirlene Holmes.

[A videotape of this performance has been donated to the *Flannery O'Connor Collection* at Georgia College & State University.]

1275   Pierce, Constance. "The Mechanical World of 'Good Country People.'" *Flannery O'Connor Bulletin* 5 (1976): 30-38.

Argues that in "Good Country People" each of the main characters has "a mechanistic way of dealing with the world, a façade that covers their underlying 'neutrality,' or 'nothingness.'" Considers each character--Mrs. Hopewell, Hulga, Manley Pointer, and Mrs. Freeman--and offers examples of their mechanistic behavior. Suggests reasons each character responds in a purely mechanical way, and contrasts Hulga and Mrs. Hopewell's approach to life with that of Manley Pointer. Observes that while "one does not admire Pointer, still he is the character in the story who, although consistently deceiving others, does not deceive himself." Concludes that O'Connor seems to be using this story to point out "that if there ever was such a thing as 'good country people,' they have been corrupted." Submits that the women lose out in this story, "for they have not even Pointer's despicable resources"; their only hope lies within the biblical quote, 'He who losest his life shall find it.'"

1276   Pitavy, François. "Through Darl's Eyes Darkly: The Vision of the Poet in
            As I Lay Dying." *William Faulkner: Materials, Studies, and Criticism*
            (Japan) 4.2 (1982): 37-62.

            Offers a reading of William Faulkner's *As I Lay Dying*. Focuses on Darl's
            voice, quality of vision, multiple identities and clairvoyance, "sense of the
            ludicrous," "'perverse' vision," "disrupted perception of space," and
            "unexpected perspectives." Contends that Faulkner's Darl exhibits a sense
            of the grotesque "not unlike the quality of Flannery O'Connor's own
            vision." Suggests that the grotesqueness exhibited in sections of the text
            "derives from what could be called a double viewpoint," qualifying Darl
            "to be what O'Connor, in her essay 'Some Aspects of the Grotesque in
            Southern Fiction,' calls a 'realist of distances.'" States that Darl's "almost
            surreal sense of the presence of beings or things . . . to the point where
            they fail to coincide with their existence physically felt and experienced,"
            may remind readers of O'Connor's view of "mystery," that which "lies
            beyond surfaces and appearances."

1277   Pitavy, François. "Walker Percy's Brave New World: *The Thanatos
            Syndrome. Walker Percy: Novelist and Philosopher.* Ed. Jan Nordby
            Gretlund and Karl-Heinz Westarp. Jackson: UP of Mississippi, 1991.
            177-88.

            Offers an explication of Percy's *The Thanatos Syndrome*. Notes that "the
            undercurrent of nostalgia that runs through Faulkner and Fitzgerald does
            not run through Percy," who "still hopes and thinks he can do something
            about man's predicament." Refers to O'Connor's fondness for quoting Saint
            Cyril of Jerusalem regarding the dragon that sits by the side of the road
            waiting to devour those who pass by. Sees Percy's view of nostalgia as
            similar to O'Connor's, as both writers look forward, not backward, and
            "attempt to come up to the threshold of transcendence" where writing
            stops, because--in their view--"what lies beyond is no longer a matter of
            fiction, but of faith, and it must remain unknowable." Ties Percy and
            O'Connor's fiction to Saint Cyril's story, suggesting that "the roadway is
            precisely the subject matter" of both writers' fiction, and both "are
            concerned with evil, with the absurdity or grotesqueness of man's
            predicament, with the dragon." Concludes that Percy, like O'Connor, "had
            to be an eccentric in the American house of fiction in order to warn us
            against the brave new worlds threatening to destroy man in this end of the
            twentieth century."

1278   Polette, Keith. "Text and Textile: Sacred and Profane Fashion Statements
            in Flannery O'Connor's 'A Good Man Is Hard to Find.'" *JAISA* 2.2 (1997):
            63-80.

Refers to Hawthorne's depiction of attire in *The Scarlet Letter* and "The Minister's Black Veil" to show how "clothing may be employed to carry and convey the freight of images and ideas that extend beyond the realm of conventional sign systems" in literature. Outlines how O'Connor "adopts and modernizes Hawthorne's pattern of outfitting a text with images of cloth and clothing" to "communicate multiple and symbolic ideas" in "A Good Man Is Hard to Find." Discusses, in this context: "the grandmother's garb for the trip south" and the "military undertones" depicted; the daughter-in-law's "cartoon-like" clothes, which mirror the "rabbit-like" image of her "spiritually slack" life; and how The Misfit is not only "too big for his britches," but is "little more than a man-beast." Comments that by "putting on Bailey's shirt," The Misfit "assumes the metaphoric role of son to the grandmother" and "takes an important first step in rejoining the human community." Concludes that the action at the end of the story and The Misfit's new garb suggest that he "may be ready to exit the *Waste Land*-like zone of the dead and enter the slowly emerging landscape of the sacred."

1279   Polter, Julie. "Obliged to See God." *Sojourners* 23.10 (1994): 16-22.

O'Connor is honored by the editors of *Sojourners* for her role as a devout Catholic and "self-taught lay theologian." Offers a biographical sketch, description of her writings, and an outline of her religious views. Discusses influences on her work, her manner of "*seeing* intensely," and how O'Connor was most concerned with "telling a good story." Asserts that the "profound action that is intrinsic to O'Connor's dramatic physical action is always the characters' recognition and acceptance of--or final defiance to--grace." Concludes that by the time she died of Lupus at 39, O'Connor was "established as one of the most technically gifted and original fiction writers of the 20th century." Includes a sidebar by Shane Helmer which briefly discusses O'Connor's intent for her writings and offers an excerpt from Alice Walker's essay "Beyond the Peacock: The Reconstruction of Flannery O'Connor." Illustrated with a photograph of O'Connor at the Russell Library of Georgia College & State University during a book-signing party.

1280   Pope, Robert. "Beginnings." *Georgia Review* 36.4 (1982): 733-51.

Discusses the art and technique writers use to begin a fictional work, their struggle to find an "immortal voice," and their search for those first few words that will speak and take the reader into a believable fictional world. Uses a variety of selections to illustrate particularly interesting "beginnings": Franz Kafka's "Metamorphosis," Jorge Luis Borges's "The Circular Ruins," Vladimir Nabokov's *Lolita*, Flannery O'Connor's *The*

Violent Bear It Away, and Gabriel García Márquez's *One Hundred Years of Solitude.* Suggests that "no writer has challenged the intellectual as much as Flannery O'Connor, for she challenges all of the changes . . . experienced, all of [the] newest and fondest insights, and points to an ancient source of light and meaning in a world that seems to contradict hope, threatening us at every step." Comments on the novel's beginning, noting the sentence length and rapid movement, and the passing of several images which speed up time. Offers an explication of the novel's beginning, discusses the role of the negro, and refers the reader to "Bishop Berkeley's infamous `Treatise on Tarwater'" as a source for the story.

1281   Portch, Stephen Ralph. "O'Connor's `A Good Man Is Hard to Find.'" *Explicator* 37.1 (1978): 19-20.

Discusses "two suggestive clues: a dirty pair of glasses and a catalytic cat, `Pitty Sing'" that may help the reader determine whether the shooting of the grandmother in "A Good Man Is Hard to Find" will "transform the murderer." Suggests that while the "trouble-causing cat" has been largely ignored by critics, in the "animal's sixth sense" and the "security of a feline's nine lives," the cat may be responding to a "changed killer."

1282   Portch, Stephen Ralph. "[Chapter 5:] Visual Flannery." *Literature's Silent Language: Nonverbal Communication.* New York: Peter Lang, 1985. 117-46.

Uses a nonverbal approach to explicate O'Connor's "Good Country People" and "The Life You Save May Be Your Own." Suggests that she uses a wide variety of nonverbal techniques in her work and is particularly fascinated by the use of "artifacts." Argues that, in "Good Country People," the "loft scene presents a rape. An expected `screw' becomes an unexpected unscrew as Hulga's venture into sexual initiation leads her to a spiritual rape." Discusses O'Connor's use of the body "primarily to show its limitations and to reveal how all too often it shapes personality and limits the spirit." Compares Hulga and Mrs. Hopewell's blindness to Manley Pointer's depravity and perversion, and notes O'Connor's use of body clues, vocal tones, and her characters' eyes and gazes to communicate meaning. Examines Hulga's "smug intellectual superiority" and comments that Pointer "use[s] his nonverbal skills to feed her natural pride." Maintains that Pointer's theft of Hulga's wooden leg "gives her a deeper understanding of life," and "the chances are good . . . that Hulga has learned something" as she "has been shaken out of her complacency." Discusses "The Life You Save May Be Your Own," focusing on how O'Connor uses appearance "to capture the essential physical and psychological qualities and limitations of her major characters," and uses color, artifacts, body clues, and vocal tones "to show readers that Shiftlet has shady motives." Refers to O'Connor criticism by Gilbert H. Muller, David Eggenschwiler, Robert Coles, Melvin Friedman, Josephine Hendin, Dorothy Walters, Dorothy Tuck McFarland, Martha Stephens, Preston M. Browning, and Carol Shloss. [Note: Appears to be based upon the author's 1982 Ph.D. dissertation completed at Pennsylvania State University: "Writing Without Words: A Nonverbal Approach to the Short Fiction of Hawthorne, Hemingway and O'Connor."]

1283   Porter, Kathleen Sullivan. "Children in Her Kingdom: The Relationship Between Touch and Health in Flannery O'Connor." *Flannery O'Connor Bulletin* 25 (1996-97): 13-29.

Contends that O'Connor's depiction of children and adolescents reflects the evidence from many studies that "adults who give their children physical, emotional, and spiritual support" not only "see them thrive," but also see them "enter adolescence and eventually adulthood with a sense of self-worth and an appreciation of their connections to others." Argues that O'Connor takes this concept a step further by showing "that spiritual development may also be either sanctioned or withheld through the mental or physical touch of adults." Examines several of O'Connor's child protagonists: Nelson in "The Artificial Nigger"; Norton in "The Lame Shall Enter First"; Harry-Bevel in "The River"; Bishop in *The Violent Bear It Away*; Mary Fortune Pitts in "A View of the Woods"; and Sally Virginia Cope in "A Circle in the Fire." Suggests that while most of O'Connor's children "who receive parental support thrive," those who are "touch-and affection-starved suffer, self-destruct, or destroy others." Concludes that the fate of these children "seems a reflection of the depravity of their adult caregivers."

1284   Powers, Douglas. "Flannery O'Connor's Treelines." *Flannery O'Connor Bulletin* 20 (1991): 54-60.

Suggests that O'Connor's recurring use of treelines indicates that "something is happening, has already happened, or is about to happen: enlightenment, a moment of being, an epiphany, the moment of truth, an impending revelation." Compares the appearance of these treelines to the natural circumstances in which they appear in mountainous regions. Notes that in these natural circumstances, "those trees and shrubs that form the treeline are often so modified that they resemble themselves very little: they are bent, warped, twisted, dwarfed." States, "O'Connor's treelines kept rising in my consciousness until they converged with my long-standing interest in prints and printmaking, and something had to happen." Illustrated with six color plates from Powers's series, *Flannery O'Connor's*

Treelines. Scenes depicted are from "The River," "You Can't Be Any Poorer Than Dead," "Parker's Back," "A View of the Woods," "The Life You Save May Be Your Own," and "Revelation."

1285   Powers, Douglas. "Ruller McFarney's Cutting Loose." *Flannery O'Connor Bulletin* 18 (1989): 70-78.

Examines selected excerpts from "The Turkey," a story originally presented by O'Connor as part of her master's thesis and later reprinted in *Mademoiselle* as "The Capture." Suggests that readers will find this story interesting because--although it presents "qualities of honesty, sharpness, humor, human weakness, and pretension . . . found in all of O'Connor's stories"--it doesn't contain "the highly implosive incendiaries common in her later [stories]" (such as grotesqueries and violence). Notes that Ruller's family is functional with "no tortured relationships," very unlike the situations she usually created, where "at least one parent is dead or absent" or where the children are reared by surrogate parents." Asserts that this story reflects O'Connor's "extraordinary understanding of the ordinary, but complex development of children and youth." Submits that "God is present in `The Turkey' . . . but He seems to be more of a big brother or guiding ancestral spirit than some terror-inducing, burning-eyed enforcer."

1286   Pratt, Mary Louise. "The Short Story: The Long and Short of It." *Poetics Journal* 10 (June 1981): 175-94.

Discusses "some of the asymmetrics in the relation between the short story and the novel, focusing on the former as a dependent and marked genre (or countergenre) with respect to the latter, now the dominant, normative genre for prose fiction." Includes two passing references to O'Connor: how she commonly used the device of "a quotation, whether a punch line, a cliché, or a proverb, which the story is understood to be illustrating" as a title; and how she, like many other noted writers, contributed a great deal of "how-to instruction" criticism for readers of her own work.

1287   Pratt, William. "The Place of the South in Contemporary Literature." *South Carolina Review* 25.1 (1992): 116-26.

Explores reasons Irish and Southern American communities, "two notorious backwaters of civilization," have been able to produce "genuinely original writers" whose art includes such deep concern for "place." Refers to comments and works by such writers as Flannery O'Connor, Frank Manley, Peter Taylor, and Robert Penn Warren to provide examples. Uses comments from O'Connor's essay "The Fiction

Writer and His Country" to illustrate her ability to draw upon "the rich imaginative resources . . . in the character, customs, religious beliefs and speech patterns indigenous to the South."

1288   Prenshaw, Peggy Whitman, ed. *Conversations with Eudora Welty.* Jackson: UP of Mississippi, 1984. 20-1, 25, 54, 80, 95, 214, 217-9, 227, 254-5, 312, 343.

Offers a collection of interviews with Eudora Welty from magazines, journals and newspapers. O'Connor is mentioned in passing in several, including Welty's remarks on O'Connor's bravery in the face of her illness; the influence of Catholicism on O'Connor's work; O'Connor's "serious" comic humor; how her own writing, along with that of Katherine Anne Porter and O'Connor, is very different; meeting O'Connor "on a program" in South Carolina in November of 1962; hearing O'Connor's lecture on "'The Catholic Writer'" at Converse College; and the existence of evil versus O'Connor's Roman Catholic view of sin. Welty remarks that while she realizes that much of O'Connor's work is unavailable to her due to her own ignorance of the Roman Catholic faith, she states that she particularly enjoys the vitality and spiritual toughness she finds in O'Connor's works. Includes a discussion of the conflict that Welty sees in O'Connor's use of symbols, focusing on how her characters often reject these very symbols. Welty indicates in one interview that she is pleased to find her own use of humor favorably compared to O'Connor's and agrees with O'Connor's position on comedy that just because something is humorous does not mean that it is not also serious.

1289   Prestianni, Vincent. "From Porter to O'Connor: Modern Southern Writers of Fiction: Seven Bibliographies of Bibliographies." *Bulletin of Bibliography* 48.3 (1991): 137-51.

Referring to bibliography as "the geography of the book world," the compiler states that the seven authors covered in this compilation "represent peaks of achievement in the post-Faulkner and Wolfe generations of story-tellers." States that each of the authors selected "is certain to endure" and that "the present effort attempts to chart the charts [of primary and secondary bibliographies] in the belief that the bibliographies need a measure of control." Entries are "'analytic' in that they identify the components of the bibliography in terms of kind, content, and arrangement. The analyses are meant to work as abstracts of books and essays . . . to provide more information than a mere title, so that the researcher can more easily decide if a certain bibliography will be useful." Authors selected include Flannery O'Connor, Katherine Anne Porter, Andrew Nelson Lytle, Eudora Welty, Walker Percy, Carson McCullers, and Peter Taylor. The O'Connor entry includes forty-three annotated citations which are first divided into two sections and then arranged in chronological order within each. Bibliographers with works cited--along with the date of publication--include: George F. Wedge (1958); Lewis A. Lawson (1966 and 1977); Joan T. Brittain (1967 and 1971); Melvin J. Friedman (1969 and 1977); Georgia Ann Newman (1970); Leon V. Driskell (1971); Walter Sullivan (1971); Allen D. Lackey (1972); Miles Orvell (1972); Dorothy Walters (1973); James E. Dorsey (1975); Michel Gresset and Claude Richard (1976); John R. May (1976); Robert E. Golden (1977); Lorine M. Getz (1980); James A. Grimshaw (1981); David R. Farmer (1981); Martha E. Cook (1983); Leo Zuber (1983); Beverly Lyon Clark and Caroline M. Brown (1985); Rosemary M. Magee (1987); Suzanne Morrow Paulson (1988); Frederick Asals (1969); Roy R. Male (1970); Stuart L. Burns (1970 and 1974); Margaret Harrison (1971); Kathleen Feeley (1972); Gerald Becham (1975); Jane Elizabeth Archer (1982); Mary Morton (1983/84); and Arthur F. Kinney (1985).

1290   Pritchard, William H. "Uncommon Common Readers." *Hudson Review* 45.2 (1992): 310-18.

Outlines the difficulties the common reader encounters when reading fiction, using Clara Claiborne Parks's *Rejoining the Common Reader* (Northwestern UP), Frank Kermode's essay "The Common Reader" in *An Appetite for Poetry* (Cambridge UP), and Harold Fromm's *Academic Capitalism and Literary Value* (U of Georgia P), as a foundation for discussion. Offers comments on Parks's essay on Flannery O'Connor, specifically her point that "while O'Connor warned against crude explanations or extractions of `meaning' from her stories, she herself regularly provided such explanations in lectures and letters." Suggests that, because of O'Connor's explanations and utilization of similar story-action devices from one story to the next, "`incursions of grace through arson and through murder and through sudden stroke become familiar to the point of predictability, [and] all moral ambiguity evaporates, leaving the stories that puzzled us all too clear.'"

1291   Pritchett, Victor Sawdon. "Flannery O'Connor: Satan Comes to Georgia." *The Tale Bearers: Literary Essays*. New York: Random House, 1980. 164-69.

Offers a review-essay of O'Connor's *Everything That Rises Must Converge* which responds to the author's own self-posed question of "Why does America produce more masters of the short story than we [the British] do?" Uses this question to explore and analyze characteristics and components of Flannery O'Connor's work, beginning with a discussion of her characters, all seen as being "abnormal: that is to say that they are normal human beings in whom the writer has discovered a relationship with the lasting myths and the violent passions of human life." Comments on how many Southern American writers "have sometimes tended to pure freakishness or have concentrated on the eccentricities of a decaying social life," then observes that the Gothic, the grotesque, even the nostalgic legend of the tragic South, are "norms" for O'Connor. Finds that passion lurks "just beneath the humdrum surface" in her stories and regards the fact that she "was an old Catholic, not a convert, in the South of poor whites, [and] of the Bible Belt," as giving her "a critical starting-point and skirmishing power" for her art. Is impressed by O'Connor's use of symbolism, stating: "whenever one finds a symbol, one is impressed by Flannery O'Connor's use of it: it is concrete and native to the text." Argues that the "symbolism of [O'Connor's] religion, rather than the acrimonies of sectarian dispute, fed her violent imagination." Discusses "Everything That Rises Must Converge," "Parker's Back," and "The Comforts of Home." Concludes that O'Connor "is at pains to make us know intimately the lives of these poor whites and struggling small-town people" that inhabit her stories; her characters "are there, as they live, not in the interest of their exposure to forces in themselves that they do not yet understand," but to find that "Satan . . . is not just a word. He has legs--and those legs are their own."

1291a   Profitt, Jennifer H. "Lupus and Corticosteroid Imagery in the Works of Flannery O'Connor." *Flannery O'Connor Bulletin* 26-27 (1998-2000): 74-93.

Contends that O'Connor "borrowed much of her unique character imagery" directly from her "debilitating, chronic, and ultimately fatal illness." Focuses on her Lupus "as a source of themes and imagery" in O'Connor's fiction and suggests that the absence of research on this topic "reflects a generalized, societal avoidance and discomfort with disability." Outlines O'Connor's health problems and the side effects of the drugs used to treat her systemic lupus erythematosus (SLS). Quotes from O'Connor's correspondence regarding her responses to her disease and treatment, and examines the effect of SLS on her daily life. Follows with an in-depth look at how the effects of her own illness figure in her fiction: "kidney function and excessive fluid retention" in "A Late Encounter With the Enemy"; swollen feet in *Everything That Rises Must Converge*; the "hunchback posture of Cushing syndrome" in *The Violent Bear It Away*; round-faced women in "Judgement Day" and "Parker's Back"; salt-free diets in "Greenleaf" and "The Enduring Chill"; nausea in *The Violent Bear It Away* and "A Stroke of Good Fortune"; facial abnormalities in "The Enduring Chill" and *The Violent Bear It Away*; inflamed joints in "A Good Man Is Hard to Find," *The Violent Bear It Away*, "A Stroke of Good

Fortune," "Parker's Back," "The Lame Shall Enter First," "Judgement Day," and "The Life You Save May be Your Own"; exhaustion in "Judgement Day" and "A Stroke of Good Fortune"; the "silence of hereditary 'disease'" in *The Violent Bear It Away*. Concludes with discussions of how O'Connor's illness affected her privacy and independence, and whether her cortisone treatments may have infused her work "with a personal sense of the grotesque and the incongruous" that she was able to pass on to her readers.

1292   Prown, Katherine Hemple. "Riding the Dixie Limited: Flannery O'Connor, Southern Literary Culture, and the Problem of Female Authorship." *Bucknell Review* 39.1 (1995): 57-78.

Notes that O'Connor "enjoyed a level of professional status that was rare among the women of her generation," as thanks to the support of powerful critics such as Andrew Lytle, she was recognized "as a bold and unique talent" destined to be "among the 'top-rate' American writers of the twentieth century." Finds it interesting that "despite her distinction as a woman writer of canonical standing, feminist critics have largely overlooked her work." Contends that readers who remain sensitive to gender-related dynamics will note that while both *Wise Blood* and *The Violent Bear It Away* are, indeed, "based on the quest narrative and the *Bildungsroman*, traditionally masculinist narrative forms, the novels defy many of the conventions around which these forms have historically centered." Points out that, in the end, both Haze and Tarwater must conform to God's will and accept "passivity and dependence as their lot, [as] they renounce all claims to a traditional masculine identity and become, in effect, 'feminized.'" Comments on O'Connor's tendency to "play by the rules established by and governing" such influential Southern writers as John Crowe Ransom, Andrew Lytle, Allen Tate, and Robert Penn Warren with whom she shared "her conservative vision of Southern culture." Notes, however, O'Connor's tendency to bury "her female identity by emphasizing masculinist plots, conventions, and characterizations," and discusses the issue of whether or not O'Connor conformed to the social role expected of a woman of her "society, class, and race" based on comments by her friends Betty Boyd Love, Maryat Lee, and correspondent "A." Declares Elaine Showalter's "'cultural' theory" as "the most useful feminist approach to O'Connor's work." Concludes that "an analysis of the ways in which gender influenced O'Connor's artistic development not only offers deeper insight into her relationship to the South and the Catholic Church, but provides a new perspective on the complexities and multiplicities of female aesthetics." [Also published in *Having Our Way: Women Rewriting Tradition in Twentieth-Century America*. Ed. Harriet Pollack. Lewisburg: Bucknell UP, 1995. 57-78.]

1293   Prunty, Wyatt. "The Figure of Vacancy." *Shennandoah* 46.3 (1996): 38-55.

Offers a comparative study of O'Connor's "A Good Man Is Hard to Find" and Peter Taylor's "A Wife of Nashville." Focuses upon each author's use of gaps and "vacancy" in their narrative in order to "to refute normal expectations and lead to what is unique and essential" about each story. Suggests that O'Connor "introduces the raw realities of life in rural Georgia, then uses wit, caricature and even cartoon-like violence to void normal expectations and achieve situations more complicated than ordinary description uncovers." Outlines how she and Taylor depict characters "stranded by elements in their lives that are as empty and inexplicable as the blank sky that characterizes the meeting between the grandmother and The Misfit." Finds Taylor's characters to be less rounded and exaggerated than O'Connor's, and notes that he tends to follow "the conventions of literary realism and avoid the religious allegory" typical of O'Connor's fiction. Refers to Kierkegaard's sense of "self" and compares his description to characters in both O'Connor's and Taylor's works. Concludes that this strategy is very effective in moving readers to look at O'Connor and Taylor's main characters from different perspectives. The "ordinary closure" that is expected from the story "is broken open and what follows is vacancy" which pushes readers to consider and confront their own bleak ends as well as those of the various characters. Sees O'Connor and Taylor as both attempting to use their themes focused on "vacancy" to represent Kierkegaard's thesis that "'no sooner has one discussed something than he is the thing himself.'"

1294   Pyron, Darden Asbury. "A Southern Mandarin." *Virginia Quarterly Review* 66.4 (1990): 740-46.

Review essay of Anne Waldron's *Caroline Gordon and the Southern Literary Renaissance* and Veronica Makowsky's *Caroline Gordon: A Biography*. Faults authors of both works as having little knowledge of regional culture and Southern history. Notes that while both deal with Gordon's friendship with O'Connor and focus on her "renderings of the bizarrest versions of Southern evangelical Protestantism," they neglect to "connect that vision with the very sort of religion that haunted [Caroline] Gordon's life."

1295   Pyron, Virginia. "'Strange Country': The Landscape of Flannery O'Connor's Short Stories." *Mississippi Quarterly* 36.4 (1983): 557-68.

Contends that by "paying attention to the landscape in Flannery O'Connor's fiction, the reader can . . . catch a glimpse of what is to come," as her natural images "bring out theological symbolism and reflect [her] characters' obsessions" while, at the same time, serving to mirror the action and assist building to the point of climax." Suggests that the "startling figures" found in O'Connor's landscapes, the "grotesque suns, trees, clouds, storms," all serve to "contribute to the shock value of her spiritual vision by their functions as indices of spiritual perception, as symbols of Divine grace or presence, and as reflections of characters' fears and tensions." Examines, in this context, "The Artificial Nigger," "The Life You Save May Be Your Own," "Greenleaf," "A Good Man Is Hard to Find," "The River," "A Circle In the Fire," "The Displaced Person," and "A View of the Woods." Concludes that O'Connor's landscapes "are so charged with vitality, and reflect so vividly the events of the stories, that nature often seems to step out of its function as mere scenery and into an active role in the drama--as a living presence, a threatening participant in the action, a conspirator against the characters' safety and security."

1296   Quinn, M. Bernetta. "Flannery O'Connor, a Realist of Distances." *Women Writers of the Short Story: A Collection of Critical Essays*. Ed. Heather McClave. Englewood Cliffs, NJ: Prentice-Hall, 1980. 136-44.

Refers to Brainard Cheney's tributeto Flannery O'Connor in the *Sewanee Review* in which he suggested that she was "the most significant writer in our time despite the slender volume she left to American letters." Follows with the statement that perhaps her "importance in contemporary criticism can be ascribed to her prophetic vision as expressed in highly individualized invention." Outlines discussions of O'Connor as a prophet "writing in a materialistic age [who] sometimes had to shout," and explores why many readers found her fiction to be "gloomy and morbid." Suggests that, upon examination, critics will find that O'Connor's "optimism decidedly outweighs her pessimism [as] more often than not, her distorted figures respond to prophecy and amend their lives." Offers brief explications in this context of "The Artificial Nigger," "The Comforts of Home," "Parker's Back," "The Partridge Festival," and "A Temple of the Holy Ghost." Finds that while O'Connor "can and repeatedly does highlight the negative," there are many examples in her stories of "a positive response to the divine invitation" while she "looks at her world with wide-open eyes and speaks about both the crude and the ugly as did Christ in his parables and she avoids any sentimental, *deus ex machina* endings." [Essay extracted from "Flannery O'Connor, a Realist of Distances" by Sister Quinn, from *The Added Dimension*, edited by Melvin Friedman and Lewis A. Lawson. 2nd. ed. (New York: Fordham UP, 1977. 157-67).]

1297 Quirk, Tom. "Realism, the `Real', and the Poet of Reality: Some Reflections on American Realists and the Poetry of Wallace Stevens." *American Literary Realism: 1870-1910* 21.2 (1989): 34-53.

Examines several passages from a variety of authors to illustrate the concept of realism in literature, which is seen as having "'nothing to do with 'reality' as such,'" but is founded instead on what Edwin H. Cady refers to as a "'Common Vision,' [that is] is rooted in and takes its authority from some shared sense of experience." Uses a passage from O'Connor's *Wise Blood* in which Hazel Motes is riding a train to discuss this topic of the difference between reality and realism in literature. Asserts that O'Connor's scene suggests to readers that Motes's perception of the movement of the train "is tempered with a modernist irony" to move her theme forward. Points out how she has "fixed objects (trees and fields) fall and curve and fade away, and [how her] hogs are transformed into stones." Contends that this allows for "the forward rush of events" to bend round and be "handed over to the past; the territory ahead is always the territory behind." Remarks that O'Connor's use of the speed and technological accomplishment of a locomotive serves as an "emblem of large cultural changes and . . . [as] the enabling agent for the experience of motion and change 'out there.'"

1298 Ragan, Sam. "Flannery O'Connor . . . *the peacocks cry all night long: help me, help me.*" *Arts Journal* (Asheville, NC) 7.7 (1982): 13.

Reports that in March, 1982, Governor Jim Hunt appointed Sam Ragan poet laureate for North Carolina. Provides a brief biographical sketch, and reprints Ragan's poem, "Flannery O'Connor . . . *the peacocks cry all night long: help me, help me.*" The poem refers to the 500 acre O'Connor family farm (Andalusia) located four miles north of Milledgeville, Georgia, Flannery O'Connor's fondness for chickens and peacocks, and to the "praying violent men" and other characters found in O'Connor's works who appear to be driven onward and inward at the same time. Alludes to O'Connor's death and absence with a reference to her crutches left leaning against a wall "unnoticed and forgotten," while peacocks strut in the shade of nearby trees. [Rpt. from Ragan's *The Tree in the Far Pasture* (Winston-Salem, NC: John F. Blair, 1964).]

1299 Ragen, Brian Abel. "'Another Room and Another Woman': Men, Women, and Flannery O'Connor." *Journal of Contemporary Thought* 4 (1994): 37-53.

Observes that while O'Connor did not try to "explore specifically female experience to any great degree," much of her work attacks the masculine myth that "celebrated the figure of the isolated, innocent man and reduced women to the roles of obstacles in his path or playthings for his use." Illustrates O'Connor's disgust with this masculine tradition--and its denial of original sin--with readings of: "The Life You Save May Be Your Own," *Wise Blood*, "The Enduring Chill," "Revelation," "Parker's Back," and "Everything That Rises Must Converge." Examines O'Connor's fictional households, focusing on those headed by a rural matriarch, and including "a self-important intellectual adult child." Sees these women as upholders of standards, and defenders "of all the values of human society." Notes that in O'Conno's explorations of gender roles, none describe successful romantic unions. Suggests that these unsuccessful episodes serve as "signposts" to the "more real and profound communion" man may find with a closer relationship with Christ. Considers also that, "Just as there is no fulfillment to be found in the arms of a lover" in her work, "there is no joyous return home to a welcoming father." Home, for O'Connor, is not an earthy dwelling place, but the heavenly domain of Christ. Concludes that O'Connor "treats all relationships as secondary to the primary relationship of the soul with God." Further, the issue of whether a man or woman accepts God's offer of grace serves as the principal concern and of O'Connor's work.

1300   Ragen, Brian Abel. "Daredevil Charity: Love and Family in O'Connor's 'The Comforts of Home.'" *Proceedings of the Northeast Regional Meeting of the Conference on Christianity and Literature, Regis College, 10-12 October 1996*. Ed. Joan F. Hallisey and Mary-Anne Vetterling. Weston, MA: Regis College, 1996. 102-07.

Offers an explication of "The Comforts of Home" focusing on how--for Thomas's mother--"charity is 'charity' in the real sense, a form of love." Points out that in this story O'Connor "does not contrast 'innocents' like Sarah with 'wicked' characters, but with the 'intelligent' characters who are 'in some measure' responsible for them . . . 'in the sense of looking after them.'" Contends that "neither Thomas nor his Mother can understand what is happening to them, much less understand the girl they are dealing with, because they ignore the fact of evil," and "forget original sin." By the end the story, however, the mother appears to gain "an even greater sense of the mystery of evil" and to recognize that the devil "is wearing Thomas's own face." Discusses animal imagery and how such imagery is used to emphasize a "dehumanizing view" of the girl. Then, considers similarities between Thomas and Saint Thomas, and compares Thomas's father with Adam. Finds that O'Connor not only uses this story to explore "what true charity is," but also to probe "the dangers of seeing either others--or oneself--as something other than a moral agent fully capable of evil."

1301 Ragen, Brian Abel. "Grace and Grotesques: Recent Books on Flannery O'Connor." *Papers on Language and Literature* 27.3 (1991): 386-98.

Observes that despite her expressed annoyance and amusement with academic literary criticism, Flannery O'Connor was "very much a product of the academic study of literature." Comments that while studying at the University of Iowa's Writer's Workshop, she "studied fiction through the lens of Brooks and Warren and was deeply influenced by the New Critics." Describes how O'Connor was "among the first important American writers whose careers were shaped by a university creative writing program," and how she "took the lessons of the New Critics and fused them with her other intellectual interests--Catholic, Thomist, Southern--to produce works unlike any others of her generation." Follows this introduction with a review essay of eight books on Flannery O'Connor published between 1985 and 1989, and devotes from one to several paragraphs to each, including: Frederick Asals's *Flannery O'Connor: The Imagination of Extremity*, Harold Bloom's *Flannery O'Connor: Modern Critical Views*, Robert H. Brinkmeyer's *The Art and Vision of Flannery O'Connor*, John F. Desmond's *Risen Sons: Flannery O'Connor's Vision of History*, Melvin J. Friedman and Beverly Lyon Clark's *Critical Essays on Flannery O'Connor*, Marshall Bruce Gentry's *Flannery O'Connor's Religion of the Grotesque*, Richard Giannone's *Flannery O'Connor and the Mystery of Love*, and Edward Kessler's *Flannery O'Connor and the Language of the Apocalypse*. Contends that the sheer volume of criticism on Flannery O'Connor's work that has been published since her death "affirms the variety of lights in which her work must be viewed . . . [as] her works demand philosophical, theological, and psychological analysis, as well as pure literary study." States that this level of response is needed "because a great mind has carefully ordered the disparate elements of her work for the reader to find." Finds that "what is most striking about the variety of commentary on O'Connor is that her stories allow, or even invite, examination from very different points of view: they are at once perfect New Critical objects, explorations of the grotesque . . . typological works like medieval mystery plays, faithful portrayals of the landscape of a region, psychological studies, dramas of the action of grace, embodiments of philosophical and theological ideas, and even dialogical interplays of voices."

1302 Rahv, Philip. "The Editor Interviews William Styron." *Conversations with William Styron*. Ed. James L.W. West, III. Jackson: UP of Mississippi, 1985. 151-61.

Quotes William Styron as stating that "much of the power of such writers as Faulkner and O'Connor" was "derived from their ability to see the bizarre connotations . . . [and] to perceive the ironies and contradictions involved when people inherited so directly the manners and mores of a nineteenth-century feudal, agrarian society" as it "collided head-on with the necessities of an industrial civilization." Comments that he found it fascinating that Walker Percy and O'Connor--"two of the very few really interesting Southern writers of the post-war period"--were "both Catholics with a skeptical turn of mind."

1303   Rajec, Elizabeth M. *The Study of Names in Literature: A Bibliography.* New York: K.G. Saur, 1978. 198.

A bibliography of articles, books, etc., concerned with "names" or "naming" in literature. Cites Dahlia Terrell's article, "Humor and Hysteria: Names in Flannery O'Connor's Fiction."

1304   Randles, Beverly Schlack. "Flannery O'Connor: The Flames of Heaven and Hell." *Poetics of the Elements in the Human Condition, Part II: The Airy Elements in Poetic Imagination: Breath, Breeze, Wind, Tempest, Thunder, Snow, Flame, Fire, Volcano.* Ed. Anna-Teresa Tymieniecka. (*Analecta Husserliana*, v. 23) Dordrecht (Netherlands): Kluwer Academic, 1988. 237-56.

Comments that while in her short lifetime Flannery O'Connor produced only two collections of stories, two short novels and a single volume of essays, "before she was killed by the fatal disease which also claimed her father's life," it may have been this very same "prolonged physical vulnerability" that molded her psyche into "one of the most unique psyches in twentieth century American literature." States that O'Connor's "harsh ontology gave her both the desire and the ability to abandon the trivial irrelevancies with which healthy, mundane beings clutter their lives in order to avoid, as she could not, the profoundest questions of human existence." Asserts that the impact of her contribution is "in the Aristotelian sense of the word *terrible*. It has great dramatic force; it is extreme, intense, severe, often stunningly funny." Suggests that "in her relentless probing of the human condition, Flannery O'Connor was always a philosopher, often a theologian, frequently a surgeon cutting through to the bone [but] -- never a cheerleader." Discusses how her work "borders everywhere on the parable . . . a species of the morality play," and in being such, reveals "the richness of her reading background" and utilizes aspects of Southern Protestant Fundamentalism. States that O'Connor uses "fire metaphors to symbolize both sin and its purgation" in "The Artificial Nigger," "A Circle in the Fire," and "The Enduring Chill." Explicates these three stories as well as "Revelation," "Parker's Back," and *The Violent Bear It Away*. Refers to the scriptural passage "that 'every man's work shall be made manifest . . . it shall be revealed by fire,'" and concludes that the "Bible's numerous associations of fire with speech, especially in the sense of fire's Pentecostal power, are as relevant to Flannery O'Connor herself as to her fictive creations."

1305   Rash, Ronald. Rev. of *Why Flannery O'Connor Stayed Home*, by Marion Montgomery. *Flannery O'Connor Bulletin* 10 (1981): 97-99.

Comments that "a good many critics have had trouble with Flannery O'Connor's view of the world," noting that "their criticism often turns out to be qualified: the standard approach is to praise the storytelling and reject the perspective." Discusses how, unlike these many scholars, Marion Montgomery accepts O'Connor not only as a fiction writer, but also heartily believes in her themes and in the territory she claims. Suggests that Montgomery sees O'Connor's world view "not as a defect but as her greatest strength." Reports that he sets out "to measure her achievement against the best that [Western literary tradition] can offer." Sees Montgomery as elevating O'Connor to being "'a prophetic poet,' one who, like such writers as Dante, sees the world in its wholeness, natural and supernatural, at once." Notes that he argues "that the criticism which has fragmented her work rises out of [the] limited and fragmented world views" of the critics, and not O'Connor herself; and because they often overlook the "depth" of her characters, critics have missed discovering where the "greatness" of her fiction lies. Rash reports that Montgomery's chapter on "A Good Man Is Hard to Find" is "the best explication" of the story that he has read. Finds Montgomery's book to be "an ambitious project" which challenges "much ill-founded criticism" and associates many of O'Connor's critics "with some of the very characters that they have been analyzing." Notes how Montgomery takes critics to task in how he "finds unsatisfactory the current tendency of critics to limit themselves to one school of critical thought when dealing with an artist as complex as O'Connor"; then describes how he fumes at the tendency of critics to "ignore such helpful materials as her letters, her essays, and even her library" when considering how O'Connor attempted to convey her view of morality." Concludes with the comment: "At last one reads a full-length study of Flannery O'Connor with the feeling that [this is one work that] maybe even O'Connor herself would have read to the end." [*Why Flannery O'Connor Stayed Home*, by Marion Montgomery. LaSalle: Sherwood Sugden & Co., 1981.]

1306   Rath, Sura P. "Changing Directions in O'Connor Criticism." *CHEERS! The Flannery O'Connor Society Newsletter* 1.2 (1993): 1, 4.

Surveys trends of criticism of O'Connor's work, decade by decade. Notes that while the focus of her contemporary critics was to analyze her use of theme and setting, by the 1960s critics had begun "to recognize the role of her faith in her poetics" and had begun examining the regional and Catholic characteristics seen in her work. Sees criticism of the 1970s as focusing on her use of "form and structure" to develop "her `redemptive' or `apocalyptic' vision." Reports that, with the publication of *The Habit of Being*, the growth of O'Connor-related articles, books, and dissertations continued "exponentially" through the 1980s, often synthesizing "previously held piece-meal perspectives" and examining "O'Connor's ideology against the larger metaphysics of life as she experienced it." Includes mention of specific critics and their books published during the 1980s, and continued interest in O'Connor as demonstrated by the receipt of the Maryat Lee-O'Connor letters by the O'Connor Collection in 1990 and establishment of the Flannery O'Connor Society in 1992.

1307   Rath, Sura P. "Comic Polarities in Flannery O'Connor's *Wise Blood*." *Studies in Short Fiction* 21.3 (1984): 251-58.

Discusses O'Connor's response to early critics of *Wise Blood*, that the book was "'a comic novel about Christian *malgre lui*, and as such, very serious, for all comic novels that are any good must be about life and death." Comments that O'Connor's critics have "since highlighted the general comic effect of the grotesque in [her] writings and her reputation as an ironist has been secured." Examines the book as an archetypal comic novel with characters resembling the three conventional archetypes as described by Northrop Frye: "the *eirons*, or self-depreciators; the *alazons*, or imposters; and the *bomolochoi*, or buffoons, clowns and fools."

1308   Rath, Sura P. "An Evolving Friendship: Flannery O'Connor's Correspondence with Father Edward J. Romagosa, S.J." *Flannery O'Connor Bulletin* 17 (1988): 1-10.

Offers a biographical sketch of Father Edward J. Romagosa, ("Father Roma") and describes his friendship and admiration for Flannery O'Connor. Provides the text of seven letters he received from O'Connor between 1959 and 1964, and states that they "complement the self-effacing, galvanic portrait of Flannery we get from her letters" previously published in *The Habit of Being* and in *The New Orleans Review*. Suggests that the letters reflect Father Roma's "critical sensibility" in recognizing "the relevance of her Catholicism to the theological training of his scholastics" as he "championed the importance of her fiction to mainstream American literature at a time when she was `trounced' by other Catholic reviewers." Mentions Father Youree Watson, Father Robert Rimes, her response to receiving a poor review of *The Violent Bear It Away*, her lecture at the University of Southwestern Louisiana (1962), preparing another for Sweet Briar College the following year, and her sense of humor as revealed in her last letter of April 11, 1964.

1309   Rath, Sura P. "Introduction." *Flannery O'Connor: New Perspectives*. Ed. Sura P. Rath and Mary Neff Shaw. Athens: U of Georgia P, 1996. 1-11.

Sees response to O'Connor's work as divided into four phases: (1) 1952-60: Reviewers praise or condemn *Wise Blood* "for its grotesquerie, violence, and other naturalistic elements." (2) 1960s: Readers "examine the role of her faith in her poetics," focusing on regional or Christian realism, while still polarized in regard to her "dramatization of plots and characters." (3) 1970s: Criticism shifts "to analyzing the function of the form and structure of her fiction in the development of her `vision.'" (4) 1980s: Scholars "question the originality of `new' insights," while books and articles continue to be written. (Lists books published during this period.) Discusses comments by Jerome Klinkowitz, Robert Coles, and Ben Satterfield suggesting that publications focused on O'Connor had perhaps become too extensive and repetitive. Then, outlines positions taken by a variety of critics in articles and books published during the last decade. Refers to the seventy-nine dissertations written during the 1980s, the unpublished letters which have become available since the publication of *The Habit of Being*, and the founding of the Flannery O'Connor Society in 1992. States that the purpose of this collection is "to bring together the major new perspectives on O'Connor of the last decade and a half and to assess the directions in which O'Connor scholarship has moved." Closes with summaries of each of the essays, and suggestions regarding topics and approaches scholars may wish to consider in the future.

1310   Rath, Sura P. "Introduction." *Journal of Contemporary Thought* 4 (1994): 6.

Lists titles and dates of publication of works by O'Connor, and refers readers to *The Flannery O'Connor Bulletin* and the *Flannery O'Connor Society*. Briefly describes six articles included in this issue of the *Journal of Contemporary Thought* as a special section on Flannery O'Connor. Acknowledges Marshall Bruce Gentry's assistance in inviting and selecting the essays.

1311   Rath, Sura P. Rev. of *Flannery O'Connor: A Memorial*, by J.J. Quinn. *Flannery O'Connor Bulletin* 24 (1995-96): 138-40.

Describes the unique nature and background of the publication of this volume and the demand for the issue of *Esprit*, published by the

University of Scranton, that this volume reprints. Outlines and describes the four sections of the book, applauds the introductory essay by J.J. Quinn, and contends that "the critical accuracy" of early readings and comments by the many contributors to the second section of tributes "has been borne out by research and the reading public of the last thirty years." Discusses O'Connor's "early critical reception" and finds it refreshing "to see some reviews . . . that foreshadow the later critics who emphasize the dramatic structure of her fiction rather than its theological content." Declares that "the revisionist readings of the mid-eighties" and the "steady flow of scholarly work" on O'Connor during the last thirty years serve as proof that this volume "will likely be appreciated for the prophetic value of the poignant tributes it offers in reprint." Concludes that this book will meet a "critical need" for access to peer reviews of O'Connor's fiction.

1312   Rath, Sura P. "Ruby Turpin's Redemption: Thomistic Resolution in Flannery O'Connor's `Revelation.'" *Flannery O'Connor Bulletin* 19 (1990): 1-8.

Reports that despite much critical commentary, Ruby Turpin's vision at the end of "Revelation" is still "problematic." States that the scene's "critical polarity hinges on the source of Ruby's epiphany: whether it is internal, the redeeming awareness emerging from the dramatic unfolding of the crisis she confronts, or whether it is external, the vision gratuitously descending upon her as a narrative *coup de grace*." Offers an analysis of the story based upon the theology of St. Thomas, and suggests that such an approach "resolves this polarity insofar as O'Connor dramatizes St. Thomas's reconciliation of opposites by drawing on external objects as a means of tracking internal growth." Outlines O'Connor's acknowledgement and interest in St. Thomas through her writings, letters, and lectures. Discusses the "aesthetic dilemma central to both St. Thomas's theology and O'Connor's poetics" and their "recognition of the supernatural in the natural world of the senses." Closes with an exploration of the eye as a recurring symbol in O'Connor's work and its role as metaphor extending "beyond the human level."

1313   Rath, Sura P. "Welcome from the Society President." *Flannery O'Connor Society Newsletter* 1.1 (1993): 1.

Recounts how the idea of forming "a Flannery O'Connor Society" came to him, and the "overwhelming" support he received from interested scholars to establish such an organization. Lists the inaugural members of the "Executive Committee," reports that Virginia Wray has agreed to serve as editor, and includes a statement regarding the Society's purpose: "to promote and assist O'Connor studies through the organization of conferences and special meetings, and to foster scholarship and academic community amongst O'Connor scholars."

1314   Redmon, Anne. "Figures for Our Displacement: An Informal Discussion of the Works of Flannery O'Connor." *The Origins and Originality of American Culture.* [Papers presented at the International Conference on American Studies, April 9-11, 1980]. Ed. Tibor Frank. Budapest (Hungary): Akademiai Kiado, 1984. 219-29.

Provides brief biographical details related to O'Connor, and suggests that "for a Southern Catholic lady, she achieves the extraordinary task of getting into the heads of people with whom she would have no obvious connection." States that readers can see the dignity O'Connor bestows on her characters and how she seizes "the image of the despised and ignorant" and gives them "a queer beauty." Refers to O'Connor's art, and asserts that she possessed "an uncommon gift--an uncommon spirituality which can mine the depths of a hostile fanaticism and find truth." Offers a reading of *Wise Blood*, focusing on the meanings in the dialogue between Hazel Motes and his landlady. Concludes that whether the reader is a believer or not, O'Connor's work divulges "Southern metaphysics at a fairly basic level in the society." Finds that in her own writings, as in O'Connor and other Southerners, there is "a sense of nameless ruin--of the Fall, perhaps," which possesses them as they practice their art.

1314a   Reem, Craig. "O'Connor's Art Changed Life of Ex-Teacher." *Savannah Evening Press* 18 Nov. 1991: 1.

Discusses Kenneth Mammel's lecture "Flannery O'Connor: Faithful Witness to Christ" presented to a gathering at the Flannery O'Connor childhood home in Savannah. Reports that Mammel said that he was so moved by O'Connor's writings that he converted from his Quaker beliefs to Catholicism. Mentions Mammel's comment that the "redemption process" is "intertwined" throughout O'Connor's stories, and his discussion of why she wrote on the theme of "when tenderness is detached from Christ, it becomes terror." Illustrations: Photograph of Flannery O'Connor's childhood home in Savannah.

1314b   Reem, Craig. "They Grew Up With O'Connor: Friends and Relatives Reminisce About Savannah-Born Author." *Savannah Morning News* 18 Dec. 1991: 29+.

Reports anecdotes by relatives and friends of O'Connor gathered at her childhood home in Savannah in early September, 1991. Among those in the gathering were Newell Parr, Tony Harty, Winnifred Persse, Margaret Persse Trexler, Miriam Tharin, and Patricia Persse. Notes comments and opinions regarding the "many levels of meaning" seen in her work, her characteristic use of violence and terror, her ability to see hypocrisy in situations at even an early age, the impact of her disease on her writing, and whether she would have been awarded a Pulitzer Prize had she lived.

1315   Reesman, Jeanne Campbell. "Women, Language, and the Grotesque in Flannery O'Connor and Eudora Welty." *Flannery O'Connor: New Perspectives.* Ed. Sura P. Rath and Mary Neff Shaw. Athens: U of Georgia P, 1996. 38-56.

Compares the opening lines of O'Connor's "Good Country People" to those of Eudora Welty's "Why I Live at the P.O." Uses these openings to illustrate both writers' interest in the grotesque. Sees their use of the grotesque as reflecting Southwestern literary folk traditions developed by Augustus Baldwin Longstreet, Johnson Jones Hooper, and Joel Chandler Harris. Suggests that grotesque Southern literature "can be tied to an individual's sense of positive power and to the celebration of individual freedom." Contends that O'Connor and Welty adapted Southern grotesque traditions for their own purposes, "which, though not identical, are parallel, especially in their invocation of a feminine grotesque." Refers to comments on the definition and use of the grotesque by a wide variety of literary critics and scholars, including Alice Walker. Indicates that "the most rewarding theorist to keep in mind in analyzing these authors is Mikhail Bakhtin," for whom "the `carnival laughter' of the grotesque is the universal laughter `of all good people.'" Concludes with an extensive discussion of each writers' use of the grotesque, along with readings--in this context--of O'Connor's "Good Country People" and "A Good Man Is Hard to Find," and Welty's "Petrified Man" and "A Worn Path."

1316   Regan, Robert. "The Legitimate Sources of Depravity in Flannery O'Connor." *Delta* (France) 2 (March 1976): 53-59.

Asserts that "A Good Man Is Hard to Find" illustrates the three elements of all of O'Connor's work: her focus on her "native South, American fiction of the nineteenth century, and her conservative Catholic Christianity." Discusses how O'Connor uses Southern diction and syntax, to provide hints to readers about the region and characters in her work. Outlines how the theme of patricide, as seen in this story, may be considered an outgrowth of "*the* dominant tradition of the American imagination." Cites a variety of examples in American literature in which a parent is murdered, including works by Ambrose Bierce, George Washington Harris, Samuel Clemens, Frederick C. Crews, and Nathaniel

Hawthorne. Closes with an examination of the impact of O'Connor's faith on her work, and concludes with the assertion that this story "reveals the Catholic dimension of her imagination" which "conversely, reveals the central meaning of the story."

1317   Reisman, Rosemary M. Canfield and Suzanne Booker-Canfield. *Contemporary Southern Men Fiction Writers: An Annotated Bibliography.* Lanham, MD: Scarecrow; Pasadena CA: Salem, 1998. 33, 53, 104, 118, 133, 136, 163, 216, 228, 231, 233, 244, 264, 381.

Offers descriptive abstracts of essays, interviews, biographical materials and bibliographies, related to the lives and work of thirty-eight contemporary Southern male writers. Notes, in the Introduction, O'Connor's quote regarding William Faulkner's work that, "'Nobody wants to be caught on the tracks when the Dixie Special comes through,'" and comments that--for contemporary Southern writers--O'Connor herself may "be moving down those tracks with equal speed" and that while for many Southern writers Faulkner may serve as a literary father, O'Connor may very well be their "literary mother." O'Connor is mentioned in abstracts of articles related to Richard Bausch, Madison Smartt Bell, Mark Childress, Harry Crews, Pete Dexter, Andre Dubus, Allan Gurganus, Barry Hannah, Madison Jones, Cormac McCarthy, and William Styron.

1317a   "Remembering Flannery." *Savannah Evening Press* 8 Nov. 1992: C7.

Photograph of "cousins and friends of writer Flannery O'Connor" unveiling a State historic marker in front of her childhood home at 207 East Charlton Street in Savannah, Georgia.

1318   "Reminder to Scholars." *Flannery O'Connor Bulletin* 20 (1991): 44.

Declares that the bibliography, "Citations to O'Connor-related Dissertations in the UMI Database," in R. Neil Scott's article, "UMI's Citations to Theses and Dissertations Related to Flannery O'Connor," in the previous issue did not include Father John J. Quinn's dissertation, "The Tragi-Comic Vision in the Writings of Flannery O'Connor: A Study of Her Analogical Imagination" (1970). Reports that the study was completed at King's College, University of London and that Father Quinn edited *Esprit*'s special issue on O'Connor in 1964. [Note: At the time of publication, British dissertations were neither cited nor listed in UMI's database index of *Dissertation Abstracts*.]

1319   Renner, Stanley. "Secular Meaning in `A Good Man Is Hard to Find.'"
            College Literature 9.2 (1982): 123-32.

Begins an analysis of "A Good Man Is Hard to Find" with a description
of a confession in a Southern murder trial of a young man accused of
murdering an eight-year-old girl who--like the grandmother--assured her
murderer that Jesus loved him. Following this example of life illuminating
literature, Renner contends that "the grandmother's last words are more
than an expression of parental love, Christian charity, and forgiveness;"
instead, they may "be taken to mean that she is responsible for The Misfit
in a causal sense."

1320   Reuman, Ann E. "Revolting Fictions: Flannery O'Connor's Letter to Her
            Mother." *Papers on Language & Literature* 29.2 (1993): 197-214.

Discusses Franz Kafka's letter to his father, which was meant to leave the
parent "with a painful realization" of what he was. States that Asbury
Fox's two-notebook long letter to his mother ("The Enduring Chill") may
be an allusion worthy of further exploration. Asserts that the very mention
of the letter by O'Connor's character may be indicative of O'Connor's own
relationship with her mother. Suggests that while their relationship has
been generally considered "loving, if difficult at times," her later stories
"strongly suggest a mother/daughter relationship which was more
troubling, crippling, and complex than conventionally assumed." Offers
a brief biographical sketch of Kafka, discusses parallels between his
portrait of his father and O'Connor's depiction of her mother (using letters
from *The Habit of Being*), and looks at circumstances in O'Connor's life
that "transformed an adolescent conflict into a tension which was as
complex as it was significant to her literary development." Examines, in
this light, "The Enduring Chill," "Everything That Rises Must Converge,"
"The Comforts of Home," "Why Do the Heathen Rage?" "A Circle in the
Fire," "Revelation" and "Good Country People." Concludes that O'Connor
may have hinted "at the ultimate irresolution of her `adolescent' conflict"
in the final scene in "Judgment Day," in which Tanner is left "grotesquely
crucified" in the staircase bannister.

1320a   Reynolds, Guy. "`There are So Many Horrible Examples of Regional
            Writers, and the South Is Loaded: Flannery O'Connor `Every Action is
            Weighted with an Eternal Consequence.'" *Twentieth-Century American
            Women's Fiction: A Critical Introduction* New York: St. Martin's Press,
            1999. 114-45.

Contends that O'Connor's visionary, allegorical and symbolic stories may
be viewed as springing directly from her "categorical adherence to the

Roman [Catholic] faith." Discusses examples of how she pitches "supposedly insightful skeptical humanists" into situations where "life contains more mysteries than rationality can account for," and offers commentary on "Revelation" and "The Artificial Nigger."

1321   Reynolds, Michael M., ed. *Guide to Theses and Dissertations: An International Bibliography of Bibliographies*. Phoenix: Oryx, 1985. 167-68.

Provides annotated references to bibliographies of dissertations and theses. Cites Robert E. Golden and Mary C. Sullivan's *Flannery O'Connor and Caroline Gordon: A Reference Guide* (Boston: G.K. Hall, 1977).

1322   Rich, Frank. "The Sound and the Fury." *Time* 25 Feb. 1980: 50.

Reviews John Huston's film version of *Wise Blood*, finding it to be "the most eccentric American movie in years." States that the material from O'Connor meant that it "was all but guaranteed to fuel the battiest recesses" of Huston's imagination. States that "Huston takes to O'Connor's hothouse style like a gambler to a royal flush," and "the inevitable results are the very essence of weird." Summarizes the plot, discusses Huston's handling of O'Connor's grotesque imagery and logic, her characters ("who are all crazy"), and their artistic theme. Concludes that "moviegoers who have a taste for *Wise Blood*" will enjoy the film "just to ride the wild imaginative waves of this singular artistic adventure."

1323   Riley, Carolyn, ed. "O'Connor, Flannery." *Contemporary Literary Criticism*. Vol. 3. Detroit: Gale Research, 1975. 365-70.

Offers excerpts from a variety of pre-1975 criticism of O'Connor's works: Saul Maloff (*Mystery and Manners*); Gene Kellogg (*The Violent Bear It Away* and "The Artificial Nigger"); Jane Carter Keller (*The Violent Bear It Away* and *Wise Blood*); John Idol (*The Complete Stories*); Preston M. Browning, Jr. (*The Violent Bear It Away*); William S. Doxey ("A Good Man Is Hard to Find"); Nancy Y. Hoffman (discusses how O'Connor is "a satirist in the savagely indignant tradition of [Roman poet] Juvenal and [Jonathan] Swift); Elmo Howell ("Everything That Rises Must Converge"); and Alfred Kazin (discusses his admiration for O'Connor's work in general).

1324   Riley, Carolyn, and Phyllis Carmel Mendelson, eds. "O'Connor, Flannery." *Contemporary Literary Criticism*. Vol. 6. Detroit: Gale Research, 1976. 375-382.

Offers excerpts of pre-1975 criticism of O'Connor's works: Thelma J. Shinn (*The Violent Bear It Away*); Leonard Casper (discusses O'Connor's view of death); Josephine Hendin (*Wise Blood* and "Everything That Rises Must Converge"); David Eggenschwiler (*Wise Blood* and *The Violent Bear It Away*); Claire Katz (*Wise Blood* and *Mystery and Manners*); Mark Edelstein (*Wise Blood*, "The Artificial Nigger," "The River," and "A Stroke of Good Fortune"); Ellen Douglas ("A Good Man Is Hard to Find"); and Alice Walker (discusses O'Connor's views on sentimentality and race).

1325   Riso, Don. "Blood and Land in 'A View of the Woods.'" *New Orleans Review* 1 (1968): 255-57.

Examines thematic relationships between "blood-loyalty and love of the land" in O'Connor's "A View of the Woods." Argues that Mr. Fortune and his granddaughter "constitute thesis and antithesis" and that their "clash results not in a new synthesis, but in self-annihilation and violence, which are in fact reversals of the 'Southern Myth.'" Suggests symbolic meanings for their names, possible explanations as to why Mr. Fortune hates his land and uses it as a weapon against the Pitts family, examples of the tension between Mary Fortune and her family and grandfather, and a symbolic interpretation of the death of the two main characters.

1326   Roberts, Diane. "Ladies of the South." *Essays in Criticism* 36.2 (1986): 180-86.

Review essay of Louise Westling's *Sacred Groves and Ravaged Gardens: The Fiction of Eudora Welty, Carson McCullers and Flannery O'Connor* (Athens: U of Georgia P, 1985). Comments on William Faulkner's influence on the three writers, and how O'Connor and McCullers can be connected "in the way they render the bleak, sterile world of the unloving, unlovely, 'unwomanly' woman in reaction to the Southern lady stereotype." Includes a discussion of O'Connor's portrayal of virtue and grace in "A Temple of the Holy Ghost."

1327   Robinson, Ella. *A Guide to Literary Sites of the South*. Northport, AL: Vision Press, 1998. xiii-xv, 64-65, 243, 250, 253, 255, 261, 263.

Designed as a literary travel guide, this book provides "detailed information about home sites open to the public and short profiles of the authors who lived in these homes." Includes a description of the Flannery O'Connor's childhood home in Savannah, Georgia and addresses of a variety of other significant sites.

1328   Robinson, Gabriele Scott. "Irish Joyce and Southern O'Connor." *Flannery O'Connor Bulletin* 5 (1976): 82-97.

Points out similarities between James Joyce's "Araby" and O'Connor's "A Temple of the Holy Ghost." Offers readings of the two stories, then discusses how: "both are intense interior dramas focusing on the inner life of the central character"; in "both children pursue their quest in an environment hostile to spiritual values and are . . . forced to live their true lives in an imaginary world of heroism and romance"; "the subject of both stories is an initiation which is in each case brought about by a fair"; and both "are built on a sequence of images and symbolic references, notably imagery of light which threads each story." Outlines how both writers appear convinced that "it is impossible to make any significant statement about life that is not closely associated with a particular place." Recognizes O'Connor and Joyce's concern with "the manifest decay of their societies," which, in turn, reveals "the social, psychological, and spiritual `paralysis' of their country." Closes with the suggestion that "Joyce's obsession with a father figure" is similar to O'Connor's focus on "parent-child relationships," and that just as Joyce has been described as "Dublin-haunted, parent-haunted, [and] God-haunted," the same "description could be applied equally well to O'Connor."

1329   Robison, James C. "1969-1980: Experiment and Tradition." *The American Short Story 1945-1980: A Critical History*. Ed. Gordon Weaver. Boston: Twayne, 1983. 77-109.

Briefly compares Joyce Carol Oates's work to that of Flannery O'Connor. States that while both writers offer strange characters and use violence, O'Connor "does so with clearly different effects." Asserts that O'Connor "suggests how things *should* be" and examines what is wrong "by means of narrative distance, irony and humor." Suggests that Oates, however, "does not offer a clear distinction between what her characters see and what their creator sees." Recalls O'Connor's comment that "`Competence by itself is deadly. What is needed is the vision to go with it.'" Offers a short review of O'Connor's *The Complete Stories*, and refers to "Why Do the Heathen Rage?" "The Geranium" and "The Partridge Festival." Concludes that "even O'Connor's weaker stories have substance."

1330   Rodgers, Audrey T. "Images of Women: A Female Perspective." *College Literature* 6.1 (1979): 41-56.

Argues that "women characters exposed by Flannery O'Connor, Dorothy Parker, Eudora Welty, and Katherine Anne Porter act out the preconceived roles of temptress, nun, or mindless romantic," and "perpetuate the fiction that women hate women."

1331   Rogal, Samuel J. *A Chronological Outline of American Literature*. New York: Greenwood, 1987. 215, 304, 311, 325, 335, 340, 352, 359.

A chronological listing of events in the lives of well-known American authors, including the year of their birth, death, and publication of works. O'Connor is mentioned on the pages cited.

1332   Roos, John. "Flannery O'Connor and the Limits of Justice." *Poets, Princes, and Private Citizens: Literary Alternatives to Postmodern Politics*. Ed. Joseph M. Knippenberg and Peter Augustine Lawler. Lanham, MD: Rowman & Littlefield, 1996. 143-67.

Considers O'Connor's fiction "as a source of insight into our contemporary search for a viable understanding of the relationship between justice and politics." Suggests that while she certainly viewed herself as an artist, as a follower of Saint Thomas Aquinas she was also a profound thinker concerned with the natural and divine governance of nature. Outlines how O'Connor's fiction "brings together themes that have powerfully re-emerged in our current reflections about the limits of politics," and refers to calls by Alexander Solzhenitsyn and Václav Haval to develop a "newly imaginative approach to politics that transcends linear Western scientific thought." Underscores the present search "for supplements to liberal individualism and its Enlightenment rationality," and the difficulty to the modern sensibility "in separating the imaginative from the dangerously romantic." Explores these themes in O'Connor's "Revelation" by combining a careful reading of the story with a consideration of the relationship of politics to revelation and poetry. Focuses upon O'Connor's response "to the question of where the boundary lies between the desire for the absolute and the possibilities of the political." Notes "parallels with two works that stand in dialectical tension with the story, the *Book of Job* and Plato's *Republic*," and sees O'Connor's "Revelation" as a response to the problems and experiences of humankind posed by these ancient authors.

1333   Roos, John. "The Political in Flannery O'Connor: A Reading of `A View of the Woods.'" *Studies in Short Fiction* 29.2 (1992): 161-79.

Asserts that in "A View of the Woods" O'Connor "brings her artistic vision to bear upon the consequences of two views of property and family." The first view is "Lockean, in which individualism and the pursuit of `life, liberty, and estate' serve as an alternative to salvation." The second view "is a Thomistic one, in which nature, including our relationship to family, community, and the world, is the analogue to the divine life and the way in which we are imperfectly drawn to the realm of grace." Suggests that O'Connor's work "is `incarnational' in the sense that whatever truth is to be found is found in the stories themselves." Explores the Lockean and Thomistic views of property, family, and progress, then offers a careful reading of the story "to see whether these elements indeed are found, and if so what light O'Connor's artistic vision sheds on this conflict." Refers to Lorine Getz, Sir Thomas Filmer and theories of the Divine Right of Kings, the writings of Thomas Aquinas, John Locke, Teilhard de Chardin, Robert Fitzgerald, and Brian Abel Ragen.

1334   Rosa, Alfred F. *Contemporary Fiction in America and England, 1950-1970: A Guide to Information Sources*. Detroit: Gale Research, 1976. 273-81.

Bibliography that includes primary sources, other bibliographies, critical books, and articles on O'Connor.

1335   Rose, Alan Henry. "Recent American Writings: The Leveling of Racial Vision." *Demonic Vision: Racial Fantasy and Southern Fiction*. Hamden, CT: Archon, 1976. 119-36.

Offers readings of *Wise Blood* and "The Artificial Nigger." Focuses on the "curious ambiguity" and "demonic narrative" in *Wise Blood*, the racial implications and symbolic meaning of the mummy ("`a dead shriveled-up part-nigger dwarf'"), and Enoch Emery's donning of the gorilla suit. Contends that O'Connor's use of the Negro in "The Artificial Nigger" is "far removed" from her "previous eruptions of demonic expression" seen in *Wise Blood*. Whereas the novel expressed an "unconscious energy of the black image [which] unstabilized the narrative," the story "leads to a resolution and spiritual enlightenment." Suggests the racial imagery in the story resembles more "the expressions of the black man in writings by northerners such as Herman Melville and Nathaniel Hawthorne" than images of the negro found in other Southern fiction. Points out parallels and comparisons to Mark Twain's *Pudd'nhead Wilson*, Henry Clay Lewis's "Stealing a Baby," Faulkner's *Light in August* and "Red Leaves," Melville's "Benito Cereno" and *Moby-Dick*, and Hawthorne's "My Kinsman, Major Molineux" and *The Blithedale Romance*. Refers to critical remarks by Martha Stephens, Preston M. Browning, Jr., Kathleen Feeley, and Gilbert Muller to clarify passages.

1336   Rosenblum, Joseph. *Masterplots II: Non-fiction Series*. Ed. Frank N. Magill. Englewood Cliffs, NJ: Salem, 1989. 630-35.

Offers a critical summary of *The Habit of Being*. Includes: a discussion of the epistolary form; lists the principal correspondents; and comments on Fitzgerald's omissions and deletions. Provides a short analytical commentary, with a section on O'Connor's critical context, and lists some of the critical sources for the work.

1337   Ross, Cheri Louise. "The Iconography of Popular Culture in O'Connor's `A Good Man Is Hard to Find.'" *Notes on Contemporary Literature* 27.1 (1997): 7-9.

Contends that O'Connor "presents a devastating critique of 1950s American society" in "A Good Man Is Hard to Find." Identifies and discusses "parodistic structures and elements of black humor" in O'Connor's depiction of the 1950s American family and in her use of "such notions of middle-class respectability" as "dressing up to travel." Concludes that O'Connor's "satire of middle-class social norms and American cultural icons provides a focus for the comic elements."

1338   Rout, Kathleen. "Dream a Little Dream of Me: Mrs. May and the Bull in Flannery O'Connor's `Greenleaf.'" *Studies in Short Fiction* 16.3 (1979): 233-35.

Argues that the bull in "Greenleaf" is a complex symbol which "combines . . . social, sexual, and religious identities in a way that allows him to represent everything that Mrs. May rejects." Concludes that the bull represents "Jesus stabbing her in the heart . . . the `bullet' of divine wrath, and Greenleaf vengeance."

1339   Rout, Kay Kinsella. "Flannery O'Connor and the Role of the Intellectual." *Intellect* 106 (April 1978): 421-22.

Describes editorials written by the editors of *Life* and *Time* magazines in 1955 and 1956 lamenting the negative attitudes of American intellectuals and supporting the ideas of Jacques Barzun. Asserts that O'Connor rejected Barzun, who appeared to support the idea that "an intellectual's proper role was to support the *status quo*," and wrote a response titled "The Place of the Intellectual" for *Commonweal*. Suggests that the "journalistic challenge may have yielded more than O'Connor's defense of her work, for, from 1958 to 1962, everything she published featured a major character who was a college graduate, if not an `intellectual.'"

Contends that "Sheppard of 'The Lame Shall Enter First,' the do-gooder who believes in a humanistic 'salvation,' could almost be O'Connor's sardonic response" to Jacques Barzun. Relates the influence on O'Connor of Pierre Teilhard Chardin's theory that "at the end of time, all creation will have returned to the creator through Christ, the Omega point." Provides an overview of O'Connor's beliefs related to society's spiritually deficient, who attempt to provide psychological and social explanations for criminals and others. Discusses O'Connor's view that these beliefs lead to "an excess of compassion called sentimentality, a distortion of sentiment usually in the direction of an overemphasis on innocence, and that innocence tends by some natural law to become its opposite." Concludes that "*Commonweal*'s statement of the problem in 1956 helped to crystalize O'Connor's attitude toward her work."

1340   Rowley, Rebecca K. "Individuation and Religious Experience: A Jungian Approach to O'Connor's 'Revelation.'" *Southern Literary Journal* 25.2 (1993): 92-102.

Asserts that Carl Jung "may have influenced O'Connor more than she acknowledged"; then, uses "a hermeneutical approach similar to Jung's interpretive method of amplification, to clarify the events in 'Revelation' through recourse to some of Jung's major tenets." Refers to O'Connor's readings of Jung's *Modern Man in Search of a Soul* and *The Undiscovered Self*, and interpretive writings by Victor White and Josef Goldbrunner. Synthesizes Jung's "diverse and often cryptic comments on religion," and suggests that his "theory of religious experience manifests itself in Mrs. Turpin's initiation to the individuation process." Discusses Mary Grace's insanity, O'Connor's use of her as a "vehicle of grace," and how she serves as a link to the Ruby Turpin's unconscious. Contends that O'Connor--like Jung--viewed evil as a viable force. Explores the symbolic meanings of images using fire, the eye, and pigs in the story. Concludes that using Jung's "psychological explanation of the dynamics of religious experience illuminates some of the darkness and profound mystery which distinguishes O'Connor's grotesque fiction."

1341   Roy, Paula A. "Flannery O'Connor and Alice Walker: Making the Connections." *Women's Studies International Forum* 10.5 (1987): 33-34.

Provides an abstract of a paper by Paula A. Roy that compares O'Connor's "Good Country People" and "A View of the Woods" with Walker's "The Child Who Favored Daughter" and "Roselily." Suggests "striking similarities between the authors" because, "despite racial and social barriers," they suggest that both white and black women become victims in ways that transcend difference." Sees women in these stories as "victims of patriarchal power in twisted parodies of southern mythology." Contends that because they are "defined by myths about female sexuality and links to the land," O'Connor and Walker's women "are powerless to form alliances, [and] without a language to call to one another at all." Sees, "within this shared vision of powerlessness," traces "of incest, sexual violence, and female complicity."

1342   Rubin, Louis D., [Jr.] "Carson McCullers: The Aesthetic of Pain." *A Gallery of Southerners*. Baton Rouge: Louisiana State UP, 1982. 135-51.

O'Connor's remarks on the use of the grotesque in Southern novels are discussed on pp. 143-44. States that O'Connor may have been suggesting "that the southern experience was still very much an affair of the complex patterns of community life, with the comings and goings of individuals taking place within a clearly recognized set of expectations and assumptions. In that kind of established social context, individual behavior ran along expected norms . . . anything truly deviant, genuinely aberrant, would therefore stand out since there was something against which it could be measured and identified." Compares O'Connor's freaks to McCullers's and finds that "McCullers focusses upon her maimed, misfitting, wounded people not as a commentary upon the complacent ʹnormality' of the community, which would term them freakish, but as exemplars of the wretchedness of the human condition."

1343   Rubin, Louis D., [Jr.] "Flannery O'Connor and the Bible Belt." *The Added Dimension: The Art and Mind of Flannery O'Connor*. Rev. ed. Ed. Melvin J. Friedman and Lewis A. Lawson. New York: Fordham UP, 1977. 49-72.

Suggests that "much of the dramatic tension that makes O'Connor's fiction so gripping and memorable lies in the insight into religious experience afforded her by her double heritage as both Catholic and Southerner." Explores this tension as seen in *Wise Blood* and *The Violent Bear It Away*, and offers explications of these two novels--works which contain some structural flaws and insufficiently developed characters, but "are remarkable" nevertheless. Compares O'Connor's use of the "strange, the grotesque, and the deformed," to that of Carson McCullers, William Faulkner, and Erskine Caldwell. Finds her use of Southern Gothic to be focused more on mental and spiritual deformity than on physical. Suggests that "it is in this light that Miss O'Connor views Southern fundamentalist Protestantism." Refers to comments by Jonathan Baumbach and Rainulf A. Stelzmann, and refers to T.S. Eliot's *The Waste Land*. Concludes that because O'Connor "is both ill at ease with the messianic fervor of the direct prophetic revelation, and profoundly suspicious of its consequences," her prophetic figures are inevitably "portrayed as grotesques." [Essay included in the first edition. [Rpt. in Rubin's *The Curious Death of the Novel: Essays in American Literature*. Baton Rouge: Louisiana State UP, 1967, 239-61.]

1344   Rubin, Louis D., Jr. "Flannery O'Connor's Company of Southerners Or, `The Artificial Nigger' Read As Fiction Rather Than Theology." *Flannery O'Connor Bulletin* 6 (1977): 47-71.

Argues against the simplistic interpretation of O'Connor's work as a forum for Catholic dogma. Establishes a congruity of character type between those in the story "The Artificial Nigger" and the average, rural Southerner. Discusses the compatibility between the religious themes of the story and the "basic social and secular attitude toward Middle Georgia humor (found in works such as those by Augustus Longstreet). Contends that O'Connor's fiction should be read as fiction, not as theology. Refers to a variety of works and authors, including: William Byrd II and the *Secret History of the Dividing Line*; Jean-Paul Sartre; François Mauriac; Erskine Caldwell; William Faulkner; John Steinbeck; Sinclair Lewis; Joel Chandler Harris; Henry W. Watterson; William Malone Baskerville; William Tappan Thompson; Richard Malcolm Johnston; Bill Arp; Johnson Jones Hooper; Augustus Baldwin Longstreet and his story, "The Horse Swap"; the Agrarian symposium: *I'll Take My Stand: The South and the Agrarian Tradition*; and remarks by David Eggenschweiler. Originally prepared for delivery at the Flannery O'Connor Conference in Milledgeville, GA in 1976. [Rpt. in *A Gallery of Southerners*. Baton Rouge: Louisiana State UP, 1982, 115-134.]

1345   Rubin, Louis D., [Jr.]. [Moderator]. "Recent Southern Fiction: A Panel Discussion: Wesleyan College/28 October 1960." *Katherine Anne Porter: Conversations*. Ed. Joan Givner. Jackson: UP of Mississippi, 1987. 42-60.

Reprints, from the *Bulletin of Wesleyan College* [Macon, GA.] 41 (Jan. 1961), the transcript of a panel discussion that included Katherine Anne Porter, Flannery O'Connor, Caroline Gordon, Madison Jones, and Louis D. Rubin as moderator. O'Connor's comments deal with: how she goes about writing; whether she considered herself to be a Southern writer; her view of the South in terms of "sense of place" and of the sense of a "Southern community"; the "Christ-haunted" nature of the South and the influence of the Bible on Southern culture; her use of symbols; her perception that many students "approach a story as if it were a problem in algebra"; her concurrence with Walker Percy's comment that the present generation of Southerners had little interest in the Civil War; and her comment that none of her generation of Southern writers were making any significant sums of money from their writings except, perhaps, William Faulkner.

1346   Russ, Don. "Pilgrimage." *Flannery O'Connor Bulletin* 25 (1996-97): 61.

A twenty-four line poem written at the Holiday Inn in Milledgeville, Georgia [across the street from Andalusia, the O'Connor family farm], which uses imagery of Flannery O'Connor's peacocks to suggest the dimension that lies beyond the activities of our daily lives.

1347   Russell, Henry M.W. "Racial Integration in a Disintegrating Society: O'Connor and European Catholic Thought." *Flannery O'Connor Bulletin* 24 (1995-96): 33-45.

Contends that "O'Connor's thoughts on race are more informed by her Christian faith than by her geographic roots." Argues that she was "an intellectual Catholic" who engaged theologians and philosophers who were in the process of defining "the implications of Church dogma for yet another era," and that it was within this context that her views on race should be seen. Refers to the writings of Jacques Maritain and Gabriel Marcel to explain why she believed that each community should gain racial integration on its own rather than endure solutions pressed by the federal government via "integrationist fiats." Concedes that O'Connor's stance "outside the Civil Rights movement has caused many of her admirers to feel a certain amount of pain," but regards her position as growing "less out of Georgia than out of a conception of society as intimately involved in the body of Christ." Comments on Ralph Wood's examination of O'Connor's views on race in his essay, "Where Is the Voice Coming From," and contends that, in Marcel's terms, "one cannot say" that she "had racist opinions." Considers whether racial comments made by O'Connor in her correspondence with Maryat Lee "justify full and separate publication," and suggests that Sally Fitzgerald consider publishing "a somewhat expanded" version of *The Habit of Being* with "the very few unpublished racial references" included. Concludes that "what is needed is a far more European and Catholic appreciation of O'Connor's ideas on race, nationalism, society, and church."

1348   Russell, Shannon. "Space and the Movement Through Space in *Everything That Rises Must Converge*: A Consideration of Flannery O'Connor's Imaginative Vision." *Southern Literary Journal* 20.2 (1988): 81-98.

Contends that "the space within and through which O'Connor's people move is neither empty nor meaningless, but rather filled with mystery." Argues that it is through movement that O'Connor reveals underlying revelation. Discusses stories from *Everything That Rises Must Converge*, and notes themes of spiritual incompleteness, seeing, motion, journeys, and O'Connor's use of cars, buses, shoes, and trains as symbols.

1349   Ryan, Elizabeth Shreve. "I Remember Mary Flannery." *Flannery O'Connor Bulletin* 19 (1990): 49-52.

Discusses memories of attending Peabody High School in Milledgeville, GA with Flannery O'Connor. Recounts attending Edward O'Connor's funeral and contends that "the intensity of [Flannery's] literary and artistic efforts in her youth might have been the result of foreknowledge perhaps prompted by the circumstances of her father's death." Describes Peabody High, its place in the community, O'Connor's personality and interests during that time, her contributions to campus publications, and the literary prize she received from Rich's department store for her essay on Marvin M. Parks titled: "The Citizen of My County Who Has Contributed the Most to the State of Georgia." Refers to her home economics teacher, Margaret Abercrombie, O'Connor's friend John M. Ryan and his mother, Roberta M. Ryan, and Betty Ferguson who were both librarians at GSCW. Includes reproductions of two cartoons and an article (with a photo of O'Connor) titled: "Peabodite Reveals Strange Hobby," from the Dec. 16, 1941 issue of *The Peabody Palladium*.

1350   Ryan, Steven T. "The Three Realms of O'Connor's `Greenleaf.'" *Christianity & Literature* 29.1 (1979): 39-51.

Contends that much of the criticism of O'Connor's "Greenleaf" has been fragmentary, offers many confusing ambiguities, and leads readers to believe that O'Connor was inconsistent in her use of symbolism. Argues that the reader's confusion results from "an over-dependence upon the violent climax and visionary denouement," which, in turn, produces "an ambiguous impression of the meaning of the bull itself, of the bull's goring of Mrs. May, and of Mrs. May whispering into the bull's ear." Suggests that the reader instead examine O'Connor's use of setting, which may be divided into three distinctive realms: "the house, the woods, and the pasture." Offers that these three settings "are as important to the story as the Heaven, Earth, Hell divisions of a medieval stage." Contends that the house "becomes the realm of mind without body . . . the woods become the realm of body without mind . . . [and] the pasture is the arena of nature, an undivided realm which openly receives God's presence." Asserts that Mrs. May's "damnation is suggested (although certainly not confirmed) when she `finds the light unbearable'" and "sinks with the bull to the earth," instead of--like the grandmother in "A Good Man Is Hard to Find"--embracing the final epiphany. Contrasts the grandmother's death posture in "A Good Man Is Hard to Find" with that of Mrs. May as evidence for this argument. Concludes with discussion of O'Connor's attempt to "place God back into the reader's reality," and placing God into the physical world to present a more accurate depiction of reality.

1351   Salem, James M. *A Guide to Critical Reviews, Part IV: The Screenplay: Supplement One 1963-1980.* Metuchen, NJ: Scarecrow, 1982. 675-77.

A guide to reviews of the screenplay for *Wise Blood*.

1352   Salzman, Jack, ed., et al. *The Cambridge Handbook of American Literature.* New York: Cambridge UP, 1986. 180-81.

Includes a short biography and list of primary sources through 1979. Refers to *Wise Blood*. Summarizes O'Connor with the following commentary: "Her vision of violent spiritual struggle in the rural south is marked by a grotesque humor and unnerving irony."

1353   Sample, Carol. "The Salvation Theme in Flannery O'Connor." *Christ in the Classroom: Adventist Approaches to the Integration of Faith and Learning.* Comp. Humberto M. Rasi. Vol. 3. Silver Spring, MD: Institute for Christian Teaching, 1991. 121-37.

Discusses O'Connor's stories as "modern parables" intended to jolt readers into recognizing "their own spiritual depravity in spite of their sometimes moral, upright lives." Contends that they "present a wealth of material" for the "christian literature teacher [who wishes to use] fiction in the same way as Jesus used it: To jar her students into an awareness of who God is and who we are in the hope that they will perceive what is valuable now and eternally." Offers a brief introduction to O'Connor's life, then outlines her theological beliefs and critical perspectives on her work. Follows with explications of "A Good Man Is Hard to Find" and "Revelation." Notes two biblical analogues to "A Good Man Is Hard to Find": the structure of the story is similar to the book of Job, and "the drama being enacted by the grandmother and The Misfit" is reminiscent of "the parable of the Pharisee and the Publican" in Luke 18:10-14. Follows a similar treatment of "Revelation," seen as having "the same salvation theme." Concludes that through her use of "black humor, the grotesque, and the absurd, O'Connor jolts the reader into a new sense of seeing and feeling in a manner quite unlike any other modern Christian writer."

1354   Samuelson, Todd. "Creating the Incommensurate God: Art and Belief in O'Connor's `Parker's Back' and Bloom's *The Book of J.*" *Literature and Belief* 17.1-2 (1997): 47-59.

Explores O'Connor's fiction alongside Harold Bloom's interpretation of the *Book of J*. Reminds readers, "J is the name assigned by biblical critics to the writer of the foundation of the Pentateuch, upon which is based the rest of the Hebrew Bible." Offers an explication of "Parker's Back," focusing on O'Connor's "insistence upon the representative position of Old Testament imagery," then explores "the relationship of belief and art through both authors' facilities for creating powerfully unpredictable characters and situations." Finds that both O'Connor and Bloom "create moments of the transcendent through scenes of normality touched by the uncanny," but concludes that "Bloom's J offers art so powerful in its intensity as to overshadow belief," while O'Connor's story "presents a unity, an art that by its very nature must contain connections to the supernatural." Includes critical remarks by: Carol Shloss, Peter Hawkins, John Burt, Sister M. Bernetta Quinn, and Joyce Carol Oates.

1355   Samway, Patrick H. *Walker Percy: A Life*. New York: Farrar, Straus and Giroux, 1997. 158-59, 161, 164, 215, 223, 196, 227-29, 234, 243, 248, 260, 264, 268, 276, 278, 283, 287, 290, 299, 314, 334, 337, 343, 359, 372, 385.

Offers, in this detailed biography of Walker Percy, numerous passing references to O'Connor's life, work, and religious views, including: Caroline Gordon's comments to O'Connor regarding Percy's work; O'Connor's praise to Percy for *The Moviegoer*; Gordon's comment to Percy that O'Connor's work was "too bare, too stripped, reduced to an essential core of action, much in the style of Kafka"; O'Connor's congratulations to Percy for winning the National Book Award; Percy meeting with O'Connor after she spoke at Loyola University in New Orleans and his difficulty in understanding her Georgia accent; Percy's comparison of *Gone With the Wind* "with O'Connor's freak-filled stories" in his essay, "Do Fictional Manners Require Sex, Horror?"; Percy's use of O'Connor's work in creative writing classes he taught at Louisiana State and at Loyola University in New Orleans; his support of John Kennedy Toole's book, *A Confederacy of Dunces*, and reference to the fact that Toole killed himself soon after visiting Milledgeville, Georgia "out of homage to Flannery O'Connor"; Percy's comment to Bob Giroux that O'Connor "`cracked some very good enduring holy jokes'" in her work; and details regarding posthumously conferring to O'Connor the National Book Award in 1972.

1356   Sanders, Andrea. "'Mirrors Arranged in a Circle Around One Center': The
            O'Connor Mystery Cycle." *Postscript: Publication of the Philological
            Association of the Carolinas* 2 (1985): 1-9.

            Argues that "the grotesque elements in O'Connor's stories *do* carry their
            aesthetic and thematic weights because the stories *must* be read in the light
            of the 'standpoint of Christian orthodoxy' from which they were written."
            Suggests that this controversial stand may also be applied to medieval
            drama, that critics examining the cycle plays and moralities "must first
            consider the world view of the society" from which they were born, "a
            society in which the Christian faith was so universal that the concept of
            'blasphemy' or 'atheism' did not exist." Cites similarities between
            O'Connor's fiction and medieval drama, and discusses the "variation of the
            ritual form of Greek drama in the Christian pattern of the medieval
            dramas," which may also be applied to O'Connor's stories. Concludes that
            "there is a valid link between the art of the medieval drama and the art of
            Flannery O'Connor; that O'Connor's art is no less viable as art because of
            the cosmic view at its center . . . and, that the reason modern readers have
            trouble recognizing--or perhaps, accepting--the nature of O'Connor's art
            is that" modern humankind's nature is no longer grounded "in a
            universally accepted belief." Mentions Josephine Hendin, *The Second
            Shepherd's Play*, *Everyman*, O.B. Hardison, Jr., Francis J. Thompson, *The
            Killing of Abel*, Clifford Davidson, and V.A. Kolve.

1357   Sanoff, Alvin P. with Mary Galligan. "Creating Literature on the Plains
            of Iowa." *U.S. News & World Report* 2 June 1986: 58.

            Offers brief references to O'Connor in a discussion of the growth and
            influence of the University of Iowa Writer's Workshop upon America's
            current generation of writers and writing programs.

1358   Satterfield, Ben. "*Wise Blood*, Artistic Anemia, and the Hemorrhaging of
            O'Connor Criticism." *Studies in American Fiction* 17.1 (1989): 33-50.

            Argues that *Wise Blood* is an "ironic study in pathology" rather than a
            novel of redemption, primarily because of the lack of meaning in Haze's
            self-inflicted suffering. Argues that no one is redeemed by Haze's
            "sacrificial" act at the end of the novel. Objects to critical views of the
            novel which purport Haze to redeem mankind--such as Jonathan
            Baumback's--and calls these types of criticism "affective fallacies." Says
            Haze's act is basically an ironic one and in keeping with the
            satirical/ironic tone of the novel. Faults the author with ambiguity, but
            points to the abundant imagery (natural, regional, animal) which tends to
            unify the novel. Discusses varying critical viewpoints by questioning

support for assertions that see Haze as a religiously successful human. Discounts O'Connor's assertion that Haze's integrity as a Christian lies in the fact that he cannot "get rid of the ragged figure who moves from tree to tree in the back of his mind." Discusses *The Violent Bear It Away* in much the same manner, and faults O'Connor's lack of artistic control.

1359   Saunders, James Robert. "The Fallacies of Guidance and Light in Flannery O'Connor's 'The Artificial Nigger.'" *Journal of the Short Story in English* (France) 17 (Autumn 1991): 103-13.

Discusses and offers a reading of "The Artificial Nigger," focusing on the grandfather's role as guide and O'Connor's use of moon and moonlight imagery at key points in the story. Notes that O'Connor believed the story to be her best work, and that readers respond to its "symbolism, imagery, thematic insight, and dichotomies ranging from rural innocence versus urban experience, on one hand, to benevolent heaven versus a lamentable hell on the other." Reviews the findings of other critics as well as O'Connor's own comments on the story from her letters. Compares the structural device of an impressionable youth with an older mentor in the "The Artificial Nigger" to a similar motif in *The Violent Bear It Away*. Concludes with discussion of O'Connor's use of the statue and asserts that it "might just be an artist's vehicle to show how grace preempts what would be dire prospects for the world." Believes that O'Connor "did with her one statue what most others won't accomplish with a thousand words or good intentions."

1360   Saunders, James Robert. "'A Worn Path': The Eternal Quest of Welty's Phoenix Jackson." *Southern Literary Journal* 25.1 (1992): 62-73.

Offers a reading of Eudora Welty's "A Worn Path," relying upon the perspectives of a wide variety of critics and Welty's own comments to convey the meaning of the story. Includes a brief discussion of Louis Rubin's recollection of a comment made by Flannery O'Connor during a symposium at Wesleyan College in Macon, Georgia, regarding the "danger in the rendering of biblical perspective" for deciphering the meaning of her work. Warns that such an approach sets limits on the level of understanding, leaving much of the depth and complexity unmined.

1361   Sayers, Valerie. "If He Wrote It, They Will Read." *New York Times Book Review* 19 Dec. 1993: 14.

Notes in a review of W.P. Kinsella's *Shoeless Joe Jackson Comes to Iowa*, mentions that Kinsella is such an admirer of Flannery O'Connor that "he once wrote a story called `Red Wolf, Red Wolf,' in which O'Connor's character Enoch Emery arrives at her Georgia house in a gorilla suit and moves in with her." Suggests that any writer--such as Kinsella--"who likes baseball and O'Connor is starting out with good material and, probably, an obsessive interest in style."

1362   "SCAD Students at Work on a Documentary." *Friends of Flannery* [Newsletter]. (April 1997): 2.

Reports that Dominique Mertens of the Savannah College of Art and Design, "is supervising the work of several of her students in the preparation of a video documentary about Flannery O'Connor and her childhood home" in Savannah, GA. States that "the project will serve as a pilot for a longer documentary which is planned."

1363   Scafidel, James R. "`It is not a bucket of Georgia Crackers.'" *Mississippi Quarterly* 47.1 (1993-94): 127-32.

Reviews *Georgia Voices: Vol. One: Fiction*, ed. Hugh Ruppersburg. Includes a brief discussion of O'Connor's "The Artificial Nigger." Finds the story to be a dramatization, through racial conflict, of Mr. Head's confrontation of a "scary new world (another trip to the city) which men who are not of his knowing have made." Suggests that Mr. Head "considers this world to be tolerable, more or less acceptable, but essentially incomprehensible."

1364   Schanche, Don. "O'Connor Bulletin Marks 25 Years of Scholarship." [Milledgeville, GA] *Union-Recorder* 22 Oct. 1998: 1A, 14A.

Offers a brief historical overview of the founding and continued rise in both subscriptions and importance of *The Flannery O'Connor Bulletin*. Describes the context of its founding at Georgia College & State University by Mary Barabara Tate and Rosa Lee Walston in 1972, and reports that the *Bulletin* is now "`the longest running journal devoted to a woman writer in American literature.'"

1365   Schaub, Thomas Hill. "Christian Realism and O'Connor's `A Good Man Is Hard to Find.'" *American Fiction in the Cold War*. History of American Thought and Culture Series. Madison: U of Wisconsin P, 1991. 116-36.

Contends that because "O'Connor's contempt for liberalism was shared by many liberals during the post-World War II period . . . her conservative fiction . . . provides a counter-example of how relevant the discourse of liberalism was to the work of a writer who had no interest in being radical." Asserts that her fiction "reinforced the `new realism' which liberalism was in the process of claiming as its own." Discusses O'Connor's debts to Henry James, William Faulkner, Cleanth Brooks's *Understanding Fiction*, and Percy Lubbock's *The Craft of Fiction*. Offers a reading of "A Good Man Is Hard to Find," beginning with a discussion of the origins of the story title (taken from a song by Eddie Green sung in 1927 by Bessie Smith). Examines the role of the ironic reversal, the violent conversions, the revisionist liberalism of the postwar era, and how the "idea of `the South'" helps to situate O'Connor's work. Discusses ideas of George Kennan, Vann Woodward and Eric J. Sandeen in regard to modern Southern history "within a specific postwar context." Suggests that the Grandmother's touching of The Misfit, "signifies two important assumptions of revisionist liberalism--human depravity and the universality of human circumstance." Describes The Misfit as a double figure, "a defenseless liberal intellectual" who also represents "the reality of violence and evil for which the liberal is unprepared."

1366   Scheick, William J. "Flannery O'Connor's `A Good Man Is Hard to Find' and G.K. Chesterton's *Manalive*." *Studies in American Fiction* 11.2 (1983): 241-45.

Suggests that O'Connor's work has been influenced not only by the Bible and "Christian thinkers," but also by the "romance tradition" handed down to American writers from England. Among the English authors who wrote in this context was Gilbert K. Chesterton, "whose Christian perspective and fictional technique would have appealed to O'Connor." Compares O'Connor's Misfit in "A Good Man Is Hard to Find" and Chesterton's Innocent Smith in *Manalive*. Concludes that "*Manalive* figured in the germinal stages of `A Good Man Is Hard to Find,' which appears to be in part a deliberate revision of Chesterton's novel.

1367   Schellenberg, Susan. "A Response to `The Displaced Person.'" *Flannery O'Connor Bulletin* 25 (1996-97): 30-32.

Discusses the context and inspiration for creating a bust of an old man's head in clay after hearing a scholar read a passage from O'Connor's "The Displaced Person" at an O'Connor Symposium at Bloor Street United Church, Toronto, Canada in 1996. A photograph of the sculpture, titled "The Displaced Person," is included on an unnumbered page that follows the text of the article.

1368   Schemmel, William ["Bill"]. "Middle Georgia Gothic." *Parade Magazine: Atlanta Weekly* 15 Jan. 1989: 8-11.

        Nearly identical to his article "Southern Comfort" (*Travel-Holiday* 169.6 (1988):70-73), but with different photographs. Illustrations: Photographs of Milledgeville's Baldwin County Courthouse, the Old Governor's Mansion, Antebellum white columns of a house, Regina Cline O'Connor's house, and memorabilia in the *Flannery O'Connor Collection* in the Russell Library of Georgia College & State University.

1369   Schemmel, [William] Bill. "Milledgeville and Its Ghosts: A Haunted and Haunting Town." *Travel & Leisure* 7.9 (1977): 594a, 594c.

        Expanded version of an article published in *Ventures* (16 August 1975: 4-5). Includes a brief biographical description of O'Connor, Milledgeville, and the influence of O'Connor's hometown on her work and life.

1370   Schemmel, [William] Bill. "Milledgeville: Flannery Lives on in Her Hometown." *Ventures: Monthly Guide to Recreation from Creative Loafing* 16 Aug. 1975: 4-5.

        Briefly describes O'Connor's visit as a guest lecturer to a class attended by the author. Discusses her reputation among both northern intellectuals and her Milledgeville, Georgia neighbors, and offers a short tourist's view of Flannery's hometown.

1371   Schemmel, William [Bill]. "Southern Comfort." *Travel-Holiday* 169.6 (1988): 70-73.

        Discusses Flannery O'Connor's career and provides historical information and anecdotes related to the Milledgeville, GA region. Schemmel states that his "most memorable tie to Milledgeville" was his visit to Andalusia to meet O'Connor three years before her death. Remembers "her sad-sweet smile as she urged our group of English majors away from futures as writers to destinies with more lucrative, less crucifying professions." Quotes Nancy Davis Bray, Curator of Georgia College & State University's *Flannery O'Connor Collection*, regarding the pride taken by Milledgeville residents as they "swear they're in Flannery's stories." Describes how O'Connor absorbed the environment around her to blend facts and personalities into her literary works. Relates a comment by Miss Katherine Scott, who taught O'Connor English Literature at Georgia State College for Women: "'Even then, it was obvious she was a genius, warped, but a genius all the same . . . when I read her first novel [*Wise*

Blood] I thought to myself that character [Hazel Motes] who dies in the last chapter could have done the world a great favor by dying in the first chapter instead.'" Illustrations: Antebellum homes (two), a "Victorian Birdmansion," and photographic portrait of Nancy Davis Bray.

1372   Schenck, Mary Jane. "Deconstructed Meaning in Two Short Stories by Flannery O'Connor." *Ambiguities in Literature and Film: Selected Papers From the Seventh Annual Florida State Conference on Literature and the Film*. Ed. Hans P. Braendlin. Tallahassee: Florida State UP, 1988. 125-35.

Discusses "how the fiction of Flannery O'Connor creates meanings in addition to or in contrast with what she herself said about her work." Argues that O'Connor's texts are "thoroughly ironic, and her use of irony creates ambiguities that undercut her own interpretations." Examines O'Connor's irony in light of Baudelaire's concept of comedy resulting "from a doubling of spectator and laughable object or person," and, being irony which is "in part an internalized doubling . . . a capacity to be at once self and other." Also examines the methods by which "characters are created and create themselves in O'Connor's fiction" in the context of Paul de Man's ironic consciousness. Discusses "A Good Man Is Hard to Find" and "The River" in the context of these assertions and finds that "at the conclusion of both stories, the reader is left with a vision of destruction of human life both literal and figurative that is absurd rather than tragic because the victims are not heroic figures reduced to misfortune." Concludes that the personalities of characters in these stories are created by language, a language which fails them because the natural world's laws "mock their interpretations" or they are confronted by another character who fully understands that "language is mere convention," not reality. Argues that readers "feel a certain shock of recognition" at the end of these stories because they find themselves witnessing "the unraveling of the characters' personalities."

1373   Schiff, Jonathan. "`That's a Greenleaf Bull': Totemism and Exogamy in Flannery O'Connor's `Greenleaf.'" *English Language Notes* 32.3 (1995): 69-76.

Notes that O'Connor's "Greenleaf" has often been discussed in regard to various classical myths. Contends that the reason for the lack of consensus of opinion may be because O'Connor may have been "less interested in specific myths than in the primitive circumstances that spawned them." Poses to readers that "the rise of closely-linked institutions of totemism and exogamy"--concerns of anthropologists and psychologists--"appear to be integral aspects of `Greenleaf.'" Suggests that Sigmund Freud's work on this subject, *Totem and Taboo*, served as O'Connor's source for the framework of "Greenleaf." Proposes that an interpretation of the cow as a totem animal for the Greenleaf clan will not only help readers better understand why the story is named after Mr. Greenleaf instead of Mrs. May, but illustrate how--by sacrificing the bull--he "ultimately rejects his primitive religion" and "he, rather than Mrs. May, serves as O'Connor's agent of grace." Concludes that, by firing the bullet which kills the bull, Mr. Greenleaf serves as instrument for O'Connor through which she "explodes, rather than borrows from, previous myths in order to propound a new myth, one in which the hero accepts a Christian grace."

1374   Schilling, Timothy P. "Trying to See Straight." *Commonweal* 122.19 (1995): 14-15.

Suggests that while O'Connor's novels, short stories, and essays are "jewels," her letters--published in *The Habit of Being*--are perhaps the "most satisfying" of her works. Uses excerpts from the letters to illustrate O'Connor's approach to "the business of writing," her sense of writing for those "`who think God is dead,'" her views of and sense of the Incarnation, her sense of responsibility to her readers, her view of reality, and her "hatred of sentimentality." Notes that the letters--when read chronologically--offer indications of the slow progress of her Lupus.

1375   Schlafer, Linda [D.] "Monitum: Beware the Getz." *Flannery O'Connor Bulletin* 11 (1982): 43-57.

Comments on Frederick Asals's "kind review" of *Flannery O'Connor: Her Life, Library and Book Reviews*, by Lorine M. Getz, which appeared in *The Flannery O'Connor Bulletin* in 1980. States that there were "a number of problems" with the bibliographic entries which comprise the mid-section of Getz's book. Contends that this section, which lists the volumes of O'Connor's own library that were moved from Andalusia to Georgia College & State University and placed in the *Flannery O'Connor Collection* of the Russell Library, has numerous errors. Provides readers with amendments to Getz's work with a list of additional annotated works, other errors noted, and "a listing of periodicals in the Collection brought from Flannery O'Connor's room at Andalusia" that have not previously been mentioned in print.

1376   Schlafer, Linda [D.] "Pilgrims of the Absolute: Léon Bloy and Flannery O'Connor." *Realist of Distances: Flannery O'Connor Revisited*. Ed. Karl-Heinz Westarp and Jan Nordby Gretlund. Aarhus (Denmark): Aarhus UP, 1987. 55-63.

Traces O'Connor's reading of French writers to find a correlation between her "handling of aesthetic distance" and "the tenor of the French writers whom she was reading at different stages in her work." Follows with an examination of the influence of Léon Bloy on the early stages of her artistic development. Focuses on how his work reinforced her use of the grotesque, violence, and the prophetic. Suggests that O'Connor must have read Bloy about the same time as she read Jacques Maritain. Mentions Bloy's *The Absolute*, Albert Béguin's *Léon Bloy: A Study in Impatience*, and Maritain's *Art and Scholasticism*. Contends that where "Maritian's work is a carefully reasoned explanation as to the *manner* in which artistic work should be pursued, Bloy, both temperamentally and topically, bears a significant relationship to the *matter* of O'Connor's fiction." Discusses how Bloy's influence provided O'Connor "with the absurdities and the extremities of which the grotesque is compounded." Touches upon how Bloy's views of Catholicism influenced O'Connor's use of "extreme measures," violence and exaggeration, and her distrust of "`compassion.'" Explores the positions of Maritian and Bloy on: the "identification of justice with mercy," anagogical vision, the view of the role of the prophet, "place and country, time and eternity, limitations and excesses, personal and vocational identity, and the `poor.'" Refers to Georges Bernanos, François Mauriac, Gabriel Marcel, Simone Weil, André Malraux, and comments by Johannes Jørgensen, Frederick Asals, Carl Hartman, Gilbert Muller, Carl Jung, Andrew Lytle, Maurice Maeterlinck and Pierre Brodin. Concludes that "an acquaintance with the work of Léon Bloy helps us to grasp significant ways in which O'Connor's work is not only unique, but also continues with a literary tradition."

1377   Schlafer, Linda D. Rev. of *Risen Sons: Flannery O'Connor's Vision of History*, by John F. Desmond. *Flannery O'Connor Bulletin* 16 (1987): 86-89.

Finds Desmond's work to be a "brief but fairly dense discussion" offering "what is perhaps, thus far, the most coherent and comprehensive published account of the metaphysical underpinnings of Flannery O'Connor's life and art." States that Desmond's thesis "is that `O'Connor's metaphysical sense, which derives from her Catholic belief, is the intrinsic foundation for both her vision of history and her artistic technique.'" Describes corresponding theological themes Desmond identifies, his use of "the medieval principle of the analogy of being," and his description of O'Connor's "turning point between her beginning writing and her mature work." Asserts that Desmond "rightly points . . . to the coherence of O'Connor's work as a whole, to its being, in a real sense, `all of a piece.'" Refers to his discussion of O'Connor's reworking of her early works as "`part of her own process of redeeming her fictional world.'" Outlines his perspective on O'Connor's "middle period," her "affirmation of . . . the communion of saints," and his discussion of historicism and "personality as expressed in the modern consciousness." States that Desmond regards O'Connor as "'a comic writer whose work is grounded in love' and whose 'best stories analogically recapitulate the redemptive act by recalling the audience to the fundamental source of being.'" Concludes that while Desmond will be criticized as dealing with philosophical issues in too cursory of a manner, his "analysis will prove to be a fruitful catalyst to further work in this area."

1378   Schleifer, Ronald. "Rural Gothic: The Stories of Flannery O'Connor." *Modern Fiction Studies* 28.3 (1982): 474-85.

Discusses the origins and meaning of Gothic fiction and how O'Connor's works fit within the context of the Gothic model. Finds that where traditional Gothic presents a "world beyond the understandings of metaphor . . . a literature of *presence* unmediated by the substitutions of language, presences which are inhuman, terrifying, *secret*," O'Connor's use of the Gothic depends upon a more literal frontier. Cites as example the fact that O'Connor often places characters between the real and the supernatural worlds, where action takes place on a journey in the rural countryside. Remarks, "This is where the supernatural is most clearly and terrifyingly encountered- on those frontiers between the country and the city, faith and faithlessness." Relates "The Enduring Chill," "Parker's Back," "Revelation," "The Artificial Nigger," and other stories to this argument. [Rpt. in *Critical Essays on Flannery O'Connor*. Ed. Melvin J. Friedman and Beverly Lyon Clark. Boston: G.K. Hall, 1985. 158-68; and, *Frontier Gothic: Terror and Wonder at the Frontier in American Literature*. Ed. David Mogen, Scott P. Sanders, and Joanne B. Karpinski. Rutherford, N.J.: Fairleigh Dickinson UP, 1993.]

1379   Schleifer, Ronald. "Rural Gothic: The Sublime Rhetoric of Flannery O'Connor." *Frontier Gothic: Terror and Wonder at the Frontier in American Literature*. Ed. David Mogen, Scott Patrick Sanders, and Joanne B. Karpinski. Cranbury, NJ: Associated UP, 1993. 175-86.

Discusses the characteristics and origins of Gothic fiction. Suggests that the Gothic novel is "haunted" by its "supernatural origin." Refers to O'Connor's comment on St. Cyril of Jerusalem and offers that "The Artificial Nigger" illustrates this parable. Asserts that O'Connor believed that both writer and reader must recognize the reality of the Devil's existence, the "poverty of our own self-sufficiency, and the necessity of grace." States that when Gothic tradition "is most serious, it offers to readers a passage to and through origin and identity to their secret cause." Argues that O'Connor placed her characters on a frontier "between the natural and the supernatural by locating them, often on a literal journey, between the cities and the rural country of the South." Contends that "the act of `facing oneself' is the recurrent action of O'Connor's stories, the action of Gothic romance." Concludes that the supernatural force O'Connor identified in fundamentalist, backwoods prophets reflected her keen interest in the supernatural "found on the edges of our culture, dark and empty as they may be, on the rural frontier."

1380   Schlueter, Paul and June, comps. and eds. *A Library of Literary Criticism: Modern American Literature.* Vol. 5. 2nd. suppl., 4th ed. New York: Frederick Ungar, 1985. 324-27.

Collection of excerpts from essays by Dorothy Tuck McFarland, Robert Brinkmeyer, and Carol Shloss.

1381   Schmitt, Deborah A., ed. "*Everything That Rises Must Converge*: Flannery O'Connor." *Contemporary Literary Criticism.* Vol. 104. Detroit: Gale, 1998. 101-203.

Offers an introductory essay which discusses the plots, major characters, themes, and critical reception of O'Connor's collection of short stories, *Everything That Rises Must Converge.* Includes a collection of twenty-two "significant passages from published criticism" related to the collection, which are presented in chronological order. Critics whose works are excerpted, include: Granville Hicks, Walter Sullivan, Webster Schott, Irving Howe, Patricia Kane, Robert Fitzgerald, Patricia Dinneen Maida, Marion Montgomery, John F. Desmond, Preston M. Browning, Jr., Robert D. Denham, Dorothy Tuck McFarland, John Ower, Jeffrey J. Folks, Alice Hall Petry, David Jauss, Harbour Winn, Bryan N. Wyatt, Michael W. Crocker, and Robert C. Evans.

1382   Schmitz, Eugenia E. Rev. of Arthur F. Kinney's *Flannery O'Connor's Library: Resources of Being. American Reference Books Annual 1986.* Ed. Bohdan Wynar, Anna Grace Atterson and Hannah L. Kelminson. Vol. 17. Littleton, CO: Libraries Unlimited, 1986. 447.

Cites, describes, and evaluates Arthur F. Kinney's *Flannery O'Connor's Library: Resources of Being.* Concludes that Kinney "has done a meticulous job on the library of one of Georgia's most significant writers."

1383   Schmude, Karl G. "The Changing Accent of Catholic Literature." *Quadrant* (Australia) 17.1 (1984): 54-59.

Discusses the "intriguing development" of the "quantity of popular literature that has been published by authors with a Catholic background" since the 1960s. Lists authors and titles of Catholic works published in England, America, and Australia and questions the meaning and implications of this phenomenon. Explores various definitions of "Catholic literature," questions what such a literature might say about "the cultural power of Catholicism," and looks for differences between contributions by those who were "born Catholics" versus converts. Offers a biographical sketch of Flannery O'Connor and a three-paragraph long explication of *The Violent Bear It Away*. Uses the work as an example of the challenges facing an author "pushing the form of the novel to see if it can bear the depiction of the supernatural without disintegrating."

1384   Schneiderman, Leo. "Flannery O'Connor: The Captive Bird." *The Literary Mind: Portraits in Pain and Creativity*. New York: Human Sciences, 1988. 84-101.

Suggests that one of the ways of truly understanding O'Connor's work "is by tracing the connection between her aesthetic aims and her emotional needs, particularly in relation to her mother, Regina." Discusses her "strong vein of skepticism," which "found expression in her fictional treatment of religious themes, in which conflict between faith and total disbelief is of central concern." Asserts that O'Connor "appears to be closely identified with the antimodernist, rebellious, and aggressive components of fundamentalism, which she uses as a vehicle for expressing her repressed hostility to authority in general, and to her mother in particular." Offers biographical details related to her father and states that her "preoccupation with death and mutilation . . . may be linked with the trauma" of his death. Argues that she used "fictional males and females interchangeably as instruments of retribution against mother figures." Finds O'Connor's work to be that "of an angry spirit," with even her early pre-lupus stories full of bitterness and anger. Offers Freudian interpretations of *Wise Blood*, *The Violent Bear It Away*, "The Life You Save May Be Your Own," "Good Country People," "The Artificial Nigger," "The Displaced Person," "A Circle in the Fire," "The Comforts of Home," "Everything That Rises Must Converge," and "Parker's Back." Concludes with a discussion of O'Connor's beloved peacock as a "symbol of rebellion and retribution." Comments on her "fear that her mother would die before her, thereby jeopardizing her dependency, and perhaps threatening to bring to the surface her dreaded ambivalence."

1385   Scholl, Diane Gabrielson. "With Ears to Hear and Eyes to See: Alice Walker's Parable *The Color Purple*." *Christianity & Literature* 40 (Spring 1991): 255-66.

Discusses Walker's admiration for O'Connor's work and how her own "biblical heritage" helped to shape and influence Walker's writing. Refers to Walker's comments on O'Connor in "Beyond the Peacock," and compares Walker's use of ironic reversals to O'Connor's use in "Parker's Back" and "The Displaced Person."

1386   Schroeder, Michael L. "Ruby Turpin, Job, and Mystery: Flannery O'Connor and the Question of Knowing." *Flannery O'Connor Bulletin* 21 (1992): 75-83.

Discusses how O'Connor uses the story of Job as a framework for constructing the character of Ruby Turpin in "Revelation." Refers to critical approaches by Richard Giannone, John R. May, Sarah Gordon, Leon Driskell, and Joan Brittain and approaches to the *Book of Job* by Nahum N. Glatzer and Moshe Greenberg. Outlines current critical perspectives and offers a new reading that focuses on the story's biblical context, specifically, the story of Job. States that by using an approach of "pursuing biblical parallels . . . readers can have a richer reading experience." Notes, and discusses, for example, that Mary Grace may be comparable with Satan or "the adversary," that both Job and Ruby Turpin "see themselves as charitable and `good,' and superior to those around them who are morally flawed; both undergo traumatic experiences that force them to lose the peace of mind they had based on their assumptions about God; both undergo a debate of sorts; . . . both directly challenge God; and both receive answers showing them that God's ways are mysterious and chastising them for presuming to know God's mind."

1387   Schroeder, Steven. "From the Church Without Christ to the Absolute Absence of God: Thinking About the First Coming." *Philosophy and Theology* 2.4 (1988): 387-98.

Suggests that one of the more striking features of reflection on and discussion about God within the Western Christian tradition "has been the unfortunate tendency to focus so heavily on the anticipated `second coming' of Christ as to virtually lose sight of the `first coming' in the person of Jesus." Argues that if one focuses instead on the first coming and its relationship to visions of the second coming, the process is "one of the most important ways for the Christian tradition to contribute to serious reflection on the structure of history, the significance of anticipation, and their importance for the structure of action." Draws upon O'Connor's *Wise Blood* and Thomas Sheehan's historical and theological study, *The Second Coming*, to lay the groundwork for such reflection. Follows the structure of Sheehan's book, but "intertwines" O'Connor's work in order to illuminate Sheehan's ideas.

1387a   Schulte, Bret. "The Price of Pride: In Banning Flannery O'Connor, a
         Catholic School Bows to Black Anger Over a Word Used by America's
         Pre-Eminent Catholic Author to Make a Moral Point." *Arkansas
         Democrat-Gazette* (17 Dec. 2000): J1, J8.

         Reports that although O'Connor's works are "taught with reverence in
         high schools and colleges across the country," English instructor Arsenio
         Orteza was forbidden by his local bishop, Edward O'Donnell, to include
         A Good Man Is Hard to Find on his required reading list at Opelousas
         Catholic School. States that, due to complaints regarding O'Connor's use
         of the word "nigger" by parents of black students, her story "The Artificial
         Nigger" would not be taught not be taught. Discusses positions of the
         students and parents, the principal, and Bishop and then offers
         commentary by O'Connor scholar Ralph Wood. Includes an explication
         of the story and concludes: "It doesn't take a literary scholar to grasp the
         irony of the O'Connor controversy . . . a group of fearful parents,
         admittedly ignorant of the author they're protesting, have succeeded in
         shelving a story about the perils of ignorance." Illustrations: photographs
         of Bishop O'Donnell, Arsenio Orteza, Flannery O'Connor (A.P. file
         photo), and the school's sign and statue of the Virgin Mary and Christ.

1388   Schwartz, Narda Lacey, comp. *Articles on Women Writers: A
         Bibliography*. Santa Barbara: ABC-Clio, 1977. 180-87.

         A selective bibliography on women writers including O'Connor. Lists
         only critical works in the following categories: bibliography, general
         works, individual works.

1389   Schwartz, Narda Lacey. *Articles on Women Writers: A Bibliography
         1976-1984*. Santa Barbara, CA: ABC-Clio, Inc, 1986. 180-87.

         Revision of 1977 entry to be more comprehensive and to delete two
         incorrectly attributed works. Organized by bibliography, general, and
         individual works.

1390   Scott, Carolynne. "The Map to Heaven." *Flannery O'Connor Bulletin* 22
         (1993-94): 75-82.

         Faux Flannery Contest: First Place Winner. Plot summary: A child, (Sarah
         Mae Brewster), accompanies her mother (Flora Mae Brewster), a "bald-
         headed preacher" (Brother Green), a Sunday School teacher, and the fat
         "Independent Lady," as they travel from Templeton to a local prison to
         conduct a service in the prison's chapel. The visit, the service, and the trip

home are all seen through Sarah's eyes as she carefully watches Brother Green pass out his tract titled *The Map to Heaven*, preach the service, and persuade a "fat young man with curly blonde hair" to convert to Christianity. Closes with Sarah Mae--a Baptist--telling everyone in the car that she hopes to become a nun. She then has a vision in which she reviews the days' events and draws crosses on her front for all to see.

1391   Scott, Katherine K. "The Mansion's First One Hundred Years - `This Calls for Pageantry.'" [Georgia College & State University] *Columns* 25.1 (1980): 16-17.

Offers a behind-the-scenes look at the centennial celebration (in 1937) which commemorated the one hundred year-old Georgia Governor's Mansion in Milledgeville. Includes a photograph of "General" William J. Bush, in Confederate officer garb. [Bush is believed to be the individual on whom O'Connor based her fictional character, General Tennessee Flintrock Sash, in "A Late Encounter With the Enemy."]

1392   Scott, R. Neil. "UMI's Citations to Theses and Dissertations Related to Flannery O'Connor." *Flannery O'Connor Bulletin* 19 (1990): 77-99.

Outlines the dissertation acquisition program of University Microfilms International (UMI) and the matching grant the company awarded the Russell Library of Georgia College & State University to fund the acquisition of 171 O'Connor-related doctoral dissertations and master's theses. Describes the UMI database, examines the recognition of dissertations and theses by members of the scholarly community, and provides two tables and a bar graph indicating which institutions have produced the most O'Connor-related dissertations and theses with dates of completion graphed. Main body of text is followed by a bibliography of 185 "Citations to O'Connor-Related Dissertations in the UMI Database." Notes at the end of the article include a list of additional sources for locating master's theses.

1393   Scouten, Kenneth. "`The Artificial Nigger': Mr. Head's Ironic Salvation." *Flannery O'Connor Bulletin* 9 (1980): 87-97.

Discusses the scene from "The Artificial Nigger," in which Mr. Head and Nelson stand gazing at the "artificial nigger." Contends that "the usual conclusion of the critics" on the meaning of the scene (that both "have been irrevocably touched and transformed by grace when they confront the stature") is debatable. Suggests instead that because true conversion "requires not only the recognition of sin, but also contrition" as well, Mr.

Head's interpretation of the meaning of this event remains unclear. Offers comments by Marion Montgomery, Louis D. Rubin, Jr., Gilbert H. Muller, Carter W. Martin, and, Preston M. Browning, Jr. Discusses a variety of related topics, including: Mr. Head's guilt in regard to the sin of pride; indications that he "possesses little ancient wisdom and is not only not `a suitable guide for the young,' he himself is lost"; how he serves as "an ironic echo of Virgil"; indications that he is a true heretic in that "instead of trying to preserve innocence, he corrupts it" (he instills his own "racist pride . . . in the form of prejudice" in Nelson); and that he "plays God throughout the story." Follows with a discussion of how the trip to the city is ironic in that "symbolically . . . they are going to the city because the old man, a fallen creature, wants his grandson to fall." In defence of this argument, points out: the "imagery of hell," in the story; the "rite of passage" experience Nelson has with the "large colored woman"; and the imagery at the end of the story which "suggests the defeat of the devil." Concludes that while Nelson's "self-confidence and pride are, in fact, chastened by the trip," and he achieves salvation, Mr. Head "goes from one kind of pride to an even more serious one," and "like Virgil, is never allowed to enter Paradise."

1394   Scouten, Kenneth. "`The Partridge Festival': Manuscript Revisions." *Flannery O'Connor Bulletin* 15 (1986): 35-41.

Notes difficulties scholars encounter when they use manuscripts housed in the *Flannery O'Connor Collection* of the Russell Library at Georgia College & State University. Suggests that they will find their task "both intriguing and frustrating," as the collection is incomplete, very well may not be in chronological order, and reflects confusion from having to deal with materials from different works containing many of the same characters. Declares that, though difficult, there are several works that are arranged in such a manner that "a study of O'Connor's creative process is possible." Focuses on "The Partridge Festival" as an illustrative example, comparing and contrasting differences found in versions in the Collection. Offers a description of the contents of various folders, and discusses the usefulness of the two-page draft in discerning O'Connor's intentions for the story. Weighs the strengths and weaknesses of her revision process and finds that the manuscripts serve as evidence that O'Connor's "problem was not one of conception but of approach." Observes that, though O'Connor considered this story to be only a "farce," she still "worked and reworked her material until she produced a polished short story with rounded characters and a consistent ironic tone."

1395   Scouten, Kenneth. "The Schoolteacher as a Devil in *The Violent Bear It Away*." *Flannery O'Connor Bulletin* 12 (1983): 35-46.

Argues that because the "burden" of *The Violent Bear It Away* "is taken up with the struggle for the boy's soul" between his great uncle and Rayber, "the schoolteacher is the most important satanic figure in the novel." Refers to O'Connor's letter to John Hawkes and critical remarks by Dorothy Walters, then offers a close reading of the text to support this assertion. Discusses how: "Rayber played the snake" in the relationship between his sister and the divinity student; represents "sterile and destructive `knowledge'"; may be compared to Mephistopheles; and sees Tarwater as a surrogate son to replace Bishop. Sees Rayber as "much more than just a modern existential man; he is the serpent who not only wants to corrupt Tarwater and weed out the word but also to destroy the garden itself." Concludes that the three manifestations of the devil in the novel "lead the boy to the light of salvation and serve the Lord's purpose-- in spite of themselves."

1396   Sederberg, Nancy B. "Flannery O'Connor's Spiritual Landscape: A Dual Sense of Nothing." *Flannery O'Connor Bulletin* 12 (1983): 17-34.

Reports that O'Connor's landscapes serve "as such an integral part of her created world that we may tend to overlook their symbolic and thematic importance, until, like the incipient violence, they erupt into meaning." Contends that O'Connor uses her fictive landscape "in every sense from the actual to the anagogical." Discusses: how the simplicity of O'Connor's landscape imagery "results from its appropriateness on a purely narrative plane"; how her settings "illuminate character and resonate with the central spiritual mystery of her fiction"; how her landscapes serve as "gauges of character" and "reflections of inadequate or inappropriate human response"; how her characters' distorted or negative reactions to nature suggest their "severely limited visions . . . and seem to indicate a deliberate use of the word *nothing* and an understanding of nothing." Notes O'Connor's use of hostile, violent, and menacing landscapes and her complicated and ambiguous treatment of the country versus the city. Explores how her landscape "functions as an inverted reflection of man's futile attempts to control or restrict . . . unwanted elements of his environment." Sees this in her use of sun and tree imagery, and in such ways as the sexual bull/bullet imagery in "Greenleaf," and fire and water in "A Circle in the Fire." Contends also that, "in addition to functioning as reflections and agents of redemption, O'Connor's landscapes serve as cosmic spectators." Refers to ideas of Martin Heidegger and remarks by: Carol Shloss, Sung Gay Chow, Jack Ashley, and Michael Cleary. Other works examined in the context of O'Connor's landscapes include: *Wise Blood*, "The Displaced Person," "Good Country People," "A View of the Woods," "Parker's Back," "A Good Man Is Hard to Find," "The Enduring Chill," and "The Life You Save May Be Your Own."

1397   See, Lisa. "PW Interviews: Barbara Kingsolver." *Publisher's Weekly* 31 Aug. 1990: 46-47.

Notes Kingsolver's remark that Flannery O'Connor was among the select group of writers who influenced her writing. Kingsolver's works include *The Bean Trees*, *Homeland and Other Stories*, and *Animal Dreams*.

1398   Seelye, John. "Georgia Boys: The Redclay Satyrs of Erskine Caldwell and Harry Crews." *Virginia Quarterly Review* 56.4 (1980): 612-26.

Briefly comments on the shared "element of religiosity" held by both Harry Crews and Flannery O'Connor.

1399   Seidel, Alison P., comp. *Literary Criticism and Authors' Biographies: An Annotated Index*. Metuchen, NJ: Scarecrow, 1978. 133.

Lists three sources for biography and criticism related to O'Connor, by Louis D. Rubin, Jr., Jonathan Baumbach, and Granville Hicks.

1400   Sessions, W[illiam]. A. "How to Read Flannery O'Connor: Passing by the Dragon." *Literature and Belief* 17.1-2 (1997): 191-215.

Uses a simile of autumn light to describe O'Connor's innocence and the loss he felt, as a personal friend, when she died in 1964. Follows with a discussion of how to "listen to O'Connor, how to read her texts not as ideological tracts working out of some self-focused thesis, . . . but to read them as bodies of mysteries, strange and real historical temples of the Holy Ghost with ultimate mystery `always showing,' in Flannery's terms, `through the texture of . . . ordinary lives.'" Illustrates this discussion with his opinion regarding her "somber theological purpose," the "influence of continental Europe upon her work," and with readings of "Revelation," "Parker's Back," and "Judgement Day."

1400a   Sessions, W.A. Rev. of *Flannery O'Connor: In Celebration of Genius*. Ed. Sarah Gordon. *Flannery O'Connor Bulletin* 26-27 (1998-2000): 196-99.

Suggests that the editor and editorial staff had to choose between offering a serious scholarly *festschrift*--which would have required considerable time to prepare and publish--or, a collection that "opted for a light touch" that would avoid "the complexity of the author" while still honoring the 75th birthday of this "obviously significant, culturally influential, and still controversial American writer." Upholds the decision to take the latter path. Discusses contributions by Guerilla Girl Alma Thomas, Fred Chappell, David Bottoms, David Madison, Mark Jarman, Maxine Kumin, Greg Johnson, Padgett Powell, Robert Coles, Lee Smith, Miller Williams, Madison Jones, Bret Lott, and Doris Betts.

1400b   Sessions, W[illiam]. A. "Sally Fitzgerald 1916-2000: The Gratitude is Ours." *CHEERS! The Flannery O'Connor Society Newsletter* 8.1 (2000): 2-5.

Eulogizes Sally Fitzgerald, commenting that her death "marks the end of an important period in American letters," and for O'Connor's readers "a moment of immense sorrow." Describes Fitzgerald's monumental contributions to O'Connor scholarship and comments on her unique friendship with the O'Connor family. Laments that, given her knowledge of O'Connor's life and work, "it is one of the great literary tragedies of our time that her biography [of O'Connor] was not finished." Remarks on Fitzgerald's sophistication, education, and background, then offers recollections of his own friendship with Sally and Robert Fitzgerald as a young Fullbright scholar in Europe in 1957-58. Describes the circumstances in which Sally Fitzgerald conceived the idea of compiling and editing O'Connor's letters for *The Habit of Being*, and recalls their last visit together only a few months before Fitzgerald's death.

1401   Sessions, William A. "Waking the Long Memory." *Georgia Review* 39.3 (1985): 629-34.

Review of Marion Montgomery's three-volume series *The Prophetic Poet and the Spirit of the Age* (LaSalle, IL: Sherwood Sugden, 1981, 1983, and 1984). Asserts that he uses Eric Voegelin as a "philosophical polestar in his trilogy of literary criticism" in an attempt to measure the loss of "'foundational'" knowledge in Western culture. Argues that Montgomery assumes "at times the mask of a persona like . . . Haze Motes . . . [to] track down the monsters of the modern world who have destroyed for human beings such primary sources of knowledge." States that Montgomery provides readers with "a long, if disjunctive, meditation on the life and fiction of Flannery O'Connor." Notes that Montgomery uses "intellectual constructs that he identifies with O'Connor" and "proceeds to write `prophetic' prose." Suggests that the result is "not so much intellectual history as a work like Carlyle's *Sartor Resartus*: rambling, diverse, with brilliant if unsystematic insights from reading and experience that at times focus into oracles from a calculated persona." Questions Montgomery's "chosen role as a kind of Southern preacher-prophet," and asserts that the rhetorical strategy employed "comes full circle and the very gnosticism he attacks haunts his own text, radiant with outrage."

1401a   "Sessions Lecture in Atlanta." *Cheers! The Flannery O'Connor Society Newsletter* 7.1 (Spring/Summer 1999): 3.

Describes a lecture given by William Sessions in Atlanta, July 25, 1999, titled "No Ordinary Life: Betty Hester, Her Cosmic Questioning, and her Friendship with Flannery O'Connor and Iris Murdoch." Reports that the lecture, co-sponsored by the Atlanta Philosophical Society and Borders Bookstore, focused on the life and interests of Hazel Elizabeth "Betty" Hester, the anonymous correspondent referred to in *The Habit of Being* as "A". Notes that Sessions "is now preparing a book about Hester, drawing upon the papers she gave him before her death, including unpublished correspondence from O'Connor and Murdoch." [Note: Betty Hester's papers are presently located in a collection of the Special Collections Department of the Woodruff Libray at Emory University closed to scholars until 2007.]

1402   Sewell, Elizabeth. "Is Flannery O'Connor a Nonsense Writer?" *Explorations in the Field of Nonsense.* Ed. Wim Tigges. Amsterdam (Netherlands): Rodopi, 1987. 183-213.

Compares writings by Edward Lear, Jonathan Swift, and Lewis Carroll to the work of O'Connor to argue that hers' is a "nonsense writer." Proposes that labeling it classic Nonsense "may afford a clue to O'Connor's work at least as helpful as the much-used `grotesque' or `Gothic' or `Southern.'" Suggests that the key to O'Connor's use of Nonsense is in her letters, "the fairly frequent comic spellings and distortions of words which she uses in letters to close friends." Compares similarities between O'Connor's life and work and Lear's. Discusses O'Connor's defensiveness and hostility toward "interlekchuls," her use of "little language," and the "many examples of violence" in her stories so characteristic of Nonsense writers. Contends that O'Connor is aligned with Nonsense writers in her use of episodic structure to maintain control of her work, and her characters' use of objects such as a wooden leg, eyeglasses, glass eyes, and hearing aids which emphasize the artificial over the natural. Concludes with extensive discussion of unifying modes and ideas that Nonsense excludes--poetry, dreams, beauty, and love--and how O'Connor dealt with these limitations. [Rpt. in *Soundings* 73.2-3 (1990): 273-302.]

1403   Sexton, Mark S. "`Blessed Insurance': An Examination of Flannery O'Connor's `Greenleaf.'" *Flannery O'Connor Bulletin* 19 (1990): 38-43.

Suggests that O'Connor "presents her readers with a narrative puzzle in regard to the insurance policy of Mrs. May" in "Greenleaf." Notes that in her first encounter with Mrs. Greenleaf, Mrs. May does not have insurance coverage, while just before her death--although she momentarily forgets it--she does. Infers that if this fact is only "an inconsistency of narrative detail, readers must infer O'Connor's intention of suggesting that something in Mrs. May's experience after her initial encounter with Mrs. Greenleaf, perhaps the encounter itself, has prompted the woman to obtain protection offered by insurance." Examines the story in the context of this inference and contends that "the inconspicuous detail of insurance may contribute significantly to the thematic and structural unity" of the story and offer insight into O'Connor's "patterns of narrative organization and meaning."

1404   Sexton, Mark S. "Flannery O'Connor's Presentation of Vernacular Religion in `The River.'" *Flannery O'Connor Bulletin* 18 (1989): 1-12.

Offers a reading of "The River" to support the argument that O'Connor uses narrative objectivity "to control reader reaction toward a purpose that ultimately transcends the perspective of vernacular religion itself." Seeks to "determine ultimate `meaning' in the story" by examining its symbols in relation to narrative structure. Finds that O'Connor's manipulation of narrative distance "controls the perception of and reaction to the believers" by readers as well as the "the kind of sympathy felt and the points at which it is experienced." Asserts that Harry's drowning is not endowed with any "special authority" because of Reverend Summers' previous attempt. Instead, it is simply a part of "the thrust of O'Connor's narrative design . . . a consummation of the `baptism' symbolism." Concludes that O'Connor uses narrative consciousness to present "the vernacular religious experience in such a way that it provides realistic motivation for the characters in the story and reveals . . . a vision powerful enough to allure a lonely little boy away from the Ashfield's home and frame of mind." Maintains that the worship service is not included "to embody ultimate religious meaning or theological belief," but only to offer a symbolic foundation for the narrative structure.

1405   Seymour-Smith, Martin. *McMillian Guide to Modern World Literature.* 3rd ed. New York: McMillian, 1985. 117-18.

Biographical/critical entry describing O'Connor as a writer who "mixes Southern Gothic . . . grotesque humor and an extremely complex and sometimes over-complicated and therefore self-defeating symbolism."

1406   Seymour-Smith, Martin. *Who's Who in Twentieth Century Literature.* New York: Holt, Rinehart, and Winston, 1976. 262-63.

Short bio-critical entry, listing four aspects of O'Connor's fiction: her Southern Gothic style; her Protestant Catholicism "(`crazy Southern Revivalist,' in fact)"; her intelligence; and her "horrible and incurable disease." Argues that O'Connor's intelligence and health influenced her fiction to a much greater extent than acknowledged. Says the works depend on "exceedingly complex and erudite theological symbolic structures," and that she is "a strange, difficult, mind-haunting case."

1407   Shackelford, Dean. "The Black Outsider in O'Connor's Fiction." *Flannery O'Connor Bulletin* 18 (1989): 79-90.

Examines the issue of whether O'Connor should be considered a racist. Offers an overview of the positions of a variety of scholars, submits possible reasons why and how O'Connor wrote about Blacks, and outlines her use of "outsider" characters. Suggests that O'Connor's most significant Black characters appear in "The Artificial Nigger," "Everything That Rises Must Converge," and "Judgement Day." Asserts that these stories imply "that social oppression and other earthly issues take second place to the individual's willingness to surrender himself, his feelings of rejection, and his pain to God." Offers readings and interpretations of the three stories, and concludes that for Flannery O'Connor, "a woman who constantly lived with the thought of death and the afterlife, earthly values, including those involving racial relations, were, in comparison to spiritual conviction, insignificant."

1408   Shackelford, Dean. "`Just Give Me Some of Him': Masculinity, Femininity, and Religious Conversion in Flannery O'Connor's *Wise Blood*." *Journal of Contemporary Thought* 4 (1994): 55-84.

Discusses *Wise Blood*, exploring such perspectives as feminist and gender issues, conventional behavior and attitudes expected of women of O'Connor's generation, and female and male stereotypes. Notes that O'Connor used foul language, violence, and sexuality to convey themes in her work, and remarks that these may reflect some of the difficulty she had in "adhering to the confining social conditions of the South of her time." Suggests that her "failure as a lady in Southern society . . . may be the origin of O'Connor's explorations of girls and women who do not fit the norms of their society." Offers a close examination of the roles each of the female characters play and contends that such examination "reveals much about O'Connor's perceptions of herself as a woman." Discusses the images of "`madonna' and `magdalen,'" and argues that while *Wise Blood* is "fundamentally a religious book," it also serves more fully than any of her other works to address the relationship between men and women. Examines the "ambiguity" noted in her portrayal of male and female characters; how heterosexuality seems for them to be "impossible"; the oedipal elements of Hazel's memories of his mother; and how Hazel seems to have to fail as a "man" in order to become a prophet. Sees the female characters as Hazel's "idols . . . temporary substitutes for God," present to tempt him as Eve tempted Adam. Further, "Hazel's possession of women through sexual acts may be related to his existential quest, a way of affirming his own existence as a separate being from his mother." Refers to critical remarks by Louise Westling, Sandra Gilbert, Susan Gunbar, Eric Trugill, Thomas LeClair, James C. McCullagh, Simone de Beauvoir, Dorothy Dinnerstein, and Steven Lynn.

1409   Sharp, Roberta. "Flannery O'Connor and Poe's `Angel of the Odd.'" *Flannery O'Connor Bulletin* 7 (1978): 116-28.

Offers evidence which indicates that O'Connor owes a debt to Edgar Allan Poe. Remarks that O'Connor, like Poe, uses "exaggerations and incongruities which violate the reader's expectations." Describes how O'Connor "fuses violence and humor, evokes eccentric images, and creates grotesque characters who often function as doubles and whose roles are sometimes reversed," to "teach that death comes in strange ways" and that "eternity waits beyond." Demonstrates O'Connor's method through readings of "Revelation," "A Good Man Is Hard to Find," and "The Comforts of Home." Then discusses: O'Connor's use of the automobile as symbol in "The Heart of the Park," *Wise Blood*, and "The Life You Save May Be Your Own"; spectacles in "A Good Man Is Hard to Find," and "Partridge Festival"; corpses in "The Train," *Wise Blood*, and "You Can't Be Any Poorer Than Dead"; "bizarre images" and characters in "Parker's Back" and "Good Country People"; and her use of doubling or the *Doppleganger* motif in "The Lame Shall Enter First," "Everything That Rises Must Converge," "Enoch and the Gorilla," "The Artificial Nigger," and "A View of the Woods." Sees O'Connor's last story, "Judgement Day," as embodying "three major elements of the `odd': violence linked with humor, bizarre images, and eccentric characterization." Concludes that knowledge of O'Connor's debt to Poe "aids in understanding" how some of her characters--like Poe's narrator in his "The Angel of the Odd--An Extravaganza"--often "find themselves in humorous situations that are sometimes violent and bizarre."

1410   Shaw, Mary Neff. "`The Artificial Nigger': A Dialogic Narrative." *Flannery O'Connor Bulletin* 20 (1991): 104-16.

Suggests that in "The Artificial Nigger," O'Connor "presents, in Mikhail Bakhtin's terms, `an unclosed whole of life itself' . . . a snippet of Mr. Head's journey of life as he develops a measure of spiritual maturity" by moving "from vanity to spiritual sensibility." Maintains that "dialogism provides the `artistic design' vital to O'Connor's dramatization of this journey," and is "an essential cipher" for fully understanding her intentions. Submits that dialogism allows readers to "attribute the pluralism of consciousness that seethes beneath the seemingly smooth surface of the story and to appreciate the rich complexity of its plot structure." Examines and compares the published story with unpublished drafts found in the *Flannery O'Connor Collection* at Georgia College & State University. Finds the manuscript drafts to be monologic narratives and only the published version to be a dialogic narrative. Argues that in her published version, O'Connor "ruptures the narrator's authority, alters the realistic opening paragraphs, and appends several paragraphs to the concluding section so that both the introductory and concluding passages are enclosed in a frame of mystery" in order to transpose the story from being a monologic to a dialogic narrative. Concludes that by doing this, "O'Connor's religious and dramatic intents" are concomitantly reached. Offers that this insight "might have surprised even O'Connor, who might not have anticipated or consciously discerned that by meeting these dual commitments she would suspend her narrator's authority and deny her narrator's omniscience." Revised version published in *Flannery O'Connor: New Perspectives*. Ed. Sura P. Rath and Mary Neff Shaw. Athens: U of Georgia P, 1996. 139-51.

1411   Shaw, Patrick W. "*The Violent Bear It Away* and the Irony of False Seeing." *Texas Review* 3.2 (1982): 49-59.

Argues that while O'Connor's insistent denial of ironic intent has made critics wary of examining *The Violent Bear It Away* from this perspective, O'Connor "does employ narrative devices which are distinctively ironic." Contends that O'Connor uses "dozens of words, phrases and passages" to reflect the use of such a "motif of vision" and that readers must carefully examine the surface reality in her fiction "lest false seeing prove habitual and fatal." Concludes that O'Connor "belongs among the best of ironists" which should not threaten her place among outstanding Christian writers.

1412   Shear, Walter. "The Sense of Fate in Mid-Century American Literature." *Journal of the Midwest Modern Language Association* 21 (1988): 38-47.

Discusses how the era which extended from the end of World War II to the early 1960s, was overly committed to "`the tragic sense of life,' a fateful determinism that affirmed the obduracy of man's nature and his surroundings." Refers to O'Connor's remarks regarding an editorial in *Life* (that "complained `our novelists are writing as if they lived in packing boxes at the edge of the dump while awaiting admission to the poorhouse,'") and her treatment, in *Wise Blood*, of "World War II as a savage cultural event that had absolutely cut her rural characters off from their true, authentic home."

1413   Sheehy, Helen and Leslie Stainton. *On Writers & Writing: 1993 Desk Calendar*. East Hartford, CT: Tide-mark, 1992.

Offers a short essay for March, 1993 which provides a brief review of O'Connor's life and work. Notes that her works are "peopled with eccentric Southern characters, packed with macabre incidents, and filled with comic, joyous life." Refers to her writing habits, that "she wrote every morning, sitting at a large brown desk amidst the clutter of books, journals and papers. She sometimes composed on an electric typewriter, even though it made her nervous to think of the electricity wasted while she thought of what to write."

1414   Shelnutt, Eve. "Contemporary Southern Fiction: *Is* It What We Recognize?" *Mississippi Quarterly* 43.1 (1989-90): 3-9.

Shelnutt discusses the influence of the South upon her own life and work, then expands her focus to include the effect upon a wide variety of other contemporary authors. Laments the similarity, predictability, and isolated nature of today's Southern writers. Includes brief references to O'Connor, including the remark that her work is "heroic" in that she expanded upon the parameters of her Southern world.

1415   Shelton, Frank W. "Harry Crews." In *Fifty Southern Writers After 1900: A Bio-Bibliographical Sourcebook*. Ed. Joseph M. Flora and Robert Bain. New York: Greenwood, 1987. 111-20.

Refers to O'Connor in a discussion of how Crews "follows an honorable Southern tradition," of "suggesting by grotesqueness, man's incompleteness and alienation and the absurdity of human existence." Contrasts Crews's use of the grotesque with that of O'Connor, Carson McCullers and Erskine Caldwell. Notes that whereas O'Connor's grotesque characters deviate from a religious norm, Caldwell's deviate from a social norm, and McCullers's deviate from a human norm, Crews "is much less sure than are these other writers of the existence of any standards by which to measure the grotesque's deviation."

1416   Shelton, Frank W. "Harry Crews: Man's Search for Perfection." *Southern Literary Journal* 12.2 (1980): 97-113.

States that Harry Crews's *purpose* for using the grotesque differs significantly from that of Flannery O'Connor and Carson McCullers, whose "grotesque characters represent deviations from some at least implicit norm." Acknowledges that "though grotesqueness may be the necessary human condition, [and] a standard does exist by which to measure such deviations," Crews's work reflects that he "is much less sure of such standards." [Rpt. in *A Grit's Triumph: Essays on the Works of Harry Crews*. Ed. David K. Jeffrey. Port Washington, NY: Associated Faculty, 1983. 21-32.]

1417   Shepherd, Allen. "`Firing Two Carbines, One in Each Hand': Barry Hannah's *Hey Jack!*" *Notes on Mississippi Writers* 21.1 (1989): 37-40.

Discusses Hannah's *Hey Jack!* as an example of his present work and compares Hannah to O'Connor. Contends that while both "are sometimes powerfully affecting," neither writer "is really at ease in constructing longer fiction." Instead, "both are notably repetitive, [and] neither [is] really persuasive in articulating positive convictions."

1418   Shepherd, Gerard W. "The Example of Flannery O'Connor As A Christian Writer." *Center Journal* 4.1 (1984): 39-63.

Lists and acknowledges some of the "many angles of approach" to O'Connor, and asserts that the common thread is her example of "a person striving earnestly to permeate all her being and doing with the riches of her Christian faith." Uses excerpts from O'Connor's letters and lectures to examine: "her stubborn pursuit of professional excellence, her refusal to dissociate her faith from the practice or vision of her craft, her lifelong effort to probe the mysteries and intellectual heritage of her faith that she might better understand, practice and explain it the better, her active concern for the spiritual welfare of her family, friends, colleagues and admirers, and her efforts toward a joyful, self-sacrificing union with Christ." Discusses O'Connor's writing habits, her view of Catholic dogma and "fidelity to the Catholic vision of reality," the views and "misconceptions" of Catholic readers, and her motives for writing. Concludes that O'Connor serves "as a notable example of a Catholic, who, drawing on the resources of the traditional faith and prayer life, felt at home in the midst of the world and used all her intelligence, heart and strength to permeate that world with Christian faith through her work, friendship, and daily tasks."

1419   Shields, John C. "Flannery O'Connor's `Greenleaf' and the Myth of Europa and the Bull." *Studies in Short Fiction* 18.4 (1981): 421-31.

Explores the significance of the myth of Europa and the bull in "Greenleaf." Contends that in using the archetypal story of the union between sky (Zeus, king of the heavens) and earth ("Europa as epiphany of Gaia or Mother Earth"), O'Connor produces "a grotesque which syncretizes the ancient myth and Christianity." Concludes that O'Connor's rewriting of the myth in this manner allows her to deal directly with the problem of good and evil and celebrate "the life, death, and rebirth rhythm of the cosmos."

1420   Shillingsburg, Miriam J. "The Ascent of Woman, Southern Style: Hentz, King, Chopin." *Southern Literature in Transition: Heritage and Promise.* Ed. Philip Castille and William Osborne. Memphis, TN: Memphis State UP, 1983. 127-140.

Outlines the neglect by critics and scholars of nineteenth-century Southern women writers, focusing on the "undercurrent of discontent" noted in their private diaries and in the popular fiction they wrote and read. Discusses Caroline Lee Hentz's *Eoline* (1852), Kate Chopin's *The Awakening* (1899), and Grace Elizabeth King's *Monsieur Motte* (1888). Includes a brief discussion of O'Connor's work on page 139, suggesting that without the early fiction of writers such as Hentz and King, "perhaps there would not have yet been a Chopin . . . and certainly not a Flannery O'Connor, whose stories simply do not have to deal with the relationships between men and women as cultural phenomena." States that O'Connor's "barnyard seductions are not sexual acts but spiritual ones" and that her characters "are not merely men and women but forces of good and evil in the world." Contends that writers such as Hentz, King, and Chopin "provide a context and a heritage in which to view the achievement and promise of their successors," such as O'Connor.

1421   Shinn, Thelma J. "A Strategic Retreat: Fiction of the 50's." *Radiant Daughters: Fictional American Women.* Contributions in Women's Studies, No. 66. New York: Greenwood, 1986. 75-124.

Examines the fiction of women writers and the cultural context in which they worked during the 1950s. Surveys a wide variety of writers and offers brief readings of their most important contributions, paying particular attention to the role and importance of their female characters. Focuses on O'Connor in a sub-section titled "Surrogate Fathers" on pages 85-90. Contends that in O'Connor's works "a good *woman* is hard to find" and the tension between female characters and their mothers (as in O'Connor's own personal life) is not resolved. Suggests that O'Connor's fiction is governed by the "tension of unresolved hatred combined with childlike dependency of young people on parents--usually mothers."

Notes that "women of any kind are few and far between" except for
"'foolish but well-intentioned elderly daughters of the old South' and a
few younger, more rebellious daughters." Discusses *Wise Blood* and "A
Good Man Is Hard to Find," "Good Country People," "Greenleaf," and
"The Comforts of Home." Concludes that O'Connor presented women in
a pessimistic, even hostile manner. Further suggests that because they
have been "deprived of a maternal heritage, the daughters haven't the
strength to face modern corruption; deprived of fathers, they turn to
religion, which offers them an eternal purity."

1422   Shloss, Carol. "Epiphany." *Flannery O'Connor: Modern Critical Views.*
Ed. Harold Bloom. New York: Chelsea House, 1986. 65-80.

Takes issue with O'Connor's use of third-person narration, insisting that
she leaves too much for the reader to infer, "to come upon through the
indirections of allusion, incongruities, and distorted hyperbole." Questions
the effectiveness of her work and suggests that her "reluctance to take full
advantage of the possibilities of omniscient narration may have been the
result of her own `double thinking'" related to her readers and their ability
to understand her fiction. Offers readings of "Revelation" and "Parker's
Back," paying particular attention to epiphanic scenes. Contends that
these scenes often leave readers wondering which of the variety of
possible interpretations O'Connor intended. Discusses her literary use of
epiphany (versus that of Virginia Woolf, Morris Beja, and James Joyce);
her ambiguous view of passivity as a virtue; her "sense of life as response
rather than action"; and her "tendency to use the same technique to
represent both potentially religious experience and decidedly nonreligious
circumstances," and its relation to her "use of the grotesque to describe
both the `sacred' and the `damned.'" Continues with a comparative reading
of "The Artificial Nigger," finding that, compared to the two other stories,
O'Connor's "willingness to assume full privilege of omniscient author has
carried through" with the story being "unambiguously rendered" and
nothing left to inference. Concludes that O'Connor would have found
more success if she had offered characters a statement of faith instead of
her "usual tendency toward oblique insult." Originally published in Carol
Shloss's *Flannery O'Connor's Dark Comedies: The Limits of Inference,*
(Baton Rouge: Louisiana State UP, 1980).

1423   Showalter, Elaine. *Sister's Choice: Tradition and Change in American
Women's Writing.* The Clarendon Lectures 1989. Oxford: Clarendon,
1991.

Through the symbolism of threads being woven into a fabric, the author
works women writers into criticism that previously represented male

authors. Focuses on Louisa May Alcott, Kate Chopin, and Edith Wharton with mention of O'Connor on pages 20, 130 and 135.

1424   Shurr, William H. *Rappaccini's Children: American Writers in a Calvinist World*. Lexington: UP of Kentucky, 1981. 101-19.

Examines the influence of Calvinism on American literature written during the nineteenth and twentieth centuries. Includes, in the chapter titled "The Southern Experience," a brief mention of O'Connor. Discusses *Everything That Rises Must Converge*, focusing on Teilhard de Chardin's influence. Contends that, instead of "the serene mystical optimism of Chardin in her work," O'Connor "remains firmly rooted in Faulkner's territory." Argues that the pattern throughout her fiction is that "what rises to the plane of action is human wickedness; when the wickedness of two human beings converges, the inevitable result is tragedy."

1425   Siegfried, Regina. "The Search for the True Self: Thomas Merton and Flannery O'Connor." *Studia Mystica* 10.1 (1987): 5-18.

Explores the level of awareness and meaning that Flannery O'Connor and Thomas Merton shared: "the search for authentic self identity." Concludes that each focused on the same truth, that "growth in true self identity is grace and gift, a process that involves the stripping away of masks, of facing the moment of truth in truth and a `hell of mercy.'"

1426   Sikora, Malgorzata. "Discovering the Grotesque in the South." *Approaches to Fiction*. Ed. Leszek S. Kolek. Pace Studies and Monographs Vol. 2. Lublin, Poland: Folium, 1996. 185-95.

Compares examples of the use of a "Northern" grotesque by Nathanael West with examples of a "Southern" grotesque in Flannery O'Connor, to "break the stereotypical image of Southern literature" and "to point out those features of the latter which justify coining the term `Southern grotesque' as a genre in American literature." Suggests that attempting to define "something as grotesque is a matter of degree--the degree to which something seems simultaneously amusing and terrifying." Further, there are borders to be observed in the use of the grotesque: "when the norm of abnomality is exceeded, the thing is no longer funny but fearsome for it [then] approaches the realm of the monstrous." Indicates that while "the thin dividing lines between the comic and the fearful cannot be crossed, it cannot be precisely defined either." Follows with an in-depth exploration of "`the profound poetry of disorder known as the American Grotesque tradition,'" resting upon Alan Spiegel's claim that "`the

Southern writer gives us the everyday world as it is experienced by a person who is mentally or physically deformed, while the Northern writer gives us a normal individual who is beset by a surrounding world that is grotesque.'" Illustrates argument with examples culled from O'Connor's fiction: *Wise Blood, The Violent Bear It Away,* "A Temple of the Holy Ghost," "The Lame Shall Enter First," "The Partridge Festival," "A Late Encounter With the Enemy," "The Displaced Person," and "A Good Man Is Hard to Find."

1427   Silk, Mark. "A Vision of Eternity and Georgia on Her Mind." *Boston Globe* 20 Aug. 1989: 2.

Remembrance of O'Connor written on the 25th anniversary of her death. Describes her place in American literature, her "memorable characters," and reflects upon the relationship between O'Connor's Catholicism and her fundamentalist heroes. Refers to O'Connor as the "last of the great Southern dialect humorists," stating that she "possessed an unerring ear for the idiom of ordinary Georgians, black as well as white . . . " Argues that she was "above all else a religious writer--probably the greatest American storyteller whose pen has been in service to orthodox Christian belief," who used "conventional and extraordinary evangelical Protestants of Georgia" serving as the role models for characters who "enlist most of her attention." Contends that the early 1950s were a "time when religion was very much on the minds of the country's literary and intellectual community" and that "O'Connor's strange tales of backwoods fundamentalists were exotic . . . but they fit in with a literary culture ready to explore stories for Christian symbols and spiritual meanings." Mentions T.S. Eliot, Graham Greene, Evelyn Waugh, Thomas Aquinas, Karl Barth, and Paul Tillich; and discusses Vatican II, *The Violent Bear It Away* and "Revelation."

1428   Simon, John. "Christ Without Christ: Nijinsky Without Nijinsky." *National Review* 2 May 1980: 543-44.

Discusses John Huston's adaptation of O'Connor's *Wise Blood.* Reports that Huston "very nearly does justice" to the novel, and suggests that, though the novel may be O'Connor's "least successful fiction, for a movie to have captured its spirit is enough to place it quite high on the film scale, and in a category of its own." Commends Huston for casting the film "with great canniness" and obtaining "a flawless performance." Concludes that the film "hops and lurches to its trivial, tremendous climax in a manner Miss O'Connor would have approved--which is praise enough."

1429   Simpson, Lewis P. "The Southern Aesthetic of Memory." *Tulane Studies in English* 23 (1978): 207-27.

Sets out "to identify an aesthetic of memory as a formative element in Southern fiction." Discusses writers who influenced Southern literature, including Marcel Proust, Thomas Mann, James Joyce, William Butler Yeats, and T.S. Eliot, and Southern writers Marion McDonnell, Eudora Welty, William Faulkner, Robert Penn Warren, Walker Percy, and Flannery O'Connor. Describes O'Connor and Percy as the most remarkable Southern writers of the past twenty-five years because of their ardent "desire to free themselves from the work of memory." States that both "are pivotal figures in the resolution of the drama of history and memory in Southern fiction." Discusses O'Connor's "A Late Encounter With the Enemy" and "Revelation" as examples of "stories that illustrate her shifting focus on the necessary aesthetic of fiction in the South."

1430   Simpson, Lewis P. "The Southern Writer and the Economy of Leisure." *Sewanee Review* 91.3 (1983): 512-18.

Considers the "relation of the southern writer to the literary marketplace." Suggests that the position of the Agrarians made it possible for Southern writers "to assert, for the first time, an overt tension between the economy of leisure and the industrialization of literature." O'Connor and Walker Percy are presented as examples of Southern writers who kept "a distance between themselves and the literary marketplace."

1431   Simpson, Lewis P. "A Vision of Flannery O'Connor's Vision." *Southern Review* 17.2 (1981): vii.

Discusses how Eric Voegelin's "massive vision of order and disorder in history" influenced Marion Montgomery's writing of his trilogy: *Why Flannery O'Connor Stayed Home* (1981), *Why Poe Drank Liquor* (1983), and *Why Hawthorne Was Melancholy* (1984). Outlines how Voegelin's writings provided Montgomery with a "context for the Southern literary mind" and enabled him to use "the guiding spirit of this quest, Flannery O'Connor," to make "a remarkable contribution to the problem of the meaning of American literature."

1432   Skaggs, Merrill. "Submission and Fidelity, Assertion and Surprise: Two `Southern Woman' Films." *Southern Quarterly* 24.3 (1986): 5-13.

Analyzes film adaptations of O'Connor's "The Displaced Person" and Katherine Anne Porter's "The Jilting of Granny Weatherall" produced for the NEH-funded "American Short Stories Series." Examines devices used "to capture the fictional purposes" of each story. Mentions Andalusia, Regina O'Connor, Horton Foote (scriptwriter), Glen Jordan (director), Shirley Stoler (actress), and Charles Bennett (art director).

1433   Skarda, Patricia. "[Mary] Flannery O'Connor (1926-1964)." *The Penguin Encyclopedia of Horror and the Supernatural.* Ed. Jack Sullivan. New York: Viking Penguin, 1986. 306-07.

Offers a brief biographical sketch, lists awards, and asserts that O'Connor was "a master at fusing horror and humor in Southern Gothic mode." Suggests that "the intensity of her strong faith, stern intellect, and economical style infuses her fiction with forceful irony and an eerie incongruity of light humor and grim horror." Mentions that O'Connor "relied on traditional sacramental symbols to show the literal minds of children and fundamentalist adults," and developed characters with crippled natures and psychic wounds to "suggest that the physical facts of her characters' lives determine and dominate their emotional lives." Asserts that "the grotesque ghosts of the `Christ-Haunted' South in O'Connor's fiction are both fierce and instructive: by distortion and exaggeration she revealed the value of belief in a `Christ-centered' universe unrestricted by regionalism." [Note: Birth date is incorrect, O'Connor was born on March 25, 1925.]

1434   Skube, Michael. "The Faith of Flannery O'Connor." *Catholic Digest* 58 (Oct. 1994): 116-21.

Discusses Flannery O'Connor's character and personality as reflected in her comments, letters, and recollections by those who knew her. Includes a briefly annotated reading list of her works and edited letters and two photographs (O'Connor seated with a book in her lap and O'Connor standing with crutches looking at a peacock on the front steps of her home at Andalusia). Refers to comments by Sally and Robert Fitzgerald, Louise Florencourt, "A," Mary Barbara Tate, and Celestine Sibley. Concludes that, after William Faulkner, "she stands with Eudora Welty, Robert Penn Warren, and Walker Percy among Southern writers of our century."

1435   Slattery, Dennis Patrick. "Evil and the Negation of the Body: Flannery O'Connor's `Parker's Back.'" *Flannery O'Connor Bulletin* 17 (1988): 69-79.

Comments on the grotesque as a theme of such 19th-century Russian writers as Gogol and Dostoevsky. Suggests that O'Connor's fiction "may be viewed as a creative product forged from the legacy of the Russian sensibility, for she deals with many of the same concerns of a post-industrial culture . . . " Argues that her short stories "powerfully and comically express the profile of a deformed soul coming to know itself." Offers "Parker's Back" as an example, stating that it "is certainly a narrative about heresy and prophecy, about ideas divorced from image, about faith rooted in the abstract, as well as about a belief grounded in sacred images . . . " Provides a close reading of the story under the premise that it "would seem to pit a modern understanding of evil against a traditional faith rooted in the flesh of the world." Further submits that "the impulse" of the story "reveals that the issue of evil may be the issue of the flesh itself." Concludes that "while Parker experiences the mystery of transfiguration offered through the icon seared into his flesh, Sara Ruth, who is without imagination, denies the flesh, denies the world as well as the reality of Christ's embodied presence."

1436   Slattery, Dennis Patrick. "Faith in Search of an Image: The Iconic Dimension of Flannery O'Connor's `Parker's Back.'" *South Central Bulletin* 41.4 (1981): 120-23.

Argues that in the Byzantine icon of Christ, which Parker has tattooed on his back, O'Connor explores "how an individual learns to focus his moral vision on the visible creation in order to apprehend . . . the invisible presence of the Creator by means of grace." Suggests that readers focus on the icon "as an embodied image of Parker's experience of grace," and ties the relationship of the New Testament Christ to the names of the couple. Concludes that Parker introduces to his wife "the mysterious paradox of the God-man, a reality too human for her to accept."

1437   Slattery, Dennis P. "In a Pig's Eye: Retrieving the Animal Imagination in Ruby Turpin's `Revelation.'" *Flannery O'Connor Bulletin* 25 (1996-97): 138-50.

Focuses on the significance of pigs in "Revelation," described as "a story that circles about the retrieval of an animal imagination, an animal way of seeing that is as important for a personal and vital incarnational theology as is the life of the spirit." Offers an explication of the story and concludes that "the pig, the sow, the warthog--are all animal images that bring Ruby Turpin to an awareness of divine justice, a way of seeing the world less through the hierarchy of her own consciousness, which tends to `hog' a worldview of her own making, and more through what might be termed an `animal' way of knowing."

1437a   Slattery, Dennis Patrick. "Wounds and Tattoos: Marking the Mystery in
             Flannery O'Connor's "Revelation" and "Parker's Back." *The Wounded
             Body: Remembering the Markings of Flesh*. Albany: State University of
             New York Press, 2000. 177-206.

             Discusses O'Connor's short story "Revelation," and notes how Ruby
             Turpin's sterile and antiseptic views reflect "a soul that has lost touch with
             the soiled and sullied qualities of the world's imperfect and often
             unpredictable unfolding." Sees Mary Grace as an angel figure whose
             action of throwing a book entitled *Human Development*, forces Ruby to
             rethink her view of herself as "unpolluted *and* innocent." Argues that by
             this action Ruby begins to realize that the "mystery of the sacred" may be
             embodied not only in herself but in such other lowly living creatures as
             "her own sleeping sow waiting to farrow." Sees Ruby's preoccupation
             "with obsessively examining people's feet" as a literalization of her
             "looking down on people." Concludes that it is only by becoming
             "marked and wounded herself" that Ruby will understand "mystery, the
             transcendent, the soiled and stained, and the ineffable origin of the
             world." Follows with a discussion of "Parker's Back," described as "a
             colorful meditation on being incarnated." Sees O'Connor as revealing
             "powerfully and comically the profile of a deformed soul [O.E. Parker]
             coming to know itself through an image it is called to have inked onto its
             back." Adds that "it is also a story about heresy and prophecy, about ideas
             divorced from image, and about faith rooted in abstract ideas against a
             belief grounded in sacred images." Offers a detailed explication of the
             story, focusing on the conflict between Parker, "whose body is
             resplendent with images," and his wife Sarah Ruth, "who is a woman not
             only without images, but who outwardly scorns them."

1438   Sloan, Gary. "The Head-Doctor in Flannery O'Connor's `A Good Man Is
             Hard to Find.'" *Notes on Contemporary Literature* 27.3 (1997): 4-5.

             Comments on the significance of The Misfit's recollection that the
             penitentiary psychiatrist had asserted that he had been imprisoned for
             killing his father. Cites articles by critics--Madison Jones, W.S. Marks,
             and Michael Bellamy--who respectively contend that The Misfit's
             inability to recall why he was sent to the penitentiary and his recollection
             of the psychiatrist's remark can be interpreted "literally, allegorically, and
             psychologically." Outlines the argument of each critic and suggests that
             "to O'Connor, The Misfit is superior to the head-doctor because The
             Misfit is not embarrassed by the supernatural. He is tortured by it."

1439   Sloan, Gary. "Mystery, Magic, and Malice: O'Connor and The Misfit."
             Journal of the Short Story in English 30 (Spring 1998): 73-83.

Notes Jill Baumgaertner's opinion that O'Connor thought that not only was God using her as a divine instrument, but that she was also "a `channel for God's grace and the Holy Spirit's breath.'" Contends that O'Connor viewed the devil not as some "wispy abstraction, diffusing into metaphor," but "like the one in Arthur Miller's *The Crucible*, palpably `precise' and indefatigably afoot." Reviews various critical responses to O'Connor's Misfit character and suggests that they are reflective of the present-day sensibilities of critics. Offers a reading of "A Good Man Is Hard to Find," discussing at length the intentions O'Connor had in mind when she created The Misfit; her use of allegory and ambiguity; The Misfit's conception of God as reflected in his comments and actions; and whether O'Connor herself was "through an unholy alliance with The Misfit, venting a pleasurable meanness of her own." Concludes that while O'Connor was "impregnably ensconced in what she called Mystery and the unbeliever calls dogmatism," it appears that she never appears to have fully grasped that "opposition to Mystery can be principled and courageous rather than vain, forward, and evasive."

1440   Sloan, Gary. "O'Connor's `A Good Man Is Hard to Find.'" *Explicator* 57.2 (1999): 118-20.

Describes a variety of perspectives which critics have offered to explain The Misfit's actions in "A Good Man Is Hard to Find," then contends that the story "offers scant support for such grandiose assessments." Argues that The Misfit's "skepticism has been greatly exaggerated," and sees him simply as "a lapsed fundamentalist locked into incarnational models of deity." Sees his concept of God as being within the "primitive mindset" that regards "deity [as] authenticated by magic feats" (specifically Jesus's ability to raise the dead). Discusses ambiguity and contradiction in The Misfit's views, his sheer meanness, and states that while he may serve as an adequate catalyst for the Grandmother's epiphany, he is woefully inadequate in the role of "informed skeptic."

1441   Sloan, LaRue Love. "The Rhetoric of the Seer: Eye Imagery in Flannery O'Connor's `Revelation.'" *Studies in Short Fiction* 25.2 (1988): 135-45.

Briefly summarizes various critical readings of "Revelation." Suggests that from beginning to end, the story's "prevailing metaphor is that of vision, or lack of it." Analyzes eye imagery in detail and concludes that O'Connor used "eyes, glances, gazes, and visions [to] form a subtle chain that inevitably leads to the final epiphany," all "while developing characters and their alliances along the way." Suggests that without these complex visual metaphors, "there would be no `Revelation.'"

1442   Sloane, Thomas O. "The Strategies of Authorial Presence: Narrators and
             Regionalism in Flannery O'Connor and Eudora Welty." *Literature in
             Performance* 2.1 (1981): 1-25.

             Discusses "the means whereby the author makes her presence known to
             us," and the proposition "that good fiction . . . must perform its meaning
             through talk." Examines how the narrator in works by O'Connor and
             Welty reveals the author's presence. Mentions Wayne Booth's "notion that
             understanding the narrator's role is crucial to understanding fiction."
             Discusses the role of the narrator, the significance of regionalism, the
             meaning and significance of belief in God and Christian orthodoxy, all in
             terms of how the two writers manage *presence*.

1443   Smith, Lee. "A Visit to Milledgeville." *Flannery O'Connor Bulletin* 24
             (1995-96): 102-03.

             Smith relates how she has "gone back to [O'Connor's] work again and
             again . . . and every time" comes away "with something different, deeper,
             [and] new." States that she could never have written her novel *Saving
             Grace* without having read O'Connor's *Wise Blood*, which she considers
             "as a kind of homage to Flannery O'Connor." Describes her visit to
             Milledgeville in 1994 during the *Flannery O'Connor Symposium*, and her
             impressions of: the local landscape; O'Connor's home; her personal library
             (in the Flannery O'Connor Room at Georgia College & State University);
             Douglas Powers's O'Connor-related art exhibit; and observations of local
             townsfolk while walking with Jill McCorkle through downtown.
             Concludes, "It was perfectly clear: O'Connor didn't make anything up."

1444   Smith, Marcus A.J. "Another Desert: Hazel Motes's Missing Years."
             Flannery O'Connor Bulletin 18 (1989): 55-58.

             Proposes that O'Connor's "reference to Hazel Motes's two deserts may
             direct readers to actual historical events, [and] it is also connected
             topologically with the star imagery near the end of *Wise Blood*."
             Discusses the lack of historical details of Motes's military background,
             and surmises that O'Connor does so "perhaps to suggest that Hazel
             Motes's situation is universal." Submits that the "two deserts" that Motes
             referred to are probably the battle for North Africa during World War II
             and the convalescent centers set up for the wounded located--in among
             other places--Palestine. Recognizes that O'Connor avoided specific textual
             clues, but believes that the suggested speculation may be further
             supported by the image of the star of Bethlehem seen by Motes near the
             end of the novel.

1445 Smith, Peter A. "Flannery O'Connor's Empowered Women." *Southern Literary Journal* 26.2 (1994): 35-47.

Challenges Mary L. Morton's contention that O'Connor's female characters in "A Circle in the Fire," "The Displaced Person," and "Greenleaf" deny their femininity. Asserts instead that they exploit it, "sometimes to the point that they seem to be parodying it." Acknowledges that while these women may appear unlikable, they still "all deserve credit for employing a clever strategy in attempting to survive in a man's world while essentially manless, and all deserve sympathy because they are faced with an impossible task in having to synthesize aspects of both gender roles in order to maintain their livelihoods." Suggests that they are justified in their use of the role of "Southern lady" as well as in the use of a masculine management style because of their common, dire economic situation. Offers readings of the stories focusing on the principal female characters, and asserts that "in the end, Mrs. Cope, Mrs. McIntyre and Mrs. May wind up losing their hold on the `places' they had managed to grab from the patriarchy because they ultimately fail to fully synthesize the necessary aspects of both traditional gender roles." Concludes that perhaps these stories are "commentaries upon the impossibility of a woman in this society successfully negotiating her way through a patriarchal power structure."

1446 Smith, Sheron. "Inauguration Poet Once Lived in Macon." *Macon* (GA) *Telegraph* 14 Jan. 1997: A1, A4.

Profiles and offers quotes from a telephone interview of, S. Miller Williams, who joined Robert Frost and Maya Angelou "as the only poets invited by U.S. presidents to compose Inauguration Day poems." Williams recounts that "one of his fondest memories . . . was getting to meet Flannery O'Connor at her Baldwin County farm."

1447 Snodgrass, Mary Ellen. "O'Connor, Flannery." *Encyclopedia of Southern Literature*. Santa Barbara, CA: ABC-CLIO, 1997. 237-40.

Describes O'Connor as a "tough-minded, unsentimental spokeswoman for the relentless seeker and an unapologetic explicator of the doctrine of human limitation." Contends that as "a purveyor of ugliness, grim retribution, and unforseen epiphanies, she achieved a remarkably high position among authors of psychological fiction and black humor." Regards O'Connor as "a visionary of the fragmented family, sullied Southern gentility, and destabilized society that preceded integration." Suggests that O'Connor's stories "profess the power of redemptive suffering, which she regularly inflict[s] on her characters." Includes a review of her childhood in Savannah and Milledgeville, a summary of major events in her personal life and career, and a list of her writings.

1448   Solotaroff, Theodore. "The Development of Flannery O'Connor." *The Red Hot Vacuum and Other Writing on the Sixties*. Boston: Nonpareil, 1979. 171-77.

Essay which describes O'Connor as one who was probably caught between Southern social realms. Sees her work as influenced by her position as a "misfit." Argues that the characters in her work have Southern speech, dress, and manners, but "their real existence is meant to lie in the eternal mysteries of sin and redemption, which they grotesquely and usually blindly enact." Remarks that the works address the conflicts of the South and transcend them.

1449   Sommer, Elyse and Mike, eds. *Similes Dictionary*. Detroit: Gale, 1988.

Offers copious citations of O'Connor's similes with a subject organization. Indexes by subject and author, but without reference to particular source.

1450   Spalding, Phinizy. "Why Atlanta Ain't Georgia." *Georgia Journal* 14.3 (1994): 61-62.

Discusses Georgia's "rural cultural roots" and contends that those "out-of-state people, unfamiliar with Georgia's past, [who] single out O'Connor as an anomaly in the state's culture" are wrong. Suggests, instead, that "no example could be less accurate." Argues that O'Connor, a "deceptively simple Georgia girl, an ardent Roman Catholic in the midst of a sea of Protestant sects, was [as] at home in Baldwin County as even the most frenetic Pentecostal or illuminated charismatic." Refers to O'Connor's forebears "associated with that little Roman Catholic enclave in Wilkes County, Locust Grove." Mentions Erskine Caldwell's Jeeter Lester, and compares Jeeter to O'Connor's characters. Offers a variety of examples of rural Georgia's offerings of culture and declares that these outlying regions have far more to offer that anything one might find in Atlanta.

1451   Spaltro, Kathleen. "When We Dead Awaken: Flannery O'Connor's Debt to Lupus." *Flannery O'Connor Bulletin* 20 (1991): 33-44.

Focuses on O'Connor's indebtedness to Lupus. Asserts that she had a deep understanding of suffering through this disease and that her views on her disability provide readers with a better understanding of her writings.

Suggests that O'Connor's belief that suffering and death are "necessary precipitants" for spiritual growth "governed her fictional use of disability and of the grotesque to depict spiritual deadness and awakening." Discusses the influence of Pierre Teilhard de Chardin's writings (such as *The Divine Milieu)* as seen in her "Introduction" to *A Memoir of Mary Ann*. Takes issue with Josephine Hendin and Clara Claiborne Park on O'Connor's reaction to suffering, stating that by focusing on O'Connor's "repression and denial, they not only misread her struggle as a disabled woman but, disjoining her art from her life, misread her stories as well." Proposes that "O'Connor's sense that we are all inherently grotesque did not simply point to our penchant for evil but derived from her belief that our destiny [is] to evolve further by accepting grace." Claims that "encounters in `A Temple of the Holy Ghost,' `Good Country People,' and `The Lame Shall Enter First' dramatize the distorted attitude toward disabled people held by physically normal people." Concludes with O'Connor's caution that "we must not `grieve for the wrong reason, for the wrong loss,' for, from the perspective of spiritual evolution, the refusal to accept unavoidable suffering creates the real loss and the real horror."

1452   Spears, Monroe K. *American Ambitions: Selected Essays on Literary and Cultural Themes.* Baltimore: Johns Hopkins UP, 1987. 187, 221, 225, 232, 249.

Contains passing references to Flannery O'Connor, most notably the suggestion that O'Connor's "grimly humorous satiric realism, which shades into the grotesque and fantastic" may be reflected in the work of some Southern artists; and, the inclusion of O'Connor's name among those writers who have portrayed black dialects in their writing.

1453   "The Special Flannery O'Connor Course." *Flannery O'Connor Bulletin* 5 (1976): 29.

Announces that the 1977 "Flannery O'Connor Course offered at Georgia College during the summers" would be taught by James A. Grimshaw, Jr. Reports that the course had been taught in the past by Stuart Burns, Sarah Gordon, Sister Kathleen Feeley, and J.O. Tate, and provides a brief two sentence description of Grimshaw's background and interests.

1454   Speigel, Blaine. "The Revealing Light: A Photographic Essay." *Flannery O'Connor Bulletin* 24 (1995-96): 76.

Offers five photographs with a short introduction "commissioned as a visual arts component for the Flannery O'Connor symposium held in

Toronto, Canada on March 22-24, 1996 at Bloor Street United Church."
Speigel comments on how "time and again" he is "struck by O'Connor's
attention to the quality of light--visionary and revelatory" in her work.
Suggests that her "every character, landscape, and emotion seems sharply
contrasted with shades and colors." The photographs are titled: "Seared
Impression," "A Sheep in the Midst of Wolves," "Ripeness Is All,"
"Landscape of the Infinite," and "Who Will Remain Whole."

1455   Spivey, Ted R. "Beyond Diabolism: Flannery O'Connor's Religious
Existentialism." *The Journey Beyond Tragedy: A Study of Myth and
Modern Fiction*. Orlando: U Presses of Florida, 1980. 139-47.

Contends that O'Connor "was a great artist who mastered the tradition of
modern symbolism through a patient study of two important masters of
the symbolist novel, [Georges] Bernanos and [François] Mauriac, and
because she based her work firmly on philosopical and theological
traditions." Notes her familiarity with the writings of such existentialists
as Sören Kierkegaard and Martin Buber, and submits that she was one of
the few writers capable of utilizing both a keen intellect and an abundant
imagination "to create some of the most powerful literary symbols in
contemporary literature." Discusses "the symbolic power" of her fiction,
focusing on how her characters must overcome diabolical influences in
order to gain God's grace. Explicates and offers examples from "The
Lame Shall Enter First," *The Violent Bear It Away*, and "A Good Man Is
Hard to Find." Concludes that not only is the power of O'Connor's work
"greater than that found in her two mentors'" (Bernanos and Mauriac), but
she is "the most important fiction writer working in the Christian tradition
in the contemporary period, if not indeed in the entire century." Refers to
remarks by Stanley Edgar Hyman, Walker Percy, and Robert Drake.

1456   Spivey, Ted R. "The Complex Gifts of Flannery O'Connor." *Essays in
Arts & Sciences* 14 (May 1985): 49-58.

Suggests that O'Connor was the South's second greatest writer and recalls
Walker Percy's comment that he, O'Connor, and Faulkner are writers of
three different time periods. Discusses why her literary influence is less
than that of other Southern literary greats--Faulkner, Wolfe--and more
than that of Nathanael West. Follows with a biographical recounting of
letters, anecdotes, etc. which portray O'Connor as God-centered, complex,
and having a keen sense of language and its power.

1457   Spivey, Ted R. "Editor's Comment." *Studies in the Literary Imagination*
20.2 (1987): 1-3.

Serves as an introduction to a special issue devoted to O'Connor. Asserts that the essays "all make the point in various ways that Flannery O'Connor is a writer of both imaginative power and mental and emotional complexity." Observes that O'Connor was also one "who was fictionally involved in the lives of various kinds of Southerners."

1458   Spivey, Ted R. "Flannery O'Connor, James Joyce, and the City." *Studies in the Literary Imagination* 20.2 (1987): 87-95.

Suggests that two aspects of O'Connor's work often overlooked are the influence of James Joyce, who "opened the door to modernism" for her, and "the meaning of the two kinds of Southern cities she writes about." The first type of city, like Savannah, Georgia, "represent[s] the order and dignity of an earlier Southern culture still hanging on." The second, like Atlanta, represents the sprawling city still seeking order and direction as part of a journey to a new order of things.

1459   Spivey, Ted R. "Flannery O'Connor: Prophetic Pilgrimage to Atlanta." *Revival: Southern Writers in the Modern City*. Gainesville: U of Florida P, 1986. 155-74.

Discusses O'Connor's life, literary career, writings, and religious and artistic legacy. Sees her characters as "caught up in a violent reaction to the general decline of cultural values" as they "stalk the city searching for new religious and social values that will turn it into a true community again." Finds her characters and letters to reflect a message of renewal, "not by remembering the past but by seeking new visions [based upon God] that cultural life will be revived." Offers a reading of *Wise Blood* and other stories with a fanatical protagonist encountering the city to bring forth "the repressed Christ in the unconscious mind." Acknowledges her debt to T.S. Eliot and James Joyce for the complexity of her religious insight. Argues that Hazel Motes incarnates O'Connor's belief that "fanaticism is the result of a religion cut off from a sustained rational Christian teaching," and sees Mrs. Flood as embodying "urban chaos and lovelessness." Discusses her expressed favorite story "The Artificial Nigger," stating "it is possibly her strongest depiction of the appearance of grace in ordinary life, and fittingly, the epiphany happens in Atlanta."

1460   Spivey, Ted R. "Flannery O'Connor, the New Criticism, and Deconstruction." *Southern Review* 23.2 (1987): 271-80.

Calls for more effective criticism concerning "the many aspects of meaning" in O'Connor's work. Says O'Connor was an intertextual critic long before deconstructive criticism, and argues by discussing O'Connor's belief that "everyone" needed to be taught how to read a text, just as deconstructionists believe "everyone" may bring meaning to a text. Discusses his correspondence with O'Connor concerning an essay he wrote/published on what he calls O'Connor's novella, "The Lame Shall Enter First." Shows how, though trained as a new critic, he gained valuable insight into O'Connor's work through biographical and deconstructive approaches.

1461   Spivey, Ted R. "Flannery O'Connor's Quest For a Critic." *Flannery O'Connor Bulletin* 15 (1986): 29-33.

Relates reasons for writing his article, "Flannery's South: Don Quixote Rides Again," published in the first issue of the *Flannery O'Connor Bulletin*, and his book *Southern Writers in the Modern City*. States that O'Connor's theme of humanity's search for religious values, "calls for much more critical attention than it has yet received." Further asserts that O'Connor was in search of a critic "who could see her work in terms of the actual experience of her time and her region." Suggests that because reviewers often misunderstand her work, O'Connor needed a critic who could explain her work in such a manner that she, herself, could "by looking at it through another's eyes, understand more of her own meaning and of her struggle to write." Quotes from a letter to the author written by O'Connor related to his own interpretation of "The Lame Shall Enter First." Indicates that her satisfaction with his views were personally meaningful and relates his subsequent successful publication effort. Concludes that works by both O'Connor and Faulkner, "await a new generation of critics who will evaluate their work judiciously and place it in the context of their thought and total life experience." Refers to comments by Jonathan Culler and O'Connor's correspondence to and from "A," Andrew Lytle, and Robert Lowell.

1462   Spivey, Ted R. "Flannery O'Connor's Vision of the Renewal of Community." *Proceedings of the Kanuga Conference for Faculty Episcopalians February 16-18, 1990.* Ed. Manning M. Pattillo, Jr. Hendersonville, NC: Kanuga Conferences, 1990. 13-21.

Discusses how stories in *Everything That Rises Must Converge* reflect the emergence of O'Connor's "apocalyptic vision of true community." Notes that while she continues with her "theme of the violent destruction of old, paralyzed worlds," the stories also demonstrate her "new sense of the renewing of a life grounded not in hate but . . . in a sympathy achieved through a renewal of community." Refers to comments by Joyce Carol Oates, Alice Walker, and Thomas Merton, on O'Connor's fiction and discusses the influence of Teilhard de Chardin's writings upon O'Connor. Follows with explications of "Revelation," "The Enduring Chill," and "Parker's Back," noting Teilhard's influence on these stories. Concludes that not only did O'Connor's "continuing interest in and the use of the ideas of Teilhard de Chardin suggest . . . that she had a romantic side that she never fully came to grips with," but it gave force to "one of the great themes at the end of her life . . . the need for a social renewal beyond the obsessive materialistic kind of Cartesian control she often satirizes."

1463   Sprieser, Martha Bell. "Flannery O'Connor in Front of the Currier Graduate House. Iowa City, February, 1947." *Flannery O'Connor Bulletin* 12 (1983): 67.

A reproduction of a photograph of Flannery O'Connor standing in front of the Currier Graduate House in Iowa City, February, 1947, courtesy of Martha Bell Sprieser. Notes that Sprieser was O'Connor's roommate at the University of Iowa.

1464   Springsteen, Bruce. "The Rolling Stone Interview: Bruce Springsteen." Interview by Kurt Loder. *Rollingstone* (6 Dec. 1984): 18-19+.

Springsteen comments in passing on his admiration for Flannery O'Connor's fiction, which he was reading while writing songs for his *Nebraska* and *The River* albums. Finds her fiction to be "just incredible."

1465   Springsteen, Bruce. "Springsteen." Interview by Kurt Loder. *Rollingstone* (Oct. 15, 1992): 130-32.

Springsteen talks about his album, *Born In the USA*, the success of his record sales and tours, the impact of becoming "a rich man," and "the danger of fame." Comments in passing on his admiration for Flannery O'Connor's fiction.

1466   Stadelman, Catherine. "O'Connor, (Mary) Flannery 1925-64." *Contemporary Authors: A Bio-Bibliographical Guide to Current Writers in Fiction, General Nonfiction, Poetry, Journalism, Drama, Motion Pictures, Television, and Other Fields*. New Rev. Series. Vol. 3. Ed. Ann Evory. Detroit: Gale Research, 1981. 402-04.

Bibliographical article on O'Connor, including a short biography, summary of her career, and listing of bibliographical sources. Includes critical commentary by: David Eggenschwiler, A.L. Rowse, Stanley

Edgar Hyman, Ted R. Spivey, Preston M. Browning, Jr., Claire Katz, Richard Poirer, Brainard Cheney, James Degan, Robert Fitzgerald, Melvin Friedman, Walter Sullivan, and Granville Hicks. An abridged version of this article appears in *Major 20th-Century Writers: A Selection of Sketches From Contemporary Authors*. Detroit: Gale Research, 1991. 2215-17. [Consult the cumulative index of this set to locate other articles related to O'Connor in other volumes and in predecessors of this title published by the same company.]

1467   Stanciu, Tanya. "Following Flannery." *Gadfly* Dec. 1998: 21, 54.

Interview of artist Laura Lasworth in question-and-answer format regarding her Flannery O'Connor-related paintings. Lasworth remarks on how easily O'Connor's stories lend themselves to artistic interpretation but details the difficulty she had in transforming images from the stories to canvas. As well, she comments on how her own Catholic beliefs have influenced her artistic perspective and career. [The previous article in this issue, "Crying in the Wilderness: The Life and Work of Flannery O'Connor," by Stanley Booth, is illustrated with photographs of four of Lasworth's paintings: "Lucette, The Child Prophetess," "Portrait of Flannery O'Connor, 1997," "Bishop," and "Dark Spot Between Two Chimneys, 1997."]

1468   Stanley, Roger. "The Efficacy of Grace in O'Connor and Cather." *Literature and Belief* 17.1-2 (1997): 259-70.

Suggests that Flannery O'Connor and Willa Cather shared a "determination to preserve basic theological orientation against the grain of their century" by seeking "to create protagonists imbued with either the power to suffuse others with grace or be radically altered by it." Outlines each writer's religious background and orientation, and discusses how each used "the grace/deliverance motif" to reflect her "theological worldview." Examines O'Connor's "A Good Man Is Hard to Find," "The Turkey," and "Wildcat," along with Cather's "Neighbor Rosicky," "Lou, the Prophet," "Eric Hermannson's Soul," "The Joy of Nelly Deane," and *Sapphira and the Slave Girl* to illustrate how each writer "bestowed gifts of grace." Suggests that O'Connor saw her central characters "as, like the secular humanist reader of the twentieth century, suffused with apathy toward the Word and matters of spirituality." Contends that she sought to "to jolt the grandmother" in "A Good Man Is Hard to Find," and "travelers (readers) like her, out of a fixation upon heritage and appearances," and into situations where they must choose whether or not to accept God's grace as offered.

1469   Stanton, William F. "Flannery O'Connor: A Biographical Analysis."
            Chronicle of Academic and Artistic Precocity 2.2 (1983): 7.

            Refers to a description of O'Connor in the March 3, 1979 issue of *New
            Republic* (pp. 33-35), lists her awards and publications, and offers a
            biographical sketch based upon other published sources noted in the
            references. The author, a "teacher of academically talented sixth graders"
            working on a Master's Degree in Education of the Gifted, then focuses on
            O'Connor's personality, her precocious and independent nature, her
            "disconcerting imagination," and her "capacity for doing the unexpected."
            Describes O'Connor's battle with Disseminated Lupus and concludes that
            while some critics may consider her output meager, "when one considers
            the pain and troubles she experienced the work . . . becomes monumental
            in proportion." [Rpt. as *ERIC* document ED 247 730.]

1470   Staton, Shirley F., ed. *Literary Theories in Praxis*. Philadelphia: U of
            Pennsylvania P, 1987.

            Offers forty-four reprinted essays as examples of "nine different types of
            contemporary criticism." Uses these to demonstrate "the ways in which
            critical theories are transformed into literary criticism and methodology."
            Three of the forty-four essays and excerpts deal with O'Connor's fiction:

            May, John R. "The Parables of Flannery O'Connor." Rpt. from *The
            Pruning Word: The Parables of Flannery O'Connor*. Notre Dame: U of
            Notre Dame P, 1976. ["Phenomenological Criticism"]. *See* entry 60.

            McFarland, Dorothy T. "Flannery O'Connor's `Revelation.'" Rpt. from
            "Chapter 3: `Everything That Rises Must Converge,'" in *Flannery
            O'Connor*. NY: Frederick Ungar, 1976. ["New Criticism"]. *See* entry 62.

            Muller, Gilbert H. "Flannery O'Connor and the Catholic Grotesque." Rpt.
            from *Nightmares and Visions: Flannery O'Connor and the Catholic
            Grotesque*. Athens: U of Georgia P, 1972. ["Archetypal and Genre
            Criticism"]. *See* Robert E. Golden's *Guide* 1972.A3.

1470a   Stefaniak, Mary Helen. "A Note to Biographers Regarding Famous Author
            Flannery O'Connor." *New Stories From the South: The Year's Best, 2000*.
            Ed. Shannon Ravenel. Chapel Hill, NC: Algonquin Books, 2000. 1-15.

            Offers a fictional recollection of a doctoral student who has written and
            burns a draft of a dissertation about O'Connor's encounter with the
            student's mother and Aunt Mimi. Uses the two as a foil to describe
            O'Connor's background, personality and interest in the grotesque.

1471   Stein, Rita. *A Literary Tour Guide to the United States: South and Southwest*. New York: William Morrow, 1979. 51-61.

Description of Southern cities and states, particularly Georgia, with reference to O'Connor in the introduction to the state. Also includes a brief biography of O'Connor under the section "Milledgeville" and mentions her four major works of fiction.

1472   Stelzmann, Rainulf A. "Two Unpublished Letters by Flannery O'Connor." *Xavier Review* 5.1-2 (1985): 49-50.

Discusses two short letters from O'Connor to the author, both of which suggest that he "broke new ground" in two articles he had written about her work. Reports that O'Connor enthusiastically approved of the interpretations and includes edited versions of the letters.

1473   Stephens, Martha. "Flannery O'Connor (1925-1964)." *Fifty Southern Writers After 1900: A Bio-Bibliographical Sourcebook*. Ed. Joseph M. Flora and Robert Bain. New York: Greenwood, 1987. 334-44.

Provides a short biographical sketch, primarily concerned with major themes of O'Connor's stories and novels, noting in many cases her own explanations. Includes a short bibliography and survey of criticism. Highlights her relationships with various literary personages, stints at Yaddo, friendship with the Fitzgeralds, and focuses on how these relationships may have influenced the writing of her novels and short story collections. Traces major themes that O'Connor said were central to her stories--the Eucharist, the presence of grace--and calls particular attention to specific works, including: "The Artificial Nigger," "The Life You Save May Be Your Own," "Revelation," "A Circle in the Fire," and "Greenleaf." Both the survey of criticism and bibliography offer little more than brief notation.

1474   Stephenson, Will and Mimosa. "Ruby Turpin: O'Connor's Travesty of the Ideal Woman." *Flannery O'Connor Bulletin* 24 (1995-96): 57-66.

Suggests that "in depicting Mrs. Turpin's self-satisfaction" in "Revelation," O'Connor "leans even more heavily on the Bible than has yet been pointed out." Contends that the biblical allusion which most "informs and gives structure" to this story is "the encomium on the ideal woman in *Proverbs* 31." Provides an explication of the story, discusses symbols in the text (eg. the sun for Christ and trees as the mystery of God's grace), and ties Mrs. Turpin to the "ideal woman" described in

Proverbs. Argues that Mrs. Turpin "is a comic version of the biblical original," one who "must learn that her price is not as great as she dreams it to be." Sees Mrs. Turpin's "compulsion for cleanliness" as a symbol of her belief that she can be made righteous by "good deeds." Adds that Mrs. Turpin lacks compassion and appears to do good deeds more from self-interest than from any other pure motive. Closes with a discussion of Mrs. Turpin's "spiritual defiance with the allusion to Baltassar." Refers to comments by Jill P. Baumgaertner, Ronald Emerick, Forrest L. Ingram, and Sura P. Rath.

1475   Stern, Daniel. "An Ambitious New Series Brings the American Short Story to TV." *New York Times* 3 Apr. 1977, sec. 3: 33.

Discusses how Arthur Barron, a documentary filmmaker, and Robert Geller, a former executive with the American Film Institute, undertook and completed a $2 million project for the National Endowment for the Humanities (NEH) to present "a six-part series" of short stories "under the umbrella title of `The American Short Story.'" Reports how ten distinguished scholars were selected and each asked to submit a list of 25 short stories that "were truly representative of the form, as well as being able to convey a sense of historical, regional, and artistic development of [the past] 100 years." Outlines how this list was narrowed down--"in the classic manner of prize juries"--to the six selected, including O'Connor's "The Displaced Person." Illustrated with a photograph of John Houseman and Irene Worth acting out a scene from the story.

1476   Stewart, Michelle Pagni. "A Good Trickster Is Hard to Find: A Refiguring of Flannery O'Connor." *Short Story* 3.1 (1995): 77-83.

Compares O'Connor's "A Good Man Is Hard to Find" with Harvest Moon Eyes's "The Day the Crows Stopped Talking," to demonstrate how "teaching ethnic stories in conjunction with more traditional stories can encourage students to rethink notions of culture and difference" and help to "make them aware of how thin the line is between canonical and noncanonical" literature. Discusses each story, focusing on the background, characters, and similarities, including: how the main character of each (the grandmother and Sky) are outsiders in their respective communities; how both refer to the importance of uncommon blood; and, how "while it seems that both The Misfit and Tom Crow have good intentions, in the end both show their self-serving sides, which allows them to do whatever it takes to make their schemes successful." Notes that Tom Crow's name ties him to traditional Native American raven stories and trickster legends, and The Misfit "has resonances of the trickster figure, even though O'Connor did not set out to create one."

1477   Stokes, David. "Grit, Grace and Miss O'Connor." *Theology* 80 (March 1977): 107-10.

Argues that O'Connor integrates manners and mystery--her names for nature and grace--and creates a fictional mode of "doing theology." The author feels critics erroneously separate theory and practice and, thus, misinterpret her fiction. Argues that O'Connor's Southernness and Roman Catholicism are married in a fiction that does not perpetuate dogma, but which credits "the whole man" of the South as being primarily theological. Discusses "The Enduring Chill" in these terms, and ends by pointing to several conclusions about Christian apologetics, humor and seriousness, and natural order.

1478   Stone, John. "The Wolf Inside." *In The Country of Hearts: Journeys in the Heart of Medicine*. New York: Delacorte, 1990. 57-64.

Describes the Lupus of one of his current patients as background to discussion of O'Connor's case. Classifies O'Connor's case as severe, and discusses the efforts her physician, Dr. Arthur J. Merrill, put forth to save her life. Remarks that "Lupus betrayed Flannery O'Connor like a sophisticated Trojan Horse, one with a wolf inside. Once within the body's gates, the enemy was everywhere . . . her life and work are a study in keeping on keeping on." [Rpt. in *The New York Times Magazine* 3 April 1988: 40-41.]

1479   Stoneback, H.R. "'Sunk in the Cornfield with His Family': Sense of Place in O'Connor's `The Displaced Person.'" *Mississippi   Quarterly* 36.4 (1983): 545-55.

Discusses the sense of place in O'Connor's fiction and argues that she does not, as some critics imply, share the "implicit values generally perceived as flowing from typically Southern topophilia." Calls attention to O'Connor's objection to becoming a "regional" writer and her comments about the writer's "true country, the place where time and place and eternity somehow meet." Discusses the theme of journeying into the true country in "The Displaced Person." Argues that Mrs. Shortley is truly an antichrist figure, though she is, in terms of place, an "earth-mother" figure. Mentions other characters (for example, the judge) who are directly and ironically opposites of other Southern place heros.

1480   Stonehill, Brian. "Memory, The Lens to Look at Life." *Los Angeles Times Book Review* 14 Aug. 1983: 5.

Reviews Andre Dubus's *The Times Are Never So Bad: A Novella and Eight Short Stories* (Godine, 1983) and comments on similarities between his fiction and O'Connor's. Reports that Dubus's "handsome fourth collection of fiction bears an epigraph about violence from Flannery O'Connor," then comments that he "resembles the great Southern gothic writer [O'Connor] in his power, [and] ability to command our attention." Suggests that he "resembles O'Connor, too, in his concern with matters spiritual," as "even more explicitly than she, he focuses on the place of faith and grace in a Catholic heart."

1481   Streight, Irwin Howard. "A Good Hypogram Is Not Hard to Find." *Literature and Belief* 17.1-2 (1997): 231-41.

Describes Michael Riffaterre's theory of the *hypogram* and suggests that O'Connor employs these absent words or phrases that have a generative effect on the text, along with "literalizing or dramatizing the figurative truths of clichés and metaphors," as fictional strategies in her stories. Contends that for O'Connor, who "uses language `incarnationally,' the hypogram abides in the heaven of the `added dimension' . . . manifest in her stories, from which the Word/word as Logos (meaning) has come down to the lexical and semantic terrain of the text." Offers readings which "examine the generative effects and hermeneutic significance of critically recognized and easily recognizable hypograms" in "Revelation" and "Good Country People." Includes in this examination, a discussion of the symbolism and significance of the sun, hogs and the term "hogwash" in "Revelation"; and of Hulga's "false leg," as a "`low joke'" and emblematic of her "very soul and self" in "Good Country People." Concludes that recognizing O'Connor's use of hypograms points the reader beyond the text and directs and enables the interpretation of meaning in her stories.

1482   Streight, Irwin Howard. "Is There a Text in This Man?: A Semiotic Reading of `Parker's Back.'" *Flannery O'Connor Bulletin* 22 (1993-94): 1-11.

Claims that the "truth of O'Connor's fiction, its mystery, is most accessible by way of a semiotic approach." Refers to O'Connor's essay "Some Aspects of the Grotesque in Southern Fiction," and discusses how "the word informs" her work. Offers a detailed reading of "Parker's Back," a story "about signs and signification, about encountering the multifold texts that need to be interpreted and the difficulties and ambiguities of interpretation." Focuses on how Parker's life has been "determined by his responses to a series of epiphanies," and how the word "`look' stresses Parker's need to move from the intuitive . . . into a sign system that is representational." Declares that Parker's whole life "is written in the text of his tattoos, and it is vital to the meaning of O'Connor's story to understand that Parker's tattoos are signs that he has *embodied*." Contends that the Byzantine Christ tattooed to his back is both a literary joke and a signifier whose meaning points toward Christ being rubbed--literally--into his flesh. Explores the significance of Parker's name and why he "has attempted to negate the presence of his true self in the initials he goes by." Argues that "the text of Parker's body is consecrated by the tattoo of Christ. A `marked' man all his life, Parker is marked with the sign of Christ, objectifying the Christian mystery that he is Christ." Concludes that "Parker's Back" is "in every sense of the word, the apotheosis of O'Connor's incarnational art."

1483   Strickland, Binky. "*Flannery O'Connor Bulletin* Celebrates Silver Anniversary." *GC&SU Connection: The Magazine for GC&SU Alumni and Friends* 90.1 (1999): 8-9.

Recounts the early history of the *Flannery O'Connor Bulletin* and the role of its editors during the scholarly journal's twenty-five year publication run. Includes quotes from Sarah Gordon, the *Bulletin*'s present editor.

1484   Strickland, Binky. "O'Connor Collection to Be Preserved." *Milledgeville (GA) Union-Recorder* 14 Sept. 1990: A1, A6.

Describes the project to preserve 6,000 pages of O'Connor's manuscripts, including drafts of *Wise Blood*, portions of *The Violent Bear It Away*, early works as a student, and most of her short stories. The National Endowment for the Humanities (NEH) approved a $29,250 grant with another $15,000 in a matching grant. Total estimated cost for the project is $87,000, and will include photocopying, treating, microfilming, and encasing the manuscripts in protective covering. Most of the manuscripts were donated to the collection in 1970 by Flannery O'Connor's mother, Regina Cline O'Connor.

1485   Strickland, Edward. "The Penitential Quest in `The Artificial Nigger.'" *Studies in Short Fiction* 25.4 (1988): 453-59.

Argues that contrary to Louis D. Rubin's analysis, the "tone of revelation in the ending" of "The Artificial Nigger" is not intended to be amusing. This story is instead, "the closest thing we have in O'Connor to specifically Catholic allegory." Refers to O'Connor's comment, "what I had in mind to suggest with the artificial nigger was the redemptive quality of the Negro's suffering for us all."

1486   Strine, Mary S. "Narrative Strategy and Communicative Design in Flannery O'Connor's *The Violent Bear it Away*." *Studies in Interpretation.* Ed. Esther M. Doyle and Virginia Hastings Floyd. Vol. 2. Amsterdam: Rodopi, 1977. 45-57.

Argues against the criticism to date of *The Violent Bear It Away* which has discussed its "improbable plot and irresponsible characters." Also argues against favorable criticism which concerns itself merely with theme rather than with what the novel is "doing." Says the novel is a "narrative transaction with a unique communicative structure . . . a structure which involves the functional inter-relationships of three formal elements: plot or action, character, and thought or theme and framed within a rhetorical situation uniting author and reader." Discusses this synthesis in the novel, which evolves from shifting points of view and the three types of narration: objective observation, limited omniscience, and conjectural commentary.

1487   Stuckey, William J. "Recent Books on Women Writers of the American South." *Modern Fiction Studies* 28.3 (1982): 507-18.

Offers a review essay of thirteen books published between 1979 and 1982 concerned with the life and writings of Ellen Glasgow, Eudora Welty, Carson McCullers, and Flannery O'Connor. Seven books related to O'Connor are discussed: Barbara McKenzie's *Flannery O'Connor's Georgia*; Lorine M. Getz's *Flannery O'Connor: Her Life, Library, and Book Reviews*; James A. Grimshaw, Jr.'s *The Flannery O'Connor Companion*; Marion Montgomery's *Why Flannery O'Connor Stayed Home*; Carol Shloss's *Flannery O'Connor's Dark Comedies: The Limits of Inference*; Robert Coles's *Flannery O'Connor's South*; and, Frederick Asals's *Flannery O'Connor: The Imagination of Extremity*. Of the lot, Stuckey finds Asals's work to be "the best book yet written" on O'Connor.

1488   Sturma, Lee. "Flannery O'Connor, Simone Weil, and the Virtue of Necessity." *Studies in the Literary Imagination* 20.2 (1987): 109-21.

Contends that O'Connor acknowledged that her character Hulga Hopewell in "Good Country People" reflected characteristics of both herself and Simone Weil. Observes that "Both Weil and O'Connor encountered crises of limitation in their lives" which "focused on personal issues of isolation and identity." O'Connor's lupus restricted her mobility and "turned her from an independent, aspiring young author into an invalid semi-confined to her mother's farm." States that while O'Connor came to terms with her situation in a positive way, Weil was unable to do so, and this inability led to her death.

1489   Sullivan, Richard. "Richard Weaver and the Bishop's Widow: A
            Cautionary Tale." *Southern Literary Journal* 20.2 (1988): 112-20.

Offers a discussion of Southern culture and the Agrarian movement in the
guise of an essay review of *The Southern Essays of Richard Weaver*,
edited by George M. Curtis, III and James J. Thompson, Jr., and Marion
Montgomery's *Possum and Other Receits for the Recovery of "Southern"
Being*. Includes discussions of: Montgomery's admiration for those
writers, such as Flannery O'Connor, who are Southerners "by birth as well
as by conviction"; the ability of O'Connor and Allen Tate to combine
Catholic and Southern traditions in their art; and, why Walker Percy's
themes, unlike those of O'Connor, William Faulkner, and Eudora Welty,
are somewhat "undeveloped."

1490   Sullivan, Walter. "About Any Kind of Meanness You Can Name."
            Sewanee Review 93.4 (1985): 649-56.

Reviews Lewis W. Green's *The Silence of Snakes*, William Hoffman's
Godfires, and Cormac McCarthy's *Blood Meridian or The Evening
Redness in the West*. Considers the influence of Flannery O'Connor upon
these and other contemporary fiction writers to be "remarkable,"
suggesting that "half of the people publishing stories today try to copy her
down-home style and her sense of the grotesque, and a good many try to
mimic her gift for writing about violence." Refers to O'Connor's view of
"good and evil" and sees similarities in their purpose for writing fiction
between O'Connor and Cormac McCarthy.

1491   Sullivan, Walter. "Rainbow's End." *A Requiem for the Renascence: The
            State of Fiction in the Modern South*. Mercer U Lamar Memorial
            Lectures, No. 18. Athens: U of Georgia P, 1976. 50-74.

Contends that the work of Southern writers who gained prominence
between World War I and II "diminishes in quality in the fifties and
sixties and early seventies." Discusses works by post-World War II
writers, Eudora Welty, Flannery O'Connor, Walker Percy, and Cormac
McCarthy in this context. Argues that this decline is based not upon the
loss of technical competence, but from living in a fragmented society
where "the uncertainty of the writer's moral vision is reflected in every
aspect of his artistic creation." Reflects upon the impact of "the decline of
myth and the dissolution of community . . . accompanied by a weakening
of moral certitude" on Welty's writing. Uses this discussion as a
springboard into O'Connor's approach: use of the grotesque to create a
distorted world "outside a conventional social context." Discusses the
influence of "the Southern scene" and imagery on "The Displaced

Person," "A Good Man Is Hard to Find," "The Enduring Chill," *The Violent Bear It Away*, and *Everything That Rises Must Converge*. Contends that after 1955, O'Connor's stories moved away from being "strictly Southern," and became "more concerned with her quarrel against the modern world and its prevailing temper, which she took to be destructively gnostic."

1492   Sullivan, Walter. "Southern Writers in Spiritual Exile." *Praise of Blood Sports and Other Essays*. Baton Rouge: Louisiana State UP, 1990. 38-48.

Refers to O'Connor's work and compares it with that of Bobbie Ann Mason. Finds both writers to have similar styles as they both consider similar situations. Regards Mason's technical virtuosity equal to O'Connor's" with the essential difference being only in their "moral commitment and religious belief." States that Cormac McCarthy appears "as if he has taken the advice of Flannery O'Connor's Misfit to do as much meanness as he can . . . [writing] like a fallen angel, lavishing on the most depraved of human actions his brilliant style, his consummate technique." Concludes that for the South's literary heritage to continue successfully, its literary artists must "recapture the sacred." [Rpt. in *The "Southern Review" and Modern Literature: 1935-1985*, edited by Lewis P. Simpson, James Olney, and Jo Gulledge (Baton Rouge: Louisiana State UP, 1988. 107-15). Updates an essay by the author entitled "Death by Melancholy" in a 1970 issue of *Southern Review*.]

1493   Sullivan, Walter. "Southerners in the City: Flannery O'Connor and Walker Percy." *The Comic Imagination in American Literature*. Ed. Louis D. Rubin. New Brunswick, NJ: Rutgers UP, 1973. 339-48.

Offers an introduction to Walker Percy and Flannery O'Connor through brief biographical notes and a discussion of *The Moviegoer* and "A Good Man Is Hard to Find." Points out O'Connor's use of superrealism, violence, and unconventional motivation, and discusses how she "searched continually for the good and evil that lurk in the depths of the human soul." Offers a close reading of "A Good Man Is Hard to Find" and follows with a discussion of *The Violent Bear It Away*. Concludes with a brief examination of "Good Country People" to illustrate that "the main differences between Walker Percy and Flannery O'Connor are temperamental and philosophical."

1494   Summer, Bob. "Collecting the Vast Brilliance of Flannery O'Connor." *Atlanta Journal-Constitution* 23 Oct. 1988: K8.

Notes comments about O'Connor by Alfred Kazin and Walter Clemons (*Newsweek*). Reviews *Flannery O'Connor: The Collected Works*, edited by Sally Fitzgerald, noting that it is the 39th volume of the Library of America series. Touts it as a collection which intersects the "outer realities of her fundamentalist, Bible Belt homeland . . . with the inner spiritual virtues of her Christendom." Notes that 21 of the 259 letters were previously unpublished and that the collection contains all the stories from her master's thesis. Discusses how, on account of the debilitating effects of lupus, O'Connor's used her region for fictive settings. Comments on O'Connor's aesthetic concerns with the writing process and ends with short comments on her novels, Walker Percy, and discussion of her lectures in which she outlined her artistic theories.

1495   Swan, Jesse G. "At the Edge of Sound and Silence: Conrad Aiken's `Senlin: A Biography' and `Silent Snow, Secret Snow.'" *Southern Literary Journal* 22.1 (1989): 41-49.

Compares the "tension" that Aiken sets up in these stories--where man is forced to accept or reject a usually vague, if not invisible, part of his being and world"--to Flannery O'Connor's "moments of grace." Refers to O'Connor's comment, "`There is a moment in every great story in which the presence of grace can be felt as it waits to be accepted or rejected, even though the reader may not recognize this moment.'" Finds that "Aiken's best work deals with such moments."

1496   Swan, Jesse G. "Flannery O'Connor's Silence-Centered World." *Flannery O'Connor Bulletin* 17 (1988): 82-89.

Finds "much of the power" of O'Connor's work to be based upon silence in her narratives. Suggests that if readers approach *The Violent Bear It Away* "silence-centrically--that is, if we realize that the novel privileges silence over words insomuch that the silences embody its meaning--we can discern two significantly distinct types of silences": secular silence and spiritual or divine silence. Sees this approach as enabling "readers to reconcile previously confusing parts without forfeiting any of the novel's mysterious power." Discusses the difficulty of "reading the silences," the distinction between the two types, and offers a reading of the novel in the context of these assertions. Finds "the silence" of Tarwater's words of revelation as providing"the mystery intrinsic to faith in a paradox, and our awareness of this silence elucidates the whole work."

1497   Swanson, Rollin A. "Truth Revealed in the Grotesque: The Writings of Flannery O'Connor." *Catholic Library World* 55.10 (1984): 449-51.

Examines the uniqueness of O'Connor's writings and points out her views of life and her themes. Suggests that her characters "take on a comic caricature-like dimension . . . as colorful as the brightly hued peacocks which surrounded O'Connor on her Georgia farm." Offers a biographical sketch and readings of "The Lame Shall Enter First," "Revelation," "The Artificial Nigger," "Parker's Back," and "The Displaced Person." Identifies some of O'Connor's dominant themes as "human lostness, misdirection, suffering and death." Remarks that she confronted the belief that an individual can be saved by good deeds alone, and addressed the problem of the human need to be freed from pride. Finds O'Connor's stories to be "neither moralistic tales or preachy sermons. They are like the parables of Jesus and must be heard." Concludes that it is "in the joy of the Gospel, boldly we celebrate with O'Connor and her people our human foolishness . . . Even in a world made grotesque by sin, she has proclaimed in her works that Jesus Christ is Lord."

1498   Sweeney, Gerard M. "O'Connor's *Wise Blood*." *Explicator* 56.2 (1998): 108-09.

Discusses the meaning behind O'Connor's description of Hazel Motes in *Wise Blood* as having "`a nose like a shrike's bill.'" Reports that the shrike, also referred to as "the butcher bird," impales its prey "on thorns and barbed wire, or wedges them in the forks of twigs." Suggests that O'Connor purposely chose this shrike imagery to foreshadow the scene in which Motes wraps barb wire around himself and is, "in some mysterious way, destined to wrap a metal `crown of thorns' around himself." Concludes that O'Connor's imagery conveys to readers Motes's inability to flee Christianity, and therefore "he cannot escape his destiny of becoming a true--albeit grotesque--type of Christ."

1499   Sweeney, Patricia, comp. *Women in Southern Literature: An Index*. New York: Greenwood, 1986. 7, 22, 26, 27, 28, 42, 43, 47, 48, 51, 52, 53, 57, 72, 78, 94.

Offers an index of female characters in Southern Literature listed by author, title and "categories" (eg. "Black Mammies," "Matriarchs," "Prostitutes," "Poor Whites," etc.) Gives descriptions of a variety of O'Connor's female characters, including: Mrs. Asbury and Mary George Asbury of "The Enduring Chill"; Sarah Ruth Cates of "Parker's Back"; Mrs. Connin of "The River"; Mrs. Pritchard, and Mrs. Cope and her twelve-year-old daughter, Miss Cope, of "A Circle in the Fire"; Mrs. Crater and her simple-minded daughter, Lucynell Crater, of "The Life You Save May Be Your Own"; Mrs. Flood, Leora Watts and and Sabbath Lily Hawks of *Wise Blood*; Mrs. Freeman of "Good Country People"; the

Grandmother in "A Good Man Is Hard to Find"; Mrs. Greenleaf of "Greenleaf"; Ruby Hill of "A Stroke of Good Fortune"; Joy-Hulga Hopewell of "Good Country People"; and, Julian's mother of "Everything That Rises Must Converge."

1500   Sweet, Glenda Y. "Old Testament Judgement Meets New Testament Grace in `Revelation.'" [16 pp.] Ms. *Flannery O'Connor Collection*, Russell Library, Georgia College & State University, Milledgeville, GA. November, 1995.

Argues that in her fiction, O'Connor seems to explore all Christian denominations in her desire to plumb the Christian Mystery. Through Ruby Turpin, the main character in "Revelation," O'Connor exposes the type of Christian who takes pride in doing for those who are in some ways "inferior." Contends that since she seems altogether unfamiliar with the New Testament concept of Grace, Ruby, as a type of Old Testament judge, metes out opinions similar to those offered to Job by his so-called friends. Having adopted the Hebrew concepts of ethnic background and prosperity as measurements of God's favor, Ruby feels it is her right and duty to rank people based, first, on skin color and, second, on wealth and outward appearance. Mary Grace, whose name and eyes identify her as a prophetess, is the only character who "sees right through" Ruby and who has the courage or the lack of social grace to say so. Concludes that after her blasphemous challenge to God, Ruby's macrocosmic vision at the end of the story is positive. By means of a heavenly revelation, God answers Ruby as he did Job--not directly but by showing her Divine Grace in action. (From author's abstract of a paper presented at the Flannery O'Connor 70th Birthday Symposium held at Brigham Young University, November 8-11, 1995.)

1501   Sweet-Hurd, Evelyn. "Finding O'Connor's Good Man." *Notes on Contemporary Literature* 14.3 (1984): 9-10.

Argues, in a highly unusual interpretation, that O'Connor's "good man" in "A Good Man Is Hard to Find" is the gasoline station--dance hall-- barbecue stand owner, Red Sammy Butts. The conclusion hinges on three points: the road signs, the name of the establishment ("The Tower") and the biblical allusion in the name of the town where the establishment is located (Timothy). The road signs contain statements such as "None like Famous Red Sammy" and "Sammy's Your Man," which Sweet-Hurd sees as authorial hints. Contends as well that there is a connection between the tower in *Piers Plowman* and Butts's store. Argues that these signs, along with O'Connor's hints in the dialogue between Red Sammy Butts and the grandmother, all point to Butts as the "good man" of the story.

1502   Swick, Thomas. "A Good Town Is Hard to Find." *Fort Lauderdale Sun-Sentinel* 30 June 1996: J1, J6.

Describes the city of Milledgeville, Georgia: its history, local sights, and features commentary on O'Connor. Discusses her reputation and interests and includes comments by Sarah Gordon, Nancy Bray, and O'Connor (from *The Habit of Being*). Includes an insert with information on lodging, restaurants, and sites to visit and photographs of Atkinson Hall of Georgia College & State University, the Cline-O'Connor house, and a slave's grave in Memory Hill Cemetery, where O'Connor is buried.

1503   Sykes, John. "Christian Apologetic Uses of the Grotesque in John Irving and Flannery O'Connor." *Literature & Theology* 10.1 (1996): 58-67.

Submits that, "in *A Prayer for Owen Meany*, John Irving proves himself to be an heir of Nathaniel Hawthorne in much the same sense as Flannery O'Connor." Compares O'Connor and Irving's use of the grotesque in their treatment of Christ and the nature of Christian conversion. Uses Karl Barth's *Church Dogmatics III* and Hans Frei's *The Identity of Jesus* to explore differences between the two authors' understanding of the supernatural. Finds that, "despite what seems to be a common purpose achieved by similar techniques, O'Connor and Irving have very different notions of the nature of Christian faith." Irving, "seems to speak for a particular kind of religious experience as the ground of Christian belief," as he urges readers to believe that "supernatural occurrences which violate naturalistic assumptions makes religious belief credible." Concludes that O'Connor's vision is, instead, largely sacramental: "personal revelation for her is a matter of seeing the whole of reality in a new trinitarian light."

1504   Takenaka, Toshiko. "An Inquiry Into Flannery O'Connor's Character Types." *Keisen Jogakuen Junior College Bulletin* (Japan) 7 (Apr. 1973): 21-52.

Sorts O'Connor's recurrent types of characters into six groups: prototypes of well-meaning vice; prophets; home-hunting people; men of despair; freaks; and, normal characters. (Abstracted by Kayoko Watanabe).

1505   Tallack, Douglas. "American Short Fiction: A Bibliographical Essay." *American Studies International* 23.2 (1985): 3-59.

Selected books and dissertations on Flannery O'Connor's life and work are included in the list of books and dissertations for the section titled: "Twentieth Century: 1950s to 1980s--Major Authors."

1506   Tallant, Carole Ellsworth. "Disjunctive Ambiguity and the Performance of Flannery O'Connor's `The Displaced Person.'" *Southern Speech Communication Journal* 51.2 (1986): 106-24.

Discusses narrative ambiguity and differentiates it from other literary devices. Analyzes "The Displaced Person" to reveal "insights into the how's and why's of performance of works exhibiting narrative ambiguity." Explores the nature of disjunctive narrative ambiguity in this text, utilizing Shlomith Rimmon's definition, and describes major sources within the narrative (plot, character, and point of view). Contends that "The Displaced Person" is a particularly appropriate example of narrative ambiguity because of O'Connor's "conscious manipulation of the point of view that renders a key scene ambiguous." Suggests techniques for solo and group performers to preserve and feature the ambiguity prevalent in the story including: "listing of clues, performing `against the line,' finding appropriate subtexts . . . slow motion, simultaneous action, split screen effects, and repeated actions." States in footnote 20 that "the Southern Speech Communication Association Convention held in Biloxi, Mississippi in April, 1979, devoted an entire afternoon seminar to exploring the treatment of ambiguity in this short story."

1507   Tanaka, Junko. "The Jesus Revolution and Flannery O'Connor." *Seishin Studies* [Bulletin of the Sacred Heart] (Japan) 38 (Dec. 1971): 31-36.

Discusses O'Connor in the context of the religious revival which swept the United States in the early 70s. Comments on the theme of baptism in *The Violent Bear It Away* and "The River," quoting from an article by Mayo Mohs, "The New Rebel Cry: Jesus is Coming," which appeared in *Time*, 21 June 1971. Asserts that Haze in *Wise Blood* is eventually conquered by the redemptive grace of Christ. (Abstracted by Kayoko Watanabe).

1508   Tanner, Stephen L. "Flannery O'Connor and Gabriel Marcel." *Literature and Belief* 17.1-2 (1997): 149-57.

Explores O'Connor's *Mystery and Manners*, to see how her imagination was complemented by her interest in the writings of Gabriel Marcel. Finds parallels "in the thought of these two Catholic artist-philosophers," and suggests that they share similar "temperaments and spiritual orientations." Sees both as "reflective empiricists who believed that concrete human experience is the only avenue to the mystery of being." Contends that Marcel's "notion of mystery enhanced and deepened [O'Connor's] preoccupation with this term; and his method of philosophizing from concrete experience, with its recognition of the revelatory nature of artistic creation, reinforced her own theory of fiction."

1509 Tarantino, Michael. "*Wise Blood.*" *Film Quarterly* 33.4 (1980): 15-17.

Offers an essay review of John Huston's film, *Wise Blood*. Praises it as "a brilliant mixture of painfully lucid and tantalizingly inexplicable elements." Describes scenes to illustrate how Huston uses obscure elements to illuminate "seemingly disparate events," and suggests that the film "is an ironic tale of believing and not believing, and how each, when taken to the precipice, results in the same type of constriction." Concludes that the film is successful "because it is able to transform the novel into its own unique, albeit sympathetic, terms."

1510 Tate, J.O., Jr. "The Essential Essex." *Flannery O'Connor Bulletin* 12 (1983): 47-59.

Discusses Stanley Edgar Hyman's "pioneering monograph," *Flannery O'Connor* (1966). Takes issue with his assertion that O'Connor's *Wise Blood* was so full of sexual references that it might be termed "pervasively sexual." Discusses Hazel Motes's sex life, Enoch's "prudishness," and Leora Watts's "sexual modes." Follows with an extensive discussion of O'Connor's use of the "Essex" automobile. Contends that it "is fundamentally significant because it is a measure of and a reproach to Haze's `existentialism.'" Sees the car not only as "the most important *thing*" in *Wise Blood* but as "the youthful O'Connor's major symbol and first unequivocal success." Provides a factual history of the production of the Essex and ties her use of the automobile to: puns and other American humor ("derived from horse-swapping stories and salesman jokes"); how Americans identify with their cars; commercialism and advertising; and, to *The Waste Land* and *Miss Lonelyhearts*. Sees Hazel as something of an anti-romantic version of Errol Flynn.

1511 Tate, J.O., Jr. "Faith and Fiction: Flannery O'Connor and the Problem of Belief." *Flannery O'Connor Bulletin* 5 (1976): 105-11.

Reviews four books on O'Connor and finds that "after reading so many pages of O'Connor criticism," he is "more forcibly struck than ever that O'Connor was (and still is) her own best critic." Finds Preston M. Browning, Jr.'s *Flannery O'Connor* (Carbondale: Southern Illinois U Press, 1974), strengthened by the author's "clear emphasis on `the time' and `current ideas,'" his economy of coverage, and "from finding his own forms for recapitulating" O'Connor's stories. Faults Browning for dissipating "power and focus when he digresses at excessive length in order to rebut Louis D. Rubin," and for unnecessarily weakening his book with his consideration of "O'Connor's relationship to the demonic mode." Suggests that Dorothy Walters tries "to have it both ways" as she argues in *Flannery O'Connor* (New York: Twayne, 1973) in favor of the presence of a "demonic thrust" in O'Connor's work, only to disavow this reading. Concludes that the author's "felicities" are "marred by some of her interpretations." Admires Dorothy Tuck McFarland's sharp eye for detail in *Flannery O'Connor* (New York: Frederick Ungar, 1976), and states that she "is a good reader, except when she is (through a failure of nerve?) insisting on the reader's right to mis-read." Finds Father John R. May's "expositions of the New Hermeneutic . . . distressingly obscure" in *The Pruning Word: The Parables of Flannery O'Connor* (Notre Dame: U of Notre Dame P, 1976). Contends that May is in too much of "a hurry to solve problems," especially in regard to how he "thinks that O'Connor's so-called ambiguity (grace versus the demon) can be dispelled by his hermeneutic interpretations." Concludes, that though "half of O'Connor's work doesn't really respond to his treatment," May's work is a book that every thoughtful student of O'Connor must read."

1512   Tate, J.O., Jr. "Flannery O'Connor's Counterplot." *Southern Review* 16.4 (1980): 869-78.

Argues against that group of critics--John Hawkes, Martha Stephens and Josephine Hendin--who claim O'Connor's work to be "demonic instead of divine" and who contend that she is of "the Devil's party without knowing it." Says that the ambiguities regarding O'Connor's spirituality have more to do with her emulation of Hawthorne and such stories of inherent mystery as "Young Goodman Brown" and "The Minister's Black Veil." States that O'Connor, as Milton with his *Paradise Lost*, has been accused of subconsciously allying herself with demonic forces. Continues the discussion by arguing that Milton and O'Connor have much in common through their use of distancing, spatial interventions, foreshortenings, and the celebration of the great theme of Creation. Discusses the novels and several of O'Connor's stories.

1513   Tate, J.O., Jr. "The Force of Example: Flannery O'Connor and Stephen Crane." *Flannery O'Connor Bulletin* 11 (1982): 10-24.

Suggests that O'Connor may have been considerably influenced by the writings of Stephen Crane. Notes Jean Wylder's comments in her memoir, "Flannery O'Connor: A Reminiscence and Some Letters," published in the *North American Review* [(Spring 1970): 58-65], which relate to O'Connor's use of elements of Crane's "The Bride Comes to Yellow Sky," especially in "The Artificial Nigger" and the similarity in her use of sun imagery in "A Temple of the Holy Ghost" with Crane's use in *The Red Badge of Courage*. Refers to comments by M. Bernetta Quinn, Frederick Asals, Louise Westling, Sally Fitzgerald, R.W. Stallman, Donald Pizer,

Edwin H. Cady, and Harold Bloom. Closes with a discussion of Crane's influence upon William Faulkner and O'Connor, with evidence supporting this contention--including a memoir by the author's own father, James Tate. Offers that O'Connor may have found *The Red Badge of Courage* to be "a motherlode of (inverted) religious imagery," and "been instructed by Crane's simplicity of syntax and circumspection of approach."

1514   Tate, J.O., Jr. "A Good Source Is Not So Hard to Find." *Flannery O'Connor Bulletin* 9 (1980): 98-103.

Examines "evidence of O'Connor's use of items from the Milledgeville and Atlanta newspapers," including items related to The Misfit in "A Good Man Is Hard to Find" and Mrs. Pritchard's anecdote in "A Circle in the Fire" about the woman who had a baby in an iron lung.

1515   Tate, J.O., Jr. "An Introduction to `An O'Connor Remembrance.'" *Flannery O'Connor Bulletin* 17 (1988): 62-64.

Offers notes to the memoir of Flannery O'Connor that his father--James Tate--wrote in 1964-65 at the request of Rosa Lee Walston. Provides the identities of and discusses the individuals who met as a literary group on Wednesday evenings at Andalusia. [The memoir is published in the same issue of *The Flannery O'Connor Bulletin*, on pages 65-68.]

1516   Tate, J.O., Jr. "A Note on O'Connor's Use of Military Names." *Flannery O'Connor Bulletin* 14 (1985): 99-102.

Suggests that O'Connor used military names "in oblique but strategic ways," Charging them with significance "in the larger context of dense, compact, and all-embracing structures of allusion and reference." Refers to: General Stonewall Jackson; the battle sites of Chickamauga, Shiloh, and Marthasville (Atlanta); General Robert E. Lee; General Robert Toombs; Francis Marion; General Daniel Harvey Hill (D.H. Hill); General Ambrose Powell Hill (A.P. Hill); and Captain Alan Bartlett Shepard, Jr.

1517   Tate, J.O., Jr. "O'Connor's Confederate General: A Late Encounter." *Flannery O'Connor Bulletin* 8 (1979): 45-53.

Sees "A Late Encounter With the Enemy" as a "direct manipulation of Southern clichés." Suggests that while O'Connor's "parodistic attack seems an outrageous comic exaggeration, [it was] . . . in truth closer to

mere transcription of homely truth." Provides evidence that O'Connor's
model for General Tennessee Flintrock Sash was William Jordan Bush,
a private during the Civil War who had won the title of "General" through
participation in the United Confederate Veterans, and that the granddaughter and graduation ceremony described was undoubtedly based
upon Bush's own young wife's graduation from Georgia State College for
Women in 1951. Suggests that examining "this documentary evidence
gives us a chance to measure *exactly* how much O'Connor felt necessary
to add to a given reality, in order to create a story." Includes photographs
of General and Mrs. Bush and the front of Loew's Grand Theatre, where
Gone With the Wind premiered. Discusses remarks by Harvey Klevar,
Paul Jones, and Celestine Sibley. Relates facts about the showing of *Two
Flags West*, at Atlanta's Fox Theatre, where Bush made an appearance,
and recounts Sibley's remarks regarding his personality in his 1952
obituary. Concludes that the story not only "contrasts the vulgarity of `a
media event' with the reality of war and history," but that "it was her
perception of absurdity, not her creation of it, that gave her the story."

1518   Tate, J.O., Jr. "O'Connor's Letters: A Preview." *Flannery O'Connor
        Bulletin* 7 (1978): 5-9.

        Offers a preliminary review of *The Habit of Being: Letters of Flannery
        O'Connor*, edited by Sally Fitzgerald. Declares that the letters "present
        more a revelation of O'Connor herself than they do an account" of her
        "methods and intentions." Reports that--as the reader follows the sequence
        of the letters published--"they take on the stature of narrative and the
        dialectic of drama." Concludes that the O'Connor letters "amount to an
        epistolary autobiography," and applauds Sally Fitzgerald's emphasis "not
        on the perfecting of the work, but the perfecting of the life and spirit."

1519   Tate, J.O., Jr. "On Flannery O'Connor: Citizen of the South and Citizen
        of the World." *Flannery O'Connor Bulletin* 13 (1984): 26-43.

        Contends that "there was a limitation to Flannery O'Connor's
        `Southernness' and her local identity, a self-imposed constraint, a
        repudiation beyond which she would not go," that--in a sense--"she wasn't
        Southern at all, and therefore not a `Southern writer.'" Supports this thesis
        with a variety of arguments including: why O'Connor ignored "a
        substantial amount of distinguished modern Southern literature";
        speculation as to why she "virtually cut herself off from Southern
        history"; her view of, and use of *Gone With the Wind*; and how images of
        death camps are conjured up in "A Good Man Is Hard to Find" and in
        "The Displaced Person." Finds that O'Connor looked at the South as an
        outsider; she did not possess, nor wish to have, "any `Southern literary

and artistic psyche' and therefore only confronted the local formulation of
`historical reality' in the form of the absurd, the discredited, the passé, the
distorted." Contends that, instead, her "historical awareness" was intuitive,
"distinctively Christian and specifically Roman Catholic."

1520   Tate, J.O., [Jr.] Rev. of *Realist of Distances: Flannery O'Connor
        Revisited*, by Karl-Heinz Westarp and Jan Nordby Gretlund. *Flannery
        O'Connor Bulletin* 16 (1987): 95-97.

Suggests that the publication of these essays indicate that "the O'Connor
industry has gone international." Lists titles, authors, and a concise
description of each of the essays included in the volume. Singles out as
"the broadest and most valuable piece," Ashley Brown's "literary memoir
of O'Connor." Describes it as "a rich and evocative summoning of a very
nearly vanished world of high culture, and a most useful corrective to any
overemphasis on O'Connor's `isolation.'" Concludes that the collection
should also be seen as a register of the "some of the impact of O'Connor's
writing here and abroad" as it reflects "how widely O'Connor spread her
narrow hands" and "how far the living power of her words has extended."

1521   Tate, J.O., Jr. "The Uses of Banality." *Flannery O'Connor Bulletin* 4
        (1975): 13-24.

Explores implications of O'Connor as "an Artist of the Banal." Considers
the range and symbolic role that everyday, banal objects play in her
works, including: Hazel Motes's "peeler," Tarwater's corkscrew, Sally
Poker Sash's Girl Scout shoes and corsage, the artificial nigger in the story
of that same name, and the purple hat in "Everything That Rises Must
Converge." Then, points out how she used news stories and everyday
sources to "make titles out of faded material." Sees *Wise Blood* as a
"savage reduction of liberalism" presented to readers "in cartoon form,"
whose theme is continued in *The Violent Bear It Away* and in a number
of other stories (e.g. "Good Country People"). Contends that her "attack
on the Gods of the Century of the Common man . . . is reminiscent of the
focus that turned the polite Fugitives into pugnacious Agrarians."
Considers how her mining of popular culture (including films such as
"Mighty Joe Young" and "Gone With the Wind") points to how she
alludes "beyond banality" to the mythology of the Old South. Refers to
works by Vladimir Nabokov, Nikolai Gogol, Gustave Flaubert, James
Joyce and Northrop Frye. Uses comments by Allen Tate and Alfred Kazin
to support claim that the "`past in the present' in O'Connor's work is not
the Southern past but the `good news' of the gospel." Concludes that her
highest achievement was--as seen in "Parker's Back" and "The Displaced
person"--her ability to transform everyday vulgarities "into sublimity."

1522   Tate, James. "An O'Connor Remembrance." *Flannery O'Connor Bulletin* 17 (1988): 65-68.

Writes of his memories of meeting and visiting with Flannery O'Connor, whom he describes as a friend and correspondent from 1957 until 1964. Describes the Wednesday evening literary group which met at the O'Connor farm near Milledgeville--Andalusia--to discuss short stories. Reviews the authors and various works the two discussed, and reports his recollection of her assessments. Mentioned are: Peter Taylor, Robie Macauley, J.F. Powers, Bernard Malamud, Madison Jones, Eudora Welty, Caroline Gordon, William Faulkner, William Butler Yeats, Frank O'Connor, Henry James, Ernest Hemingway, Andrew Lytle, William Golding, Stephen Crane, Joseph Conrad, Ford Madox Ford's *The Good Soldier*, Ring Lardner's "The Golden Honeymoon," Nathanael West's *Miss Lonelyhearts*, Max Beerbohm's *Zuleika Dobson*, Erich Auerbach's *Mimesis*, Marcel Proust's *Remembrance of Things Past*, Vladimir Nabokov's *Lolita*, the comedians W.C. Fields and Charlie Chaplin, and the CBS television show *Camera Three*.

1523   Tate, Mary Barbara. "Flannery O'Connor at Home in Milledgeville." *Studies in the Literary Imagination* 20.2 (1987): 31-36.

Describes how Milledgeville, Georgia has changed during the previous twenty-five years, but retains many similarities from O'Connor's time. Tells of meeting Flannery O'Connor in 1956 and how she and her husband became her friends. Describes the "Wednesday night group" of six to eight individuals who met at Andalusia to read each week, O'Connor's fondness for birds, impressions of those in the community, and O'Connor's funeral.

1524   Tavernier-Courbin, Jacqueline, and R.G. Collins. "An Interview with John Cheever." *Thalia: Studies in Literary Humor* 1 (1978): 3-9.

Cheever refers briefly to O'Connor, stating that she is "one of the greatest short story writer's we've ever had."

1525   Taylor, Harry H. "The University and the Writer." *Ball State University Forum* 16.2 (1975): 10-12.

Refers to O'Connor's views on writing programs and uses these views to illustrate the difficulties that writers and traditional English faculty have in valuing each others' work. Follows with quotes from O'Connor's essays, "What Is a Short Story" and "The Fiction Writer and His

Country," to emphasize that a writer should be "more interested in the mystery of being than in the publishing game in general." Asserts, in closing, that those writers who are "truly called" will "understand what O'Connor meant when she said that fiction `is an action illuminated and outlined by mystery.'"

1526   Taylor, Jacqueline. "Narrative Strategies in Fiction and Film: Flannery O'Connor's `The Displaced Person.'" *Literature in Performance* 2.2 (1982): 1-11.

Argues against contemporary criticism on the failure of film to adapt literary short stories. Says scholars not only ignore the gains made by film and regard literature as the "privileged narrative" but also suggest that film distorts good fiction. Discusses the film of O'Connor's story, "The Displaced Person" to show how film may achieve two effects--visual and aural--which fiction alone cannot. Shows how the film adds bulk and confidence to the story's opening, how long shots and point-of-view shots enhance several scenes, and in some cases, how added dialogue clarifies the prophecy Mrs. Shortley makes. Comments favorably on the filmmaker's deletion of a voice-over narrative in lieu of a more objective "imagistic" point-of-view.

1527   Tedford, Barbara Wilkie. "Flannery O'Connor and the Social Classes." *Southern Literary Journal* 13.2 (1981): 27-40.

Analyzes O'Connor's fictionalizing of "white trash," "niggers or negroes," and "good (country) people." Defends O'Connor's own attitudes about class, contending O'Connor herself was tactful in dealing with people and enlightened for her time. Points to letters in which she uses degrading terms, but the author explains them as personal correspondence and goes on to say that O'Connor's work suggests that she found all men sinful and equally dependent on God. Analyzes the matriarchal figures in several stories--primarily Mrs. Turpin in "Revelation"--for their social class consciousness. Argues that these women are satirized and often, as in Mrs. Turpin's case, suffer calamity.

1527a Templin, Charlotte. "Canons, Class, and the Crisis of the Humanities." *College Literature* 22.2 (1995): 151-56.

Discusses "interest in the academy" regarding "what books are read and why" through a review of John Guillory's *Cultural Capital: The Problem of Literary Canon Formation* (Chicago: U of Chicago P, 1993). Refers to Flannery O'Connor's *A Good Man Is Hard to Find* as an example of one of the few standard texts by a woman writer consistently included in our literary canon. Notes Frederick Asals's assertion that O'Connor's reputation "was launched by the New Critics" and that she "has not been a strong favorite of feminists." Sees her as among the "fortunate few" women writers whose works were included "in the influential anthologies created by the New Critics."

1528   TeSelle, Sallie McFague. "The Experience of Coming to Belief." *Theology Today* 32 (July 1975): 159-65.

Discusses the importance of parables and their place in our modern time. Asserts that *The Violent Bear It Away* is a good example of a "parabolic novel" since even though it "is a religious novel with a vengeance . . . the supernatural never obtrudes."

1529   "Theatrical Outfit Celebrated Flannery O'Connor with Staging of Rare `Displaced Person.'" *CHEERS! The Flannery O'Connor Society Newsletter* 6.1 (1998): 3.

Offers details from a press release from "Theatrical Outfit" describing the staging of Cecil Dawkins's adaptation of O'Connor's "The Displaced Person." Notes that while the play debuted in New York's American Place Theatre in 1968-69, this production (March 21 - April 5, 1998) is its Southern premiere. Includes information on Cecil Dawkins, Brenda Bynum ("Mrs. Hopewell"), Derek Manson ("Wesley Hopewell"), and Tom Key (the play's "producing artistic director").

1530   Thiemann, Fred R. "Usurping the Logos: Clichés in O'Connor's `Good Country People.'" *Flannery O'Connor Bulletin* 24 (1995-96): 46-56.

Contends that O'Connor's "Good Country People" is partially "an examination of the theological implications of the nature of language." Suggests that while Hulga and her mother "commit the sin of pride in their attempts to make absolute the connection between word and meaning," Manley Pointer "represents another evil, the abandonment of any connection between word and meaning." Sees in Pointer's statement that he has "been believing in nothing" since he was born, that the "two evils" are closely related. States that "some postmodern theorists, in their condemnation of the kind of `logocentrism' characteristic of the Hopewells, have fallen into the nihilism characteristic of O'Connor's Bible salesman." Concludes that "by showing the relation between the two," O'Connor illustrates for readers "the linguistic and spiritual redemption offered Hulga" as well as "an often overlooked theological dimension of linguistic theory." Focuses on how "language functions symbolically" in the story. Remarks that both Hulga and Mrs. Hopewell attempt "to define the world, perhaps even create it, by forcing being into a solidified symbol." Comments on the use of clichés by the mother and daughter as an attempt at self-deification and to dominate each other. Also argues that because Pointer "refuses to recognize the limitations and temporality of language," he is able "to hoodwink both Mrs. Hopewell and Hulga." Refers to comments and writings by: Paul Ricoeur (*The Symbolism of Evil*), Allen Tate, Walker Percy, Charles Sanders Peirce, John of St. Thomas, Frederick Asals, Lisa S. Babinec, Ralph C. Wood, John Gatta, Paul Nisly, and to works by Emily Archer and Benjamin Alexander.

1531   Thompson, James J., Jr. "Southerners Old-Fashioned and Newfangled." *Sewanee Review* 96.2 (1988): xxvi, xxviii, xxx.

In a brief review article, includes a discussion of O'Connor's view of the Southerner as alienated and "Christ-haunted." Contends that, however easily a Southern writer may have "rested with the manners and mores of his people," each "has known in his blood that the banished children of Eve suffer the curse of dividedness."

1532   Thompson, Terry. "Doodlebug, Doodlebug: The Misfit in `A Good Man Is Hard to Find.'" *Notes on Contemporary Literature* 17.4 (1987): 8-9.

Explains the process of "doodlebugging"--a pastime of Southern children that consists of enticing an ant lion, or doodlebug, to appear at the bottom of its conical-shaped trap. Notes how The Misfit in "A Good Man Is Hard to Find" replicates the process of doodlebugging, by scratching the ground with "the toe of his shoe . . . [and] the butt of his gun" in order to make a trap for the family to fall into. Also draws connections between the big, black "buglike" hearse-of-sorts from which The Misfit emerges and several physical descriptions of The Misfit as "insect-like." Concludes that The Misfit, like the ant lion, is equipped for, survival.

1533   Thompson, Terry. "The Killers in O'Connor's `A Good Man Is Hard To Find.'" *Notes on Contemporary Literature* 16.4 (1986): 4.

Analyzes the choice of names in "A Good Man Is Hard to Find." Says the name "Bobby Lee" is a direct and ironic reference to General Robert E. Lee. Sees the silver stallion on the sweatshirt, the pistol (a traditional weapon of the Southern gentleman), and the yodeling (rebel yells) as ironic contrasts to the "gallant" Lee. Notes that the second name, "Hiram," means "exalted brother" in ancient Hebrew, and reminds readers to pronounce it in the Southern idiom--"Harm." Finally, argues that the name "The Misfit" is really a tip-off that he is the "most-fit" character in the story--managing to be completely mannerly, while controlling the grandmother, the children, and even the animals, and surviving because he is able to do so.

1534   Tift, Ann. "In Search of `The Roots of the Modern South,' Duke University Comes to Macon." *Macon Magazine* 4.3 (1990): 35, 88.

Describes the "Duke Alumni College" program held in Macon, GA, October 19-22, 1989, in which 33 Duke University alumni and friends studied the life and works of Flannery O'Connor and Sidney Lanier.

1535   Tolomeo, Diane. "Flannery O'Connor's `Revelation' and the Book of *Job*." *Renascence* 30.2 (1978): 78-90.

Underscores the fact that O'Connor herself urged the reader to develop "anagogical vision" -- the kind of vision that is able to see different levels of reality in one image. This granted, Tolomeo believes that O'Connor's stories do not function in a "story = X" way. Calls attention to the way the book of *Job* may inform O'Connor's story "Revelation." One similarity the author notes between Job and Mrs. Turpin is their self-righteousness (and their need for more humility). Tolomeo notes Mrs. Turpin's reference to Job and her internalized "wrestling with God." Recalls O'Connor's comment that fiction should leave the reader, like Job, with a renewed sense of mystery. Discusses other parallels between Job and Mrs. Turpin (and to a lesser extent O.E. Parker in "Parker's Back"), most importantly that the two have seen visions and yet, are left with a greater sense of the incomprehensibleness of God, a knowledge which produces silence.

1536   Tolomeo, Diane. "Home to Her True Country: The Final Trilogy of Flannery O'Connor." *Studies in Short Fiction* 17.3 (1980): 335-41.

Views O'Connor's use of violence as indicative of the grotesque, an illustration of the Southern Gothic, and as evidence that she was fulfilling the role of a fundamentalist prophet to her generation. Seeks to prove that O'Connor was party to the Devil without her own knowledge. Notes that whereas many of her stories end in a physical or psychic assault, her last three, written during her final illness--"Parker's Back," "Revelation," and "Judgement Day"--move the moment of violence to an earlier place in the story. Suggests that this move allows the remainder of the story to be concerned with the implications of that violence. Discusses each story in detail as to its use of violence, resolution, and revelation.

1537   Tolomeo, Diane. "Letters, Parables, and Guides: Some Recent Work on
         Flannery O'Connor." *Review*. [Vol. 2] Ed. James O. Hoge and James L.W.
         West, III. Charlottesville: UP of Virginia, 1980.   271-86.

         Offers review essay on *The Habit of Being*, edited by Sally Fitzgerald,
         The Pruning Word: The Parables of Flannery O'Connor by John R. May,
         and *Flannery O'Connor and Caroline Gordon: A Reference Guide* by
         Robert E. Golden and Mary C. Sullivan. Suggests that through O'Connor's
         letters, May's "new critical study of her works" and Golden's
         bibliography, "it is now possible to know [O'Connor] better and
         understand her writing more clearly than ever before." Asserts that
         O'Connor's letters "reveal an honest sense of herself and her writing"--
         especially in regard to discussions of her faith--which "shed light on her
         writing." States that May's work, which reflects "his rigorous thinking as
         a Jesuit who is at home with literary criticism as well as with theological
         precision" may be viewed as taking "a solid stand on the side of those
         who see her theology as an essential element in her art." Compares May's
         work to that of Martha Stephens (*The Question of Flannery O'Connor*),
         Preston M. Browning, Jr (*Flannery O'Connor*), and Carter W. Martin
         (*The True Country*). Praises Golden's work as "exhaustive and
         praiseworthy," seeing it as a bibliography which will set "a high standard"
         for anyone who chooses to update it. Notes that annotations are "detailed
         and to the point," and that the chronological arrangement allows readers
         to follow O'Connor criticism from "the sparse reviews of 1952 to the
         copious number of items listed for the past decade." Closes with an
         addenda to Golden's *Guide*.

1538   Tolson, Jay, ed. *The Correspondence of Shelby Foote & Walker Percy*.
         New York: W.W. Norton, 1997.

         Index refers readers to several mentions of O'Connor in the
         correspondence between Foote and Walker. Foote's comments include:
         his opinion of O'Connor as "a minor-minor writer, not because she lacked
         talent to be a major one, but simply because she died before her
         development had time to evolve out of the friction of just living enough
         years to soak up the basic joys and sorrows"; and his suggestion that, with
         more years of experience, O'Connor would have eventually turned her
         attention to "the ordinary world, which would have been her true subject
         after she emerged from the `grotesque' one she explored throughout the
         little time she had." Percy's correspondence reveals that he attached "great
         importance to" Sally Fitzgerald's collection of O'Connor's correspondence
         in *The Habit of Being*, and that it revealed O'Connor to be "a truly
         remarkable lady, laconic, funny, tough, smart, hard-headed, no-nonsense,
         the very best of US, South, and Catholicism."

1539   Tolson, Jay. *Pilgrim in the Ruins: A Life of Walker Percy.* New York: Simon & Schuster, 1992. 219, 220, 324, 352, 426, 485, 492.

A literary biography of Percy with passing references to O'Connor: regarding Percy and O'Connor's almost simultaneous request of Caroline Gordon to read their novels (1951) and Gordon's reaction that both writers' works were "`so damned good'"; O'Connor's advice to Robert Drake that he reread Percy's *The Moviegoer*; Shelby Foote's comments to Percy regarding O'Connor's *Mystery and Manners*; Percy's letter to Bruce Springsteen regarding Springsteen's interest in O'Connor; and, Foote's comment during a memorial service that Percy, like O'Connor, "took a different path around" Faulkner to accomplish his literary art.

1540   Tomlinson, Barbara. "Cooking, Mining, Gardening, Hunting: Metaphorical Stories Writers Tell About Their Composing Process." *Metaphor and Symbolic Activity* 1.1 (1986): 57-79.

Draws from comments made in more than 2,000 published interviews to discuss figurative stories that writers use in talking about the writing process. Focuses on how writers "compare their composing with other processes: cooking, mining, gardening and hunting." Includes O'Connor's remark that she viewed her "ideas as prey of some kind," that she had to "`feel . . . out like a hound dog . . . [and] follow the scent.'"

1541   Toolan, Michael. "Compromising Positions: Systemic Linguistics and the Locally Managed Semiotics of Dialogue." *Functions of Style.* Ed. David Birch and Michael O'Toole. London: Pinter, 1988. 249-60.

A linguistic and semiotic analysis of dialogue using O'Connor's story "Greenleaf" as an example of the artificiality of fictional dialogue. Makes observations about fictional dialogue, contrasting it with transcribed spoken dialogue, noting the lack of markings for speech overlaps, interruptions, hesitations, false starts, etc. Uses Halliday's four basic speech functions--speakers either giving or demanding goods and speakers either giving or demanding information--to analyze one short exchange in the story between Mrs. May and Mr. Greenleaf for lexical and semiotic patterns.

1542   Torchia, Joseph. "Inside Flannery O'Connor." *Flannery O'Connor Bulletin* 25 (1996-97): 81-102.

Discusses his battle with the AIDS virus in the context of his respect for Flannery O'Connor's faith and how resolutely she struggled herself with the debilitating effects of lupus. Offers biographical details, commentary on his thoughts about the difficulties he is encountering, and outlines how he relies upon O'Connor's writings for guidance and strength.

1543   Trainor, Richard. "O'Connor, Lowry, Huston and Welles." *Sight and Sound* 54.1 (1984-85): 31-33.

Interview of Michael Fitzgerald (Producer) by Richard Trainor, concerning the success of his film of *Wise Blood* (1979 Cannes Festival). Notes his film *Under the Volcano*, his new picture *Rocking the Cradle*, and his association with John Huston and Orson Welles. Fitzgerald talks of his early desire to see O'Connor's novel made into a film. When asked what he looks for in screenplay adaptation of novels, Fitzgerald remarks on the "clear, dramatic lines," such as those in *Wise Blood*.

1544   Trautmann, Joanne, and Carol Pollard. *Literature and Medicine: An Annotated Bibliography*. Rev. ed. Pittsburgh: U of Pittsburgh P, 1982. 137-38.

Offers annotated references to literature involving the field of medicine. Notes the medical motifs in "Everything That Rises Must Converge," "The Lame Shall Enter First," and "Good Country People."

1545   Trimmer, Joseph F. *The National Book Awards for Fiction: An Index to the First Twenty-Five Years*. Boston: G.K. Hall, 1978. xvii, xxii, 91, 92, 141, 200, 255-69.

Lists nominees and winners of the National Book Awards from 1950 to 1974 and lists bestsellers and Pulitzer prize winners. Discusses O'Connor's *The Complete Stories*, the National Book Award winning entry for 1972. Refers, in the Preface, to Christopher Lehmann-Haupt's discussion of how *The Complete Stories* won as a "compromise candidate" over the other finalists (E.L. Doctorow's *The Book of Daniel* and Walker Percy's *Love in the Ruins*). Includes a selected critical bibliography for the winners with 17 citations to "news and comment," 7 "reviews" and 127 items of "critical commentary" related to *The Complete Stories*. Also includes citations to *A Good Man Is Hard to Find* and *The Violent Bear It Away* as nominees in 1956 and 1961 respectively.

1546   Trowbridge, Clinton W. "The Comic Sense of Flannery O'Connor: Literalist of the Imagination." *Flannery O'Connor Bulletin* 12 (1983): 77-92.

Examines O'Connor's use of humor, suggests she used it "as a two-edged sword . . . as a means of throwing the forces of evil off balance, of cutting our ties to them and theirs to us." Discusses her use of humor in: "A Late Encounter With the Enemy"; "Greenleaf"; "Parker's Back"; "A Temple of the Holy Ghost"; "The River"; *Wise Blood*; *The Violent Bear It Away*; "The Artificial Nigger"; "Good Country People"; and "Revelation."

1547   True, Michael. "The Comic Genius of Flannery O'Connor." *America* 24 Sept. 1977: 167-69.

States that O'Connor "told stories that no one else had told, profoundly comic stories, often radically conservative in their implications, shocking and disturbing and serious, as only comedy can be." Describes O'Connor's typical characters, and draws attention to her intentions and her precise definition of the term, "comic writer." Offers readings of *Wise Blood* and "Parker's Back" to get "a sense of how her stories lean on and contribute to a tradition of comedy from Aristophanes to Evelyn Waugh." Finds that *Wise Blood* provides a vision of the world that is "comic, in the classic sense: bawdy, pessimistic, [and] absurd." In a similar vein, finds that "Parker's Back" shows O'Connor as "not satisfied with merely exposing the narrow rationalists, as comic writers have done for centuries," but interested in exalting "the crazies, [and] the backwoods prophets" who possess a "unity of purpose and a consistency in point of view that more complicated, more `rational' minds are incapable of." Concludes that as readers who may feel vastly superior to grotesque characters, such as Hazel Motes or Sarah Ruth Cates, we may find that as we "confront their integrity, admire their strength and, maybe . . . fall under their spell . . . we come to realize that we, not they, are the real comic figures."

1548   True, Michael. "J.F. Powers, Flannery O'Connor and Their Satiric Muse." *America* 4 Oct. 1980: 183-88.

Asserts that "by capturing the dark side of religious belief in their stories" Powers and O'Connor "have shown the complexity of American Catholicism and given their readers a new level of Christian realism." States that even with their differing styles, "both make use of the religious tradition they share; [Powers] in his choice of material; [O'Connor] in the moral principles that inform her work." Discusses their views on the "responsibilities of the Catholic writer," and analyzes similarities of the two writers. Notes one "profound" difference: their approach to satire. Observes that "O'Connor is a comic writer and a satirist, too, but a Juvenalian satirist, more moralistic than Powers and at the same time more farcial." Explicates Powers's "Keystone" and O'Connor's "The Enduring Chill" to in an attempt to show how "Powers gives us stories and revelations about human frailty; [while] O'Connor gives us stories and revelations about the waves of God's judgement and mercy." Proposes that both stories indicate that their authors "understand the peculiar nature of the dilemma one faces in understanding the contemporary church. They do so not by theorizing about it, not by abstracting from experience, but more skillfully and humanly, by showing that church as we experience it, preparing us for disappointment and defeat."

1549   True, Michael. "The Luminous Letters of a Writer of Genius: A Splendid Collection from Flannery O'Connor." *Chronicle Review* 16 April 1979: R6.

Review essay of *The Habit of Being: Letters of Flannery O'Connor*. Asserts that O'Connor's letters are an excellent source for the reader to learn "a great deal about the particular genius that enabled O'Connor to connect the visible and the invisible, the material and the spiritual in an original, powerful, and comic way." Offers a brief biographical sketch, a review of her career, and states that "there is hardly a letter . . . that doesn't entertain, inform, or challenge the reader in a concrete way." Finds the portrait of O'Connor which emerges from this volume to be "startling in its precision, clarity and depth . . . a collage of critical comment on contemporary writers she admired." Concludes that the book is "one of the great collections of letters in American Literature, equal in range and quality to those of Hawthorne and Melville and comparable, in what they tell us about the craft of fiction, to the notebooks and prefaces of Henry James and the journals of Henry David Thoreau . . . they are among the wisest reflections we have on art, on life in these United States, and on religion . . . a university in themselves." Illustrations: Portrait photograph of O'Connor by Joe McTyre.

1550   Tullos, Allen. "Dismembering and Remembering: Embodied Experience and Oral History." *Revue Française D'Études Americaines* 44 (April 1990): 77-85.

Using their comments from the hour-long documentary film, "Being A Joines: A Life in the Brushy Mountains," Tullos discusses how the bodily injuries, physical scars, illness, and healing of John "Frail" Joines and his wife Blanche, of North Carolina, "provide narrative guides and biographical maps" of their lives. Focuses on the storytelling traditions their comments suggest and refers to examples (of these traditions) in Eudora Welty's *Losing Battles*, William Faulkner's *The Sound and the Fury* and *Light in August*, and Flannery O'Connors' *Wise Blood* and "Good Country People."

1551 Tuttle, John. "Glimpses of `A Good Man' in Capote's *In Cold Blood*." *ANQ: A Quarterly Journal of Short Articles, Notes and Reviews* 1.4 (1988): 144-46.

Tuttle sees a direct influence of O'Connor's story on Capote's novel. Compares Capote's Bonnie Clutter and the Grandmother in "A Good Man Is Hard to Find," and finds that they are both hypochondriacs and martyrs; also compares the death scenes of the two women where they appeal to the murderers' sense of decency--Bonnie Clutter calls Perry "a decent young man" and the Grandmother calls The Misfit "a good man." More importantly, the author compares the speeches of James Latham and The Misfit, which attempt to offer explanation for the murders. Tuttle says the philosophical explanation The Misfit gives--"Jesus was the only one who raised the dead . . . and he shouldn't have done it . . . no pleasure but meanness"--is echoed in Latham's speech, but falls short in the latter because the religious symbolism and inference requires too great a leap.

1552 Tynan, Daniel J. "Introduction." *Biographical Dictionary of Contemporary Catholic American Writing*. New York: Greenwood, 1989. XIII-XXIII.

Discusses O'Connor's views on the "Catholic novel" and her belief that "the Catholic writer will usually see reality from two perspectives--one focusing on the supernatural and the other on the natural--and these two ways of viewing remain always in conflict." Uses O'Connor's position on the Catholic writer's dilemma to "consider the variety of Catholic experiences" represented by writers included in the volume. States that some writers express a "reluctance" to accept the "authority of Rome," and that this reluctance is best illustrated by their treatment of sexual behavior. Compares Father Andrew Greeley's work to that of O'Connor, and asserts that "what O'Connor achieves through the use of violence and the grotesque, Greeley achieves through the use of sex." Examines O'Connor's "Good Country People" as part of a discussion of Catholic writers' exploration of "the power of sacraments to impart grace." Discusses works by Walker Percy, Mary Gordon, Robert Olen Butler, Eugene O'Neill, and Thomas Pynchon. Contains a biographical sketch by Melvin J. Friedman (221-24).

1553 Unsworth, Tim[othy]. "Flannery O'Connor's Catholic Eye." *National Catholic Reporter* 30 Nov. 1984: 8.

Essay written on the 20th anniversary of O'Connor's death lamenting her loss and praising her contribution to American and Catholic literature. Urges readers to read O'Connor's works again as "she might cause each of us to rearrange the furniture in our own soul . . . and to rise from the ashes of our own compulsive little egos."

1554   Unsworth, Timothy. "Flannery Will Get You Somewhere." *Salt* 6.9 (1986): 29-31.

Provides a biographical sketch of O'Connor and indicates the importance of her work in the context of being a Christian writer. Offers an indirect review of Fickett and Gilbert's *Flannery O'Connor--Images of Grace*, stating that this book "rescues O'Connor from the hands of some well-meaning Christians who would dub her a writer of Catholic themes . . . She is increasingly recognized as one of the finest American writers of this century." Discusses "A Temple of the Holy Ghost" and "The Displaced Person"; her approach to her art and the time she devoted to writing each day; and the fact that many of her short stories "deal with the pain that comes from the inability of people to connect." Concludes with suggestion that "O'Connor had a center from which she would not budge, a confidence that said where there is no belief there is no drama, and a sense that the best feelings stem from the realization that people cannot walk on water and are not required to in order to be Christians."

1555   Updike, John. Foreword. *Doubly Gifted: The Author as Visual Artist.* By Kathleen J. Hjerter. New York: Harry Abrahams, 1986.

O'Connor is mentioned in the foreword as a literary artist who began "surprisingly" as a cartoonist. Uses the analogy between the graphic arts and O'Connor's literary work to describe the "vivid outrageousness, [and] the definiteness of her every stroke."

1556   Uruburu, Paula M. "The Lame Shall Enter First: Flannery O'Connor." *The Grotesque Doorway: An Analysis of the American Grotesque.* New York: Peter Lang, 1987. 119-38.

Contends that in O'Connor's fiction "one can see through," to the "'outer and inner worlds' of the American Grotesque tradition.'" Connects O'Connor's use of the Grotesque with that of Edgar Allan Poe, Sherwood Anderson, Stephen Crane, Frank Norris, and Nathanael West. Suggests that O'Connor's work is proof "that a nation as fragmented as America, with no unified racial, religious, or cultural background, breeds writers with an inherent penchant for the abnormal, the unexpected, the eccentric, and the disconnected, particularly in the South, where she says they can still recognize 'freaks.'" Uses remarks from *Mystery and Manners* to outline O'Connor's "vision." Argues that her talent "lies in her ability to

articulate that which Hawthorne, Poe and others in the American
Grotesque tradition knew--that as writers and Americans, they can write
nothing else." Discusses her use of grotesque characters and violence to
"shock her readers into recognition of their flaws," and how her "fictional
qualities lean away from typical social patterns toward mystery and the
unexpected." Focuses on examples in *Everything That Rises Must
Converge*, in particular the title story and "The Lame Shall Enter First."
Concludes that as "both poet and prophet, Flannery O'Connor and her
fiction firmly declare their place in the profound poetry of disorder known
as the American Grotesque tradition."

1557   Vande Kieft, Ruth. "Flannery O'Connor: Seer of the Bible Belt." *NICM
Journal for Jews and Christians in Higher Education* 3.4 (1978): 76-92.

Argues, quoting liberally from *Mystery and Manners*, that O'Connor did
not wish her fiction to be a means of conversion, but instead, intended it
to be a means of forcing readers "to see" or "to be enlightened." Quotes
O'Connor's restatement of St. Thomas (*De Veritate*), who says "prophecy
depends on the imaginative, not the moral faculty," and her own equating
of herself with Tarwater in *The Violent Bear It Away*. Says O'Connor
juxtaposed "the word of the Lord" with contemporary social, intellectual,
moral, and religious concerns. Comments on O'Connor's attitude toward
spiritually-dead intellectuals, and her prescription for communicating with
those who were not like-minded--make the vision apparent by shock.
Illustrates with examples from various stories and the novels. Shows how
O'Connor's believers are not always "good people" and how her nonbelievers, at times, are.

1558   Vasquez, Mary S. "Two Mourners For The Human Spirit: Ana Maria
Matute and Flannery O'Connor." *Monographic Review/Revista
Monografica* 4 (1988): 51-59.

Compares and contrasts the works and artistic objectives of Flannery
O'Connor and Ana Maria Matute. Declares that both "excel in the
cultivation of the short story as a mode of expression for their dippings
into the cauldron containing the pungent, bitter broth of the human spirit."
Notes that in both writer's work violence appears frequently, human life
is taken and misused "by characters with the naturalness of breathing,"
and both share "a profoundly pessimistic view of humanity in its . . .
penchant for cruelty and the dismantling of human potential." Illustrates
discussion with citations from Matute's "Pecado de Omision" and
O'Connor's "A Good Man Is Hard to Find."

1559   Veith, Gene Edward. "Whiskey and Religion: Theoretical and Practical Notes on Teaching Literature and Religion." *Christianity and Literature* 29.3 (1980): 50-61.

Cites O'Connor's statement that "two words not allowed to be used at the University of Kansas are whiskey and religion," then discusses how he incorporates both literature and religion into his sophomore special topics classes at the University. Reports that he focuses in class on the works of four writers, Bunyan, Dante, C.S. Lewis and Flannery O'Connor. Discusses the difficulties that each of these writers had in relating to their contemporary society. Remarks of O'Connor's works, that without her "unequivocal Christian testimony," they would scarcely seem Christian. Comments on how, as Stanley Fish says of Milton and Donne, O'Connor lures the reader into making snap judgements, then dramatically judges and corrects the reader's response. Discusses "A Temple of the Holy Ghost" and *The Violent Bear It Away*. Veith concludes that, though he kept all parts of his life--religion, personal relationships, research, teaching--separate, occasionally within his class, conversions of a Christian sort took place as a result of the study.

1559a   Verderame, Carla. "A Retreat Home: Flannery O'Connor's Disempowered Daughters." *Flannery O'Connor Bulletin* 26-27 (1998-2000): 139-53.

Refers to Elaine Showalter's thesis that "domestic imprisonment confronted the American homemaker and her literary sisters of the 1950s." Contends that "while, on the surface, family life in America appeared stable and happy, there existed a dis-ease among women who were forced to assume the role of chief domestic and among writers who rendered such characters in their fiction." Suggests that women of the 1950s were imprisoned in their own homes and that contemporary women writers exposed their "latent sadness" through tales of "imprisonment and escape." Compares O'Connor to Carson McCullers, in particular *The Member of the Wedding*, and finds that both writers deal with similar themes. Discusses, in this context, a wide variety of O'Connor's female characters: Joy/Hulga Hopewell in "Good Country People"; Mary Grace in "Revelation"; the "intelligent child character" in "A Temple of the Holy Ghost"; Sally Virginia Cope in "A Circle in the Fire"; Lucynell Crater in "The Life You Save May Be Your Own"; and Ruby Hill in "A Stroke of Good Fortune." Concludes that whether her character is "a marginalized intellect such as Joy/Hulga or a disempowered daughter such as Lucynell, O'Connor's females often remain at home--forced there by a social system that undervalues and undermines them." Sees these characters as "reduced to feeble objects without resources to draw from . . . destined to live out their lives where they began their lives--at home."

1560   Vinson, James, and Greg S. Faller, eds. *The International Dictionary of Films and Filmmakers*. Vol. 5. Chicago: St. James, 1984. 265-268, 587, 319-20.

Includes references to O'Connor's work under the entries on John Huston, Harry Dean Stanton, and Alex North -- all of whom contributed to Huston's version of *Wise Blood*.

1561   Vipond, Diane. "Flannery O'Connor's World Without Pity." *Notes on Contemporary Literature* 20.2 (1990): 8-9.

Outlines an interpretation of "A Good Man Is Hard to Find" which sees the story as offering "a rapprochement between a vision of nihilism and one of spiritual redemption that takes the form of a warning." Declares that the incremental use of irony "that gathers momentum until it explodes in the final reverberating gunshot, obviates any traditional anagogical reading of the story." Concludes that the power of the story lies in O'Connor's deft use of "two elements of tragedy: pity and fear."

1562   Voelker, Joseph C. *Art and the Accidental in Anne Tyler*. Columbia: U of Missouri P, 1989. 9-10, 64, 110-13.

Offers brief discussions of Tyler's fiction and technique as compared to that of O'Connor and other writers. Contends that Eudora Welty uses "unkind events" in her fiction usually from a sense of "that's what happened," while O'Connor does the same from a sense of "authorial cruelty." Refers to Tarwater's actions in *The Violent Bear It Away* and suggests that, whereas Welty serves as "an intuitive model" for Tyler, O'Connor serves as an antitype. Compares Mrs. Emerson in Tyler's *The Clock Winder* (who has a stroke) to Julian in O'Connor's "Everything That Rises Must Converge." Sees other similarities between Miss Lorna in Tyler's "The Common Courtesies" and Mrs. Shortley in O'Connor's "The Displaced Person." Notes as well Tyler's use of "cartooning" in the same manner as O'Connor.

1563   Vollmar, Jim. "Flannery O'Connor: An Authentic Voice of the American South." *Month* (Great Britain) [Second New Series] 24.9-10 (1991): 443-47.

Review essay on the British edition of Flannery O'Connor's *The Complete Short Stories* (Faber and Faber). Provides a biographical sketch and discusses each of the stories included in the volume. Finds O'Connor's early stories to be "of variable quality," but her later works totally captivating. Regards her "eccentric characters" as "remorselessly driven by a hunger for some definitive experience--fundamentalist and transcendent--that at times verges on the psychopathic." States that the "bizarre almost ritualized behavior of the featured cast in the *Wise Blood* stories gives the reader a first taste of the intriguingly off-centre notion of spirituality which pervades the whole collection, and which is such a vital component of the very special `spirit of the place' the author conjures up." Refers to Thomas Merton, John Huston's film version of *Wise Blood*, and O'Connor's various themes. Discusses "A Stroke of Good Fortune," "Wildcat," "The Life You Save May Be Your Own," "Good Country People," "A Circle in the Fire," "The Displaced Person," "Everything That Rises Must Converge," "The Comforts of Home," "Parker's Back," "The River," "The Enduring Chill," "A Good Man Is Hard to Find," and "The Partridge Festival." Concludes that "for those who admire good story telling, and for all lovers of `Americana' especially, the stories of Flannery O'Connor make essential reading."

1564   Vonalt, Larry. "The Other End of Love: Harry Crews's *Car*." *A Grit's Triumph: Essays on the Works of Harry Crews*. Ed. David K. Jeffrey. Port Washington, NY: Associated Faculty, 1983. 132-39.

Discusses Crews's novel, *Car*, commenting on how Flannery O'Connor also expressed "some of the supernatural powers" modern man gives to the automobile. Includes a reference to Hazel Motes's remark in *Wise Blood*, that "`Nobody with a good car needs to be justified'"; and Mr. Shiftlet's claim in "The Life You Save May Be Your Own," that "`The spirit is like an automobile, always on the move . . .,' and `A man's spirit means more to him than anything else.'" Outlines how, through his novel, Crews "shows the car's power as an emblem of status, the measurer of men, and . . . suggests that the car's sexual attraction may be more actual than symbolic."

1565   Vrana, Stan A. *Interviews and Conversations with 20th-Century Authors Writing in English: An Index*. Metuchen, NJ: Scarecrow, 1982. 144-45.

Cites Granville Hicks's interview of O'Connor: "A Writer at Home With Her Heritage," *Saturday Review* 12 May 1962: 22-3. [Rpt. in Rosemary M. Magee's *Conversations With Flannery O'Connor*. Jackson: UP of Mississippi, 1987.]

1566   Vrana, Stan A. *Interviews and Conversations with 20th-Century Authors Writing in English: An Index*. Series II. Metuchen, NJ: Scarecrow Press, 1986. 176.

Offers citations to twelve interview-based articles related to O'Connor published between 1958 and 1963. [Note: all twelve interviews are cited and rpt. in Rosemary M. Magee's *Conversations With Flannery O'Connor*. Jackson: UP of Mississippi, 1987.]

1567   Wages, Jack D. and William L. Andrews. Comps. "Southern Literary Culture: 1969-1975: Flannery O'Connor." *Mississippi Quarterly* 32.1 (1978-79): 95-101, 139-40, 142-44, 146-55, 157-58.

Lists O'Connor-related master's and doctoral theses and dissertations.

1568   Wagner-Martin, Linda. "'Just the doing of It': Southern Women Writers and the Idea of Community." *Southern Literary Journal* 22.2 (1990): 19-32.

Includes a passing reference to O'Connor in a discussion of "place" and "community" of female characters in the works of Southern women writers. Works discussed include: Alice Walker's *The Color Purple* and *The Temple of My Familiar*; Sherley Anne Williams' *Dessa Rose*; Anne Tyler's *Breathing Lessons*; Lee Smith's *Fair and Tender Ladies*; Alice Adams' *Superior Women*; and Jill McCorkle's *Tending to Virginia*.

1569   Wakana, Maya Higashi. "Despair and O'Connor's Protagonists." *English and American Literature Studies in Kansai Gakuin University* (Japan) 27.1 (1982): 91-107.

1570   Walden, Daniel and Jane Salvia. "Flannery O'Connor's Dragon: Vision in `A Temple of the Holy Ghost.'" *Studies in American Fiction* 4.2 (1976): 230-35.

Discusses "A Temple of the Holy Ghost" and its twelve-year-old protagonist. Points out that the girl "shares O'Connor's situation: She is a Southern Catholic who experiences the confrontation of her religion and her region and tries to understand her world in terms of both." Analyzes the religious concerns and symbolism and concludes that her "fictional alter ego" finds that the "acceptance of mystery leads to the vision that is the basis of both creative genius and religious faith . . . a gift of God."

1571   Waldron, Ann. *Close Connections: Caroline Gordon and the Southern Renaissance*. Knoxville: U of Tennessee P, 1989. 72, 285, 286, 321-22, 328, 334, 340, 349, 352, 357, 359, 367.

Contains passing references to Flannery O'Connor in a variety of contexts, including: O'Connor's admiration for Gordon's "Summer Dust"; Gordon's interest in O'Connor's work and her editorial guidance; O'Connor's visit with Sue Jenkins while Gordon was there and comments about her reading "A Good Man Is Hard to Find" to a group which included "the Malcolm Cowleys and the Van Wyck Brooks"; comments regarding Brainard and Frances Neel Cheney's intention to visit Gordon in Rome and "perhaps bringing Flannery O'Connor along" to spend what might be her "last Christmas out of a wheelchair"; comments Gordon wrote to O'Connor in her letters about mutual friends; and, how Gordon's health began to fail soon after attending "a symposium on Flannery O'Connor" held in Georgia "in the seventies."

1572   Walker, Alice. "Beyond the Peacock: The Reconstruction of Flannery O'Connor." *Ms. Magazine* 4 (Dec. 1975): 77-79, 102, 104-06.

Walker offers her personal perspective on O'Connor's work, life-style, and cultural heritage as a Southern "lady." Describes her own now-deteriorated four-room sharecropper house and contrasts it to the homes of William Faulkner and Flannery O'Connor. Discusses biographical aspects of O'Connor's life and career, refers to "Everything That Rises Must Converge," and concludes that O'Connor's influence and courage helped Walker to truly "see." [Rpt. in *Friendship and Sympathy: Communities of Southern Women Writers*. Ed. Rosemary M. Magee. Jackson: UP of Mississippi, 1992, 172-87; in *In Search of Our Mothers' Gardens*. San Diego: Harcourt Brace Jovanovich, 1983, 42-59; in *Critical Essays on Flannery O'Connor*. Ed. Melvin J. Friedman and Beverly Lyon Clark. Boston: G.K. Hall, 1985, 71-81; and, excerpted in "A South Without Myths," *Sojourners* 23.10 (1994-95): 20.]

1573   Walker, Jeffrey. "1945-1956: Post-World War II Manners and Mores." *The American Short Story 1945-1980: A Critical History*. Ed. Gordon Weaver. Boston: Twayne, 1983. 1-34.

Briefly compares O'Connor to Eudora Welty, stating that while both use the South as their province and "liked to take chances," O'Connor's characters are more grotesque. Discusses "Good Country People" as an example of how O'Connor "blends comedy and tragedy in her depiction of people whose problems are not caused solely by their social or family upbringing, but by a basic flaw in their characters." Suggests that Hulga's disfigured body is reflectively symbolic of her "maimed soul," and that her pride and intellectual posturing only hide her "gullibility and ignorance." Summarizes the plot of "The Artificial Nigger" and claims that it focuses on distortion, estrangement, and reconciliation with a dramatic ending designed to shock "both the characters and the reader into an awareness of their infirmities."

1574   Walker, Nancy. "*Alelaste* or *Eiron*: American Women Writers and the Sense of Humor." *Studies in American Humor* 4.1-2 [New Series] (1985): 105-25.

Notes that while both "women as well as men possess the ability to appreciate and to create humor," the tradition of American humor, as reflected in "standard anthologies and critical studies, seems overwhelmingly the product of male writers." Considers why women's works have not been included in the canon of American humor and why women have "been generally regarded as humorless." Includes a brief reference to the "grim irony" in O'Connor's work, her being one of many examples of the "rich tradition of women's humor in American literature."

1575   Walker, Sue. "The Being of Illness: The Language of Being Ill." *Flannery O'Connor Bulletin* 25 (1996-97): 33-58.

Examines how O'Connor's battle with lupus is reflected in her letters, essays, stories, and novels. Uses Martin Heidegger's writings to guide readers through her "country of sickness," and suggests that, by "placing sickness within a Christian tradition, Flannery O'Connor situates the carnal body within a framework that not only allows for the presence of grace but also brings a sense of acceptance that whatever happens is part of God's ultimate purpose." Notes that "180 references to illness appear in the letters in *The Habit of Being*," the source where readers will find that O'Connor "allows herself to make her illness an actual subject of discourse." Discusses the context of O'Connor's remarks about her illness in her letters to Maryat Lee, focusing on her use of humor, perhaps "as a defense against anxiety." Follows with detailed explications of "Greenleaf," "The Enduring Chill," and "Parker's Back," to point out and discuss examples of how O'Connor's illness is reflected in her fiction.

1576   Walker, Sue. "Spelling Out Illness: Lupus as Metaphor in Flannery O'Connor's `Greenleaf.'" *Chattahoochee Review* 12.1 (1991): 54-63.

States that while O'Connor's story "Greenleaf" has been examined, from the perspectives of religion and myth, the story has been overlooked "as a metaphor of O'Connor's terminal illness." Argues that while "the overt and conscious message of `Greenleaf' may concern salvation by grace, the author's reaction both to the symptoms of lupus and to the life changes created by those symptoms seems to have influenced the action of the story; it may further serve as an unconscious motif." Provides excerpts from O'Connor's letters that describe her attitude toward the disease, offers a detailed explication in an attempt to tie aspects of "Greenleaf" to her lupus, examines the role of O'Connor's faith in adapting to her condition, and describes O'Connor's possible recognition "of unconscious forces impinging upon" her artistic work. Suggests that the bull in "Greenleaf" may symbolize O'Connor's lupus, and may be viewed as "'an unwanted, uncouth, and uninvited aspect of self. It pursues her, invades her sense of well-being, and eats away at her house, the mortal body of the Lord, until eventually, charging in sunlight, it takes her life." Refers to a connection between lupus and the legendary werewolf, and the image of the sun "as a silver bullet."

1577   Walkiewicz, E.P. "1957-1968: Toward Diversity of Form." *The American Short Story 1945-1980: A Critical History*. Ed. Gordon Weaver. Boston: Twayne, 1983. 35-76.

Discusses and characterizes the short fiction of the period 1957-68. Notes that "major figures," such as Flannery O'Connor, matured and "new and important" other writers, such as John Updike, Bernard Malamud, and John Barth, emerged. Comments on O'Connor's work, that she is "deeply concerned with ethical questions but [is] never didactic or moralistic," and outlines how her words often focus on human limitation and deformity. Discusses O'Connor's interest in the bizarre and the grotesque. Comments on the physical and spiritual condition of her characters and notes difficulties readers have with reading symbolic content in her work.

1578   Walls, Doyle W. "O'Connor's `A Good Man Is Hard to Find.'" *Explicator* 46.2 (1988): 43-45.

Notes that little attention has been paid to the scene in "A Good Man Is Hard to Find" in which "the Grandmother makes comments from the car about `the cute little pickaninny'," nor the "Christian mystery behind the Southern manners." Suggests that this passage uses biblical allusion to allow the Grandmother "to reveal her essential self and prepares the reader for the climax of the story."

1579   Walsh, William J. *Speak So I Shall Know Thee: Interviews With Southern Writers*. Jefferson, NC: McFarland, 1990. 46-47, 116-17, 130, 132, 155, 171, 179, 180, 181, 183, 269, 282, 283.

Offers a collection of interviews of poets and writers whose thoughts and ideas provide readers with a "balanced representation of writers in the

contemporary South." Passing references to O'Connor in interviews with:
Doris Betts, Clyde Edgerton, William Price Fox, Madison Jones, Terry
Kay, Marion Montgomery, John Stone, and Miller Williams.

1580   Walston, Rosa Lee. "Editor's Note." *Flannery O'Connor Bulletin* 11
         (1982): i.

         Expresses regret over the departure of Gerald Becham from Georgia
         College. Becham had served as Assistant Director of the Russell Library
         and Curator of the *Flannery O'Connor Collection* for twelve years.
         Reports that forthcoming issues of the *Bulletin* would be included in the
         MLA Directory of Periodicals and in the *MLA International Directory*;
         then, announced the formation of a new Editorial Advisory Board
         comprised of: Sally Fitzgerald, Carter Martin, Frederick Asals, J.O. Tate,
         Louise Westling, John R. May, Ralph Wood, and Marion Montgomery.

1581   Walston, Rosa Lee, Mary Barbara Tate, and Sarah Gordon. "'The Fiction
         Writer and Her Country': the Second Flannery O'Connor Symposium."
         Flannery O'Connor Bulletin 5 (1976): i, 2.

         Announces that the Second Flannery O'Connor Symposium will be held
         at Georgia College & State University, April 2-3, 1977. Slated to speak
         are: Sally Fitzgerald, Marion Montgomery, Rosa Lee Walston, Louis D.
         Rudin, Jr. [to present the O'Connor Memorial Lecture], and Glenn Jordan,
         director of the NEH-sponsored film, "The Displaced Person" [which will
         also be shown]. Reports that a prize will be awarded "for the best new
         critical paper on O'Connor's works by a young scholar."

1582   Walston, Rosa Lee. "Preface." *Flannery O'Connor Bulletin* 6 (1977): 4.

         Outlines activities and describes the presentations given during the two-
         day Flannery O'Connor symposium held at Georgia College & State
         University in April, 1977. Refers to presentations by Sally Fitzgerald,
         Melissa Hines, Marion Montgomery, Glenn Jordan (director of the NEH
         supported film, *The Displaced Person*), Louis D. Rubin, Jr., Barbara
         McKenzie, and Walston's own remarks.

1583   Walston, Rosa Lee. "1979 Visiting O'Connor Professor." *Flannery
         O'Connor Bulletin* 7 (1978): 4.

         Announces that Sally Fitzgerald will serve as Visiting Flannery O'Connor
         Professor for a four-week seminar for both undergraduate and graduate

students at Georgia College & State University during the summer of 1979. Notes that she served as co-editor with her husband, Robert Fitzgerald of *Mystery and Manners* (1969) and as editor for *The Habit of Being*. Reports that she "is continuing her study of O'Connor and has recently received a grant for this purpose from the Radcliffe Institute." A photograph of Flannery O'Connor and Brainard Cheney in the early 1950s is reproduced on the preceding page.

1584   Walston, Rosa Lee, Mary Barbara Tate, and Sarah Gordon. "From the Editors." *Flannery O'Connor Bulletin* 10 (1981): 3-4.

Acknowledges Jan Nordby Gretlund's support in acquiring permission to publish in this issue "'The Shiftlet Fragment,'" O'Connor's apparent continuation of "The Life You Save May Be Your Own." Closes with a solicitation to readers for a handscreened print of Flannery O'Connor's self-portrait. Illustration: Color photograph of "Flannery O'Connor, *Self-Portrait*, 1953."

1585   Washburn, Delores. "The `Feeder' Motif in Flannery O'Connor's Fiction: A Gauge of Spiritual Efficacy." *Realist of Distances: Flannery O'Connor Revisited*. Ed. Karl-Heinz Westarp and Jan Nordby Gretlund. Aarhus, Denmark: Aarhus UP, 1987. 123-34.

Discusses O'Connor's "treatment of the rites of feeding," focusing on the role of "wife and mother, who prepared or oversaw the preparation of life-sustaining food . . . and offered it to her family as well as to any servants, hired hands, or visitors." Suggests that authors generally place characters in this role "to provide for each individual a sense of well-being with respect to bodily and social nourishment." Cites examples from the works of William Faulkner, Carson McCullers, Katherine Anne Porter, and Eudora Welty. Analyzes the "nature of the feeders and their pattern of feeding" to illustrate how O'Connor used these observances to reflect various characters' "state of grace or absence thereof." Discusses in this context a variety of works, including: "A Good Man Is Hard to Find," "A View of the Woods," "The River," "A Stroke of Good Fortune," "The Life You Save May Be Your Own," "A Circle in the Fire," "Greenleaf," "Good Country People," "A Temple of the Holy Ghost," *Wise Blood*, and *The Violent Bear It Away*. Concludes that the feeder motif "clarifies both character and theme" in her work.

1586   Washburn, Delores. "The `Feeder' in *The Violent Bear It Away*." *Flannery O'Connor Bulletin* 9 (1980): 112-19.

Examines how the Feeder motif is applied by O'Connor "to develop character, determine conflict, and define theme" in *The Violent Bear It Away*. Argues that both Mason Tarwater and George Rayber serve as "Feeders" to Francis Marion Tarwater, that "old Tarwater function[s] as a traditional Feeder within a remnant of an agrarian culture while Rayber performs according to the new urban and technological feeding patterns." Contends that O'Connor's use of old Tarwater's stomach and "its association with bread," imply that the meals he prepared for himself and his great-nephew "are prefigurings of eternal feasts in which `the Bread of Life' is the immortal feeder." Offers an overview of sections of the book which relate to the Feeder motif.

1587   Wasserman, Renata R. Mautner. "Backwards to Nineveh." *Renascence* 32.1 (1979): 21-32.

Contends that O'Connor is "interested in the ineffectiveness of ordinary good manners when they are confronted with real evil . . . rudeness . . . betrayal . . . [and] crime." States that her work is troubling because the resolution offered is a dissonance. Mystery comes not through manners but is recognizable only when manners become absurd and "unaccountable to any human formula, or anything human." Discusses *The Violent Bear It Away*, *Wise Blood*, and O'Connor's "Introduction" to *A Memoir of Mary Ann*. Concludes that she created a world where "there is no tenderness" and characters must "separate themselves utterly from creation and fellow creatures and inhabit lands of silence and darkness."

1588   Watanabe, Kayoko. "`Grace in Nature' in the Works of Flannery O'Connor." *Alice* [Bulletin of the Graduate School of Tokyo Women's Christian University] (Japan) 9 (1988): 39-54.

Contends that O'Connor's message to readers seems to be that the South is still a place where God's grace can be felt through nature. (Abstracted by Kayoko Watanabe).

1589   Watanabe, Kayoko. "Sense of Grotesqueness in the Works of Flannery O'Connor: The `Apparent' and the `Real' Grotesque." *Tokyo Seitoku College Bulletin* 29 (1997): 73-82.

Discusses how O'Connor sees the "real" grotesque in people who have strong pride in their intelligence or practical abilities, and praises the "apparent" grotesque characters who rectify the "real" grotesque people. (Abstracted by Kayoko Watanabe).

1590   Watanabe, Kayoko. "The `Senses' in the Works of Flannery O'Connor: The South as a Sensuous Region." *Tokyo Seitoku Junior College Bulletin* (Japan) 27 (Mar. 1994): 67-85.

Contends that O'Connor was concerned about the ascendancy of reason over emotion in Western culture. Suggests that O'Connor sounds a warning to modern intellectuals--including herself--not to ignore the kind of knowledge gained through the senses. (Abstracted by Kayoko Watanabe).

1591   Watanabe, Kayoko. "*Wise Blood*: The `Double' Motif in a Wasteland." *The Tsuda Review* 41 (1996): 63-89.

Discusses the influence of Edgar Allan Poe's "William Wilson" in Haze's struggle with his "double." Sees an indication of hope of rebirth in *Wise Blood* in a manner similar to T.S. Eliot's *The Waste Land*. (Abstracted by Kayoko Watanabe).

1592   "We achieved a milestone . . . " *Friends of Flannery* [Newsletter]. 1.6 (Nov. 1992): 1.

Reports that the State of Georgia installed a historic marker in front of Flannery O'Connor's childhood home in Savannah, GA in November, 1992. Includes a photograph showing Pat Persse, Lillian Odom, Margaret Persse Trexler, and Louise Florencourt unveiling the marker.

1593   "We are combining . . . " *Friends of Flannery* [Newsletter]. 3.3-4 (June/Sept. 1994): 1.

Reports that WSAV-TV, a local Savannah, GA television station, aired a "short report" on O'Connor's childhood home, calling it "the city's major literary landmark."

1594   Weaver, Mary Jo. "Thomas Merton and Flannery O'Connor: The Urgency of Vision." *Religion in Life* 48.4 (1979): 449-61.

Suggests that Thomas Merton and Flannery O'Connor shared an "*urgency*" in their vision, "riveted on the transcendental order," and that both were driven to peculiar means of conveying their visions to an indifferent or hostile audience. Argues that the principal difference between the two is that O'Connor understood the urgency "from the beginning" and Merton "developed a sense of it only after a long time."

Concludes that some of the themes of O'Connor's work "provide interesting angles with which to view some of the angles in Thomas Merton's life and to interpret the burgeoning change in his perception of reality." [Rpt. in *Thomas Merton: Pilgrim in Process*. Ed. Donald Grayston and Michael W. Higgins. NY: Griffin House, 1983. 27-40.]

1595   Weaver, Mary Jo. "The Urgency of Vision." *Desert Call* 13.1 (1978): 3-9, 20.

Uses O'Connor's comment that she saw everything "from the standpoint of Christian orthodoxy" as a starting point from which to examine her literary strategies and view of "God's place in the Universe." Contends that O'Connor's works are "harsh and dreadful stories of life and death, economical, perceptive and gripping." Notes that O'Connor routinely used "grotesque images, characters, and situations" to pose the choice, "choose God now or never." Discusses the role of the writer and her prophetic themes. Explicates *The Violent Bear It Away* and *Wise Blood* focusing on the complexities of the works and their religious themes. Refers briefly to stories which concern death, alienation, and "the creation of the false self." Concludes that O'Connor's works serve as "urgent protests against 'fashionable' religion and notions" that propose that grace "'can be separated from nature and served . . . as Instant Uplift.'"

1596   Webb, Stephen H. "Life Over the Edges: Flannery O'Connor's Dis-Grace-Full Extremity." *Blessed Excess: Religion and the Hyperbolic Imagination*. Albany: State U of New York P, 1993. xvi, 89-111.

Explores O'Connor's "hyperbolic construal of grace" and contends that her fiction "exhibits a subtle relationship between trope and theology." Suggests that "instead of simply employing rhetoric for apologetic purposes," O'Connor's stories "move toward mystery without guaranteeing any arrival." Observes that while "hyperbole cannot deliver what it promises," it can certainly "prod and poke the reader toward unusual visions and troubling transformations." Relates that it is at this point that O'Connor's artistry is evident as she imagines "dreams of excess that nightmarishly shatter any awakening return to reality," which in turn, imposes upon her readers "the ontological question of what is really real." Concludes that O'Connor "pushes hyperbole toward its breaking point with only oblique suggestions about what lies beyond, in the aftermath of the ensuing explosion."

1597   Weber, Ronald. "The Catholic Novel Is Here to Stay (Till Spring, Anyway)." *Notre Dame Magazine* 10.4 (1981): 14-16.

Passing references to O'Connor, who thought the term Catholic "so suspect that it had to be used in quotation marks." While O'Connor acknowledged the influence of such Catholics as Léon Bloy, Georges Bernanos and Françcois Mauriac, she felt that a writer could "`get more benefit from reading someone like Ernest Hemingway, where there is apparently a hunger for a Catholic completeness in life.'" O'Connor pointed out that "`a Catholic has to have strong nerves to write about Catholics,'" because doing so might bring the wrath of pious readers and critics on the author.

1598   Weigel, George S. "Secularism R.I.P.: Reclaiming the Catholic Intellectual Tradition." *Crisis* 7 (1989): 22-31.

Offers "three lessons for modern Catholics" gleaned from *The Habit of Being*, and questions whether "the intellectual life of American Catholicism . . . could recognize, much less nurture and sustain" someone like Flannery O'Connor today. Concludes by comparing remarks by Karl Rahner on the subject "`Why I remain in the church'" to O'Connor's retort to Mary McCarthy's view of the Host as a symbol.

1599   Weiner, Alan R., and Spencer Means. *Literary Criticism Index*. Metuchen, NJ: Scarecrow, 1984. 452-53.

A guide to selected reference sources with material on O'Connor. Useful as a bibliography of bibliographical series and collections.

1600   Weinstein, Arnold. "Flannery O'Connor and the Art of Displacement." *Nobody's Home: Speech, Self and Place in American Fiction From Hawthorne to DeLillo*. New York: Oxford UP, 1993. 108-28.

Contends that O'Connor's fiction is as challenging for modern readers to understand as Kafka's, as each author struggles "to show the workings of the soul in a materialist world." Suggests that some may find O'Connor's work "too regional in its purview, and too theological, indeed too doctrinal in its assumptions." Discusses O'Connor's "relentlessly *pedestrian* concern with transcendence" which, "in her hands . . . begins to shimmer with `otherness.'" Argues that her "dark and beautiful fables are almost Edenic in their wholeness of expression," full of words which "possess a fullness of utterance that no one, including their speakers, initially sees." Analyzes O'Connor's "strategies of displacement," and states that the everyday aspects of her stories are developed to reveal to readers "the contours of that larger Passion play that is her true subject." Offers explications of "The River," "The Life You Save May Be Your Own," "Good Country People," and "The Displaced Person." Concludes that in each of her works "there is something of that `radiance of form' about which Jacques Maritain spoke, a kind of incandescence that illuminates the new circuits and lines of connection that we begin to sight as O'Connor's stories come to their odd conclusions."

1601   Weinstein, Philip M. "`Coming unalone': Gesture and Gestation in Faulkner and O'Connor." *Faulkner, His Contemporaries, and His Posterity*. Ed. Waldemar Zacharasiewicz. Transatlantic Perspectives Series, No. 2. Tübingen and Basel: A. Francke Verlag, 1993. 262-75.

Defines and compares gesture and gestation, "literally and figuratively," in works by William Faulkner and Flannery O'Connor. Focuses on "the resonance of `coming unalone.'" Discusses these themes in Faulkner's *As I Lay Dying, Go Down, Moses, The Sound and the Fury*, and *The Reivers*; and in O'Connor's "A Temple of the Holy Ghost," *Wise Blood*, "Good Country People," and "A Circle in the Fire." States that while Temple Drake may serve as the embodiment of "Faulknerian scandal," the "double-sexed circus freak" of "A Temple of the Holy Ghost" is representative of O'Connor's views of the Incarnation. Asserts that the body of O'Connor's freak is "less a site for potential and illicit subjective encounters involving the group dynamics of race and class . . . than a site of already ordained freakish opposition between the human and the divine." Sees O'Connor's "scandal," unlike Faulkner's, as a "divinely decreed" burden to be accepted and embraced. Contends that the passage in "Good Country People" in which Mrs. Freeman describes to Mrs. Hopewell Glynese's courtship is representative of the "class-coded humor that fuels O'Connor's comedy." Relates also that Glynese's sty therapy suggests "sexual intercourse, fusing the notions of illness, fornication, and the grotesque." Closes with a discussion of O'Connor's "disdain for the topical," and how she "forged her own subjective identity through participation within a host of socially constructed economies."

1602   Weisenburger, Steven. "The Devil & John Hawkes." *Review of Contemporary Fiction* 3.3 (1983): 155-63.

Briefly mentions *Wise Blood* to illustrate John Hawkes's fictional technique in his novel, *Travesty*.

1603   Weisenburger, Steven. "In-Between." *Callaloo* 7 (Winter 1984): 153-56.

Offers a review of Charles Johnson's novel, *Oxherding Tale* (Bloomington: Indiana U Press, 1982) which includes a brief comparison of his approach to satire to that of Ishmael Reed and Flannery O'Connor.

1604   Weisenburger, Steven. "Late-Modernist Disruptions: West, O'Connor, and Hawkes." *Fables of Subversion: Satire and the American Novel, 1930-1980*. Athens: U of Georgia P, 1995. 30-79.

Examines the fiction of John Hawkes, Nathanael West, and Flannery O'Connor to demonstrate how the work of these three novelists "made a clean and self-conscious break" from the conventional practice and methods of their day. Contends that this break "radically shifted the functions and form" of mid-twentieth century satire and resulted in these novelists becoming "touchstones for a generation of satirists whose work began appearing in the sixties." Examines how the work of these three also exemplifies "an experimentation with the regressive form, grotesque style, and carnivalesque *topos* that are all so distinctive to postmodern satire." Sees in their work "a steady movement away from the conventions of realism and toward a narrative poetics founded not on the serio-comic orderings of older satires but on the possibilities for structural repetition, doubling, inversion, embedding, and the like." The section on O'Connor focuses on *Wise Blood*. Uses the text of the novel, and her letters and readings during the years in which she was writing the book, to examine her "struggles" in writing this "painstakingly composed" satirical novel.

1605   Weisenburger, Steven. "Style in *Wise Blood*." *Genre* 16.1 (1983): 75-97.

Briefly describes the time, effort, and method O'Connor used to create *Wise Blood*, a work which the "first generation of critics charged "presented `a classic set of unsolved novelistic problems.'" Argues that readers can safely ignore these early critics, since "details of plot and character are themselves tangential to the writing of a *satire*." Suggests that the problems are not so much "novelistic" as stylistic. Follows with an extensive explication of *Wise Blood*'s literary style, theme, "structure of irony," eye imagery, similes, and "elegant structure of doubles and repetitions." Concludes with a discussion of each character in the novel. Mentions William Carlos Williams, Nathanael West, and John Hawkes.

1606   Weiss, Irving and Anne, comps. and eds. *Thesaurus of Book Digests 1950-1980*. New York: Crown, 1981. 146, 182, 490, 508, 528.

Short plot summaries of *Wise Blood*, *The Violent Bear It Away*, *A Good Man Is Hard to Find*, and *Everything That Rises Must Converge*.

1607   Weixlmann, Joe. *American Short-Fiction Criticism and Scholarship, 1959-1977*. Chicago: Swallow and Ohio UP, 1982. 432-45.

Provides a selected bibliography of O'Connor criticism, organized by individual stories and general studies, with ample cross-referencing.

1607a   Welborn, Amy. "Does Flannery O'Connor Show a `lack of charity'?" *Our Sunday Visitor* 10 Sept. 2000: 3.

Reports on the banning of O'Connor's short story collection *A Good Man Is Hard to Find* from Arsenio Orteza's summer reading list at the Catholic High School in Opelousas, Louisiana. States that Orteza was directed by his principal, the school's chancellor, and the Bishop of the Diocese of Lafayette, Edward O'Donnell, to drop the collection due to protests by African-American parents. Claims that complaints focused on O'Connor's Grandmother in "A Good Man Is Hard to Find" referring to black children as "pickaninnies" and her use of "`the N word'" in "The Artificial Nigger." Closes with reactions by Orteza, who is himself half-white and half-Filipino, and comments by Peter Cline, O'Connor's second cousin and English-department Chairman at Riverwood High School in Atlanta.

1608   Welling, Lloyd C. "The Catholic Vision of Flannery O'Connor." *Studies in Formative Spirituality* 1.3 (1980): 393-406.

Points out that while O'Connor is often referred to as a "Catholic writer," she attempted to distance herself from this artificial label by making it clear "that she had no intention of grinding the proselytizing ax for her particular creed." Suggests that O'Connor was, however, preoccupied with Christian themes and symbols and used her literary art as "`an instrument for penetrating reality,'" based upon her belief that "`Christian dogma is about the only thing left in the world that surely guards and respects mystery.'" Contends that O'Connor saw the Incarnation as supporting her art and that her task was to make "the word become flesh" while anchoring her stories in "the world of flesh and blood." Argues that O'Connor was a realist whose interest was in "the ultimate reaches of reality," which she attempted to represent through the Gothic and grotesque modes, appropriate symbols, and Christian and biblical archetypes. Examines *Wise Blood* in the context of the theoretical model presented. Concludes that the reader of O'Connor's works "discovers that the novel is *catholic* rather than *Catholic*, speaking to every [one] who refuses to close his eyes either to the glory or to the horror of the mysterious reality in which he lives and moves and has his being."

1609   Welling, Lloyd C. "Center of Existence: A Testament of Faith in the Letters of Flannery O'Connor." *Studies in Formative Spirituality* 3.1 (1982): 99-107.

Review essay of *The Habit of Being*. Relates an incident described in a letter in which O'Connor remarks of the Eucharist, "'Well, if it's a symbol, to hell with it,'" and asserts that "embodied in this incident is the heart of Flannery O'Connor's faith." Discusses her impatience with "saccharine piety," sentimentality, or "free-floating emotionalism." Claims that she "embraced a fully orthodox anti-dualistic view concerning nature and grace," saw the "visible universe as a reflection of the invisible universe," and was "impatient with the pseudo-mysticism touted by the so-called 'beat' writers of the late fifties." Notes that "much of the context of Miss O'Connor's letters is devoted explicitly to a discussion of her Catholic faith," focusing on "the nature of faith itself."

1610   Wells, Joel. "O'Connor, Mary Flannery (1925-64)." *The Encyclopedia of American Catholic History*. Ed. Michael Glazier and Thomas J. Shelley. Collegeville, MN: Liturgical Press, 1997. 1071-74.

Provides a biographical sketch of O'Connor's life, and considers her place in American literature. Discusses O'Connor's assertion that her commitment to Christian dogma was "actually a source of freedom, not constraint," and remarks that she lived with death as "a dark companion for all of her creative life." Declares O'Connor to be a "superbly gifted and disciplined writer" who "set her fiction mostly in the South and grounded it in her rock solid faith in the mysteries of incarnation and redemption." States that critics appreciate her "aesthetic skills, her vivid, terse descriptions, her dead-on-target ear for dialect and idiom, her irreverent humor, [and] her use of the grotesque to arrest attention and frame moral and physical tragedies." Refers to assessments by Patricia O'Connor, Granville Hicks, Katherine Anne Porter, and Thomas Merton, and to O'Connor's assessment of works by Tennessee Williams, Harper Lee, and William Faulkner.

1611   Welty, Eudora. *Conversations With Eudora Welty*. Ed. Peggy Whitman Prenshaw. Jackson: U of Mississippi P, 1984. 20-21, 25, 54, 80, 95, 214, 217-19, 227, 254-55, 312, 343.

Offers a compilation of interviews with Eudora Welty spanning forty years of her literary career. Interviews are arranged chronologically, with the full citation for the source of each interview provided. Welty responds at length to the question, "Do you have anything you would like to say about Flannery O'Connor?" and offers her views of O'Connor's religious concerns. Other passing references refer to O'Connor's remarks, life, or works to clarify a question or answer for Welty.

1612   Werner, Craig Hansen. "Dublin(er)'s Joyce: Ernest Gaines, Flannery O'Connor, Russell Banks." *Paradoxical Resolutions: American Fiction Since James Joyce.* Urbana: U of Illinois P, 1982. 34-50.

Essay on James Joyce's literary techniques, relating some of these to O'Connor. Discusses the story cycle and comments on O'Connor's development of central thematic issues from different perspectives. Discusses various stories in *Everything That Rises Must Converge*, and describes how "O'Connor, like Joyce in *Dubliners*, immerses the reader in the `thoughts of various unsavory characters.'" Suggests that while O'Connor's Catholicism may have kept her from approving of Joyce, his "techniques did not keep her from expressing her Catholicism."

1613   West, James L.W. III. *American Authors and the Literary Marketplace Since 1900.* Philadelphia: U of Pennsylvania P, 1988. 69-70, 128.

Asserts that O'Connor was an exception to the rule of young authors being "particularly vulnerable to high-handed editors because they are eager to be published and will make almost any compromise to see their work in print." Describes her conflict with Rinehart editor, John Selby, regarding her unconventional first novel, *Wise Blood*, and how her agent, Elizabeth McKee, "extricated her from her Rinehart contract and guided her to Robert Giroux at Harcourt, Brace." Includes a passing reference to O'Connor's use of the label "drugstore edition" in a discussion of early paperback editions of American fiction.

1614   Westarp, Karl-Heinz. "Flannery O'Connor's Development: An Analysis of the Judgement-Day Material." *Realist of Distances: Flannery O'Connor Revisited.* Aarhus, Denmark: Aarhus UP, 1987. 46-54.

Contends that the various versions of "Judgement Day" offer scholars an opportunity to observe "Flannery O'Connor's development as an artist and thinker." Describes the materials in the *Flannery O'Connor Collection* at Georgia College & State University in Milledgeville and addresses the question, "What are the major variants in style, structure, and message in the manuscripts?" Discusses and compares "An Exile in the East," "The Geranium," the various versions of "Getting Home," and the published version of "Judgement Day." Suggests that, "after many revisions, `Judgement Day' is not only perfect in style and structure, [but] also the characters are fully drawn." Concludes that the material discussed "epitomizes the different phases in O'Connor's development from first promises in `The Geranium' to final perfection in `Judgement Day,' both as an artist and as thinker: it `marks the distance she has traveled.'"

1615   Westarp, Karl-Heinz. "Flannery O'Connor's Displaced Persons." *The Dolphin: Publications of the English Department, University of Aarhus* (Denmark) 20 (Spring 1991): 89-98.

Offers a detailed explication of "The Displaced Person" and concludes that the theme of physical displacement includes "those who feel safely surrounded by their possessions." Considers the implications of Mr. Guizac's death, and suggests that Guizac's treatment was meant to serve as a parallel to Jesus' life story, as he too "was a displaced person, whom the pharisees regarded as a threat to their position, whom they had removed and killed." [Note: This issue of *The Dolphin* was also distributed by Aarhus UP as *Where? Place in Recent North American Fictions*, Ed. Karl-Heinz Westarp, Aarhus, Denmark: Aarhus UP, 1991.]

1615a   Westarp, Karl-Heinz. "Flannery O'Connor's Translucent Settings." *American Studies in Scandinavia* 31.2 (1999): 31-41.

Remarks that O'Connor "was fully aware of the importance of creating in her fiction a general locale and a particular physical location," described it in minute detail, and "was convinced of the truth" of the adage "`nothing in the mind unless it was first in the senses.'" Presents "a number of typical O'Connor settings as examples of focal points, where immanence and transcendence meet, and where the particular becomes translucent." Discusses the significance of setting in *Wise Blood*, "A Circle in the Fire," "A View of the Woods," *The Violent Bear It Away*, and "Revelation." Compares, briefly, O'Connor's eye for settings with Eudora Welty's and D.H. Lawrence's. Notes how she used the peacock as "an integral part of the setting and . . . a sign that a character is being offered a moment of insight." Comments on how her depiction of the sun and treeline serves "as an intersection between the immanent setting and its transcendent meaning." Concludes that O'Connor's "multifarious settings are, in the final analysis, renderings of the same country which should lead the character to a recognition of his/her `true country.'"

1616   Westarp, Karl-Heinz. "`Judgement Day': The Published Text Versus O'Connor's Final Version." *Flannery O'Connor Bulletin* 11 (1982): 108-22.

Reminds readers that "Parker's Back" and "Judgement Day" were among the last stories O'Connor worked on before her death, and suggests that they "could therefore justly be called her testament." Contends that a comparison of the published version of "Judgement Day" and late manuscript revisions reveals that "the published text is based on the version of *Dunn* 197a whereas Flannery's final emendations are found in

Dunn 197b." Poses, and offers possible answers to the question, "Why were Flannery's last minute changes not honored by the editors?" Then, describes the evidence seen in the manuscripts, and goes through the major differences between the published text and the manuscript version of *Dunn* 197b. Follows with an assessment of "how the last changes affect the story as a whole." Refers to comments by Elizabeth McKee, Sally Fitzgerald, and Catherine Carver. Concludes that "O'Connor's final [manuscript] version of `Judgement Day,' is technically . . . more satisfactory," since "its characters have more depth in their relations with each other than in the published version."

1617   Westarp, Karl-Heinz. "Lost in the Cosmos: Place in Walker Percy." *The Dolphin: Publications of the English Department, University of Aarhus.* (Denmark). 20 (Spring 1991): 108-17.

Alleges that the South is where Percy felt most at home, "his `somewhere', the place that fostered and nourished his imagination as it did the works of his contemporaries Flannery O'Connor, Eudora Welty and William Faulkner." Refers to his comment that he viewed the "New South" not as "`the South of Flannery,'" but as "`the South of Interstate 12 and Highway 190. It is the South of Los Angeles." Contrastingly, refers to how O'Connor used "the concrete Southern setting" as "`a gateway to reality', enabling her to read `a small history in a universal light,'" and allowing her to operate at "`a peculiar crossroads where time and place and eternity somehow meet.'" [Note: This issue of *The Dolphin* was also distributed by Aarhus UP as *Where? Place in Recent North American Fictions*, Ed. Karl-Heinz Westarp, Aarhus, Denmark: Aarhus UP, 1991.]

1618   Westarp, Karl-Heinz. "`Parker's Back': A Curious Crux Concerning Its Sources." *Flannery O'Connor Bulletin* 11 (1982): 1-9.

Offers substantial evidence to show that *Memoirs of a Tattooist*, compiled and edited by Peter Leighton, and published in London by Oldbourne, in 1958, heavily influenced "certain details" of "Parker's Back." Notes O'Connor's reference to *Memoirs* in a letter to "A," Leighton's description of George Burchett (the tattooist), and how O'Connor's descriptions of tattoo techniques closely resemble descriptions in Leighton's book. Follows with a discussion of possible material in *Memoirs* that O'Connor might have included in her story, in particular a list of examples of tattoos people had chosen which parallel Parker's. Offers possible reasons O'Connor chose to use the image of a Byzantine Christ. Closes with a description with an interview of Augusta tattoo artist, Ted Don Inman, Jr., published in the *Atlanta Journal and Constitution Magazine*, titled "One Night in a Tattoo Parlor," which provides strikingly similar details as well.

1619   Westarp, Karl-Heinz. Rev. of *Flannery O'Connor's Romaner*, by Erik Nielsen. *Flannery O'Connor Bulletin* 21 (1992): 140-43.

Reports that Nielsen's book, written in Danish, provides an analysis of both *Wise Blood* and *The Violent Bear It Away* as well as "a fine chapter" on O'Connor's poetics. Characterizes Nielsen's critique in thematic terms, as perceiving *Wise Blood* "as the battle of the sacred and the profane and *The Violent Bear It Away* as the victory of the sacred in that battle." Reports that Nielsen includes chapters on the sacred, Thomas Aquinas's influence on how O'Connor integrated art, and an introduction to O'Connor's world that focuses on the role of religion in her work, her relation to the South and the church, and her attitudes toward the sciences and to her readers.

1620   Westarp, Karl-Heinz. "Shades of Evil in the Fictions of Flannery O'Connor and Walker Percy." *PEO: Pre-Publications of the English Department of Odense University* (Denmark) (June 1994): 373-80.

Contends that the fictions of O'Connor and Percy are "saturated with the presence of evil," and that both authors address their fiction to a modern world "which does not want to be aware of evil" nor its power over humankind. Discusses the common backgrounds and concerns of the two authors, their mutual admiration for each other, and their struggle "against all odds to show forth the mystery of evil--and grace--in what they considered an almost completely de-mythologized world." Recounts comments by each author regarding the nature and presence of evil in the modern world, including O'Connor's comments to John Hawkes. Illustrates each author's perspective with an explication of: "The Lame Shall Enter First" for O'Connor, and the novel *Lancelot* for Percy. Concludes that in both works, "evil is present very concretely," and is "dramatized in the actions" of the protagonists, who are "increasingly possessed by the power of evil."

1621   Westarp, Karl-Heinz. "Teilhard de Chardin's Impact on Flannery O'Connor: A Reading of `Parker's Back.'" *Flannery O'Connor Bulletin* 12 (1983): 93-113.

Cites Ralph C. Wood's article: "The Heterodoxy of Flannery O'Connor's Book Reviews," in *The Flannery O'Connor Bulletin* [5 (1976): 3-21] and contends that Wood was incorrect in his conclusion that "O'Connor certainly did not have an `unbounded esteem for Teilhard de Chardin's work.'" Uses evidence from O'Connor's letters and manuscripts to support a reading of "Parker's Back" as "a poetic rendering of `Tay-ahr's' theory of evolution and convergence toward the eschatological point Omega who is Christ." Follows with a detailed and heavily footnoted explication and discussion of "Parker's Back." Concludes that, in this story, O'Connor has successfully "dramatized Teilhard's scientific-philosophical-theological vision in a unique way."

1622   Westling, Louise. "Demeter and Kore, Southern Style." *Pacific Coast Philology* 19.1-2 (1984): 101-07.

Asserts that "bookish southern girls a generation ago were likely to have saturated themselves with Greek and Roman Mythology in childhood," and suggests that this "kind of imaginative experience" is reflected in both O'Connor's and Welty's works. Declares that both "echo the Demeter/Persephone story in dramatizing strong maternal figures who preside over pastoral settings," but differ in their use of the tales. Contends that Welty "celebrates the feminine power and fertility" of the tales and appears comfortable with her femininity and is able to imagine an "attractive mother figure." O'Connor, however, "seems to have only loathing for her gender and wish[es] to deny the legitimacy of adult female authority." Discusses Welty's *Delta Wedding* and O'Connor's "A Circle in the Fire," focusing on mythical foundations and these writers' "sensitivity to landscape."

1623   Westling, Louise. "Fathers and Daughters in Welty and O'Connor." *The Female Tradition in Southern Literature*. Ed. Carol S. Manning. Urbana: U of Illinois P, 1993. 110-24.

Suggests that though authors like O'Connor and Eudora Welty "grew up in the heart of the privileged minority who dominated the South's economic life and preserved its heroic masculine myth of the Lost Cause," little has been written about the "debilitating consequences of that patriarchal heritage" on Southern women writers. Focuses on how O'Connor's stories "dramatize the cost of identification with the violent reassertion of the father's power," while Welty "uses the myths of mothers and daughters as the basis for stories of human cooperation and renewal that can serve as models for a future dominated by neither sex and freed from violent compulsion."

1624   Westling, Louise H. "Flannery O'Connor and Rebekah Poller: A Correspondence." *Flannery O'Connor Bulletin* 12 (1983): 68-76.

Provides the text of 13 letters and cards from O'Connor to Rebekah Massey Poller, and one to her parents. Describes how the two met, and provides other background information to help readers place the letters in context. Reports that the originals, along with related letters from Miriam Johnson (Rebekah Poller's sister), were donated to the *Flannery O'Connor Collection* at Georgia College & State University. Mentioned in the letters are: "Frank" ("an `elderly Negro gentleman who would act as a chauffeur for prominent Milledgeville families'"); Truman Capote; Granville Hicks; Nelson Algren; Elizabeth McKee; Lee Roy Abernathy; Rosa Lee Walston; Brainard Cheney; Katherine Anne Porter; Bernard Malamud; Cecil Dawkins; "Mr. Shannon" (chauffeur at Yaddo); and his wife "Nellie" (cook at Yaddo).

1625   Westling, Louise. "Flannery O'Connor's Hilarious Rage." *Flannery O'Connor Bulletin* 22 (1993-94): 119-32.

From an address by the author delivered at Georgia College & State University's "Habit of Art" symposium held in April, 1994. Discusses the "procession of sour `girls' who stump and march and growl their way across the pages of Flannery O'Connor's stories." Looks at the power behind the "angry passion in the portraits of these large `girls'" and suggests that it results in a "tough narrative voice never heard before O'Connor." Contends that this voice served as a foundation for a variety of modern women writers, including Alice Walker, Annie Dillard, Bobbie Ann Mason, Mary Hood, Lee Smith, Joan Didion, Louise Erdrich, Dorothy Allison, Leslie Silko, and Diana Abu-Jaber. Argues that while O'Connor may owe "some debt" to Hemingway and Faulkner for her "hard-bitten prose," it was O'Connor herself "who transformed their examples into a vehicle for women's rage, opening up a myriad of possibilities for writers who came after her." Draws parallels between O'Connor's work and that of several contemporary women writers. Relates that O'Connor's work "exploded genteel, ladylike conventions" and set women's anger free by smashing "the polite cages in which women had been forced to sing." Concludes that O'Connor "is at least as important for the development of women's literary voices in America and Europe as Hemingway is for men." [Illustrations: photographs from the "Habit of Art" symposium of Joyce Carol Oates, Lee Smith, Louise Erdrich, and Cecil Dawkins.]

1626   Westling, Louise H. "Flannery O'Connor's Mothers and Daughters." *Twentieth Century Literature* 24.4 (1978): 510-22.

Contends that although "O'Connor "seemed to think of her art as a force above or outside conditions of gender," she repeatedly relied upon a "mother-daughter pattern which seems a disturbing force often at odds with the clear purpose" of her work. Argues that in six of O'Connor's stories, the plot focuses on a mother resembling Mrs. Hopewell, a daughter like Joy-Hulga of "Good Country People," and a widowed mother and her sour daughter. Concludes that these "pictures . . . are so vivid and centrally placed that they cannot be dismissed as mere devices," and that they sometimes "confuse or negate the spiritual point O'Connor is trying to make.

1627   Westling, Louise. "Flannery O'Connor's Revelations to `A.'" *Southern Humanities Review* 20.1 (1986): 15-22.

Argues that O'Connor's "mysterious correspondent `A'" forced her to confront and accept her own womanhood by helping her to see more clearly the "violent masculine sexual attack" she utilized so often in her early stories. Contends that "A'"s influence helped O'Connor to "create more positive roles for key women characters in the late stories." Discusses O'Connor's view of sexuality as evidenced in "Greenleaf," "Good Country People," and "A Circle in the Fire."

1628   Westling, Louise. "The Perils of Adolescence in Flannery O'Connor and Carson McCullers." *Flannery O'Connor Bulletin* 8 (1979): 88-98.

Suggests that there may be some truth to Carson McCullers' claim that O'Connor may have "`learned her lesson well,'" as "A Temple of the Holy Ghost" appears to include aspects of McCullers' *The Member of the Wedding*. Compares McCullers's book to O'Connor's story, and notes similar themes, characters, events, and structural elements. Refers to remarks by "A," Ben Griffith, and Claire Katz. Discusses how O'Connor's "childhood reluctance to grow up and disgust with the behavior of teenagers" provides a context in which to better understand her story. Concludes that O'Connor's story "becomes a dialogue with Carson McCullers on the question of the choices a girl must make as she emerges from childhood and begins to construct a sense of herself as an adult."

1629   Westling, Louise. Rev. of *Flannery O'Connor: A Study of the Short Fiction*, by Suzanne Morrow Paulson. *Flannery O'Connor Bulletin* 17 (1988): 98-100.

Claims that while Paulson's book "begins with a section of critical analysis that provides some fresh readings of the stories," the first half is artificially and randomly organized, and the second, is a "hodgepodge." Commends Paulson's "emphasis on the intellectual contexts from which O'Connor emerged as a writer" during the modernist era, and asserts that this approach helps to explain why O'Connor's spiritual concerns were expressed in a manner that disturbs many readers. Laments, however, "the book's awkward construction, [which] prevents any coherent understanding of how O'Connor's modernism works."

1629a   Westling, Louise. Rev. of *Haunted Bodies: Gender and Southern Texts*, Ed. Anne Goodwyn Jones and Susan V. Donaldson. *Flannery O'Connor Bulletin* 26-27 (1998-2000): 186-89.

Recognizes this collection of essays for its examination of how gender may be seen as being "inextricably tangled with race in southern culture." Suggests that "students of Flannery O'Connor and southern culture will find" in this volume "informative and thoughtful" perspectives for consideration and comparison.

1630   White, Ray Lewis. *Index to Best American Short Stories and O. Henry Prize Stories*. Boston: G.K. Hall, 1988. 47, 106 (index), et passim.

Indexes stories, including Flannery O'Connor's, which received the *O. Henry Prize* between 1919 and 1987 and the *Best American Short Stories Award* between 1915 and 1986.

1631   White, Terry. "Allegorical Evil, Existentialist Choice in O'Connor, Oates and Styron." *Midwest Quarterly* 34.4 (1993): 383-97.

Discusses the "absolute evil and horrific suffering of female characters" in O'Connor's "A Good Man Is Hard to Find," Joyce Carol Oates's "Where Are You Going, Where Have You Been?" and in "the camp-doctor passage" of William Styron's *Sophie's Choice*. Suggests that all three works "illustrate a common allegorical technique and existentialist themes," the most prominent being the "radical evil, absolute and fixed in these story-worlds, and [how] a confrontation with this evil" forces the characters to make literal choices that "result in a physical, emotional, and psychological desecration" of the three women. Refers to the "honorable bloodlines" of American Literature for Gothic horror; the impact of moral relativism and law on the diminishment of horror when confronted by evil; and delves into how "evil in these three works is traditionally anchored in the orthodoxy of sin and guilt--the passion and suffering of our Judeo-Christianic moral values." Examines the demonic figures created--Oates's Arnold Friend, Styron's Jemand von Niemand, and O'Connor's The Misfit--as examples of "how the apotheosis of all that is violent, hateful, and cruel works." Shows how the "ego-devoured" Misfit who "cannot see beyond his own narcissism and spiritual blindness," serves as St. Cyril of Jerusalem's "dragon" for the grandmother. Finds him to be a familiar figure in O'Connor's work, whose role in this story is to "present the grandmother with a choice that will transform her from an insipid old woman to a Christian soul burnished by trial."

1632   White, William. "Profiles." *Literary Sketches* (Williamsburg, VA) 20.4 (1980): 3-4.

Profiles O'Connor, and describes her as "Southern, Catholic, enormously gifted, and unlucky." Lists and discusses each of O'Connor's works, and states that readers shouldn't "expect to be 'entertained,' for Flannery O'Connor doesn't write escape stuff or light reading." Suggests first-time readers may want to start with "A Good Man Is Hard to Find." Applauds the "stark dramatic power" of *Wise Blood*, and sees *The Violent Bear It Away* as a "macabre novel." Also refers to "A Stroke of Good Fortune," the PBS television version of "The Displaced Person," *The Complete Stories* and *The Habit of Being*.

1633   Whitehead, James. "A Recollection." *Miller Williams and the Poetry of the Particular*. Ed. Michael Burns. Columbia: U of Missouri P, 1991. 113-24.

Whitehead describes a trip that he and Miller Williams took from Nashville to Columbus, Mississippi. Includes brief references to O'Connor, including: an aside about The Misfit from "A Good Man Is Hard to Find"; Christian symbolism in her stories; and, Williams' recollections of his friendship with her when he lived in Macon, Georgia.

1634   Whiteley, Sandy. "Frances Neel Cheney: A Librarian's Literary Friendship." *American Libraries* 17 (Oct. 1986): 716-17.

Profiles Frances Neel Cheney, focusing on the literary friendship that she and her husband, Brainard Cheney, shared with Flannery O'Connor. Refers to Allen Tate, and Robert Penn Warren.

1635   Whitt, Jan. *Allegory and the Modern Southern Novel*. Macon, GA: Mercer UP, 1994. 1, 4-5, 22, 25, 28, 31, 33-34, 45, 57, 60-61, 66, 73, 78, 80, 85-97, 99-100, 134, 136.

Examines, "the violence of allegory" in Southern fiction beginning with Nathaniel Hawthorne and Herman Melville, to demonstrate "how the Southern allegorical novel is set apart from the American myth of innocence and success." Discusses, in various sections of the book, O'Connor's work, along with that of William Faulkner and Carson

McCullers, as being representative of Southern fiction in presenting characters who are "asking forgiveness for something they are unable define." Refers to the role of Calvinism in American religious history and suggests that Christianity "has become an allegory for Southern history." Contends that through the use of allegory, O'Connor, McCullers, and Faulkner were able to create larger than life characters who testify to the South's "cultural longing for redemption." Focuses on O'Connor in an essay that forms part of Chapter 3: "*Wise Blood* and the `Ragged Figure' of the Mind." Finds it ironic that it is "*because* O'Connor chose to write allegory that her work is defensible," noting that while the "blindness, denial, violence, and grace," seen in her work "take on strong New Testament overtones," her stories still function on a universal level. Suggests that to understand O'Connor's theological inflexibility in *Wise Blood* more clearly the reader must account for her "religious vision, clarify the fundamentalist Protestant spirit central to her work, and delineate new directions for allegory." Offers a reading of the novel in this context and mentions a wide variety of other authors and works, including: William Bradford's *Of Plymouth Plantation*; Nathanael Hawthorne's "The Custom-House"; Ernest Hemingway's "A Clean, Well-lighted Place"; Carson McCullers's *The Heart Is a Lonely Hunter*. Sherwood Anderson's *Winesburg, Ohio*; Sophocles's *Oedipus*; and William Shakespeare's *King Lear*. Refers also to critical commentary by: Sally Fitzgerald, Gilbert H. Muller, Louis Rubin, Miles Orvell, Robert Milder, Walter Sullivan, Stuart L. Burns, Daniel F. Littlefield, C. Hugh Holman, Carol Shloss, John R. May, and Stuart L. Burns.

1636 Whitt, Jan. "The Loneliest Hunter." *Southern Literary Journal* 24.2 (1992): 26-35.

Includes a brief comparison of O'Connor's "vision of faith and the world" with that of McCullers's, noting that while there are significant differences, both writers emphasize "the emptiness of self-reliance," and use the "grotesque portrait" as a fictional method to illustrate "the spiritual distortion of [one's] soul." Compares Hazel Motes of O'Connor's *Wise Blood* to McCullers's Jake of *The Heart Is a Lonely Hunter*.

1637 Whitt, Margaret. "Flannery O'Connor's Ladies." *Flannery O'Connor Bulletin* 15 (1986): 42-50.

Contends that O'Connor, who knew well the role and expectations of the Southern lady, "was horrified at the prospect of becoming one." Discusses her views and examines her treatment of Southern ladies in the context of "Southern manners." Focuses on O'Connor's treatment of Southern women as seen in: *Wise Blood*'s Mrs. Wally Bee Hitchcock and Sabbath

Lily Hawkes, Mrs. Hopewell in "Good Country People," Mrs. Cope in "A Circle in the Fire," the grandmother in "A Good Man Is Hard to Find," Mrs. Turpin in "Revelation," and Mrs. McIntyre in "The Displaced Person." Suggests that while the code requires men to use polite language, and to treat ladies "in keeping with the biblical teaching," the code also "dictates that men do not value ugly women." Focuses on how men treat Southern ladies as seen in: *Wise Blood*'s Hazel Motes and Mrs. Wally Bee Hitchcock, Thomas and his mother in "The Comforts of Home," Asbury and his mother in "The Enduring Chill," and Julian and his mother in "Everything That Rises Must Converge." Refers to Louise Westling's comment that Flannery O'Connor's male characters "use their manners only to seduce women into relaxing their guard so they can be exploited." Closes with a discussion of how "each daughter falls prey to matrophobia," which is described as "the fear of becoming like one's mother," and illustrates this argument through an examination of the characters of Hulga Hopewell in "Good Country People," Mary Grace in "Revelation," and Sally Virginia Cope in "A Circle in the Fire." Concludes that O'Connor's letters show that as she matured, she became less concerned with "her quarrel with being a lady," and eventually "accepted the manners of her place."

1638   Whitt, Margaret. "Letters to Corinth: Echoes from Greece to Georgia in O'Connor's `Judgement Day.'" *Literature and Belief* 17.1-2 (1997): 61-74.

Notes that criticism to date on O'Connor's "Judgement Day" has focussed on how, compared to previous versions (including "The Geranium" in her MFA thesis at the University of Iowa), the story demonstrates her "enormous growth as a writer." Offers instead a reading in light of O'Connor's own comment regarding "the importance of the writer finding knowledge in his own community, [and] operating `at a peculiar crossroads where time and place and eternity somehow meet.'" Discusses O'Connor's choice of Corinth, Georgia as locale, and notes parallels between this town and her main character T.C. Tanner, and Saint Paul and his association with Corinth, Greece. Refers to comments by Leon Driskell and Joan Brittain on ways Tanner "is an interesting combination of Peter and Paul," and how his "initial attitude toward the black Coleman is comparable to Saul's (Paul's) early persecution of the Christians." Discusses the narrative structure and time shifts of the story, the meaning of Tanner's carved eyeglasses, and how Tanner's vision of his own resurrection and death reflect "Paul's discourse in 1 Corinthians 15" to the early Christians of Corinth, Greece regarding the resurrection of Christ. Refers to critical comments by: Sister Kathleen Feeley, Miles Orvell, Ralph Wood, Carter Martin, John May, and Suzanne Morrow Paulson.

1639 Whitt, Margaret. "A Model Interterm Course in Flannery O'Connor: Fiction Study and an Odyssey Through O'Connor Country." *Flannery O'Connor Bulletin* 19 (1990): 100.

Whitt outlines an interterm class she led from the University of Denver during the 1990 Christmas break, which focused on the life and work of Flannery O'Connor. Describes the travel itinerary of the class for those *Bulletin* readers "who may be interested in following" the same trail. Mentions Sarah Gordon of Georgia College & State University, Hugh Brown of Armstrong State and the various sites visited. Whitt offered, "It was essential to me, as the group leader . . . that my students not confuse the life with the literature," and stated that she hoped that "the trip [would] serve as a model for a kind of literary inquiry that would suggest new and perhaps deeper ways to respond to O'Connor's fiction."

1640 Whitt, Margaret. Rev. of *Flannery O'Connor and Cold War Culture*, by Jon Lance Bacon. *Flannery O'Connor Bulletin* 23 (1994-95): 188-91.

Reviews Bacon's *Flannery O'Connor and Cold War Culture*, describing the content of each chapter and the methodology and illustrations used. Notes that Bacon misses "the reference to the show *Queen for a Day*" in "A Good Man Is Hard to Find" and "the fact that `The Partridge Festival' is based on Marion Stembridge's multiple murders and suicide that took place in Milledgeville in 1953." Reports that Bacon "questions O'Connor's racism before the issue was raised by Ralph Wood," and Wood's conclusion that O'Connor "`was no racist'" because she would have certainly challenged "`the ideological basis of racism.'" Finds that while Bacon "is occasionally careless in his treatment of O'Connor's stories," his book is not only "a fine contribution to O'Connor criticism," but also "an addition to the current reconception of Southern studies that employs all manner of popular culture to illuminate an author's work."

1641 Whitt, Margaret. "A Review of the 1991 *Flannery O'Connor Bulletin.* "*Flannery O'Connor Society Newsletter* 1.1 (1993): 3.

Notes that with publication of the 20th volume of the *Flannery O'Connor Bulletin*, it becomes "the longest running journal dedicated to the work and life of a 20th-century American woman writer."

1641a Whitt, Margaret. "Stopped by a Naked Woman: O'Connor's Departure from the *Kenyon Review*." *Flannery O'Connor Bulletin* 26-27 (1998-2000): 169-81.

Discusses O'Connor's publishing relationship with the *Kenyon Review* and her correspondence with its editors, John Crowe Ransom and Robie Macauley. Lists and describes each of the stories she published in the *Kenyon Review*, compares these submissions with those she sent to the *Sewanee Review* edited by her friend Andrew Lytle, and then focuses on the circumstances of O'Connor's decision to sever ties with Robie Macauley and the *Kenyon Review*. Suggests that while the "image of a naked woman" that was "whimsically" placed in the margin of O'Connor's story "The Comforts of Home" was "prompted by *her* words, [and] *her* development of a character *she herself* depicts as low and vulgar," Macauley's "decision to use the little illustration . . . should have been given more thought." Contends that while the sketch "is comically true to the language" of the story it illustrates, "the distance between O'Connor's fiction and her awareness of the power of the language in her stories appears vast." Concludes that because "the clues concerning O'Connor's reticence were always present in her fiction Robie Macauley should have known better" than to include the drawing.

1642   Whitt, Margaret. "Vapex on Her Collar: A Note." *Flannery O'Connor Bulletin* 17 (1988): 80.

Provides a photocopy of a 1932 advertisement from *Time* magazine for "Vapex, a `delightful inhalant,'" which was used by Hulga Hopewell in "Good Country People." Observes that while Hulga "considers herself above those good country people who are swayed by advertisements, her attachment to the world around her is stronger than she realizes."

1643   Whitt, Margaret. "You Will Know Them By Their Shoes." *Flannery O'Connor Bulletin* 21 (1992): 97-99.

Reports that O'Connor was careful to have her characters' shoes match their personalities. Uses as an example the bedroom slippers of the white trash woman in "Revelation," and suggests that if O'Connor placed "Girl Scout shoes" on a character's feet, it is likely that she intended "something other than affiliation with that purposeful sisterhood." Reinforces this by reporting that while O'Connor features a Boy Scout (John Wesley), none of her other characters are members of the Girl Scouts. Describes characters from "Revelation," "The Enduring Chill," and "A Late Encounter with the Enemy" who wear Girl Scout shoes, and notes that all are unattractive and "still depend on home and an older family member." Describes characteristics of these and others who wear similar shoes and recognizes that all are bookish, socially inept, and discontented. Article illustrated with an advertisement for Girl Scout shoes from the December, 1957 issue of *The Leader*.

1644   Wilbers, Stephen. *The Iowa Writers' Workshop: Origins, Emergence, & Growth*. Iowa City: U of Iowa P, 1980. 94, 106-07n3, 130.

Refers to the 1950s as a time in which the Iowa Writers' Workshop "consolidated its national reputation," noting that by 1953 Flannery O'Connor and five other Iowa Workshop students and graduates had novels either published or accepted for publication. Provides excerpts of Jean Wylder's article, "Flannery O'Connor: A Reminiscence and Some Letters," [*North American Review*, 255 (Spring 1970): 58-60] and a letter from O'Connor to Wylder. Suggests that O'Connor may have been recalling her negative experiences as a participant in Iowa Workshop sessions when she commented, "'Every time a story of mine appears in a freshman anthology, I have a vision of it, with its little organs laid open, like a frog in a bottle.'"

1645   Wilkes, Paul A. "Through a Glass Darkly: The Worlds of Flannery O'Connor & George Bernanos." *Church* 6 (Fall 1990): 5-12.

Two articles under one title, linked by how each writer dealt with a religious theme and had a readership that was not wholly sympathetic nor understanding. States that "few writers have been so loved and hated, misunderstood and overanalyzed, lionized and disclaimed, reviled and revered as Flannery O'Connor." Observes that she took it upon herself "to force us to confront our naked selves in the dehumanizing wilderness created by radical secularity." Discusses the impact of the disseminated lupus that killed her at 39 and examines the role of her faith upon her work, her theme of "individual accountability," and "her self-imposed campaign to help right the human race."

1646   Will, George F. "A Trickle-Down Culture." *Newsweek* 13 Dec. 1993, 84.

Discusses the challenges faced by America's youth from the perspective of Edwin Delattre, Dean of Boston University's School of Education. Mentions that Delattre stopped in Milledgeville, Georgia "to honor the memory of the writer Flannery O'Connor, whose words provided his theme when he later addressed a colloquium back in Boston." Cites O'Connor's remark that Delattre used: "'You have to push as hard as the age that pushes against you,'" and uses it to clarify the cultural influences on America's youth and the basis from which much of their lawlessness may be springing.

1647   Williams, David. "Flannery O'Connor and the *via negativa*." *Studies in Religion/Sciences Religieuses* (Canada) 8.3 (1979): 303-12.

Claims that the religious and philosophical components in O'Connor's work may be compared "to the so-called Pseudo- Dionysius, an extremely influential Christian Platonist of the fifth century." Contends that such a comparison retains a vision of fallen humanity while also "providing an analogy to her peculiar and sometimes troubling concept of how this fallen creature is ultimately saved." Asserts that O'Connor's writing suggests elements of a process of symbolic language referred to in the Middle Ages as the *Via Negativa*. Defines the *Via Negativa* as "a process of asserting names and stripping them away." States that "the paradigm of the *Via Negativa* may provide a possible illumination of the styles and themes" of O'Connor. Analyzes "Good Country People," "Parker's Back," *The Violent Bear It Away* and *Wise Blood* to illustrate. Concludes that the "`negative' aspect of Flannery O'Connor's work may, then, be seen as a purely formal element of her writing rather than a poorly disguised misanthropy or an unexoricised remnant of Calvinistic determinism."

1648   Williams, Mary Morris. "Biblical Echoes and Allusions in Flannery O'Connor's `Judgement Day': Also Known as Scriptural Dimensions of `Judgement Day.'" [12 pp.] Ms. [Nov. 1995] *Flannery O'Connor Collection*, Russell Library, Georgia College & State University, Milledgeville, GA.

Suggests that O'Connor "uses Biblical echoes and allusions in `Judgement Day' to remind readers of their spiritual roots." Contends that the story may be interpreted on different levels, "the material or physical, the spiritual, the psychological, and the sociological." Focuses on the story's spiritual dimension "as revealed through its Biblical reverberations." Notes that O'Connor uses the British spelling of the word "judgement" and comments on her possible reasons for doing so. Then, examines her use of the word "home," why she chose Corinth, Georgia and New York for the story's locale, notes similarities between Tanner and Christ, and refers to Dorothy Walters's view of Tanner's religious attitudes. Ties the story to the Apostle Paul's letters from *II Corinthians*, chapter 4, verses 17-18, and explains how O'Connor's genius "is clearly at work in the choice" of the name "Tanner" for the main character. Concludes that for O'Connor, like Tanner, "the end of the story . . . has been promised." Asserts that even though she may have been "twisted by illness and `wasting away' with lupus," O'Connor "met her `Judgement Day' with an intact faith." (Paper presented during Flannery O'Connor 70th Birthday Symposium held at Brigham Young University, Nov. 8-11, 1995.)

1649   Williams, Melvin G. "Black and White: A Study in Flannery O'Connor's Characters." *Black American Literature Forum* 10.4 (1976): 130-32.

Criticizes O'Connor's works for their constant portrayal of Blacks as static characters, minor, unimportant, and white-serving catalysts. Deals with the stories in *Everything That Rises Must Converge*, and says of the nine, only five contain what might be referred to as "greater roles" for Black characters. Of these five--"Greenleaf," "The Enduring Chill," "Revelation," "Judgement Day," and "Everything That Rises Must Converge"--none, however, reveal a fully developed Black character. Argues instead, that O'Connor's Black characters only serve to represent "issues" instead of people, and are used to "illuminate" white characters while not revealing themselves.

1650   Williams, Peter W. "Perceptions of Time in American Catholicism." *Journal of Religious Studies* 11 (1983): 1-13.

Examines and suggests "a typology of some of the ways in which American Catholics (broadly defined) have perceived the passage and nature of time, as a clue to better understanding the religious and cultural synthesis (or syntheses) which they were engaged in fashioning." Briefly discusses Flannery O'Connor, focusing on the fact that each of her stories present "an account of a crucial episode" of the principal character's life. Contends that the episode is "sometimes dramatic, sometimes horrifying, sometimes quiet--in which they momentarily break through the curtain of everyday mundane reality to see, often in a blinding glare, the spiritual truth about themselves."

1651   Williamson, Chilton, Jr. "The Ungarbled Word." *National Review* 28 Oct. 1988: 44-46.

Offers an review essay of *Flannery O'Connor: Collected Works*, edited by Sally Fitzgerald and published in 1988 as the second volume of the Library of America Series. Discusses whether O'Connor's work should be placed in the realm of "great" literature, and whether or not she should be referred to as a "`Catholic novelist.'" comments on her style and method of writing, the types of characters she typically created, and the "prophetic aspect of her work." Draws brief comparisons between her work and that by William Faulkner, Katherine Anne Porter, Thomas Pynchon, Raymond Carver, Graham Greene and Nathaniel Hawthorne. Refers to "A," Marion Montgomery, J.O. Tate and Eric Voegelin. Contends that O'Connor should indeed, "be placed squarely in the company of Hawthorne and James, Hemingway and Faulkner." Concludes, "I have no doubt at all: great writer or not, she was consistently one of the finest literary artists to appear in this (or any) country in this century."

1652 Willoughby, Jim. "Photographs of the 1984 Symposium." *Flannery O'Connor Bulletin* 13 (1984): 73-76.

Provides black-and-white photographs taken during the third O'Connor symposium ("Of Time and Place and Eternity"), held at Georgia College & State University, in Milledgeville, April 14-15, 1984. Among the subjects identified are: Rosa Lee Walston, Frederick Asals, J.O. Tate, Mary Barbara Tate, Bob Gorman, Sarah Gordon, Gerald Becham, Dorrie Neligan, Sarah Enos Brown, Louise Florencourt, Margaret Florencourt Mann, Frances Florencourt, Ann G. Park, Sister Rose Bowen, Sally Fitzgerald, Ralph and Suzanne Wood, and Rev. Leonard J. Tuozzolo.

1653 Wilson, Austin. "What It Means to be a Southern Writer in the '80s: A Panel Discussion with Beverly Lowry, Reynolds Price, Elizabeth Spencer and James Whitehead." *Southern Quarterly* 26.4 (1988): 80-93.

Transcript of a panel discussion at Millsaps College during the 1984 Southern Literary Festival, which focused on "what being a Southern writer means to a younger generation of writers." At one point, the moderator, Austin Wilson, asks members of the panel to react to the following statement: "Flannery O'Connor comments in any essay called `The Regional Writer' that William Faulkner was happier with his three honest, unpretentious readers in Oxford than all the Northern critics put together. `For no matter how unfavorable the critics in New York may be, they are an unreliable lot, as inescapable now as on the day they were born of interpreting Southern literature to the world.'" Includes reactions by Price, Spencer, and Lowry. Whitehead again refers to O'Connor later in the panel discussion, when he states: "I just sort of took Eudora Welty and Flannery O'Connor for granted. They were great writers."

1654 Wilson, Carol Y. "Family as Affliction, Family as Promise in *The Violent Bear It Away*." *Studies in the Literary Imagination* 20.2 (1987): 77-86.

Contends that O'Connor's fictional family members "apprehend mystery through the manners of a Southern heritage, steeped in stubbornness and stiff-necked independence, [and are] tied to each other by an endless narrative accounting." Asserts that family provides characters with little comfort and usually pull them into "a reluctant alliance where matters seethe and often explode, a means whereby conflict is advanced and the questions are asked." Suggests that the mystery of O'Connor's *The Violent Bear It Away* is based upon the unasked question of Tarwater, "Whose boy are you?" Claims that in the novel Tarwater attempts "to answer this question familially and universally." Argues that "the concept of the family is essential to the meaning of the novel, and it is founded on a reluctant sense of responsibility." Explicates the novel in this context, reprints a portion of a letter to "A" from O'Connor discussing Tarwater's future in the city, and concludes that Old Mason and Francis Marion Tarwater "are modeled on the `nobility of unnaturalness' that O'Connor prizes" and from which she derives mystery.

1655 Wilson, Charles Reagan. "William Faulkner and the Southern Religious Culture." *Faulkner and Religion: Faulkner and Yoknapatawpha, 1989.* Ed. Doreen Fowler and Ann J. Abadie. Jackson: UP of Mississippi, 1991. 21-43.

Includes a discussion of O'Connor's use of humor and how she used "rural, religiously obsessed characters [as] the raw materials of a religious message." Contends that O'Connor "made art from the specifics of the Evangelical faith," and that she, like Faulkner, often used "spiritually deformed" characters and violence to convey her message.

1656 Winchell, Donna Haisty. *Alice Walker.* New York: Twayne, 1992. 15-17, 21.

Includes a discussion of Walker's essay, "Beyond the Peacock: The Reconstruction of Flannery O'Connor" from *In Search of Our Mothers' Gardens*, which presents Walker's view of Flannery O'Connor's life and work compared to her own. Refers to O'Connor's work again as part of a discussion of Walker's review of Jean Toomer's *The Wayward and the Seeking* in her essay "The Divided Life of Jean Toomer."

1657 Winchell, Mark Royden. "Inner Dark: or, The Place of Cormac McCarthy." *Southern Review* 26.2 (1990): 293-309.

Includes three brief references to O'Connor: how McCarthy's "sense of the comic reminds one [readers] alternately of Flannery O'Connor and the best of the current `grit-lit' crowd"; her observation regarding "the mixed blessing of William Faulkner's influence"; and, how she would have approached writing McCarthy's 1973 novel, *Child of God.*

1658 Winchell, Mark Royden. "The Whole Horse: Walter Sullivan and the State of Southern Letters." *Hollins Critic* 27.1 (1990): 1-10.

Includes Sullivan's comments regarding why O'Connor's "natural metier was short fiction," and her influence upon contemporary writers who "have kept the Gothic local color and dispensed with the religious belief."

1659   Winn, Harlan Harbour. "*Everything that Rises Must Converge*: O'Connor's Seven Story Cycle." *Renascence* 42.4 (1990): 187-212.

Defines the short story cycle as a grouping of interrelated stories "too finely patterned to be described as a mere collection of stories and too dependent on individual components to be described as a novel." Offers *Everything That Rises Must Converge* as an example and discusses difficulties critics have had in labeling this collection as one because of the inclusion f two additional stories beyond those intended by O'Connor. Refers to construction of *Wise Blood* and *The Violent Bear It Away*. Mentions Teilhard de Chardin's *The Phenomenon of Man* and his influence on O'Connor. States that throughout the stories in *Everything That Rises Must Converge*, O'Connor focuses on the "struggle of rising to higher consciousness by focusing on characters whose egoism distorts their perception, blinding them to the transforming power of the divine at work in the world." Offers detailed discussions of "Everything That Rises Must Converge," "The Comforts of Home," "Greenleaf," "A View of the Woods," "The Enduring Chill," "The Lame Shall Enter First," "Revelation," "Parker's Back," "Judgement Day," and "The Partridge Festival." Concludes that the original seven stories are linked together by the use of "parallel thematic patterns" and by O'Connor varying "the location of her limited omniscient point of view."

1659a   "Winners: O'Connorland Photo Contest." *Flannery O'Connor Bulletin* 26-27 (1998-2000): [Between pages 154 and 155].

Reproduces eight black-and-white photographs depicting scenes reflective of O'Connor's characters, settings and humor. Includes submissions by David Payne, Mary De Vries, D. Michael Nifong, Margaret E. Whitt, Jane A. Rose, Donna Musil, and Brenda Lester.

1660   Winslow, William. "Modernity and the Novel: Twain, Faulkner, and Percy." *Gypsy Scholar* 8.1 (1981): 19-40.

Points out that many of O'Connor's short stories "often end with a killing or beating," and compares her use of violence with Faulkner's use in *Light in August*. Argues that, for both, violence no longer "springs out of a shared social code," but instead appears "as unexpected culminating shocks meant to secure the objectivity which narrative had placed in abeyance." Regrets how "the social foundations of such acts have thus been devalued by the ideological demands of the text."

1661   Witt, Elaine. "Play Explores Revelations of Flannery O'Connor." *Birmingham (AL) News Post-Herald* 22 Feb. 1992: C6.

Summary review of a play written by Samford University Professor of Religion and Letters, John Killinger, titled "The Mistress of Milledgeville." Reports that Killinger said that he used O'Connor's letters and fiction "to determine how the author felt, and what she might have said about her father, her work, and her faith." Quotes Killinger, an ordained United Church of Christ Minister who spent his childhood in rural Kentucky: "`These are real characters, they're not made up out of her head.'" Produced as part of Samford's "Christfest: The Gospel and the Arts in the 20th Century," the play featured Los Angeles character actress Melanie MacQueen as Flannery O'Connor and Daniel Leslie as her father. Illustrations: Photograph of Leslie and MacQueen at dress rehearsal.

1662   Witt, Jonathan. "*Wise Blood* and the Irony of Redemption." *Flannery O'Connor Bulletin* 22 (1993-94): 12-24.

Challenges Ben Satterfield's thesis--in his article published in *Studies in American Fiction* 17 (1989): 33-50--that the redemptive theme was not apparent to readers of *Wise Blood* until O'Connor pointed it out. Offers "an analysis of the novel's ambiguity that better accords with the evidence at hand," and argues that Satterfield's "`literary point of view' is clear evidence of his blindness toward his own secular ideology." Contends that Satterfield's inability to fully understand O'Connor's "tension between content and style" results in his misinterpreting other critics--such as Frederick Asals--as well. Cites John W. Simon's 1952 review of *Wise Blood* as evidence that O'Connor's redemptive theme *was* recognizable several years before O'Connor herself pointed it out. Offers a reading of the novel that examines O'Connor's choice of names for the novel's characters, and attempts to determine "whether a redemptive ending to *Wise Blood* really is non-ironic." Refers to critical commentary by André Bleikasten, Carol Shloss, Martha Stephens, Dorothy McFarland, Marshall Bruce Gentry, and John Hawkes.

1663   Witt, Margaret E. "Flannery O'Connor and the Child's Book: An Unusual Coupling." *Notes on Contemporary Literature* 22.4 (1992): 4-5.

Counters O'Connor's contention in a letter to "A" in which she states that Harper Lee's *To Kill a Mockingbird* is "a child's book . . . something like *Miss Minerva and William Green Hill*." Notes that Lee's book is "required reading in many eighth and ninth grade English classes." Asserts that while the *Miss Minerva* series is "racist, classist, and sexist," and "lacks any adult who sees the world apart from Southern Tradition," Lee's "Atticus Finch . . . is the very voice of moral consciousness." Concludes that O'Connor overlooks the basic integrity of Lee's book, and that "her odd yoking of *To Kill a Mockingbird* with *Miss Minerva* is uncharacteristically insensitive."

1664   Wolf, Michele. "Culture Gaps: Difficulties in Comprehending Minority Writers." *Le Sud et Autres Points Cardinaux*. Ed. Jeanne-Marie Santraud. Paris: Presses de l'Universite de Paris-Sorbonne, 1987. 113-21.

Examines problems posed to foreign students as they attempt to read and comprehend works by American "minority writers." Asserts that because "allusions, language, references and humor depend for their effect on a knowledge of the minority group [the] emotional response may be contrary to that desired by the writer." Discusses "Black writers," "Jewish writers," and the "Catholic Writer." Suggests that O'Connor's Southern, Baptist characters may be just as difficult to follow and understand as Black dialect or Yiddish English. Maintains that the humor in the country folk speech of characters such as the freak in "A Temple of the Holy Ghost," the preacher in "The River," and Mr. Shortley in "The Displaced Person," is difficult for such readers to grasp. Refers to the comic aspects and the "harsh, unforgiving view of human weaknesses" in "A Good Man Is Hard to Find." Concludes that with O'Connor "we see the possible lack of comprehension and sympathy of the modern secular reader . . . faced with a religious view of the world with which he cannot identify."

1665   Wood, Gerald C., and Terry Barr. "'A Certain Kind of Writer': An Interview with Horton Foote." *Literature/Film Quarterly* 14.4 (1986): 226-37.

Offers an edited transcript of an interview of Horton Foote in question-and-answer format conducted on July 18 and October 24, 1985, in which Foote discusses writers who have influenced his work. Includes two passing references to O'Connor: how he admires her work "extravagantly," and is facinated by the toughness he sees in her work.

1666   Wood, Ralph C. "The Catholic Faith of Flannery O'Connor's Protestant Characters: A Critique and Vindication." *Flannery O'Connor Bulletin* 13 (1984): 15-25.

Suggests that O'Connor's "Catholicism and her Southernness both enliven and chasten each other." Sees her Catholic vision as enabling her "to discern the universal and the eternal amidst the narrow particulars of the Southern scene, while a firm rooting in her own native soil served to enrich her faith." Offers a critique and vindication of O'Connor's work through a description of "what is irreducibly Catholic in O'Connor's theological vision," and illustrates how her Catholicism radically shaped her view of the "Southern religious scene." Discusses a variety of related topics, including: how O'Connor was "troubled by the anti-sacramental character" of Southern Protestants' brand of Christianity; the difference between "O'Connor's Catholicism and radical Protestant tradition" in *The Violent Bear It Away*; similarities "between much Southern Protestant preaching and Flannery O'Connor's fiction"; O'Connor's "Catholic understanding of baptism" in *The Violent Bear It Away* and "The River"; how Hazel Motes "is the single character in whom O'Connor's Augustinian theology is most fully realized"; and her use of a "vision of God bent more on restoration than devastation" in "Revelation," "The Artificial Nigger," "Judgement Day," and *The Violent Bear It Away*.

1667   Wood, Ralph C. "Flannery O'Connor As a Comedian of Positive Grace." *The Comedy of Redemption: Christian Faith and Comic Vision in Four American Novelists*. Notre Dame, IN: U of Notre Dame P, 1988. 107-32.

Suggests that "O'Connor's most convincing comic stories all have to do with race relations," and proves her not only to be a "truly redemptive writer," but a "comedian of positive grace." Discusses her views: of blacks; John Howard Griffin's book, *Black Like Me*; James Baldwin; the Vanderbilt Fugitives; Robert Coles's work in Mississippi; Southern "manners"; and the 1960s Civil Rights Movement to end segregation. Offers analyses of "The Artificial Nigger," "The Enduring Chill," and "Revelation." Concludes that she sought "not to wound but to heal, not to divide but to unite," and her concern with divine mercy "explains her refusal to give the standard moralistic account of black-white relations."

1668   Wood, Ralph C. "Flannery O'Connor As a Satirist of the Negative Way." *The Comedy of Redemption: Christian Faith and Comic Vision in Four American Novelists*. Notre Dame: U of Notre Dame P, 1988. 80-106.

Asserts that O'Connor's fiction "affords a fitting comic subject for theological analysis," and suggests that she may be viewed as "a comedian in both the literary and religious senses of the word." Contends that O'Connor's comic vision is more theological than ethical and that the key to her comedy "lies in her thoroughly Catholic (and specifically Thomistic) conviction that grace does not destroy but completes and perfects nature." Explores the "biographical roots" of O'Connor's comic vision, the regional aspect of her theology and humor, and attempts "to demonstrate what she discovered to be universally Catholic in her narrowly Protestant milieu." States that while O'Connor may have "suffered from an Electra complex," her resistance to self pity and her comic affirmation of both her mother and her confinement make her triumph truly impressive. Discusses *The Violent Bear It Away*. Mentions Samuel Johnson, Gerard Manley Hopkins, Jacques Maritain, T.S. Eliot, Karl Rahner, Teilhard de Chardin, Thomas Aquinas, Hans Küng, André Bleikasten, Dante, Augustine, and Reinhold Niebuhr.

1669   Wood, Ralph C. "Flannery O'Connor, H.L. Mencken, and the Southern
Agrarians: A Dispute Over Religion More Than Region." *Flannery
O'Connor Bulletin* 20 (1991): 1-21.

Examines the beliefs of H.L. Mencken and compares them to those of
O'Connor, Allen Tate, and the Southern Agrarians. Suggests that
O'Connor's beliefs placed her more on Mencken's side than with the
Agrarians because she saw, as they did not, "that the real quandary of our
time concerns not region so much as religion--and religion understood not
so much as wistful theistic faith but as radical Christological belief."
Notes, however, that O'Connor's sympathies were with the very type of
religious fundamentalist that Mencken despised. Analyzes O'Connor's
position, and reviews insights of Lewis P. Simpson, John F. Desmond,
and Robert Drake. Discusses Desmond's assertion that *The Violent Bear
It Away* demonstrates how O'Connor "successfully employed the
techniques and assumptions of modernism for her own fictional
purposes." Argues that the views held by Mrs. May of Mrs. Greenleaf in
"Greenleaf" serve as an example of "church-going atheism"; notes sexual
overtones in the story; and offers opinion as to what Mencken might have
thought of Mrs. May and Mrs. Greenleaf. Concludes that instead of
viewing the penitential Pentecostals as subjects for mockery--like
Mencken--O'Connor believed that "their skewed faith" served as "a
straight answer to the century of mass death."

1670   Wood, Ralph C. "Flannery O'Connor, Martin Heidegger, and Modern
Nihilism: A Reading of `Good Country People.'" *Flannery O'Connor
Bulletin* 21 (1992): 100-18.

Informs readers that O'Connor agreed with Walker Percy that the role of
the artist is to warn readers--in a manner not unlike the coal miners'
canary--of the "nihilistic gas of our time." Declares that she "gives our
deadly cultural ambience its rightful title: not atheism but nihilism."
Defines and describes implications of this assertion, and offers--in the
context of Martin Heidegger's writings--a reading of "Good Country
People." Argues that Hulga represents a Heideggerian figure "engaged in
metaphysical revolt against the order of the cosmos itself," and that "her
nihilism is no mere thought project" but represents an acting out of the
horrors confronting modern society. Compares characteristics shared by
both Hulga and O'Connor, and relates the significance of a passage from
Heidegger's inaugural lecture at Freiburg to Hulga. Claims that critics
have "failed to discern . . . that Hulga's nihilism is linked to her latent
pedophilia." Suggests that by the end of the story, while Hulga may not
have yet "fed on the Bread of Life . . . she has discovered at last how
bitter is the sponge of Nothingness." Offers that the story is "not finally
grim and admonitory but comic and gladdening." Concludes that Hulga's

sense of loss is "a blessed loss, a saving devastation, a deflowering not of her sexual virginity but of her virginal nihilism."

1671   Wood, Ralph C. "Flannery O'Connor's Racial Morals and Manners: Evidence from Unpublished Letters." *Christian Century* 16 Nov. 1994: 1076-81.

States that O'Connor's unpublished correspondence with Maryat Lee "will surely lead many to conclude that the novelist was a racist." Reports that-- in the letters--O'Connor "makes unsavory remarks about blacks" and provides ample evidence to indicate that she was not sympathetic with the Civil Rights crusade of her time. Assesses O'Connor's attitudes on race and asks, "What, then, does it mean if this writer was also a racist at heart?" Defines racism, and discusses O'Connor's "liberal use of the word `nigger'" and the "signs of unmistakable malignancy toward blacks" found in the letters. Notes that O'Connor did not publicly discuss her opinions on race, and suggests that this fact may indicate that she had serious doubts as to their validity. Outlines and discusses "Everything That Rises Must Converge," "The Enduring Chill," and "The Artificial Nigger." Relates possible reasons as to why O'Connor was "cool toward the Civil Rights movement," and examines O'Connor's call "for a new code of manners to help ensure mutual regard rather than internecine hatred."

1672   Wood, Ralph C. "Flannery O'Connor's Strange Alliance with Southern Fundamentalists." *Literature and Belief* 17.1-2 (1997): 75-98.

Explores how the "emerging religious pluralism of the 1950s" served as "the catalyst that helped confirm O'Connor in a radical kind of Catholic Christianity." Outlines why she as "an accomplished writer and so cultured a Catholic," looked to "Protestant fundamentalists, with all their scorn for Rome, to be her natural allies in such faith." Discusses how her "living of a disciplined Catholic life," and Catholicism seen in her fiction, "was set against the vaporized faith of the 1950s consensus religion." Reviews fundamentalist beliefs and explores how "the fundamentalist nihilism of The Misfit" in "A Good Man Is Hard to Find" serves as "a fictional instance" of this "strange alliance."

1673   Wood, Ralph C. "From Fashionable Tolerance to Unfashionable Redemption: A Reading of Flannery O'Connor's First and Last Stories." *Flannery O'Connor Bulletin* 7 (1978): 10-25.

Contends that because O'Connor "was pre-eminently a prophetic writer, a woman of apocalyptic vision," her writing "is religious to the core."

Argues that the "single religious concern woven through the tapestry of the entire O'Connor *oeuvre* is that the heedless secularity of the modern world deserves a withering judgement." Discusses: the "repetitive character" of her fiction (stories "peopled with arrogant ingrates who suffer a harrowing encounter with their own presumption"); O'Connor's focus on contemporary abandonment of faith; and how "Judgement Day" "brings her fiction full circle and yet also makes the new departure she had prayed for." Explores how in this story she made "a break with the pattern of her previous fiction," which opened up "new possibilities" that she "did not live to realize." Sees "The Geranium" (the original version), as "a rather sentimental and moralistic allegory," and "Judgement Day" as "a penetrating piece of art." Concludes that the "distance" between the early and final version of this story "is not a matter, spiritually and artistically, of decades but of light years," as in the latter, O'Connor's "vision of human communion is rooted in precisely the need which had earlier been ignored." [Also published in *Flannery O'Connor*, New York: Chelsea House, 1986. 55-64.]

1674   Wood, Ralph C. "The Heterodoxy of Flannery O'Connor's Book Reviews." *Flannery O'Connor Bulletin* 5 (1976): 3-29.

Examines the more than one hundred book reviews written by Flannery O'Connor for *The Georgia Bulletin* and the *Southern Cross* to more fully understand "the theological vision which animates her fiction." Notes that though the reviews "have a decidedly occasional tone, and they lack that sinewy perfection which characterizes her fictional prose," they are "unfailingly direct and honest" as she "attacks what is shallow and unworthy, while praising what is meritorious and profound." Finds that the reviews "are undergirded by the same heterodoxy of mind which is at work" in O'Connor's fiction. Suggests that O'Connor's reviews reveal "a religious vision so stark and original that her critics have yet to do it justice," and presents evidence that O'Connor attempted to "improve popular Catholic taste and to elevate the Church's spiritual sensibility" by taking it upon herself to instruct readers "in what constitutes good and bad writing." Remarks that "the spiritual contrariness" of her own work drew O'Connor "to fiction which has an exceptional regard for the power of evil," and that she excoriated nonfiction religious works which failed "to deal with grace in the context of the soul's real doubts and passions." Observes that she "could be as impatient with the liberal point of view which dominated the Catholic intellectual world of the 50s as with the sentimentalism of the Catholic popular press." Submits that O'Connor's "theological radicalism with regard to Catholic sensibility is less apparent when she analyzes the Church's relation to its own best traditions." Notes Miles Orvell's description that O'Connor's "orthodoxy seems to be `socially conservative and culturally enlightened,'" and asserts that "on

many occasions Flannery appears to have genuinely liberal sentiments."
Follows with a discussion of: O'Connor's "attraction to people who live
at the edge of spiritual extremity"; her "serious regard for Freud," whom
she believed, "like Hazel Motes, secretly yearned for the God he denied";
her abiding respect for the Protestant theologian Karl Barth; "her belief
that Catholicism is doctrinally closer to its traditional enemy--Protestant
conservatism--than to the liberalism of its ecumenical friends"; and her
"low regard for the youth cult of Zen Buddhism." Closes with a look at
O'Connor's interest in and eventual position on the theology and writings
of Pierre Teilhard de Chardin.

1675   Wood, Ralph C. "Letters to the Editor." *Flannery O'Connor Bulletin* 23
        (1994-95): 183.

        See entry 527. [Fitzgerald, Sally and Ralph C. Wood. "Letters to the
        Editor." *Flannery O'Connor Bulletin* 23 (1994-95): 175-83.]

1676   Wood, Ralph C. "The Long-Run Efficacy of Love: Four Books on
        Flannery O'Connor." *Flannery O'Connor Bulletin* 18 (1989): 99-105.

        Reviews Richard Giannone's *Flannery O'Connor and the Mystery of Love*,
        Brian Abel Ragen's *A Wreck on the Road to Damascus: Innocence, Guilt
        and Conversion in Flannery O'Connor*, Stephen G. Driggers and Sarah
        Gordon's *The Manuscripts of Flannery O'Connor at Georgia College*, and
        Sister Maura Eichner's volume of poetry, titled *Hope Is a Blind Bard*.
        Finds that while the four books are certainly "worthy additions" to the
        body of O'Connor studies, they--unfortunately--"enliven our
        understanding of O'Connor's fiction in uneven ways." Declares that
        Giannone's work is "far and away the most substantial" of the four.
        Reports that although it "is not easy reading," the rewards of doing so "are
        great." Implies that the content of Ragen's book may have been more
        appropriately communicated in one or more journal articles, and contends
        that it is "often theologically naive, conceptually ill-organized, and
        stylistically over-reliant on plot summaries." Outlines the content of
        Driggers and Gordon's book and maintains that while it will be used
        chiefly by librarians and scholars, "it also holds interest for . . . regular
        readers as well." Closes with commentary on excerpts of Sister Eichner's
        poetry and praises the work as having a "directness of voice" and "stark
        integrity of vision and person."

1677   Wood, Ralph C. "'Obedience to the Unenforceable': Mystery, Manners,
        and Masks in 'Judgement Day.'" *Flannery O'Connor Bulletin* 25 (1996-
        97): 153-74.

Explores the meaning of, and the human need for, manners, then uses this discussion as a context to explicate O'Connor's "Judgement Day." Connects with Henry Grunwald's definition of manners as being "`a surface sign of an underlying order,'" with the idea that Southern manners deal with "not mere politeness . . . but with the formal gestures that both bind and separate people in deeply informal ways." Suggests that O'Connor uses such concepts to demonstrate how her characters, T.C. Tanner and Coleman Parrum, "are oddly checked in their violent desire to dominate, perhaps even to murder," by "their mutual vision of Obedience to the Unenforceable" law of manners. Argues that by depicting characters who choose charity and humility over murder and racial hatred, O'Connor "succeeded in making theological mystery cohere finely with both manners and masks.

1678   Wood Ralph C. Rev. of *Flannery O'Connor: Collected Works*, Ed. Sally Fitzgerald. *Flannery O'Connor Bulletin* 17 (1988): 92-97.

Acknowledges the "virtually unanimous praise" given to the Library of America series of which this volume is a part, and submits that Sally Fitzgerald "has edited this work with her customary diligence and expertise." Declares, however, that while the book "is the nearest thing to a definitive edition of O'Connor's major fiction that we are likely to get," and certain errors have been corrected and "excellent notes" added, the choice of texts selected by Fitzgerald is lamentable and the Chronology "lacks . . . the rich interpretive insight" Fitzgerald supplied in *The Habit of Being*. Argues that, because there are "mistakes which cry out for correction," a new edition of O'Connor's letters is needed. Declares that the letters first published in this volume (22 in all) "remain a cause for great thanksgiving" because they "prove that Flannery O'Connor rarely wrote a sloppy sentence or had a lazy idea." Offers excerpts from the letters as examples, and discusses their context and importance.

1678a   Wood, Ralph C. Rev. of *Flannery O'Connor: Hermit Novelist*, by Richard Giannone. *Flannery O'Connor Bulletin* 26-27 (1998-2000): 182-85.

Suggests that this work joins Giannone's previous book, *Flannery O'Connor and the Mystery of Love*, "as two of the most provocative books yet written" on O'Connor's works. Outlines the major arguments of the work and informs readers of Giannone's thesis "that O'Connor's characters are often solitaires engaged in a spiritual combat akin to warfare waged by ancient anchorites." Affirms Giannone's approach to *The Violent Bear It Away, Wise Blood* and "Parker's Back," and agrees that "a desert kind of monasticism seems indeed to be at work" in these writings. Takes issue, however, with his use of this approach with *all* of O'Connor's fiction, stating, "By sifting all of O'Connor's work through a single sieve, he makes it seem more uniform in character and quality than it really is." Concludes, however, that Giannone "must be commended rather than chastised for his daring interpretation," because "more than any other critic, he has dealt with the terrible reality of the demonic that characterizes the whole of O'Connor's fiction."

1679   Wood, Ralph C. Rev. of *Flannery O'Connor: Images of Grace*, by Harold Fickett and Douglas R. Gilbert. *Flannery O'Connor Bulletin* 16 (1987): 90-94.

States that what appears to be "yet another coffee-table book" is instead, "a powerful interpretation of O'Connor's fiction as the spiritual distillation of her life and of her religious life as the fundament of her fiction." Describes Gilbert's photographs as "true images of her social and religious landscape," which "arrest the eye and haunt the soul." Notes that while Fickett's text offers nothing new on O'Connor's life, it is "written with . . . metaphorical richness and theological insight." Discusses and commends Fickett's interpretation of O'Connor's introduction to *A Memoir of Mary Ann*, but suggests that "there is a snarl of unexamined assumptions entangling" some of his claims, especially those related to O'Connor's views on being a writer during a time of "absence" of faith. Concludes that the book provides "an excellent verbal and visual introduction to Flannery O'Connor's world and to her work."

1680   Wood, Ralph [C.] Rev. of *The Presence of Grace and Other Book Reviews*, by Leo J. Zuber and Carter W. Martin. *Flannery O'Connor Bulletin* 12 (1983): 117-21.

Reports that these reviews, compiled by Leo J. Zuber, attest to O'Connor's "indefatigable devotion to books and ideas." Suggests that the compilation reflects her reading of "'classics' of Western literature and theology" and of current fiction, which she "scrutinized with care." Reminds readers that O'Connor chose the books she would review carefully, as she "wanted to examine the best of contemporary Roman Catholic writing" as part of her battle "against both brittle secularism and mushy faith." Compliments Carter Martin's introduction, and reports that Zuber collected "more than 50 previously unprinted letters, and notes." Notes that this volume, due to its completeness, replaces Lorine M. Getz's *Flannery O'Connor: Her Life, Library and Book Reviews* "in appearance as well as substance."

1681   Wood, Ralph C. Rev. of *Understanding Flannery O'Connor*, by Margaret Earley Whitt; *Flannery O'Connor: The Woman, the Thinker, the*

Visionary, by Ted R. Spivey; and *New Essays on Wise Blood*, Ed. Michael Kreyling. *Flannery O'Connor Bulletin* 23 (1994-95): 195-206.

Begins this lengthy, careful review by noting how "With a few exceptions, the revisionists ride triumphantly astraddle current interpretation of Flannery O'Connor's fiction." States that of the three books reviewed, only Whitt's "operates in the old mode, providing predictable religious readings of O'Connor's fiction through the lenses of her letters and essays." Suggests that "because they have become so repetitive and unimaginative, the traditionalists have been routed by a new cavalry of modernist and post-moderist critics." Claims, however, that Spivey's book and the essays on *Wise Blood* edited by Kreyling are still-- more often than not--"wide of the mark." Suggests that Spivey "misfires by trying to place O'Connor in a modernist Jungian context that will not fit," and that Kreyling's four contributors read O'Connor "in post- modernist terms that obscure as much as they illuminate."

1682   Wood, Ralph C. "Talent Increased and Returned to God: The Spiritual Legacy of Flannery O'Connor's Letters." *Anglican Theological Review* 62.2 (1980): 153-67.

Review essay of *The Habit of Being*, which attempts "to establish the essential integrity of O'Connor's life and work." Asserts that her art was inspired by "a theological conception of humor which arose out of her peculiar experience as a modern Catholic." Attempts "to demonstrate how this faithful comic vision sufficed both in her living and in her dying." Concludes that the letters complete "O'Connor's *oeuvre* in the deepest sense of the word . . . [as they] reveal how profoundly her art sprang from her spiritual life."

1683   Wood, Ralph C. "Where Is the Voice Coming From? Flannery O'Connor on Race." *Flannery O'Connor Bulletin* 22 (1993-94): 90-118.

Revised version of the author's keynote address delivered at Georgia College & State University's "Habit of Art" symposium held in April, 1994. Examines and discusses in detail the question of whether O'Connor was "a closet racist." Evaluates the assertion using evidence found in the "Maryat Lee Letters," the contents of others published in *The Habit of Being*, and from O'Connor's works. Argues that the issue is an important one because--with her strong religious convictions--if "O'Connor were a racist at heart, her stories would carry, either secretly or openly, their own racist burden." Concludes that while she sometimes "sounds like an unabashed racist in her privately expressed opinions," O'Connor was not a racist in either the political or the theological sense of the word.

Suggests instead, that her racial views reflect the "cultural conservatism" from which she skeptically viewed "self-righteous social reformers" and the Civil Rights movement as a whole. Concludes that O'Connor should not be labeled a racist, instead "she was a writer who, though not without temptation and struggle, offered the real antidote to racism," that of the path to the Cross of Jesus. Comments on racial motifs in "The Geranium," "Judgement Day," "Everything That Rises Must Converge," "Revelation," "The Enduring Chill," and "The Artificial Nigger." Refers to François Mauriac, Mississippi Governor Ross Barnett, Richard Stern, President John F. Kennedy, Clarence Jordan, Koinonia Farms, John Howard Griffin, Martin Luther King, James Baldwin, William Faulkner, Thurgood Marshall, Muhammad Ali, Alice Walker, and John Crowe Ransom.

1684   Woster, Michelle M. "Flannery O'Connor's Use of the Grotesque: From Disparity to Grace." *Wittenberg Review* 3.1 (1992): 95-102.

Discusses O'Connor's "outrageous and generally improbable" use of the grotesque "both to dismantle familiarity and to initiate a different kind of existence." Remarks that O'Connor uses this mode of character depiction to reinforce violent, tragic conclusions and to "create worlds for her characters and her readers that . . . [are] both rationally and mystically comprehensible." Concludes that while O'Connor's grotesque characters "challenge the unrealistically aesthetic, pleasing, proportionate norms of American society," she "does not just strip us of our delusions and leave us barren." Instead, she uses the grotesque to reflect our true nature and then "rejuvenates us by offering another reality, one that is rich with the hope of God's grace and the beauty of a human spirituality that no writer or worldly situation can ever defeat."

1685   Wray, Virginia F. "'An Afternoon in the Woods': Flannery O'Connor's Discovery of Theme." *Flannery O'Connor Bulletin* 20 (1991): 45-53.

Reports that O'Connor's "apprentice" short story versions of chapters of *Wise Blood*--from her University of Iowa M.F.A. thesis--differ significantly from the later novel's versions. Suggests that an examination of this difference illustrates the maturation process O'Connor underwent during the intervening period. Asserts that the most important difference between the two versions is the further development of her religious theme "that was to inform everything she wrote in the remaining thirteen years of her life." Describes O'Connor's manuscript drafts, located in the *Flannery O'Connor Collection* at Georgia College & State University, and traces the growth of O'Connor's theme from her thesis story, "The Train," into the opening chapter of *Wise Blood*. Describes communications between O'Connor and Robert Giroux related to O'Connor's "An

Afternoon in the Woods" (which was based upon her thesis story, "The Turkey" and published in *Mademoiselle* as "The Capture"), and their opinions as to whether to include the story in the collection published as *A Good Man Is Hard to Find*. Provides an explication of "The Turkey," notes and describes differences in segments revised, and compares "The Turkey" to "An Afternoon in the Woods." Concludes that the revised version is "infinitely more successful," especially when "measured against O'Connor's own often-cited critical definition of the `gesture' essential to any successful narrative."

1686   Wray, Virginia F. "An Authorial Clue to the Significance of the Title *The Violent Bear It Away.*" *Flannery O'Connor Bulletin* 6 (1977): 107-08.

Alleges that since its publication, the intended meaning of O'Connor's title for her novel *The Violent Bear It Away*, has perplexed "reviewers, critics, and teachers alike." Notes that criticism is often based upon theological scholarship, and the divided opinion of scholars on the meaning of the phrase in *Matthew* 11:12. Reports that in O'Connor's copy of Emmanuel Mounier's book, *Personalism* (New York: Grove, 1952), she had written "the violent bear it away" beside a passage "on page 49 in the subsection `Jacob's wrestling' of the second chapter, `Confrontation.'" Sees this as a "piece of evidence that is an authorial clue capable of, if not ending the critical debate, at least turning its focus away from theology back to literary analysis."

1687   Wray, Virginia F. "At Last, A Biography . . . Of Sorts." *CHEERS! The Flannery O'Connor Society Newsletter*. 2.2 (1994-95): 1, 4.

Review of *Flannery O'Connor: Literary Prophet of the South*, by Susan Balée (Chelsea House, 1995). Suggests that O'Connor would have found this book "both every bit as amusing and as appalling as she found Roy Rogers's having taken his horse Trigger to church in Pasadena." Finds Jerry Lewis's introduction bordering on "foolish, sentimental tripe"; and the beginning of the book inappropriately jocular. Refers to chapters which focus on the disability theme, O'Connor's trip to Lourdes, and contribution to *A Memoir of Mary Ann*. Relates opinion that "much of the mixed nature of this volume . . . is caused not just by the series' attitude toward disability, but also by the prescribed adolescent audience." Reports that "the book oddly does contain the fullest discussion to date of the controversy at Yaddo" but laments the lack of references. Concludes that Balée appears "trapped between her teenage audience and O'Connor scholars, whom she seems at times to want to address." The end result is a book that "serves neither audience well."

1688   Wray, Virginia F. "Flannery O'Connor In the American Romance Tradition." *Flannery O'Connor Bulletin* 6 (1977): 83-98.

Reports that since O'Connnor's death in 1964, "little has been published on either her occasional writing or her fiction's place in the American literary tradition." Laments that "there has been no serious attempt" to reconstruct from *Mystery and Manners* "the working aesthetic theory out of which her stories and novels grew." Suggests that the failure to seriously consider these essays has led to "a failure to evaluate O'Connor's claim, other than by right of birth, to the label *American* writer." Discusses how O'Connor's "conception of the nature and aim of fiction is remarkably similar to that held by nineteenth-century American precursors within the romance tradition." Outlines how American romance writers "have defined the dark tradition of American fiction," and contrasts these writers (Nathaniel Hawthorne, Herman Melville, and Henry James), with "the Happiness Boys who see only the immediate, knowable, and generally providing world about them" (Ralph Waldo Emerson and Walt Whitman). Considers O'Connor's ties to Hawthorne and James, carefully compares each of their places "in the American Romance tradition" to the other, and follows with a close examination of O'Connor as "a realist of distances," which Wray argues clearly puts her "in the school of romance writers." Refers to: comments by Robert Drake; O'Connor's comments to William Sessions and Gerard Sherry; O'Connor's introduction to *A Memoir to Mary Ann*; Hawthorne's *The House of Seven Gables* and "Sights from a Steeple" in *Twice-Told Tales*; James's *The American* and *Art of the Novel*; and Melville's *The Confidence Man*. Concludes that O'Connor's "attempts to combat the modern reader's blindness to the essential mystery of human existence and his deprivation of manners" with her use of exaggerated characters and detailed, exaggerated plots, has tended--not to result in "essential revelation"--but "to feed the fires of misreadings."

1689   Wray, Virginia [F.] "Flannery O'Connor's Long Apprenticeship: Honing the Habits of Irony and Satire." *Antigonish Review* N.S. No. 99 (Aut. 1994): 139-49.

Suggests that readers may gain a perspective of O'Connor's "developing habits" as a writer by examining her juvenile writings available in the Flannery O'Connor Collection at Georgia College & State University. Contends that her early works "document a serious emerging writer struggling toward character types, mode, and tone characteristic of her mature work." Refers to articles about O'Connor's work in her high school newspaper (*The Palladium*), a feature article on her in the *Macon Telegraph and News*, and provides a reprint of her poem "The First Book." Cites and describes several of her pieces published in College publications between 1942 and 1944, including: "Going to the Dogs"; her review of Munroe Leaf's *The Story of Ferdinand*; "Why Worry the Horse"; "Effervescence"; "Elegance Is Its Own Reward"; "Doctors of Delinquency"; "Biologic Endeavor"; "Home of the Brave"; "Fashion's Perfect Medium"; "PFTT" (a poem); "Excuse Us While We Don't Apologize"; and "Education's Only Hope." Describes other materials in the files, including unpublished fragments, class exercises, and "other pieces" from her collegiate file, including: "The Cynosure," "Interruptions Are So Exasperating," and "A Place of Action." Closes with a brief discussion of "The Coat" and its relationship to *Wise Blood*.

1690   Wray, Virginia [F.]. "Flannery O'Connor's Master's Thesis: Looking for Some Gestures." *Flannery O'Connor Bulletin* 8 (1979): 68-76.

Examines the six stories that comprise O'Connor's 1947 M.F.A. thesis completed at the University of Iowa. Suggests that while they may not be her best work, they "adumbrate the themes, the technique, and the marriage of theme and technique in the best that she began writing in the early 1950s." Contrasts these stories with O'Connor's "quantum leap in maturity only five years later with the publication of *Wise Blood*." Recognizes O'Connor's interest in racial, political, social, and artistic themes, which she later learned "to subordinate to her primary concern with man's reaction to Christian salvation." Comments that a major weakness of the stories is poor structuring of dramatic conflict. Refers to comments by Miles Orvell, Stuart Burns, and Jean Wylder. Offers readings of "The Geranium," "The Barber," "Wildcat," "The Crop," and "The Train." Concludes that the importance of O'Connor's thesis stories lies in how they introduce her major themes and "establish the pattern of the central gesture late in the plot the story into tight focus."

1691   Wray, Virginia [F.] "Flannery O'Connor's *Why Do the Heathen Rage?* and the Quotidian `larger things.'" *Flannery O'Connor Bulletin* 23 (1994-95): 1-29.

Notes that with the exception of articles by Stuart Burns and Marian Burns, "little scholarly attention" has been given to the 378 pages of manuscripts of her work--in progress at the time of her death--*Why Do the Heathen Rage?* Suggests that O'Connor's letters, "repeatedly document the uncertainty and frustration she was experiencing" with this work. Then, addresses the "obvious question of why O'Connor was unable to complete the novel." Reviews speculations by Stuart Burns and Marian Burns, then examines O'Connor's correspondence. Submits that it was O'Connor's difficulty in dealing with "issues of social justice and fairness, and love between human beings," that served as the root cause for her uncertainty and frustration with the novel in progress. Outlines the plot, characters, and issues, and discusses clues and insights gained from O'Connor's correspondence with "A," Maryat Lee, Cecil Dawkins, Sister Mariella Gable, and her interview with Gerard Sherry. Also, refers to comments by Paul Johnson, C.S. Lewis (from *The Problem of Pain*), Clara Claiborne Park, Louise Abbot, Ralph Wood, Nathaniel Hawthorne (from *Our Old Home*), Mother Alphonsa (Rose Hawthorne), and Sarah Gordon. Focuses on: O'Connor's friendship and correspondence with Maryat Lee (who may have served "as a very general model" for Sarah Gibbs); how Sarah's "fictive community [is] undoubtedly modeled after Koinonia, an interracial farm community in Americus, Georgia"; and the differing views that Lee and O'Connor held on the proper action that should be taken "to rectify the egregious injustice of racism."

1692   Wray, Virginia [F.]. "The Importance of Home To the Fiction of Flannery O'Connor." *Renascence* 47.2 (1995): 103-15.

Traces the influence of O'Connor's childhood and Southern background upon her work. Begins with a discussion of the onset of lupus erythematosus, including perspectives of her friends Sally and Robert Fitzgerald and her uncle, Louis Cline. Considers how the disease "substantially changed the circumstances of her life," but contends that it "had essentially no effect on the nature and direction of her art." Reviews her decision to change editors--from John Shelby of Rinehart to Robert Giroux of Harcourt, Brace--and refers to her reliance upon advice given by Caroline Gordon and Elizabeth McKee. Cites and offers brief descriptions of various pieces written during her school years in Savannah, Milledgeville, and at the University of Iowa Writer's Workshop, including: unpublished autobiographical pieces from her childhood years and from an Iowa journalism class; pieces from composition classes and her college's literary magazine, *The Corinthian*; her thesis stories at Iowa (focusing on "The Geranium"); and, various fragments in the manuscript files of the Flannery O'Connor Collection at Georgia College & State University, which suggest some of her later characters and plot circumstances. Concludes that only after O'Connor "had left her native South was she fully imaginatively drawn to it." Closes by pointing out indications in letters from O'Connor to Maryat Lee and Cecil Dawkins that--even before the onset of lupus--she "had undergone a slow, even gentle, imaginative turning homeward of inestimable value to her development as an artist."

1693   Wray, Virginia [F.]. "Narration in `A Good Man Is Hard to Find.'" *Publications of the Arkansas Philological Association* 14.1 (1988): 25-38.

Recalls O'Connor's definition of what makes a story work: "some gesture of a character that is unlike any other in the story, one which indicates where the real heart of the story lies." Says "A Good Man Is Hard to Find" is objectively narrated and must be so if the Grandmother's salvation is to be believable. Shows how the Grandmother's vision, though nostalgic and trivial, is still preferable to that of the rest of the family, who are blind and self-serving. Says the death scene humbles the Grandmother, and absolves her of her momentary denial: in murmuring to The Misfit "You're one of my own children," she ultimately accepts Christian grace and salvation.

1694   Wray, Virginia [F.]. Rev. of *Flannery O'Connor: New Perspectives*, by Sura P. Rath and Mary Neff Shaw. *Flannery O'Connor Bulletin* 24 (1995-96): 133-37.

Notes approvingly that Rath's introduction, "succinctly reviews four decades of O'Connor criticism in order to justify" the "claim of newness in methodology of the essays they have selected for inclusion." Notes that many "employ gender and dialogical studies," and proceeds to discuss each essay. Finds the first, by Sarah J. Fodor, to be an apt introduction to the volume as it documents the marketing strategies which resulted in the "consistently extraordinarily varied market that O'Connor has always enjoyed." Discusses the next four essays, which focus on gender: sees Richard Giannone's as the most conservative and not appropriately informed by O'Connor's letters to Maryat Lee and Ralph Wood's "analysis of O'Connor's racism"; Jeanne Campbell Reesman's examination of O'Connor's grotesqueness as being "the most general"; Marshall Bruce Gentry's as hinting at a biographical reading and offering a useful Bakhtinian approach; and, Sarah Gordon's essay as "convincingly" tying "gender questions in the fiction to biography." Comments on theoretical and interpretive problems in the three following essays by Suzanne Morrow Paulson, Mary Neff Shaw, and Laura B. Kennelly. Remarks that the essay by Robert H. Brinkmeyer, "returns to the biographical approach present in the previous essays on gender" and "analyzes the asceticism that O'Connor so frequently claimed in her letters [as] a necessity of her life as an artist." Finds Patricia Yaeger's essay not "ultimately credible" in how it posits "'a new set of connections between O'Connor's psyche and her southerness.'" Closes with a discussion of how this volume provides O'Connor's readers with "rewarding understandings of the fiction and of the artist/woman in all her human complexity, warts and all."

1694a   Wray, Virginia [F.]. Rev. of *Flannery O'Connor: A Proper Scaring* (rev. ed.), by Jill Pelaez Baumgaertner. *Flannery O'Connor Bulletin* 26-27 (1998-2000): 190-92.

Declares that the appearance of this "'revised edition' of Jill Baumgaertner's 1988 study . . . will likely be met with a mixed critical reception." Discusses the revisions and criticizes the book's "new choppy formatting, the loss of cartoons, and the authorial decision not to incorporate new critical perspectives and ideas." Concludes, however, that despite these shortcomings, "students of O'Connor's works are better off for the continued availability" of this work.

1695   Wright, Angela H. "I have a query concerning Flannery O'Connor's `Greenleaf.'" *Flannery O'Connor Bulletin* 5 (1976): 81.

Reports two contradictory statements found in "Greenleaf" concerning whether Mrs. May had insurance. Poses the question: "What purpose did O'Connor have in allowing this discrepancy?" The editors follow with a note that the Flannery O'Connor Collection does not own a draft of "Greenleaf," and is thus "unable to offer this reader any assistance."

1696   Wright, Austin M. "Recalcitrance in the Short Story." *Short Story Theory at a Crossroads*. Ed. Susan Lohafer and Jo Ellyn Clarey. Baton Rouge: Louisiana State UP, 1989. 115-29.

Examines the nature of the "two opposing forces" visible in all fictional works: "the force of a shaping form and the resistance of the shaped materials." Includes a brief discussion of how O'Connor's "The Artificial Nigger," "Parker's Back," and "Revelation" serve as examples of stories in which the reader is left to draw his or her own conclusion as to their meaning. Contends also that O'Connor's "A Good Man Is Hard to Find" and "Greenleaf" serve as important examples of a "kind of modal discontinuity" in how they abruptly switch "from comic expectations to serious violence."

1697   Wyatt, Bryan N. "The Domestic Dynamics of Flannery O'Connor: *Everything That Rises Must Converge*." *Twentieth Century Literature* 38.1 (1992): 66-88.

Refers to O'Connor's assertion that her writings reflected her "Christian orthodoxy" and discusses various reasons as to why critics have expressed reservations regarding her success. Implies that some of the reservations lie in her approach to writing, as some works may have overly emphasized the "technical demands of the stories," the utilization of "Henry James's concept of felt life," and been distracting in "the very Catholicity, the encompassing embrace, of her outlook." Suggests that "the supernatural action of grace . . . is also too often scarcely detected by her readers, unless O'Connor herself employs some seemingly obtrusive authorial device to underscore it . . . weakening [her] artistry." Examines domestic themes of "filial obligation [and] familial duty" in "Everything That Rises Must Converge," "Greenleaf," "A View of the Woods," "The Enduring Chill," "The Comforts of Home," "Revelation," "Parker's Back," and "Judgement Day."

1698   Wynne, Judith F. "The Sacramental Irony of Flannery O'Connor." *Southern Literary Journal* 7.2 (1975): 33-49.

Suggests "that `sacramentality,' when applied to literature, should be understood as an interpretive concept . . . directly dependent for its validity upon the tools of critical analysis." Then contends that while O'Connor's fiction *is* sacramental, "critics' easy reference of its literary power to the impact of its orthodoxy has robbed it of much of its inherent literary richness." Explores a use and understanding of sacramentality "as an enriching characteristic of satiric irony," and establishes "the artistic achievement of O'Connor's use of it." Submits that O'Connor's use of irony "can be seen as sacramental, not because it works with the stuff of religious belief and non-belief, which it does, but because it itself operates as a vehicle of revelation." Refers to remarks by Carter W. Martin, Northrop Frye, and I.A. Richards. Offers sacramental readings of "Revelation," "A Good Man Is Hard to Find," "Good Country People," and "A View of the Woods."

1699   Yaeger, Patricia S[mith]. "`Because a Fire Was in My Head': Eudora Welty and the Dialogic Imagination." *PMLA* 99 (1984): 955-73.

Includes a passing reference to O'Connor, noting that it was in the decade before Eudora Welty began writing, that Katherine Anne Porter, Lillian Smith, Carson McCullers, and O'Connor, produced in their novels and stories, "the `heteroglossia that rages beyond the boundaries' of a formerly sealed-off cultural universe."

1699a   Yaeger, Patricia [Smith]. *Dirt and Desire: Reconstructing Southern Women's Writing, 1930-1990*. Chicago: U of Chicago P, 2000.

Contends that the old "models of `the' Southern grotesque are due for a paradigm shift" and attempts "to examine the importance of irregular models of the body within an extremely regulated society and to focus on figures of damaged, incomplete, or extravagant characters described under rubrics peculiarly suited to Southern histories in which the body is simultaneously fractioned and overwhelmed." Refers to a variety of

O'Connor's works, characters and artistic intentions, including how ethnicity, class, and "the bizarre habitus of Jim Crow explode with premonitions of change" in "The Displaced Person"; O'Connor's attempt "to diminish our appetite" for the Southern stereotype of referring to Southern literature as Southern grotesque; how "monstrous bodies" are used to symbolize resistance to social change in "The Displaced Person"; her use of "bisected" characters, such as the freak in "A Temple of the Holy Ghost"; racial unrest in general and as depicted in "Everything That Rises Must Converge" and "Revelation"; clothing in "The Artificial Nigger"; and rags and dirt as symbols in Southern writing as evidenced in *Wise Blood* and "Revelation."

1700 Yaeger, Patricia S[mith]. "Flannery O'Connor: 1925-64." *Modern American Women Writers*. Ed. Elaine Showalter, Lea Baechler, and A. Walton Litz. New York: Charles Scribner's, 1991. 375-87.

Discusses O'Connor's "quintessential Southern lady, Mrs. Wally Bee Hitchcock" of *Wise Blood* and finds her to be "just the kind of class-obsessed Southern matriarch" that O'Connor "loves to parody." Asserts that "O'Connor's middle-class storytellers all tell the same hackneyed tale: they are preoccupied with the rules for separating and sanctioning the divisions between the South's races, genders, and classes." Examines Mary Grace and Mrs. Turpin of "Revelation" and finds similarities between Mary Grace and O'Connor herself. Points out aspects of O'Connor's relationship with her mother that may be suggested in her work; Alice Walker's perspective on O'Connor; O'Connor's status as a "Lady"; and her position on the issue of race. Analyzes the role of the South's past in "Everything That Rises Must Converge," "A Good Man Is Hard to Find," and "The River." Reports biographical details of O'Connor's childhood in Savannah, and "the orthodoxy and iconoclasm" of her Catholicism as suggested in "A Temple of the Holy Ghost." Reviews her professional career, including her undergraduate years; work with Paul Engle, Robert Penn Warren, and Andrew Lytle at Iowa; her stay at Yaddo; her battle with Lupus; and her posthumous honors. Asserts that O'Connor's stories are "aggressively spiritual . . . a direct response to the Southern cult of femininity as this cult meets the hyperbolic division of labor of postwar suburbia." Praises O'Connor's work for the way in which it "serves to break up and break open a grueling Southern tradition in which women aspire to the pedestaled passivity of beauty queens."

1701 Yaeger, Patricia Smith. "Flannery O'Connor and the Aesthetics of Torture." *Flannery O'Connor: New Perspectives*. Ed. Sura P. Rath and Mary Neff Shaw. Athens: U Georgia P, 1996. 183-206.

Addresses the question: "What happens to O'Connor's stories when we wake up the personal and political terrors of her texts?" Develops "a phenomenology of pain in O'Connor's fiction," by tracing "her literary sadism as an inchoate form of readerly torture" and examining the "relationship between this phenomenology and O'Connor's moment in history." Seeks to find "fresh terms for reading O'Connor's fiction . . . terms that refuse O'Connor's Catholicism as the pivotal focus for her grotesques," and attempts instead to use "a new set of connections between O'Connor's psyche and her southernness." Introduces this contention with a discussion of the relevancy of Lillian Smith's *Killers of the Dream*, noting how Smith "compares the experience of being southern to the anguish created by a torture instrument that turns southern children into creatures wracked by social and psychic deformities." Suggests that because O'Connor's stories "offer intricate readings of a social system gone awry," and represent the finest use "of the grotesque as a southern literary experience," they are particularly useful for "a politicized reading of the grotesque as [a] southern form." Defends this argument with the assertion that "southern literary bodies are grotesque because their authors know that bodies cannot be thought of [as] separate from the racist and sexist institutions that surround them." Refers to Lewis Carroll's *Through the Looking Glass* and critical commentary by: Mab Segrest, Katherine Anne Porter, Julius Lester, Julia Kristeva, Elaine Scarry, Roland Barthes, Robb Forman Dew, Peter Stallybrass, Allon White, and Alice Walker to support contentions.

1702   Yaeger, Patricia Smith. "The Woman Without Any Bones: Anti-Angel Aggression in *Wise Blood*." *New Essays on Wise Blood*. Ed. Michael Kreyling. New York: Cambridge UP, 1995. 91-116.

Seeks to understand the sources and meaning behind O'Connor's aggressive prose. States that by adopting "a narrative voice that is confident, aesthetically pleasing, yet deeply sadistic," and then inventing "characters who serve as foils for this voice," her works reveal a "textual schizophrenia." Examines her attempt as a writer "to remain in the tomboyish role of the angel-aggressive little girl." Finds this technique to be "a brilliant fictional strategy." Discusses how "this rebellious infantilism" is worked out in *Wise Blood* through "surrealist constructions," the use of "a child's point of view," and "disturbing resurrections of childhood aggression and anger." Notes "the pleasure O'Connor seems to take in creating the dead bodies" in the novel. Suggests that a child-like, "primitive fascination with death and bodily privation is the bedrock of O'Connor's fiction." Ties her fascination and "nearly clinical obsession with violence," physical deformities, and signs of trauma, to character types seen in horror stories and animated cartoons. Concludes that O'Connor does not represent "the portrait of an idealized female writer; she is someone more interesting, an angel-aggressive woman who uses her violent imagery and her wicked sense of humor to change the balance of social power and create a new form of writing as antiritual." Refers to Shoshana Felman's *Testimony*, Virginia Woolf's *A Room of One's Own*, Claire Kahane's essay "Flannery O'Connor's Rage of Vision," Theodor W. Adorno's *Notes to Literature* and *Negative Dialectics*, Slavoj Zizek's *The Sublime Object of Ideology*, Lillian Smith's *Killers of the Dream*, and Walter Benjamin's perspective on cartoons.

1703   Yamamoto, Yoshimi. "A Supernatural Ending: A Study of Flannery O'Connor's `A View of the Woods.'" *Tsuda Review* [Tsuda College Bulletin] (Japan) 24 (Nov. 1979): 37-46.

Examines the ending of "A View of the Woods" in light of O'Connor's correspondence with "A." Points of discussion include: whether or not Pitts is a Christ figure; and, whether Mr. Fortune should be entirely damned or not. Concludes that Flannery O'Connor's ending is certainly appropriate because it accords with her own notion that a good short story should always leave the reader with a sense of mystery. (Abstracted by Kayoko Watanabe).

1704   Yancey, Philip. "The Crayon Man." *Christianity Today* 6 Feb. 1987: 14-20.

Offers a biographical sketch of Robert Coles, prominent "child psychiatrist, lay theologian, author and teacher." Discusses Coles's use of literary works by O'Connor and other well-known writers and Christian thinkers to teach classes in Harvard College's schools of medicine, law, and business, and his admiration for O'Connor's collection of essays, *Mystery and Manners*.

1705   Yochim, Karen. "Poet's Corner: At Flannery's Grave." *Milledgeville (GA) Union-Recorder* 1 Oct. 1991: 2.

A poem which describes the scene at Memory Hill Cemetery in Milledgeville, Georgia, during the author's visit to Flannery O'Connor's grave. Text offer observations of the prisoners "trimming the graves," the sound of weedeaters, the smell of newly mown grass, and her observation of the "flying green dust" floating in the air. Writes that O'Connor's remains are now "consumed by the red clay" she so lovingly described in her works and suggests the epitaph: "She wrote the finest kind of Southern Tales. Rest in Peace."

1706   York, Lamar. "Breakfast at Flannery's." *Modern Age* 38.3 (1996): 245-52.

Notes that every story but two of the thirty-one in O'Connor's *Collected Stories* "involves at least a little eating, and often a complete meal." Offers details of each instance, including the character involved, the food consumed, and the circumstances. Reports that while O'Connor's stories "are about meals and mealtime," they focus upon the ritual of eating while not providing details about the food itself. Reports that breakfast, in her stories, appears to be a time for "dramatic resolutions," and that for each character, "resolve usually takes the place of the action of eating." Concludes that O'Connor's stories are "about a hunger that won't be satisfied at the kitchen table," but instead "at another, more important feast, when food becomes elemental, sacramental."

1707   Young, Joanna. "Habit of Art: O'Connor Symposium a Celebration in Words, Music, Drama and Art." [Georgia College & State University, School of Arts & Sciences] *Connection* 1.2 (1994): 1.

Presents an outline of activities and participants in *Habit of Art: An Interdisciplinary Celebration of the Legacy of Flannery O'Connor*, a symposium held at GC&SU in mid-April, 1994. Concludes with Sarah Gordon's comment that "'This was by far our greatest celebration.'"

1708   Young, Thomas Daniel. "Flannery O'Connor's View of the South: God's Earth and His Universe." *Studies in the Literary Imagination* 20.2 (1987): 5-14.

Argues that in "The Displaced Person" O'Connor "portrays with humor, irony, and lasting effect, the true nature of the Southern scene." Suggests that her "creative genius is demonstrated by how she presents an unforgettable image of her native region even though the thematic intent of her story is centered in another realm . . . grace offered and refused." Provides an explication of "The Displaced Person," supported with use of quotations. Concludes that O'Connor comes as close in this story as she ever does to achieving what she has called the "main business" of her story telling: "revealing the depth of God's mysteries while she is evoking the concrete particulars of her native region, middle Georgia, and presenting its inhabitants knowingly, suggestively, revealingly."

1709   Young, Thomas Daniel. "Redeeming Grace: Flannery O'Connor's *The Complete Stories*." *The Past in the Present: A Thematic Study of Modern Southern Fiction*. Baton Rouge: Louisiana State UP, 1981. 117-36.

Discusses convictions of the contributors to *I'll Take My Stand: The South and the Agrarian Tradition*, including their differences on the function of religion in modern society. Argues that O'Connor "is one of the few significant writers who lived and wrote in the South between 1925 and 1965 who accepted unquestioningly the dogma of the church of which she was a devout member." Examines the "orthodox Christian view . . . at the heart" of O'Connor's work, her "ear for Southern speech" and idiom, her perspective on the past, the "positive effect on her art of her belief in Christianity," and the role and function of various characters in her fiction. Offers brief commentary on "Good Country People," "A Temple of the Holy Ghost," "The River," and "A Circle in the Fire." Refers to Allen Tate, John Crowe Ransom, Robert Penn Warren, Eudora Welty, Sister Mariella Gable, Saint Cyril of Jerusalem, Carter Martin, Walker Percy, and John Barth.

1710   Young, Thomas Daniel. "Religion and Literature." *Mississippi Quarterly* 39.2 (1986): 126-32.

Offers a review essay of Robert H. Brinkmeyer, Jr.'s *Three Catholic Writers of the Modern South: Allen Tate, Caroline Gordon, Walker Percy* (Jackson: UP of Mississippi, 1985), which includes a comparison of Caroline Gordon's fiction with that of O'Connor. Observes how, in both writer's work, "there is often a jolt or sudden reversal to indicate the manifestation of God's grace in the world." Then suggests that the primary difference between the two writers lies in how each settles fictional conflict within their stories. Discusses how, unlike O'Connor, Gordon's "moments of conversion appear to be a means of settling the fictional conflict outside the story by Christian *deux ex machina*." Contends that this strategy weakens the conclusion of Gordon's stories, making them appear "artificial and unconvincing."

1711   Young, Thomas Daniel. "Religion, the Bible Belt, and the Modern South." *The American South: Portrait of a Culture*. Ed. Louis D. Rubin, Jr. Baton Rouge: Louisiana State UP, 1980. 110-17.

Outlines the role of religion in the South, from the customs and theology of its earliest settlers to the present. Compares the beliefs of O'Connor and Jimmy Carter and suggests that O'Connor's "`unlimited God who reveals himself specifically' is also the one responsible for Carter's being `born again.'" Offers examples of O'Connor's "arresting group of characters." Contends that it is only through close reading that readers confront her Christian message, stating: "But it's there, concealed behind some of the most polished and sophisticated writing done in America in the twentieth century." Follows with a brief discussion of her use of "warped and grotesque characters" and her unrelenting insistence on depicting "imperfect men living in a world that reflects their imperfection."

1712   Young, Thomas Daniel. "A Second Generation of Novelists." *The History of Southern Literature.* Ed. Louis D. Rubin, Jr. Baton Rouge: Louisiana State UP, 1985. 466-69.

Describes the context and approach used by post-World War II Southern writers. States that the "techniques most often employed were the grotesque--as in Flannery O'Connor's *Wise Blood* (1952) and Eudora Welty's "'Keela, the Outcast Indian Maiden' (1940)--and the existential/phenomenological."

1713   Young, Thomas Daniel and Elizabeth Sarcone, eds. *The Lytle-Tate Letters: The Correspondence of Andrew Lytle and Allen Tate.* Jackson: UP of Mississippi, 1987. 234, 238-39, 314-15.

Edited compilation of letters between Andrew Lytle and Allen Tate (1927-1968), which include passing references to O'Connor: Tate mentioning that her name appeared on a list for fellowships; Tate complimenting her use of local idiom "with the *minimum* of distorted, or phonetic spelling"; and, Lytle's suggestion that the *Sewanee Review* plan an issue highlighting O'Connor.

1714   Young, Thomas Daniel and George Core, eds. *Selected Letters of John Crowe Ransom.* Baton Rouge: Louisiana State UP, 1985. 270, 374, and 376.

O'Connor is mentioned in letters to: Monroe K. Spears (May 2, 1953) in response to his request for a recommendation in support of O'Connor for a *Sewanee Review* fellowship; Andrew Lytle (March 25, 1954) praising O'Connor's "first-rate" contributions to the *Kenyon Review*; and, Robert Penn Warren (April 14, 1955) concerning O'Connor's choice of "The Artificial Nigger" as title for a short story submitted for publication.

1715   Zacharasiewicz, Waldemar. "Flannery O'Connor Among Creative Readers Abroad: A Late Encounter With The Georgia Writer." *Studies in the Literary Imagination* 20.2 (1987): 51-65.

Reports on publication of foreign translations of O'Connor's works, their critical reception, and impact on fiction writers. Countries discussed include France, Germany, Britain and Canada. Extensive and detailed footnotes are provided. Mentions a wide variety of other writers including: Poe, Faulkner, Capote, Reynolds Price, William Styron, Hemingway, Carson McCullers, Harper Lee, William Goyen, Marshall McLuhan, and Eudora Welty. Also discussed is O'Connor's influence on Canadian writers.

1716   Zacharasiewicz, Waldemar. "From the State to the Strait of Georgia: Aspects of the Response by Some of Flannery O'Connor's Creative Readers." *Realist of Distances: Flannery O'Connor Revisited.* Ed. Karl-Heinz Westarp and Jan Nordby Gretlund. Aarhus, Denmark: Aarhus UP, 1987. 171-84.

Refers to O'Connor's influence on John Hawkes and Joyce Carol Oates in the United States, on comments by Evelyn Waugh in Britain, and efforts to translate O'Connor's work by Maurice-Edgar Coindreau (French) and Elisabeth Schnack (German). Suggests that the "affinity" between French and American Southern literature may explain why O'Connor's work has been readily acknowledged and appreciated in France, while less so in Britain and even less in Germany. Examines the extent to which Canadian authors have been influenced by O'Connor's work. Mentions a variety of Canadian critics and writers, including: Margot Northey, Anne Hebert, Marie-Claire Blais, Sheila Watson, Desmond Pacey, Bill Keith, John Metcalf, and Tim Struthers. Then, discusses in detail the influence of O'Connor on Rudy Wiebe and Jack Hodgins. [Appears to be a version of Zacharasiewicz's essay published in *Studies in the Literary Imagination* 20.2 (1987): 51-65.]

1717   Zacharasiewicz, Waldemar. "The Sense of Place in Southern Fiction by Eudora Welty and Flannery O'Connor." *AAA: Arbeiten aus Anglistik und Amerikanistik* (Germany) 10.1-2 (1985): 189-206.

Explores the significance of "place" in the work of O'Connor and Welty. Analyzes "The Displaced Person" to illustrate "how concreteness and specificity of detail evoking a sense of place enable [O'Connor] . . . to put across her vision of a transcendent reality."

1717a   Zaidman, Laura Mandell. "The Evolution of a Good Woman." *Flannery O'Connor Bulletin* 26-27 (1998-2000): 43-51.

Analyzes the evolution of O'Connor's story, "A Good Man Is Hard to Find." Reviews differences between two photocopied pages of an early working draft, the version published in a "thirty-five-cent paperback anthology published by the editors of *The Partisan Review*" titled *The*

Avon Book of Modern Writing (1953), and that seen in later reprints. Discusses variants between the two versions: the characterization of Bailey; the grandmother's role and responsibility for the incident; significant differences in the "crucial detour scene"; and "a fascinating insight" regarding Pitty Sing (the grandmother's cat). Concludes that O'Connor's revisions prove that "O'Connor constructed the grandmother in stages, revising the characterization from a woman desperately in need of God's grace to a medium of grace for The Misfit."

1718   Zaidman, Laura M. "*The Habit of Being: Letters*." *Masterplots II: Women's Literature Series*. Vol. 3. Ed. Frank N. Magill. Pasadena, CA: Salem Press, 1995. 984-88.

Provides an analysis and discussion of the form, content, and context of Flannery O'Connor's letters published in *The Habit of Being: Letters*. Finds the correspondence to "provide wonderful insight" into O'Connor's mind, and considers this "self-portrait in words" to be "a picture reflecting her true likeness, her inner self," that offers readers "an intimate glimpse of a woman perfecting her art and life despite a debilitating illness." Remarks, however, that while "reviewers have praised these letters for their wit, brilliance, intelligence, and precision of statement," the absence of her correspondence with her mother and others, coupled with the omission of selected text, make the reader's task of evaluating O'Connor's views on women's issues difficult. Concludes that, based upon the correspondence in this volume, "O'Connor remains peripheral to the feminist literary tradition . . . a woman writing about her day-to-day life without any particular focus on women's issues."

1719   Zaidman, Laura M. "Varieties of Religious Experience in O'Connor and West." *Flannery O'Connor Bulletin* 7 (1978): 26-46.

Compares and contrasts Nathanael West's *Miss Lonelyhearts* with O'Connor's *Wise Blood* to point out links which "prove that Hazel Motes's religious quest followed the same structural pattern" and contained "similar thematic motifs, metaphors, and images" as that of Miss Lonelyhearts. Sees the main characters of both novels as following similar flights from Christ and sharing "the same rejection-pursuit pattern." Further, in *Wise Blood*, O'Connor "follows West's use of satiric reduction- -an ironic voice heightening the urgency of the religious quest." Comments that West's "religious stance" closely resembles "O'Connor's religious vision," and discusses their like use of "Christian myths, rituals, and symbols to stress the need for religious experience." Notes similarities between the two main characters' facial features, background, clothing, name, and "stern, intense appearance," to the extent that "Hazel is Miss

Lonelyhearts's double." Observes that both O'Connor and West use similar language "to show violence as a prerequisite in the pilgrim's progress toward salvation": both main characters go through "a series of conscious sinning," whereby "atonement has been prepared for through violence." Refers to remarks by Stanley Edgar Hyman, John Hawkes, Frederick Asals, Robert Fitzgerald, Jay Martin, and to T.S. Eliot's *Wasteland*, West's *The Day of the Locust* and *A Cool Million*, and William James's *The Varieties of Religious Experience*. Concludes that in the writing of *Wise Blood* "there can be no question that O'Connor derived a great deal of inspiration from *Miss Lonelyhearts*."

1719a   Zenter, Joe. "Flannery O'Connor: An Irish American Literary Giant." *Irish America* 16.2 (1998): 94.

Offers a biographical sketch of Flannery O'Connor focusing upon her Irish roots. Refers to her "great-grandfather, Patrick Harry, [who] came to Georgia from county Tipperary," and notes that her father, Edward O'Connor, attended Catholic schools as a boy. States that during the time O'Connor lived in New York, she endured "a period of doubt," after which time she soon "reaffirmed her loyalty to the Catholic Church," a decision which "involved every part of her being." Discusses her battle with disseminated lupus and her reactions to her medical situation as seen in her correspondence. Refers to her move back home to Milledgeville, Georgia and suggests that while she was "jovially critical of the Irishness of her Milledgeville Irish-American pastor, [in] the way he draped the church in green on St. Patrick's Day," she was somewhat critical of "what she called the Irish cast of American Catholicism of her time." Outlines her views "on the business of writing--a business that was for her indistinguishable from the spiritual life itself." Finds her letters to "reveal a keen awareness of the absurd and an appreciation of the caprices of human personality." Contends that Milledgeville's "starchy traditionalism and its lode of Southern Gothic paradoxes were the perfect foils for Flannery O'Connor's surgical Irish Catholic wit." Concludes that, for O'Connor, "writing and faith" were "tightly bound together" as she "identified `conversion'--that is, `a character's changing'--as the only real subject of good literature."

1720   Zimbaro, Valerie P. *Encyclopedia of Apocalyptic Literature*. ABC-CLIO Literary Companion. Santa Barbara, CA: ABC-CLIO, 1996. xii, 18, 28, 144-45, 251-53, 319-20, 341-43.

Considers O'Connor's writings in entries for "O'Connor, Flannery," "Tarwater, Francis Marion," and "*The Violent Bear It Away*." Also includes passing references to O'Connor's life and work in the

Introduction and in entries for "Apocalypse: Traditional Primitive," "Babylon," "Jung, Carl Gustav" and "Grotesque." Discusses the impact on Flannery O'Connor of her father's death, and suggests that her "awareness of the gravity of her [own] illness clearly had an impact on both [her] personal and professional decisions that inevitably shaped" her work. States that although O'Connor was "frequently too ill to write" and was "acutely aware of the dwindling commodity of time" available to her, she worked hard and successfully conveyed her theme that salvation is available to all through Christ. Entries on Francis Marion Tarwater and *The Violent Bear It Away* describe the spiritual battle waged over the boy between his uncle Rayber (with his "detached scholastic life") and his great-uncle Mason (and his attempt to influence the boy to become a "fire-and-brimstone" prophet). Informs readers of O'Connor's intentions in her use of violence, and suggests that the primary theme of *The Violent Bear It Away* is to vilify "the contagious corruption of the city" and to portray American cities as modern-day Babylons.

1721   Zimmerly, Renette. "Throw Out Your Lifeline." *Flannery O'Connor Bulletin* 22 (1993-94): 83-89.

Offers the text of the Faux Flannery Contest's Second Place Winner. Plot summary: Web Duncan visits his widowed mother every Thursday to take her shopping for groceries. Because she lives in a large old house, alone, and is fearful of someone breaking in, she insists upon a prescribed ritual for knocking and entering. Action opens in her overheated kitchen, which smells of ammonia and overripe fruit, and focuses on the interaction between the dutiful but exasperated and stubborn son and his slightly senile and equally stubborn mother. On this particular Thursday--after being "pressed to the brink"--Web leaves without taking her shopping; she then calls him early the next morning to "come quick," and because he doesn't follow the usual entering ritual, he enters and disastrous, tragicomic results follow.

1722   Zoller, Peter T. "The Irony of Preserving the Self: Flannery O'Connor's `A Stroke of Good Fortune.'" *Kansas Quarterly* 9.2 (1977): 61-66.

Considers ironic technique in "A Stroke of Good Fortune," and discusses O'Connor's emphasis on spiritual values. Concludes that while "Ruby suffers from the modern form of an old sin: materialism," God still searches after her and gives her opportunities to see that she is on the wrong path and can still change and receive salvation.

1723   Zornado, Joseph. "A Becoming Habit: Flannery O'Connor's Fiction of Unknowing." *Religion & Literature* 29.2 (Summer, 1997): 27-59.

Suggests that the usual intent of O'Connor's fiction is "to introduce the reader to something other, [and] to the mystery latent and invisible in the manners." Contends that this "something other" in O'Connor's fiction may be observed "in her attempts to address the limits of fiction" through her depiction of baptism as a "sacramental ritual." Alleges that "the baptismal ritual, as St. Augustine and St. Thomas argue, is somehow a `sign for the inward thing,' and at the same moment, `the inward thing itself.'" Uses this concept to address the question: "How then can the inward thing be known if the outward thing can only fail in its representation of the inward?" Asserts that the answer "is simple" in O'Connor's work, and that is "by its failure to hold." Explores similarities in O'Connor's approach and that of Thomas Merton, and declares that "independently of one another, both writers recognized the power--and definitive limits--of text," and used "the audience's desire for a readily consumed aphorism or short story" to "communicate mystery negatively." Outlines how these "sacramental elements" operate by presenting--in the context of this discussion--detailed explications of "The River" and *The Violent Bear It Away*. Comments that while baptism may not explain Orthodoxy or sacramentalism, it does "guard these mysterious metaphysical notions from too-easy explanations." Concludes that "the gaps, fissures and differences that characterize her second novel and so much of her fiction should not be read as accidents or omissions, but rather as an attempt to articulate the inarticulatable."

1724   Zornado, Joseph. "Negative Writings: Flannery O'Connor, Apophatic Thought, and Negative Christian Criticism." *Christianity & Literature* 42.1 (1992): 117-37.

Contends that critics overlook O'Connor's "interest in apophatic thought and the `negative theology' of Pseudo-Dionysius, St. John of the Cross, and Thomas Merton." Defines apophatic thought, examines its application to O'Connor's work, and discusses the influence of negative theology. Provides a reading of "A Good Man Is Hard to Find" as illustrating "what texts cannot write" and how such a reading offers "a way of more fully experiencing the story's nagging resistance to explanation." Finds O'Connor's work to reveal "a skepticism that undermines the very intellectual constructs she relies on." Refers to her story within the story, there to "warn her audience that the ground they believe to be stable might slip out from under them at any moment." Looks at reasons for The Misfit's actions to compare him to Hazel Motes of *Wise Blood*. Contends that The Misfit's "cold-blooded need to know, his need to fill in the gaps with cognitive proof, mirrors our own need to explain a story--a tendency O'Connor fumed over." Concludes that O'Connor's fiction "leaves the reader with a heightened awareness of the gap between metaphor and meaning as well as between human intellect and divine mystery."

1725   Zubizarreta, John. "Place, Ownership, and Sin in Flannery O'Connor."
            Humanities in the South 79 (1995): 5-8.

Argues that in O'Connor's fiction, "issues of landscape, country, and
ownership include the spiritual dimensions of quest, identity, and grace
more so than the literal and topographical aspects of mapping and owning
the physical land or the socio-economic aspects of class struggle." Refers
to H.R. Stoneback's comments on "place" in "The Displaced Person," then
examines how the ownership of land becomes the context for insight and
redemption for characters in a number of O'Connor's stories. Refers to "A
Circle in the Fire," "The Displaced Person," and "Parker's Back," then
provides explications--in the context of this discussion---of "Greenleaf"
and "A View of the Woods." Concludes that O'Connor "uniquely treats
the ownership of land and the human impulse to regard oneself apart from
and above others, seeing in her characters' pride of possession and place
a token of their fallen natures."

IV Dissertations, 1961-2000

To date, almost 300 doctoral dissertations have been identified as being concerned with Flannery O'Connor. Among the first, were those by: Jonathan Baumbach at Stanford and Louise Y. Gossett at Duke in 1961; Lewis Lawson's at the University of Wisconsin in 1964; and those by Annie Louise Blackwell at Florida State, Janet Maroney Connolly at Columbia, and Sister Francis Mary Dunn at the Catholic University of America in 1966.

Since the completion of these early works, about a dozen dissertation have been produced each year involved, to a greater or lesser extent, with O'Connor's life, work and influence.

Most of the following entries are from the author's abstracts in one of the various print or electronic versions of *Dissertation Abstracts International (DAI)*. However, if a particular dissertation was not abstracted in *nor* available for purchase from University Microfilms International (UMI), an attempt was made to locate, borrow, and write abstracts and quote from the dissertation itself. Since dissertations unavailable from UMI are difficult for scholars to acquire, abstracts for these are typically longer and more detailed.

1726   Aiken, David Hubert. "Joyce, Faulkner, O'Connor: Conceptual Approaches to Major Characters." Diss. State U of New York at Stony Brook, 1975. *DAI* 36 (1975): 3680-81A.

Offers a series of related essays on Joyce's Leopold Bloom [and Stephen Dedalus], Faulkner's Jason Compson, and O'Connor's Asbury Porter Fox ("The Enduring Chill"). Sees O'Connor's character as a satiric representation of Stephen Dedalus and criticizes her attempt as "misunderstood" and "weak." Compares differences between the Stephen of *Portrait* and the Stephen of *Ulysses*. [174 pp.]

1727   Albert Marie Louise Hannibal. "Children of the Confederacy: A Study of New South Themes in Porter, Welty, McCullers, and O'Connor." Diss. U of Hawaii, 1982. *DAI* 43 (1983): 2664A.

Discusses a variety of works by Katherine Anne Porter, Eudora Welty, Carson McCullers, and Flannery O'Connor as examples of the "Southern Literary Renaissance." Focuses on the use of child characters, themes of love, good and evil, industrial progress, and on the significance of these works as cultural documents of the "New South." Asserts that the four writers "encourage a complementary blend of traditional Southern and modern industrial ways of life." Among the works examined are O'Connor's *The Violent Bear It Away*, "The Artificial Nigger," "The River," "The Lame Shall Enter First," "A Circle in the Fire," and "A View of the Woods." [340 pp.]

1728   Allen, Suzanne Thomas. "*The Mind and Heart of Love*: Eros and Agape in the Fiction of Flannery O'Connor." Diss. U of Detroit, 1976. *DAI* 38 (1978): 7330A.

Examines sexuality in O'Connor's work as a metaphor for "man's yearning for union with the divine, the erotic drive toward agape." Uses Martin C. D'Arcy's, *The Mind and Heart of Love* (1946) (found in O'Connor's personal library and annotated by her), to establish a critical vocabulary and framework for the discussion of "the sacramental view of the universe." Discusses O'Connor's fiction in terms of its "Southern, sacramental framework." [312 pp.]

1729   Aronson, Marilyn A. Carlson. "A Study for Higher Education: Themes and Narrative Methods of Flannery O'Connor Versus Eudora Welty." Diss. U of South Dakota, 1997.

Compares O'Connor and Welty's treatment of a wide variety of social issues, including: pride, prejudice, parental conflict, child abuse, secrecy, self-righteousness, crime, religion, the Southern sense of place, and femininity. Combines a historical perspective, interdisciplinary criticism, and "reader-response theory" to demonstrate from specific textual evidence how the two authors rely upon "the narrative methods of symbolism, humor, irony, and satire" to "enhance their themes." Notes that the social issues discussed by O'Connor and Welty in their fiction tend to "mirror the social concerns of the 1940s-1960s." O'Connor's fiction in particular reflects a preoccupation with issues of "feminine identity and sexuality, middle-to-lower class society, religious issues, and social injustice." Observes that, unlike Welty's, many of O'Connor's stories "show female characters negatively." Suggests that this study may be of value to those who"wish to design courses on specific short stories" by O'Connor and Welty that address social issues in modern life. [305 pp.]

1730   Asals, Frederick John, Jr. "Flannery O'Connor: An Interpretive Study." Diss. Brown U, 1967. *DAI* 33 (1973): 6897-98A.

Focussing on the theme of "development" in O'Connor's works, Asals attempts to dispel four early preoccupations: that her work can only be read in the context of Catholic orthodoxy; that her use of the grotesque and violence is merely a strategy for pointing up conventional Christian truth; that her gift is for the short story rather than the novel; and that her work is narrow in scope and limited in inspiration. [343 pp.]

1731   Au, Bobbye Green. "The Dragon by the Side of the Road: A Study of the Fiction of Flannery O'Connor." Diss. Claremont Graduate School, 1977. *DAI* 37 (1977): 6482A.

Asserts that neither O'Connor's theology nor her fiction is as consistent and simplistic as some critics claim. Calls for a close critical readings to perceive the relationship among her techniques and the larger background out of which she wrote. Divides O'Connor's works into various groups, each of which reflects her characters' progressive stages of spiritual development. [200 pp.]

1732   Austin, Emmit Wade. "Harry Crews: The Atmosphere of Failure." Diss. Middle Tennessee State U, 1984. *DAI* 45 (1984): 181A.

Examines the works of Harry Crews, concentrating on the search for meaning of his characters and the failure of religion as a theme. Traces the influence of "Southern Renaissance" writing techniques upon his work, including O'Connor's "sense of place." [111 pp.]

1733   Babich, Alan Thomas. "Crossing the Spheres: Flannery O'Connor's Catholic Imagination." Diss. State U of New York at Stony Brook, 1998. *DAI* 60.1 (1999): 126A.

Examines the role of Roman Catholicism in O'Connor's fiction. Contends that because she did not depict overtly Catholic characters such as priests or sisters, traditional Catholic settings such as the parish, convent or monastery, or "familiar moral dilemmas that have found their way into what has been designated as American Catholic fiction," readers must instead focus on her use of analogy and ritual. Sees O'Connor's works as allegories "wherein the meanings of each character and episode unfold over the course of the narratives," forcing readers "to connect multiple spheres of meaning" that bring them "to a Roman Catholic vision of reality." [159 pp.]

1734   Bacon, Jon Lance. "Invasion and Subversion: Flannery O'Connor and Cold War America." Diss. Vanderbilt U, 1991. *DAI* 53 (1992): 1910A.

Challenges the established view of O'Connor as a writer solely focused on spiritual salvation and religious aspects of Southern life. Contends that she "found reason for anxiety within American society" during the Cold War era, especially when one examines her view of the "status of the individual in a consumer culture." Contends that O'Connor approached her role as a dissenter from both religious and regional perspectives. Suggests that she exploited the "image of [the] church opposed to the American way," and "adapted a rhetoric that opposed the region to the nation on the issue of race." Concludes that O'Connor found that "religious dissent seemed the more viable approach." [254 pp.]

1735   Baker, J. Robert. "Radiant Veils and Dark Mirrors: Twentieth-Century Versions of Allegory." Diss. U of Notre Dame, 1993. *DAI* 54 (1993): 1799A.

Explores how Flannery O'Connor, Walker Percy, and Thomas Pynchon utilize the allegorical mode in their works. Reviews the definition and features of allegory, its characteristics in narrative, and difficulties posed by modern 20th-century language and authority. Examines *The Violent Bear It Away* to determine how the words, conduct, and dress of O'Connor's characters suggest biblical figures, their morality, and their spiritual end. Discusses O'Connor's distrust of allegory and her "preference for a fiction of manners . . . rooted in the medieval fourfold method of allegory." [280 pp.]

1736   Bambrick, Gail. "Trying the Borders of Realism: Selected Fiction by Flannery O'Connor, Joyce Carol Oates and Toni Morrison." Diss. Tufts U, 1990. *DAI* 51 (1991): 3740A-41A.

Examines the structure of selected works by Flannery O'Connor, Joyce Carol Oates, and Toni Morrison to demonstrate evidence of a type of two-part structure. Suggests that this structure type occurs when the work's thematic focus is on the relationship between metaphysical and physical realities in relation to characters' identities. Argues that this two-part structure is vital to, and inseparable from, the author's ability to express the dual nature of reality. Compares O'Connor's "Revelation," Oates' *Solstice*, and Morrison's *Sula*. Concludes with a discussion of the disorienting effects of this two-part structure on readers. [201 pp.]

1737   Barnes, Linda Adams. "Faith and Narrative: Flannery O'Connor and the New Testament." Diss. Vanderbilt U, 1989. *DAI* 51 (1990): 504A.

Asserts that the New Testament is not only O'Connor's theological model, but also her literary model. Sees her characters as New Testament archetypes and relates her narrative structures to Gospel accounts of Christ's life. Describes how O'Connor bases her stories on an act of violence, and how her plot structure creates a "timeless pattern of violence-suffering knowledge." [167 pp.]

1738 Barnett, Martha Floyd. "The Grotesque Southern Woman of Twentieth-Century Fiction: The Women of Kate Chopin, William Faulkner, Flannery O'Connor, and Walker Percy." Diss. U of South Florida, 1998. *DAI* 59.11 (1999): 4141A.

Utilizes a "definition of the grotesque as a person who builds a life around a guiding truth which becomes a falsehood." Applies this concept to female characters of a number of Southern authors, including Flannery O'Connor, and finds that "certain commonalities appear which explain the unique aspects of many of these women." Finds that "one of the major shaping forces in the lives of such females is the influence of patriarchal and communal forces" in shaping their beliefs. [203 pp.]

1739 Barnette, William Joseph. "Redeemed Time: The Sacramental Vision and Implicit Covenant in the Major Fiction of Richard Wright." Diss. U of Tennessee, 1981. *DAI* 42 (1982): 3997A.

Regards Richard Wright's fiction as religious, though it is often conventionally seen as anti-religious or a-religious. Suggests that Wright's notion of revelation is diametrically opposed to the views of most white, Southern writers, including Flannery O'Connor, who see human reason as leading to deception and sinfulness. O'Connor is mentioned in the introduction and conclusion. [169 pp.]

1740 Batts, Martin. "Flannery O'Connor's Art of Naming." Diss. U of Dallas, 1983. *DAI* 44 (1983): 481A.

Provides an overview of the use of significant names in literature, surveys O'Connor criticism on the topic, and discusses character names in her stories and novels. Contends that O'Connor chose proper names carefully so that each character's name might reflect his or her multi-dimensional nature, worldly yet "touched by the mysterious." Attempts to show in a systematic way how she uses names as "surface signification" in her early works, while in later works chooses names which are more complex and integral to her themes. [219 pp.]

1741   Baumbach, Georgia Anne. "The Psychology of Flannery O'Connor's Fictive World." Diss. Ohio State U, 1972. *DAI* 34 (1973): 304A.

Examines O'Connor's novels and short stories and offers a reading of each work. Takes as subject "the `psychology' of Flannery O'Connor's fiction." Asserts that the purpose in doing so is not to dismiss religious explications of her work, but "to try to provide a wider context" in which to view it. Utilizes Norman Holland's "`dictionary of childhood fantasies' to locate particular phrases of development" that O'Connor's works may proceed from, then uses these as a basis for developing subsequent analyzes. Concludes that there is much to be gained from "shifting the perspective in O'Connor criticism from the other-worldly--the religious and metaphysical--to the worldly, specifically the physical and bodily." Reviews the isolation and personality defects of her characters, those whose modern world "is dominated by assassins, con-men, by `good' people gone berserk, families collapsing, and by ever multiplying institutionalized `encounters.'" Suggests that O'Connor's stories tell us about "our flights from feeling our deep deprivation, our rages at duplicitous authorities, and also about the possibilities of gratification." Finds O'Connor's works rare, remarkable, never depressing, and commends her for refusing "to compromise the distance in showing how far we have to come." [224 pp.]

1742   Baumbach, Jonathan. "The Theme of Guilt and Redemption in the Post-Second-World-War American Novel." Diss. Stanford U, 1961. *DA* 22 (1961): 1620-21A.

Asserts that the American novel is concerned with guilt and redemption, unlike the English novel which examines and attempts to correct social behavior (according to Trilling). Offers a close reading of eight modern American novels including works by Robert Penn Warren, Bellow, Salinger, Ralph Ellison, O'Connor, (*Wise Blood*), Styron, Malamud, and Wright Morris. [244 pp.]

1743   Baxter, Harold Jason. "Touched by Fire and Laughter: The Range of Grace in the Fiction of Flannery O'Connor and Frederick Buechner." Diss. Florida State U, 1983. *DAI* 45 (1984): 179A.

Analyzes novels of O'Connor and Frederic K. Buechner for their obsession with the Christian doctrine of grace. Finds parallels and complementary themes and focuses. Suggests that both writers portray the operation of Grace through the same types of characters: grotesques, intellectuals, and children. Sees O'Connor's work to be "doctrine oriented," implying an inescapable God "of fire and dynamic activity."

Suggests that Buechner's fiction is more experience oriented, implying a God of laughter, compassion, and understanding. Contends that the work of these writers is not only complementary, but is "almost needfully linked in order to see all of God's Grace at work." [380 pp.]

1744   Becknell, Thomas Ira. "Added Dimensions: Studies in American Literary Realism." Diss. U of Iowa, 1983. *DAI* 44 (1984): 2471A-72A.

Offers essays on American literary realism. Examines selected writers "on their own terms, to underscore . . . the kaleidoscopic variety of fiction which has been written as a `realistic endeavor.'" Focuses on writings of Hamlin Garland, Sarah Orne Jewett, Harold Frederic, and William Dean Howells. Also discusses Walt Whitman, Nathaniel Hawthorne, Flannery O'Connor, and includes a variety of critical commentary regarding writers included in this study. Devotes the concluding chapter to an examination of O'Connor's views regarding realism in order "to illuminate previous essays in some startling ways." Asserts that she "felt we were losing another dimension . . . the physical as well as the spiritual." States that "her `deeper kind of realism'" sought "to restore *both* dimensions, to appeal to the kind of mind that is willing to have its sense of mystery deepened by contact with reality, and its sense of reality deepened by contact with mystery." Offers a reading of "The Lame Shall Enter First," as illustrative of O'Connor's fictional method and as showing "that a spiritual vision must begin first with a clear, natural vision." [210 pp.]

1745   Bendel-Simso, Mary Michele. "The Politics of Reproduction: Demystifying Female Gender in Southern Literature." Diss. State U of New York at Binghamton, 1992. *DAI* 53 (1993): 4318A.

Examines the American myth which "proclaims that all women innately wish to bear children and do not feel fulfilled as `real' women until they have done so." Analyzes works by Kate Chopin, Katherine Anne Porter, William Faulkner, Flannery O'Connor, and Alice Walker for themes related to the desire not to be pregnant and "the threat this `anti-desire' poses for Southern culture." Works by O'Connor discussed include: "A Stroke of Good Fortune," "A Good Man Is Hard to Find," "A View of the Woods," "The River," and "Good Country People." Concludes that "the treatment of women and motherhood" in Southern literature has been characterized by "a deep ambivalence." [222 pp.]

1746   Bennett, Barbara Anne. "Comic Visions and Female Voices: Contemporary Women Novelists and the Humor of the New South." Diss. Arizona State U, 1994. *DAI* 55 (1995): 961A.

Asserts that humor in American literature has been dominated primarily
by male writers, and that efforts by female humorists have been largely
ignored until recent criticism. Contends that contemporary Southern
women writers have carried forward the traditions of literary humor "of
the Old Southwest, continuing with Mark Twain, William Faulkner, and
more recently, Eudora Welty and Flannery O'Connor." Notes that critics
agree that Welty and O'Connor "have had the strongest influence on the
content and style of female Southern writers today." Discusses how these
roots of Southern humor have been cultivated to become a new style of
humor for women, "creating a new voice and a new vision for the South."
Finds Southern humor, as expressed by contemporary women writers, to
be so "significant and unique" that "understanding it is instrumental in
identifying and studying the voice and vision of the literature of the
contemporary South." [155 pp.]

1747   Berkowitz, Alan Steven. "Twisted Apples: Sherwood Anderson's
        Grotesque America and the Literature of Dysfunction." Diss. City U of
        New York, 1997. *DAI* 58 (1997): 1705A.

        Traces "the grotesque tradition as it was revived and re-articulated by
        Sherwood Anderson." Sees it as being "molded into a distinct literature
        of dysfunction by William Faulkner, Nathanael West, Carson McCullers,
        and Flannery O'Connor." Lists Faulkner, West, and O'Connor as "literary
        disciples" of Anderson. [437 pp.]

1748   Beutel, Katherine Piller. "Disembodied and Re-Embodied Voices: The
        Figure of Echo in American Gothic Texts." Diss. Ohio State U, 1993. *DAI*
        54 (1994): 4090A.

        Examines "disembodied and re-embodied voices" in William Faulkner's
        As I Lay Dying, Flannery O'Connor's *The Violent Bear It Away*, and Toni
        Morrison's *Beloved*. Identifies these texts as being part of the Gothic
        tradition. Uses the mythological Echo as a metaphor for the subversive,
        often feminine voices that are woven through repetition among these
        authors' characters. Associates the three novels with such traditional
        Gothic texts as *The Monk, Wieland, Melmoth, The Wanderer*, and
        Dracula. Contends that O'Connor's use of echoes in *The Violent Bear It
        Away*, "strengthens its questioning of the proper response to authority,"
        and illustrates how O'Connor balanced "the authoritative voice of the
        prophet Mason that apparently triumphs with more subversive echoes."
        Suggests that the "problematic status of voice and silence in the text
        makes finding authority behind voice difficult and ultimately shows an
        unresolved tension between accurate, prophetic echoing and revisionary,
        rebellious echoing." [241 pp.]

1749   Bieber, Christina Marie. "The Incarnational Art of Flannery O'Connor." Diss. Emory U, 1999. *DAI* 60 (1999): 2023A.

Contends that O'Connor "designed her unique sacramental aesthetic to defy the Cartesian divisions between self and other and between mind and body that have characterized American intellectual and spiritual life since Emerson." Suggests that, for O'Connor, "art, like the Incarnation, presents a grotesque body [and] instead of making an abstract argument; it reveals through the concrete, particular, untidy, and communal nature of human experience, not in spite of it." Draws upon Mikhail Bakhtin's essays to analyze the development in O'Connor's fiction of "one kind of revelatory grotesque to another." Finds that in *Wise Blood* and in her early stories, O'Connor used the grotesque "to figure the reality of human perversity that we must not ignore; [while] in *The Violent Bear It Away* and [in] the late stories she employed it to figure Christ in the body of the other that we must accept." [264 pp.]

1750   Blackwell, Annie Louise. "The Artistry of Flannery O'Connor." Diss. Florida State U, 1966. *DA* 27 (1967): 3862-63A.

Analyzes O'Connor's methods in each of her novels and short stories. Focuses on her theme of "man's alienation from God" and how she uses her characters to "dramatize the sharp dividing line which . . . exists with regard to Christianity." Examines "the fallibility of the intellectual humanist who does not believe in orthodox Christianity and the Scheme of Salvation" and "the self-righteous person, usually portrayed as a middle-aged woman, who is materialistic and selfish and suffers severe punishment for her sins." Outlines how O'Connor relies upon certain groupings of characters and deliberately exaggerates their physical appearance and behavior. Contends that O'Connor's humor is not "black humor," but "is primitivistic and traditional," with heavy reliance upon dialect, irony, and surprise. [185 pp.]

1751   Blackwell, Henry A. "Technique and the Pressure of Belief in the Fiction of Flannery O'Connor." Diss. U of Chicago, 1976.

Discusses "the development of Flannery O'Connor's system of aesthetics." Attempts to show that it was "her problem of belief, rather than her Catholic convictions," that served as the "major element affecting her conception, choice, and management of literary options." Argues that O'Connor's "problem of belief is the enabling cause of her success," then, "attempts to dispel a number of myths . . . that have been outgrowths of the fascination and repulsion, worship, and suspicion with which her admirers and detractors have responded." Asserts that much of the O'Connor criticism of the preceding ten years "has concentrated excessively on her religious beliefs, neglecting, almost entirely, the compromises, stalemates, and collisions between religious and artistic commitments that are the sources of tribulation and achievement" for her. Claims that whereas early critics misread O'Connor's works because they paid too little attention to her Catholicism, later critics "destroyed one confusion to construct another: they inflated the importance of the view of life, making it the absolute center and motivating force of her creative expression." Acknowledges that "O'Connor's Christian view of life is intrinsically relevant to her work as an artist," but "rejects the notion that it is the sole, or even the major catalyst and shaping force behind her stories." Concludes that O'Connor's critics' "emphasis upon religious devotion has retarded the recognition that the later work, not only contains richer configurations of ideas and a more cogent criticism of life, but advances within the framework of Christian ideology, a different view of the world." [337 pp. Cited in *Comprehensive Dissertation Index, Ten-Year Cumulation 1973-1982: Author Index A-Cn* 33 (1984): 414.]

1752   Bolton, Elizabeth Susan. "Transcendence and Transgression: From the Sublime to the Grotesque." Diss. Yale U, 1992. *DAI* 54 (1994): 4082A.

Examines "the obsessive and performative repetition of aggression, embodiment, and judgement in the traditions of the sublime and the grotesque." Relates the historical relationship between the terms "sublime" and "grotesque," then explores the "agonistic structure in the sublime" in Longinus' *Peri Hupsous*, and Edmund Burke's "gendered physiology of the sublime in relation to the questions of taste and exclusion." Follows with an examination of Mary Shelley's *Frankenstein*, John Ruskin's chapter on "The Grotesque Renaissance" in *Stones of Venice*, and Charles Baudelaire's carnival themes in "De l'essence du rire." Offers, in chapter seven, a reading of O'Connor's grotesque fiction "in light of the author's relationship to her characters and to her readers." Considers "parallels between O'Connor's fiction and Jacques Lacan's account of analysis in `Aggressivity and Psychoanalysis.'" [421 pp.]

1753   Boren, Mark Edelman. "Performing Anamolies: Reading, Writing, and the Extraordinary Text." Diss. U of Georgia, 1998. *DAI* 60.2 (1999): 421-22A.

Observes that "when features of a text do not correspond to the received knowledge of its current critical context, they indicate that the text's shape and knowledge exceed the limitations of that context." Argues that "Performing Anomalies constructs a methodology for exploring those aspects of texts . . . specifically, how texts generate knowledge beyond their contexts" and for distinguishing and exploring textual singularity." Examines "how powerful texts perform idiomatically, producing non-replicable, text-specific significance." Discusses a variety of authors and works, including how "the juxtapositions of incongruous contexts within the works of Flannery O'Connor . . . function in a way contrary to the modus operandi of most O'Connor critics." [210 pp.]

1754   Borgman, Paul Carlton. "The Symbolic City and Christian Existentialism in Fiction by Flannery O'Connor, Walker Percy, and John Updike." Diss. U of Chicago, 1973.

Examines the role of the "symbolic city" in fiction by Flannery O'Connor, Walker Percy, and John Updike. Suggests "both a *realistic* representation of the characteristic beliefs, attitudes, and actions of modernity and also a dramatization of a *romantic* judgement against that modernity." States that, when applied as an analytical method, "the idea of the symbolic city determines two primary goals: to identify the characteristic beliefs, attitudes and actions of the novel's represented modernity, while clarifying the normative and ontological view of man implied by the author as a basis for judging those beliefs, attitudes and actions." Uses this method to examine *The Violent Bear It Away*, *The Moviegoer*, and *Rabbit, Run*. Determines implications of Borgman's "theoretical construct" for other theories or generalizations. Subsequently attempts to "give an added significance, rather than another special meaning, to the terms `romantic' and `realistic'" and to "trace the outline for a more comprehensive theory of fictional cities which includes not only the `symbolic' city, but the `mythical' city and `allegorical' city as well." Compares the "fictional cities of `romantic realism' and `scientific realism'," and examines "the relationship between fictional cities and fictional form in the novel." Provides "a comparison of two different ontological views of man" (Sartre, in *Nausea*, and Bellow, in *Seize the Day*), and explores the "relation between these differences and the features of the symbolic city." Concludes with "a discussion of the varied forms of existentialism embodied in the fictional works explored, with emphasis on the Christian existentialism of O'Connor, Percy, and Updike." [275 pp. Cited in *Comprehensive Dissertation Index, Ten-Year Cumulation 1973-1982: Author Index A-Cn* 33 (1984): 468.]

1755   Bowen, Rose. "Christology in the Works of Flannery O'Connor." Diss. Florida State U, 1984. *DAI* 45 (1985): 2874A.

Compares the development of O'Connor's personal theological world view to the Christian theology addressed in her fiction. Suggests that

O'Connor's view of doctrine as a "developing phenomenon" influenced her openness to theological scholarship and interest in sharing her beliefs with others. Relates how "sin and grace furnish a background" against which readers might better understand her views and work. Considers Piet Schoonenberg's theory of original sin as reflected in O'Connor's "The River," the structure of "Revelation," and the iconographic image in "Parker's Back." Follows with an examination of O'Connor's book reviews and ascertains sources and influences on her theological development, including Karl Adams, Romano Guardini, Friedrich von Hügel, F.X. Durrwell, and Pierre Teilhard de Chardin. [241 pp.]

1756   Boyd, Zohara Mushinsky. "The Literary Apprenticeship of Flannery O'Connor." Diss. U of Massachusetts, 1977. *DAI* 38 (1977): 2120A.

Examines the file of unpublished material at the Russell Library of Georgia College & State University in an effort to establish its "inestimable value" to O'Connor scholarship. Discusses O'Connor's juvenilia and describes her "progress from gifted but directionless adolescent, to superb, mature author with a vision." Argues that O'Connor's work moved from satirical, educational, racial, and political issues, to compassion for the human condition while she studied at the Iowa Writer's Workshop. [333 pp.]

1757   Brewer, Kara P. "The Genesis and Development of `Parker's Back.'" Diss. U of the Pacific, 1976.

Suggests that the study of successive drafts of O'Connor's "Parker's Back" provides scholars with "significant information about [O'Connor's] mind, her craft as a writer, and about the imaginative development and meaning of her work." Contends that the drafts demonstrate how her achievements "were the results of disciplined hard work," and "extraordinary talent." Describes and compares the various drafts to illustrate how O'Connor crafted the final version of her story. Claims that although O'Connor deleted many passages of excellent writing, the single word or phrase she added here and there, almost always "resulted in enrichment of the story, and unification." Concludes that a comparison of later drafts that exist for this story, with earlier ones, shows that O'Connor's imagination carried her "deeper and deeper into the metaphysical levels of meaning" that were "earlier hidden" in earlier versions of the story. [32 pp.]

1758   Brewster, Rudolph Allen. "The Literary Devices in the Writings of Flannery O'Connor." Diss. East Texas State U, 1968. *DA* 29 (1969): 3572A-73A.

Attests to the high degree of critical success O'Connor achieved while maintaining her theme of Christian redemption. Discusses her use of allegory, symbolism, the grotesque, irony, humor, and diction in her twenty-three short stories, two novels, and three unpublished stories. Explores her interest in relating one's Christian faith to modern life while pursuing her art, and contends that O'Connor was successful in presenting "her message of redemption" by creating "another world which is beyond the meaning of the story and yet is parallel to it in situation." Suggests that while O'Connor's use of the grotesque and violence is startling, she is also very skillful "in taking readers into a world of paradoxes, opposites and surprises by use of irony and humor." Concludes that O'Connor's use of literary devices helps her to "lay down a strategy which makes her stories true works of art" and to accomplish her primary aim of shocking "an unbelieving world to return to Christ." [299 pp.]

1759 Brinkmeyer, Robert Herman, Jr. "A Crossing of the Ways: Five Catholic Writers of the Modern South." Diss. U of North Carolina at Chapel Hill, 1980. *DAI* 41 (1980): 1592A.

Claims that America's five most prominent Southern Catholic writers found solace and order in their theology at a time when modernism had collapsed the old agrarian South's emphasis on ritual and duty. Argues that Allen Tate, Caroline Gordon, and Walker Percy were "converted" to the doctrine of Catholicism and that their works reflect this; that Katherine Anne Porter's stance was one of skepticism; and that it was O'Connor alone who approached her work and the modern world via her Catholicism. Asserts that it was her faith that provided O'Connor with the context through which she was able to reach a fuller understanding of humanity. Also suggests that O'Connor's Southern background not only helped keep her work grounded in the present, but helped her "avoid the pitfalls of pious didacticism." Notes that O'Connor's use of prophetic, forceful exaggeration later influenced Walker Percy. [315 pp.]

1760 Brown, Sarah Enos. "Amazing Grace: A Study of the Means and Offer of Grace in the Short Fiction of Flannery O'Connor." Diss. Case Western Reserve U, 1987. *DAI* 48 (1987): 125A-26A.

Premised upon a belief that in every good story, there is a point where grace is apparent and must be either accepted or rejected. Discusses the means to--and offer of--grace in O'Connor's fiction as well as her theological and literary views, the relevance of her beliefs to the modern world, the narrowness of her literary work, and the reason she did not deal with many of the social issues of her time. Focuses on the short fiction, establishing the diversity of modes which O'Connor chose to use--myth, allegory, parable, and romance--and draws connections between what seems to be O'Connor's personal theology and that which is presented in her work. [253 pp.]

1761   Brown, Sheila Goodman. "A Carnival of Fears: Affirmation in the Postmodern American Grotesque." Diss. Florida State U, 1992. *DAI* 53 (1992): 809A.

Discusses the grotesque in postmodern American literature, describing the origins of the term, and the range and breadth of its applications. Examines the works of eleven American authors, including that of Flannery O'Connor, and concludes that even though many of the works invoke a sense of helplessness amid uncertainty, "they simultaneously restore human dignity by demonstrating a sense of adaptation combined with individuation." [190 pp.]

1762   Browning, Preston Mercer, Jr. "Flannery O'Connor and the Grotesque Recovery of the Holy." Diss. U of Chicago, 1969.

Examines the concept of the grotesque and the method in which it was used by O'Connor. Finds that her work "may best be understood as an effort to recover the concept of the Holy in an age in which both the meaning and the reality of this concept have been obscured." Suggests that O'Connor "perceived that loss of the Holy involved for contemporary man a concomitant loss of `depth' and a subsequent diminution of being." Asserts that she "understood that in reclaiming depth and being . . . contemporary man might very well become involved in a journey through the radically profane, embracing evil in order to rediscover good, pursuing the demonic in order to finally arrive at the Holy." Claims that O'Connor's "quest for being or the Holy" is one side of O'Connor's writing efforts, the other is "her portrayal of the world of unbelief within which that quest takes place." Discusses how O'Connor deliberately directed her satire against the shallow complacency she saw in the 1950s lifestyles around her. States that she "turned out a magnificent assortment of stories against the positivists around her, each of which might well have been entitled `The Power of Negative Thinking.'" Notes that in O'Connor's work, "the spokesmen for a self-satisfied secularism inevitably run afoul of representatives of . . . the twisted, the neurotic, the guilt-ridden and God-haunted protagonists who might best be designated `criminal-compulsive,'" who serve as spiritual catalysts in the central conflict of her fiction. Analyzes stories from *A Good Man Is Hard to Find* and *Everything That Rises Must Converge*, and the novels, *Wise Blood* and *The Violent Bear It Away*. Discusses the influence of Père Teilhard de Chardin, and asserts that O'Connor "belongs to the tradition of

Dostoevsky, Kafka, and the Conrad of *Heart of Darkness* on the European side, and Hawthorne, Melville, and (with significant qualifications) Faulkner and Nathanael West on the American side." Concludes that O'Connor reflected her times and, although she lived in a small town in middle Georgia, "her artistic (and metaphysical) vision was of such universality that her work can be rightly appreciated only when placed in a perspective that embraces not only that brooding, Christ-haunted Russian whose spirit pervades so much modern western literature--Fyodor Dostoevsky--but also such representative contemporary figures as Eugène Ionesco and Samuel Beckett." [277 pp. Cited in *Comprehensive Dissertation Index 1861-1972: Author Index A-C* 33 (1973): 578.]

1763   Brownlee, James Henry. "Limits, Risks, and Possibilities: Discourse and Religion in a Selection of Twentieth Century American Novels." Diss. U of Minnesota, 1994. *DAI* 55 (1995): 2827A.

Focuses on "the role of language to construct religious sensibility." Examines the "variety of religious experience" and the preoccupation and struggle for faith in modern times as seen in Flannery O'Connor's *The Violent Bear It Away*, Walker Percy's *The Last Gentleman*, M. Scott Momaday's *House Made of Dawn*, and in a number of Alice Walker's novels. Discusses "the pragmatic discourse theory" of Mikhail Bakhtin, C.S. Pierce, and Paul Ricoeur and suggests possibilities for meaning "when multiple voices or discourses interact." Finds that O'Connor and Percy "recognize some devaluation of religious language, but maintain[s] that this apparent devaluation lies not with the discourse itself but with how the modern age perceives it." Argues that it is through the interaction of multiple and competing voices that O'Connor and Percy "reinvest Christian orthodoxy with meaning and thus effect the restoration of the believing subject." [184 pp.]

1764   Bunch, Cecile Dianne. "Sacred Expenditure: Eroticism, Sacrifice, and Mysticism in the Fiction of Flannery O'Connor." Diss. U of Mississippi, 1998. *DAI* 60.3 (1999): 739A.

"Proposes an evaluation of Flannery O'Connor's fiction by focusing on her validation of transgression as the scintilla that leads to new understanding of a sacred economy based on non-accumulating expenditure." Uses Georges Bataille's definition of the sacred to examine O'Connor's use of eroticism, sacrifice, and mysticism to depict transgression as "the basis for the most profound spiritual insight and experience." Discusses how O'Connor appears most interested in portraying "those moments when the borders of the human body or the body of the family or the family farm are violated." Contends that she uses these moments "when individuation lost . . . through transgression" to reveal "the larger economy of the sacred, which she sees most clearly in images of destruction, waste, and personal loss." [494 pp.]

1765   Bunting, Charles Thomas. "The Christian Elements in the Writings of Flannery O'Connor." Diss. U of Southern Mississippi, 1971.

[227 pp. Not available from University Microfilms International nor via inter-library loan from U of Southern Mississippi's Library. Cited in *Comprehensive Dissertation Index 1861-1972: Author Index A-C* 33 (1973): 611.]

1766   Burns, Marian. "The Ridiculous and the Sublime: The Fiction of Flannery O'Connor." Diss. U of Manchester (Great Britain), 1984. *Index to Theses With Abstracts Accepted for Higher Degrees by the Universities of Great Britain and Ireland and the Council for National Academic Awards [ASLIB Index to Theses]* 35, Part 1:54-55.

Contends that there are two major forces in O'Connor's work: her religious vision and her comic sense. Sets out to reinstate the comic to its proper place by examining the relationship between humor and other forms of creative activity. Asserts that the range of O'Connor's work demonstrates the growth in her vision from low comedy to mysticism and examines her early work to identify the two forces. Alludes to Poe's influence and discusses traditions of American evangelism, the confidence man theme, folk motifs, regional satire, joke structures, comedy, classical paradigms, the freak in literature, original sin, farce, the problem of human suffering, race, the symbolic "other," and mysticism. Places "O'Connor's humor in the perspective of Christian comedy afforded by Wylie Sypher's comments on theory." Concludes that O'Connor offers "a radical comedy that exploits the techniques of black humor while remaining metaphysically affirmative."

1767   Burt, John Davies. "American Romance and the Bounds of Sense." Diss. Yale U, 1983. *DAI* 45 (1984): 519A-20A.

Suggests that writers of American Romance are faced with a choice regarding imaginative creation. Argues that they either give over to the impulse, thereby relinquishing control, or they reject the authority of imagination, thus risking imaginative sterility. Discusses how Hawthorne, Poe, and O'Connor respectively solve this impasse through the use of "pathological characters." [398 pp.]

1768 Butler, Rebecca Roxburgh. "The Mad Preacher in Three Modern American Novels: *Miss Lonelyhearts*, *Wise Blood*, and *Light In August*." Diss. Louisiana State U, 1977. *DAI* 38 (1978): 4164A-65A.

Offers a discussion of Nathanael West's title character of *Miss Lonelyhearts*, Flannery O'Connor's Hazel Motes of *Wise Blood*, and William Faulkner's Gail Hightower of *Light in August*. Contends that such a review invites two critical perspectives, "one urging a view of the characters as spiritually transcendent, the other documenting their mental derangement." Suggests "a more integrated view" may be determined by studying the language in each novel and by looking at each character "as typical melancholiacs whose preference for symbolic over actual reality invites a merger of the psychological and the religious elements of their characterizations." Concludes that "each man lives in an unsatisfactory present which he attempts to revitalize by way of models from the past--family, religious, aesthetic--which only confirm his defeat." Contends that "the confusion of the mad preacher is deliberately and carefully maintained, and is not intended to be resolved." Suggests that the use of such grotesque characters furthers ambiguities inherent in the conflict between the natural and supernatural worlds. [175 pp.]

1769 Caillouet, Hazel Ruth Reames. "Among Women: Toni Morrison's Mothers, Sisters, and Daughters." Diss. Louisiana State U and Agricultural and Mechanical College, 1997. *DAI* 58.9 (1997): 3522A.

Includes a chapter discussing Toni Morrison's "treatment of isolated characters who reject the community" in which comparisons are made to characters from works by Carson McCullers and Flannery O'Connor. Concludes that Morrison's female characters "find themselves in and through other women."

1770 Caputo, Peter. "Selfishness and Generosity, Isolation and Kinship: Melville, James and Flannery O'Connor." Diss. Columbia U, 1988. *DAI* 49 (1989): 3025A.

Discusses selected works by Herman Melville, Henry James and Flannery O'Connor, focusing on how each author handles the critical problems of selfishness and isolation. Examines a variety of their characters whose way of life encourages self-centeredness and results in isolation. Relates how each of the three authors is concerned with the behavior of "withholding and separating." Looks at some of the standard labels used to categorize each author and suggests that these labels tend to "camouflage" their prophetic voices. Reviews connections between theme and response, and content and form, and poses the question, "What . . . is the connection between the responses we cannot avoid and the issues we are meant to absorb?" [220 pp.]

1771   Carlson, Thomas MacNab. "Flannery O'Connor: The Manichaean Dilemma." Diss. U of North Carolina at Chapel Hill, 1973. *DAI* 34 (1973): 2613A.

Examines the Manichaean and Pelagian beliefs attacked by Flannery O'Connor. Suggests that her fiction proposes: that a lack of compassion is the main condemnation of our society; that evil exists not in objects but in the hearts of individuals; that the "tragic movement" in her fiction reflects "a slow, painful awareness;" and that ignorance rather that awareness supports the comic scenes in her fiction. [265 pp.]

1772   Caron, Timothy Paul. "'Rag-Tag and Bob-Ends of Old Stories': Biblical Intertextuality in Faulkner, Hurston, Wright, and O'Connor." Diss. Louisiana State U, 1994. *DAI* 55 (1995): 2828A.

Discusses Southern religious tradition as seen in William Faulkner's *Light in August*, Zora Neale Hurston's *Moses, Man of the Mountain*, Richard Wright's *Uncle Tom's Children*, and Flannery O'Connor's *Wise Blood*. Suggests that these authors "invoke and re-read central stories, characters, and tropes [of the Bible] in order to voice their individual contributions to the South's intracultural conversation on race." Explores questions concerned with how Southerners interpret the Bible in relation to the region's racial struggles, and speculates on the usefulness of "intertextual critical practice for Southern studies and literary investigations." [237 pp.]

1773   Carroll, R.L. "The Return of the Body in the Work of Sylvia Plath, Angela Carter, Leonora Carrington, and Flannery O'Connor." Diss. U of Newcastle Upon Tyne (Great Britain), 1996. *Index to Theses with Abstracts Accepted for Degrees by the Universities of Great Britain and Ireland* [*ASLIB Index to Theses*]. 47.2 (1998): 464.

Examines "the role of the body" in Sylvia Plath's *The Bell Jar*, Angela Carter's *Nights at the Circus*, Leonora Carrington's "fiction of 1937-41" and Flannery O'Connor's "fiction of 1949-65." Focuses upon "representations of the body and on the significance of the body as a site of crises in identity and memory." In part four of this four-part study, the author "proposes that the irrational forces of history are registered in traumatic form in the grotesque bodies of O'Connor's narratives," while addressing the "politics of origin which implicates women, as agents and victims, in the violence of an oppressive social order."

774   Case, David Allen. "American Abject, American Sublime." Diss. U of
       California, Los Angeles, 1992. *DAI* 53 (1993): 3902A.

       Analyzes ten twentieth-century American authors, including Flannery
       O'Connor, for examples of "the tradition of achieving sublime effects
       chiefly through exploitation of the Abject." Asserts that the "movement
       from Abject to Sublime brings about catharsis, but [of] a variety where
       scorn is added to terror and pity." [161 pp.]

1775   Casey, Roger N. "The Driving Machine: Automobility and American
       Literature." Diss. Florida State U, 1991.

       Examines the appearance and use of automobiles in the works of a variety
       of authors, including Flannery O'Connor (pages 156-75, 256, and 270).
       Reviews J.O. Tate's study of the Essex in *Wise Blood*, and discusses
       automobiles in "The Life You Save May Be Your Own," "Parker's Back,"
       "A Good Man Is Hard to Find," "The Displaced Person," "Greenleaf," and
       "A View of the Woods." Concludes that the automobile is a metaphorical
       engine which drives many of O'Connor's stories, and that she had "an
       overwhelming understanding of the prominence [that] automobility was
       attaining in post-war culture, particularly in the South." [284 pp.]

1776   Chanen, Audrey Wolff. "American Holocaust Novels." Diss. U of Iowa,
       1987. *DAI* 48 (1988): 1768A.

       Studies a wide and divergent group of novelists who have written about
       the Holocaust either as immediate subject or as a post-war observation.
       Suggests that a variety of literary and ethical problems become apparent
       when writers do not have a first-hand knowledge of the Holocaust and
       still attempt to fictionalize it, including the de-emphasis of the Holocaust
       as a unique Jewish tragedy and the "misconceived" universalization of it
       based upon American Democratic ideals. Includes a discussion of
       O'Connor's "The Displaced Person." Considers opinions of historians and
       theologians and excerpts from diaries and eyewitness accounts. [172 pp.]

1777   Chard, George Edward Hurd. "Flannery O'Connor's Fiction: Materials and
       Selected Structures." Diss. Northwestern U, 1975. *DAI* 36 (1976):
       8055A-56A.

       Examines O'Connor's works in terms of the materials she used: images,
       character types, qualitative progression, plot, and setting. Concludes that
       the structures and actions she chose present a clear paradigm for her
       fictional world. [260 pp.]

1778   Charnigo, Richard John. "A Structural Analysis of the Short Fiction of
            Flannery O'Connor." Diss. Bowling Green State U, 1975. *DAI* 36 (1976):
            5293A.

            Uses "Parker's Back" and "The Artificial Nigger" as touchstones to judge
            O'Connor's stories. Concentrates on how flawed characters find revelation
            in their flawed world. Discusses how the juxtaposition of antithetical
            characters often forces a violent confrontation between good and evil, and
            offers justification for the frequently shocking endings. [138 pp.]

1779   Chestnut, Allison Carol. "A Reading of *A Good Man Is Hard to Find* and
            A Curtain of Green: The Influence of Parable on Flannery O'Connor and
            Eudora Welty." Diss. Louisiana State U, 1991. *DAI* 52 (1992): 2551A.

            Submits that O'Connor's *A Good Man Is Hard to Find* and Welty's *A
            Curtain of Green* are "short story cycles harmonized by their marked
            imitation of the style and structure of the parable." Declares that the
            parabolic style and structures of the works unify each cycle and "logically
            reflect the assumptions of Hebrew myth rather than . . . Greco-Roman
            tradition." Suggests similarities between Judaic and Southern cultures, and
            analyzes how O'Connor "joins sacramental imagery and the themes of
            original sin, goodness, and grace to create parables of Southern religion
            and morality." [262 pp.]

1780   Chew, Martha Elizabeth. "Aesthetic Integration in the Works of Flannery
            O'Connor." Diss. Boston U, 1976. *DAI* 44 (1983): 1453A.

            Discusses multiple themes and their interplay among O'Connor's novels
            and short story collections. Attempts to determine if the interaction of
            these themes produces authentic thematic complexity or tends only to
            confuse readers. Suggests that O'Connor's overall intended theme,
            "workings of grace," is often at odds with the theme of human hostility
            (which also works allegorically in terms of psychic conflict to extend the
            literal conflict). Asserts that it is the conflict of her intended theme, with
            her theological intent, that so often confuses readers. Finds that
            O'Connor's reliance upon multiple themes varies from work to work and,
            while the complexity of her multiple themes sometimes subverts theology,
            it often results in conflict at the literal level as well. [268 pp.]

1781   Choi, Insoon. "The Journey Home to the True Country: A Study of
            Flannery O'Connor's Fiction." Diss. U of Wisconsin-Milwaukee, 1989.
            DAI 50 (1990): 3950A.

Argues that Flannery O'Connor belongs in the long line of American "Hawthornean Nay-Sayers." States that she uses the journey narrative (physical, climatic, visionary, circular escape, and return) as the central device in all thirty-one of her stories and both of her novels. Finds that all types culminate in her story, "Parker's Back." [279 pp.]

1782   Cioffari, Phillip Edward. "Major Themes in Southern Fiction Since World War II." Diss. New York U, 1967. *DAI* 30 (1970): 4402A.

Explores thematic patterns of Southern fiction published since World War II, and finds four principle themes: the influence of the South; treatment of the Negro; humanity's search for spiritual values; and the desire for love. Illustrates these in works by Southern writers: Carson McCullers, Truman Capote, William Styron, Flannery O'Connor, William Humphrey, and Robert Penn Warren. Concludes that "the two most striking characteristics of love as presented in Southern fiction are the element of the grotesque and the nightmarish isolation of the lover." [223 pp.]

1783   Cleveland, Carol Lynn. "Psychological Violence: The World of Flannery O'Connor." Diss. Saint Louis U, 1972. *DAI* 34 (1974): 5959A.

Examines O'Connor's major themes from the point of view of two basic theological and psychological premises: that "theological personalism" is profound and pervasive in the work and that all characters can be measured "according to the degree to which they are open to new experience and to deep relationships with other people, the physical world, and God." [256 pp.]

1784   Coale, Samuel Chase, V. "The Role of the South in the Fiction of William Faulkner, Carson McCullers, Flannery O'Connor and William Styron." Diss. Brown U, 1970. *DAI* 31 (1971): 6596A-97A.

Counters assertions in W.J. Cash's *Mind of the South* by examining the divergent (yet similar) artistic consciousness of four "Southern Renaissance" writers: Faulkner, McCullers, O'Connor, and Styron. Examines the changing role of the South, concentrating on its moral polarities, Gothic and grotesque nature, and religious awareness. [388 pp.]

1785   Cobb, Gerald Thomas. "Fictive Bodies: Representation of the Human Form in Twentieth Century American Novels." Diss. U of Washington, 1988. *DAI* 49 (1989): 2656A-57A.

Examines in detail the "fictive body" (the bodies of characters, the body politic, the body of the text, and of the reader), of seven twentieth-century American novels. Includes an analysis of O'Connor's *Wise Blood* in conjunction with Ken Kesey's *One Flew Over the Cuckoo's Nest*. Notes the demarcation of "bodily zones which address their principal thematic interests." Suggests that contemporary literary scholars can conceptualize the fictive body as a resource for integrated theory and practice of literary criticism. [252 pp.]

1786   Coghill, Sheila Renee. "Symbolism in the Fiction of Flannery O'Connor." Diss. Ball State U, 1981. *DAI* 42 (1982): 3598A.

Examines symbols and their function in the novels and short stories by Flannery O'Connor. Suggests that her ability to heighten otherwise common objects, action, people, and statements to symbolic levels "illuminates her vision of faith." Argues that O'Connor's symbolism was intended to show that evil and Grace play a vital role in uncovering the mysteries of reality. Defines and discusses symbolism, including O'Connor's own definition, in terms of three groups (dominant, recurring, and specific), and divides the stories and novels accordingly. Concludes with a discussion of the "symbolizing process" and the impact of this process on O'Connor's works. [286 pp.]

1787   Connolly, Janet Maroney. "The Fiction of Flannery O'Connor." Diss. Columbia U, 1966. *DA* 28 (1967): 670A.

Suggests that Roman Catholicism so dominated O'Connor's world that it is "responsible for the unique appeal and principal defect of her fiction." Examines *Wise Blood, The Violent Bear It Away, A Good Man Is Hard To Find*, and *Everything That Rises Must Converge*. Argues that these works reveal O'Connor's obsession with the Christian themes of a fall from innocence and the need for redemption, which substantiate her use of the grotesque. [177 pp.]

1788   Conrad, Linda. "Flannery O'Connor's Fiction: The Rhetoric of Prophecy." Diss. U of Queensland (Australia), 1987.

[Cited in *WorldCat Database*; 456 pp.]

1789   Conyers, Lisa Ann. "National Images in the Short Story: Four Motif Studies in Time." Diss. U of California, Riverside, 1989. *DAI* 51 (1990): 499A.

Studies national images in works of art, concentrating on short stories. Evaluates, in this context, several noted authors, including O'Connor. Illustrates how "these writers in capturing the themes of their respective situations (in diverse ways) and suspending them in timelessness, defined a present moment of limited duration as the predictable result of the social disintegration of contemporary life." [164 pp.]

1790   Cruser, Paul Alexander. "The Fiction of Flannery O'Connor." Diss. U of Pennsylvania, 1970. *DAI* 31 (1970): 2910A.

Summarizes current critical opinion and argues that O'Connor's fiction is not "Christian in the general sense, but a dramatization of specific points of Roman Catholic doctrine." [139 pp.]

1791   Daley, Jamie Temple. "Modern Versions of `Pilgrim's Progress': West's *Miss Lonelyhearts*, O'Connor's *Wise Blood*, and Percy's *The Moviegoer*." Diss. U of Notre Dame, 1983. *DAI* 44 (1983): 751A.

Uses *The Pilgrim's Progress* (sic) as a model for exploring the theme of pilgrimage in three modern novels: Nathanael West's *Miss Lonelyhearts*, Walker Percy's *The Moviegoer* and Flannery O'Connor's *Wise Blood*. Compares definitions of allegory by H.E. Greene and C.S. Lewis to Bunyan's. Finds Bunyan's to be a straight-forward allegory which serves in sharp contrast in diction, tone, and irony to the modern novels, though all share the pilgrimage motif. Explores the pilgrimage theme from the "perspective of ambivalence" in *Miss Lonelyhearts* and *Wise Blood*, noting that both Hazel Motes and Miss Lonelyhearts display "a pattern of pursuit and flight in their spiritual quests." Concludes that Percy's character, unlike West's and O'Connor's, "journeys toward human authenticity and wholeness." [162 pp.]

1792   Darretta, John Lawrence. "The Idea and Image of Retribution in the Fiction of Flannery O'Connor." Diss. Fordham U, 1972. *DAI* 33 (1973): 4406A-07A.

Asserts that from the writing of her first story, "The Geranium," to the completion of her final one, "Judgement Day," O'Connor's concept of retribution changed from a personal and familial theme to an interest that is eschatological. Establishes the theological movement in O'Connor's works, and suggests that it is related to Teilhard de Chardin's concept of redemptive consciousness. [242 pp.]

1793   Davis, Elizabeth Deidre. "The Effects of Lupus on Flannery O'Connor and Some of Her Works." Diss. West Virginia U, 1995. *DAI* 56 (1996): 3124A.

Using information gleaned from O'Connor's writings, interviews with Nancy Davis Bray and Sally Fitzgerald, and observations from her own battle with the disease, the author discusses O'Connor's life before and after she was diagnosed with Systemic Lupus Erythematosus to show its influence. Uses findings to show how O'Connor's life and works may be used in curriculum and instruction in a variety of disciplines and multicultural studies. Concludes that O'Connor was "a determined, intelligent writer who wants the world to realize that although disabled people may be limited physically or mentally, they are still human beings and worthy of respect and love from others." [305 pp.]

1794   Del Fattore, Joan. "The Hidden Self: A Study of the Shadow Figure in American Short Fiction." Diss. Pennsylvania State U, 1978. *DAI* 39 (1979): 6127A.

Analyzes modern novels for the Jungian archetype "shadow figure" who projects certain qualities onto others and whose wholeness is achieved only by recognition and integration of the projected traits. Discusses the "double or Doppelgänger" figure in works by Katherine Anne Porter, Henry James, Edgar Allan Poe, John Barth, Shirley Jackson, Bernard Malamud, and Flannery O'Connor ("The Artificial Nigger"). [217 pp.]

1795   Denby, Priscilla Lee. "The Self Discovered: The Car in American Folklore and Literature." Diss. Indiana U, 1981. *DAI* 42 (1982): 3703A.

Discusses the car as a symbol in American life and literature. Divides the discussion into four areas of relation: physical, spiritual self; spatial, temporal self; the powerful-powerless self; and the individual, social self. Examines folklore, humor, games, social theory, customs, music, results of informal interviews, and literary works for insights into what the automobile has come to mean to Americans. Discusses works by: Henry James, Joyce Carol Oates, Arthur Miller, William Faulkner, F. Scott Fitzgerald, John Updike, Robert Bly, Richard Hugo, and Flannery O'Connor. Concludes that the automobile is "a complex and powerful symbol of self" which, based upon Jungian theory, supplements polarities of experience which help shape a person's self-image. [439 pp.]

1796   Dennis, Joy Dee. "Tableaux, Processions, and Journeys in Flannery O'Connor's Fiction." Diss. Southern Illinois U at Carbondale, 1975. *DAI* 36 (1976): 8057A.

Suggests that O'Connor is an allegorical realist who portrays only a part of her "one notion." Discusses and analyzes her use of tableaux (fixed scenes of carefully arranged characters), processions (the formal movement of characters from one point to another), ritual processions, and journeys, not only as part of O'Connor's vision but also as formal, structural literary devices. [153 pp.]

1797   Desmond, John Francis. "Christian Historical Analogues in the Fiction of William Faulkner and Flannery O'Connor." Diss. U of Oklahoma, 1971. *DAI* 32 (1972): 3994A.

Examines four of Faulkner's novels and the entire O'Connor canon to elucidate the Christian conception of history in Southern fiction. Discusses how the Christian concept of history is used topologically, and how it is rendered dramatic through the two fictional techniques. [196 pp.]

1798   Dibble, Terry Jerome. "The Epiphanal Vision in the Short Fiction of Flannery O'Connor." Diss. U of Nebraska, Lincoln, 1971. *DAI* 32 (1971): 2681A.

Asserts that the repetitions within O'Connor's works which critics frequently comment upon are not the result of character duplication so much as the result of her habitual use of the epiphanic moment to bring about the denouement of her stories. Asserts that violence provides the modus operandi for a character's epiphany thus creating stories in which the religious message is conveyed without becoming distractingly obvious. [263 pp.]

1799   Dillard, Gail Presley. "Private Battles, Culture Wars: White Southern Writers and the Movement for Black Civil Rights." Diss. Florida State U, 1994. *DAI* 55 (1995): 963A.

Examines the response of white Southern writers to the civil rights movement in the context of two Southern traditions: the "belief in the South as a new Garden of Eden" (compared to the industrial and urban North) and the tradition of "separation of races and the relegation of all black Southerners to underclass status." Asserts that a close look at Southern writers, ranging from John Pendleton Kennedy through the Agrarians, reveals attempts "to reconcile the two traditions, largely by insisting that the paternalism of white Southern aristocrats incorporated African Americans into the Southern family." Argues that white Southern writers of O'Connor's time "found themselves under the shadow of both Faulkner's reputation and the racial dilemma of the South." Concludes that while they remained loyal to Southern life, they also "identified community, not racial segregation, as the defining quality of that life and alienation between the races, not integration, as the real threat to the South." Refers to works by Thomas Nelson Page, Mark Twain, George Washington Cable, William Faulkner, William Styron, Flannery O'Connor, and Walker Percy, among others. [389 pp.]

1800   Dinneen, Patricia Marie. "Flannery O'Connor: Realist of Distances." Diss. Pennsylvania State U, 1967. *DA* 28 (1968): 3635A.

Relates the fiction of O'Connor to Teilhard de Chardin's theories. Points out that Chardin's conception of "convergence" as the last step in the evolutionary process provided the title of the posthumous collection of O'Connor's stories, *Everything That Rises Must Converge*. Suggests that both Teilhard and O'Connor sought to make the redemptive process more meaningful. Discusses many similarities between the two, including their "Incarnational view of reality." [187 pp.]

1801   DiRenzo, Anthony. "American Gargoyles: Flannery O'Connor and the Medieval Grotesque." Diss. Syracuse U, 1990. *DAI* 51 (1991): 3742A.

Compares O'Connor's fiction "to the folk art of the Middle Ages-- to gargoyles, chimeras, miracle plays, fabliaux, woodcuts, and marginalia." Argues that when O'Connor's work is judged as medieval grotesque, it is beautiful and sophisticated. Defends aims and techniques of the grotesque using Mikhail Bakhtin's *Rabelais and His World*, especially the use of parody, mockery, and shock. Asserts that O'Connor's work exhibits a carnivalesque spirit with its gallery of bizarre characters whose repulsiveness and ludicrousness often offends readers' conventional conceptions of beauty and art. Concludes that these characters serve as gargoyles who act as "vessels of grace in her fiction." [320 pp.]

1802   Donahoo, Robert Earl. "Comic Forms and Social Meanings in the Fiction of Flannery O'Connor." Diss. Duke U, 1988. *DAI* 49 (1989): 2219A.

Discusses O'Connor's own evaluation of her work as "comic," despite critics' present rebuttal that she "appears as a flawed interpreter," not truly aware of what she accomplished. Analyzes her work in terms of what is proposed as O'Connor's "three commitments": her Catholic faith, her desire to write in the modernist tradition, and her critical vision of American society. Asserts that starting with *Wise Blood*, O'Connor's writing demonstrates that she rejected development based upon a conversion and, instead, has her characters begin a journey for their "'construction.'" Likens this to the "Christian comic form" of *The Divine Comedy*, with its descent, purgation, and journey beyond text. Follows this discussion by looking at elements from other comic forms such as those found in Aristophane's comedies. Concludes that O'Connor's vision distinguishes her work from that of her contemporaries, and considers how future writers migh view her "comedy built on hope." [362 pp.]

1803   Douglas, Thomas Edward. "The Other Side of Both Dreams: The Life and Work of Breece D'J Pancake." Diss. U of North Carolina, Chapel Hill, 1995. *DAI* 56.10 (1995): 3955A.

Examines the literary career of Breece D'J Pancake (1952-1979), a young Appalachian writer who killed himself at age 26 while completing his graduate studies at the University of Virginia. Discusses Pancake's posthumously published collection of short stories, *The Stories of D'J Pancake*, which was nominated for the *Pulitzer Prize* in 1983. Notes that Pancake reflects certain Appalachian influences and that critics often compare his work with that of Flannery O'Connor.

1804   Driggers, Stephen Gause. "Imaginative Discovery in the Flannery O'Connor Typescripts." Diss. Indiana U, 1981. *DAI* 42 (1982): 5120A.

Reviews the typescripts to note O'Connor's "progress of faith." Maintains that her main concerns were technical, combining her aesthetics in both Thomism and New Criticism. Holds that her fiction gains its structure intrinsically and that she believed that a writer could not manipulate reality in the interests of plot. Suggests that O'Connor moved without direction to find a structural center in her stories, thus "somehow mak[ing] contact with mystery." Examines her development through three stories and three novels: "The Geranium," "An Exile in the East," "Judgement Day," *Wise Blood*, *The Violent Bear It Away*, and her unfinished *Why Do the Heathen Rage?* [163 pp.]

1805   Dryden, Phylis Campbell. "Dismemberment Motifs in American Literature: The Incomplete and Homeless Body as Metaphor." Diss. State U of New York at Albany, 1988. *DAI* 49 (1989): 2657A.

Analyzes a variety of works, particularly O'Connor's "Good Country People" and "The Life You Save May Be Your Own," to examine the use of dismemberment as a recurring, rhetorical feature. Suggests that dismembered characters are used metaphorically in the context of homelessness, and that "the dismembered text" calls attention to a sense of absence and loss. [283 pp.]

1806   Dullea, Catherine M. "The Vision of Faith and Reality in the Fiction of
             Flannery O'Connor." Diss. Ball State U, 1977. *DAI* 38 (1978): 6130A.

             Analyzes O'Connor's critical essays and fiction from the standpoint of her
             own statements regarding her position as a Catholic writer. Traces
             O'Connor's development as a writer, from "young and talented" at the
             University of Iowa, to her final "remarkable" output. [305 pp.]

1807   Dunn, Francis Mary. "Functions and Implications of Setting in the Fiction
             of Flannery O'Connor." Diss. Catholic U of America, 1966. *DA* 27
             (1967): 3043A.

             Interprets O'Connor's work by emphasizing the functions and implications
             of setting, including environmental terms used to define characters,
             situations, and experiences. Suggests that O'Connor uses setting to
             dramatize--both negatively and positively--human situations viewed
             according to a religious perspective. [344 pp.]

1808   Dunn, Robert Joseph. "A Mode of Good: Form and Philosophy in the
             Fiction of Flannery O'Connor." Diss. U of Michigan, 1971. *DAI* 32
             (1972): 3995A-96A.

             Sees O'Connor's form of Catholicism as existential. Despite O'Connor's
             assertion that the grotesque mode in her fiction is a wholly accurate
             presentation of her own view of the world, similarities are established
             with theories of Gabriel Marcel, Teilhard de Chardin, Saint Paul, Saint
             Augustine, and Wolfgang Kayser. [220 pp.]

1809   Dyson, C.E. "The Form and Function of the Grotesque in the Literature
             of the American South and Its Use As a Rhetorical Strategy in the Work
             of William Faulkner and Flannery O'Connor." Diss. U of Wales (Great
             Britain), 1991. *Index to Theses With Abstracts Accepted for Higher
             Degrees by the Universities of Great Britain and Ireland and the Council
             for National Academic Awards [ASLIB Index to Theses]* 42.2 (1993): 476.

             Outlines use and definitions of "Gothic" and "grotesque" elements in
             Southern fiction. Discusses critical use of each term and analyzes
             grotesque texts using Philip Thomson's definition: "`as the unresolved
             clash between incompatibles in work and response,' and Mark Spilka's
             theory that the grotesque is the `mastering of reality through comic
             means.'" Provides a general account of the use of the grotesque in
             American literature and declares that the two principal patterns of

development of the American short story are the Tall Tale and the "symbolic mode of narration." Finds both patterns "fused" in works by Flannery O'Connor and William Faulkner, as both combine "grotesque realism with the traditional Gothic obsession with sin and death."

1810 Ebrecht, Ann Bernadette. "Flannery O'Connor's Moral Vision and `The Things of This World.'" Diss. Tulane U, 1982. *DAI* 44 (1983): 165A.

Examines Catholic theological and aesthetic elements in O'Connor's work. Offers an explication of fourteen O'Connor stories along with *Wise Blood* and *The Violent Bear It Away*. Contends that O'Connor saw herself as a "specifically Catholic" author interested in conveying her beliefs through her literary endeavors. Proposes two tenets of her faith: "her belief that man and the material world are good in and of themselves because their being comes from the creator; and, "that the Manichean temper she saw pervading the modern world is evil because it separates spirit and flesh." Discusses the influence of Saint Augustine, Saint Thomas Aquinas, Baron Frederick Von Hugel, Pierre Teilhard de Chardin, Jacques Maritain, François Mauriac, and John Lynch. [175 pp.]

1811 Elder, Harris James. "From Literature to Cinema: The American Short Story Series." Diss. Oklahoma State U, 1979. *DAI* 40 (1980): 4279A.

Examines the fidelity to the work and cinematic integrity of four adaptations produced by the "American Short Story" series: Henry James' "The Jolly Corner," Flannery O'Connor's "The Displaced Person," Ernest Hemingway's "Soldier's Home," and John Updike's "The Music School." States that O'Connor's story was highly cinematic and adapted readily to the film medium. [158 pp.]

1812 El-Kanaoui, Fatima. "Childhood, Adolescence and the Grotesque in the Fiction of Flannery O'Connor and Carson McCullers." Diss. New York U, 1990. *DAI* 51 (1991): 4121A.

Examines the nature and function of O'Connor's and McCuller's use of the grotesque in relation to their child and adolescent characters. Offers psychoanalytic insights, feminist criticism, and interpretation of the grotesque through the theories of Mikhail Bakhtin, Wolfgang Kayser, and others. Discusses how the two authors use children in their depiction of the grotesque "to make a forceful statement about human isolation, alienation, and entrapment." Asserts that O'Connor's religious grotesque depiction can be understood "as an escape from and eventual capitulation to the divine." Concludes that underlying the religious significance for these authors' adolescents is a "nihilistic strain and a preoccupation with troubled sexuality and generational conflicts." [321 pp.]

1813   Elliot, Sarah E. "Dead Bodies, Burned Letters, and Burial Grounds: Negotiating Place Through Storytelling in Contemporary Southern Fiction." Diss. Northern Illinois U, 1998. *DAI* 60.3 (1999): 741A.

Evaluates the use of regionalism in works by Clyde Edgerton, Lewis Nordan and Lee Smith and finds their use not concerned with "preserving a threatened region, but rather with redefining both historical and contemporary perceptions of that region." Traces the history of critical evaluations of regional writing, contrasting Lewis Nordan's fiction with that of other practitioners of the Southern Grotesque. Finds Nordan's use of the grotesque to contrast sharply with that of its most prominent practitioner, Flannery O'Connor. [165 pp.]

1814   Emerick, Ronald Rine. "Romance, Allegory, Vision: The Influence of Hawthorne on Flannery O'Connor." Diss. U of Pittsburgh, 1975. *DAI* 36 (1976): 4485A-86A.

Discusses Flannery O'Connor's debt to Hawthorne as a writer of Romance, with her focus on the allegorical, its blending of the natural and supernatural, and its portrayal of a world suffused with truth and mystery. Examines also the central struggle in both writers' works: the opposition between the symbolic forces of good and evil. Draws points of divergence, focusing on O'Connor's inclusion of God's grace and mercy as a means to salvation. [187 pp.]

1815   Evans, Jay Alan. "The Kierkegaardian Paradigm of the Radical Self in Flannery O'Connor's Fiction." Diss. American U, 1984. *DAI* 45 (1985): 2527A.

Juxtaposes O'Connor's fiction with Kierkegaardian philosophy to explore the existential aesthetic that "pertinently addresses" the content and structure of her stories. Concentrates on the idea of "finding the radical self" as observed in O'Connor's development from her early stories through her mature work. [45 pp.]

1816   Falnes, Mindy Lynn. "A Hall of Mirrors: Physical Doubles in the Fiction of Flannery O'Connor." Diss. Arizona State U, 1995. *DAI* 56 (1995): 1777A.

Analyzes Flannery O'Connor's work in relation to Puritan philosophy and theology and the Protestant work ethic. Sees her as adopting "the paradigm of the double as an agent of repressed elements of the self" and applying it "to the spiritual concerns that dominate her fiction." Suggests that a variety of examples appear in her works including: "faith and reason, God and the Devil, good and evil, and the old man vs. the new man." Indicates that while the doubles in her novels "focus exclusively upon spiritual issues," those in six of her short stories "expose the moral shortcomings of the stories' protagonists as well." Observes that her double relationships tend to be overwhelmingly antagonistic and that "as the tensions heighten, each self is propelled to one of two extremes." Finds that, unlike the usual modern double, O'Connor's "rarely integrate, in large part because the polarities they represent are themselves irreconcilable." Works discussed include: "A Good Man is Hard to Find," "Revelation," "A Circle In the Fire," "The Lame Shall Enter First," "Good Country People," "The Enduring Chill," "The Partridge Festival," *The Violent Bear It Away*, *Wise Blood*, "The Artificial Nigger," "A View of the Woods," "The Displaced Person," "Greenleaf," and "The Comforts of Home." [235 pp.]

1817   Falvey, Ellen Catherine. "Reconstructed Virtue: Grace King's Gothic Realism." Diss. New York U, 1998. *DAI* 59.4 (1998): 1163A.

Contends that "the Gothic is the fictional mode best suited to express the socially and psychically unsettling war-made reversals of class, race, and gender hierarchies in the post-war South." Suggests that Grace Elizabeth King's themes and meanings are not only "Gothic in scope," but may be viewed "as a precursor to later `Southern Gothic' writers such as William Faulkner, Carson McCullers, and Flannery O'Connor." [343 pp.]

1818   Feaster, Scott Vandiver. "Polemical Organization as Style: An Approach to Flannery O'Connor's *Wise Blood* and Georges Rouault's *Miserere* in Terms of a Perspective Provided by the Modern Catholic Novel." Diss. Ohio U, 1982. *DAI* 43 (1983): 3736A-37A.

Analyzes the organization and form of O'Connor's *Wise Blood* and Rouault's *Miserere* and extrapolates five modern Catholic character types. Discusses the works in literary and polemical terms and differentiates this study from other current approaches. [176 pp.]

1819   Feeley, Mary Kathleen. "Splendor of Reality: The Fiction of Flannery O'Connor." Diss. Rutgers U, New Brunswick, 1970. *DAI* 31 (1970): 1272A.

Discusses natural and supernatural reality as the unifying center of O'Connor's work. Finds three strong influences: her spiritual orientation, her eclectic reading, and her circumscribed life. Asserts that she was true to her dictum that mystery is illuminated by manners by illustrating and asserting the authenticity of manners as seen in her characters. [290 pp.]

1820   Ferguson, Penny Blackwood. "Images of the Southern White Woman in the Eleventh Grade American Literature Curriculum." Diss. U of Tennessee, 1988. *DAI* 49 (1989): 3723A.

Analyzes the content and treatment of women in works by three twentieth-century white, female fiction writers: Flannery O'Connor, Katherine Anne Porter, and Eudora Welty. Attempts to determine if the fiction examined reflects a more contemporary, androgynous view. Discusses assumptions for the study, background preparation, and the surveys and psychological tests which were administered to a select group of East Tennessee eleventh-grade teachers. States that the purpose of the study was to determine these teachers' "androgynous perception of women." Found that respondents considered the three writers to be 74 per cent androgynous in their depiction of women. [150 pp.]

1821   Finger, Larry Livingston. "Elements of the Grotesque in Selected Works of Welty, Capote, McCullers, and O'Connor." Diss. George Peabody College for Teachers, 1972. *DAI* 33 (1972): 1721A-22A.

Discusses the use of the grotesque by Eudora Welty, Truman Capote, Carson McCullers, and Flannery O'Connor. Argues for the artistic soundness of the grotesque in each writer, and pairs Capote with McCullers and Welty with O'Connor in their use of the device. [178 pp.]

1822   Fitts, Karen Louise. "Reading Flannery O'Connor by the Light of Feminist Theology: Transcendental Politics in Patriarchal Familial Structures." Diss. Texas Christian U, 1990. *DAI* 51 (1991): 3072A.

Declares that from the perspective of feminist theology and its views of familial structures, O'Connor's fiction exhibits three tenets which repress woman's ability to establish a spiritual community with others: "the ubiquity and propriety of male control in hierarchic family relations"; "the 'naturalness' of childbearing for married women with its concomitant devaluation as an act that occurs outside of culture"; and "the ideological stance that it is a pure and Godly act to punish women for resisting . . . [their] assigned role." Notes that in much of O'Connor's fiction, the father is often absent, "creating social and religious conflict." [133 pp.]

1823   Flavia, Mariapragasam. "An Analytic Study of the Existential Estrangement of Contemporary Man in Select Fiction of Flannery O'Connor." Diss. U of Madras (India), 1992.

Sister Mariapragasam explores the existential estrangement that results from human alienation from God, asserting that individuals are estranged from their family, their society, and from themselves. Argues that this estrangement introduces distortion into relationships, a distortion which "can be clearly attributed to the absence of genuine religious conviction." Finds that "such an alienation is itself evidence of Original Sin as Flannery herself believed . . . [and] can be corrected only by radical illumination which is extended to and sometimes accepted by her fictional characters." Concludes that O'Connor's faith "is seen as central to her vision enabling her to satirically present a deeply alienated world." [301 pp. The author donated a copy to the *Flannery O'Connor Collection* at Georgia College & State University, Milledgeville, GA.]

1824   Fodor, Sarah Joan. "'No Literary Orthodoxy': Flannery O'Connor and the New Critics." Diss. U of Chicago, 1994. *DAI* 55 (1995): 2389A.

Draws upon the fields of literature, sociology, and psychology to examine the impact of American New Criticism on Flannery O'Connor's career. Also examines how she "skirted the New Critical aesthetic of objectivity because of the value she placed on communicating social, racial, psychological, and religious ideas." Challenges the assumption that New Critical theories molded O'Connor work and ensured its favorable reception. Relies upon "foundational documents" by John Crowe Ransom, Robert Penn Warren, Cleanth Brooks, and Allen Tate. Argues that the version of New Criticism "as articulated by this Southern group is more complex and varied than is suggested by the stereotype that New Critics focus on the individual `verbal icon,' [while] ignoring other contexts." Contends that opposing aesthetic approaches, such as those perspectives offered by "literary historians, New Humanists, and New York Intellectuals, among others," also interacted with and impacted O'Connor's life experiences and practices as a writer. Concludes that the broader influences of O'Connor's life and career served "to help her produce fiction that readers have continued to value for varied, often contradictory reasons during a period of struggle for theoretical dominance in the field of English studies." [293 pp.]

1825   Fox, William Henry. "Opposition to Secular Humanism in the Fiction of Flannery O'Connor and Walker Percy." Diss. Emory U, 1979. *DAI* 40 (1979): 236A-37A.

Connects Percy and O'Connor in their concern with central religious and philosophical questions about human significance. Notes that their writings are professedly Christian and that both share the belief that secular humanism deludes and eventually leads the individual to alienation and despair. Outlines the premises of Erich Fromm's secular humanism to create a concrete context. [244 pp.]

1826 Fraistat, Rose Ann Cleveland. "Caroline Gordon as Novelist and Woman of Letters." Diss. U of Pennsylvania, 1980. *DAI* 41 (1981): 3105A.

Discusses Caroline Gordon as a woman of letters, a friend of writers in the Fugitive and Agrarian groups, as wife of Allen Tate, and as mentor to younger writers such as Flannery O'Connor. Closely examines Gordon's novels, and discusses her preoccupation with the role of the artist in contemporary society. [350 pp.]

1827 Friedman, Jane F. "On Developing An Affective Heuristic in Literary Response." Diss. Indiana U of Pennsylvania, 1979.

Uses the reader-response theories of Stanley Fish and David Bleich to study undergraduate student response to Joyce Carol Oates' "Where Are You Going, Where Have You Been?" and Flannery O'Connor's "A Good Man Is Hard to Find" and "Everything That Rises Must Converge." Finds that students "whose personal responses to the text had been systematically and thoroughly tapped" wrote literary essays which "evidenced enhanced command of the selection," had a "greater awareness of themselves while reading," and developed an "increased engagement with the work and [an] increased appreciation of the value of their reading experience." Includes, in the appendices, the text of each of the three stories, along with the questions posed by the author to the reader at intervals throughout each story.

1828 Gallagher, Janet M. "Telling Stories About God: Narrative Voice and Epistemology in the Hebrew Bible and in the Fiction of Flannery O'Connor, Graham Greene and Cynthia Ozick." Diss. Fordham U, 1990. *DAI* 51 (1990): 1221A.

Discusses the relationship between narrative voice and epistemology in: O'Connor's *The Violent Bear It Away*, Greene's *The Heart of the Matter*, and Ozick's *Trust* and *The Cannibal Galaxy*. Indicates perspectives of each and therelationship between reading them and the way readers are brought to knowledge. Likens the reading experience to that of readers of the Hebrew Bible who struggle to understand "the hidden God." [219 pp.]

1829 Garrett, Peggy Louise. "Flannery O'Connor's Artistry: Techniques of Characterization." Diss. Indiana U of Pennsylvania, 1975. *DAI* 38 (1978): 6119A.

Analyzes female characters in O'Connor's works and groups them into the following categories: proud, hard-working women; estranged parents and children; and intellectuals. Each of her characters is analyzed in terms of ten techniques of characterization. [220 pp.]

1830 Gattuso, Josephine Florence. "The Fictive World of Flannery O'Connor." Diss. Columbia U, 1968. *DA* 29 (1969): 3136A.

Rejects the standard criticism of O'Connor's fiction as mere exegesis. Asserts that she straddled two conflicting views of life, one traditional, and the other modern and secular. Discusses themes and imagery, and includes a section which contrasts O'Connor's work with that of William Faulkner, William Styron, and Truman Capote. Focuses on Southern preoccupations, using murder scenes as examples for discussion. [197 pp.]

1831 Gentry, Marshall Bruce. "Tracks to the Oven: Grotesque Religious Experience in the Works of Flannery O'Connor." Diss. U of Texas at Austin, 1984. *DAI* 45 (1985): 2101A.

Examines O'Connor's obsession with "redemption achieved through grotesque and unconscious means." Proposes that her protagonists rival the narrator for narrative authority, in order to free themselves of the narrator's judgement. Uses Mikhail Bakhtin's view of the grotesque to show how O'Connor's characters are rejuvenated (and degraded), thus dispelling the widespread reading of O'Connor's stories as orthodox Christian with a narrator who analyzes theological errors. Concludes that O'Connor's true focus is on her characters' "grotesque path toward redemption." [368 pp.]

1832 Getz, Lorine. "Types of Grace in Flannery O'Connor's Fiction." Diss. U of Saint Michael's College (Canada), 1979.

[329 pp. Cited in *Comprehensive Dissertation Index Ten-Year Cumulation 1973-1982: Author Index Co-Go* 34 (1984): 768. Not available from University Microfilms International nor via inter-library loan from the University of Saint Michael's College Library. Probably similar to the author's book: *Nature and Grace In Flannery O'Connor's Fiction* (New York: Edwin Mellen, 1982).]

1833   Golden, Robert Edward. "Violence and Art in Postwar American Literature: A Study of O'Connor, Kosinski, Hawkes and Pynchon." Diss. U of Rochester, 1972. *DAI* 33 (1972): 311A.

Differentiates between the nature of personal violence and massive, impersonal violence. Labels Flannery O'Connor's use as the former, Jerzy Kosinski's, John Hawkes's, and Thomas Pynchon's as the latter. Focuses on O'Connor's *The Violent Bear It Away* to establish her particular type and form of violence. [234 pp.]

1834   Goss, James. "The Assembling of the Meaning of God in the Short Stories of Flannery O'Connor, Bernard Malamud and John Updike." Diss. Claremont Graduate School, 1970. *DAI* 31 (1971): 6700A.

Presents a philosophical argument, influenced by the work of Martin Heidegger and others associated with the New Hermeneutic, to depict how a work of art may be considered as an assembling of meaning which may include an understanding of God. Uses this framework to interpret a select group of short stories by O'Connor, Malamud, and Updike. Shows parallels by use of such phrases as "radical questionableness" and "confidence and hope." [264 pp.]

1835   Gossett, Louise Young. "Violence in Recent Southern Fiction." Diss. Duke U, 1961. *DAI* 23 (1967): 233A.

States that O'Connor's concentration on her central theme accounts for much of the power of her work. Suggests that she "applies rigorously Poe's theory of relevant details," and writes an economical prose as forceful as the violence described. Argues that O'Connor refuses to bow to the critics and instead presents "to a complacent world the shocking disturbance which genuine faith creates . . ." [357 pp.]

1836   Gregory, Donald Lee. "An Internal Analysis of the Fiction of Flannery O'Connor." Diss. Ohio State U, 1967. *DA* 28 (1968): 5055A.

Argues that O'Connor has been praised and "overpraised" as an author whose technical virtuosity is enhanced by her religious view. Asserts that her fiction is marred by alternating confusion and predictability. Argues that while O'Connor's intense concern for moral implications raises her fiction to a higher level of importance, her religious point of view provides a "schematic element which frequently weakens" it. [299 pp.]

1837   Griffin, Mary N. "Coming to Manhood in America: A Study of Significant Initiation Novels, 1797-1970." Diss. Vanderbilt U, 1971. *DAI* 32 (1972): 3951A.

Examines the theme of initiation in American literature, tracing its development, defining its characteristics, and ascertaining the reasons it is such a popular structural device. Discusses thirty-six American novels: three from the Federalist period, three from the Romantic period, nine from the Realistic and Naturalistic periods, and twenty-one published since World War I. Among those discussed is O'Connor's *The Violent Bear It Away*. Offers a reading of O'Connor's work and, finds "there is more of a ritualistic nature" to the process of initiation in this novel, than in many of the others examined, including: "the use of baptism, a new name, and new clothes to signal a changed nature, the killing of another to assert one's manhood, and Tarwater's anointing of his forehead with dirt from his granduncle's grave." Notes other, more conventional aspects, including Tarwater's meeting of mentors who offer a variety of philosophies from which to choose; the fact that he must undergo an ordeal to become a different person; his realization that he has been reborn with a purpose, and--like many characters in this kind of novel-- that he heads for the city to meet his fate. Concludes that the value of *The Violent Bear It Away* "lies in the fact that Miss O'Connor has used the form to remind a jaded world of the radical alterations which faith makes in a man's life and to stress the horror which its denial brings." [381 pp.]

1838   Gulley, Ervene Frances. "Peacocks, Pigs, and Prophets: Ironic Iconography in the Short Fiction of Flannery O'Connor." Diss. Lehigh U, 1975. *DAI* 36 (1976): 6097-98A.

Establishes how O'Connor's traditional use of iconography deviates from the norm of modern American fiction, which seeks, by ironic inversion, to elevate new icons to a level of transcendence. Suggests that while most modern fiction is concerned with the "vision of a lost and chaotic society," O'Connor "resolves conflict in iconic value at the Christian pole . . . not by rational inquiry, but [by] the harsh light of revelation." [205 pp.]

1839   Ham, Marian Ellison. "Children As Victims, Demons, Seers: Flannery O'Connor's Wise Brood." Diss. U of Mississippi, 1977.

Asserts that O'Connor's characters, like other twentieth-century American fictional characters, "search powerfully, even tragically for meaning and order in a meaningless and chaotic time." Suggests that her vision "is the moral vision of Faulkner, McCullers, Fitzgerald, Welty, and Williams," and like them, "she sees the world in terms of the eternal questions which plague the greatest writers." Examines O'Connor criticism, grouping studies into three areas: among the group of "American fiction writers who prominently use violence and the grotesque character;" among those who approach her work as that of "a Christian moralist, especially as the voice of the Catholic moralist, even prophet;" and among those which explicate her work "as revelatory of existentialism." Claims that children are among O'Connor's most memorable characters, that they are "depicted with noticeable frequency, skill and perceptiveness," and that "they often are, in contradistinction to the adults, both initiates and initiators," often emerging as victims, demons, prophets, or all three. Finds that her child characters "both deny and assert the reality of the mystery of a spiritually-centered life." Postulates that they "are both inheritors of and creators of a lucidly, sometimes comically revealed bitter landscape and skyscape." Suggests that O'Connor's depiction of her "compelling brood" reveals a knowledge of rites of passage of primitive tribes which she skillfully uses for developing her structure and theme. Focusing on child characters, discusses "Good Country People," "A Good Man Is Hard to Find," "A View of the Woods," "The River," "The Artificial Nigger," "The Lame Shall Enter First," "A Circle in the Fire," and *The Violent Bear It Away*. [108 pp. Not available from University Microfilms International. A copy is in the *Flannery O'Connor Collection* of the Russell Library at Georgia College & State University, Milledgeville, GA. Cited in *Comprehensive Dissertation Index Ten-Year Cumulation 1973-1982: Author Index Gp-K* 35 (1984): 131.]

1840   Hamilton, Winifred Jean. "Fish Hooks and Desert Places: Space and the Reader in the Fiction of John Hawkes." Diss. Rice U, 1989. *DAI* 50 (1990): 3952A.

Associates John Hawkes's work with that of William Faulkner, Flannery O'Connor, and Nathanael West, each of whom uses various devices to bring the reader into the text: Faulkner, character; O'Connor, plot; and West, "empty space." [285 pp.]

1841   Han, Jae-Nam. "The Voice of One Crying in the Wilderness: T.S. Eliot and Flannery O'Connor." Diss. U of Nebraska-Lincoln, 1998.

Utilizes a historical-biographical approach to explore the "literary theory, social philosophy, and theology" of Eliot and O'Connor to "establish a firmer link" between the two as "modern Christian artists, critics, and thinkers." Explores influences that shaped their aesthetics--familial, educational, literary, and theological--then discusses how each combined "religious doctrine and literary practice" to develop their literary theories. Critiques their "social philosophies grounded in aristocratic and theocratic ideals," and suggests that both believed that "modern society was too liberal." Contends that both believed that the "order, control, and clerical hierarchy" of medieval Christendom offered a better alternative. Compares "their conceptions of Christian salvation" and its role to rescue humankind from its "alienation from God and fellow humans." Devotes a chapter to how both interweave images of animals, illness and death, deformity and debased landscape to dramatize the distortion of modern souls." Closes with a chapter which compares and contrasts their "theological use of grotesque and biblical images." Argues that both writers, "As social thinkers . . . [are] strikingly similar in their denunciation of many atheistic ideologies, in their dislike of Protestantism, in their advocacy of unified culture, and in their approval of coercion for conversion to Christ." Concludes that Eliot expressed his work as "a Christian vision mostly influenced by the Incarnation," while O'Connor emphasized damnation and judgment. [255 pp.]

1842   Hand, John Thomas. "Letters to the Laodiceans: The Romantic Quest in Flannery O'Connor." Diss. Kent State U, 1971. *DAI* 32 (1972): 5227A-28A.

Asserts that the standard of criticism since the turn of the century, "sociological realism," has done much damage to the reputations of writers whose work falls within the opposing traditions, including Flannery O'Connor's. Asserts that she used the Romance form to counter the disadvantage of being on the outside. Examines many of O'Connor's choices, including the use of violence, in order to shock what she saw as a hostile audience. [202 pp.]

1843   Hanley, Richard Eugene. "Place to Place: A Study of the Movement Between the City and Country in Selected Twentieth-Century American Fiction." Diss. State U of New York at Binghamton, 1981. *DAI* 42 (1981): 2130A-31A.

Examines works by a varied group of American writers, including Flannery O'Connor. Focuses on their concern with movement between city and country, a theme traced back to the immigration of pilgrims from Europe. Groups the writings into those concerned with: city to country movement, country to city movement, and continual movement between the two. Stresses the idea of movement from place to place, and focuses on character changes. Discusses O'Connor's works in the context of movement from country to city, noting the emotions affected: awe, confusion, and hope. Concludes that this movement back and forth is seen "as a necessary passage in the integration of the American self." [263 pp.]

1844   Hart, Gary Victor Wheatley. "The Influence of Thomistic Analogy on the
             Works of Flannery O'Connor." Diss. U of Southern California, 1984. *DAI*
             44 (1984): 3685A.

             Asserts that an examination of O'Connor's claim to Thomism may help
             resolve the question of how her religious beliefs in grace and sacrament
             function in her art. Breaks down specific aspects of Thomistic philosophy
             and discusses how each applies to her fiction. After verification of
             Thomism in O'Connor's work, the author discusses how it serves a
             number of critical objectives. Concludes that the "world and man" in her
             stories are essentially good, because they serve to "refine man's worship
             of God." [470 pp.]

1845   Hatch, Deborah Hollister. "A Reader Response Study of the Grotesque in
             the Fiction of Eudora Welty, Flannery O'Connor, and Carson McCullers."
             Diss. U of Massachusetts, 1982. *DAI* 43 (1983): 2667A.

             Rather than cataloging the use of the grotesque in the work of Eudora
             Welty, Flannery O'Connor, and Carson McCullers, this reader-response
             analysis seeks to explain how aspects which are potentially repellent
             actually create conditions which allow revelation. Employs the theories
             of Stanley Fish, Norman Holland, and Wolfgang Iser [163 pp.]

1846   Hauser, James David. "The Broken Cosmos of Flannery O'Connor: The
             Design of Her Fiction." Diss. U of Pennsylvania, 1973. *DAI* 34 (1973):
             1912A.

             Discusses the fall of humanity and society and reintegration/the grace of
             God, as opposing positions in O'Connor's dualism. Sees O'Connor's ability
             to hold the two in "rich, irrational balance" as evidence of her genius.
             Likens the fallen aspect to Kafka's stories and urges an existential
             understanding of her fiction. [321 pp.]

1847   Hegarty, Charles Michael. "Vision and Revision: The Art of Flannery
             O'Connor." Diss. U of Chicago, 1973.

             A study of O'Connor's process of writing and habit of revision. Discusses
             her self-parody in Miss Willerton from "The Crop," and examines how
             this character "continually revises her art because she always sees more
             fictional possibility in other and more distant subject matter." Asserts that,
             like Miss Willerton, O'Connor's "imaginative vision compelled her
             relentless revision," caused problems with her first publisher, and formed

the foundation of her working methodology. Attempts to "illuminate the complexity and growth of Flannery O'Connor's achievement as artist" to reveal "both her art and its residual `mystery.'" Explores how she "moved from fact to fiction" as in: her parody of the process in "The Partridge Festival;" her use of a local newspaper story for "A Late Encounter With the Enemy;" and her use of the Polish immigrant family employed on the O'Connor dairy farm as "raw materials" for "The Displaced Person." Discusses her views regarding the "role of the regional Southern writer," and her advocacy of the use of regional language and idiom. Offers detailed readings of O'Connor's works. Confirms that O'Connor's concerns were "with mystery as it is embodied in human life," the prophetic aspects of her vocation, and how to use comic effects to convey serious themes. [242 pp. Not available from University Microfilms International. Cited in *Comprehensive Dissertation Index Ten-Year Cumulation 1973-1982: Author Index Gp-K* 35 (1984): 242.]

1848   Heher, Michael E. *Flannery O'Connor on Revelation*. Diss. Pontificia Universitate Gregoriana (Rome), 1987.

Suggests a "scientific investigation and critical evaluation of the theology of revelation resident in the twenty-five short stories and two novels" of Flannery O'Connor. First, provides a statement of "convictions about methodological questions" and purpose of study, then offers a close reading of each of O'Connor's works. Uses readings of the stories and two novels to "draw together the various bits of evidence into as complete a synthesis of O'Connor's theology of revelation as the evidence allows." Places her theology of revelation "in dialogue with positions espoused by the contemporary Roman Catholic magisterium and a selection of respected Protestant and Catholic theologians." Concludes with discussion of the "originality of O'Connor's thought," and outlines "areas of concern for theologians in the area of revelation, mystery, and theological anthropology." Provides two appendices: the first presents a chronological outline of selected events of O'Connor's life and writing career; the second, "a story-by-story bibliography of sources and primary and secondary references." [504 pp. A copy is in the *Flannery O'Connor Collection* of the Russell Library at Georgia College & State University, Milledgeville, GA.]

1849   Hendricks, Fredric Jefferson. "*Accent*, 1940-1960: The History of a Little Magazine." Diss. U of Illinois at Urbana-Champaign, 1984. *DAI* 45 (1985): 3350A.

Traces the history of *Accent: A Quarterly of New Literature*. Structured chronologically, this study offers a discussion of the evolution of the magazine's critical stance and comments on a wide variety of writers, including Flannery O'Connor, who were first published there. [212 pp.]

1850   Hiers, John Turner. "Traditional Death Customs in Modern Southern Fiction." Diss. Emory U, 1974. *DAI* 35 (1974): 1103A.

Asserts that traditional death customs "are significant structural devices, climactic tableaux, and symbolic vehicles in many modern Southern novels." Selectively examines cultural attitudes, death-related rituals, family relationships, and funerals as "artistic metaphors of the ethos of a people." Suggests that some of the writings of William Faulkner, Thomas Wolfe, Robert Penn Warren, Eudora Welty, Katherine Anne Porter, William Humphrey, William Styron, Madison Jones, James Dickey, James Agee, and Flannery O'Connor, reveal "established patterns of successful narration development and full characterization" created from these attitudes and rituals. Examines O'Connor's *The Violent Bear It Away*. Argues that "Mason's death rites become Francis's initiation rites despite the youth's former prideful rebellion," and that Francis's vision at the end of the novel "illustrates his final acceptance of Mason's dark world view." Suggests that Agee, O'Connor, Wolfe, Humphrey, and Welty, exhibit "faith in the human capacity to transcend time by transcending self." Concludes that death and funeral-related lore in modern fiction of the South is "not only widespread and kaleidoscopic, but also subtle and penetrating as a cultural phenomenon for individual initiations into the ultimate mysteries of life." [149 pp.]

1851   Hoberek, Andrew Paul. "White-Collar Culture: Work, Organization, and American Fiction, 1943-1959." Diss. U of Chicago, 1998. *DAI* 59 (1998): 171A.

Argues that postwar fiction has been "shaped by concerns over the de-individualizing and mystifying effects of white-collar work." Discusses fiction by Flannery O'Connor, among others, "to show how the postwar transformation in middle-class identity, and in the relationship of intellectuals to the middle-class, constituted both a crisis and an opportunity for the production of fiction."

1852   Hobson, Linda Whitney. "Comedy and Christianity in the Novels of Walker Percy." Diss. U of Alabama, 1981. *DAI* 43 (1982): 1545A.

Discusses how Christian themes are supported by "traditional comic narrative pattern and technique" in five novels by Walker Percy, and names two influences: Sören Kierkegaard and Mark Twain. Discusses

Percy's view of his heroes, as well as his use of irony and satire. Refers to O'Connor and suggests that Percy uses shock and satire in much the same way she did. [333 pp.]

1853   Hochberg, Mark R. "Narrative Forms in the Modern Southern Novel." Diss. Cornell U, 1970. *DAI* 31 (1970): 4773A.

Discusses the work of seven major novelists classified as writers of "the Southern Gothic School," have written about the South, and are "representative of the quality and variety of contemporary Southern fiction." Examines aspects referred to as "Gothic" to determine "the function of those elements in their fiction." Contends that they "are not members of a common `school,' and that the term `Gothic' has been loosely used to describe a variety of fictional techniques used with differing effect and purpose." Suggests that because the twentieth-century South has undergone a cultural transformation, the resulting social instability has "affected the forms taken by Southern literature." Discusses works by William Faulkner, Ralph Ellison, Eudora Welty, Shirley Ann Grau, Carson McCullers, Truman Capote, and Flannery O'Connor (reviews *Wise Blood*, *The Violent Bear It Away*, several of O'Connor's short stories). Finds that O'Connor "shares with the Vanderbilt poets a strong dislike for the new urban and secular South," while holding as an ideal the dogma of orthodox Catholicism instead of mythic agrarianism. Concludes that "O'Connor's Christianity is eschatological, and the problem she faced in her work was making the reader aware of the mystery of life and transmitting to him her own sense of the awful reality of God." [185 pp.]

1854   Hoffman, Arnold Roy. "The Sense of Place: Peter De Vries, J.F. Powers, and Flannery O'Connor." Diss. Michigan State U, 1970. *DAI* 31 (1971): 6059A.

Argues that the fiction of Peter DeVries, J.F. Powers, and Flannery O'Connor is informed by both Christian theology and comic vision. Shows how thesewriters are "at variance" with the dominant strain in American fiction: humanistic absurdist literature. Equates violence in O'Connor's works with the "Good Friday-Easter sequence," seen as meant to bring readers to an awareness of their fallen state. [253 pp.]

1855   Hoffman, Eleanor Marie Riley. "A Study of the Major Structures Intrinsic to the Fiction of Flannery O'Connor." Diss. U of Texas at Austin, 1972. *DAI* 33 (1973): 3649A.

Discusses O'Connor's use of direct narration as a tool for reporting facts to her readers. Suggests that she uses "supplemental dialogue and indirect narrative" to enable main characters to "report their versions of the facts and to also set forth another contrasting value system." Argues that it is through confrontations of value systems that O'Connor's characters are often defeated and the "unacceptable value system" destroyed. Outlines how O'Connor uses the journey, that so many of her characters set out on, to place them "in an unsupportive environment," where they may be challenged to face spiritual conflict. Reviews her use of metaphor and outlines how she "seems to govern her characters rather strictly in accord with the method of narration and the basic story structure." Sees O'Connor's characters in terms of their function: system, intruder, rhetorical, and victim. [241 pp.]

1856   Hopkins, Karen Jeanne. "An Exercise in Adjudication: Interpretations of Flannery O'Connor's *The Violent Bear It Away*." Diss. Bowling Green State U, 1982. *DAI* 43 (1983): 3318A.

Analyzes the current state of practical literary criticism with regard to assumptions held and style used by critics in interpreting O'Connor's work. Discusses six representative readings of *The Violent Bear It Away* and finds none to be complete and coherent. Asserts that critics have been hindered by arbitrary professional and theoretical constraints, and proposes an alternative reader-response reading. [275 pp.]

1857   Horn, Tamara. "To Grandmother's House We Go: Modern Grandmother Archetypes in Works by Porter, Hurston, McCarthy, O'Connor, and Olsen." Diss. U of Alabama, 1997. *DAI* 58 (1997): 2209-10A.

Declares that "although the grandmother character was generally portrayed as a simplistic model of feminine empowerment," Katherine Anne Porter, Zora Neale Hurston, Flannery O'Connor, Mary McCarthy, and Tillie Olsen "were the first modernists to examine the complexities and possibilities of that role in the modern American landscape." Finds O'Connor's grandmother in "A Good Man Is Hard to Find" to be "inundated with mass produced texts defining absolute `good' in an ever-shifting society." Contends that she "overpowers her family with clichés," and that her death "is necessary to embue religious language with meaning again." Concludes that, as modern writers, these women "were instrumental in wrenching the grandmother from her position as a locus of value in American literature and society at a time when American society valued its youth." [202 pp.]

1858 Horton, James William. "Commitment and Utopia: A Liberation Theology Approach to John Dos Passos, Flannery O'Connor, and Thomas Pynchon." Diss. U of Western Ontario (Canada), 1995. *DAI* 56 (1996): 3959A.

Examines *U.S.A.* by John Dos Passos, *The Violent Bear It Away* by Flannery O'Connor and *Gravity's Rainbow* by Thomas Pynchon. Views them "from the perspective of Christianity" to consider "what the implications are of liberation theology for literature." Suggests that the work of each of these three writers casts "doubt both on the possibility of a non-religious socialism, and the possibility of a non-socialistic religion." Contends that each writer demonstrates the necessity of "a utopian commitment both artistically and politically, which focuses on this world and the next as a continuum." Offers conclusions about the religious nature and ideologies of the three works and advocates "readings which stress the reader's participation as a bearer of Christian faith." [212 pp.]

1859 Hubbard, Marion Stevens. "A View From the Outside: Robert Coles and the Power of Narrative." Diss. U of Alabama, 1996. *DAI* 58 (1997): 864A.

Examines writings of noted psychiatrist, Robert Coles, "to make the argument that the reading of literature . . . informs the 'reading' of life, and vice versa." Devotes a chapter to Coles's literary criticism, which focuses on his writings on William Carlos Williams, Walker Percy, and Flannery O'Connor. [211 pp.]

1860 Humphries, John Jefferson. "Mourning Becomes Desire: Gnosticism as an Aesthetic Principle in the Works of Proust, Flannery O'Connor and François Villon." Diss. Yale U, 1981. *DAI* 42 (1982): 5140A-41A.

Examines the concepts of violence, reading, and writing as negative acts, and the psychopathology of loss. Derives a "gnostic aesthetic" from Marcel Proust, Flannery O'Connor, François Villon, and other psychoanalytic models, including Sigmund Freud's "Mourning and Melancholia." Deals with O'Connor's use of physical violence, spiritual "aeskesis," her Catholic dualism, and "her aesthetic kinship with Proust, Georges Bataille, Maurice Blanchot, and with the revisionist psychoanalyst James Hillman." [230 pp.]

1861 Hunter, Eileen Marie. "Family, Class, and Postwar American Fiction: Three Readings and a Novel." Diss. U of Minnesota, 1999. *DAI* 60 (1999): 2026A.

Explores "the literature and culture of postwar America, focusing on the intersection between fictional and social-historical representations of the family." Examines the social history of the American family, then uses works by Flannery O'Connor, Jane Smiley, and Jane Hamilton to explore fictional representations of the relationship between class and family identity." [481 pp.]

1862   Johansen, Ruthann Knechel. "The Narrative Secret of Flannery O'Connor: The Trickster as Interpreter." Diss. Drew U, 1983. *DAI* 44 (1983): 1086A.

Asserts that O'Connor unconsciously used "trickster" elements in her narratives to embody her religious preoccupations in fiction. Traces her concept of trickster back to biblical narratives and asserts that trickster elements shape the structure, themes, and metaphors, and assist interpretation. Likens the episodic elements of the story collections to trickster cycles, and the artist herself to "a weaver of the web." [422 pp.]

1863   Johnson, Rhonda Eugene, Jr. "A Translation of Silence: The Fiction of Flannery O'Connor." Diss. State U New York at Buffalo, 1973. *DAI* 34 (1973): 3403A.

Contends that O'Connor's world is one "darkened by the continuing Fall" and that her characters attempt to deal with this by simply closing their eyes. Argues that "language exacerbates the Fall rather than heals it; but man, ignoring the fact that in a post-lapsarian existence everything is ambivalent, seizes upon words as a way to the objective knowledge which he still believes he can find." Discusses the duality of man's having to make a choice within a context which negates the grounds for any positive act and insinuates that O'Connor does what a true author must: see important issues as paradox. [203 pp.]

1864   Johnson, Rob. "The Will to Be a Writer: Caroline Gordon, Flannery O'Connor and Cecil Dawkins and Influence Among Southern Women Writers." Diss. U of Southern California, 1994.

Offers a biographical and historical study of the fiction and circumstances of three prominent Southern women and Catholic writers: Caroline Gordon, Flannery O'Connor and Cecil Dawkins. Tests the hypothesis that "the best reader of a writer is the reader who does not write like their student--in fact cannot write that way," and examines literary influences upon the three writers and whether each had a prominent and supportive "reader." Argues that O'Connor "was taught by the aristocracy of Southern letters . . . including Robert Penn Warren and Andrew Lytle."

Suggests that Caroline Gordon served as O'Connor's own gifted "'reader' for life," who "passed on to her the advice she had been given by [Ford Madox] Ford, [Allen] Tate, and others," and, by doing so, made O'Connor "heir to secrets of the craft of fiction from Ford's day and even before." Reviews the influence that O'Connor then had upon Cecil Dawkins, first as a reader and friend, then as an "'anxiety of influence'" that Dawkins had to overcome. Submits that "O'Connor's `habit of seeing'" is "directly related to Gordon's knowledge of Imagism and Henry James's theories on point-of-view." Concludes that "'the will to be a writer'" possessed all three women, and that this "will" reflects "a clear line of literary tradition and influence now well over a hundred and fifty years old."

1865   Johnson, William Lawrence. "Violence as Grace: A Theopoietic Reading of Mimetic Violence in Rene Girard and Flannery O'Connor." Diss. Syracuse U, 1992. *DAI* 53 (1993): 4366A.

Asserts that the work of Rene Girard offers a useful framework from which the reader may better understand O'Connor's fiction. Declares that O'Connor "assaults the reader by juxtaposing realistic and grotesque imagery" to evoke a vision of violence. Finds this not only appropriate but a "necessary correlation to human experience." Suggests that O'Connor's work reflects Girard's belief that violence is one of the most sacred forces. Discusses the practice of mimesis in literature and examines O'Connor's work to "identify a realism of a different order which preserves the mystery and integrity of the text and its textuality." [419 pp.]

1866   Jones, Dale Wayne. "Aesthetics of Apocalypse: A Study of the Grotesque Novel in America." Diss. U of Wisconsin, Madison, 1984. *DAI* 46 (1985): 424A.

Credits O'Connor with the writing of a unique kind of novel, "the grotesque novel," whose themes and structures are determined entirely by the "grotesque aesthetic." Names Herman Melville's *The Confidence Man* as progenitor of the type, and Nathanael West's, Flannery O'Connor's, and Thomas Pynchon's works as descendants. Refers to the popularity of this mode in the works of contemporary novelists, and its usefulness for "writers who are concerned with depicting the problematical nature of existence." Notes variance in purpose by each writer examined, and declares that O'Connor's aim is to shock readers and distort reality "in order to reveal hidden, spiritual truths." Concludes that the grotesque mode offers writers a vehicle of protest, a way "of decrying human responsibility for the evil and corruption of the world." [209 pp.]

1867   Katz, Claire Rose. "Flannery O'Connor: A Rage of Vision." Diss. U of
             California, Berkeley, 1975. *DAI* 35 (1975): 6719A.

             Discusses the secular appeal of O'Connor's work, and argues that a
             psychoanalytic exploration of the plots reveals a central conflict with
             autonomy, which is resolved only by the Christian "paradigm of
             humiliation and self-obliteration." Suggests that O'Connor's fiction directs
             a rage against characters who represent O'Connor herself: women,
             children, and intellectuals. [275 pp.]

1868   Katz, Steven Alex. "Horrifying Laughter: Improving the Teaching of
             Violent Comedy Through the Use of Theory." Diss. Memphis State U,
             1985. *DAI* 47 (1986): 109A-10A.

             Claims twentieth-century writers seem more willing to concentrate and
             elaborate on the pain that their characters feel. Notes that O'Connor's
             stories are "among the most frequently taught in college freshman and
             sophomore English courses." Analyzes trends in traditional theories of
             comedy to determine whether modern comic phenomena can be
             successfully taught and explained in those terms. Examines "Good
             Country People," "Revelation," and "A Good Man Is Hard To Find."
             Argues for a wedding of literary theory and literary criticism. Finds that
             an approach to these stories which assumes "a more psychological slant"
             offers important insights. [129 pp.]

1869   Keane, Melinda. "Structural Irony in Flannery O'Connor: Instrument of
             the Writer's Vision." Diss. Loyola U of Chicago, 1969.

             Sister Keane examines how irony informs O'Connor's work "through a
             reversal in plot, character diction, symbol and tone." Suggests that
             O'Connor uses irony to communicate "a vision of a world redeemed
             though sinful." Considers in the first chapter, O'Connor's visual
             orientation and "the importance of the concept [of] metaphor or *vision* in
             Flannery O'Connor's writing. The second chapter discusses how O'Connor
             uses ironic pattern and tradition; the third, explores O'Connor's use of
             irony in *Wise Blood, The Violent Bear It Away*, "A Good Man Is Hard to
             Find," "A Stroke of Good Fortune," "A Circle in the Fire," "Good Country
             People," "Everything That Rises Must Converge," "Revelation," "Parker's
             Back," and "Judgement Day." Closes the study with a discussion in the
             fourth chapter of O'Connor's vision, evidence of structural irony, and "the
             relation between the two in O'Connor's fiction." [258 pp. Cited in
             Comprehensive Dissertation Index 1861-1972: Author Index Hj-Mc 35
             (1973): 345.]

1870 Keessen, Jan. "Flannery O'Connor's Rhetoric of Grace." Diss. U of Chicago, 1991.

Observes that, in her speeches, correspondence, and introductions to her work, O'Connor "declared that the goal of her fiction is to teach secular audiences about the workings of grace." Discusses the problems O'Connor encountered with early critics who misunderstood her purpose in writing *Wise Blood*, and suggests that by 1949, "she had already begun writing fiction whose intent was to teach readers." Focuses on the varied response by critics to the didactic intent and redemptive nature of O'Connor's fiction, and considers whether O'Connor's own explanations and interpretations ought to be trusted. Uses Ben Satterfield's "howling complaint toward critics who he claims have `responded like so many Pavlovian dogs' to O'Connor's explanations," as a discussion point. Argues that Satterfield was "howlingly wrong" in limiting the extent to which critics should consider an authors expressed intention. Describes the characteristics of O'Connor's "didactic fiction" and how these features function rhetorically in her fiction. [272 pp.]

1871 Kelber, Barbara Neault. "Making Places: Writing Women of the American South." Diss. U of California, Riverside, 1994. *DAI* 55 (1995): 2391A.

Examines the writings of a group of Southern authors who "grew up `knowing their place,'" including: Eudora Welty, Flannery O'Connor, Alice Walker, Katherine Anne Porter, Carson McCullers, Bobbie Ann Mason, Laura Riding, and the Fugitive/Agrarian group. Sees tension in these authors' works, "created by the epistemological traditions which denigrate the authority of lived experience in favor of formal and `manageable' meanings on which systems of domination depend for their continuing powers." [228 pp.]

1872 Keller, Jane Carter. "The Comic Spirit in the Works of Flannery O'Connor." Diss. Tulane U, 1970. *DAI* 31 (1970): 2922A-23A.

Counters the prevailing view that Flannery O'Connor's work is often seen as grim and tragic. Sees the comic basis of the work to be in the movement of the plot toward pleasure. Discusses grotesquery, irony, and satire in her fiction. [291 pp.]

1873 Kent, Carol Fleisher. "Constrained Extremists: Generic Constraint and Transgression in the Work of Flannery O'Connor and Alfred Hitchcock." Diss. Brown U, 1992. *DAI* 53 (1993): 3903A.

Compares the works of Flannery O'Connor and Alfred Hitchcock, "two figures who exploit generic restrictions in an excessive way." Indicates that the most distinctive similarity is their "generic doubling: a multi-focused carnivalesque of genres." Includes discussions of the role of the "spectator," use of irony, normative versus doubling texts, literary and cinematic genres, and the omniscient point of view. [246 pp.]

1874   Kinnebrew, Mary Jane. "Dialect in the Fiction of Carson McCullers, Flannery O'Connor and Eudora Welty." Diss. U of Houston - University Park, 1983. *DAI* 44 (1983): 1454A.

Discusses the importance of dialect in the works of Carson McCullers, Flannery O'Connor, and Eudora Welty. Observes how dialect not only provides insight into characters, themes, and symbolism, but also contributes meaningful information about Southern English. [376 pp.]

1875   Kisawadkorn, Kriengsak. "American Grotesque From Nineteenth Century to Modernism: The Latter's Acceptance of the Exceptional." Diss. North Texas State U, 1994. *DAI* 55 (1995): 3190A.

Examines the history of the grotesque and arabesque in art and literature by exploring the views of a wide variety of literary theorists. Discusses the use of the grotesque in the novels and stories of: Washington Irving, Edgar Allan Poe, Nathaniel Hawthorne, Sherwood Anderson, Nathanael West, John Steinbeck, William Faulkner, Carson McCullers, and Flannery O'Connor. Contends that the grotesque, as treated by early American writers, is "often despised, feared or mistrusted by other characters, but is the opposite in modernist fiction." Suggests that "Southern grotesque writers such as Faulkner, McCullers, and O'Connor give prominence to Southern literature." Analyzes works, including O'Connor's "A Good Man Is Hard to Find," "Good Country People," "The Lame Shall Enter First," and "Parker's Back," to show how these authors portray the grotesque. Concludes that this genre is no longer deprecated "because Modernist writers, with pity and compassion for their grotesque creations," have shown them to be "ordinary and natural characters." [193 pp.]

1876   Kissel, Susan Steves. "For a `Hostile Audience': A Study of the Fiction of Flannery O'Connor, Walker Percy, and J.F. Powers." Diss. U of Cincinnati, 1975. *DAI* 36 (1975): 2824A.

Studies how three contemporary Catholic writers, Flannery O'Connor, Walker Percy, and J.F. Powers, structure their fiction for a hostile audience. Argues that "indirect communication" is used to minimize the distance between the author and the secular audience. Suggests that while the conclusions of these works may violate comic expectations created earlier, the reader is still not "cheated" intellectually, emotionally, or morally. [283 pp.]

1877   Klevar, Harvey Lee. "The Sacredly Profane and Profanely Sacred: Flannery O'Connor and Erskine Caldwell as Interpreters of Southern Cultural and Religious Traditions." Diss. U of Minnesota, 1970. *DAI* 31 (1971): 5407A-08A.

Argues that, because of their incorporation of Southern religious traditions, the fictional works of Flannery O'Connor and Erskine Caldwell offer important insights. Suggests that O'Connor elevates the profane to a sacred level and indicates that she sees humanity as dignified because it is worthy of redemption. Contends that, in contrast, because Caldwell sees a world abandoned by God, his characters' spiritual impulses turn first to sexuality, then to secular humanism. Concludes that while the two seem polarized, both employ similar methods and materials. [269 pp.]

1878   Kochanek, Patricia S. "In Pursuit of Proteus: A Piagetian Approach to the Structure of the Grotesque in American Fiction of the Fifties." Diss. Pennsylvania State U, 1972. *DAI* 33 (1973): 5729-30A.

Discusses difficulties that critics and readers have encountered in dealing with the grotesque fiction produced by American writers during the 1950s. Contends that another approach is required to permit readers to view the grotesque differently; then, suggests "an alternative theory based on the workings of the human mental processes as described" by Jean Piaget. Applies the proposed theoretical framework to explicate "hitherto puzzling aspects of grotesque imagery, characterization, and plot" in John Barth's *The End of the Road*, Paul Bowle's *The Sheltering Sky*, Norman Mailer's *The Naked and the Dead*, Joseph Heller's *Catch-22*, Ralph Ellison's *The Invisible Man*, and William Styron's *Lie Down In Darkness* and *Set This House on Fire*. Includes brief discussions of O'Connor's "The River," "Parker's Back," "Everthing That Rises Must Converge," *The Violent Bear It Away* and *Wise Blood*. [304 pp.]

1879   Kowalewski, Michael John. "Violence and Verbal Form in American Fiction." Diss. Rutgers U, New Brunswick, 1986. *DAI* 47 (1986): 2159A.

Considers the nature of the fictional representation of violence in works by James Fenimore Cooper, Edgar Allan Poe, Stephen Crane, Flannery O'Connor, Richard Wright, and Thomas Pynchon. Focuses on the ways in which the authors have constructed violence in their work. Describes conditions in the narratives needed in order for the violent action to appear realistic, then details "what happens when those conditions are subjected to the exigencies and shapings of fictional voice." [316 pp.]

1880   Lackey, Allen D. "Flannery O'Connor and Her Critics: A Survey and Evaluation of the Critical Response to the Fiction of Flannery O'Connor." Diss. U of Tennessee, 1972. *DAI* 33 (1972): 2383A-84A.

Claims that little objective criticism has been done on O'Connor's works because most critics either overemphasize or underemphasize the theological themes. Analyzes the body of present criticism (1972) and urges more which does not "resort to the subterfuge of presenting its own ideology." [292 pp.]

1881   LaCoste, André Pierre. "Mercy, Grace, and Sin in the Religious Vision of Graham Greene, Flannery O'Connor, and Walker Percy." Diss. Tulane U, 1982. *DAI* 44 (1983): 166A.

Accuses critics of Graham Greene, Flannery O'Connor, and Walker Percy as having lost--as a result of opposing ideologies--their literary judgement and being too preoccupied with the message and not the medium. Argues that religion is just a part of what these authors employ to serve artistic purposes, and demonstrates the variance in their theological focus regarding salvation. Says O'Connor "dramatizes the intrusion of a divine grace, diagnoses existentialist alienation, and offers `Marcelian intersubjectivity.'" [207 pp.]

1882   Langford, Roberta Brodie. "The Comic Sense of Flannery O'Connor." Diss. Duke U, 1973. *DAI* 35 (1974): 2995A-96A.

Distinguishes between secular and divine comedy, and establishes that O'Connor's work may be classified as among the latter, a comedy of affirmation. Examines her undergraduate satires and attempts to establish the point where her emphasis on divine comedy begins. [253 pp.]

1883   Larsen, William Val. "Manners and Mystery: Community, Economy, and Race in Flannery O'Connor's Fiction." Diss. U of Virginia, 1993. *DAI* 54 (1994): 2580A.

Contends that critics have paid little attention to manners in O'Connor's work. Focuses on broad patterns of familial conflict and "civil modes of social being," as "illuminated by Ferdinand Tönnies's *Gemeinscaft/Gesellschaft* distinction," ideas of the Agrarians, and "Gary Becker's analysis of the economics of discrimination." Suggests that "both the familial and civil modes of being are distorted" in O'Connor's stories; the familial by tribal racism, and the civil by "heartless liberal intellectualism." Examines, as a secondary focus, O'Connor's social ethic. Finds that, despite the claims of some of her critics, "O'Connor is no misanthrope." [244 pp.]

1884   Lauby, Jacqueline. "Of Like Minds: The Shared Perspectives of Flannery O'Connor and the Vanderbilt Agrarians." Diss. Loyola U of Chicago, 1990. *DAI* 51 (1990): 505A.

Discusses O'Connor's part in the "Southern Renaissance," especially her connections with the leaders of the Fugitive and other Agrarian groups. Asserts that both saw violence as a necessary force in religious understanding, and suggests that O'Connor's fiction reflects Agrarian views of the "dehumanization of the South at the hands of Northern Industrialization." [197 pp.]

1885   Lawson, Lewis Allen. "The Grotesque in Recent Southern Fiction." Diss. U of Wisconsin, 1964. *DAI* 25 (1970): 2514.

Refers to O'Connor's remark that "modern life has made grotesques of us all" as evidence that she was conscious of how her work lay within "`a school of the grotesque.'" Suggests that readers often classify her work as such even when not intended, and that her use of the grotesque was "the only mode of illusion" through which she could reach her audience. Notes that for O'Connor, as for Ihab Hassan, "the grotesque magnification of evil, as Dante knew, is a religious act." [370 pp.]

1886   Lazenbatt, William Walter George. "The Female Mind in Modern Southern Fiction: The Treatment and Expression of Female Consciousness in the Work of Flannery O'Connor, Carson McCullers, and Eudora Welty." Diss. Queen's U of Belfast (Ireland), 1984.

Discusses how women characters are portrayed in works by Flannery O'Connor, Carson McCullers, and Eudora Welty. Focuses on how the presentation of their female characters might provide a "further understanding of the nature of womanhood in the region." Contends that O'Connor, McCullers, and Welty view the stereotypical and idealized traditional Southern woman "as a restrictive influence" on their female characters "insofar as it inhibits normal sexuality." Suggests that the use of the traditional image of "demure, submissive [Southern] `ladies,'" lays the foundation for contrasting characters who are "ill-prepared to face the sexual aspects of their initiation into womanhood." Examines each of the authors' major works and outlines how "this essentially female problem" is presented. Finds that all three writers use grotesque characterization, ambiguity, and paradox to show the distorting effects "which this legacy of the past has upon women in the modern South." [347 pp. Cited in *Dissertation Abstracts International* 46 (2):306, 10/1473c.]

1887   Leaver, James Marshall. "The Finite Image: Attitudes Toward Reality in the Works of Flannery O'Connor." Diss. U of Wisconsin, Madison, 1976. *DAI* 37 (1976): 3626A-27A.

Argues that the key to the critical debate as to whether O'Connor's work is sacramental or nihilistic lies in her attitude toward human limitation. Discusses her opposition to Joyce's view of the artist as a superior rebel, hero, and mystic. Elaborates on her criticism of "the Manichaean spirit," "the naturalistic bias," and how she reconciles the finite world with the infinite. [200 pp.]

1888   Lee, Michael John. "Clowns and Captives: Flannery O'Connor's Images of the Self." Diss. U of New Hampshire, 1978. *DAI* 39 (1979): 6763A-64A.

Concentrates on what seems to be the dominant theme in O'Connor's fiction, "that people discover their own identity only when they see themselves or images of themselves reflected in the condition and experience of other human beings." Focuses away from the standard, theological approaches to insist that characters are "redeemed" from their state of being "animalistic, machinistic, or inert" and become fully human only when they unify with other people. [179 pp.]

1889   Leeson, Richard Martin. "The Iconoclastic Art of Flannery O'Connor." Diss. U of Oregon, 1982. *DAI* 43 (1982): 446A.

Discusses O'Connor's style, religious themes, and relationship to her readers. Urges a postmodern appreciation of her fiction which seeks to introduce irrational mystery into the common-sense formulaic world of a fallen, reasonable race. Seeks to undercut standard, formalistic approaches "to what are finally deconstructive, defamiliarizing texts that testify to form." [231 pp.]

1890   Leonard, Joan. "Violence and Community in the Fiction of Flannery
        O'Connor and Muriel Spark." Diss. Emory U, 1984. *DAI* 45 (1984):
        1748A.

        Remarks that Flannery O'Connor and Muriel Spark are "two Catholic
        writers whose view of violence and community reveals the limitations of
        human condition, and the possibilities for a renewed vision of
        community." Calls O'Connor's language "prophetic" and Spark's
        "parabolic" and examines both in view of three positions: reader response
        criticism, literature-theology methodology, and feminist criticism.
        Discusses O'Connor's "A Good Man Is Hard to Find," "A Temple of the
        Holy Ghost," "The Displaced Person," "Everything That Rises Must
        Converge," *Wise Blood* and *The Violent Bear It Away*. [319 pp.]

1891   Liu, Dilin. "Truth and Meaning as Fiction: A Deconstructionist Reading
        of Flannery O'Connor." Diss. Oklahoma State U, 1992. *DAI* 54 (1993):
        933A.

        Uses a deconstructionist approach to focus on signification, "an issue
        O'Connor treats continuously but critics have failed to address." Examines
        the double or paradoxical nature in her work. Concludes that O'Connor's
        writing "works as a deconstruction of many of the logocentric beliefs
        people cherish, [and also] . . . lends itself to the same deconstruction."
        Contends that her fiction effectively exposes such traditional privileged
        beliefs as "people's urge for power and control of both themselves and
        others." Suggests that while decomposing these ideas in her characters,
        O'Connor "sometimes lends herself readily to the same deconstruction by
        affirming . . . her religious vision as transcendental truth." [178 pp.]

1892   Lubin, Alice Mary. "I. Southwell's Religious Complaint Lyric. II. Becky
        Sharp's Role-Playing in *Vanity Fair*. III. Grotesques in the Fictions of
        Flannery O'Connor." Diss. Rutgers U, New Brunswick, 1973. *DAI* 34
        (1973): 2569A.

        The third part of three unrelated studies that comprise this work
        concentrates on the definition and O'Connor's use of the term "grotesque"
        in "Revelation," "The Life You Save May Be Your Own," "The Displaced
        Person," and "Parker's Back." [142 pp.]

1893   Lucas, James Lavard. "The Religious Dimension of Twentieth- Century
        British and American Literature: A Textbook in the Analysis of Types."
        Diss. Northern Illinois U, 1980. *DAI* 41 (1980): 2103A-04A.

Argues that much of the American and British literature of the 20th century "began in repudiation of religious orthodoxy" and--except for the works of T.S. Eliot, W.H. Auden, Graham Greene and Flannery O'Connor--"descended into nihilism." Defines what is meant by "religious," traces Western literature as it developed from theocentrism to anthropocentrism, and describes the resulting schools which emerged. Discusses the work of a variety of writers, including the "mystical humanists": William Butler Yeats, James Joyce, D.H. Lawrence, Eugene O'Neill, and Dylan Thomas; the "social humanists": George Bernard Shaw, Archibald MacLeish, William Faulkner, Ernest Hemingway, and Saul Bellow; the "nihilists": Robinson Jeffers and Samuel Beckett; and those representing Roman Catholic orthodoxy: Graham Greene and Flannery O'Connor. [420 pp.]

1894   Ludwig, Dale Leslie. "Controlled Distance: Internal Character Presentation in Flannery O'Connor's Short Stories." Diss. U of Illinois at Urbana-Champaign, 1988. *DAI* 50 (1989): 302A.

Studies the nature and function of narrative distance seen in O'Connor's stories. Admires her consistency of design and purpose, noting that such is "rarely found in modern literature." Discusses O'Connor's use of third-person narration, her preference for single-character focus, and her "overwhelming consistent, rhetorical thrust." Argues that O'Connor's combination of opposing, narrative techniques (figural and authorial modes of presentation), hold several tensions in balance. Illustrates how narrative fiction can be explored through oral performance. [428 pp.]

1895   MacDonald, Sara Jane. "The Aesthetics of Grace in Flannery O'Connor and Graham Greene." Diss. U of Illinois at Urbana-Champaign, 1972. *DAI* 33 (1973): 5734A.

Discusses critical reaction to the Christian aspects of Greene's and O'Connor's work. Concentrates on why and how each author uses irony. Employs Northrop Frye's terminology to discuss the process of grace in their fictional worlds. [266 pp.]

1896   Macys, Valerie Denise. "Behind the Mask: Flannery O'Connor and the Discomforts of Home." Diss. U of Maryland, 1992. *DAI* 54 (1993): 178A.

Asserts that traditional biographical portraits of Flannery O'Connor are inaccurate because they are based upon O'Connor's public posturing. Attempts to "explore the woman behind the mask," by focusing on O'Connor's life "under her mother's often tyrannical supervision and care," and examine how her suffering, anger, and pain, influenced her art. Traces Regina Cline O'Connor's heritage and "Southern belle image," and analyzes "The Enduring Chill," (describing it as "a troubling story," with "a terrifying depiction of human longing.") Suggests that O'Connor's protagonist conveys "a suffering she seldom dared to intimate in private life." [178 pp.]

1897   Magee, Rosemary McCausland. "'Ambassador of God': The Preacher in Twentieth-Century Southern Fiction." Diss. Emory U, 1982. *DAI* 43 (1982): 1973A.

Suggests that Southern literature serves to narrate the transition of the South from a traditional society to a modern one. Describes the impact that such changes have had upon the society and its citizens. Asserts that the "preacher" in Southern fiction often embodies the struggle within this movement. Examines preacher figures in Southern fiction who illustrate responses to modernity: traditional, rural preachers who affirm those within the community; isolated prophets of God who stand apart and pronounce judgement; and the seminary-trained minister concerned with the vocation of discovering and creating meaning for both himself and his congregation. Examines works by Flannery O'Connor (*Wise Blood*), Robert Penn Warren, Eudora Welty, William Faulkner, William Styron, and Carson McCullers. [198 pp.]

1898   Magistrale, Anthony Samuel. "The Quest for Identity in Modern Southern Fiction: Faulkner, Wright, O'Connor, Warren." Diss. U of Pittsburgh, 1981. *DAI* 42 (1981): 4001A-02A.

Discusses how each of four writers, William Faulkner, Richard Wright, Flannery O'Connor, and Robert Penn Warren, rejects the past due to perceptions of what evil it contained, and how each offers solutions to historical problems. Links Faulkner with Wright, and O'Connor with Warren, the latter comparison based primarily on the two authors' similar view: that knowledge of sin is the beginning of identity. [358 pp.]

1899   Mahoney, Margaret Ellen. "Flannery O'Connor and Saul Bellow: Two American Moralists." Diss. U of Delaware, 1995. *DAI* 56 (1996): 3127A.

Focuses on Bellow's *The Dean's December* and *More Die of Heartbreak* and O'Connor's short fiction to examine the "shared moral perspective" of these authors. Notes "striking similarities in their use of the literary strategies of regionalism, marginalized characters, and the comic mode." Discusses how O'Connor "uses the rural South to show family and intergenerational problems, poverty, and racial issues." Sees her characters as "obsessed by religious convictions and practices, [who] frequently encounter God's grace in extraordinary events, and are constantly searching for redemption." Reports that both O'Connor and Bellow "use the comic mode as a strategy to convey their serious moral intent." Regards O'Connor's humor as "darker and more didactic that Bellow's" and "characterized by the grotesque, by exaggeration of physical deformity, and by the juxtaposition of the genteel and the vernacular." [230 pp.]

1900 Mallon, Anne Marie G. "Mystic Quest in Flannery O'Connor's Fiction." Diss. U of Notre Dame, 1981. *DAI* 41 (1981): 4714A.

Employs the word "mystical" as a catchword for O'Connor's theme of "revelation," and notes its relevance to structure, themes, and imagery in her work. Traces her reading of mysticism--including Evelyn Underhill and Thomas Merton--and suggests that O'Connor used their ideas as models for the journey motif seen in her fiction. Contends that characters such as Hazel Motes, Francis Marion Tarwater and others are on a quest to find a "home" in the will of God. States that, along the way, these characters' hearts, minds, and souls are converted through a demanding process of purgation similar to that described in Underhill's "delineation of the 'Mystic Way.'" Explores in O'Connor's works: the motif of seeing, the imagery of light and darkness, themes of placement and displacement, imagery based on food and hunger, and dichotomies seen between her depiction of freakish and so-called normal individuals. [210 pp.]

1901 Mannis, Andrea. "These Great Christian Houses: The Ethos of Suffering in Malamud, O'Connor, and Bellow." Diss. U of Nebraska, 1996. *DAI* 57.11 (1997): 4740-41A.

Examines "the ethos of suffering" in Bernard Malamud's *The Assistant*, Flannery O'Connor's "Parker's Back," and Saul Bellow's *Herzog*. Contends that these works "present characters who are searchers [and] dreamers . . . obsessed with their desires and driven, at times, by forces unknown to themselves." Sees each of the central characters as "in the grip of a compulsion to find a higher knowledge, a new way of living." Concludes that "the spiritual journey of each character illustrates a post-modern quest for (and a questioning of) faith and survival."

1902 Marks, Margaret Louise. "Flannery O'Connor's American Models: Her Work in Relation to that of Hawthorne, James, Faulkner and West." Diss. Duke U, 1977. *DAI* 38 (1978): 4830A.

Explains how the work of Nathaniel Hawthorne, Henry James, William Faulkner, and Nathanael West served as models for O'Connor's fiction. Argues that, for O'Connor, the term "mystery" called up things that as a committed Catholic she believed in, which a secular audience did not. Reflecting O'Connor's own assertion classifies her fiction as Romance and establishes similarities: O'Connor's displaced-person character type with Henry James; her Southern historical sense with William Faulkner; and her use of the grotesque with Nathanael West. [213 pp.]

1903   Martin, Carter Williams. "The Convergence of Actualities: Themes in the Fiction of Flannery O'Connor." Diss. Vanderbilt U, 1967. *DA* 28 (1968): 4180A-81A.

Discusses the extent to which O'Connor's fiction embodies Christian themes of redemption and grace, and the degree to which her narrative technique is determined by those themes. Elaborates on the elements of grotesqueries, humor, satire, and irony in her work. [381 pp.]

1904   Martin, Karl Edward. "The Ethical Implications of Flannery O'Connor's `Prophetic Imagination.'" Diss. U of Minnesota, 1991. *DAI* 52 (1991): 972A.

Explores the ethical implications of Flannery O'Connor's prophetic vision for the modern world. Discusses her interest in and concern for the "role of the prophet." Relies upon Walter Brueggemann's studies, including his work, *The Prophetic Imagination*, as a framework with which to examine O'Connor's work. Concludes that her fiction is "consistent with the prophetic paradigm identified by Brueggemann," because her characters are repeatedly "shaken by violence and amazed to discover new ethical possibilities revealed by God." [279 pp.]

1905   Matchie, Thomas Frederick. "The Mythical Flannery O'Connor: A Psycho-Mythic Study of *A Good Man Is Hard to Find*." Diss. U of Wisconsin, Madison, 1974. *DAI* 36 (1975): 277A-78A.

Examines each of the ten stories in *A Good Man is Hard to Find*. Focuses on elements that are mythic, both in the "larger structure and in limited detail." Considers parallels between O'Connor's stories and mythic works of literature, archetypal patterns portrayed in the stories, and qualities of O'Connor's prose "which reinforce the mythic parallels and support the archetype." [376 pp.]

1906   Mathews, Marsha Caddell. "Death and Humor in the Fifties: The Ignition of Barth, Heller, Nabokov, O'Connor, Salinger, and Vonnegut." Diss. Florida State U, 1987. *DAI* 48 (1988): 1770A.

Contends that themes of death and humor constitute a major "movement" in contemporary American literature. Defines the "death and humor movement," and explores "death anxiety" as a fear in fifties novels. Discusses how this fear serves as "a primary structural device." Examines one novel of each author (*The Violent Bear It Away*, by O'Connor). Notes how death anxiety "often results in effacement of the individual" and shows how the protagonist in each of the novels discussed is "unquelled by institutions such as the law." [166 pp.]

1907   May, Elizabeth V. "Atomic Idioms: Authority, Identity, and Language in Novels by Mailer, O'Connor, Purdy, and Agee." Diss. Yale U, 1998. *DAI* 60.5 (1999): 1561A.

Examines the "American literary response to the post-atomic, post-Holocaust environment" found in four post-war novels: Norman Mailer's *Barbary Shore*; Flannery O'Connor's *The Violent Bear It Away*; James Purdy's *The Nephew*; and James Agee's *A Death in the Family*. Focuses on "the void created by the absence or distortion of putative heroes, reflecting a shared concern about notions of individual, artistic and heroic identity." Discusses whether "any literary act is sufficient to the task of representing the horror of the postwar world" and the "pervasive critical discomfort with the postwar novel as itself evidence of the difficulty of approaching imaginatively and intellectually the subject of human extinction." Notes that "paradoxically, the anxiety stirred by the contemporary climate was a creative force, generating works which illuminate the issues of moral, religious and cultural authority that dominated the postwar years." Concludes that, at least for Purdy and O'Connor, "the image of the bomb was a redemptive one, signaling elements of sublimity in an age otherwise defined by repression and scientific-rational thought." [195 pp.]

1908   May, John Richard. "Apocalypse in the American Novel." Diss. Emory U, 1971. *DAI* 32 (1972): 4009A-10A.

Suggests that the theological literary critic must be familiar "with the historical language of eschatology." Utilizes a typology of eschatology--based upon images of apocalypse--to analyze variations and innovations on the traditional apocalypse by representative American authors. Discusses apocalyptic symbolism and how "primitive religion repeats the ritual return to chaos to maintain contact with reality," while "fulfillment in Judaeo-Christian apocalypse supports a mood of genuine hope." Discusses examples from: Nathaniel Hawthorne's *The Blithedale Romance*; Nathanael West's *Miss Lonelyhearts*; William Faulkner's *As I Lay Dying*; James Baldwin's *Go Tell It On the Mountain*; Herman Melville's *The Confidence Man*; Richard Wright's *Native Son*; John Barth's *The End of the Road*; Thomas Pynchon's *The Crying of Lot 49*; Kurt Vonnegutt, Jr.'s *Cat's Cradle*; Ralph Ellison's *Invisible Man*; and O'Connor's *The Violent Bear It Away*. [201 pp.]

1909   Mayer, David Robert. "The Hermaphrodite and the Host: Incarnation as Vision and Method in the Fiction of Flannery O'Connor." Diss. U of Maryland, 1973. *DAI* 34 (1973): 3415A-16A.

Argues that O'Connor's theology gave her a way of "seeing" which she illuminated by use of her "mystery through manners" technique. Discusses her stories and novels separately, focusing on their Christian content. [189 pp.]

1910   McAllister, Jean Smith. "The End of Self: Struggles Toward Transcendence in the Fiction of Charles Williams, Flannery O'Connor, and Graham Greene." Diss. U of Washington, 1991. *DAI* 52 (1991): 1744A.

Proposes that the works of Charles Williams, Flannery O'Connor, and Graham Greene all focus on the self and its struggle for identity. Declares that all three "agree that identity is found only upon loss of self combined with an intimate union with the *other*." Suggests that each is interested in the shocks of life which allow for growth through repentance and the end of self and self-centered drives. Maintains that choice is the essential factor in determining whether a character will be able to unite with the "transcendent." Whether the transcendent be the "Omnipotence of Williams, the Mystery of O'Connor, or Greene's elusive Love, [they all] ... come to the end of themselves in that union." [228 pp.]

1911   McClain, Laurence Lee. "The Rhetoric of Regional Identity: Regional Fiction and the Politics of American Literary History." Diss. U of Texas at Austin, 1993. *DAI* 54 (1994): 3033A.

Identifies and examines theoretical issues and questions related to the history of regional American literature. Discusses Flannery O'Connor's *Wise Blood*, Ellen Glasgow's *Barren Ground*, Rolando Hinojosa's *The Valley*, and Louise Erdrich's *Love Medicine*. States that an "examination of these `regional' writings focuses a discussion of what texts might constitute a regional literary counter-tradition (or counter-traditions) and what critical problems they raise." Insists that regional literature must be discussed within the framework of "not only the politics of American literary history, but [within] the contours of literary theory as well." Suggests that while the very notion of what comprises America's national literature may be at stake, "many critics now concede the ways in which the intersections of race, class, and gender must inform the reshaping of the American canon, [and] little work has been done concerning the various regional traditions that often bridge and underpin those intersections." [287 pp.]

1912   McCullagh, James Charles. "Aesthetics and the Religious Mind: François Mauriac, Graham Greene, and Flannery O'Connor." Diss. Lehigh U, 1975. *DAI* 35 (1975): 7316A.

Examines Mauriac's *A Kiss for the Leper*, *Genitrix*, and *The Desert of Love*; Greene's *Brighton Rock*, *The Power and the Glory*, and *The Heart of the Matter*; and O'Connor's *Wise Blood* and *The Violent Bear It Away* to ascertain the relationship between religious elements and fictional techniques. Says Mauriac dramatizes the "infantile, negative, and non-symbolic attributes of Christianity," while Greene eventually repudiated that approach and moves toward O'Connor, who "represents a culmination in attempts by Catholic writers to wed religious ideas to modern secular themes." [281 pp.]

1913   McLevie, Elaine Marianne. "The Hero in the Post World War II Novel: Some Differences of Concept in the Works of English and American Novelists." Diss. Michigan State U, 1970. *DAI* 32 (1971): 391-92A.

Investigates how the conceptual "hero" of the post-World War II English novel differs from that of its American counterpart. Compares works by three English authors to those of three Americans, drawing specific contrasts between O'Connor and Graham Greene. Also examines works by: Alan Sillitoe, Lawrence Durrell, Nelson Algren, and Paul Bowles. Compares characteristics and finds differences "which similarities of language and of background culture tend to mask." [229 pp.]

1914   McMillan, Peter Aidan James. "*Illuminations*: Editing a Magazine of Contemporary Writing." Diss. U of South Carolina, 1985. *DAI* 46 (1986): 3716A.

Reprints the first four issues of *Illuminations*, a magazine designed to promote new writers. Includes an introduction with a brief history of the magazine and its editorial principles, and names a wide variety of noted authors published in it, including Flannery O'Connor. [189 pp.]

1915   McMullen, Joanne. "Writing Against God: Language and Flannery O'Connor's Literature." Diss. U of Nebraska, Lincoln, 1991. *DAI* 52 (1991): 2128A.

Argues that O'Connor's readers have a wide variety of opinions regarding the impact of her fictional message because of her linguistic choices. Suggests that her sentence structure, verb usage, and parts of speech move her work out of her own control and produce a message in conflict with the one she intended. Declares that, as she attempts to transcend time and move characters into the "eternal, heavenly now," O'Connor's "grammatical negation, passivity, and intransitivity sink . . . characters in inertia." Contends that O'Connor's imagery, symbolism, and thematic structures often fail to provide insight into her Catholic vision, and tend to confuse readers about the redemptive fates of her characters. Concludes that despite inconsistencies, O'Connor's language choices demonstrate not only her "extraordinary linguistic facility," but her "ability to manipulate doctrine through language choices as well." Suggests that it is this last trait which emerges "as the strength that will most heighten her status as an artist." [229 pp.]

1916   McShane, Zita M. "Functions of the Grotesque in Twentieth-Century American Fiction." Diss. Case Western Reserve U, 1983. *DAI* 44 (1984): 2474A.

Traces the history, development, and use of the grotesque mode in American Literature, and describes how it provides a tension between humor and terror for the reader. Points out modern uses and applies the grotesque as an interpretive tool in readings of works by six modern writers: Flannery O'Connor, Walker Percy, William Faulkner, John Irving, Nathanael West, and Jerzy Kosinski. Analyzes elements of the grotesque in works by these authors and applies analytical techniques to better understand how they "use it as a literary category offering structure to an entire work." [218 pp.]

1917   McSharry, Kathleen Jeanne. "Interracial Relations and Identity Constructions in Post-World War II American Literature." Diss. U of Wisconsin - Madison, 1994. *DAI* 55 (1995): 3191A.

Focuses on interracial relations in the works of Ralph Ellison, Saul Bellow, Flannery O'Connor, Gary Snyder, and Lucille Clifton. Finds that

Ellison, Bellow, and O'Connor "emphasize universal values in explaining human identity and community." Remarks that each develops "theories of American culture or identity that are based on or are at least related to race." Situates O'Connor's stories "within white Southern discourse on the South and segregation in the first half of the twentieth century." [217 pp.]

1918   Mehl, Duane Paul. "Spiritual Reality in the Works of Flannery O'Connor." Diss. Saint Louis U, 1974. *DAI* 36 (1975): 3716A.

Analyzes O'Connor's ability to unite natural and supernatural realities in credible settings, characterizations, and plots. Uses her essays and speeches to explore her self-proclaimed theology and its kinship to Thomism. Discusses the difficulties of making concrete and modern the theology of Saint Thomas Aquinas, and concludes that O'Connor's failure to do so produced "heretical" works, some of which are the most compelling "Absurdist" stories of the twentieth-century. [312 pp.]

1919   Mengert, George King. "The Quest for Wholeness in Three Modern Writers." Diss. Emory U, 1978. *DAI* 40 (1979): 257-58A.

Examines images and themes found in the fiction of Eudora Welty, Carson McCullers, and Flannery O'Connor who serve as representatives of the modern writer's concern with the problem of "separateness." Contends that the work of all three writers "is aligned to a journey, a journey which begins with the discovery of separateness and goes on to explore the possibilities for conquering that separateness." Asserts that while each author presents a different kind of separateness, they all imply that "man is cut off from everything but himself and that he has a desperate need to become part of something that is larger and more permanent." Declares that O'Connor perceived humanity's hunger for self-completion and suggested that the existence of this hunger was evidence of our supernatural origins. Concludes that O'Connor's work reflects her conviction that only a union with God can satisfy the hunger which is offered through God's grace. [180 pp.]

1920   Mohr, Eric Simpson. "Mystery and the Fate of Grace: Flannery O'Connor's Ironic Use of the Naturalistic Tradition." Diss. Indiana U of Pennsylvania, 1993. *DAI* 54 (1994): 4094A.

Notes that while some scholars have raised the issue of the presence of literary naturalism in O'Connor's work, it has been only briefly discussed and not resolved. Attempts to address this issue by accounting "for the apparent dichotomy existing between the naturalistic and the romance traditions" in O'Connor's work. Sets out to persuade readers that the naturalistic tradition "is at least as important as the older romance tradition, primarily because of how it encourages an interesting creative dialectic in the esthetic of O'Connor's fiction." Finds that by "applying this dialectic, O'Connor ironically uses literary naturalism to introduce the fate of grace in a mysteriously determined environment." [228 pp.]

1921   Montgomery, Elizabeth Luckett McGowan. "The Ritual of Initiation in Flannery O'Connor's Short Fiction." Diss. U of Mississippi, 1990. *DAI* 51 (1991): 3408A.

Declares that O'Connor was preoccupied with the Communion of Saints, the salvific action of grace, the theological concept of free will, and the value of purgative and expiatory suffering. Contends that these preoccupations account "for a pattern which appears in seventeen of her thirty-one short stories and affects twenty-six of the characters she created." Suggests that an encounter with salvific grace in a shocking or violent manner places a character in a position where he or she must choose to accept or deliberately reject it. Contends that the work of anthropologist Victor Turner, and ethnographer and folklorist Arnold van Gennup, may offer insights into understanding O'Connor's use of rites of passage in her short fiction. [179 pp.]

1921a   Moore, Bryan Lee. "Ecocentric Personification in American Nature Writing." Diss. Texas Christian U, 1996. *DAI* 57 (1997): 4741A.

Explores ways certain American writers utilize personification to call "for adherence to an ecocentric view of the world" and/or undermine "the anthropocentricity that legitimates the arguably excessive human industrialization of wilderness." Discusses nature writers "who employ the device frequently . . . to argue that living things and natural objects possess an intrinsic value similar to that of humans." [243 pp.]

1922   Moore, Donald Lee. "The Religious Sonnet Cycle in England, 1585-1600. Limitations in the Fiction of Flannery O'Connor? W.H. Auden's Twentieth-Century Pattern for Elegy." Diss. Rutgers U, New Brunswick, 1977. *DAI* 38 (1978): 6745A.

Suggests, in the second part of these three unrelated studies, that Flannery O'Connor's best work transcends mere theological interpretation. Argues that the universal situations in her stories such as "Judgement Day," "The Enduring Chill," and "Parker's Back" are all central themes, despite the "theological impositions" thrust upon such experience. States that the "limitations" of the works disappear when one fully and imaginatively encounters them. [192 pp.]

1923   Moran, Annette Jean. "The Church and the Fiction Writer: The Fiction of Flannery O'Connor and the *corpus Christi mysticum* ecclesiology." Diss. Graduate Theological Union, 1994. *DAI* 55 (1995): 1297A.

Attempts "to engage the reader in the complexity of the Catholicism from which O'Connor's fiction emerged." Uses an interdisciplinary study to suggest that some of O'Connor's stories may serve as a "reflection on the theology of the mystical body of Christ." Discusses twentieth-century Catholic ecclesiology and the mystical body theology in Karl Adam and Romano Guardini, and explores O'Connor's contact with this theology through the work of Léon Bloy. Contends that Bloy's influence is seen in *Wise Blood* and "A Stroke of Good Fortune," and that some of the stories from *A Good Man Is Hard to Find* give access to the tradition of the *corpus Christi mysticum*. Looks at "Parker's Back" and sees it "as illuminating for the Catholic renewal that precipitated Vatican II," then considers O'Connor's writings within the changed context after Vatican II. Concludes that her fiction engages both the *societas perfecta* and the *corpus Christi mysticum*, "which accounts to a degree for the complicated texture of the Catholic theology" found in her fiction. [309 pp.]

1924   Morefield, Kenneth Robert. "Why Christian Fiction?: Expressing Universal Truth in a Relative World." Diss. Northern Illinois U, 1998. *DAI* 59 (1998): 1567A.

Examines works by Christian authors George MacDonald, C.S. Lewis, Graham Greene, and Flannery O'Connor to discover how their narrative techniques "ensure a theological interpretation of their works." Discusses O'Connor along with Greene in the fourth chapter, focusing on how they "use epitexts, such as lectures and autobiographies, to advance specific interpretations of their own work." Contends that "as culture becomes more secular, Christian authors have increasingly turned to fiction to gain a wider audience," then offers, in the concluding chapter, his opinion as to whether or not these authors have done so successfully.

1925   Morton, Mary Lambert. "With Ground Teeth: A Study of Flannery O'Connor's Women." Diss. Louisiana State U, 1980. *DAI* 41 (1981): 3583A-84A.

Notes that the majority of O'Connor's fiction features women in leading roles or prominent supporting roles. Examines *Wise Blood* and several of her short stories to discuss how they reflect O'Connor's "special vision of comedy and horror as two sides of the same coin." Contends that while O'Connor was certainly not unique "in mixing humor and horror," she was so adept "that some critics, mired in traditional separations of tragedy and comedy," objected to her stories. Uses William F. Lynch's discussion of irony and comedy to overcome resistance in analyzing the place of women in her fictional world. Points out that the traditional role of Southern women is unsentimentalized and that O'Connor's leading female characters are often left shattered by the circumstances they attempt to overcome. Says O'Connor's women "possess imaginations inclined to reduce all of reality to the simplest, common optic," and suggests that their rigidity generates both the comedy and terror of her stories. [166 pp.]

1926   Muller, Gilbert Henry. "Flannery O'Connor and the Catholic Grotesque." Diss. Stanford U, 1967. *DA* 28 (1968): 3193A.

Argues that O'Connor is "one of the few writers of contemporary fiction to effectively integrate theology and the creative experience." Contends that her use of the grotesque is an element of her realism. Suggests her "true country" is not that of her regionalism, but that of her visionary powers of perception, which make both "religious and secular experience more meaningful." Maintains that O'Connor's principal concerns are with suffering, sin, evil, and disorder. [343 pp.]

1927   Munson, Barbara Faye. "Gates of Horn, Gates of Ivory: The Dream Motif in the Works of Elizabeth Bishop and Flannery O'Connor." Diss. U of Southwestern Louisiana, 1995. *DAI* 56 (1995): 4775A.

Alleges that "the pervasive dream motif" in Elizabeth Bishop's poetry and Flannery O'Connor's short fiction, places their work within the "Dream Vision literary tradition." Contends that "the liminal dream world of Bishop's personae and O'Connor's characters allows each writer to explore deeply felt philosophical and personal concerns without appearing confessional or didactic." Discusses a variety of related topics, including: the dreamscapes created by each writer (e.g. O'Connor's sun imagery); how both employ similar body imagery in their characters' dreams (e.g. O'Connor's "images of division and violence [which] reflect her Catholic belief that man can be whole only in Christ"); how O'Connor and Bishop each "considers the thematic treatment of home and displacement" (e.g. home, for O'Connor, "extends anagogically to refer to the after-life since Christians are displaced on earth from their true, eternal home"); and closes with a discussion of these two writers' "artistic vision." Finds that in O'Connor's stories, "dreams often foreshadow the final epiphanic plot resolution." [131 pp.]

1928   Mutkoski, Barbara Eileen. "The Teilhard Milieu: Pierre Teilhard de
        Chardin's Influence on Flannery O'Connor's Fiction." Diss. Fordham U,
        1973. *DAI* 34 (1974): 5196A.

        Discusses correlations between specific works of Teilhard de Chardin
        (those which O'Connor had reviewed or had mentioned in letters as
        having had a profound influence on her), and O'Connor's later works.
        Gleans illuminating information from the reviews, letters, and
        documented personal expressions concerning her fascination with
        Teilhard de Chardin. [237 pp.]

1929   Navarro, Mary Louise. "Departures." Diss. Carnegie-Mellon U, 1983.
        DAI 44 (1983): 481A-82A.

        A collection of five, original short stories, one of which, "The Tattoo,"
        refers to "Parker's Back." In this story, the protagonist, "an affluent,
        middle-aged mother," dissatisfied with her role in life, decides to have
        herself tattooed after reading O'Connor's story. [154 pp.]

1930   Newburger, Laurie Gurney. "Holy Violence: The Puritan Influence on
        Flannery O'Connor." Diss. Fordham U, 1995. *DAI* 56 (1995): 1780A.

        Argues that O'Connor's "disturbing view of conversion is influenced by
        a powerful, historical, and distinctly American cultural influence: the
        Puritans." Outlines how grace descends upon her flawed characters,
        "creating the intense emotional, physical, and spiritual upheavals
        necessary for conversion" and observes how her God--a God of wrath and
        vengeance instead of solace and compassion--suggests the Puritan
        perspective. Insists that this premise best explains her uses of extreme
        violence and why her characters must suffer in order to become part of the
        "new elect." [181 pp.]

1930a   Newman, Georgia A. "A `Contrary Kinship': The Correspondence of
        Flannery O'Connor and Maryat Lee, Early Years--1957-1959." Diss. U of
        South Florida, 1999.

        Reports that, among the most significant of O'Connor's correspondence,
        are the 162 letters she wrote to New York playwright, Maryat Lee. Offers
        an overview of the entire correspondence and provides biographical
        material on each writer. Proposes that the first meeting between Lee and
        O'Connor in December 1956, and the first two letters between them,
        written in January, 1957, "reflect, in microcosm, the friendship and
        correspondence as a whole." Analyzes and discusses letters exchanged

January, 1957 to December, 1959 and suggests that they not only "reflect the political and social milieu of the time," but their developing friendship as well. Refers to Lee's private journals and O'Connor's essays, lectures and other correspondence to augment the analysis. Comments that although Lee and O'Connor were "mirror opposites in many respects," they "were influenced by each other both personally and professionally." [From abstract provided by the author].

1931   Nisly, L. Lamar. "Portraying Religious Mystery in the Fiction of Malamud, Percy, Ozick, and O'Connor." Diss. U of Delaware, 1996. *DAI* 58 (1997): 168A.

Shows that "Jewish and Catholic practices of giving structure to mystery are mirrored" in how Bernard Malamud, Walker Percy, Cynthia Ozick, and Flannery O'Connor use "narrative forms that lead to the non-rational." Links Malamud with Percy and Ozick with O'Connor "because the two pairs show a similarity in their narrative portrayals of religious mystery." In the chapters focusing on O'Connor and Ozick, remarks that "these authors use the fantastic and the grotesque to transcend traditional, rational forms of fiction--and thus evoke the numinous." Concludes that the fiction of these two authors, "in its break with reason and [use of] jarring images, offers readers a physical approach to a non-rational experience." [248 pp.]

1932   Nisly, Paul Wayne. "Flannery O'Connor and the Gothic Impulse." Diss. U of Kansas, 1974. *DAI* 36 (1975): 892A-93A.

Rejects psychoanalysis, sociological regionalistic interpretation, and theological/humanistic analysis in favor of trying to understand O'Connor's works within the Gothic tradition. Defends Gothic literature by contending that it is not "lacking the high seriousness essential to significant literature," an accusation commonly applied to the genre. Defines the type by its use in Walpole's *The Castle of Otranto*, and discusses O'Connor's particular use in both her novels and some of her stories. [179 pp.]

1933   Oliver, Bill. "The Image of the Heart of Things: Contemporary American Fiction and the Catholic Novelist." Diss. U of Virginia, 1983. *DAI* 45 (1985): 2528A.

States that the Catholic imagination sees a spiritual dimension and significance which counters the idea of the world as a "deadly entrapment." Argues that J.F. Powers, Flannery O'Connor, and Walker

Percy each struggled to find artistic resolution to tensions created by personal faith in the midst of a secular audience. Holds Percy in higher esteem than the other two, suggesting that by retaining "a sacramentalist view of reality," while the others succumb to a secular dominance, he accomplishes what the others do not. [236 pp.]

1934   Olson, Barbara Kruse. "'Writing Like God' in the Twentieth Century: Theological Implications of Omniscient Narration in the Fiction of Ernest Hemingway and Virginia Woolf." Diss. Indiana U, 1991. *DAI* 52 (1992): 3924A.

Discusses various authors' styles of omniscience and the relationship of those styles to their own or their cultures' concepts of God. Focuses on Ernest Hemingway and Virginia Woolf, but also refers to the perspectives of Jean-Paul Sartre, Roland Barthes, Dorothy Sayers, Meir Sternberg, John Fowles, Ronald Sukenick, Flannery O'Connor, Graham Greene, and Muriel Spark. Contends that Fowles, Sukenick and other postmodern writers "have aimed their narrational experiments in omniscience at subverting what Fowles has called the 'Godgame' this device requires." Suggests, however, that others, such as O'Connor, Greene and Spark, "have predictably relied on the device as one consonant with their own theological assumptions." [225 pp.]

1935   Olson, Charles J. "The Dragon by the Road: An Archetypal Approach to the Fiction of Flannery O'Connor." Diss. U of New Mexico, 1975. *DAI* 36 (1975): 3698A.

Discusses O'Connor's works in light of their archetypal patterns. Focuses on how and where O'Connor attempts to fuse mystery and manners, and how and why O'Connor becomes archetypal. Notes reaction to her fiction in terms of archetypal patterns. [177 pp.]

1936   Orvell, Miles David. "An Incarnational Art: The Fiction of Flannery O'Connor." Diss. Harvard U, 1970.

Places O'Connor in the literary traditions that helped to mold and shape her artistry, and attempts to define her "distinguishing qualities." Seeks to discover what makes O'Connor's stories "run so well" through discussion of *Wise Blood, The Violent Bear It Away*, and those stories which Orvell considers O'Connor's "best, and which illustrate the diversity of the fiction," specifically: "A Good Man Is Hard to Find," "The Life You Save May Be Your Own," "Good Country People," "The Displaced Person," "The Artificial Nigger," "The Comforts of Home," "Parker's Back,"

"Judgement Day," and "The Geranium." Contends that O'Connor's own writings on fiction and the problems she encountered as a Southern Catholic writer "reinforce what the fiction itself reveals: [that] to a marked degree, she knew what she was doing." [353 pp. Published in 1972 as: *Invisible Parade: The Fiction of Flannery O'Connor* (Philadelphia: Temple UP); and reprinted in 1991 with a new preface as *Flannery O'Connor: An Introduction* (Jackson: UP of Mississippi). Cited in *Comprehensive Dissertation Index 1861-1972: Author Index Md-Sc* 36 (1973): 397.]

1937   O'Shea, José Roberto Basto. "*Wise Blood* as *Sangue Sábio*: A Literary Translation into Brazilian Portuguese." [Includes Portuguese text.] Diss. U of North Carolina at Chapel Hill, 1989. *DAI* 51 (1990): 2027A.

A study of translation theory applied to the translation of O'Connor's *Wise Blood* into Brazilian Portuguese. Asserts that the last revolution in translation theory was with John Dryden's preface to *Ovid's Epistles* (1680). Further, that Dryden's theory of "paraphrase" is still the answer to the problem of literary versus literal translation. Describes aspects of O'Connor's regionalism which present specific challenges for the translator. [329 pp.]

1938   Padgett, Thomas Eugene Jr. "The Irony in Flannery O'Connor's Fiction." Diss. U of Missouri, Columbia, 1972. *DAI* 33 (1973): 5192A.

Contends that O'Connor's fiction is significant for its moral vision and its brilliant humor. Discusses her use of irony, and the way she employs each specific type of irony: denotative and referential, connotative, situational, dramatic, and structural. [230 pp.]

1939   Palms, Rosemary Helen Grebin. "The Double Motif in Literature: From Origins to an Examination of Three Modern American Novels." Diss. U of Texas, Austin, 1971. *DAI* 33 (1972): 321A.

Examines and uses Howard Nemerov's theory that identity is the general theme of short novels, "expressed by means of dependency or attachment between A and B which must be dissolved in order that salvation be achieved." Traces the history of the double motif in folklore and literature, and discusses the double force (good and evil) warring over Tarwater's soul in *The Violent Bear It Away*. Also discusses John Knowles's *A Separate Peace* and Ralph Ellison's *Invisible Man*. [191 pp.]

1940   Patterson, Kathleen Anne. "Representations of Disability in Mid-Twentieth Century Southern Fiction: From Metaphor to Social Construction." Diss. U of California, Santa Barbara, 1997. *DAI* 58.12 (1998): 4655A.

Proposes "a sociopolitical approach to representations of disability" in selected works by Carson McCullers, Flannery O'Connor, and Harper Lee. Contends that this approach is needed because of the "limits of the conventional literary approaches to representations of disability." Investigates "how disability functions in the maintenance of identities characters attribute to others as well as the identities they assert for themselves." Explores this theme in McCullers's *The Heart Is a Lonely Hunter*, Lee's *To Kill a Mockingbird*, and O'Connor's "The Lame Shall Enter First," "The Life You Save May Be Your Own," and "Good Country People."

1941   Paulson, Suzanne Morrow. "Flannery O'Connor's Divided Vision: Apocalypse of Self, Resurrection of the Double." Diss. U of Minnesota, 1984. *DAI* 45 (1984): 1399A.

Discusses all aspects of "doubling" in O'Connor's works. Uses biographical information to justify the abundance of the motif in her fiction: O'Connor's intellect and disease; her faith and the death of her father; her mother's desire for her to be a Southern belle versus her own wish to be "like Socrates"; and other biographical aspects which may have predisposed her to "doubling." Insists that Sigmund Freud, American Romance writers, existentialism, New Criticism, Teilhard de Chardin, and Sören Kierkegaard all played a role in O'Connor's use of the doubling motif in her fiction. [351 pp.]

1942   Perunilam, Thomas Varkey. "Elements of Contemporary American Culture as Reflected in Selected Works of American Literature, 1960-1974." Diss. Rutgers U, New Brunswick, 1981. *DAI* 43 (1982): 1069A.

Points out inadequacies of the American Literature curriculum offered by the University of Kerala (South India) and offers the formulation of a new course on contemporary American literature. Includes O'Connor's story "Everything That Rises Must Converge" among the selections. [372 pp.]

1943   Piper, Wendy. "Romance or Reason: Questions of Mimesis and Methodology in Hawthorne, O'Connor, and Gadamer." Diss. State U of New York at Binghamton, 1998. *DAI* 60.1 (1999): 132A.

Compares "the modes of representation of Nathaniel Hawthorne and Flannery O'Connor and the contemporary philosophical hermeneutics of Hans-Georg Gadamer, within the context of a critique of a modern enlightenment sensibility." Suggests that O'Connor's use of the grotesque reflects how she "critically questions the sovereignty of human reason." Focuses on O'Connor's explanation and how "she distorts the physical in order to reveal its spiritual extensions or the broader context of mystery within which we live." Finds that both O'Connor and Hawthorne use their art to point toward "the finitude of human knowledge" as each "critically examines the dualism based on modern subjectivism that disrupts human community." [198 pp.]

1944 Pitts, Kathy Jean Root. "The Influence of the Book of *Revelation* and Medieval Catholic Theology on the Works of Flannery O'Connor." Diss. U of Southern Mississippi, 1994. *DAI* 56 (1995): 933A.

Proposes that Flannery O'Connor "assumes the role of a twentieth-century prophet who, through her fiction, testified [to] her faith to an antagonistic audience." Suggests that she appeals to a shared Judeo-Christian heritage of her readers to convey the working of God's mysterious actions on earth, and examines how she uses physical imagery based upon the Catholic belief that "God is a sacramental and ennobling function of material existence" to depict these actions. Discusses how O'Connor, "in the tradition of a biblically aggressive God," ends her short stories "with the paradoxical violence of a divine `love' that devastates and humbles her characters in preparation for union with God." Outlines O'Connor's emphasis on the doctrine of free will, using the medieval poem *Pearl* for comparison. Views O'Connor's perspective as Augustinian, and suggests that she believed that "twentieth-century reliance on scientific processes and analyses--to the exclusion of faith--further perpetuates the medieval fallacy that man's unaided inquiries could arrive at profound `divine' knowledge." [154 pp.]

1945 Poe, Jan E. "Allegory and the Modern Southern Novel." Diss. U of Denver, 1985. *DAI* 46 (1985): 984A.

Traces the fictional lives of Flannery O'Connor's Hazel Motes, William Faulkner's Ike McCaslin, and Carson McCullers's John Singer. Discusses the lives of these characters as allegorical in nature, focusing on Christian imagery and the Old Testament view of humankind. Begins with Puritan notions of allegory, moves on to contemporary and Southern versions, and then includes non-Americans such as Henrik Ibsen and Franz Kafka to fully explore allegory. [238 pp.]

1946   Portch, Stephen Ralph. "Writing Without Words: A Nonverbal Approach
to the Short Fiction of Hawthorne, Hemingway, and O'Connor." Diss.
Pennsylvania State U, 1982. *DAI* 43 (1983): 2349A.

Uses a theoretical framework of nonverbal communication to provide a
useful reading methodology for short stories. Establishes a framework
from psychology to physiology, and from anthropology to sociology.
Applies this framework to stories by Nathaniel Hawthorne, Herman
Melville, and Flannery O'Connor ("Good Country People" and "The Life
You Save May Be Your Own"). [202 pp.]

1947   Pridgeon, Cheryl Jean Evans. "The Influence of St. Augustine on the
Works of Flannery O'Connor." Diss. Florida State U, 1983. *DAI* 44
(1983): 754A.

Insists that the personal Catholicism and literary Protestantism of
Flannery O'Connor are not only *not* mutually exclusive, but stem from the
doctrine of Saint Augustine of Hippo, doctrine that may be traced to
particular beliefs of Protestant reformers. Regards Saint Augustine's
thought as O'Connor's "supertext," and discusses the inclusion of five
books by or about him in O'Connor's personal library. [284 pp.]

1948   Prown, Katherine Hemple. "Revisions and Evasions: Flannery O'Connor,
Southern Literary Culture, and the Problem of Female Authorship." Diss.
College of William and Mary, 1993. "Dissertations in American Studies,
1992-1993." *American Quarterly* 45.4 (1993): 695.

Suggests that O'Connor's manuscripts for *Wise Blood* and *The Violent
Bear It Away* reveal that she attempted "to remove any traces of feminine
sensibility or perspective" from her work so that she might "develop her
art within a framework acceptable to the southern new critical
establishment." Considers her unpublished works "as evidence of her
ambivalent relationship, as a woman, to a literary culture built upon
traditional southern hierarchies." Reconsiders her "published novels in
light of the manuscripts and explores the ways in which she managed to
veil her female identity through the use of male characters and masculinist
narrative conventions." [Version expected to be published as *Revising
Flannery O'Connor: Southern Literary Culture and the Problem of
Female Ownership*. Charlottesville: UP of Virginia, ca. 2001.] [239 pp.]

1949   Quinn, John James. "The Tragic-Comic Vision in the Writings of
Flannery O'Connor: A Study of Her Anagogical Imagination." Diss.
King's College, U of London, 1970.

Suggests that O'Connor used "the medieval exegetical method" in her approach to her work. Sees her fiction as lending itself "to a vertical reading of the three levels (allegorical, moral, anagogical) contained in its literal level." Finds that "the methodology of her imagination reveals that fruitful union of the *letter* with the *spirit* which yields productive insights into the human condition." States that "it is through the letter (sight) that one reaches the spirit (insight)." Argues that it is this "insight-through-sight method" which is the "chief characteristic" of her imagination's "recording reality in its various significant levels." Further, that O'Connor's imagination is "enriched with irony and grotesquerie" to help the reader encounter Christ through her work. Submits that O'Connor "uniquely balances the tension between the sensible concrete specificities of surface reality (intension) with the deeper levels illuminating that reality's multisignificance (extension)" and that it is this process which "generates the spiritual motion that makes her fiction credibly alive." Concludes that "from the surface level of plot to the depths of anagogical richness, the realm of mystery, is the path pursued by a hermeneutical approach to [O'Connor's] . . . sacramental vision of modern man." [From an abstract provided by the author.]

1950   Rabasca, Iris Conchita. "The Prophetic Voice and Vision of Flannery O'Connor: The Influence of Old Testament Prophetic Literature on Her Fiction." Diss. State U of New York at Stony Brook, 1995. *DAI* 56 (1996): 3963A.

Contends that all of O'Connor's writing "reflects the influence of Old Testament prophets on her voice and vision." Sees this influence in frequent references to these prophets in her essays and in allusions that appear in her fiction. Suggests that "her use of imagery and metaphoric language is similar to that found in the prophetic books, and many of her themes parallel those of the literary prophets." Guides interpretation, relying upon O'Connor's texts, then her essays, letters, interviews, and notes in books in her personal library in the *Flannery O'Connor Collection* at Georgia College & State University. Finds that "some of the marginal notations O'Connor made in these books and the passages she underlined add support to this study's findings." [263 pp.]

1951   Racky, Donald Joseph, Jr. "The Achievement of Flannery O'Connor: Her System of Thought, Her Fictional Techniques, and an Explication of Her Thought and Techniques in *The Violent Bear It Away*." Diss. Loyola U of Chicago, 1968.

Discusses the critical opinion as to O'Connor's place in literature at the time of her death and suggests that only a few critics "have begun that process of careful analysis which must attend the passing of any important writer." Offers a "systematic analysis of all available expository statements Flannery O'Connor made about her theories of life and art" so that readers might better understand what she was trying to accomplish through her art. Examines, in the first chapter, O'Connor's use of visual, descriptive writing and her emphasis on portraying the world "`clearly.'" Discusses, in the second chapter, arguments of critics who complained that she used distortion and the grotesque unnecessarily, and those who expected her "to be more of a propagandist for good." The third chapter examines "her positive thinking" and her use of reason ("`reason should always go where the imagination goes'"). The fourth chapter ties O'Connor's views on the meaning of life with her technique and perspective on writing fiction. Emphasizes her view that "a material object is valuable because it is matter penetrated with spirit." Illustrates how this view is applied to her work. Chapters five and six focus on *The Violent Bear It Away*, examining the novel in relation to O'Connor's "philosophy of life, theory of art, and techniques of fiction" as seen in the "symbolic patterns" and "simultaneously-true layers of textured meaning." Chapter seven concludes with a summary of the positions of "the several completely opposed camps" of critics and offers a comparison of their positions with O'Connor's expository statements. Includes an appendix, which discusses O'Connor's examination of "modern education, the plight of the negro, the cult of the `phony South,' and the gaudiness of modern life" as "important illustrations" of weaknesses in modern American society. [387 pp.]

1952   Ragen, Brian Abel. "The Motions of Grace: Flannery O'Connor's Typology." Diss. Princeton U, 1987. *DAI* 47 (1987): 4085A.

Reconstructs a theory of O'Connor's concept of fiction from her essays and lectures. Calls attention to the influence of Joseph Conrad and the New Critics, and to Saint Thomas Aquinas and other medieval commentators on scripture. Concentrates on the idea of grace in her works and how O'Connor dispels the popular American myth of the automobile and the innocent, Adamic male wandering endlessly, which she saw as subsuming any place of importance for women. [235 pp.]

1953   Rast, John Wesley. "Flannery O'Connor: Biblical Education in the Southern Home." Diss. Duke U, 1980. *DAI* 41 (1981): 5137A.

Contends that O'Connor "explores Biblical Reality through the teaching experiences embodied within selected works of short fiction." Defines "Biblical Reality" eschatologically as "the `Last Thing' a character does in the face of Mystery's increasing pressure upon his life." Works by

O'Connor discussed include: "The River," "The Lame Shall Enter First," "Everything That Rises Must Converge," "A Circle in the Fire," "A Late Encounter With the Enemy," "A Temple of the Holy Ghost," "Parker's Back," "Revelation," and "The Artificial Nigger." Outlines the "teaching experiences" in categories of: "the parent/child relationship which occurs within the Southern home"; "personal interaction on a broader scale with people, events or forces from which he absorbs some deep truth consistent with Biblical reality"; and, "individual responses to the surprising claim of Mystery upon their lives." [267 pp.]

1954   Ray, Donald Louis. "I. *Howard's End*: The Novel `Opening Out.' II. Sir Thomas Wyatt's Protestant Petrarchanism. III. Flannery O'Connor's Satires on American Liberalism." Diss. Rutgers U, New Brunswick, 1976. *DAI* 37 (1976): 300A.

In the third of these three unrelated studies, the author attempts to show how O'Connor rejects American confidence in humanity and its capacity for rational self-improvement. Examines her essays and uses story analysis to support his thesis. Notes O'Connor's defensive perspective against disbelief in evil and points out that her characters must confront its presence around them. Discusses O'Connor's rejection of the use of psychology to allow the rationalization of moral choices, and her belief that suffering is necessary. [197 pp.]

1955   Rea, Paul Wesley. "A Teacher's Guide to the Modern American Short Story." Diss. Ohio State U, 1970. *DAI* 31 (1971): 5421A.

Provides secondary school and college teachers with "stimulating critical insights into the forty-one most commonly anthologized modern American short stories." Discusses "A Good Man Is Hard to Find," focusing on how it serves as a good example of O'Connor's use of the grotesque. Examines "the characteristic pathology, violence, and horror" of the story, noting that "though its tone is basically gay, its numerous allusions to crime, criminals, graveyards, secret panels, and accidents, all foreshadow the terrible events which occur at the end." [Not Available from University Microfilms International.] [218 pp.]

1956   Rechnitz, Robert Max. "Perception, Identity and the Grotesque: A Study of Three Southern Writers." Diss. U of Colorado, 1967. *DA* 28 (1967): 2261A.

Examines the use of the grotesque in the works of Carson McCullers, Flannery O'Connor, and Eudora Welty. Indicates that grotesque objects in their works are not symbols of an actual threat indigenous in the real world, but faulty perceptions by the protagonists who have yet to find a personal identity. Asserts that while O'Connor's and Welty's characters have hope of finding themselves (O'Connor's through God and Welty's through psychological growth), McCullers's are seen as being destined to be "forever isolated." [268 pp.]

1957   Reeves, Joseph MacDonald. "An Experiment Using Fictional Literature as a Resource for Preaching with Particular Reference to Flannery O'Connor." Diss. Drew U, 1982. *DAI* 43 (1982): 1191A.

Discusses how the study of fiction might positively affect the preparation of sermons. Uses literary criticism, theories of communication, Flannery O'Connor's stories, and the "dialogue between theology and literature" to determine an approach. Utilizes readings in cultural anthropology to help define human personality in the cultural setting. Describes a group study where readings of O'Connor's fiction were discussed and used to plan, conduct, and evaluate sermons. [211 pp.]

1958   Ritchason, Shelly J. "Post-Freudian Dialogues: 'Mystery' and the Rhetorical Resistance to Meaning in Flannery O'Connor's Fiction and Jacques Lacan's Theory." Diss. U of Nebraska-Lincoln, 1996. *DAI* 57 (1997): 3009-10A.

Reports that, despite their different cultural backgrounds and "seemingly incompatible critical classifications," O'Connor and Lacan appear to have startlingly similar rhetorical goals and strategies. Contends that both sought to address the "obsession with ego-mastery and logocentrism" of their contemporaries by using rhetoric to "decenter readers from their egos and objectify them to 'mystery.'" Discusses how each uses "the art of *detournement*" with "key signals and signifiers throughout their texts" to sabotage their readers' "cognitive control." Refers to a critical framework suggested by the work of Shoshana Felman, and discusses how Lacanian theory may be used to examine O'Connor's works, and "what a rhetorical analysis of O'Connor's fiction implies about Lacanian theory." [262 pp.]

1959   Rocco, Claire Joyce. "Flannery O'Connor and Joyce Carol Oates: Violence as Art." Diss. U of Illinois at Urbana-Champaign, 1975. *DAI* 36 (1976): 6090A.

Links O'Connor to Oates, based upon their "insistence on the need for violence in their writing and because of Oates's attention to O'Connor in critical essays and interviews." Discusses the relationship between violence and power using works by Hannah Arendt and Frederick J. Hoffman. Studies two major patterns of violence: linguistic and personal. Concludes that O'Connor uses violence to stress isolation while Oates uses it to emphasize the interrelationships among her characters. [336 pp.]

1960 Rochette-Crawley, Susan Marie. "Marginal Genre, Major Form: The Twentieth-Century Short Story and the Theories of the Marginal and Minor." Diss. U of Wisconsin - Madison, 1994. *DAI* 55 (1994): 3524A.

Contends that the short story's brevity, contextual nature, and "conditions of its production and dissemination" position it as a minor genre. States that these same characteristics "enable it to challenge discursive and cultural contentions" as if it were a major form. Discusses the short story "as a deterritorialized genre, with each having an ideological immediacy" to the source in which it appears. Finds it, as a genre, "definitionally elusive and formally contradictory." Selected works by a variety of authors, including Flannery O'Connor, are used to illustrate contentions regarding complexities of the genre. [314 pp.]

1961 Root, Kathy Jean. "The Influence of the *Book of Revelation* and Medieval Catholic Theology on the Works of Flannery O'Connor." Diss. U of Southern Mississippi, 1994. *DAI* 56 (1995): 933A.

Proposes that O'Connor--as "a medievalist in her Catholic convictions and her literary inclinations"--assumes in her fiction the role of a modern prophet to declare her faith "to an antagonistic audience." Sees O'Connor's fiction as parabolically conveying God's workings on earth through a Judeo-Christian heritage. Suggests that O'Connor's Catholic belief "that God is a sacramental and ennobling function of material existence" results in "physical imagery in the form of Southern characters and settings [that] depict God." Explores her use of "the paradoxical violence of a divine `love' that devastates and humbles her characters in preparation for union with God," and uses the medieval poem *Pearl* to support discussion of O'Connor's emphasis on the Catholic doctrine of free will. Finds her perspective to be "Augustinian in its assurance that genuine truth lies beyond human perceptions and can only be had from God." [154 pp.]

1962 Rota, Charles David. "Rhetorical Irony and Modern American Fiction: The Clergy in the Novels of William Faulkner, Flannery O'Connor, and John Updike." Diss. Southern Illinois U at Carbondale, 1992. *DAI* 53 (1993): 3531A.

Explores the role of the clergy in the novels of Faulkner, O'Connor, and Updike, employing rhetorical theories of irony developed by Wayne C. Booth. Emphasizes Booth's concept of "infinite irony" as it relates to the ambiguities of the universe. Contends that, in O'Connor's novels, a grotesque clergy confronts a bizarre universe, and "despite the apparent idealism of O'Connor's surface allegory, portray[s] infinite irony, if not nihilism." [280 pp.]

1963   Rout, Kathleen Joan Kinsella. "The Development of Flannery O'Connor's Social Consciousness." Diss. Stanford U, 1975. *DAI* 36 (1976): 6103A-04A.

Analyzes distinctions between character types in *A Good Man is Hard to Find* and *Everything That Rises Must Converge*. Asserts that O'Connor's early characters are primarily concerned with money and safety, while her later ones focus on class and race. Suggests that this change reflects a change in her own moral position. Contends that O'Connor's later characters exemplify her developing awareness of the importance of social attitudes as an extension of one's moral condition. Sees these characters as not only miserable in themselves, but as inflicting misery upon others. [218 pp.]

1964   Russ, Donald Devere. "Family in the Fiction of Flannery O'Connor." Diss. Georgia State U, 1981. *DAI* 42 (1981): 705A-06A.

Discusses the use of family as metaphor in O'Connor's works. Notes changes in the way family functions, from representing only the gross, material aspects of life, to reflecting on the spiritual nature of its origin and goal. [387 pp.]

1965   Sahlin, Nicki. "Manners in the Contemporary American Novel: Studies in John Cheever, John Updike and Joan Didion." Diss. Brown U, 1980. *DAI* 41 (1981): 5102A-03A.

Discusses the concept of manners as an analytic tool for contemporary American novels. Deals in depth with the term "manners," including the novel of manners genre. Analyzes the novels of John Cheever, John Updike, and Joan Didion in these terms, and offers capsule discussions of Walker Percy, Jerzy Kosinski, and Thomas Pynchon. Theoretical approach based on discussions of manners in Flannery O'Connor, Lionel Trilling, James W. Tuttleton, and Gordon Milne. [208 pp.]

1966 Schlafer, Linda Diane. "The Habit of Becoming: Some French Influences on the Aesthetic of Flannery O'Connor." Diss. Northern Illinois U, 1983. *DAI* 45 (1984): 185A.

Contends that through the influence of certain French writers O'Connor moved from the "comedy of paradise lost" to the "comedy of paradise regained." Mentions Jacques Maritain, Teilhard de Chardin, Leon Bloy, Georges Bernanos, and François Mauriac. Discusses O'Connor's reading of Simone Weil, Andre Malraux, and Gabriel Marcel, whose emphasis on "being-with" helped O'Connor modify her aesthetic of the grotesque. Also discusses O'Connor's reading of Etienne Gilson and traces to this source O'Connor's concern with the relationship of form to matter. [274 pp.]

1967 Scott, Carol Jackson. "The Crawford Women." Diss. U of Louisville, 1981. *DAI* 43 (1982): 440A-41A.

Offers an original novel, the family saga of the history of four generations of women in the coal-mining counties of Kentucky. Credits the tradition of regionalism in William Faulkner, Thomas Wolfe, Robert Penn Warren, Eudora Welty, and Flannery O'Connor. Also, acknowledges her debt to the themes of Faulkner, O'Connor, Welty, Peter Taylor, and Carson McCullers. [354 pp.]

1968 Scott, Suzanne Wallace. "The Monkey in the Chinaberry Tree: Flannery O'Connor and the Choreography of Evolution." Diss. U of Denver, 1997. *DAI* 58 (1997): 457-58A.

"Examines the extent to which the evolutionary theory of Charles Darwin informs the choreography of evolution in the fiction of the dogmatic orthodox Christian writer, Flannery O'Connor." Notes that while other studies have focused upon O'Connor's affinities with Pierre Teilhard de Chardin, "this study traces Darwinian motif, allusion, metaphor, imagery, and thematic satire throughout O'Connor's canon." Discusses how O'Connor parodies Darwin's linking of apes and humans by having some of her characters "take on animal characteristics" and some "animals take on human characteristics." Concludes that "the evolutionary process, for O'Connor, is stagnant, until characters choose to actively participate in perceiving and believing in a spiritual destination." [219 pp.]

1969 Scudder, Janice Pryor. "The Dramatic Potential in the Adaptations of the Short Stories of Flannery O'Connor for Readers Theatre: A Case Study." Diss. Kent State U, 1982. *DAI* 43 (1982): 589A-90A.

Argues that O'Connor's short stories are easily rendered into a "Readers Theatre script." Traces some history of the Readers Theatre as an alternative to traditional staging techniques, and examines five of O'Connor's stories to ascertain elements which consistently occur and make them adaptable. Offers a step-by-step illustration of how "The Enduring Chill" might be transformed. [179 pp.]

1970   Seel, Cynthia Lynne. "The Divining Art: An Exploration of the Performance of Ritual in Flannery O'Connor's Fiction." Diss. Northwestern U, 1996. *DAI* 57 (1996): 2482-83A.

Argues for a "mythico-ritual approach" to O'Connor's fiction, contending that "the paradigm of the performance of ritual itself is an aesthetic, psychological, archetypal, and political tool" which appears "well suited to the analysis of O'Connor's multi-dimensional stories." Draws upon the work of Mircea Eliade, Teilhard de Chardin, Carl Jung, Victor Turner, Tom Driver, and Malidoma Patrice Some, among others, to explore O'Connor's use of form and narrative design, archetypal imagery, and "the Catholic or sacramental impulse" with which O'Connor infuses her Southern landscapes. Examines, "within the context of ritual transformation in a cultural, religious, and historical frame," how Jung's "individuation process" theory may be applied to O'Connor's work. Sees "an archetypal feminine force" as galvanizing the "fundamental dynamism" of O'Connor's characters and actions. Suggests that, "given the extreme theatricality of O'Connor's ritual performances," the "live staging" of O'Connor's works may produce "new revelations and sheer pleasure" for O'Connor's audience. [457 pp.]

1971   Settle, Glenn H. "Four Great Sermons: The Rhetorical Functions of the Sermons in Four Major American Novels." Diss. Regent U, 1994. *DAI* 55 (1995): 1265A.

Examines the rhetorical functions of sermons found in Nathaniel Hawthorne's *The Scarlet Letter*, Herman Melville's *Moby-Dick*, William Faulkner's *The Sound and the Fury*, and Flannery O'Connor's *Wise Blood*. Discusses relationships noted between the sermons and the novels' "respective concerns, between the sermons and American Culture, and between the sermons and character change." Refers to Arthur Dimmesdale's "Sermon as Oracle," Father Mapple's "Sermon as Show," Shegog's "Sermon as Song," and Hazel Motes's "Sermon as Search." Closes with an examination of "the concept of `character change' as it is related to the novels' sermons." [236 pp.]

1972 Sexton, Mark Stephen. "Vernacular Religious Figures In Nineteenth-Century Southern Fiction: A Study In Literary Tradition." Diss. U of North Carolina at Chapel Hill, 1987. *DAI* 48 (1988): 2339A.

Discusses the vernacular, religious figure, particularly the "rural, fundamentalist preacher," in the life and culture of the South. Analyzes such portrayals, including "character stereotyping, exaggeration, use of a trickster figure," and their "predominantly ironic narrative perspective." Suggests that this tradition was established by humorists of the Old Southwest, and offers examples from Mark Twain's *Adventures of Huckleberry Finn*, Johnson Jones Hooper's *Some Adventures of Captain Simon Suggs*, and G.W. Harris's *Sut Lovingood Yarns*. Compares the "Old Southwestern" perspective, to that of local colorists Ruth McEnery Stuart, Richard Malcolm Johnston, Mary Noailles Murfree, and John Fox, Jr. Contrasts local colorists' perspectives with the vicious, negative images of black preachers seen in the work of Elizabeth Bryant Johnston and Harry Stillwell Edwards. Contends that while these traditions were used by Will Harben in his "The Heresy of Abner Calihan" and by G.W. Cable for "Posson Jones," the characters they created transcended the "stock figures" of their predecessor, were more dramatically complex and served, in turn, to "mark the direction" of depictions by William Faulkner, Flannery O'Connor, and Erskine Caldwell. [377 pp.]

1973 Seymour, Janice Louise. "A Prophetic Model of Ministry Viewed Through the Work of Flannery O'Connor: A Lenten Study." Diss. School of Theology at Claremont, 1984. *DAI* 45 (1984): 1135A.

Provides a model for a Lenten Study Series and explores a prophetic model of ministry as an alternative to the fragmentation and compartmentalization seen in the lives of the Church's ministers and laity. Bases this model on the work of Walter Brueggemann and uses excerpts from Flannery O'Connor's stories as a theoretical basis. [127 pp.]

1974 Shackelford, Dwight Dean. "The Outsider in the Fiction of Flannery O'Connor." Diss. U of South Carolina, 1986. *DAI* 47 (1987): 3041A-42A.

Discusses the roots of the outsider archetype in O'Connor's early stories and proposes four categories of intruders in her major fiction: the outsider as social minority; the outsider as confidence man and comic figure; the outsider as existentialist; and the outsider as scourge. Traces the prototypes to Southwest humor and Herman Melville. Attempts to resolve the issue of O'Connor's identification with some of her more grotesque characters as relating to her anger over her illness and her role as a Southern woman. [240 pp.]

1975   Shaw, Joy Farmer. "The South in Motley: A Study of the Fool Tradition in Selected Works by Faulkner, McCullers and O'Connor." Diss. U of Virginia, 1977.

Discusses the fool tradition and fool figures in William Faulkner's *The Sound and the Fury*, Carson McCullers's *The Heart Is a Lonely Hunter*, and Flannery O'Connor's *The Violent Bear It Away*, and her stories, "The Life You Save May Be Your Own," "The Comforts of Home," and "Revelation." Focuses on ways each molds the fool figure "to fit the story of Southern displacement." Begins by outlining the "fundamentals of the fool tradition" and distinguishing between those characters "who are fools in a temporal sense . . . and characters who are fools in an eternal sense" (as in *The Sound and the Fury*). Follows with an examination of clown pairs and the roles of knave and dupe in *The Heart Is a Lonely Hunter*. Continues with a discussion of O'Connor's "theological use of the fool figure as a symbol of man's displacement as a result of the Fall, and as the embodiment of man's opportunity to accept God's grace." Concludes with an attempt to show how O'Connor and McCullers "have been able to build on the writings of Faulkner, whose Benjy is the fool done to completion, without being limited or overshadowed by them." [257 pp. Cited in *Dissertation Abstracts International* 38 (1978): 4162A.]

1976   Shinn, Thelma J. Wardrop. "A Study of Women Characters in Contemporary American Fiction, 1940-1970." Diss. Purdue U, 1972.

Analyzes the women characters in all the works of fourteen men and sixteen women published between 1940 and 1970 to see how they "reflect the psychological and sociological attitudes toward and development of women in contemporary America." Writers included are: Caroline Gordon, Jean Stafford, Carson McCullers, Eudora Welty, Shirley Jackson, Hortense Calisher, Flannery O'Connor, Mary McCarthy, Ann Petry, Gwendolyn Brooks, Shirley Ann Grau, Grace Paley, Katherine Anne Porter, Sylvia Plath, Susan Sontag, Joyce Carol Oates, Robert Penn Warren, James Gould Cozzens, J.F. Powers, Saul Bellow, Norman Mailer, J.D. Salinger, William Styron, Ralph Ellison, James Baldwin, Bernard Malamud, Philip Roth, John Updike, Ken Kesey, and William Gass. Finds that "the primary problems facing the women characters move [over time] from the concerns of individuals in relation to their social roles to concerns of all humanity in relation to life itself." [514 pp. Cited in *Dissertation Abstracts International* 34 (1974): 338A.]

1977   Shloss, Carol. "The Limits of Inference: Flannery O'Connor and the Representation of `Mystery.'" Diss. Brandeis U, 1974. *DAI* 35 (1975): 5427A.

Discusses O'Connor's assertion that she could not be satisfied with writing which merely recognized social situations. States that through allusion and analogy O'Connor "attempted to establish a private topology," one with which she could convey a spiritual dimension to her secular audience. Concludes that because the added dimension which O'Connor sought to include is frequently beyond what many readers can reasonably infer from the texts, some of her fiction fails. [245 pp.]

1978   Short, Donald Aubrey. "The Concrete Is Her Medium: The Fiction of Flannery O'Connor." Diss. U of Pittsburgh, 1969. *DAI* 30 (1970): 3476A-77A.

Offers readings of O'Connor's fiction and discusses the polarized readings of themes (from theological to secular). Concludes that O'Connor's themes are universal. Notes that most criticism to date uses a theological framework focusing on the "moment of grace." Suggests that a labeling of the work as "fiction of ironic vision" may be appropriate. [244 pp.]

1979   Shuman, Joel James. "Beyond Bioethics: Caring for Christ's Body." Diss. Duke U, 1998. *DAI* 59.2 (1998): 0527A.

Discusses the Christian understanding of the "Body of Christ" and how it is, by definition, reflective of the "peculiarly Christian ethic of care for the sick and the dying . . ." Contends that this concept can be better understood "by examining the life and work of the late Flannery O'Connor, who was an especially remarkable example of this sort of performance of sickness and death."

1980   Siletzky, Robert. "The Idea of a Good Man In Flannery O'Connor's Fiction." Diss. Duke U, 1999. *DAI* 60.5 (1999): 1565A.

Considers O'Connor's moral vision and the question of her relationship to goodness. Notes the concern of some critics that "her world seems unusually full of morally flawed people," while others contend that "she presents her positive moral vision by the Medieval method of the via negativa, showing us what good isn't." Argues against those who see her characters "as exhibiting only the virtue of accepting grace at the moment of an epiphany, often just preceding their own death," by illustrating how many "have their goodness grounded in several theological and non-theological forms of goodness." Concludes that, "using O'Connor's criteria for goodness, in a good number of her works a good man can indeed be found, though that person's goodness is often coated with a superficial layer of socially repugnant behavior." [308 pp.]

1981   Smiley, Pamela Marie. "In the Name of the Father: The Effects of Orthodoxy on Roman Catholic Women Authors." Diss. U of Wisconsin, Madison, 1991. *DAI* 52 (1992): 3278A.

Contends that "the Roman Catholic ideal of womanhood is silence, obedience, and self-sacrifice." Addresses the question, "How is a woman to speak as a Roman Catholic?" Outlines a response using a group of medieval and contemporary Catholic women authors -- including O'Connor. Declares that, "depending upon her Catholicism and her life events, each woman negotiates the tension between `Roman Catholic' and `woman' along a spectrum of choices stretching between the Law of the Father and a Return to the Mother." Sees O'Connor as "a conduit for the angry God of wrath," and the plurality of voices in her later work . . . disrupts narrative authority and deconstructs the Law." [293 pp.]

1982   Smith, John Charles. "`Written With Zest': The Comic Art of Flannery O'Connor." Diss. Harvard U, 1974.

Discusses how O'Connor's fiction differs from that of her contemporaries, focusing on her religious themes, regional roots, comic art, and her "startling manner of presentation." Offers a biographical sketch and suggests that her Southern childhood, family, familiarity with the "rich traditions of humorous writing and oral story-swapping," and, later, her illness, all served to produce in O'Connor a "uniqueness" which "arose from the convergence in one personality" of these influences. Discusses regional influences on Southern writers and influences on O'Connor's work by: Augustus Baldwin Longstreet, Edgar Allan Poe, Nicholai Gogol, and George Washington Harris. Traces her ability to "create linguistic comedy" to Mark Twain, Ring Lardner, and the comedy of Charlie Chaplin and W.C. Fields. Discusses how her use of the grotesque is particularly difficult to analyze, then contends that the relationship between "the sense of mystery and the sense of manners" forms the core of her art. Includes discussion of: "Revelation," "Good Country People," "A Stroke of Good Fortune," "A Good Man Is Hard to Find," "Greenleaf," "A Temple of the Holy Ghost," *Wise Blood*, and *The Violent Bear It Away*. [190 pp. Cited in *Comprehensive Dissertation Index Ten-Year Cumulation 1973-1982: Author Index P-Sm* 37 (1974): 852.]

1983   Smith, Leslie Wright. "The Elusive Confessant: A Study of Author and Character in Dostoevsky, Mauriac and O'Connor." Diss. U of Texas, Austin, 1986. *DAI* 47 (1986): 1722A.

Discusses the historical development of Christian confession and observes two prominent movements, "confession of" and "confession that."

Explains types found in Jean-Jacques Rousseau and Saint Augustine and contrasts these to Mikhail Bakhtin's model. Discusses the works of Fyodor Dostoevsky, François Mauriac, and Flannery O'Connor in terms of the prevalent type of confession. Asserts that Hazel Motes in *Wise Blood* alternates from "confession of," which leads toward mystery, to "confession that," which leads to solipsism. [227 pp.]

1984   Smith, Patrick James. "Typology and Peripety in Four Catholic Novels." Diss. U of California, Davis, 1967. *DA* 28 (1967): 2265A.

Discusses peripety and typology, defining peripety as "Aristotle's 'reversal of situation . . . a change by which the action veers round to its opposite,'" and typology as a "conception of reality which understands that past events foreshadow future ones." States that typology was used in the early primitive church to demonstrate unity between the Old and New Testament and that it offers a means of studying prefiguration. Analyzes four Catholic novels that use peripety and typology as literary techniques: Henry Longan Stuart's *The Weeping Cross*; J.F. Power's *Morte D'Urban*; Flannery O'Connor's *The Violent Bear It Away*; and Caroline Gordon's *The Strange Children*. Relates that these were chosen to "show that Aristotelian peripety and Christian typology are authentic literary methods, and that they can reflect the nature of the author's faith in God, or his vision of reality." Compares the peripety and typology of these Catholic authors to two secular writers, Ernest Hemingway (*The Sun Also Rises*) and Joseph Conrad (*Victory*). Uses this comparison "to show that peripety and typology can have religious content without ceasing to exercise the freedom of art, and that a proper structural analysis of a novel *must* observe whether or not these two devices have a religious content, because the devices . . . can exercise different effects on the form of the novel." [182 pp.]

1985   Somerville, John Nottingham, Jr. "The Significance of Space in the Fiction of Flannery O'Connor." Diss. U of North Carolina at Chapel Hill, 1991. *DAI* 52 (1992): 3605A.

Suggests that the dilemma in O'Connor criticism is "the seeming disparity between the world O'Connor portrays in her fiction and her own comments about the stories and novels." Examines the fiction and compares it to her non-fiction statements. Focuses on "her use of spatial images and descriptions as a signal to the moments of grace" which she claimed to be central to her stories. Concludes that O'Connor used these spatial images to "point her readers beyond the violence on the surface of her fiction," and on "toward the larger world of mystery," and to "the 'ultimate reaches of reality' where the grace of God is manifest." [214 pp.]

1986   Spencer, Marlene A. "The Sacred and the Profane in Flannery O'Connor's
          Fiction." Diss. Florida State U, 1984. *DAI* 45 (1984): 1780A.

          Claims that O'Connor's interjection of the sacred into a world "that
          proudly proclaims the autonomy of the profane," is not meant to shock
          and horrify the reader, but to heighten the mystery of grace. Says
          O'Connor illustrates the need for grace by her use of the grotesque, the
          violent, and the absurd. [168 pp.]

1987   Stampfl, Barry George. "Imagination's Rhetoric: Similes as Thematic
          Clues in Conrad." Diss. U of California, Santa Barbara, 1986. *DAI* 48
          (1987): 401A.

          Discusses Joseph Conrad's use of the "as if," and his modification of the
          use of simile in the broader realm of metaphor. Suggests that the "as ifs"
          may be seen as instruments of truth-seeking, enlightening the analysis of
          other "simile-addicted" authors, including Flannery O'Connor. [309 pp.]

1988   Stephens, Charles Ralph. "A `Common Bent': The Correspondence of
          Brainard and Frances Neel Cheney and Flannery O'Connor." Diss. U of
          Maryland, College Park, 1985.

          Describes the friendship between Brainard and Frances Neel Cheney and
          Flannery O'Connor, which began in 1953 after Brainard's positive review
          of *Wise Blood* in *Shenandoah*. Suggests that their correspondence reflects
          their "common interests and sympathies." Contends that the letters show
          "similarities of temperament," as both Brainard and Flannery "were
          disciplined, committed writers with a fascination for the ironic, a
          thoroughly compatible sense of humor, and a desire for the company of
          others of like values and tastes." Argues that the letters "are an important
          addition to the canon of published O'Connor letters, lending coloration
          and depth to the emerging portrait of O'Connor as a private person and
          writer." Describes, in the Introduction, O'Connor's relationship with the
          Cheneys, offers biographical and bibliographic details, reviews themes
          noted in the correspondence, and "assesses the nature of the friendship."
          The remainder of the work consists of 188 unabridged letters and carbons
          (71 from Cheney, 117 from O'Connor), transcribed, arranged
          chronologically, and annotated. [250 pp. Not available from University
          Microfilms International nor via inter-library loan from University of
          Maryland's library. Content is similar to Stephen's: *The Correspondence
          of Flannery O'Connor and the Brainard Cheneys*. Jackson: UP of
          Mississippi, 1986.]

1989   Stephens, Martha Thomas. "An Introduction to the Work of Flannery O'Connor." Diss. Indiana U, 1968. *DA* 29 (1969): 3157A.

Asserts that O'Connor's works are primarily religious in orientation, and affirm "the nobility, terror, and intensity of the true religious experience." Examines her extension of the "sanctified-sinner-tradition," relating it to T.S. Eliot's essay on Baudelaire. Discusses her perception of the "hostile audience" and procedure for writing to minimize the problems. Suggests that O'Connor is often "crudely misread." [162 pp.]

1990   Strassburg, Mildred P. "Religious Commitment in Recent American Fiction: Flannery O'Connor, Bernard Malamud, John Updike." Diss. State U of New York at Stony Brook, 1971. *DAI* 32 (1972): 6457A.

Examines works by Flannery O'Connor, Bernard Malamud, and John Updike. Labels them as "integrating figures," with O'Connor bridging the gap between Protestant and Catholic, Malamud between Christian and Jew, and Updike between Christianity and ordinary American life. Sees other correlations in their thematic and structural elements. [149 pp.]

1991   Streight, Irwin Howard. "The Word Made Fiction: The Stories of Flannery O'Connor." Diss. Queen's U (Canada), 1993.

Shows how, through the overdetermination of language and the use of internal codes, O'Connor signals and makes manifest the anagogical dimension in her art. Focuses on her stories, arguing that she employs semiotic strategies and rhetorical devices to effectively "incarnate" a sacred "presence" in the words of her texts. Draws on the critical theories and methodology of Michael Riffaterre, particularly his conception of the trope of syllepsis--the simultaneous presence of two meanings in one word--and the hypogram--an absent word or phrase that is generative of a text. Discusses these as "incarnational" strategies in the stories, as a means of "intextuating" the Word in the word. Argues for a *Logos*-centrism in O'Connor, particularly evidenced in a semiotic reading of "Parker's Back." Declares that, in her attempt to put into words the divine mystery with which she is concerned, O'Connor literally and "letterally" *put* it *into* words. [347 pp. Author's abstract. A copy is in the *Flannery O'Connor Collection* of the Russell Library at Georgia College & State University, Milledgeville, GA.]

1992   Tate, James Oliver, Jr. "Flannery O'Connor and *Wise Blood*: The Significance of the Early Drafts." Diss. Columbia U, 1975. *DAI* 36 (1975): 2828A-29A.

Analyzes the body of material in the *Wise Blood* file in the *Flannery O'Connor Collection* of the Russell Library at Georgia College & State University in Milledgeville. Traces allusions in early drafts to T.S. Eliot and William Faulkner, and comments on the genesis of characters in later works. Suggests that banality was an important issue in the drafts and discusses this topic in relation to the finished character of Enoch Emery. Asserts that "over 2,000 pages" of the drafts were, for O'Connor, "turning the soil." [241 pp.]

1993   Tate, Robert Hale. "Large and Startling Figures: The Film Adaptations of the Short Fiction of Flannery O'Connor." Diss. Florida State U 1997. *DAI* 58 (1997): 1285-86A.

Notes that O'Connor was "often recognized for the cinematic qualities of her work," especially in her stories, which "provide scenes and dialogue that have long attracted movie adapters." Analyzes six films adapted from her short fiction: *The Life You Save* (adapted by Nelson Gidding for the *Schlitz Playhouse* in 1957); *The Comforts of Home* (adapted by Jerry and Fred Shore in 1973); *Good Country People* (adapted and directed by Jeff Jackson in 1975); *A Circle in the Fire* (adapted and directed by Victor Nunez in 1976); *The Displaced Person* (adapted by Horton Foote and directed by Glenn Jordan for PBS's *American Short Story Series* in 1977); and, *The River* (produced and directed by Barbara Noble in 1978). Finds that they "range from total alterations of O'Connor's original intentions to sensitive depictions of her demanding themes." Concludes, however, that the productions are still less than satisfactory "when compared to O'Connor's ability to present [her themes] in her stories." [260 pp.]

1994   Taylor, Elizabeth Savery. "Sherwood Anderson's Legacy to the American Short Story." Diss. Brown U, 1989. *DAI* 50 (1990): 2490A.

Contends that while Sherwood Anderson's legacy to American fiction writers has generally been ignored, his style can be observed from Ernest Hemingway to Raymond Carver, and his mode of characterization can be paralleled with that of William Faulkner, Nathanael West, Flannery O'Connor, and Carver. [297 pp.]

1995   Taylor, Jacqueline Sue. "Narrative Strategies in Fiction and Film: An Analysis of 'The American Short Story Series.'" Diss. U of Texas at Austin, 1980. *DAI* 41 (1980): 1282A-83A.

A comparative study of the point of view, tone, character, and setting in film versions of stories produced as part of the "American Short Story Series." Discusses the narrative devices used in film versions as compared to the stories, and offers examples from stories by Stephen Crane, F. Scott Fitzgerald, and Flannery O'Connor ("The Displaced Person"). [320 pp.]

1996   Thomas, Kelly Lynn. "Black Sheep: Representations of Poor Whites in American Literature and Culture." Diss. U of Michigan, 1998. *DAI* 59.10 (1999): 3822A.

"Examines the discursive function of the epithet `white trash' in American culture by investigating its origins, its changing connotations in various historical and cultural contexts, and the relative absence of critical discussions of the term as an identity of poor white populations in general." Refers, in the first chapter, to works by Flannery O'Connor and Carolyn Chute, to help readers trace the historical development of the term in various contexts and to utilize methodology based upon current literary theory and cultural analysis to define concerns. [195 pp.]

1997   Thomas, Leroy. "An Analysis of the Theme of Alienation in the Fictional Works of Five Contemporary Southern Writers." Diss. Oklahoma State U, 1971. *DAI* 33 (1972): 768A.

Discusses the theme of alienation in the works of Thomas Wolfe, Robert Penn Warren, Flannery O'Connor, Eudora Welty, and Carson McCullers. Compares examples of this theme with the more general theme of existentialism in the works of Jean-Paul Sartre, Albert Camus, and Miguel de Unamuno [Y Jugo]. Traces the beginnings of existentialism as theme to Sophocles, Aeschylus, and Euripides, and to the author of the *Book of Job*. Asserts that of the five writers' works, O'Connor's stand alone in her concern with redemption. [219 pp.]

1998   Thomas, Mattie Daniels. "The Quest Motif in Flannery O'Connor's Short Stories." Diss. Purdue U, 1982. *DAI* 43 (1983): 3914A.

Asserts that the quest motif is the most prevalent in O'Connor's works. Says characters are often unaware of their religious quest and strive toward their goals while grace pulls them toward God. Analyzes the motif at literal, allegorical, moral, and analogical levels, and discusses a variety of situations, such as shock, defeat, and denial. [129 pp.]

1998a   Thornton, Debra Lynn. "The Incarnational Art of Flannery O'Connor: Grace and the Body in *A Good Man Is Hard to Find*." Diss. U of New Mexico, 1999. *DAI* 60 (2000): 2930A.

Explores "the literary modes of actual grace that evolve in Flannery
O'Connor's body of work." Refers to theological definitions of grace and
maps her "hermeneutics of the Incarnation" to "show how she fuses the
literal and the anagogical elements of her fiction." Follows with a
discussion of stories in *A Good Man Is Hard to Find* that "portray actual
operative grace," categorizing them into four categories: "the Direct Hit"
(seen in "A Late Encounter With the Enemy"); "the Unwitting Encounter"
(seen in "Good Country People" and "The Artificial Nigger"); "the Grace
Rejected Mode" (seen in "A Stroke of Good Fortune," "The Life You
Save May Be Your Own," "A Circle in the Fire," and "A Good Man Is
Hard to Find"; and, "the grace of the innocents" mode (seen in "The
River" and "A Temple of the Holy Ghost"). Finds that "all four modes of
actual grace converge in the collection's final story and masterpiece, `The
Displaced Person.'" [263 pp.]

1999   Timberlake, Jean. "`Examined, cracked, changed, made new': Conversion
Themes and Structures in American Short Fiction." Diss. U of Cincinnati,
1995. *DAI* 56 (1996): 3966A.

Examines fifteen conversion stories by five "post-war conversion
writers": James Baldwin, Bernard Malamud, Flannery O'Connor, J.D.
Salinger, and John Updike. Isolates "thematic and formal elements," and
shows how they affect the "depiction of moral freedom in the
protagonists." Compares and contrasts these fifteen stories with fourteen
pre-war conversion stories, and suggests that the pre-war conversion
stories tend to either depict "protagonists lacking in moral freedom, or
else show that freedom, but vitiate it by ending the narratives with the
protagonists suffering material disaster or deprivation." Finds post-war
conversion fiction to be perhaps "a new genre of fiction," as these
protagonists become--when given the opportunity to choose between
good and evil--"non-deterministic characters." [200 pp.]

2000   Turnbaugh, Anne. "The Enduring Chill: Mother-Child Conflict in the Life
and Work of Flannery O'Connor." Diss. U of Illinois at
Urbana-Champaign, 1983. *DAI* 44 (1983): 1739A.

Speculates that Flannery O'Connor sustained considerable conflict with
her mother. Offers as proof a Freudian psychological approach to the
stories "The Enduring Chill" and "Everything That Rises Must Converge."
Concludes that, among other possibilities, the stories function as "ego
defense mechanisms." Hypothesizes that the behavior of her characters
appears to be a "sublimation and projection of her own fantasies of
rebellion." [162 pp.]

2001   Uruburu, Paula Marie. "The Gruesome Doorway: A Definition of the American Grotesque." Diss. State U of New York at Stony Brook, 1983. *DAI* 44 (1983): 1794A.

Argues that the American Grotesque is the dominant tradition in American literature, and that it combines diverse streams of Realism, Romanticism, and Naturalism into a unified whole. Analyzes the works of Nathaniel Hawthorne, Stephen Crane, Sherwood Anderson, Edgar Allan Poe, Frank Norris, and Flannery O'Connor for their contributions to the aesthetic of the Grotesque. [350 pp.]

2002   Van Dyke, Patricia A. "Comedy in the Modern Short Story: A Study of the Interrelationship of Mode, Theme, and Genre." Diss. U of Wisconsin, 1972.

Examines "the implications of O'Connor's fundamental observation about the relationship between a reader of short stories and the outcast, rebel-victim `hero'" which are shown in dynamic correspondence with theories of comedy by Henri Bergson, Sigmund Freud, Northrop Frye, John Mortimer, and Wylie Sypher and with studies by Ihab Hassan and others. Explicates a wide range of twentieth century short stories, including O'Connor's "Everything That Rises Must Converge," to illustrate comic themes and techniques and to explore how "the comic thematic elements in invective, satire, irony, and the sardonic" reflect "work toward the development of the most inclusive and free society that can be built or maintained, granting the terms of the fiction." Concludes the study, by arguing that "the short story palliates a sense of powerlessness by creating a psychic and spiritual community of the submerged group that O'Connor notes, or the misfits, victims, fools, and rebels that Hassan describes." [259 pp. Cited in *Dissertation Abstracts International* 34 (1973): 343A.]

2003   Verderame, Carla Lee. "Making Violence in Classrooms Visible Through the Stories of Flannery O'Connor." Diss. U of Michigan, 1998. *DAI* 59 (1998): 2511A.

Contends that O'Connor's fiction is useful as a starting point for discussing "the power relations that exist in classrooms, the impact such relations have on classroom practice, and the complicated knowledge that gets produced by teachers and students." Notes that while few of O'Connor's characters are found in academic settings, several reflect her skeptical view of formal education. Uses O'Connor's depiction of gender, race, religion, and violence as "the central focus" of a qualitative study of a sophomore-level literature class. Concludes that in the classroom context it is possible to both "refute the criticism that O'Connor's project is exclusively religious, and the scholarship that writes the religion out of her texts entirely." Finds further that, "for O'Connor, education can be a site of disruption and dislocation."

2004   Vest, David Carl Quentin. "Perpetual Salvage: The Historical Consciousness in Modern Southern Literature." Diss. Vanderbilt U, 1973. *DAI* 34 (1974): 5209A-10A.

Examines representative works by William Faulkner, Allen Tate, and Flannery O'Connor and finds that they demonstrate "that the historical consciousness is the distinguishing feature of modern Southern literature." Defines "historical consciousness" and suggests that the "renaissance in Southern letters stems from the acute sense of dislocation shared by the best Southern writers with other modernists in the wake of World War I." Contends that by O'Connor's time, "the South had lost much of its regional consciousness of secular history;" she then, "in its place . . . discovered a consciousness of sacred history which `the poor hold in common.'" [189 pp.]

2005   Washburn, Delores Cole. "The `Feeder' Motif in Selected Fiction of William Faulkner and Flannery O'Connor." Diss. Texas Tech U, 1978. *DAI* 40 (1979): 861A.

Examines the character motif of "the feeder," a character, usually a mother or wife, who provided for the emotional and physical needs of the family in the works of William Faulkner and Flannery O'Connor. Analyzes various characters who reflect this role, primarily against the changing background of the South, including Faulkner's Granny Rosa Millard and Mrs. Compson, and O'Connor's Mason Tarwater and Mrs. Pitts, and discusses the ones to whom they sometimes relinquish their duties. [441 pp.]

2006   Welling, Lloyd Charles. "The Centre Cannot Hold: A Close Textual Analysis of Flannery O'Connor's *Wise Blood*, to Reveal Its Mythopoeic Dimensions and the Informing Archetypes that Create Richness and Density and Carry the Ambiguity." Diss. Carnegie-Mellon U, 1975. [Cited in *Comprehensive Dissertation Index Ten-Year Cumulation 1973-1982: Author Index Sn-Z* 38 (1975): 595.]

2007   Wendler, Linda Fine. "The Effects of Biblical Prior Knowledge and Verbal Ability on College Students' Ability to Interpret Short Stories." Diss. U of Minnesota, 1990. *DAI* 51 (1990): 773A.

Describes a study in which students were given comprehension tests, a guided prewriting assignment, and an essay exam, after having read F. Scott Fitzgerald's "Babylon Revisited" or Flannery O'Connor's "Revelation." Notes that prior biblical knowledge and verbal ability had been tested previously, and draws conclusions concerning the performance between the two sets of results. Reports results which indicate that the ability to make relevant intertextual "links" plays an important role in influencing performance, and that prior biblical knowledge did affect performance in some cases. [209 pp.]

2007a Wendorf, Thomas Allan. "The Devil and Modern Christian Realism: The Representation of Evil in Graham Greene and Flannery O'Connor." Diss. Washington U, 1999. *DAI* 61 (2000): 176A.

Focuses on selected works by O'Connor and Greene to situate "their representations of mystery, particularly involving human evil, in the context of tensions among modern psychology, literary modernism, and traditional Catholic theology." Recognizes that by using psychology but resisting its "reduction of evil to the individual human psyche," both writers restore "mystery to morality in modern narrative." Shows how their fiction "provokes a felt sense of mystery through limits of character and narrator consciousness and through grotesque character and vision that are often disturbingly aligned with the devil's perspective." [277 pp.]

2008 Whitt, Margaret Earley. "'The Meaning of Every Dim Implicit Hint': A Study of Manners in the Fiction of Flannery O'Connor." Diss. U of Denver, 1986. *DAI* 47 (1987): 3043A.

Challenges Lionel Trilling's assertion that America has no novel of manners. Recalls Flannery O'Connor's comments on the subject and proclaims her as such a writer. Discusses the qualifications, and analyzes works by Ellen Glasgow, Eudora Welty, Erskine Caldwell, and Harper Lee. Seeks to determine how these authors' characters observe "the code of Southern manners," and exactly how O'Connor perfects the fiction of manners. [177 pp.]

2009 Wilhelm, Arthur Wayne. "Maurice-Edgar Coindreau: America's Literary Ambassador to France." Diss. Georgia State U, 1992. *DAI* 53 (1993): 2819A.

Examines the career of Maurice-Edgar Coindreau, a Princeton University French professor who introduced some of America's most prominent writers to the French reading public. Describes how from 1923 to 1978, through translations, reviews, and critical essays Coindreau influenced the French reading public to first accept John Dos Passos, William Faulkner, Ernest Hemingway, Erskine Caldwell, and John Steinbeck. Declares that he later introduced another generation, including William Maxwell, William Goyen, Truman Capote, William Styron, Reynolds Price, Fred Chappell, Shelby Foote, and Flannery O'Connor. Concludes that "although Faulkner, O'Connor and Styron scholars have recognized Coindreau's contribution, the large body of Coindreau's work in American literature has been ignored in America." [545 pp.]

2010   Winn, Harlan Harbour, III. "Short Story Cycles of Hemingway, Steinbeck, Faulkner and O'Connor." Diss. U of Oregon, 1975. *DAI* 36 (1976): 4500A.

Uses Forrest Ingram's definition of the "short story cycle" to examine "groupings of interrelated stories that are too finely patterned to be described as a mere collection of stories and too dependent on individual components to be described as a novel." Advances theoretical principles, techniques, and devices of the short story genre through the examination of cycles in Ernest Hemingway's *In Our Time*, John Steinbeck's *The Pastures of Heaven*, William Faulkner's *Go Down Moses* and Flannery O'Connor's *Everything That Rises Must Converge*. Explicates each cycle, focusing on its "compositional method, its author's stated intentions, its publication history, its treatment by critics, and its interconnecting devices." Finds that in O'Connor's work there is a "recurrence of similarly treated themes in varied contexts," and that, the ordering of the final story reiterates and concludes thematic patterns developed throughout previous stories of the cycle. [183 pp.]

2011   Witt, Jonathan Ronald. "Fearless Audiences: How Modern American Literature Flatters Us." Diss. U of Kansas, 1996. *DAI* 58 (1997): 878A.

Contends that "much modern American literature, sharing romanticism's belief in the importance and authority of the individual, portrays its protagonists' pride as a virtue." Suggests that "such literature reinforces the audience's own pride by way of flattery--either by implying the audience is superior to the flawed protagonists, or by causing the audience to identify with an artificially elevated protagonist." Discusses a variety of authors's fiction in this context, including O'Connor. Remarks that she "grew increasingly proficient at using skeptical intellectual characters to unsettle her `general intelligent reader.'" Discusses *Wise Blood*, "The Barber," "You Can't Be Any Poorer Than Dead," *The Violent Bear It Away*, "The Lame Shall Enter First," "Good Country People," "The Enduring Chill," and "Everything That Rises Must Converge." [162 pp.]

2012   Woodward, Harry Loomis. "In Bold and Fearless Connection: A Study of the Fiction of Flannery O'Connor and the Photography of Diane Arbus." Diss. U of Minnesota, 1978. *DAI* 39 (1978): 3588A.

Examines the works of Flannery O'Connor and Diane Arbus. Focuses on the two artists' style and technique, rather than on interpretation. Finds parallels between the two in their use of the grotesque and use of unlikely combinations, designed to frustrate rational interpretation. [226 pp.]

2013   Wray, Virginia Field. "Flannery O'Connor in the American Romance Tradition." Diss. U of South Carolina, 1979. *DAI* 40 (1979): 1475A.

Reminds readers that O'Connor applied to herself "the one label which subsumes the rest: writer of romance." Reviews previous book-length criticism and uses O'Connor's essays, lectures, and interviews to "reevaluate" her status in terms of the American Romance tradition. Focuses on and examines O'Connor's use of central gestures. [226 pp.]

2014   Wright, Charlotte Megan. "Plain and Ugly Janes: The Rise of the Ugly Woman in Contemporary American Fiction." Diss. North Texas State U, 1994. *DAI* 55 (1995): 2837A-38A.

Examines women characters in American literature, focusing on "old maid" characters of the nineteenth century who become "not just homely, but downright ugly" in twentieth century fiction. Argues that from the 1960s forward, the ugliness of many female characters is such an intrinsic part of the story that it could not take place if [they] were beautiful." Examines works by more than thirty American authors, including that of Flannery O'Connor, for evidence. Concludes that for many of these heroines, the increase in determination over their own lives and that of others, allows them to "achieve a status more in keeping with the more 'masculine' and active role of a hero." [201 pp.]

2015   Yordon, Judy Ellen. "The Double Motif in the Fiction of Flannery O'Connor." Diss. Southern Illinois U at Carbondale, 1977. *DAI* 38 (1977): 2421A.

Examines the use of the double motif in O'Connor's fiction, recounting her interest in its Christian dualistic implications. Says the mode is exemplified in three ways: nominally, physically and psychologically. Discusses the significance of shared names, double of nicknames, and implications of the motif. [299 pp.]

2016   Zornado, Joseph Louis. "Flannery O'Connor: A Fiction of Unknowing."
        Diss. U of Connecticut, 1992. *DAI* 54 (1993): 1359A.

Examines the Western tradition of "apophatic theology known as *via
negativa* and its influence on Flannery O'Connor" in her letters and
occasional prose. Discusses *Wise Blood*, "A Good Man Is Hard to Find,"
"The Artificial Nigger," "Good Country People," "The River," "Parker's
Back," and *The Violent Bear It Away*. Suggests that the "close relationship
between deconstruction and the *via negativa* provides an approach to
O'Connor's fiction that takes into account contemporary literary theory
without rejecting her avowed religious sensibility." [284 pp.]

V Foreign Language Criticism, 1975-1999

2017   Ahrends, Gunter. "Deskriptive Theorien: Flannery O'Connor und Joyce Carol Oates." *Die Amerikanische Kurzgeschichte: Theorie u. Entwicklung.* Stuttgart: Koln, 1980. 39-44. [In German].

Explores connections between Flannery O'Connor and Joyce Carol Oates on the theory and practice of the short story. Focuses on the theme of the grotesque and the influence of Edgar Allan Poe and Nathaniel Hawthorne on O'Connor. Discusses "The Artificial Nigger," "A Good Man Is Hard to Find," and "Revelation." (Abstracted by Roger Noël).

2018   Ahrends, Gunter. "Die Analyse des Bewubsteins und der Gesellschaft: William Faulkner, Katharine Anne Porter, Eudora Welty, Flannery O'Connor und Joyce Carol Oates." *Die Amerikanische Kurzgeschichte: Theorie u. Entwicklung.* Stuttgart: Koln, 1980. 160-82. [In German].

Considers themes of the mystery of personality and the human condition in the works of O'Connor and four other American writers. (Abstracted by Roger Noël).

2019   Akai, Katsua. "A Note on Flannery O'Connor's Use of Names." *Shikoku Gakuin University Bulletin* 91 (July 1996): 145-66. [In Japanese].

2020   Alfieri, Teresa. "Por el dolor hacia la trascendencia: La biografía de Flannery O'Connor." [The Pain That Causes Transcendence: The Biography of Flannery O'Connor]. *Redes, Alambiques y Herencias.* Buenos Aires, Argentina: Editorial de Belgrano, 1981. 146-64. [In Spanish].

Biographical article relating O'Connor's life and its relation to themes in her works (Southern heritage, illness, relationship with her mother (Regina Cline O'Connor), and Catholic religion). Concludes with the thought that only God can grant salvation, and that O'Connor's work and life reflect this belief. (Abstracted by Kathleen M. Olson).

2021   Amette, Jacques-Pierre. "La spirale de la folie." ["The Spiral of Folly."] *Delta* (France) 2 (March 1976): 29-30. [In French].

Contends that O'Connor's work contains three principal types of characters: innocents, hypocrites, and prophets. Argues that each of the three frantically seeks to look truth in the face. Suggests that social relations in her stories must be either aggressive or involve a search for one's double. Discusses the role of the prophet, and states that this third type lives in a world constructed by speech. Remarks that one problem raised tirelessly by O'Connor is that of how to rid oneself of normality in order to attain one's inner truth. (Abstracted by Marguerite Bartoli).

2022   Arbeit, Marcel. "Moralni aspekty romanu Flannery O'Connorove a Walker Percyho." ["Moral Aspects of the Novels of Flannery O'Connor and Walker Percy."] *Anglisticko-Amerikanisticka Konference* ["Conference of English and American Studies."] Ed. Josef Hladky. Brno, Czech Rep.: J.E. Purkyne UP. 1985. 18, 69. [In Czechoslovakian].

[Cited in *Annual Bibliography of English Language and Literature*. London: Modern Humanities Research Assn., 1986. Item 13555.]

2023   Balgård, Gunnar. "En Södergran i Södern" [A Södergran in the South]. *Västerbottens-Kuriren* (Umeå, Sweden) 15 Feb. 1994: 3. [In Swedish].

Author reports on his Summer 1994 visit to Milledgeville, Georgia. Balgård, a poet, playwright, critic, and photographer, describes and provides photographs of Flannery O'Connor's West Green Street house and the Andalusia farm. Compares O'Connor to the Finnish-Swedish poet Edith Södergran (1892-1923) who--like O'Connor--led a short life in a rural area (outside St. Petersburg) and was cared for by her mother (Regina Cline O'Connor) during an illness which ended her life. Notes that Södergran also lived in a wooden house with a huge wild garden and that she also contributed to her country's literature with a stunning brilliance and originality. Remarks that both writers left behind a wealth of letters that have been published. Describes Andalusia as he saw it on a summer day and discusses O'Connor's birds and her relationship with her mother. Suggests that the horror in O'Connor's fiction is surpassed by her compassion and gentleness. (Abstracted by Rönnog Seaberg).

2024   Bartle, Arthur. "Der Roman des amerikanischen Sudens: Die Post-Renaissance." *Der zeitgenössische amerikanische Roman: Von der Moderne zur Postmoderne, Band 2: Tendenzen und Gruppierungen.* Ed. Gerhard Hoffman. Munich: Fink Verlag, 1988. 165-90. [In German].

Serves as a general introduction to a number of Southern Renaissance authors, including Flannery O'Connor, Robert Penn Warren, Carson

McCullers, William Styron, and Walker Percy. Focuses on the theme of religious influence and refers to the following O'Connor characters: Tarwater, Meeks, Rayber, and Hazel Motes. (Abstracted by Roger Noël).

2025	Bartle, Arthur. *Ideologeme im Amerikanischen Roman der Sudstaaten.* Wurzburg: Konigshausen und Neumann, 1980. [In German].

Provides a study of Allen Tate's *The Fathers*, Robert Penn Warren's *All the Kings Men*, Carson McCuller's *The Member of the Wedding*, and Flannery O'Connor's *The Violent Bear It Away*. Focuses on themes of disintegration, change, contrast of experience, and communication against the background of the Old South versus the New Society. [319 pp.] (Abstracted by Roger Noël).

2026	Bartle, Arthur. "Ideologemes in the Novel of the American South: A. Tate's *The Fathers*, R.P. Warren's *All the King's Men*, C. McCuller's *The Member of the Wedding*, and Flannery O'Connor's *The Violent Bear It Away*." Diss. Bayerische-Julius-Maximilians Universitat Wurzburg. 1980. [Wurzburg, Germany:] Verlag Konigshausen + Neumann, 1980. *English and American Studies in German: Summaries of Theses and Monographs, A Supplement to Anglia: 1980.* Ed. Werner Habicht. Tubingen: Max Niemeyer Verlag, 1981, pp. 139-40. [In German].

Examines four novels by Southern American authors and sets out to: 1) "elucidate the underlying semantic and narrative code of the texts"; 2) "describe the relation of the deep structure units to the observable linguistic manifestations at the surface level"; and 3) view the narrative patterns "in connection with the collective regional myths which are developed in expository texts and called ideologemes." Considers O'Connor's *The Violent Bear It Away* as illustrative of the breaking of a contract on a religious level and the use of revelation as a way of advancing the maturing process of a character. [319 pp.]

2027	Beaulieu, Paul. "Une Rencontre Privilégiée." [A Privileged Encounter]. *Écrits du Canada français* (Canada) 47 (1983): 17-34. [In French].

Examines Flannery O'Connor's work in general. Briefly describes the contents of *Mystery and Manners* and *The Habit of Being*. Comments on the origins of her titles and expounds upon her idioms and the environment from which she drew her inspiration. Notes the cruelty of her characters, specifically children, and examines her use of violence and monstrosity. Reports that although O'Connor was strictly orthodox in her beliefs, she appears broad-minded in her discussions on religion.

Discusses her recourse to the irrational, and the presence of the Christian mysteries in her work. Refers to her correspondents, her thought processes, her literary projects, and her willingness to accept criticism of her own work. Compares O'Connor to François Mauriac and Julien Green. Suggests that "The Displaced Person" illustrates O'Connor's exceptional gift for deciphering the hidden meaning of divine signs in creation. Concludes by commending O'Connor for her rejection of self-pity. (Abstracted by Marguerite Bartoli).

2028 Beck, Christiane. "Flannery O'Connor, ou la persecution." [Flannery O'Connor or Persecution]. *Recherches anglaises et américaines* 9 (1976): 197-207. [In French].

Compares Flannery O'Connor with Nathanael West. Suggests that while both writers describe a mechanized, dehumanized world, readers will find that in O'Connor's work, the world occasionally regains cohesion because of her double vision corresponding to two opposed imaginary structures. Describes the first as a schizomorphic structure of the imagination, defined as a tendency to render an abstract vision of reality. (Refers readers to Gilbert Durand's, *Les Structures Anthropologiques de l'Imaginaire*. Bordas, Paris, 1969.) Offers examples from *Wise Blood*, *The Violent Bear It Away*, and "The Displaced Person" to show this perspective to be particularly relevant in the description of characters. Proposes that O'Connor's second imaginary structure is that of reality, but only as it is lived out and transformed by the consciousness of some characters obsessed with a paranoid feeling of threat and danger. Offers as evidence examples of paranoid behavior in *The Violent Bear It Away*, "A Good Man Is Hard to Find," "Parker's Back," and "A Circle in the Fire." Challenges O'Connor's use of violence and the grotesque as a means of denouncing a world without God. Concludes that O'Connor's approach makes the Christian problem of salvation irrelevant and debases humanity. Finds "The Artificial Nigger" to be one of the very few works that expounds a Christian theme. (Abstracted by Marguerite Bartoli).

2029 Belsunce, Alicia L. de Garcia. "Flannery O'Connor: Vida, Fe, Obra." *Criterio* (Buenos Aires) 10 Sept. 1981: 526-30. [In Spanish].

Discusses Flannery O'Connor's life and work based upon her letters published in *The Habit of Being*. (Abstracted by Kathleen M. Olson).

2030 Belsunce, Alicia L. de García. "Introducción a Flannery O'Connor." *La Prensa* (Buenos Aires), "Seccion Ilustrada de los Domingos," 27 July 1975: 3. [In Spanish].

Offers a brief introduction to O'Connor, her works and her use of religion as an interwoven theme. (Abstracted by Kathleen M. Olson).

2031   Bott, François. "La demoiselle de Georgie." [The Young Lady From Georgia]. *Le Monde* [1991?]: n.p. [In French].

Reviews the publication in French of Flannery O'Connor's *Complete Works*. Compares her with other women writers who died young. Mentions the introduction by Roger Grenier, then focuses on Geneviève Brisac's biography *Loin du Paradis*. Notes that Brisac's portrayal of O'Connor is occasionally a self-portrait in disguise, and singles out particular biographical elements such as O'Connor's struggles with Lupus, her studies at the University of Iowa, and her return to Andalusia. Concludes with a comment on O'Connor's faith and her work, which perform the same task: to protect the mystery of the human soul. (Abstracted by Marguerite Bartoli).

2032   Brisac, Geneviève. *Loin du Paradis: Flannery O'Connor*. [Far From Paradise]. Paris: Gallimard, 1991. [In French].

Brisac blends fact and fiction and uses excerpts from O'Connor's short stories, novels, and letters, to construct a narrative that does not so much inform as paint a picture. Discusses O'Connor's childhood and her life and work at the University of Iowa, Yaddo (New York), and Ridgefield, Connecticut (where she lived with Sally and Robert Fitzgerald). Emphasizes her alleged self-derision, and describes her early manner as being positioned on the border between the real and the imaginary. Remarks that her illness gave O'Connor a new perception of the world. Concludes that O'Connor was an inscrutable, distant woman who first protected herself in the best way she knew (laughter, religion, reasoning, and writing), and who later evolved and eventually developed deep friendships. (Abstracted by Marguerite Bartoli).

Representative Reviews: Christine Klein-Lataud, *RFR: Resources for Feminist Research* (Canada) 21.3-4 (1992): 110-11.

2033   Broncano, Manuel. *Mundos Breves, Mundos Infinitos: Flannery O'Connor y el Cuento Norteamericano*. [Brief Worlds, Infinite Worlds: Flannery O'Connor and the American Short Story]. León, Spain: Universidad de León, 1992. [In Spanish].

Examines O'Connor's most prominent short stories to emphasize her technical skills as a writer. Includes an examination of her thoughts about the short story genre and discusses the impact and influence of O'Connor's work upon her peers. Groups O'Connor's short stories by thematic characteristics and discusses individual characters. Stories grouped under the title "The Trip" include: "A Good Man Is Hard to Find"; "The River"; and "The Artificial Nigger." Contends that the latter two stories may be read as narratives which convey the teachings of Jesus and the Catholic rite of initiation to an unbelieving world. Discusses, in a chapter titled "The Farm": "The Life You Save May Be Your Own"; "A View of the Woods"; "The Displaced Person"; "A Circle in the Fire"; and "Greenleaf." Suggests that stories in what may be described as O'Connor's "farm cycle," are morality plays constructed on sociological and ideological levels. Comments on her use of the farm as representative of the world stage and how her characters and stories serve as metaphors for individuals who end up figuratively destroying the Garden of Eden. Examines "Good Country People," "Everything That Rises Must Converge," "The Enduring Chill," "The Comforts of Home," and "The Lame Shall Enter First," as stories primarily concerned with frustrated intellectuals. Notes features of these stories and the use of emblematic names. Concurs with critics who regard "The Comforts of Home" as one of O'Connor's least successful stories. Regards this story as a melodrama of good and evil, and suggests that O'Connor seems to lose control at the end. Under the title "Gone With the Wind," discusses: "A Late Encounter With the Enemy"; "Parker's Back"; "Revelation"; and "Judgement Day." Focuses on themes of the old versus the "New South." Finds a notable absence of a religious theme in "A Late Encounter" and contends that characters in "Parkers Back" are not easily embraced. Insists that O'Connor's contribution to the American short story is distinguished by using her subject matter within a traditional style based upon a Christian point of view. [Abstracted by Jeri H. Dies and Sonia González].

2034   Broncano, Manuel. "La poética grotesca de Flannery O'Connor." *Estudios de literatura en lengua inglesa del siglo XX* (Ed. Pilar Abad, José M. Barrio, and José M. Ruiz). Valladolid, Spain: Universidad de Valladolid, 1994. 123-31. [In Spanish].

Sees two traditions present in O'Connor's literary works: romance and her use of the grotesque. Argues that she uses both to explore the mystery of human existence and to give readers a different image of everyday life. Discusses how her use of the grotesque appears to project a different light on objects, causing readers to sense that their shapes are slightly altered. Ties this idea to a definition of romance as a depiction of these objects in the process of being "defamiliarized" or made unfamiliar. Contends that while readers may encounter objects and characters commonly found in everyday life, it is O'Connor's juxtaposition of the ordinary alongside experiences that are seemingly unexpected that serves as the basis for her "realism of distances." Observes that, O'Connor relies upon two literary strategies to effectively reveal her message or intention: the use of distortion and the use of violence. Outlines how the function of distortion in Southern literature is essentially moral in nature, and ties this idea to O'Connor's use of distorted human images to emphasize the distance between humankind and our image as creatures of God. Follows with a discussion of O'Connor's use of violence and how it allows readers to see characters in extreme situations, thus showing their real personalities and behavior without societal constraints. (Abstracted by Jeri H. Dies and Raúl Llorente Parrado).

2035   Buschendorf, Christa. "Flannery O'Connor: `The River.'" *Mit Kinderaugen: zur Perspektivtechnik bei William Faulkner, Carson McCullers und Flannery O'Connor.* Epistemata Reihe Literaturwissenschaft, 28. Wurzburg: Konigshausen and Neumann, 1988. 96-117. [In German].

States that "The River" may be interpreted as a story of initiation for a youth who drowns hoping to find a better world. Focuses on O'Connor's symbolism and discusses as well, "The Comforts of Home" and *Mystery and Manners*. (Abstracted by Roger Noël). [Note: Entry in the *Library of Congress Catalog* states: "A revision and enlargement of the author's thesis (doctoral-- Universitat Dusseldorf, 1983) presented under the title `Die Funktion der Kinderperspektive in der Literatur der amerikanischen Suden anhand ausgewahlter Werke von William Faulkner, Carson McCullers und Flannery O'Connor.'"]

2036   Buschendorf, Christa. "`Mystery and Manners' oder `All was natural in a magic way.'" *Mit Kinderaugen: zur Perspektivtechnik bei William Faulkner, Carson McCullers und Flannery O'Connor.* Epistemata Reihe Literaturwissenschaft, 28. Wurzburg: Konigshausen and Neumann, 1988. 118-56. [In German].

Contends that Flannery O'Connor and Carson McCullers are typical representatives of the "Southern School," which presents humanity in all its glory and jest. Focuses on themes of the grotesque, religious influence, and family. Discusses *The Violent Bear It Away* and "A Temple of the Holy Ghost." (Abstracted by Roger Noël). [Note: Entry in the *Library of Congress Catalog* states: "A revision and enlargement of the author's thesis (doctoral-- Universitat Dusseldorf, 1983) presented under the title `Die Funktion der Kinderperspektive in der Literatur der amerikanischen Suden anhand ausgewahlter Werke von William Faulkner, Carson McCullers und Flannery O'Connor.'"]

2037   Castelli, Ferdinando. "Redenzione e Perdizione Nell'Opera di Flannery O'Connor." [Redemption and Perdition/Damnation in Flannery O'Connor's Work] *La Civiltà Cattolica* 5 March 1994: 431-44. [In Italian].

Offers a brief historical perspective on O'Connor's reception in Italy, then discusses, in detail, three essential components of her personality: her being a "Catholic, a Southerner, [and] a writer." Suggests that O'Connor's fiction illustrates her view that life is a battlefield between good and evil, with the path to salvation shrouded in mystery. Considers how she viewed humankind as fallen creatures who remain fallen if they refuse the grace offered through the redemption and salvation of Christ. Discusses, in this context, *Wise Blood*, "The Lame Shall Enter First," "A Good Man Is Hard to Find," "A View of the Woods," "Everything That Rises Must Converge," "The Enduring Chill," "The Partridge Festival" and "Good Country People," Concludes with a discussion of O'Connor's fictional device of having her characters' souls opened to God through traumatic events such as with a light that blinds but also helps them to see more clearly, or her use of a pain or disgrace that brings them to their knees so they may be able to truly live. (Abstracted by Roger Noël).

2038   Chentier, Marc. "A la recherche de l'arlésienne: `l'écriture féminine' dans la fiction américaine contemporaine." [Looking for the Arlesian Woman: `Feminine Writing' in Contemporary American Fiction]. *Revue française d'Études Américaines* 30 (Oct. 1986): 415-35. [In French].

Considers whether there is a type of writing that may be referred to as "feminine writing," and if so, what the characterisitics of its form and syntax might be. Includes brief references to works by Flannery O'Connor, Alice Walker, Jayne Anne Phillips, Mary Lee Settle, and Eudora Welty. Concludes that the assertion of an alleged "feminine writing" leads to a reghettoization that women have struggled to overcome. (Abstracted by Roger Noël).

2039   Choffrut-Faure, Patric. "Flannery O'Connor ou la vision éclatée." ["Flannery O'Connor's Fragmented Vision."] *Delta* (France) 2 (March 1976): 33-51. [In French].

Examines O'Connor's vision of the South and portrayal of Southern society. Contends that the structure of her short stories is practically immutable: a stranger enters an unstable environment, which indicates the obsessive recurrence of the cultural trauma experienced by white Southerners during the Civil War. Asserts that while blacks give the South its identity, O'Connor uses them merely as props. Argues that the theme of defeat is seen as a principal factor in revealing the contradictions of white Southern society and the disintegration of its values. Turns to the homology that can be found between the structure of Southern society and the Southern family: a stranger enters a family in order to destroy it, and men are absent, dead, or passive. Notes that matriarchy prevails in O'Connor's works and in a society governed by northern values, women cannot but adopt these same values (aggressiveness, efficiency, ownership). Finds that, as a result, O'Connor's women are unable to safeguard the identity of the group. Examines the meta-national or meta-physical answer through which O'Connor attempts to reveal her vision; that is, that the South will be deceived because it is caught in a double contradiction: Southern values are good, but in order to survive, it needs to accept Northern values. Contends that, if these values are adopted, however, the identity of the South will disintegrate. Concludes that the South ends up in sentencing itself to death in order to save itself. (Abstracted by Marguerite Bartoli).

2040   Colafato, Michele. "Il colore dell'ansia: Su Flannery O'Connor e la desegregazione." ["The Color of Anxiety: On Flannery O'Connor and Desegregation."] *Rivista di storia contemporanea* (Italy) 19.3 (1990): 412-18. [In Italian].

Offers an examination of O'Connor's views on racism. Asserts that O'Connor found creative space in the dismantling of the anti-racist optimism with sharp sarcasm and devastating comedy. Sees evidence in her characters' gestures and interior monologues that O'Connor was intent on equalizing whites, blacks, and the new immigrants from Europe. Discusses a variety of stories, including "Good Country People," "Everything That Rises Must Converge," "Revelation," "Judgement Day," "The Artificial Nigger," and--in greater detail--"The Displaced Person." Focuses on the issue of desegregation, the role of O'Connor's female characters as receptacles of anxiety, and how her traditional white Southern characters use skin color as a means of discerning social superiority. (Abstracted by Amadeo Fedeli).

2041   Dommergues, Pierre. "Flannery O'Connor." *L'aliénation dans le roman américain contemporain*. [Alienation in the Contemporary American Novel: Flannery O'Connor]. Vol. I. Paris: Union Générale d'Éditions, 1977. 7-64. [In French].

Part of a book which analyzes the work of five contemporary American novelists: Norman Mailer, Saul Bellow, Flannery O'Connor, LeRoi Jones, and William Burroughs. States that these writers were chosen not for their literary value but for the polarities they represent and for way they have influenced modern culture through their consciousness of and fight against alienation. Dommergues notes the irony that O'Connor, who lived in the conservative South, is one of the first to undermine some foundations of Western humanism (competitive individualism) and the main agent of liberalism (the education system). Explains how she went about it: by showing a state of disgrace through visible deformation, spiritual degradation, and valorization of the artificial, and by focusing on humanism and its by-products. Argues that, in a number of ways, O'Connor contends against the abstractions of liberal-humanist thought: (1) She insists that knowledge first comes through the senses and follows-up by telling stories in which she teaches the reader how to look; (2) She tirelessly talks about "mystery"; (3) She makes revelation the center of her work: instantaneous, multiple, ambiguous, or individual; (4) She contends that reality is manifold and that art must represent both mystery and manners. O'Connor then uses the grotesque to underline deformities, create perspective and distance, and prevent identification so that the reader will rebel and enter reality. Concludes that if radicalism is conceived as the will to oppose the foundations of bourgeois liberalism and to modify the mental structures that determine society, then Flannery O'Connor was a radical. (Abstracted by Marguerite Bartoli).

Representative reviews: Jean Rivière, *American Literary Scholarship: An Annual, 1976*, Durham, NC: Duke UP, 1978: 431.

2042   Eguchi, Yuko. "The Double Motif in the Works of Flannery O'Connor." *Families in American Literature*. Kyoto, Japan: Yamaguchi Shoten, 1987. 211-29. [In Japanese].

Asserts that O'Connor often uses a "double" figure to reveal the dark side of particular characters. Examines this use in "A View of the Woods" and "The Artificial Nigger." (Abstracted by Kayoko Watanabe).

2043   Eguchi, Yuko. "Flannery O'Connor's South: An Artist of the `Negative.'" *Research Report in Women's Studies in Tokyo Women's Christian University* (Japan) 5 (March 1985): 79-90. [In Japanese].

Asserts that O'Connor views the modern world as a place of evil and chaos. Suggests that her characters are all "displaced persons" alienated from their "true country." Concludes that O'Connor's "negative approach" in administering "shock therapy" to the reader seems to be the most appropriate method of presenting the mysteries of Christian truth to a modern audience. (Abstracted by Kayoko Watanabe).

2044   Engler, Bernd. "Zur Literatur katholischer Autoren im englischen Sprachraum: Kontexte--Entwicklungen--Erscheinungsformen." *Zwischen Dogma und säkularer Welt.* Ed. Bernd Engler and Franz Link. Paderborn (Germany): Ferdinand Schöningh, 1991. 9-26. [In German].

General review of the development of literature written by Catholic authors in English. Focuses on the religious theme found in O'Connor's work and refers to *Mystery and Manners*. (Abstracted by Roger Noël).

2045   Filippi, Carmen Lugo. "Alberto Moravia y Flannery O'Connor: dos aproximaciones al cuento en los anos sesenta." [Alberto Moravia and Flannery O'Connor: Two Approaches to the Short Story in the Sixties]. *Los Cuentistas y El Cuento.* San Juan, P.R: Instituto de Cultura Puertorriquena, 1991. 105-14. [In Spanish].

Examines Moravia's theory that it is difficult to give a simple definition of the short story since it demonstrates a variety and complexity as great as the novel. Follows with a discussion of O'Connor's essays in *Mystery and Manners*. Filippi contends that in these essays O'Connor is revealed as a great theorist of the short story. Outlines how O'Connor sees, in the short story, "a complete dramatic action," and her belief that, in the best short stories, the characters are drawn by means of the action and the action is controlled by the characters. Suggests that, from O'Connor's point of view, the major error that inexperienced writers commit is their attempt to use the short story to discuss psychological, philosophical, or sociopolitical problems. States that O'Connor believes that fiction relies on the senses and insists that when short stories are told, they are not meant to theorize nor to tell, but are intended to *show*. Observes that the technique of showing, instead of saying, distinguishes O'Connor's short stories. Sees indications that for O'Connor, the important thing is that the action is carried by the meaning not because the storyteller says it or establishes it, but because readers have drawn their own conclusions based on what has been shown to them. Concludes that O'Connor's objective is not merely to entertain average readers (of whom she has a very low opinion), but to offer to intelligent readers what they are looking for in fiction. (Abstracted by Jeri H. Dies and Juan A. Alcarria).

2046   Fleurdorge, Claude. "`Good Country People,' ou la visite à la vieille dame: examen d'une pratique signifiante." *Delta* (France) 2 (March 1976): 89-130. [In French].

Examines the four main characters in "Good Country People." Associates Manley Pointer with Mrs. Freeman and describes both as strangers; groups Mrs. Hopewell with Hulga as members of a family circle.

Discusses patterns of their relationships which connect them. Offers a close reading of the text supplemented with relevant biblical allusions. Suggests that Manley Pointer serves as an instrument of God's will, a human messenger of the word of Christ. Argues that it is the sexual connotations of his name which corroborate his prophetic function. Thus his unexpected arrival at the house--as well as his seduction of the daughter who lives in it--can be interpreted as a violation representing the metaphorical expression of a mystical rape, the sudden eruption of grace. Claims that, through her associations with automobiles, Mrs. Freeman is a symbolic incarnation of the movement of society and its leveling, coercive, active principle -- the law. Describes this law as a law whose spirit has disappeared. Sees Mrs. Hopewell as responsible for the perversion of a law to which she submits in order better to control it. Finds her a sterile character in that she defies a law that has become fossilized and ultimately condemns herself by refusing to hear the word of God. Focuses on Hulga and sees her nihilism as a parody of the divine order and a caricature of authentic wisdom. Maintains that Hulga's redemption depends on the discovery of Manley Pointer's true identity as a Christ-like figure and of the real content of the Book, the authentic nature and functions of God's word. Claims that the loss of her glasses and artificial leg (a substitute for spiritual convictions and faith), and the demystification of her name, are necessary stages in her healing needed before she can achieve an authentic vision of divine reality. Concludes that Hulga's regeneration, made possible by revelation and the assistance of the Spirit (Manley's breath), will enable her to face the ultimate test in her conversion -- the acceptance of Christ's love and redemption. (Abstracted by Marguerite Bartoli).

2047   Fujiyoshi, Seijiro. "Flannery O'Connor and Nathaniel Hawthorne: The Sin of Pride and Its Redemption." *Hiroshima Bunkyo Women's University Bulletin* (Japan) 28 (Dec. 1993): 15-23. [In Japanese].

2048   Gorczyþska, Renata. "Flannery O'Connor: sztuka deformacji." *Kultura: Szkice, Opowiadania, Sprawozdania* 4.511 (1990): 134-38. [In Polish].

2049   Goto, Kazuhiko. "The Violent Descendants of Ahab in Two Novels of Flannery O'Connor." *Strata* [Bulletin of Strata, Tokyo University] (Japan) 3 (Jan. 1988): 33-47. [In Japanese].

Invokes Melville's Captain Ahab in a discussion of O'Connor's violent prophet figures, Hazel Motes and Francis Marion Tarwater. Notes that where Melville's God appears "cold blooded," O'Connor's is merciful and benevolent. (Abstracted by Kayoko Watanabe).

2050   Gresset, Michel. "Entretien avec Maurice-Edgar Coindreau." [Michel
Gresset Interviews Maurice-Edgar Coindreau] *Delta* (France) 2 (March
1976): 3-11. [In French].

Maurice-Edgar Coindreau, O'Connor's French translator and a frequent
visitor at Andalusia Farm, answers questions about the novelist. Explains
how he became acquainted with O'Connor and talks about her interest in
deformed animals and people. Relates this interest to connections between
deformity and evil. Mentions Hawthorne's influence upon her. Asserts
that O'Connor disliked talking about Catholicism and never broached the
subject to him. Believes that O'Connor preferred to think of herself as a
storyteller rather than a novelist. Contends that the dominant feature in
O'Connor's personality was her sense of humor, although she rarely
laughed and she had no pity for the ludicrous side of human nature.
Claims that O'Connor admired Faulkner's technique and was in awe of
him, much like other Southern writers, such as William Goyen or Truman
Capote. Discusses O'Connor's respect for Jacques Maritain with whom
Coindreau thinks she had a lot in common. Maintains that O'Connor's did
use real people as a basis for her characters (for example, Rufus Johnson).
Finally, quotes from a letter Maritain had sent him, in which he asserts
that O'Connor was misunderstood by the critics, that she hated the devil,
pitied the evangelists, and, according to him, in fact she loved them.
(Abstracted by Marguerite Bartoli).

2051   Gross, Konrad. "Flannery O'Connor: `A View of the Woods.'" *Die
amerikanische Short Story der Gegenwart.* Ed. Peter Freese. Berlin: Erich
Schmidt, 1976. 184-93. [In German].

Asserts that "A View of the Woods" illustrates a historical perspective, or
a process of recognition, from the point of view of Mr. Fortune. Focuses
on themes of death, and on mirror and face symbolism. (Abstracted by
Roger Noël).

2052   Harada, Yuko. "The Landscape of Flannery O'Connor's `The River.'"
Bouei University Bulletin [Humanities and Sciences] (Japan) 65 (Sept.
1992): 12-28. [In Japanese].

Comments on the uniqueness of "The River" among O'Connor's stories:
the protagonist, Harry Ashfield/Bevel, has no knowledge of religion, and
the descriptions of the Southern landscapes are "exceptionally beautiful."
Discusses the woods through which innocent, young Harry passes to get
to the river, and concludes that they are a symbol of Jesus Christ.
(Abstracted by Kayoko Watanabe).

2053   Hashizume, Yumiko. "Flannery O'Connor as a Reader: The Background of the *Presence of Grace*." *Soundings* [Journal of Soundings, American and British Literature Society] (Japan) 10 (1984): 255-68. [In Japanese].

Argues that Mrs. Freeman performs a far more important role than critics have allowed. Contends that she is a person with "insight" who can see through Hulga's secret: her emptiness, naïvete, and need for love. Suggests that her name implies the liberating nature of practicality: "And ye shall know the truth, and the truth shall make you free" (*John* 8:32). (Abstracted by Kayoko Watanabe).

2054   Hashizume, Yumiko. "A Study of O'Connor's Short Stories: `The Enduring Chill,' `The Comforts of Home,' and `Everything That Rises Must Converge.'" *Sophia English Studies* (Sophia University, Japan) 7 (1982): 79-93. [In Japanese].

2055   Hashizume, Yumiko. "A Trial for Ubiquity in Flannery O'Connor's Short Stories." *Sophia English Studies* (Japan) 7 (Nov. 1982): 79-93. [In Japanese].

Analyzes "The Comforts of Home" and "Everything That Rises Must Converge." Remarks that while the characterization of Thomas is too simple and extreme, that of Julian reflects a well-developed and complicated character. (Abstracted by Kayoko Watanabe).

2056   Hattori, Akio. "Flannery O'Connor: Rhetoric of Revelation: A Reading of `A Circle in the Fire.'" *Bulletin of Notre Dame Women's College* (Japan) 9 (1979): 16-28. [In Japanese].

2057   Hattori, Akio. "A Group of Works by Flannery O'Connor: `The Geranium,' `An Exile in the East,' and `Judgement Day.'" *Insight* [Journal of Notre Dame Women's University] (Japan) 21 (March 1989): 25-41. [In Japanese].

Discusses critical comparisons of the three stories (in the title) by Miles Orvell, Ralph C. Wood, and Jan Nordby Gretlund. (Abstracted by Kayoko Watanabe).

2058   Hattori, Akio. "A Memorandum of Flannery O'Connor: A Study of `The Displaced Person.'" *Bulletin of Notre Dame Women's College* (Japan) 11 (1981): 1-11. [In Japanese].

Asserts that Mr. Guizac is the "good man," Mrs. Shortley is given to "sentimentalism," and Mrs. McIntyre to "pragmatism." Concludes that both of the women in the story are scared and insecure. (Abstracted by Kayoko Watanabe).

2059   Hattori, Akio. "A Study of Nathaniel West's *Miss Lonelyhearts* and the Works of Flannery O'Connor." *Bulletin of Notre Dame Women's Junior College* (Japan) 13 (1983): 11-21. [In Japanese].

Discusses the influence of *Miss Lonelyhearts* on *Wise Blood*. Argues that Miss Lonelyhearts and Hazel are seekers after religious truth, even if they have to find it through violence. Shrike and Rayber are hypocrites and Betty and Mrs. Flood appear as self-satisfied women. (Abstracted by Kayoko Watanabe).

2060   Heller, Arno. "'Experienced Meaning': Wirkungsasthetische Betrachtungen zur Flannery O'Connor." *Forms of the American Imagination*. Ed. Sonja Bahn. Innsbruck: Institut fur Sprachwissenschaft der Universitat Innsbruck, 1979. 165-79. [In German].

Focuses on O'Connor's story-telling technique, which encourages the reader to creatively interact with the story instead of passively deriving abstract meanings. (Abstracted by Roger Noël).

2061   Heller, Von Arno. "Zur Nachwirkung der `Southern Agrarians' im Neueren Roman des Amerikanischen Sudens." *Americana-Austriaca: Beitrage zur Amerikakunde, Band 5*. Ed. Klaus Lanzinger. Wein (Austria): Wilhelm Braumuller, 1980. 64-84. [In German].

Offers a general discussion of the "Southern Agrarians" in the literature of the South. Includes a short discussion of *The Violent Bear It Away* in the context of agrarian ideas, and religious and psychological motifs. (Abstracted by Roger Noël).

2062   Hiraishi, Takaki. "A Study of *Wise Blood*: Method and Hate." *American Literature* [Journal of the American Literature Society in Japan, Tokyo Branch] (Japan) 42 (Aug. 1983): 25-32. [In Japanese].

Asserts that *Wise Blood* is a highly ambiguous novel. Remarks that O'Connor's characters are animal-like, governed by instinct--their blood--over reason. Concludes that O'Connor appears to hate the world in this novel because she despises carnality. (Abstracted by Kayoko Watanabe).

2063   Hirose, Ryoichi. "Duality in Flannery O'Connor's *Wise Blood.*" *Shizuoka Eiwa Jogakuin Junior College Bulletin* (Japan) 5 (June 1973): 163-82. [In Japanese].

Sees a duality in Hazel Motes resulting from his conscious efforts to discard the notion of the soul while unconsciously desiring Christ's redemption. His curious behavior is derived from these opposing compulsions. Reads Enoch Emery as Hazel's carnal double and Solace Layfield as his spiritual double. (Abstracted by Kayoko Watanabe).

2064   Holmberg, Claes-Göran. *Crossroads: möten med den samtida amerikanska litteraturen.* [Crossroads: Meetings With Contemporary American Literature.] Nya Doxa (Box 113, S-713, 23 Nora, Sweden), 1994. [In Swedish].

Contains interviews with American writers, numerous book reviews by the author reprinted from *Expressen* (Stockholm's evening newspaper), a register of contemporary movements in American literature, a few illustrations, and three brief essays. O'Connor is referred to five times: (1) John Barth points out to the interviewer (Holmberg), that women writers from the South are left out of his grouping. O'Connor doesn't seem to get canonized. (2) Richard Ford remarks in his interview that he doesn't have anything to say about the South that William Faulkner, Eudora Welty, William Styron and Flannery O'Connor haven't already written about. Ford states that they wrote about the South as he knew it and took it away from him; he has to go North to find *his* material; (3) Leonard Michaels states that his favorite writers write in languages he doesn't know. He admires German and Russian writers immensely, also James Joyce and O'Connor; (4) Richard Stern outlines a tradition from Faulkner and early Welty to O'Connor and Barry Hannah; (5) Holmberg offers an overview of modern Southern novels. Claims that Faulkner, Welty, Carson McCullers, Walker Percy, Styron, and O'Connor hold a heavy tradition laid on new Southern writers. Relates that they have a strong regional identity and a sense of place and a preference for Gothic. (Abstracted by Rönnog Seaberg).

2065   Inoue, Ichiro. "Flannery O'Connor's `The Displaced Person': Jesus Christ as a DP." *Bulletin of the Faculty of Liberal Arts, Nagasaki University* [Humanities] (Japan) 33.2 (1993): 49-64. [In Japanese].

Asserts that Mr. Guizac is like Jesus in that they are both "extra." Comments on the theme of irresistible grace in the character of Mrs. McIntyre, who eventually comes to realize her own displacement. (Abstracted by Kayoko Watanabe).

2066 Inoue, Ichiro. "Flannery O'Connor's Own Virgin Landscape." *Studies in English Literature / Eibungaku kenkyu* [Journal of the English Literary Society of Japan] 67.1 (1990): 79-90. [In Japanese].

Suggests that O'Connor uses her depictions of nature to portray the dynamism and hostility that natural forces exert against humankind. Analyzes the symbolic meaning behind O'Connor's use of forests and the sun to depict the sacred meaning behind her text. (Abstracted by Chikage Toyama).

2067 Inoue, Ichiro. "The Meaning of `A View of the Woods.'" *Bulletin of the Faculty of Liberal Arts, Nagasaki University* [Humanities] (Japan) 35.1 (1994): 91-102. [In Japanese].

Asserts that Mary Fortune is another "self" for Mr. Fortune, therefore his affection toward Mary is a grotesque form of "self-love." Concludes that for Mr. Fortune, to truly recognize the meaning of the "woods," is to know himself. (Abstracted by Kayoko Watanabe).

2068 Inoue, Ichiro. "`Parker's Back' to F. O'Connor no Kadai." ["`Parker's Back' and Flannery O'Connor's Artistic Problem."] *Studies in English Literature / Eibungaku kenkyu* (Tokyo) 65 (1987): 33-45. [In Japanese].

[Cited in *American Literary Scholarship: An Annual, 1988*, 538; and in *Annual Bibliography of English Language and Literature*, 1988, entry 8400, 491.]

2069 Inoue, Ichiro. "The Problem of Expression: Flannery O'Connor's `The Artificial Nigger.'" *Nagasaki University Bulletin* [Liberal Arts] (Japan) 29.2 (1989): 21-33. [In Japanese].

Analyzes opinions of several critics about the conversion of Mr. Head and Nelson. Examines the penultimate paragraph of the story. Comments that "The Artificial Nigger" seems to be a failure, whereas O'Connor's final story, "Parker's Back," is her best. (Abstracted by Kayoko Watanabe).

2070 Inoue, Kazuko. "The World of Flannery O'Connor: A Study of *Mystery and Manners.*" *Essays in Foreign Languages and Literature* [Hokkaido University] (Japan) 20 (March 1974): 51-69. [In Japanese].

Compares two types of characters in O'Connor's fiction: the "Christ-haunted" men on one side, and the practical middle-aged women on the other. Argues that O'Connor presents them all as grotesque, because they are alienated from their true selves. In their responses to violent encounters, O'Connor gives them a chance to become decent people. (Abstracted by Kayoko Watanabe).

2071   Issenhuth, Jean-Pierre. "Flannery O'Connor m'écrit." [Flannery O'Connor Writes to Me]. *Liberté* (Canada) 28.6 (1986): 94-95. [In French].

Offers a note on the French translation of *The Habit of Being, L'Habitude d'être*. Sees O'Connor's life as prompted by love. Focuses on her lucidity and violent passion for the world, her lack of pretention, and her healthy distrust of her own ideas. Underlines appreciatively the absence of acrimony in her letters. (Abstracted by Marguerite Bartoli).

2072   Itoh, Sachiko. "`The Sacred' in *The Violent Bear It Away*." *Kitasato Journal of Liberal Arts and Sciences* [Kitasato University] (Japan) 14 (1980): 80-97. [In Japanese].

Analyses "the sacred" in *The Violent Bear It Away*. Discusses *Aufsaetze das Numinose Betreffend*, by Rudolf Otto, and categorizes Old Tarwater and Bishop as belonging to "the sacred," whereas the characters of Rayber and Young Tarwater combine both "the sacred" and "the secular." (Abstracted by Kayoko Watanabe).

2073   Iwayama, Tajiro. "A Grotesque Literature in Search of Redemption: A Study of Flannery O'Connor's `A Good Man Is Hard to Find.'" *Eigo Bungaku Sekai* [World of British and American Literature] (Japan) (Sept. 1970): 8-13. [In Japanese].

Contends that The Misfit is obsessed with the "hypostatic union" of God in Christ. Conversely, the grandmother does not abide by true religion, save when her head "clear[s] for an instant" as The Misfit shouts out in his agony to believe the Gospel. Concludes that although the grandmother is devoured by the dragon (The Misfit), she dies happily redeemed, "her face smiling up at the cloudless sky." (Abstracted by Kayoko Watanabe).

2074   Iwayama, Tajiro. "How to Find a Good Man in `A Good Man Is Hard to Find.'" *Shuryu* [Doshisha University Bulletin] (Japan) 28 (Sept. 1966): 78-80. [In Japanese].

2075   Jordis, Christine. "Flannery O'Connor: Voir ce qui crève les yeux." [Flannery O'Connor: To See What Is Staring You in the Face]. *La Nouvelle Revue Française* (France) 399 (1986): 64-73. [In French].

Focuses on O'Connor's technique of *showing*, rather than talking about people and their behavior, in order to get to the mystery of existence, as revealed by a system of beliefs. Suggests that O'Connor did not want to understand, she wanted to see and to lend a concrete form to the mystery of existence. Observes that some of her characters paid the ultimate price for this sudden discovery of the truth: death, madness, or senility. (Abstracted by Roger Noël).

2076   Kim, Kyung-Im. "A Study of the Fiction of Flannery O'Connor." Diss. Chonnam National U (Korea), [1986]. [In Korean].

[Cited in *Annual Bibliography of English Language and Literature for 1987*. (Modern Humanities Research Association), p. 709, entry 12045.]

2077   Kimishima, Kazuko. "The Structure of the Climax: How to Read Short Stories." *Bulletin of the Faculty of Liberal Arts, Hosei University* (Japan) 73 (Feb. 1990): 287-304. [In Japanese].

Discusses the climactic scene of "A Good Man Is Hard to Find." (Abstracted by Kayoko Watanabe).

2078   Kimura, Masatoshi. "A Study of *Wise Blood*: The Birth of a Christian Hero." *Bulletin of the College of Foreign Studies, Yokohama* (Japan) 7 (Feb. 1985): 1-27. [In Japanese].

Explores the "serious and tragic" aspects of *Wise Blood*. Concludes that although Hazel is a freak, he becomes a Christian hero, a modern saint who is permitted to enter the true country. (Abstracted by Kayoko Watanabe).

2079   Kimura, Yasuo. "The World of Flannery O'Connor: Revelation and Redemption." *Journal of the International College of Commerce & Economics* (Japan) 17 (1978): 1-8. [In Japanese].

Claims that O'Connor's characters are not only typically shallow-minded and stupid, but also serve as bystanders who are apathetic to evil. Contends that she gives them the chance to accept eternal redemption because she believes they are--as we are--all children of God. (Abstracted by Kayoko Watanabe).

2080   Kondo, Tadashi. "On American Short Stories: Flannery O'Connor in Search of Grace." *Journal of the School of General Education, Okayama University* (Japan) 13 (March 1977): 45-58. [In Japanese].

2081   Kumskova, E.I. "Zhanrovoe svoeobraze novelistiki Flanneri O'Konnor."
           [Genre Originality of the Short Stories of Flannery O'Connor].
           Literaturnye proizvedenia XVIII-XX vekov v istoricheskom i kul'turnom
           kontekste. [Literary Works From the 18th to the 20th Centuries in
           Historical and Cultural Context.] Moscow: Moscow UP, 1985. 137-47.
           [In Russian].

           Considers O'Connor's writings from a Soviet critic's perspective,
           acknowledging the artistic merit of her work while pointing out meanings
           which reveal antagonisms among classes in American society. Suggests
           that because of her personal circumstances--as a Southern female Catholic
           writer--O'Connor holds a unique place in American literature. Discusses
           themes in O'Connor's stories and sees them as being in opposition to the
           main trend of bourgeois mores. Argues that while she is not a
           revolutionary, O'Connor is in strong opposition to the prevailing social
           relations in American society. Contends that the vehicle for her expression
           for this opposition is her use of the grotesque. Outlines how she uses
           relations between children and parents, males and females, and between
           different classes, to exhibit her grotesque perspective. Focuses on "The
           Lame Shall Enter First," and discusses how Sheppard's egotistic
           generosity toward Rufus Johnson clashes with the egotism and self-
           centered character of his son. Offers brief discussions of "Judgement
           Day," "Everything That Rises Must Converge," "Greenleaf," "A Good
           Man Is Hard to Find," and "The Comforts of Home." Concludes that
           O'Connor's work reflects her belief that individuals must take
           responsibility for their own destiny, even if their destiny is determined or
           limited by social circumstances. (Abstracted by George S. Toth).

2082   Kusaka, Yosuke. "Haze's Dilemma: A Study of Flannery O'Connor's *Wise*
           Blood." *Studies in American Literature* (Japan) 4 (June 1982): 76-84. [In
           Japanese].

2083   Kusaka, Yosuke. "Technique and Style in Flannery O'Connor's Novels:
           A Study of *The Violent Bear It Away*." *Buntairon Kenkyu* [Studies of the
           Structure of Novels] (Japan) 33 (Nov. 1986): 8-22. [In Japanese].

2084   Kwon, Jong Joon. "The Elements of Mystery in *Wise Blood*." *Journal of*
           English Language and Literature (Korea) 37.2 (1991): 465-90. [In
           Korean].

           Investigates mystical elements of *Wise Blood* using Evelyn Underhill's
           "theory of the classic journey of the 'Mystic Way.'" Describes how
           mystics gain awareness through a conversion experience. Applies this

description to Hazel Motes in *Wise Blood* and suggests that it is only by "denying his world and committing violence" that Hazel is suddenly awakened. Contends that the image of Hazel's "external blindness and internal sight fully captures the meaning and the method of the purgative way." Argues that because the way illuminated to the mystic "reveals the soul's journey to God," the mystic is no longer of this world; and it is because of this vision that Hazel is motivated to go on to where "he will be retested in the severe trials of final purification." Suggests that when Hazel becomes merely a "'pin point of light' in the darkness," he has arrived at his "final transcendent goal of mystical union with God." Concludes that Hazel's journey reflects "classical, mystic elements which contribute to the extension of essentially effective mystery." [Based upon the author's English language abstract.]

2085   Lamontagne, Marie-Andrée. "Une lumière oblique." *Liberté* (Canada) 34.1 (1992): 163-66. [In French].

Reviews the French publication of Flannery O'Connor's novels and short stories. Notes that although the novelist left the South only three times, hers was not a narrow universe. Contends that it was in the South that she found her monsters, condemned in the name of atavism and the irresistible power of evil. Declares that at first sight, her gospel is harsh: humanity is destitute, the Bible a pretext for all kinds of excesses, and even the pleasure of reading is compromised by a feeling of unease and awe. Finds that in spite of this, O'Connor's work is, in a roundabout way, an apologia showing the disorders that pride leads to, and written with the intention of ridding Christianity of its dross. Suggests that no matter how grotesque they are, O'Connor's characters are not denied light. But it is an oblique light that appears in the darkest parts of her tales, and it is only when her characters finally seem to understand how vain their agitation is that 'Sabbath' can begin. (Abstracted by Marguerite Bartoli).

2086   Laveggi, Lucile. "Le Catholicisme de Flannery O'Connor." [Flannery O'Connor's Catholicism]. *L'Infini* (France) 10 (Spring 1985): 61-69. [In French].

Examines O'Connor's Catholicism and the way it influences her work. Contends that her universe has meaning only in relation to original sin, grace, and redemption, and that O'Connor uses violence so as to test indifferent readers in the flesh. Argues that O'Connor strongly wishes to convert the reader, through an appeal to a Catholic aesthetic, as reflected in the liturgy and formal Catholic dogmas. Notes, however, that she occasionally expresses reservations about Catholicism and has an affinity for fundamentalists. (Abstracted by Marguerite Bartoli).

2087   Lesgoirres, Daniel. "'The Displaced Person' ou `Le Christ recrucifié.'"
["The Displaced Person" or "Christ Crucified Again."] *Delta* (France) 2
(March 1976): 75-87. [In French].

Examines the parallels between "The Displaced Person" and the Gospel
story. Reads the story as a religious drama, with Guizac as a Christ figure,
Mrs. Shortley as a representation of the Pharisees, and Mrs. McIntyre as
an incarnation of the Hebrew people. Compares Guizac's life on the farm
to Christ's public life, his rise, the obstacles he meets and his fall.
Contends that by attacking an established moral order, the Pole becomes
an object of scandal deserving death. Suggests that, although Shortley is
guilty of murder, he is not as guilty as Mrs. McIntyre, who stifles her
pangs of conscience with full knowledge of the facts. Asserts that both
Astor and the priest are true prophets: the old black man because he
understands the true meaning of religious tradition and history, and the
priest because he is there to remind us that the sacrifice of Christ is
constantly renewed in the sacrifice of the righteous. Maintains that
O'Connor shows that such sacrifices must be understood as revelations of
God's grace that we must recognize if we do not want to fall into spiritual
decay. (Abstracted by Marguerite Bartoli).

2088   Lévy, Maurice. "L'éscriture catholique de Flannery O'Connor." [Flannery
O'Connor's Catholic Writing]. *Revue Française d'Études Americaines*
(France) 1 (April 1976): 125-33. [In French].

Remarks that, unlike works by Graham Greene and Georges Bernanos,
Flannery O'Connor's work bear no trace of specific Catholic concerns. In
spite of this absence, O'Connor's use of Southern, backwoods prophets is
still very effective in conveying elements of a universal, Catholic faith.
Discusses how O'Connor sidestepped the issue of being a Catholic in the
largely Protestant South, and adapted--in her writing--the local spirituality
to tell the Truth. Contends that she resorts to such methods as the breaking
down of symbols, use of the grotesque, and other techniques borrowed
from naturalistic writing to eliminate the need to focus directly on God.
Suggests instead that the aim of O'Connor's strategy was to initiate a
desire in the reader for the kinds of convergence evidenced in her work.
Suggests that O'Connor's symbols allow readers to find a Catholic reading
from the inside of the work: they function as vehicles for a homogeneous,
identifiable signified. Lists examples from "The Displaced Person" and
"A Temple of the Holy Ghost." Asserts that O'Connor's writing is Catholic
because it is ambiguous, paradoxical, and full of the equivocations of
immanence: it seizes the world in the depth of its opaqueness to drive it
to the brink of mystery. (Abstracted by Marguerite Bartoli).

2089   Link, Franz. "Erzähler des Südens: Flannery O'Connor." *Amerikanische Erzähler seit 1950: Themen, Inhalte, Formen* Paderborn, Germany: Ferdinand Schöningh, 1993. [In German].

2090   Louit, Robert. "Le Catholicisme Outrancier de Flannery O'Connor." [Flannery O'Connor's Extreme Catholicism]. *Litterature Etrangere*, [1975?]: 45-46. [In French].

Reviews the French translation of *Mystery and Manners*. Focuses on and explains O'Connor's use of violence and atonement trials. Discusses her position as a Southern American Catholic writer who denies writing strictly about the South. Explains that O'Connor's home ground is the concrete universal and why her characters need to be seen from the ethical angle. Comments that physical unsightliness is a sign of moral infirmity or of divine malediction in O'Connor's stories. Submits that for O'Connor's characters, evil is not an abstract notion but an active energy whose crude religiosity gives meaning to the universe. Finds their manners to be full of the sense of mystery which the writer can inscribe on the fabric of lived reality. Suggests that while modern ideologies have annihilated the consciousness of evil, O'Connor saw it as her duty as a novelist to restore it through violence. Proposes that O'Connor's damned characters are stronger because of their consciousness of evil which, in itself, becomes a form of faith. Recognizes that this is how these characters get the upper hand of the faint-hearted without a soul. Concludes that O'Connor's Catholicism is extreme, more willing to accept the defiance of John Milton's Satan than the orthodoxy of the modern world. (Abstracted by Marguerite Bartoli).

2091   Maeda, Ayako. "Two Georgia Writers: Carson McCullers and Flannery O'Connor." *Ferris Studies* (Japan) 20 (March 1985): 51-69. [In Japanese].

Examines McCullers's *The Member of the Wedding* and O'Connor's "A Temple of the Holy Ghost" in detail, noting their similarities and differences. Concludes that the chief difference within the two works lies in the representation of Time: McCullers's story is set in *chronos*, whereas O'Connor's story deals with *kairos*. (Abstracted by Kayoko Watanabe).

2092   Martelli, R. "Flannery O'Connor (A Southern Writer or a Catholic Writer?")" *Ponte* 52.11-12 (1996): 99-109. [In Italian].

2092a   Matsudaira, Yoko. "Chikara no toso to jenda: Amerika nanbu josei sakka kenkyu, II: Flannery O'Connor, 6." *Shoin Literary Review* 30 (1997): 17-36. [In Japanese].

2093   Matsudaira, Yoko. "Dissatisfaction and Transfiguration: A Study of Flannery O'Connor." *Shoin Literary Review* (Japan) 28 (1995): 1-16. [In Japanese].

2093a   Matsudaira, Yoko. "'Good Country People' no imi: Amerika nanbu josei sakka kenkyu II: Flannery O'Connor, II." *Shoin Literary Review* 26 (1993): 55-74 [In Japanese].

2094   Matsudaira, Yoko. "Human Classes." *Shoin Literary Review* (Japan) 27 (1994): 43-63. [In Japanese].

2095   Matsudaira, Yoko. "On Intellectual Superiority: A Study of Flannery O'Connor." *Shoin Literary Review* (Japan) 29 (1996): 21-36. [In Japanese].

2096   Matsumoto, Fusae. "The Meaning of the Grotesque in the World of Flannery O'Connor." *Bulletin of Sienan Jogakuin Junior College* (Japan) 26 (Dec. 1979): 105-11. [In Japanese].

2095a   Matsudaira, Yoko. "Ryu to osuushi: America nanbu josei sakka kenkyu, II: Flannery O'Connor, VIII." *Shoin Literary Review* 32 (1999): 1-12. [In Japanese].

2097   Matsumoto, Fusae. "Of *Wise Blood*, Part I: An Introduction to *Wise Blood*." *Seinan Jogakuin Junior College Bulletin* (Japan) 33 (Dec. 1986): 77-87. [In Japanese].

2098   Matsumoto, Fusae. *Wise Blood* and the Real Image of Flannery O'Connor." *Seinan Jogakuin Junior College Bulletin* (Japan) 31 (1984): 65-74. [In Japanese].

2099   Matsumoto, Fusae. "The World of Flannery O'Connor: The American South." *Seinan Jogkuin Junior College Bulletin* (Japan) 29 (Dec. 1982): 23-29. [In Japanese].

2100   Miyamoto, Keiko. "Flannery O'Connor's 'The Artificial Nigger': Eyes to See the Blacks." *Shikoku Gakuin University Bulletin* (Japan) 73 (March 1990): 125-40. [In Japanese].

2101   Miyamoto, Keiko. "Sacramental View in the Works of Flannery O'Connor: A Study of `The River.'" *Christian Literature* [Bulletin of the Christian Literature Society in Japan, Kyushu Branch] (Japan) 5 (May 1986): 84-72. [In Japanese].

2102   Mongin, Oliver. "L'homme qui voulait se libérer du fanatisme." [The Man Who Wanted to Free Himself From Fanaticism] *Esprit* 154 (Sept. 1989): 77-85. [In French].

Reviews John Huston's film version of *Wise Blood* (in French: "Le Malin"), and compares it to the novel. Does not see Huston as interested in deriding evangelism or fanaticism, but as setting out to focus on the possibility of creating a world in which atonement or repentance do not alienate the individual. Indicates that whereas O'Connor shows how the Antichrist becomes a fanatic through excessive sincerity, Huston describes the trials and contradictions of those who attempt an exit from religion. Maintains that ultimately the protagonist is back where he started, and Huston's skepticism demonstrates how difficult it is to free oneself from fanaticism. (Abstracted by Marguerite Bartoli).

2103   Morita, Akiharu. "Mystery and Manners in Flannery O'Connor." *Asphodel* [Doshisha Women's University Bulletin] (Japan) 14 (July 1980): 110-23. [In Japanese].

2104   Morita, Takeshi. "The World of Flannery O'Connor: A Consideration of Metaphors." *Research Bulletin C: Foreign Languages and Literature* [Bulletin of the College of General Education, Nagoya University] (Japan) 17 (March 1973): 43-66. [In Japanese].

Analyzes 180 examples of metaphors in O'Connor's works. Focuses especially on metaphors of animals, arguing that O'Connor uses beast-like figures to reveal the true nature of her characters. Concludes that though we have not blinded our eyes with lime like Haze nor had our eyes singed like Tarwater's in order to see "invisible" things, through O'Connor's many metaphors we may see what is beyond in the visionary views of the characters in her works. (Abstracted by Kayoko Watanabe).

2105   Nagatake, Yuko. "Haunted by God: Silence and Emptiness in Flannery O'Connor's *The Violent Bear It Away*." *Colloquia* [Bulletin of the Graduate School of Keio University] (Japan) 5 (1984): 1-14. [In Japanese].

Examines the motifs and silence and emptiness in *The Violent Bear It Away*, and argues that God's presence is found in the silences of the novel, while secular unbelief is figured as emptiness. Contends that Old Tarwater's fanaticism and madness is also God's domain. Concludes with a discussion of "freedom" in the novel, noting that for Rayber, freedom means being able to ignore God, while for Francis Tarwater, freedom means being free to accept God's grace in an otherwise "empty" world. (Abstracted by Kayoko Watanabe).

2106   Nielsen, Erik. "Flannery O'Connor og Thomas Aquinas." *Edda: Nordisk Tidsskrift for Litteraturforskning / Scandinavian Journal of Literary Research* (Norway) 90.4 (1990): 313-28. [In Danish].

Asserts that Flannery O'Connor was thoroughly familiar with Thomas Aquinas' writing and read from his *Summa* for a while every day during certain times in her life. States that O'Connor absorbed his philosophy creatively to the point of making it her own philosophy of writing. Aquinas' philosophy is summarized as bringing together Medieval and Aristotelian thinking resulting in the contention that the world of the senses is not seen as opposed to the spiritual world. Reports that O'Connor takes a Thomist point of view, acceptable to the Catholic Church, when she avoids abstractions and seeks to describe profane material. Maintains that in describing the sensual material she makes the supernatural world real. Discusses *The Violent Bear It Away*, focusing on Rayber's baptism of feeble-minded Bishop, and on O'Connor's use of the symbolism of water in this novel. A primary and secondary bibliography is provided. (Abstracted by Rönnog Seaberg).

2107   Nielsen, Erik. *Flannery O'Connor's Romaner*. [Flannery O'Connor's Novels]. Odense U Studies in Lit. 29. Odense, Denmark: Odense Universitetsforlag, 1992. [In Danish].

Discusses *Wise Blood*'s Hazel Motes as a "`despondent atheist'" whose conversion from fundamentalism leads to "a belief in his own soullessness," nihilism, and finally a deep faith in God. Sees *The Violent Bear It Away* as a novel where "aesthetic-nihilistic views struggle for access to the Christian universe." Suggests that O'Connor's work depicts "a worldly struggle against the persistent intrusion of the divine." Remarks that the two works should be viewed not as religious novels, but as "contributions to an idea-debating genre, initiation stories that express a philosophy of religion." Offers an overview of O'Connor's poetics. Compares her perspective of Christian alienation to Bertolt Brecht's "theory of *Verfremdung*." [From an abstract by Jan Nordby Gretlund, Elisabeth Herion-Sarafidis, and Hans Skei (in "Scandinavian

Contributions" *American Literary Scholarship: An Annual, 1992.* Ed. David J. Nordloh. Durham, NC: Duke UP, pp. 360-61), who state that this volume serves as "the first Danish study to focus exclusively on O'Connor's relatively longer works."

Representative Reviews: Karl-Heinz Westarp, *Flannery O'Connor Bulletin* 21 (1992): 140-43.

2108   Nielsen. Erik. "Ligbegaengelse - Et byproblem i urbanitetens hjørne." ["The Handling of Bodies: A City Problem in the Corner of Urbanity."] *Moderne bykultur: A Newsletter* (Denmark) 9 (1988): 16-23. [In Danish].

Focuses on the importance placed on Mason Tarwater's need for burial rather than cremation in *The Violent Bear It Away*. States that young Tarwater's refusal to carry out the old man's burial instructions is, "more than just stubborn flirting with heathenism . . . more than anti-Christian pragmatism, it is also a violation of the old-fashioned Southern ways of burying." [From citation and abstract by Jan Nordby Gretlund, Elisabeth Herion-Sarafidis and Hans Skei in "Scandinavian Contributions" in *American Literary Scholarship: An Annual, 1989*, Ed. David J. Nordloh. Durham, NC: Duke UP, 455.]

2109   Nielsen, Erik. "Sexualiteten som motiv Flannery O'Connors roman *Wise Blood*." ["Sexuality as Motive in Flannery O'Connor's Novel *Wise Blood*."] *Edda: Nordisk Tidsskrift for Litteraturforskning / Scandinavian Journal of Literary Research* (Norway) 4 (1991): 308-21. [In Danish].

Offers an analysis of the character Sabbath Hawkes in *Wise Blood*, seen as a personification of sexual desire and lust without guilt. Suggests that O'Connor uses sex in her writing mostly as a philosophical argument and not as an image of sensuality, and that erotic relations between her characters signify religious relations between humans and God. Concludes that sex needs interpretation in O'Connor's writing. Since it is never something in itself but always points outside itself, it appears to be used as a weapon in an ideological struggle. Brief bibliography included. (Abstracted by Rönnog Seaberg).

2110   Nielsen, Erik. "Om Detaljen." ["On Detail"] *Fantasi og fiktion*. Odense University Studies in Literature, Vol. 23. Ed. Erik Svejgaard and John Thobo-Carlsen. Odense (Denmark): Odense UP, 1989. 99-135. [In Danish].

Identifies eight different functions of detail as used in fiction. Examples are given from William Faulkner, Georg Lucács, Flannery O'Connor,

Walker Percy, Pat Conroy, and others. Suggests that Flannery O'Connor's use of detail is symbolic, as in Hazel Motes's rat-colored car, which he uses to preach from, and which is described as driven without a license and eventually pushed off a cliff. Discusses Mason Tarwater's wish to be buried instead of being cremated, which Nielsen argues reflects Flannery O'Connor's Southern beliefs, here in conflict with Catholic faith which is for burial without cremation. A short bibliography is included. (Abstracted by Rönnog Seaberg).

2111   Niimi, Sumiko. "Country and City." *Re-reading of American Short Stories*. Ed. Japan Bernard Malamud Association. Tokyo: Hokuseido, 1996. 295-306. [In Japanese].

Discusses "The Artificial Nigger." (Abstracted by Kayoko Watanabe).

2112   Nishikawa, Ryosuke. "'Good Country People': A World of Mirrors." *Hiyoshi Bulletin, English and American Literature* 30 (March 1997): 49-71. [In Japanese].

Analyzes the mirror images seen in Mrs. Hopewell, Hulga and Manley Pointer. (Abstracted by Kayoko Watanabe).

2113   Noguchi, Hajime. "Christian Redemption in Flannery O'Connor's `The Enduring Chill.'" *British and American Literature Studies* [Rissho University Bulletin] (Japan) 11 (1983): 1-12. [In Japanese].

Analyzes the Christian theme of this short story: Asbury's extreme confidence in his intelligence, his failure, and then God's offer of redemption. (Abstracted by Kayoko Watanabe).

2114   Noguchi, Hajime. "A Christian World in `A Circle in the Fire.'" *British and American Literature Studies* [Rissho University Bulletin] (Japan) 10 (June 1982): 1-7. [In Japanese].

2115   Noguchi, Hajime. *Flannery O'Connor Kenkyu*. [The World of Flannery O'Connor]. Tokyo: Bunnka Shobo Hakubunsha, 1992. [In Japanese].

Divided into four chapters, this eclectic book-length study of O'Connor reviews biographical details, including her two years at Iowa City (Chapter 1); examines the characters in her fiction and comments particularly on her use of the "double" motif (Chapter 2); explores

"O'Connor and Music" (Chapter 3); and, then provides a primary bibliography and chronological record of her career (Chapter 4). (Abstracted by Kayoko Watanabe).

Representative Reviews: Hiroko Sato, *American Literary Scholarship: An Annual, 1992*. Ed. David Nordloh. Durham, NC: Duke UP, 1994. 344-50.

2116   Noguchi, Hajime. "Flannery O'Connor's `Parker's Back': Parker's Pilgrimage." *Tokyo Toritsu Junior College Bulletin* 1 (1997): 3-12. [In Japanese].

2117   Noguchi, Hajime. *Furanari Okona no Sekai*. [The World of Flannery O'Connor]. Tokyo: Bunka Shobo Hakubunsha, 1988. [In Japanese].

[Cited in *American Literary Scholarship: An Annual 1988*, Durham, NC: Duke UP, 1990. p. 538.]

2118   Noguchi, Hajime. *Furanari Okona Ronko*. [A Study of Flannery O'Connor] Tokyo: Bunka Shobo Hakubunsha, 1985. [In Japanese].

A brief introduction to O'Connor's life with commentary on her major short stories. (Abstracted by Kayoko Watanabe).

2119   Noguchi, Hajime. "Manley Pointer: Image of Jesus Christ." *Tokyo Metropolitan Junior College Bulletin* (Japan) 27 (1994): 175-79. [In Japanese].

Explains how Hulga gains her spiritual "re-birth" through Manley Pointer. (Abstracted by Kayoko Watanabe).

2120   Noguchi, Hajime. "Some Christian Aspects in Flannery O'Connor's `A Good Man Is Hard to Find.'" *Journal of Yamanashi Gakuin University* (Japan) 4 (1981): 1-15. [In Japanese].

Discusses The Misfit as a typical O'Connor character, haunted by Christ and doomed to stand face to face with Christ. (Abstracted by Kayoko Watanabe).

2121   Noguchi, Hajime. "A Study of Flannery O'Connor's `Good Country People.'" *Yamanashi Gakuin University Bulletin* (Japan) 5 (1982): 29-40. [In Japanese].

Analyzes the symbolic meaning of the main characters: Hulga, Pointer, and Mrs. Hopewell. Notes that the irony lies in the fact that the real good country people are Hulga and her mother, though they think Pointer is a good country person. (Abstracted by Kayoko Watanabe).

2122   Nomura, Shizu. "Flannery O'Connor's `The Displaced Person' and Christ's Redemption." *Eigaku* [Heian Jogakuin Junior College Bulletin] (Japan) 7 (March 1975): 34-45. [In Japanese].

2123   Nylinder, Ake. "En sakramental syn pa livet: Om William Styron, Flannery O'Connor, Walker Percy och den amerikanska söden." ["A Sacramental View of Life: On William Styron, Flannery O'Connor, Walker Percy and the American South."] *Horisont* (Finland) 29.3 (1982): 84-98. [In Swedish].

Analyzes views of the South as reflected in the writings of Styron, O'Connor, and Percy. Finds Flannery O'Connor to be a straightforward, honest, unliterary and unsophisticated writer. Criticizes Caj Lundgren's translation of *Everything That Rises Must Converge* (*Bra folk fran landet*) for leaving out "Parker's Back" and "The Enduring Chill." Describes O'Connor as a Christian and Catholic writer of the mystic and ascetic tradition and finds her approach to violence and vulgarity to be comparable to that of Dostoevsky. Considers *Wise Blood* to be the story of a saint. Concludes that, as a Catholic, woman, and Southerner, Flannery O'Connor is an outsider. Illustrations: Photographs of Norman Mailer, William Styron, Flannery O'Connor, Walker Percy, and William Faulkner. (Abstracted by Rönnog Seaberg).

2124   Ochi, Hiromi. "Flannery O'Connor's `The Artificial Nigger': From Closed Self to Opened Self." *Etude* [Studies in the Graduate School of Ochanomizu University] (Japan) 19 (1989): 27-39. [In Japanese].

2125   Ochi, Hiromi. "Where Does the Conflict Go?: Flannery O'Connor and the Vision of Community." *Journal of Humanity Studies* [Ochanomizu University] (Japan) 13 (1989): 250-70. [In Japanese].

Closely compares "The Geranium" and "Judgement Day." Comments that the South to which old Tanner desperately wants to return, and where whites and blacks are socially and spiritually connected, is O'Connor's ideal community, whereas New York is a "mock society." (Abstracted by Kayoko Watanabe).

2126   Ohashi, Kichinosuke. "A World Haunted by God: A Study of *The Violent Bear It Away*." *Bengei* (Japan) 10.6 (1971): 243-44. [In Japanese].

2127   Oleneva, Valentia. "Novella SSHA. Mnogoobrazie form." ["The American Short Story: Formal Diversity"], *Zhanrovoe raznoobrazie sovremennoi prozy Zapada* ["Genre Diversity of Contemporary Western Prose"]. Kiev: Naukova Dumka. 192-299. [In Russian].

Lyra comments that despite the fact that Oleneva's work is "thoroughly grounded in Marxist literary theory," she "not only accepts Flannery O'Connor's Catholicism but emphasizes its value," stating that "it enriches the short story with new content." Contends that Oleneva reads O'Connor's work, "not as that of a Southerner but as that of an American writer." [From citation and discussion by F. Lyra in "Foreign Scholarship: East European Contributions," (in *American Literary Scholarship: An Annual 1989*. Ed. David J. Nordloh. Durham: Duke UP, 1991. 375-76).]

2128   Osada, Mitsunobu. "A Home in Literature in the South -- A Place of Death and Rebirth: Works of Tennessee Williams, Robert Penn Warren, and Flannery O'Connor." *American Literature* [Journal of the American Literature Society in Japan, Tokyo Branch] 36 (Feb. 1979): 17-24. [In Japanese].

2129   Otake, Masaru. "The Life and Works of Flannery O'Connor." *Journal of Humanities & Natural Sciences, Tokyo Keizai University* (Japan) 64 (July 1983): 173-98. [In Japanese].

Introduces the content of *Wise Blood*, *The Violent Bear It Away*, and five short stories. (Abstracted by Kayoko Watanabe).

2130   Pieiller, Evelyne. "L'univers de Flannery O'Connor." [Flannery O'Connor's Universe]. *La Quinzaine littéraire* (France) 1-15 July 1991: 8. [In French].

Reviews the publication in French of Flannery O'Connor's works as well as Geneviève Brisac's *Loin du Paradis, Flannery O'Connor*. Declares that although O'Connor is a devout Catholic, she does not write sermons or edifying parables. Describes her universe as one of passion and possession, and compares her to Dostoevsky and J.D. Salinger. Sees O'Connor's novels and stories as versions of the eternal legend that has attempted since the dawn of time to give form and meaning to the radical oddness of our presence. Suggests that *The Violent Bear It Away* may be her most beautiful tale. Praises her lightning language in which she mingles biblical flashes and everyday speech so as to conjure up an oblique, splendid anagogical vision. Contends that although the events in O'Connor's works are a real challenge to a reasonable notion of existence in that they are highly improbable, they acquire a mythical dimension through incarnations and the concrete. Reviews *Loin du Paradis*, regarding it as an exchange between Brisac and O'Connor's texts, with an emphasis on O'Connor's childhood and the rupture caused by her father's death. Regrets that no mention is made of O'Connor's splendid language, but forgives the lack of a bibliography, since the book is more a matter of fascinated tenderness than an objective assessment of a novelist neglected by fashion. (Abstracted by Marguerite Bartoli).

2131   Richard, Claude. "Désir et destin dans `A Good Man Is Hard to Find.'" [Desire and Destiny in "A Good Man Is Hard to Find"]. *Delta* (France) 2 (March 1976): 61-73. [In French].

Focuses on the character of the grandmother in "A Good Man Is Hard to Find." Contends that there are two referential systems present in the story: the cultural order and the natural order. Demonstrates that the grandmother partakes of the former and that her adventure can be defined as a passage to the latter. Suggests that through her sense of history, the grandmother knows the meaning of cultural class' values and that her crafty use of speech implies that--for her--culture pertains to the order of language. Asserts that an examination of the exercise of power through language, that is, the fulfillment of the grandmother's desires through speech, offers an method of gaining a deeper understanding of the story. Maintains that interpreting the story's meaning also hinges upon considering St. Cyril of Jerusalem's admonition: "The dragon sits by the side of the road, watching those who pass. Beware less he devour you. We go to the Father of Souls, but it is necessary to pass by the dragon." Argues that during her verbal confrontation with The Misfit/Dragon--who is shown to belong to the natural order--the grandmother gradually loses her cultural attributes, notably speech. Contends that only when this happens can the grandmother enter the natural order and have access to the prime, plurivocal language of invocation and be ready for a revelation of the natural order of God, in which her cultural concept of love gives way to an awareness of universal love. (Abstracted by Marguerite Bartoli).

2132   Richard, Claude and Michel Gresset. "Études critiques: Sélection." [Selected Critical Studies]. *Delta* (France) 2 (March 1976): 143-61. [In French].

A bibliography of critical studies on Flannery O'Connor, including: book length works, general works in periodicals, and criticism and book reviews in French. (Abstracted by Marguerite Bartoli).

2133   Richard, Claude and Michel Gresset. "Oeuvres de Flannery O'Connor." [Works by Flannery O'Connor]. *Delta* (France) 2 (March 1976): 133-42. [In French].

A classified bibliography of works by O'Connor, including: an alphabetical list of her novels and collections of short stories; a chronological list, by date of first publication, of O'Connor's stories; a chronological listing, by date of publication, of her essays and articles; O'Connor's published correspondence; her published interviews, in chronological order; and a list of French translations of her writings. (Abstracted by Marguerite Bartoli).

2134   Rigaud, Marielle. "*The Violent Bear It Away*: La Quête du Père." [*The Violent Bear It Away*: The Quest of the Father]. *Delta* (France) 27 (Feb. 1989): 45-54. [In French].

Discusses Francis Marion Tarwater's search for truth as an attempt to recover primeval speech when meaning is entangled in a multiplicity of voices. Contends that though an orphan, Tarwater still requires a relation to the father in order to enact a desired breaking of paternal law. Argues that three father figures are in his way. First, Mason Tarwater, who threatens him with passive dependence, and whose power and speech are indestructible even after his death. Second, God, whose word is transmitted by the old prophet, whereas Tarwater wants an immediate revelation that will establish him as a true prophet. Third, Rayber who wants the boy to be a substitute for his retarded son, a role and a relationship that he adamantly refuses. Submits that although Tarwater is in search of the authentic, primary word which would enable him to have access to a coherent identity, he is the victim of his desire for the absolute: one cannot fight against the father, against the dead. Describes how, ultimately, the father wins, and opens the way for the boy's new destiny. (Abstracted by Marguerite Bartoli).

2135   Riis, Torben. *Flannery O'Connor: Kristen realisme er ikke sentimental.* ["Flannery O'Connor: Christian Realism is Not Sentimental"]. *Tidens Tegn* (Copenhagen), 1984. 46-50. [In Danish].

Suggests that the absurd and evil displayed in O'Connor's work reflect her faith. Emphasizes her personal attitudes as a writer and a believing

Catholic, and offers quotes from her letters published in *The Habit of Being*. Discusses how O'Connor takes a stand against faith founded on emotions or personal experiences. Comments on the influence of the French Jesuit, Pierre Teilhard de Chardin. Reports that her letters do not reflect her severe illness, and concludes that she viewed sickness as a mystery that turned her from a subjective or sentimental worship of Christ. Illustrations: Photograph of O'Connor standing in front of her self-portrait. [From a presentation at a symposium held at Sandbjerggard, South Jutland, August, 1984, commemorating the 20th anniversary of Flannery O'Connor's death.] (Abstracted by Rönnog Seaberg).

2136   Rinaldi, Angelo. "L'autre Faulkner." [The Other Faulkner]. *L'Express* 13-19 Oct. 1975: 60-61. [In French].

Review of the French publication of *Why Do the Heathen Rage?* (In French: *Pourquoi ces nations en tumulte?*) and *Mystery and Manners*. Calls O'Connor the only high caliber Catholic writer in the United States, while underlining that she is not a church woman mixing the truth with holy water. Mentions that O'Connor's firm tone, bold images, and cruel taunts had prompted Maurice-Edgar Coindreau, who had discovered Faulkner and publicized him in France and then in America, to rush to Andalusia Farm. Sees O'Connor's characters as groping for an exit, only to find an abyss, where they topple over the edge. Compares O'Connor's vision to Faulkner's, and commends the mournful enchantment of her sentences. Focuses on her lectures, emphasizing how she differs from other Catholic writers--who tend to disguise their intentions--and how she draws from her faith the courage to expose the horror and the grotesque by forming one body with the tainted characters she creates. Describes O'Connor as a young woman from a good family, with the harshness of an exterminating angel. (Abstracted by Marguerite Bartoli).

2137   Rinaldi, Angelo. "L'évangile de sainte Flannery." [The Gospel According to Saint Flannery]. *L'Express* 25 Jan. 1985: 59-61. [In French].

Reviews the French publication of *The Habit of Being*. Regards O'Connor's correspondence as ranking with Kafka's. States that O'Connor emulates Flaubert when she tackles the mystery of artistic creation. Notes her reserve about her disease and prolixity on other subjects, literature and religion in particular. Underlines her gifts for arguing and advising. Dwells on O'Connor's broad-mindedness, irony, and self-derision. Notes that she refuses to spoil her personal expression by infusing it with theological language. Contends that the letters form a course on the novel and a chronicle of provincial life. (Abstracted by Marguerite Bartoli).

2138   Rosarossa, Maria Alejandra. "La Imagen Religiosa en Flannery O'Connor y Clarice Lispector." In *Homenaje a Marie Teresa Maiorana*. Buenos Aires: Fundacion Maria Teresa Maiorana, 1995. 98-102. [In Spanish].

Discusses religious imagery and the use of the grotesque in O'Connor's "A Good Man Is Hard to Find." Compares O'Connor's fiction to Clarice Lispector's.

2139   Roy, Claude. "Le génie au temps compté." [The Genius Whose Days Were Numbered]. *Le Nouvel observateur* (France) 18 Jan. 1985: 64-65. [In French].

Reviews the French publication of *The Habit of Being*. Selects a few incidents out of O'Connor's daily life at Andalusia. Dwells on her strict Catholic orthodoxy and her hatred of totalitarianism. Contends that her combination of somber lucidity and ultimate hope helps her to bear an unbearable universe even if she does not understand it. Sees her novels as slightly less valuable than her short stories in that they are portrayals of manners, an exploration of the disorders that heresies lead to. Asserts that there is something archaic and regionalistic about her characters' picturesque quality, and that local color prevails over the universal. Still, ranks her as high as Chekhov for her short stories, and in her masterful portrayal of pure evil. Regards "The Artificial Nigger" as one of the most beautiful tales in Western literature. (Abstracted by Marguerite Bartoli).

2140   Roy, Claude. "Sainte Flannery." *Le Nouvel Observateur* (France) 20-26 June 1991: 114. [In French].

Briefly reviews the publication in French of Flannery O'Connor's *Complete Works*. Mentions biographical elements, and regards O'Connor as a major novelist whose writings reflect human and moral comedy. Comments on O'Connor's vein of naturalism, which may be traced back to the *Bible* or Greek tragedy. Discusses her orthodox Catholicism, her belief in the Fall-Redemption-Judgement triad and mystery, and her distaste for self pity. Underlines O'Connor's talent for the comic, and sees her as the most comical of American tragic writers. Mentions Genevieve Brisac's essay on O'Connor: *Loin du Paradis*. Commends her for the audacity of her approach of blending biographical elements with the writer's prose. (Abstracted by Marguerite Bartoli).

2141   Saji, Takeshi. "The World of Flannery O'Connor: A Study of *The Violent Bear It Away*." *Shizuoka University Bulletin* [General Education Department] (Japan) 12 (1977): 31-45. [In Japanese].

2142   Saji, Takeshi. "The World of Flannery O'Connor: In Search of the Restoration of Love." *Shizuoka University Bulletin* [General Education Department] (Japan) 13 (March 1978): 157-71. [In Japanese].

2143   Sato, Haruo. "What is to See: A Study of `A View of the Woods.'" *Chyuo British and American Literature* [Bulletin of British and American Literature, Chyuo University] (Japan) 22 (Dec. 1988): 101-13. [In Japanese].

2144   Sato, Kenichi. "A Study of Flannery O'Connor's *Wise Blood*." *Research Bulletin of the Faculty of General Education of Kinki University* (Japan) 3.2 (1971): 19-38. [In Japanese].

2145   Seaberg, Rönnog. "Kapitalismens kultur." ["Culture of Capitalism."] *Var Lösen* ["Our Redeemer"] (Sweden) 8 (1993): 557-61. [In Swedish].

Flannery O'Connor is mentioned as a writer who came out of a university writing program. Her arrival at the University of Iowa is described, as her sojourn at Yaddo, the artist's retreat in New York. (Abstracted by Rönnog Seaberg).

2146   Seaberg, Rönnog and Beate Sydhoff. "USA i udda belysning." ["USA in a Different Light"]. *Var Lösen* ["Our Redeemer"] (Sweden) 8 (1993): 545-47. [In Swedish].

Editorial which addresses Toni Morrison's reception of the Nobel Prize in 1993. Flannery O'Connor is mentioned several times. (Abstracted by Rönnog Seaberg).

2147   Soneda, Kenzo. "The World of Flannery O'Connor: A Study of O'Connor's Short Stories." *Journal of Sagami Women's University* (Japan) 42 (1979): 197-205. [In Japanese].

Asserts that most of O'Connor's short stories were written to reveal the falsehood and sinfulness of humanity. (Abstracted by Kayoko Watanabe).

2148   Sorai, Yuka. "A Study of Flannery O'Connor: An Angel Among Southern Writers." *Nebyurasu* [Bulletin of the Graduate School of Meiji Gakuin University] (Japan) 15 (Feb. 1987): 233-58. [In Japanese].

Analyzes *Wise Blood*, "A Good Man Is hard to Find," and "The Enduring Chill." (Abstracted by Kayoko Watanabe).

2149   Sorai, Yuka. "Whereabouts of Self: A Study of *The Violent Bear It Away*." *Silphe Society* [Graduate School of Meiji Gakuin University] (Japan) 27 (Feb. 1988): 51-68. [In Japanese].

2150   Stelzman, Rainulf A. "Gewalt und Gnade: Die Theologie Flannery O'Connors in ihren Briefen." *Stimmen der Zeit* (Freiberg, Germany) 197 (Aug. 1979): 566-69. [In German].

Examines the concepts of evil, belief, humanity, church, and grace using examples from Flannery O'Connor's letters in *The Habit of Being*. (Abstracted by Roger Noël).

2151   Suda, Minoru. "The Theme of O'Connor's *Wise Blood*: From Grotesque to Straightness." *Tohoku Gakuin University Bulletin* (Japan) 62 (Sept. 1974): 117-33. [In Japanese].

Argues that the process of Hazel's initiation takes rather unique steps: from a grotesque fall to redeemed innocence. In the loss of his eyesight, Haze obtains spiritual vision and becomes the "new Jesus." (Abstracted by Kayoko Watanabe).

2152   Sugiura, Etsuko. "Between Belief and Art: A Study of Flannery O'Connor's *Wise Blood*." *American Literature* [Journal of the American Literature Society in Japan, Tokyo Branch] 39 (Sept. 1981): 11-19. [In Japanese].

2153   Suh, Sook. "'The Displaced Person' in Flannery O'Connor's Short Stories." *Han'guk Munhwa Yonguwon nonchong*. [Journal of the Korean Cultural Research Institute]. [Ewha Woman's University, Seoul, Korea] 59.1 (1991): 189+ [In Korean].

2154   Suh, Sook. "Flannery O'Connor's South--The Land of the Displaced Person." *Han'guk Munhwa Yonguwon nonchong*. [Journal of the Korean Cultural Research Institute]. [Ewha Woman's University, Seoul, Korea] 58 (1990): 33-48. [In Korean].

Contends that O'Connor was concerned about "the displaced person," exploring through her stories "man's suffering from the obsessive desire to forget his homelessness." Argues that her "preoccupation with man's displacement" was based upon her observation of the transition of the American South from a "cotton culture" to one based upon industrial technology. Suggests that she believed this transition meant that "the traditional South, which had been perceived in the literary imagination as a land of redemptive community," would be degraded "into the peripheral city of the modern world." Sees *Wise Blood*, as composed of grotesque, lonely characters with no relations who are "plagued by the unhappy memories of home and family." Concludes that in this novel O'Connor offers an indictment of "the emptiness of the modern life devoid of spiritual quests." (From the author's English language abstract.)

2155   Suyama, Shizuo. "Flannery O'Connor." In *God's Black Hole*. Tokyo: Kayosha, 1978. [In Japanese].

A study of four Southern writers: William Faulkner, Thomas Wolfe, William Styron, and Flannery O'Connor. Suyama discusses O'Connor's two novels, stories in *Everything That Rises Must Converge, A Good Man Is Hard to Find*, and O'Connor's occasional pieces collected in *Mystery and Manners*. (Abstracted by Kayoko Watanabe).

2156   Takahashi, Junko. "Paintings and Novels: Appreciation of Arts and Interpretation of Novels." *Chofu Gakuen Women's Junior College* (Japan) 22 (Sept. 1989): 109-18. [In Japanese].

Compares the painting, "Justice and Divine Vengeance Pursuing Crime" by Pierre-Paul Prud'hon with O'Connor's "The Life You Save May Be Your Own." (Abstracted by Kayoko Watanabe).

2157   Takahashi, Masahiko. "Alternative Judgement in the Works of Flannery O'Connor: Madness or Vanity." *Meiji Gakuin University Bulletin* (Japan) 20.4 (1983): 221-33. [In Japanese].

2158   Takenaka, Toshiko. "Enigma in Flannery O'Connor's *The Violent Bear It Away*." *Keisen Jogakuen Junior College Bulletin* (Japan) 4 (March 1969): 17-32. [In Japanese].

Admires the originality of *The Violent Bear It Away* in spite of its many defects. Finds the novel's originality to lie in how O'Connor unifies the dramatic tension with symbolization. (Abstracted by Kayoko Watanabe).

2159   Tanabe, Tamotsu. "Simone Weil and Flannery O'Connor." *Bulletin of Humanities Studies* [Osaka City University, Literature Department] (Japan) 41.6 (1990): 347-53. [In Japanese].

2160   Tanimoto, Taizo. "Flannery O'Connor's Theme and Technique: An Explication of `A Good Man Is Hard to Find.'" *Konan University Bulletin of Literature* (Japan) 3 (March 1971): 57-72. [In Japanese].

Views the grandmother as a fragile person who has not thought seriously about her life until she finds herself facing death. Contends that, unlike the grandmother, The Misfit has been contemplating the meaning of his life far longer and has concluded that either life is absurd or it is eternal. Finds The Misfit to be similar to those modern individuals who would like to believe in Christ's teachings but cannot come out of the muddy swamp of disbelief. (Abstracted by Kayoko Watanabe).

2161   Tanno, Makoto. "The Elect and the Damned: Christ's Redemption in Flannery O'Connor's Works." *Bulletin of Shizuoka University* [Education Department] (Japan) 29 (1979): 51-62. (In Japanese).

2162   Terunuma, Kahoru. "Image of Women in O'Connor's Stories of Mother and Daughter." *American Literature* 57 (1996): 7-16. [In Japanese].

Discusses O'Connor's inability to free herself of the patriarchal system of Catholicism and Southern tradition. (Abstracted by Kayoko Watanabe).

2163   Tokusue, Aiko. "An Eternal Life: A Study of Flannery O'Connor." *Nihon Women's University Bulletin* (Japan) 22 (March 1973): 10-22. [In Japanese].

Discusses O'Connor as a Southerner and Catholic. Contends that she was a writer who focused her eyes on the place of uncertainty in the seemingly perfect modern world. (Abstracted by Kayoko Watanabe).

2164   Tsuchiya, Hiroyuki. "Flannery O'Connor's `Greenleaf': The Role of the Two Mothers." *Sella* [Shirayuri English Language & Literature Association] (Japan) 12 (March 1983): 25-34. [In Japanese].

Sees Mrs. Greenleaf as a *doppelganger* representing the "dark and irrational" part of Mrs. May. (Abstracted by Kayoko Watanabe).

2165   Ueno, Naozo. "Flannery O'Connor's Novels." *Shuryu* (Japan) 28 (Sept.
              1966): 19-29. [In Japanese].

              Asserts that the religious-minded people in O'Connor's works are
              rebellious to Jesus. Observes that O'Connor appears to be asking questions
              such as, "What is truth? What is evil?" Concludes that O'Connor's works
              can be said to be "tragi-comedies." (Abstracted by Kayoko Watanabe).

2166   Uesugi, Akira. "Making an Attempt to Be Close to Flannery O'Connor."
              Shibaura Kogyo University Bulletin (Japan) 12.1 (1978): 39-46. [In
              Japanese].

2167   Umegaki, Kiyoshi. "The World of Flannery O'Connor: A Study of *The
              Violent Bear It Away*." *Joshidai Bungaku* [Osaka Women's University
              Bulletin, Foreign Literature] (Japan) 44 (1992): 57-99. [In Japanese].

              Introduces the content of *The Violent Bear It Away*. (Abstracted by
              Kayoko Watanabe).

2168   Valenti, Francisco. "Scrivere L'Incarnazione." [To Write About the
              Incarnation]. *CL: Rivista Mensile di Communione e Liberazione* (Italy)
              (June 1991): 3, 44-46. [In Italian].

              Provides a brief biographical sketch, and refers to O'Connor as one of the
              greatest writers of American literature of the last half century. Notes that
              while she has been largely ignored in Italy, her works are now being
              republished as a result of the resurgence of interest in the linguistic texture
              and themes of Southern American writers. Acknowledges the
              embarrassing silence on O'Connor in Italy during the 1960s, possibly
              based upon a misunderstanding of why as a Catholic she depicted vulgar
              characters in her work. Suggests that readers now have a better
              understanding of her motives, medieval vision, and use of symbolism.
              Discusses the allegorical nature of her work and ties this method of
              storytelling to her view of the reality of existence as based upon the
              incarnation of Christ. Refers to her sense of humor and provides excerpts
              from her letters related to her view of the Church. States that some readers
              have found her work reflective of the Christian realism of old times,
              resulting in desperate and brutal stories. Urges these readers to study the
              stories more carefully, because--on a deeper level--they will find that the
              stories deal with the action of Grace on characters who are often not
              willing to sustain it. Describes the plot, action, theme and characters of
              Wise Blood and *The Violent Bear It Away*. Focuses on the role of
              redemption and the incarnation in both novels, seeing the latter work as

a minor hymn to the Eucharist introduced by the water and bread that are Christ. Finds both works useful explorations of the abyss of Christian mystery to be discovered within each of us. (Abstracted by Amedeo Fedeli).

2169   Veat, N.P."Lekschiskie sredstva vyrazhenia avtorski i personazhnoi tochek zrenia v novellistike Flanneri O'Konnor." ["Lexical Means of Expressing Author and Character Viewpoints in the Stories of Flannery O'Connor."] *Printsipy funktsionirivania yazyka v ego rechevykh raznovidnostyakh. [Principles of the Function of Language in its Speech Varieties: A Higher Education Collection of Scientific Works.]* Ed. E.U. Matvejeva and L.G. Podorva. Perm, Russia: Perm UP], 1984. 109-15. [In Russian].

Describes various lexical means O'Connor uses to present point of view. Discusses her usage of emotional adjectives, comparison, and metaphors. Provides a detailed differentiation of her narrative viewpoints. Regards O'Connor as an outstanding example of the American Southern School, and a master of the psychological novel. (Abstracted by Timour Abdoullin).

2170   Walker, Alice. "Das letzte Wort haben die Pfauen -- eine Wiederbegegnung mit Flannery O'Connor." *Du-Die Zeitschrift Der Kultur* 7 (1988): 6-8. [In German].

2171   Watanabe, Kayoko. "The Art of Storytelling in the Works of Flannery O'Connor: The `Concrete' in the Manners of the South." *Tokyo Seitoku Junior College Bulletin* (Japan) 26 (March 1993): 245-58. [In Japanese].

Discusses the devices O'Connor uses to tell a story, including: comical dialogue, punch line humor, metaphors of grace, concise description, and narrative and dramatic irony. (Abstracted by Kayoko Watanabe).

2172   Watanabe, Kayoko. "Eyes to See the Invisible Things: Tarwater's Road to Becoming a Prophet: A Study of *The Violent Bear It Away.*" *Tsuda Inquiry* [Bulletin of the Graduate School of Tsuda College] (Japan) 10 (1989): 64-78. [In Japanese].

Compares O'Connor's backwoods prophets to the school teacher, Rayber. Though seemingly "insane," the Tarwaters lead sincere lives while Rayber attempts to find happiness in "indifference" and lives a kind of "death in life." (Abstracted by Kayoko Watanabe).

2173   Watanabe, Kayoko. "Rereading Flannery O'Connor's `Everything That
        Rises Must Converge': Issues of Gender, Race and Class." *Journal of the
        Center for Women's Studies* [Toyoko Gakuen Women's Junior College]
        (Japan) 1 (March 1990): 155-69. [In Japanese].

        Offers a reading of "Everything That Rises Must Converge" from a
        feminist viewpoint, noting O'Connor's themes of class, race, and gender.
        (Abstracted by Kayoko Watanabe).

2174   Watanabe, Kayoko. "Studies of Flannery O'Connor in the U.S. and Japan:
        With Special Emphasis on the *Flannery O'Connor Bulletin*." *Tokyo
        Seitoku College Bulletin* 30 (1997): 73-82. [In Japanese].

2175   Watanabe, Kayoko. "The Transformation of Haze and the Role of Enoch:
        A Study of *Wise Blood*." *Toyoko Gakuen Women's Junior College
        Bulletin* (Japan) 25 (Oct. 1990): 65-74. [In Japanese].

        Asserts that Hazel Motes's moment of transformation occurs when he is
        parted from the Essex. Sees Enoch Emery as largely a comic figure, and
        the novel as containing a mixture of "Romance" and "post-modern"
        narrative techniques. (Abstracted by Kayoko Watanabe).

2176   Yaguchi, Hiroo. "Flannery O'Connor's `The Lame Shall Enter First': Two
        Conflicting Visions of the World." *Sendai Shirayuri Junior College
        Bulletin* (Japan) 18 (Jan. 1990): 77-86. [In Japanese].

2177   Yagyu, Nozomu. "Religious Atmosphere in Flannery O'Connor: Irony
        and Paradoxical Symbolism Derived from Biblical Images." *Rikkyo
        Jogakuin Junior College Bulletin* (Japan) 2 (Dec. 1970): 236-74. [In
        Japanese].

        Discusses *The Violent Bear It Away*, *Wise Blood* and "A Good Man Is
        Hard to Find." Asserts that Haze can be born again by destroying the
        mummy and Solace Layfield because both are symbolic of the false half
        of Haze's divided self. Considers how Bishop's drowning signifies
        judgement and Tarwater's baptism of Bishop signifies human redemption
        by grace. Finds the simultaneous drowning and baptism to be a
        sacramental symbol, as Bishop's death reminds us of Christ's death.
        Remarks that O'Connor believed that true Christianity has a certain
        grotesqueness as readers will find that her prophetic faith
        (fundamentalism) and a sacramental, priestly faith (Catholicism) are
        fused. Contends that the former punishes sin, and then changes it,

paradoxically, into grace and redemption by the latter. (Abstracted by Kayoko Watanabe).

2178   Yamada, Fuki. "Flannery O'Connor: A Challenge to Disbelief." *Nanzan Studies in English Language & Literature* (Japan) 3 (1978): 29-46. [In Japanese].

Argues that Rayber is caught in the world of humanist "manners" and comes across as intellectually "flabby," whereas Tarwater and Bishop introduce something innocent into the world of "manners," which results in their "violent" passion. (Abstracted by Kayoko Watanabe).

2179   Yamada, Fuki. "Pastoralism in Flannery O'Connor in Relation to Southern Agrarianism." *Nanzan Studies in English Language and Literature* (Japan) 5 (1980): 61-76; 6 (1980): 93-105. [In Japanese].

2180   Yamada, Fuki. "Very Eccentric Pilgrimage of the Soul: A Consideration of the Grotesquerie in *Wise Blood*." *Nanzan Studies in English Language & Literature* (Japan) 4 (1979): 83-99. [In Japanese].

Argues that Hazel Motes gains a strong sense of integrity and becomes a prophet well-qualified to dispel the degraded mentality of secular people through the use of violence. (Abstracted by Kayoko Watanabe).

2181   Yamagata, Kazumi. "Flannery O'Connor: Vertical Transcendence." *Trace of Contemporary Literature* Tokyo: Chyukyo Shuppan, 1980. 316-48. [In Japanese].

2182   Yamagata, Ako. "Hypocrisy As a Grotesque: The Grandmother in `A Good Man Is Hard to Find.'" *Hosei University Bulletin* 39 (1997): 1-14. [In Japanese].

Asserts that The Misfit is not as grotesque as of a character as the grandmother in "A Good Man Is Hard to Find." (Abstracted by Kayoko Watanabe).

2183   Yamagata, Kazumi. "A Story of Transformation: A Study of Flannery O'Connor's Works." *Ferris Studies* [Ferris Women's College Bulletin] (Japan) 11 (April 1976): 291-308. [In Japanese].

2184   Yokoyama, Takemi. "A Study of Flannery O'Connor's `A Good Man Is Hard to Find.'" *Memoirs of the Tohoku Institute of Technology* [II: Liberal Arts and Sciences] (Japan) 10 (March 1990): 83-96. [In Japanese].

Asserts that because the grandmother is an innocent person, she has the ability to accept The Misfit as her child. Suggests that at the moment she accepts The Misfit, her superficial "goodness" is transformed into genuine "goodness." Concludes that the encounter with the grandmother will surely change the life of The Misfit. (Abstracted by Kayoko Watanabe).

2185   Yoshimura, Keiko. "Flannery O'Connor's Last Story of Home: `Judgement Day.'" *Senzoku Studies* [Senzoku Gakuen Junior College Bulletin] (Japan) 16 (1987): 19-25. [In Japanese].

2186   Yoshimura, Keiko. "Flannery O'Connor's *Wise Blood*: Eyes of the Other." *Review of the Faculty of Foreign Language, Kyorin University* (Japan) 2 (March 1990): 64-74. [In Japanese].

Explains that the name Hazel means "God sees" in Hebrew. Argues that Hazel Motes finally realizes he has been continually seen by God, who is the absolute "other person." (Abstracted by Kayoko Watanabe).

2187   Zacharasiewicz, Waldemar. "Eudora Welty's *Death of a Traveling Salesman* und Flannery O'Connor's `The Displaced Person': ein Vergleich." *Die englische und americkanische Kurzgeschiche.* Ed. Klaus Lubbers. Darmstadt: Wissenschaftliche Buchgesellschaft, 1990. 349-68. [In German].

2188   Zacharasiewicz, Waldemar. "Flannery O'Connor." *Die Erzählkunst Des Amerikanischen Südens.* Darmstadt (Germany): Wissenschaftliche Buchgesellschaft, 1990. 173-89. [In German].

Reviews criticism devoted to Flannery O'Connor's work in English, with an emphasis on the reinterpretation of her work and personality after the publication of her correspondence in *The Habit of Being* (Ed. Sally Fitzgerald. NY: Farrar, Straus and Giroux, 1979) and *The Correspondence of Flannery O'Connor and the Brainard Cheneys* (Ed. C. Ralph Stephens. Jackson: UP of Mississippi, 1986). Praises Frederick Asals's *Flannery O'Connor: The Imagination of Extremity* (Athens: U of Georgia P, 1982) as an example of the considerable progress scholars have made in discussing O'Connor's philosophical-theological foundations as well as her development as a story-teller. Concludes that there is still no consensus between the two groups of critics who devote themselves either to O'Connor's philosophy and theology, or to the problematics of her craft as a story-teller. (Abstracted by Roger Noël).

2189   Zacharasiewicz, Waldemar. "Unter der unbarmherzigen Sonne der Gnade: Flannery O'Connor's `Good Country People' and `Revelation.'" *Zwischen Dogma und Sakularer Welt*. Ed. Bernd Engler and Franz Link. Paderborn (Germany): Ferdinand Schoningh, 1991. 101-12. [In German].

Establishes parallels between "Good Country People" and "Revelation," and discusses "The Artificial Nigger." Focuses on the working of grace and use of the grotesque and religious imagery. (Abstracted by Roger Noël).

2190   Ackerman, Sarah Gene. "Creativity and Depression: An Exploration of the Lives of Four Women Writers." [Maya Angelou, Flannery O'Connor, Sylvia Plath, and Anne Sexton]. Thesis, Harvard U, 1989.

2191   Adams, Mary Helen. "Flannery O'Connor's Dragon." Thesis, Austin Peay State U, 1974.

2192   Adelman, Selma S. "A Study of the Fiction of Flannery O'Connor." Thesis, Trinity U (Texas), 1963.

2193   Aderholt, Martha J. "Flannery O'Connor's Thematic Use of Family Relationships." Thesis, U of Tennessee, 1969.

2194   Aiken, David Hubert. "New Testament Character Types in Selected Short Fiction of Flannery O'Connor." Thesis, U of Georgia, 1969.

2195   Albritton, Thomas Wellington. "Revelation or Evolution: Flannery O'Connor, Teilhard de Chardin, and the Development of the Human Spirit." Thesis, Wake Forest U, 1982.

2196   Alexander, David. "Lost in the Jungle of Shadows: Unreality in the Fiction of Flannery O'Connor." Thesis, U of South Carolina, 1992.

2197   Alford, James Curtis. "Flannery O'Connor: A Life in the Process of Death." Thesis, San Francisco State U, 1991.

2198   Allen, Lurlie Wiseman. "The Function of Symbols in the Fiction of Flannery O'Connor." Thesis, Georgia Southern College, 1982.

2199   Allen, Marjorie H. "The Religious Themes of Flannery O'Connor." M.A. Project, California State U, Sacramento, 1973.

2200   Alliston, Stephen R. "A Common Defense: The Religion and Literature of C.S. Lewis and Flannery O'Connor." Thesis, Graduate Theological Union, 1994.

2201   Alloway, Laurie Ann. "Flannery O'Connor and the Black Mask." Thesis, San Diego State U, 1991.

2202   Allsopp, Michael E. "Faces of God in the Fiction of Flannery O'Connor." Thesis, Gonzaga U, 1979.

2203   Alvis, Sara Kathleen. "Three Modes of the Grotesque in the Fiction of Flannery O'Connor." Thesis, U of Dallas, 1970.

2204   Andrews, Candace E. "Evil, Grace, and the Search for Home in the Fiction of Flannery O'Connor." Thesis, California State U, Sacramento, 1989.

2205   Andrus, Faith Posey. "`You Can't Get Ahead of Mother': An Examination of Flannery O'Connor's Relationship With Her Mother As Reflected in the Letters Collected in *The Habit of Being*, and Its Influence on Her Short Stories." Thesis, Oklahoma City U, 1997.

2206   Antle, Emily Newberry. "Novels of Vocation, Unlikely Parallels: The Fiction of Nathanael West and Flannery O'Connor." Thesis, U of Louisville, 1970.

2207   Arase, Hiroko. "Spiritual Casualties: The Mythical Hero's Night Journey Motif in Two American Narratives." [Richard Wright's "The Man Who Lived Underground" and O'Connor's *Wise Blood*]. Thesis, San Francisco State U, 1994.

2208   Archer, Patricia Faye. "Determinism in the Fiction of Flannery O'Connor." Thesis, Texas A&M U, 1970.

2209   Armitage, Shelly S. "The Dragon's Black Breath: Evil and Moral Vision in the New Gothic Novel." Thesis, Texas Technological U, 1971.

2210   Atkins, Donna Ruth. "Character and Irony in Flannery O'Connor's Stories." Thesis, U of California, Berkeley, 1986.

2211   Atkins, Erin. "Images of the Holy Trinity and the Holy Family in Flannery O'Connor's *Wise Blood*." Thesis, Appalachian State U, 1999.

2212   Ayau, Kurt Jose. "Failure and Hope: Images of the American Christian Community in Flannery O'Connor's *Wise Blood* and Walker Percy's *Love in the Ruins*." Thesis, U of Virginia, 1988.

2213   Balcer, Joan. "Flannery O'Connor's Christian Insight Revealed by Style and Content." Thesis, Aquinas College, 1966.

2214   Baldwin, Glenn E. "The Use of Conflict by Flannery O'Connor." Thesis, Stetson U, 1971.

2215   Bane, Sarah. "An Archetypal Approach to Flannery O'Connor's Fiction." Thesis, U of Wyoming, 1980.

2216   Barendse, Nancy Roberta. "Suffer the Little Children: The Role of Children in the Works of Flannery O'Connor." Thesis, Clemson U, 1976.

2217   Barfield, Ann L. "The Matriarchal Society in Flannery O'Connor's Fiction: Its Characteristics, Treatments, and Purpose." Thesis, College of William and Mary, 1981.

2218   Barnes, Patricia A. "The Problem of Evil in the Fiction of Flannery O'Connor and Eudora Welty." Thesis, Eastern Washington College, 1971.

2219   Barry, Sheila. "The Family: The Way to Christ in Flannery O'Connor's Fiction." Thesis, U de Montreal (Canada), 1989.

2220   Beard, Nila Valentine. "Freedom and Determinism As Defined in Flannery O'Connor's Fiction." Thesis, U of South Carolina, 1976.

2221   Beaty, Kelly Lynne Haggard. "Flannery O'Connor and the Reader." Thesis, College of William and Mary, 1997.

2222   Beaven, Simon W. "Terrible Swift Sword: The Action of Grace in Three Stories by Flannery O'Connor." ["A Good Man Is Hard to Find," "Greenleaf," and "Revelation."] Stanford Honors Essay in Humanities, No. 36. Stanford U, 1992.

2223   Becht, Donald Edward. "The Concept of the Ideal Self in the Fiction of Nathanael West and Flannery O'Connor." Thesis, U of Alabama in Huntsville, 1976.

2224   Bennion, Rebecca Poelman. "Flannery O'Connor and the Fiction of Mystery." Thesis, Brigham Young U, 1992.

2225   Bergup, M. Emmanuel. "Themes of Redemptive Grace in the Works of Flannery O'Connor: A Theological Inquiry." Thesis, St. John's U, 1968.

2226   Beringer, Lucinda MacDonald. "Miss Scarlett, the Cold War, and So Many Extra: The Classes Working in the Fiction of Flannery O'Connor." Thesis, Southwest Texas State U, 1993.

2227   Betsill, Catherine. "Characterization in Flannery O'Connor's *Everything That Rises Must Converge*." Thesis, Texas A&M U, 1972.

2229   Billing, Geraldine. "The Child's Spiritual Journey in Flannery O'Connor's Short Fiction." Thesis, George Washington U, 1989.

2230   Black, Janet M. "Flannery O'Connor's Fiction and Catholic Culture in Transition." Thesis, Bucknell U, 1997.

2230a   Blake, Laura Michelle. "'You Just Stay Here': Patterns of Disability, Disconnection, and Disillusionment in *The Glass Menagerie,* "Good Country People," and *The Fixer.*" Thesis, Baylor U, 1999.

2231   Blanton, William H. "The Two Modes of Vision in Flannery O'Connor's Short Fiction." Thesis, U of North Carolina at Chapel Hill, 1969.

2232   Blessing, Loren Michael. "Grace and Freedom in the Writings of Flannery O'Connor." Thesis, California State U, Sacramento, 1976.

2233   Bliss, Lowell D. "'For Christ's Sake': Flannery O'Connor and the Anagogy of Language." Thesis, Kansas State U, 1991.

2234   Bonanno, Raphael D. "Evil and the Grotesque in the Writings of Flannery O'Connor." Thesis, Saint Bonaventure U, 1963.

2235   Boone, Sherry Gilmer. "An Interpretation of the Sacramental View in the Short Stories of Flannery O'Connor." Thesis, Mississippi College, 1991.

2236   Bowman, Lee Willey. "Flannery O'Connor: A Structure of Grace." Thesis, U of Virginia, 1978.

2237   Boyer, Ken B. "The Grotesque in Flannery O'Connor's Fiction." Thesis, Saint Louis U, 1967.

2238   Bradley, William J. "Romantic Elements in Selected Writings of Flannery O'Connor." Thesis, North Texas State U, 1975.

2239   Brahaney, Carolyn. "The Theme of Spirituality in Flannery O'Connor's Work." Thesis, Rice U, 1981.

2240   Breaud, Norbert Francis. "The Quest of Flannery O'Connor's Hazel Motes: A Discussion of the Existential Implications in *Wise Blood.*" Thesis, U of New Orleans, 1975.

2241   Brechbiel, Grace R. "A Definition and Illustration of the Modern Gothic Literary Genre Based on the Selected Works of Truman Capote, Carson McCullers and Flannery O'Connor." Thesis, Millersville State College, 1967.

2242   Breckenridge, Jennifer J. "Telling It Like It Is: The Child and Revelation in Flannery O'Connor's Short Fiction." Thesis, Villanova U, 1996.

2243   Breen, Meredith A. "Flannery O'Connor and Richard Wright: Twentieth Century's Writers Use of Religion and Southern Landscapes." Thesis, U of North Carolina at Chapel Hill, 1997.

2244   Brennan, Wilma Nadine. "Children in the Short Stories of Flannery O'Connor." Thesis, Texas A&M U, 1971.

2245   Brickman, Barbara Jane. "Flannery O'Connor's Letters to `A': Visions and Adoration." Thesis, James Madison U, 1995.

2245a   Brinkerhoff, Coni Jo. "Suffering: Flannery O'Connor's Gift." Thesis, California State U, Dominguez Hills, 1999.

2246   Brittain, Joan T. "Symbols of Violence: Flannery O'Connor's Structure of Reality." Thesis, U of Louisville, 1966.

2247   Brown, Betsy Etheridge. "The Art of Flannery O'Connor: Technique and Structure in *Wise Blood*." Thesis, Ohio State U, 1974.

2248   Browne, Betty Rush. "Functions of Child Characters in the Fiction of Flannery O'Connor." Thesis, Mississippi State U, 1975.

2249   Bruce, Duane Francis. "The Regional and Religious Dimensions of Flannery O'Connor's Fiction." Thesis, U of North Carolina at Chapel Hill, 1967.

2250   Bryson, Michael Erik. "Reclaiming the Self: Transcending the Fragmentation of the Individual in Literature From the *Bhagavad Gita* to *Wise Blood*." Thesis, Northeast Missouri State U, 1996.

2251   Burns, Thomas Shannon. "Southern Evangelism and Flannery O'Connor." Thesis, U of Georgia, 1967.

2252   Burruss, John C. "The Early Development of Flannery O'Connor's *The Violent Bear It Away*." B.A. Thesis, Harvard U, 1977.

2253   Bush, George Drake. "An Author Looks at Her Work: An Approach to Flannery O'Connor." Thesis, U of Tennessee, 1965.

2254   Bush, Laura L. "The Redemptive Value of Suffering in Four Flannery O'Connor Stories." Thesis, Brigham Young U, 1989.

2255   Buturain, Leah Marie. "Determination, Crisis, and Change: Older Protagonists in Three Short Stories." Thesis, Ohio State U, 1985.

2256   Camillo, Sandra. "Flannery O'Connor, the Painter in the Portrait." Thesis, State U of New York, Brockport, 1986.

2257   Capel, Gloria Jean McGee. "Spider Web Souls and the Arabesque Christ: A Vision of Flannery O'Connor's Fictional Characters Seen Through the Incandescence of Teilhard de Chardin's Omega Point." Thesis, Clemson U, 1976.

2258   Capps, John Spencer. "'A Man Though Not Yet a Whole One': Flannery O'Connor's Vision of the Human Dilemma." Thesis, Virginia Polytechnic Institute and State U, 1977.

2259   Caputo, Donna M. "Four Major Influences on Flannery O'Connor's Fiction." Thesis, Cleveland State U, 1994.

2260   Carleton, Mark A. "Who Do You Think You Are?: Quests for Fulfillment." Thesis, Louisiana State U, 1993.

2261   Carlisle, Timothy. "The Dragon By the Side of the Road: The Devil in Flannery O'Connor's Thought and Work." Thesis, Niagara U, 1978.

2262   Carlson, Marilyn Anne. "Visions of Light: Flannery O'Connor's Themes and Narrative Method." Thesis, U of South Dakota, 1992.

2263   Carney, Virginia Moore. "Flannery O'Connor: Her Changing Perception of Blacks." Thesis, U of Alaska at Anchorage, 1990.

2264   Carroll, Linda Sue Cole. "Flannery O'Connor's Southern Children as Prophets." Thesis, Texas Women's U, 1987.

2265   Carter, Frank T. "The Use of Violence in the Works of Flannery O'Connor." Thesis, Southern Connecticut State College, 1973.

2266   Carver-Taylor, Mary Anne. "The Quest for Connection: A Comparative Analysis of the Fiction of Flannery O'Connor and Alice Munro." Thesis, Dalhousie U (Canada), 1993.

2267   Casey, Holly Sue Baynes. "The Grotesque Humor in Selected Works of Flannery O'Connor." Thesis, Northeast Louisiana U, 1971.

2268   Casey, Margaret E. "Teilhardianism in the Fiction of Flannery O'Connor." Thesis, Boston College, 1968.

2269   Champion, Lou Terrell. "Some Common Ground in Hawthorne's *The Blithedale Romance* and Flannery O'Connor's 'The Lame Shall Enter First.'" Thesis, U of Texas, 1969.

2270   Chandler, Tommie Allen. "Ironic Redemption: A Study of Flannery O'Connor's Fiction." Thesis, Emory U, 1964.

2271   Cherry, Charles Lester. "Theme, Structure, and Symbol in Flannery O'Connor's *The Violent Bear It Away*." Thesis, U of North Carolina at Chapel Hill, 1966.

2272   Cherry, Susan Blair. "An Examination of the Characteristics Commonly Referred to as Southern Gothic in the Fiction of Flannery O'Connor and Carson McCullers." Thesis, Jacksonville State U, 1970.

2273   Christenbury, Tamara O'Hearn. "The Literary Relationship of Flannery O'Connor and Caroline Gordon." Thesis, James Madison U, 1989.

2274   Christensen, Jane. "Outside the Gate: Short Stories." Thesis, Warren Wilson College, 1995. [Alternate Title: "Writing and Preaching: Flannery O'Connor."]

2275   Clark, Catherine A. "From the Country to the City: Southern Identity in the Stories of Taylor and O'Connor." Thesis, College of William and Mary, 1986.

2276   Claunch, Belinda L. "'Lady, what is a man?': Discovering the Hypostatic Union in the Writing of Flannery O'Connor." Thesis, Arkansas Tech U, 1997.

2277   Coggins, Melissa Judith. "Flannery O'Connor's Use of the Mystery and Manners of the South as the Pathway to the Action of Grace in Four Selected Works of Short Fiction." ["A Good Man Is Hard to Find," "Revelation," "Greenleaf," and "Good Country People"]. Thesis, Mississippi College, 1991.

2278   Coleman, Christy Lynn. "Bloodshed, Evil and the Forest: Hawthornian Echoes in the Short Stories of Flannery O'Connor." Thesis, Drew U, 1998.

2279   Collins, Lowrey Christopher. "Hypocrisy and Redemption in Selected Works of Flannery O'Connor." Thesis, Stephen F. Austin State U, 1992.

2280   Collins, Michael Robert. "Sin and Grace in the Fiction of Flannery O'Connor." Thesis, Indiana U, 1975.

2281   Cook, Haruko Taya. "Negative Solutions: Women in Society Through the Eyes of Three Female Authors." [Mary McCarthy, Katherine Anne Porter and Flannery O'Connor]. Thesis, Drew U, 1974.

2282   Cooper, Marie. "From Innocence to Experience in the Fiction of Four Southern Writers." [Katherine Anne Porter, Eudora Welty, Carson McCullers and Flannery O'Connor]. Thesis, Texas Women's U, 1975.

2283   Cornelison, Robert Walter. "Adaptation From Two Short Stories by
        Katherine Mansfield and Flannery O'Connor Into One-Act Play Format."
        [Mansfield's "Miss Brill" and O'Connor's "A Good Man Is Hard to Find"].
        Thesis, Eastern Kentucky U, 1995.

2284   Cotton, Alvin Horner. "The Concrete Particularity of Flannery O'Connor's
        Short Stories." Thesis, Vanderbilt U, 1980.

2285   Coulbourn, Mildred Elizabeth. "Flannery O'Connor's `Displaced Persons':
        An Interpretive Study of a Motif in Selected Works." Thesis, Duke U,
        1965.

2286   Counts, Alice Crosby. "The Grotesque in Three Southern Writers: Edgar
        Allan Poe, William Faulkner, and Flannery O'Connor." Thesis, Radford
        College, 1974.

2287   Craig, Claire G. "The Christ-Haunted Figure in the Fiction of Flannery
        O'Connor." Thesis, Mississippi State College for Women, 1972.

2288   Crump, Michele J. "An Evil Urge: The Mother-Child Relationships in the
        Short Stories of Flannery O'Connor." Thesis, San Francisco State U, 1983.

2289   Cunningham, Stanley W. "Flannery O'Connor: The Art of Redemption."
        Thesis, Southwest Texas State U, 1994.

2290   Curtis, Carol A. "The Elemental Nature of Regionalism in the Works of
        Flannery O'Connor." Thesis, Northwestern State College, 1969.

2291   Cutler, Mary Lynn. "Heresies of the Self: Displacement as Grace in the
        Short Stories of Flannery O'Connor." Thesis, Brigham Young U, 1992.

2292   Dale, Mary Ann. "This Body of My Affliction: A Study of the Motif of
        Illness in the Writings of Flannery O'Connor." Thesis, Virginia
        Commonwealth U, 1984.

2293   Daniel, Thomas M. "The Appeal of Flannery O'Connor's Distorted
        Vision." Honors Thesis, Kenyon College, 1980.

2294   Davis, Ronald Lester. "Tension in the Fiction of Flannery O'Connor."
        Thesis, U of Mississippi, 1972.

2295   Day, Mildred A. "The Significance of Flannery O'Connor: Criticism,
        1952-1969." Thesis, Samford U, 1970.

2296   Debry, Stephanie Sue. "The Role of Child Victims in the Fiction of
        Flannery O'Connor." Thesis, U of Georgia, 1976.

2297   Dehart, Robert. "An Annotated Bibliography of Flannery O'Connor." Thesis, U of Wisconsin, River Falls, 1974. [Copy in the *Flannery O'Connor Collection* at Georgia College & State U, Milledgeville, GA.]

2298   Delafield, Carter. "Flannery O'Connor: Prophet and Evangelist." Thesis, U of North Carolina at Greensboro, 1966.

2299   DeMouy, Jane Krause. "Damascus Road: Epiphany and Theme in the Works of Flannery O'Connor." Thesis, U of Maryland, 1967.

2300   Dennis, Joe. "A Study of Flannery O'Connor's Vision Revealed in Her Characters." Thesis, Mississippi State U, 1972.

2301   DeRosa, Susan. "Flannery O'Connor's Fiction As Social Criticism." Thesis, U of Rhode Island, 1990.

2302   Deutschmann, Elinor. "Reality Perceived From the Corner-of-the-Eye: An Analysis of Flannery O'Connor's Method of Presentation." Thesis, U of South Florida, 1971.

2303   Diederich, Joanne L. "The Significance of Nature in the Fiction of Flannery O'Connor." Thesis, Ohio State U, 1969.

2304   Donaghy, Joyce Aasen. "A Search For Human Significance: Flannery O'Connor and Pierre Teilhard de Chardin." Thesis, Georgia State U, 1969.

2305   Donaldson, Mara E. "Transformation: The Parable As a Genre in Contemporary Literature." Thesis, Vanderbilt U, 1974.

2306   Donner, Andrea K. "Revelations: Flannery O'Connor Manuscript Revisions for *The Violent Bear It Away*." Thesis, State U of New York at Buffalo, 1996.

2307   Dorsman-Massen, Pamela. "Violence and Redemption in Flannery O'Connor." Thesis, U of Nijmegen (Netherlands), 1994.

2308   Dow, Michelle. "Levels of Ironic Awareness in Flannery O'Connor's Stories." Thesis, California State U, Hayward, 1974.

2309   Dreyer, Ladonna J. "'The Truth Shall Make You Free': Flannery O'Connor's Ideology as Reflected in Her Prose." Thesis, West Texas State U, 1969.

2310   Dula, Martha Alice. "The State of Man as It is Portrayed in Flannery O'Connor's *Wise Blood*." Thesis, U of North Carolina at Chapel Hill, 1967.

2311   Dulworth, Deborah Quinton. "Poverty and Limitation in the Fiction of Flannery O'Connor." Thesis, Murray State U, 1981.

2312   Dupuis, John. "The Wild Look of Flannery O'Connor's Fiction." Thesis, U of Southwestern Louisiana, 1971.

2313   Dursin, Susan D. "Patterns of Violence in the Fiction of Flannery O'Connor." Thesis, U of Alaska, 1974.

2314   Durso, Robert W. "Dislocation, Violence and Revelation in the Short Fiction of Flannery O'Connor." Thesis, Adelphi U, 1972.

2315   Edge, Loretta. "Four Stories and *Wise Blood*." ["The Train," "The Peeler," "The Heart of the Park," and "Enoch and the Gorilla"]. Thesis, U of North Carolina at Chapel Hill, 1968.

2316   Edwards, Nelda Young. "Four Criminals as Religious Questors in Flannery O'Connor." Thesis, Georgia State U, 1971.

2317   Elkins, Sharon Jane. "Redemption and Associated Themes in Flannery O'Connor's Fiction." Thesis, Tulane U of Louisiana, 1964.

2318   Elwell, Evelyn. "The Devil and Flannery O'Connor." Thesis, Auburn U, 1975.

2319   Enscore, Melody Lynn. "Naturalisme Spiritualiste and Christian Realism: Thematic Strategies in Selected Novels of Joris-Karl Huysmans and Flannery O'Connor." Thesis, U of North Carolina at Chapel Hill, 1988.

2320   Eppes, Cindy. "South of Reason: Selections From a Novel." [Alternate title: "Ha Ha You're Dead: Detachment as a Source of Humor and Horror in Flannery O'Connor's `A Good Man Is Hard to Find.'" Thesis, Warren Wilson College, 1998.

2321   Evans, Carol Lynne. "Determinism in the Novels of Flannery O'Connor." Thesis, Abilene Christian U, 1991.

2322   Evans, Florence Therese. "Flannery O'Connor and Modern Man." Thesis, St. Mary's U (San Antonio), 1964.

2323   Feeley, Marie J. "The Realm of Prophets and Poets: A Study of Imagery in the Fiction of Flannery O'Connor." Thesis, Villanova U, 1967.

2324   Felts, Juanita F. "A Study of Social Classes in the American Novel." Thesis, Arkansas State U, 1970.

2325   Fitts, Karen Louise. "Reading Flannery O'Connor by the Light of Feminist Theology: Transcendental Politics in Patriarchal Familial Structures." Thesis, Texas Christian U, 1990.

2326   Flannery, Melissa C. "Certain Preoccupations: The Progression Toward Catholic Orthodoxy in the Work of Flannery O'Connor." Thesis, McGill U (Canada), 1979.

2327   Floerchinger, Sharon M. "The Rat-Gray Essex and the Wooden Leg: The Meaning of the Grotesque in Flannery O'Connor's Fiction." Thesis, Wichita State U, 1966.

2328   Flood, Kelly Joyce. "Flannery O'Connor: Artist as Healer." Thesis, Arizona State U, 1995.

2329   Forbis, Ida C. "Flannery O'Connor, Novelist and Believer: An Analysis of Her Spiritual Vision in *Wise Blood*." Thesis, Shippensburg State College, 1973.

2330   Fowler, Ruth Gwendolyn. "The Theological Moment in Eleven Short Stories of Flannery O'Connor." Thesis, California State Northridge, 1975.

2331   Franchville, Denise Ann. "From Complacency to Authenticity: Kierkegaardian Stages of Existence in Flannery O'Connor's Fiction." Thesis, U of Louisville, 1989.

2332   Franklin, Melissa Ann. "Home Again, Home Again Jiggity Jig: Mother/Adult-Child Relationships in Flannery O'Connor's `Everything That Rises Must Converge.'" Thesis, Radford U, 1992.

2333   Freeman, Warren Eugene. "The Social and Theological Implications in Flannery O'Connor's *A Good Man Is Hard to Find and Other Stories*." Thesis, U of North Carolina at Chapel Hill, 1961.

2334   Fuller, Donald Coldwell. "The Relation of Idea and Reality in the Works of Flannery O'Connor." Thesis, U of Georgia, 1966.

2335   Fuqua, Patricia Davis. "The Grotesque in Two Southern Writers." [Flannery O'Connor and Alice Walker]. Thesis, San Francisco State U, 1978.

2336   Gafford, Charlotte Kelly. "The Fiction of Flannery O'Connor: A Mission of Gratuitous Grace." Thesis, Birmingham-Southern College, 1962.

2337   Gaines, Juana Denise. "Teilhard de Chardin's Influence on Flannery O'Connor." Thesis, Florida State U, 1988.

2338   Galvin, Elizabeth Hayes. "Point of View in the Works of Flannery O'Connor." Thesis, Texas A&I U, 1968.

2339   Gamblin, Julie A. "A Good Woman Is Hard To Find: Mothers in Flannery O'Connor's Fiction." Thesis, Memphis State U, 1987.

2340   Ganley, Natalie Tholl. "Images of Desire: Echoes of the Spiritual Exercises of St. Ignatius in the Fiction of Flannery O'Connor." Thesis, Georgetown U, 1989.

2341   Gannett, Thomas M. "Epiphanies in the Invisible Church: Flannery O'Connor and the Art of Mediation." Thesis, U of Southwestern Louisiana, 1987.

2342   Garber, Charles E. "Flannery O'Connor, Catholic Fundamentalist." A.B. Honors thesis, Harvard U, 1965.

2343   Garner, Leona C. "A Study of Local Color With Emphasis on Selected Works of Three Georgia Authors [Richard Malcolm Johnston, Joel Chandler Harris, and Harry Stillwell Edwards]." Thesis, U of Georgia, 1965.

2344   Gay, Carolyn. "Sunhats and Pistols: Mother-Daughter Relationships in the World of Flannery O'Connor." Thesis, Baylor U, 1992.

2345   Gay, Julie Lane. "Grace in the Short Stories of Flannery O'Connor." Thesis, Regent College (Canada), 1983.

2346   George, Martha. "Flannery O'Connor and the Sin of Pride." Thesis, C.W. Post Center, Long Island U, 1974.

2347   Gerald, Kelly Suzanne. "The Emblematic Shoe in Flannery O'Connor's Fiction." Thesis, U of South Alabama, 1994.

2348   Gerber, Leslie E. "Flannery O'Connor and The Fugitives: A Matter of the City." Thesis, Emory U, 1967.

2349   Gibbs, Jeanne Marie. "Beyond the Absurd: Right and Wrong in the Fiction of Flannery O'Connor." Thesis, Moorhead State U, 1969.

2350   Gilbert, Mary R. "Solar and Lunar Imagery in Flannery O'Connor's Short Stories." Thesis, Boston College, 1967.

2351   Gillespie, Mary Christine. "Flannery O'Connor's Rhetoric of Ambiguity and Strategies of Explanation: The Tension Between Conflicting Fidelities." Thesis, U of Texas at Austin, 1987.

2352 Gillikin, Sandra A. "The Face of Evil: A Study of Irony in Flannery O'Connor's *The Violent Bear It Away*." Thesis, East Carolina U, 1968.

2353 Glenn, Bruce Houston. "Tenderness Leads to Terror: The Gnostic Hero in Modern Literature." Thesis, Arizona State U, 1992.

2354 Goff, Penelope Hope. "The Jehovah Imperative: Images of Incest and Blood Sacrifice in Walpole's *The Castle of Otranto* and Flannery O'Connor's *Wise Blood*." Thesis, U of Rhode Island, 1992.

2355 Goodin, Gayle. "The Protagonist in the Modern Georgia Novel." Thesis, U of Mississippi, 1966.

2356 Gott, Fleur Marie. "Clowns and Captives: A Study of Flannery O'Connor's Fiction." Thesis, La Verne College, 1972.

2357 Graham, Harriet. "The Spiritual Blindness of Modern Man: Satire and Irony in the Works of Flannery O'Connor." Thesis, Valdosta State College, 1980.

2358 Grant, Hazel Smithco. "Education: A Structural Device in the Fiction of Flannery O'Connor." Thesis, U of Georgia, 1972.

2359 Grant, Janet. "The Concept of Salvation in the Fiction of Flannery O'Connor." Thesis, U of Northern Iowa, 1972.

2360 Graves, Kay Childers. "Religious, Social and Psychological Revelations in Representative Stories of Flannery O'Connor." Thesis, U of Mississippi, 1986.

2361 Graves, Robyn Anita. "Works of Love: A Study of Kierkegaardian Themes and Style in the Works of Flannery O'Connor." Thesis, Vanderbilt U, 1977.

2362 Gray, Margaret E. "'Revelation': The Culmination of the Works of Flannery O'Connor." Thesis, Bowling Green State U, 1994.

2363 Gray, Mary Margaret Germany. "Flannery O'Connor's *Wise Blood*: Seeing Through a Glass, Darkly." Thesis, Delta State U, 1984.

2364 Greco, Joseph A. "Mind Style: Form and Meaning in *Wise Blood*." Thesis, U of South Florida, 1988.

2365 Greer, Charlotte Lou. "Mystery Versus Manners: An Examination of Selected Stories by Flannery O'Connor." Thesis, Brown U, 1972.

2366   Griffin, Debra F. "Flannery O'Connor's *The Violent Bear It Away*: The
        Growth Toward Prophecy." Thesis, State College of Arkansas, 1973.

2367   Griffin, Joan Rae. "Flannery O'Connor and the Development of the
        Grotesque in American Literature." Thesis, South Dakota State U, 1970.

2368   Griffin, Teresa E. "'Cursed With Believing': Children and Grace in the
        Fiction of Flannery O'Connor." Thesis, Wake Forest U, 1986.

2369   Griffith, Benjamin Woodward. "Two Views of Calvinism in the South:
        William Faulkner and Flannery O'Connor." Thesis, Florida State U, 1979.

2370   Guilka, Mother Therese E. "Flannery O'Connor's Violent World." Thesis,
        Boston College, 1967.

2371   Hahn, John E. "It's Only a Paper Moon: A Reading of Flannery
        O'Connor's 'The Artificial Nigger.'" Thesis, Lehigh U, 1973.

2372   Hamby, Stanley O. "Flannery O'Connor's Humor: A Study of
        Background and Approach." Thesis, Georgia Southern College, 1973.

2373   Hanks, Julie A. "Images of Southern Womanhood: A Study of the Fiction
        of Katherine Anne Porter, Eudora Welty and Flannery O'Connor." Thesis,
        U of Southwestern Louisiana, 1995.

2374   Harding, Mary Elizabeth. "Images of the Grotesque and the Myths of
        Southern Womanhood: The Female Characters of Carson McCullers and
        Flannery O'Connor." Thesis, U of North Carolina at Chapel Hill, 1988.

2375   Hardwick, Patricia A. "The Longer Fiction of Flannery O'Connor."
        Thesis, Ohio State U, 1965.

2376   Harlburt, Ronald E. "The Functions of the Child Characters in the Fiction
        of Flannery O'Connor." Thesis, Murray State U, 1969.

2377   Harrell, Jack A. "The Form and Function of the Grotesque in Flannery
        O'Connor's *Wise Blood*." Thesis, Illinois State U, 1994.

2378   Harris, Gary Marcel. "A Comparison of Adaptive Techniques for Prose
        Fiction: Representational and Chamber Theater Scripts for Flannery
        O'Connor's 'The Lame Shall Enter First.'" Thesis, U of Tennessee
        (Knoxville), 1980.

2379   Harrison, Amelia H. "Sight Imagery and the Theme of Right Versus
        Blindness in *Wise Blood*." Thesis, North Carolina State U, 1972.

2380   Hart, Gary V. "The Eucharistic Symbol and the Concept of Grace in the Works of Flannery O'Connor." Thesis, Pepperdine U, 1969.

2381   Hartin-Grysztar, Pamela. "The Voice of the Prophet: Narration in Flannery O'Connor's `The River.'" Thesis, Georgia State U, 1993.

2382   Hawley, James Russell. "As One of Faith: Reading Flannery O'Connor." Thesis, Graduate Theological Union, 1991.

2383   Hayes, George Marion. "Gesture and Grace in the Fiction of Flannery O'Connor." Thesis, Georgia State U, 1973.

2384   Hays, Sandra J. "Rhetorical Figures and Their Effects: The Theoretical Work of Mikhail M. Bakhtin and M. Fabius Quintilian as Manifested in *Wise Blood* by Flannery O'Connor and *Pequena Historia de Horror* by Maruxa Vilalta." Thesis, U of Wisconsin at Milwaukee, 1995.

2385   Hembree, Janice M. "Flannery O'Connor: `A Realist of Distances.'" Thesis, San Francisco State U, 1991.

2386   Hendrix, Ellen Hudgins. "Flannery O'Connor: Defending the Southern Sense of Self." Thesis, Georgia Southern U, 1990.

2387   Henson, Brian Keith. "Evolving With the Church: The Southern Catholic Novel in the Wake of the Second Vatican Council." Thesis, Mississippi State U, 1997.

2388   Herbkersman, Gretchen Ann. "Matrices of Paradox: The Style of Flannery O'Connor's Short Stories." Thesis, San Francisco State College, 1968.

2389   Herring, Linda. "Realm of the Peacock: Divine Grace in Flannery O'Connor's Fiction." Thesis, Sam Houston State U, 1987.

2390   Hibner, Stephanie. "Voices in the Garden: An Exploration of Gardens in the Short Stories of Eudora Welty, Flannery O'Connor, Ellen Gilchrist, and Alice Walker." Thesis, North Carolina State U, 1996.

2391   Hockensmith, David A. "Flannery O'Connor and Her Liberals." Thesis, Butler U, 1974.

2392   Hodges, Elizabeth Scott. "Variations on One Story: Habits of Art in Flannery O'Connor." Thesis, Pennsylvania State U, 1981.

2393   Hogan, Kathleen Marie. "The Moment of Grace in Flannery O'Connor's Fiction." Thesis, U of Calgary (Canada), 1983.

2394   Holbrook, Nancy L.N. "Violence and Order in the Short Stories of Eudora Welty, Flannery O'Connor, and Peter Taylor." Thesis, Vanderbilt U, 1961.

2395   Holloway, Phyllis. "The Power of Shock: A Study of the Central Figures in Flannery O'Connor's Fiction." Thesis, East Tennessee State U, 1969.

2396   Holt, Dena Novak. "Graham Greene's and Flannery O'Connor's Similar Violent Response to the Modern World in *Brighton Rock* and *Wise Blood*." Thesis, James Madison U, 1995.

2397   Homic, Maria Veres. "Finding a Place: Flannery O'Connor's M.F.A. Stories." Thesis, Southwest Texas State U, 1992.

2398   Hook, Wilma Gene. "The World of Flannery O'Connor: The Grotesque Pilgrimage." Thesis, Central Michigan U, 1966.

2399   Horton, Mary Jane. "Affective Structure in Stories by Eudora Welty, Katherine Anne Porter, and Flannery O'Connor." Thesis, U of North Carolina at Chapel Hill, 1971.

2400   Howell, Sarah Winborne. "Some Aspects of Flannery O'Connor's Humor." Thesis, U of South Carolina, 1971.

2401   Howie, Elizabeth. "Redemption of the Grotesque." Thesis, Mississippi College, 1990.

2402   Hudson, Lesley M. "The Use of Nature Imagery in the Selected Fiction of Flannery O'Connor." Thesis, U of Rhode Island, 1974.

2403   Huff, Carol Czarowitz. "Flannery O'Connor and the Technique of Characterization." Thesis, Texas Christian U, 1968.

2404   Hughes, Amanda Millay. "The Mystery of Incarnation: A Study of Incarnation in the Works of Flannery O'Connor." Thesis, U of North Carolina at Chapel Hill, 1994.

2405   Hunter, Shaun Megan. "The Apprenticeship of Alice Munro: Seeing Through the World of Flannery O'Connor." Thesis, Smith College, 1984.

2406   Hurlbert, Ronald E. "The Functions of the Child Characters in the Fiction of Flannery O'Connor." Thesis, Murray State U, 1968.

2407   Hutchinson, Mary Jo. "The Intruding Stranger in Flannery O'Connor's Fiction." Thesis, Morehead State U, 1973.

2407a   Irving, Catherine Janet Sarah. "A Jungle of Shadows: Interpretations of the Anagogical and the Grotesque in the Short Stories of Flannery O'Connor." Thesis, U of Cape Town (South Africa), 1999.

2408   Isaac, Colleen M. "Apocalyptic Vision: The Grotesque and Its Relation to Theme Development in the Fiction of Flannery O'Connor." Thesis, Holy Names College, 1971.

2409   Isaacs, Alisa Kristine. "Grace and Redemption as Offered in Violence, Prophecy, and Sacraments in the Life and Writings of Flannery O'Connor." Thesis, Garrett Evangelical Theological Seminary, 1992.

2410   Jackson, Alice Britt. "The Wise Child and the Symbolic Black: Two Character-Types in Flannery O'Connor's Short Fiction." Thesis, California State U (Sacramento), 1976.

2411   Jacobi, Laura. "From Hierarchy to Convergence in Flannery O'Connor's `Everything That Rises Must Converge,' `Revelation,' and `The Artificial Nigger.'" Thesis, U of St. Thomas, 1996.

2412   Jacobs, Robert Alan. "The Weight of Centuries Is Upon Them: The Burdens of Children in Flannery O'Connor's *The Violent Bear It Away*." Thesis, Bemidji State U, 1998.

2413   Jamieson, Janis L. "Flannery O'Connor: Her Fictive Child." Thesis, U of Texas (Arlington), 1980.

2414   Jayko, Elizabeth M. "The Glassless Spectacles: Point of View in Flannery O'Connor's *Everything That Rises Must Converge*." Thesis, U of North Carolina at Chapel Hill, 1985.

2415   Jimenez, Nilda. "The Redemptive Concern of Flannery O'Connor's Work." Thesis, U of Puerto Rico, 1972.

2416   Johnston, Carol Ann. "An Application of Simone Weil's Theories of Hunger and Vision to Selected Works of Flannery O'Connor." Thesis, Baylor U, 1980.

2417   Julienne, Marietta Lenear. "Confrontation and Redemption in Flannery O'Connor's `A Good Man Is Hard To Find.'" Thesis, U of North Carolina at Chapel Hill, 1969.

2418   Justice, Dana Alan. "O'Connor's Moments of Grace: From Bow Down Come Rise Up." Honors Thesis, Ohio U, 1989.

2419   Kane, Jennifer. "The Discomforts of Home: Parent and Child Relationships in Flannery O'Connor's Short Fiction." Thesis, Emory U, 1982.

2420   Kares, Julie L. "Flannery O'Connor: Achieving Grace?" Thesis, U of New Orleans, 1997.

2421   Kastleman, Linda Craven. "Wolfgang Iser's Reading Process Theory: A Discussion of Major Concepts and an Exploratory Study of Reader and Listener-Viewer Responses to Flannery O'Connor's `The River.'" Thesis, U of North Carolina at Chapel Hill, 1985.

2422   Kaufman, Linda Jean Watson. "Self-Deception Practiced by Intellectual Misfits in Four Flannery O'Connor Stories." ["Good Country People," "The Enduring Chill," "Everything That Rises Must Converge," and "The Comforts of Home."] Thesis, West Georgia College, 1983.

2423   Kehrer, Grace S. "Justifying Enoch Emery." Thesis, U of South Florida, 1974.

2424   Kelly, Brenda Kane. "Flannery O'Connor: Three Stories of Grace for the Individual and Hope for the Family." Thesis, U of West Florida, 1995. ["The Lame Shall Enter First," "The Enduring Chill," and "The Artificial Nigger."]

2425   Kelly, Janet Laura. "The Role of the Sponsor in Ten Flannery O'Connor Short Stories." Thesis, Trinity College (CT), 1976.

2426   Kennedy, Lisa Ann. "Flannery O'Connor: A Reference Guide, 1975-1983." Thesis, California U of Pennsylvania, 1986.

2427   Kerr, Robert Lansing. "Flannery O'Connor: Realist of Distances." Thesis, Duke U, 1966.

2428   Kerth, Thomas R. "The Intellectual in the Fiction of Flannery O'Connor." Thesis, Wake Forest U, 1976.

2429   King, Kimberly. "Living In a Material World: A Different Look at Flannery O'Connor." Thesis, Radford U, 1998.

2430   King, Liane C. "From Self-Intoxication to Salvation: A Study of the Women Characters in Selected Short Stories of Flannery O'Connor." B.A. Thesis, Tulane U, 1979.

2431   Kipp, Dorothy Hawes. "Sight Imagery and the Theme of Redemption in Flannery O'Connor's Fiction." Thesis, Indiana U of Pennsylvania, 1971.

2432   Kleinmaier, Carol Allison. "As She Lay Dying: Self-Parody in the Fiction of Flannery O'Connor." Thesis, San Francisco State U, 1983.

2433   Knutson, Linda. "Flannery O'Connor, Doppelgängers, and Grace." Thesis, Loras College, 1986.

2434   Kohman, Joan. "The Contemporary Morality Play: O'Connor's *Wise Blood*." Thesis, Wichita State U, 1976.

2435   Kolodny-Creech, Mary Ruth. "Dualism Intended: A Stylistic Analysis of the Idiolects of the Author and the Main Characters in *The Violent Bear It Away*." Thesis, U of North Carolina at Chapel Hill, 1987.

2436   Lally, Joan Marie. "Flannery O'Connor: Literary Cartoonist." Thesis, U of Utah, 1969.

2437   Lanehart, Wendy L. "Zora Neale Hurston and Flannery O'Connor: Community in Southern Literature." Thesis, College of William and Mary, 1988.

2438   Langan, Colleen P. "'And the Blind Shall See': Vision and Grace in Flannery O'Connor's Works." Thesis, Shippensburg U of Pennsylvania, 1993.

2439   Lartigue de García Belsunce, Alicia. "Flannery O'Connor." Thesis, Instituto Nacional del Profesorado de Lenguas Vivas Juan Ramón Fernández (Argentina), 1973. [Copy in the *Flannery O'Connor Collection* at Georgia College & State U, Milledgeville, GA.]

2440   Lasswell, Margaret W. "The Theme of Love and Separation in the Short Story Collections of Carson McCullers, Flannery O'Connor, and Eudora Welty." Thesis, Our Lady of the Lake College, 1968.

2441   Latham, Don Loftis. "Flannery O'Connor as Novelist." Thesis, Clemson U, 1984.

2442   Lauby, Jacqueline. "Three Studies of Literature: Revenge as Valid in Tourneur; The Problem of Suicide in Ulysses; and, Flannery O'Connor's Concept of Grace." Thesis, Pennsylvania State U, 1982.

2443   Lavin, Mary J.W. "Image and Reality: A Study of the Complete Works of Flannery O'Connor." Thesis, John Carroll U, 1962.

2444   LaVois, Caroline F. "The Theme of Death in the Works of Flannery O'Connor." Thesis, Sam Houston State U, 1969.

2445   LeBlanc, Ann McInnis. "The Devil's Territory: The Modern World in
        Flannery O'Connor." Thesis, Clemson U, 1975.

2446   Lee, Tracey Ann. "Flannery O'Connor and the Sophocles Connection."
        Thesis, Wichita State U, 1993.

2447   Lesser, Cynthia Lee. "Members Of The Wedding, The Descent of
        Immanence: Communities in the Fiction of Flannery O'Connor, Walker
        Percy, and Carson McCullers." Thesis, U of California (Berkley), 1984.

2448   Lester, Mary. "Flannery O'Connor's Young Searchers: A Study of Five of
        Her Child-Protagonists." [Bevel in "The River," Nelson in "The Artificial
        Nigger," Ruller in "The Turkey," the Child in "A Temple of the Holy
        Ghost," and Tarwater in "You Can't Be Any Poorer Than Dead"]. Thesis,
        Drew U, 1978.

2449   Lewellen, Alice D. "Violence in the Words of the World of Flannery
        O'Connor." Thesis, U of Northern Iowa, 1979.

2450   Lindsey, William D. "Story as Parable: A Parabolic Reading of Flannery
        O'Connor's `Revelation.'" Thesis, Tulane U, 1989.

2451   Lotts, Chris. "The Ironic Quest of the Modern Hero in the Fiction of
        Flannery O'Connor." Honors Project, U of Redlands, 1985.

2452   Lowe, Desiree Keena. "Art and Epiphany: A Look at Selected Short
        Stories by Flannery O'Connor and James Joyce." Thesis, U of Georgia,
        1990.

2453   Lower, Jacquelyn D. "A Study of Alienation in the Works of Flannery
        O'Connor." Thesis, U of Denver, 1969.

2454   Ludwin, Deanna L. Kern. "The Ironic Mode in Flannery O'Connor's `The
        Artificial Nigger.'" Thesis, Colorado State U, 1988.

2455   Lukas, Dorothy A. "The Dual Function of the Grotesque in Flannery
        O'Connor." Thesis, Pennsylvania State U, 1967.

2456   Lulling, Thomas William. "Purified by the Seraphim: Flannery
        O'Connor's Prophet Motif." Thesis, Arizona State U, 1995.

2457   Lutyens, Elizabeth. "Queen of the Lights: A Collection of Short Stories."
        Thesis, Warren Wilson College, 1998. [Alternate Title: "Worthy
        Opponents: Antagonists in Alice Munro's `Royal Beatings' and Flannery
        O'Connor's `The Comforts of Home.'"]

2458 Lyle, Michael L. "From `The Geranium' to `Judgement Day': The Stylistic Development of Flannery O'Connor." Thesis, Wake Forest U, 1981.

2459 Lynn, Denise D. "A Study of Certain Aspects of the Fiction of Graham Greene and Flannery O'Connor." Thesis, Iowa State Teacher's College, 1963.

2460 Maffini, William L. "A Study of Reflector Imagery in the Short Stories of Flannery O'Connor." Thesis, U of the Pacific, 1971.

2461 Mahoney, Elizabeth P. "(Un)Crowning the Modernist Mentality: Reading the Carnival in Flannery O'Connor's Fiction." Thesis, U of Vermont, 1992.

2462 Malone, Carol J. "The Religious Vision of Flannery O'Connor." Thesis, U of South Carolina, 1971.

2463 Mannmeusel, Susanne Maria. "The Religious Quest in Nathanael West's *Miss Lonelyhearts* and Flannery O'Connor's *Wise Blood*." Thesis, U of South Carolina, 1989.

2464 Marks, Gregory Angelo. "The Underworld in O'Connor's *The Violent Bear It Away*." Thesis, U of Dallas, 1991.

2465 Marlowe, Jeanne A. "A Comparison of Religious Themes in the Fiction of Graham Greene and Flannery O'Connor." Thesis, Bowling Green State U, 1969.

2466 Maroney, Janet M. "The Grotesque in Flannery O'Connor." Thesis, Columbia U, 1962.

2467 Marre, Diana Katherine. "From Hogs to Heaven: Transcendent Literalism and the Fiction of Flannery O'Connor." Thesis, Washington U, 1982.

2468 Marschel, Jacqueline A. "The Figure of Innocence in Flannery O'Connor." Thesis, Saint Louis U, 1967.

2469 Marshall, Donald R. "The Southern Quest for Identity--A Cycle: Isolation, Identity, and the Past." Thesis, Brigham Young U, 1964.

2470 Martin, Jean Colvin. "Cheer for an Invisible Parade: Humor in the Fiction of Flannery O'Connor." Thesis, Madison College, 1972.

2471 Matchette, William A. "Southern Protestantism in the Fiction of Flannery O'Connor." Thesis, North Texas State U, 1970.

2472   Matthews, Moira. "Mystery in the Works of Flannery O'Connor." Thesis, Dalhousie U (Canada), 1981.

2473   Mauck, Deanna. "The Religious Perspective of Flannery O'Connor's Fiction: A Collaboration of Roman Catholicism and Southern Protestant Fundamentalism." Thesis, Northern State U, 1992.

2474   Mayer, David R. "Flannery O'Connor's Treatment of Grace and Baptism in *The Violent Bear It Away*." Thesis, Georgetown U, 1970.

2475   McBride, Anne Keeler. "Teilhard and Maritain in O'Connor's *Everything That Rises Must Converge*." Thesis, Georgia State U, 1983.

2476   McCaffrey, Karen. "The Prophetic and Redemptive Elements in the Fiction of Flannery O'Connor." Thesis, Wesleyan U, 1980.

2477   McCullagh, James C. "Flannery O'Connor's Theology Viewed Through the Haze of the Grotesque." Thesis, Lehigh U, 1970.

2478   McFall, Todd A. "Twentieth-Century Babble: Poststructuralism and O'Connor's Poetics" Thesis, Bowling Green State U, 1994.

2479   McGinnis, Karla Ann. "The Mystical Elements in the Fiction of Flannery O'Connor." Thesis, Appalachian State U, 1986.

2480   McGrath, Mary Angeline. "A Study of the Mystery, the Fact, and the Unexpected in the Writings of Flannery O'Connor." Thesis, U of Dayton, 1966.

2481   McGurl, Katherine A. "Interpreting Flannery O'Connor: Intention and the Problem of Grace." Thesis, U of Rhode Island, 1992.

2482   McIntyre, Lynda Greene. "An Interpretation of the Revelation Imagery in the Short Stories of Flannery O'Connor." Thesis, Mississippi College, 1985.

2483   McKinney, Margaret Jordan. "Five Short Stories for Study: I and Thou in Contemporary Fiction." [D.H. Lawrence's "Two Blue Birds"; John Cheever's "The Chaste Clarissa"; Woody Allen's "Kungelmass Episode"; Joyce Carol Oates' "In the Region of Ice"; and Flannery O'Connor's "Revelation"]. Thesis, Appalachian State U, 1983.

2484   McKnight, Carol Lynn. "Tarwater's Quest for Truth: A Study of Flannery O'Connor's *The Violent Bear It Away*." Thesis, U of North Carolina at Chapel Hill, 1971.

2485   McShane, Zita. "Flannery O'Connor's Grotesque Intellectuals." Thesis, Cleveland State U, 1975.

2486   Mendez, Constance Wagner. "Signs of the Times: The Presence of the Catholic Tradition in Selected Works of Walker Percy and Flannery O'Connor." Thesis, U of Texas of the Permian Basin, 1991.

2487   Merdian, Patricia Vera DerMotta. "The Dimension of `Unspirituality' in Flannery O'Connor's Female Protagonists: A Study of Mrs. Cope, Joy-Hulga, and the Grandmother." Thesis, California U of Pennsylvania, 1985.

2488   Merryday, Ann-Jo. "Flannery O'Connor's God With Thunder." Thesis, U of Florida, 1977.

2489   Miller, Audrey I. "Chaos and Conformity: The Systematic Grotesque of Flannery O'Connor." Thesis, College of William and Mary, 1982.

2490   Miller, Marcia. "The Influence of the Apostle Paul on the Writings of Flannery O'Connor." Thesis, U of South Carolina, 1990.

2491   Mills, Elizabeth M. "Mannerist Art and the Fiction of Flannery O'Connor: A Combination of Parallels." Thesis, U of Texas (El Paso), 1967.

2492   Moore, Carol Craft. "The Victim in Flannery O'Connor's Stories." Thesis, Virginia State U, 1990.

2493   Moore, Jeffrey Scott. "Means of Communication of the Religious Dimension in Flannery O'Connor's Fiction." B.A. Thesis, Tulane U, 1988.

2494   Moore, Lofton Samuel. "Flannery O'Connor: A Descriptive Analysis of Her Fiction." Thesis, U of Idaho, 1965.

2495   Moore, Terilyn Joy. "The Poetry of Her Prose: A Critical Analysis of Flannery O'Connor's Style." Thesis, California State U, Sacramento, 1988.

2496   Morgan, Neill Sagen. "Flannery O'Connor: Images of the Holy Spirit." Thesis, Austin College, 1981.

2497   Morley, Irene. "The Unknown Self in Flannery O'Connor's Novels." Thesis, Columbia U, 1966.

2498   Morris, Mason Thomas. "In Pursuit of Self: A Study of the Process on Initiation in Four Novels." Thesis, U of Louisville, 1969. [Examines *The Violent Bear It Away*.]

2499   Morris, Michael N. "Encountering the Source of Goodness: A Study of Flannery O'Connor's `A Good Man Is Hard to Find,' `Revelation,' and `The Displaced Person.'" Thesis, East Texas State U, 1995.

2500   Morris, Robin Heather. "Silence and Savagery: The Children of Flannery O'Connor's Short Fiction." Thesis, James Madison U, 1996.

2501   Morrison, Linda Kaye McCloud. "The Devil's Territory: The Function of the Devil Figure in Flannery O'Connor's Fiction." Thesis, U of Houston, 1973.

2502   Mosher, Rachel Jennifer. "`Him and You Twins?': The Function of the Double in Flannery O'Connor's *Wise Blood*." Thesis, College of William and Mary, 1992.

2503   Mullane, Deirdre K. "`By Virtue of Kinship and Similarity and Experience': The Double Motif in Flannery O'Connor's *Wise Blood* and *The Violent Bear It Away*." Thesis, College of William and Mary, 1980.

2504   Mulrain, Mary. "The Grotesque Prophet in the Short Fiction of Flannery O'Connor." Thesis, Drew U, 1974.

2505   Muncy, Emily Maxwell. "Flannery O'Connor and [Edmund] Burke's Theory of the Sublime." Thesis, Florida Atlantic U, 1985.

2506   Murphy, Brenda C. "Flannery O'Connor: A Searing Vision." Thesis, Wagner College, 1968.

2507   Murphy, Gregory Joseph. "The Unexpected God: The Biblical Themes of Mercy and Justice in Flannery O'Connor's Later Fiction." Thesis, San Jose State U, 1984.

2508   Murphy, Michael P. "Flannery O'Connor: From Paradox to Mystery." Thesis, San Francisco State U, 1993.

2509   Nagle, Kathryn L. "Narcissistic Personality Disorder in Selected Short Stories by Flannery O'Connor." Thesis, West Chester U, 1999.

2510   Neder, Carolyn Maria. "The Nature of Knowledge: Modern Intellectualism in the Fiction of Flannery O'Connor." Thesis, Georgia Southern College, 1983.

2511   Nelson, Bobbe Smith. "God and Man in the Drama of Being: The Common Philosophical Ground of Eric Voegelin, Flannery O'Connor, and Robert Penn Warren." Thesis, Georgia Southern College, 1982.

2512   Newcomer, Grace G. "Flannery O'Connor's Stinger." Thesis, Wesleyan U, 1983.

2513   Newkirk, Terrye. "Cheers: Letters of Flannery O'Connor to Brainard and Frances Neel Cheney." Thesis, Vanderbilt U, 1984.

2514   Newman, Georgia Ann. "Flannery O'Connor: Annotated Bibliography of Secondary Sources." Thesis, Florida State U, 1970. [Copy in the *Flannery O'Connor Collection* at Georgia College & State U, Milledgeville, GA.]

2515   Newman, William S. "Flannery O'Connor's Distinctive Use of Place in Her Novels and Short Stories." Thesis, U of Tennessee, 1965.

2516   Nichols, Ellen A. "Flannery O'Connor's Intellectuals: The Stripping of Illusions." Thesis, California State College (Bakersfield), 1987.

2517   Nichols, Loxley Fitzpatrick. "`Far Things Close Up': Flannery O'Connor's Depiction of Mystery in the Banal." Thesis, U of New Hampshire, 1978.

2518   Nicosia, James. "The Misfits Bear It Away: Narrative Voice, Liminality and Comeuppance in the Short Fiction of Flannery O'Connor." Thesis, Montclair State U, 1994.

2519   Nielson, Kathleen Buswell. "Making Contact With Mystery: Christian Perspectives in O'Connor's Art." Thesis, Vanderbilt U, 1979.

2520   Nolin, Jennifer E. "Familial Relationships in Flannery O'Connor's Fiction: The Common Experience of Alienation." Thesis, U of North Carolina at Chapel Hill, 1983.

2521   Norman, Linda Carol. "Secular Protagonists in Flannery O'Connor's Fiction." Thesis, North Texas State U, 1977.

2522   Norris, Trudy Peterson. "A Study of Regionalism and Flannery O'Connor: Two Southern Character Types." Thesis, West Georgia College, 1971.

2523   Norton, Paige L. "The Family in `A Good Man Is Hard To Find.'" Thesis, Emory U, 1983.

2524   Nunley, Thelma G. "The Later Fiction of Flannery O'Connor: The Question of Chardinian Convergence." Thesis, East Tennessee State U, 1974.

2525   Oberhausen, Tammy L. "The Southern Misfit and the Dream of Escape in the Fiction of Carson McCullers and Flannery O'Connor." Thesis, Western Kentucky U, 1991.

2526   O'Brien, Conan Christopher. "The `Old Child' in Faulkner and O'Connor."
        Thesis, Harvard U, 1985. [Note: Host of NBC's late night talk show, "Late
        Night With Conan O'Brien," and former editor of *The Harvard Lampoon*.]

2527   O'Brien, John Thomas. "The Absence of Love in the Fiction of Flannery
        O'Connor." Thesis, U of Illinois (Chicago Circle), 1971.

2528   O'Connell, Mary Rose. "The Child-Figure in the Short Stories of Flannery
        O'Connor: Two Patterns of Relationship." Thesis, Catholic U of America,
        1970.

2529   O'Dell, Margaret Darlene. "The Use of Animal Imagery in the Early
        Works of Flannery O'Connor." Thesis, Clemson U, 1988.

2530   Ogawa, Yumiko. "Violence in the Works of Flannery O'Connor and
        Carson McCullers." Thesis, California State U, Sacramento, 1984.

2531   O'Keefe, Mary E. "Myth as Meaning and Structure in *The Violent Bear
        It Away*." Thesis, Boston College, 1969.

2532   Oliver, LaTrelle Blackburn. "Physical Markings in O'Connor Country:
        Flannery O'Connor's Use of Concrete Particulars from Her Region."
        Thesis, Duke U, 1968.

2533   Olivero, Mary F. "The Beacon and the Battle-ax: Catholicism in the
        Works of Flannery O'Connor and Robert Lowell." B.A. Thesis,
        Pennsylvania State U, 1986.

2534   Ontiveros, Benjamin. "Epiphany and Redemption in the Short Stories of
        Flannery O'Connor." Thesis, California Polytechnic University, 1997.

2535   Osteen, Kathy. "From Evangelists to Intellectuals: the Progression of
        Flannery O'Connor." Thesis, U of South Carolina, 1976.

2536   Ostrow, Eileen Joyce. "The Violent Reality: Alienation, Distortion, and
        Violence in the Works of Four Contemporary Women Writers: Flannery
        O'Connor, Toni Morrison, Joyce Carol Oates, Joan Didion." Thesis, Mills
        College, 1977.

2537   Ouzts, Cuyler E. "Flannery O'Connor's Use of the Grotesque." Thesis,
        Texas Christian U, 1968.

2538   Oxendine, Debbie Hutchinson. "Textual Images for Flannery O'Connor's
        Short Stories, Shakespeare's *Othello*, and Dryden's *Marriage A-La-Mode*."
        Thesis, North Carolina State U, 1989.

2539   Park, Kerry L. "The Life, Faith, and Works of Flannery O'Connor: A One-Person Play." Thesis, Regent U, 1992.

2540   Patterson, Elizabeth Linda. "The Evolution of Flannery O'Connor's Attitude Towards Southern Society." Thesis, McGill U, 1977.

2541   Payne, Pamela W. "Expressions of the Religious Imagination in the Work of Jane Austen and Flannery O'Connor." Thesis, Florida Atlantic U, 1993.

2542   Peacock, Claire R. "A Vision of Reality: Characterization in the Novels and Short Stories of Flannery O'Connor." Thesis, Vanderbilt U, 1963.

2543   Peffer, Mary Cecilia. "The Problem of Free Will in the Stories of Flannery O'Connor." Thesis, Wake Forest U, 1971.

2544   Penkala, Rosemary A. "'The Enduring Chill' and 'Revelation': Flannery O'Connor's Answer to the Problem of the Postmodern Fragmented Self." Thesis, Bowling Green State U, 1994.

2545   Perrin, Elaine. "The Unique Achievement of Flannery O'Connor." Thesis, Texas Technological U, 1969.

2546   Perry, Keith Ronald. "The Divorce of Rome and South Georgia: Mystery, Manners, and Mysticism in the Fiction of Flannery O'Connor." Thesis, Wake Forest U, 1991.

2547   Petersen, Marc Andreis. "The Parallel Mysteries of Grace and Place in Flannery O'Connor's *Wise Blood*." Thesis, San Jose State U, 1990.

2548   Pfeffer, Genevieve. "The Characterization and Thematic Use of Old Age in Selected Short Fiction of Katherine Anne Porter, Eudora Welty, and Flannery O'Connor." Thesis, Sam Houston State U, 1973.

2549   Phillips, Elizabeth Ann Aycock. "Journey Motif in the Fiction of Flannery O'Connor." Thesis, Lamar U, 1973.

2550   Phinney, Carmen Sandra. "'. . . Forever and Ever Amen': Concepts of Time in the Short Fiction of Flannery O'Connor." Thesis, Dalhousie U (Canada), 1979.

2551   Pierce, Jacklyn R. "'A Good Man Is Hard to Find': Single Southern Women and the Fiction of Flannery O'Connor." Thesis, Clemson U, 1994.

2552   Pierson, Marye. "Affirmation Through Irony: A Structural Analysis of 'The Displaced Person' by Flannery O'Connor." Thesis, Catholic U of America, 1962.

2553   Pilkington, Joyce Elaine. "The South and Christianity in Flannery O'Connor." Thesis, Clemson U, 1978.

2554   Pinnow, Jon. "An O'Connor Aviary: Notes on Birds and Bird Imagery in the Fiction of Flannery O'Connor." Thesis, U of Denver, 1997.

2555   Piper, Wendy A. "Flannery O'Connor's Concern for Truth: Aristotelian and Phenomenological Implications." Thesis, Florida Atlantic U, 1991.

2556   Pogue, Mary Beth. "The Quest for Spiritual Lucidity: The Catholic Consciousness in the Works of Allen Tate and Flannery O'Connor." Thesis, State U of West Georgia, 1997.

2557   Pope, Tilloretta Mitchell. "A Spiritual Pilgrimage with the Children of Flannery O'Connor." Thesis, Georgetown U, 1991.

2558   Pritchard, Alice S. "Violence in Flannery O'Connor's Fiction." Thesis, U of Maryland at College Park, 1967.

2559   Prochnow, Thomas Herbert. "Impressions of History in the Short Fiction of Nathaniel Hawthorne and Flannery O'Connor." A.B. Honors Thesis, Harvard U, 1989.

2560   Provost, Glen John. "Scriptural Affirmation in Flannery O'Connor's *The Violent Bear It Away*." Thesis, U of Southwestern Louisiana, 1981.

2561   Prown, Katherine Hemple. "Flannery O'Connor, Fyodor Dostoevsky, and the Antimodernist Tradition." Thesis, College of William and Mary, 1988.

2562   Psyhos, Rebecca Ruth. "The Central Mystery: Conversion Experiences in Selected Works of Flannery O'Connor." Thesis, Arizona State U, 1987.

2563   Pudas, Stacie J. "Fear and Outrage: A Study of Flannery O'Connor's Short Fiction." Thesis, California Polytechnic State U, 1999.

2564   Putnam, Thomas Wells. "Naming the Things of God." Thesis, Bucknell U, 1990.

2565   Pylate, Julia Candis. "The Omnipotent Father in Flannery O'Connor's Fictional Families." Thesis, Mississippi College, 1992.

2566   Pyle, Norma S. "Southern Gothic: A Summary of Literary Uses." Thesis, U of Illinois, Chicago Circle, 1970.

2567   Querengesser, Neil. "Flannery O'Connor's Methods of Characterization." Thesis, U of Calgary (Canada), 1984.

2568   Rainey, Carol A. "Narrative Distance in the Short Stories of Flannery O'Connor." Thesis, U of Cincinnati, 1967.

2569   Rainey, David E. "The Relationship Between Characterization and Theme in Flannery O'Connor's *The Violent Bear It Away*." Thesis, Emory U, 1968.

2570   Rannik, Stacey Ann. "Fallen Angels of Gawd: Flannery O'Connor's Paradoxical Divine Avengers." Thesis, Arizona State U, 1994.

2571   Ransom, Wayne Fletcher. "The Vision and Art of Flannery O'Connor." Thesis, West Virginia U, 1972.

2572   Rawal, Suresh. "Ritual and Violence in the Novels of Flannery O'Connor." Thesis, Louisiana State U in New Orleans, 1971. [Name changed to the U of New Orleans in 1974.]

2573   Rayburn, Kellie Renee. "'Words Moving Secretly Toward Some Goal of Their Own': The Rhetorical Use of the `As If' in the Fiction of Flannery O'Connor." Thesis, California State U (San Bernardino), 1988.

2574   Reed, Eva Laurie. "The Failure of Rationalism in the Works of Flannery O'Connor." Thesis, Southwest Texas State U, 1988.

2575   Reel, Madeleine W. "Amazing Grace: The Fiction of Flannery O'Connor." Thesis, Wesleyan U, 1973.

2576   Reeves, Rhonda. "Flannery O'Connor's Wingless Chickens: The Role of the Pseudosophisticate in Selected Short Stories." Thesis, U of Kentucky, 1992.

2577   Regin, Patsy K. "Paradox in the Works of Flannery O'Connor." Thesis, Lone Mountain College, 1970.

2578   Rhinehart, Susan. "A Comparison of Flannery O'Connor's Fictional Techniques in `The Geranium' and in `Judgement Day.'" Thesis, City U of New York, Queens College, 1974.

2579   Richard, Nora Ellen. "Human Limitations and Grace: The Influence of Flannery O'Connor's Religious Belief in Her Short Stories." Thesis, U of Wyoming, 1977.

2580   Riddick, Estelle B. "The Illumination of the Grotesque Protagonist As Seen in Selected Stories by Flannery O'Connor." Thesis, Drew U, 1980.

2581   Ridge, Donna Rebecca. "The Use of Fiction As a Religious Medium as Demonstrated in Selected Short Stories by Flannery O'Connor." Thesis, Anderson U, 1989.

2582   Riley, Eleanor M. "The Fiction and the Aesthetic Principles of Flannery O'Connor: A Study in Theory and Practice." Thesis, Creighton U, 1967.

2583   Riley, Jennifer. "The Role of Perversity in the Short Stories of Flannery O'Connor and Edgar Allan Poe." Thesis, Ohio State U, 1996.

2584   Rivard, Virginia. "Sons and Mothers: A Collection of Short Stories." [Alternate Title: "Narrative Distance in Flannery O'Connor's `The Artificial Nigger' and `Everything That Rises Must Converge.'"]. Thesis, Warren Wilson College, 1997.

2585   Roark, Dorothy Walker. "Irony, Violence, and Distortion in the Fiction of Flannery O'Connor." Thesis, U of Texas at Austin, 1981.

2585a   Roberson, Julie Ann. "A Secondary Annotated Bibliography of Flannery O'Connor's `Everything That Rises Must Converge.'" Thesis, U of South Carolina, 1999.

2586   Roberts, Bonita K. "Man as Thinker: A Study of Intellectual Character in Flannery O'Connor's Work." Thesis, U of New Orleans, 1975.

2587   Roberts, Holly. "An Application of Mikhail Bakhtin's Theory of the Grotesque to the Fiction of Flannery O'Connor." Thesis, Eastern Illinois U, 1986.

2588   Robertson, Roxzana. "Reaping What Was Sown: Searching for the Whole in the Works of Alice Walker and Flannery O'Connor." Thesis, U of Southwestern Louisiana, 1995.

2589   Robinson, Margaret. "Flannery O'Connor's Terrifying Vision." Thesis, Drake U, 1970.

2590   Rommel, Lylas Dayton. "An Examination of the Motif of Prophecy in Flannery O'Connor's Novel *The Violent Bear It Away*." Thesis, U of Kentucky, 1986.

2591   Roper, Shannon. "Flannery O'Connor's Revision of the Prophetic Tradition." A.B. Honors Thesis, Harvard U, 1988.

2592   Ruggles, Robert David. "Shocked and Altered Faces: Pride, Divine Grace, and Revelation in the Short Stories of Flannery O'Connor." Thesis, U of North Carolina (Charlotte), 1985.

2593   Russell, Mary F. "Loneliness, Violence, and Love in the Fiction of Eudora Welty, Flannery O'Connor, and Carson McCullers." Thesis, U of Massachusetts, 1965.

2594   Rutledge, Chris. "Falling Into Self: A Review of Mary McCarthy and Flannery O'Connor, and How These Two 20th Century Catholic Writers Address Catholicism and Original Sin." Thesis, City College of New York, 1997.

2595   Salibrici, Gary D. "Flannery O'Connor's *Everything That Rises Must Converge*: A Mirror of the Grotesque." Thesis, John Carroll U, 1974.

2595a   Salomone, John L. "'The Signs of the Times': The Evolution of Movement, Prophets, and Grace as Influenced by the Second Vatican Council in the Works of Flannery O'Connor." Thesis, North Carolina State U, 2000.

2596   Sanders, Diane. "Vision Imagery and its Relationship to Structure in the Novels of Flannery O'Connor." Thesis, North Texas State U, 1976.

2597   Saunders, Joan Lindsay. "Parental Instinct and Influence in Selected Works by William Faulkner, Zora Neale Hurston, and Flannery O'Connor." Thesis, Trinity College, 1982.

2598   Saussier, Corinne Madeline. "The French Critics' Reception of the Translations of Works by Flannery O'Connor and Eudora Welty." Thesis, U of Notre Dame, 1982.

2599   Savitsky, Helen Ann. "A Study of Mechanization and the Fall From Grace From Flannery O'Connor's Fiction." Thesis, Concordia U (Canada), 1986.

2600   Scalia, Linda F. "The Theological Vision of Flannery O'Connor in *Everything That Rises Must Converge*." Thesis, Northeast Louisiana State College, 1968.

2601   Scambray, Terry A. "Flannery O'Connor's Christian Vision." Thesis, Fresno State College, 1969.

2602   Schaum, Mariane Wurst. "Christian Mysticism in Flannery O'Connor's *Wise Blood*." Thesis, Georgia State U, 1983.

2603   Schenk, Susan Jean. "The Conservative, the Catholic, and the Clown: John Gardner, Flannery O'Connor, and Vladimir Nabokov on the Nature and Aim of Fiction." Thesis, U of Waterloo (Canada), 1983.

2604   Scherbel, Jenell V. "`The Savage Strategy': Communicative Functions of Grotesque Humor in Flannery O'Connor's *The Violent Bear It Away* and John Hawkes's *Second Skin*." Thesis, U of Utah, 1985.

2605   Schroeder, Sue. "The Grasp of Unreason--The Flannery O'Connor Project." Thesis, U of Arizona at Tucson, 1994.

2606   Schroeder, Vanessa M. "Flannery O'Connor and the Moral Tragedy of Modern Society." Thesis, California State U, Hayward, 1970.

2607   Scott, George R. "The Medium is Not the Entire Message." Thesis, U of Georgia, 1969.

2608   Scott, Terry Ratliff. "Flannery O'Connor's *Wise Blood*: A Key to Understanding Her Later Work." Thesis, U of Wyoming, 1979.

2609   Sears, April. "Walking With Stones in Our Shoes: Finding Comfort in Flannery O'Connor's Uncomfortable Fiction." Thesis, Southwest Texas State U, 1997.

2610   Self, Rita Jean McClelland. "Dreams in Pretty." Thesis, Lamar U, 1997.

2611   Sharian, Randall Paul. "The Bottom Rail on the Top, Social Upheaval in Four Stories by Flannery O'Connor: `Everything That Rises Must Converge,' `Greenleaf,' `Judgement Day,' and `Revelation.'" Thesis, Georgia State U, 1981.

2612   Sheahan, Diane Ross. "The Women Who Have `Everything': A Study of the Operation of Grace in Flannery O'Connor's Short Stories." Thesis, U of Denver, 1974.

2613   Shealy, Anna Kempson. "Agents of Grace in Flannery O'Connor's Fiction." Thesis, U of South Carolina, 1998.

2614   Sheehan, Daniel Brian. "Flannery O'Connor's Redeeming Art." Thesis, Christian Brothers College, 1965.

2615   Shorten, Margaret M. "A Study of Distorted Humanity Viewed in the Fiction of Flannery O'Connor." Thesis, Seton Hall U, 1971.

2616   Shroeder, Vanessa Miller. "Flannery O'Connor and the Moral Tragedy of Modern Society." Thesis, California State College (Hayward), 1970.

2617   Sidoti, M. Thomas. "Flannery O'Connor: A Study in Interpersonal Relationships." Thesis, Nazareth College of Rochester, 1967.

2618 Siletzky, Robert. "The Idea of a Good Man in Flannery O'Connor's Fiction." Thesis, Duke U, 1999.

2619 Sillaven, Christina. "A Critical Analysis of Flannery O'Connor's *Wise Blood*." Thesis, Sam Houston State U, 1973.

2620 Sims, Anne Elizabeth Shelton. "World View and the Absurd: Flannery O'Connor and Eugene Ionesco." Thesis, U of Louisville, 1973.

2621 Sitko, Barbara M. "Giant Wives of the Countryside: An Analysis of Flannery O'Connor's Women." Thesis, Bucknell U, 1975.

2621a Skillern, Ada Travelsted. "Southern Post-Modernism, Anti-Romanticism and Gender Difference in Flannery O'Connor and Some Other Southern Contemporaries." Thesis. Western Kentucky U, 1999,

2622 Skyles, Benjamin Henry. "The Lord's Supper in Flannery O'Connor." Thesis, U of Houston, 1974.

2623 Sledge, Martha Lee. "The Apocalyptic Visions of Flannery O'Connor and Walker Percy." Thesis, Ohio State U, 1983.

2624 Sloan, LaRue L. "Revelation and Relevance: The Works of Flannery O'Connor." Thesis, East Texas State U, 1970.

2625 Smietana, Patricia. "The Landless and Landed in Flannery O'Connor's Fiction." Thesis, Clemson U, 1993.

2626 Smith, Margaret M. "Redemption in the Works of Flannery O'Connor." Thesis, Sam Houston State College, 1962.

2627 Smith, Martha A. "Flannery O'Connor and Nathaniel Hawthorne." Thesis, San Diego State U, 1978.

2628 Smith, Melissa Tyler. "Violence and Vision: The Grotesque of Flannery O'Connor." Thesis, Sarah Lawrence College, 1970.

2629 Smith, Rupert LaMarr. "Flannery O'Connor in the Context of the Southern Literary Tradition." Thesis, Wake Forest U, 1963.

2630 Smith, Suzanne Ware. "Backwoods Odyssey: Flannery O'Connor's *The Violent Bear It Away*." Thesis, U of Virginia, 1968.

2631 Snow, Ollye T. "The Function of the Gothic Conventions in the Fiction of Flannery O'Connor." Thesis, Ohio U, 1963.

2632   Snyder, Barbara R. "Flannery O'Connor's Female Characters: A Feminist Reading of Selected Stories." Thesis, Southern Connecticut State U, 1991.

2633   Sorcinelli, Mary Deane Griffin. "The Peacocks Tail: A Study of Spiritual Crisis in Flannery O'Connor's Major Fiction." Thesis, Mount Holyoke College, 1972.

2634   Sprouse, Helen M. "Violence in the Work of Flannery O'Connor." Thesis, Wesleyan U, 1974.

2635   Stafford, Darrell Eugene. "The Reality of `Christian Hope': A Study of the Positive Voice in the Fiction of Flannery O'Connor." Thesis, U of Mississippi, 1978.

2636   Statelman, Peter. "Structural Elements of Flannery O'Connor's Fiction." Thesis, San Francisco State U, 1987.

2637   Stewart, Harry Dee. "Flannery O'Connor and the Parables of the Lost." Thesis, Northeast Louisiana U, 1973.

2638   Stimson, Eva Gray. "Truth as Fiction: Flannery O'Connor's Stories and New Testament Parables." Thesis, Georgia State U, 1987.

2639   Street, Ruth Roberta. "The Effect of Humor in the Works of Flannery O'Connor." Thesis, California State U (Northridge), 1978.

2640   Stumbo, Carol. "The Technique of the Grotesque in the Writings of Flannery O'Connor." Thesis, Morehead State U, 1968.

2641   Sullins, Max E. "Theological Implications in the Fiction of Flannery O'Connor." Thesis, Indiana State U, 1971.

2642   Sullivan, Anne Bowers. "The Analyzing/Adapting/Staging of Flannery O'Connor's `Good Country People' for Chamber Theatre." Thesis, California State U at Northridge, 1991.

2643   Sussman, Katherine J. "Flannery O'Connor's Religious Vision: *Everything That Rises Must Converge*." Thesis, U of North Carolina at Chapel Hill, 1973.

2644   Swan, Jesse G. "To Read Silences, Not Words: A Reading of Conrad Aiken and Flannery O'Connor." Thesis, Arizona State U, 1988.

2645   Sweezy, Patricia Ann. "Changing Perspectives on the Southern Woman: A Study of the Fiction of Chopin, Glasgow, Welty, and O'Connor." Thesis, U of Delaware, 1975.

2646   Talbird, Olga Karen. "Flannery O'Connor's Grotesque." Thesis, Stanford U, 1963.

2647   Tercek, Robert Albin. "Bedeviled by Ambiguity: Definition and Paradox in Flannery O'Connor's Writing." Thesis, Williams College, 1985.

2648   Terwillinger, Linda. "Flannery O'Connor's Alienated Characters." Thesis, U of Wisconsin (Stevens Point), 1987.

2649   Thomae, Evie Sue Sessums. "The Depiction of Women and Negroes in the Fiction of Flannery O'Connor." Thesis, North Texas State U, 1974.

2650   Thomas, Wendy Lee. "More Instructive Than a Long Trip to Europe: The Effects of Lupus on Flannery O'Connor's Short Stories." Thesis, U of New Brunswick (Canada), 1998.

2651   Thompson, Joan Elaine. "Flannery O'Connor's Prepubescents: Two On a Pedestal." Thesis, Florida Atlantic U, 1996.

2652   Thompson, Theresa C. "Enforcing Gender: Concepts of Masculinity and Femininity in Flannery O'Connor's Short Fiction." Thesis, Florida State U, 1997.

2653   Thorwaldsen, Paul R. "Illusion and Reality in *The Great Gatsby*; An Analysis of the Structure of *Dandelion Wine*; [and,] The Uses of Setting in the Selections of Flannery O'Connor." Thesis, Moorhead State College, 1971.

2654   Tierney, Marie R. "The `Displaced Person' Motif in Flannery O'Connor's Works." Thesis, Boston College, 1967.

2655   Tietjen, Mary Anne. "Toward a Psychology of Divine Grace: The Short Stories of Flannery O'Connor." Thesis, Marquette U, 1966.

2656   Tillotson, Keith L. "Flannery O'Connor's Fiction: Beyond Sociology." Thesis, Wichita State U, 1986.

2657   Toalson, Susan. "The Feminine Archetype in Selected Works by Flannery O'Connor." Thesis, Southwest Texas State U, 1988.

2658   Toombs, Sarah E. "A Parabolic Explanation of Flannery O'Connor's Short Fiction." Thesis, Incarnate Word College, (San Antonio), 1981.

2659   Tourtellotte, Jack B. "The Motif of the Intruder as an Agent of the Divine in Flannery O'Connor's `A Good Man Is Hard To Find,' `Good Country People,' and `A Circle In The Fire.'" Thesis, East Carolina U, 1984.

2660   Truffin, Sherry R. "The Identity of God and the Limits of Nihilism in Flannery O'Connor's `Good Country People': A Linguistic Experiment." Thesis, Cleveland State U, 1995.

2661   Tucker, Mary F. "Redemptive Violence in the Short Stories of Flannery O'Connor." Thesis, St. Joseph College, 1969.

2662   Tufts, Melissa Cole. "The History of the Literary Reputation of Flannery O'Connor." Thesis, U of Georgia, 1985.

2663   Vaca, Peggy Irene. "Beyond the Ironic: The Use of the Ironic Mode in Five Stories by Flannery O'Connor." Thesis, Trinity U (Texas), 1984.

2664   Vaccaro, Jean Marie. "Some Elements of the Grotesque in the Fiction of Flannery O'Connor." Thesis, DePaul U, 1975.

2664a   Vandenberg, Kathleen Marie. "Cosmological Gnostic Dualism and Flannery O'Connor's Despoiled Worlds of Fiction in *Wise Blood* and *The Violent Bear It Away*." Thesis, Winthrop U, 1999.

2665   Vassiliou, Likourgos J. "Archetypal Shadows Upon Christian Souls: A Jungian Reading of Nine Flannery O'Connor Short Stories." Thesis, Illinois State U, 1996.

2666   Vera, Peggy Diane. "Flannery O'Connor's Intellectuals." Thesis, U of Texas at El Paso, 1994.

2667   VerStrat, Patricia L. "My Body Broken for You: An Analysis of Physicality in the Fiction of Flannery O'Connor." Thesis, Northern Michigan U, 1994.

2668   Villa, Giuseppina. "Epifania e Mistero Nelle Short Stories di Flannery O'Connor." [Epiphany and Mystery in the Short Stories of Flannery O'Connor.] Thesis, Università degli Studi di Bologna [U of Bologna, Italy], 1988-89.

2669   Volk, Benita. "The Revelation of Grace in Four Stories by Flannery O'Connor." ["Greenleaf," "A View Of the Woods," "A Good Man Is Hard to Find," and "Good Country People."] Thesis, U of Denver, 1977.

2670   Wahl, Patricia. "Through the Lens of the Grotesque and Magical Realism: Flannery O'Connor and Luisa Valenzuela." Thesis, Northern Michigan U, 1990.

2671   Wakana, Maya Higashi. "`Despair' and O'Connor's Short Stories." Thesis, U of Virginia, 1982.

2672   Walker, Camille Stone. "The Possibility for Convergence of the Divided Self in the Short Fiction of Flannery O'Connor." Thesis, Mississippi College, 1991.

2673   Walker, Donna Jo. "Flannery O'Connor and the Tradition of Southwestern Humor." Thesis, Louisiana State U, 1971.

2674   Walker, Donna Lou. "Flannery O'Connor's Mystical Salvation Through External and Internal Conflicts." Thesis, U of Nebraska (Omaha), 1976.

2675   Walker, Robin Lee. "The Benevolent Violence of Flannery O'Connor, Oliver Stone, Richard Wright, and John Singleton: `A Good Man Is Hard to Find,' *Natural Born Killers*, *Native Son*, and *Boyz n the Hood*." Thesis, Winthrop U, 1995.

2676   Wallace, Richard. "Theology and Literature: Theological Themes in Two Stories by Flannery O'Connor." ["A Temple of the Holy Ghost" and "The Artificial Nigger"]. Thesis, Mount Angel Seminary, 1987.

2677   Wallis, Thomas Andrew. "Martin Scorsese's Cinema of the Grotesque: Understanding *Cape Fear* Through Flannery O'Connor's Irony." Thesis, North Carolina State U, 1994.

2678   Walters, John Paul. "Flannery O'Connor and Neo-Orthodoxy." Thesis, Oklahoma State U, 1976.

2679   Walton, Mary Mittlelee. "Flannery O'Connor's Osirian Odyssey." B.S. Thesis, U of Southern Mississippi, 1977.

2680   Ward, Mary B. "Children in the Fiction of Flannery O'Connor." Thesis, Georgetown U, 1967.

2681   Warden, Patricia B. "O'Connor's Complement: The Redeemer and the Victim as a Character Pair." Thesis, East Carolina U, 1993.

2682   Warren, Colleen. "`And Grace Will Lead Me Home': The Workings of Grace in the Mother/Child Relationships in Flannery O'Connor's Fiction." Thesis, U of Florida, 1987.

2683   Warren, F. Eugene. "God's Pursuit of Man in the Fiction of Flannery O'Connor." Thesis, Kansas State Teachers College of Emporia, 1967.

2684   Watall, Mattiel. "The Grotesque as a Portrayal of Religious Themes in the Fiction of Flannery O'Connor." Thesis, George Peabody College for Teachers, 1975.

2685   Watson, Miriam Celia. "The Africanist Presence in O'Connor's `The Artificial Nigger' and [Ellen] Douglas's `Can't Quit You, Baby.'" Thesis, North Carolina State U, 1998.

2686   Watson, William Elmo, Jr. "The Cost of Agony: The Revelation of Grace Through Violence in the Writings of Flannery O'Connor." Thesis, Southern Methodist U, 1970.

2686a   Weltmer, Jason. "Rites of Passage, Liminality, and Violence in the Novels of Flannery O'Connor." Thesis, Arizona State U, 1999.

2687   Wellington, Ann M. "Flannery O'Connor: Her Art, Her Characters, Her Self." Thesis, Southwest Texas State U, 1993.

2688   Wenz, Jennifer. "Shattering `The Peace of Perfect Order': Rethinking Critical Assumptions About Flannery O'Connor's Short Fiction." Thesis, Villanova U, 1994.

2689   Wershoven, Carol Jean. "The World Unbalanced: The Theme of Disorder in the Short Stories of Flannery O'Connor." Thesis, Florida Atlantic U, 1973.

2690   Westbrook, Thomas Gerald. "Character Types in the Fiction of Flannery O'Connor." Thesis, U of Houston, 1972.

2691   White, Beverly Leigh. "An Examination of the Constituent Elements of Interpreter's Theater As Applied to Three Short Stories by Flannery O'Connor." Thesis, U of Tennessee (Knoxville), 1978.

2692   Whitehead, Kenneth A. "A Comparative Study of Characterization in the Short Stories of Erskine Caldwell and Flannery O'Connor." Thesis, East Tennessee State U, 1962.

2693   Wikle, Michelle Hist. "Flannery O'Connor and the Spectrum of the Short Story Cycle." Thesis, Oklahoma State U, 1994.

2694   Williams, Andrea. "Who Will Remain Whole?: Five Character Types by Flannery O'Connor." Thesis, Midwestern State U, 1981.

2695   Williams, Leslie Walker. "The Quick: A Collection of Stories." [Alternate Title: "The Symbiosis of the Comic and Tragic in Flannery O'Connor's `Good Country People.'"]. Thesis, Warren Wilson College, 1994.

2696   Williams, Mary Ann. "A Study of Lyrical and Grotesque Paths Into Mystery." Honors Thesis. Kenyon College, 1982.

2697   Wilson, Harold Gregory. "Flannery O'Connor and the Difficulty of Communication." Thesis, U of Dallas, 1995.

2698   Wilson, Janice M. "Flannery O'Connor: Her Divine Perspective and Communicated Vision." Thesis, California State U (Chico), 1984.

2699   Wilson, Melony J. "Southern, Female, and Christian: A Comparative Study of Christian Orthodoxy in the Short Fiction of Flannery O'Connor and Doris Betts." Thesis, U of Mississippi, 1988.

2700   Wilson, Meredith Anita. "The Truth Told Slant: The American Literary Grotesque in Flannery O'Connor and Eudora Welty." Thesis, California State U (Sacramento), 1977.

2700a   Winkle, Laura. "From Corruption to Grace: Dark and Light Images in the Stories of Flannery O'Connor." Thesis, California State U, Dominguez Hills, 2000.

2701   Winters, Laura. "An Exploration of the Mother/Child Relationships in Six Stories by Flannery O'Connor." ["A Stroke of Good Fortune," "Good Country People," "A Circle In the Fire," "The Life You Save May Be Your Own," "Everything That Rises Must Converge," and "The Comforts of Home"]. B.A. Thesis, Drew U, 1979.

2702   Wise, Melanie Elizabeth Hoover. "Unlikely Saviors: Moving Hazel Motes Toward the Ragged Figure of Christ." Thesis, San Francisco State U, 1995.

2703   Wiseman, William J. "Idiots Clapping in the Church: The Fiction of Flannery O'Connor." Thesis, U of Tulsa, 1968.

2704   Wolff, Gay H. "The Children of Flannery O'Connor: Child of Quest and Child of Grace." Thesis, Florida Atlantic U, 1991.

2705   Wood, Ralph C. "The Scandal of Redemption: Religious Meaning in the Novels of Flannery O'Connor." Thesis, East Texas State U, 1965.

2706   Wooten, Linda West. "Three Authors in Pursuit of Writing: O'Connor, Thoreau, and Woolf." Thesis, U of North Carolina at Charlotte, 1988.

2707   Yerger, Norval Rice. "Patterns of Imagery in Flannery O'Connor's *The Violent Bear It Away*." Thesis, U of Virginia, 1966.

2708   York, Beth M. "An Ax for the Frozen Sea Within Us: Flannery O'Connor's Prose." Thesis, West Texas State U, 1965.

2709   Young, Carolyn T. "Flannery O'Connor's `Habit of Art': Marked Passages in Her Personal Library." Thesis, Auburn U at Montgomery, 1997.

2710   Zengos, Hariclea. "The Depiction of Grace in Selected Short Stories of Flannery O'Connor." Thesis, Clark U, 1985.

2711   Zhong, Ming. "The Dual Mission: The Art of Flannery O'Connor's Fiction." Thesis, Shanghai International Studies U (China), 1987.

Appendix 1

A Checklist of Representative Reviews of Flannery O'Connor's Principal Editions and Related Works

The following citations to book reviews of Flannery O'Connor's works were selected from a wide variety of bibliographic sources, including print and electronic versions of: *Book Review Digest, Book Review Index, Current Book Review Citations, The National Library Service Cumulative Book Review Index 1905-1974, American Reference Book Annual, Reference Books Bulletin, Humanities Index, Essay and General Literature Index, Readers' Guide to Periodical Literature*, the *British Humanities Index, Social Sciences Index, Access: The Supplementary Index to Periodicals* and *MLA Bibliography*.

2712   *The Complete Stories*. New York: Farrar, Straus and Giroux, 1971.

Paul Alexander, *Interview* 26.10 (Oct. 1996): 97.
Anon. *Booklist* (15 Jan. 1972): 413-14.
Anon. *Booklist* (1 Jan. 1987): 690.
Anon. *Catholic Library World* 44.6 (Feb. 1973): 425.
Anon. *Kirkus Reviews* 39 (1 Sept. 1971): 968.
Anon. *New Republic* (20 Nov. 1971): 34.
Anon. *New York Times Book Review* (5 Dec. 1971): Sec. 7, p. 83.
Anon. [London] *Observer* (6 Jan. 1991): 47.
Anon. *Review for Religious* 31.1 (Jan. 1972): 158-59.
Anon. *Virginia Quarterly Review* 48.3 (Summer 1972): ci-cii.
John Alfred Avant, *Library Journal* 97 (1 Jan. 1972): 85.
Richard J. Cattani, *Christian Science Monitor* 64.46 (20 Jan 1972) East. ed.: 7.
Walter Clemons, *Newsweek* 78 (8 Nov. 1971): 116-17.
Robert Coles, *American Scholar* 41.3 (Summer 1972): 480.
George Core, *Nashville Tennessean* (27 Feb. 1972): 10C.
Mary Silva Cosgrave, *Horn Book* 48.2 (April 1972): 171.
Guy Davenport, *National Review* 23.51 (31 Dec. 1971): 1473-74.
Robert Drake, *Modern Age* 16 (Summer 1972): 322-24.
Martha Duffy, *Time* (29 Nov. 1971): 87-88.

Richard Freedman, *Washington Post Book World* 6.5 (30 Jan. 1972): 11.
Melvin J. Friedman, *Southern Literary Journal* 5 (Spring 1973): 116-23.
Thomas A. Gullason, *Saturday Review* 54 (13 Nov. 1971): 57, 63-64.
George C. Higgins, *Commonweal* 95.21 (25 Feb. 1972): 500.
Ann Hulbert, *TLS: Times Literary Supplement* (3 May 1991): 20.
John Idol, *Studies in Short Fiction* 10.1 (1973): 103-05.
Alfred Kazin, *New York Times Book Review* (28 Nov. 1971): Sec. 7, pp. 1, 22.
Chris Savage King, *New Statesman & Society* 3.136 (1 Feb. 1991): 37-38.
Chris Savage King, *New Statesman & Society* 4 (8 Feb. 1991): 37-38.
Thomas Lask, *New York Times* (3 Dec. 1971): 37.
Saul Maloff, *Commonweal* (3 Dec. 1971): 232.
Pamela McCorduck, *Wired* 5.1 (1997): 175.
Frederick P.W. McDowell, *Southern Review* ns 9.4 (1973): 998-1013.
Edward N. Mintz, *Travel* 139 (Jan. 1973): 12-13.
Larry Powell, *Savannah News-Press* (23 April 1972): 3F.
Peter S. Prescott, *Newsweek* (27 Dec. 1971): 61.
J.J. Quinn, *America* 125.19 (11 Dec. 1971): 518-20.
J.J. Quinn, *Best Sellers* 31.16 (15 Nov. 1971): 383.
Jim Vollmar, *The Month* (Sept.-Oct. 1991): 443-47.
Joel Wells, *National Catholic Reporter* (19 Nov. 1971): 16.
Elliott Wright, *Commonweal* (3 Dec. 1971): 238.
Jonathan Yardley, *Partisan Review* 40.2 (1973): 286-93.
Donovan Young, *Atlanta Journal and Constitution* (8 April 1984): 9H.

2713   *Conversations with Flannery O'Connor*. Ed. Rosemary M.
       Magee. Jackson: UP of Mississippi, 1987.

Frederick Asals, *Canadian Review of American Studies* 21.1 (1980): 95-99.
Mary Beckner, *Southern Living* 22 (1987): 96.
Beverly L. Clark, *Resources for American Literary Study* 18.1 (1992): 113-16.
Blanche Farley, *Flannery O'Connor Bulletin* 16 (1987): 82-85.
Sandra Havener, *Women's Studies International Forum* 11.1 (1988): 87.
Brad Hooper, *Booklist* 83.13 (1 March 1987): 974.
Patrick Kelly, *Canadian Catholic Review* 5.3 (March 1987): 107.
William Monroe, *South Central Review: The Journal of the South Central MLA*
       5.1 (1988): 101-03.
Starr E. Smith, *Library Journal* (1 April 1987): 150.

2714   *The Correspondence of Flannery O'Connor and the
       Brainard Cheneys*. Ed. C. Ralph Stephens. Jackson: UP
       of Mississippi, 1986.

Anon. *Kirkus Reviews* 54.9 (1 May 1986): 711.
Frederick Asals, *Canadian Review of American Studies* 18.2 (Summer 1987): 231-33.
Robert H. Brinkmeyer, *Southern Literary Journal* 20.1 (Fall 1987): 145-48.
Virginia Spencer Carr, *American Literary Scholarship: An Annual 1986.* (Durham, NC: Duke UP, 1988): 269.
Beverly Lyon Clark, *New York Times Book Review* (24 Aug. 1986): 19.
John F. Desmond, *Modern Age* 30.3-4 (Summer-Fall 1986): 331-33.
Joe Dewey, *Modern Fiction Studies* 33.2 (Summer 1987): 323-26.
Stephen G. Driggers, *Southern Humanities Review* 22.3 (Summer 1988): 291-92.
Sarah Gordon, *Flannery O'Connor Bulletin* 15 (1986): 92-95.
Jan Nordby Gretlund, *Mississippi Quarterly* 40.3 (Summer 1987): 349-52.
Darlene Kelly, *Canadian Catholic Review* 5.3 (March 1987): 106-07.
Russell Kirk, *Reflections: The Wanderer Review of Literature, Culture, the Arts* 7.1 (Winter 1988): 8.
Loxley F. Nichols, *National Review* 38.24 (19 Dec. 1986): 54-55.
Miles D. Orvell, *Journal of Modern Literature* 13 (1986): 519.
Nancy M. Tischler, *Choice* 24.3 (Nov. 1986): 479.
Sandy Whiteley, *American Libraries* 17.9 (Oct. 1986): 716-17.
Lawrence Willson, *Sewanee Review* 96.2 (April-June 1988): 283-86.

2715 *Everything That Rises Must Converge.* Intro. Robert Fitzgerald. New York: Farrar, Straus and Giroux, 1965.

Anon. *Booklist* 61.21 (1 July 1965): 1015.
Anon. *Choice* 2.7 (Sept. 1965): 387.
Anon. *Kirkus* 33 (25 May 1965): 338.
Anon. *Newsweek* (31 May 1965): 85-86.
Anon. *Newsweek* (27 Dec. 1965): 73.
Anon. *Publisher's Weekly* 191.19 (8 May 1967): 63.
Anon. *Time* 85.24 (4 June 1965): 92.
Anon. *TLS: Times Literary Supplement* (24 Mar. 1966): 242.
Anon. *Virginia Quarterly Review* 41 (1965): lxxxiv.
William Barrett, *Atlantic Monthly* 216.1 (July 1965): 139-40.
Harold Beaver, *TLS: Times Literary Supplement* (21 Nov. 1980): 1336.
Ralph Bergamo, *Atlanta Journal and Constitution* (23 May 1965): B2.
Naomi Bliven, *New Yorker* (11 Sept. 1965): 220-21.
Larry Earl Bone, *Library Journal* 90 (1 May 1965): 2160-61.
Anthony Burgess, *Listener* (7 April 1966): 515.
James Campbell, *New Statesman* 100.2590 (7 Nov. 1980): 26-27.
R.V. Cassill, *Chicago Sun-Times* (13 June 1965): sec. 3: 2.
Warren Coffey, *Commentary* 40.5 (Nov. 1965): 93-99.
John Coleman, *Observer* 27 Mar. 1966: 27.

Richard, Coleman, *News and Courier* [Charleston, SC] (20 June 1965): B5.

Cressida Connolly, *Books and Bookmen* (Aug. 1985): 36.

Edith Copeland, *Books Abroad* 39.4 (Autumn 1965): 461.

Patrick Cruttwell, *Hudson Review* 18.3 (Autumn 1965): 442-50.

Guy Davenport, *National Review* 17.30 (27 July 1965): 658-59.

James P. Degnan, *Commonweal* 82.16 (9 July 1965): 510-11.

Robert Drake, *Christian Century* 82.20 (19 May 1965): 656.

Richard A. Duprey, *Catholic World* 202.1207 (Oct. 1965): 54.

James F. Farnham, *Cross Currents* 15.3 (Summer 1965): 376-78.

Dale Francis, *America* (5 June 1965): 821-22.

Mariella Gable, *Critic* 23.6 (June-July, 1965): 58-60.

Paul J. Hallinan, *Georgia Bulletin* [Archdiocese of Atlanta] (12 Aug. 1965): 8.

Alex Hamilton, *Books and Bookmen* (June 1966): 45.

Granville Hicks, *Saturday Review* (29 May 1965): 23-24.

Thomas Hoobler, *Ave Maria* 102.3 (17 July 1965): 18-19.

Edward M. Hood, *Shenandoah* 16.4 (Summer 1965): 109-14.

Irving Howe, *New York Review of Books* 5.1 (30 Sept. 1965): 16-17.

Riley Hughes, *Columbia* 45.7 (July 1965): 34, 36.

Stanley Edgar Hyman, *New Leader* (10 May 1965): 9-10.

Katherine Gauss Jackson, *Harper's Magazine* 231.1382 (July 1965): 112.

Rene Jordan, *British Association for American Studies Bulletin* Nos. 12-13 (1966): 99-101.

Patricia Kane, *Critique: Studies in Modern Fiction* 8.1 (Fall 1965): 85-91.

Robert Kiely, *Christian Science Monitor* 57 (17 June 1965): 7.

Lewis A. Lawson, *Studies in Short Fiction* 3.3 (1965-66): 374-76.

Paul Levine, *Jubilee* (Oct. 1965): 52-53.

Eric Lloyd, *Wall Street Journal* (9 July 1965): 8.

Saul Maloff, *Commonweal* (3 Dec. 1965): 287-88.

Alice Mayhew, *Commonweal* (3 Dec. 1965): 288-89.

Julian Moynahan, *New York Times Book Review* (5 Dec. 1965): 4.

Malcolm Muggeridge, *Esquire* (May 1965): 44, 46, 48.

Joyce Carol Oates, *Southern Humanities Review* 7 (Summer 1973): 235-46.

Robert Ostermann, *National Observer* (28 June 1965): 19.

Richard Poirier, *New York Times Book Review* 70 (30 May 1965): 6, 22.

Charles Poore, *New York Times* (27 May 1965): 35; Rpt. *Atlanta Journal and Constitution* (28 May 1965): 34.

V.S. Pritchett, *New Statesman* (1 April 1966): 469, 472.

Alan Pryce-Jones, *New York Herald Tribune* (25 May 1965): 23.

John J. Quinn, *Best Sellers* 25.5 (1 June 1965): 124-25; Rpt. *Catholic Week* (9 July 1965): 12.

M. Bernetta Quinn, *Boston Sunday Herald* (13 June 1965): Sec. 6, p. 8.

Hilary Reynolds, *Dublin Magazine [Ireland]* (Summer 1966): 89-90.

Louis D. Rubin, Jr., *Southern Review* 2 (1966): 697-713.

Webster Schott, *Nation* 201.7 (13 Sept. 1965): 142-44, 146.

Lillian Smith, *Chicago Sunday Tribune Book Section* (6 June 1965): 5.

Theodore Solotaroff, *New York Herald Tribune Book Week* 2.38 (30 May 1965): 1, 13.
Walter Sullivan, *Hollins Critic* 2.4 (Sept. 1965): 1-8, 10.
Stanley Trachtenberg, *Yale Review* 55.1 (Oct. 1965): 144-49.
Joel Wells, *U.S. Catholic* 31.3 (July 1965): 62-63, 65.
Kenneth L. Woodward, *Commonweal* (3 Dec. 1965): 291.

2716   *Flannery O'Connor: Collected Works*. Ed. Sally
       Fitzgerald. New York: Library of America, 1988.

Anon. *Christian Century* (1 Feb. 1989): 150.
Anon. *Southern Living* (Dec. 1989): 86.
Anon. *Time* (3 Oct. 1988): 90.
Bruce Bawer, *New Criterion* 7.5 (Jan. 1989): 35-41.
Robert Brinkmeyer, *Southern Reader* 1.1 (Summer 1989): 173-75.
Tony Brown, *Charlotte (NC) Observer Book Week* (25 Sept. 1988): F5.
Gail Caldwell, *Boston Sunday Globe* (21 Aug. 1988): A14-A15.
Joseph Coates, *Chicago Tribune Books* (14 Aug. 1988): Sec. 14, pp. 1, 4.
Frederick Crews, *New York Review of Books* 37 (26 Apr. 1990): 49-55.
Thomas D'Evelyn, *Christian Science Monitor* 80 (24 Aug. 1988): 17-18.
Melvin J. Friedman, *International Fiction Review* 16.2 (1989): 139-42.
Benjamin Griffith, *Sewanee Review* 97.4 (Fall 1989): 575-80.
George F. Hawkins, *School Library Journal* 35.5 (Jan. 1989): 107.
Brad Hooper, *Booklist* (1 Sept. 1988): 39.
Brad Leithauser, *New Yorker* 64 (7   Nov. 1988): 154-58.
Henry McDonald, *American Scholar* 58.4 (Autumn 1989): 622-25.
Ralph McInerny, *Crisis* 6.9 (Oct. 1988): 42-43.
Brian Moore, *New York Times Book Review* 93 (21 Aug. 1988): 1, 30-31.
Don O'Briant, *Atlanta Journal and Constitution* (28 Aug. 1988): M1.
Isie Peat and Diane Young, *Southern Living* (May 1990): 87-92.
Larry Powell, *Savannah News-Press* (25 Sept. 1988): 4F.
William Robertson, *Macon (GA) Telegraph and News* (18 Sept. 1988): E10, E12.
William Robertson, *Milledgeville (GA) Union-Recorder* (14 Sept. 1988): A6.
Mary Jo Salter, *New Republic* 200 (24 April 1989): 34-38.
Larry Sibley, *Christianity Today* (17 Nov. 1989): 39.
Raymond Sokolov, *Wall Street Journal* (25 Oct. 1988): A24.
Nancy M. Tischler, *Choice* 26 (Feb. 1989): 942.
Chilton Williamson, Jr., *American Spectator* (Dec. 1988): 21.
Chilton Williamson, Jr., *National Review* 40 (28 Oct. 1988): 44-46.
Ralph C. Wood, *Flannery O'Connor Bulletin* 17 (1988): 92-97.
Jonathan Yardley, *Washington Post Book World* 18 (4 Sept. 1988): 3.

2717   *A Good Man Is Hard to Find and Other Stories.* New
York: Harcourt Brace, 1955. *The Artificial Nigger and
Other Tales.* London: Spearman, 1957.

Anon. *Best Sellers* 30 (15 Sept. 1970): 238.
Anon. *Booklist* 51.20 (15 June 1955): 428.
Anon. *Bookmark* 14 (July 1955): 246.
Anon. *Grail* 38 (Jan. 1956): 59.
Anon. *Harper's Bazaar* (July 1955): 72.
Anon. *Kirkus* 23 (15 April 1955): 290-91.
Anon. *New Yorker* (18 June 1955): 105.
Anon. *Newsweek* (26 Dec. 1955): 68-70.
Anon. *Time* (6 June 1955): 114.
Anon. *TLS: Times Literary Supplement* (12 Sept. 1968): 975.
Robert Martin Adams, *Hudson Review* 8 (1956): 627-32.
William Bonney, *Studies in Short Fiction* 27.3 (Summer 1990): 347-56.
Fred Bornhauser, *Shenandoah* 7.1 (Autumn 1955): 71-81.
Malcolm Bradbury, [Manchester, England] *Guardian Weekly* (12 Sept. 1968): 14.
Ashley Brown, *Spectator* (6 Sept. 1968): 330, 332.
Anatole Broyard, *New York Times* (5 Sept. 1977): 15.
Fanny Butcher, *Chicago Tribune Magazine of Books* (3 July 1955): Part 4, p. 3.
Thomas H. Carter, *Accent* 15.4 (Autumn 1955): 293-97.
Ray Dilley, *Savannah Evening Press* (4 June 1955): B16.
Walter Elder, *Kenyon Review* 17 (Autumn 1955): 661-70.
Dale Francis, *Commonweal* 62.19 (12 Aug. 1955): 471.
Caroline Gordon, *New York Times Book Review* (12 June 1955): 5.
Kenneth Graham, *Listener* 80 (5 Sept. 1968): 313.
James Greene, *Commonweal* (22 July 1955): 404.
Ben Griffith, Jr., *Savannah Morning News* (5 June 1955): G60.
Gary R. Grund, *Studies in Short Fiction* 32.1 (Winter 1995): 121-22.
Granville Hicks, *New Leader* (15 Aug. 1955): 17.
Riley Hughes, *Catholic World* 182.1087 (Oct. 1955): 66-67.
John A. Lynch, *Today* 9 (Oct. 1955): 30-31.
John David Marshall, *Library Journal* 80.10 (15 May 1955): 1217.
Geoffrey Norman, *Forbes: FYI The Good Life Supplement* (Winter, 1997): 186.
Mario Praz, *Studi Americani* 2 (1955): 207-18.
Orville Prescott, *New York Times* (10 June 1955): 23.
R.G.G. Price, *Punch* (4 Sept. 1968): 346.
Louis D. Rubin, Jr., *Sewanee Review* 63.4 (Oct.-Dec. 1956): 671-81.
Celestine Sibley, *Atlanta Journal and Constitution* (17 May 1955): 24.
Sylvia Stallings, *New York Herald Tribune Book Review* (5 June 1955): 1.
Frank X. Steggert, *Books on Trial* 14 (Dec. 1955): 187.
Charlotte Templin, *College Literature* 22.2 (June 1995): 151-56.
Gillian Tindall, *New Statesman* 76 (6 Sept. 1968): 292.
Francis J. Ullrich, *Best Sellers* 15.6 (15 June 1955): 59.

Lewis Vogler, *San Francisco Chronicle "This World"* (10 July 1955): 19.
John Cook Wyllie, *Saturday Review* (4 June 1955): 15.

2718   *The Habit of Being: Letters of Flannery O'Connor.*
        Ed. and intro. Sally Fitzgerald. New York: Farrar, Straus
        and Giroux, 1979.

Anon. *Atlanta Journal-Constitution* (4 March 1979): 24-25, 27-29.
Anon. *Atlantic Monthly* 243.6 (June 1979): 96.
Anon. *Choice* 16.5-6 (July-Aug. 1979): 670.
Anon. *Christian Science Monitor* (14 Apr. 1980): B2.
Anon. *Kirkus Reviews* 47 (15 Jan. 1979): 109.
Anon. *National Review* (16 Feb. 1979): 246.
Anon. *New Republic* 182.23 (7 June 1980): 39.
Anon. *New York Times Book Review* (9 March 1980): 31.
Anon. *New York Times Book Review* (25 Nov. 1979): 15.
Anon. *New York Times Book Review* (30 Dec. 1979): 10.
Anon. *Progressive* 43.5 (May 1979): 60.
Anon. *Publisher's Weekly* 216.3 (15 Jan. 1979): 120.
Anon. *Publisher's Weekly* 217.3 (25 Jan. 1980): 339.
Anon. *Sign* 58.8 (June 1979): 18-22.
Anon. *Wall Street Journal* (13 Dec. 1979): 26.
Paul Bailey, [London] *Observer* (2 Dec. 1979): 37.
Harold Beaver, *TLS: Times Literary Supplement* 4051 (21 Nov. 1980): 1336.
Robert H. Brinkmeyer, *Southern Quarterly* 18.2 (1980): 92-94.
Richard H. Brodhead, *Yale Review* 69.3 (Spring 1980): 451-56.
David Bromwich, *Listener* 103 (14 Feb. 1980): 220-21.
Martha Frances Brown, *Georgia Life* (Autumn 1979): 46.
Elena Brunet, *Los Angeles Times Book Review* (19 June 1988): 14.
Edward Butscher, *Booklist* 75 (1 Apr. 1979): 1195.
Constance Casey, *San Francisco Review of Books* 8 (May 1983): 6.
John L. Casteel, *Review for Religious* 40.6 (Nov.-Dec. 1981): 947-49.
Jane Clapperton, *Cosmopolitan* (May 1979): 70.
Lindley H. Clark, Jr., *Wall Street Journal* (13 Dec. 1979): 26.
Walter Clemons, *Newsweek* 93.12 (19 Mar. 1979): 87-88.
George Core, *Sewanee Review* 87.3 (1979): R68-R69 [lxviii-lxix].
Eugene Current-Garcia, *Southern Humanities Review* 14 (1979): 373-75.
Janet Demowitz, *Christian Science Monitor* (12 Mar. 1979): B5.
John F. Desmond, *World Literature Today* 54.2 (1980): 288-89.
Michael Dirda, *Washington Post Book World* 23.50 (12 Dec. 1993): 11.
Robert Drake, *Christian Century* 96.18 (16 May 1979): 557-58.
S.F., *Atlanta Journal and Constitution* (4 March 1979): 24-25, 27-29.
Sally Fitzgerald, *Flannery O'Connor Bulletin* 6 (Autumn 1977): 5-16.
Melissa Conway Flannery, *Best Sellers* 40.3 (June 1980): 109.

Melvin J. Friedman, *Southern Literary Journal* 12.2 (1980): 114-24.

Edmund Fuller, *Wall Street Journal* 193 (12 March 1979): 18.

Kenneth L. Gibble, *Christianity Today* 26.7 (9 April 1982): 78.

Richard Gilman, *New York Times Book Review* (18 March 1979): 1, 32-33.

Mary Gordon, *Saturday Review* (14 Apr. 1979): 42-45. Rpt. *Dialogue* 52.2
    (1981): 56-59; Rpt. *Good Boys and Dead Girls and Other Essays* [by Mary
    Gordon]. (NY: Viking, 1991): 37-44.

Thomas F. Gossett, *Southwest Review* 65.3 (Summer 1980): 335-36.

Shirley Anne Grau, *Chicago Tribune Book World* (25 Mar. 1979): 1.

Paul Gray, *Time* 113.10 (5 Mar. 1979): 86-87.

Graham Greene, [London] *Observer* (7 Dec. 1980): 27.

Jan Nordby Gretlund, *South Carolina Review* 12.2 (Spring 1980): 61-63.

Janet Groth, *Commonweal* 106 (7 Dec. 1979): 695-96.

Janet Varner Gunn, *American Literature* 53.3 (Nov. 1981): 522-24.

Josephine Hendin, *New Republic* 180.10 (10 Mar. 1979): 33-35.

George Hendrick, *Studies in Short Fiction* 16.4 (Fall 1979): 358.

Douglas Hill, *Books in Canada* 8.5 (May 1979): 16-17.

Thomas Howard, *Christian Scholar's Review* 10.2 (1981): 180-81.

Bette Howland, *Ms.* 8.1 (July 1979): 39-40.

Thomas Hubert, *Christianity & Literature* 29.3 (Spr. 1980): 73-74.

Jonathan Keates, *Spectator* 243 (22-29 Dec. 1979): 28-29.

Warren Leamon, *Western Humanities Review* 35.2 (Summer 1981): 177-79.

Hermione Lee, *New Statesman* 98.2542 (7 Dec. 1979): 895-96.

John Leonard, *New York Times* (9 March 1979) [Weekend]: C-23; Rpt. *Books of
    the Times* 2 (March 1979): 116-17.

David Livingstone, *Maclean's* (23 April 1979): 64.

R.J. MacSween, *Antigonish Review* 39 (Autumn, 1979): 103-04.

Marilyn Chapin Massey, *Commonweal* 108.4 (27 Feb. 1981): 125.

John R. May, *America* 140 (16 June 1979): 498-99.

John R. May, *Horizons* 7.1 (Spring 1980): 95-99.

William McPherson, *Washington Post Book World* (11 Feb. 1979): F1, F3.

Annabelle M. Melville, *Catholic Library World* 56.1 (July-Aug. 1984): 38-43.

Nolan Miller, *Antioch Review* 37.3 (1979): 373-74.

Catherine Risingflame Moirai, *Feminary* 12.1 (1982): 129-46.

Arthur J. Moore, *Commonweal* 107 (29 Feb. 1980): 119-20.

Susan Moore, *Quadrant* (Australia) 30.7-8 (July-Aug. 1986): 111-13.

Frank E. Moorer and Richard Macksey, *Modern Language Notes* 94.5 (Dec.
    1979): 1272-75.

Donald R. Noble, *Southern World* 3.1 (March-April 1981): 73-79.

David O'Brien, *Commonweal* 106 (7 Dec. 1979): 698-99.

Adrian Oktenberg, *New Letters* 47.1 (Fall 1980): 121-23.

Miles Orvell, *American Scholar* 48.4 (Autumn 1979): 562-65.

Virginia Oxford, *Campus Report* [Emory University] (15 March 1982): 4.

Agnes Ann Pastva, *English Journal* 69.8 (Nov. 1980): 70-72.

Robert Phillips, *Commonweal* (13 Apr. 1979): 216-20.

Larry Powell, *Savannah News-Press Sunday Magazine* (8 April 1979): 5G.

John Raymond, *Atlanta Journal and Constitution* (11 March 1979): E4.
Pamela Schwandt, *Manitou Messinger* [Saint Olaf College, Northfield, MN] (13 Nov. 1980): 12.
Robert B. Shaw, *Nation* 228.16 (28 Apr. 1979): 472-74.
Carol Shloss, *Massachusetts Review* 20.2 (Summer 1979): 387-91.
William J. Stuckey, *Modern Fiction Studies* 25.4 (Winter 1979-80): 737-40.
Stephen L. Tanner, *Chronicles of Culture* 4.3 (May-June 1980): 8-10.
J.O. Tate, *Flannery O'Connor Bulletin* 7 (Autumn 1978): 5-9.
J.O. Tate, *National Review* 31.11 (16 Mar. 1979): 364, 366, 368.
Jean M. Thorpe, *National Catholic Reporter* (7 Sept. 1979): 25.
Diane Tolomeo, *Review* (Charlottesville: UP of Virginia) 2 (1980): 271-86.
Robert Towers, *New York Review of Books* (3 May 1979): 3-6.
F. Thomas Trotter, *Christian Century* 99.19 (26 May 1982): 645.
Michael True, *Chronicle of Higher Education* (16 Apr. 1979): R6.
Helen Ruth Vaughn, *New Catholic World* 222 (July/Aug. 1979): 188.
Quentin Vest, *Library Journal* 104 (15 Jan. 1979): 194.
W.L. Webb, [Manchester England] *Guardian Weekly* (19 Aug. 1979): 23.
Lloyd C. Welling, *Studies in Formative Spirituality* 3.1 (Feb. 1982): 99-107.
Joel Wells, *Critic* 37.18 (1 April 1979): 2-3.
Ralph Wood, *Anglican Theological Review* 62.2 (April 1980): 153-67.
Ralph Wood, *Wake Forest Magazine* 42.1 (Sept. 1994): 24-28.
Donovan Young, *Atlanta Journal and Constitution* (8 April 1984): 9H.
Laura M. Zaidman, *Masterplots II: Women's Literature Series* Ed. Frank N. Magill. Pasadena, CA: Salem, 1995. 984-88.

2719   "Introduction." *A Memoir of Mary Ann*. Dominican Nuns of Our Lady of Perpetual Help Home Atlanta, Georgia. New York: Farrar, Straus & Cudahy, 1961, 3-21.

Charlotte H. Corrigan, *Daily Times* [Melbourne, FL] (13 Dec. 1961): 5.
Anne Fremantle, *Commonweal* 75.21 (16 Feb. 1962): 545-46.
Harold C. Gardiner, *America* (13 Jan. 1962): 474.
John J. Quinn, *Best Sellers* 21.18 (15 Dec. 1961): 394.
Celestine Sibley, *Atlanta Journal and Constitution* (5 Nov. 1961): 7B.
Ester Thomas, *Atlanta Journal* (12 Aug. 1961): 37.

2720   *Mystery and Manners: Occasional Prose*. Ed. Sally and Robert Fitzgerald. New York: Farrar, Straus, and Giroux, 1969.

Anon. *Antioch Review* 29.2 (Summer 1969): 262.
Anon. *Booklist* 66 (1 Sept. 1969): 25.

Anon. *Chicago Tribune Book World* 3 (29 June 1969): 8.

Anon. *Choice* 6.10 (Dec. 1969): 1398.

Anon. *Kirkus [Reviews] Bulletin* (1 March 1969): 289-90.

Anon. *National Observer* 8 (5 May 1969): 21.

Anon. *New York Times Book Review* (8 June 1969): 56.

Anon. *New Yorker* 45 (19 July 1969): 84.

Anon. [London] *Observer* (5 Feb. 1984): 52.

Anon. *Publisher's Weekly* (3 Mar. 1969): 55.

Anon. *Publisher's Weekly* (10 Nov. 1969): 51.

Anon. *Time* 93 (30 May 1969): 70.

Anon. *TLS: Times Literary Supplement* (25 Feb. 1972): 213.

Anon. *Virginia Quarterly Review* 45.4 (Autumn 1969): R137.

Frederick Asals, *Novel* 4.1 (Fall 1970): 92-96.

David Blewitt, *Times Educational Supplement* 4006 (11 May 1984): 29.

Francis F. Burch, *America* 121.1 (5 July 1969): 16.

Robert Coles, *Harvard Educational Review* 40.1 (Winter 1970): 130-35.

Robert Drake, *CEA Critic* 32.7 (April 1970): 13.

Leon V. Driskell *Louisville (KY) Courier Journal & Times* (15 June 1969): G5.

James F. Farnham, *Cross Currents* 20.2 (Spring 1970): 252-56.

Melvin J. Friedman, *Journal of Modern Literature* 1 (1970): 288-92.

Richard Gilman, *New York Review of Books* 13 (21 Aug. 1969): 24-26.

Granville Hicks, *Saturday Review* 52 (10 May 1969): 30.

Charles J. Huelsbeck, *Catholic World* 210.1257 (Dec. 1969): 128-29.

Catherine Jackson, *Harper's Magazine* (June 1969): 94.

Jean Kellogg, *Christian Century* 86.27 (9 July 1969): 927.

John Leonard, *New York Times* (13 May 1969): 45.

Saul Maloff, *Commonweal* 90.18 (8 Aug. 1969): 490-91.

D. Keith Mano, *New York Times Book Review* (25 May 1969): Sec. 7: 6-7, 20.

Frederick P.W. McDowell, *Southern Review* ns 9.4 (Oct. 1973): 998-1013.

Ralph McInerny, *American Spectator* 16.7 (July 1983): 22-23.

Minnie Hite Moody, *Columbus (OH) Dispatch* 15 June 1969: 14.

John Morressy, *Sign* (Dec. 1969): 53.

Elizabeth R. Nelson, *Library Journal* 94 (15 May 1969): 1994.

Joyce Carol Oates, *Southern Review* ns 7.1 (Jan. 1971): 295-313.

Miles D. Orvell, *Sewanee Review* 78.1 (Jan. 1970): 184-92.

Howell Pearre, *[Nashville] Banner* (16 May 1968): [n.p.]

John J. Quinn, *Best Sellers* 29.4 (15 May 1969): 76.

A.L. Rowse, *Books and Bookmen* 17.8 (May 1972): 38-39.

Charles T. Samuels, *Chicago Tribune Book World* (4 May 1969): Part 1, Sec. 9: 1, 3.

William A. Sessions, *Studies in Short Fiction* 8.3 (1971): 491-94.

Jonathan Yardley, *Greensboro Daily News* (27 July 1969): B3.

2721 *The Presence of Grace and Other Book Reviews by Flannery O'Connor.* Comp. Leo J. Zuber. Ed. and intro. Carter W. Martin. Athens: U of Georgia P, 1983.

Anon. *American Literature* 56.1 (March 1984): 136.
Anon. *Virginia Quarterly Review* 60.1 (Winter 1984): 7.
John L. Casteel, *Review for Religious* 42.6 (Nov.-Dec. 1983): 937-38.
Sheila Coghill, *Library Journal* 108.14 (Aug. 1983): 1484.
Thomas J. Corr, *College Literature* 11.3 (1984): 293-96.
John F. Desmond, *Modern Age* 28.2-3 (Spring-Summer 1984): 296-98.
Laurence Dorsey, *Southern Partisan* (Summer 1984): 44-45.
Patrick Jordan, *Commonweal* 110.20 (18 Nov. 1983): 637-38.
Joan Leonard, *Journal of the American Academy of Religion* 52.4 (1984): 793.
Rosemary M. Magee, *Christianity and Literature* 33.3 (1984): 76-77.
Anne Marie Mallon, *Religion and Literature* 17.3 (1985): 64-65.
W.J. Stuckey, *Modern Fiction Studies* 30.4 (Winter 1984): 832-34.
John Sykes, *Religious Studies Review* 13.1 (Jan. 1987): 63-64.
Michael True, *Cross Currents* 33.4 (Winter 1983-84): 493-94.
Ralph Wood, *Flannery O'Connor Bulletin* 12 (Autumn 1983): 117-21.

2722 *Three by Flannery O'Connor.* New York: Signet, 1967.

Anon. *New York Times Book Review* (7 Aug. 1983): 31.
Thomas Reeves, *American Spectator* (Dec. 1991): 16.
Donovan Young, *Atlanta Journal and Constitution* (8 April 1984): 9H.

2723 *The Violent Bear It Away.* New York: Farrar, Straus and Cudahy, 1960.

Anon. *Booklist* 56 (1 April 1960): 478.
Anon. *Christian Century* (1 June 1960): 672.
Anon. *English Journal* 49 (1960): 275.
Anon. *Information: The Catholic Church in American Life* 74.4 (1960): 57-58.
Anon. *Kirkus Bulletin* 27 (15 Dec. 1959): 931.
Anon. *New Yorker* (19 March 1960): 179.
Anon. *Punch* 239.6263 (5 Oct. 1960): 505.
Anon. *Spectator* 223 (16 Aug. 1969): 210-11.
Anon. *Time* (29 Feb. 1960): 118-19.
Anon. *TLS: Times Literary Supplement* (14 Oct. 1960): 666.
Anon. *TLS: Times Literary Supplement* (10 July 1969): 745+.
Algene Ballif, *Commentary* 30 (Oct. 1960): 358-62.
Barbara Bannon, *Publisher's Weekly* (27 June 1966): 102.

Harold Beaver, *TLS: Times Literary Supplement* (21 Nov. 1980): 1336.
Robert O. Bowen, *Renascence* 13 (Spring 1961): 147-52.
James Campbell, *New Statesman* 100.2590 (7 Nov. 1980): 26-27.
Francis X. Canfield, *Critic* 18.5 (Apr.-May 1960): 45.
Gerda Charles *New Statesman* (24 Sept. 1960): 445-46.
Noel Coman, *Crux* (29 May 1962): 3.
Cressida Connolly, *Books and Bookmen* (Aug. 1985): 36.
Hubert Creekmore, *New Leader* (30 May 1960): 20-21.
Pat Somers Cronin, *Ave Maria* 92.1 (2 July 1960): 25.
Ben Czaplewski, *Nexus* (St. Mary's College) (Oct. 1960): 7.
Donald Davidson, *New York Times Book Review* (28 Feb. 1960): 4.
Joan Didion, *National Review* 8.15 (9 Apr. 1960): 240-41.
Louis Dollarhide, *Jackson (Miss.) News-Clarion Ledger* (27 Mar. 1960): D6.
Bill Dorr, *Publisher's Auxilary* (Chicago) (28 May 1960): 2.
Robert Y. Drake, Jr., *Modern Age* 4 (Fall 1960): 428-30.
P. Albert Duhamel, *Catholic World* 190.1139 (Feb. 1960): 280-85.
Donald C. Emerson, *Arizona Quarterly* 16.3 (Autumn 1960): 284-86.
Paul Engle, *Chicago Tribune Magazine of Books* (6 Mar. 1960): Part 4, p. 3.
Sumner J. Ferris, *Critique: Studies in Modern Fiction* 3.2 (1960): 11-19.
R.W. Flint, *Partisan Review* 27 (1960): 374-78.
Harold C. Gardiner, *America* 102.28 (5 Mar. 1960): 682-83.
Thomas F. Gossett, *Southwest Review* 46 (Winter 1961): 86-87.
James Greene, *Commonweal* 72.3 (15 Apr. 1960): 67-68.
Eileen Hall, *[The Georgia] Bulletin* [Official Newspaper of the Archdiocese of Atlanta] (5 March 1960): 5.
Granville Hicks, *Saturday Review* (27 Feb. 1960): 18.
William Hogan, *San Francisco Chronicle* (25 Feb. 1960): 31.
Edward M. Hood, *Kenyon Review* 23.1 (Winter 1961): 170-72.
Anna C. Hunter, *Savannah (GA) Morning News* (21 Feb. 1960): 13.
Bud Johnson, *Catholic Messinger* (Davenport, IA) (2 June 1960): 15.
Frederick S. Kiley, *Clearing House* 36.3 (Nov. 1961): 188.
Paul Levine, *Jubilee* 8.1 (May 1960): 52.
David Lodge, *Tablet* 214 (17 Dec. 1960): 1175-76.
Vivian Mercier, *Hudson Review* 13 (1960): 449-56.
Nolan Miller, *Antioch Review* 20.2 (Summer 1960): 248-56.
Arthur Mizener, *Sewanee Review* 69.1 (Jan.-March 1961): 154-64.
Susan Myrick, *Macon* [GA] *Telegraph* (25 Jan. 1960): 2.
Dorothy Nyren, *Library Journal* 85.1 (1 Jan. 1960): 146.
Vince Passaro, *Harper's Magazine* 293.1756 (Sept. 1996): 64-71.
Paul Pickrel, *Harper's Magazine* 220.319 (April 1960): 114.
Orville Prescott, *New York Times* (24 Feb. 1960): 35.
John J. Quinn, *Best Sellers* 19 (1 March 1960): 414-15.
W.G. Rogers, *Augusta (GA) Chronicle-Herald* (13 Mar. 1960): 3C.
Coleman Rosenberger, *New York Herald Tribune Book Review* (28 Feb. 1960): 13.
Marjory Rutherford, *Atlanta Journal and Constitution* (28 Feb. 1960): E2.
Webster Schott, *Kansas City Star* (5 Mar. 1960): 7.

Norman Shrapnel, [Manchester, England] *Guardian Weekly* (10 July 1969): 15.
Thomas F. Smith, *Pittsburgh Catholic* (28 March 1963): 1, 3.
Bede Sullivan, *Catholic Library World* 31.8 (1960): 518, 521.
Bede Sullivan, *Today* 15 (March 1960): 36-37.
John J. Traynor, Jr. *Extension* 55 (July 1960): 26.
Frank J. Warnke, *New Republic* (14 Mar. 1960): 18-19.

2724 *Wise Blood.* New York: Harcourt, Brace, 1952.

Anon. *Colonnade* [Georgia State College for Women] (15 May 1952): 1, 4.
Anon. *Kirkus* 19 (1952): 252.
Anon. *Library Journal* 77.4 (15 Feb. 1952): 354.
Anon. *New Yorker* (14 June 1952): 106.
Anon. *Newsweek* (19 May 1952): 114-15.
Anon. *Milledgeville (GA) Union Recorder* (25 Apr. 1952): 1.
Anon. *Publisher's Weekly* 191.18 (1 May 1967): 57.
Anon. *Savannah Evening Press* (20 May 1952): 5.
Anon. *Time* (9 June 1952): 108, 110.
Anon. *TLS: Times Literary Supplement* (2 Sept. 1955): 505.
Anon. *TLS: Times Literary Supplement* (1 Feb. 1968): 101.
Anon. *United States Quarterly Book Review* 8 (Summer 1952): 256.
Paul Bailey, [London] *Observer* (11 Feb. 1968): 27.
Harold Beaver, *TLS: Times Literary Supplement* (21 Nov. 1980): 1336.
Melwyn Breen, *Saturday Night* [St. Lawrence University] (19 July 1952): 22-23.
Milton S. Byam, *Library Journal* 77 (15 May 1952): 894-95.
James Campbell, *New Statesman* 100.2590 (7 Nov. 1980): 26-27.
Linda Connolly, *Books and Bookmen* (Aug. 1985): 36.
Joe Lee Davis, *Kenyon Review* 15.2 (Spring 1953): 320-26.
William Goyen, *New York Times Book Review* (18 May 1952): 4; Rpt. (6 Oct. 1996): 78.
M. Greenberg, *American Mercury* 75.343 (July 1952): 111-13.
Doris Grumbach, *Critic* 21.2 (Oct.-Nov. 1962): 95.
Carl Hartman, *Western Review* 17 (Autumn 1952): 76-80.
Ihab Hassan, *English Journal* 51.1 (Jan. 1962): 1-8.
Oliver LaFarge, *Saturday Review* 35.21 (24 May 1952): 22.
Paul Levine, *Jubilee* 10.8 (Dec. 1962): 47.
R.W.B. Lewis, *Hudson Review* 6 (Spring 1953): 144-50.
Leonard F.X. Mayhew, *Commonweal* (22 Feb. 1963): 57.
Hoke Norris, *Chicago Sun-Times* (2 Sept. 1962): Sec. 3: 2.
Robert Nye, *Manchester Guardian Weekly* (2 Feb. 1968): 7; Rpt. (8 Feb. 1968): 12.
Dan Peerman, *Christian Century* (14 Aug. 1963): 1008-09.
Isaac Rosenfeld, *New Republic* 127.1 (7 July 1952): 19-20.

John W. Simons, *Commonweal* 56.12 (27 June 1952): 297-98.
Martha Smith, *Atlanta Journal and Constitution* (18 May 1952): F7.
Thomas F. Smith, *Pittsburgh Catholic* (28 March 1963): 1, 3.
Bonnie Smothers, *Booklist* 94.9-10 (Part 2) (1-15 Jan. 1998): 872.
Sylvia Stallings, *New York Herald Tribune Book Review* (18 May 1952): 3.
Harvey C. Webster, *New Leader* (23 June 1952): 23-24.

Appendix 2

A Checklist of Motion Pictures and Videos Based Upon Flannery O'Connor's Works

With the exception of the representative film reviews cited for *Wise Blood*, information related to the following motion pictures and videotapes is taken from the *EUREKA* database of bibliographic data and the *U.S. Copyright File* database, both of which are accessible at U.S. Library of Congress.

In addition to the commercial motion pictures cited and described below, the Flannery O'Connor Collection at Georgia College & State University owns two additional items that may be of interest to scholars: A news film-clip titled "Unique Chicken Walks in Reverse," (Pathé News Reel Series, 1931), which portrays Flannery O'Connor as a child in Savannah, Georgia with a pet chicken shown walking backwards; and, a clip of a television broadcast of *Galleyproof*, a television show produced by WRCA-TV which aired in 1955. This show includes an interview of O'Connor by Harvey Breit and an enactment of a portion of "The Life You Save May Be Your Own," with Mary Perry as "the old woman," Mildred Coole as "the girl," and Sandy Kenyon as "the visitor."

2725 *A Circle in the Fire*. [Motion Picture]. Chicago: Perspective Films, [16 mm., 1 reel, 50 min.], 1976.

An adaptation of Flannery O'Connor's story of the same title. "Shows how the security of the Cope farm is shattered when three teenage boys cruelly destroy what they cannot possess." Cast includes: Betty Miller, Ingred Schweska, Katherine Miller, Mark Hey, Casey Donovan and Tom Horken.

2726 *The Comforts of Home*. [Motion Picture]. Leonard Lipson. Released by Phoenix Films, [40 min., color, 16 mm.], 1974.

Directed by Jerome Shore, this production, based upon O'Connor's story of the same title, "presents a story about the relationship of a mother and son in a household which is disrupted by the arrival of a young girl." Cast includes: Graham Jarvis, Kate Harrington, and Stockard Channing.

2727   *The Displaced Person: A Short Story by Flannery O'Connor.* [Motion Picture]. Chicago: Perspective Films, [16 mm. 1 reel, 58 min.], 1977; & [Videorecording, 58 min.] Northbrook, IL: Learning in Focus, 1976 [Distributor] and Woodland Hills, CA: Monterey Monterey Home Video, 1987.

Portrays "the difficulties of integration experienced by a Polish refugee who arrives with his family at a Georgia farm in the 1940s."

Notes indicate that this production, part of the *The American Short Story Series*, was produced by Robert Geller and Matthew Herman, and directed by Glenn Jordan. The cast includes: John Houseman; Irene Worth; Shirley Stoler; Lane Smith; Colleen Dewhurst; and, Robert Earl Jones.

A filmstrip [2 35 mm. rolls, 108 frames & 113 frames, 2 cassettes, 29 min., of the same title and based upon this version of the motion picture, was produced and distributed in 1978 by [Chicago] Coronet Instructional Media as part of their *American Short Story Filmstrip Program* series. Database notes indicate that the script was adapted by Richard P. Creyke and the finished production packet included a program guide, four worksheet masters and sound accompaniment.

Videorecorded versions [1/2 inch] which--because they are of the same length (58 min.) and production date (1977)--appear to be identical to the motion picture, were distributed by Coronet Films & Video in 1978 and 1985 and Monterey Home Video in 1976.

2728   *Good Country People.* [Motion Picture]. Agoura, CA: Jeffrey F. Jackson Films, Inc., [16 mm., 32 min., color], 1975.

An adaptation of O'Connor's story of the same title "about a sullen, 36-year-old girl with a wooden leg, a Ph.D. in philosophy, and a heart condition who is out to pasture on her mother's farm waiting to die, until a traveling Bible salesman takes her on a picnic." Produced by Anderson G. House and directed, edited and written by Jeff Jackson. Cast includes: Johnnie Collins, III; Shirley Slater; June Whitley Taylor; and, Sue Marrow. The musical score is by Dale Derda.

2729   *The Life You Save May Be Your Own.* [Motion Picture]. Philadelphia: Movies Unlimited, 1957.

An adaptation of O'Connor's story of the same title. First shown on the television show *Schlitz Playhouse of Stars* on March 1, 1957. Cast includes: Gene Kelly, Agnes Moorehead and Janice Rule.

2730   *The River.* [Motion Picture]. Beverly Hills, Calif.: The [American Film] Institute, [1 reel, 26 min., 35 mm.], 1976; New York: Phoenix Films, [Made 1976, 1 reel, 29 min., 16 mm.], 1978.

An adaptation of O'Connor's story of the same title "about a neglected young boy . . . [whose] babysitter takes him to a religious healing by a river. After he returns to his unloving parents, he decides he must go back to the river." Produced and directed by Barbara Noble. Cast includes: Robby Paris, Dran Hamilton, Shelby Leverington, James Eric, Martin Nicholson, and Tiger Jo Marsh.

Also distributed in 1983, by Phoenix Films, as a segment of *The American Short Story Series* [2 videocassettes, 1/2 inch VHS format, color] which--in addition to *The River*--included dramatizations of: Stephen Crane's "Three Miraculous Soldiers"; Willa Cather's "Jack-A-Boy"; Ray Bradbury's "The Murderer"; Kurt Vonnegut's "Next Door"; Edgar Lee Masters' "Spoon River Anthology"; and, Carson McCullers' "A Tree, a Rock, a Cloud."

2731   *Wise Blood.* Released by New Line Cinema. 108 min. [Videorecording]. Universal City, Calif.: MCA Home Video, [1 videocassette, 106 min., color, 1/2 inch], 1985.

Based upon Flannery O'Connor's novel of the same title, the screenplay was written by Benedict and Michael Fitzgerald, directed by John Huston, and produced by Michael and Kathy Fitzgerald. The work was released as a motion picture in 1979. Depicts "religious fundamentalism, fanaticism, charlatanism and chicanery, Southern style," with characters "ranging from bizarre to crazy." Cast includes: Brad Dourif, Ned Beatty, Harry Dean Stanton, Dan Shor, Amy Wright, and Mary Nell Santacroce.

Representative Reviews of the Film and Video:
Anon. *Film Comment* 15 (1979): 63-4.
Roger Angell, *New Yorker* (Feb. 25, 1980): 114-17.
David Ansen, *Newsweek* (March 17, 1980): 101.
Gary Arnold, *Washington Post* (May 7, 1980): C-1.
Joy G. Boyum, *Wall Street Journal* (Feb. 22, 1980): 21.
Vincent Canby, *New York Times* (Mar. 2, 1980): II-19, 25; (Feb. 17, 1980): 68; (Oct. 7, 1979): II-1+; (Sept. 29, 1979): 12.

Charles Champlin, *Los Angeles Times* (Dec. 12, 1979): IV-1.
Harold Clurman, *Nation* (Oct. 27, 1979): 409-10.
David Denby, *New York* (Mar. 10, 1980): 85.
Rob Edelman, *Films in Review* (Jan. 1980): 115.
James R. Fultz, *Purdue University Fifth Annual Conference on Film* (1980):
    117-23.
Robert Hatch, *Nation* (Mar. 8, 1980): 283.
Stanley Kauffman, *New Republic* (Mar. 15, 1980): 24-25.
Alex Keneas, *Newsday* (Feb. 18, 1980): II-30.
Judith Martin, *Washington Post* "Weekend," (May 9, 1980): 17.
Michael Mason, *Times Literary Supplement* (11 Jan. 1980): 36.
Geoffrey Nowell-Smith, *New Statesman* (Jan. 18, 1980): 102.
Tim Pulleine, *Sight and Sound* (Winter, 1979-80): 56.
Frank Rich, *Time* (Feb. 25, 1980): 50.
Andrew Sarris, *Village Voice* (Feb. 25, 1980): 39.
J. Simon, *National Review* 32 (May 2, 1980): 543-44.
David Sterritt, *Christian Science Monitor* (Ap. 7, 1980): 19.
Michael Tarantino, *Film Quarterly* 33.4 (Sum. 1980): 15-17.
Fancher Winsten, *New York Post* (Feb. 18, 1980): 26.

Author Index

Includes entry numbers for authors of books, articles, dissertations, theses and other works cited and abstracted in this guide. Also includes entry numbers for: authors of reviews cited (# r); master's theses cited (# t); editors of works abstracted (# ed); and, works reprinted in critical anthologies. Letters "a" and "b" indicate late additional entries added.

Authors of works cited in the text of critical abstracts are included in the *Name Index* (# c). Works by Flannery O'Connor are included as subject terms in the *Subject Index*.

Abad, Pilar 2034ed
Abadie, Ann J. 1059ed, 1655ed
Abbot, Louise H. 23r, 82
Ackerman, Sarah Gene 2190t
Adair, Sally 83
Adams, Mary Helen 2191t
Adams, Robert Martin 2717r
Adelman, Selma S. 2192t
Aderholt, Martha J. 2193t
Ahrends, Gunter 2017, 2018
Aiken, David Hubert 84, 1726, 2194t
Aiken, Robert 42r
Akai, Katsua 2019
Albert, John 85
Albert, Marie Louise Hannibal 1727
Albritton, Thomas Wellington 2195t
Alessio, Carolyn 86
Alexander, Alice 87
Alexander, Benjamin B. 88, 89, 90
Alexander, David 2196t
Alexander, Paul 2712r
Alfieri, Teresa 2020
Alford, James Curtis 2197t
Alkire, Leland G., Jr. 91
Allen, Diogenes 53r
Allen, Lurlie Wiseman 2198t
Allen, Marjorie H. 2199t
Allen, Reynolds 92
Allen, Suzanne [Thomas] 93, 1728
Allen, Walter 94

Allen, William Rodney 95, 96, 97
Allison, John M. 98
Allison, Stephen R. 2200t
Alloway, Laurie Ann 2201t
Allsopp, Michael E. 2202t
Als, Hilton 98a
Alther, Lisa 99, 941
Alvis, Sara Kathleen 2203t
Amette, Jacques-Pierre 2021
Anastaplo, George 100
Anderson, Roger K. 101
Andreas, James 102
Andretta, Helen R. 102a
Andrews, Candace E. 2204t
Andrews, William L. 80r, 1567
Andrus, Faith Posey 2205t
Angell, Roger 2731r
Angle, Kimberly Greene 103
Ansen, David 2731r
Antle, Emily Newberry 2206t
Anzalone, John 54r
Arase, Hiroko 2207t
Arbeit, Marcel 2022
Arbery, Glenn Cannon 105
Archer, Emily 106, 107
Archer, Jane Elizabeth 108
Archer, Patricia Faye 2208t
Armitage, Shelly S. 2209t
Arnold, Edwin T. 109
Arnold, Gary 2731r

Arnold, Marilyn 110, 111, 112, 113
Aronson, Marilyn A. Carlson 1729
Asals, Frederick [John], Jr. 23r, 29,
    30ed, 35, 46, 47r, 48r, 56r, 68a,
    70r, 71, 80r, 114, 115, 116, 117,
    118r, 119r, 120, 1730, 2713r,
    2714r, 2720r
Aschkenasy, Nehama 246ed
Ashley, Jack Dillard 79, 121
Association of American Book
    Publishers 122
Atkins, Donna Ruth 2210t
Atkins, Erin 2211t
Atterson, Anna Grace 1382ed
Au, Bobbye Green 1731
Austin, Emmit Wade 1732
Avant, John Alfred 17r, 21r, 2712r
Ayau, Kurt Jose 2212t
Aycock, Wendell 124

Babich, Alan Thomas 1733
Babinec, Lisa S. 125
Bach, Peggy 231ed
Bacon, Jon Lance 31, 58, 126, 1734
Baechler, Lea 1700ed
Bahn, Sonja 71ed, 2060ed
Bailey, Paul 2718r, 2724r
Bain, Robert 98ed, 127, 533ed,
    791ed, 1415ed
Baker, J. Robert 50r, 128, 1735
Baker, William 129
Balazy, Teresa 32, 130
Balcer, Joan 2213t
Baldanza, Frank 131
Baldeshwiler, Eileen 62r
Baldwin, Dean 132
Baldwin, Glenn E. 2214t
Balée, Susan 33, 133
Balgård, Gunnar 2023
Ballif, Algene 2723r
Bamberg, Marie Louise 134
Bambrick, Gail 1736
Bandy, Stephen C. 135
Bane, Sarah 2215t
Banner, Keith 135a

Bannon, Barbara 2723r
Barendse, Nancy Roberta 2216t
Barfield, Ann L. 2217t
Barnes, Linda Adams 59, 136, 1737
Barnes, Patricia A. 2218t
Barnett, Floyd 58r
Barnett, Martha Floyd 1738
Barnette, William Joseph 1739
Barr, Terry 1665
Barrett, William 2715r
Barrio, José M. 2034ed
Barry, Sheila 2219t
Bart, Robert S. 137
Bartle, Arthur 2024, 2025, 2026
Bartley, Numan V. 138
Bass, Eben 139
Bassan, Maurice 23r
Bassett, Beth Dawkins 140, 141
Batts, Martin 142, 1740
Bauer, Margaret D. 143
Baumbach, Georgia Anne 1741
Baumbach, Jonathan 144, 1742
Baumgaertner, Jill Peláez 34, 35a,
    41r, 81r, 145
Bawer, Bruce 146r, 2716r
Baxter, Harold Jason 1743
Bazzanella, Carla 704ed
Beacham, Walter 424ed
Beacham, Walton 147ed
Beard, Nila Valentine 2220t
Beasley, David 148
Beaty, Kelly Lynne Haggard 2221t
Beauchamp, Wilton 149, 990
Beaulieu, Paul 2027
Beaven, Simon W. 2222t
Beaver, Harold 38r, 150, 151, 2715r,
    2718r, 2723r, 2724r
Becham, Gerald 42r, 44r, 152, 153,
    154
Becht, Donald Edward 2223t
Beck, Charlotte 155
Beck, Christiane 79, 156, 2028
Becker, Isidore H. 157
Becker, Leslee 158
Becknell, Thomas Ira 1744
Beckner, Mary 2713r

Beeching, Paul Q. 159

Beets, Richard Van Der 22r

Behrendt, Stephen C. 160

Beiswanger, George 161

Belflower, Robert 29r

Bellamy, Michael O. 30, 68a, 162

Belsie, Laurent 163

Belsunce, Alicia L. de García 2029, 2030

Ben-Bassat, Hedda 164, 164a

Bendel-Simso, Mary Michele 1745

Benedict, Stewart 212ed

Bennett, Barbara Anne 1746

Bennion, Rebecca Poelman 2224t

Benoit, Raymond 165

Beppu, Keiko 166

Bergamo, Ralph 2715r

Bergstrom, Robert F. 167

Bergup, Bernice 44r, 168

Bergup, M. Emmanuel 2225t

Beringer, Cindy 169a

Beringer, Lucinda MacDonald 2226t

Berkowitz, Alan Steven 1747

Berret, Anthony J. 169

Betsill, Catherine 2227t

Betts, Doris 170, 171, 172, 173

Beutel, Katherine Piller 174, 1748

Bevilacqua, Winifred Farrant 1181

Bieber, Christina Marie 174a, 1749

Billing, Geraldine Mart 2229t

Binding, Paul 175

Bixby, George 44r

Black, Janet M. 2230t

Blackwell, Annie Louise 1750

Blackwell, Henry A. 1751

Blake, Laura Michelle 2230at

Blanch, Mae 176

Blann, Robinson 36r

Blanton, William H. 2231t

Blasingham, Mary V. 79, 177

Bleikasten, André 46, 71, 178, 179

Blessing, Loren Michael 2232t

Blewitt, David 2720r

Bliss, Lowell D. 2233t

Bliven, Naomi 2715r

Bloom, Harold 35, 35a ed, 180ed, 268ed, 1422ed

Blythe, Hal 181, 182, 183, 184

Bolton, Betsy 185

Bolton, Elizabeth Susan 1752

Bolton, Philip 186, 187

Bonanno, Raphael D. 2234t

Bond, Adrienne 188

Bone, Larry Earl 2715r

Bonetti, Kay 189

Bongartz, Roy 190

Bonner, James C. 690

Bonney, William 191, 2717r

Booker-Canfield, Suzanne 1317

Boone, Sherry Gilmer 2235t

Boos, Florence 192

Booth, Mark 193

Booth, Stanley 194

Boren, Mark [Edelman] 195, 1753

Borgman, Paul [Carlton] 196, 1754

Bornhauser, Fred 2717r

Bott, François 2031

Bourne, Paul 197

Bowen, Rose 198, 199, 1755

Bowen, Robert O. 2723r

Bowman, Lee Willey 2236t

Bowman, Michael S. 200

Boyum, Joy G. 2731r

Box, Terry 201

Boyd, L.M. 202

Boyd, Zohara Mushinsky 1756

Boyer, Ken B. 2237t

Boyles, Mary 203

Boyum, Joy Gould 204

Bracken, James K. 205

Bradbury, Malcolm 206, 558ed, 2717r

Bradley, William J. 2238t

Brady, Charles A. 18r, 19r

Braendlin, Hans P. 30ed, 1372ed

Brahaney, Carolyn 2239t

Brandolino, Gina 207

Brantley, Richard E. 208

Brantley, Will 31r, 209

Bray, Nancy Davis 210, 488

Breaud, Norbert Francis 2240t

Brechbiel, Grace R. 2241t
Breckenridge, Jennifer J. 2242t
Breen, Melwyn 2724r
Breen, Meredith A. 2243t
Brennan, Wilma Nadine 2244t
Brewer, Kara P. 1757
Brewer, Nadine 211
Brewster, Rudolph Allen 1758
Brewton, Butler 212
Brickman, Barbara Jane 2245t
Bridges, Phyllis 213
Bright, Nancy 47r
Brinkerhoff, Coni Jo 2245at
Brinkmeyer, Robert H[erman]., Jr.
    31r, 35a, 36, 39r, 47r, 56r, 57r, 58,
    70r, 71r, 74, 80r, 215, 216, 217,
    218, 219, 1759, 2714r, 2716r,
    2718r
Brisac, Geneviève 2032
Brito, Manuel 79r
Brittain, Joan T. 17, 71, 2246t
Brittin, Ruth L. 220
Brodhead, Richard H. 221r, 2718r
Bromwich, David 2718r
Broncano, Manuel 2033, 2034
Brooks, Cleanth 222, 223
Brown, Ashley 79, 224, 225, 2717r
Brown, Beatrice 1076ed, 1077ed
Brown, Betsy Etheridge 2247t
Brown, Betsy Rush 2248t
Brown, Caroline M. 46, 313
Brown, Dorothy H. 57r
Brown, Hugh R. 226, 227
Brown, Jerry Elijah 228, 229
Brown, Mary Ward 230
Brown, Martha Frances 2718r
Brown, Rosellen 231
Brown, S.C. 1270ed
Brown, Sarah Enos 1760
Brown, Sheila Goodman 1761
Brown, Terrence N. 34r
Brown, Thomas H. 232
Brown, Tony 34r, 232a, 2716r
Brown, W. Dale 233
Brown-Guillory, Elizabeth 39r

Browning, Preston M[ercer]., Jr. 15,
    17r, 18r, 19r, 21r, 24r, 25r, 27r,
    35a, 71, 234, 235, 1762
Brownlee, James Henry 1763
Broyard, Anatole 2717r
Bruccoli, Matthew J. 1065ed
Bruce, Duane Francis 2249t
Brunet, Elena 2718r
Bruss, Neal H. 236
Brussat, Frederic and Mary Ann 237
Bryant, Hallman B. 30, 68a, 238
Bryant, J.A., Jr. 239
Bryer, Jackson R. 340ed, 432ed
Bryfonski, Dedria 240ed, 241ed
Bryson, Michael Erik 2250t
Buchalter, Gail 242
Buchanan, James H. 243
Buck, Claire 244
Buckley, James J. 245
Budick, Emily Miller 246, 247, 248
Budy, Andrea Hollander 249
Buechner, Frederick 250
Bukovinsky, Janet 251
Bunch, Cecile Dianne 252, 1764
Bunting, Charles Thomas 1765
Burch, Francis F. 2720r
Burgess, Anthony 2715r
Burke, Daniel 253
Burke, William 39r, 59r, 254, 255,
    256
Burkle, Howard R. 257
Burkman, Katherine H. 258
Burns, Dan G. 259
Burns, Margie 260
Burns, Marian 46, 261, 262, 1766
Burns, Michael 1633ed
Burns, Shannon 263, 264
Burns, Stuart L. 17r, 18r, 24r, 25r,
    27r, 28r, 265
Burns, Thomas Shannon 2251t
Burr, Nelson R. 266, 267
Burruss, John C. 2252t
Burt, John 35, 268
Burt, John Davies 1767
Buschendorf, Christa 2035, 2036
Bush, George Drake 2253t

Bush, Laura L. 2254t
Butcher, Fanny 2717r
Butler, Rebecca Roxburgh 34r, 68a, 269, 270, 271, 1768
Butscher, Edward 2718r
Butler, Robert James 272
Butterworth, Nancy K. 273
Buturain, Leah Marie 2255t
Buzan, Mary 274
Byam, Milton S. 2724r
Byars, John A. 275, 276, 277
Byerman, Keith E. 278
Byrd, Rudolph P. 279, 280
Byrne, Mary Ellen 281

Caillouet, Hazel Ruth Reames 1769
Caldwell, Gail 2716r
Calish, Richard 282
Campbell, Debra 283
Campbell, James 2715r, 2723r, 2724r
Camillo, Sandra 2256t
Canby, Vincent 2731r
Canfield, Francis X. 2723r
Canfield, John 284
Capel, Gloria Jean McGee 2257t
Capps, John Spencer 2258t
Caputo, Donna M. 2259t
Caputo, Pete 1770r
Carey, Patrick W. 39r
Carleton, Mark A. 2260t
Carlisle, Timothy 2261t
Carlson, Marilyn Anne 2262t
Carlson, Thomas MacNab 1771
Carney, Virginia Moore 2263t
Caro, Frances A. de 285
Caron, Timothy Paul 1772
Carr, Pat 286
Carr, Virginia Spencer 47r, 56r, 70r, 80r, 2714r
Carrigan, Henry 34r
Carroll, Linda Sue Cole 2264t
Carroll, Rachel 286a
Carroll, R.L. 1773
Carruth, Gorton 447
Carson, Ricks 287

Carter, David 287a
Carter, Frank T. 2265t
Carter, Thomas H. 2717r
Carver-Taylor, Mary Anne 2266t
Case, David Allen 1774
Casey, Constance 2718r
Casey, Holly Sue Baynes 2267t
Casey, Margaret E. 2268t
Casey, Roger N. 288, 1775
Cash, Jean W. 289, 290, 291, 292, 293, 294, 295, 296, 297
Cassill, R.V. 2715r
Casteel, John L. 69r, 2718r, 2721r
Castelli, Ferdinando 2037
Castex, Peggy Hanemann 298
Castille, Philip 1420ed
Castronovo, David 299
Cattani, Richard J. 2712r
Cavnar, Cindy M. 300
Chamlee, Kenneth D. 301
Champion, Lou Terrell 2269t
Champlin, Charles 2731r
Chandler, Tommie Allen 2270t
Chanen, Audrey Wolff 1776
Chapin, John D. 302
Chappell, Fred 303
Chard, George Edward Hurd 1777
Charles, Gerda 2723r
Charney, Mark J. 304
Charnigo, Richard John 1778
Chauhan, Posh Charak 37
Cheatham, George 305
Cheney, Brainard 70
Cheney, Lynne V. 306
Chentier, Marc 2038
Cherry, Caroline L. 1133
Cherry, Charles Lester 2271t
Cherry, Susan Blair 2272t
Chestnut, Allison Carol 1779
Chew, Martha [Elizabeth] 63r, 307, 1780
Childress, Mark 307a
Choffrut-Faure, Patric 2039
Choi, Insoon 1781
Chow, Sung Gay 308
Christenbury, Tamara O'Hearn 2273t

Christensen, Jane 2274t
Church, Joseph 309
Cioffari, Phillip Edward 1782
Ciuba, Gary M. 41r, 50r, 310, 311,
    311a, 312r
Clapperton, Jane 2718r
Clarey, Jo Ellyn 909, 1214ed, 1696ed
Clark, Beverly Lyon 29r, 46, 68r,
    70r, 80r, 313, 435ed, 564ed, 670ed,
    811ed, 963, 2713r, 2714r
Clark, C.E. Frazer, Jr. 1065ed
Clark, Catherine A. 2275t
Clark, John R. 314
Clark, Lindley H., Jr. 2718r
Clark, Michael 315
Clasby, Nancy T. 316
Claunch, Belinda L. 2276t
Clayton, J. Douglas 1228ed
Clayton, Lauren 317
Cleary, Michael 318
Clemons, Walter 2712r, 2718r
Cleveland, Carol [Lynn] 17r, 19r,
    25r, 1783
Clift-Pellow 319
Cline, Peter 320
Clurman, Harold 2731r
Coale, Samuel Chase, V. 321, 322,
    1784
Coates, Joseph 2716r
Cobb, Gerald Thomas 73r, 1785
Cobb, James C. 323
Cobb, Joann P. 324
Coffey, Warren 46, 2715r
Coggins, Melissa Judith 2277t
Coghill, Sheila [Renee] 29r, 53r, 69r,
    1786, 2721r
Colafato, Michele 2040
Cole, Letha B. 1092ed
Coleman, Christy Lynn 2278t
Coleman, John 2715r
Coleman, Kenneth 138ed, 643ed
Coleman, Richard 2715r
Coles, Robert 38, 63, 325, 326, 327,
    328, 329, 330, 331, 332, 333, 334,
    335, 2712r, 2720r
Collins, Glenn 336

Collins, Lowrey Christopher 2279t
Collins, Michael Robert 2280t
Collins, R.G. 1524
Collum, Danny Duncan 337
Coman, Noel 2723r
Combs, Diana Williams 63r, 338
Combs, Richard E. 339
Conarroe, John 38r
Connell, Sandra B. 33r
Connolly, Cressida 2715r, 2723r
Connolly, Janet Maroney 1787, 2715r
Conrad, Linda 1788, 2724r
Conyers, Lisa Ann 1789
Cook, Haruko Taya 2281t
Cook, Martha E. 340, 341
Cooper, Edith 2715r
Cooper, Marie 2282t
Cooper, Stephen 342
Copeland, Jennifer 342a
Core, Deborah 343
Core, George 344, 1714ed, 2712r,
    2718r
Corn, Alfred 345
Cornelison, Robert Walter 2283t
Corr, Thomas J. 29r, 69r, 2721r
Corrigan, Charlotte H. 2719r
Corse, Larry B. and Sandra 346
Cosgrave, Mary Silva 2712r
Coshnear, D. 55r
Cotton, Alvin Horner 2284t
Coulbourn, Mildred Elizabeth 2285t
Coulthard, A.R. 29r, 47r, 68a, 347,
    348, 349, 350, 351, 352
Counts, Alice Crosby 2286t
Cox, James M. 353
Craig, Claire G. 2287t
Creekmore, Hubert 2723r
Crews, Frederick 29r, 36r, 354r,
    2716r
Crocker, Michael W. 355
Cronin, Gloria L. 356
Cronin, Pat Somers 2723r
Crowley, J. Donald 357, 359
Crowley, P. 838ed
Crowley, Sue Mitchell 358, 359
Crump, Michele J. 2288t

Cruser, Paul Alexander 1790
Cruttwell, Patrick 2715r
Cummings, Thomas W. 23r
Cunningham, David S. 360
Cunningham, John 18r, 19r, 21r, 23r, 24r, 25r, 29r, 53r, 76r, 361
Cunningham, Lawrence S. 60r, 362
Cunningham, Stanley W. 2289t
Curley, Dan 71
Current-García, Eugene 363r, 2718r
Currie, Sheldon 71, 79, 364, 365
Curtis, Carol A. 2290t
Cutler, Mary Lynn 2291t
Czaplewski, Ben 2723r

Dale, Mary Ann 2292t
Daley, Jamie Temple 1791
Daniel, David 367
Daniel, Thomas M. 2293t
Darretta, John Lawrence 59, 368, 369, 1792
Dart, Bob 370
Daunt, Chris 371, 372
Davenport, Guy 2712r, 2715r
Davidson, Cathy N. 1195ed
Davidson, Donald 2723r
Davies, Horton 374
Davies, Horton and Marie-Helene 375
Davis, Alan 376
Davis, Cynthia J. 377,
Davis, Elizabeth Deidre 1793
Davis, Joe Lee 2724r
Davis, Joseph K. 378
Davis, Rebecca 379ed
Davis, Ronald Lester 2294t
Davis, Thadious M. 380
Davis, William V. 381
Davison, Richard Allen 20r
Dawkins, Cecil 382
Dawson, Edward B. 690
Dawson, Jan C. 383
Day, Mildred A. 2295t
Day, Susan M. 384, 385
Debry, Stephanie Sue 2296t

Deeken, Agnese 386
Degnan, James P. 2715r
Dehart, Robert 2297t
Delafield, Carter 2298t
Delattre, Edwin J. 387
Del Fattore, Joan 1794
Demers, Patricia 45r
Demory, Pamela H. 388
DeMouy, Jane Krause 2299t
Demowitz, Janet 2718r
Denby, David 2731r
Denby, Priscilla Lee 1795
Denham, Robert D. 389
Dennis, Joe 2300t
Dennis, Joy Dee 1796
DeRosa, Susan 2301t
Desmond, John F[rancis]. 29r, 35a, 39, 53r, 60r, 65r, 69r, 70r, 81r, 390, 391, 392, 393, 394, 395, 396, 397, 398, 399, 400, 401, 402, 403, 404, 2714r, 2718r, 2721r
Dessommes, Nancy Bishop 405
Dettelbach, Cynthia Golomb 406
Detweiler, Jane A. 407
Deutschmann, Elinor 2302t
D'Evelyn, Thomas 366r, 2716r
Dewey, Joseph 36r, 45r, 56r, 70r, 2714r
Dibble, Terry Jerome 40, 1798
Didion, Joan 2723r
Diederich, Joanne L. 2303t
Dillard, Annie 408
Dillard, Gail Presley 409, 1799
Dillard, Martha 410
Dilley, Ray 2717r
DiLorenzo, Ronald 15r, 27r
Dimié, Milan 782ed
Dinger, Ed 411
Dinneen, Patricia Marie 1800
Dirda, Michael 2718r
DiRenzo, Anthony 35a, 41, 1801
Ditsky, John 60r, 412
Divay, Gaby 991ed
Doll, Howard D. 413
Dollarhide, Louis 2723r

Dommergues, Pierre 2041
Donaghy, Joyce Aasen 2304t
Donahoo, Robert [Earl] 31r, 414,
    415, 416, 417, 418, 419, 420, 1802
Donaldson, Mara E. 2305t
Donaldson, Scott 17r
Donnelly, Daria 421
Donner, Andrea K. 2306t
Donohue, Agnes McNeill 422
Dorr, Bill 2723r
Dorsey, James E. 423
Dorsey, Laurence 2721r
Dorsman-Massen, Pamela 2307t
Dougherty, David C. 147, 424
Douglas, Thomas E[dward] 425,
    1803
Dow, Michelle 2308t
Downs, Gene 425a
Doxey, William S. 30
Doyle, Esther M. 1486ed
Drake, Robert 16, 18r, 19r, 24r, 34r,
    35a, 39r, 65r, 71, 79, 426, 427, 428,
    429, 2712r, 2715r, 2718r, 2720r
Drake, Robert Y., Jr. 2723r
Dreyer, Ladonna J. 2309t
Driggers, Stephen G[ause] 42, 70r,
    430, 1804, 2714r
Driskell, Leon V. 17, 71, 2720r
Dryden, Phylis Campbell 1805
Duckworth, C. Victoria 431
Duffy, Martha 2712r
Duhamel, P. Albert 46, 2723r
Duke, Maurice 340ed, 432ed
Dukes, Thomas 433
Dula, Martha Alice 2310t
Dullea, Catherine M. 1806
Dulworth, Deborah Quinton 2311t
Dunaway, John M. 434ed
Dunleavy, Janet Egleson 35a, 46, 435
Dunn, Francis Mary 1807
Dunn, Joe P. 436ed
Dunn, Robert J[oseph]. 27r, 42, 437
438r, 1808
Dunwell, Lara 785ed
Duprey, Richard A. 2715r
Dupuis, John 2312t

Durian, David 708
Dursin, Susan D. 2313t
Durso, Robert W. 2314t
Dyer, Joyce C. 439
Dyson, C.E. 1809
Dyson, J. Peter 30, 440

East, Charles 441
Ebner, Dean 60r
Ebrecht, Ann [Bernadette] 79, 442,
    1810
Eckert, Edward K. 38r
Edelman, Rob 2731r
Edelstein, Mark G. 443
Edge, Loretta 2315t
Edmondson, Henry T., III 42a, 443a
Edmunds, Susan 444
Edwards, Bruce L., Jr. 445, 446
Edwards, Nelda Young 2316t
Egan, Kimberly 446a
Eggenschwiler, David 18, 27r, 71
Eguchi, Yuko 2042, 2043
Ehrlich, Eugene 447
Eifrig, Gail McGrew 34r, 448
Eigen, Michael 449
Elder, Harris James 1811
Elder, Walter 2717r
El-Kanaoui, Fatima 1812
Elkins, Mary J. 450
Elkins, Sharon Jane 2317t
Elledge, Jim 80r
Elliot, Sarah E. 1813
Elliott, Emory 380ed, 451
Ellis, Grace W. 452
Ellis, James 453
Ellis, Juniper 454
Elrod, John W. 455
Elwell, Evelyn 2318t
Emerick, Ronald Rine 456, 457, 1814
Emerson, Bo 458
Emerson, Donald C. 2723r
Emerson, O.B. 16r, 459ed
Emmens, Carol A. 461
Emmett, Paul J. 460
Engell, John 462

Emmett, Paul J. 460
Engell, John 462
England, Eugene 463
Engle, Paul 2723r
Engler, Bernd 2044, 2189ed
Enjolras, Laurence 43
Enscore, Melody Lynn 2319t
Enser, A.G.S. 464
Ensor, Allison R. 465
Eppes, Cindy 2320t
Ericson, Edward E. 427ed
Ettin, Andrew V. 467
Evans, Carol Lynne 2321t
Evans, Elizabeth 76r, 468, 468a, 469r
Evans, Florence Therese 2322t
Evans, Jay Alan 1815
Evans, Robert C. 355, 470, 471, 1163
Evory, Ann 1466ed
Ewell, Barbara C. 472

Fairbanks, Carol 474
Faller, Greg S. 1560ed
Falnes, Mindy Lynn 1816
Falvey, Ellen Catherine 1817
Fancher, Betsy 475
Fanknitz, Mark A.R. 476
Farley, Blanche 68r, 477, 478a, 478r,
     2713r
Farmer, David R. 44
Farmer, Joy A. 479
Farnham, James F. 480, 481, 2715r,
     2720r
Faust, Langdon Lynne 286ed
Feaster, Scott Vandiver 1818
Feeley, Kathleen J. 19, 29r, 34r, 45r,
     73r, 79, 483, 484, 485
Feeley, Margaret Peller 486
Feeley, Marie J. 2323t
Feeley, Mary Kathleen 1819
Felder, Deborah G. 487
Felton, Sharon 35r, 79r
Felts, Juanita F. 2324t
Fennell, Janice C. 488
Fennick, Ruth 489
Fenster, Valmai Kirkham 490

Ferguson, Paul F. 491, 492
Ferguson, Penny Blackwood 1820
Ferraté, Juan 782
Ferris, Sumner J. 46, 2723r
Ferris, William 874ed, 964ed
Fialka, Elaine 1178
Fialka, Maurice 1178
Ficken, Carl 493, 494
Fickett, Harold 34r, 45, 495
Field, James A. 496
Field, Leslie 60r
Fike, Francis 45r, 50r
Filippi, Carmen Lugo 2045
Fincher, Cheryl 497
Finger, Larry Livingston 1821
Finholt, Richard 498
Finley, Mitch 499
Finn, James 500
Fiondella, Maris G. 501
Fishman, Jane 501a
Fitch, Robert E., 16r
Fitts, Karen [Louise] 50r, 1822, 2325t
Fitzgerald, Robert, 9ed, 35, 71, 502,
     503
Fitzgerald, Sally, 4ed, 7ed, 9ed, 39r,
     47r, 56r, 79, 504, 505, 506, 507,
     508, 509, 510, 511, 512, 513, 514,
     515, 516, 517, 518, 519, 520, 521,
     522, 523, 524, 525, 526, 527,
     1090ed, 1119, 1120ed, 1675, 2718r
Fitzgerald, Sheila 713ed
Fitzpatrick, Ruth McDonough 528
Flaig, Bonnie 529
Flannery, Melissa Conway, 38r,
     2326t, 2718r
Flavia, Mariapragasam 1823
Fleenor, Juliann E. 814ed
Fleissner, Robert F., 16r, 20r, 531
Fleming, Thomas J. 532
Fleurdorge, Claude 2046
Flint, R.W. 2723r
Floerchinger, Sharon M. 2327t
Flood, Kelly Joyce 2328t
Flora, Joseph M. 98ed, 127, 533ed,
     791ed, 1415ed
Flower, Dean 534, 535

Floyd, Virginia Hastings 1486ed
Fodor, Sarah J[oan]. 74, 536, 537,
    538, 539, 540, 1824
Folks, Jeffrey J. 541, 542, 543, 544
Fontes, Montserrat 545
Foote, Horton 1665
Forbis, Ida C. 2329t
Forkner, Ben 546
Foster, Edward Halsey, 73r
Foster, Shirley 547
Foust, Ronald E. 548
Fowler, Doreen Ferlaino 549, 550,
    1059ed, 1655ed
Fowler, Jennifer 550a
Fowler, Ruth Gwendolyn 2330t
Fowlie, Wallace 551
Fox, William Henry 1825
Fraistat, Rose Ann C[leveland]. 552,
    1826
Franchville, Denise Ann 2331t
Francis, Dale 2715r, 2717r
Frank, Edwin 503
Frank, Tibor 1314ed
Franklin, Melissa Ann 2332t
Freedman, James O. 553
Freedman, Richard 2712r
Freeman, Mary Glenn 554, 555
Freeman, Warren Eugene 2333t
Freemantle, Anne 2719r
Freese, Peter 2051ed
French, Patricia Ross 557
French, Warren 558, 856
Friebert, Lucy M. 556
Friedman, Jane F. 1827
Friedman, Melvin J., 15r, 20ed, 25r,
    27r, 29r, 38r, 39r, 44r, 46, 48r, 50r,
    51r, 52r, 56r, 57r, 60r, 62r, 63r, 71r,
    76r, 313ed, 435ed, 559, 560, 561,
    562, 563, 564, 565, 566, 567,
    619ed, 670ed, 811ed, 963, 1343ed,
    2712r, 2716r, 2718r, 2720r
Fromm, Harold 569
Frost, Wendy 570
Fuglie, Gordon 571
Fujiyoshi, Seijiro 2047
Fuller, Donald Coldwell 2334t

Fuller, Edmund 38r, 2718r
Fultz, James R. 572, 2731r
Fuqua, Patricia Davis 2335t

Gable, Mariella 2715r
Gafford, Charlotte Kelly 2336t
Gaines, Juana Denise 2337t
Gale, Steven H. 573ed
Gallagher, Janet M. 1828
Gallagher, Michael Paul 574, 575
Galligan, Mary 1357
Galloway, Lewis F. 576
Galvin, Elizabeth Hayes 2338t
Gamber, Matthew T. 577
Gamblin, Julie A. 2339t
Gandolfo, Anita 578
Ganley, Natalie Tholl 2340t
Gannett, Thomas M. 2341t
Garber, Charles E. 2342t
Garbett, Ann D. 579
Gardiner, Harold C. 35a, 2719r,
    2723r
Garmon, Gerald 203ed
Garner, Leona C. 2343t
Garrett, Peggy Louise 1829
Garson, Helen S., 79, 580
Gates, Fan Mayhall, 34r
Gatta, John 581
Gattuso, Josephine Florence 1830
Gay, Carolyn 2344t
Gay, Julie Lane 582, 2345t
Gelley, Alexander 54r
Geng, Veronica 583
Gentry, Marshall Bruce, 29r, 31r,
    35a, 36r, 41r, 45r, 47, 56r, 59r, 64r,
    71r, 74, 77r, 78r, 79, 80r, 81r, 584,
    585, 586, 587, 588, 589, 590, 591,
    592r, 593r, 594r, 595r, 596, 597,
    1831
George, Martha 2346t
Gerald, Kelly Suzanne 599, 2347t
Gerber, Leslie E. 2348t
Gernes, Sonia 600, 601, 602
Getz, Lorine M., 48, 49, 1832

Giannone, Richard, 50, 50a, 59, 74, 369, 603, 604, 605, 606, 607, 608, 609, 610, 611, 612, 613

Gibble, Kenneth L. 2718r

Gibbs, Jeanne Marie 2349t

Gibson, Mary Ellis, 25r, 614

Gidden, Nancy Ann 615

Gilbert, Douglas R., 45

Gilbert, Mary R. 2350t

Gilbert, Rick 616

Gilbert, Sandra M. 617

Gilbert, Susanna 617a

Giles, Paul 618

Gillan, M., 50r

Gillespie, Mary Christine 2351t

Gillespie, Michael Patrick 619

Gillikin, Sandra A. 2352t

Gilman, Richard 620, 2718r, 2720r

Gilmore, Haydn L., 16r

Gioia, Dana 376ed

Givner, Joan 928ed, 1345ed

Glazier, Michael 1610ed

Glenn, Bruce Houston 2353t

Goff, Penelope Hope 2354t

Gohdes, Clarence 621

Golden, Robert Edward 51, 1833

Goldfield, David R. 622

Goldstein, Bill 623

Gombar, Christina 624

Gonzales, Sarah 625

Goodin, Gayle 2355t

Gorak, Jan 626

Gorczyþska, Renata 2048

Gordon, Carolyn 46, 941, 2717r

Gordon, Mary 627, 628, 629, 2718r

Gordon, Sarah 24r, 42, 46r, 51a ed, 55r, 70r, 71, 74, 104a, 488, 630, 631, 632, 633, 634, 635, 636, 637, 637a, 638, 639, 640, 641, 642, 643, 644, 645, 646r, 647r, 648r, 649, 650, 780a, 1119, 1581, 1659a, 2714r

Goss, James 651, 652, 1834

Gossett, Louise Y[oung]. 17r, 19r, 20r, 23r, 24r, 52r, 76r, 653, 1835

Gossett, Thomas F. 654, 655, 2718r

Goto, Kazuhiko 2049

Gott, Fleur Marie 2356t

Goyen, William 656, 2724r

Graham, Harriet 2357t

Graham, Kenneth 2717r

Grallafent, Edward 56r

Grant, Hazel Smithco 2358t

Grant, Janet 2359t

Gratton, J. 54r

Grau, Shirley Anne 2718r

Graulich, Melody 657

Graves, James B. 65r

Graves, Kay Childers 2360t

Graves, Phyllis 33r

Graves, Robyn Anita 2361t

Gray, Dabney 658

Gray, Jeffrey 659

Gray, Mary E. 2362t

Gray, Mary Margaret Germany 2363t

Gray, Paul 660, 661, 2718r

Gray, Richard 38r, 76r, 662, 663

Greco, Joseph A. 2364t

Gregory, Donald [Lee] 21r, 1836

Green, Eddie 68a

Green, Carol Hurd 520ed

Greenberg, M. 2724r

Greenburg, Paul 664, 665

Greene, Graham 2718r

Greene, Helen I. 666

Greene, James 2717r, 2723r

Greenhouse, Karen 667

Greer, Charlotte Lou 2365t

Gregory, Donald 668

Greiff, Louis K. 669

Gresset, Michel 35a, 46, 71, 670, 2050, 2132, 2133

Gretlund, Jan Nordby 29r, 30, 45r, 70r, 79, 121ed, 156ed, 177ed, 224ed, 358ed, 442ed, 484ed, 580ed, 590ed, 671, 672, 673, 674, 675, 676, 784ed, 977ed, 1102ed, 1127ed, 1277ed, 1376ed, 1716ed, 2714r, 2718r

Griffin, Debra F. 2366t

Griffin, Joan Rae 2367t

Griffin, Julie Lynn 677

Griffin, Mary N. 1837
Griffin, Teresa E. 2368t
Griffith, A.J. 47r, 73r, 80r
Griffith, Benjamin 36r, 678, 679,
    2369t, 2716r, 2717r
Grimes, Ronald L. 680
Grimshaw, James A., Jr. 52, 681,
    682, 683
Grobel, Lawrence 684
Groover, Joel 685
Gross, Konrad 2051
Groth, Janet 2718r
Grumbach, Doris 2724
Grund, Gary R. 30r, 2717r
Gubar, Susan 617
Guest, David 686
Gulika, Therese E. 2370t
Gullason, Thomas A. 2712r
Gulley, Ervene Frances 1838
Gunn, Janet Varner 2718r
Gunton, Sharon R. 687ed, 688ed
Gurr, Charles Stephen 643ed

Habicht, Werner 2026ed
Hahn, John E. 2371t
Hair, William Ivey 690
Halio, Jay L. 356ed
Hall, Donald 691ed
Hall, Eileen 2723r
Hall, J.W. 41r
Hall, Wade 123 9ed
Hallinan, Paul J. 2715r
Hallisey, Joan F. 142ed, 734ed,
    735ed, 1300ed
Hallissy, Margaret 692
Halsall, Jalaine 693
Halvorson, Arndt 34r
Ham, Marian Ellison 1839
Hamby, Stanley O. 2372t
Hamelman, Steven 693a
Hamilton, Alex 2715r
Hamilton, Barbara Tunnicliff 694
Hamilton, Winifred Jean 1840
Hammen, Scott 695
Hampl, Patricia 696

Han, Jae-Nam 697, 1841
Hand, John Thomas 1842
Handa, Sakae 698, 699
Hanke, Toney 700
Hanks, Julie A. 2373t
Hanley, Richard Eugene 1843
Hannon, Jane 701
Hannon, Patrick 702
Hanson, Stephen L. and Patricia King
    949ed
Harada, Yuko 2052
Harding, Mary Elizabeth 2374t
Hardwick, Elizabeth 703
Hardwick, Patricia A. 2375t
Hardy, Donald E. 704, 705, 706, 707,
    708
Hardy, John Edward 709
Harlburt, Ronald E. 2376t
Harmon, Justin 710
Harmsel, Henrietta Ten 34r, 711
Harrell, Jack A. 2377t
Harris, Gary Marcel 2378t
Harris, Laurie Lanzen 688ed, 712,
    713ed
Harrison, Amelia H. 2379t
Hart, Gary Victor Wheatley 1844,
    2380t
Hart, James D. 714
Hart, Patrick 715ed, 1066ed
Hartin-Grysztar, Pamela 2381t
Hartley, Lois 20r
Hartman, Carl 2724r
Hashizume, Yumiko 716, 717, 718,
    2053, 2054, 2055
Hassan, Ihab 2724r
Hatch, Deborah Hollister 1845
Hatch, Robert 2731r
Hatcher, Lint 719
Hattori, Akio 2056, 2057, 2058, 2059
Hauser, James David 1846
Havazelet, Ehud 720
Havely, Cicely Palser 721
Havener, Sandra 68r, 2713r
Havighurst, Craig 721a
Havird, David 722
Hawkes, John 35, 46

Hawkins, George F. 2716r

Hawkins, Peter S. 45r, 53, 723, 724, 725

Hawley, James Russell 2382t

Hayes, George Marion 2383t

Haykin, Marti 726

Hays, Sandra J. 2384t

Hegarty, Charles M[ichael]. 17r, 1847

Heher, Michael E. 727, 1848

Heine, Max 728

Heller, Von Arno 71, 2060, 2061

Helmer, Shane 729

Helprin, Mark 729a

Hembree, Janice M. 2385t

Hemming, Roy 730

Hendin, Josephine 21, 731, 2718r

Hendrick, George 2718r

Hendricks, Fredric Jefferson 1849

Hendrix, Ellen Hudgins 2386t

Henson, Brian Keith 2387t

Herbkersman, Gretchen Ann 2388t

Herring, Gina 732

Herring, Linda 2389t

Herrscher, Walter 733

Hewitt, Avis 734

Hewitt, Eben 735

Heymann, C. David 736

Hibner, Stephanie 2390t

Hickey, Marcella 1053

Hicks, Granville 2715r, 2717r, 2720r, 2723r

Hiers, John T[urner]. 1194ed, 1850

Higdon, David Leon 737

Higgins, George C. 2712r

Higgs, Robert J. 738, 739

Highsmith, Dixie Lee 68a, 740

Hill, Dorothy Combs 741

Hill, Douglas 2718r

Hillis, Charlton 742

Hines, Melissa 743

Hiraishi, Takaki 2062

Hirose, Ryoichi 2063

Hirsch, David H. 246ed

Hjerter, Kathleen J. 1555

Hladky, Josef 2022ed

Hoberek, Andrew Paul 1851

Hobson, Fred C. 744, 745r, 746, 747, 748

Hobson, Linda Whitney 34r, 749, 750, 1852

Hochberg, Mark R. 1853

Hockensmith, David A. 2391t

Hodges, Elizabeth Scott 2392t

Hoffman, Arnold Roy 1854

Hoffman, Daniel 751

Hoffman, Eleanor Marie Riley 1855

Hoffman, Frederick J. 35a

Hoffman, Gerhard 2024ed

Hoffman, Nancy Y. 28r

Hogan, Kathleen Marie 2393t

Hogan, Michael 752

Hogan, Patrick G. 38r

Hogan, William 2723r

Holbrook, Nancy L.N. 2394t

Holfeltz, Heidi 753

Hollandsworth, Linda P. 754

Holloway, Phyllis 2395t

Holman, Clarence Hugh 35a, 755, 756, 757

Holmberg, Claes-Göran 2064

Holmes, John R. 758

Holsen, Ruth M. 759

Holt, Dena Novak 2396t

Homans, Michael 759a, 759b, 759c, 759d

Homic, Marie Veres 2397t

Honaker, Lisa 50r

Hoobler, Thomas 2715r

Hood, Edward M. 2715r, 2723r

Hood, Mary 760

Hook, Wilma Gene 2398t

Hooper, Brad 2713r, 2716r

Hooper, William Bradley 52r

Hopkins, Karen Jeanne 1856

Hopkins, Mary Frances 761, 762

Horn, Tamara 1857

Horton, James William 763, 1858

Horton, Mary Jane 2399t

Howard, Maureen 22ed, 764, 778ed

Howard, Rosanne 764a

Howard, Thomas 2718r

Howarth, William 765
Howe, Irving 766, 2715r
Howe, Susan Elizabeth 767
Howell, Elmo 768
Howell, Sarah Winborne 2400t
Howie, Elizabeth 2401t
Howland, Bette 2718r
Hubbard, Marion Stevens 1859
Hubert, Linda 769
Hubert, Thomas 2718r
Hudson, Lesley M. 2402t
Huelsbeck, Charles J. 23r, 2720r
Huff, Carol Czarowitz 2403t
Hughes, Amanda Millay 2404t
Hughes, Richard E. 770
Hughes, Riley 2715r, 2717r
Hulbert, Ann 36r, 2712r
Hulbert, Dan 771
Hulick, Diana Emery 772
Humphries, Jefferson 35, 54, 773,
    774, 775, 1860
Hunter, Anna C. 2723r
Hunter, Eileen Marie 1861
Hunter, Shaun Megan 2405t
Hurd, Myles Raymond 776
Hurlbert, Ronald E. 2406t
Hurst, Mary Jane 777
Hutchinson, Mary Jo 2407t
Huttar, Charles A. 16r
Hyman, Stanley Edgar 22, 778, 2715r
Hynes, Joseph 779

Idol, John L. 15r, 27r, 780, 2712r
Inge, M. Thomas 340ed, 432ed
Inge, Tonette Bond 781ed
Ingram, Forrest L. 782
Inoue, Ichiro 2065, 2066, 2067, 2068,
    2069
Inoue, Kazuko 2070
Ireland, Patrick J. 79, 783, 784
Irving, Catherine Janet Sarah 2407at
Irving, Janet 785
Isaac, Colleen M. 2408t
Isaacs, Alisa Kristine 2409t
Issenhuth, Jean-Pierre 2071

Itoh, Sachiko 2072
Iwayama, Tajiro 2073, 2074

Jackson, Alice Britt 2410t
Jackson, Catherine 2720r
Jackson, O. Kay 785a
Jacobi, Laura 2411t
Jacobs, Robert Alan 2412t
Jacobsen, Josephine 786
Jamieson, Janis L. 2413t
Janowski, Lawrence 788
Janssen, Marian 789
Jarman, Mark 790
Jarrett, Beverly 791
Jarvis, Thea 792, 793
Jasnowski, Tony 794
Jasper, David 1271
Jauss, David 795
Jayko, Elizabeth M. 2414t
Jefferson, Douglas 721ed
Jeffrey, David K. 220ed, 796, 1126ed
Jenkins, Keith A. 47r
Jensen, Gendron 797
Jensen, Joseph E. 18r
Jevens, Lisa 798
Jewell, Elizabeth 799
Jimenez, Nilda 2415t
Johansen, Ruthann Knechel 35a, 55,
    800, 1862
Johnson, Bud 2723r
Johnson, Christiane 178ed
Johnson, Greg 800a, 800b
Johnson, Ira. D. 178ed
Johnson, Mark 801
Johnson, Rhonda Eugene, Jr. 1863
Johnson, Rob 802, 1864
Johnson, William Lawrence 1865
Johnston, Carol Ann 2416t
Joiner, Dorothy M. 157ed
Joiner, Lawrence D. 24r
Jones, A. Alling 63r, 338
Jones, Bartlett C. 71
Jones, Dale Wayne 1866
Jones, Madison 30, 68a, 803, 804
Jones, Phillip 804a

Jones, Sonya 805
Jordan, Michael 65r, 67r, 806
Jordan, Patrick 69r, 2721r
Jordan, Rene 2715r
Jordis, Christine 2075
Jorgenson, Eric 807
Julienne, Marietta Lenear 2417t
Justice, Dana Alan 2418t

Kadlecek, Jo 808
Kahane, Claire Katz 27r, 35a, 46, 71, 80r, 809, 810, 811, 812, 813, 814, 815, 1867
Kane, Jennifer 2419t
Kane, Patricia 2715r
Kane, Richard 815
Kaplan, Carola 816
Kaplan, Fred 817ed
Kaplan, Steven 388ed
Karam, Sharon 818
Kares, Julie L. 2420t
Karl, Frederick R. 819, 820
Karpinski, Joanne B. 1379ed
Kass, Jerome 821
Kastleman, Linda Craven 2421t
Katz, Claire. *See* Kahane, Claire Katz
Katz, Steven Alex 1868
Kaufman, Linda Jean Watson 2422t
Kaufman, Stanley 2731r
Kazin, Alfred 46, 822, 823, 824, 2712r
Keane, Melinda 1869
Keates, Jonathan 2718r
Keessen, Jan 1870
Kehl, D.G. 825, 826
Kehrer, Grace S. 2423t
Keillor, Garrison 583
Kelber, Barbara Neault 1871
Keller, Jane Carter 1872
Keller, Karen 827
Kellogg, Jean D. 20r, 2720r
Kelly, Brenda Kane 2424t
Kelly, Darlene 70r, 2714r
Kelly, Janet Laura 2425t
Kelly, Patrick 68r, 2713r

Kelminson, Hannah L. 1382ed
Keneas, Alex 2731r
Kennedy, Arthur L. 828
Kennedy, Eileen 18r
Kennedy, J. Gerald 546, 829
Kennedy, Lisa Ann 2426t
Kennelly, Laura B. 74, 79r, 830
Kenney, Catherine 50r, 73r
Kent, Carol Fleisher 1873
Kerr, Robert Lansing 2427t
Kerth, Thomas R. 2428t
Kessler, Edward 35a, 56, 71
Ketchin, Susan 831, 832
Khawaja, Mabel 832a
Kidd, Harriet 833
Kidd, John 1068
Kiell, Norman 834
Kiely, Robert J. 835, 2715r
Kiernan, Robert 836
Kikkawa, Junichi 837
Kilcourse, George 838, 839, 840
Kiley, Frederick S. 2723r
Kilmer, Anne 841
Kim, Chrysostom 842
Kim, Kyung-Im 2076
Kimball, Sue Leslie 367ed
Kimishima, Kazuko 2077
Kimmey, John L. 843
Kimura, Masatoshi 2078
Kimura, Yasuo 2079
King, Chris Savage 844, 2712r
King, Josephine 845r
King, Kimberly 2429t
King, Liane C. 2430t
King, Richard 38r, 846, 847
King, Robert W. 848
King, Thomas Mulvihill 849
Kinnebrew, Mary Jane 850, 1874
Kinney, Arthur F. 36r, 56r, 57, 79r, 851, 852, 853, 854
Kipp, Dorothy Hawes 2431t
Kirk, Russell 2714r
Kirkland, William M. 855
Kirkpatrick, D.L. 756ed, 757ed, 856ed
Kirsch, Jonathan 45r

Kisawadkorn, Kriengsak 1875
Kissel, Susan Steves 857, 1876
Klein, Michael 858
Klein-Lataud, Christine 2032r
Kleinmaier, Carol Allison 2432t
Kleppe, Sandra Lee 858a, 859
Klevar, Harvey Lee 860, 1877
Klinkowitz, Jerome 861, 862
Klug, M.A. 71, 863
Knapp, Bettina L. 864
Knauer, David J. 41r, 55r, 78r, 865,
    866
Knippenberg, Joseph M. 1332ed
Knutson, Linda 2433t
Knutson, Roslyn Lander 867
Koch, Claude 868
Kochanek, Patricia S. 1878
Koelb, Clayton 869
Koenenn, Connie 870
Kohman, Joan 2434t
Kolar, Carol Koehmstedt 871
Kolb, Harold H., Jr. 872
Kolek, Leszek S. 1426ed
Kolin, Phillip 873ed
Kolodny-Creech, Mary Ruth 2435t
Kondo, Tadashi 2080
Koon, G.W. 80r, 874
Koon, William 29r, 38r, 51r, 76r, 875
Koontz, Christian 876
Koster, Donald N. 877
Kowalewski, Michael John 39r, 878,
    879, 1879
Kraft, Stephanie 880
Kramer, Victor A. 903ed
Kretzoi, Charlotte 973ed
Kreyling, Michael 58, 126ed, 218ed,
    881, 882, 883, 1702ed
Krickel, Edward 16r
Kuehl, John 884
Kugelmann, Robert 885
Kumin, Maxine 886
Kumskova, E.I. 2081
Kunkel, Francis L. 887
Kurmmel, Fusako 888
Kusaka, Yosuke 889, 2082, 2083
Kwon, Jong Joon 2084

Labrie, Ross 890
Lackey, Allen D. 1880
LaCoste, André Pierre 1881
LaFarge, Oliver 2724r
Lally, Joan Marie 2436t
Lamontagne, Marie-Andrée 2085
Landy, Robert 891
Lane, Belden C. 892
Lanehart, Wendy L. 2437t
Lang, John 893
Langan, Colleen P. 2438t
Langford, Roberta Brodie 1882
Langland, Elizabeth 894
Langman, Larry 895
Larsen, [William] Val 896, 897, 1883
Lask, Thomas 2712r
Lasseter, Victor 898, 899
Lasswell, Margaret W. 2440t
Lasworth, Laura 899a
Latham, Don Loftis 2441t
Lauby, Jacqueline 1884, 2442t
Laveggi, Lucile 2086
Lavin, Mary J.W. 2443t
LaVois, Caroline F. 2444t
Lawler, Peter Augustine 1332ed
Lawson, Lewis A[llen]. 20ed, 35,
    39r, 65r, 451ed, 565, 566, 900, 901,
    902, 903ed, 1343ed, 1885, 2715r
Lazenbatt, W[illiam]. W[alter].
    G[eorge]. 1886
Leamon, Warren 21r, 2718r
Leary, Lewis 856, 904
Leaver, James Marshall 1887
LeBlanc, Ann McInnis 2445t
Leckey, Dolores 905
LeClair, Thomas 906
Le Clézio, J.M.G. 71
Lee, A. Robert 36r
Lee, Hermione 2718r
Lee, Maryat 907
Lee, Michael John 1888
Lee, Tracy Ann 2446t
Lesser, Cynthia Lee 2447t
Leeson, Richard Martin 1889
Leitch, Addison H. 908
Leitch, Thomas M. 909

Leithauser, Brad 910, 2716r
Leon, Philip W. 911
Leonard, Douglas Novich 912, 912
Leonard, Joan 69r, 913, 1890, 2721r
Leonard, John 2718r, 2720r
Lesgoirres, Daniel 2087
Lester, Mary 2448t
Levine, Paul 2715r, 2723r, 2724r
Levy, Andrew 915
Lévy, Maurice 71, 2088
Lewellen, Alice D. 2449t
Lewis, R.W.B. 2724r
Lhamon, W.T., Jr. 916, 917
Lindberg-Seyersted, Brita 27r
Lindroth, James R. 918
Lindsey, William D. 919, 920, 2450t
Lineham, Thomas M. 921
Link, Franz 2089, 2189
Little, Anne C. 471
Litz, Walton 1700ed
Liu, Dilin 922, 1891
Livingstone, David 2718r
Lloyd, Eric 2715r
Loder, Kurt 1464, 1465
Logan, Jan H. 923
Lodge, David 2723r
Logsdon, Loren 59ed, 136ed, 368ed,
    369ed, 608ed, 925ed
Lohafer, Susan 909ed, 1214ed,
    1696ed
Long, J.V. 924
Lonnquist, Barbara C. 59, 925
Loomis, Jeffrey B. 926
Lopez, Enrique Hank 927, 928
Lorentzen, Mel 45r
Lotts, Chris 2451t
Louit, Robert 2090
Love, Betty Boyd 929
Lowe, Desiree Keena 2452t
Lower, Jacquelyn D. 2453t
Lowry, Beverly 1653
Lubin, Alice Mary 1892
Lucas, James Lavard 1893
Luddy, Thomas E. 18r
Ludwig, Dale Leslie 1894
Ludwig, Richard M. 930ed

Ludwin, Deanna L. Kern 931, 2454t
Lukas, Dorothy A. 2455t
Luker, Ralph E. 932
Lulling, Thomas William 2456t
Lundmark, Leonard 933
Lutyens, Elizabeth 2457t
Lyle, Michael L. 2458t
Lynch, John A. 2717r
Lynn, Denise D. 2459t
Lyons, Bonnie 50r, 934
Lyons, Grant 935
Lyra, F. 2127
Lytle, Andrew 936

MacDonald, Sara Jane 1895
MacKethan, Lucinda H. 937, 938,
    939
Macksey, Richard 2718r
MacSween, R.J. 2718r
Macys, Valerie [Denise] 42r, 1896
Madden, David 231ed
Maddux, Stephen 940
Maeda, Ayako 2091
Maffini, William L. 2460t
Magee, Rosemary M[cCausland].
    1ed, 68ed, 69r, 99ed, 941ed, 1897,
    2721r
Magill, Frank N. 445ed, 529ed,
    579ed, 596ed, 942ed, 943ed,
    944ed, 945ed, 946ed, 947ed,
    948ed, 949ed, 1718ed
Magistrale, Tony [Anthony Samuel]
    950, 951, 952, 953, 954, 955, 956,
    1898
Magliola, Robert 957, 958
Mahoney, Elizabeth P. 2461t
Mahoney, Margaret Ellen 1899
Maida, Patricia D. 959
Mainiero, Lina 286ed
Mairs, Nancy 959a
Makowski, Elizabeth 960
Makowsky, Veronica A. 961
Male, Roy R. 962
Malin, Irving 18r, 22r, 35a, 46,
    911ed, 963

Mallard, William 964

Mallon, Anne Marie [G.] 29r, 38r, 57r, 65r, 69r, 76r, 965, 1900, 2721r

Maloff, Saul 19r, 46, 2712r, 2715r, 2720r

Malone, Carol J. 2462t

Maloney, Anne M. 966

Mann, Susan Garland 967

Manning, Carol S. 170ed

Mannis, Andrea 1901

Mannmeusel, Susanne Maria 2463t

Mano, D. Keith 2720r

Mariani, Paul 968, 969, 970r, 971

Marinovich, Sarolta 972, 973

Marks, Gregory Angelo 2464t

Marks, Margaret Louise 1902

Marks, W.S., III, 30

Marlowe, Jeanne A. 2465t

Maroney, Janet M. 2466t

Marovitz, Sanford E. 621

Marre, Diana Katherine 2467t

Marschel, Jacqueline A. 2468t

Marshall, Donald R. 2469t

Marshall, John David 2717r

Marston, Jane 974

Martelli, R. 2092

Martin, Carter W[illiams]. 10ed, 23, 30, 35a, 69ed, 79, 975, 976, 977, 978, 1903

Martin, Graham 721ed

Martin, Jean Colvin 2470t

Martin, Judith 2731r

Martin, Karl Edward 979, 980, 1904

Martin, Regis 59a, 981, 982, 983

Martin, W.R. 984, 985

Martinez, Inez 986

Martyn, J. Louis 987

Marx, Lesley 785ed

Maschinot, Michael 988

Mason, Michael 989, 2731r

Massey, Marilyn Chapin 2718r

Matchen, David E. 149, 990

Matchette, William A. 2471t

Matchie, Thomas Frederick 991, 1905

Mathews, Marsha Caddell 1906

Matsudaira, Yoko 2092a, 2093, 2093a, 2094, 2095, 2095a

Matsumoto, Fusae 992, 993, 2096, 2097, 2098, 2099

Matthews, Moria 2472t

Matvejeva, E.U. 2169ed

Mauck, Deanne 2473t

May, Elizabeth V. 1907

May, John R. 29r, 30r, 52r, 60, 994, 995, 996, 997, 998, 999, 1000r, 1001r, 1002, 1470, 2718r

Mayberry, Susan Neal 1003

Mayer, Charles W. 59ed, 136ed, 238ed, 369ed, 608ed, 925ed, 1004

Mayer, David R[obert]. 61, 1005, 1006, 1007, 1008, 1009, 1010, 1011, 1012, 1013, 1014, 1909, 2474t

Mayer, Suzanne 1015, 1016

Mayhew, Alice 2715r

Mayhew, Leonard F.X. 2724r

McAlexander, Hubert H. 1017

McAllister, Jean Smith 1910

McBride, Anne Keeler 1018, 2475t

McBride, Mary 19r, 60r, 62r, 1019

McBrien, William 29r

McCaffrey, Karen 2476t

McCaffery, Larry 1020ed

McCarthy, Coleman 1021

McClain, Laurence Lee 1911

McClave, Heather 1067ed

McCombs, Phil 1022

McCord, Andrew 503

McCorduck, Pamela 2712r

McCorkle, Jill 1023

McCormick, Patrick 1023a

McCown, James H. 1024

McCullagh, James Charles 1912, 2477t

McDermott, John V. 1025, 1026, 1027, 1028, 1029

McDonald, Henry 1030, 2716r

McDonald, Russ 1031

McDonnell, Thomas P. 1032

McDowell, Frederick P.W. 17r, 19r, 21r, 2712r, 2720r

McElderry, B.R. 23r
McEntyre, Marilyn Chandler 1033
McFague, Sallie 1034
McFall, Todd A. 2478t
McFarland, Dorothy Tuck 35a, 62, 1470
McFee, Michael 1035
McGifford, Diane 38r, 63r, 76r, 1036
McGinnis, Karla Ann 2479t
McGowan, Cecilia 1037
McGrath, Mary Angeline 2480t
McGurl, Katherine A. 2481t
McHaney, Thomas L. 63r
McInerny, Ralph M. 65r, 1038, 1039, 1040, 2716r, 2720r
McIntyre, Lynda Greene 2482t
McKenzie, Barbara 63, 1041, 1042, 1043, 1044, 1045
McKeon, Zahava 1046
McKinney, Margaret Jordan 2483t
McKnight, Carol Lynn 2484t
McLellan, Amy Louise 1047
McLevie, Elaine Marianne 1913
McMahon, Patrick 1048
McMillan, Norman R. 1049, 1050, 1051
McMillan, Peter Aidan James 1914
McMullen, Joanne Halleran 35a, 64, 1052, 1915
McNamee, M.B. 29r
McNiff, John 1053
McPherson, William 2718r
McShane, Zita M. 1916, 2485t
McSharry, Kathleen Jeanne 1917
Means, Spencer 1599
Meehan, Elizabeth 1053a
Meek, Kristen 1054
Meese, Elizabeth A. 1055
Mehl, Duane Paul 1056, 1918
Meindl, Dieter 1056a
Mellard, James M. 36r, 53r, 54r, 58, 1057, 1058, 1059, 1060, 1061
Meloy, J. Reid 258
Melville, Annabelle M. 1062, 2718r
Mendelson, Phyllis Carmel 1324ed
Mendez, Constance Wagner 2486t

Menendez, Albert J. 1063
Mengert, George King 1919
Menides, Laura Jehn 1064
Méras, Phyllis 1065
Mercier, Vivian 2723r
Merdian, Patricia Vera DerMotta 2487t
Merryday, Ann-Jo 2488t
Merton, Thomas 46, 1066, 1067
Mesner, Susan 379ed
Meurs, Jos Van 1068
Meyer, Alvis 1069
Meyer, William E.H., Jr. 1070, 1071, 1072, 1073, 1074, 1075
Meyering, Sheryl L. 73r
Meyers, Bertrande 1076, 1077
Michael, Marion C. 459ed
Michaels, J. Ramsey 45r, 1078, 1079
Middleton, David L. 1080, 1081
Milder, Robert 1082
Miller, Audrey I. 2489t
Miller, Lynn 192
Miller, Marcia 2490t
Miller, Nolan 2718r, 2723r
Mills, Elizabeth M. 2491t
Mills, Jerry Leath 1083, 1084
Mills, William 1085
Ming, Zhong 1086
Mintz, Edward N. 2712r
Mitchell, Garry 1087
Mitchell, Timothy A. 26r
Miyamoto, Keiko 2100, 2101
Mizener, Arthur 2723r
Moddelmog, Debra A. 1088
Mogen, David 1089, 1379ed
Mohr, Eric Simpson 1920
Moirai, Catherine Risingflame 1090, 2718r
Mongin, Oliver 2102
Monroe, William F. 68r, 1091, 1092, 1093, 1093a, 2713r
Monteiro, George 59r, 1094
Montgomery, Elizabeth Luckett
McGowan 1921

Montgomery, Marion 16r, 20r, 22r, 65, 66, 67, 79, 1095, 1096, 1097, 1098, 1099, 1100, 1101, 1102, 1103, 1104, 1105, 1106, 1107, 1108, 1109, 1110, 1111, 1112, 1113, 1114, 1115, 1116, 1117, 1118, 1119

Moody, Minnie Hite 2720r

Moore, Arthur J. 2718r

Moore, Brian [Lee] 1120, 1921a

Moore, Carol Craft 2492t

Moore, Donald Lee 1922

Moore, Jeffrey Scott 2493t

Moore, Lofton Samuel 2494t

Moore, Susan 1121, 2718r

Moore, Terilyn Joy 2495t

Moose, Ruth 1122

Moorer, Frank E. 2718r

Moran, Annette Jean 1923

Morefield, Kenneth Robert 1924

Morgan, Neill Sagen 2496t

Morita, Akiharu 2103

Morita, Takeshi 2104

Morley, Irene 2497t

Morressy, John 2720r

Morris, Gregory L. 132

Morris, Helen 1182ed

Morris, Mason Thomas 2498t

Morris, Michael N. 2499t

Morris, Robert K. 911ed

Morris, Robin Heather 2500t

Morris, William E. 314

Morrison, Linda Kaye McCloud 2501t

Morse, Pamela 1123

Mortimer, Gail 47r

Morton, Mary L[ambert]. 19r, 29r, 52r, 54r, 63r, 71, 76r, 1124, 1125, 1925

Mosher, Rachel Jennifer 2502t

Moss, William M. 1126

Mott, Sara 79, 1127

Moynahan, Julian 2715r

Muggeridge, Malcolm 2715r

Mulder, Karen 1129

Mullane, Deirdre K. 2503t

Mullen, Christopher 1129a

Muller, Gilbert H[enry]. 24, 1470, 1926

Mulrain, Mary 2504t

Muncy, Emily Maxwell 2505t

Munk, Linda 1130, 1131

Munson, Barbara Faye 1927

Murphy, Brenda C. 2506t

Murphy, Carol R. 1132

Murphy, George D. 1133

Murphy, Gregory Joseph 2507t

Murphy, John J. 1134

Murphy, Michael P. 2508t

Mutkowski, Barbara E[ileen]. 18r, 19r, 1928

Muþina, Matej 79, 1135, 1136

Myers, David A. 71, 1137

Myers, Michael 1138

Myrick, Susan 2723r

Nagatake, Yuko 2105

Nagle, Kathryn L. 2509t

Napier, James J. 1139, 1140, 1141, 1142, 1143, 1144

Nas, Loes 785ed

Nash, Charles C. 36r

Nash, Jay Robert 1145

Natoli, Joseph 1146

Nault, Clifford A., Jr. 930ed

Navarro, Mary Louise 1929

Neder, Carolyn Maria 2510t

Neligan, Patrick, Jr. 1147

Nelson, Bobbe Smith 2511t

Nelson, Edward B. 1148, 1149, 1150

Nelson, Elizabeth R. 23r, 2720r

Nesbitt, Laurel 1150a

Neubauer, Alexander 1151

Neuleib, Janice Witherspoon 1152

Newburger, Laurie Gurney 1930

Newcomer, Grace G. 2512t

Newkirk, Terrye 2513t

Newman, Georgia Ann 1154, 1930a, 2514t

Newman, William S. 2515t

Nichols, Ellen A. 2516t

Nichols, Loxley Fitzpatrick 70r, 1156, 1157, 1158, 1159, 2517t, 2714r
Nicosia, James 2518t
Niederauer, George H. 1160
Nielsen, Erik 1161, 2106, 2107, 2108, 2109, 2110
Nielson, Kathleen Buswell 2519t
Nifong, D. Michael 1162
Niimi, Sumiko 2111
Niland, Kurt R. 1163
Nilsen, Don Lee Fred 1164
Nishikawa, Ryosuke 2112
Nisly, L. Lamar 1931
Nisly, Paul W[ayne]. 18r, 27r, 45r, 52r, 65r, 71r, 1165, 1166, 1167, 1168, 1169, 1170, 1171, 1932
Noble, Donald R. 63r, 796, 1172, 2718r
Noguchi, Hajime 2113, 2114, 2115, 2116, 2117, 2118, 2119, 2120, 2121
Nolan, Mary Lou 1173
Nolin, Jennifer E. 2520t
Nomura, Shizu 2122
Nordloh, David J. 2127ed
Norman, Geoffrey 1174, 2717r
Norman, Linda Carol 2521t
Norris, Hoke 2724r
Norris, Trudy Peterson 2522t
Norton, Jody 1175
Norton, Paige L. 2523t
Nowell-Smith, Geoffrey 2731r
Noya, José Liste 1176
Noyles, Tom 78r
Nuñez, Victor 1147
Nunley, Thelma G. 2524t
Nuwer, Hank 1177
Nye, Robert 2724r
Nye, Valerie 75a, 1177a, 1177b
Nylinder, Ake 2123
Nyren, Dorothy 1178, 2723r

Oates, Joyce Carol 35, 1179, 1180, 1181, 2715r, 2720r

Oberhausen, Tammy L. 2525t
Obriant, Don 2716r
O'Brien, Conan Christopher 2526t
O'Brien, David 2718r
O'Brien, Geoffrey 1182ed
O'Brien, John Thomas 2527t
O'Brien, William J. 45r
Ochi, Hiromi 2124, 2125
Ochshorn, Kathleen G. 1184
O'Connell, Mary Rose 2528t
O'Connor, Flannery 1, 2, 3, 4, 5, 6, 7, 8, 9, 10, 11, 12, 13, 14, 68, 68a, 69, 70, 1185, 1186, 1187, 1188, 1189, 1190, 1191, 1192, 1193, 1194
O'Connor, Margaret Anne 1195
O'Connor, Patricia 1196
O'Dell, Margaret Darlene 2529t
O'Donnell, Patrick 1200
Oe, Kenzaburo 1201
Ogawa, Yumiko 2530t
Ohashi, Kichinosuke 2126
O'Keefe, Mary E. 2531t
Okeke-Ezigbo, Emeka 1203
Oktenberg, Adrian 2718r
Oleksy, Elzbieta H. 451ed
Oleneva, Valentia 2127
Oliver, Bill 1204, 1205, 1933
Oliver, LaTrelle Blackburn 2532t
Olivero, Mary F. 2533t
Ollman, Leah 1206
Olschner, Leonard M. 1207
Olson, Barbara Kruse 1934
Olson, Charles J. 1935
Olson, Steven 1208
O'Mara, Phil 1209
Ontiveros, Benjamin 2534t
Opdahl, Keith 1211
Oram, Richard W. 1212
Oreovicz, Cheryl Z. 1213
O'Rourke, William 1214
Orr, John 1215
Orvell, Miles D[avid]. 20r, 23r, 25, 47r, 70r, 1936, 2714r, 2718r, 2720r
Osada, Mitsunobu 2128
Osborn, Chris 1216
Osborne, Linda Payne 1217

Osborne, William 1420ed
O'Shea, José Roberto Basto 1937
Osinski, Bill 1218, 1218a, 1219
Osteen, Kathy 2535t
Ostermann, Robert 2715r
Ostrander, Betty 1220
Ostrow, Eileen Joyce 2536t
Otake, Masaru 2129
Ouzts, Cuyler E. 2537t
Owen, Nancy 339
Owens, Collie 1221
Owens, Mitchell 1222
Owens, Virginia Stem 1223
Ower, John 1224
Oxendine, Debbie Hutchinson 2538t
Oxford, Virginia 2718r
Ozaki, Shunsuke 1225
Ozer, Jerome S. 1226

Pace, Barbara 1227
Pachmuss, Temira 1228
Padgett, Thomas Eugene, Jr. 1938
Paige, Linda Rohrer 1229
Palmer, Louis H., III, 1230
Palms, Rosemary Helen Grebin 1939
Parini, Jay 1231
Park, Clara Claiborne 1232, 1233
Park, Kerry L. 2539t
Parker, Peter 1234ed
Parker, Susan 1235
Parks, Cynthia 1236
Parks, John G. 1237
Parlato, Salvatore J., Jr. 1238
Parrish, Tim 1239
Passaro, Vince 1240, 2723r
Pastva, Agnes Ann 2718r
Patrick, Anne E. 48r
Patterson, Elizabeth Linda 2540t
Patterson, Kathleen Anne 1940
Patterson, Margaret C. 1241, 1242
Patterson, Tom 1243, 1244
Pattillo, Manning M., Jr. 1462ed
Paulson, Suzanne Morrow 71, 74, 1246, 1941
Payne, David H. 1247, 1248

Payne, Ladell 1249
Payne, Nancy 1250
Payne, Pamela Wood 2541t
Peacock, Claire R. 2542t
Pearre, Howell 2720r
Pearson, Michael 1251, 1252, 1253, 1254
Peat, Isie 1255
Peerman, Dan 2724r
Peffer, Mary Cecilia 2543t
Pelfrey, David 1256
Penkala, Rosemary A. 2544t
Pepin, Ronald E. 1257
Pepper, Sheila 51r
Pepperdene, Margaret W. 1258
Percy, Walker 1259
Percy, Will 1260
Perisho, Steve 1261
Permut, Joanna Baumer 1262
Perrin, Elaine 2545t
Perry, Keith Ronald 2546t
Perunilam, Thomas Varkey 1942
Petersen, Marc Andreis 2547t
Petry, Alice Hall 50r, 1263ed, 1264, 1265, 1266, 1267, 1268, 1269
Pfeffer, Genevieve 2548t
Phelan, Carolyn 33r
Phillips, D.Z. 1270, 1271, 1272
Phillips, Elizabeth Ann Aycock 2549t
Phillips, K.J. 1273
Phillips, Robert 2718r
Phinney, Carmen Sandra 2550t
Pici, Frances Anne 1274
Pickett, T.H. 65r, 67r
Pickrel, Paul 2723r
Pieiller, Evelyne 2130
Pierce, Constance 1275
Pierce, Jacklyn R. 2551t
Pierson, Marye 2552t
Pilkington, Joyce Elaine 2553t
Pinnow, Jon 2554t
Piper, Wendy 1943, 2555t
Pitavy, François 1276, 1277
Pitts, Kathy Jean Root 1944
Podorva, L.G. 2169ed
Poe, Harry L. 34r

Poe, Jan E. 1945
Pogue, Mary Beth 2556t
Poirier, Richard 35a, 46, 2715r
Polette, Keith 1278
Polk, Noël 80r
Pollard, A. 53r
Pollard, Carol 1544
Polter, Julie 1279
Poore, Charles 2715r
Pope, Robert 1280
Pope, Tilloretta Mitchell 2557t
Portch, Stephen Ralph 1281, 1282, 1946
Porter, Katherine Anne 46, 941
Porter, Kathleen Sullivan 1283
Powell, Larry 2712r, 2716r, 2718r
Powers, Douglas 1284, 1285
Pratt, Mary Louise 1286
Pratt, William 1287
Praz, Mario 2717r
Prenshaw, Peggy Whitman 1288ed,
Prescott, Orville 2717r, 2723r
Prescott, Peter S. 2712r
Prestianni, Vincent 1289
Preston, Howard L. 436ed
Price, Reynolds 1653
Price, R.G.G. 2717r
Pridgeon, Cheryl Jean Evans 1947
Pritchard, Alice S. 2558t
Pritchard, William H. 1290
Pritchett, Victor Sawdon 1291, 2715r
Prochnow, Thomas Herbert 2559t
Profitt, Jennifer H. 1291a
Provost, Glen John 2560t
Prown, Katherine Hemple 1292, 1948, 2561t
Prunty, Wyatt 1293
Pryce-Jones, Alan 2715r
Psyhos, Rebecca Ruth 2562t
Pudas, Stacie J. 2563t
Pulleine, Tim 2731r
Putnam, Thomas Wells 2564t
Pylate, Julia Candis 2565t
Pyle, Norma S. 2566t
Pyron, Darden Asbury 1294
Pyron, Virginia 1295

Querengesser, Neil 2567t
Quinn, Edward 39r
Quinn, J[ohn] J[ames]. 15r, 19r, 25r, 38r, 45r, 60r, 72ed, 1949, 2712r, 2715r, 2720r, 2723r
Quinn, M. Bernetta 35a, 71, 1296, 2715r
Quirk, Tom 1297

Rabasca, Iris Conchita 1950
Racky, Donald Joseph, Jr. 1951
Ragan, Sam 1298
Ragen, Brian Abel 29r, 35r, 36r, 39r, 46r, 47r, 50r, 56r, 73, 1299, 1300, 1301, 1952
Rahv, Philip 1302
Rainey, Carol A. 2568t
Rainey, David E. 2569t
Rajec, Elizabeth M. 1303
Randles, Beverly Schlack 1304
Rannik, Stacey Ann 2570t
Ransom, Wayne Fletcher 2571t
Rash, Ronald 67r, 1305r
Rasi, Humberto M. 1353
Rast, John Wesley 1953
Rath, Sura Prasad 47r, 72r, 74ed, 536ed, 606ed, 630ed, 1306, 1307, 1308, 1309, 1310, 1311r, 1312, 1313, 1315ed, 1701ed
Rawal, Suresh 2572t
Rawlings, Peter 58r
Ray, Donald Louis 1954
Rayburn, Kellie Renee 2573t
Raymond, John 2718r
Rea, Paul W[esley]. 1955
Reardon, Patrick Henry 18r
Rechnitz, Robert Max 1956
Redmon, Anne 1314
Reed, Eva Laurie 2574t
Reel, Madeleine W. 2575t
Reem, Craig 1314a, 1314b
Reesman, Jeanne Campbell 35a, 74, 1315
Reeves, Joseph MacDonald 1957
Reeves, Rhonda 2576t

Reeves, Thomas 2722r

Regan, Robert 1316

Regin, Patsy K. 2577t

Reisman, Rosemary M. Canfield
     1317

Reiter, Robert E. 26

Renner, Stanley 1319

Reuman, Ann E. 1320

Reynolds, Hilary 2715r

Reynolds, Michael M. 1321ed

Reynolds, Guy 1320a

Rhinehart, Susan 2578t

Rhodes, Royal 53r

Rich, Frank 1322, 2731r

Richard, Claude 71, 2131, 2132,
     3133

Richard, Nora Ellen 2579t

Riddick, Estelle B. 2580t

Ridge, Donna Rebecca 2581t

Rigaud, Marielle 2134

Riis, Torben 2135

Riley, Carolyn 1323ed, 1324ed

Riley, Eleanor M. 2582t

Riley, Jennifer 2583t

Rinaldi, Angelo 2136, 2137

Riso, Don 1325

Ritchason, Shelly J. 1958

Rivard, Virginia 2584t

Rivière, Jean 2041r

Ro, Sigmund 558ed

Roark, Dorothy Walker 2585t

Robbins, J. Albert 862ed

Roberson, Julie Ann 2585at

Roberts, Bonita Koehler 2586t

Roberts, Diane 80r, 1326

Roberts, Holly 2587t

Robertson, Roxzana 2588t

Robertson, William 2716r

Robinson, Ella 1327

Robinson, Gabriele Scott 1328

Robinson, Margaret 2589t

Robison, James C. 1329

Rocco, Claire Joyce 1959

Rochette-Crawley, Susan Marie 1960

Rodgers, Audrey T. 1330

Rogal, Samuel J. 1331

Rogers, W.G. 2723r

Roller, David C. 131ed

Rommel, Lylas Dayton 2590t

Roos, John 1332, 1333

Root, Kathy Jean 1961

Roper, Shannon 2591t

Rosa, Alfred F. 1334

Rosarossa, Maria Alejandra 2138

Rose, Alan Henry 1335

Rosenberger, Coleman 2723r

Rosenblum, Joseph 1336

Rosenfeld, Isaac 2724r

Ross, Cheri Louise 1337

Ross, Stanley Ralph 1145

Rota, Charles David 1962

Rout, [Kay] Kathleen Joan Kinsella
     1338, 1339, 1963

Rowe, Anne 55r

Rowley, Rebecca K. 1340

Rowse, A.L. 2720r

Roy, Claude 2139, 2140

Roy, Paula A. 1341

Rubin, Louis D., Jr. 46, 71, 127,
     222ed, 653ed, 1119, 1342, 1343,
     1344, 1345, 1493ed, 1712ed,
     2715r, 2717r

Ruggles, Robert David 2592t

Ruiz, José M. 2034ed

Ruoff, Gene W. 25r

Rusch, Frederik L. 1146

Russ, Don[ald Devere] 1346, 1964

Russell, Henry M.W. 1347

Russell, Mary F. 2593t

Russell, Shannon 1348

Rutherford, Marjory 2723r

Rutledge, Chris 2594t

Ryan, Elizabeth Shreve 1349

Ryan, Maureen 34r, 50r

Ryan, Steven T. 1350

Ryken, Leland 908ed, 1189ed

Saal, Rollene W. 22r

Sadler, Lynn Veach 367ed

Saji, Takeshi 2141, 2142

Salem, James M. 1351

Salibrici, Gary D. 2595t
Salomone, John L. 2595at
Salter, Mary Jo 2716r
Salvia, Jane 1570
Salzman, Jack 1352ed
Sample, Carol 1353
Samuels, Charles T. 2720r
Samuelson, Todd 1354
Samway, Patrick H. 1355
Sanders, Andrea 1356
Sanders, Diane 2596t
Sanders, Scott Patrick 1379ed
Sanoff, Alvin P. 1357
Santraud, Jeanne-Marie 1664ed
Sarcone, Elizabeth 1713ed
Sarris, Andrew 2731r
Sato, Haruo 2143
Sato, Hiroko 2115r
Sato, Kenichi 2144
Satterfield, Ben 1358
Saunders, James Robert 1359, 1360
Saunders, Joan Lindsay 2597t
Saunders, Kay 75
Saussier, Corinne Madeline 2598t
Savitsky, Helen Ann 2599t
Sayers, Valerie 1361
Scafidel, James R. 1363
Scalia, Linda F. 2600t
Scambray, Terry A. 2601t
Schaap, James C. 53r
Schaarschmidt, Gunter 1228ed
Schanche, Don 1364
Schaub, Thomas Hill 31r, 1365
Schaum, Konrad 920ed
Schaum, Mariane Wurst 2602t
Scheick, William J. 30, 1366
Schellenberg, Susan 1367
Schemmel, William "Bill" 1368, 1369, 1370, 1371
Schenck, Mary Jane 30, 1372
Schenk, Susan Jean 2603t
Scherbel, Jenell V. 2604t
Schiff, Jonathan 1373
Schilling, Timothy P. 1374
Schlafer, Linda D[iane]. 39r, 48r, 79, 1375, 1376, 1377, 1966

Schleifer, Ronald 35, 35a, 46, 1378, 1379
Schlueter, June 48r, 1380ed
Schlueter, Paul 1380ed
Schmitt, Deborah A. 1381ed
Schmitz, Eugenia E. 57r, 1382r
Schmude, Karl G. 1383
Schneiderman, Leo 1384
Scholl, Diane Gabrielson 1385
Schott, Webster 2715r, 2723r
Schroeder, Michael L. 1386
Schroeder, Steven 1387
Schroeder, Sue 2605t
Schroeder, Vanessa M. 2606t
Schulte, Bret 1387a
Schwandt, Pamela 2718r
Schwartz, Narda Lacey 1388, 1389
Scott, Carol Jackson 1967
Scott, Carolynne 1390
Scott, George R. 2607t
Scott, Katherine K. 1391
Scott, R. Neil 75a, 488, 1392
Scott, Suzanne Wallace 1968
Scott, Terry Ratliff 2608t
Scouten, Kenneth 1393, 1394, 1395
Scudder, Janice Pryor 1969
Seaberg, Rönnog 2145, 2146
Sears, April 2609t
Sederberg, Nancy B. 1396
See, Lisa 1397
Seed, David 76r
Seel, Cynthia Lynne 75b, 1970
Seelye, John 1398
Seidel, Alison P. 1399
Self, Rita Jean McClelland 2610t
Senick, Gerard J. 687ed
Sessions, William A. 65r, 66r, 67r, 1400, 1400a, 1400b, 1401, 2720r
Settle, Glenn H. 1971
Sewell, Elizabeth 1402
Sexton, Mark Stephen 1403, 1404, 1972
Seymour, Janice Louise 1973
Seymour-Smith, Martin 1405, 1406
Shackelford, [Dwight] Dean 1407, 1408, 1974

Shapiro, C. 27r

Shapiro, Herbert E. 25r

Sharian, Randall Paul 2611t

Sharp, Roberta 1409

Shaw, Joy Farmer 1975

Shaw, Mary Neff 74, 536ed, 606ed, 630ed, 1309ed, 1315ed, 1410, 1701ed

Shaw, Patrick W. 1411

Shaw, Robert B. 2718r

Sheahan, Diane Ross 2612t

Shealy, Anna Kempson 2613t

Shear, Walter 1412

Sheehan, Daniel Brian 2614t

Sheehy, Helen 1413

Shelley, Thomas J. 1610ed

Shelnutt, Eve 1414

Shelton, Frank W. 1415, 1416

Shepherd, Allen 1417

Shepherd, Gerard W. 1418

Sheridan, Daniel P. 848

Sherman, Carl R. 60r

Shields, John C. 1419

Shillingsburg, Miriam J. 1420

Shinn, Thelma J. Wardrop 1421, 1976

Shloss, Carol 35, 76, 1422, 1977, 2718r

Short, Donald Aubrey 1978

Shorten, Margaret M. 2615t

Showalter, Elaine 1423, 1700ed

Shrapnel, Norman 2723r

Shroeder, Vanessa Miller 2616t

Shuman, Joel James 1979

Shurr, William H. 1424

Sibley, Celestine 2717r, 2719r

Sibley, Larry 2716r

Sicherman, Barbara 520ed

Sidoti, M. Thomas 2617t

Siegel, Ben 356ed, 619ed

Siegfried, Regina 1425

Sikora, Malgorzata 1426

Siletzky, Robert 1980, 2618t

Silk, Mark 1427

Sillaven, Christina 2619t

Simon, John 1428, 2731r

Simons, John W. 46, 2724r

Sims, Anne Elizabeth Shelton 2620t

Simpson, Lewis P. 1429, 1430, 1431

Sitko, Barbara M. 2621t

Skaggs, Calvin 353ed

Skaggs, Merrill 1432

Skarda, Patricia 1433

Skillern, Ada Travelsted 2621at

Skube, Michael 1434

Skyles, Benjamin Henry 2622t

Slattery, Dennis Patrick 1435, 1436, 1437, 1437a

Sledge, Martha Lee 2623t

Sloan, Gary 1438, 1439, 1440

Sloan, LaRue Love 1441, 2624t

Sloane, Thomas O. 1442

Smietana, Patricia 2625t

Smiley, Pamela Marie 1981

Smith, Harold J. 991ed

Smith, Jessie Carney 319

Smith, John Charles 1982

Smith, Lee 1443

Smith, Leslie Wright 1983

Smith, Lillian 2715r

Smith, Marcus A.J. 1444

Smith, Margaret M. 2626t

Smith, Martha A. 2627t, 2724r

Smith, Melissa Tyler 2628t

Smith, Patrick James 1984

Smith, Peter A. 1445

Smith, Rupert LaMarr 2629t

Smith, Sheron 1446

Smith, Starr E. 2713r

Smith, Suzanne Ware 2630t

Smith, Thomas F. 2723r, 2724r

Smothers, Bonnie 2724r

Snodgrass, Mary Ellen 1447

Snow, Ollye T. 2631t

Snyder, Barbara Royalty 2632

Snyder, Marc 726

Sokolov, Raymond 2716r

Solotaroff, Theodore 1448, 2715r

Somerville, John Nottingham, Jr. 42r, 50r, 73r, 1985

Sommer, Elyse and Mike 1449ed

Soneda, Kenzo 2147

Sonnenfeld, Albert 46
Sorai, Yuka 2148, 2149
Sorcinelli, Mary Deane Griffin 2633t
Spalding, Phinizy 1450
Spaltro, Kathleen 1451
Spears, Monroe K. 1452
Speigel, Blaine 1454
Spencer, Elizabeth 1653
Spencer, Marlene A. 1986
Spivey, Ted R. 56r, 71r, 77, 1455, 1456, 1457, 1458, 1459, 1460, 1461, 1462
Sprieser, Martha Bell 1463
Springsteen, Bruce 1464, 1465
Sprouse, Helen M. 2634t
Stadelman, Catherine 1466
Stafford, Darrell Eugene 2635t
Staggs, Sammy 24r, 27r
Stainton, Leslie 1413
Stallings, Sylvia 46, 2717r, 2724r
Stampfl, Barry George 1987
Stanciu, Tanya 1467
Stanley, Roger 1468
Stanton, William F. 1469
Statelman, Peter 2636t
Staton, Shirley F. 1470ed
Stefaniak, Mary Helen 1470a
Steggert, Frank X. 2717r
Stein, Rita 1471
Stelzmann, Rainulf A. 1472, 2150
Stephens, Charles Ralph 2ed, 70ed, 1988
Stephens, Martha [Thomas] 15r, 27, 1473, 1989
Stephenson, M.S. 74r, 77r
Stephenson, Will and Mimosa 1474
Stern, Daniel 1475
Sterritt, David 2731r
Stewart, Harry Dee 2637t
Stewart, Michelle Pagni 1476
Stimson, Eva Gray 2638t
Stokes, David 1477
Stone, John 1478
Stoneback, H.R. 1479
Stonehill, Brian 1480
Strassburg, Mildred P. 1990

Strauss, Harriett 15r
Street, Ruth Roberta 2639t
Streight, Irwin Howard 1481, 1482, 1991
Strickland, Binky 1483, 1484
Strickland, Edward 1485
Strine, Mary S. 1486
Stuckey, William J. 29r, 38r, 48r, 49r, 50r, 52r, 63r, 65r, 69r, 76r, 1487, 2718r, 2721r
Stumbo, Carol 2640t
Sturma, Lee 1488
Suda, Minoru 2151
Sugiura, Etsuko 2152
Suh, Sook 2153, 2154
Sullins, Max E. 2641t
Sullivan, Anne Bowers 2642t
Sullivan, Bede 2723r
Sullivan, Jack 1433ed
Sullivan, Mary C. 51
Sullivan, Richard 1489
Sullivan, Walter 21r, 1490r, 1491, 1492, 1493, 2715r
Summer, Bob 1494
Sussman, Katherine J. 2643t
Suyama, Shizuo 2155
Svejgaard, Erik 2110
Swan, Jesse G. 1495, 1496, 2644t
Swanson, Rollin A. 1497
Sweeney, Francis 19r
Sweeney, Gerard M. 1498
Sweeney, Patricia 1499
Sweet, Charlie 181, 182, 183, 184
Sweet, Glenda Y. 1500
Sweet-Hurd, Evelyn 1501
Sweezy, Patricia Ann 2645t
Swick, Thomas 1502
Sydhoff, Beate 2146
Sykes, John D., Jr. 53r, 69r, 1503, 2721r

Takahashi, Junko 2156
Takahashi, Masahiko 2157
Takenaka, Toshiko 1504, 2158
Talbird, Olga Karen 2646t

Tallack, Douglas 1505
Tallant, Carole Ellsworth 1506
Tanabe, Tamotsu 2159
Tanaka, Junko 1507
Tanimoto, Taizo 2160
Tanner, Stephen L. 1508, 2718r
Tanno, Makoto 2161
Tarantino, Michael 1509, 2731r
Tassin, Anthony G. 36r, 64r
Tate, Allen 46
Tate, J.O. 15r, 28r, 30, 38r, 60r, 62r,
    79r, 2718r
Tate, J[ames] O[liver], Jr. 68a, 1510,
    1511, 1512, 1513, 1514, 1515,
    1516, 1517, 1518, 1519, 1520,
    1521, 1992
Tate, James 1522
Tate, Mary Barbara 1523, 1581
Tate, Robert Hale 1993
Tavernier-Courbin, Jacqueline 1523
Taylor, Elizabeth Savery 1994
Taylor, Harry H. 1525
Taylor, Henry 23r
Taylor, Jacqueline [Sue] 1526, 1995
Tedford, Barbara Wilkie 1527
Templin, Charlotte 30r, 1527a, 2717r
Tennyson, G.B. 427ed
Tercek, Robert Albin 2647t
Terunuma, Kahoru 2162
Terwillinger, Linda 2648t
TeSelle, Sallie McFague 1528
Thiemann, Fred R. 1530
Thobo-Carlsen, John 2110
Thomas, Ester 2719r
Thomae, Evie Sue Sessums 2649t
Thomas, Kelly Lynn 1996
Thomas, Leroy 1997
Thomas, Mattie Daniels 1998
Thomas, Wendy Lee 2650t
Thompson, James J., Jr. 53r, 1531r
Thompson, Joan Elaine 2651t
Thompson, Richard 20r
Thompson, Terry 1532, 1533
Thompson, Theresa C. 2652t
Thornton, Debra Lynn 1998a
Thorpe, Jean M. 2718r

Thorwaldsen, Paul R. 2653t
Tierney, Marie R. 2654t
Tietjen, Mary Anne 2655t
Tift, Ann 1534
Tigges, Wim 1402ed
Tillotson, Keith L. 2656t
Timberlake, Jean 1999
Tindall, Gillian 2717r
Tischler, Nancy M. 39r, 70r, 80r,
    2714r, 2716r
Toalson, Susan 2657t
Tokusue, Aiko 2163
Tolomeo, Diane 51r, 60r, 1535, 1536,
    1537, 2718r
Tolson, Jay 1538ed, 1539
Tomlinson, Barbara 1540
Toolan, Michael 1541
Toombs, Sarah E. 2658t
Torchia, Joseph 1542
Tourtellotte, Jack B. 2659t
Towers, Robert 2718r
Trachtenberg, Stanley 2715r
Trainor, Richard 1543
Trautmann, Joanne 1544
Traynor, John J., Jr. 2723r
Trimmer, Joseph F. 1545
Trotter, F. Thomas 2718r
Trowbridge, Clinton W. 1546
True, Michael 1547, 1548, 1549,
    2718r, 2721r
Truffin, Sherry R. 2660t
Tsuchiya, Hiroyuki 2164
Tucker, Mary F. 2661t
Tufts, Melissa Cole 2662t
Tullos, Allen 1550
Turnbaugh, Anne 2000
Tuttle, John 1551
Tuttleton, James W. 884
Twyman, Robert W. 131ed
Tymieniecka, Anna-Teresa 1304ed
Tynan, Daniel J. 1552

Ueno, Naozo 2165
Uesugi, Akira 2166
Ullrich, Francis J. 2717r

Umegaki, Kiyoshi 2167
Unsworth, Tim[othy] 45r, 1553, 1554
Updike, John 1555
Uruburu, Paula Marie 1556, 2001

Vaca, Peggy Irene 2663t
Vaccaro, Jean Marie 2664t
Valenti, Francisco 2168
Valiquette, Michele 570
Vande Kieft, Ruth M. 63r, 1557
Vandenberg, Kathleen Marie 2664at
Van Dyke, Patricia A. 2002
Vasquez, Mary S. 1558
Vassiliou, Likourgos J. 2665t
Vaughn, Helen Ruth 2718r
Veat, N.P. 2169
Veith, Gene Edward 1559
Vera, Peggy Diane 2666t
Verderame, Carla Lee 1559a, 2003
VerStrat, Patricia L. 2667t
Vest, David Carl Quentin 2004,
    2718r
Vetterling, Mary-Anne 142ed, 734ed,
    735ed, 1300ed
Villa, Giuseppina 2668t
Vinson, James 756ed, 757ed, 1560
Vipond, Diane 1561
Voelker, Joseph C. 1562
Vogler, Lewis 2717r
Volk, Benita 2669t
Vollmar, Jim 1563, 2712r
Vonalt, Larry 1564
Vrana, Stan A. 1565, 1566

Wages, Jack D. 1567
Wagner-Martin, Linda 1195ed, 1568
Wahl, Patricia 2670t
Wakana, Maya Higashi 1569, 2671t
Walden, Daniel 1570
Waldron, Ann 1571
Walker, Alice, 46, 68a, 941, 1572,
    2170
Walker, Camille Stone 2672t
Walker, Donna Jo 2673t

Walker, Donna Lou 2674t
Walker, Jeffrey 1573
Walker, Nancy 1574
Walker, Robin Lee 2675t
Walker, Sue 1575, 1576
Walkiewicz, E.P. 1577
Wallace, Richard 2676t
Wallach, Rick 1239ed
Wallis, Thomas Andrew 2677t
Walls, Doyle W. 1578
Walsh, Thomas F. 20r
Walsh, William J. 1579
Walston, Rosa Lee 1119, 1580, 1581,
    1582, 1583, 1584
Walters, Dorothy 28, 71
Walters, John Paul 2678t
Walton, Mary Mittlelee 2679t
Ward, Mary B. 2680t
Warden, Patricia B. 2681t
Warnke, Frank J. 46, 2723r
Warren, Colleen 2682t
Warren, F. Eugene 2683t
Warren, Robert Penn 1194
Washburn, Delores [Cole] 79, 1585,
    1586, 2005
Wasserman, Stephen 1182ed, 1587
Watall, Mattiel 2684t
Watanabe, Kayoko 1588, 1589, 1590,
    1591, 2171, 2172, 2173, 2174,
    2175
Watkins, Floyd C. 1194ed
Watson, Miriam Celia 2685t
Watson, Noelle 357ed
Watson, William Elmo, Jr. 2686t
Weaks, Mary Louise 36r, 80r, 1194ed
Weaver, Mary Jo 1594, 1595
Webb, Stephen H. 1596
Webb, W.L. 2718r
Weber, Brom 21r
Weber, Ronald 1597
Webster, Harvey C. 2724r
Weigel, George S. 1598
Weiner, Alan R. 1599
Weinstein, Arnold 1600
Weinstein, Philip M. 1601

Weisenburger, Steven 1602, 1603,
    1604, 1605
Weiss, Irving and Anne 1606ed
Weixlmann, Joe 1607
Welborn, Amy 1607a
Welling, Lloyd C[harles] 1608, 1609,
    2006, 2718r
Wellington, Ann M. 2687t
Wells, Joel 1610, 2712r, 2715r, 2718r
Weltmer, Jason 2686at
Welty, Eudora 1611
Wendler, Linda Fine 2007
Wendorf, Thomas Allan 2007a
Wenz, Jennifer 2688t
Werner, Craig Hansen 1612
Wershoven, Carol Jean 2689t
West, James L.W., III, 1302ed, 1613
West, Kathryn 377
Westarp, Karl-Heinz 30, 78, 79,
    121ed, 156ed, 177ed, 224ed,
    358ed, 442ed, 484ed, 580ed,
    590ed, 676ed, 784ed, 977ed,
    1102ed, 1127ed, 1277ed, 1376ed,
    1614, 1615, 1615a, 1616, 1617,
    1618, 1619, 1620, 1621, 1716ed,
    2107r
Westbrook, Thomas Gerald 2690t
Westerman, Cheryl I. 91
Westling, Louise 71, 80, 1622, 1623,
    1624, 1625, 1626, 1627, 1628,
    1629, 1629a
White, Beverly Leigh 2691t
White, Ray Lewis 1630
White, Terry 1631
White, William 1632
Whitehead, James 1633, 1653
Whitehead, Kenneth A. 2692t
Whiteley, Sandy 1634, 2714r
Whitfield, Stephen J. 80r
Whitt, Jan 1635, 1636
Whitt, Margaret [Early] 81, 1637,
    1638, 1639, 1640, 1641, 1641a,
    1642, 1643, 2008
Whyte, S.W. 34r, 46r
Wiedemann, Barbara 471
Wikle, Michelle Hist 2693t

Wilbers, Stephen 1644
Wilhelm, Arthur Wayne 2009
Wilkes, Paul A. 1645
Will, George F. 1646
Williams, Andrea 2694t
Williams, David 1647
Williams, Leslie Walker 2695t
Williams, Mary Ann 2696t
Williams, Mary Morris 1648
Williams, Melvin G. 1649
Williams, Peter W. 1650
Williamson, Chilton, Jr. 1651, 2716r
Willoughby, Jim 1652
Willson, Lawrence 70r, 2714r
Wilson, Austin 1653
Wilson, Carol Y. 1654
Wilson, Charles Reagan 874ed,
    964ed, 1655
Wilson, Harold Gregory 2697t
Wilson, Janice M. 2698t
Wilson, Melony J. 2699t
Wilson, Meredith Anita 2700t
Wimsatt, Margaret 38r
Winchell, Donna Haisty 1656
Winchell, Mark Royden 1657, 1658
Winifred, Mary 53r
Winkle, Laura 2700at
Winkler, Mary G. 1092ed
Winn, Harlan H., III, 1659, 2010
Winslow, William 1660
Winsten, Fancher 2731r
Winters, Laura 2701t
Wise, Melanie E. Hoover 2702t
Wiseman, William J. 2703t
Witt, Elaine 1661
Witt, Jonathan [Ronald] 1662, 2011
Witt, Margaret E. 1663
Wolf, Michele 1664
Wolfe, Gregory 34r
Wolff, Gay H. 2704t
Womack, Kenneth 129
Wood, Gerald C. 1665
Wood, Ralph C. 15r, 31r, 35, 36r,
    38r, 41r, 42r, 45r, 48r, 50r, 53r, 55r,
    56r, 69r, 73r, 76r, 527, 1666, 1667,
    1668, 1669, 1670, 1671, 1672,

1673, 1674, 1675, 1676r, 1677, 1678a, 1678r, 1679r, 1680r, 1681r, 1682r, 1683, 2705t, 2716r, 2718r, 2721r

Woodress, James 861ed

Woodward, Harry Loomis 2012

Woodward, Kenneth L. 2715r

Wooten, Linda West 2706t

Woster, Michelle M. 1684

Wray, Virginia Field 74r, 1685, 1686, 1687r, 1688, 1689, 1690, 1691, 1692, 1693, 1694a, 1694r, 2013

Wright, Angela H. 1695

Wright, Austin M. 1696

Wright, Charlotte Megan 2014

Wright, Elliott 2712r

Wright, Will 388ed

Wyatt, Bryan N. 1697

Wyllie, John Cook 2717r

Wynar, Bohdan 1382ed

Wynne, Judith F. 1698

Yaeger, Patricia Smith 35a, 58, 74, 1699, 1699a, 1700, 1701, 1702

Yaguchi, Hiroo 2176

Yagyu, Nozomu 2177

Yamada, Fuki 2178, 2179, 2180

Yamagata, Ako 2182

Yamagata, Kazumi 2181, 2183

Yamamoto, Yoshimi 1703

Yancey, Philip 495ed, 1704

Yardley, Jonathan 2712r, 2716r, 2720r

Yerger, Norval Rice 2707t

Yochim, Karen 1705

Yokoyama, Takemi 2184

Yordon, Judy Ellen 2015

York, Beth M. 2708t

York, Lamar 1706

Yoshimura, Keiko 2185, 2186

Young, Carolyn T. 2709t

Young, Diane 1255, 2716r

Young, Donavan 2712r, 2718r, 2722r

Young, Joanna 1707

Young, Thomas Daniel 341ed, 1708, 1709, 1710r, 1711, 1712, 1713ed, 1714ed

Zacharasiewicz, Waldemar 79, 1601ed, 1715, 1716, 1717, 2187, 2188, 2189

Zaidman, Laura Mandell 1717a, 1718, 1719, 2718r

Zengos, Hariclea 2710t

Zenter, Joe 1719a

Zhong, Ming 2711t

Zimbaro, Valerie P. 1720

Zimmerly, Renette 1721

Zimmerman, D.W. 56r

Zoller, Peter T. 1722

Zophy, Angela Howard 644ed

Zornado, Joseph 1723, 1724, 2016

Zuber, Leo J. 10ed, 69ed

Zubizarreta, John 1725

Name Index

Includes entry numbers for all proper names--except Flannery O'Connor's and those of fictional characters--mentioned in the titles or descriptive abstracts of books, articles, dissertations, and other works described or cited in this guide.

The letters "a" and "b" indicate that the item was a late entry added after numbering was set. Also, works cited which include the mention of a name and the title of a work by that person (e.g. in abstract # 1801, Mikhail Bakhtin's *Rabelais and His World* is discussed), have the designation of the letter "c" following the entry number (e.g. 1801c) to indicate to the reader that a work is cited in this entry.

"A." *See* Hester, "Betty" Hazel
  Elizabeth
Abbot, Louise H. 82, 87, 172, 645,
  723, 724, 800a, 1691
Abercrombie, Margaret 1349
Abernathy, Lee Roy 1624
Abrahams, Roger D. 800
Abu-Jaber, Diana 1625
Adam, Karl 199, 1923
Adams, Alice 1568c
Adams, Henry 1097
Adams, Karl 1755
Adorno, Theodor W. 1702c
Aeschylus 1997
Agee, James 265c, 331c, 970, 1850,
  1907
Aiken, Conrad 1495, 2644
Aiken, David 241, 313
Aiken, Susan Hardy 174
Alcott, Louisa May 415, 1423
Aldridge, John W. 536, 882
Alexander, Benjamin 1530
Algren, Nelson 854, 1139, 1624,
  1913
Ali, Mohammad 1683
Alice, Sister 481
Alighieri, Dante 90c, 137c, 274,
  282c, 368, 395c, 416, 479, 551c,
  718c, 931c, 1080, 1102, 1559,
  1668, 1885

Allen, Dick 87
Allen, Reynolds 87
Allen, Suzanne 861
Allen, Walter 339c
Allen, William Rodney 218, 939,
  1264
Allen, Woody 2483
Allison, Dorothy 1625
Alphonsa, Mother. *See* Hawthorne,
  Rose.
Alther, Lisa 533
Ames, Elizabeth 33
Amis, Martin 101
Andersen, Hans Christian 869c
Anderson, Sherwood 246, 248c, 561,
  1556, 1635c, 1747, 1875, 1994
  2001
Andre, Judith 1092
Andreas, James 1054
Andreev, Leonid 1136
Angelou, Maya 1446, 2190
Ansen, David 1226
Anthony, Saint 532
Anthony the Great 612
Apollo (God) 615
Aquinas, Saint Thomas 38, 42a, 77,
  102a, 174a, 385c, 571, 575c, 697,
  977, 1030, 1096, 1098, 1102, 1332,
  1333, 1427, 1619, 1668, 1810,
  1918, 1952, 2106

Arbiter, Petronius 975c
Arbus, Diane 61, 892, 1007, 2012
Archer, Emily 1530
Archer, Jane Elizabeth 1164
Arcimboldo, Giuseppe 454
Arendt, Hannah 481, 760, 1107, 1116c, 1959
Aristophanes 416, 975c, 1547
Aristotle 1080, 1984
Arp, Bill 217, 1344
Arvin, Newton 126
Asals, Frederick 104, 152, 218, 313, 354c, 396c, 424c, 454, 470, 489, 562, 638, 878, 882, 979, 999, 1001c, 1092, 1125c, 1167, 1264, 1301c, 1375, 1376, 1487c, 1513, 1527a, 1530, 1580, 1652, 1662, 1719, 1730, 2188
Ashley, Jack 1396
Assisi, Saint Francis of 611
Atwood, Margaret 972
Auden, W.H. 365, 977, 1893, 1922
Auerbach, Erich 1522c
Augustine, Saint 360, 499, 501, 851, 1030, 1181, 1668, 1723, 1808, 1810, 1947, 1983
Austin, Jane 662, 2541

Babcock-Abrahams, Barbara 800
Babinec, Lisa S. 1530
Bachelard, Gaston 858a
Bacon, Jon Lance 209c, 415, 1153c, 1640c, 1672
Baez, Joan 1271
Bakhtin, Mikhail 36, 354, 454, 587, 590, 597, 762, 832a, 859, 882, 1175, 1315, 1410, 1749, 1763, 1801c, 1812, 1831, 1983, 2384, 2587
Balázs, Béla 342
Baldwin, James 481, 527, 1055, 1139, 1667, 1683, 1908, 1976, 1999
Baldwin, Joseph Glover 755
Balée, Susan 845c, 1687c

Balgård, Gunnar 2023
Balzac, Honoré de 140
Banks, Russell 1612
Banner, Keith 135a
Barfield, Owen 391c
Barnes, Linda Adams 594, 604
Barnes, Roslyn 802
Barnett, Ross 1683
Barron, Arthur 1475
Barrus, Paul 1177a
Barth, John 1577, 1709, 1794, 1878c, 1906, 1908, 2064
Barth, Karl 208, 245, 1427, 1503c, 1674
Barthelme, David 59, 594, 618
Barthelme, Donald 784, 816
Barthes, Roland 1130, 1701, 1934
Barzun, Jacques 1339
Baskerville, William Malone 1344
Bassan, Maurice 687
Bataille, Georges 775, 1764, 1860
Baudelaire, Charles 234, 365, 1372, 1752c, 1989
Bauer, Dale M. 587
Baumbach, Jonathan 1343, 1358, 1399
Baumgaertner, Jill 174, 250c, 269c, 448c, 749c, 1439, 1474, 1694a
Bausch, Richard 1317
Bawer, Bruce 541
Bayly, Joseph 1240c
Beardsley, Monroe C. 536
Beattie, Ann 59, 594
Beatty, Ned 342, 684, 2731
Beauvoir, Simone de 972, 1408
Beaver, Harold 687
Becham, Gerald 154, 437, 1119, 1580, 1652
Beck, Charlotte 414
Beck, Christiane 393
Becker, Ernest 255
Becker, Gary 1883
Becker, Isidore H. 1164
Beckett, Samuel 75a, 1762, 1893
Becknell, Thomas 945
Beerbohm, Max 1522c

Béguin, Albert 1376c
Beiswanger, George 293, 414c, 509, 666, 1177a
Beja, Morris 1422
Bell, Elizabeth S. 939
Bell, Madison Smart 1317
Bell, Marvin 553
Bellamy, Michael O. 470, 1438
Bellow, Saul 213, 779, 823, 1742, 1754c, 1893, 1899, 1901c, 1917, 1976, 2041
Benjamin, Walter 185c, 1702
Bennett, Charles 1432
Bennett, John C. 126
Bergson, Henri 275, 364, 477, 800, 975, 2002
Bern, Walter 1107
Bernanos, Georges 38, 178, 326, 998, 1024, 1240, 1376, 1455, 1597, 1645, 1966, 2088
Berry, Chuck 916
Berry, Wendell 893
Betts, Doris 51a, 535c, 637, 781, 1035c, 1400a, 1579, 2699
Bierce, Ambrose 1316
Binswanger, Ludwig 1200
Bion, Wilfred R. 449
Bishop, Elizabeth 84a, 688, 910, 1127, 1139, 1927
Bishop, J.P. 224
Bivins, Stephen T. "Pete" 1247
Bivins, Thomas 976
Black, Edwin 830c,
Blackwell, Henry 393
Blais, Marie-Claire 1716
Blake, William 56, 160c, 316, 977
Blanchot, Maurice 775, 1860
Blasingham, Mary V. 393
Bleich, David 1827
Bleikasten, André 174, 241, 457, 564, 618, 713, 878, 1662, 1668
Bliven, Naomi 713
Bloom, Harold 164a, 979, 1092, 1239, 1301c, 1354, 1513
Bloy, Léon 79, 1024, 1376c, 1597, 1923, 1966

Bluestone, George 342, 1041c
Bly, Robert 1795
Boccaccio, Giovanni 869c
Bond, Adrienne 641c
Bonetti, Kay 382
Bonner, Carl 1247
Bonner, James 1251, 1177a
Booth, Stanley 1467
Booth, Wayne 979, 1442, 1962
Borges, Luis 1280c
Bosch, Heironymous 454
Bottoms, David 51a, 1400a
Bourne, Paul 197
Bowen, Robert O. 687
Bowen, Rose 1652
Bowles, Paul 1878c, 1913
Boyd, Betty 290, 509
Boyd, Turner F. 319c
Bradbury, Ray 2730
Bradford, M.E. 532c
Bradford, William 1070, 1635c
Bradley, Malcolm 536
Bray, Nancy Davis 488, 1251, 1371, 1502, 1793
Brecht, Bertolt 2107
Breit, Harvey 68, 478
Breslin, Jimmy 1014
Brinkmeyer, Robert H., Jr. 97, 354c, 383c, 470, 587, 679, 800a, 882, 1301c, 1380, 1694, 1710c
Brisac, Geneviève 2031c, 2032c, 2130c, 2140c
Brittain, Joan T. 471, 979, 999, 1026, 1166c, 1208c, 1386, 1638
Broadway, J. William 1017
Brodhead, Richard 415
Brodin, Pierre 1376
Brontë, Emily 894c
Brooks, Cleanth 415c, 540, 826, 1092, 1097c, 1108, 1365c, 1824
Brooks, Gwendolyn 1976
Brooks, Van Wyck 1571
Broughton, Panthea Reid 946
Brown, Ashley 224, 225, 261, 393, 976, 1520
Brown, Charles Brockton 246

Brown, Hugh 226, 227, 501a, 530, 742, 759c, 759d, 764a

Brown, Larry 533

Brown, Mary Ward 51a, 230

Brown, Sarah Enos 1652

Brown, Susan Jenkins 225

Browning, Preston M., Jr. 313, 471, 565c, 687, 996, 999, 1069, 1127, 1282, 1323, 1335, 1381, 1393, 1466, 1511c, 1537c

Browning, Robert 977

Brownson, Orestes 1014

Bruccoli, Matthew J. 997c

Brueggemann, Walter 979, 980, 1904c, 1973

Brunson, Beverly 599

Bryant, Hallman B. 471

Brzenk, Gene 295

Buber, Martin 77, 979, 1455

Buchanan, Harriette 781

Buck, Pearl S. 370

Budy, Andrea Hollander 51a, 637

Buechner, Frederick K. 169c, 250, 375, 1743

Bulfinch, Thomas 80c

Bunyan, John 53c, 162c, 1559, 1791

Burchett, George 1012c, 1618

Burford, Kay 295

Burke, Edmund 1752, 2505

Burke, Kenneth 225, 789, 1092

Burke, William 419c

Burnett, Robert ("Bob") 501a, 227, 764a

Burns, Marion 262, 1691

Burns, Stuart L. 261, 409, 489, 896, 1453, 1635, 1690, 1691

Burrell, David 618

Burroughs, William 2041

Burt, John 1354

Bush, ["General"] William J. 468a, 690, 1391, 1517

Butler, Jack 591

Butler, Robert Olen 1552

Buzan, Mary 174

Bynum, Brenda 1529

Bynum, Caroline Walker 1092

Byrd II, William 1344c

Byron, Lord (George Gordon) 122

Cabell, James Branch 755

Cable, George Washington 105c, 1264c, 1799, 1972c

Cady, Edwin H. 1513

Cahill, Susan 1014

Caldwell, Erskine 56, 220, 573, 630, 662, 663, 745c, 755, 1126, 1253c, 1343, 1344, 1398, 1415, 1450, 1877, 1972, 2008, 2009, 2692

Caldwell, Mark 586

Calisher, Hortense 1976

Callahan, Barry 120

Calvin, John 1100

Campbell, Donald 1107c

Campbell, Kate 721a

Campbell, Will 233

Camus, Albert 816, 1997

Cannella, Anthony R. 72

Capote, Truman 551, 686c, 1139, 1174c, 1249, 1551c, 1624, 1715, 1782, 1821, 1830, 1853, 2009, 2050, 2241

Carey, Peter 1121

Cargill, Oscar 1105

Carlyle, Thomas 263, 1401

Carrington, Leonora 1773

Carroll, James 1014

Carroll, John 1062

Carroll, Lewis 1402, 1701c

Carter, Angela 973c, 1773c

Carter, Jimmy [James Earl] 1711

Caruth, Cathy 286a

Carver, Catherine 1177a, 1616

Carver, Raymond 59, 476, 594, 925c, 1651, 1994

Cash, Jean W. 414, 584, 587

Cash, W.J. 1784c

Casper, Leonard 1178, 1324

Cather, Willa 176c, 370, 1014, 1468, 2730

Catherine of Genoa 1129a

Catherine of Siena, Saint 965c, 1129a

Cawthon, Raad 180
Champin, Robert 868
Champlin, Charles 1226
Channing, Stockard 2726
Chaplin, Charlie 1522, 1982
Chappell, Fred 51a, 1400a, 2009
Chardin, Pierre Teilhard de 75b, 77,
    79, 199, 215, 273, 345c, 442, 729a,
    738, 782, 820, 849, 851, 1163,
    1181, 1333, 1339, 1424, 1451,
    1462, 1621, 1659, 1668, 1674,
    1755, 1762, 1792, 1800, 1808,
    1810, 1928, 1941, 1966, 1968,
    1970, 2135, 2195, 2257, 2304,
    2337, 2475
Chase, Richard 247, 1167, 1169
Chaucer, Geoffrey 53c, 183, 184c
Cheever, John 59, 594, 1524, 1965,
    2483
Chekhov, Anton 519, 720, 2139
Cheney, Anne 781
Cheney, Brainard 2, 70, 149, 224,
    225, 273, 477, 502, 687, 802, 806,
    854, 1034, 1177a, 1466, 1571,
    1583, 1624, 1634, 1988, 2513,
    2714
Cheney, Frances Neel 2, 70, 149,
    854, 1571, 1634, 1988, 2513
Cherry, Caroline L. 588
Chesnutt, Charles Waddell 1249c
Chesterton, G.K. 793, 1112, 1240,
    1366
Chew, Martha 570, 587
Childress, Mark 623c, 677c, 1317
Chopin, Kate 472, 824, 996, 1420c,
    1423, 1738, 1745, 2645
Chow, Sung Gay 1396
Christ. See Jesus Christ
Chung-yuan, Chang 958
Chute, Carolyn 1996
Cisnero, Sandra 1175c
Cixous, Hélène 420
Clark, Beverly Lyon 646c, 1301c
Clark, Kenneth 1060
Cleary, Michael 1396
Clemens, Samuel. See Twain, Mark

Clemons, Walter 1494
Clifton, Lucille 1917
Cline, Katie 929
Cline, Louis 1692
Cline, Mary 929
Cline, Peter 320, 502, 1607a
Cobb, James B. 436
Cofer, Judith Ortiz 1154c
Coffey, Warren 687, 1100
Cohn, Dorrit 597
Coindreau, Maurice-Edgar 561, 851,
    1188, 1716, 2009, 2050, 2136
Coleman, Korva 466c
Coleridge, Mary Elizabeth 973c
Coles, Robert 51a, 150c, 306, 313,
    323, 330, 332, 335, 339c, 567c,
    641c, 647, 713, 784, 802, 851, 862,
    878, 879, 882, 1036c, 1127, 1182c,
    1218a, 1270, 1282, 1309, 1400a,
    1487c, 1667, 1704, 1859
Collins, Johnnie, III 2728
Collum, Danny Duncan 337
Colson, Charles 1240c
Combs, Diana Williams 338
Connolly, John 72
Conrad, Joseph 72, 167c, 258c, 443a,
    514, 522c, 531c, 553, 670c, 720,
    1084c, 1139, 1522, 1762c, 1952,
    1984c, 1987
Conroy, Pat 2110
Cooper, James Fenimore 1879
Cooper, Reginald 759b
Corey, Deborah Joy 120
Corn, Alfred 345, 508, 637, 723, 724,
    1185, 1196
Corrington, John William 1085
Coulthard, A.R. 347, 351, 591, 599
Cowan, Louise 383c
Cowley, Malcolm 225, 1571
Cozzens, James Gould 1139, 1976
Crane, George W. 1158c
Crane, Hart 225
Crane, R.S. 389
Crane, Stephen 146, 519, 522c, 878,
    1513, 1522, 1556, 1879, 1995,
    2001, 2730

Cresap, Paul 293
Crews, Frederick 444, 454, 536, 587, 588, 865, 878, 882, 1174c, 1316
Crews, Harry 189, 220c, 533, 796, 1020, 1126, 1177, 1317, 1398, 1415, 1416, 1564, 1732
Creyke, Richard P. 2727
Crocker, Michael W. 471, 1381
Crossan, John Dominic 1034
Culbertson, Diana 838
Culler, Jonathan 1461
Cunningham, Frank R. 591
Currie, Sheldon 393
Curtis, George M., III 1489c
Cyril of Jerusalem, Saint 59a, 385, 718, 851, 983, 1277, 1379, 1631, 1709, 2131

Dali, Salvador 454
Daniel, Frank 68
Daniell, Rosemary 693c
Dante. *See* Alighieri, Dante
D'Arcy, Martin C. 1728
Darretta, John L. 59, 369c, 594
Darwin, Charles 1137, 1968
Daunt, Chris 371, 372
Davidson, Clifford 1356
Davidson, Donald 536, 744, 854
Dawkins, Cecil 111, 133, 218, 261, 382, 524, 563, 564, 723, 760, 771, 788, 976, 1165, 1177b, 1198, 1529, 1624, 1625, 1691, 1692, 1864
Dawson, Jan 383
Day, Dorothy 499
Degan, James 1466
Delattre, Edwin J. 387, 1646
Delbanco, Andrew 612c
Denby, David 1226
Denham, Robert D. 1381
Derda, Dale 2728
Derrida, Jacques 1034
Desmond, John F. 218, 393, 471, 541, 882, 979, 1092, 1301c, 1377c, 1381, 1669
Dessommes, Nancy Bishop 591

devil, the (Lucifer) 131, 178, 211, 234, 268, 274, 329, 354, 378, 470, 487, 551, 612, 884, 918, 1005, 1054, 1096, 1105, 2501
Devlin, Albert J. 344c
De Vries, Mary 1659a
De Vries, Peter 208, 1854
Dew, Robb Forman 1701
Dewhurst, Colleen 2727
Dexter, Pete 336, 802, 1247c, 1251c, 1317
Dickens, Charles 291
Dickey, James 175, 206, 436, 625, 1850
Dickinson, Eleanor Creekmore 846
Dickinson, Emily 977, 1123
Didion, Joan 1271, 1625, 1965, 2536
Dillard, Annie 1223, 1625
Dillard, Martha 410
Dinesen, Isak 973
Dinger, Ed 915
Dinnerstein, Dorothy 1408
Dionysus 615, 1647, 1724
DiRenzo, Anthony 312c, 471, 866c
Doctorow, E.L. 59, 594, 1545c
Donadio, Candida 1177a
Donahoo, Robert 584, 589
Doner, Lois 482
Donne, John 1102, 1559
Donner, Robert 68
Donovan, Casey 2725
Dostoevsky, Fyodor Mikhaylovich 77, 94, 234, 235, 1049c, 1228c, 1240, 1435, 1762, 1983, 2123, 2130, 2561
Doty, William 800
Dougherty, David C. 147c
Douglas, Ellen 1324, 2685
Dourif, Brad 684, 2731
Dowd, Sharyn 788
Dowell, Bob 687, 1257
Downey, Michael 892c
Doxey, William S. 471, 1323
Drake, Robert 152, 393, 426, 427, 428, 543, 687, 713, 728, 851, 882, 979, 1069, 1455, 1539, 1669, 1688

Dreiser, Theodore 1014
Driggers, Stephen G. 42, 154c, 430c, 488, 649, 1177a, 1676c
Driskell, Leon V. 471, 976, 979, 999, 1026, 1166c, 1208c, 1386, 1638
Driver, Tom 75b, 1970
Drury, M. O'C. 1271
Dryden, John 1937c, 2538c
Dubus, Andre 533, 1317, 1480c
Duhamel, P. Albert 979
Dunleavy, Janet Egleson 46, 646
Dunn, Robert J. 42, 152, 154c, 430c, 438, 649, 674, 1177a
Durand, Gilbert 2028c
Durrell, Lawrence 1913
Durrwell, Francis 199, 1755
Dyson, J. Peter 120

Ebrecht, Ann 393
Eckardt, A. Roy 126
Eco, Umberto 571
Eddy, Mary Baker 1132
Edelman, Rob 1226
Edelstein, Mark 1324
Edgerton, Clyde 533, 1035c, 1254c, 1577, 1813
Edwards, Betty 103
Edwards, Bruce 945
Edwards, Harry Stillwell 1972, 2343
Edwards, Jonathan 422c, 830, 1072
Eggenschwiler, David 247, 361c, 565c, 996, 999, 1282, 1324, 1344, 1466
Eichmann, Adolf 1116
Eichner, Maura 1676c
Eisenstein, Sergei 342
Eliade, Mircea 75b, 288, 345c, 400, 800, 851c, 1970
Eliot, George 574
Eliot, T.S. 37, 56, 77, 178, 215, 365, 502, 514c, 522c, 608, 662, 669c, 767c, 826c, 854, 977, 999c, 1014, 1098, 1101, 1115, 1159c, 1343c, 1427, 1429, 1460, 1591, 1668, 1719c, 1841, 1893, 1989, 1992

Ellis, Kate 174
Ellison, Ralph 752, 829, 916c, 1215, 1249c, 1742, 1853, 1878c, 1908, 1917, 1939, 1976
Elmore, A.E. 89c
Embree, Charles 295, 411
Emerick, Ronald 1474
Emerson, O.B. 1177a
Emerson, Ralph Waldo 599, 1032, 1070, 1072, 1688
Emmanuel, Pierre 524
Engle, Paul 45, 295, 514, 521, 536, 538, 553, 764, 1020, 1177a, 1232, 1700
Ennis, Marion 976, 1247
Erdrich, Louise 59, 133, 594, 991c, 1625, 1911c
Eric, James 2730
Estes, David 437
Esty, William 687
Euripides 1997
Evans, Elizabeth 469
Evans, Robert C. 414, 471, 1381
Evans, Walker 1172c
Eyes, Harvest Moon 1476c

Facknitz, Mark 925
Fancher, Betsy 68, 475c, 478
Fara, Rudolph 72
Farley, Blanche 477, 478
Farmer, David 153c, 168c, 205c, 490, 560, 564c, 566c, 567c, 1125c, 1212c
Farnham, James F. 481c
Farrell, James 1014
Faulkner, William 35a, 80, 105c, 110, 140, 143, 151, 159, 175, 206, 213, 222, 225, 232a, 247c, 260c, 265, 310, 314c, 321, 355c, 378, 418, 481, 529, 538, 542, 543, 559, 561, 573, 619, 624, 653, 663, 664, 665, 670, 671, 678, 720, 737, 741, 745, 747, 748, 752, 755, 777c, 781, 810c, 819, 820, 826, 842, 848, 881, 919c, 943, 962c, 975c, 977, 988,

1017, 1034, 1056, 1059, 1085,
1104c, 1107, 1111, 1115c, 1116,
1139, 1173, 1174c, 1215, 1233,
1249, 1255, 1269, 1276c, 1277,
1289, 1302, 1317, 1326, 1335c,
1343, 1344, 1365, 1424, 1429,
1434, 1456, 1489, 1513, 1522,
1539, 1550c, 1572, 1585, 1601,
1610, 1617, 1625, 1635, 1651,
1653, 1655, 1657, 1660, 1683,
1715, 1726, 1738, 1745, 1746,
1747, 1748c, 1762, 1768, 1772c,
1784, 1795, 1797, 1799, 1809,
1817, 1830, 1839, 1850, 1853,
1875, 1893, 1897, 1898, 1902,
1908, 1916, 1945, 1962, 1967,
1971, 1972, 1975, 1992, 1994,
2004, 2005, 2009, 2010c, 2018,
2035, 2036, 2050, 2064, 2110,
2123, 2136, 2155, 2286, 2369,
2526, 2597

Federman, Raymond 536

Feeley, Kathleen 313, 361c, 383c,
393, 424c, 457, 471, 564c, 565c,
713, 882, 999, 1010, 1125c, 1161,
1335, 1453, 1638

Feeney, Father 516

Felder, Deborah G. 487

Felman, Shoshana 1702c, 1958

Fennell, Janice C. 488, 1251

Fennick, Ruth 587

Fenwick, Elizabeth 509

Ferguson, Betty 1177a, 1349

Ferguson, Elizabeth 293

Ferrell, Mary Key 636

Ferris, Sumner J. 687

Ficken, Carl 494

Fickett, Harold 1015, 1170r, 1554c,
1679c

Fiedler, Leslie 739, 809

Fields, W.C. 1522, 1982

Filippi, Carmen Lugo 2045

Filmer, Thomas 1333

Fish, Stanley 1559, 1827, 1845

Fitts, Karen 587

Fitzgerald, Benedict 141, 572, 978,
2731

Fitzgerald, F. Scott 167c, 265c, 669c,
1014, 1070, 1277, 1795, 1839,
1995, 2007

Fitzgerald, Kathy 2731

Fitzgerald, Michael 141, 684, 695,
1543, 2731

Fitzgerald, Robert 33, 80, 254, 273,
502, 503, 509, 511, 513, 519, 524,
536, 553, 565c, 643, 682, 688, 713,
789, 805, 879, 970c, 977, 1037,
1133, 1150, 1333, 1381, 1400b,
1434, 1466, 1473, 1583, 1692,
1719, 2032

Fitzgerald, Sally 33, 57, 77, 79, 104,
133, 140, 141, 155, 186, 215, 232a,
273, 366, 393, 424, 477, 499, 502,
509, 511, 513, 517, 518, 521, 524,
527, 527a, 553, 563, 564, 565, 586,
638, 640, 643, 724c, 767, 780a,
788, 792, 805, 839, 910c, 913, 961,
1018, 1037, 1062, 1090c, 1092,
1119, 1120c, 1122c, 1172r, 1243,
1336, 1347, 1400b, 1434, 1473,
1494c, 1513, 1518c, 1537c, 1538c,
1580, 1581, 1582, 1583, 1616,
1635, 1651, 1652, 1678, 1692,
1793, 2032, 2188c

Flanders, Lorene 1128

Flaubert, Gustave 140, 215, 429, 519,
553, 559, 560, 564, 923c, 1263c,
1521, 2137

Fletcher, Alan J. 599

Fleurdorge, Claude 561

Florencourt, Louise 1199, 1251,
1434, 1592, 1652

Flynn, Errol 1510

Fodor, Sarah 84a, 414, 1694c

Foley, Martha 100

Folks, Jeffrey J. 544, 1381

Fontes, Montserrat 545

Foote, Horton 1432, 1665, 1993

Foote, Shelby 1174c, 1255, 1538,
1539, 2009

Ford, John 1064
Ford, Maddox Ford 343, 553, 961,
    1522c, 1864
Ford, Richard 747, 2064
Forkner, Ben 883c, 903c, 942
Forster, E.M. 559
Foster, Shirley 586
Foucault, Michel 1034
Foulkes-Taylor, David 292
Fowler, Doreen 384, 471
Fowles, John 167c, 1934
Fox, John, Jr. 1972
Fox, William Price 1579
Fraistat, Rose Ann C. 343c
Francis of Assisi, Saint 611
Frankfort, Henri 218
Franklin, Ben 263
Frederic, Harold 1744
Freeman, Douglas Southall 665
Frei, Hans 1503c
Freud, Sigmund 38, 71, 234, 236,
    255, 286a, 316, 326, 477, 659c,
    826, 1057, 1373, 1674, 1860, 1941,
    2002
Frieden, Betty 213
Friedman, Ellen G. 591
Friedman, Melvin J. 288, 424c, 492,
    566, 646c, 882, 1178, 1282, 1296c,
    1301c, 1466, 1552
Frieling, Kenneth 240
Frisbie, Richard P. 68, 478
Frisch, Max 1088
Frohock, W. 621
Fromm, Erich 1135
Fromm, Harold 1290c
Frost, Robert 868, 878, 879, 1446
Frye, Northrop 443, 498, 680, 718,
    975, 1131, 1307, 1521, 1698, 1895,
    2002
Fugin, Katherine 68
Furlong, Monica 524

Gable, Mariella 261, 977, 1691, 1709
Gadamer, Hans-Georg 1943
Gaddis, William 884

Gaines, Ernest 542, 1612
Galdon, Joseph 1131
Gamber, Matthew 414
Gardiner, Harold 1024
Gardner, John 110, 2603
Garland, Hamlin 1744
Garner, Catherine 437
Garrison, William Lloyd 830
Gass, William 752, 1976
Gasset, José Ortega y 1135
Gates, Henry Louis, Jr. 800
Gatta, John 1530
Gay, Volney 680
Geimer, Rob 945
Geller, Robert 1475, 2727
Genet, Jean 618
Geng, Veronica 583
Gennup, Arnold van 1921
Gentry, Marshall Bruce 84a, 393,
    415, 454, 471, 539, 589, 762, 826,
    882, 999, 1301c, 1310, 1662, 1694
Gerber, Merrill Joan 289
Gernes, Sonia 602c
Getz, Lorine M. 118c, 153c, 424c,
    564c, 567c, 999, 1209c, 1333,
    1375c, 1487c, 1680c
Giannone, Richard 59, 164a, 369c,
    471, 594, 826, 1301c, 1386, 1676c,
    1678a, 1694c
Gibbons, Kaye 533, 1255
Gidding, Nelson 1993
Gide, 234
Gilbert, Douglas R. 1170r, 1554c,
    1679c
Gilbert, Sandra 536, 1408
Gilbert, Susan 781
Gilbert, William S. 440
Gilchrist, Ellen 533, 2390
Giles, Paul 129c
Gilkey, Langdon 979
Gill, Eric 1096
Gilman, Richard 68, 452, 478, 620
Gilson, Etienne 400, 1966
Gingher, Marianne 533
Girard, René 114c, 130, 311a, 403c,
    838, 1239, 1865

Giroux, Robert 261, 517, 519, 839, 976, 1015, 1177a, 1355, 1613, 1685, 1692

Glasgow, Ellen 433, 755, 1487, 1911c, 2008, 2645

Glatzer, Nahum N. 1386

Gleason, Philip 618

Goethe, Johann Wolfgang von 316, 867

Gogol, Nikolai 1435, 1521, 1982

Goldbrunner, Josef 1340

Golden, Robert E. 51, 72c, 153c, 205c, 563c, 566c, 597, 1321c, 1537c

Golding, William 816, 1522

Goodman, Allegra 356

Godwin, Gail 170, 781

Goodwin, Stephen 1017

Goody, J. 897

Gordon, Caroline 30c, 72, 100, 131, 152, 155, 205, 219, 222, 224, 225, 229, 273, 343, 383, 434, 502, 514, 515, 517, 518, 519, 521, 524, 527, 536, 538, 540, 546, 552, 553, 554, 560, 563, 564, 618, 643, 687, 688, 713, 748, 882, 941, 961c, 976, 1122, 1139, 1177a, 1178, 1188, 1212, 1232, 1294, 1321, 1345, 1355, 1483, 1522, 1539, 1571, 1710, 1759, 1826, 1864, 1984c, 2273

Gordon, Jaimy 1154c

Gordon, Mary 169c, 627, 628, 629, 1552

Gordon, Sarah 51a, 84a, 148, 152, 154c, 342a, 414, 430c, 497, 527, 633, 634, 635, 638, 646, 650, 1119, 1128, 1154a, 1154b, 1154c, 1177a, 1218a, 1236, 1386, 1453, 1483, 1502, 1639, 1652, 1676c, 1691, 1694, 1707

Gorman, Robert "Bob" 148, 1652

Gossett, Louise 878

Gossett, Thomas F. 671, 1164

Goyen, William 536, 656, 1715, 2009, 2050

Graff, Gerald 979

Graham, Billy 1188

Gratz, David 591

Grau, Shirley Ann 284, 307a, 380, 781, 1853, 1976

Gray, Richard 883c

Greeley, Andrew 283, 1552

Green, Eddie 738, 1365

Green, Henry 152

Green, Julien 2027

Green, Lewis 1490c

Green, Russell 293

Greenberg, Moshe 1386

Greenberg, Paul 665

Greene, Graham 618, 816, 831, 998, 1240, 1427, 1651, 1828, 1881, 1893, 1895, 1910, 1912, 1913, 1924, 1934, 2007a, 2088, 2396, 2459, 2465

Greene, H.E. 1791

Greene, Helen I. 290

Gresset, Michel 46, 561, 2050

Gretlund, Jan Nordby 393, 428, 593, 1187c, 1192c, 1584, 2057

Griffin, Ben 218, 1628

Griffin, John Howard 527, 839, 1667c, 1683

Griffith, Benjamin 678, 679, 1140

Griffith, Paul 509

Grimshaw, James A., Jr. 205c, 567c, 787, 1000c, 1125c, 1453, 1487c

Grossman, Allen 996

Grossman, Robert 583

Grunwald, Henry 1677

Guardini, Romano 199, 1755, 1923

Gubar, Susan 420, 536, 1408

Guillory, John 1527a

Guntrip, Harry 986

Gurdjieff, George Ivanovich 279

Gurganus, Allan 411, 832, 1317

Hall, Eileen 826, 1177a

Hall, James B. 289, 290, 295, 411

Hall, Martha Lacy 692c

Halliday, Michael Alexander

Kirkwood 1541
Hamblen, Abigail Ann 687
Hamill, Pete 1014
Hamilton, Barbara Tunnicliff 694
Hamilton, Dran 2730
Hamilton, Jane 1861
Hannah, Barry 304, 533, 747, 848,
    859, 881c, 1317, 1417
Hannibal, Edward 1014
Hannon, Jane 384c
Harben, Will 1972c
Hardin, John Wesley 898
Hardison, O.B., Jr. 1356
Hardwick, Elizabeth 33, 688, 736,
    842
Hardy, Thomas 531c
Harpham, Geoffrey Galt 215, 218
Harrington, Kate 2726
Harris, George Washington 739c,
    755, 1316, 1972c, 1982
Harris, Joel Chandler 217, 270, 1218,
    1315, 1344, 2343
Harrold, DeVene 1177a
Hart, Jane 308
Hartman, Carl 724, 1376
Hartman, Geoffrey 1130
Harty, Tony 1314b
Hasel, Gerhard F. 979
Hassan, Ihab 536, 1092, 1885, 2002
Haval, Václav 1332
Hawkes, John 70, 174, 234c, 297,
    354, 420, 443a, 495, 536, 564, 595,
    612, 626c, 775, 776, 784, 838, 851,
    878, 882, 884c, 918, 1056, 1105,
    1139, 1171, 1200, 1270, 1395,
    1512, 1602, 1604, 1605, 1620,
    1662, 1716, 1719, 1833, 1840,
    2604
Hawkes, Terence 922
Hawking, Stephen 905
Hawkins, Peter S. 648c, 999, 1354
Hawthorne, Nathaniel 62, 66, 96c,
    140, 146, 234, 246, 247c, 253c,
    264c, 321, 365, 456, 457, 462, 514,
    538, 581c, 678, 801, 820, 826, 890,
    1011, 1034, 1039, 1056, 1089,

1096, 1101, 1105, 1112, 1113,
    1115c, 1133, 1139, 1240, 1264,
    1278c, 1316, 1335c, 1503, 1512,
    1549, 1635c, 1651, 1688, 1691,
    1744, 1762, 1767, 1814, 1875,
    1902, 1908, 1943, 1946, 1971,
    2001, 2017, 2047, 2269, 2278,
    2559, 2627
Hawthorne, Rose 1039, 1691
Haynes, Alta 1177a
Hearst, Patty 1120
Hebert, Anne 1716
Hecker, Isaac 1014
Hegharty, Charles M. 154, 437
Heidegger, Martin 599, 725, 958,
    977, 1101, 1056a, 1213, 1396,
    1575, 1670, 1834
Heller, Joseph 816, 1139, 1906
Hemingway, Ernest 100c, 213, 365,
    618, 1014, 1066, 1070, 1085, 273c,
    1522, 1597, 1625, 1635c, 1651,
    1715, 1811c, 1893, 1934, 1946,
    1984c, 1994, 2009, 2010c
Hendin, Josephine Gattuso 218, 240,
    313, 339c, 361c, 424c, 440, 471,
    563c, 564c, 565c, 640, 660, 687,
    691c, 713, 751, 826, 882, 996, 999,
    1127, 1133, 1141, 1265, 1282,
    1324, 1356, 1451, 1512
Henley, Beth 873
Henry, O. 1053a
Hentz, Caroline Lee 1420c
Herberg, Will 126c
Herman, Matthew 1147, 2727
Hester, "Betty" Hazel Elizabeth 57,
    102a, 111, 261, 290, 325, 458, 509,
    517, 521, 563, 564, 632, 685, 723,
    724, 802, 966, 976, 1140, 1165,
    1292, 1401a, 1434, 1461, 1627,
    1628, 1651, 1654, 1663, 1691,
    1703, 2245
Hey, Mark 2725
Heyward, DuBose 231c
Hicks, Granville 68, 427c, 536,
    1077c, 1381, 1399, 1466, 1565,
    1610, 1624

Hiers, John T. 129c
Hill, A[mbrose]. P[owell]. 1516
Hill, D[aniel]. H[arvey]. 1516
Hill, James Frances [aka "Maniac
  Hill" or "Three Gun Hill"] 512, 899
Hillman, James 1860
Hinckley, John 1120
Hines, Melissa 1582
Hinojosa, Rolando 1911c
Hirsch, E.D. 958, 996
Hitchcock, Alfred 618, 1873
Hitler, Adolf 1116
Hobson, Fred 881
Hodgins, Jack 120, 1716
Hoffman, Eva 1269
Hoffman, Frederick J. 316, 688, 826,
  1959
Hoffman, Nancy Y. 1323
Hoffman, William 1490c
Holland, Norman 1741, 1845
Hollander, John 174
Holman, C. Hugh 172, 313, 748, 856,
  872c, 1635
Holmberg, Claes-Göran 2064
Holquist, Michael 587
Honig, Edwin 276
Hood, Hugh 120
Hood, Mary 479c, 760, 1625
Hood, Ruth Walker 1218
Hooper, Johnson Jones 418, 674c,
  755, 1315, 1344, 1972c
Hopkins, Gerard Manley 362, 977,
  1102, 1103, 1668
Hopkins, Mary Frances 393, 471
Horker, Tom 2725
House, Anderson G. 2728
Houseman, John 1147, 1475, 2727
Howard, Maureen 915
Howe, Irving 536, 802, 1381
Howe, Susan Elizabeth 51a
Howell, Elmo 1323
Howells, William Dean 1744
Hoyt, Charles Alva 339c
Hügel, Baron Freidrich von 599, 855,
  1755, 1810
Huggan, Isabel 120

Hughes, Langston 777c
Hugo, Richard 1795
Hume, Robert D. 1167
Humphrey, William 533, 1782, 1850
Humphries, Jefferson 586, 648c, 784,
  1125c
Hunt, Jim 1298
Hunter, Holly 497
Hurley, D.F. 591
Hurston, Zora Neale 209, 370, 614,
  960, 1173, 1174c, 1772c, 1857,
  2437, 2597
Huston, John 53, 141, 187, 204, 341,
  232a, 342, 373, 558, 572, 684, 695,
  730, 732, 858, 978, 989, 1018,
  1064, 1081, 1145, 1226, 1243,
  1322, 1428, 1509, 1543, 1560,
  1563, 2102, 2731
Hutcheon, Lina 881
Huysmans, Joris-Karl 2319
Hyman, Stanley Edgar 41, 313, 713,
  1133, 1455, 1466, 1510, 1719

Ibsen, Henrik 1945
Idol, John 1323
Ignatius, Saint 2340
Imthorn, Aleid 788
Ingram, Forrest L. 985, 1474, 2010
Inman, Ted Don, Jr. 1618
Inman, Ted Don, Sr. 480
Ionesco, Eugène 1762, 2620
Ireland, Patrick 393
Irving, John 784, 1503, 1916
Irving, Washington 1875
Iser, Wolfgang 247, 1175, 1845,
  2421
Ivey, Caroline Lawson 228, 1177a

Jackson, Jeff 1147, 1993, 2728
Jackson, Jesse 897
Jackson, Shirley 973c, 1794, 1976
Jackson, "Stonewall" [Thomas
  Jonathan] 1516
Jacobsen, Josephine 637, 760

James, Henry 139, 146, 366, 392, 429, 514, 519, 553, 560, 688, 779, 958, 1023, 1070, 1139, 1365, 1522, 1549, 1651, 1688, 1697, 1770, 1794, 1795, 1811c, 1864, 1902
James, William 418, 1719c
Jameson, Fredric 881
Janeway, Elizabeth 751
Jarman, Mark 51a, 637, 1400a
Jarrell, Randall 970, 1097
Jarvis, Graham 2726
Jaspers, Karl 400, 1135
Jauss, David 471, 1257, 1381
Jauss, Hans Robert 1175
Jeffers, Robinson 1893
Jenkins, Sue 1571
Jennings, Willie James 133, 788
Jensen, Gendron 797
Jerome, Saint 262
Jesus Christ 62, 77, 110, 131, 268, 305, 375, 450, 496, 643, 978, 987, 1040, 1054, 1056, 1160, 1353, 1387, 1427, 1436, 1507, 1551, 1615, 1720, 1737, 2168
Jewett, Sarah Orne 1744
Job 1100, 1353, 1386, 1500, 1535, 1997
Johanson, Ruthann 398c, 866c
John, Saint 1135
John of the Cross, Saint 965, 1724
John the Baptist 174a
Johnekin, Emma 1247
Johnson, Amy Edith 1120
Johnson, Charles 1603c
Johnson, Denis 421c
Johnson, Elizabeth Bryant 1972
Johnson, Greg 51a, 591, 1400a
Johnson, Miriam ("Mimi") 1177a, 1624
Johnson, Paul 1691
Johnson, Richard Malcolm 1344, 1972
Johnson, Samuel 1668
Johnston, Richard Malcolm 2343
Joines, John "Frail" and Blanche 1550

Jonas, Hans 1092
Jones, A. Alling 338
Jones, Anne 847
Jones, Gayl 278c
Jones, Jim 1116
Jones, LeRoi 2041
Jones, Madison 51a, 220, 383, 533, 591, 673c, 675c, 803, 1317, 1345, 1400a, 1438, 1522, 1579, 1850
Jones, Paul 1517
Jones, Robert Earl 1147, 2727
Jones, Tommy Lee 242, 497
Jonson, Ben 975
Jordan, Clarence 1683
Jordan, Glenn 1044, 1432, 1581, 1582, 1993, 2727
Jorgensen, Johannes 1376
Joselyn, M., Sr. 313
Joyce, James 77c, 84, 241, 608c, 785c, 975, 1103, 1111, 1115c, 1139, 1168c, 1215, 1328c, 1422, 1429, 1458, 1460, 1521, 1612, 1726, 1887, 1893, 2064, 2452
Judd, Sylvester 1112
Judge, John J., Jr. 72
Julian, [the Apostate] Emperor 984, 1265
Julian, [the Hospitaller] Saint 795, 984
Jung, Carl 38, 71, 75b, 102a, 316, 326, 990, 1056a, 1135, 1340c, 1376, 1720, 1970
Justus, James 536
Juvenal [Roman poet] 1323

Kaelin, Eugene F. 958
Kafka, Franz 463, 519, 522c, 1139, 1181, 1280c, 1320, 1355, 1600, 1762, 1846, 1945, 2137
Kahane, Claire 313, 444, 564, 570, 587, 826, 882, 1702
Kane, Patricia 1381
Kaplan, Carola M. 945
Katz, Claire Kahane 164a, 174, 541 586, 879, 1324, 1466, 1628

Kay, Terry 1579
Kayser, Wolfgang 454, 590, 892, 1135, 1808, 1812
Kazin, Alfred 536, 601, 823, 1323, 1494
Keane, Philip 385c
Keillor, Garrison 583, 988
Keith, Bill 1716
Keller, Jane Carter 1323
Kellogg, Gene 1323
Kelly, Frank 72
Kelly, Gene 33, 2729
Kempe, Margery 1129a
Keneas, Alex 1226
Kennan, George 1365
Kennedy, J. Gerald 903c
Kennedy, John F. 1683
Kennedy, John Pendleton 1799
Kennelly, Laura B. 1694
Kermode, Frank 1290c
Kerr, Walter 1144
Kesey, Ken 1785c, 1976
Kessler, Edward 541, 586, 618, 762, 1177a, 1301c
Kettle, Arnold 721
Key, Tom 1529
Kidd, Hariett 833
Kieft, Ruth M. Vande 1178
Kiely, Robert 332
Kierkegaard, Sören 165c, 455, 642, 735, 1137, 1455, 1852, 1941
Kilcourse, George 838c
Killinger, John 1661c
Killinger, Sam 1123c
King, Grace Elizabeth 1420c, 1817
King, Martin Luther, Jr., 444, 622, 1683
Kingsolver, Barbara 1397
Kinney, Arthur F. 641c, 853, 878, 879, 1054, 1177a, 1382c
Kinsella, W.P. 1361c
Kirk, Russell 713, 854
Kirkland, William M. 293, 855
Klevar, Harvey 1517
Klinkowitz, Jerome 562, 1309
Knapp, Bettina L. 339c, 749c

Knowles, John 1939c
Kolve, V.A. 1356
Koon, William 1177a
Kosinski, Jerzy 1833, 1916, 1965
Kracauer, Siegfried 1041c
Kraft, Stephanie 339c
Kramer, Stephen 293
Kreyling, Michael 58, 1681c
Kristeva, Julia 1701
Kronenberger, Louis 126
Kugelmann, Robert 794
Kumin, Maxine 51a, 641c, 1400a
Kundera, Milan 1200
Küng, Hans 826, 1668
Kuryluk, Ewa 454

Lacan, Jacques 71, 236, 826, 1057, 1058, 1059, 1752, 1958
Lackey, Allen D. 996
LaFarge, Oliver 882
Landt, Elizabeth 800a
Langkjaer, Erik 287a, 292, 509, 666
Lanier, Sidney 1534
Lardner, Ring 1522c, 1982
Larsen, Val 419c
Lasseter, Victor 591
Lasworth, Laura 194, 571, 616, 637a, 899a, 1197, 1206, 1218a, 1467
Lauter, Paul 536
Lawrence, D.H. 122, 213, 826, 1215, 1615a, 1893, 2483
Lawrence, Roberta 1177a
Lawson, Lewis A. 136c, 424c, 457, 532c, 1296c
Lax, Robert 839
Layman, Richard 997c
Leaf, Munroe 1689c
Lear, Edward 1402
Le Clair, Thomas 240, 1408
Lee, Harper 677, 1610, 1663c, 1715, 1940, 2008
Lee, Hermione 688
Lee, Maryat 261, 290, 292, 293, 509, 517, 538, 564, 584, 589, 640, 788, 802, 907, 914, 1155, 1165, 1177a,

Lee, Maryat (con't) 1202, 1292, 1306, 1347, 1575, 1671, 1683, 1691, 1692, 1694, 1930a
Lee, Robert E. 290, 1516, 1533
Leffland, Ella 535c
Lehmann-Haupt, Christopher 1545
Leighton, Peter 1618
Leo XIII, Pope 618
Leonard, B.J. 418
Leslie, Daniel 1661
Lessing, Doris 972
Lester, Brenda 1659a
Lester, Julius 1701
Leverington, Shelby 2730
Leviton, Jay 1120
Lewis, C.S. 446, 1014, 1097, 1112, 1152c, 1559, 1691, 1791, 1924, 2200
Lewis, Jerry 845, 1687
Lewis, Henry Clay 1335c
Lewis, R.W.B. 536, 882
Lewis, Sinclair 1344
Liesman, Paul D. 72
Liggett, Sarah 595
Lindaman, Edward B. 103
Lindley, Denver 1177a
Lindsay, Vachel 970
Linehan, Thomas M. 921c
Lipson, Leonard 1147
Lish, Loretta 1212
Lispector, Clarice 2138
Littlefield, Daniel F., Jr. 308, 979, 1635
Lochridge, Betsy 68
Locke, John 1333
Logsdon, Loren 594c
Long, Beverly 393
Long, Mary Ann 1163, 2719
Longfellow, 263
Longinus 1752c
Longstreet, Augustus Baldwin 217, 270, 477, 755, 1253c, 1315, 1344c, 1982
Lonnquist, Barbara C. 476, 594
Lorentzen, Mel 724
Lott, Brett 51a, 1218a, 1400a

Love, Betty Boyd 218, 929, 1177a, 1292
Lowe, John 209c
Lowell, Amy 736
Lowell, Robert 33, 140, 503, 509, 514, 521, 536, 618, 736, 823, 842, 969, 970, 1053a, 1097, 1461, 2533
Lowry, Beverly 1653
Lowry, Paul W. 72
Lubbock, Percy 1365c
Lucács, Georg 2110
Lukas, Dorothy A. 946
Lundgren, Caj 2123c
Lunz, Elisabeth 913
Lynch, John 1127, 1810
Lynch, William F. 72, 400, 618, 1925
Lynn, Steven 1408
Lyra, F. 2127
Lytle, Andrew [Nelson] 88c, 89, 222, 289, 290, 295, 502, 536, 643, 936, 1289, 1292, 1376, 1461, 1522, 1641a, 1700, 1713, 1714, 1864

Macauley, Robie 289, 290, 509, 1212, 1522, 1641a
MacDonald, George 1924
MacLeish, Archibald 1893
MacLeod, Joan 120
MacQueen, Melanie 1123, 1661
Madden, David 51a
Madison, David 1400a
Maeterlinck, Maurice 1376
Magee, Rosemary M. 68, 478c
Maida, Patricia D. 241, 471, 1381
Mailer, Norman 213, 481, 826c, 1139, 1878c, 1907, 1976, 2041, 2123
Mairs, Nancy 51a, 959a, 1218a
Maisel, Edward 509
Makowsky, Veronica 1294c
Malamud, Bernard 720, 816, 934, 1056, 1522, 1577, 1624, 1742, 1794, 1834, 1901c, 1931, 1976, 1990, 1999

Malebranche, Nicolas 1213

Malin, Irving 46, 621, 1127, 1230

Mallard, William 913

Maloff, Saul 1323

Malraux, André-George 1139, 1376, 1966

Mammel, Kenneth 1314a

Man, Paul de 1200, 1372

Manley, Frank 1287

Mann, Margaret Florencourt 1199, 1652

Mann, Sally 98a

Mann, Thomas 1429

Manning, Carol S. 129c

Mansfield, Katherine 285c, 781, 927, 2283

Manson, Charles 1116, 1120

Manson, Derek 1529

Marcel, Gabriel 77, 642, 1347, 1376, 1508, 1808, 1966

Mariani, Paul 637, 641c

Mariapragasam, Flavia 1250

Marion, Francis 1516

Marion, John H. 126

Maritain, Jacques 84a, 102a, 174a, 215, 400, 434, 511, 513c, 553, 839, 851, 1040, 1102c, 1103c, 1105, 1347, 1376c, 1600, 1668, 1810, 1966, 2050, 2475

Maritain, Raïsa 434

Marks, W.S., III 912, 1438

Marlowe, Christopher 867

Márquez, Gabriel García 1280c

Marrow, Sue 2728

Marsh, Tiger Jo 2730

Marshall, Thurgood 1683

Martin, Carter W. 153c, 308, 361c, 393, 454, 471, 564c, 565c, 999, 1125c, 1133, 1257, 1393, 1537, 1580, 1638, 1680c, 1698, 1709

Martin, Jay 1719

Martin, Karl 539

Martin, Renae 68a

"Mary Ann" [See Long, Mary Ann]

Mason, Bobbie Ann 59, 136, 533, 594, 604, 1492, 1625, 1871

Master, Edgar Lee 2730

Masters, Olga 1121

Matthew, Saint 770

Matthews, Jack 477

Matute, Ana Maria 1558

Mauriac, François 178, 998, 1024, 1240, 1344, 1376, 1455, 1597, 1683, 1810, 1912, 1966, 1983, 2027

Maxwell, Allen 1177a

Maxwell, William 2009

May, Charles E. 445c, 942

May, John R. 313, 471, 563c, 826, 882, 979, 1386, 1511, 1537c, 1580, 1635, 1638

Mayer, Charles W. 594c, 861

Mayhew, Leonard 851

McAlexander, Hubert H. 1017

McCaffrey, Larry 536

McCarthy, Cormac 533, 1083c, 1230c, 1239, 1317, 1490c, 1491, 1492, 1657

McCarthy, Mary 618, 702, 1014, 1032, 1598, 1857, 1976, 2281, 2594

McCorkle, Jill 1443, 1568c

McCown, James 292, 527, 654, 802, 935, 1024, 1087, 1127, 1165

McCown, Robert 687

McCullagh, James C. 1408

McCullers, Carson 56, 71, 80c, 94, 119, 138, 150, 180, 206, 225, 247c, 284, 301c, 321, 412, 423, 436, 527c, 556, 662, 721c, 741, 748, 752, 769, 781, 800a, 1228c, 1249, 1269, 1289, 1326, 1342, 1343, 1415, 1416, 1487, 1559a, 1585, 1628, 1635c, 1636, 1699, 1715, 1727, 1747, 1769, 1782, 1784, 1812, 1817, 1821, 1839, 1845, 1853, 1871, 1874, 1875, 1886, 1897, 1919, 1940, 1945, 1956, 1967, 1975, 1976, 1997, 2024, 2025c, 2026c, 2035, 2036, 2064, 2091c, 2241, 2272, 2374, 2440, 2447, 2525, 2530, 2593, 2730

McDermott, John V. 471
McDonnell, Marion 1429
McFarland, Dorothy Tuck 313, 563c,
    999, 1282, 1380, 1381, 1511, 1662
McInerny, Ralph 1014
McIntosh, Mavis 1177a
McKane, Janet 57, 261, 521
McKee, Elizabeth 517, 521, 1122,
    1177a, 1613, 1616, 1624, 1692
McKenzie, Barbara 338c, 567c, 641c,
    858c, 861, 1036c, 1045c, 1125c,
    1172r, 1487c, 1582
McLuhan, Marshall 31, 126c, 1139,
    1715
McMillan, Norman 584
McMullen, Joanne Halleran 595c
McMurtry, Larry 747
McNeil, David 939
McTyre, Joe 1549
Meatyard, Ralph Eugene 772c, 891c
Mellard, James M. 354, 454, 541,
    659, 882
Melville, Herman 164a, 246, 678,
    820, 962c, 1056, 1075c, 1089,
    1094c, 1335c, 1549, 1635, 1688,
    1762, 1770, 1866, 1908, 1946,
    1971, 1974, 2049
Mencken, H.L. 1669
Meredith, George 975
Meridith, George 524c
Merrill, Arthur J. 502, 1478
Mertens, Dominique 1362
Merton, Thomas 77, 100, 165c, 524,
    607, 713, 715, 839c, 965, 1015,
    1066, 1167, 1259, 1425, 1462,
    1563, 1594, 1610, 1723, 1724,
    1900
Meryash, Arthur 1154c
Messick, Hank 295
Metcalf, John 1716
Meyers, Bertrande 1077
Michael, Leonard 2064
Midler, Robert 240
Milder, Robert 162c, 1635
Miller, Arthur 1439, 1795
Miller, Betty 2725

Miller-Budick, Emily 164a
Miller, Catherine 2725
Miller, J. Hillis 218
Miller, James E. 1092
Miller, Margaret 83
Millichap, Joseph R. 588
Mills, C. Wright 126c
Milne, Gordon 1965
Milton, John 53c, 926c, 1102c,
    1512c, 1559, 2090
Ming, Zhong 174
Minor, Jeanne 1177a
Mirandola 968
Mitchell, Margaret 800a, 1266c
Mohs, Mayo 1507
Molloy, Robert 755
Momaday, M. Scott 1763c
Moncrieff, George Scott 854
Montgomery, Marion 83, 152, 175,
    244c, 399c, 743, 984, 999, 1038c,
    1100, 1119, 1127, 1177a, 1305c,
    1381, 1393, 1401c, 1431, 1487c,
    1489c, 1579, 1580, 1581, 1582,
    1651
Mooney, Harry S. 339c
Moore, Brian 574
Moore, Marianne 524
Moorhead, Agnes 2729
Moran, Annette 838
Moravia, Alberto 1088, 2045
Morgan, Berry 533
Morisset, Henri 561
Morris, Alice 261
Morris, Ann Orr 83
Morris, Joe 759b
Morris, Wright 1742
Morrison, Toni 278c, 370, 802, 939,
    1736, 1748c, 1769, 2146, 2536
Mortimer, John 2002
Morton, Mary L. 1445
Moser, Barry 133
Mosley, Deborah 638
Mounier, Emmanuel 1686c
Muecke, D.C. 832a

Muller, Gilbert 361c, 431, 454, 565c, 588, 713, 878, 879, 999, 1127, 1282, 1335, 1376, 1393, 1635
Mullins, C. Ross, Jr. 68
Munk, Linda 120
Munro, Alice 84a, 120, 412c, 720, 2266, 2405, 2457
Murdoch, Iris 53, 685, 1401a
Murfree, Mary Noailles 1972
Murphy, George D. 588
Murphy, John J. 1134
Musil, Donna 1659a

Nabokov, Vladimir 826c, 1139, 1280c, 1521, 1522c, 1906, 2603
Nash, Ogden 538
Needleman, Jacob 1200
Neligan, Dorrie 152, 743a, 1652
Neligan, Patrick, Jr., 1147
Nemerov, Howard 789, 1939
Nettels, Elsa 781
Nevins, Allan 666
Newkirk, Terrye 70c
Newman, Georgia A. 1154
Newman, John Henry 499
Nicholson, Martin 2730
Niebuhr, Reinhold 1668
Nielsen, Erik 1619c, 2110
Nietzsche, Friedrich 977, 1030, 1137
Nifong, D. Michael 1659a
Nijinsky, Vaslav 1428
Nin, Anais 973c
Nipson, Herbert 295
Nisly, Paul W. 1140c, 1530
Noble, Barbara 1993, 2730
Nordan, Lewis 1813
Norman, Geoffrey 1174, 1255
Norris, Frank 1556, 2001
Norris, Helen 533
North, Alex 1560
Northey, Margot 1716
Nowell-Smith, Geoffrey 1226
Null, Martha Pennington 1177a
Nuñez, Victor 1147, 1993

Nunn, Kem 870c
Nye, Valerie 550a

Oates, Joyce Carol 180, 339c, 405, 591c, 784, 878, 878, 879, 1329, 1354, 1462, 1625, 1631c, 1716, 1736, 1795, 1827, 1959, 1976, 2017, 2018, 2483, 2536
O'Brien, Conan 2526
O'Connor, Edward F., Jr. 51a, 75, 502, 515, 523, 526, 643, 1384
O'Connor, Edwin 620
O'Connor, Frank 1522
O'Connor, Joan 1177a
O'Connor, Patricia 1610
O'Connor, Regina Cline 140, 148, 173, 292, 387, 437, 502, 510, 511, 515, 521, 602, 649, 667, 690, 764a, 929, 935, 1092, 1122, 1128, 1147, 1172, 1177a, 1199, 1210, 1236, 1251, 1368, 1384, 1432, 1484, 1896, 2020, 2023
Odom, Lillian 1592
O'Donnell, Edward 1387a, 1607a
Oe, Kenzaburo 1201
Oetgen, Janey 232a
O'Faolain, Sean 752
Oleneva, Valentia 2127
Olsen, Tillie 1857
Olson, Steven 599
O'Neill, Eugene 1552, 1893
Ong, Walter J. 618, 897
Oreovicz, Cheryl Z. 861
Orteza, Arsenio 1387a, 1607a
Ovid 174
Orvell, Miles 263, 264, 276, 313, 354, 361c, 397c, 471, 564c, 565c, 740c, 882, 897, 979, 996, 999, 1127, 1208c, 1635, 1638, 1690, 2057
Otto, Rudolf 2072
Ovid, 174
Ower, John 1381
Ozick, Cynthia 59, 594, 1828, 1931

Pacey, Desmond 1716
Packard, Vance 126c
Page, Marion Peterman 1177a
Page, Thomas Nelson 1799
Pagels, Elaine 1092
Paley, Grace 59, 594, 720, 1976
Palmer, John 536
Pancake, Breece D'J 1803
Paris, Robby 2730
Park, Ann G. 1652
Park, Clara Claiborne 912, 1246c,
    1290c, 1451, 1691
Parker, Dorothy 1330
Parks, Marvin 1349
Parr, Newell 1314b
Pascal, Blaise 324
Passos, John Dos 561, 1858, 2009
Patrick, Anne 979
Patterson, Tom 1243
Paul, Saint 232a, 444, 611, 711, 987,
    1101, 1648, 1808, 2490
Paulson, Suzanne Morrow 586, 591,
    1232, 1246, 1629c, 1694
Payne, David 1659a
Peale, Norman Vincent 126c
Pearce, Richard 339c, 946
Pearson, Michael 641c
Peden, William 136c
Peirce, Charles Sanders 1530
Pelton, Robert 800
Percy, Walker 53, 77, 97c, 106, 208,
    219, 222, 229, 310c, 323, 334, 337,
    358c, 359c, 363c, 391c, 402, 404c,
    446, 451, 519, 532, 543, 546, 567,
    618, 619, 642c, 648, 703c, 709,
    740, 747, 750, 779, 801c, 831, 835,
    842, 857c, 861, 862, 883, 900c,
    903, 932, 939c, 961, 966, 970,
    1014, 1022, 1023a, 1024, 1034,
    1174c, 1204c, 1252c, 1255, 1259,
    1260, 1277c, 1289, 1302, 1355,
    1429, 1434, 1455, 1456, 1489,
    1491, 1492, 1494, 1530, 1538,
    1539, 1545c, 1552, 1617, 1620,
    1660, 1670, 1709, 1710, 1735,
    1738, 1754, 1759, 1759, 1763c,

1791c, 1799, 1825, 1852, 1859,
    1876, 1881, 1916, 1931, 1933,
    1965, 2022, 2024, 2064, 2110,
    2123, 2212, 2447, 2486, 2623
Percy, William Alexander 932, 1260
Perelman, S.J. 583
Peretti, Frank 1240c
Perpetua, Sister 1079
Persse, Patricia 1183, 1314b, 1592
Persse, Winnifred 1314b
Peter, Saint 1185
Peterson, Levi 463
Petry, Alice Hall 1381
Petry, Ann 1976
Phillips, Jayne Anne 1020, 2038
Phillips, Lance 293
Phillips, Mary 293
Phillips, William 536
Piaget, Jean 1878
Pickney, Josephine 755
Pieper, Josef 1110c
Pierce, C.S. 1763
Pius XII, Pope 33, 502
Pizer, Donald 1513
Plath, Sylvia 1773c, 1976, 2190
Plato 968, 1101, 1141, 1332
Platzner, Robert L. 1167
Poe, Edgar Allan 67, 146, 159, 322,
    396, 470, 477c, 514, 522c, 538,
    561, 569, 909, 1056, 1089, 1101,
    1105, 1109c, 1118c, 1409, 1556,
    1591, 1715, 1766, 1767, 1794,
    1835, 1875, 1879, 1982, 2001,
    2017, 2286, 2583
Poggioli, Renato 783
Poirier, Richard 713, 1130, 1466
Pollack, Harriet 1292
Poller, Rebekah Massey 1177a, 1624
Polycarp, Saint 1079
Pope, Alexander 975
Portch, Stephen R. 688
Porter, Helen 120
Porter, Katherine Anne 72, 143, 209,
    213c, 273, 324c, 383, 412, 429,
    433, 513, 618, 671, 748, 826, 847,
    927, 928, 970, 1014, 1066, 1139,

1177a, 1288, 1289, 1330, 1345,
1432, 1585, 1610, 1624, 1651,
1699, 1701, 1727, 1745, 1759,
1794, 1820, 1850, 1857, 1871,
1976, 2018, 2281, 2373, 2399,
2548
Porter, Kathleen Sullivan 414
Portis, Charles 533
Pound, Ezra 970, 977, 1098, 1115c
Powell, Padgett 51a, 533, 1400a
Powers, Douglas 639, 1284, 1443
Powers, J.F. 71, 159, 169c, 285c,
514, 620, 857c, 924, 970, 1014,
1023a, 1024, 1139, 1204c, 1522,
1548, 1854, 1876, 1933, 1976,
1984c
Powers, Jessica 1015c
Powers, John R. 1014
Praz, Mario 618
Prescott, Peter S. 431
Prewitt, James 441
Price, George 502
Price, Reynolds 180, 367c, 537, 831,
881, 1653, 1715, 2009
Pritchett, V.S. 339c, 687
Proust, Marcel 35, 54, 236c, 519,
538, 648, 773, 775, 1125, 1139,
1429, 1522c, 1860
Prud'hon, Pierre-Paul 2156
Pulleine, Tim 1226
Purdy, James 206, 819, 1139, 1907
Pynchon, Thomas 816, 1552, 1651,
1735, 1833, 1858, 1866, 1879,
1908, 1965

Quinn, John J. 72, 1311c, 1318c
Quinn, M. Bernetta 1296c, 1354,
1513
Quinn, Richard W. 72
Quintilian, M. Fabius 2384

Rad, Gerhard von 979
Ragen, Brian Abel 288, 1092, 1333,
1676c

Rahner, Karl 618, 1598, 1668
Rahv, Philip 536
Ramsey, Alta 290
Rand, Ayn 1139
Ransom, John Crowe 80, 222, 514,
527, 536, 678, 789, 1159, 1292,
1641a, 1683, 1709, 1714, 1824
Raper, Julius Rowan 881
Rath, Sura P. 639, 1245c, 1474,
1694c
Rawlings, Marjorie Kinnan 433
Raybon, Patricia 466
Reesman, Jeanne Campbell 1694
Reindl, Frank 1219
Reising, Russell 979
Reisman, David 126c
Renner, Stanley 1319
Rice, Phillip Blair 527
Rich, Adrienne 370
Rich, Frank 1226
Richard, Claude 313
Richards, I.A. 1698
Richardson, H. Edward 109c
Ricoeur, Paul 1034, 1530c, 1763
Riding, Laura 1871
Riffaterre, Michael 1481, 1991
Rimes, Robert 1308
Rimmon, Shlomith 1506
Rivard, Faye 68
Rivers, Caryl 1014
Rogers, Roy 1687
Romagosa, Edward J. 1308
Rooke, Leon 120
Rose, Jane A. 636, 788, 1659a
Rosen, Norma 826
Rosenfeld, Isaac 502, 882
Rosenmeier, Rosamond 420
Rossetti, Christina 973c
Roth, Henry 777c
Roth, Philip 591, 1976
Rouault, Georges 1818
Rousseau, Jean-Jacques 1983
Rout, Kathleen 688
Rowse, A.L. 1466
Roy, Paula A. 1341
Rubin, Larry 591

Rubin, Louis D., Jr. 313, 339c, 383,
    477, 536, 713, 748, 881, 882, 1014,
    1119, 1127, 1133, 1345, 1360,
    1393, 1399, 1485, 1511, 1581,
    1582, 1635
Ruether, Radford 1092
Rule, Janice 2729
Runyan, Mary 764a
Rupp, Richard H. 1178
Ruppersburg, Hugh 939, 1363
Rushton, John 373
Ruskin, John 1752c
Russell, Henry 133, 384, 584, 788
Russell, James 736
Russell, Richard 1177a
Russell, Mary Virginia 87
Ryan, Abram 1014
Ryan, Elizabeth Shreve 1349
Ryan, John 1349
Ryan, Roberta M. 1349
Ryan, Steven T. 861

Salinger, J.D. 669, 826c, 1742, 1906,
    1976, 1999, 2130
Sallee, Mary 293
Samway, Patrick 883c
Sandeen, Eric J. 1365
Santacroce, Mary Nell 2731
Santayana, George 1135
Sarris, Andrew 1226
Sartre, Jean Paul 774, 816, 1066,
    1101, 1344, 1754c, 1934, 1997
Satterfield, Ben 536, 1221, 1309,
    1662, 1870
Satterfield, Virginia 1177a
Saussure, Ferdinand de 549
Savory, Jerold 1127
Sayers, Dorothy 1934
Scarry, Elaine 218, 1701
Schaub, Thomas Hill 415, 591, 592c
Schemmel, William [Bill] 1371
Schenck, Mary Jane 471
Schepis, Tallulah 1128
Schiller, Johann 467
Schimanski, Stefan 599

Schlafer, Linda 393
Schliefer, Ronald 174, 646
Schmude, Karl 1121
Schnack, Elisabeth 1716
Schneidau, Herbert 218
Schoonenberg, Piet 1755
Schott, Webster 1381
Schweska, Ingred 2725
Scorsese, Martin 2677
Scott, Katherine 1177a, 1371
Scott, Nathan A., Jr. 751
Scott, R. Neil 550a, 1202, 1318c
Scouten, Kenneth 1140c
Scura, Dorothy M. 781
Segrest, Mab 478a, 1701
Seidel, Kathryn Lee 587
Selby, John 1613
Semmes, Kate Flannery 292, 502
Semmes, Mrs. Raphael 764a
Sessions, William ["Bill"] 342a, 527,
    599, 685, 792, 800a, 913, 1401a,
    1688
Settle, Mary Lee 2038
Sexton, Anne 2190
Shakespeare, William 236c, 1080,
    1635, 2538c
Sharp, Becky 1892c
Sharp, Paula 591c
Shaw, George Bernard 1893
Shaw, Mary Neff 1245c, 1694
Sheehan, Thomas 1387c
Shelby, John 92, 1692
Shelley, Mary 1752c
Shelnutt, Eve 1414
Shepard, Alan Bartlett, Jr. 1516
Shepard, Claire 133
Sherry, Gerald E. 68, 1688, 1691
Shields, John C. 1054
Shinn, Thlma J. 587, 1324
Shkovsky, Victor 446
Shloss, Carol 424c, 469c, 564c, 567c,
    595, 862, 878, 882, 999, 1036c,
    1125c, 1282, 1354, 1380, 1396,
    1487c, 1635, 1662
Shor, Daniel 342, 684, 2731
Shore, Fred 1993

Shore, Jerome 1147, 2726
Shore, Jerry 1993
Showalter, Elaine 420, 1292, 1559a
Sibley, Celestine 68, 1434, 1517
Sidney, Sir Philip 868
Sieh, Margaret 68
Silko, Leslie 59, 594, 1625
Sillitoe, Alan 1913
Simon, Andre 561
Simon, John W. 1662
Simons, John 536
Simpson, Lewis P. 400c, 748, 751, 881, 1669
Singleton, John 2675
Slater, Shirley 2728
Slattery, Dennis P. 414
Sloane, Thomas O. 586
Smedley, Agnes 33
Smelstor, Marjorie 945
Smiley, Jane 1861
Smith, Bessie 1365
Smith, Jonathan Z. 680
Smith, Lane 2727
Smith, Lee 51a, 86c, 637, 741, 747c, 781, 1400a, 1443, 1568c, 1625, 1813
Smith, Lillian 527, 1699, 1701c, 1702c
Smith, Lucy Nell Cunningham 152
Smith, Marcus 1177a
Smith, Robert N. 437
Snipes, Katherine 945
Snyder, Gary 1917
Snyder, Marc 726
Södergran, Edith 2023
Solomon, Rhoda 1177a
Solotaroff, Theodore 339c
Solzhenitsyn, Alexander 1108, 1113, 1117, 1332
Somé, Malidoma Patrice 75b, 1970
Sontag, Susan 1976
Sophocles 282c, 715, 1066, 1105, 1997, 2446
Southwell, Robert 1892
Spark, Muriel 1890, 1934
Spears, Monroe 536, 1714

Speigel, Blaine 637
Spellman, Cardinal 1102c
Spencer, Elizabeth 1233, 1653
Spenser, Edmund 53c
Spiegel, Alan 1426
Spilka, Mark 1809
Spitler, Jim 1147
Spivey, Ted R. 261, 541, 723, 851, 883c, 1456, 1461, 1466, 1681c
Sprieser, Martha Bell 1463
Springsteen, Bruce 497, 1260, 1464, 1465, 1539
Stafford, Jean 1976
Staley, Thomas F. 339c
Stallings, Sylvia 536
Stallman, R.W. 1513
Stallybrass, Peter 587, 1701
Stanton, Elizabeth Cady 1092
Stanton, Harry Dean 684, 1560, 2731
Starr, Belle 898
Steele, Jeffrey 339c
Stein, Edith 632
Stein, Gertrude 370, 1092
Steinbeck, John 408, 1344, 1875, 2009, 2010c
Steinberg, Leo 247
Stelzmann, Rainulf A. 1343, 1472
Stembridge, Marion 1640
Stephens, C. Ralph 1157c, 2188c
Stephens, Martha 313, 438c, 471, 564c, 565c, 595, 713, 791, 878, 882, 979, 996, 999, 1069, 1166c, 1282, 1335, 1512, 1537c, 1662
Stern, Richard 1683, 2064
Sternberg, Meir 1934
Sterritt, David 1226
Stevens, Wallace 56, 1297
Stevenson, Elisabeth 913
Stillwell, Cynthia 759d
Stoler, Shirley 1147, 1432, 2727
Stone, John 1092, 1579
Stone, Oliver 2675
Stone, Robert 819
Stoneback, H.R. 1725
Stout, Janis P. 209c
Stowe, Harriet Beecher 247c

Streight, Irwin 120, 419c, 838c
Stritch, Thomas 465
Strozier, Robert ("Bob") 501a, 227, 764a
Struthers, Tim 1716
Stuart, Henry Logan 1984c
Stuart, Jesse Hilton 109
Stuart, Ruth McEnery 1972
Sturma, Lee 541
Styron, William 80, 321, 322, 418, 561, 703c, 911, 1139, 1174c, 1215, 1302, 1317, 1631c, 1715, 1742, 1782, 1784, 1799, 1830, 1850, 1878c, 1897, 1976, 2009, 2024, 2064, 2123, 2155
Suckow, Ruth 285c
Sukenick, Ronald 1934
Sullivan, John 287a, 509
Sullivan, Mary C. 51, 72c, 153c, 563c, 566c, 1321c, 1537c
Sullivan, Walter 152, 290, 687, 748, 1127, 1147, 1381, 1466, 1635, 1658
Suyama, Shizuo 2155
Sweeny, Steve 1172
Swift, Jonathan 740c, 1103, 1112, 1323, 1402
Sypher, Wylie 1766, 2002

Tabb, John Banister 1014
Tanizaki, Jun'ichiro 1138c
Tarantino, Quentin 388
Tate, Allen 30c, 80, 105c, 219, 222, 224, 225, 229, 261, 434, 477, 540, 543, 618, 789, 842, 932, 1292, 1489, 1530, 1634, 1669, 1709, 1710, 1713, 1759, 1824, 1826, 1864, 2004, 2025c, 2026c, 2556
Tate, Caroline Gordon. *See* Gordon, Caroline.
Tate, J.O. 104, 240, 288, 468a, 470, 471, 522, 591, 638, 979, 1453, 1580, 1651, 1652, 1775
Tate, James 87, 293, 1513, 1515, 1522

Tate, Mary Barbara 87, 152, 293, 541, 1251, 1364, 1434, 1652
Tate, Sue Fan 83
Taylor, Edward 1070
Taylor, June Whitley 2728
Taylor, Peter 94, 225, 527, 781, 789, 881c, 1017, 1287, 1289, 1293c, 1522, 1967, 2275, 2394
Teresa of Avila, Saint 499
Terrell, Dahlia 1303c
Terry, Grace 297, 1177a
Tharin, Miriam 1314b
Theresa of Avila, Saint 965
Theroux, Alexander 884
Thieman, Fred R. 384
Thomas, Alma (aka "Guerilla Girl Alma Thomas) 51a, 1400a
Thomas, Dylan 1893
Thomas, Saint 588, 1103, 1135, 1300, 1312, 1530, 1557, 1723
Thompson, Francis J. 1356
Thompson, James J., Jr. 1489c
Thompson, Kristin 342
Thompson, Mary Jo 87
Thompson, William 217, 400, 1344
Thomson, Philip 1809
Thoreau, Henry David 1549, 2706
Thornton, Jack 1251
Thorpe, Thomas Bangs 755, 1094
Thorpe, Willard 536
Tillich, Paul 979, 999, 1427
Tilman, Walter 262
Tindall, George B. 746c
Tolkien, J.R.R. 1102, 1112
Tolomeo, Diane 687, 1535
Tolstoy, [Leo] Nikolaevich 977, 1139
Tomkievicz, Shirley Abbott 1177a
Tomkins, Jane 420
Tönies, Ferdinand 1883c
Toole, John Kennedy 148c, 262c, 533, 619c, 791, 939c, 1198a, 1355c
Toombs, Robert 1516
Toomer, Jean 279c, 1249c, 1656
Torchia, Joseph 414, 497, 1542
Tournier, Paul 905
Towers, Robert 240, 882

Townend, Joseph C. 72
Trachtenberg, Alan 751
Tracy, David 618, 1237c
Trainor, Richard 1543
Trawick, Jessie 1177a
Treanor, Mrs. Hugh 502
Treanor, Kate L. 502
Treanor, Margaret Ida 502
Tresmontant, Claude 400, 979
Trexler, Margaret Persse 1314b, 1592
Trilling, Lionel 1965, 2008
True, Michael D. 240, 687, 979
Trugill, Eric 1408
Tucker, Sophie 738
Tullos, Allen 1550
Tuozzolo, Leonard J. 1652
Turner, Margaret 68
Turner, Victor 75b, 1921, 1970
Tuttleton, James W. 1965
Twain, Mark 448c, 663, 678, 737,
    962c, 1316, 1334c, 1660, 1746,
    1799, 1852, 1972c, 1982
Tyler, Anne 468, 781, 1263c, 1269c,
    1562, 1568c

Uhler, Margaret 87
Ulanov, Ann Belford 420
Unamuno, Miguel de 1997
Underhill, Evelyn 965c, 1132, 1900,
    2084
Updike, John 164a, 208, 283, 1056,
    1577, 1754, 1795, 1811c, 1834,
    1962, 1965, 1976, 1990, 1999

Valenzuela, Luisa 2670
Valéry, Paul 854
Van Doren, Carl 100
Van Doren, Mark 100
Van Gogh, Vincent 499
Vaughn, Ellen 1240c
Vawter, Bruce 575
Vilalta, Maruxa 2384
Villon, François 54, 648, 773, 775,
    1125, 1860

Vizenor, Gerald 59, 594
Voegelin, Eric 400, 1098c, 1101c,
    1105, 1108, 1110c, 1401, 1431,
    1651, 2511
Vonnegut, Kurt, Jr. 816, 1906, 1908,
    2730

Wagner-Martin, Linda 781
Waldron, Anne 1294c
Walker, Alice 143c, 272c, 280c, 281,
    431c, 472, 500c, 556, 570, 614,
    638, 641c, 678, 713, 765, 769,
    800a, 878, 879, 960, 1218, 1231c,
    1279c, 1315, 1324, 1341c, 1385c,
    1462, 1568c, 1572, 1625, 1656,
    1683, 1700, 1701, 1745, 1763,
    1871, 2038, 2390, 2588
Walker, Margaret 556
Walker, Sue 414
Walpole, Horace 2354
Walpole, Hugh 1932c
Walsh, [Sister] Jude 764a
Walston, Rosa Lee 152, 228, 1119,
    1177a, 1364, 1515, 1580, 1581,
    1582, 1624, 1652
Walters, Dorothy 424c, 438, 471,
    565c, 588, 621, 882, 979, 999,
    1127, 1282, 1395, 1511, 1648
Walton, Beacham 424
Warner, Mary Lambert 489
Warren, Robert Penn 109, 129c, 222,
    225, 415c, 536, 624, 787, 911,
    1097, 1174c, 1194, 1255, 1287,
    1292, 1429, 1434, 1634, 1700,
    1709, 1714, 1742, 1782, 1824,
    1850, 1864, 1897, 1898, 1967,
    1976, 1997, 2024, 2025c, 2026c,
    2128, 2511
Washburn, Dolores 393
Wasserman, Renata R. Mautner 313
Waters, John 497
Watkins, Floyd C. 129c
Watson, Sheila 1716
Watson, Youree 724, 995, 1308
Watt, Alan 103

Watt, I. 897
Watterson, Henry W. 1344
Waugh, Evelyn 618, 779, 910, 1024,
    1427, 1547, 1716
Way, Elizabeth Fenwick 297
Weaks, Mary Louise 129c
Weaver, Richard 1095c, 1107c, 1489
Weigel, Gustave 345c, 979
Weil, Simone 38, 325, 326, 407, 632,
    1132, 1135, 1271, 1376, 1488,
    1966, 2159, 2416
Weiman, Henry 1127
Weisenburger, Steven 762, 878, 879
Welles, Orson 1543
Wells, Joel 68, 288
Wells, Kellie 51a
Welty, Eudora 56, 59, 71, 74, 80,
    140, 143, 180c, 200, 206, 213, 225,
    301, 314c, 323, 344c, 370, 394,
    412, 426, 429, 433, 436, 468, 472,
    534, 594, 614, 641c, 653, 671, 677,
    721a, 737, 741, 747, 748, 780, 781,
    847, 881c, 927, 1011, 1017c, 1092,
    1173, 1255, 1263, 1269, 1288,
    1289, 1315c, 1330, 1360, 1429,
    1434, 1442, 1487, 1489, 1491,
    1522, 1550c, 1562, 1573, 1611,
    1615a, 1617, 1622, 1623, 1653,
    1699, 1709, 1712, 1715, 1717,
    1727, 1729, 1746, 1779, 1820,
    1821, 1839, 1845, 1850, 1853,
    1871, 1874, 1886, 1897, 1919,
    1956, 1967, 1976, 1997, 2008,
    2018, 2038, 2064, 2187, 2218,
    2373, 2390, 2394, 2399, 2440,
    2548, 2593, 2598, 2645, 2700
Wesley, John 418
Wesley, Marilyn 591
West, Lloyd 986
West, Nathanael 35a, 56, 396c, 522c,
    878, 884, 887c, 1105, 1426, 1456,
    1522c, 1556, 1604, 1605, 1719c,
    1719c, 1747, 1762, 1768c, 1791c,
    1840, 1866, 1875, 1902, 1908,
    1916, 1994, 2028, 2059, 2206,
    2223, 2463c

West, Robert 83
Westarp, Karl-Heinz 428, 480, 541,
    593c, 866c, 1061c, 1153c
Westling, Louise 119c, 133, 313,
    420, 586, 587, 636, 826, 878, 879,
    882, 999, 1326c, 1408, 1513, 1580,
    1637
Wharton, Edith 370, 1423
White, Allon 587, 1701
White, Fannie 87
White, Hayden 1034
White, Patrick 1137c
White, Victor 1340
Whitehead, James 1633, 1653
Whitman, Walt 467, 1070, 1688,
    1744
Whitt, Margaret 584, 599, 1639,
    1659a, 1681
Whyte, William H. 126c
Wiatt, Mary Mudge 295
Wiebe, Rudy 1716
Wilbers, Stephen 290
Wilcox, James 98, 533
Wilkinson, Sylvia 533
Williams, Charles 1910
Williams, Melvin G. 319c
Williams, Miller 1400a
Williams, S. Miller 51a, 1154c, 1446,
    1579, 1633
Williams, Sherley Anne 1568c
Williams, Tennessee 873, 1003c,
    1139, 1610, 1839, 2128
Williams, William Carlos 321, 1605,
    1859
Wills, Garry 932
Wilmsatt, W.K. 536
Wilson, Austin 1653
Winn, Harbour 1381
Winnicott, D.W. 449
Winsten, Archer 1226
Woiwode, Larry 784
Wolfe, Thomas 663, 1070, 1174c,
    1215, 1289, 1456, 1850, 1967,
    1997, 2155
Wood, Ralph C. 104, 133, 208c, 245,
    292, 354c, 371, 414, 419c, 527,

589, 599, 618, 636, 638, 788, 793,
839, 840, 1347, 1387a, 1530, 1580,
1621, 1638, 1640, 1652, 1691,
1694, 2057
Wood, Suzanne 1652
Woodward, C. Vann 481, 1365
Woolf, Virginia 213, 960, 1422,
1702c, 1934, 2706
Worth, Irene 1147, 1475, 2727
Wray, Virginia 539, 584, 896, 1313,
1685, 1688
Wright, Amy 342, 684, 2731
Wright, Clifford 509
Wright, Richard 542, 748, 1215,
1249c, 1739, 1772, 1879, 1898,
1908, 2243, 2675
Wyatt, Bryan N. 1381
Wyatt, Thomas 1954
Wylder, Jean Williams 295, 411, 915,
1513, 1644, 1690

Yaeger, Patricia 1694
Yanavich, Bernard A., Jr. 72
Yeats, William Butler 77, 183c, 277c,
1522, 1893
Young, Marguerite 884
Young, Thomas Daniel 748
Yount, John 533

Zaidman, Laura 1177a
Zeiss, Kenneth 72
Zizek, Slavoj 1702c
Zuber, Leo 153c, 564c, 1125c, 1177a,
1191, 1680c
Zweig, Paul 1092

Subject Index

This index refers users to subjects discussed in descriptive abstracts of books, articles, dissertations, theses, reviews and other works described in this reference guide. Readers are also encouraged to consult the subject indexes of books that are cited and described in Parts I and II of this guide as well.

Note that references are to *entry numbers* not pages. Also, the designation of the letter "r"following an entry number indicates that the item is a review. Other designations such as "a"or "b" or "c" following a number indicate that these citations and abstracts were inserted after initial indexing and alphabetization.

"A"
> *See* Correspondence, Flannery O'Connor's--Correspondents--Hester,
> Hazel Elizabeth "Betty"

Absurd
> *See* Symbols and images--absurd

Accent: A Quarterly of New Literature 1849

Adaptations 75b, 44, 153, 1506, 1969, 2283, 2539, 2642
> Interpreter's theatre 2691
> Permission for 649
> Plays
>> "The Displaced Person" *Theatrical Outfit* [Atlanta] 771, 1198,
>> 1506, 1529
>>> Brenda Bynum [as Mrs Hopewell] 1529
>>> Cecil Dawkins [playwright] 1529
>>> Tom Key [producer] 1529
>>> Derek Manson [as Wesley Hopewell] 1529
>> "The Enduring Chill" 225, 1969
>> "Everything That Rises Must Converge" 761
>> "Flannery: A Life in Words" 1050
>> "Good Country People" 2642
>> "A Good Man Is Hard to Find" 225
>> "The Habit of Being: A Solo-Biographical Drama on Flannery
>> O'Connor" 1274
>> "The Lame Shall Enter First" 2378
>> "The Mistress of Milledgeville" 1123, 1123r, 1661r
>>> Daniel Leslie [as Edward F. O'Connor] 1661
>>> Melanie MacQueen [as Flannery O'Connor] 1661
>>> John Killinger [scriptwriter] 1661r
>> "A Return to the South" 1047
>> "Revelation" 808
>> "Shouting to the Deaf" 373

(Con't) Adaptations
        Oral interpretation 200, 704, 1550, 1894
        Parodies 1337, 1470a
            Sarah Gordon 633, 634, 635
            Self-parody in "The Crop" 1847
            Veronica Geng 583
            Garrison Keillon 583
            Flannery O'Connor 1517
        Reader's Theatre 1969
        Recordings of 413
        Ritual performances 75b, 1970
        Television
            "The Life You Save May be Your Own." *Schlitz Playhouse*
               [1957] 33, 153, 158, 1993
        See also Films
Advertising and marketing
        See Style--advertising and marketing, use of
Aesthetics of O'Connor's art 29, 31, 32, 36, 38, 39, 45, 49, 53, 54, 55, 56, 57,
        60, 62, 66, 71, 73, 78, 80, 84, 106, 107, 108, 110, 111, 112, 130, 131,
        135, 145, 146, 164, 169, 171, 178, 199, 215, 257, 258, 272, 291, 292,
        316, 334, 347, 348, 358, 360, 362, 366, 368, 374, 375, 376, 390, 391,
        400, 417, 420, 422, 427, 437, 442, 446, 456, 457, 469, 479, 484, 487,
        491, 492, 493, 495, 523, 538, 540, 541, 545, 554, 564, 569, 575, 576,
        579, 580, 588, 592, 597, 599, 600, 601, 603, 607, 618, 619, 626, 627,
        628, 629, 630, 632, 661, 662, 664, 670, 727, 732, 766, 775, 791, 823,
        828, 839, 851, 860, 863, 864, 866, 876, 878, 910, 912, 931, 943, 962,
        977, 996, 998, 1014, 1023, 1035, 1058, 1065, 1073, 1074, 1086, 1097,
        1103, 1105, 1113, 1133, 1142, 1189, 1195, 1208, 1258, 1270, 1277,
        1279, 1280, 1291a, 1293, 1312, 1345, 1347, 1348, 1358, 1374, 1376,
        1377r, 1383, 1384, 1409, 1418, 1429, 1451, 1494, 1495, 1509, 1525,
        1548, 1554, 1586, 1604, 1614, 1626, 1651, 1655, 1688, 1692, 1694r,
        1697, 1700, 1701, 1749, 1751, 1777, 1780, 1804, 1810, 1824, 1834,
        1841, 1846, 1847, 1860, 1895, 1912, 1920, 1927, 1949, 1951, 1952,
        1963, 1977, 2001, 2045, 2060, 2086, 2135, 2158, 2247, 2309, 2312,
        2356, 2392, 2571, 2582, 2614, 2687, 2711
African American writers 1249, 1664
African Americans
        See Characters--types of--African American
        See also Civil Rights Movement, the
        See also O'Connor, Flannery--views and opinions--African Americans
Agent [McKee, Elizabeth] 1613, 1692
Agnosticism 619
Agrarian
        See Southern agrarian
        See also Intellectual(s)--Southern agrarian

Alienation
    See Style--alienation, use of
    See also Characters--types of--alienated
    See also God--alienation from
    See also Hero(ines)--alienation from community
    See also South, the--alienation of
Allegory
    See Style--allegory, use of
"American Short Story Film Series"
    See Films--"American Short Story Film Series"
Allusion
    See Style--allusion, use of
Ambiguity
    See Style--ambiguity, use of
American Dream, the
    See Symbols and images--American dream, the
The American Short Story Film Series 237, 1432, 1475, 1811, 1993, 1995
"An Afternoon In the Woods" 1685
    See also "The Capture"
    See also "The Turkey"
Anagogy 73, 128, 374, 469, 610, 680, 785, 921, 1038, 1103, 1396, 1535, 1561,
    1949, 1991, 1998a, 2130, 2233, 2407a
Analogies 76, 785, 884, 1141, 1977
Andalusia
    See O'Connor, Flannery--biographical details--homes--Milledgeville
Animal
    See Symbols and images--animal
Anxiety
    See Style--anxiety, use of
Apocalypse
    See Style--apocalyptic context, use of
Apophatic thought 1724, 2016
Appalachian writers 739, 1230, 1972
Archetypes
    See Style--motifs and archetypes, use of
Armstrong Atlantic State University 530, 568, 764a, 1639
Art
    See O'Connor, Flannery--art, interest in
The Artificial Eye
    See Films--*The Artificial Eye*
"The Artificial Nigger" 31, 33, 34, 36, 38, 40, 41, 47, 49, 50a, 53, 75b, 77, 96,
    137, 155, 193, 253, 258, 261, 265, 282, 305, 318, 319, 352, 391, 395,
    396, 427, 443, 466, 479, 501, 511, 513, 523, 527, 529, 540, 546, 549,
    556, 557, 575, 601, 603, 607, 610, 624, 651, 676, 678, 718, 725, 752,
    778, 788, 809, 815, 840, 859, 890, 909, 910, 916, 917, 922, 925, 931,
    937, 939, 943, 945, 991, 1018, 1069, 1093, 1140, 1150a, 1169, 1176,

(Con't) "The Artificial Nigger"
1179, 1203, 1205, 1208, 1221, 1249, 1272, 1283, 1295, 1304, 1320a,
1335, 1344, 1359, 1363, 1378, 1379, 1384, 1387a, 1393, 1407, 1409,
1410, 1422, 1459, 1473, 1485, 1497, 1513, 1521, 1527, 1546, 1573,
1607a, 1666, 1667, 1671, 1683, 1696, 1699a, 1714, 1727, 1778, 1794,
1816, 1839, 1936, 1953, 1998a, 2016, 2017, 2028, 2033, 2040, 2042,
2069, 2100, 2111, 2124, 2139, 2189, 2371, 2411, 2424, 2454, 2584,
2676, 2685
See also Characters, O'Connor's--specific--Mr. Head
See also Characters, O'Connor's--specific--Nelson
See also Characters--O'Connor's--specific
"Artificial nigger" [statue]
See Symbols and images--artificial nigger [statue]
Artistic interpretations of O'Connor's work 194, 371, 372, 410, 502, 554, 571,
583, 616, 637a, 639, 721a, 726, 767, 773, 797, 800a, 899a, 964,
977, 1007, 1102, 1103, 1110, 1113, 1133, 1197, 1206, 1284, 1367,
1443, 1454, 1464, 1467, 1584, 1641a, 2115, 2156, 2491
See also Folk art
See also O'Connor, Flannery--art, interest in
Asceticism 50a, 215, 218, 607, 612, 613, 1091, 1092, 1694r, 2123
See also O'Connor, Flannery--ascetic artist, as an
"as if" contructions
See Style--"as if" constructions, use of
Atheism 1669, 1670, 2107
Atlanta, Georgia
See Georgia--cities and towns--Atlanta
Atlanta Constitution 468a, 899, 1158, 1514, 1618
Atonement
See Redemption
Authority, response to 174, 587, 813, 1384, 1741, 1748, 1907
Automobile
See Symbols and images--automobile
Awards 598, 757, 1433, 1469, 1592
Best American Short Story Award 1630
Georgia Writer's Association Scroll 72
Historic marker 501a, 743a, 1317a, 1592
Kenyon Review Fellowship 502, 789
National Book Award 163, 377, 927, 1247, 1355, 1545
O. Henry Prize 1630
Nation's Most Influential Women 370, 487
Rich's Department Store Prize 1349
Sewanee Review Fellowship 1713, 1714
See also Pulitzer Prize

Banal
    See Symbols and images--banal[ity]
Baptism
    See Symbols and images--baptism
"The Barber" 29, 31, 34, 60, 419, 435, 897, 1690, 2011
    See also Characters, O'Connor's--specific--Joe
Berea College 516
Bible, The Holy 298, 332, 378, 403, 491, 492, 608, 697, 727, 735, 770, 785,
    890, 926, 979, 1008, 1015, 1025, 1034, 1053, 1054, 1082, 1130, 1148,
    1150, 1223, 1275, 1304, 1444, 1635, 1684, 1737, 1772, 1862, 1945,
    1950, 1953, 1984, 2085, 2140, 2194, 2507, 2638
    Apocrypha 282
    II Corinthians, Book of 1648
    Gospels 1185, 1497, 2087
    Hebrew 1354, 1500, 1533, 1779, 1828, 2186
    Job, Book of 1332, 1353, 1386, 1500, 1535
    Luke, Book of 1353
    Matthew, Book of 818, 966, 1686
    Proverbs, Book of 734, 1474
    Psalms, Book of 609
    Revelation, Book of 1944, 1961
    Student's knowledge of 2007
    I & II Timothy, Books of 315, 1501
    See also Characters--types of--Biblical
    See also Symbols and images--Biblical
Bibliographies and critical overviews
    O'Connor criticism, of 51, 60, 61, 74, 81, 129, 132, 147, 192, 193, 205,
        266, 267, 313, 339, 340, 346, 357, 409, 423, 424, 471, 474,
        490, 506, 533, 536, 562, 566, 570, 576, 577, 585, 586, 597,
        646, 687, 688, 713, 748, 800a, 855, 861, 862, 876, 877, 882,
        902, 904, 941, 1036r, 1068, 1125, 1242, 1248, 1282, 1289,
        1301, 1306, 1309, 1311, 1321, 1323, 1324, 1334, 1358, 1375,
        1380, 1381, 1388, 1389, 1438, 1461, 1466, 1470, 1487, 1505,
        1511, 1512, 1520r, 1537r, 1567, 1607, 1676, 1681r, 1694r,
        1697, 1730, 1740, 1751, 1785, 1790, 1824, 1839, 1848, 1856,
        1880, 1881, 1908, 1951, 1978, 2013, 2132, 2133, 2188, 2295,
        2297, 2301, 2426, 2514, 2585a, 2688
    O'Connor's personal library, of 57, 641, 649, 671, 851, 853, 1177a,
        1375, 1382r, 1443, 1947, 1950, 2709
    O'Connor's works, of 44, 153r, 205, 424, 432, 490, 533, 560, 566, 650,
        757, 817, 836, 1212, 1220, 1289, 1310, 1544, 1599, 1848,
        2106, 2115, 2132, 2133
Biography
    See O'Connor, Flannery--biographical details
"Biologic Endeavor" 1689

Bird
>   *See* Symbols and images--animal--bird

Bizarre
>   *See* Style--bizarre, use of the

Black characters
>   *See* Characters--types of--African American
>   *See also* O'Connor, Flannery--views and opinions--African Americans

Black writers
>   *See* African American writers

Blasphemy
>   *See* Style--blasphemy, use of

Blood
>   *See* Symbols and imagery--blood

Body, the human
>   O'Connor's depiction of 43, 659, 763, 972, 1282, 1575, 1764, 1785,
>   2667
>   O'Connor's regard for 41, 1091, 1092, 1773

Book reviews and criticism [by O'Connor of other writers] 10, 47, 65, 69, 118,
>   199, 575, 855, 1097, 1098, 1129a, 1139, 1191, 1209, 1610, 1663,
>   1674, 1680r, 1755

Boundaries
>   *See* Symbols and images--boundaries

Bridgewater State College 1062

Buddhism, Zen 1138, 1674

Bull
>   *See* Symbols and images--animal--bull

Bush, "General" William Jordan [character Gen. Poker Sash based upon] 468a,
>   690, 1391, 1516, 1517

Canadian writers, O'Connor's influence on 1715, 1716

Calvinism 926, 1096, 1100, 1424, 1635, 2369

Camera Three [television show] 1522

Canterbury Tales [Geoffrey Chaucer] 53, 184

"The Capture" 268, 1094, 1285, 1685
>   *See also* "An Afternoon In the Woods"
>   *See also* "The Turkey"

Caricature
>   *See* Symbols and images--caricature

Carnival
>   *See* Style--carnival , use of

Catherine of Genoa, Saint 1129a

Catherine of Siena, Saint 965, 1129a

Catholic(ism) 75b, 417, 496, 516, 577, 578, 618, 619, 638, 655, 662, 701, 774,
>   840, 842, 843, 926, 943, 1040, 1079, 1096, 1119, 1127, 1129a, 1195,
>   1196, 1209, 1240, 1308, 1316, 1344, 1347, 1376, 1383, 1427, 1477,

(Con't) Catholic(ism)
  1548, 1552, 1598, 1650c, 1666, 1672, 1674, 1724, 1733, 1755, 1759,
  1787, 1790, 1808, 1810, 1848, 1853, 1893, 1923, 1931, 1947, 1961,
  1981, 2007a, 2020, 2086, 2106, 2162, 2177, 2230, 2230a, 2326, 2473,
  2486, 2533, 2556, 2594
  French 1209, 1966
  Second Vatican Council 578, 998, 1195, 1923, 2387, 2595a
  See also Theology--Calvinist versus Catholic
Catholic faith, Flannery O'Connor's 37, 59a, 135a, 169, 197, 211, 272, 281,
  292, 327, 337, 353, 356, 375, 400, 403, 417, 443a, 446, 505, 507, 511,
  512, 516, 523, 524, 526, 564, 575, 576, 577, 578, 578, 579, 592, 600,
  601, 618, 619, 620, 626, 627, 628, 629, 632, 654, 655, 661, 662, 679,
  701, 735, 741, 774, 791, 792, 794, 800b, 818, 823, 831, 839, 840, 842,
  843, 844, 855, 868, 875, 890, 910, 918, 920, 925, 926, 932, 943, 953,
  959a, 966, 981, 998, 1022, 1023a, 1037, 1038, 1040, 1053, 1054,
  1062, 1070, 1087, 1090, 1103, 1119, 1120, 1127, 1129a, 1132, 1149,
  1160, 1165, 1180, 1189, 1195, 1196, 1204, 1209, 1216, 1240, 1258,
  1277, 1279, 1287, 1288, 1299, 1302, 1308, 1316, 1320a, 1339, 1343,
  1347, 1353, 1376, 1377r, 1383, 1384, 1406, 1418, 1427, 1468, 1477,
  1497, 1503, 1519, 1548, 1552, 1576, 1595, 1598, 1608, 1609, 1610,
  1612, 1619r, 1645, 1647, 1648, 1650, 1666, 1668, 1672, 1674, 1682r,
  1700, 1709, 1719a, 1731, 1733, 1751, 1755, 1759, 1766, 1787, 1790,
  1802, 1808, 1810, 1816, 1823, 1835, 1841, 1844, 1848, 1853, 1864,
  1893, 1896, 1902, 1909, 1923, 1927, 1931, 1941, 1944, 1947, 1961,
  1981, 1984, 1990, 2027, 2050, 2081, 2086, 2088, 2090, 2106, 2110,
  2123, 2127, 2135, 2136, 2139, 2140, 2162, 2163, 2230a, 2326, 2329,
  2342, 2359, 2360, 2473, 2493, 2533, 2556, 2579, 2581, 2594
  See also O'Connor, Flannery--views and opinions--religious
  See also O'Connor, Flannery--views and opinions--Sacrament, the
Catholic fiction 1023a, 1113, 1204, 1240, 1302, 1308, 1344, 1383, 1548, 1552,
  1597, 1608, 1664, 1674, 1680, 1697, 1733, 1759, 1790, 1808, 1818,
  1848, 1864, 1893, 1912, 1923, 1931, 1933, 1936, 1961, 1981, 1984,
  1990, 2044, 2088, 2230a, 2326, 2387, 2486, 2533, 2556, 2594, 2230
Catholic Index of Forbidden Books 935
"The Catholic Novelist in the Modern South" 291
Celibacy 505
Characters, O'Connor's 32, 34, 35a, 36, 38, 41, 43, 47, 50a, 52, 99, 117, 135,
  139, 143, 161, 169a, 204, 230, 252, 256, 263, 287, 317, 318, 335, 381,
  407, 449, 470, 507, 520, 523, 540, 551, 554, 576, 587, 597, 612, 644,
  653, 657, 661, 667, 676, 712, 720, 722, 727, 747, 808, 809, 811, 827,
  850, 867, 890, 909, 940, 951, 953, 956, 962, 974, 983, 986, 997,
  1000r, 1006, 1009, 1011, 1013, 1014, 1025, 1033, 1045, 1066, 1067,
  1069, 1091, 1099, 1111, 1120, 1127, 1135, 1140, 1229, 1234, 1237,
  1263, 1282, 1283, 1293, 1314, 1330, 1339, 1343, 1354, 1371, 1372,
  1379, 1394, 1413, 1422, 1427, 1448, 1459, 1468, 1497, 1500, 1504,
  1547, 1557, 1563, 1612, 1614, 1616, 1635, 1649, 1651, 1659, 1664,

(Con't) Characters, O'Connor's
     1684, 1692, 1702, 1706, 1709, 1711, 1719, 1743, 1762, 1767, 1768,
     1777, 1778, 1783, 1829, 1831, 1839, 1855, 1857, 1868, 1874, 1875,
     1888, 1894, 1899, 1921, 1954, 1961, 1963, 1976, 2000, 2011, 2021,
     2045, 2050, 2062, 2070, 2079, 2115, 2210, 2227, 2257, 2403, 2410,
     2522, 2525, 2542, 2567, 2569, 2687, 2690, 2692, 2694, 2703
     Distance between readers and 167, 172, 185, 203, 216, 245, 257, 260,
          268, 273, 276, 308, 309, 389, 443, 448, 523, 582, 590, 631,
          648, 657, 705, 706, 830, 1272, 1329, 1876, 1894
     Knowledge of 705, 706, 708, 953, 962, 974, 990, 1011, 1093, 1203,
          1401, 1901, 2041, 2510
     Language to show contrast of 1135, 1200, 1372, 1378, 1533, 1600,
          1719, 1855, 1857
     Manners of 37, 1819, 1883, 1935, 1965, 2008, 2090, 2178, 2277, 2365
     Music as part of the lives of 465, 1013, 2115
     Names of 898, 912, 985, 1079, 1257, 1265, 1482, 1516, 1533, 1740,
          2015, 2019, 2046, 2050, 2053
     Personality types 956, 962, 1025, 1133, 1741, 1901, 2509, 2522, 2525
     Psychological well-being of 164a, 617a, 955, 986, 1083, 1133, 1213,
          1245, 1283, 1339, 1384, 1474, 1536, 1670, 1701, 1702, 1780,
          1783, 1812, 1860, 1867, 1868, 1878, 1946, 1976, 2000, 2028,
          2061, 2360, 2509
     Space, impact of 156, 1060, 1348, 1985
     Specific
          Abram ["The Coat"]1186
          Ashfield, Harry ["The River" aka "Bevel"] 349, 465, 590, 669,
               726, 1073, 1283, 1404, 2052, 2448
          Astor ["The Displaced Person"] 435, 1131, 2087
          Bible Salesman, the ["Good Country People"] 317, 654, 755,
               908, 1019, 1213, 1530
          Bailey ["A Good Man Is Hard to Find"] 182, 309, 776, 1278,
               1717a
          Black [African American] cook ["A Temple of the Holy
               Ghost"] 93, 763
          Black [African American] mother ["Everything That Rises
               Must Converge"] 455, 531, 640, 864
          Butts, Red Sammy ["A Good Man Is Hard to Find"] 776, 1501
          Calhoun ["The Partridge Festival"] 36, 252, 963, 1171
          Carmody, Lucette [*The Violent Bear It Away*] 36, 420
          Carver ["Everything That Rises Must Converge"] 864, 1163
          Cates, Sarah Ruth ["Parker's Back"] 268, 717, 1008, 1435,
               1436, 1437a, 1499, 1547
          Chestny, Julian ["Everything That Rises Must Converge"] 36,
               231, 252, 299, 323, 331, 389, 455, 531, 550, 640,
               734, 795, 864, 909, 984, 1026, 1163, 1265, 1562,
               1637, 2055

(Con't) Characters, O'Connor's--Specific

Chestny, Mrs. ["Everything That Rises Must Converge"] 231, 317, 389, 455, 531, 550, 640, 761, 795, 864, 984, 1163, 1265, 1266, 1267, 1499, 1637

Connin, Mrs. ["The River"] 1499

Cope, Mrs. ["A Circle in the Fire"] 467, 597, 909, 1078, 1124, 1445, 1499, 1637, 1487

Cope, Sally Virginia ["A Circle in the Fire"] 1283, 1499, 1559a, 1637

Crater, Lucynell ["The Life You Save May Be Your Own"] 80, 166, 307, 371, 772, 891, 1499, 1559a

Crater, Mrs. ["The Life You Save May Be Your Own"] 962, 1499

Daughter ["An Exile in the East"] 1187

Drake, Temple ["A Temple of the Holy Ghost"] 1601

Dudley ["The Geranium"] 896, 1171

Emery, Enoch [*Wise Blood*]126, 218, 287, 364, 439, 457, 465, 657, 668, 726, 770, 810, 850, 911, 990, 1010, 1025, 1058, 1169, 1335, 1361, 1510, 1992, 2063, 2175, 2423

Flood, Mrs. [*Wise Blood*]196, 1073, 1459, 1499, 2059

Fortune, Mr. ["A View of the Woods"] 248, 606, 950, 1057, 1060, 1325, 1703, 2051, 2067

Fox, Asbury Porter ["The Enduring Chill"] 36, 84, 169a, 241, 252, 262, 331, 410, 523, 734, 773, 785, 1168, 1320, 1637, 1726, 2113

Fox, Mary George ["The Enduring Chill"] 1499, 2113

Mrs. Fox ["The Enduring Chill"] 169a, 1499, 2113

Freak, the ["A Temple of the Holy Ghost"] 1664, 1699a

Freeman, Mrs. ["Good Country People"] 587, 1275, 1499, 1601, 2046, 2053

Gabriel ["Wildcat"] 858a

Gibbs, Sarah [*Why Do the Heathen Rage?*] 1691

Grace, Mary ["Revelation"]257, 528, 727, 808, 1078, 1130, 1340, 1386, 1437a, 1500, 1559a, 1637, 1700

The Grandmother ["A Good Man Is Hard to Find"] 30, 36, 47, 135, 162, 182, 201, 249, 309, 315, 317, 365, 416, 453, 460, 512, 590, 731, 754, 764a, 776, 804, 832a, 850, 898, 909, 912, 1013, 1056a, 1067, 1184, 1196, 1222, 1278, 1293, 1319, 1350, 1353, 1365, 1440, 1468, 1476, 1499, 1501, 1551, 1578, 1607a, 1631, 1637, 1693, 1717a, 1857, 2073, 2131, 2160, 2182, 2184, 2487

Greenleaf, Mr. ["Greenleaf"]1373, 1541

Greenleaf, Mrs. ["Greenleaf"]1078, 1129a, 1403, 1499, 1669, 2164

(Con't) Characters, O'Connor's--specific

Guizac, Mr. ["The Displaced Person"] 298, 353, 485, 622,
    642, 658, 676, 980, 1051, 1073, 1131, 1207, 1264,
    1615, 2058, 2065, 2087
Ham, Sarah ["The Comforts of Home" aka Star Drake] 371,
    588, 1300
Hawks, Sabbath Lily [*Wise Blood*]105, 611, 1229, 1499, 1637,
    2109
Head, Mr. ["The Artificial Nigger"] 96, 137, 253, 258, 305,
    395, 466, 501, 549, 651, 718, 909, 931, 1069, 1140,
    1169, 1179, 1203, 1249, 1272, 1359, 1363, 1393,
    1410, 2069
Hermaphrodite, the ["A Temple of the Holy Ghost"] 157, 158,
    505, 763, 1909
Hill, Ruby ["A Stroke of Good Fortune"]41, 972, 973, 1004,
    1028, 1499, 1559a, 1722
Hitchcock, Mrs. Wally Bee [*Wise Blood*] 1069, 1637, 1700
Holy, Onnie Jay [*Wise Blood* aka Hoover Shoats] 126, 277,
    465, 1099
Homosexual, the [*The Violent Bear It Away*] 165, 297, 818
Hopewell, Joy/Hulga ["Good Country People"] 36, 126, 166,
    169a, 198, 307, 331, 364, 384, 592, 595, 597, 617a,
    632, 654, 755, 759, 780, 824, 831, 850, 908, 909,
    986, 1073, 1078, 1099, 1171, 1208, 1213, 1275,
    1282, 1488, 1499, 1530, 1559a, 1573, 1626, 1642,
    1670, 2046, 2053, 2112, 2119, 2121, 2487
Hopewell, Mrs. ["Good Country People"] 36, 166, 169a, 384,
    1069, 1275, 1282, 1530, 1601, 1626, 1637, 2046,
    2112, 2121
Joe ["The Barber"] 897
Johnson, Rufus Florida [*The Violent Bear It Away*] 682, 1150,
    1255, 2050, 2081
Judge, the ["The Displaced Person"] 1131
Layfield, Solace [*Wise Blood*] 126, 277, 1118, 2063, 2177
Mary Elizabeth ["The Partridge Festival"] 36, 1171
May, Mrs. ["Greenleaf"]157, 169a, 349, 360, 405, 609, 721,
    974, 1027, 1054, 1078, 1124, 1129a, 1273, 1338,
    1350, 1373, 1403, 1445, 1541, 1669, 1695, 2164
    See also Hero(ines)--Mrs May as
McFarney, Ruller ["The Turkey"] 268, 1094, 1285, 2448
McIntyre, Mrs. ["The Displaced Person"]47, 353, 485, 642,
    653, 658, 733, 909, 962, 980, 1051, 1078, 1124,
    1131, 1445, 1637, 2058, 2065, 2087
The Misfit ["A Good Man Is Hard to Find"] 30, 36, 47, 59a,
    94, 135, 142, 159, 162, 182, 183, 201, 249, 263, 309,
    315, 324, 365, 388, 416, 436, 460, 465, 470, 498,

(Con't) Characters, O'Connor's--Specific--The Misfit
512, 535, 591, 592, 654, 703, 731, 754, 774, 776,
779, 800, 816, 822, 832a, 888, 898, 899, 912, 1013,
1016, 1019, 1059, 1069, 1073, 1099, 1104, 1105,
1106, 1107, 1117, 1118, 1144, 1184, 1196, 1222,
1264, 1270, 1281, 1293, 1319, 1353, 1365, 1366,
1438, 1439, 1440, 1476, 1492, 1514, 1532, 1533,
1551, 1633, 1672, 1693, 1717a, 1724, 2073, 2120,
2160, 2182, 2184, 2422, 2518, 2525
Anti-hero, as 402, 804
"Big Bad Wolf," as 827
Dragon, as St. Cyril's 2131
Ego-devoured, as 1631
Evil and 201, 388, 470, 776, 815, 816, 1118, 1167,
1196, 1365, 1379, 1587, 1631, 1926
Hill, James Frances [aka "Maniac Hill" and "Three-
Gun Hill"] as prototype for 512, 899
Intellectual, as a liberal 1365
Linked to Faulkner's "Popeye" 1059
Linked to J.F. Powers's "Perry" 1551
Linked to Roman law, as 776
Manners of 1104, 1533, 1587
Name, meaning of 912
Nihilism of 1672
Personality 1013, 1133, 1533, 1631
Pride and 1107
Recollections of 776, 1438
Serial killer, as 182, 436, 460, 686, 816
Signatures and 1222
Spiritual twin to the grandmother, as 365
Sympathy for 816
Trickster, as 1476
Violence and 1106
Yeat's "Beast," as 183
Motes, Hazel [*Wise Blood*] 36, 50a, 62, 67, 97, 113, 167, 204,
262, 263, 268, 271, 275, 277, 287, 288, 329, 341,
364, 385, 406, 431, 439, 444, 450, 457, 481, 486,
516, 571, 572, 585, 591, 611, 638, 659, 668, 697,
726, 732, 767, 770, 779, 810, 840, 850, 857, 863,
867, 878, 881, 887, 888, 906, 911, 927, 989, 1010,
1025, 1040, 1058, 1060, 1069, 1071, 1072, 1073,
1074, 1078, 1080, 1099, 1100, 1116, 1118, 1152,
1161, 1169, 1216, 1225, 1229, 1292, 1297, 1314,
1358, 1371, 1401, 1408, 1444, 1459, 1498, 1507,
1510, 1521, 1547, 1564, 1591, 1636, 1637, 1666,
1674, 1719, 1724, 1768, 1791, 1900, 1945, 1971,

(Con't) Characters, O'Connor's--Specific--Motes, Hazel
    1983, 2024, 2049, 2059, 2063, 2078, 2082, 2084,
    2104, 2107, 2110, 2151, 2175, 2180, 2186, 2240,
    2702
    See also Hero(ines)--Hazel Motes as
Mother, the child's ["A Temple of the Holy Ghost"] 93
Mother, Thomas's ["The Comforts of Home"] 954, 1300,
    1637
"The Mummy" [*Wise Blood*] 990, 1335, 2177
Munson, Buford [*The Violent Bear It Away*] 311a, 1280
Nelson ["The Artificial Nigger"]41, 137, 253, 258, 395, 466,
    549, 718, 909, 1169, 1179, 1203, 1272, 1283, 1393,
    2069, 2448
Norton ["The Lame Shall Enter First"] 1283
Nun ["A Temple of the Holy Ghost"] 587
Paradise, Mr. ["The River"] 317
Parker, O.E. ["Parker's Back"] 117, 179, 195, 202, 268, 345,
    381, 420, 457, 493, 683, 717, 735, 807, 840, 909,
    1008, 1012, 1030, 1148, 1268, 1435, 1436, 1437a,
    1482, 1535, 1618, 2116
Perpetua, Sister ["A Temple of the Holy Ghost"] 1079
Parrum, Coleman ["Judgement Day"] 1187, 1638
Pitts, Mary Fortune ["A View of the Woods"] 606, 950, 1057,
    1283, 1325, 1703, 2005, 2067
Pitty Sing ["A Good Man Is Hard to Find"] 440, 1281, 1717a
Pointer, Manley ["Good Country People"] 94, 780, 1069,
    1275, 1282, 1530, 2046, 2112, 2119, 2121
Preacher, the ["The River"] 1664, 1897
Priest, the ["The Displaced Person"] 733, 1051, 2087
Pritchard, Mrs. ["A Circle in the Fire"] 587, 1078, 1499, 1514
Rayber, Bishop [*The Violent Bear It Away*] 66, 174a, 274,
    311a, 610, 878, 1283, 1395, 1467, 2072, 2106, 2177,
Rayber, George [*The Violent Bear It Away*] 36, 37, 66, 128,
    165, 174a, 311a, 613, 744, 747, 818, 850, 878, 889,
    897, 952, 1030, 1067, 1073, 1158, 1196, 1216, 1245,
    1395, 1586, 1720, 2024, 2059, 2072, 2105, 2106,
    2134, 2172, 2178
Rosa ["The Coat"] 1186
Sash, Sally Poker ["A Late Encounter With the Enemy"]1521
Sash, [General] Tennessee Flintrock "A Late Encounter With
    the Enemy"] 468a, 690, 1069, 1391
See also Bush, "General" William Jordan
Sheppard ["The Lame Shall Enter First"] 36, 642, 1073, 1158,
    1339, 2081
Sheriff, the ["The Comforts of Home"] 954

(Con't) Characters, O'Connor's--Specific

Shiftlet, Tom T. ["The Life You Save May Be Your Own"] 364, 401, 406, 465, 591, 674, 726, 962, 1019, 1069, 1171, 1282, 1564

Shortley, Chancey ["The Displaced Person"] 733, 1019, 1131, 1664

Shortley, Mrs. ["The Displaced Person"] 41, 47, 59a, 353, 485, 597, 658, 909, 962, 980, 1051, 1073, 1078, 1131, 1207, 1479, 1562, 2058, 2087

Singleton ["The Partridge Festival"] 36

Starr, June ["A Good Man Is Hard to Find"] 898, 954, 1069

"The Stranger-Friend" [*The Violent Bear It Away*] 311a, 818, 952

Stripper, the [*Wise Blood*] 906

Sulk ["The Displaced Person"] 435, 485

Summers, Rev. ["The River"] 1404

Tanner, Old ["An Exile in the East"] 1187, 1638, 2125

Tanner, T.C. ["Judgement Day"] 1171, 1320, 1638, 1648, 1677

Tarwater, Francis Marion [*The Violent Bear It Away*] 37, 41, 62, 76, 128, 134, 165, 174, 174a, 232a, 247, 262, 263, 274, 297,311a, 400, 403, 420, 457, 481, 610, 613, 653, 818, 850, 857, 863, 889, 952, 965, 1029, 1069, 1078, 1208, 1216, 1245, 1292, 1395, 1496, 1557, 1562, 1586, 1654, 1720, 1837, 1850, 1900, 1939, 2024, 2049, 2072, 2104, 2105, 2108, 2134, 2172, 2178, 2448, 2484

See also Hero(ines)--Frances Marion Tarwater as

Tarwater, Mason [*The Violent Bear It Away*] 36, 37, 41, 76, 77, 128, 134, 174a, 247, 274, 311a, 360, 610, 1079, 1216, 1245, 1557, 1586, 1654, 1720. 1748, 1850, 2005, 2024, 2072, 2105, 2108, 2110, 2134

Teagarden, Edgar Atkins ["A Good Man Is Hard to Find"] 453, 1222

Thomas ["The Comforts of Home"] 588, 734, 909, 954, 1300, 1637, 2055

Tilman, Walter [*Why Do the Heathen Rage?*] 262

Truck driver, the [*The Violent Bear it Away*] 165

Turpin, Claud ["Revelation"] 808

Turpin, Ruby ["Revelation"] 255, 257, 435, 446a, 528, 597, 652, 705, 800b, 805, 808, 985, 1049, 1069, 1073, 1078, 1130, 1141, 1171, 1261, 1312, 1340, 1386, 1437, 1437a, 1441, 1474, 1500, 1527, 1535, 1637, 1700

Twelve-Year Girl, the ["A Temple of the Holy Ghost"] 41, 257, 1073, 1328, 1570

(Con't) Characters, O'Connor's--Specific
> Watts, Mrs. Leora [*Wise Blood*] 1152, 1229, 1499, 1510
> Wesley, John ["A Good Man Is Hard to Find"] 898, 1069,
>> 1643
> Willerton, Miss ["The Crop"] 630, 1847
> Spiritual hunger of 394, 576, 658, 706, 763, 850, 867, 890, 940, 955,
>> 959, 1283, 1353, 1451, 1564, 1655, 1706, 1749, 1855, 1900,
>> 1919, 1977, 2416, 2633
Thoughts of 1612
Types of
> African-American 105, 137, 157, 319, 380, 435, 444, 455,
>> 466, 485, 549, 557, 603, 638, 640, 778, 788, 809,
>> 896, 931, 939, 1056a, 1127, 1140, 1142, 1150a,
>> 1186, 1203, 1335, 1393, 1407, 1485, 1578, 1638,
>> 1649, 1667, 1671, 1683, 1699a, 1951, 1972, 2125,
>> 2263, 2410, 2649, 2685
> Alienated 457, 576, 732, 863, 897, 1053, 1293, 1531, 1750,
>> 1782, 1881, 1919, 1997, 2041, 2043, 2070, 2102,
>> 2453, 2520, 2536, 2648
> Ambiguous 55, 298, 312, 321, 540, 657, 738, 974, 1268,
>> 1372, 1408, 1506, 2351, 2647
> Archetypal
>> *See* Style--motifs and archetypes, use of--characters,
>>> archetypal
> Arrogant 420, 734, 1659
> Artistic 43, 84, 734, 758, 773, 1168
> Bestial 218
> Biblical 800, 2194
>> Abraham 735
>> Daniel 610
>> Isaac 735
>> Jacob 1130, 1686
>> Job 1535
>> Jonah 232a, 807, 1225
>> Paul 232a, 1648, 2490
> Bigoted 550, 733, 916, 1257
> Bizarre 203, 302, 710, 908, 1563, 1801
> Blind 959, 1088, 1161, 1659, 2104, 2379
> Catholic 1733, 1818
> Child 43, 80, 125, 139, 143, 157, 160, 177, 257, 355, 479,
>> 550, 580, 669, 734, 763, 814, 874, 899a, 1028,
>> 1088, 1119, 1283, 1285, 1337, 1421, 1628, 1727,
>> 1729, 1743, 1812, 1829, 1839, 1867, 2000, 2027,
>> 2216, 2229, 2242, 2244, 2248, 2264, 2288, 2296,
>> 2368, 2376, 2406, 2410, 2412, 2413, 2448, 2500,
>> 2526, 2528, 2557, 2651, 2680

(Con't) Characters, O'Connor's--Types of

Christian 43, 247, 1129a, 1500

College graduates 1339

Controlling 501, 1088, 1530, 1891

Country 286a, 605, 703, 939, 1664, 1725, 2121

Crazy 1067, 1768

Criminals 1013, 2316

Cripples 1013

Cruel 2027

Cunning 703

Damned 2090

Daughters 80, 166, 244, 307, 758, 1217, 1530, 1559a, 1623, 1626, 1637, 1829, 2162

    See also Style--mother-child relationships, use of

Demonic 956, 962, 1135, 1136, 1335, 1511, 1512, 1839

Disciple(s) 493, 607

Dismembered 1805

Disturbed 1019

Double(s) 55, 115, 116, 164, 164a, 179, 258, 275, 396, 658, 659, 668, 754, 896, 967, 1057, 1072, 1109, 1124, 1245, 1365, 1372, 1409, 1591, 1604, 1605, 1719, 1794, 1816, 1873, 1891, 1939, 1941, 2015, 2021, 2042, 2063, 2115, 2502, 2503

    See also Style--motifs and archetypes, use of--double

Dreamers 1901, 1927

Eccentric 851, 1563

Egotistical 1659, 2000

Employers 962

Evil 443a, 470, 491, 605, 612, 652, 658, 727, 775, 815, 816, 838, 884, 890, 919, 1019, 1022, 1029, 1033, 1067, 1093a, 1107, 1116, 1118, 1127, 1152, 1167, 1196, 1270, 1277, 1300, 1340, 1365, 1379, 1424, 1451, 1490, 1530, 1587, 1620, 1631, 1727, 1762, 1786, 1810, 1816, 1866, 1885, 1898, 1926, 1954, 2043, 2079, 2085, 2204, 2218, 2234, 2278, 2288, 2352

    See also O'Connor, Flannery--views and opinions of --evil

Existential 157, 165, 329, 361, 367, 502, 816, 1067, 1395, 1455, 1510, 1631, 1754, 1808, 1815, 1823, 1839, 1846, 1941, 1974, 1997, 2331, 2361

Faces of 311, 342, 973, 2051

Fanatic 1013, 1459, 2102, 2105

Fathers 245, 588, 735, 743, 777, 954, 1299, 1421, 1822, 2134, 2565

Female 1559a, 1738, 2040

Fetishists 255, 419

(Con't) Characters, O'Connor's--Types of
        Flat 156, 667
        Flawed 1778, 1980
        Fools 1975
        Freaks 59a, 93, 136, 157, 178, 203, 211, 308, 361, 364, 505,
              514, 520, 617, 703, 812, 850, 851, 887, 1007, 1080,
              1090, 1135, 1136, 1150, 1172, 1194, 1342, 1343,
              1355, 1504, 1601, 1699a, 1766, 1900, 2078
        Gamblers 324
        Gospel singer(s) 465
        Greedy 703
        Grotesque 138, 143, 203, 235, 244, 278, 286, 298, 308, 312,
              316, 321, 357, 443, 454, 489, 585, 590, 657, 662,
              710, 763, 810, 813, 814, 822, 840, 851, 852, 884,
              901, 937, 991, 1019, 1053, 1080, 1086, 1291, 1342,
              1343, 1376, 1426, 1435, 1470a, 1536, 1552, 1556,
              1573, 1577, 1589, 1595, 1684, 1701, 1711, 1738,
              1743, 1749, 1752, 1758, 1768, 1812, 1821, 1831,
              1841, 1866, 1875, 1878, 1885, 1892, 1899, 1902,
              1903, 1916, 1926, 1955, 1956, 1974, 2001, 2007a,
              2070, 2073, 2085, 2182, 2234, 2237, 2327, 2335,
              2367, 2374, 2377, 2505, 2580
              See also Grotesque, the
        Haunted 800, 890, 1040, 1107, 1116, 1328, 1345, 1358, 1433,
              1531, 2070, 2120, 2287
        Hypochondriacs 1551
        Hypocrites 1314b, 2021, 2059, 2279
        Identity of 164a, 956, 1601, 1907
        Idolatrous 391
        Immoral 1019
        "indignant young watcher" 139
        Innocent 318, 394, 395, 759, 1111, 1339, 1393, 2021, 2184,
              2468
        Intellectual 43, 139, 167, 247, 252, 299, 307, 348, 326, 457,
              581, 716, 734, 758, 763, 956, 1099, 1135, 1216,
              1299, 1339, 1365, 1557, 1573, 1589, 1743, 1829,
              2011, 2033, 2178, 2422, 2428, 2485, 2510, 2516,
              2586
        Jesus freaks 887
        Killer(s) 182, 403, 436, 460, 470, 668, 686, 776, 816, 1186,
              1316, 1319, 1533, 1830, 1837, 2087
        Liberal 323, 584, 592, 640, 768, 932, 1365, 1521, 1954, 2041,
              2391
        Liberated 953
        Lonely 1071, 1169, 2593
        Male 80, 139, 247, 734, 1078, 1637, 1948, 2039, 2618

(Con't) Characters, O'Connor's--Types of

Marginalized 1899

Martyrs 1551

Matriarchs 139, 1700, 2039, 2217

Mediator 962, 2341

Medieval 184, 262, 312, 697, 743, 1356, 1801, 1944, 1949, 1961

Melancholiacs, as 1768

Mentors 1837

Miserable 1963

Mother(s) 80, 125, 139, 169a, 317, 460, 472, 523, 531, 667, 670, 731, 734, 758, 778, 795, 813, 814, 864, 935, 954, 1168, 1217, 1299, 1320, 1384, 1421, 1626, 1745, 1829, 2000, 2005, 2332, 2339, 2344, 2584, 2682, 2701

Mythological 800, 827, 1088, 1373, 1419, 1905

Nuns 1079

Obsessed 128, 457, 1563, 1655

Odd 362, 443

Other, The [the Devil] 164a, 174, 178, 211, 234, 268, 274, 276, 287, 311a, 329, 378, 406, 421, 528, 549, 551, 581, 612, 652, 658, 659, 727, 775, 776, 818, 820, 867, 884, 890, 918, 952, 972, 1005, 1054, 1057, 1096, 1120, 1171, 1189, 1216, 1239, 1270, 1291, 1300, 1379, 1386, 1395, 1439, 1536, 1600, 1631, 1749, 1762, 1766, 1816, 1910, 2007a, 2050, 2090, 2102, 2261, 2318, 2501
See also Symbols and images--"The Other"

Outsider 618, 972, 1407, 1476, 1519, 1974

Overbearing 667

Pilgrim(s) 1019, 1719, 1791, 1843

Priests 1087

Prophet(ic) 37, 62, 131, 164a, 174a, 257, 274, 276, 329, 439, 529a, 613, 683, 767, 807, 818, 979, 1072, 1079, 1082, 1120, 1216, 1343, 1376, 1379, 1408, 1435, 1437a, 1500, 1504, 1673, 1720, 1839, 1847, 1897, 1904, 1944, 1950, 1961, 2021, 2049, 2088, 2134, 2172, 2180, 2264, 2298, 2323, 2366, 2381, 2476, 2504

Protestant fundamentalist 131, 145, 162, 211, 217, 356, 418, 619, 644, 655, 717, 778, 779, 800, 890, 964, 1014, 1063, 1070, 1082, 1132, 1258, 1294, 1304, 1343, 1379, 1384, 1427, 1536, 1635, 1655, 1664, 1666, 1669, 1672, 1841, 1972, 2086, 2107, 2471, 2473

Pseudosophisticates 2576

Psychotic 1013, 1563, 1701

(Con't) Characters, O'Connor's--Types of

         Reactionary 956

         Rebellious 77, 618, 888, 1169, 1906

         Religious 956, 1972

         Repulsive 1801

         Rural 818, 939, 1078, 1253, 1378, 1379, 1412, 1899,
               1972

         Salesmen 126, 962

         Searchers 1901

         Selfish 733, 951, 1019, 1770

         Self-satisfied 705

         Servant 1131

         Shallow-minded 2079

         Sinful 50, 50a, 101, 130, 176, 178, 198, 211, 253, 302, 312,
               318, 368, 371, 395, 406, 501, 529, 551, 592, 651,
               754, 804, 811, 840, 851, 852, 857, 867, 879, 887,
               898, 908, 1010, 1033, 1049, 1056, 1116, 1135, 1189,
               1205, 1255, 1260, 1288, 1299, 1300, 1304, 1393,
               1424, 1448, 1527, 1631, 1719, 1764, 1869, 1898,
               1926, 2177, 2280, 2594

         Skeptical 1440, 2011

         Social scientists 638, 640, 890, 1270

         Sodomists, satanic 887

         Solitary 50a, 501, 857, 1071, 1169, 1293, 1678a

         Sons 248, 670, 864, 1395

         Southern 93, 169a, 217, 267, 299, 418, 453, 619, 638, 747,
               815, 896, 939, 956, 975, 1080, 1111, 1127, 1187,
               1217, 1302, 1342, 1344, 1365, 1445, 1531, 1588,
               1623, 1654, 1666, 1692, 1699a, 1700, 1708, 1772,
               1799, 1830, 1877, 1897, 1961, 1972, 2039, 2040,
               2154

         Spectator 1873

         Sponsor 2425

         Stranger 311a, 962, 2407

         Struggling 733

         Stupid 2079

         Surrogate 939

         Teachers 174a

         Trickster 800, 1476, 1862

         Ugly 166, 308, 311, 520, 659, 1009, 1257, 2014

         Unbeliever, as 775, 1384

         Violent 617a, 1019, 1033, 1106, 1127, 1135, 1239, 1365,
               1459, 1536, 1558, 1655, 1684, 1702, 1833, 1835,
               1837, 1868, 1879, 1890, 1959, 2049, 2370, 2396,
               2449

         Vulgar 2168

(Con't) Characters, O'Connor's--Types of
    White-collar 1851
    White trash 916, 939, 1229, 1527, 1996
    Widows 80, 1078
    Wives 2005
    Wolf, big bad 827
    Women 75b, 80, 114, 117, 119, 139, 166, 307, 405, 420, 453, 474, 485, 529, 587, 667, 722, 731, 824, 954, 973, 1078, 1124, 1127, 1140, 1217, 1227, 1275, 1299, 1330, 1341, 1408, 1421, 1445, 1474, 1499, 1527, 1559a, 1568, 1625, 1631, 1637, 1738, 1750, 1820, 1822, 1829, 1867, 1886, 1925, 1976, 2014, 2039, 2070, 2162, 2281, 2373, 2374, 2430, 2551, 2621, 2632, 2645, 2649
    Workers 962
    Writers 588, 716
  Vision of 50a, 196, 203, 206, 241, 272, 273, 276, 321, 349, 379, 400, 431, 468a, 554, 576, 679, 708, 718, 732, 778, 940, 951, 956, 959, 1029, 1049, 1069, 1161, 1229, 1237, 1312, 1372, 1396, 1436, 1638, 1693, 1850, 1869, 2041, 2075, 2084, 2300, 2357, 2416

Chardin, Pierre Teilhard de--theory of evolution of 62, 442, 738, 1621, 1800, 1968, 2195, 2257, 2268, 2524, 2672
  See also Influence--of other writers and artists on O'Connor--Chardin, Pierre Teilhard de
Charity
  See Symbols and images--charity
Cheers! The Flannery O'Connor Society Newsletter 568, 589, 639, 1313
Chicago Tribune Tower 798
Chickens
  See Peacocks, chickens and other fowl
Child
  See Characters--types of--child
  See also Style--motifs and archetypes--child and childhood motif
  See also Symbols and images--child[ren]
Christ, Jesus
  Belief in 496, 987, 1025, 1160, 1185, 1384, 1459, 1528, 1841, 1858, 2160, 2165, 2219
  Body of 1979
  Byzantine 381, 807, 1012, 1482
  Crucifixion of 987, 1027
  Denial of 754, 1435, 1693, 1719, 1837
  Displaced person, as a 1615, 2065
  Divinity of 840
  Embodiment of 735, 1027, 1056, 1092, 1436, 1482, 1498, 2087
  Eucharist as body of 50a, 702, 1032, 1598, 1609, 1979, 2380

(Con't) Christ, Jesus
  Following 1150, 1160, 1347, 1459, 1683, 1719, 2219
  Image of 652, 767, 838, 840, 887, 1009, 1054, 1070, 1148, 1150, 1338,
        1350, 1435, 1436, 1498, 1503, 1615, 1703, 1737, 1838, 1841,
        1915, 2119, 2189, 2257, 2273
  Mythology of 770, 827, 1054
  Name of 1148
  Presence of 839, 1009, 1029, 1040, 2046
  Redeemer, as
        See Redemption
  Saint Matthew's depiction of 770
  Second Coming of 1387, 1638
  Sinner's appearance to 851, 1393, 1435, 1527, 1869, 1898, 2120
  Suffering of 697
  Tattoos of 480, 493, 717, 807, 840, 1008, 1012, 1148, 1268, 1436,
        1482, 1618
  Teachings of 1353, 2033
  See also God
  See also Grace
  See also Hero(ines)--Christ as
  See also Style, Flannery O'Connor's--Christian Mystery, use of
  See also Style, Flannery O'Connor's--Grace, use of
  See also Symbols and images--Christ, Jesus
Christian community 701, 792, 1102, 1897, 1944, 2212
Christian fiction 1240, 1307, 1320a, 1353, 1411, 1418, 1635, 1709, 1790, 1854,
        1858, 1924, 1945
Christian humanism
  See Humanism
Christian mystery
  See Style--Christian mystery, use of
Christianity
  Ethics of 1979
  Loss of 53, 126, 181, 418, 445, 493, 496, 701, 710, 774, 950, 996,
        1270, 1401, 2230
  Myths of 1719, 1905
  Protestant view of 1666, 1672, 1674, 1816, 1841, 1947, 2471
  Reality of 174a, 901, 908, 964, 1034, 1038, 1053, 1072, 1080, 1102,
        1103, 1107, 1112, 1129a, 1137, 1138, 1150, 1152, 1160,
        1237, 1271, 1299, 1350, 1374, 1418, 1419, 1435, 1436, 1491,
        1498, 1500, 1503, 1535, 1548, 1552, 1595, 1596, 1608, 1733,
        1750, 1763, 1786, 1800, 1810, 1854, 1858, 1887, 1908, 1918,
        1933, 1944, 1953, 1984, 2319, 2443, 2635
  Southern history and 1635, 1708, 1711, 1772, 1779, 1784,
        1797, 1799, 1877, 1902, 1972, 2004, 2039, 2131, 2553
  See also Critical approaches to O'Connor's fiction--specific--Christian
        dogma

(Con't) Christ, Jesus
 See also O'Connor, Flannery--views and opinions--religious
 See also Symbols and images--Christian
"The Church and the Fiction Writer" 935, 1024
"A Circle in the Fire" 31, 34, 41, 47, 50a, 75b, 80, 108, 125, 211, 318, 392, 443,
 467, 529, 587, 597, 800, 815, 826, 890, 909, 962, 991, 1005, 1052,
 1086, 1124, 1133, 1217, 1221, 1283, 1295, 1304, 1320, 1384, 1396,
 1445, 1473, 1514, 1559a, 1563, 1585, 1601, 1615a, 1622, 1627, 1637,
 1709, 1725, 1727, 1816, 1839, 1869, 1953, 1998a, 2028, 2033, 2056,
 2114, 2659, 2701
 See also Characters, O'Connor's--specific--Cope, Mrs.
 See also Characters, O'Connor's--specific--Cope, Sally Virginia
 See also Characters, O'Connor's--specific--Pritchard, Mrs.
 See also Films--*A Circle in the Fire*
"The Citizen of My County Who Has Contributed the Most to the State of
 Georgia" 1349
City
 See Symbols and images--city[scape]
Civil rights movement, the 38, 68a, 380, 436, 444, 455, 579, 781, 1090, 1132,
 1195, 1347, 1407, 1667, 1671, 1683, 1799
Civil War, the American 815
 Defeat of the South in the 822, 890, 2039
 Influence of the 1104, 1233, 1345, 1516, 1517, 1623
 See also South, the--post-Civil War
Class structure
 See O'Connor, Flannery--views and opinions of--class structure
 See also Symbols and images--class structure
Cliches
 See Style--cliches, use of
Cline, Louis [Flannery O'Connor's uncle] 1692
Cloistral fiction 962
"The Coat" 1186, 1689
 See also Characters, O'Connor's--specific--Abram
 See also Characters, O'Connor's--specific--Rosa
Cold War, the 31, 68a, 209r, 228, 592, 1640r, 1734, 2226
 See also Communism
Collected Works [Library of America edition] 146, 354r, 366r, 678r, 910r, 946,
 1039r, 1120r, 1182, 1255, 1494r, 1651r, 1678r, 1706, 2031, 2444
The Colonnade
 See Georgia College & State University--*The Colonnade*
Color
 See Symbols and images--color
Columbia University 525
Comedy, O'Connor's work as 56, 62, 111, 117, 121, 131,136, 149, 157, 169,
 172, 178, 196, 203, 208, 220, 260, 270, 271, 275, 351, 416, 443, 477,
 484, 486, 495, 523, 543, 544, 572, 579, 581, 654, 668, 670, 674, 755,

(Con't) Comedy, O'Connor's work as
827, 832, 842, 875, 888, 918, 937, 939, 975, 1004, 1012, 1031, 1081,
1144, 1152, 1158, 1159, 1205, 1209, 1225, 1253, 1288, 1293, 1307,
1315, 1337, 1372, 1426, 1462, 1510, 1546, 1547, 1548, 1573, 1574,
1601, 1603r, 1604, 1605, 1610, 1655, 1657, 1667, 1668, 1682r, 1689,
1696, 1698, 1700, 1702, 1719, 1726, 1746, 1758, 1762, 1766, 1771,
1802, 1809, 1847, 1852, 1854, 1868, 1872, 1876, 1882, 1899, 1903,
1906, 1916, 1925, 1938, 1954, 1966, 1968, 1972, 1974, 1982, 2002,
2171, 2320, 2357, 2372, 2400, 2436, 2470, 2639, 2673
See also Symbols and images--comic
See also Georgia--middle--humor in
See also Grotesque, the--humor and
"The Comforts of Home" 34, 49, 50a, 77, 103, 108, 155, 230, 288, 514, 580,
588, 734, 826, 909, 954, 1076, 1133, 1167, 1291, 1300, 1320, 1384,
1409, 1421, 1563, 1637, 1641a, 1659, 1697, 1816, 1936, 1975, 2033,
2035, 2054, 2055, 2081, 2422, 2457, 2701
See also Characters, O'Connor's--specific--Ham, Sarah
See also Characters, O'Connor's--specific--Mother, Thomas's
See also Characters, O'Connor's--specific--Sheriff, the
See also Characters, O'Connor's--specific--Thomas
See also Films--*The Comforts of Home*
Commonweal 1339
Communism 33, 1858
See also Cold War, the
Community
See Symbols and images--community
Comparisons [of O'Connor's work] with work(s) by
Adams, Alice 1568c
Agee, James 1850, 1907
Aiken, Conrad 1495, 2644
Alcott, Louisa May 415
Allen, Woody 2483
Andersen, Hans Christian 869
Anderson, Sherwood 248, 561, 1635, 1875, 1994, 2001
Andreev, Leonid 1136
Angelou, Maya 2190
Aquinas, Saint Thomas 1030
Arbus, Diane 1007, 2012
Aristophanes 416, 975, 1547, 1802
Aristotle 774, 830, 1080, 2106, 2555
Artaud, Antonin 75b
Atwood, Margaret 972
Auden, W.H. 1893
Augustine, Saint 1030
Austen, Jane 2541
Baldwin, James 1908, 1999

(Con't) Comparisons [of O'Connor's Work] With Work(s) By
    Barth, John 1577, 1794, 1878, 1906, 1908
    Barth, Karl 1503
    Bataille, Georges 775
    Beckett, Samuel 75b, 1762
    Beja, Morris 1422
    Bellow, Saul 779, 823, 1899, 1901, 1917, 2041
    Bergson, Henri 275, 364
    Bernanos, Georges 1645, 2088
    Berry, Wendell 893
    Betts, Doris 781, 2699
    Bierce, Ambrose 1316
    Bishop, Elizabeth 910, 1927
    Blake, William 160, 316
    Blanchot, Maurice 775
    Bloom, Harold 1354
    Bly, Robert 1795
    Boccaccio, Giovanni 869
    Bowle, Paul 1878
    Bradford, William 1635
    Brontë, Emily 894
    Brooks, Cleanth 540
    Buechner, Frederick 250, 375, 1743
    Bunyan, John 162, 1559
    Burroughs, Willam 2041
    Byron, Lord 122
    Cable, Thomas Nelson 1799
    Caldwell, Erskine 573, 630, 662, 663, 745, 755, 1253, 1343, 1415, 1450, 1877, 2008, 2692
    Campbell, Kate 721a
    Capote, Truman 552, 686, 1249, 1782, 1821, 1830, 1853, 2241
    Carrington, Leonora 1773
    Carroll, Lewis 1402
    Carter, Angela 973, 1773
    Carter, Jimmy 1711
    Carver, Raymond 594, 925, 1651
    Cather, Willa 176, 1468
    Chardin, Pierre Teilhard de 345
    Cheever, John 2483
    Chekhov, Anton 720, 2139
    Chesnutt, Charles Waddell 1249
    Chopin, Kate 472, 824, 1738, 2645
    Clemens, Samuel.
        See Twain, Mark
    Clifton, Lucille 1917
    Coleridge, Mary Elizabeth 973

(Con't) Comparisons [of O'Connor's Work] With Work(s) By

    Conrad, Joseph 258, 531, 554, 670, 1762, 1984, 1987
    Cooper, James Fenimore 1879
    Corrington, John William 1085
    Crane, Stephen 878, 1879, 2001
    Crews, Frederick 1316
    Crews, Harry 189, 220, 1020, 1126, 1398, 1415, 1416, 1564
    Dante 368, 395, 416, 479, 551, 718, 1080, 1559, 1802
    Dawkins, Cecil 1864
    DeVries, Peter 1854
    Dexter, Pete 802, 1247
    Dickens, Charles 291
    Dickey, James 1850
    Dickinson, Eleanor 846
    Didion, Joan 1271, 2536
    Dinesen, Isak 973
    Doctorow, E.L. 1545
    Donne, John 1559
    Dostoevsky 77, 94, 235, 1049, 1228, 1435, 1762, 1983, 2123, 2130,
        2561
    Douglas, Ellen 2685
    Dubus, Andre 1480
    Edgerton, Clyde 1035, 1254, 1813
    Edwards, Harry Stillwell 2343
    Edwards, Jonathan 422, 830
    Eliade, Mircea 345
    Eliot, George 574
    Eliot, T.S. 37, 56, 77, 316, 502, 662, 669, 826, 1115, 1510, 1591,
        1841, 1893, 1989
    Ellison, Ralph 829, 916, 1215, 1853, 1878, 1908, 1917, 1939
    Emerson, Ralph Waldo 1032
    Erdrich, Louise 991, 1911
    Eyes, Harvest Moon 1476
    Faulkner, William 151, 159, 206, 232a, 265, 355, 378, 418, 481, 529,
        542, 543, 559, 561, 573, 619, 624, 631, 53, 663, 664, 670,
        678, 720, 737, 741, 747, 748, 777, 10, 819, 820, 919, 943,
        962, 975, 1034, 1056, 1104, 1111, 1115, 1116, 1173, 1249,
        1255, 1276, 1302, 1317, 1335, 1343, 1434, 1456, 1461,
        1550c, 1572, 1585, 1601, 1617, 1635, 1651, 1655, 1660,
        1726, 1738, 1747, 1748, 1762, 1768, 1772, 1784, 1795, 1797,
        1799, 1809, 1830, 1839, 1850, 1853, 1875, 1897, 1898, 1902,
        1908, 1916, 1945, 1962, 1971, 1975, 2004, 2005, 2010, 2018,
        2136, 2286, 2369, 2526, 2597
    Fitzgerald, F. Scott 669, 1795, 1839, 2007, 2653
    Flaubert, Gustave 554, 559, 564, 2137
    Foote, Shelby 1255

(Con't) Comparison [of O'Connor's Work] With Work(s) By
  Ford, Ford Maddox 554
  Ford, Richard 747
  Forster, E.M. 559
  Frei, Hans 1503
  Frost, Robert 878
  Gadamer, Hans-Georg 1943
  Gaddis, William 884
  Gaines, Ernest 542
  Gardner, John 110, 2603
  Garrison, William Lloyd 830
  Gilbert and Sullivan [Sir William S. Gilbert and Sir Arthur Sullivan]
    440
  Gilchrist, Ellen 2390
  Girard, Rene 311a, 1865
  Glasgow, Ellen 1911, 2008, 2645
  Goethe, Johann Wolfgang von 316, 867
  Golding, William 816
  Goodman, Allegra 356
  Gordon, Caroline 540, 552, 748, 1294, 1710, 1864, 1984, 2273
  Grau, Shirley Ann 307a, 380, 781, 1853
  Green, Julien 2027
  Greene, Graham 816, 831, 1651, 1828, 1881, 1893, 1895, 1910, 1912,
    1913, 1924, 2007a, 2088, 2396, 2459, 2465
  Hall, Martha Lacy 692
  Hannah, Barry 304, 747, 848, 859, 1417
  Hardy, Thomas 531
  Harris, George Washington 1316, 1972
  Harris, Joel Chandler 1218, 2343
  Haval, Václav 1332
  Hawkes, John 443a, 626, 884, 1056, 1602, 1604, 1833, 1840, 2604
  Hawking, Stephen 905
  Hawthorne, Nathaniel 253, 264, 321, 401, 456, 457, 462, 581, 678,
    801, 890, 1011, 1039r, 1056, 1096, 1105, 1113, 1133, 1278,
    1316, 1335, 1512, 1549, 1635, 1651, 1762, 1767, 1875, 1902,
    1908, 1943, 1946, 1971, 2001, 2047, 2269, 2559, 2627
  Heller, Joseph 1878, 1906
  Hemingway, Ernest 1273, 1635, 1946, 1984, 2010
  Hinojosa, Rolando 1911
  Hirsch, Marianne 125
  Hitchcock, Alfred 618, 1873
  Hopkins, Gerard Manley 362, 1103
  Hughes, Langston 777
  Hugo, Richard 1795
  Humphrey, William 1782, 1850
  Hurston, Zora Neale 1173, 1772, 1857, 2437, 2597

(Con't) Comparisons [of O'Connor's Work] With Work(s) By
> Huysmans, Joris-Karl 2319
> Ionesco, Eugène 1762, 2620
> Irving, John 1503, 1916
> Irving, Washington 1875
> Jackson, Shirley 973, 1794
> James, Henry 554, 779, 1549, 1651, 1770, 1794, 1795, 1902
> Johnson, Charles 1603
> Johnson, Richard Malcolm 2343
> Jones, LeRoi 2041
> Jones, Madison 1850
> Joyce, James 77, 241, 608, 1103, 1111, 1168, 1328, 1422, 1612, 1726,
>   2452
> Kafka, Franz 1320, 1355, 1600, 1762, 1846, 2137
> Kennedy, John Pendleton 1799
> Kesey, Ken 1785
> Kierkegaard, Sören 165, 455, 642, 735, 2361
> King, Martin Luther, Jr. 444, 622
> Knowles, John 1939
> Kosinski, Jerzy 1833, 1916
> Kugelmann, Robert 794
> Lacan, Jacques 1958
> Lanier, Sidney 1534
> Lawrence, D.H. 122, 1615a, 2483
> Lear, Edward 1402
> Lee, Harper 1940, 2008
> Lessing, Doris 972
> Lewis, C.S. 446, 1152, 1559, 1924, 2200
> Lewis, Henry Clay 1335
> Lispector, Clarice 2138
> Lowell, Robert 618, 1053a, 1209, 2533
> Lytle, Andrew 1292
> MacDonald, George 1924
> Mailer, Norman 826, 1878, 1907, 2041
> Malamud, Bernard 720, 816, 934, 1056, 1577, 1794, 1834, 1901, 1931,
>   1990, 1999
> Mann, Sally 98a
> Mansfield, Katherine 927, 2283
> Marcel, Gabriel 1508
> Maritain, Jacques 2050
> Marlowe, Christopher 867
> Mason, Bobbie Ann 594, 604, 1492, 1871
> Matute, Ana Maria 1558
> Mauriac, François 1912, 1983, 2027
> McCarthy, Cormac 1083, 1230, 1239, 1490, 1491, 1492, 1657
> McCarthy, Mary 618, 1857, 2281, 2594

(Con't) Comparisons [of O'Connor's Work] With Work(s) By

McClanahan, Ed 988

McCorkle, Jill 1568c

McCullers, Carson 284, 301, 436, 556, 662, 721, 741,748, 781, 800a, 1228, 1234, 1249, 1342, 1343, 1415, 1416, 1559a, 1585, 1635, 1636, 1727, 1747, 1782, 1784, 1812, 1821, 1839, 1845, 1853, 1871, 1874, 1875, 1886, 1897, 1919, 1940, 1945, 1956, 1975, 1997, 2024, 2025, 2026, 2036, 2091, 2241, 2272, 2374, 2440, 2447, 2525, 2530, 2593

McLuhan, Marshall 126

Melville, Herman 164a, 678, 962, 1056, 1075, 1094, 1335, 1549, 1762, 1770, 1908, 1971, 2049

Mencken, H.L. 1669

Merton, Thomas 77, 524, 607, 839, 965, 1015, 1425, 1594, 1723, 1724

Miller, Arthur 1439, 1795

Milton, John 926, 1512, 1559, 2090

Mitchell, Margaret 468a, 800a, 1266, 1355, 1517, 1519, 1521, 2226

Morrison, Toni 1736, 1748, 1769, 2146

Munro, Alice 720, 2266, 2457

Nabokov, Vladimir 826, 1906, 2603

Nemerov, Howard 789

Nietzsche, Friedrich 1030

Nin, Anais 973

Nordan, Lewis 1813

Norris, Frank 2001

Nunn, Kem 870

Oates, Joyce Carol 405, 591, 731, 1329, 1631, 1736, 1795, 1959, 2017, 2483, 2536

O'Connor, Edwin 620

Olsen, Tillie 1857

Ovid [Publius Ovidius Naso] 174

Ozick, Cynthia 1828, 1931

Page, Thomas Nelson 1799

Paley, Grace 720

Pancake, Breece D'J 1803

Parker, Dorothy 1330

Passos, John Dos 561, 1858

Percy, Walker 53, 77, 97, 106, 219, 310, 323, 358, 359, 363, 391, 404, 446, 532, 543, 546, 619, 642, 648, 703, 740, 750, 765, 779, 801, 831, 835, 857, 862, 883, 900, 932, 939, 966, 1014, 1022, 1023a, 1034, 1204, 1231, 1255, 1277, 1302, 1429, 1430, 1434, 1456, 1489, 1491, 1493, 1494, 1539, 1545, 1617, 1620, 1670, 1735, 1738, 1754, 1791, 1799, 1825, 1852, 1876, 1881, 1916, 1931, 1933, 2022, 2024, 2123, 2212, 2447, 2486, 2623

Percy, William Alexander 932

Peterson, Levi 463

(Con't) Comparisons [of O'Connor's Work] With Work(s) By

    Phillips, Jayne Anne 1020, 2038
    Plath, Sylvia 1773, 2190
    Plato 1332
    Poe, Edgar Alan 159, 470, 477, 561, 569, 909, 1056, 1105, 1109, 1118,
        1794, 1875, 1879, 2001, 2583
    Porter, Katherine Ann 429, 671, 748, 847, 1288, 1329, 1432, 1585,
        1727, 1794, 1820, 1850, 1857, 1871, 2018, 2281, 2286, 2373,
        2399, 2548
    Powers, J.F. 159, 620, 857, 924, 1014, 1023a, 1204, 1548, 1854, 1876,
        1933, 1984
    Price, Reynolds 367
    Proust, Marcel 775, 1860
    Prud'hon, Pierre-Paul 2156
    Pseudo-Dionysius 1647, 1724
    Purdy, James 1907
    Pynchon, Thomas 1200, 1651, 1735, 1833, 1858, 1879, 1908
    Ransom, John Crowe 1292
    Rawlings, Marjorie Kinnan 433
    Riding, Laura 1871
    Rossetti, Christina 973
    Roth, Henry 777
    Rouault, Georges 1818
    Ruddick, Sara 125
    Salinger, J.D. 669, 826, 1906, 1999, 2130
    Sartre, Jean Paul 774
    Scorsese, Martin 2677
    Settle, Mary Lee 2038
    Sexton, Anne 2190
    Shakespeare, William 1080, 1635
    Singleton, John 2675
    Smith, Lee 741, 747, 781, 1568c, 1813
    Smith, Lillian 1701
    Snyder, Gary 1917
    Södergran, Edith 2023
    Solzhenitsyn, Alexander 1114, 1117, 1332
    Sophocles 282, 715, 1066, 1105, 1635, 2446
    Spark, Muriel 1890
    Spencer, Elizabeth 781, 1233
    Steinbeck, John 408, 1875, 2010
    Stone, Oliver 2675
    Stuart, Henry Logan 1984
    Styron, William 322, 418, 561, 703, 911, 1631, 1782, 1784, 1799,
        1830, 1850, 1878, 1897, 2024, 2123
    Swift, Jonathan 740, 1103, 1402
    Tanizaki, Jun'ichiro 1138

(Con't) Comparisons [of O'Connor's Work] With Work(s) By

    Tarantino, Quentin 388

    Tate, Allen 540, 543, 932, 1292, 1489, 2004, 2025, 2026, 2556

    Taylor, Peter 881, 1293, 2394

    Theroux 884

    Thoreau, Henry David 1549, 2706

    Thorpe, Thomas Bangs 1094

    Toole, John Kennedy 262, 619, 939

    Toomer, Jean 279, 1249

    Twain, Mark 663, 678, 737, 962, 1316, 1335, 1799, 1972

    Tyler, Anne 468, 781, 1263, 1269, 1562, 1568c

    Updike, John 1056, 1577, 1754, 1795, 1834, 1962, 1990, 1999

    Valenzuela, Luisa 2670

    Villon, François 1860

    Voeglin, Eric 1098, 2511

    Vonnegutt, Kurt, Jr. 1906, 1908

    Walker, Alice 143, 272, 280, 281, 431, 472, 500, 556, 638, 640, 641,
        678, 800a, 960, 1218, 1341, 1568c, 1572, 1656, 1871, 2038,
        2390, 2589

    Walpole, Horace 2354

    Warren, Robert Penn 787, 911, 1255, 1292, 1434, 1782, 1850, 1897,
        1898, 1997, 2024, 2025, 2026, 2128, 2511

    Waugh, Evelyn 779, 910, 1547

    Weigel, Gustave 345

    Weil, Simone 2416

    Welty, Eudora 80, 111, 119, 180, 206, 323, 344, 394, 429, 436, 468,
        472, 534, 631, 641, 653, 737, 741, 748, 780, 781, 847, 881,
        927, 1011, 1173, 1255, 1288, 1315, 1329, 1434, 1442, 1491,
        1550c, 1562, 1573, 1585, 1615a, 1617, 1622, 1623, 1699,
        1712, 1717, 1727, 1729, 1746, 1779, 1820, 1821, 1839, 1845,
        1850, 1853, 1871, 1874, 1886, 1897, 1919, 1956, 1997, 2008,
        2018, 2038, 2187, 2218, 2373, 2390, 2394, 2399, 2440, 2548,
        2593, 2598, 2645, 2700

    West, Nathanael 878, 884, 887, 1105, 1426, 1456, 1510, 1604, 1719,
        1747, 1762, 1768, 1791, 1875, 1902, 1908, 1916, 2028, 2206,
        2223, 2463

    White, Patrick 1137

    Williams, Charles 1910

    Williams, Sherley Anne 1568c

    Williams, Tennessee 1003, 1839, 2128

    Wills, Garry 932

    Wolfe, Thomas 663, 1215, 1456, 1850, 1997

    Woolf, Virginia 1422, 2706

    Wright, Richard 542, 748, 1215, 1249, 1739, 1772, 1879, 1898, 1908,
        2243, 2675

    Yeats, William Butler 77, 183, 277 1137

(Con't) Comparisons [of O'Connor's Work] With Work(s) By
        Young, Marguerite 884
Compassion
        See Style--compassion, use of
Conferences, lectures and symposia
        American Literature Association [1999] 84a
        Christfest: The Gospel and the Arts in the 20th Century [Samford
                Univ.] 1661
        *The Communities of Flannery O'Connor: The Enigma of a Georgia
                Writer* [April 30, 1980; Emory Univ.] 792, 913
        Conference on Christianity and Literature [Oct. 1996; Dayton, Ohio]
                793
        Flannery O'Connor: A Celebration [1974; Georgia College & State
                Univ.] 152
        *Flannery O'Connor and the Christian Mystery Seventieth Birthday
                Symposium* [Brigham Young Univ.] 214, 1134, 1648
        Flannery O'Connor Commemorative Symposium [Aug. 1984;
                Denmark] 393, 506
        Flannery O'Connor Summer Seminar [Georgia College & State Univ.]
                1018, 1453
        Flannery O'Connor Symposium [Mar. 1996; Bloor Street United
                Church; Toronto, Canada] 1367, 1454
        Flannery O'Connor's 75th Birthday Celebration [Mar. 2000; Georgia
                College & State Univ.] 51a, 1154a, 1218a, 1400a
        Georgia Festival of Arts and Letters [Mar. 2000; Georgia College &
                State Univ.] 1154c
        *The Habit of Art: An Interdisciplinary Celebration of the Legacy of
                Flannery O'Connor* [April 1994; Georgia College & State
                Univ.] 104, 133, 273, 527, 589, 638, 689, 788, 1250, 1443,
                1625, 1683, 1707
        Homeplace: A Celebration of Family [April 22, 1995; Athens, Ga.]
                633, 634, 635
        Loyola University [New Orleans] 1355
        *Old Capital Historical Society and Georgia College Architectural
                Seminar* [June, 1975; Savannah, Ga.] 1149
        Second Flannery O'Connor Symposium [April, 1977; Georgia College
                & State Univ.] 1119, 1581
        Southern Speech Communication Association Convention [April, 1979;
                Biloxi, Miss.] 1506
        Third Flannery O'Connor Symposium: Of Time and Place and Eternity
                [April, 1984; Georgia College & State Univ.] 1652
        Vanderbilt University Symposia [1959] 109, 1194
        Wesleyan College [Macon, Ga.] 654
                Panel discussion [Oct. 1960] 383, 1345, 1360
        See also Lectures and readings, Flannery O'Connor's
Confession, Christian 1983 1582

Conflict and contrast 116, 196, 256, 257, 271, 396, 422, 450, 455, 477, 540, 544, 606, 611, 733, 785, 814, 950, 953, 967, 1025, 1209, 1343, 1495, 1511, 1654, 1662, 1780, 1816, 1822, 1846, 1855, 1868, 1883, 1894, 1916, 2158, 2214, 2294, 2351, 2674

Types of

Artificial/natural 1402, 1918

Autonomy 1867

Black and white 809, 896, 916, 931, 939, 1056a, 1150a, 1186, 1203, 1207, 1215, 1335, 1341, 1407, 1649, 1667, 1671, 1683, 1699a, 1996, 2040, 2125, 2263

Characters and 1080, 1372, 1379, 1654, 1762, 1855, 1971

Class 71, 446a, 733, 800b, 1159, 1215, 1229, 1337, 1527, 1601, 1699a, 1700, 1725, 1729, 1817, 1851, 1963, 2081, 2094, 2131, 2173, 2226, 2324

Conscious/unconscious 286a, 1133, 1340, 1372, 1576, 1792

Empirical reality and spiritual truth 1137, 1138, 1152, 1167, 1213, 1229, 1270, 1271, 1350, 1365, 1372, 1411, 1425, 1435, 1436, 1491, 1503, 1508, 1535, 1595, 1596, 1608, 1650, 1684, 1717, 1730, 1733, 1744, 1749, 1786, 1810, 1814, 1819, 1846, 1855, 1865, 1866, 1887, 1891, 1908, 1918, 1933, 1949, 1951, 1953, 1961, 1977, 1984, 2021, 2041, 2059, 2090, 2130, 2302, 2334, 2443, 2542, 2555, 2633, 2635

Europe and America 392, 618, 733, 1207, 1400, 1843

Familial 1559a, 1764, 1883, 2325, 2520

Good/evil [demonic/holy] 71, 107, 142, 162, 174, 193, 201, 211, 256, 257, 276, 297, 300, 317, 321, 322, 337, 368, 378, 388, 392, 396, 404, 406, 450, 605, 612, 652, 658, 718, 727, 733, 784, 785, 815, 816, 818, 823, 838, 855, 863, 884, 890, 998, 1006, 1019, 1022, 1033, 1067, 1083, 1093a, 1103, 1107, 1118, 1127, 1152, 1171, 1270, 1300, 1335, 1340, 1365, 1419, 1420, 1435, 1451, 1490, 1493, 1495, 1511, 1512, 1530, 1546, 1587, 1620, 1631, 1674, 1762, 1778, 1786, 1810, 1814, 1816, 1839, 1866, 1885, 1898, 1939, 1954, 1999, 2033, 2043, 2352

Male/female 71, 606, 617, 1207, 1299, 1330, 1341, 1445, 1637, 1822, 2081

Economy of leisure and industrialization of literature 1430, 1435

Material/spiritual 950, 963, 980, 1051, 1600, 1749, 1846, 1951, 1964, 2430

Natural/supernatural worlds 858a, 1768, 1814, 1819, 1918, 1919, 1920, 1931, 2062, 2106

North/south 896, 938, 1187, 1215, 1270, 1448, 1799, 1884, 2039, 2154

(Con't) Conflict and Contrast--Types of
> Parent/child 139, 160, 166, 257, 273, 348, 479, 523, 550, 580,
>> 606, 617a, 669, 670, 734, 763, 776, 777, 814, 831,
>> 951, 967, 1088, 1283, 1285, 1328, 1337, 1421, 1628,
>> 1654, 1729, 1812, 1953, 2000, 2081, 2288, 2368,
>> 2376, 2419, 2597
> Polemical 1818
> Political 897, 980, 1107, 1153, 1332
> Protestant election/Catholicism 162, 211, 618, 638, 655, 1082,
>> 1096, 1096, 1100, 1666, 1672, 1674, 1841, 1930,
>> 1947
> Psychosexual 954, 1670
> Racial 71, 133, 328, 353, 380, 384, 419, 435, 444, 455, 466,
>> 527, 549, 557, 603, 607, 622, 640, 678, 705, 781,
>> 788, 793, 802, 809, 831, 897, 898, 1055, 1168, 1176,
>> 1187, 1203, 1207, 1224, 1335, 1347, 1363, 1393,
>> 1407, 1500, 1607a, 1667, 1671, 1683, 1690, 1691,
>> 1699a, 1700, 1701, 1734, 1766, 1772, 1782, 1883,
>> 1899, 1917, 1963, 2003, 2173
> Reason/emotion 1590, 1609, 1943, 1951, 2062
> Seeing/hearing 1073, 1402
> Skeptical adults/faith of children 160, 257, 1283
> Skepticism and faith 164, 450, 619, 735, 887, 890, 897, 1185,
>> 1320a, 1378, 1384, 1435, 1724, 1816, 2011, 2102
> Social classes 446a, 800b, 897, 980, 1159, 1207, 1215, 1227,
>> 1229, 1337, 1527, 1559a, 1601, 1699a, 1700, 1701,
>> 1725, 1729, 1773, 1817, 1851, 1861, 1963, 1976,
>> 1977, 2040, 2081, 2094, 2131, 2173, 2226, 2324,
>> 2333, 2611
> Social justice 1691, 1977
> Strong/weak 181, 606, 985, 986, 122

Connecticut
> *See* O'Connor, Flannery--biographical details--homes--Connecticut

Conscience 1152

Conservatives 163, 327, 607, 896, 1316, 1365, 1547, 1674, 1683
> *See also* Values, traditional

Consumer culture
> *See* Popular culture

Converse College 1288

Conversion Experience
> *See* Redemption

Corinth, Georgia
> *See* Georgia--cities and towns--Corinth

The Corinthian
> *See* Georgia College & State University--*The Corinthian*

Correspondence, Flannery O'Connor's 2, 7, 14, 59a, 145, 289, 292, 350, 432, 481, 508, 509, 510, 513, 517, 527, 550a, 563, 583, 602, 613, 627, 628, 629, 640, 649, 667, 671, 723, 724, 753, 788, 789, 849, 851, 907, 914, 929, 965, 966, 995, 1002, 1050, 1090, 1130, 1131, 1155, 1156, 1158, 1160, 1165, 1177a, 1180, 1185, 1188, 1202, 1212, 1232, 1308, 1309, 1320, 1336, 1347, 1359, 1374, 1402, 1418, 1434, 1459, 1472, 1494, 1518, 1527, 1549r, 1575, 1576, 1604, 1609, 1621, 1624, 1627, 1637, 1661r, 1671, 1678, 1680, 1682r, 1683, 1691, 1692, 1703, 1713, 1714, 1718, 1988, 2023, 2027, 2072, 2168, 2513
 Christmas cards 473, 481
 Collections of 550a, 1177a, 1177b
 The Correspondence of Flannery O'Connor and the Brainard Cheney's [C. Ralph Stephens] 2188
 Correspondents
  "A" *See* Hester, Hazel Elizabeth "Betty"
  Abott, Louise 723, 724
  Barrus, Paul 1177a
  Beiswanger, George 1177a
  Bonner, James 1177a
  Boyd, Betty 290
  Brown, Ashley 224, 225, 261
  Brown, Susan Jenkins 225
  Carver, Catherine 1177a
  Chardin, Pierre Teilhard de 782
  Cheney, Brainard and Frances Neel 2, 70, 149, 273, 477, 806r, 1157r, 1177a, 1634, 1988, 2188, 2513
  Coindreau, Maurice-Edgar 1188
  Corn, Alfred 345, 508, 723, 724, 1185, 1196
  Dawkins, Cecil 111, 261, 563, 564, 723, 1165, 1177b, 1691, 1692
  Donadio, Candida 1177a
  Emerson, O.B. 1177a
  Engle, Paul 521, 1177a
  Farnham, James F.
  Fitzgerald, Robert and Sally 502, 511, 519, 529a, 682, 724, 805
  Furguson, Betty 1177a
  Gable, Mariella 261, 1691
  Giroux, Robert 261, 517, 519, 1177a
  Gordon, Caroline 517, 519, 521, 552, 563, 564, 1122, 1177a, 1212
  Griffin, Benjamin 678, 1140
  Hall, Eileen 1177a
  Harrold, DeVene 1177a
  Hartman, Carl 724 481

(Con't) Correspondence, Flannery O'Connor's--Correspondents

Hawkes, John 297, 495, 564, 612, 775, 776, 784, 838, 884,
      918, 1270, 1395
Haynes, Alta 1177a
Hester, Hazel Elizabeth "Betty" ["A" in *The Habit of Being*]
      57, 102a, 111, 125, 261, 290, 325, 58, 517, 518, 521,
      563, 564, 632, 685, 723, 724, 1140, 1165, 1401a,
      1461, 1618, 1627, 1654, 1663, 1691, 1703, 2245
Ivey, Caroline Lawson 228, 1177a
Johnson, Miriam 1177a, 1624
Jones, Madison 803
Kessler, Edward 1177a
Koon, William 1177a
Lawrence, Roberta 1177a
Lee, Maryat 261, 290, 292, 293, 509, 517, 564, 584, 589,
      640, 788, 907, 914, 1155, 1165, 1177a, 1202, 1306,
      1347, 1575, 1671, 1683, 1691, 1692, 1694r, 1930a
Lindley, Denver 1177a
Lish, Loretta 1212
Lorentzen, Mel 724
Love, Betty Boyd 1177a
Lowell, Robert 521, 736, 969, 1053a, 1461
Lytle, Andrew 1461
Macauley, Robie 1212, 1641a
Maxwell, Allen 1177a
McCown, James H. 1024, 1165
McIntosh, Mavis 1177a
McKane, Janet 261, 521
McKee, Elizabeth 517, 521, 1122, 1177a, 1613
Minor, Jeanne 1177a
Montgomery, Marion 1177a
Morris, Alice 261
Null, Martha 1177a
O'Connor, Joan 1177a
O'Connor, Regina Cline
Page, Marion Peterman 1177a
Perelman, S.J. 583
Poller, Rebekah Massey 1177a, 1624
Porter, Katherine Anne 671, 1177a
Ransom, John Crowe 527, 789, 1641a
Romagosa, Edward J. ["Father Roma"] 1308
Russell, Richard 1177a
Satterfield, Virginia 1177a
Scott, Katherine 1177a
Smith, Marcus 1177a
Solomon, Rhoda 1177a 1177a

(Con't) Correspondence, Flannery O'Connor's--Correspondents
        Spivey, Ted R. 261, 723, 1460, 1461
        Stelzmann, Rainulf A. 1472
        Stern, Richard 731
        Tate, Allen 261
        Terry, Grace 297, 1177a
        Tomkievicz, Shirley Abbott 1177a
        Trawick, Jessie 1177a
        Walston, Rosa Lee 1177a
        Watson, Youree 724, 995
        Way, Elizabeth Fenwick 297
        Wilburs, Stephen 290
        Wylder, Jean 1644
        Zuber, Leo 1177a
    See also Adaptations--plays--"Flannery: A Life in Words"
    See also The Correspondence of Flannery O'Connor and the Brainard
        Cheney's
    See also The Habit of Being
Country[side]
    See Symbols and images--country[side]
Craft
    See Technique and craft, Flannery O'Connor's
Creative writing programs
    See O'Connor, Flannery--views and opinions of--creative writing
        programs
Cremation 2108, 2110
Critic, O'Connor as
    See Book reviews and criticism
Critical approaches to O'Connor's fiction
    Attacks on, as 1221, 1417, 1477, 1605, 1607a, 1662
    Directions of 71, 74, 108, 129, 135, 164a, 270, 273, 276, 315, 354,
        361, 390, 393, 409, 415, 419, 454, 455, 536, 563, 564, 565,
        566, 567, 577, 580, 586, 597, 621, 624, 646, 671, 687, 693a,
        797, 725, 748, 800a, 804a, 861, 862, 865, 879, 882, 920, 943,
        994, 996, 999, 1001, 1013, 1063, 1073, 1075, 1100, 1125,
        1133, 1136, 1141, 1178, 1215, 1246, 1270, 1290, 1301, 1309,
        1311, 1418, 1438, 1439, 1461, 1470, 1511, 1512, 1520r,
        1537r, 1605, 1674, 1698, 1839, 1856, 1870, 1880, 1881,
        1951, 1978, 1985, 2013
    Exasperation with, O'Connor's 150, 915, 1653, 1948
    Specific
        Archetypal 75b, 1470, 1794, 1935, 1970, 1974, 2215, 2657,
            2665
            See also Style--motifs and archetypes, use of
        Artistic 454, 554, 773, 977, 1097, 1113, 1847
        Bakhtinian 1694r, 1812, 2587

(Con't) Critical Approaches to O'Connor's Fiction--Specific
       Biographical and bio-bibliographical 232a, 640, 756, 757,
            836, 864, 910, 1037, 1042, 1053a, 1062, 1090, 1127,
            1180, 1460, 1466, 1469, 1473, 1694r, 1719a, 1841,
            1864, 1896, 1941, 2020, 2115
       Casual inquiry 389
       Christian dogma, based upon 75b, 135, 266, 267, 270, 276,
            315, 493, 495, 536, 577, 578, 579, 618, 619, 626,
            627, 628, 629, 638, 655, 679, 697, 701, 725, 729,
            839, 840, 842, 843, 844, 851, 875, 890, 893, 908,
            918, 920, 932, 939, 940, 953, 957, 966, 998, 999,
            1006, 1014, 1022, 1023a, 1040, 1054, 1056, 1079,
            1096, 1127, 1129a, 1160, 1165, 1195, 1196, 1204,
            1209, 1237, 1240, 1288, 1299, 1302, 1307, 1316,
            1344, 1347, 1356, 1376, 1383, 1386, 1406, 1418,
            1427, 1477, 1500, 1548, 1552, 1598, 1608, 1650,
            1666, 1668, 1672, 1682r, 1701, 1709, 1733, 1755,
            1759, 1787, 1790, 1808, 1810, 1818, 1839, 1848,
            1853, 1854, 1858, 1893, 1908, 1923, 1927, 1931,
            1933, 1936, 1944, 1947, 1961, 1970, 1979, 1981,
            1984, 1990, 2007a, 2044, 2081, 2086, 2088, 2090,
            2106, 2127, 2140, 2162, 2163, 2230, 2230a, 2326,
            2473, 2486, 2533, 2556, 2594
       Comparative analysis 1046, 1075, 1247, 1558, 1729, 2266
            See also Comparisons [of O'Connor's work] with
                 work(s) by
       Cultural 75b, 693a
       Cyclical 2010
       Deconstruction 865, 693a, 1001r, 1460, 1889, 1891, 2016
       Dialogism 74, 704, 1410
       "empathetic understanding" 1051
       Existential 1839, 1846, 1941, 1997, 2240, 2331, 2361
       Feminist 74, 75b, 80, 119, 125, 420, 570, 587, 589, 606, 617,
            693a, 812, 813, 864, 876, 941, 1055, 1078, 1119,
            1124, 1227, 1292, 1341, 1408, 1527a, 1622, 1718,
            1812, 1820, 1822, 1890, 1948, 1976, 2038, 2173,
            2325, 2632
            See also Identity--female
       Freudian
            See Psychoanalytic
       Game, as literary 548
       Gender studies 74, 420, 536, 586, 587, 588, 606, 617, 763,
            847, 941, 1292, 1299, 1408, 1445, 1626, 1629a,
            1694r, 1745, 1817, 1976, 2173, 2621a, 2652
            See also O'Connor, Flannery--views and opinions of
                --gender

(Con't) Critical Approaches to O'Connor's Fiction--Directions of--Specific
   Genre 1470, 1999
   "Hard No" classification [Leslie Fiedler's] 739
   Heideggerian theory 958, 1056a, 1670, 1834
   Historical context 286a, 882, 1444, 1729, 1797, 1841, 1864,
         2004, 2051, 2559
   "insight-through-sight" 1949
   Interdisciplinary 999, 1036r, 1772
   Ironic vision 1978, 2663
   Jungian
         See Psychoanalytic
   Lacanian 1057, 1058, 1958
   Linguistic 64, 897, 1093, 1915, 1991, 2660
   Literary history 75b, 1911
   Marxist 693a, 2127
   Material-rationalist 55, 216, 246, 263, 286a, 329, 443a, 529,
         741, 818, 865, 890, 962, 1012, 1029, 1093, 1907,
         1221, 1320a, 2574
   Modernist 286a, 564, 586, 618, 863, 953, 1056a, 1102, 1221,
         1297, 1384, 1802, 2004, 2461
   Motion studies 765
   New Criticism 74, 469, 536, 538, 540, 693a, 882, 1179, 1339,
         1460, 1470, 1527a, 1804, 1824
   Nonverbal communication 1282, 1946
   Parabolic 920, 2658
   Performance of ritual approach 75b, 1970
   Peripety, Aristotelian 1984
   Phenomenological 1470, 2555
   Piety, as an act of 743
   Political 847, 1332
   Post-modern 564, 618, 1889, 2175, 2621a
   Poststructural 865, 2478
   Protestant 912, 1947, 2471
   Psychoanalytic 74, 75b, 116, 128, 164, 164a, 175, 177, 220,
         255, 257, 270, 286a, 316, 327, 331, 335, 350, 354,
         396, 420, 449, 460, 496, 538, 541, 544, 551, 590,
         617a, 640, 651, 652, 658, 659, 667, 674, 680, 693a,
         706, 732, 749, 766, 809, 810, 811, 812, 813, 816,
         834, 864, 865, 896, 910, 954, 955, 986, 990, 1056a,
         1057, 1058, 1059, 1068, 1088, 1133, 1146, 1161,
         1189, 1213, 1245, 1339, 1340, 1373, 1384, 1438,
         1681r, 1701, 1702, 1741, 1780, 1783, 1794, 1795,
         1812, 1816, 1860, 1867, 1868, 1878, 1905, 1932,
         1946, 1954, 1958, 1970, 1976, 2000, 2007a, 2061,
         2169, 2190, 2360, 2509, 2665
   Qualitiative 2003

(Con't) Critical Approaches to O'Connor's Fiction--Directions of--Specific
     Racial 802, 809, 1203, 1347, 1407, 1607a, 1667, 1671,
          1683, 1699a, 1883, 1917, 2003
     Reader response theory 557, 631, 680, 725, 830, 958, 1004,
          1265, 1290, 1729, 1827, 1845, 1856, 1890, 2421
     Reader/text relation, theory of 1175, 1290, 1753
     Regionalism 1813, 1911, 1926, 1932, 1937, 1967, 2249,
          2290, 2522, 2532
     Rehetorical theory 74, 1046
     Semiotic strategies 1991
     Social criticism 418, 548, 603, 630, 640, 676, 680, 705, 712,
          793, 802, 980, 1136, 1215, 1227, 1559a, 1861, 2301
     Socio-political 1940
     Statistical 708
     Textual 286a, 994, 1153, 1460, 1753, 1772
     Theological 164a, 454, 590, 603, 650, 725, 800b, 818, 918,
          954, 957, 964, 966, 999, 1000r, 1030, 1070, 1119,
          1150a, 1299, 1312, 1347, 1384, 1477, 1731, 1836,
          1839, 1844, 1848, 1890, 1908, 1909, 1912, 1922,
          1924, 1932, 1947, 1978, 1981, 1989, 2016, 2177,
          2226, 2243, 2249, 2330, 2333, 2359, 2360, 2462,
          2493, 2519, 2541, 2579, 2581, 2600, 2641, 2676,
          2684
     Typology typological 1131, 1952, 1984
     via negativa 1980, 2016
   See also Bibliographies--O'Connor criticism
Critics, challenges O'Connor's work posed to 50, 55, 60, 150, 164a, 270, 276,
     536, 693a, 793, 800a, 804a, 1205, 1290, 1301, 1372, 1439, 1477, 1511,
     1512, 1607a, 1653, 1870, 1880, 1881, 1891, 1908, 1985, 2050
     See also Bibliographies--O'Connor criticism
Criticism
     See Critical approaches to O'Connor's fiction
"The Crop" 29, 34, 60, 489, 587, 630, 826, 1690, 1847
     See also Characters, O'Connor's--specific--Miss Willerton
Cross tattoo
     See Symbols and images--cross tattoo
Cycles and patterns
     See Style--cycles and patterns, use of
Cyril, Saint--of Jerusalem 59a, 385, 718, 983, 1015, 1277, 1379, 1570, 1631,
     1935, 2073, 2131, 2191, 2261

Darkness
     See Symbols and images--darkness
Daughters
     See Characters--types of--daughters

Death 274, 300, 349, 389, 580, 597, 608, 617a, 622, 668, 669, 697, 710, 757, 778, 812, 864, 887, 892, 906, 1006, 1031, 1054, 1060, 1078, 1135, 1163, 1168, 1186, 1204, 1384, 1409, 1451, 1497, 1551, 1595, 1610, 1638, 1660, 1669, 1693, 1702, 1809, 1841, 1850, 1857, 1906, 1980, 2444
   See also Cremation
   See also O'Connor, Flannery--death and funeral
   See also O'Connor, Flannery--views and opinions of--death
   See also Style--death, use of
Deconstruction
   See Critical approaches to O'Connor's fiction--specific--Deconstruction
Deeds, good 1474, 1497, 1816, 2499
Deformity
   See Symbols and images--deformity
Demonic
   See Symbols and images--demonic
Denver, University of 1639
Devil, the [Satan] 111, 131, 142, 162, 164a, 174, 178, 201, 234, 268, 274, 276, 287, 297, 311a, 329, 378, 406, 551, 581, 612, 652, 658, 776, 818, 820, 867, 884, 890, 918, 952, 1005, 1054, 1096, 1120, 1171, 1189, 1216, 1239, 1270, 1291, 1300, 1379, 1386, 1395, 1439, 1536, 1631, 1816, 2007a, 2102, 2261, 2318, 2501
   See also Characters--O'Connor's--types of--"The Other"
Dialogism
   See Critical approaches to O'Connor's fiction--specific--dialogism
Dialogue 55, 165, 180, 189, 270, 366, 704, 1541, 1855
Dignity 613
Disability
   See Symbols and images--disability
Discourse, free indirect 704, 705, 707
Disorder 1926, 2394, 2689
"The Displaced Person" 31, 33, 34, 38, 40, 41, 45, 47, 50a, 59a, 76, 77, 108, 114, 164, 185, 191, 211, 254, 263, 286a, 288, 298, 323, 328, 330, 353, 392, 417, 427, 445, 465, 485, 495, 529, 595, 597, 621, 624, 632, 642, 653, 658, 676, 711, 712, 733, 774, 778, 783, 809, 815, 838, 860, 909, 925, 943, 945, 949, 962, 980, 991, 1005, 1009, 1019, 1043, 1048, 1051, 1052, 1061, 1073, 1124, 1131, 1137, 1150a, 1207, 1221, 1264, 1295, 1367, 1384, 1385, 1396, 1426, 1445, 1479, 1491, 1497, 1506, 1519, 1521, 1526, 1554, 1562, 1563, 1600, 1615, 1637, 1699a, 1708, 1717, 1725, 1775, 1776, 1816, 1847, 1890, 1892, 1902, 1936, 1998a, 2027, 2028, 2033, 2040, 2058, 2065, 2087, 2088, 2122, 2153, 2154, 2187, 2285, 2499, 2552, 2654
   See also Adaptations--plays--"The Displaced Person"
   See also Characters, O'Connor's--specific--Astor
   See also Characters, O'Connor's--specific--Guizac, Mr.
   See also Characters, O'Connor's--specific--Judge, the

(Con't) "The Displaced Person"
 See also Characters, O'Connor's--specific--McIntyre, Mrs.
 See also Characters, O'Connor's--specific--Priest, the
 See also Characters, O'Connor's--specific--Shortley, Chancey
 See also Characters, O'Connor's--specific--Shortley, Mrs.
 See also Characters, O'Connor's--specific--Sulk
 See also Films--*The Displaced Person*
 See Style--motifs and archetypes--displaced persons
 See also Symbols and images--displaced persons
Displacement
 See Symbols and images--displacement
Dissertations, [discussion of] Flannery O'Connor-related 51, 423, 459, 1202,
 1250, 1318, 1321, 1392, 1470a, 1505, 1567
Distortion
 See Style--distortion, use of
Divine
 See Symbols and images--divine
Divine Comedy 551, 718, 931, 1802
Divorce
 See O'Connor, Flannery--views and opinions of--divorce
"Doctors of Delinquency" 1689
Dominican Nuns of Our Lady of Perpetual Help Cancer Home [Atlanta,
 Ga.] 194, 1039r, 1209, 1219
Donkey, O'Connor's ["Earnest"] 833
Dopplegänger motif
 See Style--motifs and archetypes--Dopplegänger motif
Doubles
 See Characters--types of--double(s)
 See also Style--motifs and archetypes--double motif
Dragon
 See Cyril, Saint--of Jerusalem
 See also Symbols and images--dragon
Dream vision literary tradition 1927
Dreams
 See Symbols and images--dreams
"Driggers' Catalog," [Stephen] 488, 649, 1177a
Dualism
 See Symbols and images--dualism
Duke University Alumni College 1534
"Dunn's Catalog," [Robert J.] 649, 1616

Eatonton, Georgia
 See Georgia--cities and towns--Eatonton
Echo
 See Symbols and images--echoing voices

Eden, The Garden of 318, 394, 401, 735, 815, 1393, 1600, 1799, 1863, 1975, 2033
Editors 1616
 Giroux, Robert [Harcourt, Brace] 1613, 1692
 Selby, John [Rinehart] 804a, 1613, 1692
Education
 See O'Connor, Flannery--views and opinions of--education
"Education's Only Hope" 1689
"Effervescence" 1689
Egypt 607, 613
"Elegance Is Its Own Reward" 1689
Emblem(s) 34, 418, 448, 599, 889, 1060, 1564, 2033
 See also Symbols and images
Emory University 345, 508, 792, 913, 1185
"The Enduring Chill" 31, 34, 36, 37, 38, 41, 47, 50a, 54, 77, 103, 143, 155,
 169a, 172, 195, 223, 225, 261, 262, 265, 326, 331, 435, 465, 514, 523,
 541, 580, 586, 597, 654, 716, 722, 734, 767, 773, 785, 819, 890, 923,
 945, 995, 1076, 1168, 1181, 1217, 1291a, 1299, 1304, 1320, 1378,
 1396, 1462, 1477, 1491, 1548, 1563, 1575, 1637, 1643, 1649, 1659,
 1667, 1671, 1683, 1697, 1726, 1816, 1896, 1922, 1969, 2000, 2011,
 2033, 2054, 2113, 2148, 2422, 2424, 2544
 See also Adaptations--plays- "The Enduring Chill"
 See also Characters, O'Connor's--specific--Fox, Asbury Porter
 See also Characters, O'Connor's--specific--Fox, Mary George
 See also Characters, O'Connor's--specific--Fox, Mrs.
Enlightenment, the 165, 959, 1110, 1332, 1943
"Enoch and the Gorilla" 60, 143, 465, 665, 770, 1361, 1409, 2315
Epiphany
 See Symbols and images--Epiphany
Equality 800b
Eschatology 1908, 1953
Eucharist, the Holy 50a, 93, 496, 505, 702, 1032, 1132, 1473, 1598, 1609, 2168,
 2380
 See also Christ, Jesus--the Eucharist as body of
 See also Symbols and images--Eucharist, the
Evangelists 104a, 1188, 1766, 1768, 1897, 1957, 1962, 1973, 2050, 2274, 2535
Everything That Rises Must Converge [collection]
 37, 50a, 55, 60, 62, 102, 114, 351, 502, 507, 514, 541, 544, 561, 565,
 617a, 653, 671, 738, 758, 766r, 768, 849, 871, 930, 943, 946, 967, 985,
 1181, 1348, 1381, 1424, 1462, 1612, 1649, 1659, 1697, 1800, 1963,
 2010, 2155, 2227, 2475, 2600, 2643
"Everything That Rises Must Converge" [story] 31, 33, 34, 35a, 36, 37, 40, 47,
 49, 50a, 114, 143, 172, 195, 203, 231, 251, 263, 265, 281, 299, 317,
 331, 355, 371, 377, 389, 435, 442, 455, 471, 507, 514, 531, 546, 550,
 580, 623, 624, 640, 648, 676, 678, 712, 716, 729a, 734, 738, 749, 761,
 783, 795, 802, 809, 817, 838, 849, 864, 909, 923, 943, 945, 949, 1026,

(Con't) "Everything That Rises Must Converge" [story]
          1052, 1053, 1109, 1133, 1150a, 1163, 1208, 1224, 1265, 1266, 1267,
          1291, 1291a, 1299, 1320, 1348, 1381, 1384, 1407, 1409, 1491, 1521,
          1544, 1556, 1562, 1563, 1572, 1606, 1612, 1637, 1649, 1659, 1671,
          1683, 1697, 1699a, 1700, 1762, 1787, 1827, 1869, 1878, 1890, 1942,
          1953, 2000, 2002, 2011, 2033, 2040, 2054, 2055, 2081, 2173, 2332,
          2411, 2414, 2422, 2475, 2584, 2585a, 2595, 2611, 2701
          See also Adaptations--plays--"Everything That Rises Must Converge"
          See also Characters, O'Connor's--specific--black mother
          See also Characters, O'Connor's--specific--Carver
          See also Characters, O'Connor's--specific--Chestny, Julian
          See also Characters, O'Connor's--specific--Chestny, Mrs.
Evil
          See O'Connor, Flannery--views and opinions of--evil
          See also Characters--types of--evil
Exaggeration
          See Style--exaggeration, use of
"Excuse Us While We Don't Apologize" 1689
"An Exile In the East" 78, 261, 265, 593, 608, 672, 1187, 1614, 1804, 2057
          See also Characters, O'Connor's--specific--daughter
          See also Characters, O'Connor's--specific--Tanner, Old
          See also Characters, O'Connor's--specific--Tanner, T.C.
Existentialist writers 130, 157, 165, 816, 1137, 1455, 1815, 1941, 1997, 2331,
          2361
Existentialists
          See Characters--types of--existential
Exogamy 1373
Eye(sight) 34, 231, 241, 255, 371, 374, 431, 454, 477, 554, 555, 575, 576, 585,
          755, 778, 812, 840, 858, 863, 889, 959, 968, 977, 1006, 1040, 1041,
          1044, 1058, 1060, 1072, 1073, 1074, 1075, 1088, 1282, 1312, 1340,
          1436, 1441, 1482, 1555, 1605, 1869, 1943, 2151, 2186, 2379, 2431
          See also Symbols and images--eyes
          See also Characters--vision of

Fairy tales, influence of 827, 973
          See also Style--fable, use of
Faith
          See Catholic faith, Flannery O'Connor's
          See also O'Connor, Flannery--views and opinions of--religious
Families
          See Style--families, use of
          See also Symbols and images--family
Fantasy, childhood 1741
"Fashion's Perfect Medium" 1689
Faust legend 867

Faux Flannery Contest 1390, 1721
Feminine
    See Style--motifs and archetypes--feminine
    See also Symbols and images--feminine
Feminist
    See Critical approaches to O'Connor's fiction--specific--feminist
    See also Critical approaches to O'Connor's fiction--specific--gender
        studies
"The Fiction Writer and His Country" 427, 514, 980, 1043, 1076, 1077, 1287,
        1525
"The Fiction Writer in the South" 291
Films 108, 124, 153, 286a, 461, 536, 558, 695, 978, 1074, 1081, 1147, 1362,
        1432, 1526, 1560, 1811, 1993, 1995
    The Artificial Eye [*Wise Blood*] 464
    A Circle in the Fire 108, 461, 1147, 1238, 1993
    The Comforts of Home 108, 413, 461, 1147, 1238, 1993
    Comparisons [to other films]
        Boyz n the Hood 2676
        Cape Fear 2677
        Mighty Joe Young 1521
        Natural Born Killers 2676
        Silence of the Lambs 100
        Two Flags West 1517
    The Displaced Person 108, 124, 237, 461, 1044, 1147, 1238, 1432,
        1475, 1526, 1581, 1582, 1632, 1811, 1993, 1995
        Actors/actresses 1147
            John Houseman [as Father Flynn] 1147, 1475
            Robert Earl Jones [as Astor] 1147
            Shirley Stoller [as Mrs. Shortley] 1147, 1432, 1526
            Irene Worth [as Mrs. McIntyre] 1147, 1475
        Art director
            Charles Bennett 1432
        Director
            Glenn Jordan 1432, 1581, 1582
        Filming techniques 1432, 1526
        Screenplay
            Horton Foote 1432
        Visual effects 1526
    Good Country People 108, 413, 461, 1147, 1993
    Revelation 413
    The River 225, 1993
    Wise Blood 53, 141, 187, 204, 232a, 342, 373, 558, 572, 601, 684, 695,
        730, 732, 858, 895, 978, 989, 1018, 1041, 1064, 1081, 1145r,
        1226, 1322, 1351, 1428, 1509r, 1543, 1563, 2102
        Actors/actresses 684
            Ned Beatty [Onnie Jay Holy] 342, 684

(Con't) Films--Wise Blood--Actors/actresses
      Brad Dourif [as Hazel Motes] 684
      Dan Shor [as Enoch Emory] 342, 684
      Harry Dean Stanton [as Asa Hawks] 684, 1560
      Amy Wright [as Sabbath Lily] 342, 684, 1064
    Comedy, as 1081
    Director
      Huston, John 695, 732, 858, 978, 989, 1018, 1064,
        1243, 1322, 1428, 1509r, 1543, 1560, 2102
    Filming techniques 695, 858
    Naturalistic style of 1041
    Reviews 1226, 1509r
    Screenplays 1243
      Benedict Fitzgerald 572, 978
      Michael Fitzgerald 684, 695, 1543
      Jerome Kass 821
    Visual effects 1064
  The World of Flannery O'Connor 152, 1147
  See also The American Short Story Film Series
  See also Symbols and images--film imagery
Fire
  See Symbols and images--fire
"The First Book" [poem] 1689
Fitzgerald, Sally
  See Correspondence, Flannery O'Connor's--specific correspondents--
    Fitzgerald, Sally and Robert
  See Recollections and comments about Flannery O'Connor--Fitzgerald,
    Sally
Flannery O'Connor Bulletin
  See Georgia College & State University--*Flannery O'Connor Bulletin*
Flannery O'Connor Childhood Home Foundation
  See O'Connor, Flannery--biographical details--homes--Savannah
Flannery O'Connor Collection
  See Georgia College & State University--Russell Library--*Flannery*
    O'Connor Collection
Flannery O'Connor: The Complete Stories 81, 122, 377, 565, 630, 823, 844r,
  930, 1182, 1329r, 1545, 1563r, 1632
Flannery O'Connor Professorship in Letters [University of Iowa] 553
Flannery O'Connor Review
  See Georgia College & State University--*Flannery O'Connor Review*
Flannery O'Connor Society 639, 1306, 1309, 1310, 1313
Folk art 41, 128, 1012, 1801
  See also Artistic interpretations of O'Connor's work
Folklore 55, 277, 1939
Food
  See Symbols and images--food

Fool tradition 1975
Formal thought in teaching literature 167
Fowl
       See Peacocks, chickens and other fowl
Fox Theatre [Atlanta, Ga.] 1517
"The Freak in Modern Literature" 291
Freaks
       See Characters--types of--freaks
       See also Symbols and images--freaks
Free will
       See Style--free will, use of
Freedom 32, 73, 75b, 164a, 727, 800, 1005, 1315, 1610, 1815, 1921, 1999,
       2105, 2131, 2220, 2232
       See also O'Connor, Flannery--views and opinions of--freedom
French Catholicism
       See Catholic--French
French literature 1716, 1966, 2009
Frontier literature 1089
Fundamentalism, religious 38, 126, 131, 145, 217, 272, 318, 418, 495, 532, 619,
       644, 778, 779, 890, 964, 1063, 1070, 1072, 1082, 1093, 1258, 1304,
       1343, 1379, 1384, 1427, 1536, 1635, 1655, 1666, 1669, 1672, 1972,
       2086, 2107, 2177, 2251, 2473
       See also Characters--types of--Protestant fundamentalist
       See also Theology--fundamentalist

Gargoyles 41, 1801
Gender
       See O'Connor, Flannery--views and opinions of--gender
       See also Critical approaches to O'Connor's fiction--specific--gender
       See also Identity
Gender studies
       See Critical approaches to O'Connor's fiction--specific--gender studies
Georgia 181, 207, 526, 607, 792, 793, 977, 1062, 1063, 1471
       Authors 2343, 2355
       Cities and towns
              Atlanta 883, 938, 1253, 1450, 1458, 1459
              Corinth 1638, 1648
              Eatonton 886, 1218, 2343
              Locust Grove 1450
              Macon 684, 978
              Milledgeville 31, 133, 148, 158, 250, 293, 336, 387, 545, 641,
                   650, 691, 802, 822, 823, 833, 853, 855, 858, 886,
                   976, 1018, 1023, 1044, 1065, 1218, 1236, 1247,
                   1370, 1371, 1443, 1471, 1523, 1624, 1639, 1646,
                   2023

(Con't) Georgia--Cities and Towns--Milledgeville
     Central State Hospital 1093a
     Courthouse 1368
     Governor's Mansion 1251, 1368, 1391
     Holiday Inn 1251, 1346
     Mary Vinson Public Library 1090
     Memory Hill Cemetery 1502
     Sacred Heart Catholic Church 1090
     The Union-Recorder 468a, 860, 899, 1128, 1514
     See also O'Connor, Flannery--biographical details--
      homes--Millegeville
    Savannah 501a, 1362, 1458, 1592, 1593
    Toombsboro 858
   Middle 641, 886, 991, 1708
     Humor in 217, 270, 314, 362, 477, 631, 674, 678, 1344, 1746,
      1972
     Photographs of 63, 173, 338r, 637a, 1043, 1044, 1045, 1162,
      1170, 1172r, 1251, 1368, 1371, 1592, 1659a, 1679r
     Racist traditions of 1055, 1090, 1671
   See also Koinonia [Americus, Ga.]
   See also Region
   See also South, the
Georgia Bulletin 1674
Georgia College & State University 435, 497, 625, 641, 690, 788, 886, 929,
   1150, 1193, 1243, 1250, 1349, 1371, 1502, 1517, 1637
   Alumni Association 743a
   Arts & Letters 1154c
   Atkinson Hall 1502
   The Colonnade 454, 599
   The Corinthian 273, 690, 1120, 1692
   Flannery O'Connor Bulletin 104a, 205, 384, 414, 419, 490, 497, 527,
    538, 565, 589, 636, 637a, 639, 1119, 1154a, 1218a, 1241,
    1310, 1364, 1461, 1483, 1580, 1641, 2174
   Flannery O'Connor Review 104a, 637a, 1154a
   Flannery O'Connor Scholarship Fund 1210
   Flannery O'Connor Visiting Professor 787, 1453, 1581, 1583
   Flannery O'Connor Writer's Forum 625
   Russell Library, Ina Dillard 57, 152, 387, 437, 649
    Flannery O'Connor Collection at 42, 148, 152, 210, 387, 437,
     473, 488, 545, 589, 640, 649, 671, 719, 743a, 760,
     787, 797, 1122, 1155, 1202, 1236, 1244, 1306, 1368,
     1371, 1375, 1382r, 1484, 1580, 1614, 1624, 1689,
     1695, 1947, 2709
    Correspondence in 1177a
    Curators 1580
    Dissertations in 1202, 1392

(Con't) Georgia College & State University--Russell Library--Flannery O'Connor Collection

> Preservation of 1202
> Flannery O'Connor Room 152, 501a, 693, 742, 1042, 1198a, 1244, 1251, 1368, 1443
> Flannery O'Connor's desk 797, 1413
> Flannery O'Connor's personal library 44, 48, 57, 65, 118, 148, 152, 641, 649, 671, 851, 853, 1129a, 1177a, 1375, 1382r, 1443, 1947, 1950
> Periodicals in 1375
The Spectrum 454, 690

Georgia Historical Society 526

Georgia State College for Women [GSCW]
> *See* Georgia College & State University

"The Geranium" 29, 33, 34, 60, 78, 368, 369, 377, 435, 608, 672, 896, 1171, 1187, 1329, 1614, 1638, 1673, 1683, 1690, 1692, 1792, 1804, 1936, 2057, 2125, 2458, 2578
> *See also* Characters, O'Connor's--specific--Dudley

Gestures
> *See* Style--gestures, use of

"Getting Home" 78, 1614

Gnosticism 1860, 2353, 2664a

God
> Absence of 407, 445, 648, 697, 800b, 850, 1270, 1374, 2440
> Action of 59a, 727, 790, 987, 1010, 1261, 1339, 1386, 1722, 2330, 2488, 2683
> Alienation from 37, 800b, 974, 1005, 1053, 1107, 1169, 1272, 1386, 1415, 1531, 1535, 1554, 1595, 1741, 1750, 1770, 1782, 1799, 1812, 1823, 1825, 1841, 1881, 1910, 1919, 1959, 1997, 2034, 2041, 2102, 2107, 2440, 2453, 2469, 2520, 2536, 2648
> "Bread of Life" and 1586
> Call of 1078, 1299
> Creation and 800b, 1080, 1124, 1189, 1339, 1512, 2027
> Damnation of 1841, 1930, 1981
> Death of 697, 953, 966, 1374
> Depiction of 800b, 1285, 1436, 1708, 1743, 1816, 1834, 1934, 1944, 2046, 2049, 2105, 2496, 2511, 2660
>> O'Connor's 831, 1053, 1722, 1816, 1961, 1981, 2202
> Divinity of 722, 779, 918, 1012, 1037, 1437, 1812
> Humankind's relationship with 763, 778, 800b, 864, 876, 887, 893, 974, 978, 987, 1010, 1038, 1046, 1053, 1080, 1094, 1096, 1101, 1268, 1272, 1299, 1332, 1350, 1353, 1365, 1386, 1407, 1415, 1500, 1527, 1535, 1575, 1595, 1601, 1608, 1620, 1645, 1647, 1691, 1722, 1783, 1807, 1823, 1844, 1846, 1853, 1854, 1877, 1900, 1904, 1910, 1930, 1933, 1949, 1954, 1956, 1957, 1976, 2018, 2046, 2084, 2109, 2134, 2147, 2186, 2511

(Con't) God
    Immanence of 1008, 1034, 2447
    Judgement of 59a, 164a, 1056, 1149, 1189, 1548, 1841, 1930, 1981,
            2157
    Love of 166, 274, 403, 512, 523, 579, 591, 606, 607, 608, 609, 818,
            933, 944, 1109, 1216, 1261, 1782, 2079, 2131, 2142, 2440,
            2527
    Meaning of 1834
    Mercy of 1548, 1667, 1814, 2079, 2507
    Prayers to 1185
    Rescue from damnation 890, 1080, 1841, 2020
    Revealed to man 1009, 1853
    Search for, man's 770, 818, 890, 940, 1461, 1782, 1910, 1919
    Transcendence of 268, 388, 390, 401, 606, 607, 608, 610, 648, 697,
            1008, 1046, 1080, 1189, 1350, 1354, 1437a, 1600, 1838,
            1850, 1910, 2020, 2181
    Will of 708, 790, 807, 944, 987, 1037, 1292, 1575
    Worship of 1844
"Going to the Dogs" 1689
Gone With the Wind
    See Comparisons [of O'Connor's work] with work[s] by--Mitchell,
            Margaret
"Good Country People" 31, 34, 35a, 38, 40, 47, 50a, 77, 80, 94, 108, 116, 125,
            126, 143, 166, 169a, 195, 198, 203, 255, 256, 288, 307, 317, 318, 326,
            331, 364, 384, 396, 477, 478ar, 529, 547, 580, 581, 587, 590, 592, 595,
            597, 617a, 624, 654, 672, 696, 722, 740, 755, 759, 775, 778, 780, 814,
            824, 826, 838, 884, 887, 890, 908, 909, 922, 925, 939, 943, 945, 949,
            962, 986, 1019, 1052, 1053, 1069, 1073, 1135, 1171, 1172, 1213,
            1217, 1221, 1275, 1282, 1315, 1320, 1341, 1384, 1396, 1409, 1421,
            1451, 1481, 1488, 1493, 1521, 1527, 1530, 1544, 1546, 1550, 1552,
            1559a, 1563, 1573, 1585, 1600, 1601, 1626, 1627, 1637, 1642, 1647,
            1670, 1698, 1709, 1745, 1805, 1816, 1839, 1868, 1869, 1875, 1936,
            1940, 1946, 1982, 1998a, 2011, 2016, 2033, 2040, 2046, 2112, 2121,
            2189, 2277, 2422, 2659, 2660, 2669, 2695, 2701
    See also Adaptations--plays--"Good Country People"
    See also Characters, O'Connor's--specific--Bible salesman, the
    See also Characters, O'Connor's--specific--Freeman, Mrs.
    See also Characters, O'Connor's--specific--Hopewell, Joy/Hulga
    See also Characters, O'Connor's--specific--Hopewell, Mrs.
    See also Characters, O'Connor's--specific--Pointer, Manley
    See also Films--*Good Country People*
A Good Man Is Hard to Find [collection] 37, 50a, 55, 59, 60, 62, 99, 144, 155,
            191, 198, 273, 318, 351, 377, 428, 507, 529, 552, 559, 560, 561, 565,
            591, 592, 594, 671, 672, 738, 850, 871, 899, 922, 925, 926, 930, 943,
            946, 1013, 1053, 1174, 1387a, 1527a, 1545, 1607a, 1685, 1762, 1779,
            1787, 1905, 1923, 1963, 1998a

"A Good Man Is Hard to Find" [story] 30, 31, 32, 34, 35, 35a, 40, 41, 47, 50a,
53, 59a, 62, 65, 68a, 77, 94, 100, 109, 135, 142, 162, 180, 181, 183,
184, 191, 194, 201, 203, 211, 225, 238, 249, 256, 260, 264, 281, 285,
288, 309, 315, 317, 324, 349, 365, 376, 386, 388, 392, 415, 416, 427,
436, 440, 448, 460, 465, 471, 498, 512, 529, 535, 540, 547, 557, 576,
580, 590, 591, 592, 595, 601, 619, 624, 648, 654, 676, 686, 703, 707,
711, 712, 731, 738, 740, 751, 754, 764a, 775, 776, 779, 783, 800, 804,
815, 819, 822, 827, 828, 832a, 850, 888, 890, 898, 899, 909, 910, 911,
912, 922, 934, 943, 945, 949, 977, 1005, 1013, 1019, 1023, 1053,
1056a, 1059, 1067, 1069, 1073, 1084, 1085, 1104, 1105, 1106, 1118,
1133, 1144, 1167, 1172, 1177a, 1184, 1196, 1204, 1208, 1217, 1221,
1222, 1253, 1254, 1270, 1278, 1281, 1291a, 1293, 1295, 1305, 1315,
1316, 1319, 1337, 1350, 1353, 1365, 1366, 1372, 1396, 1409, 1421,
1426, 1438, 1439, 1440, 1455, 1468, 1491, 1493, 1501, 1514, 1519,
1532, 1533, 1551, 1558, 1561, 1563, 1578, 1585, 1606, 1607a, 1631,
1632, 1637, 1640r, 1664, 1672, 1693, 1696, 1698, 1700, 1717a, 1724,
1745, 1775, 1816, 1827, 1839, 1857, 1868, 1869, 1875, 1890, 1905,
1936, 1955, 1982, 1998a, 2016, 2017, 2028, 2033, 2073, 2074, 2077,
2081, 2120, 2131, 2138, 2148, 2155, 2160, 2177, 2184, 2222, 2277,
2320, 2333, 2417, 2499, 2523, 2551, 2618, 2659, 2669
See also Adaptations--plays--"A Good Man Is Hard to Find"
See also Characters, O'Connor's--specific--Bailey
See also Characters, O'Connor's--specific--Butts, Red Sammy
See also Characters, O'Connor's--specific--The Grandmother
See also Characters, O'Connor's--specific--The Misfit
See also Characters, O'Connor's--specific--Pitty Sing
See also Characters, O'Connor's--specific--Starr, June
See also Characters, O'Connor's--specific--Wesley, John
A Good Man Is Hard to Find [musical score by Eddie Green] 68a, 512
Bessie Smith, as sung by 1013, 1365
Gorilla
See Symbols and images--animal--gorilla
Gothic
See Symbols and images--Gothic
Gothic literature 1932, 2241, 2631, 1817
Grace, action of 50a, 59a, 64, 103, 111, 112, 113, 130, 135, 159,
160, 164a, 169, 176, 185, 198, 203, 208, 211, 274, 281, 291, 315, 321,
337, 352, 357, 359, 378, 416, 469, 481, 489, 501, 547, 550, 551, 577,
615, 618, 622, 627, 628, 629, 648, 651, 683, 708, 729, 729a, 754, 779,
818, 838, 840, 852, 869, 879, 884, 892, 893, 908, 909, 912, 931, 940,
966, 987, 1009, 1010, 1053, 1056, 1073, 1080, 1082, 1094, 1100,
1103, 1105, 1111, 1130, 1134, 1149, 1152, 1160, 1165, 1176, 1204,
1272, 1279, 1290, 1295, 1326, 1340, 1359, 1373, 1393, 1425, 1436,
1451, 1455, 1459, 1468, 1473, 1477, 1495, 1500, 1576, 1585, 1588,
1595, 1596, 1609, 1620, 1667, 1668, 1674, 1684, 1693, 1697, 1708,
1709, 1717a, 1725, 1743, 1755, 1760, 1779, 1786, 1801, 1814, 1832,

(Con't) Grace, Action of
     1844, 1846, 1870, 1881, 1895, 1899, 1903, 1919, 1920, 1921, 1930,
     1952, 1975, 1978, 1980, 1985, 1986, 1998, 1998a, 2046, 2065, 2080,
     2168, 2189, 2204, 2222, 2225, 2232, 2236, 2277, 2280, 2291, 2330,
     2336, 2345, 2368, 2380, 2383, 2389, 2393, 2409, 2418, 2420, 2424,
     2433, 2438, 2442, 2474, 2481, 2592, 2595a, 2599, 2612, 2613, 2682,
     2700a
     Augustinian 49, 335, 360, 501, 1666, 1944, 1961
     Jansenistic 49, 335, 100
     Language of 53, 281, 358, 404, 546, 657, 740, 852, 922, 931, 998,
          1009, 1204, 1213, 1378, 1481, 1596, 1600, 1719, 1801, 1870,
          2575
     Nature and 32, 73, 106, 169, 181, 318, 321, 359, 361, 394, 399, 403,
          457, 615, 893, 974, 991, 1333, 1396, 1477, 1588, 1609, 1668,
          1921a, 2066, 2402
     Offer of 50a, 547, 622, 627, 628, 629, 651, 1111, 1149, 1152, 1217,
          1379, 1455, 1495, 1500, 1585, 1596, 1717a, 1743, 1919,
          1930, 1975, 1978, 1985, 2087, 2105, 2150, 2204, 2232, 2393,
          2418, 2547, 2655, 2669, 2686, 2700a, 2704, 2710
     Thomistic 49, 102a, 335, 697, 1038, 1102, 1103, 1668, 1844, 1918,
          2106
     See also Style--motifs and archetypes--grace and deliverance motif
     See also Themes, Flannery O'Connor's--specific--Grace
Grammar
     See Style--grammar, use of
Great Awakening, the American 1072, 1074
"Greenleaf" 31, 34, 47, 49, 50a, 76, 77, 80, 157, 169a, 261, 263, 265, 288, 349,
     360, 392, 405, 514, 547, 580, 595, 609, 612, 615, 648, 711, 721, 722,
     770, 789, 800, 822, 826, 838, 878, 942, 943, 945, 974, 1005, 1027,
     1033, 1052, 1054, 1124, 1133, 1221, 1253, 1264, 1273, 1295, 1338,
     1350, 1373, 1396, 1403, 1419, 1421, 1445, 1473, 1541, 1546, 1575,
     1576, 1585, 1627, 1649, 1659, 1669, 1695, 1696, 1697, 1725, 1775,
     1816, 1982, 2033, 2081, 2222, 2277, 2611, 2669
     See also Characters, O'Connor's--specific--Greenleaf, Mr.
     See also Characters, O'Connor's--specific--Greenleaf, Mrs.
     See also Characters, O'Connor's--specific--May, Mrs.
Grotesque, the
     Concept of, O'Connor's 38, 111, 136, 206, 278, 286, 298, 316, 321,
          443, 545, 552, 574, 575, 585, 590, 611, 667, 737, 743, 754,
          784, 810, 837, 848, 851, 874, 884, 892, 900, 901, 911, 937,
          975, 991, 1003, 1053, 1056a, 1073, 1086, 1111, 1112, 1126,
          1136, 1137, 1150, 1152, 1180, 1249, 1270, 1277, 1291, 1315,
          1322, 1342, 1356, 1376, 1415, 1416, 1419, 1426, 1435,
          1470a, 1491, 1503, 1536, 1552, 1556, 1589, 1595, 1601,
          1604, 1608, 1684, 1694r, 1699a, 1701, 1712, 1720, 1730,
          1749, 1752, 1758, 1761, 1762, 1782, 1787, 1808, 1809, 1812,

(Con't) Grotesque, the--Concept of, O'Connor's
1813, 1821, 1831, 1841, 1845, 1866, 1872, 1875, 1878, 1885,
1892, 1899, 1902, 1903, 1916, 1926, 1966, 2007a, 2012,
2034, 2073, 2096, 2177, 2203, 2234, 2237, 2267, 2327, 2335,
2367, 2374, 2377, 2398, 2401, 2407a, 2408, 2466, 2489,
2587, 2595, 2628, 2684, 2700
Debt to other writers, O'Connor's 29, 235, 552, 684, 884, 975, 1556
Depiction of, O'Connor's 43, 94, 131, 143, 175, 178, 206, 308, 311,
321, 454, 575, 822, 850, 851, 884, 1019, 1080, 1086, 1091,
1152, 1228, 1237, 1249, 1285, 1573, 1577, 1636, 1699a,
1752, 1787, 1845, 1916, 1926, 1931, 1951, 1955, 1956, 1982,
1986, 2001, 2028, 2036, 2182, 2189, 2286, 2327, 2477, 2537,
2640, 2646, 2664, 2670
Freudian view of 286a, 693a, 810, 813, 814, 1088
Hawthorne, Nathaniel and 62, 96, 264, 321, 401, 456, 457, 462, 581,
801, 1278, 1503, 1512, 1556
Humor and 102, 111, 136, 157, 178, 195, 196, 203, 260, 270, 312, 314,
329, 333, 359, 388, 443, 454, 457, 572, 573, 574, 575, 631,
654, 657, 674, 678, 737, 739, 762, 788, 827, 842, 843, 937,
975, 1009, 1195, 1288, 1337, 1352, 1353, 1482, 1510, 1545,
1547, 1655, 1702, 1729, 1746, 1758, 1766, 1903, 1906, 1916,
1938, 1972, 2171, 2320, 2400, 2469, 2604
Horror and 260, 316, 321, 395, 601, 659, 1076, 1181, 1255, 1433,
1631, 1702, 1907, 1925, 1955, 1986, 2023, 2320
Medieval 41, 128, 312, 697, 743, 785, 1356, 1735, 1801, 1944, 1949,
1961, 2168
Purpose for using, O'Connor's 41, 53, 94, 113, 162, 178, 240, 241,
244, 273, 298, 300, 308, 358, 367, 385, 427, 454, 481, 541,
550, 574, 590, 611, 683, 743, 754, 762, 763, 774, 784, 813,
837, 840, 851, 852, 861, 911, 937, 991, 1009, 1091, 1111,
1137, 1152, 1270, 1353, 1497, 1503, 1589, 1610, 1636, 1761,
1762, 1845, 1916, 2017, 2041, 2081, 2088, 2455
Religious, O'Connor's 24, 47, 131, 138, 162, 240, 241, 281, 300, 318,
321, 324, 385, 493, 574, 710, 852, 887, 1051, 1320a, 1340,
1477, 1619r, 1682r, 1926
Southern Fiction and 32, 136, 206, 260, 323, 802, 1111, 1426, 1782,
1699a, 1784, 1813, 1850
See also Characters--types of--grotesque
See also Illness-grotesque
Guilt 96, 389, 608, 617, 809, 864, 887, 906, 919, 1205, 1631, 1742, 2109
See also Sin
Guys and Dolls 117

The Habit of Being 45, 57, 81, 122, 145, 149, 150, 158, 185, 199, 221r, 232a,
261, 296, 325, 327, 335, 340, 342a, 488, 494, 499, 509, 510, 511, 513,

(Con't) The Habit of Being
        517, 518, 519, 521, 541, 550a, 563, 564, 602, 613, 627, 628, 629, 632,
        640, 643, 724, 753, 780a, 791, 803, 836, 861, 899, 918, 930, 935r, 981,
        995, 998, 1002, 1018, 1050, 1090r, 1121r, 1122r, 1172r, 1177b, 1180r,
        1185, 1306, 1308, 1309, 1320, 1336, 1347, 1374, 1400b, 1401a, 1502,
        1518r, 1538, 1549r, 1575, 1583, 1598, 1609r, 1632, 1678, 1682r,
        1683, 1718, 2027, 2029, 2071, 2135, 2139, 2150, 2188, 2205
        See also Adaptations--plays--"The Habit of Being: A Solo-Biographical
                Drama on Flannery O'Connor"
        See also Correspondence, Flannery O'Connor's
Harcourt-Brace 92
Hat
        See Symbols and images--hat
Harvard University 330, 332, 333, 334
Hearing 1073, 1402
"The Heart of the Park" 60, 1409, 7315
Heathenism 2108
Hell 368, 395, 416, 718, 1026, 1120, 1350, 1393
        See also Devil, the
Hermeneutic patterns 60, 697, 785, 921, 957, 958, 1200, 1340, 1834, 1943,
        1949
Hero(ines) 887, 1328, 1372, 1373, 1427, 1479, 1907, 1913, 2207, 2353, 2451
        Alienation from community 1113, 1462, 1769, 1782, 1799, 1823, 1841,
                2453
        Christ as 41, 131, 134, 166, 176, 211, 216, 247, 381, 493, 720, 838,
                887, 888, 943, 978, 1435
        Dedalus, Stephen--as artist hero 84, 241, 1168, 1726, 1887
        Mrs. May as 405
        Hazel Motes as 204, 268, 271, 329, 450, 571, 585, 611, 659, 668, 770,
                887, 1025, 1072, 1900, 2049, 2078, 2180, 2702
        Post-World War II novels, in 1907, 1913, 1999
        Tarwater, Francis Marion--as 37, 274, 297, 403, 610
Hill, James Francis
        See Characters--O'Connor's, Flannery--specific--The Misfit--Hill,
                James Francis
History
        See Themes--specific--history
History, sacred 286a, 1764, 2004
        See also Critical approaches to O'Connor's fiction--specific--historical
                context
        See also Themes, Flannery O'Connor's--specific--history, of
Hog
        See Symbols and images--animal--hog
Holocaust 1776, 1907
        See also Symbols and images--Holocaust

Holy Ghost
        See Symbols and images--Holy Ghost
"The Home of the Brave" 538, 1689
Homes
        See O'Connor, Flannery--biographical details--homes
Hope
        See Style--hope, use of
Horror
        See Grotesque, the--Horror and
"Hound of Heaven" [poem] 684
Humanism 18, 37, 130, 131, 162, 367, 592, 732, 733, 855, 1320a, 1339, 1468,
        1750, 1825, 1854, 1877, 2041, 2178
Humor
        See Georgia--middle--humor in
Hypograms 1481, 1991

Identity
        Change of 778, 1843, 1851, 1907, 1910, 2025
        Female 472, 617, 667, 670, 722, 813, 1090, 1292, 1299, 1330, 1421,
                1445, 1474, 1527, 1559a, 1568, 1625, 1637, 1729, 1738,
                1822, 1886, 1948, 2632
        Loss of 286a, 1159, 1292, 1805, 1851, 1860, 1910
        Masculine 1292, 1299, 2014, 2652
        Place on, influence of 37, 286a, 829, 860, 932, 977, 1107, 1116, 1127,
                1150a, 1207, 1287, 1328, 1345, 1479, 1516, 1568, 1615a,
                1635, 1638, 1717, 1725, 1843, 1854, 1871, 1996, 2515
        Search for 164a, 1425, 1461, 1468, 1601, 1736, 1773, 1782, 1851,
                1898, 1907, 1910, 1917, 1956, 2134, 2469
        Sexual 80, 420, 599, 606, 763, 813, 826, 906, 954, 973, 1341, 1601,
                1627, 1728, 1812, 1886, 2109
        Southern 37, 286a, 938, 939, 1080, 1111, 1116, 1127, 1194, 1195,
                1207, 1217, 1287, 1302, 1314, 1316, 1325, 1342, 1343, 1344,
                1345, 1365, 1408, 1414, 1445, 1458, 1489, 1492, 1519, 1531,
                1572, 1588, 1690, 1623, 1654, 1666, 1692, 1694r, 1699a,
                1700, 1701, 1708, 1711, 1772, 1784, 1853, 1871, 1877, 1888,
                1897, 1948, 1972, 1996, 2039, 2154, 2275, 2469, 2540
        True 840, 1425, 1910, 1917
Illness
        AIDS Virus 1542
        Grotesque 541, 580, 709, 775, 892, 1091, 1575, 1576, 1601, 1841,
                1979, 2020, 2328
        Lupus Erythematosus 33, 45, 59a, 75, 82, 140, 186, 194, 221,
                243, 273, 287a, 327, 335, 414, 502, 514, 520, 523, 524, 541,
                545, 584, 607, 617a, 624, 627, 628, 629, 640, 643, 667, 709,
                757, 792, 822, 833, 841, 843, 855, 880, 892, 905, 910, 936,

(Con't) Illness--Lupus Erythematosus
        959a, 961, 981, 1002, 1037, 1053a, 1065, 1090, 1091, 1092, 1132,
        1142, 1172, 1188, 1218a, 1234, 1258, 1262, 1288, 1291a, 1314b,
        1374, 1406, 1451, 1469, 1478, 1488, 1494, 1542, 1575, 1576, 1645,
        1648, 1668, 1687r, 1692, 1700, 1718, 1720, 1793, 1896, 1941, 1974,
        1979, 1982, 2020, 2031, 2032, 2135, 2137, 2292, 2650
        See also Style--motifs and archetypes--illness
Illuminations [magazine] 1914
Illustrations
        See Photographs and illustrations
        See also Georgia--middle--photographs of
        See also O'Connor, Flannery--photographs and illustrations of
Imagery
        See Symbols and images
Incarnation 55, 73, 93, 106, 174a, 345, 392, 398, 866, 893, 1008, 1010, 1056,
        1111, 1115, 1181, 1333, 1374, 1437, 1481, 1482, 1601, 1608, 1610,
        1749, 1800, 1909, 1936, 1991, 1998a, 2168, 2404
        See also Language--Incarnational
        See also O'Connor, Flannery--views and opinions of--Incarnation, the
Individualism 919, 1006, 1169, 1332, 1333, 1340, 1764, 1851, 1906, 1970,
        1976, 2011, 2041
The Inferno [Dante Alighieri] 931
Influence 149, 508, 533, 1371, 1658, 2033
        Of other writers and artists on Flannery O'Connor
                Adams, Karl 199, 1755
                Alighieri, Dante 90, 137, 274, 282, 395, 416, 479, 551, 718,
                        931, 1802
                Anderson, Sherwood 1556, 1747
                Aquinas, Saint Thomas 102a, 174a, 1332, 1619r, 1810, 1918,
                        1952, 2106
                Arp, Bill 217
                Auden, W.H. 365
                Augustine, Saint 1810, 1947
                Bakhtin, Mikhail M. 832a, 2384, 2587
                Barth, Karl 208, 245, 1674
                Barzun, Jacques 1339
                Baudelaire, Charles 365
                Bernanos, Georges 326, 1455, 1597, 1966
                Bloy, Léon 1376, 1597, 1923, 1966
                Brooks, Cleanth 1365
                Buber, Martin 77
                Burke, Edmund 2505
                Cable, George Washington 1264, 1972
                Carey, Peter 1121
                Chaplin, Charlie 1982

(Con't) Influence--Of Other Writers and Artists on Flannery O'Connor

Chardin, Pierre Teilhard de 59a, 75b, 77, 199, 215, 273, 442, 729a, 738, 820, 849, 1163, 1181, 1339, 1424, 1451, 1462, 1621, 1659, 1674, 1755, 1762, 1792, 1800, 1810, 1928, 1941, 1966, 1968, 2135, 2268, 2304, 2337, 2475, 2524

Chaucer, Geoffrey 184

Chesterton, Gilbert K. 1366

Conrad, Joseph 443a, 514, 522, 720, 1084, 1952

Crane, Stephen 522, 1513, 1556

D'Arcy, Martin C. 1728

Darwin, Charles 1968

Dostoevsky 234, 1049

Dryden, John 2538

Durrwell, Francis X. 199, 1755

Eliade, Mircea 75b, 400

Eliot, T.S. 365, 514, 522, 608, 662, 669, 767, 1159, 1459, 1591, 1992

Engle, Paul 232a, 538, 1021, 1232

Faulkner, William 35a, 37, 355, 538, 624, 664, 671, 819, 975, 1059, 1317, 1326, 1365, 1424, 1610, 1625, 1657, 1799, 1902, 1992, 2050

Fields, W.C. 1982

Fitzgerald, Robert and Sally 643, 970

Flaubert, Gustave 560, 923, 1263

Ford, Ford Madox 1864

Freud, Sigmund 286a, 326, 1057, 1088, 1373, 1674, 1941

Gilson, Etienne 400, 1966

Girard, René 114, 130, 311a, 403, 838

Gogol, Nikolai 1435, 1982

Goldbrunner, Josef 1340

Gordon, Caroline 155, 343, 538, 546, 552, 554, 560, 563, 643, 961, 1539, 1571, 1826, 1864

Guardini, Romano 199, 1755

Harris, George Washington 1982

Harris, Joel Chandler 217, 270, 1315

Hawthorne, Nathaniel 66, 96, 234, 253, 264, 321, 365, 456, 457, 462, 514, 538, 581, 801, 820, 1089, 1264, 1278, 1503, 1635, 1688c, 1781, 1814, 1902, 2017, 2050, 2278, 2627

Hemingway, Ernest 77, 100, 365, 618, 1597, 1625

Hentz, Caroline Lee 1420

Honig, Edwin 276

Hooper, Johnson Jones 674, 1315, 1972

Hugel, Baron Fredrick Von 1810

Ignatius, Saint 2340

(Con't) Influence--Of Other Writers and Artists on Flannery O'Connor
Inman, Ted Don, Jr. 161
James, Henry 139, 366, 392, 514, 519, 560, 1023, 1365,
        1688c, 1697, 1902
Jaspers, Karl 400
Joyce, James 77, 84, 241, 608, 785, 1458, 1459, 1612,
        1726
Jung, Carl 75b, 326, 1056a, 1340, 1720, 1794, 1970
Kafka, Franz 522, 1181, 1320
Kempe, Margery 1129a
Kierkegaard, Sören 1941, 2331, 2361
King, Grace Elizabeth 1420, 1817
Lacan, Jacques 1057, 1752, 1958
Lardner, Ring 1982
Lee, Harper 1610, 1663
Lee, Maryat 538, 584
Leighton, Peter 1618
Longstreet, Augustus Baldwin 217, 270, 477, 1253, 1315,
        1344, 1982
Lowell, Robert 823, 1053a
Lubbock, Percy 1365
Lynch, John 1810
Lynch, William 400
Lytle, Andrew 289, 643, 1864
Malraux, Andre 1966
Marcel, Gabriel 77, 642, 1347, 1508, 1966
Maritain, Jacques 102a, 174a, 215, 400, 511, 513, 554, 839,
        1040, 1103, 1347, 1376, 1810, 1966, 2475
Mauriac, François 1455, 1597, 1810, 1966
McCullers, Carson 1628
Melville, Herman 820, 1089, 1635, 1688c, 1974, 2049
Merton, Thomas 1900
Milton, John 926
Mitchell, Margaret 1266
Mounier, Emmanuel 1686
Nash, Ogden 538
Norris, Frank 1556
Paul, Saint 2490
Percy, Walker 970
Poe, Edgar Allan 67, 322, 396, 470, 477, 514, 522, 538,
        569, 1089, 1409, 1556, 1591, 1766, 1835, 1982,
        2017
Porter, Katherine Anne 928, 970
Powers, J.F. 970
Proust, Marcel 538, 642, 773
Quintilian, M. Fabius 2384

(Con't) Influence--Of Other Writers and Artists on Flannery O'Connor
     Ransom, John Crowe 1159
     Shakespeare, William 2538
     Sophocles 1088, 2446
     Stein, Edith 632
     Tate, Allen 1864
     Tate, Caroline 1232
     Thompson, William Tappan 217, 400
     Tresmontant, Claude 400
     Twain, Mark 1982
     Underhill, Evelyn 1900
     Voegelin, Eric 400, 1101, 1110, 1431
     von Hügel, Baron Friedrich 855, 1755
     Warren, Robert Penn 624, 1864
     Weil, Simone 326, 407, 632, 1132, 1135, 1488, 1966, 2159, 2416
     Welty, Eudora 671, 1017
     West, Nathanael 35a, 396, 522, 1556, 1902, 2059
     White, Victor 1340
     Williams, Tennessee 1610
     Yeats, William Butler 277
   On other writers and artists by Flannery O'Connor
     Abu-Jaber, Diana 1625
     Allison, Dorothy 1625
     Alther, Lisa 533
     Banner, Keith 135a
     Bausch, Richard 1317
     Bell, Madison Smartt 1317
     Betts, Doris 51a, 171, 172, 535, 637
     Bond, Adrienne 641
     Bottoms, David 51a
     Brown, Larry 533
     Brown, Mary Ward 51a
     Budy, Andrea Hollander 51a, 637
     Callaghan, Barry 120
     Capote, Truman 1551c
     Carver, Raymond 476, 925
     Chappell, Fred 51a
     Cheever, John 1524
     Childress, Mark 623, 677, 1317
     Cofer, Judith Ortiz 1154c
     Coles, Robert 51a, 306, 330, 332, 333, 334, 335, 1218a, 1704
     Corey, Deborah Joy 120
     Corn, Alfred 508, 637, 1185
     Corrington, John William 1085
     Crews, Harry 533, 796, 1177, 1317, 1732

(Con't) Influence--On Other Writers and Artists by Flannery O'Connor
              Dawkins, Cecil 1864
              Dexter, Pete 336, 802, 1317
              Dickey, James 625
              Dickinson, Eleanor 846
              Didion, Joan 1625
              Dillard, Annie 1625
              Drake, Robert 426, 1539
              Dubus, Andre 533, 1317
              Edgerton, Clyde 533, 1254, 1813
              Erdrich, Louise 991, 1625
              Fickett, Harold 495
              Foote, Horton 1665
              Giardina, Denise 425
              Gibbons, Kaye 533
              Gilchrist, Ellen 533
              Gingher, Marianne 533
              Godwin, Gail 781
              Gordon, Jaimy 1154c
              Gordon, Sarah 51a
              Green, Lewis W. 1490
              Gurganus, Allan 1317
              Hannah, Barry 304, 533, 848, 881, 1317
              Hawkes, John 1716
              Henley, Beth 873
              Heyward, DuBose 231
              Hodgins, Jack 120, 1716
              Hoffman, William 1490
              Hood, Hugh 120
              Hood, Mary 479, 1625
              Howe, Elizabeth 51a
              Huggan, Isabel 120
              Humphrey, William 533
              Jacobsen, Josephine 637
              Jarman, Mark 51a, 637
              Johnson, Denis 421
              Johnson, Greg 51a
              Jones, Madison 51a, 533, 673, 675, 803, 1317
              Kingsolver, Barbara 1397
              Kinsella, W.P. 1361
              Kumin, Maxine 51a, 641
              Lane, Beldon C. 892
              Lasworth, Laura 637a, 899a, 1218a, 1467
              Leffland, Ella 535
              Lott, Brett 51a, 1218a
              MacLeod, Joan 120

(Con't) Influence--On Other Writers and Artists by Flannery O'Connor

Madden, David 51a
Mairs, Nancy 51a, 959a, 1218a
Mariani, Paul 637, 641
Mason, Bobbie Ann 136, 533, 604, 1625
McCarthy, Cormac 533, 1083, 1317, 1490
Meatyard, Ralph Eugene 772, 891
Merton, Thomas 839
Morgan, Berry 533
Munro, Alice 120, 412, 2405
Norris, Helen 533
Oates, Joyce Carol 591, 1716
Percy, Walker 310, 358, 402, 451, 546, 642, 750, 1252, 1259, 1539, 1759
Porter, Helen 120
Porter, Katherine Anne 213, 273, 671
Portis, Charles 533
Powell, Padgett 51a, 533
Price, Reynolds 537
Purdy, James 819
Saunders, Kay 75
Scott, Carol Jackson 1967
Sharp, Paula 591
Silko, Leslie 1625
Smith, Lee 51a, 86, 637, 781, 1443, 1625, 1813
Springsteen, Bruce 1260, 1464, 1465, 1539
Stone, Robert 819
Styron, William 1317
Thomas, Alma 51a
Toole, John Kennedy 533, 1198a, 1355
Torchia, Joseph 1542
Tyler, Anne 1269
Walker, Alice 614, 638, 640, 769, 1385, 1572, 1625, 1656
Wells, Kellie 51a
Whitehead, James 1653
Wiebe, Rudy 1716
Wilcox, James 98, 533
Wilkinson, Sylvia 533
Will, George 1646
Williams, Miller 51a, 1154c
Williams, Tennessee 873, 1003
Yount, John 533

See also Canadian writers, O'Connor's influence on
Ingersoll Foundation, The 163
Initiation
See Style--use of Innocence

Insurance 1403, 1695
Intellectual(s)
        Catholic 1598
        Children as 763, 1299, 2410
        Grotesque 1749, 2485
        Northern 536, 850, 1270, 1370, 2039
        O'Connor as an 38, 48, 77, 291, 326, 701, 920, 998, 1005, 1040, 1180,
                1185, 1332, 1339, 1347, 1406, 1455, 1519, 1598, 1629r,
                1692, 1841, 1867, 2095
        O'Connor's attacks on and challenges to 73, 252, 326, 331, 348, 457,
                581, 716, 809, 850, 956, 1099, 1135, 1280, 1339, 1402, 1557,
                1573, 1589, 1590, 1739, 1749, 1867, 1883, 2113, 2422, 2428,
                2510, 2516, 2586
        O'Connor's interest in 407, 1339, 2535, 2666
        Religion and 842, 998, 1110, 1185, 1320a, 1384, 1669, 1981
        Skeptics, as 160, 647, 890, 1185, 1216, 1384, 1724, 2011
        Southern agrarian 77, 89, 299, 323, 399, 564, 718, 919, 938, 939, 1302,
                1430, 1521, 1669, 1799, 1853, 1871, 1883, 1884, 2061, 2348
        See also Characters--types of--intellectual
Interviews [of Flannery O'Connor] 1, 68, 509, 1065, 1194, 1565, 1566, 1691,
        2064
        See also Recollections and comments about O'Connor
Iowa
        See O'Connor, Flannery--biographical details--homes--Iowa
Iowa Writer's Workshop 289, 295, 354, 514, 538, 553, 624, 671, 764, 915, 936,
        1021, 1151, 1357, 1644, 1692, 1756
        See also O'Connor, Flannery--views and opinions of--creative writing
                programs
Irish Catholic heritage
        See Catholic faith, Flannery O'Connor's
Irony
        See Style--irony, use of
        See also Symbols and images--ironic
Isolation
        See Style--isolation, use of

Jesus
        See Christ, Jesus
John, Saint 1135
John of the Cross, Saint 965, 1724
Journals
        Maryat Lee 290
        Alta Ramsey 290
Journey
        See Style--motifs and archetypes, use of--quest motif

Judaism 1779
"Judgement Day" 31, 33, 34, 40, 41, 42, 47, 49, 50a, 77, 78, 114, 265, 318, 363,
        368, 369, 435, 477, 514, 593, 608, 672, 793, 809, 943, 985, 1142,
        1153, 1171, 1187, 1205, 1291a, 1320, 1400, 1407, 1409, 1536, 1614,
        1616, 1638, 1648, 1649, 1659, 1666, 1673, 1677, 1683, 1697, 1792,
        1804, 1869, 1922, 1936, 2033, 2040, 2057, 2081, 2125, 2185, 2458,
        2611
        See also Characters, O'Connor's--specific--Parrum, Coleman
Julian the Apostate [Roman Emperor] 984, 1265
Julian the Hospitaller, Saint 795, 984
Justice 1332, 1437, 2507
Justification 651, 1564

Kansas, University of 1559
Kenyon Review 789, 1641a, 1714
Killer
        See Characters--type of--killers
Kindness, acts of 733, 734
"The King of the Birds" 1009, 1219, 1272
Klu Klux Klan 781
Knowledge
        See Style--knowledge, use of
Koinonia [interracial farm community in Americus, Ga.] 1691

"The Lame Shall Enter First" 34, 36, 38, 49, 50a, 75b, 77, 155, 211, 318, 363,
        443a, 465, 514, 523, 541, 580, 587, 595, 617a, 624, 642, 777, 819,
        826, 838, 859, 878, 887, 890, 955, 966, 1005, 1033, 1043, 1046, 1073,
        1094, 1150, 1158, 1167, 1181, 1221, 1256, 1270, 1283, 1291a, 1339,
        1409, 1426, 1451, 1455, 1460, 1461, 1497, 1544, 1556, 1620, 1659,
        1727, 1744, 1816, 1839, 1875, 1940, 1953, 2011, 2033, 2081, 2176,
        2269, 2378, 2424
        See also Characters, O'Connor's--specific--Norton
        See also Characters, O'Connor's--specific--Sheppard
Landscape
        See Symbols and images--landscape
        See also Adaptations--plays--"The Lame Shall Enter First"
        See also Place--depiction of--landscapes
Language
        Inadequacy of 1378, 1664, 1724, 1863, 1890
        Incarnational 174a, 1481, 1482, 1601, 1749, 1909, 1936, 1991, 2404
                See also Incarnation
        Internal codes and 1991
        Misuse of religious 1159

(Con't) Language
>   Narrator's 931, 942, 1486, 1625, 1693, 1702, 1809, 1855, 1894, 2007a,
>   2381
>   Nature of 1530, 1600
>   O'Connor's use of 1200, 1533, 1596, 1719, 1763, 1768, 1847, 1857,
>   2130, 2131, 2134, 2169
>   Oral 897, 922, 1550, 1894, 1982
>   Power of 998, 1115, 1135, 1213, 1372, 2131
>   Prophetic 164a, 174a, 529a, 1437a, 1890, 1904, 1944, 1950, 1961,
>   1973, 2381
>   *See also* Prophetic role, the
>   Women's lack of a common 1341, 1423
>   Written 897, 922
>   *See also* Characters, Flannery O'Connor's--language to show contrast
>   *See also* Grace--action of--language
"A Late Encounter With the Enemy" 31, 34, 37, 40, 41, 47, 50a, 230, 465, 468a,
>   529, 676, 826, 838, 860, 865, 881, 899, 922, 1069, 1249, 1291a, 1391,
>   1426, 1429, 1517, 1546, 1643, 1847, 1953, 1998a, 2033
>   *See also* Characters, O'Connor's--specific--Sash, Sally Poker
>   *See also* Characters, O'Connor's--specific--Sash, Tennessee Flintrock
Laughter
>   *See* Style--laughter, use of
Lectures and readings, Flannery O'Connor's 291, 345, 553, 828, 1150a, 1288,
>   1290, 1308, 1355, 1370, 1371, 1494, 1571, 1604, 1918, 1924, 1952,
>   2136
>   *See also* Conferences, lectures and symposia
Leg(s)
>   *See* Symbols and images--leg(s)
Lent 609, 1973
Letters
>   *See* Correspondence, Flannery O'Connor's
Liberals 163, 323, 584, 592, 640, 768, 788, 844, 896, 932, 1095, 1332, 1365,
>   1521, 1674, 1841, 1954, 2041, 2391
>   *See also* Characters--types of--liberal
Library, Flannery O'Connor's personal
>   *See* Georgia College and State University--Russell Library--Flannery
>   O'Connor's personal library
Life Magazine 1339, 1412
"The Life You Save May Be Your Own" 31, 32, 34, 40, 47, 50a, 73, 80, 158,
>   166, 211, 255, 288, 307, 316, 364, 401, 406, 443, 465, 503, 529, 542,
>   591, 674, 751, 772, 826, 890, 891, 962, 977, 991, 1005, 1019, 1069,
>   1167, 1171, 1217, 1227, 1282, 1284, 1291a, 1295, 1299, 1384, 1396,
>   1409, 1473, 1559a, 1563, 1564, 1584, 1585, 1600, 1775, 1805, 1892,
>   1936, 1940, 1946, 1975, 1998a, 2033, 2156, 2701
>   *See also* Adaptations--television--"The Life You Save May Be
>   Your Own"

(Con't) *"The Life You Save May Be Your Own"*
> *See also* Characters, O'Connor's--specific--Crater, Lucynell
> *See also* Characters, O'Connor's--specific--Crater, Mrs.
> *See also* Characters, O'Connor's--specific--Shiftlet, Tom T.

Light
> *See* Style--motifs and archetypes--light-shadow motif
> *See also* Symbols and images--light

Linguistic
> *See* Critical approaches to O'Connor's fiction--specific approaches--
> > linguistic

Literature
> *See* Theology--Literature and

Locust Grove, Georgia
> *See* Georgia--cities and towns--Locust Grove

Logismos 613
Loin du Paradis [Geneviéve Brisac's French biography] 2031, 2032, 2130, 2140
"The Lord's Supper" 1032, 2622
Los Angeles Times 929
Lourdes, France 33, 1687r
Lupus Erythematosus
> *See* Illness--Lupus Erythematosus

Macon, Georgia
> *See* Georgia--cities and towns--Macon

Male
> *See* Characters--types of--male
> *See also* Symbols and images--masculine

"Maniac Hill"
> *See* Characters, Flannery O'Connor's--specific--The Misfit--Hill, James
> > Frances

Manichaean 39, 49, 66, 162, 321, 396, 406, 863, 1115, 1771, 1810
> *See also* Themes, Flannery O'Connor's--specific--Manichaean

Manners
> *See* Style--manners, use of
> *See also* Characters, Flannery O'Connor's--manners of
> *See also* South, the--manners in

Manuscripts
> "autobiographical pieces" 1692,
> Flannery O'Connor Collection at Georgia College & State University, in
> > the 14, 42, 148, 152, 154, 210, 261, 262, 340, 430, 432, 437,
> > 473, 488, 490, 545, 649, 674, 690, 719, 760, 787, 1155,
> > 1177a, 1202, 1244, 1375, 1394, 1410, 1484, 1580, 1685,
> > 1689, 1692, 1695, 1756, 1804
> Juvenilia, in 1756

(Con't) Manuscripts
    Specific works
        "An Afternoon In the Woods" 1685
        "The Artificial Nigger" 1410
        "The Coat" 1186, 1689
        "The Cynosure" 1689
        "Dunn 156a" 1192
        "Dunn 197" 1616
        "An Exile in the East" 78, 608, 672, 1187, 1614, 1804
        "The Geranium" 78, 608, 1614, 1692, 1804
        "Getting Home" 78, 1614
        "A Good Man Is Hard to Find" 1717a
        "Interruptions Are So Exasperating" 1689
        "Judgement Day" 78, 593, 608, 1153, 1614, 1616, 1804, 2578
        "The Life You Save May be Your Own" 674, 1584
        Notebooks, O'Connor's personal 767
        "The Partridge Festival" 802, 976, 1394, 1847
        "A Place of Action" 1689
        "The Shiftlet Fragment" 674, 1192, 1584
        "The Train" 1685
        Violent Bear It Away 1804, 1948, 2306
        Why Do the Heathen Rage? 261, 262, 265, 1691, 1804
        Wise Blood 764a, 1804, 1948, 1992
Marketplace, the literary 1430, 1694r
Mary Flannery O'Connor Charitable Trust 1199
Maryland, University of--McKeldin Library 671
Masculine
    See Symbols and images--masculine
Master's thesis, Flannery O'Connor's MFA [Univ. Of Iowa] 37, 630, 694, 897,
    915, 1285, 1494, 1638, 1685, 1690, 1692, 2397
Material-rationalist
    See Critical approaches to O'Connor's fiction--specific approaches--
    material-rationalist
Materialism
    See Style--materialism, use of
Matthew, Saint 770
McKee, Elizabeth
    See Agent [McKee, Elizabeth]
Mechanization
    See Symbols and images--mechanization
Medical documentation skills for nurses 555
Medicine and literature 1544
Medieval period 102, 128, 184, 312, 697, 743, 785, 1356, 1735, 1801, 1841,
    1944, 1949, 1961, 2106
    See also Characters--types of--medieval
    See also Grotesque, the--medieval

(Con't) Medieval Period
  See also Style--medieval gothic, use of
  See also Style--motifs and archetypes--medieval
The Member of the Wedding [Carson McCullers] 80
A Memoir of Mary Ann, O'Connor's "Introduction" to 33, 45, 194, 300, 358,
  379, 404, 427, 456, 541, 581, 900, 1039r, 1150, 1163, 1209, 1451,
  1587, 1679, 1687r, 1688
  Mary Ann Long's cancer 900
  See also Dominican Nuns of Our Lady of Perpetual Help Cancer Home
Memoirs of a Tatooist [Peter Leighton] 1618
Memory, aesthetic of 1429
Mercy, Divine
  See Style--mercy, use of divine
Metaphor
  See Style--metaphor, use of
"Midday crisis"
  See Style--motifs and archetypes--"midday crisis" motif
Middle Ages, the 785, 943, 1115, 1129a, 1647
Middle-class respectability 1056a, 1337, 1851, 2131
The Mikado [Sir William S. Gilbert and Sir Arthur Sullivan] 440
Milledgeville, Georgia
  See Georgia--cities and towns--Milledgeville
  See also O'Connor, Flannery--biographical details--homes--
    Milledgeville
Millsaps College 1653
Minority writers 1664
Miracle plays 1801
Mirroring
  See Style--mirroring devices, use of
  See also Symbols and images--mirrors
Mississippi 1667
"The Mistress of Milledgeville"
  See Adaptations--plays--"The Mistress of Milledgeville"
Modern age, the 32, 37, 38, 65, 71, 106, 113, 114, 126, 130, 138, 164, 181, 184,
  193, 195, 206, 216, 218, 219, 222, 228, 285, 286a, 323, 329, 353, 362,
  375, 385, 390, 391, 399, 400, 404, 415, 443, 444, 472, 542, 544, 564,
  574, 586, 618, 642, 710, 741, 783, 832, 839, 855, 857, 863, 883, 939,
  953, 991, 1005, 1102, 1159, 1189, 1209, 1221, 1297, 1384, 1458,
  1491, 1528, 1604, 1620, 1629r, 1660, 1669, 1670, 1673, 1729, 1754,
  1759, 1760, 1763, 1802, 1841, 1846, 1851, 1875, 1885, 1897, 1906,
  2004, 2007a, 2043, 2090, 2154, 2322, 2357, 2396, 2445, 2606
  See also South, the--1950s
  See also Critical approaches to O'Connor's fiction--specific--modernist
  See also O'Connor, Flannery--views and opinions--modern world, the
Monastery of the Holy Ghost [Conyers, Ga.] 1219

Moonlight
        See Symbols and images--moonlight
Moral compulsion
        See Themes, Flannery O'Connor's--specific--moral compulsion
Mothers
        See Characters--types of--mothers
        See also Style--mother-child relationships, use of
        See also Symbols and images--mothers
Motifs
        See Style--motifs and archetypes, use of
Music, role of--in OConnor's life 465, 738, 1013, 2115
        "A Good Man Is Hard to Find" [music score by Eddie Green] 68a, 512
        See also Characters, Flannery O'Connor's--music as part of the lives of
        See also Style--music, use of
Mysteries at Eleusis 75b
Mystery, Christian
        See Style--Christian mystery, use of
Mystery and Manners 31, 37, 45, 81, 199, 342a, 415, 487, 511, 561, 565, 653,
        739, 780a, 801, 804, 871, 885, 930, 942, 946, 949, 1018, 1023, 1038,
        1082, 1129, 1189, 1190, 1191, 1539, 1556, 1557, 1583, 1688, 1704,
        2027, 2035, 2044, 2045, 2070, 2103, 2155
Mysticism 965, 1010, 1037, 1129a, 1225, 1609, 1684, 1764, 1766, 1887, 1893,
        1900, 1923, 2084, 2123, 2479, 2546, 2602, 2674

Names
        See Style--names and naming techniques, use of
        See also Characters, Flannery O'Connor's--names of
        See also Symbols and images--name(s)
Narrative structure
        See Style--narrative structure, use of
Narrator
        Authorial 234, 534, 878, 1200, 1442, 1697, 1831
        Knowledge of 706, 974, 1011, 1831
        Omniscient 586, 974, 1422, 1486, 1873, 1934
        Parent, as 811
        Role of O'Connor's 36, 41, 47, 55, 139, 540, 587, 590, 811, 1195,
                1410, 1693, 1809, 1831, 1855, 1894, 2007a, 2381
        "*see* tokens" and the 708
        Strategy of 1486, 1496, 1855
        Third person 1422
        Violence by the 811
        Voice of O'Connor's 53, 121, 164a, 174, 420, 534, 587, 590, 800, 811,
                884, 918, 931, 942, 1056a, 1280, 1625, 1702, 1763
National Endowment for the Humanities 488, 1147, 1202, 1432, 1475, 1484
Natural law 1339, 1372, 2131

Natural world 1030, 1372, 1402, 1814, 1819, 1918, 1921a, 2066, 2402
Naturalism 783, 921, 1019, 1105, 1127, 1309, 1887, 1920, 2001, 2088, 2140
Nature
        See Style--nature, use of
        See also Grace, action of--nature and
        See also Natural world
        See also Symbols and images--natural
"The Nature and Aim of Fiction" 391, 460, 588, 1023, 1115
Nature writing 1921a
Negation
        See Style--negation, use of
Negative space theory
        See Style--negative space theory, use of
New critical
        See Critical approaches to O'Connor's fiction--specific--New Criticism
New South
        See South, the--New South
"New World norms" 1073, 1074, 1075
New York Times 452
The Nigger of the "Narcissus" [Joseph Conrad] 258, 670
Nihilism
        See Style--Nihilism, use of
Nobel Prize 1201
Nonsense writers 1402
Nostalgia
        See South, the--nostalgia for
Notre Dame College 760
Novel, the
        American 1908, 1913, 1939, 2041
        British 1913
        Catholic 1023a, 1733
        Conversion fiction 1999
        Georgia 2355
        Grotesque 1699a, 1866, 1875, 1878, 2001, 2367, 2377, 2587, 2700
        Initiation 1837, 1850, 2498
        Manners genre 1965, 2008
        New Gothic 2209, 2241
        Psychological 164a, 2169
        Religious 1320a, 1828, 1912, 1962, 1984, 2049, 2107
        Sermons in the American 1971
        Southern 1635, 1850, 1853, 1945, 2026, 2036
        See also Catholic fiction

O'Connor, Edward F., Jr. 75, 502, 515, 523, 526, 643, 1053a, 1349, 1384, 1661,
        1720, 1941, 2130

O'Connor, Flannery
        Accent, Georgia 507, 1355
        Art, interest in 173, 410, 454, 507, 575, 599, 666, 690, 767, 830, 914,
                977, 1193, 1349, 1555, 1562, 1702, 2436
                Self-portrait 629, 788, 997, 998, 1123, 1584, 2256
                See also Artistic interpretations of O'Connor's work(s)
                See also Folk art
        Ascetic artist, as an 50a, 215, 218, 554, 607, 612, 613, 773, 792, 1091,
                1092, 1132, 1694r, 2123
        Astrological sign 927
        Biographical details 30, 33, 45, 48, 59a, 63, 68a, 70, 81, 87, 92, 118,
                119, 127, 131, 132, 133, 138, 150, 170, 194, 207, 212, 232a,
                237, 239, 243, 244, 251, 273, 287a, 292, 325, 327, 357, 424,
                432, 487, 496, 500, 507, 509, 510, 515, 517, 520, 526, 529a,
                533, 553, 560, 563, 564, 575, 576, 598, 601, 621, 624, 630,
                643, 644, 666, 710, 714, 724, 731, 747, 753, 756, 757, 764a,
                778, 800a, 843, 845r, 874, 876, 880, 910, 943, 983, 997,
                1015, 1037, 1039r, 1042, 1042, 1050, 1053a, 1062, 1090,
                1091, 1120, 1121, 1132, 1165, 1170, 1172, 1173, 1177a,
                1180, 1183, 1195, 1196, 1218, 1220, 1234, 1235, 1236, 1243,
                1251, 1272, 1279, 1314, 1331, 1349, 1352, 1353, 1369, 1371,
                1382, 1384, 1399, 1400b, 1406, 1433, 1447, 1450, 1459,
                1466, 1469, 1473, 1488, 1497, 1549, 1552, 1554, 1563, 1572,
                1610, 1632, 1668, 1687r, 1692, 1700, 1719a, 1896, 1930a,
                1941, 1982, 1989, 2020, 2031, 2032, 2115, 2117, 2118, 2168
                Adolescence 45, 792, 1180, 1183, 1320, 1349, 1628, 1692,
                        1756, 1812, 2130
        Autobiography 1924
        Catholic faith
                See Catholic faith, Flannery O'Connor's
        Chronology of life and career 71, 513, 1700, 1848, 2115, 2133
        Contemplative gifts 839, 1037, 1132
        Death and funeral 82, 149, 243, 287a, 475, 574, 625, 694,
                849, 892, 928, 967, 1039r, 1400, 1427, 1523 , 1538,
                1553, 1610, 1616, 1951, 2197
        Education 194, 553, 1139, 1183, 1349
        Estate of 764a
        Father
                See O'Connor, Edward F., Jr.
        Georgia State College for Women [GSCW], at 33, 538, 599,
                624, 690, 1172, 1193, 1700
        Grave [Memory Hill Cemetery, Milledgeville, Ga.] 886, 1502,
                1705
        Homes 447, 1090
                Connecticut 140, 513, 524, 553, 970, 1172, 1243,
                        2032

(Con't) O'Connor, Flannery--Biographical Details--Homes
    Iowa 33, 45, 289, 295, 327, 482, 514, 538, 553, 624,
       666, 671, 694, 764, 915, 1017, 1021, 1037,
       1172, 1463, 1644, 1692, 1700, 1756, 2031,
       2032, 2115, 2145
    Milledgeville ["Andalusia" and "Green Street"] 51a,
       70, 77, 82, 85, 133, 140, 148, 173, 207, 212,
       221, 250, 273, 291, 293, 327, 336, 387, 500,
       502, 504, 507, 511, 513, 523, 524, 553, 607,
       641, 645, 654, 666, 671, 678, 691, 742,
       764a, 787, 788, 792, 803, 822, 823, 833,
       880, 886, 929, 976, 997, 998, 1018, 1050,
       1053a, 1065, 1090, 1093a, 1147, 1172,
       1173, 1188, 1199, 1218, 1219, 1251, 1298,
       1349, 1368, 1369, 1370, 1371, 1375, 1432,
       1443, 1446, 1502, 1515, 1522, 1523, 1692,
       1847, 2023, 2139
    New York City 929
    Savannah [207 East Charlton; includes Flannery
       O'Connor Childhood Home Foundation] 33,
       226, 227, 232a, 273, 425a, 447, 482, 501a,
       530, 568, 598, 742, 759a, 759b, 759c, 759d,
       785a, 1053a, 1172, 1314a, 1314b, 1317a,
       1327, 1362, 1447, 1458, 1592, 1593, 1692,
       1700
    Yaddo 33, 45, 158, 190, 503, 524, 666, 736, 823,
       929, 969, 1053a, 1473, 1624, 1687r, 1700,
       2032, 2145
    See also Iowa Writer's Workshop
  Lupus Erythematosus
    See Illness--Lupus Erythematosus
  Mother
    See O'Connor, Regina Cline
  Name 420, 722, 929
  Pathé news clip with chicken, in 194
  Peabody High School [Milledgeville, Ga.] 1349, 1689
  Personality and sense of humor 287a, 325, 366, 458, 478,
     478ar, 481, 513, 515, 524, 537, 545, 553, 572, 573,
     574, 575, 584, 598, 631, 640, 654, 666, 667, 678,
     694, 728, 731, 767, 788, 792, 803, 806, 823, 831,
     833, 845r, 854, 864, 915, 927, 929, 935, 981, 1017,
     1021, 1037, 1039r, 1042, 1065, 1087, 1090, 1133,
     1150, 1156, 1180, 1183, 1191, 1196, 1288, 1304,
     1308, 1349, 1355, 1371, 1384, 1434, 1462, 1469,
     1470a, 1527, 1538, 1668, 1682r, 1692, 1700, 1702,
     1718, 1896, 1941, 1982, 1988, 2032, 2050, 2168,

(Con't) O'Connor, Flannery--Biographical Details--Personality and Sense of
        Humor
                        2400, 2639
                        See also Intellectual(s)--O'Connor as an
                Physical description of 140, 1065
                Readings [what O'Connor read] 68a, 140, 194, 224, 345, 671,
                        823, 855, 965, 1024, 1049, 1139, 1304, 1376, 1680,
                        1819, 1966, 2053, 2106,
                Recluse [isolated artist], depiction as a 77, 186, 545, 607, 612,
                        742, 792, 829, 830, 953, 1819
                Response and influence of of community and family 232a,
                        630, 792, 1065, 1090, 1243, 1369, 1370, 1371, 1523,
                        1692, 1700
                Romantic possibilities 133, 290, 736, 767, 1055
                        Erik Langkjaer 287a, 292, 509, 666
                        John Sullivan 287a
                Self-projections 617a, 630, 766, 829, 864, 986, 1042, 1136,
                        1217, 1349, 1408, 1888, 1941, 2386
                        Electra complex 1668
                Sex life 290
                Southerner, as a 37, 99, 131, 170, 207, 212, 244, 257, 272,
                        292, 323, 328, 335, 337, 444, 468, 507, 532, 564,
                        567, 574, 575, 630, 660, 792, 843, 883, 920, 932,
                        936, 975, 1066, 1080, 1111, 1116, 1127, 1195, 1217,
                        1254, 1287, 1302, 1314, 1316, 1343, 1344, 1365,
                        1408, 1414, 1457, 1477, 1489, 1492, 1519, 1521,
                        1572, 1617, 1623, 1666, 1692, 1694r, 1700, 1701,
                        1708, 1759, 1871, 1877, 1896, 1948, 1982, 2123,
                        2162, 2163, 2540
                        Stereotypes of 500, 584, 638, 676, 809, 1326, 1972
                Spirit of 927, 1023, 1384
                Travels 502, 1400, 1571
                See also Critical approaches to O'Connor's fiction--specific--
                        biographical and bio-bibliographical
        Correspondence, Flannery O'Connor's
                See Correspondence, Flannery O'Connor's
        Intellectual, as
                See intellectual--O'Connor as an
        Interviews of
                See Interviews
        Photographs and illustrations of 51a, 63, 173, 207, 273, 292, 329, 372,
                422, 454, 458, 487, 502, 507, 513, 583, 629, 671, 759b, 759d,
                764a, 788, 792, 800a, 835, 880, 899a, 929, 997, 998, 1005,
                1018, 1042, 1053a, 1120, 1172, 1173, 1218, 1219, 1235,
                1243, 1251, 1279, 1387a, 1434, 1463, 1467, 1549, 1583,
                1584, 2123, 2135

(Con't) O'Connor, Flannery
    Views and opinions of
        African Americans 70, 133, 292, 328, 353, 380, 384, 435, 444,
            455, 527, 549, 584, 589, 603, 607, 622, 640, 678,
            750, 765, 781, 788, 793, 802, 809, 844, 896, 897,
            1055, 1056a, 1090, 1093, 1150a, 1176, 1179, 1203,
            1205, 1224, 1335, 1347, 1393, 1407, 1500, 1601,
            1607a, 1640r, 1667, 1671, 1683, 1690, 1691, 1694r,
            1699a, 1700, 1701, 1734, 1766, 1772, 1782, 1817,
            1883, 1899, 1917, 1951, 1963, 2003, 2040, 2125,
            2173, 2263, 2410
            See also Critical approaches to O'Connor's fiction--
                specific--racial
            See also Themes, Flannery O'Connor's--specific--
                racial
        Class structure 263, 333, 800b, 1159, 1215, 1229, 1337, 1527,
            1601, 1699a, 1700, 1725, 1729, 1817, 1851, 1861,
            1963, 2081, 2094, 2131, 2173, 2226, 2324
        Creative writing programs 1151, 1301, 1525, 2145
        Death 468a, 512, 711, 757, 892, 987, 1006, 1135, 1204, 1384,
            1407, 1409, 1451, 1497, 1610, 1660, 1669, 1693,
            1702, 1809, 1850, 1906, 1980, 2197, 2444
        Divorce 1188
        Education 2003, 2358
        Evil 59a, 66, 77, 101, 142, 162, 164a, 174, 193, 206, 276,
            297, 300, 322, 337, 368, 378, 388, 392, 404, 443a,
            479, 491, 575, 605, 612, 652, 658, 718, 727, 760,
            775, 784, 815, 816, 823, 838, 855, 884, 890, 919,
            983, 998, 1006, 1019, 1022, 1029, 1033, 1067, 1083,
            1093a, 1107, 1116, 1118, 1127, 1152, 1167, 1196,
            1270, 1277, 1300, 1340, 1365, 1379, 1424, 1435,
            1451, 1490, 1530, 1546, 1587, 1620, 1631, 1674,
            1727, 1762, 1771, 1786, 1810, 1814, 1866, 1885,
            1898, 1926, 1954, 2043, 2079, 2085, 2090, 2135,
            2139, 2150, 2204, 2209, 2218, 2234, 2278, 2288,
            2352
        Freedom 73, 800, 1005, 1030, 1610, 1921, 1999, 2105, 2220,
            2232
        Gender 586, 587, 588, 606, 617, 1299, 1408, 1445, 1694r,
            1700, 1745, 1817, 1976, 2003
            See also Critical approaches to O'Connor's fiction--
                specific--gender studies
            See also Identity
        Incarnation 39, 174a, 345, 392, 398, 866, 893, 1008, 1010,
            1056, 1111, 1115, 1181, 1374, 1437, 1481, 1482,
            1601, 1608, 1610, 1749, 1800, 1909, 1936, 1991,

(Con't) O'Connor, Flannery--Views and Opinions of--Incarnation
1998a, 2168, 2404
Modern world, the 59a, 106, 113, 130, 138, 164, 181, 193,
195, 218, 285, 286a, 323, 329, 333, 353, 362, 375,
385, 391, 400, 402, 404, 443, 444, 472, 544, 574,
575, 642, 710, 741, 832, 839, 855, 857, 863, 883,
908, 939, 953, 991, 1005, 1102, 1159, 1189, 1209,
1221, 1384, 1458, 1491, 1528, 1620, 1660, 1669,
1670, 1673, 1729, 1741, 1754, 1759, 1760, 1810,
1841, 1846, 1851, 1885, 1897, 1904, 1906, 2028,
2043, 2090, 2154, 2163, 2322, 2357, 2396, 2445,
2606
Pornography 111, 741
Reality 37, 59a, 130, 142, 144, 162, 169, 174a, 181, 193,
237, 255, 258, 260, 264, 316, 349, 362, 386, 390,
394, 442, 457, 475, 484, 501, 523, 538, 575, 576,
592, 611, 622, 631, 672, 674, 720, 740, 762, 770,
773, 783, 784, 801, 802, 828, 843, 850, 851, 858,
858a, 860, 868, 894, 901, 908, 922, 937, 956, 964,
977, 1004, 1011, 1013, 1034, 1038, 1053, 1072,
1080, 1102, 1103, 1105, 1107, 1109, 1112, 1135,
1137, 1138, 1150, 1152, 1160, 1167, 1176, 1189,
1203, 1258, 1271, 1297, 1350, 1365, 1372, 1374,
1411, 1418, 1436, 1491, 1503, 1535, 1552, 1595,
1596, 1608, 1617, 1650, 1684, 1717, 1733, 1736,
1744, 1786, 1800, 1804, 1806, 1809, 1810, 1819,
1855, 1865, 1866, 1871, 1887, 1908, 1918, 1925,
1933, 1949, 1953, 1984, 2021, 2028, 2041, 2090,
2130, 2196, 2246, 2302, 2334, 2443, 2536, 2542,
2635
Religious 36, 53, 57, 60, 62, 64, 66, 77, 81, 112, 126, 135,
138, 144, 145, 162, 170, 174, 175, 178, 184, 194,
199, 232a, 240, 266, 267, 272, 273, 281, 292, 298,
318, 324, 333, 353, 385, 388, 390, 400, 446, 478ar,
493, 505, 516, 524, 538, 575, 576, 592, 595, 632,
701, 753, 767, 800a, 800b, 811, 818, 823, 831, 839,
866, 887, 890, 898, 910, 925, 940, 953, 964, 966,
981, 998, 999, 1006, 1037, 1051, 1053, 1057, 1070,
1119, 1120, 1127, 1129a, 1132, 1138, 1150a, 1160,
1189, 1195, 1209, 1288, 1299, 1320a, 1339, 1340,
1353, 1377r, 1384, 1418, 1468, 1477, 1497, 1513,
1519, 1559, 1619r, 1647, 1673, 1759, 1766, 1802,
1830, 1844, 1848, 1881, 1909, 1912, 1918, 1941,
1972, 1981, 2016, 2177, 2330, 2359, 2360, 2462,
2519, 2541, 2579, 2581
See also "The Church and the Fiction Writer"

(Con't) O'Connor, Flannery--Views and Opinions--Religious

      See also Grotesque, the--O'Connor's Religious

      See also Reputation, Flannery O'Connor's--Catholic
          writer, as a

    Prophetic 65, 79, 121, 164a, 257, 274, 276, 329, 385, 439,
          475, 529a, 575, 576, 578, 613, 683, 767, 807, 818,
          868, 979, 998, 1015, 1053, 1072, 1079, 1082, 1104,
          1110, 1112, 1120, 1216, 1343, 1376, 1379, 1408,
          1435, 1437a, 1500, 1536, 1651, 1673, 1720, 1759,
          1770, 1788, 1839, 1847, 1897, 1904, 1944, 1950,
          1961, 1973, 2049, 2088, 2134, 2180, 2264, 2298,
          2323, 2366, 2381, 2409, 2476, 2504, 2591

      See also Prophetic role, the

    Sacraments, the 34, 93, 128, 218, 357, 358, 359, 362, 576,
          1433, 1552, 1666, 1698, 1706, 1723, 1728, 1779,
          1844, 1887, 1944, 1949, 2101, 2235, 2409

    Science 1619r

    Sentimentality 59a, 65, 111, 159, 195, 270, 272, 347, 404,
          703, 732, 750, 1033, 1046, 1184, 1196, 1339, 1374,
          1376, 1609, 1674, 1925, 2135, 2353

    Skepticism 1185, 1384, 1724, 2011,

    Suffering 56, 162, 195, 198, 300, 358, 379, 441, 496, 576,
          603, 611, 659, 733, 734, 851, 864, 876, 887, 892,
          922, 931, 934, 980, 987, 1037, 1038, 1091, 1272,
          1332, 1342, 1358, 1365, 1415, 1451, 1485, 1497,
          1620, 1645, 1647, 1737, 1766, 1773, 1785, 1807,
          1846, 1896, 1901, 1921, 1926, 1930, 1949, 1954,
          1976, 2154, 2245a, 2254, 2258, 2310

      See also Style--suffering, use of

    Thomism 77, 102a, 697, 1038, 1102, 1103, 1668, 1804, 1844,
          1918, 2106

    Violence 68a, 164a, 286a, 617a, 800a, 816, 818, 890, 977,
          1031, 1033, 1053, 1106, 1127, 1133, 1136, 1159,
          1181, 1186, 1239, 1273, 1293, 1314b, 1350, 1376,
          1409, 1459, 1462, 1490, 1493, 1536, 1552, 1556,
          1627, 1655, 1696, 1702, 1719, 1720, 1798, 1833,
          1835, 1837, 1854, 1860, 1865, 1868, 1879, 1884,
          1890, 1904, 1927, 1930, 1944, 1955, 1959, 1985,
          2003, 2027, 2034, 2049, 2070, 2084, 2086, 2180,
          2246, 2265, 2307, 2313, 2314, 2370, 2394, 2396,
          2409, 2449, 2530, 2536, 2558, 2572, 2585, 2686a

      See also Symbols and images--violence

      See also Violence

O'Connor, Regina Cline 45, 57, 140, 148, 173, 292, 387, 437, 502, 510, 511,
    515, 521, 602, 630, 640, 649, 666, 667, 690, 742, 753, 864, 929, 935,
    1090, 1122, 1128, 1132, 1172, 1180, 1199, 1210, 1236, 1251, 1320,

(Con't) O'Connor, Regina Cline
        1384, 1421, 1432, 1484, 1668, 1700, 1718, 1896, 1982, 2000, 2020,
        2023, 2205
Oedipus Rex [Sophocles] 282
        See also Themes, Flannery O'Connor's--specific--Oedipal
Old Capital Historical Society [Milledgeville, Ga.] 743a
Old South
        See South, the--Old South
Oral interpretation
        See Adaptations--oral interpretation
"Other," the [the Devil]
        See Characters--types of--"the Other" [the Devil]
        See also Symbols and images--"the Other"

Palestine 607
Panel discussions
        See Interviews
Parables
        See Style--parables, use of
Paradigms
        See Style--paradigms, use of
Paradise Lost [John Milton] 53, 926, 1966
Paradox
        See Style--paradox, use of
Paris Trout [Pete Dexter] 802, 1247
"Parker's Back" 32, 34, 37, 38, 40, 41, 42, 47, 49, 50a, 53, 73, 77, 117, 155,
        179, 195, 202, 211, 256, 259, 265, 268, 288, 345, 348, 352, 381, 419,
        420, 480, 483, 493, 495, 514, 540, 576, 587, 676, 683, 717, 735, 743,
        766, 778, 783, 807, 826, 840, 890, 909, 943, 945, 985, 1006, 1008,
        1012, 1014, 1030, 1046, 1056, 1091, 1092, 1094, 1142, 1143, 1148,
        1181, 1205, 1268, 1284, 1291, 1291a, 1299, 1304, 1354, 1378, 1384,
        1385, 1396, 1400, 1409, 1422, 1435, 1436, 1437a, 1462, 1482, 1497,
        1521, 1535, 1536, 1546, 1547, 1563, 1575, 1616, 1618, 1621, 1647,
        1659, 1678a, 1696, 1697, 1725, 1755, 1757, 1775, 1778, 1781, 1869,
        1875, 1878, 1892, 1901, 1922, 1923, 1929, 1936, 1953, 1991, 2016,
        2028, 2033, 2068, 2069, 2116
        See also Characters, O'Connor's--specific--Cates, Sarah Ruth
        See also Characters, O'Connor's--specific--Parker, O.E.
Parody
        See Style--parody, use of
        See also Adaptations--parodies
Parricide 776
"The Partridge Festival" 41, 47, 49, 60, 155, 230, 265, 288, 716, 802, 963, 976,
        995, 1076, 1093a, 1133, 1171, 1247, 1329, 1394, 1409, 1426, 1563,
        1640, 1659, 1816, 1847

(Con't) "The Partridge Festival"
    See also Characters, O'Connor's--specific--Calhoun
    See also Characters, O'Connor's--specific--Mary Elizabeth
    See also Characters, O'Connor's--specific--Singleton
Pastoral genre 467, 1622, 2179
Patriarchal culture
    See Symbols and images--patriarchal culture
Patricide 1316, 1623
Paul, Saint 987, 1638, 1648, 2490
Peacocks, chickens and other fowl 33, 70, 123, 174, 298, 336, 513, 554, 599,
    736, 765, 786, 792, 835, 881, 925, 929, 980, 998, 1009, 1016, 1018,
    1065, 1137, 1190, 1219, 1384, 1434, 1523, 1615a
    See also Symbols and images--animal--peacock
Pedophilia 1670
"The Peeler" 31, 60, 2315
Pelgaian beliefs 1771
Penthos 612
Performing literature 200, 1442, 1506, 1541, 1894, 1970
Perpetua, Saint 1079
Peter, Saint 1185, 1638
"PFTT" [poem] 1689
Photographs and illustrations 45, 51a, 52, 63, 72, 173, 207, 227, 251, 273, 292,
    307a, 329, 338r, 371, 410, 422, 454, 458, 487, 501a, 502, 507, 583,
    599, 629, 637, 637a, 671, 742, 743a, 759d, 764a, 788, 792, 800a, 835,
    880, 890, 899a, 913, 929, 997, 998, 1005, 1018, 1042, 1043, 1044,
    1045, 1053a, 1120, 1162, 1173, 1218, 1219, 1235, 1243, 1244, 1251,
    1279, 1284, 1317a, 1349, 1368, 1371, 1387a, 1391, 1434, 1454, 1463,
    1467, 1475, 1517, 1549, 1583, 1584, 1592, 1625, 1652, 1659a, 1661,
    1679, 2012, 2123, 2135
    See also O'Connor, Flannery--photographs and illustrations of
    See also Georgia--middle--photographs of
Pilgrim's Progress [John Bunyan] 53, 1791
Place
    Dependence upon 860, 1287, 1328, 1345, 1479, 1568, 1615a, 1717,
        1725, 1843, 2515
    Depiction of
        City, the 174a, 217, 308, 318, 337, 395, 406, 479, 605, 651,
            718, 939, 1021, 1187, 1194, 1230, 1253, 1359, 1363,
            1378, 1379, 1393, 1396, 1458, 1459, 1461, 1586,
            1654, 1720, 1754, 1799, 1837, 1843, 1853, 2111,
            2154, 2275, 2348
        Corinth, Greece 1638
        Country, the 318, 395, 426, 605, 703, 939, 1359, 1378, 1379,
            1725, 1843, 2111
        Farms 80, 114, 980, 1078, 1127, 1764, 2033
        Groves 80

(Con't) Place

        Landscapes 80, 119, 161, 178, 308, 321, 329, 338r, 385, 501,
              653, 785, 977, 991, 1060, 1295, 1325, 1341, 1350,
              1396, 1622, 1725, 1839, 2052, 2066, 2243
        Meadows 80
        New York City 1187, 1648, 2125
        Pastures 80
        Pool hall 807
        Powderhead 613
        Sky 329, 365, 1419, 1839
        Sun 134, 156, 329, 359, 921, 959, 980, 1295, 1396, 1481,
              1576, 1615a, 1927, 2066, 2350
        Taulkinham 161, 611, 668, 726
        Treelines 1284, 1396, 1615a
        Woods 80, 321, 329, 785, 921, 991, 1284, 1297, 1350, 1396,
              1615a, 2052, 2066, 2067, 2278
        World 851, 937, 1030, 1048, 1060, 1109, 1135, 1363, 1636,
              1778, 1869, 2062
    Dislocation and 260, 1207, 1843, 2004, 2314
    Female use of 80, 119, 617, 1568, 1637, 1822
    Names of 238, 270, 350, 378, 491, 492, 493, 735, 1131, 1482
    Sense of 56, 272, 394, 426, 641, 653, 709, 775, 822, 829, 932, 1044,
        1107, 1116, 1127, 1345, 1479, 1638, 1717, 1729, 1813, 1843,
        1854, 2515
    Transformation of 1061, 1600
    See also Identity--place on, influence of
"The Place of the Intellectual" 1339
Plots
    See O'Connor, Flannery--works--plots
Poetry
    Flannery O'Connor's 529a, 1689
    Inspired by Flannery O'Connor's writings 75, 85, 188, 641, 645, 693,
        700, 786, 790, 805, 841, 886, 968, 971, 1016, 1154, 1298,
        1346, 1705
Point of view
    See Style--point of view, use of
Poland
    O'Connor criticism in 32
Polycarp, Saint 1079
Popular culture 68a, 73, 126, 418, 539, 548, 1337, 1521, 1734, 1851, 1996
Pornography
    See O'Connor, Flannery--views and opinions of--pornography
Portrait of the Artist As A Young Man [James Joyce]
    See O'Connor, Flannery--influence of other writers--Joyce, James
Potato
    See Symbols and images--potato peeler

Preachers
> *See* Evangelists

The Presence of Grace and Other Book Reviews by Flannery O'Connor 1097, 1191, 1674, 1680r, 2053

Pride
> *See* Style--pride, use of

Progress
> *See* Symbols and images--progress

Projections
> *See* O'Connor, Flannery--self-projections

Prophetic role, the 32, 62, 164a, 174a, 257, 274, 276, 329, 385, 439, 475, 529a, 576, 578, 613, 683, 767, 807, 818, 868, 879, 979, 998, 1015, 1053, 1072, 1073, 1079, 1082, 1104, 1110, 1112, 1121, 1216, 1343, 1376, 1379, 1408, 1435, 1437a, 1500, 1536, 1651, 1673, 1720, 1770, 1788, 1839, 1847, 1897, 1904, 1944, 1950, 1961, 1973, 2049, 2088, 2180, 2264, 2298, 2323, 2366, 2381, 2409, 2476, 2504
> *See also* Characters--types of--prophetic
> *See also* Language--prophetic
> *See also* O'Connor, Flannery--views and opinions of--prophetic
> *See also* Style--motifs and archetypes--prophet motif

Protestant Election
> *See* Style--Protestant Election, use of

Protestant fundamentalist
> *See* Characters--types of--Protestant fundamentalist

Psychoanalysis
> *See* Critical approaches to O'Connor's fiction--specific--psychoanalytic
> *See also* Characters, Flannery O'Connor's--psychological well-being of
> *See also* Theology--Psychoanalysis and

Pulitzer Prize 163, 927, 1314b

Pulp Fiction [Quentin Tarantino] 388

Purgatory 395, 1130

Puritanism 66, 1816, 1930, 1945

"Queen for a Day" [television show] 1640r

Quest
> *See* Style--motifs and archetypes, use of--quest motif

Quotations 379, 499, 750, 760, 764, 788, 791, 796, 798, 851, 885, 938, 1023a, 1024, 1043, 1065, 1070, 1076, 1107, 1113, 1114, 1132, 1154, 1214, 1219, 1223, 1233, 1235, 1271, 1277, 1286, 1317, 1345, 1360, 1451, 1480, 1502, 1540, 1564, 1646, 1653, 1688, 1708, 1806, 2135

Race and racism
> *See* O'Connor, Flannery--views and opinions on--race
> *See also* Critical approaches to O'Connor's fiction--specific--racial

(Con't) Race and Racism
> *See also* Georgia--middle--racist traditions of
> *See also* Symbols and images--racial
> *See also* Themes, Flannery O'Connor's--specific--racial
Radcliffe University 1583
Radical, Flannery O'Connor as a 2041
Rape
> *See* Symbols and imagery--rape
Reader response theory
> *See* Critical approaches to O'Connor's fiction--specific--reader
>> response theory
Readings
> *See* O'Connor, Flannery--Readings
Readers
> Catholic 1002, 1023a, 1232, 1240, 1308, 1383, 1418, 1598, 1608,
>> 1864, 1893, 1933, 1981, 2230
> Impact of O'Connor's fiction on 60, 148, 160, 162, 164a, 172, 178,
>> 179, 203, 211, 239, 245, 257, 276, 311a, 353, 362, 390, 443,
>> 495, 498, 501, 509, 511, 547, 559, 575, 582, 591, 593, 595,
>> 603, 619, 631, 648, 650, 659, 680, 741, 743, 778, 818, 828,
>> 851, 865, 879, 892, 910, 937, 953, 958, 964, 998, 1013, 1023,
>> 1042, 1049, 1076, 1105, 1121, 1159, 1170, 1176, 1232, 1237,
>> 1246, 1258, 1265, 1290, 1350, 1353, 1359, 1372, 1409, 1422,
>> 1451, 1511, 1559, 1594, 1596, 1600, 1608, 1629r, 1632,
>> 1645, 1696, 1716, 1718, 1724, 1801, 1827, 1828, 1859, 1876,
>> 1885, 1889, 1915, 1924, 2043, 2221, 2609, 2617
> Secular 1867, 1924, 1944
> Strategies to reach 53, 56, 61, 76, 113, 131, 160, 164, 174a, 176, 178,
>> 179, 185, 211, 216, 245, 257, 264, 268, 298, 308, 309, 347,
>> 357, 385, 389, 415, 420, 446, 448, 469, 481, 493, 538, 554,
>> 575, 590, 631, 657, 704, 705, 741, 743, 828, 830, 884, 898,
>> 912, 920, 926, 931, 975, 980, 1004, 1007, 1011, 1013, 1033,
>> 1056, 1057, 1103, 1109, 1112, 1152, 1175, 1204, 1261, 1268,
>> 1270, 1286, 1290, 1293, 1316, 1347, 1350, 1353, 1400, 1404,
>> 1495, 1496, 1535, 1559, 1573, 1594, 1664, 1688, 1703, 1723,
>> 1840, 1842, 1853, 1864, 1870, 1876, 1889, 1933, 1944, 1949,
>> 1958, 1961, 1970, 1977, 1985, 2011, 2045, 2086, 2088
> Views of OConnor of her 36, 38, 47, 60, 164a, 273, 631, 679, 760, 762,
>> 801, 934, 1097, 1176, 1184, 1191, 1345, 1374, 1468, 1989,
>> 2045
> *See also* Characters, O'Connor's--distance between readers and
Reader's theatre
> *See* Adaptations--Reader's theatre
Realism [Flannery O'Connor's fiction as] 41, 53, 76, 136, 161, 316, 575, 592,
> 630, 631, 672, 674, 783, 801, 802, 890, 918, 921, 1102, 1103, 1121,
> 1136, 1149, 1297, 1309, 1365, 1493, 1604, 1608, 1744, 1754, 1796,

(Con't) Realism [Flannery O'Connor's Fiction as]
1809, 1817, 1842, 1865, 1926, 2001, 2007a, 2034, 2135, 2168, 2319, 2670

Reality
See O'Connor, Flannery--views and opinions of--reality
See also Christianity--reality of

Recluse
See O'Connor, Flannery--recluse, depiction as a

Recollections and comments about Flannery O'Connor 478, 509, 691, 1434
"A" *See* Hester, Betty
Abbot, Louise 87
Allen, Reynolds and Dick 87
Alther, Lisa 941
Barth, John 2064
Bonner, James 1251
Bourne, Paul 197
Bray, Nancy Davis 1251
Brzenk, Gene 295
Burford, Kay 295,
Cash, Jean W. 293
Daniell, Rosemary 693
Dawkins, Cecil 382, 524, 760
Dinger, Ed 915
Doner, Lois 482
Drake, Robert 428, 543, 728
Embree, Charles 295, 411
Emmanuel, Pierre 524
Engle, Paul 295, 553, 764, 1021
Fancher, Betsy 475, 478
Farley, Blanche 478
Fennell, Jan 1251
Fitzgerald, Benedict 978
Fitzgerald, Robert 502, 503, 511, 970, 1150
Fitzgerald, Sally 140, 232a, 342a, 393, 477, 510, 511, 513, 527, 529a, 638, 780a, 792, 913, 961, 1018, 1062, 1119, 1243, 1400b
Florencourt, Louise 1251
Ford, Richard 2064
Frisbie, Richard 478
Furlong, Monica 524
Gilman, Richard 478
Giroux, Robert 1015
Gordon, Caroline 515, 524, 941, 961, 1571
Greene, Helen I. 290, 666
Gurganus, Allan 411, 832
Hall, James B. 290, 295, 411
Hamilton, Barbara Tunnicliff 694

(Con't) Recollections and Comments About Flannery O'Connor
Hardwick, Elizabeth 842
Harty, Tony 1314b
Hendin, Josephine 751
Hester, Betty 1292
Holmberg, Claes-Göran 2064
Hood, Mary 760
Howard, Maureen 915
Jacobsen, Josephine 760
Jones, Madison 803
Kazin, Alfred 823
Kidd, Hariett 833
Kinney, Arthur F. 853
Kirk, Russell 854
Kirkland, William M. 855
Lee, Maryat 1292
Lee, Robert E. 290
Love, Betty Boyd 929, 1292
Lowell, Robert 969
Lunz, Elisabeth 913
Lytle, Andrew 290, 295, 936
Macauley, Robie 290
Mallard, William 913
McCorkle, Jill 1023
McCown, James 935, 1024, 1087
Méras, Phyllis 1065
Merton, Thomas 1066
Messick, Hank 295
Michaels, Leonard 2064
Miller, Margaret 83
Montgomery, Marion 83
Moore, Marianne 524
Morris, Ann Orr 83
Murphy, John J. 1134
Nipson, Herbert 295
Oates, Joyce Carol 878
O'Connor, Regina 515, 1251, 1896
Parr, Newell 1314b
Percy, Walker 903, 1022
Persse, Patricia 1314b
Persse, Winnifred 1314b
Porter, Katherine Anne 927, 928, 941
Prewitt, James 441
Price, Reynolds 831
Russell, Mary Virginia 87
Ryan, Elizabeth Shreve 1349

(Con't) Recollections and Comments About Flannery O'Connor
      Schemmel, [William] Bill 1370
      Scott, Katherine 1371
      Sessions, Bill 792, 913, 1400, 1400b, 1401a
      Stern, Richard 2064
      Stevenson, Elisabeth 913
      Sullivan, Walter 290
      Tate, Allen 219, 224, 229
      Tate, James and Mary Barbara 87, 293, 1251, 1515, 1522, 1523
      Tate, Sue Fan 83
      Taylor, Peter 1017
      Tharin, Miriam 1314b
      Thompson, Mary Jo 87
      Thornton, Jack 1251
      Trexler, Margaret Persse 1314b
      Uhler, Margaret 87
      Walker, Alice 878, 941, 960, 1656
      Walsh, Sister Jude 764a
      Welty, Eudora 1611
      West, Robert 83
      White, Fannie 87
      Whitehead, James 1633
      Wiatt, Mary Mudge 295
      Williams, S. Miller 1446, 1633
      Wood, Ralph 793, 1387a
      Wylder, Jean Williams 295, 411, 915, 1513, 1644
      See also Interviews [of Flannery O'Connor]
      See also Reputation, Flannery O'Connor's
Readings
      See Adaptations--recordings of
Redemption 32, 39, 43, 47, 59a, 66, 73, 96, 103, 110, 111, 113, 121, 128, 130,
      131, 134, 135, 145, 159, 166, 176, 203, 208, 216, 248, 258, 259, 268,
      272, 273, 274, 276, 281, 291, 302, 305, 317, 348, 349, 352, 381, 392,
      394, 401, 404, 418, 431, 443, 446, 481, 486, 496, 501, 546, 551, 576,
      590, 591, 597, 603, 608, 611, 648, 651, 652, 653, 683, 697, 698, 699,
      710, 717, 727, 729, 729a, 743, 754, 757, 770, 776, 795, 811, 816, 828,
      832, 838, 839, 840, 852, 866, 867, 888, 890, 908, 931, 943, 983, 985,
      987, 998, 1008, 1010, 1019, 1027, 1031, 1033, 1034, 1051, 1053,
      1072, 1149, 1150, 1160, 1167, 1179, 1189, 1091, 1196, 1216, 1217,
      1239, 1299, 1314a, 1333, 1339, 1353, 1358, 1365, 1393, 1395, 1396,
      1503, 1507, 1530, 1557, 1559, 1561, 1576, 1595, 1600, 1610, 1635,
      1662, 1667, 1690, 1693, 1719, 1720, 1722, 1758, 1760, 1787, 1792,
      1800, 1802, 1814, 1831, 1841, 1869, 1870, 1877, 1881, 1888, 1899,
      1900, 1903, 1910, 1915, 1921, 1930, 1939, 1989, 1997, 1999, 2020,
      2028, 2046, 2047, 2063, 2073, 2079, 2084, 2090, 2102, 2107, 2113,
      2122, 2161, 2168, 2177, 2225, 2254, 2279, 2289, 2307, 2317, 2359,

(Con't) Redemption
    2360, 2401, 2409, 2415, 2417, 2431, 2476, 2534, 2562, 2626, 2661,
    2681, 2705
Region 45, 98a, 99, 133, 175, 181, 207, 211, 272, 323, 338r, 353, 380, 523, 536,
    622, 703, 785, 964, 1014, 1035, 1053, 1080, 1116, 1126, 1127, 1233,
    1316, 1371, 1442, 1461, 1479, 1617, 1623, 1669, 1700, 1766, 1784,
    1813, 1853, 1899. 1911, 1926, 1967, 1982, 2249, 2290, 2522, 2532
    See also Critical approaches to O'Connor's fiction--specific--
        regionalism
    See also South, the
Regional fiction 1813, 1911, 1926, 1937, 1967, 1982, 2522
"The Regional Writer" 938, 1653
Relationships, subject/object 763
    See also Style--mother-daughter relationships, use of
Relativism
    Moral 347, 612
    Romantic 783
Religion
    Art and 876, 963, 964, 1097, 1113, 1133, 1138, 1454, 1467, 1619r,
        1912
    Failure of organized 842
    Hindu 1009
    Judaism 1779
    Questions addressed by 998
    The Violent Bear It Away as an examination of 164a, 944, 1669, 1686,
        1735, 1837
    Vaporization of 1032
    See also Intellectuals--religion and
    See also Symbols and images--religious
    See also Theology
Religious vision
    See O'Connor, Flannery--themes--religious
    See also O'Connor, Flannery--views and opinions of--religious
    See also Symbols and images--religious
    See also Themes, Flannery O'Connor's--specific--religious
    See also Theology--literature and
Republic [Plato] 1333
Reputation, Flannery O'Connor's 37, 46, 51a, 59a, 65, 72, 77, 79, 81, 127, 131,
    146, 150, 151, 165, 175, 180, 200, 211, 212, 215, 230, 232a, 235, 239,
    248, 250, 273, 283, 289, 291, 307a, 310, 320, 332, 354, 366, 387, 408,
    429, 449, 452, 475, 478, 482, 485, 493, 514, 517, 529, 536, 537, 543,
    553, 556, 559, 560, 574, 575, 576, 579, 582, 588, 598, 601, 620, 624,
    627, 628, 629, 631, 643, 644, 647, 657, 661, 663, 664, 665, 670, 703,
    710, 715, 748, 757, 766, 768, 775, 781, 783, 789, 800a, 803, 812, 818,
    820, 822, 831, 832, 835, 843, 862, 868, 874, 876, 878, 882, 890, 910,
    928, 931, 936, 943, 983, 996, 997, 1036, 1037, 1040, 1057, 1066,

(Con't) Reputation, Flannery O'Connor's

1077, 1080, 1117, 1121, 1125, 1129, 1130, 1134, 1149, 1174, 1209, 1211, 1232, 1234, 1236, 1240, 1248, 1249, 1255, 1279, 1301, 1304, 1311, 1314, 1317, 1329, 1352, 1359, 1370, 1371, 1374, 1377r, 1400a, 1405, 1406, 1411, 1413, 1427, 1429, 1433, 1434, 1447, 1448, 1455, 1456, 1457, 1502, 1520, 1524, 1527a, 1538, 1549, 1553, 1554, 1556, 1563, 1610, 1625, 1645, 1651, 1653, 1674, 1682, 1688, 1708, 1715, 1716, 1741, 1756, 1806, 1836, 1842, 1915, 1918, 1951, 1977, 2033, 2081, 2139, 2140, 2168, 2545, 2662,

Abroad

Australia 1121,

Canada 120, 412, 1715, 1716

Denmark 1619r

France, in 559, 560, 561, 774, 1715, 1716, 1966, 2009

Germany 1715, 1716

Great Britain 721, 1715, 1716

India 1250

Soviet Union 2081

Catholic writer, as a 52, 99, 151, 164, 170, 178, 211, 218, 281, 353, 354, 383, 417, 429, 505, 574, 575, 577, 578, 579, 590, 602, 618, 619, 620, 626, 627, 628, 629, 638, 655, 661, 662, 679, 697, 701, 717, 729, 774, 835, 840, 843, 844, 851, 875, 890, 893, 908, 926, 932, 939, 943, 953, 966, 996, 997, 998, 1006, 1014, 1022, 1023a, 1040, 1056, 1062, 1079, 1087, 1096, 1103, 1113, 1119, 1127, 1165, 1180, 1189, 1195, 1196, 1204, 1209, 1237, 1240, 1248, 1279, 1288, 1302, 1307, 1308, 1316, 1343, 1344, 1347, 1353, 1356, 1376, 1377r, 1383, 1406, 1411, 1418, 1427, 1455, 1477, 1548, 1552, 1553, 1554, 1597, 1598, 1608, 1612, 1635, 1650, 1651, 1664, 1666, 1672, 1674, 1697, 1709, 1733, 1755, 1759, 1787, 1790, 1806, 1808, 1810, 1848, 1853, 1864, 1893, 1912, 1923, 1927, 1931, 1933, 1936, 1944, 1945, 1947, 1961, 1981, 1984, 1990, 2044, 2081, 2086, 2088, 2090, 2092, 2106, 2123, 2127, 2135, 2136, 2162, 2168, 2213, 2230, 2230a, 2326, 2387, 2473, 2486, 2533

Conservative writer, as a 163, 327, 607, 896, 1316, 1365, 1547, 1674, 1683

Correspondent, as a 59a, 221, 325, 327, 473, 481, 513, 563, 640, 1177a

Growth in, 352, 1910

Short story writer, as a 265, 389, 582, 644, 661, 710, 818, 909, 942, 943, 997, 1063, 1065, 1286, 1577, 1658, 1659, 1730, 1955, 1960, 1991, 2010, 2033, 2045, 2050, 2081, 2127

Southern writer, as a 37, 52, 77, 98a, 99, 121, 131, 138, 151, 170, 175, 206, 212, 219, 267, 272, 292, 323, 380, 390, 422, 429, 436, 452, 468, 472, 475, 483, 493, 532, 533, 534, 536, 542, 559, 561, 575, 614, 630, 662, 665, 703, 747, 748, 754, 781, 783, 802, 843, 862, 874, 883, 932, 936, 938,

(Con't) Reputation, Flannery O'Connor's--as a Southern Writer
975, 998, 1014, 1043, 1066, 1080, 1107, 1111, 1116, 1121,
1174, 1249, 1255, 1287, 1302, 1314, 1316, 1343, 1345, 1365,
1414, 1430, 1434, 1456, 1457, 1479, 1489, 1492, 1519, 1600,
1617, 1623, 1653, 1692, 1701, 1705, 1708, 1711, 1784, 1799,
1813, 1847, 1871, 1877, 1911, 1948, 2036, 2039, 2061, 2092,
2123, 2168, 2169, 2540, 2629, 2699
    Twentieth-century writer, as a 52, 74, 77, 136, 142, 230, 357, 393, 487,
493, 710, 820, 823, 835, 996, 1455, 1547, 1604, 1977
    Woman writer, as a 52, 77, 99, 166, 370, 383, 468, 472, 487, 529, 536,
614, 630, 640, 660, 667, 731, 781, 941, 943, 960, 1055, 1227,
1263, 1292, 1299, 1364, 1420, 1421, 1527a, 1568, 1574,
1622, 1886, 1948, 1974, 2699
    See also Aesthetics of Flannery O'Connor's art
    See also Comparisons [of O'Connor's work] with work(s) by
    See also Critical approaches to O'Connor's fiction
    See also Recollections and comments about Flannery O'Connor
"A Return to the South"
    See Adaptations--plays--"A Return to the South"
Revelation
    See Style--revelation, use of
"Revelation" 34, 35a, 37, 40, 41, 45, 47, 50a, 53, 60, 77, 80, 125, 176, 245, 256,
263, 281, 295, 352, 366, 396, 410, 414, 435, 446a, 465, 514, 528, 537,
540, 574, 576, 580, 590, 597, 631, 638, 652, 670, 676, 678, 701, 705,
722, 727, 751, 766, 783, 788, 800b, 805, 808, 838, 859, 923, 937, 940,
943, 945, 985, 987, 1015, 1033, 1049, 1053, 1069, 1078, 1093a, 1127,
1130, 1133, 1141, 1142, 1171, 1181, 1217, 1243, 1253, 1257, 1261,
1271, 1284, 1299, 1304, 1312, 1320, 1320a, 1332, 1340, 1353, 1378,
1386, 1400, 1409, 1422, 1427, 1429, 1437, 1437a, 1441, 1462, 1473,
1474, 1481, 1497, 1500, 1527, 1535, 1536, 1546, 1559a, 1615a, 1637,
1643, 1649, 1659, 1666, 1667, 1683, 1696, 1697, 1699a, 1736, 1755,
1816, 1868, 1869, 1892, 1953, 1975, 1982, 2007, 2017, 2033, 2040,
2189, 2222, 2277, 2362, 2411, 2450, 2499, 2544, 2592, 2611
    See also Adaptations--plays--"Revelation"
    See also Characters, O'Connor's--specific--Grace, Mary
    See also Characters, O'Connor's--specific--Turpin, Claud
    See also Characters, O'Connor's--specific--Turpin, Ruby
    See also Films--*Revelation*
Reversal
    See Style--reversal, use of
Revivals, religious 1072, 1507
Rhetorical theory
    See Critical approaches to O'Connor's fiction--specific--rhetorical
theory
    See also Style--rhetorical devices, use of
Rinehart Publishing Company 92, 627, 628, 629, 1209, 1613, 1847

(Con't) Rinehart Publishing Company
>   Selby, John [editor] 1613

Rites of passage
>   *See* Style--rites of passage, use of

Rituals
>   *See* Style--rituals, use of

"The River" 32, 34, 40, 41, 45, 47, 50a, 75b, 77, 160, 211, 225, 302, 314, 317,
>   349, 465, 495, 523, 529, 580, 596, 652, 669, 711, 751, 775, 869, 890,
>   922, 957, 958, 966, 991, 1005, 1043, 1053, 1073, 1175, 1283, 1284,
>   1295, 1372, 1404, 1507, 1546, 1563, 1585, 1600, 1664, 1666, 1700,
>   1709, 1723, 1727, 1745, 1755, 1839, 1878, 1953, 1998a, 2016, 2033,
>   2035, 2052, 2101, 2381, 2421
>   *See also* Characters, O'Connor's--specific--Ashfield, Harry
>   *See also* Characters, O'Connor's--specific--Connin, Mrs.
>   *See also* Characters, O'Connor's--specific--Paradise, Mr.
>   *See also* Characters, O'Connor's--specific--Preacher, the
>   *See also* Characters, O'Connor's--specific--Summers, Rev.
>   *See also* Films--*The River*

Roman world 607, 776, 1265, 1779

Romantic tradition 931, 1115, 1332, 1366, 1379, 1754, 1760, 1767, 1814, 1842,
>   1902, 1920, 1943, 2001, 2011, 2013, 2034, 2175, 2238, 2621a
>   American historical 248, 318, 462, 783, 942, 1169, 1688, 2013, 2559
>   Nathaniel Hawthorne, and 62, 321, 456, 457, 462, 801, 1814

Rural
>   *See* Characters--types of--rural

Sachet, the Grandmother's 776

Sacraments
>   *See also* O'Connor, Flannery--views and opinions of--Sacraments, the
>   *See also* Symbols and images--Sacraments, the

Sacred
>   *See* Symbols and images--sacred

Sacrifice
>   *See* Symbols and images--sacrificial

Saint Teresa, College of 1134

Salvation
>   *See* Redemption

Samford University 1123, 1661r

Sanctification 651

Satire
>   *See* Comedy, O'Connor's work as

Savannah, Georgia
>   *See* Georgia--cities and towns--Savannah
>   See also O'Connor, Flannery--biographical details--homes--Savannah

Savannah College of Art and Design 1362

The Scarlet Letter [Nathaniel Hawthorne] 581, 1278
Science
        See O'Connor, Flannery--views and opinions of--science
Scientific thought 1332, 1944
"The Second Coming" [William Butler Yeats] 183
        See also Christ, Jesus--Second Coming of
Second Vatican Council
        See Catholic(ism)--Second Vatican Council
Secularism 165, 321, 358, 375, 618, 739, 744, 953, 1159, 1319, 1598, 1645,
        1762, 1924, 2521
Seduction
        See Style--seduction, use of
        See also Style--sexuality, use of
Seeing
        See Style--motifs and archetypes--seeing
Self
        Depiction of 164a, 1749, 1816, 1888, 1910, 2223, 2386, 2497, 2498
        Divided 75b, 2177, 2544
        Radical 1815
        Reliance upon 1636
Sentences
        Length of 1280
        Simple, use of 64
        Structure of 1109, 1915
        Titles 738, 1268, 1286, 1521, 1686, 2027
Sentimentality
        See O'Connor, Flannery--views and opinions of--sentimentality
Sermons
        Based upon Flannery O'Connor's life and work 1148, 1149, 1150,
        1957
        Wise Blood, in 1971
Sewanee Review 1641a, 1713
Sexuality
        See Style--sexuality, use of
        See also Body, human
        See also Identity, female
        See also Symbols and images--sexual
Shock
        See Style--shock, use of
Shoe
        See Symbols and images--shoe
Short story, the 59, 389, 471, 594, 909, 925, 942, 967, 1286, 1475, 1577, 1723,
        1730, 1789, 1809, 1946, 1955, 1960, 1991, 2010, 2017, 2033, 2045,
        2050, 2081, 2127
        Christian 193, 493, 943, 1240, 1435
        Cycle, as a 1659, 1779, 2010, 2033, 2693

(Con't) Short Story, the
        Experimental 59, 206
        Realistic 59, 672, 1493, 1754, 2007a
        Southern 942
        Women, and link with American 59, 119, 206, 383, 472, 529, 587, 614,
                630, 943, 1227, 1292, 1568, 1625, 1925, 2014
"Shouting to the Deaf"
        See Adaptations--plays--"Shouting to the Deaf"
Signification
        See Style--signification, use of
Similes
        See Style--similes, use of
Sin
        See Characters--types of--sinful
        See also Christ, Jesus--sinner's appearance to
Skepticism
        See O'Connor, Flannery--views and opinions of--skepticism
Smith, Bessie
        See A Good Man Is Hard to Find [musical score by Eddie Green]--
                Bessie Smith
Social status
        See Style--social status, use of
Sociology 744, 747, 1107, 1189, 1842, 1946, 1976, 2033, 2656
"Some Aspects of the Grotesque in Southern Fiction" 737, 801, 980, 1115,
        1276, 1342, 1482
South, the [American] 523, 613, 647, 703, 785, 815, 1080, 1853, 2099, 2540
        African Americans in 435, 444, 455, 549, 622, 638, 788, 802, 809, 931,
                939, 1127, 1207, 1667, 1671, 1699a, 1782, 1799, 2039, 2040,
                2125, 2263
        Alienation of 38, 181, 222, 323, 455, 638, 732, 863, 890, 1053, 1415,
                1531, 1588, 1700, 1750, 1782, 1799, 1897, 2453, 2520
        Ambiguities of the 1066, 1207, 1342, 1408, 1531, 1623, 1666, 1700,
                1877, 2039
        Bible Belt in 68a, 169, 175, 211, 267, 272, 332, 356, 662, 887, 964,
                970, 1082, 1127, 1148, 1258, 1343, 1345, 1666, 1711, 1772
        Catholics in the 717, 774, 842, 843, 845r, 932, 939, 953, 970, 1062,
                1127, 1195, 1207, 1302, 1343, 1347, 1477, 1519, 1666, 1936,
                2088, 2162
        Change in 323, 436, 550, 622, 638, 676, 781, 1194, 1207, 1342, 1365,
                1617, 1699a, 1700, 1853, 1897, 2025, 2026, 2039, 2154
        "Christ-haunted" 638, 1040, 1107, 1116, 1328, 1345, 1358, 1531,
                1708, 1784, 1972, 2070, 2287
        Culture and heritage of 37, 222, 272, 286a, 307, 337, 550, 606, 622,
                638, 703, 705, 744, 815, 829, 881, 890, 897, 938, 975, 980,
                1066, 1116, 1148, 1159, 1194, 1207, 1270, 1287, 1292, 1302,
                1314, 1316, 1342, 1343, 1365, 1371, 1408, 1414, 1421, 1450,

(Con't) South, the [American]--Culture and Heritage of
          1468, 1492, 1516, 1519, 1521, 1531, 1572, 1588, 1590, 1617,
          1623, 1654, 1655, 1666, 1692, 1700, 1701, 1708, 1711, 1725,
          1745, 1772, 1779, 1784, 1799, 1843, 1853, 1871, 1877, 1897,
          1898, 1917, 1948, 1972, 1996, 2039, 2108, 2123, 2131, 2154
     Desegregation in 802, 1207, 1667, 1799, 1917, 2040
     Foreign refugees, and 1207
     Future of 436
     Humor in 314, 333, 362, 477, 573, 575, 631, 654, 674, 678, 737, 755,
          827, 1059, 1195, 1337, 1510, 1655, 1668, 1746, 1766, 1972
     Image of 662, 703, 785, 1116, 1521, 1590
     Industrialization of 874, 1302, 1727, 1884, 1921a
     Landowners 330, 1325, 1333, 1725, 2039, 2625
     Literary tradition 783, 932, 975, 1116, 1174, 1287, 1414, 1489, 1492,
          1617, 1623, 1700, 1701, 1716, 1897
     1950s, the 31, 68a, 126, 206, 219, 239, 273, 323, 328, 380, 455, 592,
          676, 781, 820, 917, 939, 1194, 1207, 1211, 1337, 1412, 1421,
          1427, 1559a, 1672, 1762, 1853, 1878, 1897
     Manners in 37, 81, 114, 128, 142, 299, 307, 337, 416, 435, 453, 622,
          638, 660, 661, 731, 792, 793, 929, 936, 1104, 1116, 1217,
          1258, 1271, 1342, 1408, 1477, 1531, 1578, 1587, 1637, 1654,
          1671, 1677, 1700, 1735, 1819, 1883, 1965, 2008, 2108, 2277
     New South, the 31, 136, 181, 228, 323, 436, 455, 542, 544, 622, 676,
          732, 744, 1700, 1727, 1746, 1853, 1897, 2033, 2154
     Northerners in 938, 1270, 1884, 2039
     Nostalgia for 30, 219, 231, 323, 550, 638, 1111, 1291, 1521, 2125
     Old South 41, 217, 676, 1267, 1314, 1521, 2025, 2125
     Peculiarities of 79, 207, 638, 781, 815, 881, 1342, 1531, 1588, 1590,
          1623, 1700, 1701, 1784, 1799
     Phony 1951
     Poor whites in, 353, 549, 550, 809, 939, 1215, 1899, 1996, 2311
     Post-Civil War 80, 815, 890, 1104, 1517
     Post-World War II 114, 138, 219, 228, 288, 323, 329, 544, 601, 703,
          781, 783, 784, 823, 835, 939, 980, 1207, 1230, 1249, 1302,
          1365, 1412, 1491, 1617, 1623, 1700, 1712, 1727, 1775, 1782,
          1784, 1817, 1833, 1851, 1853, 1861, 1897, 1907, 1913, 1917,
          2024
     Race in the 337, 353, 380, 435, 436, 444, 455, 527, 622, 638, 765, 781,
          809, 897, 1090, 1195, 1203, 1347, 1407, 1601, 1671, 1683,
          1700, 1799, 1817, 2040
     Racists in 809, 1671, 1701
     Religion in the 175, 239, 267, 272, 281, 318, 328, 337, 638, 717, 846,
          964, 1082, 1116, 1127, 1216, 1655, 1666, 1668, 1669, 1708,
          1711, 1729, 1772, 1779, 1784, 1877, 1897, 1972
     Rural 131, 217, 353, 380, 939, 977, 1021, 1048, 1078, 1194, 1253,
          1293, 1378, 1379, 1412, 1899, 1972

(Con't) South, the [American]--Culture and Heritage of

Segregation in 622, 1667, 1671, 1917, 2040

Setting, as 175, 206, 272, 301, 321, 328, 355, 613, 785, 975, 1116,
1230, 1342, 1371, 1414, 1521, 1615a, 1692, 1700, 1777,
1784, 1961, 2123

Slavery in 822

Social stratification in 676, 705, 733, 744, 747, 802, 897, 980, 1207,
1227, 1527, 1559a, 1623, 1691, 1700, 1701, 1773, 1799,
1861, 1976, 1977, 2040, 2333, 2360, 2611

Story-telling in 332, 587, 1116, 1126, 1204, 1279, 1287, 1427, 1547,
1813, 1871, 1982, 2050, 2060

See also Characters--types of--Southern

See also Christianity--Southern history and

See also Georgia

See also Identity--Southern

See also Intellectual(s)--Southern Agrarian

See also Region

See also Southern literature

Southern agrarian 169a, 356, 564, 673, 938, 939, 1005, 1194, 1302, 1430, 1521,
1586, 1669, 1759, 1799, 1853, 1871, 1883, 1884, 2061, 2179, 2348

See also Intellectual(s)--southern agrarian

Southern Cross 1674

Southern literature 41, 180, 206, 222, 260, 303, 323, 332, 357, 399, 428, 452,
468, 483, 532, 533, 536, 542, 556, 559, 561, 575, 662, 703, 746, 747,
748, 754, 774, 781, 783, 802, 809, 813, 820, 847, 874, 876, 883, 932,
938, 939, 972, 975, 1044, 1080, 1116, 1174, 1195, 1215, 1230, 1287,
1291, 1302, 1316, 1342, 1343, 1365, 1378, 1379, 1406, 1414, 1426,
1429, 1433, 1489, 1492, 1519, 1536, 1623, 1653, 1699a, 1700, 1701,
1708, 1711, 1712, 1716, 1745, 1748, 1782, 1784, 1797, 1799, 1809,
1817, 1830, 1835, 1850, 1853, 1871, 1875, 1877, 1885, 1897, 1932,
1940, 1948, 2004, 2026, 2034, 2036, 2061, 2123, 2168, 2169, 2272,
2540, 2566, 2631

See also Grotesque, the--Southern fiction and

Southern speech 223, 230, 281, 333, 399, 454, 468, 475, 477, 501, 511, 534,
546, 548, 549, 557, 581, 595, 643, 666, 800, 850, 896, 897, 936, 1041,
1258, 1287, 1316, 1378, 1427, 1452, 1530, 1533, 1610, 1664, 1709,
1713, 1750, 1847, 1874, 1877, 1915, 2021, 2027, 2130, 2131, 2168

Nigger [the word] 557, 561, 572, 788, 1093, 1187, 1231, 1335, 1387a,
1527, 1607a, 1671, 1714

Southerners, types of 231, 272, 286a, 299, 323, 399, 453, 550, 619, 638, 660,
744, 781, 809, 939, 1116, 1127, 1344, 1408, 1445, 1531, 1666, 1700,
1711, 1784, 1799, 1877, 1897, 1972, 2039

See also Identity--Southern

See also O'Connor, Flannery--Southerner, as a

Space

See Style--space, use of

The Spectrum
> *See* Georgia College & State University--*The Spectrum*
Spelling
> *See* Style--spelling, use of
Spring Hill College [Mobile, Ala.] 1087
Stone Mountain Park [Atlanta, Ga.] 1219
"A Stroke of Good Fortune" 50a, 75b, 80, 318, 465, 529, 595, 676, 812, 813,
> 814, 826, 972, 973, 991, 1004, 1028, 1052, 1291a, 1559a, 1563, 1585,
> 1632, 1722, 1745, 1869, 1923, 1982, 1998a, 2701
> *See also* Characters, O'Connor's--specific--Hill, Ruby
Structure.
> *See* Style--narrative structure, use of
Style, [Flannery O'Connor's] 64, 547, 1052, 2361, 2458, 2495
> Advertising and marketing, use of 126, 929, 1510, 1642
> Aggression, use of 814, 2021, 2039
> Alienation, use of 142, 457, 617a, 576, 732, 816, 863, 897, 1005, 1053,
>> 1415, 1531, 1595, 1750, 1782, 1799, 1812, 1823, 1881, 1997,
>> 2041, 2043, 2070, 2102, 2107, 2453, 2520, 2536, 2648
> Allegory, use of 128, 162, 676, 890, 921, 936, 939, 1054, 1060, 1439,
>> 1485, 1631, 1635, 1673, 1733, 1735, 1758, 1760, 1780, 1791,
>> 1796, 1814, 1945, 1949, 1962, 1998, 2168
> Allusion, use of 96, 183, 501, 795, 898, 1320, 1422, 1474, 1501, 1516,
>> 1648, 1664, 1950, 1955, 1968, 1977, 1992, 2046
>> Biblical 53, 55, 172, 246, 332, 492, 493, 608, 610, 614, 668,
>>> 727, 800, 926, 1474, 1578, 1648, 1953, 2046, 2177
> Ambiguity, use of 868, 974, 1140, 1268, 1372, 1408, 1439, 1506,
>> 1886, 1962, 2062, 2351, 2647
> Anagrams, use of 64
> Antagonism, use of 253, 2457
> Anxiety, use of 255, 445, 888, 1153, 1734, 1906, 2040
> Apocalyptic context, use of 164a, 818, 987, 1462, 1720, 1866, 1908,
>> 2623
> "as if" constructions, use of 55, 56, 342, 374, 501, 1011, 1225, 2573
> Bizarre, use of the 53, 103, 175, 203, 218, 302, 710, 908, 1007, 1302,
>> 1577, 1801, 1962
> Blasphemy, use of 41, 97, 703, 1356, 1500
> Carnival, use of 41, 93, 1315, 1604, 1801, 2461
> Christian mystery, use of 53, 60, 73, 81, 85, 107, 114, 130, 131, 134,
>> 142, 160, 166, 174a, 181, 185, 219, 237, 247, 260, 274, 281,
>> 305, 321, 328, 333, 337, 362, 392, 395, 398, 401, 403, 407,
>> 440, 445, 446, 449, 457, 469, 483, 493, 523, 549, 575, 608,
>> 647, 669, 697, 706, 716, 720, 727, 729, 739, 740, 743, 754,
>> 796, 800, 815, 832, 838, 840, 851, 860, 887, 888, 893, 901,
>> 908, 921, 940, 943, 966, 996, 998, 1006, 1008, 1010, 1053,
>> 1103, 1109, 1111, 1116, 1124, 1126, 1129a, 1137, 1150,
>> 1181, 1204, 1217, 1225, 1237, 1270, 1271, 1276, 1299,

(Con't) Style, [Flannery O'Connor's]--Christian Mystery, Use of
1320a, 1340, 1348, 1356, 1396, 1418, 1435, 1436, 1437a, 1439, 1477, 1482, 1496, 1498, 1500, 1508, 1525, 1535, 1556, 1570, 1578, 1587, 1596, 1608, 1620, 1654, 1677, 1723, 1724, 1740, 1744, 1786, 1804, 1814, 1819, 1839, 1847, 1848, 1850, 1853, 1858, 1889, 1902, 1909, 1910, 1920, 1931, 1935, 1943, 1944, 1945, 1949, 1953, 1958, 1977, 1982, 1983, 1991, 2007a, 2018, 2027, 2034, 2041, 2043, 2075, 2084, 2168, 2224, 2277, 2365, 2472, 2480, 2508, 2517, 2519, 2562, 2668, 2696

Clichés, use of 384, 740, 1033, 1116, 1286, 1481, 1517, 1530, 1857
Comedy
    See Comedy, O'Connor's work as
Compassion, use of 1205, 1215, 1339, 1376, 1474, 1771, 2023
Cycles and patterns, use of 125, 275, 298, 495, 559, 564, 580, 595, 597, 599, 608, 617a, 765, 766, 814, 850, 864, 889, 897, 925, 956, 967, 977, 985, 998, 1011, 1052, 1127, 1130, 1268, 1541, 1612, 1626, 1659, 1673, 1719, 1779, 1798, 1805, 1850, 1869, 1905, 1935, 1951, 2010, 2026, 2033, 2313, 2469, 2528
Death, use of 255, 300, 349, 389, 468a, 512, 580, 597, 608, 622, 668, 669, 697, 711, 757, 778, 812, 864, 887, 906, 1006, 1031, 1054, 1060, 1078, 1135, 1163, 1168, 1179, 1186, 1204, 1325, 1384, 1403, 1409, 1451, 1497, 1551, 1595, 1610, 1638, 1660, 1669, 1693, 1702, 1809, 1850, 1857, 1906, 1980, 2051, 2073, 2075, 2087, 2134, 2172, 2197, 2444
Determinism, use of 272, 1106, 2208, 2220, 2255, 2321
Distortion, use of 53, 73, 454, 457, 601, 657, 734, 758, 775, 802, 851, 884, 1120, 1152, 1237, 1252, 1339, 1433, 1491, 1519, 1573, 1636, 1823, 1841, 1866, 1883, 1886, 1943, 1951, 2034, 2536, 2585, 2615
Evolution, use of 1968
Exaggeration, use of 53, 67, 203, 311, 454, 839, 1409, 1433, 1517, 1759, 1899, 1972
Fable, use of 345
Families, use of 617a, 1285, 1559a, 1764, 1822, 2193, 2325, 2520
    Abusive 125, 169a
    Aristocratic, 874, 898
    Fragmented 951, 1299, 1741
Father-son communication, use of 777, 1395, 2134
Fear, use of 611, 810, 892, 1561, 1916, 2563
Fragmentation, use of 547, 1025
Free will, use of 450, 779, 944, 1025, 1029, 1030, 1100, 1921, 1944, 1961, 2105, 2543
Gaps and vacancy, use of 1293
Gestures, use of 56, 73, 1168, 1601, 1677, 1685, 1690, 1693, 2013, 2383

(Con't) Style [Flannery O'Connor's]
    Grace, use of
        See Grace, action of
    Grammar, use of 61, 708, 752, 763, 850, 1375, 1915
    Heresy, use of 1435, 1437a
    Heteroglossia, use of 762
    Homelessness, use of 1805, 1927, 2154
    Hope, use of 113, 402, 838, 855, 1026, 1834, 1843, 1908
    Humiliation, use of 722, 811, 1867
    Humor
        See Comedy, O'Connor's work as
    Ignorance, use of 157, 1387a, 1573
    Illusion, use of 800, 1004, 1184, 1885
    Inference, use of 76
    Initiation, use of 253, 355, 529, 531, 1328, 1837, 1839, 1850, 1886, 1921, 2033, 2151, 2498
    Innocence, use of 160, 394, 395, 759, 919, 1111, 1339, 1359, 1393, 1635, 1787, 2151, 2184, 2282, 2468
    Irony, use of 55, 56, 98a, 116, 121, 157, 164, 259, 273, 285, 319, 350, 352, 396, 422, 501, 587, 592, 654, 705, 706, 737, 762, 766, 795, 800b, 820, 832a, 839, 840, 844, 890, 897, 931, 956, 989, 1060, 1073, 1179, 1181, 1200, 1203, 1297, 1329, 1358, 1365, 1372, 1385, 1393, 1394, 1411, 1433, 1561, 1574, 1605, 1662, 1689, 1698, 1722, 1729, 1750, 1758, 1838, 1869, 1872, 1873, 1895, 1903, 1920, 1925, 1938, 1949, 1962, 1972, 1978, 1988, 2121, 2171, 2177, 2210, 2270, 2308, 2352, 2357, 2451, 2454, 2552, 2585, 2663, 2677
    Isolation, use of 668, 953, 974, 1169, 1230, 1520r, 1554, 1741, 1770, 1782, 1812, 1959, 2469
    Knowledge, use of 160, 501, 706, 708, 953, 962, 974, 989, 1011, 1093, 1203, 1401, 1753, 1901, 1943, 2041, 2510
    Laughter, use of 178, 195, 280, 364, 937, 1315
    Limitation, use of 2311
    Manners, use of 37, 128, 142, 416, 622, 638, 661, 731, 793, 936, 1104, 1116, 1217, 1258, 1271, 1477, 1531, 1578, 1587, 1637, 1654, 1671, 1677, 1723, 1735, 1819, 1883, 1935, 1965, 1982, 2008, 2090, 2178, 2277, 2365
    Materialism, use of 131, 191, 246, 263, 329, 367, 418, 529, 599, 669, 741, 770, 865, 874, 950, 980, 1051, 1113, 1600, 1615, 1722, 1750, 1963, 1964, 2430
    Medieval gothic, use of 102, 128, 159, 184, 262, 312, 697, 743, 785, 1356, 1735, 1801, 1944, 1949, 1961, 2106
    Mercy, divine 111, 112, 128, 193, 274, 331, 405, 576, 608, 892, 986, 1033, 1037, 1099, 1179, 1205, 1425, 1437, 1548, 1667, 1812, 1814, 2507
    Metaphor, use of 56, 64, 76, 161, 179, 254, 256, 275, 302, 342, 365,

(Con't) Style, [Flannery O'Connor's]--Metaphor, Use of
418, 523, 541, 599, 729, 762, 772, 778, 800, 838, 860, 878,
879, 955, 1041, 1056, 1061r, 1089, 1100, 1109, 1141, 1150a,
1203, 1278, 1312, 1378, 1441, 1576, 1719, 1724, 1728, 1748,
1775, 1805, 1850, 1855, 1862, 1869, 1940, 1950, 1964, 1968,
2033, 2104

Metonymy, use of 256

Mimicry, use of 275

Mirroring devices, use of 275, 444, 658, 829, 896, 955, 973, 1057,
1080, 1230, 1273, 1295, 2051, 2112

Mother-child relationships, use of 80, 125, 169a, 166, 244, 307, 472,
523, 580, 617a, 670, 731, 758, 812, 814, 864, 935, 954, 1156,
1168, 1217, 1299, 1320, 1384, 1421, 1530, 1623, 1626, 1637,
2000, 2162, 2205, 2332, 2344, 2584, 2682

Motifs and archetypes, use of 75b, 316, 437, 550, 716, 887, 977, 990,
1092, 1307, 1359, 1411, 1419, 1608, 1719, 1789, 1791, 1794,
1900, 1905, 1935, 1970, 2215, 2285, 2292, 2456

Characters, archetypal 1307, 1379, 1419, 1659, 1737, 1738,
1743, 1762, 1767, 1777, 1805, 1855, 1875, 1901,
1974, 1976, 2005

Child and childhood motif 177, 257, 550, 580, 669, 1283,
1337, 1421, 1745, 1812, 1867, 2000, 2229, 2242,
2244, 2264, 2288, 2296, 2368, 2376, 2406, 2410,
2412, 2413, 2448, 2500, 2526, 2528, 2557, 2651

Darwinian 1968

Displaced persons 1615, 2065, 2285, 2314, 2654

Doppleganger motif 116, 1409, 1794, 2164, 2433

Double motif 1939, 1941, 2015, 2021, 2042, 2063, 2115
2502, 2503

See also Characters--types of--double(s)

Dream motifs 1927

"Everyman" motif 888

Feeder motif 1585, 1586, 2005

Feminine 75b, 1970, 2038, 2657

Folk motifs 1766

Grace and deliverance motif 1468, 1576, 1585, 1743, 1846,
1881, 1899, 1903, 1921, 1930, 2393

Illness 1576, 1979, 2020, 2292, 2328

Jonah motif 807

Journey 1900, 1919, 2549

Light-shadow motif 1141, 1161, 1328, 1454, 1794, 1900,
2700a

Medieval 184, 262, 312, 697, 785, 1356, 1735, 1801, 1944,
1949, 1961, 2106, 2168

"Midday crisis" motif [sun motif] 134, 156, 359, 921, 959,
1396, 1927, 2350

(Con't) Style, [Flannery O'Connor's]--Motifs and Archetypes, Use of
        Prophet motif 164a, 1437a, 2456, 2476, 2590
        Quest motif 32, 34, 106, 144, 162, 204, 258, 395, 396, 404,
            431, 439, 486, 632, 717, 718, 931, 965, 1080, 1169,
            1200, 1229, 1230, 1292, 1348, 1378, 1379, 1408,
            1410, 1461, 1485, 1719, 1725, 1762, 1781, 1791,
            1796, 1837, 1839, 1855, 1900, 1901, 1919, 1971,
            1998, 2134, 2154, 2207, 2240, 2260, 2316, 2451,
            2463, 2469, 2556, 2704
        Shadow figure 1794
        Swine motif 1257, 1261, 1340
        Taboo motif 477
        Trickster motif 55, 398, 477, 800, 1476, 1862
        Would-be writers 716, 1371
    Music, use of 465, 738, 1013, 2115
    Mutilation, use of 638, 884, 1384
    Names and naming techniques, use of 64, 106, 107, 117, 259, 270, 281,
        350, 378, 420, 491, 492, 493, 595, 681, 683, 722, 735, 759,
        761, 795, 840, 898, 912, 985, 1079, 1130, 1257, 1265, 1303,
        1325, 1482, 1516, 1533, 1740, 2015, 2019, 2046, 2053, 2064
    Narrative structure, use of 121, 139, 217, 262, 273, 281, 540, 586, 587,
        590, 642, 670, 683, 704, 706, 762, 800, 802, 918, 956, 977,
        1058, 1080, 1096, 1343, 1404, 1411, 1486, 1638, 1690, 1693,
        1702, 1724, 1736, 1737, 1804, 1809, 1828, 1837, 1850, 1853,
        1855, 1862, 1866, 1869, 1894, 1900, 1916, 1924, 1931, 1948,
        1970, 1995, 2271, 2358, 2381, 2399, 2518, 2552, 2596, 2636
        Affirmative 956
        Ambiguity and 1506, 2351, 2647
        Circular 55, 216, 360, 1203
        Distance 2568
        Masculine 1948
        Mystic 965, 1129a, 1225, 1764, 1766, 1887, 1893, 1900,
            2084, 2479, 2674
    Nature, use of 934, 974, 1159, 1333, 1396, 1477, 1588, 1609, 1668,
        2066, 2303, 2402,
    Negation, use of 64, 116, 450, 486, 657, 707, 775, 800, 896, 1092,
        1915
    Negative space theory, use of 103, 156, 486, 1980
    Nihilism, use of 42a, 268, 774, 934, 1161, 1216, 1239, 1530, 1561,
        1670, 1812, 1887, 1893, 1962, 2046, 2107, 2660
    Nonsense, use of 1402
    Nonverbal techniques, use of 1282, 1946
    Omission, use of 802
    Opposites, use of 1758
    Parables, use of 60, 245, 345, 352, 374, 785, 878, 920, 940, 1034,
        1141, 1179, 1304, 1353, 1379, 1497, 1528, 1760, 1779, 2305,

(Con't) Style, [Flannery O'Connor's]--Motifs and Archetypes--Parables, Use of
2450, 2637, 2638, 2658
Paradigms, use of 653, 1088, 1766, 1815, 1816, 1867, 1970
Paradox, use of 547, 550, 657, 820, 901, 965, 1223, 1229, 1496, 1758,
1863, 1886, 1891, 1961, 2177, 2388, 2508, 2570, 2577, 2647
Parody, use of 54, 275, 331, 401, 502, 551, 881, 931, 1266, 1337,
1341, 1445, 1470a, 1517, 1700, 1847, 2432
Pity, use of 1561, 1774
Point of view, use of 139, 498, 501, 507, 763, 783, 1156, 1486, 1506,
1659, 1702, 1864, 2169, 2338, 2414
Polarization, use of 1025
Popular sayings, use of 740, 1521
Poverty, use of 2311
Power and powerlessness, use of 640, 916, 1005, 1891, 2131
Prejudice, use of 157, 253, 832a, 1393, 1729
Pride, use of 157, 191, 244, 253, 348, 457, 495, 529, 581, 599, 611,
722, 734, 939, 985, 1005, 1049, 1053, 1093, 1099, 1107,
1163, 1205, 1282, 1393, 1497, 1530, 1573, 1589, 1725, 1729,
2011, 2047, 2085, 2346, 2592
Processions, use of 1796
Proverbs, use of 285, 734, 1286
Protestant election, use of 162, 655, 1930, 1947
Punishment, use of 776
Puns, use of 738, 1510
Rebellion, use of 611, 618, 1850
Reconciliation, use of 321, 809, 1573
Repetition, use of 348, 617a, 704, 772, 1086, 1604, 1605, 1798
Retribution, use of 368, 1792
Revelation, use of 1033, 1053, 1109, 1216, 1284, 1348, 1441, 1485,
1500, 1535, 1536, 1698, 1778, 1838, 1845, 1848, 1900, 2026,
2041, 2056, 2079, 2131, 2195, 2242, 2314, 2360, 2482, 2624
Reversal, use of 389, 592, 1034, 1365, 1409, 1710, 1869
Rhetorical devices, use of 76, 106, 271, 762, 830, 869, 918, 1046,
1093, 1441, 1486, 1596, 1958, 1962, 1991, 2171, 2351, 2358
Rites of passage, use of 1839, 1850, 1921, 2686a
Rituals, use of 75b, 144, 169, 360, 599, 619, 668, 680, 770, 811, 864,
990, 1014, 1159, 1702, 1706, 1719, 1723, 1733, 1796, 1837,
1839, 1850, 1908, 1921, 1970, 2572
Sadism, use of 175, 811, 1701
Sarcasm, use of 766
Seduction, use of 80, 1021, 1176, 1420, 1637, 2046, 1209
Sexuality, use of 80, 116, 255, 287, 350, 420, 454, 505, 599, 606,
668, 722, 763, 778, 789, 813, 818, 826, 887, 906, 934, 954,
974, 1021, 1229, 1282, 1342, 1396, 1408, 1420, 1510, 1552,
1601, 1627, 1669, 1728, 1729, 1812, 1886, 2046, 2109
Shame, use of 331

(Con't) Style, [Flannery O'Connor's]--Motifs and Archetypes, use of
    Shock, use of 50a, 164, 176, 179, 216, 270, 477, 489, 574, 612, 741,
        1008, 1033, 1086, 1104, 1109, 1112, 1252, 1295, 1372, 1556,
        1557, 1573, 1660, 1758, 1778, 1835, 1842, 1852, 1866, 1910,
        1921, 1931, 1986, 1998, 2043, 2395
    Signatures, use of 1222
    Signification, use of 549, 858, 864, 897, 916, 917, 922, 966, 1011,
        1222, 1278, 1482, 1740, 1891, 2088
    Silence, use of 1496, 1535, 1587, 1748, 1981, 2105, 2500, 2644
    Similes, use of 50, 73, 76, 96, 101, 130, 176, 198, 211, 253, 302, 312,
        314, 368, 371, 395, 406, 501, 529, 551, 592, 651, 722, 754,
        804, 811, 822, 840, 851, 852, 857, 867,878, 879, 887, 898,
        908, 974, 1010, 1033, 1041, 1049, 1056, 1082, 1116, 1135,
        1149, 1172, 1189, 1205, 1260, 1288, 1299, 1300, 1304, 1393,
        1424, 1449, 1527, 1605, 1631, 1719, 1722, 1725, 1739, 1750,
        1755, 1766, 1779, 1809, 1823, 1869, 1898, 1926, 1987, 2177,
        2280, 2346, 2349, 2594
    Slogans, use of 740
    Smugness, use of 631
    Social status, use of 350, 443, 455, 548, 599, 613, 618, 638, 640, 676,
        705, 733, 744, 747, 802, 896, 897, 980, 1005, 1207, 1227,
        1527, 1559a, 1564, 1691, 1701, 1773, 1861, 1976, 1977,
        2040, 2333, 2360, 2611
        See also Middle-class respectability
    Sorrow, use of 864
    Space, use of 156, 859, 869, 1060, 1348, 1985
    Spelling, use of 57, 75, 1402, 1648
    Stupidity, use of 794, 885
    Suffering, use of 43, 64, 300, 358, 379, 576, 603, 611, 734, 931, 1037,
        1358, 1485, 1497, 1631, 1737, 1766, 1896, 1901, 1921, 1926,
        1930, 1954, 2154, 2245a
        See also O'Connor, Flannery--views and opinions of--suffering
    Suppression, use of 814
    Tableaux 1796
    Time, use of 360, 378, 595, 676, 775, 802, 859, 1052, 1159, 1280,
        1339, 1479, 1650, 1768, 1789, 1850, 1898, 1915, 2091, 2548,
        2550
    Topical, the 802, 1601
    Touch, use of 1283
    Truth the, use of 107, 457, 581, 588, 608, 657, 785, 812, 816, 837, 867,
        868, 937, 953, 977, 1015, 1026, 1072, 1152, 1213, 1229,
        1270, 1333, 1425, 1517, 1650, 1730, 1814, 1891, 1953, 1961,
        2021, 2059, 2134, 2309, 2484, 2555, 2700
    Unconscious, the 116, 286a, 990, 1057, 1340, 1372, 1576
    Understatement, use of 298, 1131
    Value systems, use of 1855, 1917, 2039

(Con't) Style, [Flannery O'Connor's]--Motifs and Archetypes, Use of
        Vengeance, use of 1338
        Victims, use of 257, 1054, 1839, 1855, 2296, 2492, 2681
        Word choice, use of 161, 657, 922, 966, 1025, 1073, 1111, 1135, 1402,
            1481, 1482, 1496, 1530, 1648
Suffering
        See Style--suffering, use of
        See also O'Connor, Flannery--views and opinions of--suffering
Sun
        See Symbols and images--sun
        See also Place--depiction of--sun
        See also Style--motifs and archetypes--"midday crisis" motif
Supernatural
        See Symbols and images--supernatural
Symbols and images 34, 37, 45, 52, 61, 64, 76, 94, 102, 128, 137, 150, 161, 169,
        177, 204, 211, 236, 262, 265, 268, 284, 288, 305, 316, 319, 333, 341,
        345, 349, 351, 353, 358, 376, 394, 395, 418, 427, 454, 489, 505, 515,
        523, 527, 595, 599, 610, 615, 618, 626, 771, 778, 789, 800, 811, 842,
        858, 889, 916, 925, 937, 967, 974, 989, 990, 1009, 1015, 1054, 1061r,
        1070, 1091, 1109, 1204, 1208, 1222, 1224, 1229, 1267, 1291, 1335,
        1338, 1340, 1345, 1350, 1358, 1396, 1404, 1405, 1427, 1433, 1455,
        1474, 1481, 1510, 1530, 1533, 1608, 1609, 1719, 1729, 1758, 1777,
        1786, 1789, 1830, 1841, 1850, 1869, 1874, 1900, 1908, 1915, 1919,
        1951, 1968, 2035, 2052, 2088, 2158, 2168, 2177, 2198, 2271, 2323,
        2467, 2707
        Specific types of
        Abstract 472, 747, 932, 1093, 1208
        Absurd 901, 1225, 1353, 1372, 1376, 1415, 1517, 1519, 1587, 1918,
            1986, 2135, 2349, 2620
        Accident 541
        Action 575, 869, 884, 897, 1054, 1094, 1104, 1105, 1133, 1486, 2045,
            2330
        Affliction 407, 1654
        American Dream, the 164a, 618, 1153, 1337
        Angels 1437a
        Animal 95, 181, 275, 364, 365, 414, 440, 454, 652, 827, 858a, 884,
            1094, 1257, 1278, 1281, 1300, 1358, 1533, 1717a, 1841,
            2062, 2104, 2189, 2529
            Bird 776, 785, 1168, 1498, 2554
            Bull 609, 615, 838, 1054, 1264, 1273, 1338, 1350, 1373,
                1396, 1419, 1576
            Cow 1373
            Dog 365, 776
            Gorilla 143, 770, 776, 990, 1335, 1361, 1968
            Hog 1130, 1297, 1340, 1437, 1481
            Lion 610

(Con't) Symbols and Images--Animal

        Peacocks 123, 298, 485, 500, 554, 765, 774, 778, 786, 881,
            925, 980, 1009, 1016, 1018, 1137, 1298, 1384,
            1615a, 2633

        Snake 776

        Werewolf 1576

        Wolf 827

Ant lion 1532

Apocalyptic 164a, 1908, 2623

Artificial nigger [statue] 137, 305, 395, 479, 501, 523, 527, 549, 557,
    610, 931, 1176, 1203, 1359, 1393, 1485, 1521

Atomic bomb 1907

Automobile 73, 255, 288, 364, 406, 516, 591, 674, 805, 874, 963,
    1005, 1060, 1064, 1131, 1229, 1348, 1409, 1510, 1532, 1564,
    1775, 1795, 1952, 2046, 2110, 2175, 2327

Banal(ity) 388, 703, 977, 1159, 1521, 1992, 2517

Baptism 128, 145, 198, 345, 599, 680, 858, 966, 1404, 1507, 1666,
    1723, 1837, 2474

Beauty 977, 1009, 1402, 2014

Biblical 137, 246, 259, 332, 492, 608, 610, 614, 727, 1072, 1648,
    1841, 1953, 2177, 2194

Bigot 550, 1257

Birth 972, 973

Blood 617a, 800, 833, 985, 1476, 2062, 2278, 2354

Body parts 126, 1785

Bottle-opener 889, 1521

Boundaries 549, 611, 613, 618, 708, 785, 838, 1927

Boxing ring 618

Bread 128, 1586

Brutal 617

Bullet, silver 1576

Burial 599, 2108, 2110

Caricature 37, 271, 311, 326, 550, 592, 599, 619, 638, 674, 758, 1278,
    1293

Castration 864

Cave 1141

Charity 135, 403, 793, 800b, 926, 1048, 1049, 1094, 1300, 1607a,
    1677

Child[ren] 177, 257, 316, 479, 500, 550, 580, 669, 734, 763, 814,
    1088, 1283, 1285, 1337, 1421, 1628, 1727, 1729, 1812, 1867,
    2000, 2216, 2229, 2242, 2244, 2264, 2288, 2296, 2368, 2376,
    2406, 2410, 2412, 2448, 2500, 2526, 2528, 2557, 2651, 2680

Christ, Jesus 130, 131, 134, 166, 201, 211, 247, 268, 493, 643, 720,
    735, 838, 888, 943, 1040, 1054, 1056, 1204, 1299, 1350,
    1435, 1436, 1608, 2052, 2341
    See also Christ, Jesus--image of

(Con't) Symbols and Images

Christian 652, 720, 735, 767, 807, 838, 840, 887, 1056, 1179, 1299,
        1427, 1436, 1498, 1500, 1635, 1638, 1719, 1944, 1945
Cigarette 669
City(scape) 605, 718, 939, 1021, 1253, 1363, 1378, 1379, 1393, 1396,
        1458, 1459, 1461, 1720, 1754, 1799, 1837, 1853, 2111, 2275,
        2348
Class structure 263, 446a, 800b, 1159, 1215, 1229, 1337, 1527, 1601,
        1699a, 1700, 1725, 1729, 1817, 1851, 1861, 1963, 2081,
        2094, 2131, 2226, 2324
Cleanliness 255, 1474
Clothing 778, 889, 1278, 1699a, 1719, 1837
Coca-Cola 453
Color 156, 374, 959, 985, 1006, 1092, 1131, 1282, 1454, 2110
Comic 364, 407, 477, 484, 543, 581, 668, 692, 810, 827, 842, 888,
        937, 939, 975, 1004, 1012, 1081, 1144, 1152, 1159, 1225,
        1253, 1293, 1546, 1547, 1668, 1696, 1700, 1854, 1899, 1906,
        1925, 1982, 2002, 2372
Community 254, 399, 401, 444, 585, 597, 792, 897, 962, 1102, 1104,
        1107, 1113, 1116, 1278, 1342, 1345, 1459, 1462, 1568, 1623,
        1769, 1799, 1822, 1823, 1846, 1883, 1890, 1897, 1917, 1943,
        2125, 2212, 2447
Compulsion 457, 1474, 1901
Control 472, 1088, 1891
Corsage 1521
Country(side), the 395, 426, 605, 703, 1378, 1379, 1725, 2111
Cross 134, 611, 781, 1186
Cross tattoo 840, 1012, 1148, 1268, 1482, 1618
Darkness 617a, 739, 939, 1040, 1587, 1900, 2700a
Darwinian universe 181, 1968
Death camp 1519, 1669
Decadence 206
Deformity 312, 667, 1010, 1343, 1426, 1435, 1577, 1655, 1702, 1841,
        1899, 2041, 2050, 2090
Demonic 321, 378, 612, 613, 818, 962, 1136, 1335, 1511, 1512, 1839
Dependence 809, 954, 1292, 2134
Desert 50a, 607, 612, 1444
Destruction 1764
Detachment 2320
Detail 2110
Dignity 613
Dirt 1699a
Disability 94, 541, 775, 1291a, 1451, 1793, 1940
Disease 617a, 1291a
Displaced persons 286a, 353, 485, 642, 1207, 1615, 1902, 2004, 2043,
        2154, 2285, 2314, 2654

(Con't) Symbols and Images

    Displacement 185, 642, 774, 1207, 1600, 1900, 1902, 1927, 1975,
        2004, 2043, 2065, 2291, 2314

    Disruption 585

    Divine 515, 608, 779, 990, 1010, 1012, 1037, 1437, 1728, 2107

    Division 1927

    Doodlebug 1532

    Dragon 1079, 1277, 1570, 1631, 1731, 2073, 2131, 2190, 2209, 2261

    Dreams 858a, 980, 1058, 1402, 1927, 2525

    Dualism 29, 396, 652, 754, 778, 1092, 1609, 1846, 1860, 1863, 1943,
        2664a

    Earth 889, 921, 1350, 1837

    Eating 955, 1706

    Echoing voices 164a, 174, 198, 973, 1029, 1266, 1393, 1648, 1748,
        1763

    Entrapment 973, 1812

    Epiphany 268, 395, 495, 1111, 1137, 1284, 1312, 1350, 1422, 1441,
        1459, 1482, 1798, 1980, 2299, 2341, 2534, 2668

    Eucharist, the 50a, 345, 496, 702, 1032, 1132, 1473, 1598, 1609, 1909,
        2168, 2380

    Eye[sight/seeing] 94, 161, 164, 185, 196, 203, 218, 232, 241, 255, 374,
        391, 431, 477, 505, 554, 555, 576, 585, 595, 602, 657, 679,
        755, 778, 800, 802, 840, 881, 889, 959, 968, 1058, 1060,
        1071, 1073, 1074, 1075, 1088, 1109, 1237, 1279, 1281, 1282,
        1312, 1340, 1348, 1402, 1409, 1411, 1437, 1441, 1500, 1605,
        1638, 1864, 1900, 2046, 2151, 2186, 2379, 2414, 2431

    Faces 311, 342, 973, 2051

    Fairness 1691

    Family 169a, 611, 617a, 778, 951, 1230, 1285, 1333, 1559a, 1654,
        1697, 1741, 1764, 1799, 1822, 1850, 1861, 1964, 2036, 2039,
        2193, 2424, 2520, 2523

    Feminine 75b, 316, 420, 617, 812, 813, 864, 1078, 1124, 1292, 1445,
        1622, 1729, 1820, 1822, 2038, 2652

    Fetishism 255, 419

    Film imagery 185, 286a, 858, 1044

    Fire 680, 800, 889, 1290, 1304, 1340, 1396

    Fish 128, 800

    Flashback 1143

    Florida 394

    Food 955, 1585, 1706, 1900

    Football 618

    Forgiveness 331, 1319, 1635

    Freaks 59a, 136, 157, 178, 203, 211, 361, 364, 475, 505, 617, 703, 812,
        850, 851, 1007, 1080, 1136, 1150, 1172, 1194, 1342, 1343,
        1355, 1601, 1699a, 1766, 1900, 2078

    Games 618

(Con't) Symbols and Images

    Gluttony 859, 955

    Gothic 102, 159, 180, 206, 260, 303, 357, 462, 536, 556, 746, 812,
        813, 820, 972, 1020, 1044, 1089, 1167, 1215, 1230, 1291,
        1343, 1378, 1379, 1536, 1608, 1631, 1748, 1809, 1853, 1932,
        2209, 2241

    Gun 954, 1532, 1533

    Hat 595, 778, 889, 1109, 1208, 1266, 1521

    Holiness 613, 1762

    Holocaust 185, 286a, 353, 404, 597, 632, 638

    Holy Ghost 34, 505, 735, 1762, 2211

    Homogeneous 472

    Horizon 838

    Hyperbole 901, 1596

    Idols 391

    Incest 2354

    Incompleteness 374, 1415

    Incubus 287

    Ironic 259, 319, 350, 352, 396, 501, 654, 705, 706, 737, 766, 890, 931,
        956, 1060, 1073, 1200, 1329, 1358, 1365, 1372, 1385, 1393,
        1394, 1411, 1722, 1838, 2270, 2663

    Jefferson nickel 1224

    Jerome, Saint 262

    John the Baptist 174a

    Jonah 232a

    Jungle, world as 181

    Landscape 1060, 1295, 1325, 1350, 1396, 1725, 1839, 1841, 2052,
        2066, 2243

    Leg(s) 94, 126, 255, 364, 365, 477, 824, 1282, 1402, 1481, 2046, 2327

    Light 156, 281, 342, 739, 959, 1141, 1161, 1328, 1350, 1454, 1600,
        1900, 2084, 2085, 2700a

    Lime 881

    Lincoln penny 1224

    Loneliness 457, 732, 1169, 2593

    Lust 1159, 2109

    Macabre 663, 711

    Marriage 345

    Martyrdom 550, 611, 1551

    Masculine 316, 420, 460, 587, 722, 1292, 1299, 2014, 2652
        See also Male

    Mechanization 542, 544, 874, 1275, 1435, 1727, 1884, 1921a, 2599

    Minstrel 916

    Mirror(s) 444, 658, 896, 973, 1057, 1230, 1273, 1295, 2051, 2112

    Mobility 1005, 1278

    Moonlight 96, 137, 921, 1359, 2350

    Mother(s) 460, 472, 531, 670, 734, 758, 778, 795, 812, 814, 864, 935,

(Con't) Symbols and Images--Mother(s)
                954, 1168, 1217, 1299, 1320, 1384, 1421, 1626, 1745, 2000,
                2005, 2332, 2339, 2344
        "Mother Earth" 864, 1419
        Movement 156, 800, 1006, 1297, 1348, 1843
        Multicultural 693a, 777
        Name(s) 259, 270, 350, 378, 420, 491, 492, 493, 595, 681, 683, 735,
                759, 761, 795, 840, 849, 898, 912, 985, 1079, 1130, 1257,
                1265, 1325, 1482, 1516, 1533, 1740, 2015, 2046, 2053
        Narcissism 501, 1057, 1631
        National 1789
        Natural 959, 1402, 1819, 1918, 2066
        Nightmarish 405
        1950s 1153, 1337, 1412, 1427, 1559a, 1609, 1672, 1762, 1878, 1907
        Ordination 345
        "The Other" 1749, 1910
        Pain 1701
        Pastoral 467, 610, 1622, 2179
        Patriarchal culture 549, 587, 606, 618, 777, 1341, 1445, 1623, 1738,
                1822, 1948, 2162, 2325
        Paul, Saint 232a
        Penance 599
        Phallic 1229
        Piety 618, 1609
        Polemical 1818
        Pool hall 618
        Potato peeler(s) 418, 770, 1521
        Profane situations 599, 1148, 1161, 1278, 1877
        Progress 544, 644, 741, 1005, 1106, 1107, 1727
        Property 255, 1325, 1333, 1341
        Proverbs 285, 734, 1286
        Purgation 599, 1900
        Purse 954
        Racial 444, 466, 536, 549, 557, 588, 606, 622, 678, 802, 1168, 1176,
                1203, 1292, 1335, 1347, 1393, 1500, 1667, 1671, 1683, 1690,
                1700, 1745, 1917, 2173, 2621a
        Rags 1699a
        Rape 80, 274, 722, 818, 952, 1282
        Rats 805
        Realistic 1865
        Reflective 2460
        Rejection 486
        Religious 29, 45, 61, 112, 126, 128, 135, 144, 145, 174, 178, 184, 266,
                272, 281, 318, 324, 493, 595, 632, 735, 818, 828, 831, 887,
                898, 910, 925, 940, 953, 959, 990, 1051, 1054, 1072, 1204,
                1291, 1339, 1384, 1404, 1421, 1427, 1477, 1513, 1844, 1848,

(Con't) Symbols and Images--Religious
       1908, 1909, 1912, 1915, 1972, 2138, 2177, 2330
  Resurrection 201, 1127, 1638
  Roman wall paintings 454
  Sacraments, the 1749, 1779, 1887, 1944, 1949, 2101, 2235
  Sacred 255, 316, 361, 739, 743, 775, 1161, 1278, 1492, 1619r, 1764,
      1986, 2066, 2072
  Sacrificial 248, 617, 864, 1358, 1764, 1981, 2087
  Sainthood 1163, 1921, 2123
  Salesmen 126
  Sambo figures 916, 917
  Seeds 800
  Sexual 826, 887, 906, 954, 973, 974, 1021, 1229, 1282, 1341, 1396,
      1408, 1420, 1510, 1552, 1564, 1601, 1627, 1669, 1728, 1729,
      1812, 1886, 2046, 2109
  Shirt [Bailey's] 1222, 1278
  Shoe(s) 599, 1348, 1521, 1532, 1643, 2347
  Sister 588
  Sky 921, 1419, 1839
  Solitary man, The 73, 1169
  Solitude 613, 857, 887
  "something" 439
  Sound 858a
  South 785
  Star of Bethlehem 1444
  Starvation 676, 955
  Stick 1229
  Succubus 287
  Suits 778
  Sun 134, 156, 359, 505, 615, 778, 921, 959, 980, 1295, 1396, 1474,
      1481, 1576, 1615a, 1927, 2066, 2350
      See also Place--depiction of--sun
      See also Style--motifs and archetypes--"midday crisis" motif
  Superficial 850, 980, 1184, 2184
  Supernatural 386, 457, 887, 963, 1204, 1312, 1354, 1378, 1379, 1383,
      1438, 1503, 1528, 1552, 1564, 1697, 1703, 1768, 1814, 1819,
      1918, 1919, 1920, 1931, 2106
  Superrealism 1493
  Surrealism 454
  Tattoos 179, 202, 261, 268, 345, 381, 480, 493, 683, 717, 807, 840,
      1008, 1012, 1148, 1268, 1436, 1482, 1618, 1929
  Tears 259, 612
  Technology 185, 644, 1586, 1907
  Tomb 973
  Torture 1701
  Train[s] 97, 286a, 523, 597, 651, 1161, 1297, 1348

(Con't) Symbols and Images
  Trees and woods 959, 991, 1284, 1297, 1396, 1474, 1615a, 2052,
      2066, 2067, 2278
  Trespass 591
  True image, our 800
  Underworld, the 2464
  Unicorn 1054
  Violence 29, 43, 54, 73, 97, 100, 103, 111, 112, 113, 114, 128, 131,
      160, 164a, 176, 185, 216, 218, 270, 273, 281, 286a, 300, 348,
      353, 357, 361, 362, 388, 403, 431, 460, 477, 489, 545, 606,
      614, 617a, 622, 659, 668, 683, 720, 722, 754, 762, 767, 775,
      800, 800a, 811, 815, 816, 818, 838, 844, 878, 888, 890, 912,
      967, 977, 1009, 1019, 1033, 1053, 1106, 1127, 1133, 1136,
      1159, 1181, 1186, 1239, 1258, 1273, 1290, 1293, 1314b,
      1325, 1329, 1341, 1350, 1352, 1365, 1376, 1396, 1402, 1409,
      1459, 1462, 1490, 1493, 1536, 1552, 1556, 1558, 1627, 1635,
      1655, 1660, 1684, 1696, 1701, 1702, 1719, 1720, 1730, 1737,
      1758, 1773, 1778, 1798, 1833, 1835, 1837, 1842, 1854, 1860,
      1865, 1868, 1878, 1884, 1890, 1904, 1921, 1927, 1930, 1944,
      1955, 1959, 1985, 2003, 2027, 2028, 2034, 2049, 2070, 2084,
      2086, 2090, 2123, 2180, 2246, 2265, 2307, 2313, 2314, 2370,
      2394, 2396, 2409, 2449, 2530, 2536, 2558, 2572, 2585, 2593,
      2628, 2634, 2661, 2686, 2686a
  Water 680, 889, 1130, 1396, 2106
  Watermelon 453
  Wholeness 1919, 2588
  Womb 973
  Women 587, 722, 973, 1078, 1124, 1127, 1227, 1275, 1299, 1330,
      1341, 1408, 1421, 1445, 1474, 1527, 1559a, 1568, 1625,
      1627, 1631, 1637, 1738, 1750, 1820, 1822, 1867, 1886, 1925,
      1976, 2014, 2070, 2162, 2373, 2374, 2430, 2621, 2632, 2645
  World, the 818, 908, 937, 1048, 1060, 1109, 1135, 1363, 1530,
      1636, 1783, 1869, 1933, 2062, 2106
  YWCA 1267

Tattoos
  See Symbols and images--tattoos
Teaching Flannery O'Connor's works 167, 281, 347, 376, 469, 489, 496, 543,
      555, 557, 631, 648, 827, 966, 1018, 1023, 1048, 1093, 1218a, 1223,
      1227, 1242, 1250, 1353, 1355, 1387a, 1453, 1476, 1534, 1559, 1639,
      1664, 1704, 1729, 1793, 1827, 1868, 1942, 1953, 1955, 2003, 2007
Technique and craft, Flannery O'Connor's 55, 91, 145, 161, 173, 215, 265, 271,
      273, 276, 279, 281, 296, 303, 308, 311, 328, 352, 354, 388, 409, 492,
      498, 501, 513, 540, 547, 548, 664, 588, 592, 593, 608, 609, 610, 619,
      631, 667, 696, 716, 727, 794, 800, 802, 822, 831, 836, 837, 850, 851,

(Con't) Technique and craft, Flannery O'Connor's
885, 896, 897, 911, 920, 922, 940, 956, 959, 981, 986, 1011, 1013,
1023, 1042, 1043, 1109, 1120, 1143, 1144, 1151, 1159, 1171, 1189,
1194, 1204, 1213, 1225, 1264, 1280, 1282, 1290, 1293, 1345, 1348,
1359, 1371, 1372, 1374, 1377r, 1379, 1383, 1394, 1402, 1409, 1410,
1413, 1418, 1481, 1486, 1496, 1517, 1525, 1540, 1554, 1586, 1605,
1614, 1650, 1669, 1685, 1690, 1693, 1697, 1717, 1722, 1723, 1731,
1757, 1763, 1777, 1781, 1786, 1796, 1835, 1837, 1839, 1842, 1847,
1862, 1876, 1906, 1912, 1916, 1921, 1924, 1949, 1951, 1985, 1992,
2000, 2026, 2039, 2045, 2060, 2110, 2145, 2158, 2171, 2262, 2302,
2358, 2403, 2640, 2646
Technology
See Symbols and images--technology
"A Temple of the Holy Ghost" 34, 45, 47, 49, 50a, 75b, 80, 93, 157, 257, 288,
352, 417, 427, 465, 496, 505, 523, 529, 576, 587, 763, 767, 812, 813,
814, 887, 890, 922, 991, 1073, 1078, 1079, 1205, 1217, 1326, 1328,
1426, 1451, 1513, 1546, 1554, 1559, 1559a, 1570, 1585, 1601, 1628,
1664, 1699a, 1700, 1709, 1890, 1953, 1982, 1998a, 2036, 2088, 2091,
2676
See also Characters, O'Connor's--specific--black cook
See also Characters, O'Connor's--specific--Drake, Temple
See also Characters, O'Connor's--specific--Freak, the
See also Characters, O'Connor's--specific--Hermaphrodite, the
See also Characters, O'Connor's--specific--Mother, the child's
See also Characters, O'Connor's--specific--Nun, the
See also Characters, O'Connor's--specific--Perpetua, Sister
See also Characters, O'Connor's--specific--Twelve-year-old girl, the
Texas at Austin, University of--Henry Ransom Humanities Research Center--
O'Connor-related holdings 1212
Themes, Flannery O'Connor's 23, 37, 50a, 52, 65, 71, 238, 256, 281, 299, 303,
348, 353, 376, 379, 392, 400, 429, 437, 468a, 484, 489, 523, 533, 540,
551, 554, 559, 575, 576, 588, 595, 597, 653, 672, 679, 701, 708, 720,
728, 732, 735, 739, 741, 757, 758, 768, 778, 785, 800a, 800b, 806,
809, 815, 828, 853, 863, 868, 901, 910, 925, 937, 940, 950, 951, 956,
959, 965, 973, 974, 980, 986, 997, 1015, 1030, 1031, 1038, 1053,
1061, 1066, 1069, 1070, 1082, 1086, 1091, 1093a, 1102, 1103, 1109,
1112, 1115, 1149, 1195, 1206, 1225, 1237, 1258, 1309, 1312, 1320a,
1332, 1372, 1381, 1384, 1418, 1436, 1473, 1497, 1535, 1559a, 1563,
1570, 1585, 1594, 1595, 1600, 1604, 1608, 1635, 1636, 1645, 1648,
1666, 1668, 1673, 1674, 1685, 1690, 1693, 1700, 1719, 1720, 1729,
1730, 1734, 1743, 1744, 1756, 1766, 1770, 1780, 1782, 1783, 1786,
1787, 1798, 1802, 1806, 1810, 1814, 1816, 1830, 1835, 1839, 1847,
1850, 1854, 1862, 1866, 1869, 1874, 1888, 1889, 1891, 1899, 1900,
1903, 1906, 1912, 1915, 1919, 1922, 1926, 1949, 1950, 1978, 1982,
2020, 2028, 2030, 2039, 2051, 2075, 2081, 2160, 2168, 2231, 2262,
2293, 2300, 2309, 2317, 2329, 2357, 2361, 2408, 2438, 2440, 2506,

(Con't) Themes, Flannery O'Connor's
        2542, 2569, 2571, 2589, 2596, 2601, 2623, 2628, 2643, 2698
    Specific
            Confidence man 1766, 1974
            Domestic 1559a, 1697
            Escape 1559a
            Grace 50a, 59a, 468a, 729a, 1717a, 1780, 1844, 1978, 1980,
                1997, 2336, 2409, 2418, 2420, 2424, 2438, 2440,
                2595a, 2612, 2613, 2682, 2700a
            History, of 39, 248, 286a, 390, 394, 400, 415, 444, 1207,
                1429, 1431, 1444
            Hostility, human 1780
            Imprisonment 1559a
            International 392
            Manichean 39, 162, 321, 396, 406, 863, 1115, 1771, 1810
            Moral compulsion, works as 146, 352, 612, 659, 1067, 1901,
                1949, 1954, 2022
            Morality plays, works as 936, 2033, 2434
            Oedipal 906, 954, 1064, 1088, 1161, 1408
            Pregnancy 972, 1745
            Racial 800a, 1224, 1347, 1407, 1607a, 1667, 1671, 1683,
                1690, 1699a, 1700, 1766, 1782, 1883, 1899, 1917,
                1963
            Religious 38, 45, 60, 77, 84, 106, 112, 117, 126, 131, 135,
                144, 145, 146, 160, 164, 171, 174, 175, 178, 184,
                185, 198, 215, 216, 217, 218, 232a, 239, 240, 241,
                262, 266, 267, 272, 273, 281, 292, 298, 318, 321,
                324, 337, 357, 358, 366, 368, 384, 385, 392, 400,
                405, 407, 417, 427, 443, 443a, 446, 469, 493, 505,
                511, 523, 524, 540, 551, 554, 575, 576, 592, 595,
                597, 599, 602, 612, 632, 653, 659, 662, 680, 701,
                708, 718, 720, 732, 735, 778, 785, 791, 794, 800a,
                800b, 806, 809, 811, 818, 823, 828, 831, 844, 853,
                855, 858a, 863, 866, 867, 868, 869, 887, 890, 898,
                901, 910, 918, 925, 936, 937, 940, 953, 956, 959,
                964, 965, 966, 981, 986, 998, 1006, 1030, 1031,
                1037, 1038, 1051, 1053, 1057, 1067, 1069, 1070,
                1072, 1082, 1091, 1093a, 1102, 1103, 1112, 1115,
                1119, 1120, 1127, 1129a, 1132, 1138, 1150a, 1160,
                1185, 1189, 1194, 1195, 1196, 1221, 1224, 1237,
                1258, 1277, 1288, 1299, 1309, 1316, 1320a, 1339,
                1347, 1384, 1418, 1435, 1436, 1468, 1477, 1497,
                1503, 1513, 1519, 1535, 1559, 1570, 1576, 1594,
                1595, 1608, 1609, 1610, 1619r, 1635, 1636, 1645,
                1647, 1648, 1666, 1673, 1674, 1693, 1719, 1731,
                1744, 1751, 1755, 1756, 1759, 1766, 1780, 1786,

(Con't) Themes, Flannery O'Connor's--Religious
1802, 1810, 1814, 1816, 1823, 1836, 1837, 1841,
1844, 1848, 1869, 1881, 1891, 1902, 1909, 1912,
1915, 1918, 1938, 1944, 1949, 1950, 1980, 1981,
1989, 2016, 2024, 2028, 2036, 2050, 2113, 2135,
2177, 2199, 2209, 2231, 2239, 2249, 2262, 2300,
2309, 2329, 2330, 2333, 2342, 2357, 2359, 2360,
2382, 2462, 2465, 2493, 2506, 2519, 2541, 2579,
2581, 2596, 2684, 2684
See also O'Connor, Flannery--views--religious
Social 1224, 2333
Theology
Augustinian 1666, 1944, 1961
Calvinist versus Catholic 926, 1096, 1100, 1424, 1650, 1666, 1672,
1923, 1947, 1990, 2369
Death-of-God 697
Emotional versus intellectual in 842, 850, 1099, 1133, 1590, 1609,
1749
Feminist 1822, 2325
Fiction and 29, 32, 34, 84, 164a, 174, 199, 407, 697, 725, 729, 818,
926, 964, 979, 1030, 1312, 1320a, 1347, 1816, 1822, 1848,
1854, 1858, 1922, 1923, 1926, 1947, 1957, 1972, 1981, 2600
Fundamentalist 717, 778, 779, 800, 890, 964, 1063, 1070, 1082, 1093,
1258, 1304, 1343, 1384, 1427, 1536, 1635, 1655, 1666, 1669,
1672, 1972, 2086, 2473
Jewish 1990
Liberation 1858
Literature and 164a, 725, 818, 964, 979, 999, 1107, 1312, 1347, 1559,
1837, 1848, 1854, 1858, 1922, 1926, 1957, 2333, 2641
Mystical body 1764, 1923
Negative 1724
Psychoanalysis and 1057, 1133, 1167, 1189, 1339, 1438, 1474, 1670,
1701, 1702, 1741, 1783, 1860, 1954, 2360
Puritan 1816, 1930, 1945
Via negativa 1647, 1980, 2016
See also Critical approaches to O'Connor's fiction--specific--
theological
See also Intellectual(s)--religion and
Theresa of Avila, Saint 965
Theses, checklists of O'Connor related 423, 459, 1392, 1567
Thomas, Saint 1135, 1300, 1312, 1557
Thomistic grace
See Grace, action of--Thomistic
See also O'Connor, Flannery--views and opinions of--Thomism
Time
See Style--time, use of

Time Magazine 1339, 1642
Toombsboro, Georgia
          See Georgia--cities and towns--Toombsboro
"Total Effect and the Eighth Grade" 311a
Totemism 1373
"The Train" 29, 60, 140, 435, 514, 592, 1409, 1685, 1690, 2315
Trains
          See Symbols and images--train
Transcendence
          See God--transcendence of
Translations 1715
          Brazilian Portuguese 1937
          French 561, 1188, 1716, 2009, 2050, 2085, 2130, 2132, 2133, 2598
                    Complete Works 2031, 2130, 2140
                    Everything That Rises Must Converge 561
                    A Good Man Is Hard to Find 561
                    The Habit of Being 2071, 2137, 2139
                    Mystery and Manners 561, 2090, 2136
                    Why Do the Heathen Rage? 2136
                    Wise Blood 1188
          German 1716
          Italian 2168
          Swedish 2123
                    Everything That Rises Must Converge 2123
Translators 561, 1716, 2050
          Coindreau, Maurice-Edgar 561, 2050, 2136
          Fleurdorge, Claude 561
          Morisset, Henri 561
          Simon, Andre 561
Trees and woods
          See Symbols and images--trees and woods
Tributes
          See O'Connor, Flannery--reputation of
Trickster
          See Style--motifs and archetypes--trickster motif
Truth
          See Style--truth, use of the
"The Turkey" 29, 34, 60, 268, 704, 1094, 1285, 1468, 1685
          See also "An Afternoon in the Woods"
          See also "The Capture"
          See also Characters, O'Connor's--specific--McFarney, Ruller

The Union Recorder
          See Georgia--cities and towns--Milledgeville--*The Union Recorder*

Values, traditional 163, 550, 587, 932, 1222, 1267, 1455, 1461, 1700, 1855
Vanderbilt University
      Fugitives at 1667, 1853, 1871, 1884, 2348
      Jean and Alexander Heard Library 70, 149
Vapex 1642
Victims
      See Style--victims, use of
"A View of the Woods" 34, 35, 50a, 77, 116, 176, 246, 248, 255, 263, 351, 442,
      514, 523, 544, 606, 617a, 676, 767, 838, 950, 1005, 1043, 1052, 1057,
      1060, 1076, 1133, 1167, 1217, 1221, 1283, 1284, 1295, 1325, 1333,
      1341, 1396, 1409, 1585, 1615a, 1659, 1697, 1698, 1703, 1725, 1727,
      1745, 1775, 1816, 1839, 2033, 2042, 2051, 2067, 2143, 2669
      See also Characters, O'Connor's--specific--Fortune, Mr.
      See also Characters, O'Connor's--specific--Pitts, Mary Fortune
Violence
      See also Characters--types of--violent
      See also O'Connor, Flannery--views and opinions of--violence
      See also Symbols and images--violence
Violence and the Sacred [René Girard] 114, 403
The Violent Bear It Away 29, 31, 32, 33, 34, 35, 36, 37, 38, 41, 45, 46, 47, 50a,
      54, 55, 56, 60, 62, 76, 77, 97, 111, 112, 128, 131, 134, 144, 146, 164a,
      165, 174, 174a, 175, 178, 216, 232a, 239, 247, 261, 262, 273, 274,
      297, 308, 311a, 312, 318, 321, 326, 360, 367, 377, 380, 396, 400, 402,
      403, 407, 420, 421, 427, 479, 503, 507, 514, 516, 523, 529a, 559, 576,
      587, 595, 610, 613, 619, 624, 653, 670, 671, 680, 682, 698, 701, 712,
      744, 778, 815, 817, 818, 819, 826, 835, 838, 850, 859, 863, 871, 878,
      887, 889, 890, 918, 930, 933, 944, 946, 947, 949, 952, 965, 977, 978,
      994, 995, 1005, 1029, 1030, 1033, 1034, 1046, 1063, 1067, 1069,
      1073, 1079, 1086, 1093a, 1109, 1111, 1158, 1196, 1208, 1216, 1221,
      1228, 1239, 1245, 1280, 1283, 1291a, 1292, 1304, 1308, 1343, 1358,
      1359, 1383, 1384, 1395, 1411, 1426, 1427, 1455, 1484, 1486, 1491,
      1493, 1496, 1507, 1521, 1528, 1545, 1546, 1557, 1559, 1562, 1585,
      1586, 1587, 1595, 1606, 1615a, 1619r, 1632, 1647, 1654, 1659, 1666,
      1668, 1669, 1678a, 1686, 1720, 1723, 1727, 1735, 1743, 1748, 1749,
      1754, 1762, 1763, 1787, 1804, 1810, 1816, 1828, 1833, 1837, 1839,
      1850, 1853, 1856, 1858, 1869, 1878, 1890, 1906, 1907, 1912, 1932,
      1936, 1939, 1948, 1951, 1975, 1982, 1984, 2011, 2016, 2025, 2026,
      2028, 2036, 2061, 2072, 2083, 2105, 2106, 2107, 2108, 2126, 2129,
      2130, 2134, 2141, 2149, 2158, 2167, 2168, 2172, 2177, 2252, 2271,
      2306, 2352, 2366, 2375, 2412, 2435, 2441, 2464, 2474, 2484, 2498,
      2503, 2531, 2560, 2569, 2590, 2591, 2604, 2630, 2664a, 2707
      See also Characters, O'Connor's--specific--Carmody, Lucette
      See also Characters, O'Connor's--specific--Homosexual, the
      See also Characters, O'Connor's--specific--Johnson, Rufus Florida
      See also Characters, O'Connor's--specific--Munson, Buford
      See also Characters, O'Connor's--specific--Rayber, Bishop

(Con't) The Violent Bear It Away
    See also Characters, O'Connor's--specific--Rayber, George
    See also Characters, O'Connor's--specific--"The Stranger-Friend"
    See also Characters, O'Connor's--specific--Tarwater, Francis Marion
    See also Characters, O'Connor's--specific--Tarwater, Mason
    See also Characters, O'Connor's--specific--truck driver, the
Vision
    See Eyesight
    See also Characters--vision of
Voice
    See Narrator--voice of O'Connor's

"The War of Northern Aggression"
    See Civil War, the American
The Wasteland [T.S. Eliot] 37, 522, 669, 767, 1343, 1591c
"What Is a Short Story?" 1525
"Why Do the Heathen Rage?" 60, 80, 155, 261, 262, 265, 584, 826, 1320, 1329,
    1691, 2136
    See also Characters, O'Connor's--specific--Gibbs, Sarah
    See also Characters, O'Connor's--specific--Tilman, Walter
"Why Worry the Horse?" 1689
"Wildcat" 29, 60, 435, 465, 858a, 1468, 1563, 1690
    See also Characters, O'Connor's--specific--Gabriel
Wise Blood 29, 31, 32, 33, 34, 36, 37, 38, 41, 45, 46, 47, 50a, 54, 55, 58, 60, 62,
    65, 73, 77, 92, 95, 97, 105, 111, 113, 126, 130, 131, 140, 141, 143,
    144, 146, 155, 161, 164a, 167, 169, 178, 187, 190, 194, 195, 196, 204,
    211, 218, 224, 232, 232a, 239, 255, 262, 268, 271, 272, 273, 275, 277,
    287, 288, 289, 308, 311, 318, 329, 335, 340, 342, 364, 371, 377, 380,
    385, 396, 406, 418, 431, 439, 443, 444, 445, 450, 454, 457, 465, 486,
    492, 495, 507, 514, 516, 519, 522, 523, 524, 529a, 532, 542, 546, 548,
    551, 552, 554, 558, 559, 561, 572, 576, 579, 585, 587, 591, 595, 611,
    624, 652, 656, 657, 659, 662, 668, 670, 697, 699, 712, 732, 762, 764,
    764a, 767, 770, 778, 804a, 805, 810, 812, 813, 814, 815, 817, 826,
    830, 833, 839, 840, 850, 858, 860, 863, 867, 871, 879, 882, 884, 887,
    888, 890, 901, 906, 911, 927, 930, 939, 944, 948, 949, 961, 978, 989,
    991, 995, 1005, 1010, 1018, 1021, 1025, 1040, 1041, 1043, 1052,
    1058, 1060, 1063, 1071, 1072, 1073, 1074, 1075, 1080, 1081, 1086,
    1091, 1092, 1104, 1109, 1113, 1115, 1116, 1118, 1119, 1135, 1138,
    1152, 1161, 1188, 1200, 1215, 1216, 1221, 1225, 1228, 1229, 1230,
    1239, 1292, 1297, 1299, 1307, 1309, 1314, 1335, 1343, 1352, 1358,
    1371, 1384, 1387, 1396, 1408, 1409, 1412, 1421, 1426, 1443, 1444,
    1459, 1484, 1498, 1509, 1510, 1521, 1543, 1546, 1547, 1550, 1563,
    1564, 1585, 1587, 1591, 1595, 1601, 1602, 1604, 1605, 1606, 1608,
    1609, 1615a, 1619r, 1632, 1635, 1636, 1637, 1647, 1659, 1662, 1678a,
    1681r, 1685, 1689, 1690, 1699a, 1700, 1702, 1712, 1719, 1724, 1742,

(Con't) Wise Blood

       1743, 1749, 1762, 1768, 1775, 1785, 1787, 1791, 1802, 1804, 1810,
       1816, 1818, 1853, 1869, 1870, 1878, 1890, 1897, 1911, 1912, 1923,
       1925, 1932, 1936, 1937, 1948, 1971, 1982, 1983, 1992, 2011, 2016,
       2028, 2059, 2062, 2063, 2078, 2082, 2084, 2097, 2098, 2102, 2109,
       2123, 2129, 2144, 2148, 2151, 2152, 2154, 2168, 2175, 2177, 2180,
       2186, 2211, 2212, 2240, 2247, 2250, 2310, 2315, 2329, 2363, 2364,
       2375, 2377, 2379, 2384, 2396, 2434, 2441, 2502, 2503, 2547, 2602,
       2608, 2619, 2664a

       See also Characters, O'Connor's--specific--Emery, Enoch
       See also Characters, O'Connor's--specific--Flood, Mrs.
       See also Characters, O'Connor's--specific--Hawks, Sabbath Lily
       See also Characters, O'Connor's--specific--Hitchcock, Mrs. Wally Bee
       See also Characters, O'Connor's--specific--Holy, Onnie Jay
       See also Characters, O'Connor's--specific--Layfield, Solace
       See also Characters, O'Connor's--specific--Motes, Hazel
       See also Characters, O'Connor's--specific--"The Mummy"
       See also Characters, O'Connor's--specific--Stripper, the
       See also Characters, O'Connor's--specific--Watts, Mrs. Leora
       See also Films--*Wise Blood*

"Woman On the Stairs" 1004

Women

       Southern 75b, 80, 114, 244, 272, 307, 383, 453, 529, 550, 587, 630,
          660, 731, 813, 824, 1078, 1090, 1127, 1217, 1292, 1299,
          1326, 1408, 1421, 1445, 1527, 1559a, 1568, 1572, 1622,
          1625, 1637, 1692, 1700, 1701, 1745, 1750, 1820, 1822, 1867,
          1871, 1886, 1925, 1948, 2162, 2373, 2374, 2551, 2632, 2645,
          2649
       Writers 206, 383, 436, 468, 472, 529, 536, 614, 630, 640, 662, 731,
          781, 814, 876, 941, 943, 960, 972, 973, 1020, 1227, 1263,
          1292, 1343, 1364, 1388, 1389, 1420, 1421, 1423, 1568, 1574,
          1622, 1623, 1625, 1702, 1746, 1820, 1871, 1886, 1925, 1948,
          1974, 1981, 2373, 2374, 2536, 2645, 2699
       See also Symbols and imagery--women

Women's rights 579, 1078, 1341, 1408, 1718, 1822, 1948, 2014

"The Word" 1025, 1070, 1073, 1482, 1530, 1608, 2134

Word choice

       See Style--word choice, use of

Works, Flannery O'Connor's

       Background of, social and historical 930
       Endings 512
       Literary history of 536, 650, 1911
       Plots of 43, 52, 216, 422, 445, 697, 712, 811, 817, 871, 897, 956, 997,
          1381, 1606, 1777, 1804, 1867, 1869, 1872
       Settings of 100, 134, 181, 184, 301, 321, 417, 457, 559, 712, 931,
          1230, 1350, 1378, 1379, 1422, 1615a, 1733, 1777, 1807,

(Con't) Works, Flannery O'Connor's--Settings of
                1855, 1918, 1961, 2003
        Specific
                    See "An Afternoon In the Woods"
                    See "The Artificial Nigger"
                    See "The Barber"
                    See "Biologic Endeavoi"
                    See "The Capture"
                    See "The Catholic Novelist in the Modern South"
                    See "The Church and the Fiction Writer"
                    See "A Circle in the Fire"
                    See "The Citizen of My County Who Has Contributed the
                            Most to the State of Georgia"
                    See "The Coat"
                    See Collected Works [Library of America edition] *See*
                            Flannery O'Connor: The Complete Stories
                    See "The Comforts of Home"
                    See "The Crop"
                    See "The Displaced Person"
                    See "Doctors of Delinquency"
                    See "Education's Only Hope"
                    See "Effervescence"
                    See "Elegance Is Its Own Reward"
                    See "The Enduring Chill"
                    See "Enoch and the Gorilla"
                    See Everything That Rises Must Converge [collection]
                    See "Everything That Rises Must Converge" [story]
                    See "Excuse Us While We Don't Apologize"
                    See "An Exile in the East"
                    See "Fashion's Perfect Medium"
                    See "The Fiction Writer in the South"
                    See "The Fiction Writer and His Country"
                    See "The First Book" [poem]
                    See "The Freak in Modern Literature"
                    See "The Geranium"
                    See "Getting Home"
                    See "Going to the Dogs"
                    See "Good Country People"
                    See A Good Man Is Hard to Find [collection]
                    See "A Good Man Is Hard to Find" [story]
                    See "Greenleaf"
                    See "The Heart of the Park"
                    See "Home of the Brave"
                    See "Judgement Day"
                    See "The King of the Birds"
                    See "The Lame Shall Enter First"

(Con't) Works, Flannery O'Connor's--Specific
        See "A Late Encounter With the Enemy"
        See "The Life You Save May Be Your Own"
        See Master's thesis, Flannery O'Connor's MFA
        See Mystery and Manners
        See "The Nature and Aim of Fiction"
        See "Parker's Back"
        See "The Partridge Festival"
        See "The Peeler"
        See "PFTT" [poem]
        See "The Place of the Intellectual"
        See The Presence of Grace and Other Book Reviews by
                Flannery O'Connor
        See "The Regional Writer"
        See "Revelation"
        See "The River"
        See "Some Aspects of the Grotesque in Southern Fiction"
        See "A Stroke of Good Fortune"
        See "A Temple of the Holy Ghost"
        See "Total Effect and the Eighth Grade"
        See "The Train"
        See "The Turkey"
        See "A View of the Woods"
        See The Violent Bear It Away
        See "What Is a Short Story?"
        See "Why Do the Heathen Rage?"
        See "Why Worry the Horse"
        See "Wildcat"
        See Wise Blood
        See "Woman on the Stairs"
        See "Writing Short Stories" [*Mystery and Manners*]
        See "You Can't Be Any Poorer Than Dead"
The World of Flannery O'Connor
        See Films--*The World of Flannery O'Connor*
Work ethic, American 263, 1078, 1816
Writing programs
        See O'Connor, Flannery--views and opinions of--creative writing
        See also Iowa Writer's Program
"Writing Short Stories" [in *Mystery and Manners*] 942
WSAV-TV (Savannah) 1593

Yaddo
        See O'Connor, Flannery--biographical details--homes--Yaddo
"You Can't Be Any Poorer Than Dead" 60, 514, 1284, 1409, 2011, 2448
Yügen 1138

Photograph Courtesy of NYT Pictures

You do not write the best you can for the sake of art but for the sake of returning your talent increased to the invisible God to use or not use as he sees fit.

Flannery O'Connor

About the Author

R. Neil Scott was born on Maxwell Air Force Base in Montgomery, Alabama. Educated in public schools near military installations in Georgia, Illinois, Texas, and Florida, he received his B.A. in English from the University of South Florida in 1975, his M.S. in Library Science from Florida State in 1976, and his M.B.A. from Stetson University in 1982.

Professor Scott has worked as Technical Writer for the Unisys Corporation (1976-77); Instructor and Public Services Librarian for William Carey College (1978-80); Associate Professor and Head of Reference Services for Stetson University (1980-86); and, as a Management Consultant in the Washington, D.C. office of KPMG Peat Marwick (1987-88).

From 1988 to 1996 Scott served as Associate Professor and Coordinator of Information Services--which included responsibility for the *Flannery O'Connor Collection*--at the Russell Library of Georgia College & State University (GC&SU). In 1996 he accepted his present appointment as Associate Director for Library Operations and Administrative Services at GC&SU and was promoted to Professor of Library Science in 1998. He has published articles in a wide variety of scholarly journals.

Professor Scott lives with his wife Sheila, and their three children, Stephanie, Sherry and David in Milledgeville, Georgia.

About the Editor

Irwin Streight teaches courses in literature and writing at Queen's University and the Royal Military College in Kingston, Ontario.

He completed a dissertation on Flannery O'Connor *The Word Made Fiction: The Stories of Flannery O'Connor* (Queen's 1993) and has published articles on O'Connor, socio-linguistics, and contributed substantially to the *Guide to Canadian English Usage* published by Oxford University Press (1997).

Dr. Streight and his wife Susan manage a household of five children: three sporty boys--Jarius, Aaron, and Jesse--and twin daughters Sage Margaret and Flannery Evangeline.